A Companion to Research in Teacher Education

Michael A. Peters · Bronwen Cowie
Ian Menter
Editors

A Companion to Research in Teacher Education

 Springer

Editors
Michael A. Peters
Faculty of Education
University of Waikato
Hamilton
New Zealand

Ian Menter
Department of Education
University of Oxford
Oxford
UK

Bronwen Cowie
Faculty of Education
University of Waikato
Hamilton
New Zealand

ISBN 978-981-13-5041-2   ISBN 978-981-10-4075-7   (eBook)
DOI 10.1007/978-981-10-4075-7

Printed on acid-free paper

This Springer imprint is published by Springer Nature
The registered company is Springer Nature Singapore Pte Ltd.
The registered company address is: 152 Beach Road, #21-01/04 Gateway East, Singapore 189721, Singapore

Acknowledgements

The editors would like to acknowledge the generous funding of the Faculty of Education at Waikato University and the Wilf Malcom Institute of Educational Research and also thank Richard Heraud for his work in the administration of this project. He provided the necessary support at critical points during the composition of this volume and did so with unfailing politeness and good humour.

Endorsements

This *Companion to Research in Teacher Education*, assembled by skilled and knowledgeable experts in teacher education and research in teacher education, is an important resource to practitioners, researchers and policy makers. With an ever-expanding number of international researchers in teacher education, such a Companion offers a useful guide to what matters in the field.

—D. Jean Clandinin

This book marks a coming of age for the scholarship of teacher education; an essential resource for everyone seriously interested in the field.

—John Furlong

Contents

Editors and Contributors

About the Editors

Michael A. Peters is Professor in the Wilf Malcolm Institute for Educational Research at Waikato University, Emeritus Professor at the University of Illinois at Urbana-Champaign. He is the executive editor of *Educational Philosophy and Theory* and has written over 75 books. He was made an Honorary Fellow of the Royal Society of New Zealand in 2010 and awarded honorary doctorates by State University of New York (SUNY) in 2012 and University of Aalborg in 2015.

Bronwen Cowie is Professor of Education and Director of the Wilf Malcolm Institute of Educational Research at the Faculty of Education: Te Kura Toi Tangata, The University of Waikato New Zealand. Her research interests span assessment for learning, science education, student voice, curriculum implementation and teacher education/professional learning.

Ian Menter is a Fellow of the Academy of Social Sciences in the UK and was President of the British Educational Research Association (BERA), 2013–15. He is Emeritus Professor of Teacher Education at the University of Oxford and was a member of the Steering Group of the BERA Inquiry into Research and Teacher Education (2014).

Contributors

Bobby Abrol University of Houston, Houston, USA

Daniela Acquaro University of Melbourne, Melbourne, VIC, Australia

Alison L. Bailey University of California, Los Angeles, CA, USA

Poonam Batra University of Delhi, Delhi, India

Clive Beck University of Toronto, Toronto, Canada

Leon Benade Auckland University of Technology, Auckland, New Zealand

Ghazala Bhatti Bath Spa University, Bath, England, UK

Gert Biesta Brunel University, Uxbridge, England, UK

Simon Bott Swansea University, Swansea, Wales, UK

David Bridges University of East Anglia, England, UK

Katharine Burn University of Oxford, Oxford, England, UK

Helen Cahill University of Melbourne, Melbourne, Australia

Jeffrey M. Choppin University of Rochester, Rochester, USA

Allie Clemans Monash University, Clayton, Australia

Julia Coffey University of Newcastle, Callaghan, Australia

Beverley Cooper University of Waikato, Hamilton, New Zealand

Bronwen Cowie University of Waikato, Hamilton, New Zealand

Cheryl J. Craig Texas A&M University, College Station, USA

Larissa McLean Davies University of Melbourne, Melbourne, Australia

Nesta Devine Auckland University of Technology, Auckland, New Zealand

Pooja Dharamshi Simon Fraser University, Burnaby, Canada

Valerie Drew University of Stirling, Stirling, Scotland, UK

Anne Edwards University of Oxford, Oxford, England, UK

Sue Ellis University of Strathclyde, Glasgow, Scotland, UK

Debbie Epstein University of Roehampton, London, England, UK

Paige Evans University of Houston, Houston, USA

Sandy Farquhar University of Auckland, Auckland, New Zealand

Odilla E. Finlayson Dublin City University, Dublin, Ireland

Christine Forde University of Glasgow, Glasgow, Scotland, UK

Rachel Forgasz Monash University, Melbourne, Australia

Trevor Gale University of Glasgow, Glasgow, Scotland

Andrew Gibbons Auckland University of Technology, Auckland, New Zealand

Donald Gillies University of the West of Scotland, Ayr, Scotland, UK

Merrilyn Goos University of Queensland, Brisbane, Australia

Judith Green University of California, Santa Barbara, CA, USA

Lexie Grudnoff University of Auckland, Auckland, New Zealand

Qing Gu University of Nottingham, Nottingham, England, UK

Hazel Hagger University of Oxford, Oxford, England, UK

Judith Harford School of Education, University College Dublin, Dublin, Ireland

Hannu L.T. Heikkinen University of Jyväskylä, Jyväskylä, Finland

Margaret Heritage WestEd, San Francisco, CA, USA

Steven Hodge Griffith University, Brisbane, Australia

Bill Hubbard Rosehill College, Auckland, New Zealand

Anne Hume University of Waikato, Hamilton, New Zealand

Barbara Kameniar University of Melbourne, Melbourne, Australia; University of Tasmania, Tasmania, Australia

Laurie Katz Ohio State University, Columbus, OH, USA

Alison Kearney Massey University, Palmerston North, New Zealand

Aileen Kennedy University of Edinburgh, Edinburgh, Scotland, UK

Jefferson Kinsman University of Melbourne, Melbourne, Australia

Clare Kosnik University of Toronto, Toronto, Canada

Jeana Kriewaldt University of Melbourne, Melbourne, VIC, Australia

Duck-Joo Kwak Seoul National University, Seoul, South Korea

Leanne Lamb Auckland University of Technology, Auckland, New Zealand

John Loughran Monash University, Clayton, Australia

Andreas Lund University of Oslo, Oslo, Norway

Mieke Lunenberg University Amsterdam, Amsterdam, Netherlands

Julianne Lynch Deakin University, Warrnambool, Australia

Meg Maguire King's College, London, England, UK

Eilish McLoughlin Dublin City University, Dublin, Ireland

Gail McEachron College of William and Mary, Williamsburg, USA

Colleen McLaughlin University of Cambridge, England, UK

Larissa McLean Davies University of Melbourne, Melbourne, VIC, Australia

Margery A. McMahon University of Glasgow, Glasgow, Scotland, UK

Lydia Menna University of Alberta, Edmonton, Canada

Ian Menter University of Oxford, Oxford, England, UK

Mandia Mentis Massey University, Palmerston North, New Zealand

Kevin W. Meuwissen University of Rochester, Rochester, USA

Martin Mills University of Queensland, Brisbane, Australia

Jean Murray University of East London, London, UK

Rosa Murray University of Edinburgh, Edinburgh, Scotland, UK

Trevor Mutton University of Oxford, Oxford, England, UK

Birgitte Lund Nielsen VIA University College, Aarhus, Denmark

Pernilla Nilsson Halmstad University, Halmstad, Sweden

Alis Oancea University of Oxford, England, UK

Mark Olssen University of Surrey, Guildford, UK

Janet Orchard University of Bristol, England, UK

Justen O'Connor Monash University, Clayton, Australia

Teresa O'Doherty Mary Immaculate College, Limerick, Ireland

John O'Neill Massey University, Palmerston North, New Zealand

Stephen Parker University of Glasgow, Glasgow, Scotland, UK

Lorraine Pau'uvale Auckland University of Technology, Auckland, New Zealand

Michael A. Peters University of Waikato, Hamilton, New Zealand

Carey Philpott (Deceased) Leeds Beckett University, Leeds, UK

Mark Priestley University of Stirling, Stirling, Scotland, UK

Richard Pring Oxford University, Oxford, England, UK

Catherine Reid University of Melbourne, Melbourne, Australia

Suzanne Rice University of Melbourne, Melbourne, VIC, Australia

Field Rickards University of Melbourne, Melbourne, VIC, Australia

Jessica Ringrose University College London, London, England, UK

Herner Saeverot Western Norway University of Applied Sciences, Bergen, Norway

Andrew Skourdoumbis Deakin University, Burwood, Australia

Kari Smith Norwegian University of Science and Technology, Trondheim, Norway

Paul Stephens University of Stavanger, Stavanger, Norway

Donna Stokes University of Houston, Houston, USA

Carl Anders Säfström Södertörn University, Stockholm, Sweden

Maria Teresa Tatto Arizona State University, Tempe, USA

Jeanne Pau'uvale Teisina Auckland University of Technology, Auckland, New Zealand

Marek Tesar University of Auckland, Auckland, New Zealand

Martin Thrupp University of Waikato, Hamilton, New Zealand

Tom Are Trippestad Western Norway University of Applied Sciences, Bergen, Norway

Debra Tyler University of Melbourne, Melbourne, Australia

Jon Magne Vestøl University of Oslo, Oslo, Norway

Simone White Monash University, Melbourne, Australia

Geoff Whitty University of Newcastle, Callaghan, Australia; Bath Spa University, Bath, England, UK

Chapter 1
A Companion to Research in Teacher Education

Ian Menter, Michael A. Peters and Bronwen Cowie

1.1 Introduction

During the early part of the twenty-first century teacher education has been the subject of much change in many countries around the globe. From Australia to Austria, from Norway to Scotland, we have seen reviews, reports and reforms. Within the UK, all four jurisdictions—as well as the Republic of Ireland—have seen major reports that have led to changes of various sorts in the provision for initial teacher education (Teacher Education Group 2016).

The reasons that there has been so much concern with teacher education are in part an element of the wider concern about education that has led to the 'Global Education Reform Movement'—the GERM, as Sahlberg (2011) calls it. But the particular focus on teacher education has arisen because of the widespread realisation that the quality of teaching does matter! And of course if the quality of teaching matters, then the ways in which teachers are prepared to undertake their work is a key consideration. So this welter of reform is perhaps not a real surprise. Indeed, what may be the real surprise is that it has taken so long for there to be so much policy interest in the area.

In a fascinating review of developments in the USA, Cochran-Smith and Fries (2008) have traced a number of phases, culminating—for the present time at least—in the definition of teacher education as 'a policy problem'. In previous phases, they argue it was variously defined as a curriculum problem (1920s–1950s), as a training

I. Menter (✉)
University of Oxford, Oxford, England, UK
e-mail: ian.menter@education.ox.ac.uk

M.A. Peters · B. Cowie
University of Waikato, Hillcrest, New Zealand
e-mail: mpeters@waikato.ac.nz

B. Cowie
e-mail: bcowie@waikato.ac.nz

© Springer Nature Singapore Pte Ltd. 2017
M.A. Peters et al. (eds.), *A Companion to Research in Teacher Education*,
DOI 10.1007/978-981-10-4075-7_1

problem (late 1950s to early 1980s) and then as a learning problem (early 1980s to early 2000s). It was in the 1990s that teacher education became defined as a policy problem, especially in the USA.

However, although the political interest—both in the USA and the UK—is relatively recent, there are several questions that have been central to the development of teacher education from the nineteenth century through the twentieth century and which still pertain to this day, within this more volatile context. The purpose of this *Companion to Research in Teacher Education* is to provide a range of evidence that can be called upon to inform the debates and arguments that continue in many parts of the world about these matters.

In this introduction, we seek to explore these questions and show how they are significant to current developments, especially within the UK and in New Zealand, the countries in which the editors of the book are based. We do this because we think that careful analysis of nation-based developments in teacher education tend to demonstrate some of the wider themes that are of international significance. It is something of a paradox in these days of globalised education (Rizvi and Lingard 2010; Peters 2001; Simons et al. 2009), that teacher education systems remain (almost) resolutely national in their organisation and dispositions. Nevertheless, as you read the contributions to this companion you will see themes recurring in different ways in different contexts. There are plenty of examples in the field of teacher education of 'travelling policy' being transmuted into contexts where aspects of policy are already 'embedded' (Ozga and Jones 2006).

In relation to the UK, part of this discussion necessarily needs to differentiate between what has been happening to the four main jurisdictions—England, Northern Ireland, Scotland and Wales—for in spite of the globalising influences, there appears to have been some divergence between the trajectories of the four countries in relation to developments in teacher education.

In the following section, we discuss models of teaching and teacher education and how they have developed across the UK and how they relate to differing conceptions of the work of a teacher. The second section sets out the key elements of a 'clinical practice' approach to teacher education.

Throughout this discussion we draw on a range of sources, including our own experiences in teacher education, a wide range of research that has been carried out and ideas that have emerged from the work undertaken by the British Educational Research Association with the Royal Society for the Arts in an inquiry into research and teacher education (BERA-RSA 2014a, b), as well as on a collectively written book on teacher education across the UK and Republic of Ireland (TEG 2016).

1.1.1 Models of Initial Teacher Education

In 2010, a team at the University of Glasgow carried out a literature review on teacher education in the twenty-first century. This had been commissioned by the Scottish Government as part of Graham Donaldson's review of teacher education in

Scotland, subsequently published as *Teaching Scotland's Future* (Donaldson 2011; see below as well). In this literature review it was suggested that it was possible to identify four significantly different paradigms of teaching and the nature of teachers' work.

These we called (Menter et al. 2010; also Menter 2010):

1. The effective teacher—emphasising skills, content, performativity and measurement.
2. The reflective teacher—skills and content again, but with the addition of knowledge about learners, and consideration of the values underlying and the purposes of education.
3. The enquiring teacher—systematic enquiry into all of the above; deploying research and evaluation methods and techniques.
4. The transformative teacher—adopting a 'critical enquiry' approach, looking beyond the classroom, considering social context, moral and ethical issues, developing alliances (adopting a 'stance').

These paradigms can be seen as ranging across a continuum from a limited or 'restricted' view of teacher professionalism to a more expansive or 'extended' model (Hoyle 1974). Clearly the challenge of preparing someone to become a teacher will vary according to which paradigm is aspired to.

In a paper prepared for the BERA-RSA inquiry into research and teaching, a team of philosophers suggested, in somewhat similar vein, that there were three aspects of knowledge that contribute towards teaching—practical wisdom, technical knowledge and critical reflection (Winch et al. 2015; BERA-RSA 2014a). Again, the approach taken towards initial teacher education is likely to be strongly shaped by the particular balance of these forms of knowledge that are believed to be important in preparing the best quality of teacher.

It is valuable therefore to consider how major policy statements have defined teaching and models of learning to become a teacher. As was mentioned earlier, there has been a steady stream of policy reviews and documents emerging around the world concerning these matters and it has been very illuminating to compare some of them with each other. In particular, the contrasts between recent statements in England and Scotland show a very marked contrast.

In November 2010, the Department for Education at Westminster published a White Paper entitled *The Importance of Teaching*. The then Secretary of State, Michael Gove, used this document to set out the main plans of his intended policy in relation to teaching and teacher education. A close reading of the paper shows quite clearly that teaching is seen as being essentially a craft that is best learned through an apprenticeship model set within a school. The contribution to be made by studying education or by researching education was limited or non-existent. Teachers' main tasks were to convey subject knowledge and to manage children's behaviour. Subject knowledge was to be learned through study certainly—usually through pursuing an honours degree in that subject. But the management of behaviour and other matters such as literacy and numeracy teaching, as well as responding to learners' special educational needs were to be learned through working alongside experienced teachers in school. Schools themselves should be encouraged to take a much more leading role—indeed a pre-eminent role—in the provision of teacher education and the White Paper announced the creation of a new approach, to be called 'School Direct' in which schools would be allocated training places by government and would select candidates and organise the programme of learning. This approach fitted with the wider mantra that was adopted by this government of education becoming a 'school-led system'. Mr Gove aimed to have at least half of beginning teachers being trained by school-led approaches by the time of the next election—that is by 2015, a target that was indeed achieved.

In January 2011, the Scottish Government published the report written by the former Chief Inspector of Education, Graham Donaldson, notably a professional educator rather than a politician. Nevertheless, his report had been commissioned by a politician, the Cabinet Secretary for Education. The ensuing report *Teaching Scotland's Future* (Donaldson 2011) was based on a very different view of teaching. It set out a model of teaching as a complex and intellectually challenging occupation, requiring practical learning experience in schools certainly, but also requiring significant study in higher education. It also saw teachers as active decision makers in schools who would need to be able to exercise leadership in their work. The report emphasised the contribution of the university and indeed challenged the universities to offer more than they had done to enhance the quality of teacher education.

We thus saw within the space of a few months in these contiguous parts of the United Kingdom fundamentally different accounts of the nature of teaching and fundamentally different views about the best approaches to initial teacher education (although it was called initial teacher training in the English White Paper). Hulme and Menter (2011) have carried out a detailed analysis of some of the key differences between the two documents. Simply setting out different views in policy statements such as these does not of course directly or necessarily lead to an equivalent variation in the practices of teacher education that are carried out. Nevertheless in Scotland the Government did accept all fifty of Donaldson's recommendations and set about implementing them. In England the White Paper policy proposals became enacted in practice. However in both settings, there was a process of mediation—a process of 'enactment' that in both cases has the effect of 'softening the edges' on the extremes of the policy approaches. Indeed in England there has been a subsequent review, more similar in approach to that of Donaldson, a review carried out by a primary school head teacher, Sir Andrew Carter, who with the support of an advisory group produced a report early in 2015 on effective approaches to initial teacher training. Although Carter was appointed to this role by Michael Give, by the time his report was produced Gove had been replaced by Nicky Morgan and this may be part of the explanation of why this report seems much more nuanced and less polemical than the 2010 White Paper (see Mutton et al. 2016). It may also of course relate to the fact that Carter is himself a professional educator rather than a politician.

One of the key concerns that underlies all of these reviews and discussions is the question of teachers' professional knowledge and skills. What is it that a good teacher should know and be able to do? Once that question has been discussed there is then subsequently a further key question which is how best the beginning teacher learns and/or develops those skills and knowledge.

Whatever age range the teacher is working with it is now widely acknowledged that there are going to be at least three major elements of professional knowledge that will be needed. The first is curriculum knowledge, that is knowing and understanding what it is that is to be taught—the appropriate knowledge, concepts, understandings and skills, as well arguably, as values and/or dispositions. Secondly, there is what has been called 'professional content knowledge'—PCK—that is, knowing and understanding the subject content in such a way that it can actually be taught. This implies knowing something about how knowledge in a particular field is constructed and how a learner best comes to understand and know it. The third aspect of professional knowledge is what might best be dubbed professional knowledge and understanding of teaching. This would range from theories of learning, through theories of classroom management (including behaviour management), the philosophy and sociology of education and schooling and much else besides. This element also of course includes much that is skills based and requires the learner to be able to 'translate' theory into practice—although many would argue that that distinction is not a helpful one.

Indeed, it is because of the complex nature of professional learning that recent research has increasingly emphasised the need for integrated models of professional learning, which break down the distinction between theory and practice and which emphasise the link between cognition and experience. The models that perhaps best demonstrate such an approach are sometimes called clinical practice models and such an approach is what emerged strongly as the favoured model within the BERA-RSA inquiry.

1.1.2   Research-Based Clinical Practice in Teacher Education

Drawing on the paper written for the inquiry by Burn and Mutton (2013), the interim report from the inquiry offered the following definition of research-informed clinical practice:

> Although the precise terminology varies, the notion of 'clinical practice' in education essentially conveys the need to bring together knowledge and evidence from different sources, through a carefully sequenced programme which is deliberately designed to integrate teachers' experiential learning at the 'chalk face' with research-based knowledge and insights from academic study and scholarship. Inspired by the medical model, the goal is to refine particular skills and deepen practitioners' knowledge and understanding, by integrating practical and academic (or research-based) knowledge, and to interrogate each in light of the other.

The meaning of 'clinical practice' is potentially ambiguous, since 'practice' can be understood both as a deliberate process of rehearsal for beginners or novices, and as routine or established ways of working for experienced practitioners. While this review focuses on clinical preparation for novice teachers in programmes of initial teacher education, it is also possible to apply the principles of 'research-informed clinical practice' to professional learning for experienced practitioners as well as new recruits.

We see therefore that this approach is not just relevant to pre-service teacher education but can be invoked more generally as a model for professional learning throughout the career.

There have been several examples around the world of these kinds of approaches, including aspects of Professional Development Schools in the USA, projects in Scotland (Scottish Teachers for a New Era and The Glasgow West Teacher Education Initiative) and in Australia (see Hooley 2013, although different terminology is adopted in this context). But one of the most sustained examples of this kind of approach is that developed at Oxford. Initiated in the 1980s the Oxford Internship Scheme set out to establish a full partnership between the University and a number of local state schools. The scheme was developed collaboratively by the various partners including the local education authority and has been operating successfully ever since. An early account is provided in the collection of articles edited by Benton (1980) but subsequent developments can also be seen in the accounts from Hagger and McIntyre (2006). A sustained analysis of the nature of beginning teachers' learning in this context has been undertaken by Burn, Hagger and Mutton in their Developing Expertise of Beginning Teacher (DEBT) project, an overview of which can be found in Burn et al. (2015).

What is common to all of these schemes is a sustained attempt to integrate theory and practice in professional learning. Indeed Hagger and McIntyre (op. cit.) talk of 'practical theorising' and 'theorising practice' to emphasise the dialectical relationship between these elements. A further common feature is the sustained effort to make explicit the contribution that each participant makes to the learning processes. For example, in the Oxford scheme, university staff are designated, respectively, as curriculum tutors or as general tutors, with the former taking responsibility for ensuring the students have access to appropriate subject knowledge and to the distinctive elements of their own subject's pedagogy. The latter staff are responsible for the development of the wider professional knowledge of the student in terms of national and local policies as well as general aspects of learning theory and other research. In the schools where students are placed, teachers who work with the trainees may be either Professional Tutors or Subject mentors. The Professional Tutors play a very significant role in ensuring the coordination of the programme within the school as well as in supporting the students in understanding the ways in which general professional matters are implemented in the particular school context. The subject mentors on the other hand ensure that the student has access to resources within the subject department and is supported in their planning, preparation and teaching. All of the staff working on the scheme experience considerable professional development themselves through their engagement and this again is a common feature of clinical practice models.

In recent years the Oxford scheme has been developing further, initially with just a limited number of schools, within the City of Oxford, to become part of a wider more broadly conceived partnership, which has been called The Oxford Education Deanery. This has again been developed on a collaboration basis between the schools and the University. There are two elements to this expansion of the longstanding partnership within the internship scheme. The first is that the Deanery seeks to establish activity on three 'levels', not only initial teacher education (ITE), but also continuing professional development (CPD) and research. The CPD partnership includes a range of interactions between the Department and the schools, including a Master's programme—the M.Sc. in Learning and Teaching. This programme recruits openly, nationally and internationally, but there is a strand within it which is focused on local schools and provides an opportunity for collaborative endeavour for registered teachers to focus on matters of common concern in these schools. The research element has led to the identification of 'Research Champions' on the staff of each school and to a range of significant joint activities between the academic staff of the Department of Education and teachers within the schools. Some of this activity also involves the pre-service interns. One such example, indeed focussing on an aspect of science education, is written up by Childs et al. (2014).

However, the second aspect of the expansion of the longstanding partnership is the range of partners—as well as being 'multi-levelled'—the Deanery is 'multi-relational'. In a spirit of sharing and exploiting the full range of resources available in the wider community of learning represented by the City of Oxford, the Deanery is a partnership with the wider university and with a number of other partners. So, the Oxford University Vice-Chancellor very explicitly offered the University's support—not least because the University sees the Deanery as an alternative to the establishment of a University of Oxford Academy (school), along the lines taken by some other English higher education institutions. It is seen as an element in the University of Oxford's deep commitment to widening access and participation in higher education generally and in the University itself. So several central departments of the University as well as a range of colleges and other subject departments are playing a role in the Deanery. There is growing involvement also of the University's museums, of the Students' Union as well as a partnership with some primary schools, student volunteering bodies (The Student Hub) and the local authorities.

In the context of wider education policy in England therefore, we can see how the partnership stemming from a longstanding commitment to high quality initial teacher education has been developing an alternative trajectory to that being promoted by central government, an alternative which is based on principles of social justice and high quality educational provision (Fancourt et al. 2015). Furthermore, we can see that in terms of the four paradigms of teaching that were identified earlier in this chapter, we can place these approaches very much in the third and fourth categories of 'enquiring' and 'transformative' teaching. Whilst teachers working in the scheme are becoming both effective and reflective, it is clear that the approach seeks to move them well beyond these qualities.

Fig. 1.1 Dimensions of
teacher effectiveness and
teachers' professional identity

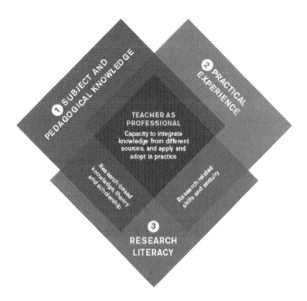

The relationship with educational research is an especially critical element of this approach. There are signs that there is increasing recognition of this in England, with moves towards 'evidence-based teaching' being encouraged by government and investment in school-based research by bodies such as the Education Endowment Foundation. The proposed College of Teaching would have a strong emphasis on teachers having access to published research (as Scottish teachers do through their General Teaching Council), as well as encouraging an enquiry orientation in their own work.

The final report from the BERA-RSA inquiry (BERA-RSA 2014b) adopted the following model of the requisite knowledge and experience for a teacher (Fig. 1.1).

Here we see all of the traditional elements of teacher education but the addition of the research strand, such as does indeed happen in clinical approaches of the kind referred to above. This is framed in terms of 'research literacy' which is defined in the BERA-RSA report as being a combination of an ability to be able to read and critically evaluate research carried out by others, as well as possessing the capacity and skills to engage in appropriate school-based enquiry.

1.1.3 Quality in Teacher Education in New Zealand

The then Minister of Education in 2010, Anne Tolley commissioned and released a discussion document after receiving an independent report on how to attract, train and retain high quality teachers entitled *A Vision for the Teaching Profession.*

The Education Workforce Advisory Group report noted that there are approximately 51,000 teachers in more than 2500 schools throughout New Zealand. The report argued:

> To ensure that the teaching profession can attract and retain high quality individuals, broad changes are needed in the way that the profession is perceived. Teachers cannot afford to be isolated practitioners working within a single classroom. If teaching is to be seen as a high status profession much greater emphasis is needed on continued learning by teachers within schools supported by clear and strong professional leadership and the sharing of effective practice across schools. (p. 2)

The report focused on teacher education and in particular initial teacher education (ITE); recognition, reward and progression of teachers within the profession; professional leadership; and diversity. An understanding of 'theories of teaching, learning and development and the skills necessary to operate effectively within teaching environments' was seen as a key determinant of raising the quality and status of the teaching profession. Professional leadership and leadership development were recognised as key to raising the quality of teaching.

The Advisory Group made several sets of recommendations for ITE including:

- moving towards initial teacher education being provided only at postgraduate level (so that entry into teaching is dependent on holding a postgraduate qualification)
- addressing the balance between the number of teachers being trained and the number of appropriate placements available for trainee and beginning teachers
- ensuring that trainee teachers are accepted into ITE programmes only after being assessed with a 'disposition to teach' through a formal selection process
- strengthening links between trainee and beginning teachers, and teacher education providers and schools, by altering the structure of ITE and provisional registration (Executive Summary, p. 4).

The report argued for increasing flexibility to support, recognise and reward teaching excellence and educational leadership as well as strengthening professional leadership across teaching by establishing compulsory training and development for aspiring and new principals. More controversially the report introduced a system of 'distributive leadership within schools' and sought to refocus the Teachers' Council in order to set clear entry requirements to the profession, develop continuing professional development and enhance the ethical accountability of teachers.

The report was soon followed by a Discussion Paper released in June 2010 that characterized the approach as follows:

The Advisory Group's vision for the teacher workforce is one where:

- high quality, capable people enter the profession
- the best and most capable become leaders in the profession
- ongoing professional learning and development supports effective teaching

- high levels of exibility for school leaders supports the growth and capability of teachers within their schools and profession to raise student achievement. (Education Workforce Advisory Group Report)

Secretary to the Treasury, Gabriel Makhlouf, waded into the debate on the quality of teacher writing for *Dominion Post* on 27 March 2012 making the following statement:

High quality teachers produce better-performing students who go into the workforce and make a significant contribution to economic growth. If we lift student achievement to match the top performing OECD countries, we could raise GDP by 3 to 15% by 2070.… So is the performance and value-for-money of taxpayer-funded services; education is the third largest area of government expenditure, and we need get the best results from this investment. Treasury's vision is higher living standards for New Zealanders. Education is a key economic lever. It's also a critical way to give disadvantaged children a better chance in life.

Reviewing international surveys of student achievement Makhlouf finds that the NZ's system does 'fair to good' but as he indicates far too many students are failing and NZ has more low-scoring students than other high-performing countries. He puts the argument very simply:

Education spending has increased by 20% for every pupil in the past 10 years, yet our performance by international comparisons remains stagnant. So what do we need to do? We need to invest in quality teaching.

Makhlouf also suggests that while class size matters the quality of teaching matters more. Even if the measurement of the quality of teaching is not straightforward there is 'pretty good understanding of the kinds of skills and competencies that characterise good teaching'. In this regard he makes some interesting claims on the basis of an OECD report:

We have variable teacher assessment, and poor linkages between assessments, professional and school development. There appears to be no formalised career path to support our good teachers to stay in the classroom.

At the same time he acknowledges, 'Different students respond to different teaching styles, and student achievement is influenced by factors beyond the school gate', and 'assessing the quality of teaching is not just about student test scores'.

Two research papers have been influential in the NZ context: 'Initial Teacher Education Outcomes: Standards for Graduating Teachers' (Aitken et al. 2013) and 'Learning to Practice' (Timperley 2013). Both were seen as attempts to guide and inform policy. The former proposed 'standards', or the graduate profile, that is expectations of graduate teachers on entry to the profession including: 'what they should be able to do, and the knowledge, competencies, dispositions, ethical principles, and commitment to social justice that they should possess'.

Both Aitken et al. (2013) and Timperley (2013) adopt an inquiry-oriented model for graduate teaching called the 'Teaching for Better Learning' model including standards structured around a series of inquiries 'designed to establish learning priorities and teaching strategies, examine the enactment of strategies and their impact, determine professional learning priorities, and critique the education system'.

The companion paper develops a notion of 'adaptive expertise' as the hallmark of a professional teacher. Timperley (2013) remarks:

> Much traditional teacher education literature has been based on models in which the teacher progresses from novice to routine expert (Dreyfus & Dreyfus, 1986), not adaptive expert. Although not mutually exclusive, routine and adaptive expert models represent fundamentally different views of what it means to be professional.

Routine expert models emphasis practice and procedural efficiency whereas adaptive expert models recognise great complexity in professional identity, school interactions and relationships, and in the teaching and learning that emerges in the co-construction of knowledge and joint identification of learning that reflects earlier work on teacher professional learning and development including best evidence synthesis. Timperley et al. (2007) identify a set of five principles: (1) Develop knowledge of practice by actively constructing conceptual frameworks; (2) Build formal theories of practice by engaging everyday theories; (3) Promote metacognition and self-regulated learning; (4) Integrate cognition, emotion, and motivation; (5) Situate learning in carefully constructed learning communities.

Timperley (2013) identifies and discusses the kinds of teacher education experiences that capture and endorse the vision of the inquiry-base model called 'Teaching for the Better' that is structured around six inquiry elements: deciding on learning priorities; deciding on teaching strategies; enacting teaching strategies; examining impact; deciding on and actioning professional learning priorities; critiquing the education system.   These inquiries are guided by a set of elements designed to strengthen the quality of inquiry and practice:

- *education's body of knowledge* about all learners, learning, society and culture, content, pedagogy, content pedagogy, curriculum and assessment and *knowledge* of *te reo me ona tikanga*
- cultural, intellectual, critical, relational and technical *competencies* and, in particular, the cultural competencies outlined in *Tātaiako*, namely: *wānanga, whanaungatanga, manaakitanga, tangata whenuatanga and ako*
- *dispositions* of open-mindedness, fallibility, discernment and agency
- *ethical principles* and commitment to learners, families/*whānau*, the profession and society
- commitment to *social justice* by challenging racism, inequity, deficit thinking, disparity and injustice (Fig. 1.2).

In 2013 the Ministry selected Universities of Auckland, Waikato and Otago as preferred providers of ITE for exemplary postgraduate programmes to start in 2014. These programmes are deemed to differ in approach from the clinical practice/practicum components of teaching providing a much more integrated and collaborative approach between the ITE provider and the school. This is a Ministry initiative to improve the expertise of graduating teachers and to strengthen their practice as part of the Government's Quality Teaching Agenda. A recent report of the New Zealand Council of Deans of Education (2016) has endorsed the model of adaptive expertise and maintained that universities should be accountable for

Fig. 1.2 Teaching for better learning model

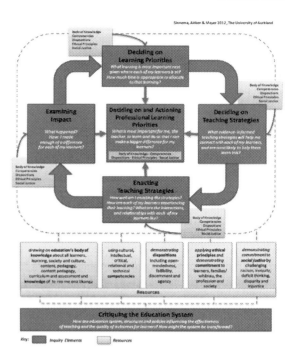

graduating teachers as well as 'close and continuous integration of practice and research' in programme design. The report also proposes that teaching should become a postgraduate profession managed through the support of different pathways into teaching.

1.1.4 Conclusion

Although the man focus of this discussion has been on initial teacher education (or what in England the policymakers insist in calling Initial Teacher Training), the ongoing professional learning and development of teachers as they progress through their careers is also a matter of considerable significance and is the focus for a significant number of contributions to this volume.

Teacher education and professional development have become something of a political battleground since the 1980s. In order to ensure that we continue to prepare teachers of the highest quality in all phases of schooling and college and across all curriculum areas it is crucial to take great care over the arrangements for professional preparation and training. There is a danger in politicians exerting their ideological prejudices, which may well be partly based on their own experiences of school, as a pupil. Rather, educationists should be examining the evidence to make judgements about the most appropriate forms of teacher preparation and indeed should be seeking to maximise the opportunities for all concerned to be engaged in professional development, not focusing entirely on the beginning teachers but thinking about staff at all levels both in the schools and the universities.

Elsewhere (Menter 2015) one of us has sought to identify 'enduring themes' in teacher education and these are certainly all relevant in the discussions that ensure in this book:

- The relationship between theory and practice
- The nature of professional knowledge
- The sites of professional learning
- The pedagogical contributions of the school and of the university
- Curriculum and assessment within teacher education
- The extended continuum of professional learning

In this introduction, we have referred to all of these in some way or other and you may find all of them, picked up elsewhere in this volume, in different ways and in different contexts.

And we would add to this list a concern with the relationships between research, policy and practice in teacher education. Ensuring that each informs the other is critical to the development of a healthy, constructive and productive approach to teacher education and it is here that we hope this volume can make a significant contribution.

1.1.5 The Structure of a Companion to Research in Teacher Education

As editors of this project we have been delighted at the range of contributions we have been able to gather together. They come from many parts of the world where teacher education is being researched and they cover a wide range of important topics. The studies reported also draw on a wonderful diversity of research methods.

We have grouped the submissions around some of the important themes in teacher education and have offered a brief introduction to each of the sect.

1. Becoming a Teacher: Teacher Education and Professionalism
2. Initial Teacher Education
3. Teacher Education, Partnerships and Collaboration
4. Global Education Reform and Teacher Education
5. Teacher Education as a public good
6. Research, institutional evaluation and evidence-based research
7. Pedagogy in action.

References

Aitken, G., Sinnema, C., & Meyer, F. (2013). *Initial teacher education outcomes: Standards for graduating teachers*. Wellington: Ministry of Education. http://www.educationcounts.govt.nz/publications/ECE/2511/initial-teacher-education-outcomes

Benton, P. (Ed.). (1980). *The Oxford internship scheme*. London: The Gulbenkian Foundation.

BERA-RSA. (2014a). *The role of research in teacher education. Reviewing the evidence. interim report of the BERA-RSA inquiry*. London: BERA. Retrieved from https://www.bera.ac.uk/wp-content/uploads/2014/02/BERA-RSA-Interim-Report.pdf

BERA-RSA. (2014b). *Research and the teaching profession. Building the capacity for a self-improving education system. Final report of the BERA-RSA Inquiry into the role of research in teacher education*. London: BERA. Retrieved from https://www.bera.ac.uk/wp-content/uploads/2013/12/BERA-RSA-Research-Teaching-Profession-FULL-REPORT-for-web.pdf

Burn, K., Hagger, H., & Mutton, T. (2015). *Beginning teachers' learning—Making experience count*. Northwich: Critical Publishing.

Burn, K., & Mutton, T. (2013). *Review of 'research-informed clinical practice' in initial teacher education. Research and teacher education: The BERA-RSA Inquiry*. Retrieved from https://www.bera.ac.uk/wp-content/uploads/2014/02/BERA-Paper-4-Research-informed-clinical-practice.pdf

Cochran-Smith, M., & Fries, K. (2008). Research on teacher education: Changing times, changing paradigms. In M. Cochran-Smith, S. Feiman-Nemser, D. McIntyre, & K. Demers (Eds.), *Handbook of research on teacher education: Enduring questions in changing contexts* (pp. 1050–1093). New York: Routledge.

Department for Education (DfE). (2010). *The importance of teaching. White paper*. London: DfE.

Donaldson, G. (2011). *Teaching Scotland's future: A report of the review of teacher education in Scotland*. Edinburgh: Scottish Government.

Fancourt, N., Edwards, A., & Menter, I. (2015). Reimagining a school—University partnership: The development of the Oxford education deanery narrative. *Education Inquiry, 6*(3), 353–373.

Hagger, H., & McIntyre, D. (2006). *Learning teaching from teachers: Realizing the potential of school-based teacher education*. Buckingham: Open University Press.

Hilds, A., McNicholl, J., & Edwards, A. (2014). Developing a multi-layered system of distributed expertise: What does cultural historical theory bring to understanding of workplace learning in school-university partnerships? In O. McNamara, J. Murray, & M. Jones (Eds.), *Workplace learning in teacher education: International practice and policy*. Dordrecht: Springer.

Hooley, N. (2013). Exposing the intricacies of pre-service teacher education: Incorporating the insights of Freire and Bourdieu. *Review of Education, 1*(2), 125–158.

Hoyle, E. (1974). Professionality, professionalism and control in teaching. *London Education Review, 3*(2), 13–19.

Hulme, M., & Menter, I. (2011). South and North—Teacher education policy in England and Scotland: A comparative textual analysis. *Scottish Educational Review, 43*(2), 70–90.

Menter, I. (2010). *Teachers: formation, training and identity (A literature review for Culture, Creativity and Education)*. Newcastle-upon-Tyne: CCE.

Menter, I. (2015). Teacher education. In J. D. Wright (editor-in-chief), *International encyclopedia of the social & behavioral sciences* (2nd ed., Vol. 24, pp. 51–55). Oxford: Elsevier.

Menter, I., Hulme, M., Elliot, D., & Lewin, J. (2010). *Literature review on teacher education in the 21st century*. Edinburgh: The Scottish Government.

Mutton, T., Burn, K., & Menter, I. (2016). Deconstructing the Carter review: Competing conceptions of quality in England's 'school-led' system of initial teacher education. *Journal of Education Policy* (in press).

New Zealand Council of Deans of Education. (2016). Summary recommendations on future directions for initial teacher education in New Zealand.

Ozga, J., & Jones, R. (2006). Travelling and embedded policy: The case of knowledge transfer. *Journal of Education Policy, 21*(1), 1–17.

Peters, M. A. (2001). Globalisation and the knowledge economy: Implications for education policy. *International Journal of Learning, 8*. The Learner Collection, ISBN 1863353720. Article: Electronic (PDF File; 141.325 KB), ISBN 1863353739. http://ijl.cgpublisher.com/product/pub.30/prod.307

Rizvi, F., & Lingard, B. (2010). *Globalizing education policy*. London: Routledge.

Sahlberg, P. (2011). *Finnish lessons: What can the world learn from educational change in Finland?*. New York: Teachers College Press.

Simons, M., Olssen, M., & Peters, M. A. (Eds.). (2009). *Re-reading education policies a handbook studying the policy agenda of the 21st century*. Rotterdam, The Netherlands: Sense.

Teacher Education Group. (2016). *Teacher education in times of change*. Bristol: Policy Press.

Timperley, H. (2013). *Learning to practice*. Wellington: Ministry of Education. http://www.educationcounts.govt.nz/publications/ECE/2511/learning-to-practise

Timperley, H., Wilson, A., Barrar, H., & Fung, I. (2007). Teacher professional learning and development: Best evidence synthesis iteration Wellington. New Zealand: Ministry of Education http://educationcounts.edcentre.govt.nz/goto/BES

Winch, C., Orchard, J., & Oancea, J. (2015). The contribution of educational research to teachers' professional learning—Philosophical understandings. *Oxford Review of Education, 41*(2), 202–216. doi:10.1080/03054985.2015.1017406

Author Biographies

Ian Menter is a Fellow of the Academy of Social Sciences in the UK and was President of the British Educational Research Association (BERA), 2013–15. He is Emeritus Professor of Teacher Education at the University of Oxford and was a member of the Steering Group of the BERA Inquiry into Research and Teacher Education (2014).

Michael A. Peters is Professor in the Wilf Malcolm Institute for Educational Research at Waikato University, Emeritus Professor at the University of Illinois at Urbana-Champaign. He is the executive editor of *Educational Philosophy and Theory* and has written over 75 books. He was made an Honorary Fellow of the Royal Society of New Zealand in 2010 and awarded honorary doctorates by State University of New York (SUNY) in 2012 and University of Aalborg in 2015.

Bronwen Cowie is Professor of Education and Director of the Wilf Malcolm Institute of Educational Research at the Faculty of Education: Te Kura Toi Tangata, The University of Waikato New Zealand. Her research interests span assessment for learning, science education, student voice, curriculum implementation and teacher education/ professional learning.

Part I
Becoming a Teacher: Teacher Education and Professionalism

Introduction

Teaching is no simple matter. It is hard work, part craft, part art, part technique, part politics, and it takes time to develop ease within such a complex role. However, for many of us the effort makes sense, for one gets the opportunity to see young people grow while one has a positive and caring role in their lives.

Kohl (1976), *On Teaching*, p. 13

What is a Teacher?

In the twenty-first century the meaning of 'teacher' internationally has settled around the notion of a person working within schools, with responsibility for the learning of young people. State education, as it has developed from the late eighteenth century onwards is now recognised as a crucial element in the development of societies and economies. This has led to the creation of a global occupational cadre of people sharing a common purpose, that of educating the young, being teachers.

Historically in the western world and more recently in 'underdeveloped' societies, the provision of formal education was much more limited in its availability, being the domain of those with the wealth and/or power to secure it. Even at that stage, the significance of education as a means of individual improvement was recognised and this of course continues to be the case to this day. But what happened during the late eighteenth century in the industrial world and more recently in the efforts to develop less 'advanced' societies, was that the social and economic advantages of education came to be acknowledged (not without serious struggle). Thus we saw the 'universalisation' or 'massification' of education. In many countries, parallel education systems still operate for the benefit of the social elite (e.g. the so-called 'public schools' in the United Kingdom) but in nations around the world we have seen the development of systems for preparing teachers to work in genuinely public schools and the bulk of what is discussed in this book is concerned with that provision.

As Kohl indicates above, the occupation of teaching is a complex and contested one, perhaps more now in the twenty-first century than ever before. In the early days of public schooling, the role of the teacher, often referred to as the schoolmaster or schoolmistress, was more straightforward. It was to provide a grounding in the basic skills of literacy and numeracy, provide some knowledge of the world (nature, science), some practical skills (handicrafts) and a strong sense of morality—often based in a particular religion. While elements of all of these responsibilities continue to exist in the work of the teacher, the subsequent development of several phases of schooling (from 'early years' through to tertiary provision) and the augmentation of the curriculum by a range of new subjects, some of which are quite specialised, has led to much greater specialisation and greater complexity in the roles and responsibilities of the public school teacher.

The Professionalisation of Teaching

Given this increasing complexity and diversity in the nature of teaching over the past century it is only to be expected that the ways in which teachers are prepared for their work have also developed over the same period. But this history has been far from straightforward. There have been very vociferous arguments over the years about the nature of teaching—as implied by Kohl, above. Is it an art, a craft, a science or even a 'calling'? Or what combination of these? Is the work of teachers a profession akin to medical or legal practice or is it perhaps a 'semi-profession', perhaps more aligned to social work or nursing? What are the moral or ethical responsibilities and obligations of teachers to their students and/or to the students' parents/carers? What is it that teachers need to know and be able to do? Should it be a requirement that teachers have a distinctive qualification before they are permitted to teach in the state sector?

It is questions such as these that have been debated and answered in many different ways over the past decades, with notable struggles between different interest groups, notably including teachers themselves, teacher educators, parents, politicians and sometimes the young people—the learners.

Early in the twentieth century during a period of trade unionisation of teachers, we saw both in England and elsewhere, struggles over the payment, terms and conditions of teachers, running in parallel to debates about the nature of the school curriculum. Over the twentieth century as a whole it can be argued that teaching was increasingly professionalised, in spite of the pressures from what Ozga and Lawn (1981) have called 'proletarianisation'.

In the late twentieth century, as global politics took an increasingly significant role in education policy and the significance of 'the knowledge economy' was identified, we have seen the increasing direct intervention of politicians into the previous professional arena of education—including the school curriculum—

described by one British Prime Minister as teachers' 'secret garden'. And if politicians have become increasingly interventionist in what should be taught and learned in schools (the curriculum), they have also become increasingly interventionist in the 'how' of teaching (the pedagogy). As many transnational reports including several from global consultancies have drawn attention to the proposition that the most significant determinant of educational outcomes is 'the quality of teaching' (Barber and Mourshed 2007; OECD 2005), so we have seen much more centralised control of many aspects of teacher preparation and development. As becomes clear in several chapters in this book (and not only in Part I) the policies around teaching quality have been very fraught and often characterised by deep contradictions and paradoxes.

Given the history of professionalisation of teaching, outlined above, one of the most glaring paradoxes, at least in some settings, has been the simple view of the nature of teaching asserted by a number of mainly right-wing politicians. Such views suggest that all that is required for effective teaching is good subject knowledge and a passion for the transmission of that subject knowledge to the next generation. These views therefore downplay the element of professional knowledge that teachers require in order to carry out their work successfully. On this view, the most effective form of teacher preparation is a simple modelling of existing teachers, an apprenticeship approach, implying indeed that teaching is simply a craft.

The Institutionalisation of Teacher Education

Views such as these have been in deep tension with the development of teaching as a profession. Widely accepted definitions of 'professionalism' often centre around the notion of a core of distinctive professional knowledge that is 'owned' by members of the profession concerned. In the case of teaching, that specialist professional knowledge would include not only knowledge of the subject being taught (although that is of course crucial), but also knowledge about teaching and learning generally (often described as general pedagogical knowledge). Furthermore, there is also what Shulman (1987) has helpfully called 'pedagogical content knowledge', which might be simply described as knowing how the content of a subject is best conveyed to learners. Additionally, there is a range of knowledge about the structures of the curriculum, the legal responsibilities of teachers and many other matters that might be called general professional knowledge.

Depending on where one stands in relation to these views of teaching and teachers, differing views are likely to follow about how those with an interest in becoming a teacher may best achieve that aim. However, in many countries what we saw during the twentieth century was a steady 'academisation' of teacher education. From its origins in 'pupil teachers' and the largely apprenticeship approaches of 'normal schools' (Dent 1977) for an account of the history in England), the study of education as a field or discipline and the growing amount of research in and on education, gradually led to an increasing role for higher education institutions in teacher education. Although this took many different forms in different settings, from specialist teacher education 'monotechnics', especially where the preparation of teachers for younger ages was concerned, through to provision within university departments of education ('UDEs'), especially for the preparation of subject specialists in the secondary school sector, preparation for teaching moved towards being a professional qualification associated with an academic qualification (see Furlong 2013, for a very through account of these developments in the UK). In the UK, by the late 1970s, entry into teaching was entirely through graduate routes—either a postgraduate qualification or a first degree—typically a BEd (Alexander et al. 1984).

However, this enhanced role for higher education was increasingly contested by people such as those alluded to earlier, who saw such an approach as overelaborate and (sometimes) expensive. In countries around the world, but most notably in England and in some parts of the USA, it was suggested that the place for teachers to learn how to teach was 'on the job', that is from other teachers—and that school-based teacher education or training was likely to be more effective. Proponents of this approach have not been able to offer any evidence that teachers prepared in this way are better prepared than those coming through a route that involves Higher education as well as school experience. However, proponents of the HE Partnership approaches have also found it difficult to sustain their case that this is a superior approach—hence the establishment in the UK of an inquiry into the relationship of research and teacher education (BERA-RSA 2014). The report from this inquiry does offer evidence that research and the contribution of Higher Education are key components of high-quality teacher education.

The other major trend in the recent development of institutionalised teacher education has been the introduction of 'standards', as a benchmark against which to judge teacher performance. Sometimes originally framed as teaching 'competences', statements about the knowledge, skills and dispositions (sometimes values) that beginning teachers are required to demonstrate have swept the world of teacher education with manifestations of some sort in the majority of nations around the world. The specifics of these standards do vary in some regards—even within the UK for example (see Kennedy 2016)—but they are all based on a view that if teaching quality is a matter of such importance, then it is crucial to have some explicit criteria by which to judge readiness for teaching. One effect of this 'standardisation' could be seen to be to reduce the autonomy of the actual provider of teacher education in making decisions about the aims and content of specific courses, but such has been the consensual view of the national significance of teaching that the universities and other providers have not resisted this incursion into their academic freedom to any great extent (see Ellis and McNicholl 2015, for an account of the 'proletarianisation' of teacher education in the UK).

Teachers' Careers

The ways in which beginning teachers join the profession indubitably have a sig-nificant influence on the construction of their professional identity. Much research over many years in many different contexts has examined the aspirations and self-identity of teachers and has explored how policy interventions have enhanced or undermined these identities. Early work tended to demonstrate that teachers felt the core of their identity was the pedagogical relationship with the learner (see Nias 1989 for example). Some of the policy developments associated with neoliberalism and the 'New Public Management' have undermined this relationship and replaced it variously with key relationships with school management and with the (national) curriculum. Teachers have increasingly found themselves cast as servants of the state rather than servants of the learner (Helsby 1999). From the view of a teacher as some kind of 'organic intellectual' that emerged from Huberman's classic study (Huberman 1993) we see a much more institutionalised pattern of career progres-sion for many twenty-first century teachers, as described by Day and Gu, some 20 years later (Day and Gu 2010).

The development of educational leadership as a major field of study and as a major area for professional development has also had some interesting effects on professional identity. In many countries we have seen opportunities appearing for the development of 'accomplished teaching' as a career stage that does not nec-essarily involve moving into school management. Designations such as chartered teacher, advanced skills teacher and (the rather tautologous!) master teacher have appeared in many national systems (and are addressed in one of the chapters in this section).

Teaching In/Teachers for the Twenty-First Century

By way of conclusion to this introduction to Part I, it is worth considering the current direction of travel in becoming a teacher. As we have already observed, teaching and teacher education continue to figure very prominently in political debate. The days of 'leaving it to the professionals' are certainly behind us, although the impact of this is far weaker in some contexts than in others.

However at a time of ecological threat and of continuing global inequality, it is possible to suggest that the moral responsibilities of teachers are greater now than ever before (Menter 2009). These teachers are working with the adult citizens of tomorrow who will have to live with the consequences of contemporary policies and of global phenomena such as climate change and insecurity.

How might the development of new technologies change the work of teachers? Can digital technology facilitate more effective teaching? Some have suggested that the very essence of teaching and of the teacher may change to such an extent that we will no longer recognise the teacher as a person working with a group of children in a classroom, but rather will see the teacher as a facilitator of 'blended learning' supporting young people gain access to digital resources through electronic networks, including a range of social media.

References

Alexander, R., Craft, M. & Lynch, J. (Eds.). (1984). *Change in teacher education—Context and provision since Robbins.* London: Holt, Rinehart and Winston.

Barber, M. & Mourshed, M. (2007). *The McKinsey report: How the world's best performing school systems come out on top.* London: McKinsey and co.

British Educational Research Association—Royal Society for the Arts (BERA-RSA). (2014). *Research and the teaching profession—Building the capacity for a self-improving education system.* London: BERA.

Day, C. & Gu, Q. (2010). *The new lives of teachers.* London: Routledge.

Dent, H. (1977). *The training of teachers in England and Wales 1800–1975.* London: Hodder and Stoughton.

Ellis, V. & McNicholl, J. (2015). *Transforming teacher education: Reconfiguring the academic work.* London: Bloomsbury.

Furlong, J. (2013). *Education—The anatomy of a discipline.* London: Routledge.

Helsby, G. (1999). *Changing teachers' work.* Buckingham: Open University.

Huberman, M. (1993). *The lives of teachers.* New York: Teachers' College.

Kennedy, A. (2016). Standards and accountability in teacher education. In Teacher Education Group, *Teacher education in times of change.* Bristol: Policy Press.

Kohl, H. (1976). *On teaching.* London: Methuen.

Menter, I. (2009). Teachers for the future: What have we got and what do we need? In S. Gewirtz, P. Mahony, I. Hextall & A. Cribb (Eds.), *Changing teacher professionalism: International trends, challenges and ways forward* (pp. 217–228). London: Routledge.

Nias, J. (1989). *Primary teachers talking.* London: Routledge.

OECD. (2005). *Teachers matter: Attracting, developing and retaining effective teachers.* Paris: OECD.

Ozga, J. & Lawn, M. (1981). *Teachers, professionalism and class: A study of organized teachers.* London: Falmer.

Shulman, L. (1987). Knowledge and teaching: Foundations of the new reform. *Harvard Educational Review, 57*(1), 1–22.

Chapter 2
Developing the Thoughtful Practitioner

Donald Gillies

2.1 Introduction

The concept of the 'reflective practitioner' has been prominent in educational discourse for some decades. Within initial teacher education, students are often encouraged to engage in 'reflection' but rarely is this theorised effectively or operationalised meaningfully. At times, 'reflective practice' reduces to an exercise in cursory self-evaluation. The theoretical work of Hannah Arendt (1906–75) on 'enlarged thought', however, offers opportunities for both clarifying the nature of professional reflection and for aiding the development of sound practice.

It is a truth, if not universally acknowledged then at least of widespread disciplinary concern, that the link between theory and practice in professional education remains as contested as it has ever been. The *longue durée* of teacher education could well be this clunky dispute about the extent to which theory does, or should, influence classroom practice. Yet, in one basic sense at least, this debate is inadequately grounded. Theory is silently present, however, much we imagine that we are free of it: it precedes, constricts and infuses our observation. And, of course, the very notion that theory has no useful place in the classroom is, itself, a theory—and one that is irreparably self-contradictory. Thus, we come always to our professional practice guided and informed by theory however unconscious, inchoate, or flimsy its omnipresence may be.

In this chapter, the work of Hannah Arendt, her thinking around the concept and exercise of judgement, is employed, without apology, as a means of illuminating what 'reflective practice' means in action and how it may be better developed. If theory is ever present in our professional lives, then it seems eminently reasonable to endeavour to seek out the most robust and persuasive examples to make sense of our work and to improve our practice.

D. Gillies (✉)
University of the West of Scotland, Ayr, Scotland, UK
e-mail: donald.gillies@uws.ac.uk

© Springer Nature Singapore Pte Ltd. 2017
M.A. Peters et al. (eds.), *A Companion to Research in Teacher Education*,
DOI 10.1007/978-981-10-4075-7_2

In addition to this defence of the place of theory in education, a further warrant for the particular approach—eclectic and selective—deployed in this chapter comes from the work of Hannah Arendt herself where she talks of the value of explorations into the past which seek to illuminate the present. Arendt uses the image of the pearldiver to illustrate this idea of seeking out something 'rich and strange' from the depths of published thought which may transform our current thinking—something lasting, 'immune to the elements' which can be recovered to assist pressing concerns (Arendt 1999, pp. 54–55). In what follows, only a small part of Arendt's work will be referred to and no attempt will be made to cover her work as a whole nor to argue that this is either typical or representative of her output. The key positional belief underpinning this approach, therefore, is that if we are unavoidably influenced by theory, then we should employ those that are of value, which have been tried and tested by deep human thought and informed action. Arendt's work on judgement is claimed in this chapter to be such a treasure.

2.2   The Reflective Practitioner

The concept of the reflective practitioner is one that is very prevalent within teacher education and within the profession itself. It re-emerged most powerfully in recent decades through the highly influential work of Schön (1983), but from there its roots can be traced back to Dewey (1916). More recently, influenced by Schön's attack on technical rationalism, others have turned to Aristotle's concept of *phronesis*—practical wisdom—as a source of inspiration on the topic.

Its prevalence cannot be doubted. In 2014, Google Analytics show that about 33,100 research outputs dealing with reflection and teaching were published, equivalent to around 22% of all teacher-related research. Some 1560 articles on *phronesis* and teaching were published that year, and around 1660 which addressed both reflection and *phronesis*. Such data do suggest that the topic is of widespread interest and importance and, given the scale of the interest, an issue which remains live and contested rather than settled and agreed.

When Zeichner (1994) first critiqued the concept, he argued, amongst other things, that it was a 'slogan' which had been embraced worldwide and that 'everyone, no matter what his or her ideological orientation, has jumped on the bandwagon' (pp. 9–10). Given that in 1994 only 107 of the 114,000 research outputs on teachers that year referred to the concept of the 'reflective practitioner', one can state that current publication statistics suggest any 'bandwagon' that existed 20 years ago is miniscule in comparison to what is evident now.

This chapter is also positioned from a critical standpoint by questioning what is understood by reflection and questioning the capacity of beginning teachers, in particular, to reflect effectually on their practice without there being a context established within which it is to be conducted, and a knowledge base, a range of reflective resources, available to assist such activity. The danger is that we replicate what is happening currently in social media and elsewhere, where opinion, neither considered nor informed, is expressed boldly and authoritatively. Thus, the risk is of beginning teachers, pre-service teachers, being encouraged to pass judgement on their practice without sufficient care being taken to ensure that such judgements are soundly based. In addition, reflection without wider reference-points risks becoming 'ritualistic' (Moore 2004, p. 105), 'pseudo-reflection' (p. 109), solipsistic navel-gazing, or an exercise in narcissistic self-affirmation. If reflection is to be purposive, then it needs to be set up in such a way as to allow chosen ends to be realised. The literature base would seem to suggest that the main aim of teacher reflection, either implied or expressed, is that of improved practice, howsoever understood. In that sense, therefore, there is a professional imperative to see that such activity is set up in a way that would enable such an outcome to follow. This chapter suggests that the work of Hannah Arendt, drawing on her Kantian affinities, offers some suggestions about ways in which teacher professional reflection could be undertaken in a more robust and coherent manner.

2.3 Reflection

Although the work of Schön (1983) only deals fleetingly with teaching, it is considered to be the source of the current fascination in the concept of the reflective practitioner within educational literature. Schön's critical focus was what he labelled 'technical rationality', an essentially positivist stance, which judged that professions, including teaching, required robust improvement through 'instrumental problem solving made rigorous by the application of scientific theory and technique' (p. 15). This approach suggested that the teacher, for example, simply required to learn a series of actions which could be applied in given situations to achieve desired results. Schön claimed that this not only reduced the professional to the role of a skilled worker or functionary but also failed to acknowledge and take into account the nature of the context within which teachers work. Schön argued that the professional context could not provide the invariable site for a scientist approach because, firstly, the pace of technological change was such that it required of professionals 'adaptability that is unprecedented' (p. 15), and, secondly, that it was marked by 'uncertainty, complexity, instability, uniqueness and value conflict' (pp 16–17)

Schön set out to show how professionals worked in reality and analysed various aspects of reflection which were identified by him as being central to their practice. Schön's work on reflection-in-action showed how professionals constantly reviewed the situations that they found themselves in and considered their choices of action in the light of these evolving understandings. This underpinning of the key role of professional judgement, founded on a form of continuous action research, clearly struck a nerve and over the decades since, the importance of reflection in teacher education has never waned, as the volume of journal articles and books cited above would indicate.

Although Schön never referred to the work of Dewey, nor, indeed, to Aristotle, his concept of the reflective practitioner can be seen to resonate with the work of these two. For Dewey, thinking was the key ingredient which turned mere activity into experience, and thus something from which teachers could learn. Dewey's concept of thinking in teaching (1916) is focused on how the teacher thinks through potential actions by replaying and anticipating the causal connections evident in any given situation, the key factors and the potential effects. Dewey argues that it is this applied thought, grounded in professional knowledge, which avoids the haphazard risk of trial and error. The opposites to 'thoughtful action' are caprice and routine (p. 74) where the teacher engages in activity either merely through habit or without thinking through issues of purpose and effectual means. 'Thought', Dewey argues, is 'the sole method of escape from purely impulsive or purely routine action' (2012, p. 14). 'Reflective thought' aims at 'reasoned conclusions' (p. 5) and consists of 'active, persistent and careful consideration of any belief or supposed form of knowledge in the light of the grounds that support it, and the further conclusions to which it tends' (Dewey 2012, p. 6).

In recent times, researchers, as has been noted, have returned to the work of Aristotle and his concept of *phronesis* as a way of further understanding professional practice. *Phronesis*—practical wisdom—combines both the selection of virtuous goals and the means to achieving them. Thus, it elevates the teacher from merely being concerned with the instrumentality typified in technical rationality and, instead, stresses how practical wisdom is about the selection of virtuous ends, or goals, as well as the choice of effective means to their realisation. It is in Aristotle's distinction of *phronesis* from scientific knowledge (*episteme*) and craft knowledge or skill (*techne*) that further value is seen in his work. *Techne*, which is art or skill, can be seen to be typical of the technical rationalist approach to teaching which Schön rejected.

The work of Brookfield (1995) stresses the element of criticality in reflective practice, highlighting the importance of reflection going beyond the immediate classroom experience to consider wider issues about systemic goals, policy context, power relations and governance arrangements. Drawing on the critical theory tradition, it sees reflective action as positioned in an emancipatory role.

2.4   Perceived Strengths and Weaknesses of Reflective Practice as Concept

The perceived strengths of reflective practice as concept within teacher professionalism can be summarised as having five main elements: it places 'thoughtful action' at the heart of teaching and so elevates the notion and importance of professional judgement; it provides the basis for rejecting the claims of technical rationalism and its twin risks of limiting teachers to a functional role and misrepresenting the contexts of teaching as invariable and so susceptible to a scientist model; it reasserts the moral aspect of teaching in relation to the choice of virtuous ends and means; it enhances, and entrenches, the professionalism of teaching by seeing it as not something for which one can be merely 'trained' but rather as a practice where nuanced judgement is required on a daily basis; and, finally, it lends itself well to the current model of continuing professional learning, where reflection is seen as a crucial ingredient, from the novice to the expert levels, from the unpromoted to the most senior rank.

From the very beginning, a number of critics took issue with the way in which reflective practice came to assume such a central role within teacher education. Zeichner (1994), an early and repeated critic, argues that is used in an imprecise and fuzzy manner, and so it is unclear on what exactly the practitioner should be reflecting; it is unclear which tools and processes should be deployed in this reflection; and, it is similarly unclear as to the purpose of the reflective activity. Further critics observed that reflection which was limited to thinking was quite a different exercise from that which was focused on action. It is possible to reflect on practice, and even come to an evaluation of it, without that being further utilised to affect future action. They also show how the use of different time-frames can create quite different models so that reflection-in-action can lead to ad hoc, instant changes in practice whereas other forms of reflection may gestate for some time before any resultant action is appropriate or envisaged. As with Brookfield (1995), they also point out how different levels of criticality can affect the range of issues considered in the reflection and so produce radically different responses.

Without clarity on the nature and aims of reflection, therefore, it is hard to see how beginning professionals can engage in it in any systematic and purposive manner. The concepts of single-loop and double-loop learning can be used to illustrate how one form of reflection may involve consideration of the means or methods employed to reach a planned goal (single-loop), whereas a second form of reflection will call into question not just the methods but the very goals themselves (double-loop). This distinction serves to stress just how diverse the possible approaches to professional reflection are, from that which leads to some minor adjustment and tinkering to reflection which can lead to radical transformation.

A further criticism is founded on the lack of clarity about the practice so that at times, and especially with early professionals, it can seem to involve merely a superficial exercise in self-evaluation, which Moore (2004) terms pseudo-reflection: often self-congratulatory without an obvious evidence-base.

2.5 Hannah Arendt

In addressing the concept of reflective practice, particularly in relation to beginning teachers, this chapter will deploy some of the ideas of Hannah Arendt, as has been indicated, to illuminate what is involved in professional reflection, and to suggest how the exercise of judgement, central to reflective practice, can be developed.

Hannah Arendt was born into a secular Jewish family in Hanover, Germany in 1906. She studied philosophy at the University of Marburg under Martin Heidegger, with whom she formed a passionate, if brief, relationship. She moved later to the University of Heidelberg where she completed her doctorate in 1928 under the supervision of Karl Jaspers. Following the rise of the Nazi party in 1933, she fled Germany and finally settled in America in 1941, gaining citizenship some ten years later. She taught at a number of universities in the USA, latterly at the New School of Social Research in New York City. Despite the importance to her work of the world of classical philosophy, she declined the designation 'philosopher' herself, apparently preferring to be described as a 'political theorist' (Strong 2012, p. 328). Amongst her published works are *The Origins of Totalitarianism*, *The Human Condition*, and *Eichmann in Jerusalem*. Her final, unfinished work—*The Life of the Mind*—returned to the Kantian focus on thought, the will, and judgement. Devoted to caffeine and nicotine throughout her adult life, she suffered heart trouble in her latter years and died in 1975, aged 69.

Her work is marked by clarity of thought, and conceptual rigour, but also by a commitment to addressing genuine political and moral issues in their social reality, in actual human experience rather than as theoretical abstractions. Her work is disparate but could be seen to have a central attachment to maintaining a notion of humanity and democratic co-existence within a world tormented by totalitarian excess and post-modern uncertainty. She thus probes how communal existence—political life—can survive in a world where we have lost the 'yardsticks' and 'rules' which once guided us (Arendt 1994, p. 321).

2.6   Kant, Arendt and Judgement

Arendt draws her work on judgement—the key ingredient of reflective practice—from the work of Immanuel Kant, one of whose three great works was devoted to the topic: *A Critique of Judgement* (1790). What Arendt's work does is to suggest a way of understanding judgement that both gives it strength and avoids the risk of subjective whim. In other words, for teacher reflection to overcome the risks identified above that teacher reflection is shallow or narrow or lightweight, Arendt's analysis of judgement offers a way forward, a means by which judgement can be developed and better enacted.

Arendt touches on the nature of judgement in a number of her published works, often in the context of the 'crisis' of late modernity, as she sees it, where there is a struggle amongst humans to find common ground, to achieve agreement, in a world where the old fundamentals of religion and society have gone. Without the shared orthodox beliefs of the past, humans struggle to find anything permanent and fixed upon which to rely: she terms this development as necessitating 'thinking without a banister' (Strong 2012, p. 334), where one has nothing external to rely on but where humans need to work together instead to achieve common understanding and mutual recognition in a world without fixed truths. Arendt sees in Kant's work on judgement the potential for establishing stronger foundations for our thinking and beliefs, a means of progressing beyond the despair of judgemental relativism or the abandonment of any hopes of rapprochement or overlapping consensus. It is in her lectures on Kant's political philosophy (Arendt 1992) that she devotes most attention to the issue of judgement but it also arises in a number of her other works on philosophy and politics. In outlining Arendt's treatment of judgement, some of Kant's ideas are subsumed within but it is easier to deal with the issue in this singular, interpreted form rather than to have to alternate repeatedly between the two theorists.

In the *Critique of Judgement*, Kant outlines two mental operations in judgement. The first is operation of imagination so that we can represent in our minds an object or experience even although it is no longer present with us. The second part of judgement is identified as 'the operation of reflection' (Arendt 1992, p. 68). This establishes very clearly, therefore, how pertinent and relevant is this discussion of judgement to the concept of the 'reflective practitioner'. In approving or disapproving that which is brought into the mind's eye through the process of imagination, one is no longer directly finding the object or experience pleasing, but rather one is judging it to be, or to have been, pleasing or not. In a somewhat difficult argument (p. 69) Arendt claims that the act of approbation creates pleasure in the one judging and that we judge between approval or disapproval on the 'criterion of communicability or publicness'. The criterion for approval or disapproval is said, therefore, to be communicability 'and the standard for deciding about it is common sense' (p. 69). This term has a particular meaning for Kant and is central to his discussion of judgement. The expression of judgement is dependent upon a community of humans that one has confidence share the same faculty of judgement. One appeals to 'common sense' when one makes a judgement 'and it is this possible appeal that gives judgements their special validity'. We feel that our judgements are valid if they attract community agreement—'common sense'. The insane may be quite capable of communication: it is the fact that their expressed judgements are alien to common sense, that they do not square with those of others, that is a significant criterion for suspecting them to be mad, or at least strange or eccentric.

In coming to make, and communicate, a judgement, therefore, one considers its likely worth in relation to an appreciation of its expected reception: our anticipation of what 'common sense' would suggest. It is from this phenomenon that Kant develops his concept of 'enlarged mentality' which he explains as the capacity to put oneself in others' standpoints and compare one's judgement with what one imagines would be theirs. The faculty of judgement, therefore, takes account of 'the collective reason of humanity', as envisaged (p. 71). Persons of 'enlarged thought' are capable of overcoming their own biased or partial judgements by disregarding 'the subjective private conditions' of their own judgements (p. 71) and, instead, by reflecting on the issue from the perspective of others, and so establishing a *general* standpoint from which to judge.

It is this concept of the 'enlarged mentality' which especially appeals to Arendt. Her related idea of 'enlarged thought' is used by her in a number of her works and needs also to be understood for one to make sense of her claim that at the root of Eichmann's crime is 'thoughtlessness', a failure to reflect *thought-fully* on action and a failure to either develop or make use of an 'enlarged mentality'. Arendt deviates in an important way from Kant in her conceptualisation of 'enlarged thought'. In a sense, it can be considered as more a political than a moral judgement. For Kant, the person of 'enlarged mentality' attempts to stand in the place of all others when making a judgement; the person of 'enlarged mentality' adopts 'the standpoint of the world citizen' (Arendt 1992, p. 44). Arendt does not subscribe to this 'universal' position but rather prefers the 'general'. By this is meant, that while Kant sees sound judgement and enlarged mentality as seeking validity for 'every single judging person', Arendt instead narrows this to those who judge, in other words, to those who have an interest in the particular instance of judgement (Strong 2012, p. 344). Arendt thus lays stress on intersubjective validity to counter subjective vagaries but without any claim to Kantian certainty.

Representative thinking is the key to enlarged thought. It involves the capacity to bring to one's mind the potential perspectives of all who would have a claim to be judges in the specific instance.

> Political thought is representative. I form an opinion by considering a given issue from different viewpoints, by making present to my mind the standpoints of those who are absent; that it, I represent them ... The more people's standpoints I have present in my mind while I am pondering a given issue, and the better I can imagine how I would feel and think if I were in their place, the stronger will be my capacity for representative thinking and the more valid my final conclusions, my opinion. (Arendt 2006, p. 237)

Thus, Arendt moves forward in this world without banisters on the basis that, in a world lacking objective moral standards, we need not be at the mercy of subjective whim but rather have the potential to use Kant's insights on taste and judgement to create moral boundaries based on communication, intersubjectivity and shared judgement.

Arendt makes two further key points on the implications of the centrality of enlarged thought in coming to sound judgement. She uses two related but distinct metaphors to convey how enlarged thought can be developed. The first of these is the concept of 'visiting': 'To think with an enlarged mentality means that one trains one's imagination to go visiting' (Arendt 1992, p. 43). Thus, the development of enlarged thought is achieved through its very practice: by visiting the viewpoints of others one increases one's capacity for enlarged thought and representative thinking. Arendt, however, adds a second metaphor by which to add a qualitative element to this 'visiting'. Indiscriminate 'visiting' may not assist our goal of sound judgement unless those whom we visit comprise 'good company'. The cultivated person, the person of sound judgement, Arendt asserts will be the one 'who knows how to choose his [sic] company among men, among things, among thoughts, in the present as well as in the past' (Arendt 2006, p. 222). It is those whose thinking we visit who must be good company themselves if our judgements are to be sound, either morally or politically: '...our decisions about right and wrong will depend upon our choice of company, of those with whom we wish to spend our lives. And again, this company is chosen by thinking in examples, in examples of persons dead or alive, real or fictitious, and in examples of incidents, past or present' (Arendt 2003, pp. 145–6).

Arendt, therefore, drawing on Kant's concepts of taste and judgement, presents the possibility of circumstances where judgement, by reaching out to the plural, by anticipating and weighing up relevant potential perspectives, has the capacity to reach a form of intersubjective validity, rooted in the notion of common sense.

2.7 Implications for Reflective Practice

This brief excursion into Arendtian thought can be brought to bear on the problematic aspects of reflective practice as outlined earlier. The basic principle underlying a putative Arendtian viewpoint on reflective practice would be that the possibility of such reflection being soundly based and of its having the potential for improving practice depend upon the extent to which it is rooted in a broad spectrum of relevant perspectives and of having been subject to this form of communal consideration, which in turn gives rise to a form of intersubjective validity.

Smith (2001) argues persuasively that the implications of this for (initial teacher) education are twofold. The first consequence is that learners need to be exposed to a wide, and growing, spectrum of potential viewpoints and perspectives. Smith, in dealing with school education per se, suggests that this means—as has been the case generally in schools, even if not explicitly so labelled—that students are introduced, through literature, and through the study of history and the humanities in general, to different people, to different outlooks, to different cultural, social and moral values. The role of education involves this introduction to human plurality in all its forms. An Arendtian outlook would suggest that this should be pursued strenuously so that the capacity for representative thought, of being able to anticipate and reflect upon what a wide range of others would think in a given situation, is extended and maximised.

If applied to teacher education, then one can suggest that the capacity for improved reflective practice will be increased through the exposure of beginning teachers to as wide a range as possible of relevant voices and views on education and schooling. The more relevant perspectives that the beginning teacher can bring to bear on their own practice, then the greater the prospect for that reflection to be soundly based and to be effectual in relation to desired improvement.

The second implication for education of Arendt's concept of judgement (Smith 2001, p. 86) is that learners, in addition to developing the capacity for enlarged thought, need to have opportunities to exercise related judgement. As learners develop the capacity for representative thinking, so they need opportunities to practise making judgements. As with all sound pedagogical practice, this needs to be enacted in a graduated way, so that the scenarios in which judgement is exercised develop from the basic and relatively inconsequential to the more complex and more significant. After all, the purpose of enlarged thought is to enhance the capacity for exercising sound judgement and so the two, it would appear, ought to be developed in tandem. Exercising judgement would develop, one would expect, from activity which is more concrete, more explicit and more staged, to that which becomes increasingly implicit, 'natural' and embedded. As with all such activity, expertise at the highest level seems more effortless and spontaneous, but this impression belies all that has gone before in terms of development and activity.

If applied to teacher education, then one would expect to see beginning teachers having the opportunity to exercise judgement, and to share and discuss such decisions, on a regular basis, again starting from more simple and inconsequential issues before progressing to the more complicated and weighty. It is perfectly feasible for these opportunities for practice to be undertaken in relation to hypothetical situations which still require the professional to consider the reported facts of the matter, contemplate different potential perspectives and viewpoints, and then make a judgement. In some ways, this sort of activity is of double benefit as the debate and discussion with peers thereafter also contributes to the growth of representative thinking, and so to enlarged thought.

It is important to stress that all of this, for Arendt, is assumed to be conducted in a world 'without banisters'. There is no secret truth about professional practice to be unearthed, no immutable laws of practice to be discovered. Instead, our judgement is not just required in terms of reflection on practice, but even in terms of the viewpoints and perspectives which we choose to deploy in our internal consideration prior to a judgement being made. There is an inherent paradox within this concept of professional judgement in that to make sound judgement, the chances are improved through considering as wide a range of perspectives and potential viewpoints as possible and, yet, judgement is also required in terms of selecting those perspectives which are deemed to be relevant and valued in the first place. As Arendt says, our decisions depend upon 'our choice of company' (2003, p. 145–6)—in other words on the viewpoints which we select as being important and helpful.

Thus, one could add to the position of Smith (2001) that part of developing sound judgement is not just developing enlarged thought, through encounters with myriad outlooks and viewpoints, nor having opportunities to practise making judgements, but also the development of a set of values and professional principles which would enable one to sift through these viewpoints and decide which to choose to be influential and on what basis. As Arendt indicates, at bottom this is a matter of choice: from all the 'visiting' we do, we have to choose the 'company' we wish to keep, those to whom we will elect to refer when judgements have to be made.

2.8   A Developmental Approach to Teacher Reflective Judgement

This study has been conceptual and nothing yet has been said, or claimed, about current professional practice itself: what teachers actually do when reflecting on practice and how they come to the decisions they make and the corrective actions which result. Nevertheless, even in the absence of such data, in applying Arendt's views on judgement to teacher professional practice, one can make some tentative suggestions about how this might operate in relation to initial teacher education.

The first issue, as was recognised above, is that beginning teachers need to be encouraged to develop a moral stance in relation to their professional responsibilities. It is this overall moral outlook which will be key to selecting the 'company' they will frequent when reflecting on practice and when making related judgements. One would expect these to reflect democratic values suited to the social and political context within which schooling is undertaken, and to have been encouraged already through previous educational experiences prior to entering the teaching profession.

Of more direct significance to the issue of reflective practice, however, the development of enlarged thought would involve exposure to, and increasing familiarity with, a range of relevant viewpoints and perspectives. To be enabled to make sound judgements about their work, beginning teachers would need to bring into professional consideration outlooks drawn from three broad categories: self; others; and literature. In relation to self, reflective practice would involve consideration of prior experience, values, principles, and how they relate to the situation in question. Drawing on the thinking of others would be that of such relevant persons as peers, professional colleagues, tutors, pupils, parents, other stakeholders. In terms of literature, what would be considered is evidence from relevant research, relevant educational theory, policy of various forms, insights from philosophy, psychology, sociology, history and pedagogy. In addition, personal reading of all forms could be relevant and applicable. As the professional develops, more and more of these insights become part of the practitioner's enlarged thought and so the need to seek out external sources to bolster reflection would recede as more of this professional knowledge and expertise is assimilated and internalised. For the beginning teacher, however, the need to go visiting for such insights is more pressing and a teacher education programme endeavouring to apply Arendtian principles would need to be explicit about how this was to be practised, and developed in a graduated manner.

Thus, for the beginning teacher, going visiting could involve the following:
Self

Personal experience—*drawing on situations and circumstances already encountered which provide insight to the matter in question; drawing on relationships, advice, memory,*

Personal reading—*applying insights from one's own reading—personal, pleasure, academic, journalistic, professional, practical to instances from practice;*

Principles and values—*considering how these personal views position the situation in question; reflecting if these are helpful or require refinement;*

Others

Peers—*eliciting the opinion of others in a similar situation, either generally or as observers of own practice;*

Partners—*seeking views from others involved in one's context—support staff, parents, external and internal stakeholders;*

Pupils—*eliciting the views of those taught, of those for whose ultimate benefit teachers are employed;*

Professionals—*eliciting and drawing from tutors, from the views of the wider profession, from written and spoken data, and from wider relevant professional standpoints.*

Literature

Publications—*applying evidence from research studies of various forms and from various contexts such as philosophy, psychology, sociology, politics, and history; applying theory and research evidence from such;*

Pedagogy—*considering and applying to context, learning theory and debate on teaching methods;*

Policy—*drawing from policy and guidelines relevant data, and subjecting it to critique, where appropriate;*

Such a list is by no means exhaustive but indicates the complexity, indeed, of teacher professional practice and, given the extent of potential perspectives, the need for beginning teachers to be introduced gradually and systematically into such reflective practice. The beginning teacher would need to be encouraged to articulate in specific detail the sources which were deemed to be relevant, the ideas being drawn on, and why, when reflecting on a particular professional issue or experience. At the earliest stages, this might involve a very few factors. Over time, that range would be extended as they became more familiar with different thinkers, different research evidence and with wider social and cultural viewpoints. As more of this breadth of thought is assimilated so there reduces the need to be explicit and detailed in citing the sources being deployed. As Schön suggests, the experienced professional reflects-in-action, drawing almost unconsciously on this body of knowledge; it becomes part of their daily, hourly, professional practice.

However, what an Arendtian perspective also indicates is that this introduction to sound professional judgement is also an introduction to the very leadership practice so valorised in current policy. If leadership is a combination of vision and influence, then it is through the development of sound professional judgement that the capacity for 'vision' is also developed—the ability to identify and select sound educational goals. Thus, the encouragement of a systematic approach to professional reflection ought also to sow the seeds for increased leadership capacity—not in the generic skills of influencing and motivating, but in the far more important and crucial area of developing sound professional judgement in relation to the problems and puzzles of professional life and the contested world of educational values, aims and ultimate goals.

References

Arendt, H. (1992). *Lectures on Kant's political philosophy*. Chicago: University of Chicago Press.

Arendt, H. (1994). *Essays in understanding*. New York: Random House.

Arendt, H. (1999). Walter Benjamin 1892–1940. In W. Benjamin (Ed.), *Illuminations* (pp. 7–55). London: Pimlico.

Arendt, H. (2003). *Responsibility and judgment*. New York: Random House.

Arendt, H. (2006). *Between past and future*. New York: Penguin.

Brookfield, S. (1995). *Becoming a critically reflective teacher*. San Francisco: Jossey-Bass.

Dewey, J. (1916). *Democracy and education*. New York: Macmillan.

Dewey, J. (2012 {1910}). *How we think*. Mansfield Centre CT: Martino Publishing.

Kant, I. (2007 {1790}). *Critique of judgement*. New York: Oxford University Press.

Moore, A. (2004). *The good teacher*. Abingdon: Routledge.

Schön, D. (1983). *The reflective practitioner*. USA: Basic Books.

Smith, S. (2001). Education for judgement: An Arendtian paradox? In M. Gordon (Ed.), *Hannah arendt and education* (pp. 67–92). Boulder, CO: Westview Press.

Strong, T. (2012). *Politics without vision*. Chicago: University of Chicago Press.

Zeichner, K. M. (1994). Research on teacher thinking and different views of reflective practice in teaching and teacher education. In I. Carlgren, G. Handal, & S. Vaage (Eds.), *Teachers' minds and actions: Research on teachers' thinking and practice* (pp. 9–28). Bristol, PA: Falmer Press.

Author Biography

Donald Gillies has been Dean of the School of Education at the University of the West of Scotland since 2014. From 2012–14 he was Professor of Education Policy at York St John University. He is compiler of *A Brief Critical Dictionary of Education*, a free online resource for students www.dictionaryofeducation.co.uk.

Chapter 3
Variations in the Conditions for Teachers' Professional Learning and Development: Teacher Development, Retention and Renewal over a Career

Qing Gu

3.1 Introduction

Every student in every school in every country of the world has an entitlement not only to the provision of educational opportunities but also to be taught by teachers who, as well as being knowledgeable about curriculum and pedagogically adept, are constant and persistent in their commitment to encouraging their students to learn and achieve; and who are themselves demonstrably passionate about their own learning. In one sense, these are self-evident truths about the core task of every teacher to engage students in learning which will assist them in their personal, social and intellectual development. In another sense, however, the ambitions which are embedded in these truths will not always be easy to achieve consistently over a 30-year career span.

Teachers' work is carried out in an era of testing times where the policy focus in many countries has shifted from provision and process to outcomes. The OECD's Programme for International Student Assessment (PISA), for example, is having an unprecedented influence on national policies for improvement and standards across many nation states. The rapidly growing international interest in 'surpassing Shanghai' and outperforming the world's leading systems (Tucker 2011) has contributed to intensify further national and international emphases upon standards, performativity and accountability. For many schools in many countries, this means that their educational values and practices, particularly in relation to the progress and achievement of their students, are now under increased public scrutiny. At the same time, widespread movement of population in many countries has seen the

---

This paper is drawn from Day and Gu (2014) and Day and Gu (2010).

Q. Gu (✉)
University of Nottingham, Nottingham, England, UK
e-mail: qing.gu@nottingham.ac.uk

© Springer Nature Singapore Pte Ltd. 2017   37
M.A. Peters et al. (eds.), *A Companion to Research in Teacher Education*,
DOI 10.1007/978-981-10-4075-7_3

makeup of the local communities which schools serve become more diversified (OECD 2010). Couplled with this change in student populations are the broader, more explicitly articulated social and societal responsibilities that schools are expected to have in supporting their communities, other schools and other public services (OECD 2008). In many countries, also, schools are expected to manage a concurrent movement towards the decentralisation of financial management and quality control functions to schools (OECD 2008, 2010). Thus, to be successful in these testing times, teachers and their schools need to be forward thinking, outward looking, optimistic, hopeful and above all, resilient.

This chapter will examine what it is that enables teachers to sustain the quality of their passion and commitment through good times and bad and what might prevent them from doing so over the course of their professional lives. Evidence shows that teachers do not necessarily learn through experience, that expertise is not acquired in an even, incremental way and that they are at greater risk of being less effective in later phases of their professional lives. Variations in professional, personal and workplace conditions in different professional life phases affect these. Moreover, the contexts for teacher' professional learning and development are, by definition, different from those who do not work in human service organisations, since teachers are essentially engaged in work which has fundamental moral and ethical as well as instrumental purposes. Their capacity to exercise these effectively relates to their ability to manage positive and negative 'scenarios' in different professional life phases. It suggests, therefore, that to be effective, professional learning opportunities must be designed which take account of the personal, workplace and external scenarios which challenge their commitment to these core purposes.

3.2   Variations in the Conditions for Teachers' Professional Learning

Previous studies on teachers' professional learning and development tend to focus on one particular aspect of learning and development, such as teacher knowledge construction (Shulman 1987) or the development of teacher identity through participation in a learning community (Lave and Wenger 1991), and thus they have failed to address the complexity of the conditions in which teachers' professional learning and development take place which enhances their commitment and effectiveness.

The VITAE research (Day et al. 2007) investigated teachers' work, lives and effectiveness from a holistic perspective. This holistic perspective provided richer insights into the complex and dynamic nature of the conditions for teachers' learning and development throughout their professional lives than previous research. The research revealed the tensions for professional learning and development caused by workplace conditions and interactions between these and personal and professional scenarios experienced by teachers in different professional life phases. It found that while CPD (continuing professional development) is a necessary and important component of professional learning, it is likely to be less effective in all its forms if the professional life phase scenarios which teachers experience and which influence their attitudes to and motivation for learning are predominantly negative. In other words, the success of professional development (planned interventions in teachers' learning lives) is dependent upon the opportunities for professional learning (unplanned, unrewarded and often implicit) which occur in their everyday context.

3.3 Professional Life Phases: Characteristics and Trajectories

There are different ways to analyse and define the characteristics of teachers' work and lives. We found distinctive phases over the course of teachers' professional lives where groups of teachers demonstrated similar professional needs and concerns and characteristics of professional identities. These concerns and characteristics were shown to be associated with their length of service in the profession, rather than chronological age. They revealed not only different levels of psychological, spiritual and emotional strength in the inner landscape of their professional selves (Palmer 2007), but also the influence of their ability to manage (or not manage) successfully the complex internal and external influences which threatened to impact negatively on their commitment, resilience and capacity to teach to their best.

'Professional life phase' refers to the number of years that a teacher has been teaching, rather than age or responsibilities. Teachers are likely to experience different challenges in different professional life phases and the ways in which they— and their leaders—are able to manage these are likely to affect their job satisfaction and fulfilment. We know from a range of research, for example, that teachers may lose heart over time as a result of: (i) tensions in relations with pupils and parents; (ii) excessive externally imposed initiatives and reforms; (iii) increases in bureaucracy; and (iv) negative images of teaching in the media.

The analysis of teachers' professional life phases and identity scenarios revealed that they are an important influence in their work, lives and effectiveness; and that variations in teachers' perceived effectiveness can be understood by examining teachers and groups of teachers who are experiencing different scenarios within and between particular phases of their professional lives. We identified key influences on teachers' work in different professional life phases and the differential impact of these on teachers' commitment and effectiveness. Understanding the impact of such interaction between the influences of teachers' professional life phases and identities and the mediating factors in these, i.e. the situated (workplace), the professional (ideals and polices), and the personal (life experiences and events), was central to achieving an understanding of what causes variations in the conditions for teachers' professional learning and development over the course of their careers and the impact of these variations on their effectiveness. Our interpretations of teachers' professional learning and development trajectories and identification of the nature of their professional lives over time thus were primarily concerned with the impact of these on their commitment and well-being in the particularities of the social, political and personal environments in which they lived and worked.

For the purpose of this chapter, short stories of one beginning teacher, one middle career teacher and one veteran teacher have been selected in order to illustrate their remembered experiences of peaks and troughs in their professional lives and the ways in which various personal, professional and workplace-related factors had supported or hindered their commitment to learn and develop and their capacity to teach to their best.

3.4 Learning to Build Identity in Classrooms and Schools in the First 7 Years: Schools Matter

On entry, most teachers have a strong sense of vocation (Day et al. 2007; Hansen 1995), and at the beginning of their professional lives their work is underpinned by their intrinsic motivation and emotional commitment to provide the best service for their students. Like those in other human services professions, teachers' emotional commitment is an important element of their ability to teach to their best and is associated with an ethic of care for the well-being of their students. For new teachers especially, support in managing the emotional unpredictability of classroom teaching and learning is as important as support in developing their pedagogical and classroom management skills; and the availability, extent and appropriateness of such support in the workplace are likely to be key influencing factors in retaining their commitment to the school and to their decisions about remaining in the profession over the long term.

Compared with their more experienced colleagues, beginning teachers' challenges primarily stem from two distinct but interrelated realities: one is to develop a sense of professional self in their interactions with their colleagues, pupils and parents; and the other is to develop a sense of belonging during their socialisation into the school community and the profession. As a result, many new teachers often find themselves immersed in complex social relations and sophisticated professional roles inherent within established school communities (Lee et al. 1993), whilst at the same time fighting to make sense of their own experiences and understand what it means to be a teacher.

Over the last two decades there has been ample evidence in the literature which shows that new teachers are more likely to stay in teaching and also develop greater commitment to teaching if their school organisations provide them with access to intensive mentoring and professional learning opportunities and through these, help them to focus on tasks that improve their teaching competence and performance efficacy. The quality of professional cultures in schools is, therefore, central in supporting and retaining able, enthusiastic and committed new teachers, and plays a key mediating role in influencing their decision to leave or stay in the school or the profession. In addressing the critical challenge of supporting new teachers and enhancing their enthusiasm in the profession, Kardos and Johnson (2007) urged policy makers and school leaders to create an 'integrated professional culture' in schools—a culture of professional support and commitment that 'promotes frequent and reciprocal interaction among faculty members across experience levels; recognises new teachers' needs as beginners; and develops shared responsibility among teachers for the school' (ibid.: 2083).

In the VITAE project (Day et al. 2007), the large majority (75%) of teachers in the first 7 years of their professional lives remained highly committed and motivated. However, one in four found it difficult to cope with the social and cultural realities of teaching and were at risk of being lost to the profession.

3.4.1 Professional Life Phase 0–3 Years—Learning Which Builds Identity and Classroom Competence

The outstanding characteristic of the large majority of teachers (85%) was their high level of commitment to teaching. Two sub-groups were observed within this professional life phase: one with a developing sense of efficacy and the other with a reducing sense of efficacy. Teachers who had an 'easy beginning' benefited from a combination of influences that were more positive than those for teachers who experienced 'painful beginnings'. Teachers in both groups reported the negative impact of poor pupil behaviour on their work. For new teachers who were struggling to survive the challenges of a new professional life in the reality of the classroom, the impact of combined support from the school/departmental leadership and colleagues was highly significant in helping to build their confidence and self-efficacy and deciding the direction of their next professional life path.

CPD activities in relation to classroom knowledge were most frequently reported as having a positive impact on their morale and as being significant to the stabilisation of their teaching practice. These activities included school/department-based training and INSET days, external newly qualified teacher (NQT) conferences, and visiting and working with teachers in other schools.

The key influences on these teachers' potential professional life trajectories were found to be the level of support, recognition of their work and the school culture. However, it was the influences of head teachers, colleagues and cultures in the school that were crucial to their learning about how to behave and how to be as a professional. Thus, in terms of professional learning and development activities, it would seems that those which focus upon building a sense of professional identity and classroom competence are likely to be most effective for the development of these teachers.

3.4.2 Professional Life Phase 4–7 Years—Developing Professional Identity

Promotion and additional responsibilities had now begun to play a significant role in teachers' motivation, commitment and sense of effectiveness. Most VITAE teachers (78%) in this phase had additional responsibilities and particularly stressed the importance of promotion to their growing professional identity. This suggests that for many teachers this professional life phase is not a stabilisation period. Rather, it is a period in which teachers, whilst consolidating their professional identities in their classrooms, also have challenges beyond these.

Three sub-groups of teachers were identified: (a) those who were sustaining a strong sense of identity, self-efficacy and effectiveness; (b) those who were coping/managing identity, efficacy and effectiveness; and (c) those whose identity, efficacy and effectiveness were at risk. An important difference between sub-groups (a) and (b) was that the latter group had a stronger concern over their ability to manage their heavy workloads. Teachers in sub-group (c) felt that their identity, efficacy and effectiveness were at risk because of workload and difficult life events.

Support from the school/departmental leadership, colleagues and pupils continued to be of importance to teachers in this phase who demonstrated a primary concern about their confidence and feelings of being effective. In contrast with professional life phase 0–3, there were more frequent references made to heavy workload, which was seen as reducing their teaching effectiveness. The need for classroom knowledge and knowledge of external policies was markedly less, role effectiveness similar, and CPD which focused upon professional and personal development needs had become more important.

3.4.3 Pat's Story: The Leadership Effect

Pat was 36 years old, a classroom teacher and science coordinator at her first school, where she has taught for 3 years. Prior to this she had run a 'parent and toddler' (small child) group.

Pat had always enjoyed teaching and working with the children, who she described as, 'delightful'. She gained immense pleasure and satisfaction from her pupils' good results, progress and achievements. Her confidence and sense of efficacy had greatly increased as a consequence of their good results. Pat's workline shows that support and recognition from strong leadership and the transformation of negative cultures in her school had solidified her long-term commitment to teaching. Not surprisingly, she had highly positive views on the school leadership. She described the new head as 'exceptional':

With our new head there is a lot more support for your own development in the sense of your position in the school. It's the encouragement or making decisions for the school, also the literacy adviser from the LA [school district] is wonderful; team teaching, observations together, very good. She's exceptional.

Pat consistently described the staff at her school as extremely supportive of one another, both professionally and socially. Her teaching colleagues help to keep her commitment strong. As part of her growing self-efficacy, she had become more aware of not letting herself slip behind because 'If you let something slip, it builds up and builds up—so you don't feel good about yourself anyway.' As such, she set herself targets and was getting more organised. Her upward trajectory, as shown in her workline, suggests that the impact of combined support from her school leadership and colleagues is crucial to her learning about how to behave, how to belong, how to teach well and how to be as professionals (Fig. 3.1).

It just gives you a buzz to keep going, even when a lesson that has been terrifically planned goes pear shaped. It's enjoyable, but it is also exhausting. It's not having enough hours in the day, but you want it to be right.

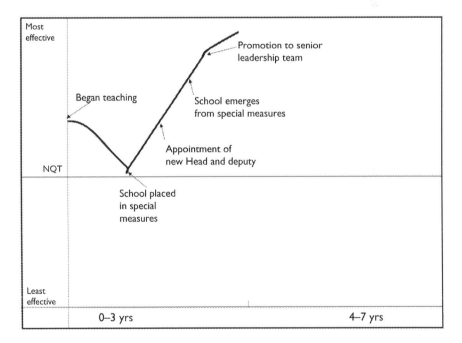

Fig. 3.1 Pat's workline (professional life phase 0–3)

3.5   Managing Tensions and Transitions in the Middle Years of Teaching: Teachers at the Crossroads

The discrepancies in the categorisation of 'mid-career' may have, to a greater or lesser extent, contributed to two different researcher perspectives on teachers in this phase. One tends to suggest that they are experiencing a relatively stable period in their professional lives, with the lowest attrition rates, growing competence and enhanced confidence, resilience and efficacy. Other studies, however, have characterised teachers in mid-career as being at a transitional phase in which they experience new challenges and tensions. In his seminal work on the lives of teachers, Huberman (1993) found that teachers with 11–19 years of experience in particular tended to have a latent fear of stagnating. Many of these teachers reported moments of reassessment or 'crisis' and attributed these to changes within the school system, poor workplace environments, family events, difficult classes and heavy investments in curriculum and pedagogical changes that had little or no beneficial effects.

Whilst mid-career may not be a distinctive phase of self-questioning or 'crisis' for all teachers, for many it is an important watershed in their professional lives, which presents, on the one hand, greater career progression opportunities, but on the other, greater challenges to manage the tensions between two equally important teaching and personal lives. This led Huberman and other scholars internationally to argue that '[While difficult moments can crop up at any phase of the career, there are periods of greater vulnerability' (ibid. 1993: 255)]. We found that it is in this 8–15-year phase of their professional lives when work–life tensions are most likely to test their sense of resilience. However, it also suggested that where there is appropriate personal and professional support from school leaders and colleagues, many teachers are able to build upon their experience, energy and enthusiasm, respond positively to their internal 'quest for stimulation, for new ideas, challenges and engagement' (Huberman 1989: 352) and continue to pursue a professional life path in which they develop and deepen their capacity to teach to their best.

3.5.1   Professional Life Phase 8–15 Years—Defining Work–Life Tensions

This professional life phase, described by some as being populated by 'the most overlooked group in the entire teaching profession' (Hargreaves and Fullan 2012: 72), marks a key watershed in teachers' professional development. Although they are likely to more established, confident and competent, these teachers are beginning to face additional tensions in managing change in both their professional and personal lives. The majority of teachers in VITAE, for example, were struggling with work–life tensions. Most of these teachers had additional (79%) out-of-classroom and out-of-school responsibilities and had to place more focus upon their management roles. Heavy workloads also worked against the continuing improvement of their classroom teaching.

We identified two sub-groups of teachers in this professional life phase. Sub-group (a) contained teachers who were *sustaining their engagement* and whose expected trajectories were career advancement with increased self-efficacy and commitment (human capital investment). The combined support from leadership, staff collegiality (high social capital), rapport with the pupils and engagement in CPD were contributing factors in this sub-group's positive sense of effectiveness. Teachers' professional learning within the first sub-group were related to the needs of (i) those with aspirations for further promotion who were primarily concerned about the effectiveness of their managerial responsibilities and extending these; and (ii) those intending to remain in the classroom, fulfilling the original 'call to teach', and developing and refining their knowledge repertoires for teaching and learning. Professional learning opportunities, therefore, need to target at their differentiated professional learning needs and help enhance their role effectiveness either as managers or as classroom teachers.

Around half of the teachers in sub-group (b) *'Detachment/loss of motivation'* reported a lack of support from leadership (50%) and colleagues (60%)—low social capital. Adverse personal events and tensions between work and life were also important issues. Professional and personal support and care within and outside the workplace which focussed upon improving their self-efficacy, morale and emotional well-being would be of particular value.

Getting professional learning and development relating to these two sub-groups right for this key cohort of mid-career teachers is crucial because, more than in any other phases, it will influence their final commitment and effectiveness trajectories.

3.5.2 Professional Life Phase 16–23 Years—Managing Work–Life Tensions

After the crossroads experience of the previous phase, teachers in this professional life phase benefited from having a more clearly defined sense of professional identity. In common with the previous two professional life phases (4–7 and 8–15), excessive paperwork and heavy workload were seen as key hindrances to their effectiveness. In contrast with teachers from the earlier professional life phases, events in personal lives, coupled with additional duties, had a stronger impact on the work of this phase, and as a consequence, a larger proportion of teachers were struggling with a negative work–life balance. Teachers in this phase were categorised into three sub-groups on the basis of their management of the challenges of work life and home events:

Three sub-groups were identified: (a) those who were likely to see their motivation and commitment continue to grow; (b) those who maintained their motivation, commitment and effectiveness and who were likely to cope with work–life tensions in their next professional life phase; and (c) those whose heavy workloads, lack of management of competing tensions and career stagnation had led to their decreased motivation, commitment and effectiveness.

Professional learning opportunities that enhanced teachers' role effectiveness were of value. However, greater support from knowledgeable head teachers and colleagues in whom they could trust which focussed upon maintaining and increasing teachers' morale and capacities to manage work–life tensions and sustaining their commitment and effectiveness was important also.

3.5.3 Alison's Story: Managing Personal and Professional Challenges

Alison was 30 years old and had taught for 11 year. She had been teaching in her current primary school for 9 years, having previously worked in one other as a temporary 'supply' teacher. Her workline indicates that her two promotions over a 3-year period positively impacted on her work life as a teacher. However, because of a challenging class, coupled with her failure to obtain an internal promotion and her stressful experience with an Ofsted inspection, Alison experienced a dip in her motivation and job satisfaction. A year later, her success in gaining further promotion in the school and her new 'lovely' class re-ignited her motivation and self-esteem and ultimately made a significant contribution to the rise in her sense of efficacy and commitment. Reflecting on her recent divorce, Alison felt that she had

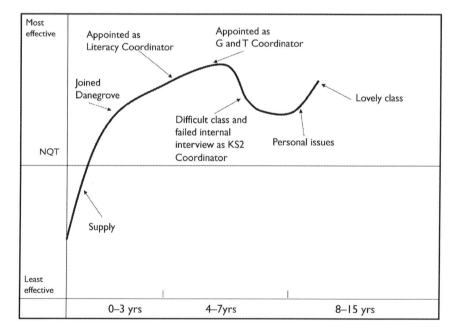

Fig. 3.2 Alison's workline: moving onwards and upwards

grown stronger as a person—because being a single parent meant that she had to push herself to become more organised in her personal life (Fig. 3.2).

Alison felt that the current phase of her professional life was notably different from the previous ones. Then, she had enjoyed the professional recognition that her early promotions had brought about and gained immense satisfaction from her rapidly growing sense of efficacy. However, at the beginning of this phase, she felt unsettled and 'dithery' and could not help wondering what steps she ought to take to advance her career path: 'Should I go or should I stay at this school?'; 'Is it time for me to be looking for deputy headships?'. She went through an unsuccessful period of seeking promotion. She now felt more 'settled' and content and was no longer looking for further promotion within the school. She enjoyed leading a 'big and exciting push' on literacy and knew that she would be teaching a new year group the following year—another, different challenge ahead!

After 11 years of teaching, then, Alison continued to feel 'engaged' and 'committed'. She felt that she had a 'new lease of life', but understood that, if she wanted to become a deputy head, she would have to leave her current school when the right opportunity arose.

3.6 Veteran Teachers: Adaptation, Regeneration and Hardiness

Throughout their professional lives these teachers will have been confronted by professional, workplace and personal pressures and tensions which, at times at the very least, are likely to have challenged and perhaps ultimately eroded their values, beliefs and practices: for some, their willingness to remain in the job, and for others, their capacity to continue to teach to their best in the classroom as commitment becomes eroded.

There is a real sense, then, that physical retention, whilst important, is no more so than the retention of teacher quality. At a time when the age profile of teachers in many countries is skewed towards those with more than 20 years of experience, and in which most of these would be unlikely to feel able to change career for financial and domestic reasons, we believe that it is important, also, to investigate whether the demands and challenge over time have dimmed these teachers' sense of well-being and commitment and thus their capacity to teach to their best. We see retention, therefore, as a process rather than a result. We know that these teachers have survived to become veterans, but we know relatively little about the conditions which have added to or diminished their sense of commitment and well-being, and the relationship of these to their felt capacities to teach to their best. As teachers grow older, so do the challenges of maintaining energy increase in the complex and persistently challenging work of teaching children and young people, whose attitudes, motivations and behaviours may differ widely from those with whom veteran teacher began their careers. Moreover, teachers' own professional agendas may have changed in response to their experiences of many policy and social reforms, school leaders, and cohorts of students, as well as the ageing process and unanticipated personal circumstances. The persistence of such combination of challenges, which are part of the experience of most of those who work for prolonged periods of their lives in one occupation, may have begun to take its toll on the motivation, commitment and resilience which are essential to the willingness and capacity of veteran teachers to maintain teaching at its best.

Huberman's (1993) research on secondary and middle school teachers' lives in Switzerland found that teachers in the later stages 2 of their career became either 'disenchanted' or 'serene' as they approached retirement. The VITAE research provided broad confirmation of this picture, but also more nuanced portraits of teachers' lives and work, finding that a distinctive sub-group of the teachers in the final two phases of their professional lives (24–30 years and 31+ years) demonstrated, alongside 'serenity' and 'positive focusing', a high level of motivation and commitment and a strong sense of 'active' engagement in the profession. However, it showed, also, differences in the relative proportions of teachers in each group who were sustaining their commitment, motivation and sense of efficacy.

3.6.1 Professional Life Phase 24–30 Years—Adjusting to Change

Teachers in this phase were facing more intensive challenges to sustaining their motivation in the profession. Eighty-eight per cent had additional leadership responsibilities. Deteriorating pupil behaviour, the impact of personal life events, resentment at 'being forced to jump through hoops by a constant stream of new initiatives', taking stock of their careers (and lives) and length of service in the school were key influences on the effectiveness of teachers in this cohort. However, not all teachers were disenchanted. Two sub-groups were identified: (a) those with improved work–life balance and sustained motivation and; and (b) those who were holding on but losing motivation and commitment.

Teachers' identities in this phase were constantly challenged by the need to adjust. For those who still had additional out-of-classroom responsibilities (58%), professional learning opportunities which targeted at strengthening their effectiveness as managers continued to be of importance. However, for those who struggled to manage extreme fluctuations caused by combined negative influences from outside and within the workplace and their professional and personal lives, in-school support focussing upon mediating the effects of unsolicited and undesired external policy initiatives and assisting them in adjusting successfully to these, had a significant role to play in sustaining their motivation and commitment and enabling them to teach at their best.

3.6.2 *Professional Life Phase 31+—Sustaining Commitment*

Pupils' progress and positive teacher–pupil relationships were the main source of job satisfaction for these teachers. However, ill health was also a primary personal concern.

Teachers in this phase were categorised into two subgroups: (a) Teachers whose motivation and commitment remained high despite or because of changing personal, professional and organisation contexts and whose expected trajectories were strong agency, efficacy and achievement; and (b) Teachers whose motivation was declining or had declined and whose expected trajectories were increased fatigue, disillusionment and exit.

Not only were supportive school cultures of crucial importance to teachers' sense of effectiveness across all six professional life phases but, for teachers in this professional life phase, in-school support (high social capital investment) which provided for professional care and emotional well-being played a major part in teachers' continued engagement in the profession. These were of crucial importance to teachers' commitment and sense of effectiveness in this final phase.

3.6.3 *Andrew's Story*

Andrew was 53 years old and had taught for 33 years, 16 of them in his current primary school of 200+ pupils. He was a member of the school leadership team, responsible for maths, design and technology and physical education.

Andrew came into teaching because he had 'hated' school and thought that he could do better. He was still enjoying teaching in the school. Andrew's workline shows his sense of effectiveness over time following an initial entry period in which he built his classroom management and teaching skills and established his sense of professional identity. It shows, also, that in the mid-career, 'watershed' phase, he sought new professional challenges through promotion to a different school. His renewed enthusiasm, commitment and strong sense of self-efficacy were maintained until an adverse external inspection report placed his school on 'special measures'. However, within a year the school had recovered under the leadership of a new head: 'There have been quite big changes in the school. Management have got an awful lot sorted out and have worked hard. Everything is working well at the moment.'

This had resulted in a change of teaching group for Andrew, significant in that he no longer taught the year group that was subject to national testing. This had a positive effect on his work life. As the workline was 'unpacked' during further conversations, it became clear that Andrew continued to be devoted to his pupils, despite his distaste for the effects of reforms upon his work (Fig. 3.3).

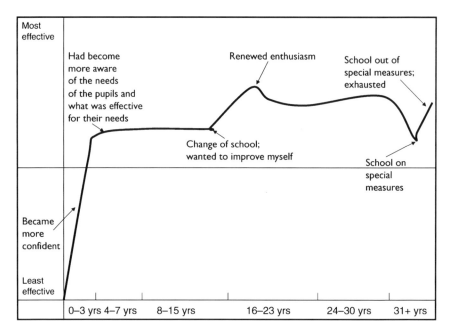

Fig. 3.3 Andrew's workline: renewed commitment

3.7 Conclusions: Teacher Development, Retention and Renewal over a Career

Understanding variations in the conditions for teachers' professional learning and development which enhance their sense of positive professional identity and well-being requires more than a consideration of the functional needs of organisations and needs arising from teachers' personal lives. It requires, also, a consideration of how tensions within and between these interact and how they might be managed by organisations and teachers in ways which build commitment and maintain and enhance effectiveness. Schools need to develop 'expansive' rather than restrictive learning cultures and practices which pay attention to individual differences, needs and preferences.

Moreover, the differences in teachers' trajectories and professional learning and development needs within and between each professional life phase confirm the significant impact that certain key influences can have on teachers' sense of identity, commitment and effectiveness. Such diverse life trajectories had led Huberman (1993: 263) to conclude that 'we do not claim to be able to qualitatively or statistically to 'predict' professional satisfaction'. The VITAE research, however, suggests that the provision of responsive and differentiated support to meet teachers' professional and personal learning needs at different times in their work and lives can help counter declining commitment trajectories, enhance the continuity of positive development of teachers' professional commitment and, thus, their effectiveness. The key influences provide a departure point for teachers, school/departmental leaders and policy makers to understand and acknowledge teachers' needs and to identify appropriate support for these needs. To provide favourable conditions for teachers' professional learning and development within the same and across different phases of their professional lives means understanding and taking into account the different positive and negative scenarios which affect teachers' identities, and which, therefore, affect their sense of commitment and effectiveness.

The professional and personal experiences of the majority of VITAE teachers can be seen as being reflected in their journeys of self-adjustment and professional growth within these professional life phase scenarios. In all their journeys the teachers were confronted by professional and personal pressures, tensions, and challenges to their values, beliefs and practices. However, what shone through for most was their capacity to learn to build upon favourable influences and positive opportunities in their work and life contexts, overcome the emotional tensions of the scenarios in the environments which they experienced, and maintain the sense of vocation—an "inner motivation to serve" (Hansen 1995: 6)—which had initially attracted them into teaching. They were able to continue to learn and develop their professional assets whilst at the same time meet the challenges of the changing environments in which they worked. Whilst this was the case for the majority (74%), it was not so for a sizable minority (26%). Put another way, approximately 1 in 4 students were receiving teaching from teachers who were not as effective as they might be.

Support by head teachers and other colleagues which focuses upon creating and maintaining a learning climate and professional learning opportunities for teachers which relate to the core needs to sustain commitment and, through this, effectiveness, is a key mediating factor in building and supporting the classroom and school improvement. The kinds of support and professional relationship which teachers experience, for them, as with their students, have important positive or significant negative effects upon their motivation, commitment and effectiveness trajectories in each phase of their professional lives. As the VITAE research shows, teachers do not necessarily become more effective with age and experience. Because the scenarios which they experience vary in kind and complexity during their working lives, teachers need to be resilient if their pupils are to receive their best teaching. Just as the best teaching 'personalises' students' learning agendas, so the best professional learning and structures and cultures will differentiate between the learning agendas of teachers in order to sustain their resilience, commitment and effectiveness which are fundamental to classroom and school effectiveness and improvement.

References

Day, C., & Gu, Q. (2010). *The new lives of teachers*. Abingdon, Oxon: Routledge.

Day, C., & Gu, Q. (2014). *Resilient teachers, resilient schools: Building and sustaining quality in testing times*. Abingdon and New York: Routledge.

Day, C., Sammons, P., Stobart, G., Kington, A., & Gu, Q. (2007). *Teachers matter: Connecting lives, work and effectiveness*. Maidenhead: Open University Press.

Hansen, D. T. (1995). *The call to teach*. New York: Teachers College Press.

Hargreaves, A., & Fullan, M. (2012). *Professional capital: Transforming teaching in every school*. New York, NY: Teachers College Press.

Huberman, M. (1989). On teachers' careers: Once over lightly, with a broad brush. *International Journal of Educational Research, 13*(4), 347–362.

Huberman, M. (1993). *The lives of teachers*. London: Cassell.

Kardos, S. M., & Johnson, S. (2007) On their own and presumed expert: New teachers' experience with their colleagues. *Teachers College Record, 109*(9), 2083–2106 (Lave and Wenger 1991).

Lave, J., & Wenger, E. (1991). *Situated learning: Legitimate peripheral participation*. Cambridge: Cambridge University Press.

Lee, V. E., Bryk, A. S., & Smith, J. B. (1993). The organization of effective secondary schools. In L. Darling-Hammond (Ed.), *Review of research in education,* (Vol. 19, pp. 171–267). Washington, DC: American Education Research Association.

OECD. (2008). *Improving school leadership*. Paris: OECD.

OECD. (2010). *Education Tody*. Paris: OECD.

Palmer, P. J. (2007). *The courage to teach: Exploring the inner landscape of a teacher's life* (The 10th Anniversary edition). San Francisco: Jossey-Bass.

Shulman, L. S. (1987). Knowledge and teaching. *Harvard Educational Review, 57,* 1–22.

Tucker, M. (2011). *Surpassing Shanghai*. Harvard: Harvard Educational Publishing Group.

Author Biography

Qing Gu is Professor of Education in the University of Nottingham, UK. She is author of *Teacher Development: Knowledge and Context* (Continuum 2007), and co-author of *Teachers Matter* (OUP 2007), *The New Lives of Teachers* (Routledge 2010), *Successful School Leadership* (OUP 2011), and *Resilient Teachers, Resilient Schools* (Routledge 2014).

Chapter 4
Clinical Praxis Exams: Linking Academic Study with Professional Practice Knowledge

Barbara Kameniar (✉) · Larissa McLean Davies, Jefferson Kinsman, Catherine Reid, Debra Tyler and Daniela Acquaro

4.1 Introduction

One of the more salient challenges facing teacher educators and curriculum leaders in schools is how to assist beginning teachers to link their academic studies with professional practice knowledge. Traditionally, the role of universities and colleges in teacher education has been to provide both theoretical and practical under-standings of curriculum and pedagogy, as well as to administer the placement and mentoring of pre-service teachers in schools; however, whilst the remit may have been to provide both theoretical and practical understandings, the overall emphasis was largely on the provision of theoretical and decontextualised, laboratory-based perspectives (Darling-Hammond and Bransford 2005). This emphasis was balanced by a belief that teaching of much of the requisite professional practice knowledge would be taken up by teachers in schools. From a university perspective, practice

B. Kameniar (✉) · L.M. Davies · J. Kinsman · C. Reid · D. Tyler · D. Acquaro
University of Melbourne, Melbourne, Australia
e-mail: b.kameniar@unimelb.edu.au

L.M. Davies
e-mail: l.mcleandavies@unimelb.edu.au

J. Kinsman
e-mail: jkinsman@unimelb.edu.au

C. Reid
e-mail: crcid@unimelb.edu.au

D. Tyler
e-mail: d.tyler@unimelb.edu.au

D. Acquaro
e-mail: d.acquaro@unimelb.edu.au

B. Kameniar
University of Tasmania, Tasmania, Australia

© Springer Nature Singapore Pte Ltd. 2017
M.A. Peters et al. (eds.), *A Companion to Research in Teacher Education*,
DOI 10.1007/978-981-10-4075-7_4

was generally seen as the 'poor cousin' of theory and the emphasis on extant practice by classroom teachers was frequently cited as a key explanation for why the lofty ideas put forth in the academy did not work in schools.

Over the years, this model of teacher education has been criticised for creating an unfavourable divide between academic studies and professional practice knowledge, tertiary institutions and schools. Each generation of teacher educators has attempted the exigent task of linking theory to practice in the learning experiences of pre-service teachers (teacher candidates). Solutions from within the university frequently emphasise links between theory and practice through university-based tasks requiring teacher candidates to trial an idea in the classroom and report back in university classes. This approach can be seen as intrusive by classroom teachers or as decontextualised by teacher candidates and students in schools. On occasions, teacher candidates have reported complaints from schools about this approach, as well as feeling the need to 'take sides' in a perceived debate between academic studies and professional practice knowledge; however, the relationship between the two is more nuanced, complex, and multi-dimensional than a simple theory-practice divide might suggest. While the impact of university programmes on teachers has proved difficult to measure, many commentators have questioned the efficacy of the dominant models of teacher education (Darling-Hammond and Bransford 2005).

4.2 The Challenge of Linking Theory to Practice

The failure to adequately merge academic studies and professional practice knowledge in the learning experience of teacher candidates has characterised teacher education programmes for longer than we like to think. Malcolm Vick has shown that, for more than a century, the coordination of responsibilities for educators between the schools and teaching colleges has been fraught with problems, including teacher education staff not being sufficiently experienced in contemporary school teaching, the imposition of conflicting requirements on teacher candidates and the timing of programme elements to work against the reflective linking of theory and practice (Vick 2006). The last of these conundrums has usually been ascribed to teacher mistrust of university methods, which discourages teacher candidates from attempting to translate theoretical perspectives and other elements of their academic studies into classroom practice, and the expectation of the universities that their teacher candidates will transform their new schools, rather than reproduce prevailing practices (Vick 2006, p. 191).

The inability of generations of teacher educators to devise a satisfactory programme linking knowledge *about* teaching and learning, to knowledge *of* teaching and learning (Loughran 2010) led some commentators to question the theoretical competence of the teacher educators themselves (Zeichner et al. 2015). On the other hand, more sanguine researchers continue to claim that the fundamental feature of any education programme design is the need for a unified programme where teacher candidates are taught a clear conception of what is needed in order to be a successful practitioner (Darling-Hammond and Bransford 2005). The unification of a programme necessitates the development of shared understanding of what excellent teaching and learning look like, the development of a shared metalanguage, and a genuine integration of these across the programme. Importantly the professional practice placement also requires re-envisioning as a 'hybrid [space] where academic, practitioner and community-based knowledge come together in new ways to support the development of innovative and hybrid solutions to the problem of preparing teachers' (Zeichner et al. 2015, p. 124).

Darling-Hammond and Bransford (2005) likewise describe the need for teachers to access 'shared understandings and practices'. They argued for the need of education to learn from other professions: as is the case for law and medicine, that have 'evolved from a consensus about what professionals need to know and be able to do if they are to profit from profession-wide knowledge and if they are to have the diagnostic and strategic judgment to address the needs of those whom they serve' (Darling-Hammond and Bransford 2005, p. 9). Teacher education, then, becomes a matter of encouraging the concrete application of broad principles, followed by reflection on the experience (Darling-Hammond and Bransford 2005).

The approach was broadly endorsed in the Australian Learning and Teaching Council's (ALTC) report (2009) exploring different professional placement models for teacher education courses. The ALTC report concluded that teacher candidate placements should be concurrent with the academic and theoretical component of the programme (ALTC 2009, p. 14). It also identified the need for further evidence-based research into the coherence and quality of academic study and professional practice links to determine how programme design promotes teaching practice, acknowledging that there remains a lack of understanding about how teacher candidates draw on their academic studies or how their placement experiences contribute to their professional development (ALTC 2009, p. 25). This challenge of negotiating the theory/practice nexus, and need for teacher education programmes to more meaningfully engage with the sites of practice have led to what Mattsson et al. (2011) have described as the 'Practicum turn' in teacher education. This 'Practicum turn' is a recognition that theorised 'practicum knowledge', which takes a variety of forms, is the key to developing understandings of pre-service teachers. Burn and Mutton (2013) show in their recent survey of clinical models of pre-service teacher education, that clinical programmes, which are invested in strong partnerships between schools and university, are particular examples of this practicum turn.

In the following section, we will turn our attention to the ways in which an assessment and curriculum innovation, the Clinical Praxis Exam (CPE), sought to leverage the close partnerships between schools and the university facilitated by a clinical model, in order to facilitate and mobilise the meaningful interplay between theory and practice, and ground theoretical understandings in school experience. The CPE is described and the theoretical basis for the innovation is outlined. Particular attention is paid to the way in which the content of each CPE is drawn from the classroom practice of individual teacher candidates and their negotiations with students, mentor teachers, and school-based university staff. The chapter then outlines responses from teacher candidates, mentor teachers, teaching fellows (see below) and university teachers who participated in two qualitative research projects examining the efficacy and impact of the CPE. Findings are then summarised and the next steps in the ongoing refinement of the CPE are outlined.

4.3 The Innovation of a Promising Assessment Approach —The Clinical Praxis Examination

In 2008, MGSE introduced the pre-service Master of Teaching degree. Discussions about the design of the degree considered contemporary debates about the relationship between academic studies and professional practice experiences. The final design drew inspiration from research into teacher education programmes across the English-speaking world to construct an academically taught, clinical practice programme in which keen skills of observation, the gathering and analysis of evidence, and the capacity to make reasoned judgements and take action, were developed. In the first instance, the design drew heavily on the Stanford Teacher Education Programme (STEP) from Stanford University in California, as well as programmes implemented at the University of Virginia and Bank Street Teachers' College, New York, each of which emphasised a strong relationship among knowledge about teaching and learning, and knowledge of teaching and learning, albeit in their own ways. Each of these programmes also emphasised the importance of discipline-specific knowledge experts' input into programming. Accordingly, MGSE academics redesigned subjects to take account of the increased time in schools and to assist teacher candidates to make meaningful links between their academic studies and professional practice through a range of practice-based tasks within each subject.

New placement structures such as the clustering of schools into partnership networks and the introduction of teaching fellows (school-based expert teachers able to provide strong contextual knowledge and support for both teacher candidates and mentor teachers) and clinical specialists (university-based clinical experts involved in the teaching of academic subjects who work with teaching fellows to provide a school-based seminar programme) were designed to support the bringing together of academic studies and professional practice knowledge (McLean Davies et al. 2013). While the additional time in schools and the revised structures produced some significant gains, particularly in the overall relationship between schools and the university, some teacher candidates found the links between academic subjects and practicum experience difficult to make. In response, a Clinical Praxis Exam (CPE) was designed with the explicit intention of integrating learning from amongst the academic subjects with professional practice knowledge developed during placements (Fig. 4.1). The intention was also to provide a form of assessment and feedback conducive to learning in a clinical model.

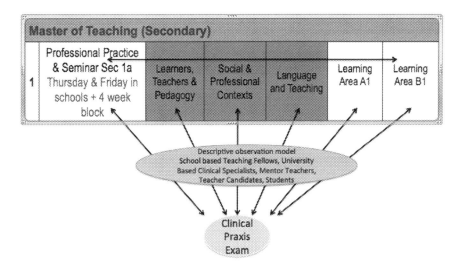

Fig. 4.1 This figure shows the elements and participants within the first semester of study in the Master of Teaching (Secondary), highlighting their relationship to each other and to the Clinical Praxis Exam

4.3.1   Why Clinical Praxis?

In bringing together the terms 'clinical' and 'praxis' the academic team responsible for its design and implementation, aimed to denote a set of practices that draw upon productive elements from both 'clinical' and 'praxis' approaches to teacher education. While each approach aims to link theory and practice, academic studies and professional practice knowledge in productive ways, they each do so with different emphases, both of which the team felt were important. The use of 'clinical' was intended to draw attention to the importance of learning in situ from experienced practitioners and from interactions with students as well as the need to develop a repertoire of strong technical, practical and reasoning skills from which to draw when making judgments (Kriewaldt and Turnidge 2013) about student progress and how best to intervene to meet individual learning needs. The use of 'praxis' was intended to draw attention to the impossibility of our interventions and actions being neutral or inherently benign, and to the reality that actions have both short and long-term ontological, epistemological, political, cultural and material consequences for students, families, communities, teachers, schools and the broader world. Therefore, any interventions should be undertaken with care and consideration of broader consequences including those that may not be immediately apparent.

Clinical approaches to education offer structures, processes and procedures to assist with the development of diagnostic skills and informed choices for action; however, the strength offered by their structures could result in rigid or unreflective practices that reproduce existing injustices and curtail agency. On the other hand, praxis models of teacher education are concerned with empowerment and transformation of both the individual and the world. For teacher candidates, this means learning to assess '*their conduct and its consequences*, not just what they or others say about their conduct' (Kemmis and Smith 2008, p. 32; emphasis in original). For teacher educators and mentor teachers this means examining established power relations for the ways in which they inhibit democratic dialogue and diminish the agency of teacher candidates, communities and the students in schools for whom we share responsibility. As Zeichner et al. note, it is the 'quality of the knowledge and power relationships that exist, not the structure of the programme' (2015, p. 131) that are the important factors in teacher education. A clinical praxis approach in teacher education both appropriates and adapts medical frameworks and discourses (Kreiwaldt and Turnidge 2013), and strengthens these through incorporation of praxis approaches which are explicitly 'morally committed, and oriented and informed by tradition' (Kemmis and Smith 2008, p. 4).

4.4   The Clinical Praxis Exam

The CPE is an oral assessment task that involves a cyclical process of analysis and reflection, integrating theory, evidence, practice and evaluation. The purpose of the task is for teacher candidates to show evidence of clinical thinking and judgement in relation to student learning, by reporting on their experience of clinical praxis during their placement. The CPE assesses the teacher candidates' planning, implementation and evaluation of their practice, based on their deliberations with other educators (including mentor teachers, clinical specialists, teaching fellows, families and community organisations), their analysis of evidence, their consideration of contextual factors and their attention to the content and language demands of *what* they are teaching in relation to *who* they are teaching.

To develop and demonstrate clinical praxis, each teacher candidate is required to select a student, or small group of students, in conversation with their mentor teacher. This student or group of students may have specific learning needs or may be students for whom the teacher would like additional information about their learning. The teacher candidate then plans, implements, reflects upon and evaluates a series of learning 'interventions'. The term 'intervention' is used to denote action on the part of a teacher to assist a student to go beyond their current level of knowledge or skill; furthermore, the interventions are to take place during the course of regular classroom instruction and activities. The assessment of the needs of the student and the subsequent pedagogical responses are to be informed by research and relevant theories. In this sense, the task involves the integration of the teacher candidate's understanding of learning and teaching gained through their academic studies and their professional practice experience. The intended result is an authentic linking of teaching practice to teaching theory.

The CPE was also designed to foster close cooperation between teacher candidates, mentor teachers and university staff. The exam was piloted in 2010 and formed a key part of assessment within the core subjects. Individual oral assessment was carried out for each of the 420 teacher candidates in the secondary programme. An oral examination was chosen as the medium for assessment in recognition that teachers, more often than not, appear to have a propensity for talking about their work, however, this talking is not always undertaken in ways that are informed by research and theoretical perspectives. The oral examination was designed to build on, and enhance, this propensity by encouraging the development of descriptive rather than judgemental language, the capacity to utilise valid evidence to support claims, and the capacity to use the theoretical and research discourses of the profession when speaking about practice. An oral examination also opened up assessment to professional dialogue between teacher candidates and assessors from the university and school sectors in the form of clinical questions that would probe and discuss the decisions made by the teacher candidates. Following Burbules' note that '[d]ialogue is ... more an expression of *praxis* than of *techne*' (1993, p. xi) the designers worked closely with assessors to assist them in asking questions that were cumulative (Alexander 2008), building on what was already known and giving rise to deeper thinking and other questions. An emphasis was placed on the content of the dialogue as well as the form. This required a shift in understanding of assessment from a final judgement of a past practice to an understanding of assessment as fundamental to ongoing development and the strengthening of critical thinking and clinical reasoning.

A rubric based on the SOLO taxonomy (Biggs 2003) was designed to assist assessors in making judgements about the level to which teacher candidates were able to draw together their academic studies with professional practice knowledge so as to improve the learning outcomes for students. The design team found the SOLO taxonomy well suited to the task of assessing the CPE because of its description of levels of increasing complexity in thinking and understanding. It was not expected that teacher candidates' efforts to improve learning would necessarily produce identifiable results during their extended placement (4 weeks), however, the teacher candidates' reasoning and pedagogical choices, and their capacity for informed reflection and action, were assessed.

The inclusion of the CPE at the heart of the Master of Teaching model reflected the commitment of course designers to the belief that teaching practice must be guided if teachers are to have reference points when developing and evaluating their teaching. It supported the claim that good teaching practice is mindful of a relatively confirmable and highly functional body of knowledge while being heavily reliant on sophisticated levels of reflexivity and an ongoing resistance to any easy determinism amongst its practitioners. Furthermore, the CPE was very much an expression of support for the notion that universities and experienced school teachers not only can but must work together to generate a more academic-minded corps of professionals.

4.5 Researching the Efficacy of the CPE

To examine the extent to which the CPE was helping to bridge the relationship between academic studies and professional practice experiences and knowledge we conducted a series of questionnaires, focus groups and interviews in 2011 before undertaking further research in 2012. In 2011, participants from the different levels of engagement with the CPE were asked to examine beliefs and understandings about: (i) the nature of teaching and learning; (ii) the form and implementation of the CPE; (iii) the importance of language and literacy to teaching and (iv) the impact of social and policy contexts to teaching. No questions asked directly about the impact of the CPE on bringing academic studies together with professional practice knowledge. Many of the questions were structured in such a way, though, that conclusions could be drawn about the teacher candidates' capacity to link the two.

Data were gathered from teacher candidates and mentor teachers via separate online questionnaires that were both voluntary and anonymous. Data were also gathered from clinical specialists and teaching fellows during small focus group discussions.

Responses were recorded, coded and categorised according to three broad areas: understandings of the nature of teaching and learning; the relationship among research, theory and practice; and the implementation of the CPE. Analysis occurred through an iterative process of examining the data as it first appeared, then comparing the data with theory and other research before returning to the data again. This process gave rise to a number of themes, some of which included concerns about the impact of the CPE on workload, gaps in understanding, and areas for improvement. In this chapter we have limited our reporting to participant responses regarding the impact of the CPE on bringing theory and practice closer together.

4.6 Research Findings

The following discussion explores the potential of the clinical praxis exam to assist teacher candidates in linking university studies and professional practice knowledge, among three key groups of participants in teacher education: (1) teacher candidates; (2) school-based staff including teaching fellows and mentor teachers; and (3) university-based staff including academics and clinical specialists.

4.6.1 Teacher Candidates

As noted, teacher candidates were not asked directly about how the CPE assisted them in linking education theory and classroom practice. However, when asked: 'What was the most rewarding aspect of undertaking the CPE? Or what was the most valuable thing you learnt through undertaking the CPE?' almost one third chose to talk about this linking, with many indicating it was *the* most valuable thing they learnt through the process.

> I thought the most valuable part was seeing how it all connected together, and really putting into practice what we had learnt from Uni. I thought it was a good indication of using all knowledge from each area and applying it.

> Reading what the research said on my methodology and analysing deeply why I used the strategy I used made me understand a bit more what kind of teacher I am. It also helped me find resources that are appropriate for me and will help me design better ... lessons.

> Being able to directly link theory, research and practice and to try and articulate that in one case

> I found the CPE valuable in relating educational theory into classroom practice. Having the opportunity to voice my experiences and pedagogical approach was incredibly rewarding and helped me to identify my own pedagogical approach.

Many teacher candidates also spoke about the impact of the CPE on the students with whom they had worked and identified this as the most rewarding aspect of the CPE. Some then went on to explain that it was the bringing together of theory and practice that assisted in working with students.

> After speaking all about different theorists, this CPE really made the link between knowing a student's learning need and a learning theorist. I had felt lost until it was time to plan and organise this CPE.

> [Seeing] the difference my intervention made in the learning of my focus students. Tying theory and practice together in a hands-on exercise allowed me to better understand the link.

A number of teacher candidates also wrote about the impact the CPE had on their understanding of their academic studies, in particular, highlighting the way in which the CPE assisted them in bringing together the different elements across the programme of study at the university.

> Making sure I fully understood the concept/literature and was able to put that knowledge to use in a real situation.

> The most valuable thing gained from the CPE is being forced to see how the three subjects interrelate.

This last point was particularly interesting for the academic team who had worked on development of the CPE. Until the CPE, very little discussion had occurred among academics teaching in the fields of educational psychology, sociology and education, language and literacy, and the various learning areas. Each subject was taught separately and it was assumed teacher candidates would, and could, make sense of the contradictions and tensions that existed between the different fields and the conflicting demands of each subject. There also existed an unarticulated assumption that teacher candidates would be able to incorporate elements from each of these fields into their daily practice during their professional placements. However, no formal structures existed to facilitate dialogue about how this might occur. With its emphasis on highlighting the complexity of any educational encounter and subsequent intervention, the CPE encouraged and supported conversations among university staff and school-based staff in ways that developed deeper clarity about the purposes of a clinically based programme of study. This, in turn, provided teacher candidates with strong support in developing deep understandings about the complex intellectual, diagnostic, planning, intervention, and evaluative aspects of teaching practice. The CPE also encouraged them to engage with, and respond to, the social and cultural realities of students' lives, and the linguistic and literacy demands of the subjects they were teaching. As one teacher candidate noted, 'making the links with theory encourages a more reflective approach to teaching'.

4.6.2   School-Based Teaching Fellows

Many of the school-based teaching fellows spoke about the additional time demands the CPE added to their work and the difficulty the task presented for some of the mentor teachers. These difficulties appeared to result from the shift in focus brought about by the CPE. Previously, mentor teachers and teaching fellows had understood a large part of their support for teacher candidates was to focus on the mechanics of teaching and the teacher candidate's capacity to perform in the classroom. The assumption was that if teacher candidates planned methodically, managed classroom behaviour and delivered lessons in an engaging manner, they were doing well and students were learning. The CPE focused attention on student learning as the principal aim of teacher candidates' professional placement experience. This required teacher candidates, and those with whom they worked, to develop close knowledge about each student's current levels of knowledge, understanding and skills, as well as an intimate knowledge of the content they were teaching, appropriate pedagogical content knowledge and sophisticated skills of assessment and evaluation. A number of teaching fellows described the impact of the CPE on the teacher candidates in the following ways:

> The CPE focuses practice on the skill of diagnosis and intervention. It moves TCs away from content teaching to focus on process and student learning.

> The CPE improves the TC's ability to plan their teaching. It hones the TC's awareness of planning and implementing an intervention strategy that genuinely integrates the three core subjects.

> The course is brave enough to try something new to reinforce understanding in totality – not just in isolated subjects, as is often the case.

While some school-based teaching fellows described a number of teachers as seeing the CPE 'as another "ivory tower" task and gave minimal help' to the teacher candidates, other teaching fellows spoke about the positive impact of the task on many mentor teachers.

The CPE improves mentor teacher and teacher candidate practice. Mentors are challenged to re-think current actions.

Mentor teachers can see it as an opportunity to get the teacher candidates to work with an 'at risk' or high needs student.

Professional dialogue is enhanced

Quite a number of teaching fellows spoke about the way in which the CPE altered the relationship between mentor teachers and teacher candidates in positive ways:

The CPE strengthened professional conversations between teaching fellows and mentor teachers. [The CPE] affirmed the mentor teacher's role as important to development of teacher candidates. Some mentor teachers learned from teacher candidate's research.

One teaching fellow noted that some mentor teachers 'can resent teacher candidates who intervene with a student who the mentor teacher is not handling well'. Other teaching fellows spoke about the impact of the CPE on their own practice indicating that it 'enhanced' and 'improved' their understanding of the university programme.

[I developed a] new awareness of the integration and the overall clinical intervention teaching practice model of the M. Teach.

Now see the need for teacher candidates to address each of the core subjects in balanced way.

Some teaching fellows described feeling 'more connected to the university' and felt that the task promoted greater 'reflection on their own teaching' and helped develop their 'understanding of the individual needs [of] students'.

4.6.3 School-Based Mentor Teachers

A number of mentor teachers indicated that the task facilitated relationship building between themselves and the teacher candidates through shared collection of data, choice of focus student and shared decision-making of pedagogical interventions. Almost one in five mentor teachers indicated that the CPE had had a positive impact on their own teaching,

Further to this, most respondents expressed interest in training and education associated with the CPE: as professional development; to further the partnerships between schools and the university; to develop mentoring skills; and to enhance the relationships with the teacher candidates.

Of particular note is that most mentor teachers indicated the need for further work to ensure that all mentor teachers were fully cognisant of the ways in which the task could support the linking of theory and practice. These data were instructive for the academic team of researchers, whose intention was to design a task that would essentially draw on the daily work teacher candidates were undertaking with students in classrooms, and not additional work. Data emphasised the imperative of working closely with mentor teachers around teacher candidate assessment, and more broadly the vision of the Master of Teaching. These data provided impetus for the revision of the task, and in particular the development of professional learning initiatives for mentor teachers around clinical praxis imperatives.

4.6.4   University-Based Academics and Clinical Specialists

In 2012, a further project was undertaken to gain an understanding of the ways in which academic staff working in the Master of Teaching (Secondary) were experiencing the connections between theory and practice facilitated by the clinical model, and leveraged by the CPE. This project involved 12 in depth semi-structured interviews with a range of staff either supporting candidates in schools as clinical specialists or working in the academic programme, either in discipline specific learning areas, or a range of academic subjects, including the core subjects in which the CPE is assessed. While the results and analysis of this project are the focus of a separate article in preparation, and the CPE was not the focus of this research per se, it is worth noting that of the staff members interviewed, all those working in both the academic and school-based programme (eight participants) identified the CPE as a catalyst for shifting their thinking about teacher preparation. Participants also identified ways in which the CPE had impacted on the delivery and content of their academic subjects in assisting with the linking of theory and practice. One academic, who works as both a school-based teaching fellow and an academic learning area specialist said:

> The CPE is fundamentally important – from the point of view of seeing the outcome students are moving towards at the end of semester. It is instrumental in my discussions with mentor teachers, as to what TCs may be wanting to research [and] why they are collecting data. In terms of the learning area it has helped me to really emphasise what we do need to focus on in semester.

The notion that the CPE was providing a link between the university and the site of practice was also emphasised by another academic who was working as a learning area specialist on campus, and also one day a week in a school as a clinical specialist. For this academic, the CPE oriented the academic subjects towards the school, and served as an example of how assessment in the Master of Teaching might be considered differently:

> I think the CPE is a key – significant- not so much that it is [drawing together] three common subjects, but because it is absolutely grounded in school, and on an individual in a school. I think it has shifted everyone's thinking.

As will be discussed more fully in a forthcoming article focussed on this project, this 'shift in thinking' pertained most strongly to those who had access to the CPE, through either teaching in a core subject or through a school-based clinical role. For these academics, the CPE offered a framework for thinking differently about the integrated nature of theory and practice in a clinical model of pre-service teacher education, and revealed that these staff members saw themselves as occupying and nurturing the space of praxis. For those whose roles did not provide the opportunity to facilitate or assess this task, understandings of clinical praxis were more varied and diffused. This has pointed to both the value of a shared articulation of the nexus between theory and practice, and the value of curriculum and assessment innovations drawing together academic study and placement sites.

4.7   CPE Developments Since 2012

Since 2012, the CPE has been a significant factor in furthering the partnerships between the university and schools and consolidating the ways in which both university and school-based staff view the links between academic studies and professional practice knowledge. The inclusion of school-based staff (teaching fellows) on CPE assessment panels (from 2011) and the professional development associated with this involvement has been a factor in a number of school-based staff attaining university-based employment as teachers in the Master of Teaching coursework subjects. Conversely, the CPE has provided an impetus for school-based professional development, run by university staff. The CPE has also provided a focus for clinical specialists, teaching fellows and mentor teachers to frame their discussions of classroom observations; furthermore, significant numbers of teacher candidates have commented that their interviews for employment comprised discussion of their approaches to the CPE. All of these factors have contributed to the CPE becoming more understood in the partnership schools. One illustration of this is the way in which a number of partnership schools have adapted the CPE as a vehicle for staff appraisal. In one such school, the teacher performance review process utilises the CPE format so that practising teachers reflect on their use of classroom data and framing theory as a means to evaluate their own professional development. Associated with this growing understanding of clinical praxis in partnership schools has been the development of two university courses aimed at practising teachers: the Professional Certificate of Clinical Teaching, first implemented in 2012; and the online Master of Clinical Teaching, offered for the first time in 2016. While both of these courses explore clinical practice broadly, the links between theory and practice are fundamental to their design, with CPE examples providing useful modelling for course participants.

4.8   Conclusion

Increased attention to the educational performance of nations has resulted in international concern with the quality and relevance of teacher preparation programmes. In Australia, governmental interest in pre-service teacher education programmes resulted in the formation of a Teacher Education Ministerial Advisory Group, and the subsequent publication of a report (2015) emphasising the need for pre-service teachers to be *classroom ready* at the conclusion of their pre-service preparation. Clearly, the key to classroom readiness lies in the ways in which pre-service programmes are able to offer teacher candidates opportunities to negotiate the nexus between their academic studies and professional practice knowledge—to embrace praxis—and ensure that rich professional practice experiences are supported by rigorous investigations of relevant theory and research.

The research conducted in conjunction with the implementation of the CPE has revealed that while there are challenges and complexities in implementing curriculum and assessment items that transcend and redefine the traditional boundaries of school and university, the affordances for teacher candidates are significant. In his paper for the Australian Institute for Teaching and School leadership (AITSL), *Standardised Assessment of Initial Teacher Education: Environmental Scan and Case Studies*, William Louden concluded that the CPE is reflective of best practice in teacher education assessment, and could be extended nationally (Louden 2015, p. 33). Further to this, the CPE innovation in the Melbourne Master of Teaching has shown the potential for assessment undertaken during a pre-service programme to not only leverage the potential of a clinical model of teaching for teacher candidates, but to enhance the praxis of all concerned with the programme, including university academics and school-based staff.

References

Alexander, R. J. (2008). *Essays on pedagogy*. London: Routledge.

Australian Learning and Teaching Council. (2009). *Practicum partnerships: Exploring models of practicum organisation in teacher education for a standards-based profession* (Final Report).

Biggs, J. B. (2003). *Teaching for quality learning at university*. Buckingham, UK: The Society for Research into Higher Education and Open University Press.

Burbules, N. C. (1993). *Dialogue in teaching: Theory and practice*. New York: Teachers College Press.

Burn, K., & Mutton, T. (2013). Review of research informed clinical practice in initial teacher education. *British Education Research Association* (*Bera*). Retrieved from http://Www.Bera.Ac.Uk/Wp-Content/Uploads/2014/02/Bera-Paper-4-Research-Informed-Clinical-Practice.Pdf

Darling-Hammond, L., & Bransford, J. (Eds.). (2005). *Preparing teachers for a changing world: What teachers should learn and be able to do*. San Francisco: Jossey Boss.

Kemmis, S., & Smith, T. J. (2008). Personal praxis: Learning through experience. In S. Kemmis & T. J. Smith (Eds.), *Enabling praxis: Challenges for education*. Rotterdam, The Netherlands: Sense Publishers.

Kriewaldt, J., & Turnidge, D. (2013). Conceptualising an approach to clinical reasoning in the education profession. *Australian Journal of Teacher Education, 38*(6), 102–115. doi:10.14221/Ajte.2013v38n6.9

Louden, W. (2015). *Insights—Standardised assessment of initial teacher education: Environmental scan and case* studies. A paper prepared for the Australian Institute for Teaching and School Leadership (AITSL). http://Www.Aitsl.Edu.Au/Docs/Default-Source/Initial-Teacher-Education-Resources/Standardised-Assessment-Of-Ite_Environmental-Scan-And-Case-Studies.Pdf

Loughran, J. (2010). *What expert teachers do: Enhancing professional knowledge for classroom practice*. London: Routledge.

Mattsson, M., Eilertson, T. V., & Rorrison, D. (Eds.). (2011). *A practicum turn in teacher education*. Rotterdam: Sense Publishers.

Mclean Davies, L., Anderson, M., Deans, J., Dinham, S., Griffin, P., Kameniar, B., et al. (2013). Masterly preparation: Embedding clinical practice in a graduate pre-service teacher education programme. *Journal of Education for Teaching: International Research and Pedagogy, 39*(1), 93–106. doi:10.1080/02607476.2012.733193

Teacher Education Ministerial Advisory Group (TEMAG). (2015). *Action now: Classroom ready teachers*. Canberra: Department of Education.

Vick, M. (2006). 'It's a difficult matter: Historical perspectives on the enduring problem of the practicum in teacher preparation'. *Asia-Pacific Journal of Teacher Education, 34*(2), 181–198.

Zeichner, K., Payne, K. A., & Brayko, K. (2015). Democratizing teacher education. *Journal of Teacher Education, 66*(2), 122–135.

Author Biographies

Barbara Kameniar is Senior Fellow in the Melbourne Graduate School of Education and Adjunct Senior Lecturer in the Faculty of Education at the University of Tasmania. The primary focus of her research and teaching is improvement of teacher practice to support the learning outcomes of power-marginalised young people.

Larissa McLean Davies is an Associate Professor in Language and Literacy, and Associate Dean, Teacher Education Research in the Melbourne Graduate School of Education. Larissa's current research is concerned with teacher education effectiveness, clinical teaching, and the role of literature in subject English.

Jefferson Kinsman is a teacher educator in the Melbourne Graduate School of Education. After studying Philosophy, Law and Literature, he taught for 14 years in high schools in Melbourne. He now specialises in preparing Humanities teachers for the classroom, in relation to which he is currently undertaking a Ph.D.

Catherine Reid is a lecturer in the Melbourne Graduate School of Education. Catherine lectures in a number of Masters programs, and most recently, was part of a team who developed an online Master of Clinical Teaching. Catherine's research interests include school- university partnerships, and 21st century literarcies across the curriculum.

Debra Tyler lectures in Sociology of Education at the Melbourne Graduate School of Education. Debra, in particular, is involved in the rural teaching program and the coordination of both an international and Aboriginal and Torres Strait Islander teaching placement for pre-service teachers.

Daniela Acquaro is the Program Coordinator of the Master of Teaching Secondary in the Melbourne Graduate School of Education. As a Senior Lecturer in Teacher Education, her research focuses on initial teacher education, teacher effectiveness and teachers' lives. She is also interested in teacher preparation for alternative and global educational settings.

Chapter 5
A Role of Doing Philosophy in a Humanistic Approach to Teacher Education

Duck-Joo Kwak

5.1 Introduction: A Humanistic Approach to Teacher Education

In teaching a philosophy of education course within teacher training program, we are often challenged by self-assertive student-teachers with questions like: "What is the relevance of philosophy to teacher training?" or more specifically, "What is the relevance of 'philosophy of education' to the (professional) life of teachers?" Knowing that any attempt to respond to such questions in the form of justificatory claims—i.e., giving the account of how useful it may be—will sound unconvincing to them,[1] I tend to throw the question back at them, asking what sort of relevance they can conceive of in terms of its preparation for their professional lives. Very often, doubtful silence follows. The raising of this relevance-question by students over the role of philosophy of education in teacher education program has always haunted me, but with a sense of frustration as well as a sense of fascination: it frustrates me because I do not have any magical answer for them, and it fascinates me because it suggests to me that they may at least be beginning their journey to an answer. How exasperating yet deeply intriguing this challenge is to us!

An earlier version of this essay, "Stanley Cavell's Ordinary Language Philosophy as an Example of Practicing Philosophy in the Essay-form: In Search of a Humanistic Approach to Teacher Education," was published in *Teachers College Record*, 113:8 (2011). I am grateful for permission to use this material here.

[1]What is assumed here is that practically minded students will be looking for some instrumental connection between philosophy and their professional lives. That is, they will want to know what skills and competences philosophy will equip them with.

D.-J. Kwak (✉)
Seoul National University, Seoul, South Korea
e-mail: djkwak@snu.ac.kr

M.A. Peters et al. (eds.), *A Companion to Research in Teacher Education*,
DOI 10.1007/978-981-10-4075-7_5

There is a distinctive line of response to this kind of challenge that I find quite attractive. This is from the view of philosophy of education as "practical philosophy" (Carr 1995, 2005; Dunne 1993), a view that emerged as a decisive alternative to the analytic tradition of philosophy of education, alongside the postmodernist critique of philosophy as an epistemology-oriented theoretical project. What I find interesting and instructive about the "practical" nature of this line of response is twofold. One is that it is based on the view of education as a human practice with its own tradition and integrity long embedded in educational communities through the accumulated *practical* wisdom of teachers. The other is that philosophy of education as "practical philosophy" is expected to be not so much "philosophy *of* education" as "philosophy *for* education," in the sense that it is "explicitly committed to promoting the integrity of education as a practice by cultivating the educational practitioner's natural human capacity of *phronesis* (*practical knowledge*)" (Hirst and Carr 2005, pp. 625–626). This means that the teaching of philosophy of education is in itself expected to be *educative* by producing not theoretically justified propositional knowledge but "reflectively acquired self-knowledge" *in* student-practitioners. Thus, the idea of teaching or doing philosophy of education as practical philosophy can pre-empt the relevance-question that can be raised by student-teachers because the whole approach is designed to begin with students' direct engagement in the understanding of their own educational practice.

Wilfred Carr, one of the main advocates of this view of philosophy of education, aims to enable student-practitioners to engage in a form of reflective philosophy that makes them more self-consciously aware of the prejudices embedded in their pre-philosophical practical understanding of education and the historical and cultural contexts of their lives. Combining this reflective philosophy with "action research" as a form of practitioner research, Carr presents his action research as a kind of inquiry that enables practitioners to test the historically embedded assumptions implicit in their practice in such a way as to improve their practice (Carr 2007, p. 145). Thus, we can say that philosophy of education as practical philosophy begins with a full acknowledgement of its dependence on the willingness of student-practitioners to recover reflectively the unacknowledged prejudices at work in their practical knowledge as a way of improving the practical knowledge exercised in their educational practice.

While being sympathetic to the "practical" nature of this view of philosophy of education—in the sense of its being "explicitly committed to promoting the integrity of education as a practice"—I wonder if there may be another form of reflective philosophy that can contribute to "cultivating the educational practitioner's natural human capacity of *phronesis* (*practical knowledge*)," *in Carr's words. Practical philosophy as action research may* prepare would-be teachers to be historically conscious and reflective professionals, but it would fall short of enabling them to be morally mature and emotionally literate *humanistic* professionals. I want to hold on to the word "humanistic" in order to differentiate what I am doing most obviously from technicist approaches to teacher education but also from those forms of practical philosophy associated with Carr and Dunne.

As David Hansen (Hansen 2001, p. 21) suggests in his emphasis on "the person" in the role of the teacher,[2] I think the cultivation of this humanistic orientation for teachers is more urgent today than ever. It is an orientation that can be sensitive to the predicament of being human in the face of the conflicts of modern life and that can respond to the increasing yet unpredictable complexity of social relations and human emotions. This is even more important when unprecedented changes in our educational environment, against the background of economic globalization, tend to challenge and frustrate classroom teachers, sometimes to the point of breakdown.[3] Questions that might touch a person's soul—questions about their sensibility, their fate, wholly conflicting world-views, the vanity of human existence and so on— have rarely been the object of ethical or educational reflection with teachers. But it is precisely this sort of ethical and educational reflection that would *deepen* their self-understanding—of the emotions, desires and opinions whose innumerable cross-currents give point, purpose, and meaning to their lives. And I think this kind of self-understanding constitutes a core to the kind of humanistic practical wisdom that teachers need to deal with the difficulties in their everyday school lives.

In contrast to reflective philosophy in the form of action research, I would call this new form of humanistic practice "philosophy in the form of essay." As men- tioned in the earlier chapters, the term "essay" has its origin in the title of the sixteenth century French Renaissance humanist Michel de Montaigne's book *Essais* (1958), where its literal meaning is "attempt" or "test." Montaigne is known for popularizing the essay as a literary genre in which serious philosophical speculation is merged with anecdotes and autobiography. Montaigne identifies the essay as a philosophical form for "trying-oneself-out" or "putting-oneself-to-the-test" or "self-study" in which philosophical reflection and personal story-telling are held in balance in such a way as to uncover a deeper sense of things. I take inspiration from this idea of the essay because it exemplifies the *classical* relation of philosophy to life but refracted through the *modernist* sensibility. It is *classical* in the sense that the essay as a philosophical practice is also an educational practice in which what we know of the world is turned to the problem of how to conduct ourselves, as shown in Socratic soul-searching. It is *modernist* in the sense that the essay's openness to the unsettling and the unorthodox reflects our modern sense of

---

[2]In his book *Exploring the Moral Heart of Teaching* (2001), David Hansen refreshingly explores the nature and predicament of teaching that can be well articulated and responded to by the humanistic sensibility.

[3]Think, for example, of the kind of classroom setting with students from different ethnic and cultural backgrounds that is seen in the recently released French film, *The Class* (2009), and the kinds of challenges that these rebellious students present to the teacher. These wild and uncon- ventional, yet curious and self-assertive students seem to represent a new kind of challenge to teachers today. Even in Korea today, well-intentioned young teachers often leave their teaching career after the disillusionment they experience when confronted by wild teenage students, who seem completely unintelligible to them.

insecurity—an insecurity that is the price we pay for our newly acquired freedom, in a world with no fixed points of support.[4]

In this chapter, I shall explore whether this original sense of the essay can be recovered for the purpose of cultivating a humanistic orientation in our student-teachers. I will take here Stanley Cavell's notion of ordinary language philosophy as an exemplary case of the essay-form of writing and thinking, and examine its underlying method and aspiration to see if it can be developed into a humanistic approach to teacher education. Here I will focus on whether his ordinary language philosophy is a plausible way of recovering the aspiration of the classical relation of philosophy to life, at the same time considering how far its method realizes the modernist sensibility. This will, I hope, pave the way for a rich response to the relevance-question raised by student-teachers, addressed at the beginning of this introduction.

5.2   The Methodological Characteristics of Cavell's Ordinary Language Philosophy

In the introduction to his work *Must We Mean What We Say?* (Cavell 1976), Cavell attempts to articulate the beliefs underlying his way of philosophizing and explain why it takes such a form. While acknowledging that different aspects of his writing can be categorized under such different headings as philosophy, literature or criticism, Cavell confesses his wish to call them all *philosophical* works. I take this as saying that what he does, across different genres of writing, is always "philosophical" in a different sense from that in which we normally understand the word. But then what does he mean by "philosophy" or "the philosophical"? It seems to take the whole book for him to explain the kind of philosophy he does. In fact, what he seems to intend is not to explain this directly but rather to *show* it through different styles of his writings, with sporadic comments about it; in other words, the way he explains it is very allusive and elusive, turning a number of corners and taking many detours. This means that it is not easy for readers to grasp the nature of his philosophical work in a systematic way. So let me reconstruct his account of the kind of philosophy he is doing, mainly drawing upon his book *Must We Mean What We Say?* since this early work does seem to give a more or less explicit account of what he is doing.

Cavell makes it clear from the beginning that he does not see philosophy as a form of science. I think this can be read as a way of distancing himself from the tradition of analytic philosophy in which he was academically trained. In fact, Cavell tries to describe his complex relationship with this analytic tradition in terms of what he calls "the modern," similar to the problem of the modern in the modern

---

[4]Emphasizing this modernist aspect of Montaigne's philosophy, Hartle calls it 'accidental philosophy', implying the radically contingent and created order of the world (Hartle 2003, pp. 3–27).

art,[5] and he devotes some space to an account of this term. According to Cavell, the essential feature of "the modern" lies in "the fact that the relation between the present practice of an enterprise and the history of the enterprise" has become problematic (Cavell 1976, p. xix). Here he formulates the problem of "the modern" in relation to his philosophical practice in two ways. First, anyone committed to the enterprise tends to be placed in a *paradoxical* position in which he or she needs to *repudiate* the history, and yet his or her practice and ambition within the enterprise can be identified only against the continuous experience of the past. Second, the past here does not refer merely to the historical past, but "to one's own past, to what is past, or what has passed, within oneself". Cavell adds: "in a modernist situation 'past' loses its temporal accent and means anything 'not present' (Cavell 1976, p. xix)." Thus, for Cavell, "the modern" means that "what one says becomes a matter of making one's sense present to oneself." I would call the first element of the modern "the historical turn" and the second element of it "the intra-personal turn." Cavell finally announces that Wittgenstein's philosophical practice and J.L. Austin's philosophical teaching are exactly what taught him how to do philosophy in this *modernist* sense, incorporating these two turnings. This is why Cavell describes his philosophy as "ordinary language philosophy, following the spirit of these two philosophers. We can also notice here that Cavell's ordinary language philosophy is a form of philosophy that has come out of serious confrontations with two elements: one's tradition and one's self.

How, then, should we understand Cavell's ordinary language philosophy in this modernist sense? How can it be characterized? What is its distinctive philosophical procedure? Cavell takes pains throughout the book to show the main characteristics of ordinary language philosophy. He sometimes complains about his teacher Austin's not giving an accurate account of his philosophical procedures; at other times, he ponders the thought that Austin's apparent reluctance to do this may itself be a way of saying something about ordinary language philosophy. For example, in the middle of discussing *King Lear*, Cavell suddenly mentions the difficulty of "discovering when and how to stop philosophizing" (Cavell 1976, p. 269). It seems that Cavell writes in this way about *King Lear* as if to show the nature of his ordinary language philosophy. In this sense, we may even say that Cavell's entire texts are designed to make our reading of them challenging and demanding, to remind us constantly as *readers* of this difficulty of "discovering when and how to stop philosophizing".

---

[5]The term 'modern art' is usually associated with art in which, in a spirit of experimentation, the traditions and conventions of the past are no longer taken for granted, and it refers to artworks produced during the period extending roughly from the 1860s through to the 1970s. Modern artists experimented with new ways of seeing and with fresh ideas about the *nature* of materials and the functions of art, being highly conscious of the nature of their own practice. A salient characteristic of modern art is self-consciousness. This often led to experiments with form and work that draw attention to the processes and materials used. I think that the same thing can be said about the nature of what Cavell attempts to do in his practice of philosophy.

What sort of difficulty is this? Why is it so difficult for us to know "when and how to stop philosophizing"? To unpack what this phrase means seems critical to the understanding of Cavell's notion of ordinary language philosophy. So let me take it as a starting-point for our enquiry. I think this difficulty has deep connections with what Cavell describes below as ordinary language philosophy:

> there[in ordinary language philosophy] the problem is also raised of determining data from which philosophy proceeds and to which it appeals, and specifically the issue is one of placing the words and experiences with which philosophers have always begun in align-ment with human beings in particular circumstances who can be imagined to be having those experiences and saying and meaning those words. This is all that "ordinary" in the phrase "ordinary language philosophy" means, or ought to mean... It reminds us that whatever words are said and meant are said and meant by particular men, and that to understand what they (the words) mean you must understand what they (whoever is using them) mean, and that sometimes men do not see what they mean, that usually they cannot say what they mean, that for various reasons they may not know what they mean, that when they are forced to recognize this they feel they do not, perhaps cannot, mean anything, and they are struck dumb. (Cavell 1976, p. 270)

The passage above points to the two distinctive features of the practice of ordinary language philosophy. First, ordinary language philosophy is usually triggered by something we are tempted to say about particular persons in particular circum-stances, the meaning of which can be brought out by appealing to widely shared, or easily imaginable, circumstances. This means that the ordinary language philoso-pher claims to know only what an ordinary human being can know and that this is what "ordinary" means in "ordinary language philosophy." Second, the ordinary language philosopher seems to take seriously the fact that, sometimes when asked, the speaker of an utterance does not know how to "place" the ordinary words and experiences in relation to her own particular circumstance, even when she is the one who has uttered the words. For we ourselves sometimes do not seem to know, when we are asked, what we meant when we said the words. This is exactly the state that the ordinary language philosopher intends to throw us into, i.e., the state of "being struck dumb" when faced by the question "What do you mean by what you said?"[6] But, how is it that we can say words without knowing what we mean by them? We have to ask, then, *what sort of meaning* the ordinary language philosopher is concerned with in asking the speaker what she means by her words.

According to Cavell, in asking what the speaker means by her words, the ordinary language philosopher does not expect her to *explain* or *paraphrase* the

---

[6]Now it may be objected that this is a slight variation on the formulation of words with which ordinary language philosophy is most commonly associated, which is "When we say..., we mean..." And indeed Cavell makes much of the importance of this being both first person and plural, indicating first that we are required to say how things seem *to us*, and second that in so doing we are trying to speak for others too, making an appeal *to community*. But it is this very point that legitimates my expressing this in the second person: in doing ordinary language phi-losophy with others (and how else could it be done?), I must take the other's first person expression as at the same time an address to me, to see if this is what I mean by the words I use.

meaning of her words. As an example, let us take the case where I ask a close friend of mine what she means when she says of Jane, who I know lives next-door: "Jane is a student at the school where I am teaching." In response to my question, my friend may well respond, with some surprise: "What do *you* mean by the question? You don't know who Jane is?" Or considering that I am not a native English speaker, she may try to explain the words "student" or "school" or some aspect of her expression that may have caused my trouble in understanding her words. According to Cavell, what my friend is trying to do for me, in such a scenario, is precisely to *explain* the meaning of her words; here what is at stake is the *literal* meaning of the words. So, if my friend can explain things to me *this* way in response to my question, she can be said to know what she means by her words.

We can imagine another context in which I ask another friend of mine what she means when she says: "Juliet is the sun to Romeo." Unlike the earlier case, the first response of my friend is not likely to be one of surprise; for what is at stake here is the *metaphorical* meaning of the words. According to Cavell, what is expected from the speaker in this case is *not* that she explain the words by, say, offering dictionary-type definitions of them, but rather that she *paraphrase* the expression; for in metaphorical expressions "meaning is bound up in the very words they [the expressions] employ" (Cavell 1976, p. 78). Thus, my friend might say: "To Romeo Juliet is the warmth of his world, his day begins with her, and so on. This is why Juliet is the sun to Romeo." If she cannot provide some kind of answer along these lines for me, we can say she does not know what she means by the words she has said. An interesting point that Cavell makes in regard to the metaphorical expression of words is that to understand a metaphor, or to be able to give its paraphrase, we need to understand the ordinary meanings of the words first, *and then* we are able to see that the words are not there being used in their ordinary sense; we are now invited to look for the meanings of the words *imaginatively*. What is unique about the function of metaphor as an expressive form of words is that it opens up the meanings of words in a more or less indefinite way, so that the words can mean as much as the speaker can imagine. Thus, Cavell says, "metaphors are paraphrasable" (Cavell 1976, p. 79).[7]

In the light of this, then, we can say that it is neither the *literal* nor the *metaphorical* meanings of the words that ordinary language philosophers are concerned with in asking the speaker what she means by her words; for philosophers are interested in the case in which the speaker does not know what she means,

---

[7]Some people are very good at explaining what they mean by their words, putting their thoughts another way, perhaps referring to a range of similar or identical thoughts that have been expressed by others, depending upon who the listeners are. These good explainers are those who are quick to notice what prevents the listeners from understanding the meaning of their words, whether this is their presuppositions, their prejudices and so forth. But to *explain* what I mean by my words is basically to *reproduce* the *literal* meaning of the words; nothing is to be added to the original meaning of them. On the other hand, in the case of metaphor, in giving the paraphrase, we are *free to create* meaning in an indefinite way. According to Cavell, this is the very attraction of metaphor as a form of expression, even if there is always the danger of over-reading (Cavell 1976, p. 79).

even if she knows what the words mean to her in the literal or metaphorical sense. In fact, Cavell brings up the point that there are some modes of figurative language in which what the expression means cannot be stated at all, at least not in any conventional way. According to Cavell, one example in such a use of language is the style of poetry known as "Symbolist", "Surrealist," or "Imagist."[8] Cavell describes the kind of dumbness that strikes us in such a case when we find ourselves lacking the language to express what we mean by the words we use:

> I know what it means but I cannot say what it means. And this would no longer suggest, as it would if said about a metaphor, that you really do not know what it means—or; it might suggest it, but you couldn't be sure...

> Paraphrasing the lines, or explaining their meaning, or telling it or putting the thought another way—all these are out of the question. One may be able to say nothing except that a feeling has been voiced by a kindred spirit and that if someone does not get it he is not in one's world, or not of one's flesh. The lines may, that is, be left as touchstones of intimacy. Or one might try describing more or less elaborately a particular day or evening, a certain place and mood and gesture, in whose presence the line in question comes to seem a natural expression, the only expression. (Cavell 1976, p. 81)

The moment of dumbness Cavell describes in the earlier citation seems to refer here to the moment when we feel something deep, rich or powerful inside us, which cannot be put into words. For Cavell, this is not a *failing* of language but a feature of a specific approach of language. As Cavell suggests above, in poetry of certain kinds the words are used *not to mean* something, but *to show* something, as if they were *gestures* of pointing to something happening deep inside us.

But what exactly is Cavell trying to say when he talks about the nature of "this dumbness" that ordinary language philosophers tend to evoke in us? What does he imply about the connection between using words and meaning what they say? Normally what is said is what is meant; when being forced to explain the meaning of what we say, we can explain what we mean by the words we use. But there are a number of specific ways in which one's words do not say what one means, as in the more deliberate cases of lying, feigning, or misleading, and as also in those less obvious cases of self-deceiving and "bad faith." Thus, the connection between using words and meaning what they say is not inevitable or automatic; it looks more like a matter of convention or convenience. Yet, for Cavell, this is not the sort of convention we would know how to get rid of. For "it is not a matter of convention or ritual unless having language is convenience or unless thinking and speaking are ritual" (Cavell 1976, p. 271). This would mean that having language (i.e., thinking and speaking) must be a very special kind of ritual (if it could be said to be a ritual at all), outside which we could not imagine what human life would be like, or without which there could be no human life at all. Likewise, if the connection between using words and meaning what they say is a matter of convention at all, this would be a very special kind of convention, in the absence of which we could

---

[8]Cavell cites as examples of poetic expression of this kind "The mind is brushed by sparrow wings," and "as a calm darkens among water-light" (Cavell 1976, p. 81).

not be the linguistic creatures as we are, and without which we could not even make sense of what we say. So what is the point of Cavell's pointing to the possibility of the disassociation between what we say and what we mean by what we say? Or what is the point of ordinary language philosophers' wish to "strike us dumb" with the annoying question of "What do you mean?"?

We may find some clue to Cavell's answer from the following passage:

> But Wittgenstein is also concerned with forms of words whose meaning cannot be elicited in this (ordinary) way—words we sometimes have it at heart to say but whose meaning is not secured by appealing to the way they are ordinarily (commonly) used, because there is no ordinary use of them, in that sense. It is not, therefore, that I mean something other than those words would ordinarily mean, but rather that what they mean, and whether they mean anything, depends solely upon whether I am using them so as to make my meaning... In general, Part II of the Philosophical Investigations moves into this region of meaning. It is a region habitually occupied by poetry. (Cavell 1976, p. 271)

Ordinary language philosophers tend to ask: "What do *you* mean by the words you use?" Of course, in response, I may be able to answer by saying what I meant by referring to the way they are ordinarily used. But being interested in forms of words in which there is a chasm between what we say and what we mean by it, ordinary language philosophers raise the question, "What do you mean?," in a *specific* way, to which the (ordinary) response I have just given is not quite on target—very much in the way that Plato's Meno, when he gives to Socrates all the answers he knows to the question, "What is virtue?," is thrown by Socrates. The passage tells us that the question raised by ordinary language philosophers, "What do you mean?," can be read to have a certain force in it, which gives us the impression that we are supposed to have our *own* meaning in saying the words we use, as if we *ought to* have a special relation to the words we say. This relation may be of a kind that could not be replaced by the conventional relation between using the words and meaning what they say, as if I *ought to* interfere between the two to create my own meaning. What is surprising is that Cavell says above that this demand is not meant to make us create a meaning for the words that is somehow other than what they ordinarily mean; there is no other meaning for them. The demand is rather meant to lead us to see the condition of what makes the words mean what they ordinarily mean or of what makes them mean anything at all: that is, to understand my capability in using words to say what I mean. But what does this mean?

As Cavell makes clear in the passage above, the moment when I find a disassociation between using words and meaning what they say, which is as much as to strike me dumb, is the moment when I am called upon to make my *own* meaning of the words, by intervening between the words I use and the meaning they have. But, as Cavell also says, this meaning that is my own creation cannot be other than what they ordinarily mean; in other words, there cannot be a special or private meaning that only I can attach to the words I use. Then what is the *use* of making my own meaning of the words? I think that, even if the meaning of the words I use remains the same, my relation to the words will be changed when I am able to make my own meaning of the words I use. In other words, I am forced to establish a new relation to the words I use and, thereby, a new relation to myself, as well as to the world around me. Cavell describes above the meaning involved here as akin to the meaning that poetry is usually concerned with.

Let me further elaborate on this point. One way of understanding "making my meaning" may be that I can say now that the words, whose meaning I already knew before, come to me in a new light, concrete and alive: "Now I know what the words mean *to* me, which is the same as what I knew before *objectively*, but not exactly the same *subjectively*." To put it another way, the same ordinary meaning of the words has come alive for me, and I can see now what the ordinary meaning of the words exactly means: now I am living through the words. I think this is exactly what Cavell means when he says above: "What they mean, and whether they mean anything, depends solely upon whether I am using them so as to make my meaning." Echoing the words of Michael Oakeshott that "Philosophical reflection is recognized here as the adventure of one who seeks to understand in other terms what he already understands and in which the understanding sought is a disclosure of the conditions of the understanding enjoyed and not a substitute for it" (Oakeshott 1975, p. vii), Cavell concludes, "their (ordinary philosophers') philosophical procedure is designed to bring us to a *consciousness* of the worlds we must have and hence of the lives we have" (Cavell 1976, p. xxv). In other words, ordinary language philosophy "strikes us dumb" only to lead us to become aware of what we already know through our *lived experience* of it.

To explore further the nature of this awareness that ordinary language philosophers try to realize for us, let me quote more of Cavell's words:

> The philosophy of ordinary language is not about language, anyway not in any sense in which it is not also about the world. Ordinary language philosophy is about whatever ordinary language is about.

> The philosopher appealing to everyday language turns to the reader not to convince him without proof but to get him to prove something, test something, against himself. He is saying: Look and find out whether you can see what I see, wish to say what I wish to say. (Cavell 1976, pp. 95–96)

From the passage above we may draw out three distinctive features about what ordinary language philosophy is about. First, we can confirm that ordinary language philosophy is about understanding the ordinary meaning of the language we use, but only in relation to *oneself*. In other words, it may be said that it is about the understanding of what we already know, but only to *deepen* its meaning in relation to oneself. Thus, we can say that ordinary language philosophy is, first and foremost, directed to one's self-knowledge as the first-person knowledge of one's inner experience. Second, the kind of self-knowledge that ordinary language philosophy is concerned with is, given the passage above, not a matter of knowing, but a matter of *seeing*: "Look, and find out whether you can *see* what I can *see*." I think this indicates a crucial aspect of what Cavell's ordinary language philosophy aspires to, which has to do with its primary concern with first-person self-knowledge, since seeing is exclusively a first-person activity. Third, Cavell's ordinary language philosopher seems to have a wish to subscribe to a kind of realism: she assumes that what she sees could be also seen or shared by others, even if this is not something that could ever be a matter of objective proof or certainty of knowing.

5.3   The Educational Aspiration of Cavell's Ordinary Language Philosophy

We may now wonder: if ordinary language philosophy is a matter of seeing, "Seeing exactly what?" In fact, Cavell gives us a short response to this in the passage above, when he says that ordinary language philosophy is not about language, nor about the world, but "about whatever ordinary language is about." This means that ordinary language philosophy is about the way we ordinarily use language to mean what we say—i.e., about our "language games," in Wittgenstein's terms. And Wittgenstein describes what the ordinary language philosopher does as "the grammatical investigation" of the language game, which means unpacking the grammar of the way we ordinarily use language. This indicates that there is a special grammar or pattern in the ways we ordinarily use language, which ordinary language philosophers are supposed to make stand out for us. To make this grammar or pattern stand out for ourselves, we need the form of account that ordinary language philosophers provide. What form would that be? In fact, describing ordinary language philosophers' job as "the grammatical investigation" of the way we use language gives us the impression that this project attempts to do something similar to what "transcendental argument" attempts to do.[9] But, following Wittgenstein, Cavell clearly denies this view. To get a clearer understanding of what is meant by "grammatical investigation," let me quote Wittgenstein's words directly:

> A main source of our failure to understand [our use of language] is that we do not command a clear view of the use of our words.—our grammar is lacking in this sort of perspicuity. A perspicuous representation produces just that understanding which consists of 'seeing connexions'. Hence the importance of finding and inventing intermediate cases.
>
> The concept of a perspicuous representation is of fundamental significance for us. It earmarks the form of account we give, the way we look at things. (Is this a 'Weltanschauung'?) (Wittgenstein 1958, #122)

From the passage above we can say that Wittgenstein does not presume that his grammatical investigation can provide a transcendental account of the grammar of

---

[9]'Transcendental argument' refers to a kind of philosophical inquiry that seeks to spell out all the presuppositions that are necessary to make sense of experience, or all the objective conditions that are necessary to make our experience at all. The first technical distinction between the terms 'transcendent' and 'transcendental' was made by Kant. Kant reserved the term 'transcendent' for entities such as God and soul that are said to be beyond human experience and to be unknowable. The term 'transcendental' Kant reserved to signify prior thought forms: the innate principles that give the mind the ability to formulate its perceptions and to make experience intelligible.

how we use language because "we do not command a clear view of the use of our words." He finds that we cannot ground or justify the grammar, nor explain it *for certain*. The grammar underlying the way we use language cannot afford the form of account his grammatical investigation requires. So, for Wittgenstein, the best thing we can do is to give an "intermediate case" that enable us to *see* the connections between things, for this will be the best means of attaining "a perspicuous representation," not of the whole but of that segment of reality, of the language game, that is under scrutiny. Thus, the offering of careful descriptions of intermediate cases that guide us to see connections would be the form of account that Wittgenstein or ordinary language philosophers would give in such grammatical investigations.

What should be noted here is that Wittgenstein says of his "form of account" that it is "the way we look at things" in the passage above. What does this mean? How should we understand it? One way of understanding it may be that his form of account (of the way we use language)—namely, the perspicuous representation—*reveals* (or shows) the way we look at things. Wittgenstein then asks himself in parenthesis at the end of the passage above, whether it (the way we look at things revealed here) is a *Weltanschauung*, a German word usually translated into English as "world view," referring to a comprehensive framework of ideas and beliefs through which we as individuals interpret the world and interact with it. Cavell's answer to this question of Wittgenstein's is insightful: "The answer to that question is, I take it, not No. Not, perhaps, Yes; because it is not a special, or competing, way of looking at things. But not No; because its mark of success is that the world seem—be—different" (Cavell 1976, p. 86).

Cavell characterizes "the way we look at things," revealed by Wittgenstein's form of account of the way we use language, as twofold. First, his answer is "not Yes"; this means that "the way we look at things" cannot be said to be a Weltanschauung because it is not a particular—i.e., Christian or Muslim, etc.—way of looking at things, which is what Weltanschauung usually means. Now looking at the term in a different way, Cavell's "the way we look at things" might be taken to refer to the human's way of looking at things, as opposed to, for example, the bird's way of looking at things, if this can be called a Weltanschauung at all. Second, Cavell's answer is "not No" because "the way we look at things" can be changed as a result of our grammatical investigation, not because we are now allowed to choose another way of looking at things—indeed we are not—but because things now seem different, the world becomes different. But what do all these points add up to? What do they mean? Cavell seems to say: we come to live in the (same) world in a different spirit (Cavell 1976, p. 86).

Thus, we may conclude that, when ordinary language philosophers ask us "What do you mean by the words you use?," they do not mean to test out empirically the extent of our agreement; nor are they setting out to strike us dumb. They mean rather to exert a certain pressure on us to make us see "the way we look at things." In other words, ordinary language philosophers try to challenge our very condition in using language as a whole, or our power to use language at all, by making us confront the gap between the words we say and what we mean by them, only to lead us to see the language game in which we live, i.e., its limitation as well as its possibility. This seems to be a kind of realization that there is nothing that grounds our language except for our form of life, contingent though this inevitably is; and this seems also to be a kind of realization that leads us to see that it is only I who can decide to participate in this form of life to make sense of my life as human at all. This self-knowledge as a human being as well as a subject is exactly what makes the way we inhabit the world become different. And this is a self-knowledge that is derived not so much from introspection as from attending better to the way things are.

Why is this kind of self-knowledge-as-seeing so important for education? I think this is because it makes us go back to our everyday life in a different spirit or as a different being; we are different now. Let me quote the way Cavell describes this:

> The more one learns, so to speak, the hang of oneself, and mounts one's problems, the less one is able to say what one has learned; not because you have forgotten what it was, but because nothing you said would seem like an answer or a solution; there is no longer any question or problem which your words would match. You have reached conviction, but not about a proposition; and consistency, but not in a theory. You are different, what you recognize as problems are different, your world is different. ("The world of the happy man is a different one from that of the unhappy man" (Tractatus; 6.43).) And this is the sense, the only sense, in which what a work of art means cannot be said. Believing it is seeing it. (Cavell 1976, pp. 85–86)

The above passage can be read as describing what the ordinary language philosopher aspires towards for us: a certain state of our being. Can we call it a state of "being educated"? We may describe "a state of being educated" in various ways: being equipped with high-level knowledge, being competent to think critically, being developed in moral ways, and so on. But I think that this list cannot be complete without that kind of happiness that involves a sense of being in harmony with oneself as well as with the world, which the passage above seems to refer to. Cavell also describes this state of being as a state in which human beings' "passion for their lives is at one with their lives" (Cavell 1976, p. xxviii). For Cavell, when one has reached this state of being, philosophy is not useful any more: its job for the moment is done.

What is noteworthy about Cavell's ordinary language philosophy as indicated in the above passage is that "saying" or "theory" matter less than "having conviction" or 'seeing' aright. I think this aspect of Cavell's ordinary language philosophy is closely connected to his confession of the difficulty of "discovering when and how to *stop* philosophizing," which I raised early on in my discussion. Philosophizing consists of activities of speaking and thinking, typically taking the form of arguing, reasoning and justifying. But what ordinary philosophers aspire towards for us is a state of being that can be reached not by "theory" or "proposition," but by "conviction" or "seeing." Cavell makes an analogy between our way to this state of being and our way to the meaning of an artwork. This means that, no matter how powerful my philosophical argument for the truth of "the way we look at things" may be, or no matter how elaborate my explication about "the note of F# minor" may be, it will fall short of bringing the reader to *see* (or *hear*) it.[10] For seeing or having a conviction is ultimately a nonmediated and only personally accessible first-person action.

However, the emphasis on seeing or personal conviction in doing ordinary language philosophy, as opposed to public persuasion or objective proof, should not be understood as a sign of subjectivism or of the impossibility of communication. It should be rather understood as an indication of the distinctively different way of communication that is needed in ordinary language philosophy. For, when a person has come to see something and tries to communicate it to her interlocutor, what it is that is to be communicated cannot be directly said, no matter how hard she tries to convey it; she may be able only to circle around it in her words as a way of pointing towards it. This is not because what is meant to be conveyed is in principle something that cannot be put into words, but because, if it is put into words, the very nature of what is meant to be conveyed—i.e., *my seeing* it or *your seeing* it—will be ruined or obstructed; what matters is one's special relation to it. This is the very reason why Cavell says that ordinary language philosophers have difficulty in knowing "when and how to stop philosophizing"; they can exert upon us pressure to feel or act in a certain way, but they cannot deliver this directly to us.

I think that from this fact we can draw out two important educational implications about ordinary language philosophy as a form of educational practice. One is that ordinary language philosophers must, in a sense, take a *nonauthoritative* approach in their teaching. The other is that the aim of ordinary language philosophy as an educational practice is to transform the reader's (or the interlocutor's) *sensibility*, rather than to equip him or her with a certain set of abilities and competences. Understood this way, Cavell's ordinary language philosophy can be described as an educational practice that promotes the essay in Montaigne's sense as a kind of "trying-oneself-out" or "putting-oneself-to-the-test" or, in a sense, "self-study." Cavell as an ordinary language philosopher tends to start with examples from literature, film or even normal everyday circumstances, but only so as to bring the reader into a philosophical reflection on what is meant by someone when she says a certain a thing in a particular circumstance. In doing this, he often

---

[10]In *A Pitch of Philosophy* (1994), Cavell introduces an autobiographical example that shows vividly the way we have an access to the meaning of a work of art. According to Cavell, in his college music class, a famous teacher, Ernest Bloch, often introduced an exercise to the students by playing something simple at the piano, for instance, a Bach four-part chorale, with one note altered by a half step from Bach's rendering, and then with the Bach unaltered. Introducing these two versions, he asked the students if they could hear the difference. And then he went on to say: "my version is perfectly correct; but the Bach, the Bach is perfect; late sunlight burning the edges of a cloud. Of course, I do not say you must hear this. Not at all. No. But, if you do not hear it, do not say to yourself that you are a musician. There are many honorable trades, Shoe-making for example (Cavell 1994, pp. 49–50). Cavell confesses that he heard the difference, supposing that not everybody did, and describes how thrilled he was by the drama of this teaching because it made him interested in the understanding of what he heard as well as in the rightness and beauty of what he heard. I think that this sense of a private triumph about what we experience is exactly what ordinary language philosophy aspires towards for our education.

strikes the reader dumb by provoking her to respond in her own voice as a way of *recovering* the ordinary meaning of her words—that is, by becoming able to understand the ordinary words in a *different spirit*. In fact, Cavell's well-known philosophical writings on Emerson and Thoreau are examples of the essay as his own testing of himself (Cavell 1988, 1990). We can always hear his voice, which is triggered by some specific example and which is constantly engaged in a conversation with itself (much as is realized by the presence in the *Investigations* of Wittgenstein's interlocutor)—sometimes in a self-confessing way, at other times in a self-testing way, on the journey towards a kind of self-enlightenment in the face of the familiar and everyday.

5.4 Conclusion: A Role for Philosophy in Teacher Education

Going back to our question in the introduction, we may now need to ask ourselves how the practice of ordinary language philosophy can contribute to teacher education. That is, what is its relevance to the (professional) lives of (would-be) teachers? Highlighting "the contested and often ambiguous nature of the work" in the delivery of teaching as one of the conditions that may drive teachers to philosophical abstraction, Hansen points out how philosophy can *humanize* teachers in such a way as to be responsive to the contested and ambiguous nature of teaching (Hansen 2001, p. 6). I think this view can be a good way of making sense of Cavell's ordinary language philosophy in regard to its contribution to the life of teachers.

Cavell points out that, unlike in other disciplines where a teacher of literature is a professor of English and a professor of anthropology is an anthropologist, in philosophy a professor of philosophy is not necessarily a philosopher. This impish remark underscores the point that being a philosopher or being philosophical need not require us to write philosophical works or to study serious philosophical literature. I think what is assumed here is the classical relation between philosophy and life, which is implied in an expression such as: "since ancient times, what theory (philosophy) was supposed to do was not to make life possible but to make it happy" (Blumenberg 1983, p. 232). Pierre Hadot, well-known French scholar of the ancient philosophy, also says that for the ancient "theory is never considered an end in itself; it is clearly and decidedly put in the service of practice" (Hadot 1995, p. 60). When Cavell says, "If silence is always a threat in philosophy, it is also its highest promise" (Cavell 1976, p. xxi), he seems to express the wish to recover this healthy relation between philosophy and life, a relation that has been jeopardized by the narrow professionalization of academic philosophy, far away from the wider problems of human culture or human life as classically understood.

On the other hand, Cavell agrees with Socrates and Nietzsche who thought that good old men have no need of philosophy, not necessarily because they are old but because their passion for their lives is at one with their lives through the *experience* of a long life; their private passion is well spent, and spent without rancor (Cavell 1976, p. xxviii). Cavell holds that philosophy *must* be useful to life, for otherwise it will be harmful; this is why, where philosophy is not needed for life, it should be silent. Thus, we may need philosophy only as a way of recovering and enlivening our everyday life that has been flattened and alienated from us, and this is exactly the role that Cavell thinks his ordinary language philosophy is committed to: by making us more attentive to the familiar and everyday, so that we develop an existential and esthetic sense of life that allows us to relish what exists in all its particularity and complexity, in its excellence, in the depth of things.

This relation between philosophy and life has a number of practical implications for teacher education and education in general. First, when the ordinary language philosopher as teacher-educator attempts to invite student-teachers to participate in doing philosophy, she does it as an ordinary person without any privileged position. She knows that she cannot have for her students the self-knowledge they need for themselves, and we are all placed equally in relation to it. Thus, Cavell says, "No man is in any better position for knowing it than any other man unless *wanting* to know is a special position," and he goes on to conclude: "this discovery about oneself is the same as the discovery of philosophy" (Cavell 1976, p. xxviii). I think this tells us how humble we should be not only as teacher educators but also teachers in regard to what we *can* (and *cannot*) do for the growth of our students as persons. What is educationally significant about this self-discovery is that it can be a source of our genuine respect for our students *as* persons *with* the possibility of their own inner depth, no matter how young they would be.

Second, while teachers and students stand equal in the quest for self-knowledge, the awakened desire of teachers for self-knowledge puts them in a special position, that is, the position of being able to see the point of philosophical enterprise for their students, and thereby being obliged to take up an educational responsibility to *awaken* the students' desire to know themselves. However, the kind of self-knowledge at stake here is distinct from what is emphasized in the current educational discourse of "emotional intelligence" or "emotional literacy" that is directed to the cultivation of students' ability to understand their own as well as others' emotions and desires.[11] The latter psychological approach has its own merit in giving teachers and students technical prescriptions on what we should do in order to understand better their emotions, heighten their self-esteem, and attain balanced emotional control. But Cavell's philosophical practice aspires after a different kind of self-understanding for both teachers and students. It is the kind that is accompanied by a long-lasting *ethical* or *spiritual* effect on us, derived from our deepened self-understanding of what is true about ourselves.

---

[11]The recent discourse of 'emotional intelligence' or 'emotional literacy' in the practice of teaching and learning tends to highlight interpersonal sensitivity and emotional responsiveness not only as an effective pedagogical virtue but also as an educational aim. The term 'emotional literacy' was coined and popularized in the 1990's in the field of positive psychology, especially in the UK, whereas the term 'emotional intelligence' became popularized in the US by Daniel Goleman's book *Emotional Intelligence* (1995).

Third, it is the case that, in this sense, everybody is in need of philosophy; it is almost inescapable because it is about our lives and about happiness, in a deep sense. Thus, Cavell adds: "If philosophy is esoteric, that is not because a few men guard its knowledge, but because most men guard themselves against it" (Cavell 1976, p. xxvii). This means that what makes philosophy look so irrelevant to student-teachers in the first place is not so much philosophy itself as the students themselves, who tend sweepingly to dismiss wonder and hope, confusion and pain, caused by philosophical questions, as irrelevant to their lives. Thus, what teachers as ordinary language philosophers should do is to lead students to take seriously the complex and ambiguous nature of their pain, wonder, confusion and hope they encounter in their everyday lives as a way of understanding themselves. This requires teachers to have courage to question their own teaching-and-learning experiences in company with their students. This aspect of Cavell's philosophical practice leads teachers to build up a kind of friendship with their students, at least in the sense that they are helping each other for the others to take a step into their own inner journey into self-knowledge.

Fourth and lastly, it was said that Cavell's philosophical practice can be best delivered and expressed in the essay-form of writing as "trying-oneself-out." For Cavell, philosophy is a form of writing (or reading) of someone else's work, such as a philosophical or literary text, or a works of art including film or painting. This means that philosophy as writing about (or reading) someone else' work is a way to self-understanding. What kind of constitutional features does this philosophical writing imply? And what sort of text or works of art are more appropriate for this kind of practice? These are the key questions we need to pursue for the future to make Cavell's ordinary language philosophy more employable for teacher education or education in general.

Unlike "philosophical reflection as a form of action research," philosophical reflection as a form of essay is not concerned directly with educational practitioners' practical knowledge; it tends to view student-teachers primarily as free learners rather than as would-be professionals. While philosophical reflection as action research is interested in promoting self-knowledge as historical consciousness—that is, in coming to recognize our educational beliefs as historically constrained and culturally embedded—philosophical reflection as the essay-form is directed to self-knowledge as philosophical consciousness, that is, to a knowledge of ourselves as human subjects obliged to find and speak in our own voices. In addition, philosophical reflection as action research is understood to be the practice of *public* discourse in which dialogical inquiry among practitioners is promoted, whereas philosophical reflection as the essay-form must be a *personally engaged* practice in which an inner conversation with oneself is stimulated. The former is focused on the formation of professional identity, the latter on the cultivation of one's humanistic sensibility as a human being. No matter how different the two forms of philosophical reflection may be, I think that they can contribute to improving would-be teachers' practical knowledge in a complementary way. But, providing student-teachers with a more intense and focused experience of being free learners themselves is something that has been widely neglected in teacher training programs, even though this seems essential to the formation of that humanistic orientation that will help them face today's unprecedented educational problems and challenges with courage, imagination and vision.

References

Blumeberg, H. (1983). *The legitimacy of the modern age* (R. M. Wallace, Trans.). Cambridge, Massachusetts: MIT Press.
Carr, W. (1995). *For education: Towards critical educational research*. Buckingham: Open University Press.
Carr, W. (2005). Philosophy of education. In W. Carr (Ed.), *Philosophy of education*. London & New York: Routledge.
Carr, W. (2007). Philosophy, methodology, and action research. In D. Bridges & R. Smith (Eds.), *Philosophy, methodology and educational research*. Oxford: Blackwell Publisher.
Cavell, S. (1976). *Must we mean what we say?* Cambridge: Cambridge University Press.
Cavell, S. (1988). *In quest of the ordinary: Lines of scepticism and romanticism*. Chicago: University of Chicago Press.
Cavell, S. (1990). *Handsome and unhandsome: The constitution of emersonian perfectionism*. Chicago: University of Chicago Press.
Cavell, S. (1994). *A pitch of philosophy*. Cambridge, Massachusetts: Harvard University Press.
Dunne, J. (1993). *Back to the rough ground: Practical judgment and the lure of technique*. Notre Dame, Indiana: Notre Dame University Press.
Goleman, D. (1995). *Emotional intelligence*. New York: Bantam Books.
Hadot, P. (1995). (M. Chase, Trans.). In A. I. Davidson (Ed.), *Philosophy as a way of life*. Oxford: Blackwell Publishing.
Hansen, D. (2001). *Exploring the moral heart of teaching*. New York: Teachers College, Columbia University.
Hartle, A. (2003). *Michel de Montaigne: Accidental philosopher*. Cambridge: Cambridge University Press.
Hirst, P. H., & Carr, W. (2005). Philosophy of education—A symposium. *Journal of Philosophy of Education, 39*(4), 615–632.
Montaigne, M. (1958). *The essays* (J. M. Cohen, Trans.). London: Penguin.
Wittgenstein, L. (1958). *Philosophical investigation* (3rd. G. E. M. Anscombe, Trans.). New York: Macmillan Publishing Company.

Author Biography

Duck-Joo Kwak is a professor at the Department of Education, Seoul National University in Seoul, Korea. Her research interests are, broadly speaking, in esthetics, postmodern concept of education, and teacher education. She has written numerous articles on Stanley Cavell, especially his existential interpretation of later Wittgenstein and its implications on teacher education and civic and moral education in the post-liberal Confucian culture.

Chapter 6
The Development of Accomplished Teaching

Margery A. McMahon, Christine Forde and Rosa Murray

6.1 Introduction

In efforts to raise pupil attainment, the question of teacher quality has become a key policy concern (Schleicher 2011). A range of strategies has been used by different educational systems to raise teaching quality including reforms to the initial preparation of teachers, raising the entry requirements, the development of teacher induction schemes and improving school leadership. Increasingly the focus has turned to the effectiveness of serving teachers where initiatives for teacher appraisal and accountability have been established alongside strategies to promote ongoing professional development. However, the anticipated improvements that such measures would bring have not been realised particularly in reforming and enhancing practice in the classroom. The question of how you improve and sustain pedagogic practice over a teacher's career is an issue currently being grappled with in Scottish education, mirroring similar concerns in other education systems. Much of these efforts have been on upskilling teachers (Schleicher 2011) to enable them to deliver reforms in the curriculum and assessment programmes. Scottish education is an example of a system trying to put in place strategies to sustain teachers in their development over a lengthy career as the means of enhancing pedagogic practice and motivation thereby, improving the quality of teaching in order to raise the achievement and attainment of diverse groups of learners.

M.A. McMahon (✉) · C. Forde
University of Glasgow, Glasgow, Scotland, UK
e-mail: Margery.McMahon@glasgow.ac.uk

C. Forde
e-mail: cforde@educ.gla.ac.uk

R. Murray
University of Edinburgh, Edinburgh, Scotland, UK
e-mail: rosa.murray@ed.ac.uk

© Springer Nature Singapore Pte Ltd. 2017   87
M.A. Peters et al. (eds.), *A Companion to Research in Teacher Education*,
DOI 10.1007/978-981-10-4075-7_6

The concepts of 'career long teacher education' and 'accomplished teaching' are central to a national review of teacher education in Scotland, *Teaching Scotland's Future* (Donaldson 2011), in which professional learning has been reconceptualised. Professional development in Scottish education has long been associated with continuing professional development, 'CPD', largely short awareness raising or skills based courses conducted either in school or by a local provider, frequently the Local Authority. Such provision is often fragmented and does not lead to sustained change in practice across a school. Nevertheless, teachers are expected to engage in professional learning and demonstrate their ongoing development against a professional standard through a programme of professional re-certification, *Professional Update,* administered by the General Teaching Council Scotland (GTCS). Within this process there is a tension between maintaining the required level of performance against the professional standard which all teacher are required to demonstrate on entry into the profession and enhancing the quality of practice progressively across a career. There are then, a number of issues around the relationship between the ongoing professional learning of teachers and the development of accomplished teaching. The chapter begins with a discussion of the development of policy in Scotland around the continuing development of serving teachers since 1997 and critically appraises the strategies used to foster teacher learning as part of efforts to improve attainment and achievement. Of particular note is the Chartered Teacher Scheme in Scottish education where we consider some of the lessons to be learned from this approach to developing accomplished teaching. Then we turn to the question of teacher expertise. We conclude by considering the role of professional learning and the relationship between the development of accomplishment and the construction of a teaching career.

6.2 Teacher Development and Teacher Quality in Scottish Policy

The question of ongoing teacher development has been an issue much debated in Scotland over two decades and there has been a number of key milestones. Prior to 1998 there was little discussion of the need for a national approach to teacher development. Instead there had been a substantial investment in firstly, a management development programme to support serving head teachers to implement a wave of reforms in relation to the governance and management of schools and secondly, a formal appraisal process for all teachers. A national framework for the continuing development of teachers was proposed in 1998 and this idea has been grappled with in Scottish educational policy in different ways over the intervening period. In the proposal for a National CPD Framework a teaching career had two broad pathways: that of teaching and that of management. The next major development followed on from the establishment of the Scottish Parliament in 1999 and after a period of industrial unrest in the teaching profession. A committee of enquiry was set up to review the teaching profession that sought to reaffirm the status of the teaching profession. In this process of 're-professionalisation' professional development was a key defining feature. In the subsequent agreement reached between central government, the local authorities (the employers) and the teacher unions, *The Teachers' Agreement* (Scottish Executive 2001), professional development remained a key dimension. Thus, all teachers were contractually obliged to (1) engage in an additional thirty five hours professional learning per annum, (2) contribute to the school's development through collegiate activities and (3) take part in the annual professional review and development process. To support this programme of reform, substantial effort was put into enabling schools to create programmes of CPD for their staff. In addition, all teachers at the top to the main grade scale (six years service) could enrol on the Chartered Teacher Programme, a form of incentivized professional learning whereby, through successful completion of the programme, teachers were able to apply for Chartered Teacher status and gain significant salary increments.

In 2010 a review of teacher education was set up by Scottish Government and part of the impetus had been a concern that the pace of implementation of the major reform of the school curriculum, the Curriculum for Excellence. *Teaching Scotland's Future* had some harsh criticisms of much of the provision of CPD, characterising this as 'mass "force-feeding"' (Donaldson 2011: 10) related to either a particular national or local priority or the transmission of guidance for a particular area. This approach did not foster sustained engagement and ongoing teacher development and so the impact on practice and therefore on pupil learning, was severely limited. The Report called for a re-professionalisation of teaching, an 'extended professionalism' (Donaldson 2011: 15) where the impetus for change and improvement comes from inside the profession and teachers become the prime agents for change. *Teaching Scotland's Future* presented a vision of the teaching profession of the twenty-first century:

> Education policy should support the creation of a reinvigorated approach to twenty-first century teacher professionalism. Teacher education should, as an integral part of that endeavour, address the need to build the capacity of teachers, irrespective of career stage, to have high levels of pedagogical expertise, including deep knowledge of what they are teaching; to be self-evaluative; to be able to work in partnership with other professionals; and to engage directly with well-researched innovation (Donaldson 2011: 15).

This new policy focus looks to 'career long professional learning' across the profession and as a consequence, the Chartered Teacher Programme was discontinued. However, there remain issues about how you engage a critical mass of the profession in forms of professional learning that will have a systemic impact. From this brief overview of policy on teacher development over the last twenty years in Scottish education, we can see that it has been a series of 'starts and stops'. There have been a number of attempts to re-professionalise the teaching profession with different initiatives launched to engage the critical mass of teachers in professional learning to bring about system level improvement in pupil learning outcomes.

This raises questions about the purposes of professional learning, particularly for serving experienced teachers.

6.3 Purposes of Professional Learning

The OECD background report (Schleicher 2011), written in preparation for the first international summit of education ministers on the teaching profession, illustrates some of the tensions embedded in the current constructions of professional learning. The report echoes some of the criticisms Donaldson (2011) made of professional learning in Scottish education:

> schools and systems need to better match the costs and benefits of, and supply and demand for, professional development. Results from Talis [The OECD's *Teaching and Learning International Survey*] show that, across countries, relatively few teachers participate in the kinds of professional development they believe has the largest impact on their work, namely qualifications programs and individual and collaborative research. (Schleicher 2011: 27)

The report identified a range of purposes for the development of teachers beyond their initial teacher education:

- updating individuals' knowledge of a subject in light of recent advances in the area;
- updating individuals' skills and approaches in the light of the development of new teaching techniques and objectives, new circumstances, and new educational research;
- enabling individuals to apply changes made to curricula or other aspects of teaching practice;
- enabling schools to develop and apply new strategies concerning the curriculum and other aspects of teaching practice;
- exchanging information and expertise among teachers and others, e.g. academics and industrialists; or
- helping weaker teachers become more effective (Schleicher 2011: 24).

While critical of extant provision, what is noteworthy in this list is the focus on updating and application of ideas generated elsewhere rather than in the immediate site of practice. This construction of the purposes of continuing professional learning reflects much of the provision in Scottish education. There has been a focus on looking for effective forms of professional learning whereby policy priorities and associated practices are applied to the setting of the classroom. In the purposes above there is one reference to schools developing strategies and teachers exchanging expertise. In Scottish education insufficient attention has been paid to the position of teachers to move from them being the recipients of professional learning opportunities to active constructors in the process of professional learning.

Accordingly, we need to move from seeing such programmes as updating to a much richer notion of professional learning as being about developing and recognising a high level of expertise. In the next section we examine some of the programmes that different systems have established in order to recognise and build this high level of expertise in teachers. We begin with the Chartered Teacher Scheme established in Scotland and then consider some examples from other systems.

6.4 Lessons Learned: The Chartered Teacher Programme

The *Teachers' Agreement* (Scottish Executive 2001) was intended as generational review that considered the teacher contract and conditions of service alongside the issue of the re-engagement and revitalization of the teaching profession. The *Teachers' Agreement* underscored two key aspects of the changing construction of what it means to be a teacher in Scotland, that of the 'developing professional' and of 'the collegiate professional'. It was anticipated that particularly the Chartered Teacher Scheme would be a means of improving the quality of teaching. However, the Chartered Teacher Scheme was much debated particularly the question of the role of the chartered teacher and their impact on teaching and learning across the school. Progression to the status of Chartered Teacher was through qualification, largely the completion of a masters programme whereby teachers demonstrated their achievement of the professional standard, set out by the GTCS, the *Standard for Chartered Teacher*. The programme was open to all teachers: entry was by individual application with no obligation on the part of the applicant to inform their school or employer though the employer had to meet the extra salary costs. The two criteria for selection were that teachers were at the top of the main grade scale and had maintained a CPD portfolio. Thus, the Chartered Teacher Scheme was a form of incentivized continuing professional learning.

For many serving teachers participating in the programme was transformational (McMahon and Reeves 2007). There was evidence of the impact of the programme on the practice of individual teachers as well as evidence of those pursuing the chartered teacher programme working collaboratively with colleagues in improving teaching and learning. However, there was an uneasy relationship between the role and contribution of chartered teachers and the established structures in school relating to leadership hierarchies that shape and direct school improvement processes and professional learning. Further, there was also evidence of some of the barriers the chartered teachers experienced in school, which limited their contribution and influence (McMahon and Reeves 2007).

It had been anticipated that the Chartered Teacher Scheme would be attractive to serving teachers particularly given the significant financial incentive. Indeed, following the launch of the *Chartered Teacher Scheme*, over 6000 teachers applied for their 'certificate of eligibility' (which indicated that they were at the top of the main grade salary scale). However, participation on Chartered Teacher programmes did not reflect this initial interest and remained low overall. Out of a profession of over

56,000 by session 2010–11 there were only 1107 chartered teachers in Scotland with approximately a further 2000 pursuing the Chartered Teacher programme. Of the 1107 chartered teachers, 615 are between the ages of 51 and 65 (General Teaching Council Scotland 2010) which raised questions about the long term development and impact of the Chartered Teacher Scheme. The grade of chartered teacher attracted a higher salary than that of main grade teacher but there were no additional responsibilities for chartered teachers (Scottish Executive 2001). This raised a concern about a limited contribution on the part of chartered teachers to their school and this concern reached its peak in the establishment of a Ministerial Review of the Chartered Teacher Programme from which a code for chartered teachers was agreed. This code set out expectations with regard to chartered teachers working with and leading other teachers in the development of teaching and learning in the school. However, this did not quell the criticism and the scheme closed in 2012.

The Chartered Teacher Scheme as an incentivised programme of professional learning in Scotland is one example of a range of strategies used in different educational systems to build the quality of teaching across the system. The recognition of high performance is the approach adopted in one of the longest established programmes, that of National Board Certification in the USA. Here through a substantial portfolio of evidence individual teachers are recognised as having met the standards (Forde and McMahon 2011). A set of professional standards underpins the National Board Certification programme and this use of professional standards to raise the quality of teaching is another approach adopted. A key element in the Chartered Teacher Scheme in Scotland was also the development of the *Standard for Chartered Teacher* that set out the professional actions, values, knowledge and skills expected of high level performance. The Australian professional standards for teaching is structured through successive standards for teaching which articulate the development of teaching: graduate, proficient, highly accomplished and lead teacher. Another approach used in some systems has been the establishment of specific roles based on teaching merit. This was a strategy adopted across the different systems in the UK for example: Advanced Skills Initiative and Excellent Teacher status and latterly the London Chartered Teacher. Singapore introduced a more structured career structure where teachers could progress from senior, lead master and finally principal master teacher (Forde and McMahon 2011). There are three issues that are noteworthy here, firstly the variety of different approaches that have been trialled, secondly, many of these initiatives, like the Chartered Teacher Scheme, are relatively short lived and thirdly, it is only a small proportion of teachers who engage in these programmes. While systems level improvement ultimately comes down to individual teachers working with colleagues in their school to improve the conditions for effective learning, the Chartered Teacher Scheme in Scotland highlights the need for a critical mass of teachers operating at this high level to achieve improvement. The difficulties of developing high level skill and expertise across a critical mass of teachers is an issue common to many of the schemes established to drive improvements to the quality of teaching. Therefore, a different conceptualisation of the role and development of experienced teachers and a different approach to the development of these teachers is needed. The purpose of the project, *Accomplished Teaching* (Forde and McMahon 2011) was to explore the issue of the development of accomplished teaching across an educational system.

6.5   The Concept of Accomplished Teaching

The origins of the project on accomplished teaching were firstly, in a series of research studies (McMahon and Reeves 2007) on the role and impact of the chartered teachers in Scotland and secondly, in a series of symposia that brought together stakeholders in Scotland with international partners including academics and professional associations to examine the issues related to the recognition and development of expertise and accomplishment in teaching. This model of drawing together academics and professional groups was used as the basis for the project on *Accomplished Teachers and Teaching*. Two International Symposiums *on Developing Accomplished Teachers and Teaching (ISAT&T)* (June 2010 and September 2012) brought together researchers, teacher educators, policy makers and teaching councils drawn from England, Australia, Wales, USA, New Zealand and Scotland. A key outcome of the symposia was to inform thinking in Scotland on the development of accomplished teaching. Among others, two key issues emerged in this discussion firstly, the concept of accomplished teaching and the issue of the development of accomplished teaching and a teaching career (Forde and McMahon 2011).

The term of 'accomplished teaching' was used in the first *Standard for Chartered Teacher* (General Teaching Council Scotland 2002: 3):

> Accomplished teaching of the kind reflected in the Standard for Chartered Teacher is teaching in which four central values and commitments permeate the work of the teacher in the classroom, the school, and beyond. The Chartered Teacher will be effective in promoting learning and committed to the development of all forms of professional action.

In this standard four central values characterised a Chartered Teacher and in these we can see a form of the extended professionalism: effectiveness in promoting learning in the classroom; critical self-evaluation and development; collaboration and influence and educational and social values. However, the term 'accomplished' did not gain any real currency in Scottish education where, as we have seen, debates focussed on the role and impact of the chartered teacher.

One of the tensions is using a mandated programme where the outcomes are shaped a professional standard while at the same time fostering a transformational process of engaging in coherent and critical professional learning (McMahon and Reeves 2007). This again brings the question back to the purposes of professional learning—whether teachers are to be updated to come up to an externally imposed policy or standard or whether professional learning is the means for teachers to develop and share their expertise as practitioners. The Accomplished Teaching project had as its focus an exploration of teaching expertise: what high level practice is and more importantly how might this been developed across an education system and across a teacher's career (Forde and McMahon 2011). A key element was an exploration of the concept of expertise.

6.6   The Concept of Expertise

The notion of accomplishment relates to the wider concept of expertise and there is a range of definitions we can draw on here. A 'stage model' of expertise is one construction where the acquisition of expertise is through a series of developmental stages. Dreyfus and Dreyfus's (1986: 19) model is one of the best known models of expertise. They argue that:

> A careful study of the skills acquisition process shows that a person usually passes through at least five stages of qualitatively different perceptions of his (sic) task and/or mode of decision-making as his (sic) skill improves.

In this model there are five sequential stages and in the final stage of expert, the practitioner sees what needs to be done and decides how to go about this. Rather than follow routines, an expert is able to draw from a rich repertoire to determine the course of action.

> An expert knows what to do based on mature and practiced understanding [...] While most expert performance is ongoing and non-reflective, when time permits and outcomes are crucial, an expert will deliberate before acting [...] which involves critically reflecting on one's intuition (pp. 30–32).

Dreyfus and Dreyfus have generated a continuum that moves from the detached rule-following beginner to the involved, intuitive expert at the final stage of expertise. It is the ability to perceive subtle distinctions and make decisions or take courses of action, which forge new ways or practices that distinguishes between proficient and expert performance.

There has been much critical appraisal of Dreyfus and Dreyfus's (1986) model. Its strength is that it illustrates two aspects: firstly, the importance of learning through experience to a point where the 'flow' of practice seems to be seamless and almost unknowable and secondly, the importance of tacit knowledge and 'intuition' in skilled practice. However there are limitations in that firstly the process of learning from experience is not explored and secondly, this framework suggests that expertise is simply the accumulation of years of experience rather than outstanding performance.

An alternative approach has been to identify and describe the characteristics of expert practice. Building on the idea of 'tacit knowing' that experienced practitioner display, Schon (1985) developed his notion of 'reflection-in-action'. This concept allows us to think about the process of expert practice: 'reflection-in-action' refers to the process whereby the expert practitioner constantly reads the environment or problem and makes subtle adjustments to ensure a successful outcome whether this is to resolve an engineering problem, make a medical diagnosis or teach a group of learners. Schon's work begins to open up the question of how an experienced practitioner acquires expertise. He argues that mastery is acquired through practice and reflection. While practice and reflection are vital, new ideas and insights are not necessarily drawn on; there is a strong danger of over-routinisation. Therefore, Schon's model too is not fully adequate. Expertise is not just the process of becoming more skilled and so more efficient in the same sets of practices because there seems to be a generative dimension.

Some of the most comprehensive studies related to the question of teacher expertise have been conducted by Berliner (2001) and in these discussions we see a tension between routinisation of practice and the ability to make subtle changes according to the immediate circumstance. Thus Berliner (2004: 200) argues that expert teachers:

- often develop automaticity and routinization for the repetitive operations that are needed to accomplish their goals
- are more sensitive to the task demands and social situations when solving pedagogical problems, are more opportunistic and flexible in their teaching than are novices
- represent problems in qualitatively different ways than do novices
- have fast and accurate pattern-recognition capabilities (whereas novices cannot always make sense of what they experience)
- perceive meaningful patterns in the domain in which they are experienced, they may begin to solve problems slower but they bring richer and more personal sources of information to bear on the problem they are trying to solve.

Hammerness et al. (2005) also point to what might seem to be paradoxical in the practice of expert teachers: they display high degrees of efficiency as they perform variety of activities skilfully but at the same time they readily break these routines and rules by being innovative and so move beyond their existing expertise. Therefore, expertise is not simply about skill and efficiency but there are questions about motivation, engagement and commitment. Further, in Hammerness et al.'s construction expertise is about a constant process of development. Opfer et al. (2011) identified this issue of teacher development as central in looking at the building of teacher expertise. Opfer et al. explored the relationship between a teacher's individual orientation to learning and their practice and identified a continuum of five broad orientations towards learning. At the opposite ends of this continuum were firstly, teachers who were in the 'engaged learners' category and secondly, teachers who were in the 'infrequent learners' category. Whereas for the engaged learners, there was a high alignment in both their beliefs and practices related to learning, this alignment was not evident in the practice of the 'infrequent learners'. Thus, there seems to be a critical relationship between teacher effectiveness and their attitude and approaches to their own development as learners. Teachers who are engaged as learners with regard to their own learning are more ready and effective in fostering the learning of their pupils. These studies of teacher expertise illustrate the critical relationship between professional learning and practice. However, these constructions still focus on the work and abilities of the individual teacher and overlook the social dimensions of practice that have a critical influence over the length of a teaching career.

6.7 Accomplished Teaching Across a Teaching Career

The development of expertise is often associated with more experienced practitioners. However, there has been debate about whether this is a characteristic to be nurtured early in professional life. Levin's (2003) longitudinal study of teacher development does suggest that there is growth over a career where thinking becomes more complex and there is a greater congruency between understanding and actions. However, discussions have pointed to the difficulty of constructing a linear framework for career long teacher education. Levin (2003) also highlights the grounded quality of expert practice where teachers display a rich understanding of the context and the learning needs of the particular groups of pupils they work with. Alongside this we need to be conscious of career cycles. Day and Gu (2010) point to critical periods in a teacher's career in terms of motivation/demotivation and engagement/disengagement but opportunities to develop and more importantly to contribute to the school and pupil learning can build resilience. Here the social context of practice, that is the culture of the school, is critical in determining whether teachers engage or disengage.

Collins and Evans (2007) in their book *Rethinking Expertise*, looked at expertise in science and though this is in a different domain from education, there is a strong analogy to be drawn in that science, like teaching, can be characterised as a practice. Collins and Evans (2007: 14) propose a 'Periodic Table of Expertise', which helps us to consider further the nature of expertise including the relationship between the tacit knowledge of the individual practitioner and the wider social context of practice. The process of developing expertise has to be about developing sophisticated and flexible forms of tacit knowledge but there is an important social dimension to this. Collins and Evans identified two categories of specialist expertise. One of the categories is 'contributory expertise' which is akin to the one that we commonly think of as expertise—the leading scientist in a particular field. Their proposal includes specialist expertise and this sits alongside that of 'interactional expertise', which comes from being immersed in a community of practice:

> Enculturation is the only way to master an expertise, which is deeply laden with tacit knowledge because it is only through common practice with others that the rules that cannot be written down can come to be understood. (p. 24)

Collins and Evans (2007) demonstrate that expertise is not simply accumulated experience. Within science the relationship between interactional expertise and contributory expertise is fundamental to the generation of ideas and practices—a combination of peer exploration, review and the individual and collective creative and generative thinking. However, in education we have broken that relationship which fosters and refines expertise. Instead expertise is commonly understood to lie in academic work, in research or in theory. Thus part of the development of tacit knowledge critical to expertise in practice is through participation in genuine communities of practice where ideas and practice is explored. We need to consider the intersection of professional learning, working in communities of practice in the development of expertise.

6.8   Accomplished Teaching and Career Long Teacher Learning

Career long teacher education cannot be conceived of as a linear process: there is no single process or typical career trajectory that can be identified. Instead it is important to recognise the non-linear and sometimes fluctuating nature of teachers' careers. A career long approach to teacher education and the development and sustaining of accomplished teaching requires commitment and participation from all with the strengthening of existing partnerships and the establishment of new partnerships. Building capacity at school level will foster knowledge exchange between practitioners and researchers and ground practice securely in theory and practice. This process would also strengthen research and its roots in the profession. Education systems need accomplished teachers, teachers who are not only expert in their practice and ensuring effective learning experiences for pupils but who can also support the development of other teachers. Consequently, an education system needs to develop strategies and processes to identify, support and sustain those teachers who can benefit other teachers. In order to realise this there are a number of issues we need to consider.

Firstly, we need to distinguish between expertise and experience: some experience is a necessary component of expertise but not sufficient. There is the question about how much experience is necessary: is this a characteristic that we should recognise and nurture early in professional life or should we be focussing on engaging experienced mid-career teachers in the development of teaching expertise.

Secondly, we need to consider when we should focus on developing the high level of skill necessary for accomplished teaching as a facet of all levels of teacher education so that as teachers progress through their career they can develop and display a high level of expertise. We need to be sensitive to career stage in the development and particularly the recognition of accomplished teaching. Day and Gu (2010) point to critical periods in a teacher's career but professional learning including school-based collaborative approaches can help support and extend skills and maintain teachers' engagement. In this we have to grapple with professional attitudes and cultures which limit aspiration and expectations. The limited uptake of the Chartered Teacher Programme can in part be explained by a significant disincentive to teachers from going forward to be accredited as accomplished teachers found in existing professional norms.

Thirdly, we need to explore the scope of accomplished teaching. Motivated and engaged teachers are essential for the generation and exemplification of interactional and contributory expertise. However, we need to consider whether we follow Berliner's (2004) proposition that expert teachers will be a small cadre of highly skilled teachers or should whether we should be aspiring to a critical mass of teachers demonstrating accomplished teaching. In Scottish education there is a clear move towards looking at accomplished teaching as the building of a critical mass of highly skilled and effective teachers that will have a system level impact. If that is the case, then we need to establish ways of developing, recognising and if necessary, rewarding expert practice particularly in mid-career for teachers who are not pursuing promotion through the management structure. However, this has implications for career long professional learning.

If we are to raise the quality of teaching and build greater capacity and capability for accomplished teaching across the education system, we need to consider the design of professional learning. One of the early theorists on expertise is Glaser who addressed the issue of the agency of the learner as part of the processes of developing expertise. In this he proposes a developmental process:

- externally supported: taught coherent and structured programmes of development
- transitional: decrease in the structured learning and more emphasis on 'guided' learning
- self-regulatory: in this stage a developing expert controls much more of their own learning environment. Here the conditions for deliberate practice are arranged. The emerging expert receives the feedback they need, and also chooses the level of challenge for their own development (Glaser cited in Berliner 2001: 478).

6.9 Conclusion

Using the idea of expertise helps to consider the intersection between experience, practice and ongoing professional learning. It seems essential that we move away from that idea that continuing professional learning is about keeping teachers up-to-date and instead consider professional learning as a means of fostering expertise. Therefore, there clearly needs to be a practice-based learning element but side by side with this, there needs to be opportunities for teachers focus on and reflect deeply on their practice and the impact this has on the learners. This exploration of and reflection on practice is not a solitary process but is very much a process of development that takes place within a community of practice. In this, however, we have to be cautious of the dangers of conformity within an inward looking culture and of the over routinsation of practice. The building of interactional expertise has to be a collective enterprise to build knowledge and commitment within the specific contexts of practice but where the processes found by

Collins and Evans (2007) are adopted: the gathering and analysing of evidence especially of the impact of teaching on pupil learning, peer review and exchanges ideas, and different practices are tried out, critiqued and refined.

References

Berliner, D. (2001). Learning about and learning from expert teachers. *International Journal of Educational Research, 35*, 463–482.

Berliner, D. (2004). Describing and documenting the accomplishments of expert teachers. *Bulletin of Science, Technology & Society, 24*(3), 200–212.

Collins, H., & Evans, R. (2007). *Rethinking expertise*. Chicago: University of Chicago Press.

Day, C., & Gu, Q. (2010). *The new lives of teachers*. London: Routledge.

Dreyfus, H. L., & Dreyfus, S. E. (1986). *Mind over machine: The power of human intuition and expertise in the era of the computer*. Oxford: Basil Blackwell.

Donaldson, G. (2011). *Teaching Scotland's future—Report of a review of teacher education in Scotland* (Donaldson Report). Edinburgh: Scottish Government.

Forde, C., & McMahon, M. (2011). *Accomplished teaching, accomplished teachers in Scotland: A report submitted to the review of teacher employment in Scotland*. Glasgow: University of Glasgow, from http://eprints.gla.ac.uk/61304/. Accessed June 16 2015.

General Teaching Council Scotland. (2002). *The Standard for chartered teacher*. Edinburgh: GTCS.

General Teaching Council Scotland. (2010). *Chartered teacher programme*. Edinburgh: GTCS.

Hammerness, K., Darling-Hammond, L., Bransford, J., Berliner, D., Cochran-Smith, M., McDonald, M., et al. (2005). How teachers learn and develop. In L. Darling-Hammond & J. Bransford (Eds.), *Preparing teachers for a changing world: What teachers should learn and be able to do* (pp. 358–389). San Francisco: Wiley.

Levin, B. (2003). *Case studies of teacher development*. Mahwah, New Jersery: Lawrence Erlbaum.

McMahon, M., & Reeves, J. (2007). *Evaluating the impact of chartered teacher: The perceptions of chartered teachers*. Report submitted to GTCS and Scottish Government. Glasgow: University of Glasgow.

Opfer, V. D., Pedder, D. G., & Lavicza, Z. (2011). The role of teachers' orientation to learning in professional development and change: A national study of teachers in England. *Teaching and Teacher Education, 27*(2), 443–453.

Schleicher, A. (2011). *Building a high-quality teaching profession: Lessons from around the world*. Paris: OECD.

Schon, D. (1985). *The reflective practitioner*. Aldershot, Hants: Ashgate.

Scottish Executive. (2001). *A teaching profession for the 21st century: Agreement reached following the McCrone report*. Edinburgh: HMSO.

Author Biographies

Dr. Margery A. McMahon is Director of Professional Learning and Leadership, School of Education, University of Glasgow, co-chair of the International Professional Development Association and co-founder of the Leadership in Scottish Education Network. In 2013–2014 she led the scoping and set up of the Scottish College for Educational Leadership.

Christine Forde is Emeritus Professor at Glasgow University where she held a personal chair in Leadership and Professional Learning. Her research interests include leadership, professional learning and accomplished teaching. An important element of Professor Forde's work has been working with policy communities to develop policy and programmes in teacher development.

Rosa Murray is currently working in Teacher Education at the University of Edinburgh developing strategic partnerships with the University, local authorities and schools to develop the concept and model of a Professional Learning Continuum designed to meet the aspirations of teachers throughout their professional career.

Part II
Initial Teacher Education

Introduction

Waterman (2015) reports on a conference lecture with Geoff Whitty, the former Director of the Institute of Education in London and now a research professor across universities at Bath, New York and Newcastle, Australia. He begins with the contrast that Whitty makes between Andreas Schleicher, of the OECD and Michael Gove, the former English Secretary for Education. Schleicher is quoted as saying:

Many of the [most successful] countries studied have moved from a system in which teachers are recruited into a larger number of specialized, low-status colleges of teacher education, with relatively low entrance standards, into a relatively smaller number of university-based teacher education colleges with relatively high entrance standards and relatively high status in the university.

This remark is then contrasted with Gove's view:

Teaching is a craft and it is best learnt as an apprentice observing a master craftsman—or woman. Watching others and being rigorously observed yourself as you develop is the best route to acquiring mastery in the classroom.

These two views have dominated the policy landscape and demonstrate the ways in which teacher education, and especially initial teacher education, have become politicized since the rise of neoliberalism in the 1980s. Whitty is reported as addressing the way in which the education establishment in UK has been singled out for criticism by New Right pressure groups that also feed into the ensuing policy changes designed to weaken the influence of the left or social democratic teacher educators in universities responsible for the training of teachers. Whitty (2014) addresses "modes of teacher education" in England in an earlier paper where he distinguishes three main routes: Partnerships led by higher education institutions (HEIs); School-centred initial teacher training schemes (SCITTs), and; Employment-based routes (EBITTs). Remarking on the Coalition's reforms, Whitty (2014: 468) remarks

The Coalition Government's White Paper 2010 on The Importance of Teaching encouraged more school-led initial teacher training in England, including the creation of around 500 Teaching Schools, schools rated by Ofsted as outstanding in teaching and learning that could potentially take over leadership of teacher training from the universities.

He leaves us in no doubt about the orchestrated attack on teacher professionalism and autonomy that emerged in a set of teacher training policies is best described as "another example of the neoliberal combination of the strong state and the free market" (p. 471). One, of the results has been that some universities have begun to abandon teacher education while others have embraced School Direct, a scheme in which schools undertake the recruitment of trainee teachers themselves and may then choose which universities to work with.

Drawing on the work of Furlong (2013) in the UK and Labaree (2004) in the US, and the official criticisms of university-based teacher education, Whitty makes the case for the importance of a professionally oriented "discipline" of Education, although not necessarily involving a commitment to one model. Whatever the long term outcome it certainly also looks likely that private providers will become part of a more differentiated "market" in the not too distant future, as they already are in some other parts of the world.

The concerns that Whitty raises have also been felt in the Nordic countries, Canada, Australia, New Zealand and around the world, as contributors to this section amply demonstrate.

If there is one knock-down argument to Gove's craft-based view of teaching mastery learned on-site in the classroom, it is that even best practice schools and teachers today require a research and innovative approach to teaching and to an understanding of the future world of work. As Schleicher (2012) argues,

Perhaps the most challenging dilemma for teachers today is that routine cognitive skills, the skills that are easiest to teach and easiest to test, are also the skills that are easiest to digitize, automate and outsource. A generation ago, teachers could expect that what they taught would last for a lifetime of their students. Today, where individuals can access content on Google, where routine cognitive skills are being digitized or outsourced, and where jobs are changing rapidly, education systems need to place much greater emphasis on enabling individuals to become lifelong learners, to manage complex ways of thinking and complex ways of working that computers cannot take over easily. Students need to be capable not only of constantly adapting but also of constantly learning and growing, of positioning themselves and repositioning themselves in a fast changing world (p. 13).

Schleicher (2012) puts the argument on even firmer ground when he suggests:

The kind of teaching needed today requires teachers to be high-level knowledge workers who constantly advance their own professional knowledge as well as that of their profession. But people who see themselves as knowledge workers are not attracted by schools organized like an assembly line, with teachers working as interchangeable widgets in a bureaucratic command and control environment (p. 13).

This is perhaps the reason that in some settings what have been called 'clinical' models of teacher education are emerging. These are models which emphasize the importance of learning to teach through a systematic process of enquiry that includes the careful analysis of teaching episodes and involves considerable dialogue between beginning and experienced teachers, as well as input from educational researchers and theorists (Burn and Mutton 2014). In settings as diverse as Finland, Scotland and Australia, there are important examples of such approaches which completely reject the assembly line approach to schools and to teaching which Schleicher so roundly criticizes

References

Burn, K. & Mutton, T. (2014). *Review of 'research-informed clinical practice' in initial teacher education*. London: British Educational Research Association. Available at bera.ac.uk

Furlong, J. (2013). *Education—An anatomy of the discipline: Rescuing the university project?* London: Routledge.

Labaree, D. (2004). *The trouble with Ed Schools*. New Haven, CT: Yale University Press.

Schleicher, A. (2012). "Introduction". In. A. Schleicher (Ed.), *Preparing teachers and developing school leaders for the 21st century: Lessons from around the world*. OECD Publishing. http://dx.doi.org/10.1787/9789264174559-en

Waterman, C. (2015). "Universities and teacher education in a new era" *Education Journal*, Issue 223, 13.

Whitty, G. (2014). Recent developments in teacher training and their consequences for the 'University Project' in education, *Oxford Review of Education, 40*(4), 466–481. http://dx.doi.org/10.1080/03054985.2014.933007

Chapter 7
Towards a Principled Approach for School-Based Teacher Educators: Lessons from Research

Katharine Burn, Trevor Mutton and Hazel Hagger

This chapter has its origins in our attempt to provide a summary of key insights into teacher education, written for teachers in school who are increasingly taking responsibility for designing (and not merely implementing) curricula for beginning teachers' school-based professional learning. Although the distinctive roles of particular partners and the precise designs of course structures vary significantly between and within different countries, the 'practicum turn' (Mattsson et al. 2011) taken by initial teacher education (ITE) in recent years is an international phenomenon.

As teacher educators within one of the earliest ITE partnership models—the Oxford Internship Scheme—we fully endorse the principle that teachers should assume significant responsibility for the education of new entrants to the profession. Such responsibility means providing far more than real classrooms in which to practise: accomplished practitioners have a wealth of professional expertise, underpinned by richly contextualised understandings of specific learners. This is knowledge that academic outsiders, however substantial their research-base, simply cannot replicate and it is essential to find ways of making it accessible to beginners.

We are aware, however, that despite a research focus on the use of specific mentoring *strategies*, rather less attention has been paid to mentors' understanding of beginning teachers as learners and to the broader challenge of constructing a curriculum for their school-based learning. Rapid increases in the numbers entering teaching through employment-based routes with a limited or non-existent role for higher education have increasingly focused our attention on making research into

K. Burn (✉) · T. Mutton · H. Hagger
University of Oxford, Oxford, England, UK
e-mail: katharine.burn@education.ox.ac.uk

T. Mutton
e-mail: trevor.mutton@education.ox.ac.uk

H. Hagger
e-mail: hazel.hagger@education.ox.ac.uk

© Springer Nature Singapore Pte Ltd. 2017
M.A. Peters et al. (eds.), *A Companion to Research in Teacher Education*,
DOI 10.1007/978-981-10-4075-7_7

the nature of beginning teachers' learning accessible to teachers in school who are taking on new, or more extensive, mentoring roles.

In light of that concern, this chapter reports the decisions that we took in seeking to distil and make available to school-based teacher educators the range of research findings that we believed would prove most useful to them. The guide that we produced (Burn et al. 2015) drew extensively on insights from our own empirical work, particularly the Developing Expertise of Beginning Teachers (DEBT) Project. This was a longitudinal study of the learning of 24 beginning teachers whom we tracked for 3 years, interviewing them at least once a term (following an observed lesson) to explore their accounts of the thinking that underpinned their planning and teaching decisions and their reflections on their ongoing learning. But our selection of references also ranged more widely as we sought to identify those research insights (some new and some long established) that would provide the strongest foundations for mentors' own professional learning.

Teacher education reform, driven more often by policy imperatives than by research, tends to be focused on structural or regulatory issues (such as partnership arrangements), on the specific content of ITE programmes and on meeting statutory national teaching standards. It is our contention, however, that it is only by paying serious attention to the nature of teaching itself and to the ways in which beginning teachers engage in the process of learning to teach that school-based teacher educators can enable novices to capitalise on the main source from which they expect to learn: their classroom experience.

7.1 Understanding the Challenges of Learning to Teach

Our first priority was to help mentors to understand the challenges that beginners face in learning to teach. In distilling wider research evidence as well as the findings of the DEBT project we suggested that these challenges derive from three sources:

- the nature of teachers' knowledge and expertise
- the ways in which learning to teach differs from other kinds of learning
- the tensions inherent in sustaining a dual identity as teacher and learner.

7.1.1 The Nature of Teachers' Knowledge and Expertise

Although the framework of knowledge, skills and dispositions that teachers need can be categorised in relation to three basic dimensions (Bransford et al. 2005)—knowledge of learners and learning; knowledge of subject matter and curriculum goals; and knowledge of teaching—the range of different aspects that each encompasses make getting to grips with them a formidable undertaking.

Knowledge of how young people learn within the social context of the class-room requires an understanding both of general developmental progression and of individual differences in learning, shaped by pupils' increasingly diverse cultural backgounds. This calls for highly developed diagnostic abilities, informed by an appreciation of what young people have learned previously (and are continuing to learn outside school).

Content knowledge—an understanding of what is to be taught—is obviously essential, but insufficient. Teachers also require a developed awareness of the underlying concepts and organisational structures within a particular subject domain, and of the most effective steps by which knowledge within that domain may be built. Such pedagogical content knowledge encompasses not only clearly framed, well-justified goals and models of progression, but also familiarity with those mis-conceptions that often prevent pupils from developing more powerful ideas.

The range of teaching strategies that beginners need to master are concerned with the processes of 'motivating and organizing students' work in settings that provide access to challenging content and frequent assessments of their progress, coupled with feedback and opportunities to revise and improve (Bransford et al. 2005, p. 35). Effective classroom management is obviously essential, but this extends far beyond rules for classroom conduct and procedures to deal with misbehaviour; it draws, for example, on motivation theory and the management of groups to create a psycho-logically safe and productive learning environment. Beyond this general repertoire of strategies, teachers need a storehouse of representations and analogies for teaching specific topics. To judge their effectiveness, they need a similar range of formative assessment strategies, allowing them to tap into pupils' current thinking and levels of understanding, and to adapt their teaching accordingly.

Moreover, the fact that teaching and learning are social processes involving a diverse range of individuals means there is a constant interplay between the dif-ferent knowledge bases on which teachers need to draw. Teachers have to juggle the immediate and longer term needs of up to 30 individuals who are interacting (with the teacher and with each other) in complex ways. Doyle famously summarised these challenges in terms of beginning teachers' encounters with the 'multi-dimensionality, simultaneity and unpredictability' of the classroom. It is not just the need to deal with numerous things at once; the range of different purposes being served and the variety of events and processes are 'not all necessarily related or even compatible' (Doyle 1977, p. 52). Indeed, Kennedy (2005), examining experienced teachers' ways of thinking, concludes that teachers are actually trying to address no fewer than six different, competing concerns, often simultaneously:

- covering desirable content;
- fostering student learning;
- increasing students' willingness to participate;
- maintaining lesson momentum;
- creating a civil classroom community; and
- attending to their own cognitive and emotional needs.

This complex picture is consistent with our own examination of the planning and teaching decisions reported by beginning teachers within the DEBT project. Explaining their practice in particular lessons, trainees referred to six different types of goal: four related to the pupils (determining their existing knowledge, promoting their achievement and influencing their affective state or their actions/behaviour) and two related to their own learning or performance. In seeking to achieve these objectives or to arbitrate between them, they also reported taking into account up to 12 different kinds of factor: most obviously the pupils and the content (often with reference to examination or curricular requirements) but also a wide variety of contextual factors (concerned with the timing and the sequence of learning, the resources available, particular material conditions and established routines) as well as specific factors derived from their own position as trainees.

Once this complexity is acknowledged, it also becomes clear why teaching cannot be reduced to a set of prescriptions. It depends fundamentally on a process of selection (determining which features of the situation are most pertinent in deciding what to do), interpretation and judgment.

The first challenge for teacher educators in supporting trainees' school-based learning is thus to ensure that they are aware of the demands that they face, without being overwhelmed by them. Designing an effective programme depends on finding ways of managing that complexity so that trainees remain confident that they can succeed, without distorting or denying its reality in ways that ultimately inhibit their learning.

7.1.2   The Ways in Which Learning to Teach Differs from Other Kinds of Learning

At the heart of that learning is experience. Of all the specific instances of their own learning to which trainees within the DEBT project attributed a source, 72% were ascribed to direct engagement in the processes of planning and teaching. While other sources undoubtedly inform what they do, it is only in action that those ideas come together and acquire meaning. The fact that trainees are seeking both to learn from experience (from others' practice as well as their own) and to demonstrate their learning in action presents significant challenges. Successful graduates, used to high achievement, may be unprepared for the degree of difficulty they encounter in the public arena of the classroom.

While the expertise of practising teachers offers a rich resource from which to learn, it is not easily accessed. As Kennedy (2006, p. 206) has observed, experienced teachers tend to handle the complexity of teaching by devising collections of ready-made responses to events—habits or 'rules of thumb'—that reduce the need for extensive thought about each event as it unfolds. Unfortunately, if the 'rule of thumb' is all that is articulated, the novice will lack essential knowledge of the underlying principles on which it is based. Ignorance of those principles, and of the nature and strength of the evidence that underpins them, deprives beginners of any warrant for the practice and of the capacity to diagnose why it may not prove effective in particular circumstances or how it could be adapted to accommodate them. Rules of thumb promise 'efficiency', but they cannot address the other essential dimension of 'adaptive expertise', which is 'innovation'—the capacity to 'move beyond existing routines… to rethink key ideas, practices, and even values in order to respond to novel situations' (Hammerness et al. 2005, pp. 358–359).

'Rules of thumb' can also obscure the nature and foundations of the experts' own expertise. What they now do so efficiently can seem so obvious and uncomplicated to them that they struggle to identify what it is they could usefully share. This helps to explain why experienced practitioners, when they *do* talk about their practice, often discuss it in terms of 'espoused-theories' (the principles that they believe they are following or assume will give credibility to their practice) rather than the nuanced, highly contextualised 'theories-in-use' on which they actually rely (Eraut 2000). While research shows that trainees can overcome these problems by asking specific questions about what they observe, seeking detailed explanations of the teachers' interpretation of the situation and the rationale for their decisions (Hagger and McIntyre 2006), it is difficult for beginners to frame such questions positively and sensitively.

The second challenge for skilful professionals is thus to find ways of making their expertise accessible to beginners, not simply as practices to be replicated nor as espoused theories, but as a process of well-informed analytical reasoning.

7.1.3 The Tensions Inherent in Sustaining a Dual Identity as Teacher and Learner

Even this is not enough, however, unless beginning teachers *remain* committed to learning from that expertise. Trainees who have achieved a basic level of competence are often reluctant to go on engaging in activities that mark them out as novices. The need to demonstrate competence, a requirement of *all* teachers within a 'culture of performativity' (Ball 2003), makes it unsurprising that beginners should focus on demonstrating what they believe is currently required of them, rather than engaging in observation or in critical evaluation of the impact of their own actions. While this may enable them to develop 'an initial level of teaching competence' sufficient for them to practise in that particular context, it tends to impede development of the capacities needed 'for continued professional development enabling them to go on learning as a teacher in new contexts, and for critical engagement with suggested innovations in classroom practice' (Hagger and McIntyre 2006, p. 37).

The third challenge for mentors is thus to find ways of validating trainees' emerging identity as teachers that do not impede their ongoing learning. Asking specific questions of experienced teachers' practice, planning collaboratively with them, continuing to be observed and discussing those observations with experienced colleagues are the best ways both of gaining access to the professional knowledge of experienced teachers, and of learning to ask critical questions about their own teaching. Sustaining such practices is only possible if school-based teacher educators can help trainees to reconcile the tension between being seen as a teacher and continuing to act as a learner.

7.2 Understanding Beginning Teachers as Learners

Having established the complex nature both of teaching and of learning to teach, we considered what is known about beginning teachers themselves *as learners*. We wanted school-based teacher educators to be aware that beginning teachers may not necessarily follow common stages of development. While extensive research has revealed a number of typical features in trainees' development over time, exemplified in Fuller and Bown's (1975) model—suggesting that trainees move from an initial preoccupation with themselves, through a concern with managing the class to an eventual focus on the impact of their actions on pupils' learning—others have expressed a cautionary note. Findings from the DEBT project suggest that while these issues may all feature at some point in an individual's learning trajectory, few trainees actually work through them in a neatly ordered sequence. A distinctive feature of trainees' learning was the complexity of their thinking, indicated by the range of issues with which they were grappling at any one point. Although the proportion of the trainees' aims concerned with pupil progress did increase over time, it was also true that more than half of their aims were, from the very beginning, concerned with pupil progress or achievement.

Rather than assuming that all trainees would go through a series of sequential stages, we concluded that it would be more helpful for mentors to focus on two significant facets of beginning teachers' learning (drawn from the research) and on the interactions between them:

- the preconceptions that trainees bring with them;
- their particular orientations towards learning from experience.

7.2.1 The Preconceptions that Trainees Bring with Them

Personal classroom experience over many years as a pupil gives many beginning teachers a firmly rooted sense of their ability to judge the nature of effective teaching. Such experience can generate many positive images, but may also give rise to deeply entrenched, negative images—models of teaching that are passionately rejected. Experience gained in previous teaching roles, assumed formally or informally, will also influence trainees' subsequent assumptions, shaping the lens through which they view not only the nature of teaching and the value of specific pedagogical strategies but also the pupils that they encounter.

Most common among trainees in the DEBT project was a tendency to conceive of 'good teaching' in terms of teachers' personal characteristics (such as enthusiasm or compassion) and to talk about teachers' practices in terms of an undifferentiated 'teaching style'—demonstrating little awareness of the need for a flexible repertoire of teaching strategies or careful judgment about when and how to apply them. Some trainees rejected certain teaching strategies outright in light of particular individual experiences.

The idea that we need to take account of beginning teachers' preconceptions is by no means new, but it is of vital importance. Unless mentors engage appropriately with their trainees' initial understandings then any advice or guidance they give is likely to be less effective. Trainees may appear to acquiesce when offered suggestions for practice, but if those suggestions do not resonate with their own assumptions, they are much less likely to understand or adopt them with any conviction.

Beginning teachers often hold strong ideas about the most effective ways of *learning* to teach and these assumptions also need to be explicitly acknowledged and examined. The notion of learning from experience is a particularly powerful (and well-justified) preconception, but it can have quite particular meanings and not all of the different ways in which it is understood prove equally helpful.

7.2.2 Trainees' Orientations Towards Learning from Experience

Within the DEBT project, trainees' references to 'learning from experience' actually encompassed a wide variety of learning processes. Analysis revealed that their approaches to those processes could be helpfully categorised in relation to five key dimensions, or opposable orientations, each representing different aspects of the trainees' approach. These dimensions are summarised in Table 7.1. In using the term 'orientations', we do not mean to suggest that these are fixed characteristics, rather that they reflect the current disposition of the particular trainee at a particular point in time.

In identifying and mapping the attitudes revealed in each interview over the course of the training year (and over the subsequent two years), we were able to discern both specific differences on particular occasions and, in certain cases, clear trends over time. It is precisely because of this potential for change that teacher educators need to be able to identify their trainees' current dispositions towards learning from experience, and, where necessary, seek to promote more positive orientations.

We have discussed these dimensions in greater detail elsewhere (see for example Hagger et al. 2008) but wish to emphasise here their importance in determining the

Table 7.1 Learning from experience: five dimensions according to which trainees' orientations may differ

Dimension	Orientation			
Aspiration *The extent of the trainee's aspirations for their own and their pupils' learning*	Satisfaction with current level of achievement	←	→	Aspirational both as learners and teachers
Intentionality *The extent to which the trainees' learning is planned*	Reactive	←	→	Deliberative
Frame of reference *The value that the trainee ascribes to looking beyond their experience in order to make sense of it.*	Exclusive reliance on the experience of classroom teaching	←	→	Drawing on a range of sources to shape and make sense of experience
Response to feedback *The trainee's disposition towards receiving feedback and the value that they attribute to it*	Tendency to be disabled by critical feedback	←	→	Effective use of feedback to further learning
Attitude to context *Attitude to the positions in which trainees find themselves and the approaches that they take to the school context*	Tendency to regard the context as constraining	←	→	Acceptance of the context and ability to capitalise on it

Table adapted from Hagger et al. (2008)

ways in which teacher educators both understand and respond to particular aspects of their trainees' learning. It is particularly important for mentors to understand their trainees' aspirations and to recognise that the relationship between aspiration and action is not entirely straightforward. While there is often an inevitable gap (in the early stages, especially) between an aspiration to achieve things in certain ways and the level of competence needed to realise that aspiration, what really matters is that the ambition and desire to improve are accompanied by 'intentionality': the capacity and commitment of the trainee to plan systematically for their own learning. While it may be useful for mentors to continue to provide feedback and establish new targets, it is also important to look beyond simply supplying the trainees with what the mentors can see that they need next. The real challenge is to enable the trainees to identify and begin to address those developmental needs themselves. This may also depend on broadening the trainees' frame of reference— alerting them to the other resources on which they can draw, which includes seeing their *pupils* as valuable sources from which they could potentially learn.

While the nature of feedback on trainees' teaching and the way in which it is given will obviously have an important impact on the way in which it is received, there are also marked differences in beginning teachers' dispositions towards feedback, regardless of its quality. For many, the process is a highly emotive one that serves to highlight their vulnerability. Perceptions of success and failure, when faced with the challenges of establishing a new identity as a teacher and building productive relationships with both pupils and colleagues, tend to be powerfully amplified. What is important is the trainees' capacity to *make use* of the feedback in developing their practice, which may, in turn, be determined by their attitude to the particular context in which they are placed.

In considering the different orientations of beginning teachers towards their current context, we define that context quite broadly to include the nature of the school, the subject department and the particular classes and pupils that they are teaching, as well the role and status of the trainees themselves. A trainee's acceptance of the given context, notwithstanding the particular challenges that it presents, and a desire to exploit its particular features to promote their professional learning, is clearly linked to the other dimensions; it is likely to depend on the extent of the trainee's aspiration and their capacity to identify the first steps towards its realisation, again revealing the interconnections between each of the different dimensions.

7.3   Developing Research-Informed and Practice-Sensitive Principles

Taking account of what research has revealed about teaching, learning to teach and beginning teachers as learners, we sought to formulate a series of key principles to underpin the practice of school-based teacher educators. These principles are concerned with

- eliciting trainees' preconceptions
- structuring trainees' access to the curriculum of ITE
- sustaining the trainees' dual identity as teacher and learner
- promoting a deliberative orientation towards learning from experience
- expanding trainees' frame of reference.

Principle 1: *Trainees need to be given the opportunity to articulate their pre-conceptions and so acknowledge their influence and begin to subject them to critical scrutiny*

Given the power that they exercise over beginning teachers' development, it is essential for mentors to elicit their trainees' preconceptions, enabling the trainees to acknowledge their influence and so begin to subject them to critical scrutiny. The trainees' prior experiences serve not only to provide them with models of teaching to which they aspire (or perhaps emphatically reject), but also to shape the lens through which they view their subsequent experience and the advice and suggestions for practice offered to them. Eliciting these roots through careful questioning will help teacher educators both to appreciate the emotional attachment that trainees might have to those ideas and enable them to support trainees in evaluating their relevance and meaning in the new context in which they are now learning to teach.

Being able subsequently to link any advice given to images that they already hold, or to explicitly acknowledge the fact that what is being suggested might seem counter-intuitive in light of their ideals, means that trainees will be helped to connect those new insights to their existing ideas, thereby making the prospect of critical evaluation and subsequent development much more likely.

Principle 2: Careful attention needs to be given to the way in which the curriculum for ITE is structured, given that the competing demands of teaching are encountered simultaneously, not in a carefully staged sequence

The trainees' need to learn to draw flexibly on a wide range of knowledge bases as they are confronted by the complexity of the classroom, coupled with the fact that beginners do not all follow neatly ordered trajectories means that any attempt to structure their learning into a coherent programme faces a number of challenges. Mentors need to prevent trainees from feeling overwhelmed by all that they need to learn, but the very nature of what they are trying to learn means that it cannot be neatly packaged into a series of discrete units. Such packages risk diverting them from their current priorities and the realities of working life in a school.

In thinking about how to structure trainees' learning in school, it quickly becomes clear that most of the curriculum that they need is, in fact, already laid out in the realities of teachers' practice and pupils' learning as they happen in classrooms. Rather than focusing on constructing a curriculum' for trainees' school-based learning, the emphasis needs to be on organising or structuring trainees' access to that curriculum. While observation and learning by doing both have a critical role to play neither of them are straightforward or guaranteed to prove effective: prior experience as a pupil can obscure rather than help beginners to interpret experienced teachers' classroom decision-making; simple imitation of others' practice will never give rise to the sort of expertise that teachers actually need. A number of processes can be used to maximise the learning opportunities presented to trainees during the practicum experience, including:

- designing a timetable which reflects the fact that they need time to learn as well as to teach;
- creating opportunities for collaborative planning and teaching;
- ensuring within lesson feedback that trainees assume increasing responsibility for leading the evaluation of their teaching;
- providing opportunities *throughout* the programme for focussed observation of experienced teachers and subsequent discussion with them; and
- encouraging trainees to consult pupils, eliciting feedback on their experience of learning.

Consulting pupils about their learning is, of course, only likely to be embraced by trainees if they think that experienced teachers also regard it as an important source for their own learning. If pupils' views are not recognised as important and valued by qualified practitioners, then trainees, anxious to establish their professional credibility, are unlikely to want to distinguish themselves as novices by drawing pupils' attention to their interest in learning from them. This focuses attention on our third essential principle—sustaining the trainee's dual identity as both teacher and learner.

Principle 3: *Trainees need support to help them to embrace and sustain a dual identity as both teacher and learner, thereby establishing a sustainable commitment to continued professional learning*

The most effective way of doing this, as already suggested, is for mentors to demonstrate their own commitment to continued professional learning, embodying precisely those orientations towards learning from experience that play such a crucial role in trainees' development. If trainees are aware of the professional development priorities of experienced teachers, and of the steps that those teachers have identified to enable them to work towards their achievement, they are much more likely to regard the process of target-setting not simply as a requirement of their training programme but as an essential component of a deliberative approach to future development. Given its potential impact on the formation of trainees' professional identity, we should not under-estimate the value of experienced teachers clearly modelling to beginners their own engagement in enquiry-oriented practice (BERA-RSA 2014).

Principle 4: *Trainees need to be encouraged to adopt a deliberative approach towards their own learning, enabling them to take increasing responsibility for directing their own development*

The notion of engaging in 'enquiry-oriented practice' is essentially an extension of what we have described among beginners as a deliberative orientation towards learning from experience, with both terms implying an explicit commitment to the process of continuing professional development, and to the kinds of action necessary to bring this about. Modelling such an orientation and alerting trainees to ways in which it may be embodied in specific professional development initiatives within a school offers one way of promoting it. Another effective strategy is to invite trainees to contribute *first* whenever they are given feedback on their teaching. Persisting with such a strategy, even if some trainees find it difficult to begin with, will encourage them to recognise their responsibility to make their own professional judgements and to identify the implications of those judgements for their future development, rather than simply relying on experienced teachers for affirmation and direction.

It is also important to ensure that any discussion of observed teaching concludes not simply with a number of points for future development but with the identification of particular ways in which the trainee can begin to address them. This range of suggestions, some of which are clearly focused within the trainee's own classroom while others direct them to look beyond it, serves to demonstrate the importance of our final principle: the importance of expanding the frame of reference on which trainees draw.

Principle 5: *Trainees need to be supported in drawing on a range of sources in order to make sense of their experience, equipping them to learn effectively from the full range of learning opportunities available to them within school and beyond.*

Professional learning needs to happen in both directions—reaching deep *within* the trainees' classroom teaching to ensure, for example, that they recognise the range of insights that they can gain from the pupils themselves, as well as looking *beyond* that particular context to draw on ideas and practices developed and refined by experienced colleagues or more systematically analysed and evaluated through different kinds of research. Again the most important contribution probably derives from the way in which mentors model an open-minded and enquiring disposition. Mentors should also identify *other* colleagues who may be particularly able to help with specific developmental needs. Observing and asking questions of a range of different teachers will give trainees a much more developed appreciation of the role of interpretation and judgement in teachers' decision-making. Particular course demands (especially where courses are offered in partnership with universities) may also direct trainees to certain literature or require systematic investigation of specific issues. Although these demands can sometimes appear as distractions from the 'real' business of teaching, the way in which mentors respond to them is crucial in ensuring that those wider sources of learning are actually brought to bear on the issues that confront their trainees.

7.4 Framing the Future Research Agenda

Our concern to elaborate the research-informed and practice-sensitive principles that we believe should underpin the practice of school-based teacher educators, was rooted in our long engagement in an established ITE partnership. It derived its sense of urgency, however, from two important stimuli. One is the 'practicum turn' in ITE, examined by Mattsson et al. (2011). The other, which preceded and, in many ways, drove the trend towards school-based and school-led provision, was the international policy turn, to which Cochran-Smith has drawn attention: the way in which teacher education is now defined as a 'policy problem' rather than the learning problem that it was previously conceived to be. Instead of trying to understand 'how prospective teachers learn the 'knowledge, skills and dispositions needed to function as school professionals' (Cochran-Smith 2005, p. 4), the focus of the 'new teacher education' emphasises those parameters that can be controlled by policy-makers—the 'broad structural arrangements and teacher education regulations'. It is in seeking to redress this balance that we have highlighted research insights into the learning of beginning teachers, informed by detailed analysis of what it is they are trying to learn.

This is not to claim that the 'new teacher education' has no place for research. As Cochran-Smith has pointed out, the appeal to research and evidence is, in fact, another of its most salient features, although the focus of that research is almost exclusively on outcomes as measured by pupils' attainment in standardised tests. Thus, while policy-makers' reduction or rejection of a role for universities in ITE does not necessarily imply a rejection of research itself, the research that is promoted tends to be narrowly conceived as identifying 'what works' in producing teachers who raise pupils' test scores.

In concluding with reflections on the implications of our work for future research, we are therefore compelled to consider two fundamental questions: not merely 'What kind of research is needed to strengthen the quality of beginning teachers' school-based learning?' but also 'Who should conduct that research?' While our answer to the second question—that teachers should play a prominent role in conducting the research that is needed—is not at odds with the views of policy-makers, our conception of the purpose and nature of that research is much wider and more complex than the 'new teacher education' would admit.

In setting out that research agenda, we begin with the central preoccupation of this chapter—the beginning teachers themselves—but we also believe that there are important questions to be asked about the kinds of changes that are required of schools, or that might arise in schools, if they were to take engagement in school-based teacher education as seriously as we have suggested. There are also questions to be asked about the impact on the mentors who work most closely with beginning teachers in the ways in which we have described.

7.4.1 How Do Beginning Teachers Solve the Dilemmas and Deal with the Dichotomies They Face?

As we have explored, beginning teachers face two particular kinds of challenges: the range of simultaneous and essentially competing demands that teaching itself presents and the particular tensions inherent in establishing and sustaining a dual identity as teacher and learner. While stage theories of development have been shown to be of limited value in conceptualising the ways in which their concerns shift over time, much more needs to be known about how beginners learn to prioritise, both in their planning and interactive decision-making and in apportioning their time and energy, and about how they learn to manage the emotional demands inherent in making the conscious compromises that are always necessary. We have argued that one of the most effective ways of helping beginners to embrace continued learning as part of their teacher identity is for those supporting and guiding them to adopt precisely that orientation themselves. A sustained commitment of that kind could play a fundamental role in the transformation of schools as learning environments.

7.4.2   How Might Schools Be Transformed as Learning Environments for Teachers?

There is much more to learn about the nature of the attitudes and practices that could emerge in schools that take teachers' learning seriously as a core part of their professional identity and invest significantly in it. To what extent, and in what ways, is it possible to develop an ethos within schools that acknowledges the full complexity of teaching and is prepared to problematize the development of practice rather than seeking to identify and implement apparently simple solutions? Consideration, of course, also needs to be given to pupil outcomes, but these should be defined more widely than test scores, encompassing even the nature of pupils' attitudes to teachers' learning and the kinds of responsibility that they might assume for helping beginners (and more experienced practitioners) to learn from pupils' perspectives.

7.4.3   How Does Acting as School-Based Educator Impact on the Practice of Experienced Teachers?

The transformation of schools will, of course, depend on and be driven by the transformation of those leading the schools' engagement with ITE. While there is considerable anecdotal evidence about the benefits for mentors arising from their engagement with beginners—not least the stimulus it provides for them to articulate and reflect in some detail on their interactive decision-making—it is important that research goes beyond mentors' self-reporting, to examine whether and in what ways their thinking and practice actually change. This raises questions about how such changes can be effectively identified and tracked over time. If mentors are themselves committed to their own professional learning, new questions also arise about the use that they themselves make of research, as teachers and as teacher–educators.

7.4.4   What Role Should School-Based Teacher Educators Play in Further Research?

As we have already suggested, school-based teacher educators' engagement with research should certainly not be confined to the critical use of others' research findings. Just as effective ITE depends on accessing the distinctive knowledge bases to which expert teachers have unique access, so effective ITE research also depends on an appreciation of the distinctive insights to be gained from practitioners' own research. That is not to suggest that *all* such research should be practitioner-led, nor is it to overlook either the practical challenges associated with adding further to the agendas of school-based teacher educators or the acknowledged limitations of the inevitably small-scale studies that would be feasible for them. It is, however, an argument for multi-method research-designs that are at least co-constructed with school-based teacher educators, and allow for the accumulated insights that can be generated through multiple cases, drawn from different contexts.

References

Ball, S. (2003). The teacher's soul and the terrors of performativity. *Journal of Education Policy, 18*(2), 215–228.

BERA-RSA. (2014). *Research and the teaching profession: Building the capacity for a self-improving education system*. London: British Education Research Association.

Bransford, J., Darling-Hammond, L., & LePage, P. (2005). Introduction. In L. Darling-Hammond, J. Bransford, P. LePage, K. Hammerness, & H. Duffy (Eds.), *Preparing teachers for a changing world: What teachers should learn and be able to do* (pp. 1–39). San Francisco: Jossey-Bass.

Burn, K., Hagger, H., & Mutton, T. (2015). *Beginning teachers' learning: Making experience count*. Northwich: Critical Publishing.

Cochran-Smith, M. (2005). The new teacher education: For better or for worse? *Educational Researcher, 34*(7), 3–17.

Doyle, W. (1977). Learning the classroom environment: An ecological analysis. *Journal of Teacher Education, 28*(6), 51–55.

Eraut, M. (2000). Non-formal learning and tacit knowledge in professional work. *British Journal of Educational Psychology, 70*(1), 113–136.

Fuller, F., & Bown, O. (1975). Becoming a teacher. In K. Ryan (Ed.), *Teacher education: The seventy-fourth yearbook of the National Society for the Study of Education*. Chicago, IL: University of Chicago Press.

Hagger, H., Burn, K., Mutton, T., & Brindley, S. (2008). Practice makes perfect? Learning to learn as a teacher. *Oxford Review of Education, 34*(2), 159–178.

Hagger, H., & McIntyre, D. (2006). *Learning teaching from teachers: Realizing the potential of school-based teacher education*. Maidenhead: Open University Press.

Hammerness, K., Darling-Hammond, L., Bransford, J., Berliner, D., Cochran-Smith, Mc Donald, & Zeichner, K. (2005). How teachers learn and develop. In L. Darling-Hammond, J. Bransford, P. LePage, K. Hammerness, & H. Duffy (Eds.), *Preparing teachers for a changing world: What teachers should learn and be able to do* (pp. 358–389). San Francisco: Jossey-Bass.

Kennedy, M. (2005). *Inside teaching: How classroom life undermines reform*. Cambridge, MA: Harvard University Press.

Kennedy, M. (2006). Knowledge and vision in teaching. *Journal of Teacher Education, 57*(3), 205–211.

Mattsson, M., Eilertson, T., & Rorrison, D. (Eds.). (2011). *A practicum turn in teacher education*. Rotterdam: Sense.

Author Biographies

Katharine Burn is Associate Professor of Education at the University of Oxford, with particular interests in history education and teachers' professional learning. She is also Director of the Oxford Education Deanery—a multi-strand partnership between the university and local schools that encompasses initial teacher education, teachers' continuing professional development and research collaboration.

Trevor Mutton is Associate Professor of Education at the University of Oxford, works as PGCE Course Director at the University of Oxford and contributes to the Master's programme in Learning and Teaching. He has been involved in a range of research into language teaching, teacher education policy and the nature of beginning teachers' learning.

Hazel Hagger was Director of Professional Programmes at the University of Oxford and co-director of the Developing Expertise of Beginning Teachers project. She has researched and written extensively about beginning teachers' learning with a particular interest in ways of making practising teachers' expertise accessible to beginners.

Chapter 8
The Strathclyde Literacy Clinic: Developing Student Teacher Values, Knowledge and Identity as Inclusive Practitioners

Sue Ellis

8.1 Background: The Problems of Initial Teacher Education

There remains much debate about the features of initial teacher education (ITE) programmes that will produce effective professionals, able to exercise the agency and values that promote flexible, adaptive self-expanding and evidenced-informed professional knowledge. There is particular concern about how to develop teachers who understand inclusion, social disadvantage and who can deliver educational equity through their teaching. Research approaches have drawn attention to the design principles and organisation of ITE programmes that develop knowledgeable, effective and reflective practitioners. The most convincing research approaches use impact evidence to identify those programmes that produce effective teachers and analyse their features (see for example Darling-Hammond 2012). From such analyses we have learned that there can be many pathways to successful outcomes, but that the quality of opportunities to make sense of placement experiences and apply academic knowledge matters.

To develop student teachers' professional efficacy and their commitment to social justice, ITE programmes need to provide varied opportunities that develop professional identity and professional knowledge. 'Clinical' approaches, which bring university academics and professional staff into partnership, are considered effective ways forward, but there is often little specific analysis of how such approaches actually work in practice to develop student teachers' professional knowledge and identity. This lack of analysis matters: in England, the Secretary of State for Education has promoted 'clinical' solutions that widen the routes for achieving qualified teacher status. Traditional university-based ITE courses

S. Ellis (✉)
University of Strathclyde, Glasgow, Scotland, UK
e-mail: sue.ellis@strath.ac.uk

© Springer Nature Singapore Pte Ltd. 2017
M.A. Peters et al. (eds.), *A Companion to Research in Teacher Education*,
DOI 10.1007/978-981-10-4075-7_8

continue to exist, but more favoured approaches fund schools (or academy chains of schools) directly to 'train' their own staff. Schools may choose to buy specific services from universities or commercial training organisations or not. In Scotland, policy makers have chosen to retain universities as centrally involved in the teacher qualification process, but have strengthened the requirements for school–university partnership working. There are just two main routes to becoming a qualified primary teacher: a four-year undergraduate degree that confers a Teaching Qualification with Education and/or other areas of study, and a one-year postgraduate diploma that also confers such a teaching qualification. Both qualifications require a minimum number of weeks spent on 'teaching practice' with assessment by both school and university staff. Candidates then enter a one-year probationary teacher period, with structured assessments by school staff, which must be satisfactory to achieve qualified teacher status. The system is overseen by a professional body, the General Teaching Council for Scotland, which keeps a register of all teachers qualified to work in Scotland. However, despite the different approaches in England and Scotland there have been few descriptions of the affordances and constraints within each system to develop the professional knowledge and identity of student teachers. Both systems are premised on the assumption that school placement, with supervision by the school, provides the type of practical experience that student teachers need.

Various theoretical models describe how student teachers develop a professional identity by gradually becoming encultured into the profession (see for example, Cochran-Smith et al. 2008 and many chapters in this volume). Whilst clinical models solve some problems, it is likely that they may bring others to the fore. It is important to understand the affordances and constraints that different kinds of school placement experience provide, and the extent to which traditional school placements may simply encourage student teachers to accept and reproduce the inequities that already exist in the system. To explore this we need to examine how student teachers negotiate a positive and productive professional identity by participating in school placements. Several studies of both student teachers on placement and early-career teachers indicate the challenges this involves. One challenge highlights the delicate balance student teachers must strike between the desire to present themselves as competent professionals and the need to be allowed to be seen by others, and themselves, as learners. This is a unique and crucial 'dance of identity' (Boaler 2003) because to access the nuanced knowledge of more experienced professionals student teachers must be able and willing to initiate and sustain in-depth professional discussions about practice and to acknowledge what is complex, difficult or unjust. Socio-cultural theorists position these very early-career experiences as ones in which student teachers through participatory activities, learn to exercise agency and negotiate the 'landscapes of practice' (Wenger 1998). They learn to align different kinds of knowledge, envisage new professional applications, contexts and roles and, through this negotiate their identity. Lave and Wenger (1991) present a model in which the student teachers' participation may begin at the periphery of the organisational action, but it is facilitated by the context in which it takes place and looks to gradually develop more central involvement.

Empirical research into student experiences on placement, however, indicates that this may not be exactly what happens in practice (e.g. Bartow-Jacobs 2014; Huntly 2008). Hall et al. (2012), studying Irish student teachers, found that the power relations in schools and student teachers' desire to be seen as competent professionals, constrained them from exercising any agency to present themselves as learners. Instead of engaging in the sort of rounded 'legitimate peripheral participation' that would gradually deepen their understanding of teaching and learning, the student teachers adopted, and strove to satisfy, narrow and sometimes superficial conceptions of teaching, learning and of being a teacher. Whilst this served an immediate purpose, it meant they forged professional identities that made it difficult to admit to uncertainty, and conversations that may have challenged and deepened their professional understanding and developed a broader cultural script about teaching, learning and about being professional, did not take place.

The four-year ITE course at Strathclyde has developed several initiatives to help student teachers develop an early professional identity that is agentic, focused on students understanding themselves as learners, and strives to make it the norm for students to seek social justice and to problematize and enquire into professional practice. Many of these initiatives are located outside traditional 'teaching placement' experiences. For example, when students start their course, they are introduced to the principle of students as leaders of learning. They are told that the collective knowledge of all those in the room far exceeds the knowledge of a single person and that their professional training will involve learning to debate and share all sorts of knowledge that may be useful to primary teachers. Some of the University structures that can make this happen include the Student Teacher Continuing Professional Development (CPD) Society, run by students, for students encourages students to offer workshops on their own areas of expertise (recent workshop topics included 'Christmas Traditions in Germany'; 'British Sign Language for Teachers'; 'What it Means to Be a Muslim'; 'Drumming for Beginners' and 'Scottish Country Dancing'). They are encouraged to join student-driven community projects such as the Homework support club that serves local disadvantaged communities, and are encouraged to attend regular Teach-Meet meetings, where practitioners from Directors of Education and top Inspectors to first year students will share recent experiences, questions, projects and professional learning.

All these initiatives are designed to create an engaged, knowledgeable, inquiring and pro-active student body, committed to principles of inclusion and social justice. They offer opportunities for student teachers who are at the very start of their professional journey to begin to develop positive professional values and identities by participating in a range of activities and contexts, and to see themselves as competent, socially engaged and well-networked learners. Although participation offers no academic credit (a founding principle being that student teachers should engage because the activities are, in themselves, worthwhile) they offer distinct advantages for student learning. Driven by students, the power relationships are often more equitable and participation is outside the official course, so membership can be less formal. There is no assessment or close-scrutiny so students can engage on their own terms, be driven by their own motivations and are free to try things out and experiment.

8.2 Strathclyde Literacy Clinic: Theoretical and Professional Knowledge

The Strathclyde Literacy Clinic was born from this context but stands in different relation to the other student activities. It is a distinct collaboration between university academics, local school management teams and the Strathclyde student body, and is specifically designed to help student teachers understand how poverty impacts on literacy. Although it involves student teachers teaching in schools, it is not a traditional school placement because it does not directly involve the class teachers, and nor is it a club. It makes explicit use of the academic research expertise that resides in the university to enhance the professional knowledge of student teachers and impact on the lives of local children who are experiencing difficulties in learning to read. Students in the third or fourth year of Strathclyde's 'BA in Primary Education with Teaching' course can sign up to work in the literacy clinic for a 10-week block. In the clinic, the students work in teams of four and each team works with one pupil from a disadvantaged community who has had difficulty learning to read. The lesson is a half-hour, one-to-one withdrawal lesson. This means that one student teacher in the team goes on Monday, one on Tuesday, one on Wednesday and so on, so that the pupil gets four lessons per week.

The student teams do not follow a programme. Instead, they must work as a team to share their professional observations of the pupil's learning and, in discussion with university academics who have research expertise in literacy and understand the mechanisms whereby poverty impacts on literacy, agree the learning and teaching mix that is likely to give the biggest payoff for the child. Once this is agreed, all student teachers in the team work to deliver it. The focus is on fast, responsive teaching, closely tailored to the knowledge of the child that emerges as each lesson unfolds. All sessions will involve the child reading continuous text—sometimes more than one text—and the ITE students taking a running record and miscue analysis of this. They coach the child into using reading cues and strategies efficiently and check that the text offers the child an appropriate level of interest, challenge and agency. All sessions will also encourage comprehension in the form of Reader Response conversations (Rosenblatt 1978). Beyond these basic elements, the student team decides what takes place in the sessions, in consultation with the child; it may involve writing or drawing, reading to the child for relaxation, oral storytelling, phonics, spelling, handwriting or comprehension skills practice. The child can express an opinion about what happens (one child asked to learn to read the menu from a popular Hamburger chain so he 'didn't look stupid' when he went out with his friends, for example). The team members source (and share and discuss) appropriate activities and resources. They do not write lesson plans, but write brief notes after each lesson in a folder, which is kept in school. These notes record the activity (in brief) plus important observations about the child as a reader that might be significant for the child's future learning. All team members, the university academics, the class teachers and the Head Teachers have access to this folder. Team members also telephone the student teacher who will go in the following day and give a brief oral report of what they did, what they noticed and what they think the next priority should be. The focus is on fast, interactive teaching and on fluent pedagogies that are responsive to real-time observations. All third year students and some fourth year students participate in the clinic on a voluntary basis but fourth year students can also choose to write up their clinic experiences as a case study for academic credit towards their final degree classification. Some students participate on a non-credit basis in Year 3 and then for credit in Year 4. All student groups are supported by a weekly tutorial with a university academic. Each tutorial contains 3–4 groups, who each present and analyse evidence, discuss their thoughts about the diagnosis, the learning mix that is likely to work, and the range of practical activities that could take this forward. The students talk about the knowledge that emerges during their teaching, what they have tried, what worked and what needed to be adapted or abandoned.

Although the student teachers do not follow a set programme, their observations, analysis and diagnosis are all informed by the same *3 Domains of Knowledge* model for thinking about what matters in becoming literate and how experiences of literacy at home, in the community and in school impact on young children. The model makes explicit the need for professionals to negotiate multiple paradigms if they to understand the whole child as a learner at school and in the family and community. Theoretically, it is underpinned by an explicit acceptance that literacy is not autonomous skill and that becoming literate is a process that is both social and cognitive. The model is designed to help our ITE students think about the key influences on literacy, and work out what educators need to notice and do to design a learning mix that is likely to work. It is presented as a 'Venn Diagram' that brings together three domains, each representing a domain of professional knowledge. These domains are not precisely defined for the student teachers, but offer an intuitive validity.

The first domain asks them to think about the child's cultural capital for, and their socio-cultural understanding of, literacy. This includes the child's funds of knowledge from outside school, the frequency and nature of the literacy experiences they have, and with which important people in their family and the wider community. The student teachers have to think about what the child has experienced, what they know and can do outside school in relation to literacy as well as the child's wider interests, what they believe literacy to be for, and the specific literacy practices in which they will have engaged. This is the child's starting point. The student teachers then have to think about how well this matches with the assumptions that may have been made by the school system, and whether there are experiences, knowledge or understandings that they can provide which may benefit the child.

The second domain asks the student teachers to think about the child's identity as a learner in general, as a literate being and as a literacy learner. They must consider the sorts of things the child would like to be able to read, how the child sees himself/herself as a reader, how they would like to be seen by others and how others do see them. They need to gather evidence about the extent to which a child has a 'growth mindset' (Dweck and Rule 2013) about being a reader, what the child believes it might be possible to achieve in relation to becoming literate, what they believe they need to do, and think about how they are socially and academically positioned by others in the classroom in relation to literacy, and how much this matters. They then have to think about how well all this contributes to helping the child learn effectively, whether some beliefs, practices or attitudes need to be addressed, and how this might be done.

The third domain concerns the child's cognitive skills and knowledge about reading. This involves their concepts about print, their phonological awareness, phonic and letter knowledge, their sight vocabulary, comprehension, the cues and strategies they use for working out unknown words when they encounter them in continuous text, as well as their reading behaviours, stamina and persistence.

The two biggest factors that impact on how quickly and easily children learn to read in school, not just in Scotland but internationally, are poverty and gender. Evidence from longitudinal studies, attainment surveys and cohort studies shows that these two factors are systematically and consistently associated with literacy attainment. Explanations for this draw on sociological concepts and theories that speak directly to the first two domains, cultural capital and identity. However, the vast majority of intervention programmes that teachers are directed to use for children struggling to read draw almost entirely on psychology theories and the cognitive knowledge and skills embodied in the third domain. One important factor therefore in the design and use of the *3 Domains* model is that it prompts emerging professionals to negotiate across different knowledge domains to understand the whole child. Each domain has a different evidence-base, different theoretical frameworks and different kinds of explanations for how and why disadvantage arises, and the model is an explicit prompt to consider each and bring them into some sort of alignment. This model of professional learning draws on Wenger-Trayner et al. (2014) that acquiring professional knowledge involves learning to negotiate a complex landscape of practice that looks seamless but actually brings different kinds of knowledge into focus at different points. Through participation, professionals learn to understand each domain, to negotiate across the boundaries of practice that they present and to bring them into alignment. Appreciating the insights each individual domain affords to understand a particular context and juxtaposing the insights from several domains, allows professionals to make nuanced decisions as they operate in complex landscapes of practice and provides a basis for professional refection and learning.

8.3   The Study

ITE students from one Literacy Clinic cohort were interviewed about the process of working in the literacy clinic and about what they had learnt. The interviews were conducted by researchers who did not know the ITE students, were not connected to the course, and who were not connected with the schools in which the clinics took place. The interviews lasted between 25 and 40 min, were conducted by telephone and took the form of semi-structured conversations with pre-identified lead questions and sub-questions that could be used to prompt further explanation or examples. The ITE students were drawn from both third and fourth year, had all volunteered to be interviewed and knew that the interviews were anonymised and would have no impact on their academic grades. The interviewer took copious notes and typed these up immediately after the interview, using wherever possible the interviewees own words. These transcripts were sent to the interviewees for checking and interviewees were invited to add further clarification or additional examples and information if appropriate. The interviews were then subjected to iterative coding processes by two researchers. The data reported here relates to the categories of professional agency, collaborative enquiry, professional identity and professional knowledge.

8.4   Results and Discussion

Several themes from the analysis indicated that the Literacy Clinic experience impacts on student teachers' emerging professional identities in ways that are different from traditional school placements. One strong theme was the opportunities that working in the Literacy Clinic provided for student teacher agency. Because participation was located outside the usual placement experience, the Literacy Clinic offered new and different opportunities for professional discussion and learning. It was clear from almost all the interviewees that in traditional school placement contexts, student teachers are highly mindful of the pedagogical and conceptual priorities and practices of both their supervising teacher and of the wider school. They have limited freedom to question or challenge dominant practices and assumptions (even when they are patently unjust), or to introduce and try out their own ideas because they are, in effect, working under licence in another person's professional space. Introducing new practices or doing things differently requires a careful dance of courtship, where the student teacher must 'sound out' the supervising teacher to see how the new activity or ideas fit within the teacher's own plans, priorities and the established routines and practices. Some teachers make this easier than others, but all students were clearly aware of the delicacy of such negotiations, were cautious about how they innovated and for some any innovation was a considerable source of anxiety. Working in the Strathclyde Literacy Clinic afforded students a new kind of freedom to exercise professional agency. This was evidenced in several ways. For some it involved the freedom to try out new ideas, quickly and without having to expend emotional energy thinking about how to 'prepare the ground' or convince a more experienced professional that this was a potentially fruitful way forward. In the Clinic context, actions could be prompted simply by the student teacher's judgement that it might address some of the child's needs. For example, one student described how she noticed that the child did not expect reading to make sense. She felt that this was partly because his reading scheme books were designed for much younger readers and did not offer age-appropriate meaning-making opportunities. She decided to take the child off the official reading scheme and teach him using an age-appropriate Joke Book instead. She used this to coach the child to use a range of strategies to decode the text, and they talked about the jokes—which ones were funny and not funny, how the humour was created; they talked about puns, about syntactic 'garden-path' jokes, about the child's home life and family jokes. The child spontaneously began writing his own book of jokes, based on those he collected from friends and family. This was the first time that this child had ever voluntarily initiated a literacy activity. The interviewee said that she would not have dared to suggest this on a normal school placement, although she might now feel more confident because of this positive experience. Of course, not all activities were successful, but the Clinic context supported innovative teaching because the students were aware that if an idea did not work, the only people to know would be the child and the other students in the team. This gave student teachers the confidence to innovate, and some support to reflect on why their innovations were successful or unsuccessful, to learn from this and from the innovations of others. Freedom to innovate is an important part of developing professional agency and identity; it allows student teachers to envisage the sort of teacher they want to be, to think about how they use evidence, to apply their knowledge and try out different kinds of action to create new professional understandings.

Several interviewees also raised a much more fundamental point about agency and the range of pedagogical activities that engage student teachers on traditional school placements. When a student teacher arrives in a class, they are told the teacher's attainment groupings that facilitate appropriate delivery of teaching and learning. These are commonly called the 'ability groups' in the class. Inevitably there is a small group of 'strugglers', sometimes called 'individuals', whose literacy is so poor they cannot follow the work of the class. Several interviewees pointed out that these individuals were invariably on an intervention programme chosen by the teacher. As students, apprenticed to the teacher, they were expected to follow this programme. They had no licence to make their own diagnosis, to question the evidence-base on which the diagnosis had been made, or to adapt the programme that had been chosen. Interviewees who were in their fourth and final year of their ITE course pointed out that they had never been asked to diagnose why an individual reader might be struggling to learn and to come up with their own suggestions about what could be done, and (several were quick to point out) they could not think of a single friend on the course who had been asked to do this either. If we do not give student teachers opportunities to engage in these types of decision as part of their ITE course, the first time they make them is in the relatively unsupported context as a probationary teacher, with many calls on their time and attention, and possibly scant access to experienced literacy practitioners (Shoffner 2011).

The interviewees also described some distinctive elements of the agency and knowledge exercised through collaborative discussions with their peers to determine the learning mix that would give the biggest payoff for their child. Negotiating across the different knowledge domains of the *3 Domains of Knowledge* involves balancing different kinds of evidence and it offers no single way forward. Some students were clearly more familiar and comfortable working within just the cognitive domain. As a consequence, there was strong professional debate, and occasionally heated arguments, about what should be prioritised and why. Taking explicit account of the evidence-based amassed across all the domains was, for most students, a new way of thinking about teaching. Although the university ITE course covers sociological concepts and both school and national policy documents routinely acknowledge the importance of homes and families, many students had absorbed the idea that this implied a line of impact that went in just one direction—from 'school to home'. This was the first time they had been asked to think about how a child's experiences outside school might impact on the learning mix provided in school. Some student teachers embraced the idea that schools might adapt to children more easily than others, and for some it challenged institutionalised views that 'good teaching' is rooted in prescriptive programmes of study, delivered as specified by the publisher. Several interviewees described heated debates taking place within the group about whether to move the child away from reductive and skill-based approaches such as teaching decoding through phonics, or comprehension through reciprocal reading and introduce more contextualised, meaningful approaches, what these might look like and how they might relate to the evidence collected around the *3 Domains* model.

The 'Clinic' context gave these decision-making processes a hard emotional and professional edge. Whereas the university parts of the ITE course often involve collaborative discussion and joint projects, the Literacy Clinic discussions were not just of theoretical interest, but offered a real opportunity to impact on a child's life. The one-to-one context captured the ITE students' emotional energies, which drove the discussions and helped to cement their commitment to social justice. One interviewee explained that the more equal power-dynamics of the peer group and the absence of an inherited historical pedagogy in the Literacy Clinic group allowed them to exercise their pedagogical imaginations, envisage new teaching approaches and to challenge each other freely. There were many instances of professional learning from the Literacy Clinic discussions, both within the group and also in the tutorial discussions with the university academic and other groups.

Of course some groups collaborated more frequently and meaningfully than others. Those teams that worked most closely together reported generating ideas and understandings in formal pre-arranged meetings, but also through informal conversations amongst friends. These often started with one or two group members chatting (sometimes with friends who were not participating in the Literacy Clinic), but then fruitful ideas were then taken to the group. Not all groups worked closely together, but there was evidence that the weekly commitment of working with the child created an imperative that meant that there were no instances where groups did not collaborate or a where a single student 'opted out'. Those working in friendship groups were able to 'hit the ground running' in terms of establishing communication networks and dialogue, but several interviewees said that they had enjoyed working with people outside their established friendship networks. They felt they had gained different insights from this. Interestingly, even students working with their friends felt that they discussed teaching in a new way. Previously, discussions had focussed on generic issues; the 'correct' format for planning documents, classroom organisation and school expectations whereas the joint endeavour, focused on a specific child, prompted 'in depth' discussion of literacy teaching and learning issues, and sharing of resources and knowledge that they had not previously experienced.

The learning the interviewees reported came from their own participation in teaching and from discussion of how other students taught. It included learning about persistence, timing, adaptation of activities to make them meaningful to make them work in the context of use, and to address particular learning goals. Student teachers described paying new attention to the children's lives, interests and aspirations, to observations and evidence that emerged during the teaching, and they described becoming more responsive during lessons (they talked about learning to "teach on the hoof" and "dealing with what the child needed to know") and more thoughtful between sessions. The fact that each student was only teaching for 30 min, once each week, created a new dynamic for reflection. It offered important 'cooking time' for ideas; student teachers could assimilate what had happened, think about what it meant, engage in some research and discussion and allow new interpretations and understandings of the child as a learner to grow. This balance between participation or activity, vicarious learning from the participation and activities of other students, and unpressured opportunities to think, reflect and read about issues before the next participatory session seemed to be important, and an area for wider discussion, particularly given the increasingly content-heavy nature of many ITE courses.

8.5   Final Word

It has not been the intention of this chapter to suggest that traditional school placements should be replaced by a Literacy Clinic model. Instead it has tried to suggest that offering ITE students a variety of contexts for professional participation in teaching and learning activities can afford different opportunities to exercise agency, challenge the status quo and develop professional knowledge. Different contexts for professional learning can present student teachers with different scripts for understanding what it means to be a professional. All of this is important for developing strong, rounded professional identities.

Identity is a complex and multi-faceted beast, hard to pin down. Professional identities are developed across the context of a person's life and may present in different ways in different contexts to different groups. There is no sure-fire way to ensure that student teachers on ITE courses develop positive and productive professional identities. This makes it all the more important for ITE courses to pay explicit attention to the affordances that different contexts offer for developing professional identity. It is certainly an area that needs close attention and further research.

Of course, a profession is defined by the knowledge its members hold, but this knowledge is not exact. It is complex, drawing on different disciplines with different epistemologies, understandings of evidence and definitions of what matters. Prioritising different knowledge domains creates different views of the child, and different agendas for action. It is important that ITE courses embrace this complexity and do not to present professional knowledge in reductive or superficial ways. To do this, we need to continue to provide contexts for student teachers to freely engage with the different domains in practice, and we need an explicit 'theory of change' about how the planning, implementation and assessment tools we provide help ITE students to participate in ways that deepen understanding within and across knowledge domains.

All knowledge has an emotional and social dimension, and the act of learning new knowledge cannot be divorced from the contexts in which it takes place. It is important that ITE research recognises the emotional and social context of student teacher learning, both in the formal learning structures ITE courses present and the informal networks created by student teachers themselves. Doing so does not diminish the importance of professional knowledge, but positively enhances it. Shulman, writing about his early model of professional knowledge reflects that, whilst it successfully captures some aspects of professional knowledge, it fails to capture other significant elements, namely the "…emotions, affect, feelings and motivations that underpin wider concepts of professional identity, moral judgement and reasoning" (Shulman 2015, p. 9).

Wenger-Trayner and Wenger-Trayner (2015) identify participation, alignment and imagination as central to identity formation, but it is easy to make assumptions about the opportunities that student teachers have to exercise agency through participation. Any hierarchical system—and Scotland like most countries has deeply hierarchical power relations in its schools—feels more equitable and accessible to those at the top. Research on ITE courses needs to play explicit attention to how different contexts of implementation affect student teacher values and agency. We need to listen closely to what the student teachers themselves say about how the power relationships on traditional placements actually feel and how this affects their agency. We need to think about the social and emotion context for student teacher learning, and about how effectively we enable them to negotiate their own pathway in the complex landscape of professional practice that literacy teaching involves. These points are important, not just for university-based ITE courses, but for school-based ones. We need information about the affordances and constraints of school-based training and how affects student teacher identities and knowledge.

We have no evidence for the long-term effects of student teacher participation in the Strathclyde Literacy Clinic, and make no claims about this. Identities develop and change over time and ITE courses do not offer a life-long inoculation against powerlessness or ignorance. However, putting educational conversations onto a professional, more clearly evidence-based (and perhaps therefore a more neutral), basis can support student teachers in becoming more agentic and in initiating conversations that both help them to learn and encourage them to evolve practices that better-address children's needs. An anecdotal event serves as a post-script to this. A Head Teacher recently rang us to say she had one of our Literacy Clinic student teachers on her final placement. The student teacher had approached her with *3 Domains* evidence of the negative consequences for two children of the school's policy preventing children from borrowing 'reading for pleasure' books from class. The student teacher asked that the policy be reconsidered. The Head Teacher was impressed with the professionalism, agency and commitment to making a difference this small act demonstrated. It is anecdotal evidence, but illustrates how professional knowledge can drive agency, and create professionals who take full responsibility for ensuring that schooling meets the needs of every child.

References

Bartow-Jacobs, K. (2014). The role of field experiences in the professional socialization of early career literacy teachers. *LEARNing Landscapes, 8*(1), 173–191.

Boaler, J. (2003). Studying and capturing the complexity of practice—The case of the "dance of agency". *International Group for the Psychology of Mathematics Education, 1,* 3–16.

Cochran-Smith, M., Feiman-Nemser, S., McIntyre, D. J., & Demers, K. E. (Eds.). (2008). *Handbook of research on teacher education: Enduring questions in changing contexts.* London: Routledge.

Dweck, C., & Rule, M. (2013). Mindsets: Helping student to fulfill their potential. Smith College Lecture Series, North Hampton, MA: Smith College.

Darling-Hammond, L. (2012). *Powerful teacher education: Lessons from exemplary programs.* Hoboken: Wiley.

Hall, K., Conway, P., Murphy, R., Long, F., Kitching, K., & O'Sullivan, D. (2012). Authoring oneself and being authored as a competent teacher. *Irish Educational Studies, 31*(2), 103–117.

Huntly, H. (2008). Teachers work: Beginning teachers conceptions of competence. *The Australian Educational Researcher, 35*(1), 125–145.

Lave, J., & Wenger, E. (1991). *Situated learning: Legitimate peripheral participation.* Cambridge: CUP.

Rosenblatt, L. (1978). *The reader, the text, the poem: The transactional theory of the literary work.* Carbondale, IL: Southern Illinois University Press.

Shoffner, M. (2011). Considering the first year: Reflection as a means to address beginning teachers' concerns. *Teachers and Teaching, 17*(4), 417–433.

Shulman, L. S. (2015). PCK: Its genesis and exodus (Chap. 1). In A. Berry, P. Friedrichsen & J. Loughran (Eds.), *Re-examining pedagogical content knowledge in science education* (pp. 3–14). London: Routledge.

Wenger, E. (1998). *Communities of practice: Learning, meaning and identity.* Cambridge, MA: CUP.

Wenger-Trayner, E., Fenton-O'Creevy, M., Hutchinson, S., Kubiak, C., & Wenger-Trayner, B. (Eds.). (2014). *Learning in landscapes of practice: Boundaries, identity, and knowledgeability in practice-based learning.* London: Routledge.

Wenger-Trayner, E., & Wenger-Trayner, B. (2015). Learning in landscapes of practice: A framework. *Learning in landscapes of practice boundaries, identity and knowledgeability.* London, United Kingdom: Routledge.

Author Biography

Sue Ellis is Professor of Education at the University of Strathclyde and Co-Director of its Centre for Education and Social Policy. She researches effective literacy teaching and policy development, working with student teachers, qualified teachers and local policy makers on projects that improve literacy outcomes for pupils.

Chapter 9
You Teach Who You Are Until the Government Comes to Class: A Study of 28 Literacy Teacher Educators in Four Countries

Clare Kosnik, Lydia Menna, Pooja Dharamshi and Clive Beck

> Something dramatic has happened to teacher education policy in the last 30 years. Up until
> the 1980s, in virtually every country around the world, teacher education was a relative
> backwater in terms of educational policy … Today as one international report after another
> makes clear (Barber and Mourshed 2007; Mourshed et al. 2010; Organisation for Economic
> Co-Operation and Development [OECD] 2005), teachers are now seen as *the* key resource
> in ensuring global competitiveness … In a world of intense competition among nations,
> education increasingly plays a key role. National prosperity, social justice, and social
> cohesion are all seen to rest on the shoulders of education (Lauder et al. 2007) … (Furlong
> 2013, p. 29)

As reform efforts in education continue at a rapid and seemingly unrelenting rate, teachers and teacher educators must navigate the choppy waters of education by reconciling a plethora of initiatives. For example, in Australia "[t]here have been 101 government inquiries of one sort or another into Australian teacher education since 1979" (Louden 2008, p. 357). Beside the sheer number of reports and initiatives, the rhetoric around education is polarizing especially for those working in literacy education: on the one hand there is former British Secretary of State for Education, Michael Gove, advocating that literacy instruction is "about the preservation of the nation's cultural heritage" (Furlong 2013, p. 40), while UNESCO is promoting literacy for all with awareness and sensitivity to cultural needs (2006). Wading through this vitriolic and contradictory mine field is difficult

C. Kosnik (✉) · C. Beck
University of Toronto, Toronto, Canada
e-mail: clare.kosnik@utoronto.ca

C. Beck
e-mail: clive.beck@utoronto.ca

L. Menna
University of Alberta, Edmonton, Canada
e-mail: lidia.menna@utoronto.ca

P. Dharamshi
Simon Fraser University, Burnaby, Canada
e-mail: poojadharamshi@gmail.com

© Springer Nature Singapore Pte Ltd. 2017
M.A. Peters et al. (eds.), *A Companion to Research in Teacher Education*,
DOI 10.1007/978-981-10-4075-7_9

135

for teacher educators because they must often negotiate government initiatives with their own views.

If, as Furlong (2013) noted in the opening quote, teachers are *the* key to education then teacher educators have an equally important role. Goodwin and Kosnik (2013) note "Simply put, it is reasonable to assume that quality teacher preparation depends on quality teacher educators" (p. 334). The research being reported in this chapter contributes to the growing understanding of teacher educators because it systematically examined 28 literacy teacher educators (LTEs) in four countries (Canada, U.S., England, and Australia). The overall goal of this multi-year research study is

- to study in depth a group of literacy/English teacher educators (LTEs), with special attention to their backgrounds, knowledge, research activities, identity, view of current government initiatives, pedagogy, and course goals.

Three specific questions guided this phase of the research with data drawn from the three interviews conducted over 3 years:

- What are the influences on the LTEs' practices?
- What goals do LTEs have for their literacy courses?
- How are government initiatives affecting LTEs?

9.1   Research on Teacher Educators

Over the last two decades there has been a growing body of research specifically on teacher educators. One aspect of the research examines the transition from classroom teacher to teacher educator (Murray and Male 2005). New teacher educators need to repackage and extend their knowledge because preparing student teachers is quite different from teaching primary or secondary age pupils. New teacher educators must acquire "a more generalized and scholarly knowledge of education" (Murray and Male 2005, p. 73). Murray and Male (2005) argue that there is no direct application of the skills used for teaching children to teaching adults.

Teaching in a teacher credential program is quite a different enterprise than teaching children because there is such a range of content to be addressed: pedagogical approaches must be tailored for working with adults; the diverse needs of the student body must be considered; and student teachers want practical strategies for immediate application in the classroom. Loughran (2006) calls for a pedagogy of teacher education which "involves a knowledge of teaching about teaching and a knowledge of learning about teaching and how the two influence one another in the pedagogic episodes that teacher educators create to offer students of teaching experiences that might inform their developing views of practice" (p. 118). What should teacher educators try to achieve?

As research on teacher educators becomes more sophisticated, aiming to uncover the nuances of their work, a clearer picture of this heterogeneous group is emerging. For example, as they gain experience in higher education both their practice and

Fig. 9.1 Spheres of
knowledge

identity must evolve. They need to see themselves as researchers yet they must remain connected to schools. Adding to the growing body of research, Ellis et al. (2014, p. 37) call attention to the work intensification teacher educators are experiencing. They identify 10 dimensions of teacher educator's work which include course management, relationship maintenance, and external examination at another institution. Their elaboration shows the multifaceted work of teacher educators, which extends far beyond just teaching courses.

The consideration of how teacher educators manage and fulfil their demanding role prompts the logical question: What do teacher educators need to know? The work of LTEs is complex because they "must bridge theory and practice; attend to the requirements of a number of external bodies (e.g. college of teachers; government departments); be cognizant of new school district/government initiatives; connect academic courses to practice teaching (over which they often have little control); develop a coherent course for student teachers who come to the program with markedly different prior experiences; and model effective teaching". In order to meet these extensive requirements, Kosnik et al. (2015) identified four spheres of knowledge required for those teaching literacy methods courses (Fig. 9.1).

LTEs must be familiar with government initiatives in order to address them with student teachers. Their knowledge of literacy theory and literacy teaching will guide their pedagogy. Conducting research will deepen their knowledge and enhance their identity as researchers. Their knowledge of pedagogy in higher education must be extensive because they must design opportunities for learning, select appropriate readings, set useful assignments, and create a supportive environment. The knowledge required to be an effective LTE extends far beyond knowing how to be a good classroom teacher.

9.2 Politicalization of Teacher Education

As Furlong (2013) noted in the opening quote, the stakes in education have been raised because it is seen to be one of the saviours for society and the economy. This stance has led to significant interference from governments. For example, in

England the government determined the number of days student teachers must spend in practice teaching schools (Murray and Passy 2014, p. 497) which diminished their connection to the university. Gilroy (2014) wryly observed that in 1992 the Secretary of State "launched a ferocious attack on university teacher education … where he made it clear that only a tiny rump of courses would be left in the hands of higher education, with teacher education quickly to be moved to schools" (p. 623). Following suit, the U.S. governments (federal and state) are increasingly inserting themselves into teacher education. The proposed new Teacher Preparation Regulations:

> requires states to assess and rate every teacher preparation program every year with four Performance Assessment Levels (exceptional, effective, at-risk, and low-performing), and states must provide technical assistance to "low-performing" programs. "Low-performing" institutions and programs that do not show improvement may lose state approval, state funding, and federal student financial aid. (Kumashiro 2014, p. n/a)

White et al. (2010) describe the Australian scene as an audit culture:

> At a broad level, neoliberalism elicits a climate of 'governmentality' that is articulated through systems of centrally managed regulation. Outcomes, in this case of education, are not only prescribed, but are also monitored and assessed through regulatory frameworks. Professional standards frameworks linked to accreditation requirements underpin an 'audit' culture in which structures and processes of centralised regulation are paradoxically 'de-centralised' as institutions and individuals are made responsible for self-evaluation and meeting specified quality assurance requirements (p. 185).

Reforms have "played themselves" out differently across many countries leading to a plethora of initiatives, models, and practices. In Australia there have been 101 government reports on teacher education over the past three decades (Louden 2008). In Australia and England there has been greater oversight by governments to ensure adherence to the national mandates for education. In England OFSTED carefully monitors programs to ensure they are addressing the National Curriculum. Ironically these same governments and the US are allowing for alternative certification providers. The US the government has gone so far to "support" alternative certification programs by giving them financial incentives and loosening the rules for "highly qualified" teachers for those who complete an alternative certification program. Many American states have adopted the EdTPA (exit portfolio) while others are framing their programs around Core Competences. Canada with its decentralized education system has had the least interference although there is slightly more monitoring of programs. An additional problem with the English, Australia, and US governments is that they conceptualize literacy teaching as a mechanistic process and learning to become a teacher through an apprenticeship model is rooted in a nineteenth century conception of schooling. In the midst of this political maelstrom teacher educators are preparing student teachers to work in the schools as they are currently organized which may not be congruent with their beliefs. Reconciling the differences raises both practical and moral issues.

9.3   Methodology

To put together the sample of 28 LTEs, lists of literacy teacher educators in Tier 1 (research-intensive) and Tier 2 (teaching-focused) institutions were complied. Some were invited because they taught literacy methods courses, others because they had published research in literacy. Initially, invitations to participate were sent to 15 LTEs. This led to "snowball sampling" whereby some LTEs who had accepted the invitation then suggested a colleague who might be relevant for the study. Punch (2014) describes "snowball sampling as identifying 'cases of interest from people who know people who know what cases are information rich" (163). After reviewing the suggested individuals' faculty profiles on their university websites to ensure they were teaching literacy they were invited. To make the sample was consistent only those who had a doctorate were invited. Efforts were made to ensure a range of experience (e.g. elementary/primary and secondary teaching), and a gender representation comparable to that in the profession as a whole. Six declined the invitation to participate for a variety of reasons (e.g. assuming a new administrative position and so not teaching literacy methods courses). None declined because of lack of interest. Figure 9.2 shows the sample included LTEs with a range of experience both as classroom teachers and university faculty.

Each participant was interviewed three times over the period April 2012 to March 2015. Each semi-structured interview was approximately 60–90 min in length. The same questions were asked of all participants but probe questions were added when necessary. Most of the questions were open-ended in that they sought more than a yes/no or simple factual answer. The first interview had five parts: background experiences; qualities (in their view) of an effective literacy educator; identity (e.g. your academic community); turning points in your career (personal and professional); and research activities. The second interview had four parts: framework and goals for your literacy course(s); pedagogies used and reasons for using them; assignments and readings; and how and why your views and practices have changed over the years. The third interview focused on use of digital technology and future plans. However, the issue of politics arose in the first and second interviews (even though there were no specific questions on the political context). In the third interview some questions addressed the political situation. Interviews were done either face to face or on Skype and were audio-recorded and transcribed.

Much of the methodology was qualitative as defined by Merriam (2009) and Punch (2014). Qualitative inquiry is justified as it provides depth of understanding and enables exploration of questions that do not on the whole lend themselves to quantitative inquiry (Merriam 2009). It opens the way to gaining entirely unexpected ideas and information from participants in addition to finding out their opinions on simple pre-set matters. A grounded theory approach was employed, not beginning with a fixed theory but generating theory inductively from the data using

Experience as a classroom teacher	0 years = 1
	1-5 years = 3
	6-10 years = 12
	11-20 years= 6
	21+ years = 6
Rank at the university	Assistant Professor (Lecturer in UK and AU) = 6
	Associate Professor =5
	Senior Lecturer = 7
	Full Professor = 5
	Other =1
	Contract = 4
Experience as a teacher educator	1-5 years = 7
	6 -10 years = 10
	11-15 years = 2
	16 -20 years= 5
	21+ years = 4
Countries	Canada - 7
	US - 11
	England - 5
	Australia -5

Fig. 9.2 Background of participants (as of 2013)

a set of techniques and procedures for collection and analysis (Punch 2014). As the analysis progressed, key themes were identified and refined—adding some and deleting or merging others—through "constant comparison" with the interview transcripts.

For data analysis NVivo 9 was used, going through a number of steps:

i. Initial coding of the transcripts was fairly broad, leading to 100 + nodes/themes. Some arose simply as answers to interview questions (e.g. background experience as a classroom teacher) while others emerged unexpectedly (e.g. fell into doing a PhD).

ii. After two rounds of coding the 100+ nodes/themes were collapsed into 40 nodes; however, within these there were sub-nodes (e.g. gaps in knowledge had sub-nodes of knowledge of research, knowledge of schools). NVivo allows for double- and triple-code certain content (e.g. the same material might relate to influence on practice, classroom teacher experience, and pedagogy).

iii. As the quotes, annotations, and memos were analyzed summary findings in three key areas were identified: influences on practice; goals for courses; and impact of politics. Given the sophistication of NVivo, queries were conducted to see relationships between the biographical data and other data (e.g. PhD area of study and current research activities). With NVivo both qualitative and quantitative data can be drawn upon.

9.4 Findings

The findings discussed in the following sections contribute to the understanding of the central influences on the LTEs' practices and considers how these guide priorities established for their literacy courses. First, their personal backgrounds as well as classroom teaching experiences are presented, followed by a discussion of their goals and pedagogies in higher education, and finally the impact of increasing government intervention is described.

9.5 Influences on Practices

To understand the LTEs as individuals, participants were asked to create a timeline identifying personal and professional turning points. In analyzing the data, three key influences on their current practices were identified, see Fig. 9.3.

9.5.1 Influence of Early Life Experiences

Interestingly, almost all LTEs identified a profound experience from their early childhood which influenced them as classroom teachers and continued to shape their work as teacher educators. There was a direct link between these early childhood experiences and their current goals for their course. In recounting these stories, it was as if these pivotal experiences had happened yesterday. For example, Maya[1] (US) recalled as an English Language Learner (ELL) she was considered a "poor" student in her regular English program but was a high achieving student in her Saturday heritage classes, which were taught in Spanish. As a teacher educator she focused on helping student teachers acquire both the skills to meet the needs of ELL students and cultivate a disposition that values the rich linguistic resources they bring to the classroom. Sara (Australia) was raised in a poorly resourced rural community; however, she was offered a scholarship to attend teacher's college. As a teacher educator she aimed to help her student teachers understand issues pertinent to rural education and her research is also focused on rural education. Jessie (Canada) recounted the story of her sixth-grade teacher Mr. Ward who was the first teacher who believed in her. As a teacher educator she emphasized to her student teachers that one teacher can make a difference in the life of a child.

---

[1]Pseudonyms used for participants.

Fig. 9.3 Influences on
practice

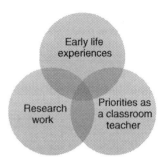

9.5.2   *Influence of Work as a Classroom Teacher*

Another key turning point for the LTEs was their work as classroom teachers. When asked if they model their work as teacher educators on their work as a classroom teacher 23 responded yes, but all noted they used a different pedagogy. However, for the most part they had the same priorities as teacher educators that they had had as classroom teachers. As a classroom teacher, Giovanni (US) worked in schools with high immigrant populations. He continued his work with this population as an LTE so far as to involve his student teachers in a church-based community outreach program for immigrants. Drama and storytelling were central to the classroom teaching work of Jane and Lance (both from Canada) and was an emphasis in their literacy methods courses. Lance (Canada) organized a trip to a local theatre production for his student teachers while storytelling was central to Jane's pedagogy. The continuity of priorities allowed the LTEs to provide many relevant classroom-based examples (from their own practice) thus giving their courses in higher education authenticity.

9.6   **Influence of Research**

Not surprisingly, the LTEs' research was very influential in determining the goals for their courses and, to a degree, their pedagogies. By running queries through NVivo a direct link between the topics of the LTEs' research and goals for their courses was identified. Sharon's (Canada) research on adolescents' writing led to the writing process as the focus of her course. Her student teachers were required to go through the entire writing process from conception of a piece of writing to the completed piece of work (one third of course hours were devoted to the writing process). Amelia and Jessie (both from Canada) who both currently research the use of digital technology in schools had multiliteracies as the framework their courses. Jessie (Canada) had student teachers tutor a child using iPads, while Amelia had student teachers complete an assignment focused on technology. Both shared examples of their research (raw data) with their student teachers. Stella's (England) research was concerned with poetry which was the central focus of her English methods course. Student teachers engaged with and often contributed to an online poetry archive which she created and studied. Drawing on their research meant the LTEs were teaching from their strength and interests.

Government mandates notwithstanding, each LTE created a unique course. The LTEs' prior experiences significantly influenced their priorities for their courses and their pedagogies. They come to their work as "whole" individuals whose successes, challenges, interests, and commitments shaped their courses and interactions with others.

9.7   Developing a Pedagogy

As Loughran (2006) notes, a pedagogy of teacher education is distinct from a pedagogy for teaching children. Both goals and practices need to be appropriate for those learning to become teachers.

Using a Personalized Approach. When describing their work as classroom teachers it was clear the LTEs were very committed to their pupils: getting to know them individually and tailoring curriculum for individual needs. This personalized approach continued into their work in higher education because almost all felt that in order to teach well they needed to know their student teachers as individuals. Figure 9.4 shows the importance of developing a relationship with their student teachers which was a top priority.

Some LTEs engaged in social activities with their student teachers (e.g. going to the pub, inviting student teachers to their home for a potluck dinner) while others spent time beyond class hours meeting with students. Bob's (Australia) beliefs summarized the views of many when he stated you need to have "productive relationships" with student teachers. A number involved their student teachers in their research and a few included student teachers in their work in the community. Hope (US) said "dear to my heart is a relationship with students that invites them to co-construct a community space. And what that means to me is being honest, being transparent, being vulnerable, being willing to change and knowing how to listen. And to expect the same, that same kind of professional integrity from them as they respond to me". By building relationships and a supportive community the LTEs were modelling a particular kind of teacher, one that Lance (Canada) described as "creating caring classrooms … building healthy relationships with kids" (Fig. 9.5).

Although learning about literacy and acquiring pedagogical strategies were common goals, interpretations of what student teachers need to know about literacy theory and teaching strategies varied. Some like Melissa, Dominique, and Maya (all from US) focused on critical literacy while Amelia and Jessie (both from Canada) had multiliteracies as the framework for their courses. Jane and Lance (both from Canada) focused on children's literature, while Sharon and Margie (both from

Fig. 9.4 Hold dear to your heart

What do You Hold Dear to Your Heart?	Number who identified this element
Relationship with your student teachers	26
Focusing on children	25
Literature	23
Social Justice	12
Writing process	11

Fig. 9.5 Goals for literacy courses

Goals for course	Number who identified this goal
Build knowledge of literacy	28
Build knowledge of pedagogy	25
Student teachers adopt a professional role	18
Student teachers develop a critical stance	16
Build knowledge of government initiatives	13
Build knowledge of digital technology	11
Focus on student teacher growth	10

Canada) had the writing process as their priority. Rachel's (Australia) broad view of literacy influenced her course goals:

> I want them to understand that Literacy is not a single, global skill that once you have it, you have it forever. I want them to understand that it's … increasingly complex and is a whole lot of different literacies. I want them to understand that they need to develop an integrated program with literature and other real texts at the centre of what they are programming and learning and implementing. I want them to develop a passion for children's literature.

Regardless of their particular interpretation of literacy (e.g. critical literacy, multiliteracies) there was a common belief among the LTEs that they needed to prepare student teachers to teach all children. Bob (Australia) elaborated "One would be wanting to support the student teachers in such a way that they would develop a growing capacity to be responsive to the students in their care. And that's not an easy thing to do". Carolina told her student teachers that "teaching is not about you, it's actually about the students and the contexts and all of those sorts of things".

Many of the participants conceptualized teaching beyond a mechanistic task. Justin's (England) aims were broad, not simply preparing student teachers to teach the current mandated curriculum.

> I see our work as being about the development of teachers as public intellectuals … not simply to prepare beginning teachers for whatever the particular curricular or pedagogic demands of policy here now are but for a lifetime in teaching and this involves them being able to be both critical of initiatives that are thrust on them and creative in their approaches.

Although all stated that knowledge of government initiatives was essential, few stated explicitly that the goal for their course was to teach the official curriculum! None of the participants from England echoed Gove's goals of "the preservation of the nation's cultural heritage" (Furlong 2013, p. 40). Similarly, the Australian LTEs did not conceptualize their courses around the narrow set of goals (phonics and grammar) that the government proposed. Across the participants many stated they addressed the formal curriculum but when teaching it they also intentionally critiqued it. Sharon (Canada) had her student teachers try to figure out the goals of the official curriculum while considering the limitations of the government's position; Bob (Australia) and his student teachers critiqued the curriculum to expose the view of literacy that underpins it. Those in England felt the pressure to teach synthetic phonics, but did so in a way that showed this is not the only way to teach literacy because it does not work for all children. Although many governments have developed agencies (e.g. OFSTED in England) to ensure teacher educator compliance, the 28 LTEs intentionally found ways to go beyond simply and uncritically teaching the national curriculum.

9.7.1 Designing Responsive Courses

Moving from the goals for their courses to course design further illustrates the complexity of the work of LTEs. Although all spent time preparing a formal course syllabus enacting it was not straightforward. Given their focus on their student teachers as individuals courses had to be somewhat flexible. Discussing issues student teachers were facing in their teaching (e.g. pupil lack of interest in content, pressure of standardized testing) was deemed a priority by most. The LTEs felt that connecting the academic program with practice teaching was essential to help student teachers understand the complexity of teaching and navigate their journey in teacher education. In order to create a place for these relevant and timely discussions, the LTEs could not adhere to a rigid syllabus. When asked if their courses were organic, pre-set, or a combination of both many explained that the course has to be flexible (organic) in order to meet the needs of the students and address issues as they arise, see Fig. 9.6.

Misa (US) described the importance of being flexible/organic. "I'm not someone that goes there with a prepared lecture but I love to engage in conversational dialogue … sometimes those digressions are where some of the most powerful learning happens". While Maya (US) conceptualized her approach as "I see my role as facilitating conversations between the readings and then providing particular examples and scaffolds so that we can inquire together and they can arrive at just different understandings [of children]". Giovanni (US) said that some of topics

Fig. 9.6 Approach to
developing your course

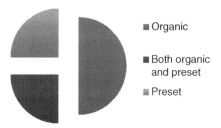

raised by his student teachers "related to everything from issues of power or racism
or class… it also could be how issues related to the erosion of the public education
system or the large discourse about disrespecting teachers. It could be about mental
health issues, test anxiety in classrooms, and sometimes these issues are pretty
heavy". Giovanni (US) like many of the other LTEs felt he needed to create space
for discussion of issues student teachers were facing.

The findings above reveal that the LTEs developed courses that were responsive
to their student teachers' needs. Flexibility and a personalized approach characterized their work.

9.8 Influence of Political Context

In an earlier section, the politicization of education was described. In all three
interviews most LTEs repeatedly referenced the political context in which they
worked. Most felt they were being jockeyed about by their governments which
impacted on them in various ways.

Required changes to structure and content of the program. With governments
increasingly setting program requirements many LTEs felt the impact both directly
and in less obvious ways. Some in the U.S. found the new education teacher
performance assessment (edTPA) exit portfolio was causing stress for student
teachers, which was having a ripple effect onto their courses (see http://www.edtpa.
com). Although they were not supposed to directly teach to the edTPA requirements, many revised their courses to ensure student teachers were prepared for it.
Those in England, where the government has mandated the number of days spent in
practice teaching, found that the practice teaching component started to overshadow
the academic program. With student teachers in university-based programs
spending up to two-thirds of their program in schools (Murray and Passy 2014, p.
497) some courses had to be eliminated and other courses had to be compressed.
With student teachers spending less time in academic courses (and with their
instructors) the LTEs noted the university had less significance for them. As a
consequence the student teachers did not identify as strongly with the university and
their particular cohort of fellow student teachers as those had in previous years.

Recognizing they must prepare student teachers to work in schools as they are currently organized LTEs needed to rethink some of their goals and practices. Marisa (US) was torn

> knowing that yes, student teachers are going to be asked to do things and they need to be considering how far they'll go, and how they'll take it up. One example, for me, is test prep. Not my favorite thing in the world, but children are taking tests regularly and [student teachers] need to be exposed to how that looks and what kind of thinking they should consider.

Hailey (US) felt the tension in another way. Her course goals were based on an understanding of literacy teaching (e.g. use of children's literature and making literacy relevant) which she felt was becoming less common in many schools (e.g. schools are worksheet driven with a focus on phonics). She wondered if she was doing her student teachers a disservice by presenting an approach to literacy they may not see in schools. Similarly, Rachel (Australia) who was a strong advocate of the arts and children's literature despaired because these were vanishing from the formal government curriculum. From her teaching experience and her research she knew the value of both and wanted these to continue to be pivotal to her literacy courses; however, with time at a premium and student teachers wanting many strategies to teach the formal curriculum she experienced significant tension in designing her course. She wondered how much should she compromise? Demerra (US) stated "What we know about literacy learning and what we know about understanding how children read and write, and what the State is now moving toward do not match. So what they're going to see in the schools and what we espouse as most valuable don't necessarily match". Given these tensions and discrepancies the divide between the university and schools seemed to be increasing which raises a host of questions.

9.8.1   Increased Vigilance

To ensure compliance, many governments created external agencies to monitor teacher education programs. For example in England:

> The Blair government continued with the Conservative government redesign of teacher education through "quangos" (quasi-autonomous government organisations) such as the Teacher Training Agency, the QCA, and OFSTED [Office for Standards in Education] which ensured that little would escape (MacBeath 2012, p. 73)

Many of the participants described these external reviews as stressful, demeaning, and time consuming. Justin from England felt

> the whole process was run by bureaucrats who literally went around with clipboards and when they asked you questions, unless what you said was something that they could fit into the box on the clipboard, there was no response whatsoever. There wasn't hostility, there was just blank incomprehension. The only thing that they wanted was words to fill in the right space to answer the questions that they had in advance.

Juliana from England noted that the OFSTED visit divided the faculty: some wanted to comply, while others felt it should be boycotted. While Stella (England) a Director of a teacher education program described the high stakes of an OFSTED visit and the dire consequences of a poor OFSTED report as follows:

> I suppose I've become more critically aware of pressures on me … to make sure that what I do is going to be compliant or not found wanting of any of kind of OFSTED regulation. Because I am very clear that … they could say our course [program] didn't fit the bill and that would be curtains [for the program]. And that's terrifying.

The stress of these high stakes external reviews cannot be underestimated. Nor can the logistical, conceptual, and moral challenges be dismissed as the LTEs faced as a result of government agendas. One participant described the situation as "soul destroying" while others were choosing to leave teacher education and/or their faculty position because they simply could no longer endure what some described as the "destruction of teacher education".

9.9 Discussion

The LTEs showed themselves to be hard-working, thoughtful, and knowledgeable. Their commitment to their student teachers and sheer ingenuity were impressive. Although there were some common practices and beliefs (e.g. importance of getting to know their student teachers) they clearly were individuals. As Dominique (US) noted, "I really, really believe you teach who you are so I really just try to stay true to that".

There was substantial evidence the 28 LTEs had extensive knowledge spanning many key areas. They demonstrated knowledge of the four spheres identified by Kosnik et al. (2015): knowledge of research, pedagogy of higher education, literacy and literacy teaching, and current school and government initiatives. Evidence of including the four spheres was found in the design and delivery of their courses and in their course syllabi. Using the four spheres to assist with the data analysis it is evident that teacher educators drew on their knowledge and further, they require a vast knowledge in order to capably fulfil their work.

The LTEs' pedagogy of teacher education was based on their research, their work as classroom teachers, and their own early childhood experiences. As a result, each course was unique which has both merit and drawbacks. By working from their individual strengths and interests even in the confines of government oversight there was not a great deal of consistency in literacy courses. However, there is some concern in the variability of courses. With governments monitoring many teacher education programs, this range could inadvertently lead to further control by governments.

Determining what student teachers need to know about literacy can be interpreted differently. To help assuage the differences LTEs need to come together to discuss goals and pedagogies so they can start to come to some agreement on a pedagogy of *literacy* teacher education. What do beginning teachers need to know if they are to teach well? What are some teaching strategies LTEs could use in their literacy courses? Induction courses for new teacher educators and ongoing inservice for experienced LTEs could be places to discuss the four spheres of knowledge, including sharing course syllabi, discussing goals for courses, pedagogies, and assignments. Both a university forum for LTEs and cross-university forums would provide places for these discussions and learning. Social media might be useful such as the website (https://literacyteaching.net/) devoted to literacy teacher educators where issues are discussed, course syllabi are shared, and research findings are disseminated which may lead to a community of LTEs.

A glaring oversight in governmental approaches to teacher education seems to be the complete dismissal of the importance of teacher educators getting to know their student teachers and in building a strong community. The 28 LTEs truly believed that knowing their student teachers well was essential as shown on Fig. 9.4: Hold Dear to Your Heart. This less tangible goal has potentially huge benefits: student teachers have a sense of belonging which may increase their learning, issues that are genuinely important to the student teachers are addressed, and the LTEs' personalized approach provide a model for them as future teachers. Trying to teach a generic literacy methods course as many governments advocate while ignoring the interpersonal aspect of teaching is folly!

These 28 LTEs had a clear view of effective literacy teaching but this has collided with the government's view that literacy teaching be narrowed to phonics and grammar and assessment done by standardized tests. The government's belief that teaching is a craft learned through apprenticeship in schools downplays the importance of the academic program, while the LTEs still conceptualized teaching as an intellectual and reflective endeavour with a role for higher education. As a result many were having tremendous difficulty reconciling government directives with their priorities which were based on their research and experiences. Knowing that their student teachers will be going into schools where the curriculum is mandated to what extent do they prepare them to teach in the way the government advocates? This was a conundrum faced by many with no easy answer.

The sheer number of policy briefs and initiatives were troublesome because they were often contradictory with insufficient time to implement them. With surveillance of programs and mandated content for teacher education courses, there were fewer and fewer "places" for teacher educators to have "important" discussions with student teachers. The sheer ingenuity of these LTEs to carve out space in their course for these important discussions was impressive; however, it was demanding and difficult. Although the situation is discouraging, LTEs need to continue to try to engage with government officials and policy developers so their voices are heard and their research is used as a basis for policy development. Their knowledge of teacher education and of literacy education is essential if we are to improve literacy instruction at both preservice and school levels.

Surveillance by governments is affecting LTEs' views of themselves as autonomous and informed academics. Having to "teach to the national curriculum" erodes their independence with some seeing themselves as pawns for the government. When asked about future plans eight said they plan to retire. Being an LTE as many of our participants noted was a privilege but was demanding physically, intellectually, and emotionally. How long can LTEs continue to work under conditions which they feel dismiss their knowledge/expertise and question their ability?

Teacher educators are charged with guiding their student teachers through the roiling waves of education. This is not an easy task given work intensification, competing demands, levels of compliance imposed on them, short timelines, limited funding, and hierarchy within schools of education. Studying the multifaceted work of teacher educators should continue because it is hoped that the neoconservative trend in education will eventually subside and teacher educators will once again be at the decision-making table. Research on them through these troubled times makes explicit their difficult reality.

Acknowledgements We wish to thank the Social Sciences and Humanities Research Council of Canada for their generous support of this research.

References

Ellis, V., McNicholl, J., Blake, A., & McNally, J. (2014). Academic work and proletarianisation: A study of higher education-based teacher educators. *Teaching and Teacher Education, 40*, 33–43.

Furlong, J. (2013). Globalisation, neoliberalism, and the reform of teacher education in England. *The Educational Forum, 77*(1), 28–50.

Gilroy, P. (2014). Policy interventions in teacher education: Sharing the English experience. *Journal of Education for Teaching, 40*(5), 622–632.

Goodwin, L. A., & Kosnik, C. (2013). Quality teacher educators = quality teachers?: Conceptualizing essential domains of knowledge for those who teach teachers. *Teacher Development: An International Journal of Teachers' Professional Development, 17*(3), 334–346.

Kosnik, C., Menna, L., Dharmashi, P., Miyata, C., Cleovoulou, Y., & Beck, C. (2015). Four spheres of knowledge required: An international study of the professional development of literacy/English teacher educators. *Journal of Education for Teaching, 4*(1), 52–77.

Kumashiro, K. (2014). *Review of proposed 2015 federal teacher preparation regulations*. National Education Policy Centre. Retrieved January 29, 2015. http://nepc.colorado.edu/thinktank/review-proposed-teacher-preparation

Louden, L. (2008). 101 Damnations: The persistence of criticism and the absence of evidence about teacher education in Australia. *Teachers and Teaching: Theory and Practice, 14*(4), 357–368.

Loughran, J. (2006). *Developing a pedagogy of teacher education: Understanding about teaching and learning about teaching*. London: Routledge.

MacBeath, J. (2012). Teacher training, education of learning by doing in the UK. In L. Darling-Hammond & A. Lieberman (Eds.), *Teacher education around the world: Changing policies and practices* (pp. 66–80). New York: Routledge.

Merriam, S. (2009). *Qualitative research: A guide to design and implementation*. San Francisco: Jossey-Bass.

Murray, J., & Male, T. (2005). Becoming a teacher educator: Evidence from the field. *Teaching and Teacher Education, 21*(2), 125–142.

Murray, J., & Passy, R. (2014). Primary teacher education in England: 40 years on. *Journal of Education for Teaching, 40*(5), 492–506.

Punch, K. (2014). *Introduction to social research: Quantitative and qualitative approaches*. London: Sage.

UNESCO. (2006). *Literacy for life: Education for all*. Retrieved from http://www.unesco.org/new/en/education/themes/leading-the-international-agenda/efareport/reports/2006-literacy/

White, S., Bloomfield, D., & Le Cornu, R. (2010). Professional experience in new times: Issues and responses to a changing education landscape. *Asia-Pacific Journal of Teacher Education, 38*(3), 181–193.

Author Biographies

Clare Kosnik is Director of the Dr. Eric Jackman Institute of Child Study at the Ontario Institute for Studies in Education, University of Toronto (OISE/UT). Her area of research is teacher education which she has systematically studied. She is currently conducting a large-scale study of 28 literacy/English teacher educators in four countries.

Lydia Menna is an Assistant Professor in the Department of Elementary Education at the University of Alberta. Her research interests are in the areas of teacher education, multiliteracies, critical literacy, and teacher identity construction.

Pooja Dharamshi is Assistant Professor of Teacher Education at Simon Fraser University. Her research is in the areas of critical literacy and teacher education. She recently completed her doctorate at the Ontario Institute for Studies in Education/UofT exploring the practices and pedagogies of literacy teacher educators with a critical stance.

Clive Beck teaches in the Curriculum Department at OISE/University of Toronto. He is conducting an ongoing 12-year longitudinal study of 40 teachers. His books include *Better Schools* (1990), *Innovations in Teacher Education* (2006), and *Growing as a Teacher* (2014). He is a past-President of the American Philosophy of Education Society.

Chapter 10
Clinical Practice in Education: Towards a Conceptual Framework

Jeana Kriewaldt, Larissa McLean Davies, Suzanne Rice, Field Rickards and Daniela Acquaro

10.1 Introduction

Clinical practice has recently emerged as a promising approach that is being applied to teaching and teacher education. Despite this growing interest, however, conceptual and practical ambiguities continue to surround the term. This chapter provides a critical and comprehensive review of how clinical practice is being conceptualised in education by: (a) identifying the core components that characterise clinical practice in education; and (b) discussing the complexities and possibilities of clinical practice in theory and practice. The chapter begins by forging a conceptual framework for understanding clinical practice by identifying three core components that are central to characterising teaching as a clinical practice profession: (1) a focus on student learning and development; (2) evidence-informed practice; and (3) processes of reasoning that lead to decision-making. In summary, we argue that clinical practice offers important possibilities for deepening the theoretical and practical aspects of teaching and teacher education, but that several cautions need to be born in mind in order for it to continue to develop into a meaningful and sustainable concept. While adapting a medical model to teaching

J. Kriewaldt (✉) · L. McLean Davies · S. Rice · F. Rickards · D. Acquaro
University of Melbourne, Melbourne, VIC, Australia
e-mail: jeana@unimelb.edu.au

L. McLean Davies
e-mail: l.mcleandavies@unimelb.edu.au

S. Rice
e-mail: s.rice@unimelb.edu.au

F. Rickards
e-mail: f.rickards@unimelb.edu.au

D. Acquaro
e-mail: d.acquaro@unimelb.edu.au

© Springer Nature Singapore Pte Ltd. 2017   153
M.A. Peters et al. (eds.), *A Companion to Research in Teacher Education*,
DOI 10.1007/978-981-10-4075-7_10

should be done with caution and a number of caveats, on balance it offers an approach that has the capacity to strengthen teaching and teacher education.

10.2 Conceptualising Clinical Practice for Teaching

The past decade has seen an amplified interest within education research and policy in the notion of 'clinical practice' as it relates to teaching and teacher education (Burn and Mutton 2013). Most discussions about clinical teaching have centred on the education of pre-service teachers, and characteristics of particular programs which self-identify as clinical (e.g. Conroy et al. 2013; McLean Davies et al. 2013; Burn and Mutton 2013). Central to these programs is the close connection between theory and practice, sustained and substantive time spent in clinical sites and the explicit development of pre-service teachers' capacity to make evidence-informed judgments. In these ways, these programs appropriate and adapt a model of medical education to the school education context. While program-based research is important in advancing an understanding of the enactment of clinical judgment and clinical practice, it is also imperative to advance thinking regarding the conceptual frameworks underpinning notions of clinical teaching that are made possible through clinical practice models. Research and scholarship has also directed attention to this process of adapting a model of medical education for teacher education, and the affordances and complexities of this in terms of conceptualising the way teachers conceive their work with students and advance learning (Alter and Coggshall 2009; Kriewaldt and Turnidge 2013; McLean Davies et al. 2015). This chapter builds on this conceptual work, and presents a framework for understanding the central tenets of clinical teaching and their interrelationship; these extend beyond the pre-service phase and can be understood as the basis of a broader conceptualisation that frames *all* teachers' work as having a clinical foundation. That is, clinical teaching is not just about a model of teacher preparation, but rather, is an approach that encompasses and informs teacher practice on a daily basis.

Central to the medical professional's thinking is that all decisions must be made with an overriding concern for the best interests of the person whose health or well-being is charged to their care. In education, we argue that this translates into a clinical model of teaching that has the following features:

- The student and their learning needs are pivotal to all decision-making about what, when and how to teach;
- The teacher uses evidence about the student, what they already know and what they are ready to learn to make decisions about subsequent teaching;
- The teacher draws on current research evidence about effective practice in making decisions about how to work with a student or group of students;
- The teacher integrates knowledge about who the student is, including knowledge of their characteristics, circumstances and prior experiences, into decision-making about the student and their own teaching;

- The teacher evaluates their own impact on student learning on a regular basis; and
- The teacher exercises professional judgement involving all these elements.

In light of this, in this chapter we identify three core components that are central to characterising teaching as a clinical practice profession: (1) a focus on student learning and development; (2) evidence-informed practice; and (3) processes of reasoning that lead to decision-making. In the following sections, we will explore these central tenets of clinical teaching; bringing together, where appropriate, research in the fields of medicine and education to illustrate this framework. A conceptual framework for clinical teaching can be seen as a contribution more broadly to developing teaching as a profession, as it offers ways in which theory and practice are integrated and evidence-based judgements are made in the daily work of teachers. At a time when teachers are increasingly called to account for their impact, and policy imperatives such as high-stakes testing present often limited ways of understanding this, a framework for clinical teaching offers ways of responding to, negotiating, contesting and reclaiming the professional work of teachers.

10.3   Characteristics of Clinical Practice for Teaching

10.3.1   Focus on Learning and Development

A defining feature of a clinical approach to teaching is that of purpose: all teacher interpretation, decision-making, action and reflection are centred on fostering students' learning and development. Other writers have noted that the centrality of the client is fundamental to all clinical practice (Alter and Coggshall 2009). While this may seem a rather self-evident point to make about any approach to teaching, there are demands on teachers and opinions on what and how they should teach that are multifaceted and come from many sources—government, media, parents, school leadership—and these may constrain and shape teacher behaviour.

The hallmark of the professional clinician, whether in education or medicine, is that the student or patient's needs are placed above all these competing demands in importance (Alter and Coggshall 2009; Burn and Mutton 2013; Ure 2010). In a school setting, these needs are conceptualised largely in terms of student learning, with a focus on ensuring that all students have the conditions and support needed to excel as learners. 'Learning' here refers not only to academic skills and knowledge, but to the broad range of capabilities students need to flourish in the twenty-first century, including aspects such as interpersonal, problem-solving and self-management skills.

In teacher education, and in particular, the initial preparation of teachers, a clinical approach makes the students' learning central to observation, feedback and formation of teacher candidates. Pre-service teacher candidate assessment and observation can very easily slide to an emphasis on what the teacher is doing ('Try to speak more clearly', 'Don't hand out the worksheets until you've finished giving instructions', 'Make sure you control students' entry to the classroom'), rather than what the students are doing and learning. Though the connection between teacher action and student learning may be inferred, it is through the examination of products of learning that student growth can be directly assessed.

At the level of the individual teacher, then, a clinical approach is characterised by a number of qualities. First, ensuring that actions within and outside the classroom are done with the primary and central focus of improving student learning requires an unremittingly inquiring and reflective stance on the part of the teacher, and an awareness of the complexity of the teaching situation. If a teacher is to place students' learning needs as the central driving force for their decisions and actions, they need a self-awareness of motives and needs, and a thorough and nuanced understanding of all the competing pressures on them to act and teach in given ways in response to various situations. So a clinical teacher, then, will need to be aware of these influences on their teaching, and their own reactions to them. They will need to be able to recognise the degree to which the demands of various stakeholders are related to improved student learning, and will prioritise their time and efforts accordingly.

Second, while the lens of clinical practice focuses sharply on student learning and development, this does not imply an approach driven by test scores and other student performance measures. A clinical model in medicine is based on the understanding that physical, mental and social aspects all underpin and together interact to influence patient health, so that it is not possible to diagnose and treat patients effectively without a broad vision of what constitutes patient wellbeing. Similarly, a clinical approach to education conceptualises student learning and development in terms not just of the individual knowledge or skills that can be assessed in a written test, but also in terms of the broader aptitudes, attitudes and understandings that will enable students to flourish in a diverse and rapidly changing world. So a clinical practitioner in education, in focusing on student learning and development, is not simply considering student achievement in isolation. Broad-based questions such as, 'Does this student drive their own learning?' 'Why doesn't this student persist in the face of a setback?' and 'How well does this student work in a team?' are integral to a clinical teaching perspective. Clinical teaching practitioners work to understand the answers to these questions so as to support the development of the whole student. As well, classroom teachers are alert to physical, cognitive and social factors that affect student learning and liaise with a system of services to support student development. Student learning and development is at the centre of clinical teaching with full recognition of the influence of physical, cognitive and social factors at play, just as medical models place patient wellbeing at the centre.

10.3.2 *Evidence and Research-Informed Practice*

In this section, we turn attention to the second of the central tenets of clinical teaching—a focus on data, evidence and research in order to determine the next stage or step to advance student's learning. Arguably, defining what constitutes evidence-informed practice in teaching is essential in this era of policy focus on teacher education and professionalism. On one level, an interest in and commitment to evidence-informed practice might be seen as a part of a general move in teacher education to a greater emphasis on basing decisions on data and knowledge that extends beyond an individual teacher's intrinsic understanding, and more broadly the development of teaching as a profession. This reflects Timperley's edict that teachers need to shift their mindset, as historically, teacher training and practice 'did not require [teachers] them to interpret and use evidence because assessment information was about labelling and categorising students, not about guiding and directing teaching practice' (Timperley 2010, p. 5).

On another level, though, clinical understandings of the uses of evidence and research extend beyond general principles of good practice, and offer ways of identifying how the various forms of evidence and research can be used to inform the development of learning interventions designed and enacted by teachers in classrooms. Fundamental to this enterprise is the notion that clinical teachers are interventionist practitioners capable of using data to meet the needs of individual learner, and that, importantly these interventions are designed to promote growth—all evidence is used to support learners to move along a developmental continuum. Pavlovic et al. (2014) note that framing student learning in terms of a developmental continuum does not refer to

> a cognitive, Piagetian style of development but to the accumulation of skills, knowledge and attitudes that accrue as a result of exposure to new ideas, new procedures and new opportunities to learn. (Pavlovic et al. 2014, p. 61)

In light of this, a central premise of clinical teaching models is that with a data-driven, evidence-based approach to teaching and learning, teachers can create productive learning environments and scaffold learning for every student, regardless of the student's development or intellectual capacity (Griffin 2007; cited in McLean Davies et al. 2013).

Data and other forms of evidence are only useful if students' learning goals are understood and shared. Having said this, it is important to emphasise that evidence itself cannot be used without judgment, and that the collection of evidence in no way compromises teachers' professional responsibility to analyse, synthesise and make decisions about the relevance of the data they have collected. In what follows, we will explore the different forms of evidence that clinical teachers draw on in order to make professional judgements about the individual needs of learners. In their research and analysis of the way evidence was conceptualised in their clinical pre-service teacher education program, Cochran-Smith and The Boston College

Evidence Team (2009) argue for a nuanced and context-sensitive understanding of evidence that is relevant to both pre-service and in-service teachers and teaching:

> …we have found that there is a difference between a culture where evidence 'drives' decisions and a culture where evidence 'informs' decisions. The former suggests a narrow almost empiricist focus and a linear, uncomplicated conception of the relationship between evidence and policy/practice. On the other hand, the latter acknowledges that evidence alone can never tell us what to do. Rather, evidence always has to be interpreted. (Cochran-Smith and The Boston College Evidence Team 2009, p. 466)

Mindful of this caution, in what follows we offer a framework which identifies levels of evidence that clinical teachers negotiate in supporting student learning. The levels of evidence we have identified are as follows:

- Classroom-based evidence—the data gathered in the classroom context and as a result of verifiable observations, and formal and informal assessments;
- para-classroom evidence—data about the student's out-of-school life that may be impacting on their capacity to undertake tasks and meet learning outcomes;
- external assessment evidence—summative assessment measures determined by governments and fed back to school leadership and teachers; and,
- research evidence—knowledge about learning acquired through refereed research that informs teacher understandings of the efficacy of various interventions and suitability for their context.

The levels listed above start with the evidence teachers utilise that is most closely derived from the interactions between students and teachers, and move to the evidence that is least context dependent; to put this another way, this framework recognises the way in which it is assessment practices (informal, formal, formative, summative) that provide evidence, and that this evidence is both generated within and outside a teacher's immediate work with students. Moreover, we see distinctions between the role of teacher knowledge (disciplinary/pedagogical) in working with the different levels of evidence and data. While classroom-based evidence and para-classroom evidence require teachers to draw on their own professional knowledge to make sense of the data they receive, and even determine what constitutes data, external assessment evidence and research evidence present packages of data that draw on bodies of knowledge which bring other classrooms and contexts into teachers' and students' experiences. This is not to suggest that some forms of evidence are more or less relevant than others, but rather that all levels and forms are constantly in play in the work of clinical teachers. While clinical models do not advocate a rigid framework for addressing student needs, they do highlight the need to consider multiple variables when planning for learning; as Alter and Coggshall (2009) assert, an evidence-informed approach involves understanding the needs of clients [students], observation, questioning, diagnostic evidence and research on what works. Although it is most likely that classroom-based evidence will impact on teachers' in-the-moment responses, decisions taken at the point of need are therefore informed by the other forms of evidence that influence the clinical teacher's professional practice.

In the material which follows, we will provide further details about the levels of evidence clinical teachers collect, synthesise, interrogate and negotiate. We will draw attention to how clinical teachers use evidence to inform practice, and also acknowledge the challenges of using and understanding evidence in this way.

10.3.3   Classroom-Based Evidence

Classroom-based evidence can take a variety of forms, from the work samples collected by teachers, to the answers given during class discussions. Following Griffin's insights, classroom evidence can be understood as anything students 'do, say, make or write' (Griffin 2007). In response to definitions of data and evidence that focus primarily on external high-stakes assessment evidence, we argue that importantly teachers can gather data that surrounds them in classroom contexts. The paradigm through which clinical teachers synthesise data is also important, and teacher knowledge of students and the possibilities of learning are paramount. Just as surgeons must understand anatomy and physiology, so too teachers must understand how students learn and how approaches to learning and teaching can vary to meet the needs of individuals. This knowledge provides the context and focus of the ways in which evidence is gathered and understood in the classroom, and thus points to the need for clinical teachers to have both sound pedagogical content knowledge, but also a knowledge of student learning that is regularly updated, tested and developed.

10.3.4   Para-Classroom Evidence

The importance of knowing students' beyond classroom experiences, in order to best target learning is a well-established teaching practice. Indeed, para-classroom evidence about what learning experiences they have had in life provides the teacher with stronger evidence of what they know. Moreover the student's immediate domestic circumstances—family composition, recent arrival to a country or family member illness—can assist clinical teachers to appropriately adjust and target learning instruction. An understanding of the challenges students may be facing in the classroom context as a result of family experiences of education, socioeconomic status, ethnicity, language learning or special needs, for example, can also assist clinical teachers to design suitable learning interventions, and improve the educational outcomes for all students.

Clinical teachers must be mindful, though, of the need to use this evidence in order to enhance student learning and enable them to grow and progress along a learning continuum. As has been documented, teachers' conscientious and well-intentioned efforts to modify learning according to para-classroom evidence can result in differentiation practices that continue to marginalise some groups of students, and result in lower educational expectations and outcomes.

10.3.5 External Assessment Evidence

Most educators are familiar with the Global Educational Reform Movement (GERM) and the influence this has had on policy and practice, in particular through the increasing use of high-stakes testing (Sahlberg 2012). In the country from which we write, Australia, high-stakes testing now provides a key form of data about student achievement regarding literacy and numeracy across the compulsory years of schooling. Aggregate data for Australian schools has been published online since 2010, and this practice increasingly determines parental perceptions of schools and teachers (Frawley et al. 2015). The imperative for clinical teachers is to make appropriate use of this data, and to synthesise this with other forms of data collected over longer periods of time that reflect a more comprehensive view of student learning. Moreover, the clinical teacher also needs to be aware of the limitations of achievement data drawn from formal high-stakes tests if they are to use this data appropriately to inform their teaching practice. Clinical teachers therefore need to develop and maintain a level of data literacy that enables them to understand, interpret and critique high-stakes test data.

10.3.6 Research-Informed Evidence

While the forms of evidence we have described have to different degrees often been intrinsically, if not explicitly mobilised by governments, school leaders and teachers, research evidence—encountered at universities—can remain outside teachers' daily practice once they commence autonomous teaching. Research has often been seen to be the business of university-based teacher education programs focussed on theoretical or empirical work while the real learning is seen to emerge from the lived experiences of teachers in the trenches developed through an apprenticeship model based on trial and error. While practice is undeniably important in any service profession, a clinical model for teaching presupposes an iterative dialogue and synthesis of classroom and para-classroom-based evidence, and research-based knowledge. Together, these constitute evidence-informed practice focussed on students' learning and development.

Indeed, in determining how best to advance learning for a student or group of students, the clinical teacher makes ongoing reference to current research-based knowledge about effective teaching practices. Clinical teachers have a broad understanding around what the research literature says about effective teaching and learning, and use this knowledge to decide how to proceed in the classroom. The clinical teacher adopts a stance of openness to new research evidence about quality teaching and student learning, and a commitment to maintain and refresh their knowledge around this.

10.3.7 Using Evidence and Research-Informed Practices

While identification of the various forms of evidence available to teachers goes some measure towards explaining the work of clinical teaching, the challenge for teachers working in this paradigm is to incorporate different forms of evidence into their practice to make best judged decisions to advance each student's learning. While processes of reasoning will be addressed in the following section, it is worth emphasising here that a clinical teacher's commitment to using evidence also means that she/he collects evidence around impact of her/his own teaching, and uses this to inform future teaching and their own professional learning. Clinical teachers monitor and evaluate their impact regularly, seek to understand the reasons behind what the evidence suggests, and make plans to maintain, change or learn further about their practice based on these evaluations. It is important to note that this focus on impact and on using evidence to improve teaching and learning is distinct from often punitive approaches to teacher accountability driven by top-down political imperatives (see Cochran-Smith and The Boston College Evidence Team 2009); rather, this analytical and reflective work is designed to develop teachers' agency around evidence, and enable them to be both effective clinical teachers, and part of a broader learning focussed profession. The notion that teachers' ability to draw on various sources of evidence gives them access to a professional community is something that has been elucidated by Sahlberg (2012), who argues that teachers need to integrate 'scientific educational knowledge, didactics and practice in a manner that enables [them] to enhance their pedagogical thinking, evidence-based decision making and engagement in a scientific community of educators' (2012, p. 6).

10.4 Processes of Reasoning that Lead to Decision-Making

We now come to third tenet of clinical practice in education—the use of processes of reasoning that lead to decision-making. Teachers use a range of specific and broader reasoning processes to decide how to improve student learning. These processes are described in various terms, including hypothesis-testing, problem solving, critical thinking, and particularly as reflective practice. For more than a century, Dewey's conceptions of how teachers think using a reflective process have had a distinctive influence in the education field. Education has a long history of describing the key reasoning processes of teachers as reflective practice which emphasises the reflective stage of thinking about practice within a cyclic model of planning, acting, collecting, analysing and evaluating data to reflect and begin the cycle again. The key dimension in all of these approaches is a foundational belief that teaching is a profession that uses analyses to form judgment for action, 'rather than the routinised application of learned repertoires' (Burn and Mutton 2013, p. 4).

Significantly, three key theorists in education, John Dewey, Donald Schön and David Boud all begin with a situation or experience and reasoning processes are applied to the experience to develop professional knowledge. It is an event that is the starting point. This is an important component of reasoning processes though it lends itself to a focus on teaching without fully connecting reflection to the consequences for learning. This longstanding reflective tradition is important in improving practice, yet 'reflective practice often defaults to little more than lay thinking' (Ure 2010, p. 463) or trial and error. Reorienting teacher thinking to clinical reasoning draws explicit attention to a focus on student learning informed by evidence. This will consider ways in which different levels of evidence might be used to identify areas of teacher knowledge that need to be extended and expanded, for example, if a teacher is working with a student with a particular learning need and his/her current interventions are not advancing learning, then seeking research evidence to inform ensuing interventions is warranted. Clinical processes of reasoning are designated differently as clinical reasoning as it is centrally student-focused, while not overlooking teaching.

We argue that clinical teaching uses clinical reasoning processes to make decisions. Clinical reasoning describes the analytical processes that professionals systematically use to decide on their course of action in a specific practice-based context (Kriewaldt and Turnidge 2013). Teachers integrate knowledge of student characteristics, curriculum frameworks, school and broader policy to frame their clinical reasoning. The term clinical reasoning is sometimes used interchangeably with clinical judgment or decision-making, though reasoning describes the process and judgement describes the result. Thus clinical reasoning is a complex and multifaceted process that professionals use to decide what the best judged action is to take next. This cyclic system of reasoning comprises gathering evidence to form a diagnosis, selecting and undertaking an intervention, evaluating and reflecting upon the outcomes, and this cycle is then repeated. Clinical judgments are the result of an unremitting focus on student learning and growth, and draw on evidence at multiple stages in a cyclic process.

Clinical teaching uses processes of clinical reasoning to identify, collect and analyse evidence to determine students' learning needs to plan and implement teaching interventions. Subsequent clinical reasoning is employed to evaluate the outcomes of teacher action using evidence and to initiate a new cycle of clinical reasoning. Therefore clinical reasoning becomes situated in practice in which teacher actions are the result of critical deliberations about options and predicted effects. As we have argued, clinical teaching is learner-focussed and requires a culture of evidence by 'making evidence central to decision-making' (Cochran-Smith and The Boston College Evidence Team 2009, p. 458).

Teachers make decisions by employing clinical reasoning in which they seek and use evidence to guide their practice by asking and integrating these questions into their thinking processes:

- What does the student already know and what can they do?
- What does each individual student need to advance their learning?
- What are effective practices according to the evidence base from research?
- What evidence of learning can be gathered during and after the teaching intervention?
- What happened and how can this be interpreted, or what does it show?
- What does this mean for future interventions?

Clinical teachers view their practice from an inquiring stance (Cochran-Smith and The Boston College Evidence Team 2009) and use student evidence generated by observing, questioning and formatively and summatively assessing student performance. By giving emphasis to clinical reasoning this drives a forward-thinking orientation to teaching in which each student's development is brought sharply into focus, which in turn drives powerful planning. It works hand in hand with reflective practice that focuses on learning from teaching episodes. Clinical reasoning puts learning first as it begins with a focus on individual learning. This reorients teachers to examine learning and teaching through the lens of learning.

10.5   Conclusion

Conceptualising clinical teaching as a clinical practice profession offers a powerful means of reconceptualising practice in ways that better support teachers to understand student learning and how to develop it. In contrast to clinical practice in the medical field which normally addresses the clients' illness, clinical practice in education focuses on enhancing learning and growth of the whole student. Clinical teachers seek and use a range of evidence employing clinical reasoning and judgment to guide their practice by asking and integrating questions into their thinking processes to arrive at best judged ethical responses. In adapting a medical education model, it is through clinical reasoning that robust evidence-informed interventions are developed that precisely build from what each student already knows and can do in order to advance their learning.

In addition to providing a robust framework for conceptualising teachers' work with students, the notion of clinical practice has important implications for teacher preparation. Clinical models of teacher education are characterised by the following:

- Close partnerships between schools and universities that inform practice in both sites (Grossman 2010; Conroy et al. 2013);

- Strong articulation between coursework and professional practice founded on a shared understanding and commitment to clinical reasoning and practice;
- Professional conversations between novice and mentor that pose questions and probe to make reasoning explicit (Kriewaldt and Turnidge 2013); and
- A shared community of practice who are committed to a clinical approach.

By interweaving these four elements, a strong model of teacher preparation is built. Clinical models of teacher education, while incorporating the above elements, also draw on medical education models of doctor preparation in which universities, current practitioners and those studying to become a practitioner work together to support the application of knowledge and the development of clinical judgement. Educators in the relational professions share in the challenging quest to develop graduates' processes of reasoning to successfully enable them to engage in complex practices. In broad terms, this can be seen as the capacity to use complex and interlocking processes of reasoning to exercise judgement. Such ways of thinking or habits of mind go beyond technical or instrumental responses, to encompass dialogic and critical dimensions. By using explicit clinical reasoning processes, teachers are better able to understand their own and other teachers' ways of thinking and acting enabling them to work individually and collaboratively.

Using clinical models of education to frame and inform the work of teachers presents challenges that need to be borne in mind as there are limits to the extent to which it is both possible and reasonable to *apply* models from other fields of practice to teaching. For example, aligning teaching and teacher education too closely with medical models may run the risk of ignoring the centrality of relationships and values to effective teaching and learning (Grossman et al. 2009). In utilising medical models and language to reconceptualise teaching, it is vital for both practitioners and theorists to think critically about how broadly such models and language apply. In this chapter, we have argued that there are important prospects for education in conceptualising teaching as a clinical practice profession notwithstanding that cross-professional comparison also pose risks. However, *adapting* clinical models to frame and inform the work of teachers offer significant affordances for teacher practice.

References

Alter, J., & Coggshall, J. (2009). *Teaching as a clinical practice profession: Implications for teacher preparation and state policy*. New York: National Comprehensive Center for Teacher Quality.

Burn, K., & Mutton, T. (2013). Review of 'research informed clinical practice' in initial teacher education. *British Education Research Association (BERA)*. Retrieved from http://www.bera.ac.uk/wp-content/uploads/2014/02/BERA-Paper-4-Research-informed-clinical-practice.pdf

Cochran-Smith, M., & The Boston College Evidence Team. (2009). "Re-culturing" teacher education: Inquiry, evidence, and action. *Journal of Teacher Education, 60*(5), 458–468. doi:10.1177/0022487109347206

Conroy, J., Hulme, M., & Menter, I. (2013). Developing a 'clinical' model for teacher education, *Journal of Education for Teaching: International Research and Pedagogy, 39*(5), 557–573. doi:10.1080/02607476.2013.836339

Frawley, E., & McLean Davies, L. (2015). Assessing the field: Students and teachers of writing in high-stakes literacy testing in Australia. *English Teaching: Practice & Critique, 14*(2), 83–99. doi:10.1108/ETPC-01-2015-0001

Griffin, P. (2007). The comfort of competence and the uncertainty of assessment. *Studies in Educational Evaluation, 33,* 87–99. doi:10.1016/j.stueduc.2007.01.007

Grossman, P. (2010). *Learning to practice: The design of clinical experience in teacher preparation.* Washington DC: American Association of Colleges for Teacher Education & National Education Association.

Grossman, P., Hammerness, K., & McDonald, M. (2009). Redefining teaching, re-imagining teacher education. *Teachers and Teaching, 15*(2), 273–289. doi:10.1080/13540600902875340

Kriewaldt, J., & Turnidge, D. (2013). Conceptualising an approach to clinical reasoning in the education profession. *Australian Journal of Teacher Education, 38*(6), 103–115. doi: 10.14221/ajte.2013v38n6.9

McLean Davies, L., Anderson, M., Deans, J., Dinham, S., Griffin, P., Kameniar, B., et al. (2013). Masterly preparation: Embedding clinical practice in a graduate pre-service teacher education programme. *Journal of Education for Teaching: International Research and Pedagogy, 39*(1), 93–106. doi:10.1080/02607476.2012.733193

McLean Davies, L., Dickson, B., Rickards, F., Dinham, S., Conroy, J., & Davis, R. (2015). Teaching as a clinical profession: Translational practices in initial teacher education—An international perspective. *Journal of Education for Teaching: International Research and Pedagogy, 41*(5), 514–528. doi:10.1080/02607476.2015.1105537

Pavlovic, M., Awwal, N., Mountain, R., & Hutchinson, D. (2014). Conducting assessments. In P. Griffin (Ed.), *Assessment for teaching* (pp. 58–68). Port Melbourne, Australia: Cambridge University Press.

Sahlberg, P. (2012). The most wanted: Teachers and teacher education in Finland. In L. Darling-Hammond & A. Lieberman (Eds.), *Teacher education around the world: Changing policies and practices.* Abingdon: Routledge.

Timperley, H. (2010). *Using evidence in the classroom for professional learning.* Paper presented to the Ontario research symposium. Retrieved at https://cdn.auckland.ac.nz/assets/education/about/schools/tchldv/docs/Using%20Evidence%20in%20the%20Classroom%20for%20Professional%20Learning.pdf

Ure, C. (2010). Reforming teacher education through a professionally applied study of teaching. *Journal of Education for Teaching, 36*(4), 461–475. doi:10.1080/02607476.2010.513860

Author Biographies

Dr Jeana Kriewaldt is a Senior Lecturer in the Melbourne Graduate School of Education, University of Melbourne. Her research interests include professional learning in initial and in-service teacher education and the development of clinical reasoning in teachers' practice. She is currently Senior Leader: Clinical Teaching Practice.

Larissa McLean Davies is an Associate Professor in Language and Literacy, and Associate Dean, Teacher Education Research in the Melbourne Graduate School of Education at the University of Melbourne. Larissa's current research is concerned with the teacher education effectiveness, clinical teaching and the role of literature in subject English.

Dr Suzanne Rice is a Senior Lecturer in the Melbourne Graduate School of Education, University of Melbourne. Her research interests include clinical models of teacher education, student engagement and retention, and teacher pathways. She has led the development of the MGSE's Master of Clinical Teaching.

Professor Field Rickards has been Dean of the Melbourne Graduate School of Education since 2004. He has guided the development of the new clinical Master of Teaching program which develops graduates with the capabilities to meet the needs of individual learners. His background is auditory neuroscience, audiology and deaf education.

Dr Daniela Acquaro is the Program Coordinator of the Master of Teaching Secondary, MGSE, The University of Melbourne. As a Senior Lecturer in Teacher Education, her research focuses on initial teacher education, teacher effectiveness and teachers' lives. She is also interested in teacher preparation for alternative and global educational settings.

Chapter 11
Initial Teacher Education in Ireland—A Case Study

Teresa O'Doherty and Judith Harford

This chapter examines how international research and the literature on good practice in initial teacher education has been reflected and refracted within a national policy. Influenced by the Global Education Reform Movement, control of teacher education curriculum has shifted from the higher education institutions to the Teaching Council and government agencies. Reflecting the turn to practice within the literature, the role and place of school placement and partnership with schools is now a dominant feature within ITE programmes. In parallel, influenced by the need to achieve critical mass to support and maintain educational research, partnership between institutions has also been mandated, resulting in further loss of institutional autonomy for ITE providers. Within this chapter, partnership in Irish education is reviewed from two specific aspects

1. The reconceptualised curriculum of ITE, where university-schools partnerships are now a mandated requirement for accreditation/recognition of programmes, and significant portions of ITE programmes must be school-based;
2. The revision of the infrastructure of ITE provision, where in a bid to reduce fragmentation, create a critical mass and thereby sustainable and research led and driven high quality ITE provision, traditionally autonomous institutions are currently engaged in a process of amalgamation, incorporation or creating strategic 'partnerships' and alliances.

Ensuring high-quality initial teacher education is a key concern across the OECD (Schleicher 2012). The emphasis on and visibility of ITE on the policy landscape is a relatively recent development, resulting from the confluence of a

T. O'Doherty (✉)
Mary Immaculate College, Limerick, Ireland
e-mail: Teresa.ODoherty@mic.ul.ie

J. Harford
School of Education, University College Dublin, Dublin, Ireland
e-mail: judith.harford@ucd.ie

© Springer Nature Singapore Pte Ltd. 2017
M.A. Peters et al. (eds.), *A Companion to Research in Teacher Education*,
DOI 10.1007/978-981-10-4075-7_11

number of factors described as 'the perfect storm' (Conway and Murphy 2013). Influenced by a multiplicity of external and internal factors, the reform of the nature, content, duration and structure of teacher provision and providers in recent years, provides an interesting case study of change in teacher education. Following a long period of stability where the structure of teacher education had remained unchanged for many decades, the establishment of the Teaching Council, the statutory body with responsibility for regulating the teaching profession, in 2006, was a significant development on the education landscape. Traditionally universities and colleges exercised high levels of institutional autonomy in relation to the content and nature of teacher education programmes with little state intervention or regulation. This situation has changed considerably, and teacher education has become the object of state intervention and regulation, at a period when the government is seeking to recapture economic prosperity and competitiveness.

Ireland's poor national performance in PISA, and influenced by economic regeneration and perceptions about our international competitiveness, the Department of Education and Skills [DES] decided to extend the duration of ITE programmes to provide additional time for the development of teachers' skills in teaching literacy and numeracy (DES 2011, July). Led by the then reform-oriented Minister for Education and Skills (Ruairí Quinn), supported by a vigorous Department, building on the foundation established by the Teaching Council, and facilitated by a period of austerity and financial rectitude, the time was ripe for the reform of long established processes and institutions.

Working within a state where teachers and teaching are highly valued, the Teaching Council has espoused a particular set of values and aspirations for Irish teacher education. The reform agenda is carefully balanced between preserving the commitment to high-quality teacher education and centralising control over the content, and management, of ITE. Consequently, partnership, which assumes equality and mutual respect built up voluntarily over a sustained period of time, has taken on new shades of understandings within the Irish landscape.

11.1   School-University Partnerships and the Professional Preparation of Student Teachers

The issue of where student teachers are most effectively prepared for the profession is one of the 'most vigorously debated' issues throughout the history of formal teacher education (Zeichner 2008, p. 263). As Robinson (2008, p. 385) notes, 'the history of teacher preparation provides ample evidence of tensions between the liberal arts and professional conceptions, between theoretical and clinical preparation, between university-based and school-based approaches'. More recently, however, the universitisation of teacher education has emerged as a dominant trend internationally, with teacher education being increasingly university-led, with concomitant implications for partner schools involved in initial teacher education.

This development is indicative of both of the drive for quality, and the perceived need to promote the professionalisation of teaching (Harford 2010).

Teacher education programmes in top-performing countries emphasise the significance of preparing teachers in structured, appropriate and supportive clinical settings. A robust clinical component and a research base are core elements of the Finnish teacher education system, which has been a key influence in driving the teacher education reform agenda in Ireland as elsewhere (OECD 2011). Reflecting international trends, the centrality of the school as a key learning site for student teachers is embedded in teacher education provision in Ireland.

Further reflecting international best practice, there is universal agreement surrounding the fundamental need for student teachers to be adequately supported at this critical formative phase and thus for the need to ensure meaningful relationships between universities and schools in the achievement of this objective. Nonetheless, there is concern at EU level that ITE in a number of European countries needs to be upgraded and that the school-university transition requires attention and support via effective mentoring, induction and school leadership (Sahlberg et al. 2012, p. 14). The recent policy agenda in Ireland reflects concerns over the quality of teacher professional development and over the informal nature of the relationship between schools and teacher education institutions.

11.2   A Vision for the Future: Policy Honoured More in the Breach Than in the Observance?

Recent reform of teacher induction in Ireland has resulted in a more formal approach to the mentoring of newly qualified teachers requiring a more structured partnership between schools and teacher education providers. The need to ensure that such a partnership begins in initial teacher education, running smoothly through to induction and CPD phases has thus not been lost to policy makers. The Teaching Council has, through its recent policy agenda, highlighted the issue of fragmentation across the continuum of teacher education, with insufficient linkages being made between the stages of the continuum. It is also cognisant of the persistence of a model of teacher education which relies too heavily on initial teacher education.

In its efforts to bring greater coherence to provision across all stages of the continuum, the Council has observed that 'the time is now right for a fresh and thorough look at teacher education to ensure that tomorrow's teachers are competent to meet the challenges that they face and are lifelong learners, continually adapting over the course of their careers to enable them to support their students' learning' (Teaching Council 2011a, p. 6). Regarding the ITE phase as 'the foundation of the teacher's career', the Council also recognises that historically, ITE has relied on informal, ad hoc relationships between HEIs and schools often as a result of 'good will' (Teaching Council 2011a, p. 11) with school-university partnerships thus varying considerably in structure and effectiveness. The lack of any formalised structure and the absence of any quality assurance framework have meant that some students experience placement in schools where support structures are minimal (Long et al. 2012, p. 620).

> Internationally, it is common for formal partnership arrangements to be developed between higher education institutions and schools to provide structured support and a gradual increase in classroom responsibility for student teachers. However, these arrangements vary along a continuum from the school playing a host role (work placement model), to shared responsibility between the school and higher education (collaborative model) to the school providing the entire training (training school model). In Ireland, school/higher education partnerships in ITE are typically at the work placement end of the continuum. (Conway et al. 2009, p. xviii)

As Young et al. note

> In an Irish context, schools accept student teachers on a voluntary basis and cooperating teachers do not have a formal role in the supervision of student teachers, instead following an 'informal support and guidance' role. While many cooperating teachers provide tutorial assistance to student teachers allocated to their classes, a system of structured supervision has yet to be formalised between the school and university. (Young et al. 2015, p. 27)

As such the school-university partnership model historically is reflective of a 'work placement model' as opposed to a 'training school model' (Young et al. 2015). Indeed a recent report into the landscape of ITE in Ireland registered surprise at the rather informal relationship that exists between schools and university education departments, in particular regarding the issue of school placement

> The Review Panel was surprised that, on the whole, the responsibility for finding placements for students on teaching practice rested with the students themselves. Based on their experience, the Panel is of the view that placements should be allocated by the ITE provider, either in the university teacher training schools or other schools, on the basis of partnerships between the provider and schools. (Sahlberg et al. 2012, p. 22)

Hence, cognisant of the need to provide a more structured framework for initial teacher education and in particular for the generation of effective school-university partnerships, the Council has called for the development of 'new and innovative school placement models... developed using a partnership approach, whereby HEIs and schools actively collaborate in the organisation of the school placement' (Teaching Council 2011a, p. 15). The cornerstone of the reform agenda is a more sophisticated experience of the practicum which requires a more structured relationship between schools and university education departments. In order to advise, guide and oversee the school-university dimension of all teacher education provision, the Teaching Council issued a set of guidelines for schools in 2011. The title of the guide, *Guidelines on School Placement*, reflects a move from the narrower concept of 'teaching practice' to 'school placement' which presupposes a deeper and richer experience of school life on the part of the student teacher, and not merely teaching experience. The guidelines note that

> School placement is designed to give the student teacher an opportunity to learn about teaching and learning, to gain practice in teaching, to apply educational theory in a variety

of teaching and learning situations and school contexts and to participate in school life in a way that is structured and supported. It replaces the term "teaching practice" and more accurately reflects the nature of the experience as one encompassing a range of teaching and non-teaching activities. (Teaching Council 2013, p. 6)

The *Guidelines* are underpinned by three key assumptions concerning the benefits of reconceptualising the school placement experience, namely

It will enhance the school placement experience for student teachers

It will enrich learning outcomes for both current and future learners

It will deepen the professional satisfaction and improve the status of teachers.

(Teaching Council 2013, p. 7)

The *Guidelines*, while detailed and the result of extensive consultation, are largely aspirational, however, with little or no mention of exactly how any sea change in the school-university partnership model is to be realised, operationalised or resourced—'host schools are encouraged to be communities of good professional practice and to engage of their own accord with ITE,' (Ibid., p. 8).

11.3   The Elephant in the Room: The Professional Development of Cooperating Teachers

The issue of the selection and professional development of cooperating teachers in particular is an obvious gap in current policy and provision. Currently cooperating teachers are selected by school principals to work alongside student teachers. The criteria for this selection may be linked to their professional and personal capacity to undertake this role, yet it may also be linked to other variables, such as time-tabling issues or the need to supplement an ineffective experienced teacher with a student teacher. Also, the lack of a more formal relationship between university personnel (tutors and supervisors who supervise school placement) and cooperating teachers who work alongside student teachers in school is again a glaring deficit in existing provision. The context of becoming a teacher is a critical variable in shaping student teachers' professional identity and the absence of a universal framework which supports a professional conversation between university and school personnel challenges the potential of this resource to empower student teachers to deconstruct their apprenticeship of observation and build a strong professional identity which is central to teachers' self-efficacy, motivation and job satisfaction. Despite the central role that cooperating teachers play in the professional formation of student teachers, they have no role in the evaluation of school placement. Assessment of this practicum is typically undertaken by HEI personnel and while school-based personnel play a key role in the professional formation of student teachers, they have a largely silent role in the area of assessment. The Sahlberg report (2012) also drew attention to the issue of assessment of students on school placement and the lack of any real partnership approach between school personnel and university personnel in this activity noting that 'ideal partnerships involve shared responsibility between the school and the university for the assessment of student competence.'

This is not to underestimate the complex process involved in fostering authentic partnership models based on trust and meaningful collaboration but in the absence of a comprehensive and detailed framework which addresses all of the key issues, notably the role, professional development and accreditation of cooperating teachers, this policy change will only result in superficial change and not in any meaningful deep-seated reform.

Despite the increased level of prescribed school placement within initial teacher programmes where 25% of the duration of undergraduate programmes and 40% of postgraduate programmes must be dedicated to practicum or school experience, the concept of school-based teacher education has not become a feature of the Irish landscape. In contrast to developments in other jurisdictions (Britain, Sweden), recent policy decisions have reaffirmed the primary role in and contribution of universities and higher education institutions to Irish teacher education.

11.4   The Place of University Education Within Teacher Education

The establishment of the Teaching Council in 2006 heralded the first formal encroachment of the state into the autonomy of teacher educators within the universities and colleges of education. Previously, while the Inspectorate maintained a brief to review the performance of 10% of primary-level student teachers during their final practicum, other than the quality assurance processes within higher education carried out by external examiners and peer review, decisions on the content and nature of initial teacher education programmes were the preserve of university staff. While one of the first activities of the Council was to articulate the core values and standards within the teaching profession, it soon turned its attention to the review of initial teacher education programmes. Established providers were asked to volunteer to pilot the accreditation process in 2009 and four colleges/departments, two primary level and two second-level providers, engaged in the process. Review panels were established by the Council comprising representatives of the teaching profession and the Inspectorate, and chaired by a leading teacher educationist. While the reports on each piloted programme contained specific programme-related recommendations, they also referred to potential system level reforms which the panels deemed desirable. The Council, under the aegis of the Department of Education and Skills and as an advisory body to the Minister, did not have the authority to fundamentally reshape the structure and content of initial teacher education. However, it had created a platform for engagement with the continuum of teacher education and following the disappointing results of Irish 15-year-old students in PISA, the DES sought to avail of an opportunity to address perceived short-comings in ITE. The policy document *Literacy and Numeracy for Learning and for Life* (DES 2011) identified the need to 'improve the quality and relevance of initial teacher education' (p. 32). Furthermore it stated,

> It is possible, for example, to obtain a BEd qualification (for primary teaching) in some colleges without completing intensive modules in the teaching of literacy and numeracy. The low mathematical ability among a number of students entering undergraduate initial teacher education courses at primary level and the more general weaknesses in many students' conceptual understanding in mathematics are also causes of concern. (DES 2011, p. 32)

Embedded within the policy statement on the enhancement of literacy and numeracy, the DES subsumed responsibility for initial teacher education and the decades of benign neglect which the DES had displayed towards ITE were at an end. The DES announced its decision to extend the duration of concurrent ITE for primary level education to four years and postgraduate ITE programmes for primary and post-primary to be extended to two years. In addition, the structure of concurrent programmes for primary teachers was to be radically revised; the policy where 40% of the programme was committed to studies in arts/humanities was at an end. Within the new four-year programme, which was to be implemented the following academic year (2012), 'electives' could comprise a maximum of 20% of the programme. Where included, electives were to be more closely related to education and relevant to the curriculum (DES 2011, p. 34). The DES policy became the springboard for the publication of the *Criteria Guidelines for Programme Providers* (Teaching Council 2011b) which defined the content of teacher education programmes, outlined mandatory elements of all ITE programmes and identified some 65 learning outcomes to be achieved. The Council specified that foundation studies, professional studies and school placement should be at the heart of the programmes; within foundation studies it stipulated that all ITE programmes should include the study of curriculum studies, the history and policy of education, philosophy of education, psychology of education and sociology of education. Reaffirming the centrality of these subject areas to prepare the beginning teachers to 'critically engage with curriculum aims, design, policy, reform, pedagogy and assessment' and to "enhance students" understanding of the Irish education system,' (Teaching Council 2011b, p. 13), the Teaching Council firmly rooted teacher preparation within the university/academy and advocated that teacher educators be research active and student teachers research literate. Despite the move to closely define, manage and control centrally the content and structure of ITE, and contrary to developments in Britain where the locus of teacher education has been transferred to schools, the Teaching Council safeguarded education as a discipline within programmes and emphasised the important contribution of the university in the professional formation of teachers.

11.4.1 Partnership, Mergers and Incorporations

Pre-2000 alliances of higher education institutions in Ireland were rare and where they did exist, they were generated on a voluntary basis between institutions and individual researchers (Harkin and Hazelkorn 2015). Where these academically and strategically motivated alignments occurred, the autonomy of the partners was not disputed. However, the 2004 OECD review of the Irish higher education sector became the catalyst for significant change in the sector. Greater collaboration between higher education institutions and a closer alignment of the work of these institutes with national planning objectives was leveraged through the Programme for Research in Third-Level Institutions (PRTLI) and the Strategic Innovation Funding (SIF). Incentivised funding mechanisms challenged institutions to develop regional collaboration in research and areas such as access, lifelong learning, and teaching and learning. Regional clusters, such as the Shannon Consortium which included the University of Limerick, Mary Immaculate College and Limerick Institute of Technology, were established. While motivated by additional functionality and funding, a significant level of inter-institutional collaboration was generated.

As the economic crisis in Ireland intensified, the Higher Education Authority published the *National Strategy for Higher Education to 2030* (HEA 2011) which provided the platform for a root-and-branch review of all higher education provision. With a view to enhancing the 'quality and cost-effectiveness of provision through shared collaborative provision' (HEA 2012, p. 9), this strategy heralded the end of voluntary bottom-up collaboration and the beginning of an 'amalgamate or perish' (Hinfelaar 2012) approach to higher education. In particular, the HEA targeted the structures of teacher education, 'to identify possible new structures for teacher education ... to envision innovative strategies so that Ireland can provide a teacher education regime that is comparable with the world's best' (Hyland 2012). The perceived messy and fragmented problem of 19 autonomous state-funded providers of teacher education was addressed by an international panel comprising Professors Pamela Munn and John Furlong, and chaired by Professor Pasi Sahlberg. The resulting Sahlberg Report (2012), cognisant of international trends in ITE, advocated the locating of teacher education within the university with high-quality instruction in both pedagogy and pedagogical content knowledge, where graduates would have access to masters and doctoral awards, as well as having the capacity to engage in research as a basis of teaching and learning. Recognising the importance of creating a critical mass to achieve the optimum context for ITE, the Panel recommended that teacher education be consolidated into six centres/clusters, and that two providers of teacher education be discontinued. With a mixed agenda of rationalisation and efficiency gains on one hand, and an upgrading of the quality and status of the institutions on the other (Hinfelaar 2012, p. 5), thus began the process whereby levels of 'partnership' between institutions became mandated.

The first merger of an ITE provider, initiated by the institution itself and pre-dating the Sahlberg Report, occurred when Froebel College, an autonomous college offering ITE for primary-level teachers and affiliated to Trinity College, agreed to merge with Maynooth University (MU) which offers second-level and adult teacher education programmes. Froebel began the process of transitioning its programmes to MU in September 2011 and its staff and students are now full members of the MU community. Following the publication of the Sahlberg Report four Dublin teacher education institutions agreed to amalgamate creating the DCU Incorporation. Following an intensive two-year planning process, St Patrick's College Drumcondra (primary, Catholic college), the Church of Ireland College of Education (primary, Anglican college), Mater Dei Institute (post-primary, Catholic college) and Dublin City University (post-primary, civic university) merged to establish an Institute of Education within Dublin City University in September 2016. Also in Dublin, Trinity College Dublin (post-graduate studies in education, Anglican), Marino Institute of Education (primary, Catholic College), University College Dublin (post-primary, civic) and the National College of Art and Design (post-primary) have agreed to participate in the formation of a new Institute of Education. Greater collaboration has been achieved between the School of Education in University College Cork and Cork Institute of Technology (art and design education, post-primary), while a decision has been made to incorporate St Angela's College (home economics, post-primary, Catholic college) into NUI Galway (post-primary, civic). This imposed integration is an example of direct HEA involvement and has been the source of considerable disquiet for staff.

Mary Immaculate College (MIC, primary, Catholic college), the University of Limerick (UL, post-primary, civic) and Limerick Institute of Technology (art and design, post-primary, civic), identified by the Sahlberg Report as a 'Centre of Excellence for Teacher Education' have collaborated to establish the National Institute for Studies in Education (NISE); while retaining institutional autonomy, this trans-sectoral and regional cluster, building on a decade of bottom-up relationship building within the Shannon Consortium, is committed to ensuring that greater academic coherence is attained. While initially it was advocated that MIC would merge with UL, this merger did not occur. Instead, MIC has retained its autonomy and St Patrick's College, Thurles (post-primary, Catholic), one of two providers which was earmarked to be discontinued, was incorporated into MIC in 2016.

11.5 Conclusion

The lexicon of partnership in teacher education in Ireland has developed and expanded over the last five years to reflect the increasingly complex array of relationships between institutions involved in initial teacher education; discussions of integration, incorporation, merger, alliance and clustering predominate where teacher educators gather. In some instances these developments were initiated by the actors themselves, who have invested significant time in the management of the transitions, and form the basis for positive and enriching new contexts for teacher education; in others, the mandatory nature of the mergers and the inadequacy of the time and opportunity to establish a shared vision for teacher education, suggests that the process may be less than beneficial for all concerned.

Building partnership in Irish teacher education has assumed new and challenging meanings in recent years; within the context of programmatic reforms, the extension of the relationship between initial teacher education providers and schools has been mandated by the Teaching Council. While all providers have built strong relationships with schools, the nature of the partnership now required by the Council will take time and resources to establish. Recognising all cooperating teachers in schools as 'teacher educators' and sharing ownership of the lifelong 'teacher education project', will require a significant mind-shift on the part of teachers and teacher educators alike. Simultaneously, institutional partnership required of teacher education providers challenges the institutional autonomy and identity of teacher educators. Deconstructing a web of relationships and discontinuing institutions which have persisted for decades is not a simple undertaking. Merging institutions, irrespective of size, requires considerable planning and dialogue. Where these institutions have conflicting ethos or denominational identity, these reforms challenge the core of the institutions and the integration process requires depths of trust and confidence which demand time and commitment from all involved. The impact of institutional change on the identity of teacher educators, and its influence on the nature, content and approach to teacher education across the state has yet to be seen. While undoubtedly these partnerships can provide new energies and opportunities for all the actors involved, and may enable a new and dynamic form of teacher education to develop, the policy of imposed 'partnership' within and between institutions, be that university-schools in relation to school placement, or university-higher education college, may have questionable outcomes for Irish education.

Structural change in teacher education is commonplace internationally, even where teachers' education seems to be world class (Sahlberg et al. 2012, p. 7); the merging of smaller colleges is deemed essential to create units capable of leading research-based teacher education. The increased focus on facilitating theory and practice within clinical settings is also evident. Developments in the Republic of Ireland in many ways reflect the changes occurring elsewhere; however, set in a context where policy and practice in ITE has remained stationary for many decades, the level and rate of change is unprecedented. The increased state interest in and surveillance of ITE through the work of the Teaching Council, at a time when all higher education institutions have experienced significant reductions in state funding, has further influenced the nature of change. While ambitious plans for the future of ITE in Ireland have been made, the actuality of imposing radical reforms to both the content and structure of teacher education with much reduced resources does not augur well for these developments. Without adequate investment in our relationships with schools and with partner institutions, delivering real and authentic partnership is severely challenged.

References

Coonway, P. F., Murphy, R., Rath, A., & Hall, K. (2009). *Learning to teach and its implications for the continuum of teacher education: A nine-country cross-national study.* Maynooth: Teaching Council.

Conway, P. F., & Murphy, R. (2013). A rising tide meets a perfect storm: New accountabilities in teaching and teacher education in Ireland. *Irish Educational Studies, 32*(1), 11–36.

Department of Education and Skills. (2011). *Literacy and numeracy for learning and for life: The national strategy to improve literacy and numeracy among children and young people 2011–2020.* Dublin: Department of Education and Skills.

Harford, J. (2010). Teacher education policy in Ireland and the challenges of the 21st century. *European Journal of Teacher Education, 33*(4), 349–360.

Harkin, S., & Hazelkorn, E. (2015). 'Institutional mergers in Ireland'. In A. Curai, L. Georghiou, J. C. Harper, R. Pricopie, & E. Ergon-Polak (Eds.), *Mergers and alliances in higher education: International practice and emerging opportunities* (pp. 105–121). SpringerLink.com.

Higher Education Authority. (2011). *National strategy for higher education to 2030.* Dublin: The Higher Education Authority.

Higher Education Authority. (2012). *Towards a future higher education landscape.* Dublin: The Higher Education Authority.

Hinfelaar, M. (2012). Emerging higher education strategy in Ireland: Amalgamate or Perish. *Higher Education Management and Policy, 24*(10), 1–16. doi:10.1787/17269822

Hyland, A. (2012). *A review of the structure of initial teacher education provision in Ireland: Background paper for the international review team.* Dublin: Department of Education and Skills.

Long, F., Hall, K., Conway, P., & Murphy, R. (2012). Novice teachers as 'invisible' learners. *Teachers and Teaching: Theory and Practice, 18,* 619–636.

OECD. (2011). *Lessons from PISA for the United States, strong performers and successful reformers in education.* Paris: OECD Publishing. doi:10.1787/9789264096660-en

Robinson, W. (2008). 'England and Wales'. In T. O'Donoghue & C. Whitehead, (Eds.), *Teacher education in the English-speaking world: Past, present and future* (pp. 45–60). USA: Information Age Publishing.

Sahlberg, P., Munn, P., & Furlong, J. (2012). *Report of the international review panel on the structure of initial teacher education provision in Ireland: Review conducted on behalf of the department of education and skills.* Dublin: Department of Education and Skills.

Schleicher, A. (Ed.). (2012). *Preparing teachers and developing school leaders for the 21st century: Lessons from around the world.* Paris: OECD Publishing.

Teaching Council. (2011a). *Policy on the continuum of teacher education.* Maynooth: Teaching Council.

Teaching Council. (2011b). *Initial teacher education: Criteria and guidelines for programme providers.* Maynooth: Teaching Council.

Teaching Council. (2013). *Guidelines on school placement.* Maynooth: Teaching Council.

Young, A. M., O'Neill, A., & Mooney Simmie, G. (2015). Partnership in learning between university and school: Evidence from a researcher-in-residence. *Irish Educational Studies, 34* (1), 25–42.

Zeichner, K. (2008). 'The United States'. In T. O'Donoghue & C. Whitehead, (Eds.), *Teacher education in the English-speaking world: Past, present and future* (pp. 7–22). USA: Information Age Publishing.

Author Biographies

Teresa O'Doherty is Dean of Education, Mary Immaculate College, Limerick. Her research interests are in the history and policy of education. She is a member of SCoTENS, an all-Ireland association of teacher educators, Teacher Education Policy in Europe Network and the UK-based Teacher Education Group.

Judith Harford is Associate Professor and Director of the Professional Master of Education at the School of Education, University College Dublin. She is Co-Ordinator of the Teacher Education Policy in Europe Network, a Fellow of the Royal Historical Society (London) and an International Clinical Practice Fellow of the American Association of Teacher Educators.

Chapter 12
Doing Harm to Educational Knowledge: The Struggle over Teacher Education in Sweden and Norway

Carl Anders Säfström and Herner Saeverot

12.1 Introduction

In the Scandinavian countries, particularly Sweden and Norway, the concept of educational sciences (in Swedish: utbildningsvetenskap; in Norwegian: utdanningsvitenskap) has, over the last 20 years, emerged as an overarching and unifying concept, which has subjugated pedagogik and other disciplines. For this reason we wish to analyse this particular concept. But before we do that, we need to know what the concepts of 'utbildning' and 'utdanning' signify.

Both concepts consist of a combination of the preposition 'ut' [out] and the verbal nouns 'bildning' and 'danning'. The preposition 'ut' signifies a direction, i.e. 'out from' and 'out towards' (see Wivestad 2015: p. 115). In this way, we see that 'utbildning' and 'utdanning' have a beginning (out from) and an end (out towards), that is to say that 'utbildning' and 'utdanning' are something that take place within a particular period of time. Something will happen during this time period. When the education or 'utbildning' and 'utdanning' is over, the person involved is considered to be either 'utbildad' or 'utdannet'. The person is in other words formed into something specific.

Could we then say that 'utbildning' and 'utdanning' are connected to the concepts of 'bildning' and 'danning', what is known as *Bildung*? Not quite, as 'utbildning' and 'utdanning' are directed towards specific goals, within a certain period of time. On the other hand, if we turn to Goethe's prototypical *Bildungsroman—Wilhelm Meister* (1795–96)—we may see that *Bildung* is basically understood as an education or 'utbildning'/'utdanning' of man's inner and

C.A. Säfström (✉)
Södertörn University, Stockholm, Sweden
e-mail: carl.anders.safstrom@sh.se

H. Saeverot
Western Norway University of Applied Sciences, Bergen, Norway
e-mail: Herner.Severot@hvl.no

© Springer Nature Singapore Pte Ltd. 2017   179
M.A. Peters et al. (eds.), *A Companion to Research in Teacher Education*,
DOI 10.1007/978-981-10-4075-7_12

natural abilities. So in that respect, we can see a connection between the different concepts. Nonetheless, 'utbildning' and 'utdanning' are primarily concerned with that which happen within a formally organized institution, either the school, the university or the university college. That which happens outside of such institutions; or, that which happens informally in daily life, is more or less neglected.

Henceforth, we shall investigate the concept of educational sciences. We wish to do so by way of four points. First, we view the concept of utbildningsvetenskap/utdanninsgvetenskap in relation to the educational system. Second, we ask which discipline(s) is/are the most relevant when it comes to utbildningsvetenskap/utdanninsgvetenskap. Third, we ask what has happened to the discipline pedagogik (Swedish)/pedagogikk (Norwegian) within utbildningsvetenskap/utdanninsgvetenskap? Finally, we take a look at the concept of time in relation to utbildningsvetenskap/utdanninsgvetenskap.

12.2   A Science of the System Itself

The first point can be described thus: Utbildnings-vetenskap in Swedish and Utdannings-vitenskap in Norwegian, both connote to an educational system, that is, utbildning/utdanning as an administrative body, a set of rules and regulations, a particular institution in society. So, if utbildning/utdanning means the system itself, then to add science to it means that what is required is a science of the system itself. What becomes 'natural' educational issues within such an understanding are questions of how to 'steer' the system, its history and social and political formations, how knowledge are represented by the system and what is learnt within the confines of the system.

A problem with such an understanding is that utbildningsvetenskap/utdanninsgvitenskap becomes normative in its entirety. That is a social system as the educational system is an institution in society which means that it cannot be in the hands of researchers and scientists—it is rather a system for reproducing the state, to form a certain public, for socialization, professionalization, etc., that is for making labour and distributing labour in the society. It is in any case a basic system/institution in society for which politics is absolutely necessary. It is simply not possible to separate the 'educational system' from its political underpinnings—it is not possible to think an educational system outside a particular society. An educational system outside politics is an anomaly. It is therefore not possible to separate 'the system' from its political normative functions in society—it is saturated with values, norms and interests. It is nothing else than those norms, interests, values formulated in administrative, bureaucratic language, in rules and regulations, in gestures as well as buildings.

If 'science' is to take place within such a context, then there is no base from which science can perform its critical task, which is not already deeply involved in those interests, values and norms. The science itself *is* the science of the system of values norms and values making up the system of utbildnings/utdanning.

For politics proper this is deeply troublesome and points to a kind of 'scientification' of politics, meaning that political problems are transformed into scientific problems, that is, into seemingly neutral problems. This can work in two 'directions', that is, when the research conducted within such an understanding goes along with the politics of the day, it confirms and neutralizes through truth claims, what is political ideology (Bengtsson 2010). Second, if research does not confirm the politics of the day, then it is pointed out as biased (Säfström 2010).

For example, since the first White Paper in Norway 30 years ago, *Datateknologi i skolen* (St.meld. nr. 39, 1983–84) [Computer technology in school (White Paper no. 39, 1983–1984)], nearly 20 national policy documents for the use of ICT in education have been published. As a consequence of policy guidelines, there have been a shift towards more use of digital learning materials. The Norwegian government has pumped billions of kroner into hardware and software, with the result that Norway is one of the countries in the world with the highest technology density at schools (*European Survey of Schools: ICT in Education* 2013).

This shows that political constraints do affect the research. In many cases, Norwegian research has emphasized a socio-cultural approach when it comes to research on digital learning materials. An important theoretician within the socio-cultural milieu is the Russian psychologist Lev Vygotsky (1896–1934), who focused on learning occurring in a social interaction between the environment and the individual. One should take into account, however, that Vygotsky had never seen nor touched a computer. Today's technology has completely different structures and educational possibilities than Vygotsky could ever imagine, far beyond the intentions of his overall learning models. One must also keep in mind that Vygotsky's research is connected to the Soviet social situation, in the years just after the Russian revolution and World War 1.

Even though today's technology and education are significantly different and complex, substantial governmental research millions have in recent years been given to such socio-cultural based educational research. Both researchers and politicians have 'believed' that such outdated psychological principles can be used more directly on new digital learning materials.

Furthermore, the 'results' of this research has been used in the teacher education departments, among teachers and within other educational institutions. This may be one explanation as to why the Norwegian schools have had such a poor progress when it comes to educational use of digital tools. The problem is that a number of politicians and researchers have had such a strong and certain belief on the idea that ICT in itself will automatically improve the learning outcomes for all students. But the focus has in many ways been unsuccessful, because it is not based on pedagogical research. Instead, the plans have focused on the technology itself surrounded by sets of normative assumptions within the political sphere, rather than pedagogikk knowledge. Thus, Norwegian schools have a lot of technological equipment, along with ideological approaches to knowledge, yet very little educational insight and awareness.

Both of those 'directions' mentioned above, i.e. that research either replaces political will or are considered obsolete if it does not, are highly problematic from a democratic point of view, since the most important questions of an educational system are not to be solved by science, but are to be 'voted' for by the people. That is, what do we want the educational system for? What is, as Biesta (2010) formulates it, good education? What kind of society do we want to live in—through our educational systems? All these kinds of questions are political questions that need to be on the table for democratic considerations. To leave them to 'science' is deeply troublesome for democratic reasons. But it is also troublesome for the field of pedagogik(k)—since it deprives the field from its insights based on traditions and research outside the ideology of 'scientification of politics', which ironically tend to destroy both science and politics proper.

12.3   Towards Psychology, Away from Pedagogik(k)

One of the main arguments for establishing utbildningsvetenskap/ utdanningsvitenskap, and this is part of our second point, was that it was supposed to be a 'wider' concept than 'pedagogik' and therefore could host all disciplines that had any kind of connection to 'educational systems'. The change to utbildningsvetenskap/utdanningsvitenskap was needed, so it was argued, in order to give teacher education a sound base in science. Somewhat ironically was that it was suppose to happen through the different disciplines themselves and their subjects and not by, for example, strengthen the already existing and internationally established field of teacher education research. It was claimed that pedagogik(k) could not fulfil all the requirements for what a teacher needed. Instead of for example philosophy of education teaching about ethics of teaching—one should have a 'real' philosopher teaching about ethics. Instead of having a 'pedagog' trained in history of education studying the history of schooling, one should have a 'real' historian studying the same things, etc., and that regardless if the philosopher or historian or any other subject specialist had any knowledge of educational traditions of thought or traditions of research in 'pedagogik(k)'. For example, traditions of pedagogik(k) can at least be traced back to the ancient Greek formulation of paideia, and the idea that the citizen needed education in its role *as* citizen in order to form a public that could recognize itself as such.

The material basis for this somewhat new attitude of 'anything goes' in educational research as long as it is not exclusively based in pedagogik(k) can be found in two circumstances, first The Swedish Research Council (VR) in March 2001 established a Committee for Educational Sciences 'utbildningsvetenskapliga kommittén' entirely dedicated to such research; that produced a need at Swedish universities to identify research that could be considered for being funded.

Second, all universities in Sweden were by directives from the state obliged to establish a faculty board for 'utbildningsvetenskaplig' research. These two factors were decisive for the birth of 'utbildningsvetenskap'. It was though unclear at the time for its birth what exactly it could be which was not already covered by traditions of knowledge within 'pedagogik'. Largely this unclearness remains being a distinct feature of utbildningsvetenskap/utdanningsvitenskap. So two years after the decision to establish the committee at VR, Lundgren and Fransson (2003) published a report, financed and published by VR in which 'utbildningsvetenskap' '-its concepts and their context' were explained. Their conclusion was that "a clear tendency that 'utbildningsvetenskap' forms a collective term, that includes different directions of research about education" (p. 105). They also somewhat confess in the report that their conclusion is not satisfactory since, we will say, it does not add any clearness to the situation of exactly what utbildningsvetenskap/utdanningsvitenskap could be which is not already part of educational traditions of thought covered by the disciplines of pedagogik and pedagogikk.

At Uppsala University, Lidegran and Broady (2003: 2) produced a report on what was said to be possibly going on at the university under the heading of 'utbildningsvetenskap'. They found that such research was indeed going on in all of the faculties including medicine and science. As a basis for their survey, they used a definition established by the newly established faculty board of 'utbildningsvetenskap':

> ...the board chooses to understand 'utbildningsvetenskap' as a broad term for a kind of research within a multiplicity of disciplines at the university which is directed to - or could be directed to - 'bildning' [Bildung], 'utbildning' [institutionalised education], 'fostran' [value based upbringing] and 'lärande' [learning]. At least in principle 'utbildningsvetenskap' thereby has a place in all areas of research, faculties and departments, and are at the same time - with its outspoken foci on schools and society - deeply engaged in a practice outside the university. (Lidegran and Broady 2003: p. 2)

This would result, so was the hope, in stronger knowledge base for different types of educational systems and thereby give teacher education a base in research. We can indeed see that utbildningsvetenskap/utdanningsvitenskap is research that mainly is concerned with systems of education, and/or their contents over time. Ironically, though, this had led to a situation in which what is considered educational research in other faculties than educational ones, essentially is formed within traditions of knowledge and research within those faculties and then applied to educational issues. Disciplines such as medicine, law, sociology, psychology, etc., are of course formed in relation to issues of medicine, law, socialization and what Rose (1998) called sciences of the 'psy-', and then *applied* to educational issues. In consequence alienating those issues from long standing traditions of knowledge and research in pedagogik(k) in which they have their rightful place. But also, and this is maybe worse, reduce those issues to other issues than educational ones. In effect depriving teacher education of educational knowledge.

A similar tendency can be seen in Norway, when, for example, the educational historian Alfred Oftedal Telhaug was head of the National Academic Committee for pedagogikk under the auspices of The Research Council of Norway from 1995 to 2001. One of his objectives as leader was to create a multidisciplinary profile in terms of educational research, i.e. he wished to give room for multiple fields and disciplines other than pedagogikk concerning the research field of education, such fields and disciplines as economics, law, political science, sociology, anthropology and history (Saeverot 2014). By doing so he wanted to share the financial resources between many disciplines, instead of just giving them to pedagogikk, as had traditionally been done. In other words, pedagogikk should have a minor role with regard to research on education. Beyond this, Telhaug suggested that sociologists should take care of sociology of education, psychologists should do the same with psychology of education, while philosophers should attend philosophy of education. As a consequence, educational research and educational practice could be based on sociological, psychological and philosophical norms.

As pleasant as the argument may sound it also comes with some unforeseen consequences more than what already have been mentioned above. First and taking Sweden as an example: Pedagogik was established as a discipline in 1907 at Uppsala University as a response to the need to give teaching and teachers a base in science. Its first professor was Bertil Hammer (installed in 1910) who was firmly based in a hermeneutic tradition of educational thought and who dismissed the idea that the new type of experimental psychology (inspired by Wilhelm Wundt) was doing any good for education (Säfström 1994). As for Norway, Pedagogisk seminar (seminar for pedagogikk) was established the very same year, and only two years later, in 1909, Otto Anderssen was appointed as the first Professor of pedagogikk in Norway. For over 100 years, countless of people trained in research have spent entire carriers and life times, studying, thinking and writing about educational issues. This means that there literally is a tradition of knowledge accumulated as disciplines of pedagogik(k) for over 100 years. To simply replace this tradition of educational [pedagogik] knowledge with traditions of thought formed around other issues than education—but applied to educational systems, is to deny the power of history as well as how scholarly traditions are formed and developed over time.

Also, with some time passed we can now see that the promise of improving educational research for the benefit of school systems simply is not happening. Sweden, for example, have never been lower ranked in PISA than in 2013. When it comes to Norwegian pupils their math skills are at the lowest level since Norway started testing pupils for Pisa. In science, too, there is a negative change, while the results in reading remain quite stable.

But maybe more important is what tended to happen in teacher education in relation to the massive critique of poor quality of teacher education in Sweden orchestrated by the state department of education from 2006 onwards (see Säfström 2014 for a response to this critique). What tended to happen, among other things, was that a wide variety of disciplines were taking up 'didaktik' as a way of moving into the centre of teacher education. Reasons for doing this were not only a newly awaken interest for 'ämnesdidaktik' (subject didactics) within the subject disciplines but also economical. The basic funding for the disciplines at the univeristies became from the beginning of the 1990s and on directly related to a system of funding based on full time equivalents and student completions rates, meaning that it suddenly became clear that teacher education programs was a major financial contributor to the economy of the universities and university colleges. Small disciplines, with few students became all the more motivated to take active part in teacher education, and to develop ways of legitimizing this by developing 'ämnesdidaktik', or other inventions. They tended to do this though often without connecting themselves either to traditions of 'didaktik' (content focused) research developed within pedagogik(k) over the years or international educational research, even though one can find exceptions to the rule. Through the new teacher education launched in Sweden in 2009 ('Bäst i klassen' [Best in class] Bill 2009/10:89), the different subject disciplines are further 'strengthened', for example, by only allowing students final papers in their respective programs in other disciplines than pedagogik, depriving teacher students from more fully engaging in traditions of knowledge formed within traditions of educational thought (pedagogik[k]). This is more than alarming for the possibility to educate competent teachers in Sweden in the future.

As for the Norwegian teacher education, it has for a long time been marked by an official report—NOU 1996: 22 Lærerutdanning—mellom krav og ideal [Teacher Education—Between Demand and Ideal]. The majority in this committee wanted increased number of lessons for pedagogikk in the teacher education, while the minority (in which the educational historian Telhaug was part of) wanted to reduce pedagogikk. What happened is almost indescribable, but it was the minority that won acceptance for its view. Thus, pedagogikk was reduced by one third, from three quarters to half a year. At the same time, the minority decided that the subject Christianity with religion and life orientation should have its credits doubled in the teacher education. Thus, pedagogikk suffered for many years in the Norwegian teacher education, while the subjects and subject didactics (in Norwegian: fagdidaktikk) had strengthened their positions.

In 2010, another important event took place around the Norwegian teacher education. Norwegian politicians had long looked to Finland to strengthen the teacher education. What they found was that there was quite a lot of pedagogik in the Finnish teacher education. Thus, upon the completion of the GLU-reform in 2010, the Norwegian politicians increased the scope of pedagogikk to 60 credits. At first glance this looks like good news for pedagogikk, but upon closer inspection it is not. Why might that be so? First, the politicians had made a change of term. What has always been called pedagogikk should now be called pedagogikk og elevkunnskap (PEL) [Pedagogikk and student knowledge]. Second, the state politicians had not earmarked that pedagogikk should get all the 60 credits. Consequently, there was a struggle regarding which subjects that could teach PEL. In several teacher educations in Norway, different subjects are involved with the teaching of PEL, ranging from drama, to social studies, physical education and more. Thus, pedagogikk is slowly but surely 'eaten up' by other subjects that claim to teach pedagogikk.

A recent example of this "strengthening of the disciplines in teacher education trend" is the newly established HUMTANK in Sweden, which has as its main task to strengthen the status of humanist disciplines within Swedish universities. Even though we would be more than sympathetic to this initiative, not the least since our understanding is that pedagogik(k) has its proper grounding within a humanist strand of thinking, we are still a bit hesitant for the argument that humanist disciplines (in Swedish and Norwegian; humaniora) need to engage more fully in teacher education for their own benefit. That is the need for strengthening 'humaniora' in teacher education seems *not* be based on an analysis of how that would

186 C.A. Säfström and H. Saeverot

improve teacher education, but entirely on the needs of humanistic disciplines themselves.

As a result those disciplines in themselves or through 'subject didactics' (in Swedish: ämnesdidaktik) risks forcing educational research backwards, moving into picturing educational issues mainly as instrumental problems to be solved instrumentally. That is if subject didactics is to be understood as the knowledge accumulated by the disciplines and teacher education as learning teacher students how this knowledge is 'learnt' by the pupils in schools, focusing on what methods that are subject specific and which most effectively enhance 'learning', then teacher education easily becomes reduced to an administration without any significant meaning for educating teachers. Teacher education then becomes reduced to a system for channelling money for the benefit of all disciplines at the university regardless if they have any idea or not about the field of teacher educational research or educational traditions of thought. In effect reducing educational issues to the application of subject knowledge through the concept of learning. But 'learning' is a process itself empty of content, which means that if learning is that which make issues educational, nothing makes them educational.

And second, if those disciplines do not engage in educational traditions of thought but see their involvement in teacher education as based on subject specific methods combined with theories of learning, they push utbildningsvetenskap even further into the hands of psychology instead of pedagogik(k).

As 'learning' is a psychological concept, 'utbildningsvetenskap' is ironically not dependent on pedagogical knowledge but psychological. Through the ignorance of traditions of educational thought, 'utbildningsvetenskap' tends to defining the entire scope of 'utbildningsvetenskap' in terms of 'learning'.

'Psychology of learning' is also what tends to dominate educational research that wants to be funded by the Committee for educational sciences. This is more than clear if one takes the description of what constitutes the field of 'utbild-ningsvetenskap' at the home webpage of the Committee for educational sciences (UVK) at Swedish research council (VR) as a legitimate description of the field. 'Utbildningsvetenskap' is defined in a short text of eight and a half lines, in which learning is mentioned seven (7!) times, and always as a concept framing all other possible themes and concepts (see also Säfström and Månsson 2015). It is therefore questionable if it is *educational* sciences at all that are defined—but rather 'learning sciences'.

When in 2008 the report on 'Sustainable teacher education' (SOU 2008: 109) was presented by the main investigator Sigbritt Franke—it could more than any-thing else be read as a blueprint of how educational research was perceived at the point in time by those in power to define the field of 'utbildningsvetenskap' from the 'outside', including researchers of neuroscience as well as the political sphere. That the new subject 'the core of educational sciences' (Den utbildningsveten-skapliga kärnan) as the new 'subject' in teacher education programs in Sweden replacing pedagogik was called, could be read as a mix of partly outdated educa-tional research with neuroscience and a political will to transform the entire edu-cational system from its core. The result, as we understand it, is a particular kind of reification and reduction of educational thought which together with the trend that an expertise in pedagogik is not needed in order to teach within 'the core of educational sciences', is an obvious risk that a reductionist understanding of education for teachers becomes solidified.

12.4   The Marginalization of Pedagogik(K)

As for our third point, modern education in Sweden as well as in Norway is a combination of educational psychology and social engineering (Säfström 1994). It was established as a response to the need to build a new society after the Second World War, a society for the (liberal) democratic man, and the 'welfare' state. Influences come mainly from United States of America, and Swedish social researchers were trained in the emerging field of statistical based research in the USA. In Sweden, the prominent social engineers in education come from military psychology and the solutions they established on the problem of building a school system for the new age, were based in what was called differential psychology (see further Säfström 1994). For Torsten Husén, a major figure in establishing modern pedagogik, pedagogik was not at all a science in its traditional sense, that is, it was not a 'discipline' forming traditions of thought and knowledge but rather a response to pressing societal problems that needed to be solved by scientific methods (see Husén 1988).

The Anglosaxian tradition of education, in contrast to the tradition of pedagogik (k), is not an independent and autonomous academic discipline, it is rather dependent on other disciplines, in particular psychology, sociology, philosophy and history. Neither Hammer (in Sweden) nor Anderssen (in Norway) considered pedagogik(k) as a hyphen-subject in which pedagogik was completely dependent on other disciplines. True, they both used different philosophers in their theoretical works, but that did not transform the works into some kind of philosophy of education. The reason being that their theorizing was not philosophical by nature. Rather than theorizing on the terms and premises of philosophy, they theorized on the terms and premises of pedagogik(k). They simply made use of pedagogical thinking, which is a completely unique way of thinking, quite different from other discipline's ways of thinking, including philosophy (Saeverot 2014). In contrast to the Anglosaxian tradition of education, where it is impossible to examine education based on pedagogik(k) the Hammer-Anderssen tradition of pedagogik(k) makes it possible to investigate education based on pedagogik(k). It is the language of pedagogik(k) that steers the thinking. Unlike the Anglosaxian tradition of education, where the validization of education so to speak goes through the four major disciplines mentioned above, the Hammer-Anderssen tradition of pedagogik(k) is structured in such a way that the validization of education goes directly through pedagogik(k).

Since the mid 1990s, however, this way of structuring pedagogik(k) has become marginalized in Sweden and Norway. The reason for this is that pedagogik(k) has, as already mentioned, become a multidisciplinary field under educational sciences. Due to the hybrid and interdisciplinary structure of educational sciences, pedagogik (k) has come closer to the structure of education. Indeed, politicians and certain academics almost take for granted that pedagogik(k) is a multidisciplinary field, rather than an independent discipline which is formed and developed in such a way as to being able formulate educational problems and questions.

Pedagogik(k) may be harmed by this, as other disciplines, including philosophy of education, is undermining pedagogik(k) as an independent academic discipline and therefore hinders the development of educational knowledge. Ironically, the consequence of such state of affairs tends to be that an increased focus on educational research decreases the production of educational knowledge based in traditions of educational thought. Consequences for teacher education tend to be that instead of being able to base 'the idea of teacher eduaction' its 'ethos' as well as its practical undertakings in educational thought other disciplines than pedagogik are legitimized to teach courses at teacher education traditionally taught by teacher educators coming from pedagogik(k) based in traditions of educational thought. The irony is that by doing this the knowledge proper for teacher education is at best dated and at worst wrong. Of course there are exceptions to this state of affairs—but then always as other disciplines have managed to take up traditions of educational knowledge. Ironically, by so doing those disciplines either have to admit that they are producing 'second hand knowledge' in education or refute the argument for utbildningsvetenskap, that each discipline produces 'better' knowledge within the confine of itself. Or, which is not that uncommon refute pedagogik(k) as a valuable discipline at all for teacher education (see for example article in Dagens 2008 signed by Ebba Bratt-Wittström, Martin Ingvar et al.).

12.5   A Quantitative Conception of Time

Our fourth and final point leads us back to the introduction where we pointed out that utbildning/utdanning has a beginning and an end, and takes place within an institutional framework. As a basis of this, we find a conception of time where beginning and end, and everything in between, lie on a straight line, where old and new incidents move forward, in a pretty much predetermined progression and subsequent order. This is a quantitative understanding of time, which is characterized by homogeneity and succession, in which events follow successively after each other, making it possible to measure that which occurs within the given timeframe. Today's education is by many described as 'the age of measurement', where teachers and others focus on measuring learning outcomes and similar areas. In the age of measurement, utbildningsvetenskap/utdanningsvitenskap plays an important role as it provides legitimacy to evidence-based research, i.e. rigorous outcome-oriented research, which can then be transferred more or less directly to the practice field. The goal being to ensure that the research can lead to certain knowledge about the educational practice. Thus, we end up with a positivist approach to research, and we are back where Husén (and Johannes Sandven in Norway) started, with the belief that reality can be grasped in full.

This is why the modern education researcher is concerned with concrete and visible results, with the consequence that psychology, yet again, becomes a role model. Not only does the researcher seek to reach certain knowledge, but also that which is considered as useful. Everything that falls outside of the scope of usefulness, are therefore considered to be useless. For example, discussions on attitudes and values have little or no value when it comes to the positivist way of thinking. Rather, the researcher sticks to the belief that research data can depict reality, whereupon these data can be translated directly into practical pedagogical situations. The thinking turns into an instrument or a tool, in which measures, often combined with efficient organization, can anticipate and control the (predetermined) future. As a result of the enormous focus on utbildning/utdanning and utbilningsvetenskap/utdanningsvitenskap, the schools have been governed by non-pedagogical issues, which are based on homogeneity and quantity, as shown through the overarching question of today's education: How to educate from immature to mature state/child to adult/non-graduate to graduate?

Such questions are bound by a concept of time characterized by measurement and extension but if we take a close look in the rear-view mirror we may see that pedagogik(k) from the very beginning, as for example, perceived by Herbart in Germany and Hammer in Sweden, was not particularly concerned about such questions. They did not relate to time conceived as a straightforward line of development, as does developmental psychology or progressive education. Right up to the present time, many have believed that the task of education has consisted in an upbringing towards something specific, for example democracy, as if the student initially lacked something, of which the teacher—through educational processes—is supposed to give this not-yet-mature individual. But this has not always been the concern of pedagogik(k).

Way back to Rousseau's time pedagogik was related to a different understanding of time, i.e. time as quality and heterogeneity. Instead of taking for granted that the students lack something, the teacher may, for example, assume that something ought to be removed. Therefore, the teacher puts more emphasis on disruptions and unforeseen events; in short, everything that interferes with existence, in a surprising and non-calculable way. At the same time, one turns away from psychological, sociological and philosophical questions, where the main concern often is to evolve and improve, climbing towards perfection, presumably in an epistemological and moral perspective. In fact, this so-called educational idea is similar to the basic idea of sports, where the athletes are constantly practicing to develop and improve their skills. As already mentioned, this has not always been the concern of pedagogik(k). Pedagogik(k) has also focused on that which could bring students away from prejudices, delusions, egocentric desires, etc., and thereby challenge the students, without knowing what the outcome will be (Saeverot 2013). In this sense, pedagogik(k) is related to a different concept of time than the homogeneous one, which probably is needed in certain situations, but not as an overarching concept, as utbildningsvetenskap/utdanningsvitenskap proposes.

12.6 Conclusion

We have argued in conclusion that the struggle over teacher education in politics as well as research has caused damage to not only the discipline of pedagogik(k), but maybe more seriously the possibility to produce knowledge concerning teacher education that actually has anything to do with education. The situation we are in is that the system of education has taken precedence over the entire field of educational research through utbildningsvetenskap/utdanningsvitenskap, depriving the field of educational knowledge that is not already normatively attached to the system as such. There is an obvious risk that what we get instead of pedagogik(k) research based on traditions of educational thought and research is a serious de-scientification of educational knowledge as such, coupled with a scientification of politics as the basis for knowledge production within teacher education in Sweden and Norway. That will do no good in any PISA evaluation, and maybe worse, it would not give us any extra points when it comes to democracy either. And finally, it certainly will do no good in educating teachers who know their trade.

References

Bengtsson, J. (2010). Qualifications of future teachers. ideas and ideals in the liberal discourse about teachers and teacher education in Sweden. *Utbildning & Demokrati*, *19*(1), 59–67.

Biesta, G. J. J. (2010). *Good education in the age of measurement: Ethics, politics, democracy.* London: Paradigm Publishers.

Bill. (2009/10:89). Bäst i klassen—en ny lärarutbildning. http://www.regeringen.se/content/1/c6/13/93/30/100696be.pdf

Dagen, N. (2008). Klasstillhörighet styr när elever sållas ut. Dagen Nyheter, September 20. http://www.dn.se/debatt/klasstillhorighet-styr-nar-elever.sallas-ut/[20150526]

Husén, T. (1988). *Skolreformerna och forskningen: psykologisk pedagogik under pionjäråren.* (Educational reforms and research: Educational psychology under the early years). Stockholm: Verbum Gothia.

Lidegran I. & Broady D. (2003). Forskning och forskarutbildning av utbildningsvetenskaplig relevans vid Uppsala Universitet: inventering våren 2003 på uppdrag av Utbildningsvetenskapliga fakultetsnämnden (Research and doctoral programs with relevance for educational sciences at Uppsala university…). (Rapport 2003: 2.): Uppsala Universitet.

Lundgren U. P. & Fransson K. (2003). *Utbildningsvetenskap: ett begrepp och dess sammanhang.* (Educational sciences: One concept and its context). Vetenskapsrådet/Uppsala Universitet.

NOU. (1996: 22). Lærerutdanning—mellom krav og ideal (Teacher education—Between demand and ideal). Oslo: Kunnskapsdepartementet.

Rose, N. (1998). *Inventing ourselves: Psychology, power and personhood.* Cambridge: Cambridge University Press.

Säfström, C. A. (1994). *Makt och mening. Om innehållsfokuserad pedagogisk forskning* (Power and meaning. About the prior conditions for content focused educational research). Doctoral thesis, Uppsala universitet.

Säfström, C. A. (2010). Vad kan utbildning åstadkomma? En kritik av idealiserade föreställningar om utbildning. *Utbildning & Demokrati, 19*(3), 11–22.

Säfström, C. A. (2014). The passion of teaching at the border of order. *Asia−Pacific Journal of Teacher Education.* doi:10.1080/1359866X.2014.956045

Säfström, C. A., & Månsson, N. (2015). The ontology of learning, or teaching the non-person to learn. *Interacçöes 11*(37).http://www.revista.recaap.pt

Saeverot, H. (2013). *Indirect pedagogy: Some lessons in existential education*. Boston & Rotterdam: Sense Publishers.

Saeverot, H. (2014). Den pedagogiske vendingen (The Pedagogic Turn). *Nordic Studies in Education, 34*(4), 235–246.

SOU. (2008:109). En hållbar lärarutbildning. (A sustainable teacher education). Regeringskansliet. http://www.sweden.gov.sr/sb/d/10005/a/116737[20150526]

Wivestad, S. (2015). Utdanningsbegrepet—I dag, I går og I morgen (The concept of "Utdanning"—Today, yesterday and tomorrow). In P. O. Brunstad, S. M. Reindal, & H. Saeverot (Eds.), *Eksistens og pedagogikk (Existence and education)*. Oslo: Universitetsforlaget.

Author Biographies

Professor Carl Anders Säfström School of Culture and Education, Södertörn University, Stockholm, his research focuses on issues of responsibility for the other, justice, equality and freedom in educational relations. His current research deals with the theory, practice and policy of teacher education.

Herner Saeverot is professor of education at Western Norway University of Applied Sciences. His research focuses on existential education, literature and education, international perspectives of educational research and educational policy. He is the editor-in-chief of *Nordic Studies in Education* and member of the editorial board of Studies in Philosophy and Education.

Chapter 13
The Pre-service Education of Disability Pedagogues in Norway: Maximising Social Pedagogic Ambition

Paul Stephens

> *You [disability pedagogues].... are a human rights profession.*
> (Norwegian Solidarity Union 2013, no pagination)

13.1 Introduction

Outside Continental Europe, it is quite common to connect education with cognitive knowledge that educators teach, such as English and Mathematics. In the Nordic countries, the idea of education is broader. This is particularly noteworthy when the adjective "social" is placed before the noun, "education" (or as it is more commonly termed, "pedagogy", also a noun). Put "social" and "pedagogy" together and the result is "social pedagogy". The social aspect complements the cognitive dimension. In short, social pedagogues are interested in social learning and social development.

I teach and conduct research at the University of Stanger in Norway, where I was appointed to the Inaugural Chair of Social Pedagogy in 2007. The subject is central in the pre-service education of child welfare pedagogues and disability pedagogues.

My focus is on disability pedagogues because what they study and do is a bit of a mystery. I think that this might stir curiosity among other social professionals. In turn, inquisitiveness may stimulate cross-national learning, particularly in professions that uphold advocacy work with people who have disabilities. The enhancement of pedagogic capacity, in its broadest sense, is a key objective in that context.

In this chapter, I concentrate on what the policymakers in Norway want and expect from aspiring disability pedagogues. The journey from the campus to professional practice would make an interesting subject for another study.

P. Stephens (✉)
University of Stavanger, Stavanger, Norway
e-mail: paul.stephens@uis.no

© Springer Nature Singapore Pte Ltd. 2017
M.A. Peters et al. (eds.), *A Companion to Research in Teacher Education*,
DOI 10.1007/978-981-10-4075-7_13

13.2 Background

In the UK, there is an increasing interest in Continental European social pedagogy, a field and a practice that openly investigates and supports social justice (Cameron et al. 2011; Coussée et al. 2010; Stephens 2009); especially as an adjunct to social work. The conviction is that social, physical and spatial challenges can often be prevented and tackled by pedagogic means, as well as through health and welfare casework.

Before going further, I should state that my argument is forthrightly normative. In my defence, I look to Max Weber (1864–1929) (1949, p. 60), who famously wrote that, 'An attitude of moral indifference has no connection with scientific "objectivity"'. Afterwards, it is surely fitting to states one's own values honestly and openly. This is particularly cogent in the context of contemporary social pedagogy, which, with few exceptions, is _for_ social justice, as am I. Ethical conviction admitted allow me to be more specific. I believe that social pedagogic work, including disability pedagogy, should commit itself to the furtherance, until this is finally achieved, of social justice.

13.3 Disability Pedagogy: Origins and Progress

As a profession, disability pedagogy in Norway is young, being traceable to the post Second World War period. The education of disability pedagogues was initially inspired by Ole B. Munch, a consultant physician, who worked in the country's first and, until 1917, only care home for people with developmental difficulties: Emma Hjorth's Home. In 1947, just one year after he began working there, Dr. Munch launched the first disability pedagogy course in the country. This innovative project addressed the physical, psychological and social needs of its residents, pedagogic measures playing a pivotal role.

Today, the state-mandated role of the intending disability pedagogue in Norway —a renaissance figure of sorts, part pedagogue/teacher, part clinician—is found in a policy document (the so-called _Framework_), published in 2005. Its mandate, as at 2016, is unchanged. I shall be referring to this document throughout the chapter. Although the brief of the disability pedagogue is wide, many of them work with people who have intellectual difficulties. The settings vary and include community living services, inclusive work places, own homes and schools. Central institutions, once common, are less often used and disability pedagogues are quite ambulant, often supporting service users in mainstream settings.

This de-institutionalisation, which began in earnest during the early 1990s, promotes inclusion by offering appropriately adapted—but not overly protective— settings where maximum capacity building in natural surroundings is prized (see, e.g. Tollefsen 2006). Diverse pedagogic and spatial landscapes provide cognitive challenges and foster pedagogic ambition. For this reason, aspiring disability pedagogues undergo a 3-year bachelor degree course, during which time they learn much about promoting perceived self-efficacy (see Bandura 1997). There is an important message here. People, all people, can only make the best possible progress when social and physical environments are enabling, not disabling.

Given the important role they have in Norwegian society, I am surprised that many Norwegians do not know what disability pedagogues actually do. Even some employers in the health and social sectors seem to know little about the profession (see Tollesfsen 2006). Yet the country educates more disability pedagogues than it does nurses and child welfare pedagogues. Moreover, disability pedagogues often express strong solidarity with other occupations in the public sector. For example, many of them are members of FO (Fellesorganisasjonen; [Solidarity Trade Union], in English translation), alongside, for example, social workers, child welfare pedagogues and nurses.

In addition, disability pedagogues candidly support the International Federation of Social Workers' global goal of promoting, 'social change and development, social cohesion, and the empowerment and liberation of people' (IFSW 2014, no pagination).

Without wanting to balkanize professional boundaries involving pedagogic and social and health professions in Norway, if disability pedagogy has a distinctive signature, then it is this. A disability pedagogue is educated to prevent and/or respond in a solution-focused way to the particular problems facing many disabled children and adults. These persons often find it impossible or difficult to plot and cross a course through routine physical and social spaces in a particular setting or in society at large. Social pedagogic and clinical dexterity are essential tools if the job is to be done properly. So too is the dialogue between disabled and professional communities. Yes, disability pedagogues do help some disabled people to reposition cognitive capacity in a positive way. But the disabled community has a right to engage in this process. Better than anyone, disabled people know and experience the real structural obstacles that so often foil their "get-up-and-go" resolve. As part of their job, educators of all stripes must lobby the policymakers to get rid of these barriers.

13.4   Study Focus

In this study, I investigate the pre-service education of disability pedagogues, as set out in *Section 3 Goals* in accordance with a state-mandated document (briefly referred to earlier): *Rammeplan for vernepleierutdanning* [*The Framework for the Education of Disability Pedagogues*; in Norwegian]. The year of implementation was 2005, but the criteria in the document still hold today (2015). The *Framework* (2005) contains two main parts

1. General criteria for the education of, among others, disability pedagogues, child welfare pedagogues, social workers and nurses. This sets out the common content for the education of all these professions.

2. Specific criteria for the education of disability pedagogues. This sets out specific content for the education of disability pedagogues.

For now, I concentrate almost exclusively on the *Section 3 Goals*, which contains specific criteria for the education of disability pedagogues. Disability pedagogy, I should add, is commonly referred to as a social pedagogic profession, but involves some clinical work too. Although the *Framework* (2005) explicitly refers to social pedagogy, it also—and this is a bit confusing—refers to psychosocial environmental rehabilitation. The latter designation broadly refers, but in unnecessarily complex language, to social pedagogic work.

I am especially interested in the social pedagogic aspects of the *Framework*'s (2005) content. There are two reasons: first, my chapter is part of an international anthology on comparative pedagogy; second, a distinguishing feature of disability pedagogy is its anchorage in social pedagogy. A tentative definition of the discipline is therefore appropriate. Following Natorp (1904, p. 94), a founding thinker:

> 'The social aspects of education, broadly understood, and the educational aspects of social life constitute this science' [social pedagogy].

In a stroke of genius, Natorp (1904) has spotted the *social in the educational* and the *educational* in the *social*. This might sound obvious. Yet the dichotomization of the "social" and the "educational" into separate spheres has strong roots because social care and schooling have often been regarded as separate functions. Yet for Natorp (1904, p. 94), 'The concept of social pedagogy recognises that the education of the individual … is socially conditioned'. For all the discernment in Natorp's (1904) work, his position is a finding, not a discovery. The educational and the social spheres have always been interlocked, but this relationship has frequently been overlooked (Stephens 2013).

Like other social scientific disciplines, social pedagogy has been used for benign and malign aims: for example, promoting perceived collective efficacy among oppressed groups (Freire 1996); and indoctrinating the Hitler Youth into Nazi ideology (Sünker and Otto 1997). I often think of social pedagogy as a rose with many names. These names include "emancipatory pedagogy" and "critical pedagogy". Having said that, *you know social pedagogy when you see it*, because it is a discipline always present in the dance between the social and the pedagogic. The two are inseparable.

13.5 Norwegian Disability Pedagogy: The Political Mandate

The preparation of pedagogues who will later help people who are disabled to understand, in union and solidarity with them, that they can reach beyond the limits of agency they bravely fight is a prodigious task. I am reminded of Habermas's (2005, p. 56) conviction that, 'The concept of humanity obliges us to take up the "we"-perspective from which we perceive one another as members of an *inclusive* community no person is excluded from.' In that regard, the Norwegian Framework (2005) has gone a long way—but still has a longer way to go—in putting what Florian and Linklater (2010, p. 372) speak of as the 'ethic of everybody' into tangible practice. I am, without apology, impatient about speeding up the journey; notwithstanding, it is encouraging to see that the politicians understand how important it is to turn rhetoric into action. I shall say more about the practical side of things later.

The good news is that the state-sanctioned directive for intending disability pedagogues is unequivocal. The edict is articulated in a parliamentary document, *Rammeplan for vernepleierutdanning* (*The Framework for the Education of Disability Pedagogues*; in Norwegian 2005). Disability pedagogy educators have got what they want: a mandate from the Department of Research and Education (Utdannings- og forskningsdepartementet) to prepare disability pedagogues for work that is based, 'on egalitarian principles', as well as a clear 'focus on service user influence and participation' (*Framework* 2005; 3). The aim is ambitious; but why settle for "less bad" instead of "much better"? The compilers of the *Framework* (2005) understand this, by establishing common disciplinary [in the subject sense] standard, regardless of the course provider. Common purpose must be maintained and protected throughout the country.

I know this might sound rather prescriptive. However, the politicians have delineated fundamental markers without filling in details. The upshot is enough wiggle room for disability pedagogue educators to exercise reasonable judgment regarding finer points, so long as they keep to the bold outlines. That said, certain criteria are non-negotiable. For example, student disability pedagogues are expected to, 'Identify interests, resources & limitations in cooperation with service users' (ibid, 3).

In addition, the *Framework* (2005, 3) requires disability pedagogy students to show the, 'Ability to analyse and map the relationship between societal conditions and individual service user circumstances'. If the policymakers achieve the outcome they seek, the removal, or at least the amelioration, of potential obstacles to inclusive policy will get the chance it deserves.

There are echoes of radical sociology and emancipatory social pedagogy in these enunciations, and that inspires me. Later in the chapter, I have constructed a more systematic oversight of the specific criteria that apply to the education of disability pedagogue students, as prescribed in the Section 3 goals of the *Framework* (2005). I have used document analysis and semantic coding for the purpose. For now, though, I shall consider words and (some) action in policymaking circles.

13.6 Time to Walk the Walk

It is all very well to make grandiose statements, but if they count for nothing, then the words are just words. The important issue of the extent to which the stated intentions of the Framework have brought about inclusive action on the ground, while not the focus of my study, certainly merits further research. Yet even though I am not able to say whether or not political prose and inclusive pedagogic practice are in harmony, it is pertinent to note that Norway invests quite heavily in Universal Design (UD). This, in turn, surely enhances the parity between systemic enablement and the individual experience of inclusivity. At this suture, disability pedagogues are usually adept at finding the right balance between support and bossiness. The emphasis is always though on bringing social justice into social structure. The rationale is persuasive. Many disabled people actually become experts in UD through hit-and-miss encounters. That sounds positive, but in a civilised society like Norway, it is unacceptable. Why, for example, fit button door openers—not always easy for wheelchair users to access—after the fact? It would be better to instal electronic sensors right from the start. This would benefit everyone, including wheelchair users and professors carrying bundles of books. Forgive the cliché, but surely this is "win, win". Equally important, the design is inclusive and respectful, and it does reverberate with Framework (2005) aspirations.

Once UD becomes "normalised", that is, made mainstream, practical benefits aside, it reduces social stigma. In addition, many non-disabled people can gain from UD, as briefly exemplified above, even though it generally targets the disabled community. Consider voice command software, for instance. A simple oral command—'Fix slow download'—would surely appeal to all PC and Mac users. Similarly, curb cuts are a helpful and an inclusive UD innovation. Disability groups introduced them in the city of San Francisco on a 1970s "peace and love" wave. The primary aim was to improve wheelchair user mobility in urban areas. Today, this innovation is quite widespread in urban areas. Cheap and easy to produce, curb cuts improve mobility for those who use grocery carts, wheeled luggage and other forms of pedestrian transport.

Another enabling device, closed-caption decoder TVs, also assist diverse populations: not only those who are hard of hearing or deaf, but for people for whom English is a second language and early readers. Although the advancement of UD in Norway is an unfinished project, publicly funded assistive design and technology is establishing itself as a cornerstone of disability policy. I am optimistic that this investment will further the social pedagogic aim of raising pedagogic capacity because UD holds great potential for lifting perceived self-efficacy. It is also a compassionate form of engineering, uniting Heart and Head in the service of kind acts. That way, the circle is rounded, so to speak.

To round off this section on an up-beat note, public spending on top quality assistive technology has become a major priority, to the extent that Nordic nations are often seen as role models in the development of new and innovative UD. The accolade is deserved because Norway is slowly but surely moving towards a society in which the empowerment of disabled people is taking hold. Disability pedagogy is an important part of this story. Students and practitioners of the discipline study and work in a country in which the welfare state spends relatively more on families, unemployment, sick leave, disability support and health than most other OECD countries (OECD 2014). This is the "walking the walk" part.

It is evidence of government policy that places principle over mere profit, of understanding in policymaking circles that platitudes about good public services are no substitute for responsible social investment. There is an important rider here, and it is this. Such investment is not charity, but rather an outlay that holds the promise of rich returns. The bounty is a future in which, for example, all people can uncomplicatedly get to and from work on public transport (and contribute to economic growth) because universal design—the authentic, complete kind—is put in place. It also signals the triumph of magnanimity over pettiness in public affairs. Even more importantly, generous spending is a pre-emptive rather than an after-the-fact measure. It helps disabled people to get up and going on their own terms right from the starting block, not from way behind it.

Another encouraging finding, which should please disability pedagogues, is reported in a cross-national comparison of social justice in the member states of the OECD (Schraad-Tischler 2011). The investigation found that these nations are well ahead on a Justice Index which uses six criteria: poverty prevention, access to education, labour market inclusion, social cohesion and non-discrimination, health, and intergenerational justice (e.g. consistency in family and pension policies). Overall, Iceland and Norway were judged to be the most socially just countries, ranking first and second, respectively.

It is now time to look at the core principles that disability pedagogy educators are obliged to follow, as approved in the *Framework* (2005), a thin document (just 12 pages in total, most of them devoted to the specific content for the education of disability pedagogues), but with words carefully and sincerely chosen.

13.7   The Remit

See Table 13.1.

Table 13.1 Specific content for the education of disability pedagogues: section 3: goals

Semantic codes	Illustrative text
Able & keen to support needs & protect rights	Possess knowledge, skills and attitudes that support the needs of varying types of disability Attend to service user interests through multi-professional cooperation In accordance with institutional principles and law, protect service users' needs and rights Mentor, teach, tend to and care for people who want and need support
Respect for human dignity	Ensure that professional practice is based on egalitarian values and respect for the service user's integrity

(continued)

Table 13.1 (continued)

Semantic codes	Illustrative text
Show empathy, respect and equality	Engage the service user with empathy, respect and as an equal, irrespective of age, sex, culture, belief and interpretation of reality
Foster perceived self- and collective efficacy ("mastery")	Plan and conduct practical & methodical psycho-social environmental [i.e., social pedagogic] work, emphasising well-being and optimal mastery Ability to foster agentic change in the best interests of individual service users & groups of service users
Cooperation, user participation and user influence	Identify interests, resources and limitations in cooperation with service users Focus on service user influence and participation
Possess necessary clinical skills	Understand the consequences of different performance challenges and the most common somatic and psychological disorders Provide appropriate medication Understand normal development and developmental disabilities
Communicate and negotiate ethically	Communicate and negotiate in an ethical way with service users and affected parties, such as relatives
Critique ideologies in policy circles, comply with local and national decisions, & map societal/individual circumstances	Appraise ideologies and resources in the health and social apparatus and act on decisions made at local and national levels Ability to analyse and map the relationship between societal conditions and individual service user circumstances
Critique own practice	Document, evaluate and secure high quality professional work
Handling conflict	Prevent and deal with different types of conflict

13.8 Discussion

Throughout its 50-year long history in Norway, the education and training of disability pedagogues has been and still is primarily focused on supporting people who have developmental difficulties of one kind or another. At the same time, disability pedagogues have extended their social pedagogic and clinical skills to other areas of care. Arguably, the main function of the disability pedagogue is to nurture perceived individual and collective efficacy. On the societal level, this involves standing up for people who are rarely given the chance to assert their right to active user participation and to do this in cooperation with disability pedagogues.

Provided that clinical and social/pedagogic support from disability pedagogues is available, people who have developmental difficulties can learn, rehearse and practise change agency in order to improve life quality. The fostering of pedagogic ambition is vital here because it can sustain optimal performance, even when things get tough. The celebration of empathic forms of communication, signals the concern that the disability pedagogue is expected to have as regards personhood and the will to cooperate rather than, except on rare occasions, to "force" a position. …. Bernstein's (2000, p. 201) distinction between 'official pedagogic modalities' and 'local pedagogic modalities' comes to mind here. Furthermore, the inclusion of the user's view (stated in the user's language) places necessary limits on what Lewis (2003, p. 23) calls, 'doing-to, rather than doing-for or doing-with the client', or on, to cite Bourdieu et al. (1999, p. 2), 'setting up the objectivising distance that reduces the individual to a specimen in a display case.'

There is a clear recognition in the *Framework* (2005) that expert knowledge not only resides in knowledgeable care professionals, but also with the disabled person. Moreover, the anticipation is that the two different kinds of expert will engage in respectful, cooperative dialogue, each having a voice that should be taken seriously by the other. Sure, the voices might not always concur. Nevertheless, the aim is to nurture democratic discourse instead of letting the disability pedagogue trump the other party through professional misuse of communicative weight. It is pertinent to note here that some people with intellectual disabilities are not always aware of their rights, in which case disability pedagogues might sometimes have to support those rights by proxy.

When **conflict** does arise, as it surely does, handling the situation in a conciliatory manner is essential. **Respect for the human dignity of the other person** is considered paramount here. The *Framework* (2005) puts great stock too on critical judgment, both through **self-scrutiny** and by engaging in **debates on the political level**. Permit me a short comment on this last matter. The expectation that disability pedagogues should get involved in political debate and also follow a "curriculum" comprised by the political elite, rings a bit hollow. Indeed, it seems something of an oxymoron.

In conclusion, it appears to me that the call to serve people who are marginalised—in this particular example, those with disabilities—is sealed by the political imprimatur of the Norwegian welfare state. It is a plea based on the mutually supporting values of empathy, solidarity and social justice, which together shore up the principle of *ego sum meus frater custodies* ("I am my brother's/sister's keeper"). In this regard, the *Framework* (2005) holds the student disability pedagogue accountable for social justice-based practice. For all that, it is salutary to reiterate, once again, that the document announces a political goal, not a guaranteed outcome. If political rhetoric alone could turn the heart towards righteous action, then there would be cause for celebration. In this concise chapter, I have cited some real examples of inclusive practice, notably, UD, that certainly do align with political intentions. The next step might be to conduct a quantitative study in order to find out if the *Framework* (2005) can be considered as an independent predictor of certain envisaged outcomes. But that's another story for another time!

References

Bandura, A. (1997). *Self-efficacy*. New York: W.H. Freeman and Company.
Bernstein, B. (2000). *Pedagogy, symbolic control and identity*. Lanham, Maryland: Rowman & Littlefield Publishers Inc. (Revised Edition).
Bourdieu, P., et al. (1999). *The weight of the world*. Cambridge: Polity Press.
Cameron, C., Petrie, P., Wigfall, V., Kleipoedszus, S., & Jasper, A. (2011). *Final report of the social pedagogy pilot programme: Development and implementation*. London: Thomas Coram Research Unit, Institute of Education, University of London.
Coussée, F., Bradt, L., Roose, R., & Bouverne-De Bie, M. (2010). The emerging social pedagogical paradigm in UK child and youth care: Deus Ex machina or walking the beaten path? *British Journal of Social Work, 40*, 789–805.
Florian, L., & Linklater, H. (2010). Preparing teachers for inclusive education: using inclusive pedagogy to enhance teaching and learning for all. *Cambridge Journal of Education, 40*(4), 369–386.
Habermas, J. (2005). *The future of human nature*. Cambridge: Polity Press.
International Federation of Social Workers' (IFSW). (2014). *Global definition of social work*. Accessed 4 November 2014. http://ifsw.org/policies/definition-of-social-work/ (no pagination).
Lewis, H. (2003). In M. Reisch (Ed.), *For the common good*. New York: Brunner-Routledge.
Natorp, P. (1904). *Sozialpädagogik. Theorie der Willenserziehung auf der Grundlage der Gemeinschaft* [*Social Pedagogy: The theory of community will*; in German]. Stuttgart: Fr. Frommann Verlag (E. Hauff).
OECD. (2014). *Society at a glance 2014. Norway*. Accessed November 3, 2014. http://www.oecd.org/norway/OECD-SocietyAtaGlance2014-Highlights-Norway.pdf
Schraad-Tischler, D. (2011). *Social justice in the OECD—How do the member states compare? Sustainable governance indicators 2011 Gütersloh*. Germany: Bertelsmann Stiftung.
Stephens, P. (2009). The nature of social pedagogy: An excursion into Norwegian territory. *Child & Family Social Work, 14*, 343–351.
Stephens, P. (2013). *Social pedagogy: Heart and head*. Bremen: Europäischer Hochschulverlag GmbH & Co. KG.
Sünker, H., & Otto, H.-U. (1997). Foreword. In H. Sünker & H.-U.Otto (Eds.), *Education and fascism: Political identity and social education in Nazi Germany* (pp. vii–viii). London: Falmer Press.
Tollefsen, N. (2006). Foreword. In B. Horndalen & Rynning Torp (Eds.). *Vernepleier – utdanning og yrke i et faglig og etisk perspektiv* [*Disability social pedagogues—Education and profession in an academic and ethical perspective*; in Norwegian]. Kjeller, Norway: Høgskolen i Akershus, Skriftserien (no pagination).
Utdannings- og forskningsdepartementet. (2005). *Rammeplan for vernepleierutdanning* [*The Framework for the Education of Disability Pedagogues*]; (in Norwegian).

Author Biography

Paul Stephens is Inaugural Professor of Social Pedagogy at the University of Stavanger, Norway. He published the first known English textbook of Social Pedagogy in 2013. Currently, he is writing an academic book on Social Pedagogy and social justice. He received a B.Sc. Hons and a Ph.D. in Sociology from the University of London.

Part III
Teacher Education, Partnerships and Collaboration

Introduction

The common law of partnership is a general form of organization for the pursuit of mutual interest and now very common also in government as a means for engaging citizens in governance activities which is a collaboration permitted and enabled through new forms of digital open government based on co-creation, co-design, and co-evaluation of public services and public goods.[1] Education fits into this schema and offers important opportunities for partnerships. The overwhelming question that needs to be addressed is the question of power relations between parties, especially when the relationship is between the State and a people, constituency, or institution.

It is possible to distinguish three main notions of partnership as they affect education policy (Peters 2015). The first is strongly connected to the notion of "community" and "governance" when viewed from the perspective of a liberal democratic theory of governance; the second is the notion of partnership inherent in the notion of "public private partnerships" (PPP); and the third is a concept of partnership construed as "collaboration". The first two notions are notions that have surfaced within neoliberal and Third Way politics. In general, these terms mask power relations. The third is more visionary and arises in the context of the social knowledge economy as a form of collaboration that builds on the principles of social media.

The principles of consultation, participation and informed consent are useful operating principles for partnership but the critical discourse of partnership in policy terms requires an understanding of the political context. As Fairclough (2008) notes in his presentation "Participation and partnership: a critical discourse analysis perspective on the dialectics of regulation and democracy":

The first part of this introduction is based on Peters (2014) 'Education as the Power of Collaboration.'

---

[1]See e.g. http://www.opengovpartnership.org/ and http://www.p21.org/.

- Participants bring different construals of the event/process, expectations about how to proceed and orientations to being a participant, from official sources or experiences.
- They bring different semiotic resources: discourses, genres and styles; intertextual and interdiscursive chains, relations of recontextualization.
- 'Pre-constructed' resources are drawn upon plus articulated together in potentially innovative, novel, creative, surprising ways.

He goes on to conclude that that "regulated forms of participation/partnership may be spaces of dialectic between democracy and regulation and of emergence of democratic moments".

"Partnership" as conceived by the neoliberal policy regime is intended to draw together state, market, and civil society in pursuit of entrepreneurial goals which really means that the rhetoric of governance and partnership actually shifts responsibility from states onto communities. We might see official rhetoric about partnership as part of government technology or technocracy, Foucault might use the term "governmentality" as a means of describing the coordinating grassroots social democratic community action with capacity-building from above. Under managerialism this kind of partnership bypasses community partnership and replaces genuine local democracy with performance management techniques often dressed up in terms of "empowerment" and "engagement". Often the language of partnership is policy speak for "working together" with no specification of shared partnership responsibilities or processes for decision-making.

A dominant neoliberal form of partnership, the so-called public–private partnership (PPP), is relevant to the policy discourse of partnership, although it can simply be a term for a government service funded through the private sector. In the period 1999–2009 some 1400 PPP deals were brokered in the EU with capital value of €260 billion, however, since the global financial crisis of 2008 these deals have declined by about 40% (Kappeler and Nemoz 2010). Fennell (2010) reports that PPP has been embraced by agencies such as the World Bank as a possible way to ensure access to education by bolstering demand-driven provision as well as more cost-effective supply of education (World Bank 2004, 2005; Tooley and Dixon 2003). Fennell focuses on how such partnerships affect the educational experience and outcomes of the poor. She notes that PPP as a means of promoting universal access has "added to the number of non-state providers of schools in the last two decades" and seems quite sanguine about this prospect. By comparison Ball suggests: "The 'reform' of the public service sector is a massive new profit opportunity for business... the outsourcing of education services is worth at least £1.5 billion a year" (Ball 2007, pp. 39–40). Others have asked why PPP have become "a favoured management tool of governments, corporations, and international development agencies" (Robertson and Verger 2012) and they remark:

when governance is located in multiple sites, both the governance of educational PPPs, and PPPs as a tool of governance over the education sector, becomes problematic. Who is the relevant authority? Who is affected by decisions of various governments, transnational firms, foundations, international agencies or consultants? From whom should those affected by decisions seek account? Is the managerial discourse on risk taking appropriate for the distribution of a public good as education? Does managerial governance, with its focus on outputs and efficiency pay sufficient attention to the complexity of education processes? (p. 15).

The notion of co-production, which has gained currency in the last 10 years, offers another perspective on the nature of and possibilities arising from partnerships across sectors, institutions, and individuals. Peters (2015) challenges us to think of partnerships as "co-labor-ation" in the co-production of public goods. In their manifesto for co-production, the New Economics Foundation (2008) suggested that the traditional public economy of service is failing because "Neither markets nor centralised bureaucracies are effective models for delivering public services based on relationships" (p. 8); … "Professionals need their clients as much as the clients need professionals" and "Social networks make change possible" (p. 8). The Foundation defined the concept of co-production in the following way: "Co-production means delivering public services in an equal and reciprocal relationship between professionals, people using services, their families and their neighbours" (Slay and Robinson 2010, para. 2).

The term co-production was first developed by Ostrom (1996) who used it "to explain to the Chicago police why the crime rate went up when the police came off the beat and into patrol cars," "explaining why the police need the community as much as the community need the police" (Stephens et al. 2008, para. 1). Anna Coote and others (Coote 2002) at the Institute for Public Policy Research use the concept to explain "why doctors need patients as much as patients need doctors and that, when that relationship is forgotten, both sides fail" (para. 2). Cahn (2000) used it to explain how critical family and community relationships were part of a core economy, originally called *oekonomika* (para. 3). This reciprocity and mutual help and exchange at the very heart of the social economy is built upon principles that view citizens as equal partners in the design and delivery of services, not passive recipients of public services. Co-production is about a mutual and reciprocal partnership between professionals and citizens who engage and make use of peer, social and personal networks as the best way of transferring knowledge and supporting change. As the New Economics Foundation's (2008) manifesto suggested, co-production "devolve[d] real responsibility, leadership and authority to 'users', and encourage[d] self-organization rather than direction from above" (p. 13). This understanding has much to offer to our understanding and enactment of partnership and collaboration in education.

This aspect of co-production while enhanced and facilitated by new social media, has its home in a theory of the commons, a policy of personalization and a political theory of anarchism that collectively forms around peer-to-peer relationships and that replaces the old emphasis on the autonomous individual. This conception becomes even more helpful as the new logic of the public sphere when the notion of co-creation and co-design sit alongside co-production.

Partnerships and collaboration are two ideas that have transformed teacher education and enhanced teacher professional learning, enquiry and research. The Association for Teacher Education in Europe, 40th Annual Conference, in Glasgow (2015) on "Teacher Education through Partnerships and Collaborative Learning

Communities" recognized "the complex, diverse and changing contexts in which teachers work means that they need to revise, add to and enhance their knowledge and skills continually throughout their careers and engage in different forms of professional development according to their own and their pupils' needs." The conference web site unpacks the theme further recognizing the need for "blended professional learning" that demands collaborative approaches and calls "for stronger partnerships that help connect teachers with their peers in their own school and in other schools and enable greater interaction and interdependence between different teacher education providers and stakeholders". The conference organizers refer to The Council of the European Union's conclusions to its 20th May 2014 statement on effective teacher education (2014/C 183/05) that recognizes the potential of enhanced cooperation, partnership and networking with a broad range of stakeholders. The Council's conclusions acknowledged that teacher education programmes: *"should draw on teachers' own experience and seek to foster cross-disciplinary and collaborative approaches, so that education institutions and teachers regard it as part of their task to work in cooperation with relevant stakeholders such as colleagues, parents and employers."*

How to establish and sustain partnerships between teacher education providers and schools, across the different levels of the education sector, amongst clusters of schools at the same and different schooling levels, and between schools and their communities—is currently a focus for policy development and research worldwide. This section illustrates some of the diverse ways this can be achieved. The chapters provide an indication of the breadth of possibilities—the breadth of theoretical and practical foci that are available and can usefully be taken up as a forum for partnership and collaboration.

References

Association for Teacher Education in Europe, The. (2015). *Teacher education through partnerships and collaborative learning communities* [Conference Theme] at the 40th Annual Conference, Glasgow. Retrieved from http://www.gla.ac.uk/schools/education/atee2015/conferencetheme/

Ball, S. J. (2007). *Understanding private sector participation in public sector education.* New York, NY: Routledge.

Cahn, E. (2000). *No more throwaway people: The co-production imperative.* Washington, DC: Essential Books.

Coote, A. (2002, May). *Claiming the health dividend: Unlocking the benefits of NHS spending* [Report Summary]. Retrieved from https://www.kingsfund.org.uk/sites/files/kf/field/field_publication_file/claiming-health-dividend-unlocking-benefits-nhs-spending-summary-anna-coote-kings-fund-1-may-2002_0.pdf

Council of the European Union, The. (2014, May). *The conclusions to its 20th statement on effective teacher education, 2014/C 183/05.* Retrieved from http://eur-lex.europa.eu/legal-content/EN/TXT/?qid=1480301117938&uri=CELEX:52014XG0614(05)

Fairclough, N. (2008). *Partnership, governance and participatory democracy: A critical discourse analysis perspective on the dialectics of regulation and democracy[PowerPoint slides].*

Coimbra, Portugal: Centro de Estudos Sociais, Universidade de Coimba. Retrieved from http://www.ces.uc.pt/eventos/passados2008.php

Fennell, S. (2010). Public-private partnerships and educational outcomes: New conceptual and methodological approaches [RECOUP Working Paper No. 37]. *Research consortium on educational outcomes and poverty WP10/37*. Retrieved from http://ceid.educ.cam.ac.uk/researchprogrammes/recoup/publications/workingpapers/WP37-PPP_and_Educational_Outcomes.pdf

Kappeler, A., & Nemoz, M. (2010). *Public-private partnerships in Europe—Before and during the recent financial crisis* (Economic and Financial Report 2010/04, July, European Investment Bank). Retrieved from www.eib.org/epec/resources/efr_epec_PPP_report.pdf

New Economics Foundation. (2008). *Co-production: A manifesto for growing the core economy*. Retrieved from http://www.stockport.gov.uk/2013/2996/41105/nefcoproduction

Ostrom, E. (1996). Crossing the great divide: Coproduction, synergy and development. *World Development, 24*(6), 1073–1087.

Peters, M. A. (2014). Education as the Power of Collaboration

Peters, M. A. (2015). Education as the power of partnership: The context of co-labor-ation. *Knowledge Cultures, 3*(5), 2327–5731.

Robertson, S. L., & Verger, A. (2012). *Governing education through public private partnerships*, published by the Centre for Globalisation, Education and Societies, University of Bristol, Bristol BS8 1JA, UK at: Retrieved from http://susanleerobertson.com/publications/

Slay, J. & Robinson, B. (2010). *In this together: Building knowledge about co-production*. London: New Economics Foundation.

Stephens, L., Ryan-Collins, J., & Boyle, D. (2008). *Co-production: A manifesto for growing the core economy*. London: New Economics Foundation.

Tooley, J., & Dixon, P. (2003). *Private schools for the poor: A case study from India*. [Research Paper]. Reading, UK: CfBT. Retrieved from http://www.centralsquarefoundation.org/wp-content/uploads/2016/02/Private-Schools-For-The-Poor-A-case-study-from-India.pdf

World Bank. (2003). *World development report 2004: Making services work for poor people*. Washington, DC. Retrieved from https://openknowledge.worldbank.org/handle/10986/5986

World Bank. (2005). *Mobilizing the private sector for public education*. A PEPG —World Bank Conference, A Harvard—World Bank Conference, October 5–6, 2005 Kennedy School of Government, Harvard University. Retrieved from http://www.ksg.harvard.edu/pepg/conferences/MPSPEpapers.htm

Chapter 14
Repositioning, Embodiment and the Experimental Space: Refiguring Student–Teacher Partnerships in Teacher Education

Helen Cahill and Julia Coffey

14.1 Introduction

This chapter provides an introduction to the feminist post-structuralist theory of change used to inform the pedagogical design of the Learning Partnerships program. It analyses data gathered from surveys, focus groups and in-depth interviews with the school students and trainee teachers involved in various iterations of the program. The respondents cite the humanising effect of the encounter and point to the way in which it builds their confidence to communicate with and understand each other's perspectives. The process has them rethink who each other are and who they can 'be' in their encounters. Findings from this research include recommendations for use of a 'third space' for exploratory exchange between client and professional as an element within teacher education. It highlights the need to foster socially critical thinking as well as knowledge and skill development as core to the teacher development process.

Participants in the Learning Partnerships workshops are positioned as co-investigators considering matters of shared concern. In this they are positioned in a way which disrupts the confining binary of teacher–student. They engage in a number of drama-based tasks in which they depict and deconstruct common patterns of interaction that occur between teachers and students. This process provides an opportunity for them to examine the discourses that work to limit honest and helpful exchange in teacher–student relationships. The shared engagement in deconstruction has a connective and humanising effect. Working in partnership helps to generate new possibilities in relation to help-seeking and problem-solving.

H. Cahill (✉)
University of Melbourne, Melbourne, Australia
e-mail: h.cahill@unimelb.edu.au

J. Coffey
University of Newcastle, Callaghan, Australia
e-mail: julia.coffey@newcastle.edu.au

© Springer Nature Singapore Pte Ltd. 2017
M.A. Peters et al. (eds.), *A Companion to Research in Teacher Education*,
DOI 10.1007/978-981-10-4075-7_14

As they embody and articulate the internal dialogue of thoughts and feelings which shape their interactions, the participants engage in a form of identity work, and come to recognise themselves and each other differently. As they embody and enact the underpinning fears, hopes and desires that sit behind the performance of the teacher–student role-set, they rethink what is possible in teacher–student relations, and come to understand the two parties as being 'on the same side' rather than as existing in opposition.

14.2 Working with Theory

Post-structural theory is brought to analysis of teacher development to direct attention to the ways in which discourses, institutional regimes and dividing practices work to shape what is possible in relationships.

Post-structural theory offers an ongoing critique of humanism, including the understanding of the self or subject. Drawn largely from the work of Foucault (1980) and expanded numerous feminist authors (St. Pierre and Pillow 2000; Butler 1993; Davies 1993), this approach contends that people inherit a way of understanding the world established in the discourses or sets of cultural ideas, explanatory models and practices that preexist and surround them. Through the concept of subjectivity, post-structural theories highlight the influence of social norms upon attitudes, practices and behaviours. However the 'individual' is not understood to be fixed or static within this process of shaping; but rather is fluid, with an ongoing capacity for change.

Foucault (1980) argues that the production of our sense of who we are involves learning key categories that include and exclude. We learn to categorise and play into binaries such as teacher–student. As people observe the patterns around them, they internalise social norms and expectations and learn to self-monitor and enact the categories that pertain to themselves and others. From this theory it can be seen that teachers and students will be shaped by the practices of the institution as well as by their notions of what it means to be student or teacher. They will play into (or resist) their understood positions and confer the appropriate status and expectations upon the other. Thus to change the teacher–student relationship, it will be important to address the defining discourses which help to hold them in place.

14.3 Positioning

A key concept garnered from feminist post-structural theory is that of positioning (see Davies 2006). The concept of positioning is a way of understanding the formation of subjectivity as an ongoing process of taking up and/or resisting of the various subject positions, patterns and storylines available within the discourses and practices of a society. Thus teacher is not only a role—but also a position—defined by the interlocking binary of teacher–student.

The concept of positioning opens the idea that one's sense of self is shaped by broader social discourses about who and how to be. One of the pedagogical implications arising from a shift from a focus on role to a focus on positioning is the presumption that it will not be sufficient to focus only on developing the skills and knowledge associated with performing the role of teacher. Rather there will also be a need to critically engage with the way in which social norms, and discourses influence their very sense of what is possible and desirable. A post-structural feminist model of change presumes that a collective process, incorporating critical engagement, will assist the participants to articulate and recognise the shaping discourses, conditions and practices that hold things in place. This suggests the importance of emphasising the constructions of the thinking spaces that underpin the binaries of teacher/learner, expert/novice which tend to infuse teacher–student interactions.

14.4 Post-structural Theory of Change

Consequently, it is important to engage teachers in examining the influence of the traditions and discourses that preexist their position. This requires a pedagogical design which structures opportunities for critical thought, and methods for catching the discourses at work in shaping desires, presumptions, perceptions and behaviour.

Davies argues that for people to create change in patterns of behaviour they must engage in a threefold task through which they (a) identify the shaping discourses which influence their senses of what is acceptable or appropriate; (b) catch these discourses at play in shaping their responses; and (c) work collectively with others to imagine and enable new possibilities (Davies 1993). The work of deconstruction is posited to open the space for reconstruction, generating the possibility that things can be done differently. Davies argues that the conditions of possibility affect the choices people make: "choice stems not so much from the individual, but from the conditions of possibility—the discourses which prescribe not only what is desirable, but what is recognisable as an acceptable form of subjectivity" (Davies et al. 2001, p. 172). From this theoretical premise, approaches to improving teacher–student relationships will need to engage with the social discourses that influence the "conditions of possibility" in interactions between students and teachers.

One of the challenges educators face in engaging participants in the process of deconstruction is that dominant discourses tend to remain unnoted and therefore pass by without critique. A key challenge for the educator, then, is to find pedagogical strategies which assist students to detect the shaping influence of dominant stories.

Working from this premise, it is important to find pedagogical strategies which help to make visible the ways in which hegemonic cultural stories "teach" ways to understand the "problem" and suggest "conclusions" about the possibility of taking action.

In response to this challenge, the *Learning Partnerships* program works from the premise that teachers need to learn *with* and *from* rather than just *about* young people. The program brings classes of school students into the academy to engage in workshops with pre-service teachers. Workshops are usually of around 1.5–2 h in length and combine a class of around 25 school students with a class of approximately 30 pre-service teachers. School students may be drawn from any year level, though typically high school students are drawn from Years 7 to 10 (ages 12 to 16).

The students are positioned as advisors and as co-investigators. This process repositions both students and trainee teachers, locating them as co-investigators. The parties are invited out of their binary roles as providers-recipients and located in an exploratory learning space.

The *Learning Partnerships* program sets out to straddle the theory–practice divide by demarcating a space for exploration and experiment. It uses a participatory pedagogical approach to provide a 'third space' for learning in which school students and pre-service teachers can explore issues pertaining to student engagement and well-being. This third space is designed to disrupt the dominant relational binaries of teacher–student and youth-adult and the traditional institutional binary of theory–practice, school-university.

14.5 The Program and Research Methods

Learning Partnerships was initiated by the first author as a Ph.D. research project (2002–2008). It has been implemented within the medical curriculum and in pre-service teacher education at the University of Melbourne in the period of 2003–2014. The methods and resultant data are described in more detail elsewhere (Cahill 2011, 2012, 2015; Cahill et al. 2011, 2015; Cahill and Coffey 2013b).

The data used here draws both from the initial Ph.D. research and from a subsequent study. In the 'first wave', the Ph.D. study (2002–2008) the workshops involving 30 pre-service teacher and 25 Year 9/10 students were led by the first author and took place within a core subject in the Diploma of Education (Secondary) at the University of Melbourne. The first author uses her reflective notes and video-taped recordings of the 2003 workshop as source of data for the workshop narrative, and audio-taped interviews with students and teachers conducted post-workshop. The Learning Partnership workshop of 1.5 h included 30 pre-service teachers training to become secondary teachers (aged 23–45 years) and a Drama class of 25 Year 9/10 students (aged 15–16 years). It was conducted within a core subject in the Diploma of Education called *Education Policy, Schools and Society*. The subject addresses the role of schooling in society and explores issues of equity and inclusion. Interviews were conducted with nine students (five females and four males) and nine teachers (eight females and one male) from the 2003 cohort. Ethics approval was provided for this research by University of

Melbourne, and by the Education Department of Victoria. The data was collected as part of the first author's Ph.D. research.

In the 'second wave' of data collection (2013), the *Learning Partnerships* workshops were housed within an elective subject *Promoting Student Wellbeing* provided within The Master of Teaching (Secondary) at the University of Melbourne, Australia. These workshops were led variously by the first author and four colleagues, each of whom conducted workshops with their own classes of around 30 pre-service teachers and 20–25 school students. The second author gathered the data from the subsequent study, conducting post-workshop focus groups with teacher trainees (11 females, four males) and school students from Years 7–9 (47 females, 22 males). Focus groups were audio-recorded and transcribed verbatim. Using techniques described by Willis (2006), and focus group data was thematically analysed with two researchers cross-checking themes to ensure rigour (Alsford 2012).

Survey data was also collected post-workshop in the second wave of the study. Data was collected from 120 pre-service teachers and 125 secondary school students from four schools in metropolitan Melbourne, Australia. The research participants were members of five different *Learning Partnerships* workshops which took place in the *Promoting Student Wellbeing* elective. Two of the workshops were run with Year 10 students (aged 15–16), two with Year 9 students (aged 14–15), and one with Year 7 students (aged 12–13). Each workshop of around 2 h in length included approximately 25 school students with a class of approximately 30 pre-service teachers. Full details about the instruments and the data collected are available elsewhere (Cahill and Coffey 2013a, b). Ethics approval study was obtained from the University of Melbourne (2012 study: HREC 1237767.1) and the Department of Education and Early Childhood Development in July 2012. The second wave of the research was conducted with financial support in the form of a grant from the CASS Foundation.

In the following section, we focus on techniques used during both waves of research to involve participants in detecting and deconstructing the discourses that inform teacher–student relations, with the aim of shaping more generous modes of interaction between the two parties. In doing so, we highlight the role that theory can play in informing teacher education practice and analysis of participants responses both within and after the workshops.

14.6 Pedagogical Approach Used in the Learning Partnerships Workshops

The workshops employ a dialogic pedagogy to bring students and teachers variously into pairs and small groups in which students contribute as key informants providing their advice to teachers. Participants also engage in collaborative tasks in which they work to document and describe both the factors that enhance and those that detract from learning and connectedness. A series of paired sharing, small group and plenary exchanges provide opportunity for the pre-service teachers to consult students about what they find contributes to their well-being and engagement in learning. A further series of short performative tasks are used as a medium to investigate the concerns that influence teacher and student behaviours. These short role-plays are then used as the context within which to explore how teachers can effectively intervene in response to the issues within the scenario. The students provide formative feedback and advice to those in role as teacher, as well as demonstrations to communicate what they find to be effective forms of intervention or support on the part of the teacher. Common issues used as the basis for these problem-solving exercises include failure to submit assignments on time, experiences of peer bullying or emotional distress, and student manifestations of boredom, misbehaviour or lack of application to set tasks. For a more detailed account of the workshop methodology see (Cahill 2011, 2012, 2015; Cahill et al. 2011, 2015; Cahill and Coffey 2013b).

A narrative is provided below which describes some of the interactions in a typical workshop. It is drawn from the first wave of the research. It is followed by analysis of the qualitative data that was gathered in post-workshop interviews with the participating students and teachers. This narrative is provided to illustrate the way in which post-structural theory was translated into pedagogical practice, and to show how theory was used to critique or analyse practice. The workshop format was closely replicated in subsequent workshops in the second wave of the study, with similar responses from participants. A subsequent round of data collected in this second wave shows that although led by different facilitators, working with different groups of students and teachers, the workshops were similarly appraised, indicating that the intervention can be readily replicated.

14.6.1 Workshop Narrative from First Wave of the Study

An initial meet and greet exercise has teachers and students paired, and set the task of finding some things they have in common. The students are then asked to comment on what contribution teachers can make by engaging in simple small talk with their students. This activity builds relationships, and helps students to develop the sense that their teachers are approachable.

The next task is a paired role-play exercise, in which the student-teacher dyads are asked to engage in a 'Complaints Game'. First they play in role as teachers complaining about the tough week they have had. After a few minutes of play, they are asked to replay a snippet of their scene in a 'channel surfing' exercise whereby the class gets a quick look at each of the scenarios, lingering just long enough on each to gain a flavour of the encounter. A ten second glimpse at each of the pairs allows just enough time for the audience to encounter their complaints. The sweep around the room fulfils the role of a brainstorm. A listing and echoing of complaints is heard. The scene is then inverted, with players asked to repeat the exercise but this time taking the roles of two Year 10 students. Another channel surfing shows the student side of the complaints 'story'.

The parody invited via 'The Complaints Game' invites exaggeration and distortion. Though the performances are a distortion, they reveal a pattern that operates beyond the personal. What is exaggerated here is the opposition between students and teacher. Made to loom large the scenarios seem to be both true (teachers and students do feel aggrieved) and not true (but not to this heightened extent).

The next task invites participants to deconstruct the patterns that they heightened in the parody. They gather in groups of four to 'reality-test' the scenarios and they talk together about what they actually think teachers and students find hard. They are called on to reality test what has been seen in the complaints game by comparing it to what they believe to be real-life concerns. There is a serious quality to this enquiry that sits upon the previous playfulness of 'The Complaints Game'. After talking in their buzz groups, students and teachers engage in dialogue about what students find stressful or challenging about school life, and about what they believe their teachers can do to help. The students are positioned as key informants, reporting on their world. The teachers work as investigators, seeking the students' views and advice.

Later in the workshop the players work in small groups to create a scene in which something is happening at school which negatively affects the student. They show their selected scene as a freeze frame, and the group reads its message. The students then speak to the message of the scene, using it to help them articulate the effect on their learning, engagement or well-being. They use the fiction to help them describe the reality.

Student is to approach the *Teacher* to seek help in relation to the bullying that he or she has been subjected to. After a few minutes to improvise their scene one pair volunteers to show their work. The scene is replayed. The performance shows the hesitancy in the Student and the tension in the Teacher. Neither wants this moment in their life. They are pinned into a story they do not want. The teacher is abrupt. The student assumes that the teacher does not care.

Volunteers are asked to add to this scenario by stepping into the role of the 'Hidden Thoughts' of the characters. They are asked *What might this person be thinking or feeling but not saying out aloud? What is s/he hoping for? What is s/he afraid of?* the following response is created as the student's hidden thoughts

He is thinking that he should be able to handle this by himself

he is weak if he can't

He is feeling ashamed

like it is all his fault.

He is hoping the teacher will understand,

hoping someone can stop this,

He is afraid that telling will make it worse,

that people will talk about him and think there is something wrong with him,

afraid that the teacher won't take him seriously,

that there will be nothing any one can do to help

and it will just go on and on …

As the players verbalise the hidden thoughts of the character, they fashion a complex and compassionate interpretation of the character. The questioning device presumes a multiplicity of answers and hence a poly-vocal response is created. The class re-teaches the persona of 'student' and the position of the help-seeker who struggles with the barriers of shame and hopelessness.

The Teacher's Hidden Thoughts follow:

She thinks she hasn't got time for this.

She is ashamed because she doesn't know what to do.

She is afraid that she will mess this up,

that she will let the kid down,

that even if she tries to help she will be no use.

She is wishing she could help,

wishing someone could tell her what to do,

wishing the problem could just have a happy ending,

wishing that the student did not have to suffer

wishing that school could just be about learning,

wishing they had taught her how to deal with this when she was still at Uni …

The text of the Hidden Thoughts both emerges from and disrupts the stereotype of unsupportive teacher that we had previously seen played. The Hidden Thoughts reveal that the teacher too is afraid. She feels under-prepared, and concerned because she wants to help but does not know how. The collective re-interpretation speaks a different teacher into being. She is re-fashioned, shifting from unsupportive or not-caring, to unsupported and caring.

Where the naturalistic paradigm favours a more logically coherent and unitary sense of the individual and tends to replicate the type, the "Hidden Thoughts Game" invites an embodied poly-vocality. In this is a particularly powerful mechanism for deconstruction and reconstruction. The players work to speak wide the possibilities of the self. This assists in the crossing of the victim–villain definitional boundary. Rather than demonise, valorize, or patronise the characters, this device assists players to humanise them. In this way, use of a learning activity inspired by post-structuralist theory evokes a more generous understanding of the characters.

14.7 Research Findings from First Wave Study

The interview data collected in the first wave illustrates that the pedagogies in the workshop assisted teachers and students to work beyond the usual 'roles' of teacher and student, enabling new possibilities for interaction. Liz (teacher) found that the workshops provided a levelling reprieve from the institutionalised relationships. She found that once on *an equal footing*, and freed from her confining role as *disciplinarian*, a *more honest* exchange became possible.

> … every interaction that you have with students you are in this role as the teacher and to some degree or another you're a disciplinarian, and then to be able to meet and interact with them as people instead. … I got a lot out of it in terms of being able to talk to them on equal footing and find out what their point of view was in that kind of perspective. (Liz, teacher)

The *levelling* experience interrupts the institutionalised nature of the teacher–student relationship. Julia (teacher) points to the way in which the repositioning permits a humanising exchange.

> It is a great leveler, because it is not a power relationship that is set up … It kind of humanised both the role of the teacher and the role of the student. And that can tend to be de-humanised in institutions because you are so busy with your agenda. (Julia, teacher)

The students found that it was an uplifting affective experience for them to be re-positioned from student to advisor.

> It's a lot more like satisfying because it's like—yes—I'm being listened to, my opinions are being heard you know, and you feel really important—like—this is something that's really good for the community, it's going to benefit everybody … It's really good, it's really morale boosting… (Susie, student)

This process of embodying the characters assists the players to create new interpretive 'stories' through which to explain school relationships. Krissy (student) points to the explanatory default whereby students ascribe negative motive to teachers. This default is informed by the cultural discourse about who teachers and students 'are'.

> You see kind of the teachers whinging, and the student just thinks that the teacher doesn't care, you know… whereas the teacher is worrying about it on the other side. (Krissy, student)

The assumption that the teacher is whinging, rather than worried, arises from a discourse that demonises teachers. Within this presumption, the teacher is likely to be *interpreted* in a negative light. Natalie (student) describes the way in which she re-stories from *teacher is the enemy* to *teacher as tolerant*.

> I guess in a school environment you don't normally think about, you know, the teachers' perspectives, it is just they're the enemy and I'm right. And, you know, it is kind of teaching you to see the other side of the story in a way. (We saw) how tolerant they could be to certain stuff, whereas we don't see that side of it prior because we just assume that they're not (Natalie, student).

Krissy's previous reading of teachers as *whingeing* and Natalie's perception of them as *enemies* had prevented them from seeing the *tolerance* of teachers or the way in which they *worry* about their students. However, engaging in the workshop exchange produces a shift in this interpretation, unsettles the dominant story, and allows a new one to form.

This rethinking of teacher operates in parallel with a rethinking of student on the part of the trainee teachers. Jane (teacher) describes how she becomes able to see the *person* where previously she saw the *scary mob.*

> … it gave you a chance to meet them as a person, and see Them, not this scary group of students. … On rounds I used to go in and they were just this mob of people who I was scared of basically… (Jane, teacher)

This is an embodied and experiential form of learning. Jane appreciates the located and kinaesthetic nature of the work, making a distinction between theory (talk) and practice (doing), and between the verbal forms of knowing and an embodied form of knowing.

> I think you needed to do the role-play because a lot of times you can talk and talk about something but until you actually see it or feel yourself in that situation you don't have an understanding of it. (Jane, teacher)

Gina finds that the Hidden Thoughts Game *makes* the person go on a deeper level. The questions inherent in the form not only position, but also *require* the players to think in a certain way and to extract a different sort of knowledge.

> I really liked the hidden fears. So making not only fears come out, but also making the person go on a deeper level because you really have to think and go "Ohh, what is beneath that for me?" and that kind of process was beneficial not only for the individual, but for the people watching. Because you don't always think about what is actually causing your behaviour and what is actually underneath it. (Gina, teacher)

Butler argues that "that new norms are brought into being when unanticipated forms of recognition take place." (Butler 2007) (31). When there is a 'rupture' in our recognition, or when the familiar is disturbed, uprooted, or contradicted, we can come to see or understand someone or something differently. Potentially, the encounters in the Learning Partnerships workshops provide this rupture or at least the opportunity to recognise the other. If so, the pedagogy can potentially help to generate new norms in the student–teacher interaction. These findings from the initial wave of the study are echoed in the second wave, discussed below.

14.8   Research Findings from the Second Wave of the Study

The survey data from both teachers and students following the 2013 workshops with four classes makes clear that they valued the experience very highly. The teacher survey showed that 96% rated as highly useful the opportunity to get feedback and advice. Most (87%) found the workshop to be highly useful in giving them a better insight into the needs of students, with 86% saying it enhanced their motivation to initiate helping conversations with students and 83% saying it was highly useful in increasing their capacity to build positive relationships with students.

The student survey results also showed highly positive responses with 90% of students rating the workshops as highly useful for gaining a better understanding of what it is like for teachers; and 86% rating the workshop as highly useful in increasing their confidence that teachers could be helpful for teenagers' experiencing personal problems; and 78% indicating that the workshops increased the likelihood that they would talk to a teacher if they had a problem. All of the student respondents identified that it was highly valuable to listen to the contributions of their peers. This data suggests that not only did the experience provide an opportunity for them to connect with adults, but it also provided them with a chance to reimagine each other. Student perspectives and findings from this research are discussed in greater detail elsewhere (Cahill and Coffey 2013a).

14.8.1 'In the Workshop You Feel like You're Actually Working with Them'

Whilst the survey data shows the consistency of response and the high value ascribed by both parties to this learning experience, as with the first study, the qualitative data collected in focus group discussions shines greater light on the relationship between the method and the learning. Here, just as in the first study, the participants highlighted the participatory, consultative and 'humanising' effect of the exchange.

> I think it was good because we got to be interactive, and we both—the teacher and the student—got to be able to work together. Cos like, when you think of being at school, you don't really think of working with your teacher. You think of them being your 'teacher'. But in the workshop you feel like you're actually working with them. (Post-interview, School student 8, male)

These students, just as the others, believed that the process helped both parties to build a better understanding each other better.

> In that workshop the teacher understood how we felt, then we understood how they react, so we understand what they are going through. (Post-interview, School student 33, female)

The teachers too found that the workshop provided a rare 'third space' within which to explore the relational domain of their professional responsibilities—one which was harder to focus on when in the practicum domain where their attention was caught up with issues of pedagogy and content delivery, rather than on development of relationship skills.

> I think it was the best session we've had so far—hands down. Because when you're teaching, building rapport isn't your main focus so it was great getting a chance to focus on that. (Pre-service teacher 11, female)

The 'third space' of the workshop provided opportunity for rehearsal and feedback as well as more generic advice.

> The reflection on the role-play was also really very useful. After the first feedback, they said I had a lot to work on and then we had a second go, and second feedback and this was so valuable! To have two 'goes' at practicing it; I was really able to improve. (Pre-service teacher 1, male)

The participants valued their *positioning* as equals, the function of the *participatory* methodology in orchestrating the exchange, and the use of *embodied performative* tasks to assist them to enquire deeply into the discourses and presumptions that inform their interactions. They believed that they had gained a greater confidence in the possibility of honest and helpful communication between students and teachers.

Data collected across the waves of this program show that the workshop provides a beneficial alternative space in which participants can work beyond the usual binaries and limiting discourses of teacher–student. This space enables a more honest and humanising exchange. As a result the participants seem to be able to *conceptualise* each other differently. They understand each other not just from a different angle, but *within a different story*. Inside of the layered stories constructed via the Hidden Thoughts device, inside of their *affective* engagement generated by learning *with* each other, and in the face of *credible* nature of the co-created and embodied data, the participants can see things they did not see before. Students can see that the teacher *cares* about them. Teachers can see that the students *care* about their learning. In this way the process assists participants to 'stretch' the categories which confine their understandings of each other and their resultant interactions. This rethinking is important as from a post-structuralist perspective, the process of re-classification, reimagining or re-storying is necessary if we are to create change. Here change is held to not only require a shift in a skillset—with the teachers *able* to communicate effectively with students, but also a shift in *mindset*—whereby they imagine it to be *possible* to speak differently with their students.

14.9   Conclusion

This chapter provides an example of the way in which post-structuralist theory can be used to help explain the way in which individuals are shaped by the stories and discourses that precede them. It demonstrates that this theoretical frame can be harnessed to inform the design of a pedagogy for change. It suggests the use of learning activities which engage players in detecting patterns, categories and discourses. It calls for strategies which help participants to notice the way in which these patterns influence what is held to be possible or desirable in teacher–student relations. It emphasises the importance of collective engagement in reconstruction or the creation of a new imaginary, in which change is held to be possible.

Inspired by a post-structural logic of change, it can be seen that the binaries can be bridged by the invention of new pedagogical spaces. A bridge does not dismantle the old structures. Rather it straddles and connects them. The position of co-investigator creates a bridge between the binary of student–teacher.

The collective embodied play in the bridging space helps to create a humanised community of learners. Repositioned on the levelled playing space, they are able to perform themselves differently. In performing themselves differently, and in working as audience learning with and from each other, they co-create evidence that change is possible.

References

Alsford, S. (2012). An educational development student forum: Working partnerships with students. *Journal of Applied Research in Higher Education, 4,* 186–202.

Butler, J. (1993). *Bodies that matter: On the discursive limits of "sex".* London: Routledge.

Butler, J. (2007). An account of oneself. In Davies, B. (Ed.), *Judith Butler in conversation: Analyzing the texts and talk of everyday life.* New York: Routledge.

Cahill, H. (2011). Drama for deconstruction. *Youth Theatre Journal, 25,* 16–31.

Cahill, H. (2012). Form and governance: Considering the drama as a 'technology of the self'. *RiDE: The Journal of Applied Theatre and Performance,* 1–20.

Cahill, H. (2015). Playing at being another we: Using drama as a pedagogical tool within a gender rights and sexuality education program. In Finneran, M. & K. Freebody (Eds.), *Drama and social justice.* London: Taylor and Francis.

Cahill, H., & Coffey, J. (2013a). *Learning partnerships.* Melbourne: Youth Research Centre.

Cahill, H., & Coffey, J. (2013b). Young people and the "Learning Partnerships" program: shifting negative attitudes to help-seeking. *Youth Studies Australia, 32,* 1–9.

Cahill, H., Coffey, J., & Sanci, L. A. (2015). 'I wouldn't get that feedback from anywhere else': Learning partnerships and the use of high school students as simulated patients to enhance medical students' communication skills. *BMC Medical Education, 35,* 1–9.

Cahill, H., Murphy, B., & Pose, M. (2011). Learning partnerships: Positioning students as co-investigators, coaches and actors. In S. Beadle, R. Holdsworth, & J. Wyn (Eds.), *For we are young and ...?* Melbourne: Melbourne University Press.

Davies, B. (1993). *Shards of glass: Children reading and writing beyond gendered identities.* St Leonards: Allen & Unwin.

Davies, B. (2006). Subjectification: The relevance of butler's analysis for education. *British Journal of Sociology of Education, 27,* 425–438.

Davies, B., Dormer, S., Gannon, S., Laws, C., Rocco, S., Taguchi, H., et al. (2001). Becoming schoolgirls: The ambivalent project of subjectification. *Gender and Education, 13*(2), 167–182.

Foucault, M. (1980). *Power/knowledge. Selected interviews and other writings 1972–1977.* Brighton, Sussex: Harvester Press.

St. Pierre, E., & Pillow, W. (Eds.). (2000). *Working the ruins: Feminist poststructural theory and methods in education.* New York: Routledge.

Willis, K. (2006). Analysing qualitative data. In M. Walter (Ed.), *Social research methods.* Oxford: Oxford University Press.

Author Biographies

Helen Cahill is the Deputy Director of the Youth Research Centre in the Melbourne Graduate School of Education at the University of Melbourne, Australia. She specialises in arts-based pedagogies in the development and research of school and community education programs designed to promote well-being and participation.

Julia Coffey is a lecturer in sociology in the School of Humanities and Social Sciences, University of Newcastle, Australia. Her research is in the field of health sociology, focussing on youth, the body, and gender. Her book, *Body Work: Youth, Gender and Health* has been recently published by Routledge.

Chapter 15
Redesigning Authentic Collaborative Practicum Partnerships: Learnings from Case Studies from Two New Zealand Universities

Beverley Cooper and Lexie Grudnoff

15.1 Introduction

For a number of years, initial teacher education (ITE) has faced criticism for not adequately preparing teachers for the realities of teaching. Such criticism has intensified in the context of widespread recognition that teacher quality is the major in-school influence on student achievement (Hattie 2009) and the drive to improve the education outcomes and opportunities for increasingly diverse student populations (UNESCO 2014). It is therefore not surprising that policy aimed at reforming ITE in order to improve teacher quality has been at the top of many nations' policy agendas.

Underpinning much of the reform is the widely held concern that teacher education programmes, especially those based in universities, prioritise theory over practice. There is a belief that the (over) emphasis on theory results in a disconnect between what students learn in teacher preparation programmes and what they need to do as teachers, particularly in terms of being effective with, and responsive to, a wide range of learners (UNESCO 2014). Hence the focus of reform efforts in many countries is on strengthening the practice components of teacher preparation programmes.

The emphasis on practice, coupled with policy attention on the link between teacher quality and student achievement, has resulted in a greater value being placed on student teachers' experiential learning in practicum settings than on their university-based learning. For example, the American National Council for the Accreditation of Teacher Education Report (NCATE) report of an expert Blue

B. Cooper (✉)
University of Waikato, Hamilton, New Zealand
e-mail: bcooper@waikato.ac.nz

L. Grudnoff
University of Auckland, Auckland, New Zealand
e-mail: l.grudnoff@auckland.ac.nz

© Springer Nature Singapore Pte Ltd. 2017
M.A. Peters et al. (eds.), *A Companion to Research in Teacher Education*,
DOI 10.1007/978-981-10-4075-7_15

Ribbon Panel (2010) recommended a restructuring of teacher education around clinical practice and partnerships as a way to improve the quality of teacher preparation and teacher effectiveness. Similarly, the UK's recent Carter Review of Initial Teacher Education (2015) reinforced the importance of effective school-based experiences and the value of robust school-provider partnerships, but also pointed to the need to increase mentoring capability through a more rigorous process of identification, selection, training and resourcing of mentor teachers.

Notwithstanding the findings from recent reviews of ITE, universities have for a number of years attempted to address the theory-practice 'gap' by developing partnerships with schools. While some argue that collaboration between universities and schools in teacher preparation programmes enhances the relationship between theory and practice and provides benefits to all concerned: student teachers, mentor teachers and teacher educators (e.g. Allen et al. 2013), others claim that collaborative relationships between schools and universities are weak and ineffective (Zeichner 2010). A number of studies have identified difficulties associated with developing and maintaining strong school-university partnerships. For example, Bloomfield (2009) points to the time and resource pressures experienced by both school and university staff while Allen (2011) notes that typically there is very limited communication between providers and schools which can increase the disconnect student teachers face between the practicum and on-campus components of their programme. Allen argued that such limited communication can result in lack of clarity regarding the roles and responsibilities of university and school staff in terms of supporting student teachers on practicum.

There has also been criticism of the power relationships involved in school-university partnerships. According to McIntyre (2009) much of the research suggests that the principles of collaboration, equity and respect that often frame such partnerships are often more visible in rhetoric rather than in reality. McIntyre contended that in most cases university knowledge is privileged over practising teacher expertise, and that the emphasis is on ensuring that student teacher practice is aligned with what is taught on campus rather than offering anything fundamentally innovative in school-university partnerships.

To address such power imbalances, some scholars have argued for a transformative change in school-university relationships. Zeichner (2010), for example, believed that practicum roles, relationships and sites needed to be radically rethought. He asserted that schools, not classrooms, should be the sites for professional learning and that university and school staff should be co-learners, along with the student teachers, in the practicum partnership. According to Ziechner, a non-hierarchical interplay between academic, practitioner and community expertise would create expanded learning opportunities for prospective teachers that would better prepare them to be successful in enacting complex teaching practices. Bringing practitioner and academic knowledge together has the potential to create, "a transformative space where the potential for an expanded form of learning and the development of new knowledge are heightened" (Gutiérrez 2008, p. 152). Such views are in stark contrast to the way practicum has traditionally been structured, that is, around hierarchical relationships between university staff, school supervisors and student teachers, where the prospective teacher is positioned as the sole learner, guided by the teacher as expert (Bloomfield 2009).

This chapter reports on work undertaken in two New Zealand universities whose goal was to re-conceptualise and reinvigorate university-school partnerships. The two case studies contribute specifically to an understanding of how genuinely collaborative school-university partnerships can establish shared goals and processes to support the professional learning of student teachers. The authors argue that such partnerships can help to address the disconnect between school and university, and between theory and practice, that is a feature of much of the criticism of university-based ITE.

15.2 Background and Context

Currently, over 90% of primary and secondary teachers graduate from one of the seven main New Zealand universities. The traditional route into teaching is either through an undergraduate teacher education degree or, for those holding an existing degree, through a one-year Graduate Diploma in Teaching.

New Zealand policy makers, in common with other countries, have identified ITE as being key to the quest to improve the educational outcomes for diverse students by improving teacher quality. For example, in 2009 the Minister of Education established the Workforce Advisory Group to advise her on ways of improving the quality of ITE in order to raise the overall quality of teaching across the school system. In their subsequent report, *A Vision for the Teaching Profession* (Ministry of Education 2010), the advisory group recommended substantial changes be made to ITE, including requiring a postgraduate qualification to enter teaching and the need to significantly strengthen university-school practicum relationships.

These ideas resurfaced in 2013, with the New Zealand Ministry of Education's competitive tendering process for 'exemplary postgraduate initial teacher education (EPITE) programmes' that were more 'practice focused' and grounded in rich partnerships with schools (Ministry of Education 2013). Selected programmes received additional funding of approximately NZ $6000 per student teacher. The programmes are being trialled over an initial 3-year period and are intended to lift the quality of graduating teachers practice and contribute to raising student achievement, particularly that of priority student groups (Maori and Pasifika learners, those from low socio-economic backgrounds, and students with special education needs). Three universities were selected to implement 'exemplary programmes' in 2014.

This chapter reports work undertaken in two universities with the goal of re-conceptualising and reinvigorating university-school partnerships by intentionally bringing school and university communities together to establish shared goals and processes to support student teacher learning. The following sections outline two case studies of masters' ITE programmes from universities from different parts of New Zealand that were selected in the first round of the competitive tendering process. Also discussed are the two undergraduate level practicum projects that informed the development of the two masters' programmes.

15.3 Case Study: The University of Waikato

15.3.1 Background

In New Zealand, normal schools were mandated in the Education Act in the 1870s to support Teacher Training Colleges. The University of Waikato has always valued its relationships with its six local normal primary schools who have supported the Faculty of Education to deliver a practicum programme which involved students engaging in microteaching in a range of curriculum learning areas. This model involved the university requesting times that student teachers could teach groups of children prescribed lessons with a particular class level, and lecturers observing student teachers interact with small groups of children. While well supported by the normal schools this process disrupted classroom programmes and focussed on student teachers as learners rather than the children as learners and was often referred to by schools as 'child banking'. A revision of the New Zealand Curriculum, coupled with the introduction of National Standards in Numeracy and Literacy implemented in 2010, impacted on school programmes and the delivery of curriculum, which led to schools' reluctance to disrupt programmes to meet university practicum and coursework needs.

15.3.1.1 Collaborative University Partnership (CUSP)

In 2011, university staff and school leaders from the six normal schools met regularly over a 6-month period to co-construct a new school placement/practicum programme. The development provided opportunities for shared meaning making through co-generative dialoguing (Tobin and Roth 2005) and an opportunity for differences in agendas and perspectives to be shared and acknowledged. The first step was to establish principles that underpinned the CUSP initiative. Principles centred on the central focus on children's learning, shared decision-making and shared responsibilities. Schools also insisted that the development be researched.

The co-construction of the CUSP programme resulted in student teachers in the first year of the 3-year Bachelor of Teaching programme being placed in pairs in classrooms for one day per week for the academic year. Three schools in addition to the six normal schools were recruited to accommodate the student teacher numbers. The programme's first professional practice paper was co-taught in the school context in the first 6-months and a 4-week practicum block was completed at the end of the year in the same placement school. The schools were agreeable to taking responsibility for the assessment of the final practicum block because they believed that they would have established a long-term relationship with the students and an understanding of their learning trajectories.

Schools were very positive towards the proposed changes because of the flexibility it provided to the school to accommodate university tasks, the fit for purpose and authentic experience for the student teacher, and the genuine relationship the student teacher would develop with the class and the classroom teacher (Table 15.1).

> I actually think it's wonderful. I am very excited about it. I love the way that we have flexibility to fit it around our programme. It will lift the bar, and it focuses on the professional edge and why we are learning, what we are doing in our teaching, as well as how it fits into learning programme for the students to see the relevance. It's authentic learning, awesome! (School A Principal, 2012)

> I think it will mean authentic learning, with no mini lessons, where the pupils are used as a child-bank. There can be a genuine relationship resulting in better learning. The student teachers will see the progression of the term, for example in the reading groups. They will understand for example, how science comes out of the classroom programme. (School B Principal, 2012)

Table 15.1 Summary of key differences between the reframed and traditional practicum models: University of Waikato

Reframed placement/practicum model	Traditional placement/practicum model
• School selects one teacher as Associate Lecturer (AL) to have overall professional responsibility for all student teachers in the school and to work with mentor teachers	• School selects one teacher as Liaison Teacher to have overall professional responsibility for all student teachers in the school and to work with the Faculty of Education
• University selects one lecturer (Faculty mentor) to work with the school to works with the AL to co-deliver the professional practice programme. They co-design the school-based programme	• University lecturer responsible for the teaching task and attends while student teachers carry out tasks and supervises groups
• Groups of 30 student teachers placed in pairs in a range of classrooms with mentor teacher selected by school for one day per week for the academic year	• Groups of 30 students teachers visit the school for 1 h blocks and work with a specific year level to carry out a specified teaching task with a group of 4–5 children
• Teaching tasks are completed when appropriate in the classroom programme	• Teaching Tasks completed at time dictated by university
• Mentor teacher and AL comments on student teacher lesson reflections	• University lecturer assesses student teacher work
• Student teachers complete a 4 week practicum block at the end of the year in the classroom they have worked in over the year	• 4 week practicum completed in new school. Student teachers have no knowledge of the context
• Associate Lecturer observes and assesses student teacher. Joint summative decision by school and university	• Assessment carried out by university lecturer

The initiative has been fully researched for four years over two programme cycles, through a developmental evaluation approach (Harlow et al. 2014). Data generation has included document analysis, researcher attendance at planning and review meetings, case studies of two partner schools, focus group interviews of student teachers, associate lecturers, faculty lecturers and surveys of mentor teachers and student teachers over the three year's of the programme.

Several practices have supported the development of the partnership between schools and university. Partner school leaders are appointed as Associate Lecturers of the university and listed in the official university calendar to give status to the positions. A formal memorandum of understanding which sets out the responsibility of the faculty, the school and the student teachers has been developed for each school. Subsidised postgraduate study has been provided to school mentors. The faculty lecturer and the associate lecturer take joint responsibility for the school programme and decisions around student teacher placement in classes. This has facilitated close working relationships between university and schools.

> [The professional practice lecturer] and I have gone back to the programme overview and worked out a plan for the semester in-school tutorials with different people coming into speak to the students. I think it's wonderful for her to be coming and planning with me. She is amazing to work together with to plan ahead. If she can't be there I will carry on under her guidance, and if I can't be there she will do the same. I thought it would be huge amounts of work and I'd be busy, I was expected to cancel everything on a Wednesday and it's not like that at all. (School A Associate lecturer, 2012)

> I think there now seems to be a shared responsibility between placement schools, the associates and the university for the professional development of future teachers. I think it is a positive move for all. I do feel it adds a greater depth to the programme. (School B Associate lecturer, 2012)

Ninety-seven percent of the first-year student teachers surveyed reported that their practicum experience had helped them to have a better understanding of what it means to be a teacher. They reported that had gained an insight into the workload and life of a teacher, had been able to learn from their mistakes, to gain confidence in a safe environment, and to link the theory they had learnt to the practice of teaching and learning.

> I was involved with the class learning everyday which allowed me to see the progress the children were making and helped me understanding where a teacher would go next with their teaching. (Student Teacher A, 2013)

> It taught me that teachers need to have good organization and a good plan is essential. A teacher needs to put herself to the front line and set a role model for the students and scaffold the children through their learning. (Student Teacher E, 2013)

> I got to make mistakes and learn what works and what doesn't. I got to experience a full day of being a teacher - not just the 9am - 3 pm part. It really helped put into perspective what a teachers job is, what they do all day, and get a sense of the workload. I got to put into practice some of the ideas and techniques I had learnt in university papers. (Student Teacher K, 2013)

The research on CUSP has highlighted: the importance of developing mutually respectful and trusting relationships among faculty and schools; the value of sustained practice for student teachers, mentor teachers, and learners; and, the importance of seamless learning to break down the perception of the theory/practice divide. The research has also highlighted the issues in developing a shared understanding across all individuals in the partnership, particularly mentor teachers, and the commitment and persistence needed by key members in the partnership to support deeply embedded cultural shifts by both the university and schools.

Both school and university staff, four years into the partnership, are positive and committed to the initiative and recognise the positive difference the programme has made to student teacher learning, relationships between the schools and university, and the benefits to children in classrooms.

15.3.2 Master of Teaching and Learning

Building on this initiative, in 2013 we designed an exemplary postgraduate initial teacher education (EPITE) programme in response to the Ministry of Education's tendering process noted above. This programme, which began delivery in January 2014, is intended for high achieving students with highly developed dispositions for teaching. The one-year Master of Teaching and Learning (MTchgLn) degree involves student teachers being placed in one partner school context for 4 days in a 10-day cycle for 6 months followed by a 10-week full-time experience in another partner school. The intention of the programme was to have a closer link between school practice and academic learning through student teachers' sustained relationships with partner schools over the academic year.

A similar process to the CUSP programme occurred involving meeting with schools over a 6-month period to co-construct the practicum component of the programme. The first practicum experience is pivotal to the programme. It involves sustained guided engagement with groups of students including those from priority groups (Māori and Pasifika learners, those from low socio-economic backgrounds, and students with special education needs) centred around teaching as an inquiry stance, building of relationships with students and their community, using research informed pedagogy, gathering evidence related to achievement and developing adaptive expertise.

Cohorts of student teachers are placed in partner schools in pairs with selected mentor teachers. A senior staff member from within each school has been appointed as an Associate Lecturer to the faculty. Faculty lecturers, the school-based Associate Lecturer and mentor teachers, work together on the school site to assist the student teachers to problematise the issues relating to their group of students through a teaching as inquiry process.

As with the CUSP programme, MTchgLn partner schools were enthusiastic to work with these student teachers as they saw a mutual benefit to both student teacher and their own staff learning. The conceptual framework of the programme is very much in line with the current focus of schools to build capacity within their own staff in the targeted areas due to government priorities.

This programme is under intense scrutiny and is being monitored by four separate processes—Ministry of Education contract monitoring, independent monitoring by an external agency appointed by the Ministry of Education, external monitoring by the Education Council New Zealand and an embedded developmental evaluation funded by the university. Evaluations are indicating we are delivering high-quality programmes at the appropriate postgraduate level and student teacher quality is high. However these evaluations are highlighting the importance of building mentor teacher and lecturer capacity, developing a shared vision and understanding of the conceptual framework between schools and university and the intensive and time-consuming process required by schools and university to implement the programme in its true spirit.

The evaluations are also highlighting the tensions between concurrently developing a practice base and supporting academic work at postgraduate level.

Providing time and resources to build capacity and establish roles of school mentors and university lecturers in the school context is a difficult process when these people are responsible for running their own teaching programmes which have high contact and assessment loads. Building capacity is not an overnight process and we are certainly undergoing a steep learning curve to ensure we enact the programme in the way it is intended.

15.4 Case Study: University of Auckland

15.4.1 Background

The practicum has long been considered to be a critical component of the University of Auckland's ITE programmes. However, while the faculty has enjoyed positive relationships with its practicum schools we were also aware that student teachers' practicum experiences could be variable and that there was often a disconnect between the campus and practicum components of teacher education programmes.

15.4.1.1 Reframing Practicum Project (RPP)

Our response to addressing such issues was the Reframing Practicum Project (RPP), which began in 2008. Over the course of that year we worked with 20 primary principals with whom we had long-standing practicum relationships to develop a different approach to the final practicum in a 3-year undergraduate primary teacher education degree. The focus of the project was on rethinking roles, relationships and sites for the practicum with the aim of the more effective preparation of beginning teachers through the development of more robust and authentic school-university partnerships. The principals were excited about the opportunities afforded through working together to enhance the practicum as they believed that

> It was a chance to bring the best of school and the best of university together in a way that's collaborative and co-constructed. For once it's a joint thing, as opposed to the university over there and the school over here. (Principal, School D).

We have outlined elsewhere the outcomes of the development process that contributed to the design of practicums that would align with a school's professional culture and meet university credentialing requirements (Grudnoff and Williams 2010).

Table 15.2 provides a summary of the key differences between the reframed approach to the practicum and the university's traditional practicum model.

Data on the RPP have been gathered primarily from individual and focus group interviews of student teachers and associated school and university staff, and from meeting documentation. The evidence indicates that the aims of the project were being enacted in practice. For example

> There's a much closer working relationship between the university and the school and … that's the way it should be. The project has built relationships between us so that the links between what happens here in theory and what happens in practice in schools are much clearer. (Principal, School C)

> It is about co-construction in a really authentic sense - about co-constructing powerful teaching between expert and novice on the basis of knowledge and big goals from both the university and the school. It is a real collaboration and it's authentic. (Principal, School A)

Table 15.2 Summary of key differences between the reframed and traditional practicum models University of Auckland

Reframed practicum model	Traditional practicum model
• Group of 4–6 student teachers assigned to a school which then selects an appropriate mentor teacher for each student teacher	• University assigns student teacher to an Associate Teacher in an individual classroom
• School selects one teacher (Adjunct lecturer —AL) to have overall professional responsibility for all student teachers in the school and to work with the mentor teachers	• School identifies contact person for practicum administrative purposes within the school
• University selects one lecturer (university liaison lecturer—ULL) to work with School/AL	• University supervisor is allocated an individual student teacher to observe and assess their performance against university practicum requirements
• The principal is involved in designing the practicum that is appropriate for their school	• The principal's focus is administrative e.g. oversight of mentor payments
• The AL and the ULL have the prime responsibility of designing a practicum that meets school culture and university requirements for that group of student teachers	• Associate teacher is responsible for providing the conditions to enable the student teacher to meet university practicum requirements
• Practicum assessment practices involve a range of professional participants depending on the elements of the practicum design	• Student teacher, mentor teacher and university supervisor meet in a triadic assessment discussion

The mentor teachers also valued the collaboration that was a feature of the new approach to the practicum:

> When you [work with] other people to support the students and their teaching… you notice things that you might overlook because you are in your own little world. I think the whole thing [the new model] has made us think more broadly and we have benefitted as a team. (Mentor, School E)

Student teachers also noted the benefits of collaboration. For example

> This practicum was a partnership between the associate and the others [the ULL and AL] and us [student teachers] so that we were always working together and alongside each other modelling what good practice looks like. (Student teacher, School D)

The key collaborative relationship was, however, between the school-based Adjunct Lecturer and the University Liaison Lecturer

> We [the AL and ULL] worked very closely … and we looked at usual practices and the strengths/minuses and interesting points and advantages/disadvantages of the usual practice and looked very carefully at where we could make dramatic change … We spent a long time trying to debunk our usual practice. (AL and ULL, School C)

Over the last six years, the faculty has worked closely with principals and staff from eighteen Auckland primary schools who are now involved in the RPP. Two factors have been critical to the success of the project. First, explicit recognition that teacher professional knowledge and university theoretical knowledge are complementary and are of equal value

> [The practicum] is now about co-constructing powerful teaching between an expert and a novice on the basis of knowledge from both the university and the school. (Principal, School D)

Second, empowering the schools to develop contextually relevant ways of working with student teachers

> We (the principal, the AL and ULL) interpreted the [practicum] learning outcomes for us as a school: What do they look like in the context of [the] school? What does effective teaching look like in the context of our school. So we've have worked with the students together in terms of contextualising the practicum learning outcomes. (Principal, School C)

While the aims and outcomes of the RPP are viewed positively, what cannot be underestimated is the amount of hard work and commitment that the school principals, and those undertaking the new roles of school-based adjunct lecturer (AL) and the university-based liaison lecturer (ULL) have put into making the new practicum partnerships work successfully.

15.5 The Master of Teaching (Primary)

We have built on the understandings developed through the Reframing Practicum Project in the design and development of a new one-year Master of Teaching (Primary) programme, which began in July 2014. The overarching goal of the

Master of Teaching (MTchg) programme is to prepare teachers who engage in practice that promotes equitable outcomes and opportunities for disadvantaged students from priority learner groups. In New Zealand, these include learners from low socio-economic communities who are often Maori and Pasifika students. The aim is to develop student teachers' complex understandings of practice combined with strong commitments to social justice.

The schools that are part of the MTchg are viewed as 'learning hubs' because they are intended to provide sustained and systematic opportunities for student teachers to practise and hone the required skills, knowledge and professional practice. Currently there are 12 schools involved in the programme. Student teachers work intensively in two different schools over the year. The intention is to address what Darling-Hammond (2006) has identified as being the central issue confronting ITE: how to foster learning about and from practice *in* practice. The schools are considered to be 'learning hubs' for two main reasons.

First, the schools provide opportunities for MTchg students to begin to develop the expertise necessary to work effectively with all learners. In the first six months of the programme, in addition to a three-week practicum, a maximum of ten student teachers work in one school for two days a week. While the student teachers work primarily in one classroom with an experienced mentor teacher, the Adjunct Lecturer has oversight of the group and designs professional learning experiences to meet student teacher needs and requirements. In the last six months of the programme, another group of four to six student teachers are deliberately placed in a school situated in a low socio-economic community with a high proportion of priority learners. In addition to being in the school for two days a week, the MTchg students undertake a 3-week practicum at the beginning of the school year so they can experience and participate in the establishment of class learning environments and whole school activities connected with the start of the teaching year.

The MTchg students are in the same school for the summative 6-week practicum, three weeks of which they take full responsibility for the class as mandated by policy. During this practicum the student teachers also undertake site-based supervised research into an aspect of their practice. Over the six months, a University Liaison Lecturer works with the school's Adjunct Lecturer to ensure that MTchg students are provided with an effective professional learning environment and that they are meeting university and school expectations and requirements. The mentor teacher, Adjunct Lecturer and University Liaison Lecturer collaboratively undertake the summative assessment of the student teacher's practicum and their readiness to start teaching.

Second, participating schools are viewed as learning hubs because they facilitate a different and more collaborative way of teaching the programme. The new courses in the Master of Teaching were co-constructed by interdisciplinary faculty and school teams, and they combine campus and school-based teaching and learning. The aim of this approach is to help make explicit the links between theory and practice and to support student teachers to teach in ways that promote equitable outcomes for all learners. For example, in two courses that combine mathematics and literacy teaching, student teachers conducted observations and tasks in partner schools and critically examined these with teachers and faculty staff. Another course combines the expertise of assessment, literacy, mathematics and arts specialists with the knowledge and experience of teachers and school leaders to explore how to accelerate progress for disadvantaged learners.

The Master of Teaching (Primary) is very new and we have already identified a number of challenges to the 'learning hub' partnership model. First, the enormous amount of time and energy required to build relationships and develop understandings around a new approach to ITE in a truly collaborative manner. The school and university participants have committed many hours to partnership building and problem solving, all on top of busy and demanding university and school roles and responsibilities. Finding time for collaboration was a major challenge and raises the question about the level of resourcing required for teacher education programmes to support the development of authentically collaborative university-school practicum partnerships. Second, while the Adjunct Lecturers were fully engaged in the programme, this was not the case for all of the mentors. Hence, a key focus for the next iteration of the programme is ensuring that the mentor teachers understand the aims of the programme and the role they play in achieving these aims. Third, as the numbers of schools partnering with the faculty in teaching the programme grow, so will the demands on the time and energy of those building relationships and capability with new partners, while at the same time as sustaining established partnerships. Issues to do with scalability and sustainability will become more confronting as the programme becomes more established with an increase in student teacher numbers. Finally, we do not know enough about whether or in what ways the 'learning hub' approach model has influenced MTchg graduates' practice as beginning teachers. This is an area for future research.

15.6 Conclusion

The University of Waikato and University of Auckland case studies are examples of how schools and universities have worked together to design and implement programmes to support student teacher learning through partnership arrangements. In the two contexts there has been a genuine commitment between the stakeholder schools and university to raise the expertise of beginning teachers through the design and co-construction of fit for purpose ITE programmes.

Both universities built on established long-term relationships with their local schools. The practicum innovations have both built on and contributed to mutual professional respect and trust between all participants—student teachers, school and university-based participants. The university and school partners have confirmed their shared commitment to high-quality teacher education programmes and to high-quality resourcing and have established the long-term shared vision of what is to be achieved. The new practicum partnership arrangements are still evolving and all parties recognise that the time, commitment and energy to support this evolution is significant and should not be underestimated. As Darling Hammond (2006) pointed out, establishing a shared vision between school and university is only the starting point. The implementation of this vision is a complex and long-term process to create expanded learning opportunities for prospective teachers that will better prepare them to be successful in enacting complex teaching practices.

We have gone someway to breaking down the traditional hierarchy between university and school. However, the transformative spaces (Gutiérrez 2008; Zeichner 2010) conceptualised by the developers of these programmes are yet to become fully realised as school and university capacity is still being developed. The outstanding classroom teachers we have identified are not necessarily skilled mentors nor are they familiar with the academic work student teachers are expected to undertake. At the same time, our university academic staff may have had little experience in working alongside teachers in classroom contexts, or be unfamiliar with recent schooling initiatives. Hence both school and university need support to develop the additional skills required to work as collaborative partners. For true innovation to occur we need to be continually mindful of McIntyre's (2009) warning to ensure that the masters' programmes do not privilege university knowledge over practising teacher expertise nor emphasise the alignment of school practice with what is taught in the university setting.

Making time and space for university-school conversations and clarifying the mix of university and school roles and responsibilities while enacting and innovating a strong university-school partnership is a challenge, as others have found (e.g. Allen 2011; Bloomfield 2009). These studies have alerted us to the potential for limited communication between schools and universities in a partnership model to increase, rather then decrease, the disconnect between the two partners. As these EPITE are scaled up with more student teachers, schools and university staff involved, we need to pay careful attention to these issues. Developing shared understanding and capacity across all stakeholders is essential if we are to maintain authentic partnerships, effect innovation and support the academic and practice rigour intended of these exemplary programmes.

References

Allen, J., Howells, K., & Radford, R. (2013). A 'partnership in teaching excellence': Ways in which one school-university partnership has fostered teacher development. *Asia-Pacific Journal of Teacher Education, 41*(1), 99–110.

Allen, J. M. (2011). Stakeholders' perspectives of the nature and role of assessment during practicum. *Teaching and Teacher Education, 27*, 742–750.

Bloomfield, D. (2009). Working within and against neoliberal accreditation agendas: Opportunities for professional experience. *Asia-Pacific Journal of Teacher Education, 37*, 27–44.

Carter, A. (2015). *Review of initial teacher training (ITT)*. Retrieved from www.gov.uk/government/publications

Darling-Hammond, L. (2006). *Powerful teacher education: Lessons from exemplary programmes*. San Francisco, CA: Jossey-Bass.

Grudnoff, L., & Williams, R. (2010). Pushing boundaries: Reworking university-school practicum relationships. *New Zealand Journal of Educational Studies, 45*(2), 33–45.

Gutiérrez, K. (2008). Developing a sociocritical literacy in the third space. *Reading Research Quarterly, 43*(2), 148–164.

Harlow, A., Cooper, B., & Cowie, B. (2014). *Collaborative university school partnerships research brief: Hamilton—The first-year practicum experience*, 2013. (pp. 1–11). (Research brief). http://www.waikato.ac.nz/wmier/research/projects/collaborative-university-school-partnerships/_recache:TheUniversityofWaikato

Hattie, J. (2009). *Visible learning*. London: Routledge.

McIntyre, D. (2009). The difficulties of inclusive pedagogy for initial teacher education and some thoughts on the way forward. *Teaching and Teacher Education, 25*(4), 602–608.

Ministry of Education. (2010). *Education workforce advisory group. A vision for the teaching profession*. New Zealand Government: Wellington.

Ministry of Education. (2013). Provision of exemplary post graduate initial teacher education. Retrieved from http://www.mindedu.govt.nz/theMinistry/EducationInitiatives/QualityOfITE-Provision.aspx

National Council for Accreditation of Teacher Education. (2010). *Transforming teacher education through clinical practice: A national strategy to prepare effective teachers. Report of the blue ribbon panel on clinical preparation and partnerships for improved student learning*. Washington, DC: NCATE.

Tobin, K., & Roth, W.-M. (2005). Implementing coteaching and cogenerative dialoguing in urban science education. *School Science and Mathematics, 105*, 313–322.

UNESCO. (2014). Teaching and learning: Achieving quality for all. Author.

Zeichner, K. (2010). Rethinking the connections between campus courses and field experiences in college-and university-based teacher education. *Journal of Teacher Education, 6*(1–2), 89–99.

Chapter 16
Researching the Intersection of Program Supervision and Field Placements: Interactional Ethnographic Telling Cases of Reflexive Decision-Making Process

Laurie Katz and Judith Green

16.1 Introduction

Today, in the US (and other countries), teacher education programs are faced with a range of policy mandates to transform their programmatic practices in order to enhance the development of teaching competencies by teacher-candidates in field placements as well as those supervising these candidates. Such mandates have led to the development of a range of research initiatives, as teacher educators seek to study the impact of such transformations on existing teacher education programs as well as on the candidates within those programs (e.g., Avalos 2011; Murray et al. 2009; Joram 2007). In this chapter, we seek to contribute to this growing body of work by making transparent the interactional ethnographic logic of inquiry (Green, Skukauskaite & Baker 2012) that is guiding, and has guided, an ongoing research program of an early childhood teacher education program (ECTE) with PreK-3rd grade licensure in the Midwest United States. This research program was designed to support a reflexive process, through which the program director (Katz, first author) sought to systematically explore the impact of particular changes being considered within the teacher education program, before scaling the change to the full program (e.g., Katz and Green 2012; Katz and Isik-Ercan 2015).

L. Katz (✉)
Ohio State University, Columbus, OH, USA
e-mail: katz.124@osu.edu

J. Green
University of California, Santa Barbara, CA, USA
e-mail: judith.green@gmail.com

© Springer Nature Singapore Pte Ltd. 2017
M.A. Peters et al. (eds.), *A Companion to Research in Teacher Education*,
DOI 10.1007/978-981-10-4075-7_16

16.2 Why Interactional Ethnography as a Basis for a Reflexive Research Program

The discussion of Interactional Ethnography as a logic of inquiry, and how it supported reflexive actions and understandings within the ECTE program, is presented through a new study undertaken by the embedded ethnography team. This study was a response to the need that the embedded ethnography team identified in two previous studies—i.e., a clash in expectations about what constitutes the practice of lesson planning that was identified in previous studies. The initial study by Katz and Green (2012) had identified a conflict that occurred between the supervisor from the ECTE program and the field-based team of two teacher-candidates and one mentor-teacher. That study was extended by a second one by Katz and Isik-Ercan (2015), as embedded ethnographers, who returned to data associated with the point of conflict to further analyze the dialogues between the supervisor and field-based team, to see if they could identify the roots of the conflict in the dialogues. This level of analysis, while extending their understanding of elements of the conflict, also led to the need to gather additional information to trace sources of influence on the supervisor's interactions during the supervisory conference, sources not directly visible in the dialogues.

Based on her understanding that the supervisor was part of a larger program, the director decided to invite Green [second author] to engage with her team in a new way, that is, to serve as a virtual external ethnographer, given that Green had worked with her on the initial study (Katz and Green 2012). Based on her past experience with Green, the director understood that Green would be able to ask questions previously unasked by the embedded (internal) ethnography team to enable her to identify and trace potential program actors, who influenced the supervisor's actions and to explore how these led to the frame clash between the supervisor and the field-based team. In taking this reflexive action, the director made visible her recognition that as an embedded ethnographer she needed further support to step back from what Heath (1982) calls *ethnocentrism* in order to explore further the sources of influence of different actors within the ECTE program; that is, to create the possibility of identifying program factors that were invisible to her at that time.

By creating an internal–external ethnographic study with members, who shared a common *logic of inquiry*, she was able to formulate a phase for her study and to seek new ways of uncovering factors that supported and/or constrained what guided the supervisor's interactions with the field-based team. By making visible the logic that the internal–external ethnography team developed for this phase of the study, we make visible what is involved in taking an interactional ethnographic perspective, and how this process supported required additional data collection and analysis processes, ones that moved the inquiry process from analyses of the moments of interaction to exploring layers of contexts and actors within and across contexts (e.g., the classroom, supervisory meetings, university courses, and administrative contexts). By (re)constructing the logic-in-use, we seek to make visible how, and in what ways, an interactional ethnographic logic of inquiry created a foundation for reflexive decision-making about future actions within the ECTE Program.

16.3   Theoretical Arguments Guiding the Dialogic Process of the Ethnography Team

Three conceptual arguments were central to the logic of inquiry that guided the insider–outsider ethnographers' approach: *Telling cases* (Mitchell 1984), *langua-culture* (Agar 1994, 2006), and *intertextuality as socially constructed* (Bloome and Egan-Robertson 1993).

Telling Cases: The concept of telling cases is grounded in an anthropological perspective framed by Mitchell (1984), a British anthropologist, who argues that ethnographic accounts constitute case studies of

> … some sequence of events from which the analyst seeks to make some theoretical inference. The events themselves may relate to any level of social organization: a whole society, some section of a community, a family or an individual. What distinguishes [telling] case studies from more general ethnographic reportage is the detail and particu-larity of the account. Each case study is a description of a specific configuration of events in which some distinctive set of actors have been involved in some defined situation at some particular point of time. (p. 237)

From this perspective, by engaging in the process of tracing the roots of episte-mological differences between actors in the field-based team and the university-supervisory team previously identified, the embedded ethnography team constructed a research design that was based on a set of telling cases of the sources of influence on different actors. By tracing the actors (i.e., school-based team and university-supervisory team), the insider–outsider ethnographers were able to identify what counted as (Heap, 1985) *lesson planning*.

Therefore, by tracing different actors and analyzing what different actors defined as *lesson planning*, the internal–external team created a series of telling cases of particular chains of activity by particular groups of actors at particular points of contact with each other and with other actors in their primary contexts (e.g., classroom, university). Through this process, the insider–outsider analysis team was able to lay a foundation for a process of triangulation to build a telling case study of what counted as *lesson-planning* and how it was conceptualized by each group of actors, located in different institutional settings (i.e., classroom field-based and university-supervisory teams).

By tracing points of contact among particular groups of actors, two telling cases were constructed. The first telling case was constructed by identifying all references to email exchanges in the archive between the Supervisor (Denise) and student-teacher (Brad) as a tracer unit in order to explore what the university-supervisory team *counted as lesson-planning*. This telling case, therefore, was constructed to make visible the processes involved in identifying a defined situation, and in identifying what was learned about what the supervisory team expected to see in Brad's lesson plans. This telling case, therefore, focused on uncovering the university expectations about lesson planning.

The second telling case shifts the angle of analysis of factors contributing to the differences in perspectives on lesson planning from the point of view of the supervisory team to a focus on the development of an approach to lesson-planning as team—building activity for the third grade instructional team. This analysis involved identifying what was inscribed in both an email from the mentor-teacher to the supervisor, and in an interview of Brad by an embedded ethnographer. By shifting this angle of analysis and sources of data, we constructed a contrastive telling case in which we held the phenomena of interest constant—i.e., lesson planning dialogues between and among different sets of actors in order to construct more complex understandings of previously observed epistemological differences by Katz and Isik-Ercan (2015).

16.4 Languaculture

Central to the exploration of the roots of epistemological and conceptual differences identified in the Katz and Isik-Ercan (2015) study, and underlying the conceptualization of the nature of emic-etic/insider–outsider points of contact, is Agar's argument about actors as bringing different languacultures to new social spaces, whose cultural processes and practices the ethnographer-as-an-outsider seeks to enter and understand. For Agar (1994) "[c]ulture is a conceptual system whose surface appears in the words of people's language" (p. 79).

Agar (1994) captures the underlying theoretical arguments about language–culture relationships in the following:

> Language, in all its varieties, in all the ways it appears in everyday life, builds a world of meanings. When you run into different meanings, when you become aware of your own and work to build a bridge to the others, "culture" is what you're up to. Language fills the spaces between us with sound; culture forges the human connection through them. Culture is in language, and language is loaded with culture. (p. 28)

This relationship between different languacultures, as the analyses in this study will show, was a central construct to uncovering what was happening at points of contact between actors from different systems (classroom/field placement and university ECTE program) or roles within a common system (university ECTE supervisor and other members of the supervisory team). From this perspective, what becomes potentially visible when there is a difference in meanings of common concepts is not merely a personal perspective; rather it is one grounded in, and guided by, particular roles and relationships as well as institutional norms and expectations for particular actors (e.g., supervisor within the ECTE program). Thus, when differences become visible to one or more of the actors, and the actor(s) (and/or ethnographer) begin to wonder what is happening and/or what led to the puzzling situation, Agar argues, *culture happens*. At such points, differences in interpretation of a common phenomenon (e.g., lesson-planning), as argued in the previous section, create a potential anchor for tracing the roots leading to the differences.

With this process of tracing roots of the observed phenomenon, and the routes taken in relationship to this phenomenon by particular actors, the ethnographer creates a process for exploring the roots of the phenomenon grounded in the different languacultures. While Agar used this argument to address what happens when an ethnographer enters a new social group, we argue that in the present study, the concept of languaculture was a critical argument to understanding the observed actions and references used in relationship to the professional practice that both groups understood as lesson-planning. The initiating question for this chain of analysis, however, came from the external ethnographer, who raised the need for the insider team to locate additional records that made visible what people perceived as important to identify and assess as the practices and processes of lesson planning. By identifying the email trail and by examining other points of contact (e.g., supervisory interview with Brad, the plans themselves, and email exchanges), the external ethnographer enabled the internal team to further examine what counted as lesson planning, to whom, in what ways, for what purposes, and with what outcomes and consequences for different actors within and across the two systems—i.e., the classroom as a professional practice space, and the university team as a different space with professional practices guided not only by internal dialogues and goals but as a space embedded in larger dialogues and practice spaces (i.e., national policy dialogues, dialogues in professional organizations, international policy dialogues). By conceptualizing each as a languaculture and tracing points of contact where actors with different languacultures met, the internal–external ethnography team transformed their conceptualization from a dyadic relationship to one in which intercultural dialogues made visible both common and clashing understandings of common phenomena, *lesson planning*, in these telling case analyses.

16.5 Intertextuality as a Social Construction

While the previous two arguments were critical to framing how we theoretically defined the purpose of the research and ways of viewing the historical roots of the actors at points of contact, in this section we present the concept of intertextuality to frame two additional angles of analysis. Intertextuality was critical to identifying emails and other archived records in which the actors inscribed (spoken or written) a common reference—*planning/lesson-planning*. The identification of this reference across archived records, as indicated previously, provides an empirical grounding for the construction of the two telling cases, each focusing on, and tracing what this term referred to, and how it formed an anchor for constructing two data sets, each framing the basis for examining the point of view of particular actors in particular roles, interacting in particular spaces.

Bloome and Egan-Robertson's research (1993) on intertextuality as a social accomplishment made visible how in and through the discourse (oral and written), actors inscribe historical contexts, meanings as well as actions. This argument, and related research builds on, and provides evidence of Bakhtin's (1986) theoretical argument that "Any utterance is a link in a very complexly organized chain of other utterances," (p. 60). Bloome and Egan-Robertson (1993) further argue that, in and through discourse, actors in a particular event, propose, recognize, acknowledge, and interactionally accomplish what is socially significant, and by extension, academically significant to know, understand, and do.

Bloome et al. (2005) take this argument further by making visible how intertextuality is socially constructed in and through the everyday discourse in which particular events of social life are being constructed. They present how, in and through moment-by-moment interactions in particular events, actors construct local and situated identities, what counts as literacy processes and meanings as well as how in such interactions they make visible locally situated power relationships that define whose perspectives count, when and where, for what purposes and under what conditions.

By grounding the analysis of records from the archive in these conceptual arguments, we created a basis for identifying intertextual references that were then used to bound particular levels and angles of analysis (Green et al. 2012). These conceptual arguments also framed the need to examine roles and relationships being constructed in the local situations among different configurations of actors, not just the official positions each held. This angle of analysis, as the telling cases that follow will show, provided an empirical grounding for examining how, not just what, each actor proposed to others as counting as *professional practices of lesson planning*. It also frames the need to trace the chain of proposed actions to examine how, and in what ways, those with whom the actor was interacting, whether in a common languaculture or in an intercultural space, responded to the email queries and comments sent to them from particular actors in particular social situations, for particular purposes. In this way, these chains of interaction made visible the sources of influence and local inscriptions of what was proposed, recognized, and interactionallly accomplished grounded in collective decisions with others in their official work sites (i.e., the classroom and ECTE program). This logic of inquiry was held constant along with the focus on lesson planning references, while the actors, points of contact, and their frames of reference varied. Through *triangulating differences* in reference, actions, and interactions, as the telling cases will show, the internal–external ethnography team laid a foundation for reflexive decision-making processes that will be discussed in the final section of this paper.

16.6 Telling Case I

An email trail forms the foundation for Telling Case 1. From this email trail, we present a series of analyses of references to lesson-planning processes and performances identified through a form of discourse analysis of chains of interaction between and among particular configurations of actors. By identifying all instances of reference to lesson-planning in emails to both sets of actors (teacher-candidates and supervisory team members), across the six-month period of the second field placement for the teacher-candidates, we constructed a data set focusing on an intertextual web of email exchanges between February 28 and May 17. The assembly of this data set formed a basis for the insider–outsider ethnographic analysis team to (re)examine what happened, who participated in decision-making, and whose particular interpretations of what counted as lesson-planning led to the epistemological differences observed previously. Table 16.1 (re)presents a purposeful set of email exchanges identifed.

To analyze what particular actors inscribed in these email exchanges, we constructed three columns. Column 1 marks the date in which the emails were sent. This column supported analysis of response time among intertextually tied email exchanges. Column 2, Observation Visits Related to Email Exchanges About Lesson-Planning, indicates who sent emails to whom, creating a basis for identifying intertextually tied cycles of interaction among particular configurations of actors. Column 3, Context and referential content of texts (re)presents the referential content and focus of the emails. The intertextually tied exchanges were separated by blank rows, creating a visual chain for analysis that parallels work on transcribing as theoretically guided action (Ochs 1979). Each chain, therefore, is bounded by blank rows to make analysis of the referential information by particular actors visible.

At the beginning, and throughout the ECTE program, teacher-candidates were provided with a specific set of practices and a template regarding lesson planning. One of the university-supervisor's roles is to review and provide feedback to the teacher-candidates on their lesson planning. As indicated in Table 16.1, Column 1, the earliest inscription of a frame clash in lesson-planning was identified in a reflective email (February 28) to the other embedded ethnographer, in which Denise, the supervisor, referenced a growing awareness about "*missing lesson plans for teaching from both candidates*". What this email also made visible was that Denise had received "*scarce written reflections from Brad*, although weekly reflections were required of both teacher-candidates. This growing awareness, therefore, served as a rich point for further exploration of what Brad-as-a-tracer-unit took up, or not, and what kinds of responses to requests for information or missing lesson plans were made by each student.

The next reference to missing assignments, field journal (reflective logs), was identified in email exchanges (March 4–7) between Denise and Brad. In this exchange, she once again referenced missing assignments; however, in this exchange with Brad, she also inscribed not only a request for the missing records

Table 16.1 Observations and email exchanges focusing on lesson-planning

Dates	Observation visits related to email exchanges about lesson-planning	Context and referential content of texts
Feb. 28	*Denise* reflective email to the other embedded ethnographer	*I am beginning to see missing lesson plans for teaching from both candidates and scarce written reflections from Brad*
Mar 4	Denise emails Brad	Denise reminds Brad of doing his missing field journals Asks for missing journals in email. Denise assigns several questions to be considered
Mar 7	Brad answers and sends his requested reflection. Denise responds	Brad makes great progress. Denise makes suggestions and adds ideas
Mar 18a	Brad responds to email from Denise	To inform Denise that he is missing his lesson plans due to job interviewing
Mar 18b	Denise sends reminder emails to all of her assigned candidates	Restating program norm and expectations about policies on lesson plan preparation and absences
Mar 19	Denise visits both candidates and has three way conferences each: Brad, Mentor-Teacher and Supervisor; Amy, Mentor-Teacher and Supervisor	Checking progress for individual teacher-candidates [does not meet as whole with full team]
Apr 27	Brad sends email to Denise	Required weekly email reflection of lessons taught
Apr 28	Denise emails Brad	Denise responds to his reflection Denise notices his lesson plans lacks several components of required format Denise send him some good sample lesson plans
Apr 29a	Denise emails Brad	Asks for week's lesson plans
Apr 29b	Brad emails Denise	Sends last week's lesson plans
Apr 29c	Denise emails Brad	Asks for the current week's plans
Apr 30a	Brad sends the current week's plans	Denise sees many missing pieces in thinking and thorough planning for lessons
Apr 30b	Denise contacts program manager for feedback	
May 1	Program manager emails supervisor with feedback	Agrees with Denise's concerns that lesson plans need attention. Requests additional information
Apr 30	Amy also sends in her plans	
May 11a	Denise emails program manager and director	Informs them of missing lesson plans and Amy's absence Provides information about Amy's pattern of absence
May 11b	Denise emails Amy	Reminds her again about program norms about absence
May 11c	Denise emails Brad	Requests lesson plans

(continued)

Table 16.1 (continued)

Dates	Observation visits related to email exchanges about lesson-planning	Context and referential content of texts
May 12	Brad responds in email to Denise	Informs her that he places past lesson plans in a folder in the classroom
May 12	Amy sends her lesson plans	For the past weeks, even though they are required in advance
May 14	*Denise observes Brad*	
May 17	Brad sends Denise his lesson plans	

but also actions she proposed to guide his writing of the missing reflections. As indicated in the chain, Brad then responded by sending the requested reflections. Denise's response is both critical and supportive in multiple ways, leading her to conclude that Brad was "*making great progress.*"

The ways in which she provided feedback made visible how she sought to support his growth in reflecting on his teaching, while also providing areas for further exploration. This email chain, therefore, provided evidence of how the supervisor understood her role as support for the Brad's learning as well as how he took up her suggested questions to complete the assignment at this point in time. However, as a later exchange indicates (March 18), Brad once again failed to submit his lesson plans. This time, however, the omission was not due to a lack of understanding of the required content but because of external factors, i.e., job search.

On April 28, the issue of missing components was also raised in the chain between April 29 and 30, in which she sent a request to Brad for missing lesson plans. This latter exchange made visible how Brad elected to respond to this request. One way of interpreting his initial response to the supervisor was that she was not specific about which plans to submit, since she did not reference past or present plans that were missing. Given this was approximately four months into the program, and a recurrent theme, we argue that Brad was aware of the requirement for weekly submission of lesson plans and that his failure to send in his plans deserved further exploration, one not possible solely from the email trail.

The analysis of Brad's email exchanges formed a rich point, one that raised questions for the external ethnographer about the reporting system within the ECTE program and the relationship among actors in the chain of supervision. This question led to identification of a chain of interactions between the program manager and Denise, as indicated in her emails on April 30b/May 1. In this email chain, Denise raised concerns about how she should address Brad's growing pattern of action (failure to submit lesson plans until requested), and how to assess his competence in lesson-planning, which was a program requirement for her work. This shift in interactional actors made visible to whom Denise was accountable within the larger ECTE program. Denise sent another email on May 11 to the program manager, and this time included the program director. Email exchanges prior to May 11 between Denise and Amy Ithe female teacher-candidate) had focused on a concern of Amy's absences from her placement. In this email, Denise shifts her concern from Brad to Amy's pattern of absences. This shift became a rich point for further analysis of the chain of these interactions. Like Brad, Amy was not following the program's policies on how to inform the program when she would be absent.

The repeated nature of both exchanges to Brad, and then to her supervisory team members, led to identification of indicators of points of tension between the field-based team and the university program's expectations. The requests to her own supervisor and program director identified a tension that the students' actions, or rather lack of action, had for her in fulfilling her positions as support for these students as well as assessor of their performances.

At this point in the analysis, therefore, we, in our role as analysts, faced a challenge in explaining how to understand the significance of these chains of analyses. While they made visible a tension between the perspectives of different actors, they did not provide sufficient contextual information on which to build warranted claims about sources of the epistemological differences. This led us to seek additional sources of information. One such source was identified when, on May 12 (see Table 16.1) Brad "Informs her that he places past lesson plans in a folder in the classroom," suggesting there was a norm at the classroom level that was agreed to by the instructional team in the classroom as to what to do with lesson plans and where they should be placed.

This message, therefore, created an anchor for the second telling case. This telling case required us, as the insider–outsider ethnography team, to (re)enter the archive in order to identify additional records where classroom processes and practices related to team planning were referenced. This second telling case, therefore, was undertaken to provide further contextualized information about the students' work in planning from the angle of classroom actors in order to identify how these classroom actions related to the requirement demonstrating competence in lesson-planning and teaching from the lesson plans.

16.7   Telling Case 2

Based on analyses of the exchanges described in Telling Case 1, our first step was to return to the archive to identify any references in emails from the teacher at, or, around this particular point in time (May 12) that might provide contextual information about what was happening in the classroom that might have led Brad to keep the plans in the classroom, even though he knew that he was expected to send them to the university-supervisor prior to her observations (1–2 times per week). At the same time, we sought to identify potential records from interviews with Brad or Amy that could add further evidence into the relationship between teacher-candidate actions and university requirements from the perspective of the mentor-teacher and/or teacher-candidates.

The search of the archive for mentor-teacher emails related to lesson-planning and other classroom processes led to the identification of an email in which mentor-teacher inscribed what the supervisor should expect to see. This email was sent just prior to observations that the supervisor would undertake during student teaching, which began approximately on May 14. On this date, Denise was to observe Brad's teaching in the classroom.

As indicated in the email, the mentor-teacher explained how she, and the teacher-candidates, functioned as a team, not just in planning but also teaching. Below she explicitly foreshadowed for the supervisor what she should expect to see in her observations during their student teaching period.

> Keep in mind that when you are observing, you might see one or two of us in "helper" positions while one teaches. We agreed that the lead teacher would be the one who makes these "on your feet" decisions based on the needs of the students for that particular part of the lesson. A few students enter the room after a transition period ... and are having problems settling down and focusing on the lesson; students sometimes enter the room needing special attention ...; there often are several needy situations occurring simultaneously. Getting a high percentage of engagement sometimes takes a while. This is when the lead teacher might decide to change the way the lesson is delivered and the roles of the other two teachers. It should be noted in your plan that they function as co-teachers who support the instruction.

What she inscribed in this text was an ongoing process of planning and teaching that had been purposefully developed among these actors to support student learning in this urban classroom. In this email, she also inscribed the history of the team, and processes and practices that defined what constitutes lead teaching for this team as well as planning. In framing the fact that the supervisor may observe changes in the plan that were reflected in "on your feet" decisions by the lead teacher, she made visible why the "planned" lesson might be modified and that the others on the team would respond to this modification in the moment. She also framed how actions of students, who would be returning to the class, made such in-the-moment modifications necessary to support these students in "settling down" and or respond to those students who had "special needs."

Her email, therefore, can be interpreted as making visible prior conversations among the team about work together, and also how to communicate to the supervisor (and by extension the university team) areas in which the supervisor had previously raised questions of the teacher-candidates. Her email also showed that she was experienced in communicating about her classroom processes and practices that foregrounded how she worked with her third grade urban students, and by extension, how she was engaging the teacher-candidates in developing a responsive planning process in which the planned curricular activities was subject to revision in the face of the responses and actions of students. In this email, she also inscribed a process of lead teaching within this team as one in which the actors negotiate in the moment as well as in preplanned ways. This process framed who would do what, when and where, with whom, in response to what they were observing in relationship to students in the developing activity (lesson). In her text to the supervisor, therefore, she framed the team's situated approach to planning–teaching relationships, and indicated how the candidates were meeting expectations of the program in ways unanticipated by the program, as indicated in the frame clashes related to lesson-planning identified in Telling Case 1.

This email, therefore, served as the roots of the collection of additional records in this second telling case. This analysis of what was inscribed in her email framed the need for the insider–outsider ethnography team to return to the archive in order to locate, through a process of backward mapping processes (Green et al 2012) from this email, previous discussions of the planning and teaming process at other points of contact between the teacher-candidates and university-supervisor. This backward mapping process led to one additional source of information that could then be triangulated with the teacher's inscription of the team's working process. This record was an interview on February 28, by the embedded ethnographer with Brad about how the team was engaging in a process of lesson-planning.

16.8 Triangulation as a Nonlinear Process—Analysis 2 in Telling Case 2

Once the interview was identified as an anchor for further exploration about how, and in what ways, the teacher-candidates inscribed a process of planning within a team context, we constructed a transcript of the interview. Given the repeated contacts Brad had about missing elements in his lesson plans as well as missing lesson plans, the insider–outsider ethnography team decided to focus on Brad's interview. This decision extended Brad's role as a tracer unit to this phase of the research, building on Mitchell's argument presented previously that an individual could be the focus of a telling case. In selecting Brad's early interview, as a point of triangulation, we were able to identify the actors with whom he worked in the class and other spaces, to construct a point for reflexivity for the insider–outsider ethnography team.

In this transcript, Brad discussed an ongoing nature of planning; i.e., Thursdays the team reflected on activities they conducted that week and then, would plan for activities they would implement the following Wednesday and Thursday in the actual third grade class. He then indicated their ideas would be brought to a team discussion with Megan, the mentor-teacher. Following the teaching of the plan, Brad stated that he and Amy would discuss with Megan what was accomplished in the teaching and propose ideas for the following week's activities with students in the class. Following this, they went home and individually wrote down some of their ideas of what they each wanted to do and discussed those ideas with each other on Tuesdays between university courses. They would then further discuss them, with the mentor-teacher on Wednesday, in their field placement. For example, in Table 16.2, he indicated possible content areas that each would develop plans for the team to explore. Additionally, he indicated that they would identify students who had special needs that would require specific support from one or all of the

Table 16.2 Transcript of February interview with Brad

Brad	Amy and I would meet on Tuesday in between (university) classes
	And we would bring ideas together
	what we need to discuss with Megan
	And on Thursday,
	we would all meet to reflect on the week
	and then discuss what was going on next week,
	as far as,
	I would try a math lesson
	and Amy would try a social studies lesson,
	or what kinds of assignments we would be working on
	and who would need to pull out students for assignments

team members to successfully work with the content. This latter description, when triangulated with the teacher's email around May 14, provides further clarification of what the teacher meant by "students often entered the room needing special attention." Finally, in the chain of activity and planning actions Brad inscribed, he made visible the basis for the mentor-teacher's claim that they were meeting the university's expectations for competent performance in planning and teaching.

As this brief analysis of Table 16.2 was contrasted with the mentor-teacher's description of what the supervisor could expect to see, Brad's description provided convergent validation of the chain of actions that the supervisor would be able to see. The backward mapping process, therefore, provided a means of triangulating inscribed activity in the classroom by the team as well as the ways in which planning was a process among the actors that served particular purposes that were undertaken by the teacher-candidates in multiple spaces at multiple times. This process was not captured in the required lesson plan that the ECTE program introduced to, and expected from, the teacher-candidates. This distinction was one not visible in the analysis of email conversations, providing further evidence that the epistemological differences were rooted in different assumptions about what counts as evidence of planning and teaching competencies grounded in different institutional spaces.

16.9 Discussion and Implications

In this study, we demonstrated how an interactional ethnographic analysis of points of contact between a field-based team and university actors, each representing a different languaculture, made visible a series of frame clashes. These frame clashes were grounded in differing expectations for what should be happening in the classroom, or should be displayed as meeting standards and requirements of the program. These frame clashes made visible differences in cultural expectations of the institutionally based actors. These frame clashes were often bidirectional; that is, the clash had consequences for how each actor viewed their work, met their responsibilities, and took up, or not, what the other proposed.

The findings identified an unanticipated contradiction with the ECTE program—while the program's early childhood pedagogy is based on student-centered, culturally relevant, hands-on activities, and ways of accommodating to diverse needs of students. This model was not visible in the ways in which the program expected candidates to adhere to state standards for demonstration of teacher competencies. As indicated in the analysis, the field-based team (re)formulated, and provided a rationale for what counted as appropriate ways of planning and teaming. However, the university-supervisory program did not adjust to their rationale and continued to use standards to assess teacher competencies that conflicted with the field placement's standards for instructing third graders.

Although Amy and Brad did not complete requirements according to the university-supervisory program, they both met the graduating teacher competencies. The following year both secured elementary teaching positions. Brad who is teaching near the ECTE Program has returned to the program to share his experiences as a practicing teacher and what he learned from the program.

The unanticipated findings of the impact of competing policies contributed to a decision within the program leadership to (1) focus more on student learning and not just teacher performance, (2) rethink program requirements for lesson-planning to further align with the languaculture of the field-based placement, and (3) rethink supervisory practices that support teacher-candidate(s) as being part of a school-based team with their mentor-teacher. These unanticipated findings were influenced by the insider–outsider ethnography team by creating a reflexive stance for further in-depth analysis. Green, as the outsider, was able to make visible from the archive of data, in this case email trails, the roots and routes taken by the actors between the languacultures that were not visible from only an insider perspective. In summary, this insider–outsider approach is critical for teacher education programs as they continue addressing the challenges of preparing competent teachers for Twenty-First Century Learning.

References

Agar, M. (1994). *Language shock: Understanding the culture of conversation* (pp. 140–163). New York, NY: Wm. Morrow.

Agar, M. (2006). Culture. Can you take it anywhere? *International Journal of Qualitative Methods, 5*(2), 1–12. Retrieved from http://www.ualberta.ca/ ~ iiqm/backissue/5_2PDF/agar.pdf

Avalos, B. (2011). Teacher professional development in teaching and teacher education over ten years. *Teaching and Teacher Education, 27,* 10–20.

Bakhtin, M. (1986). *Speech genres and other late essays.* Austin: University of Texas Press.

Bloome, D., Carter, S. P., Otto, S., & Shuart-Faris, N. (2005). *Discourse analysis and the study of language and literacy events: A microethnographic perspective.* Mahwah, NJ: Lawrence Erlbaum.

Bloome, D., & Egan-Roberston, A. (1993). The social construction of intertextuality in classroom reading and writing lessons. *Reading Research Quarterly, 28*(4), 304–333.

Green, J. L., Skukauskaite, A., & Baker, W. D. (2012). Research methodologies and methods in education.

Heap, J. (1985). Discourse in the production of classroom knowledge: Reading lessons. *Curriculum Inquiry, 15*(3), 245–279.

Heath, S. B. (1982). Ethnography in education: Defining the essentials. In P. Gillmore & A. A. Glatthorn (Eds.), *Children in and out of school: Ethnography and education* (pp. 33–55). Washington, D.C.: Center for Applied Linguistics.

Joram, E. (2007). Clashing epistemologies: Aspiring teachers', practicing teachers', and professors' beliefs about knowledge and research in education. *Teaching and Teacher Education, 23*, 123–135.

Katz, L., & Green, J. (2012). Exploring continuities and discontinuities for teacher candidates between university and early childhood classrooms. In M.-S. Honig & S. Neumann (Eds.), *(Doing) Ethnography in early childhood education and care*. Proceedings of an International Colloquium at the University of Luxembourg.

Katz, L., & Isik-Ercan, Z. (2015). Challenging points of contact among supervisor, mentor teacher and teacher candidates: Conflicting institutional expectations. *Pedagogies: An International Journal, 10*(1), 54–69.

Mitchell, J. C. (1984). Typicality and the case study. In R. Ellen (Ed.), *Ethnographic research: A guide to general conduct* (pp. 238–241). New York: Academic Press.

Murray, J., Swennen, A., & Shagrir, L. (2009). Understanding teacher educators' work and identities. In A. Swennen & M. van der Klink (Eds.), *Becoming a teacher educator: Theory and practice for teacher educators* (pp. 29–44). Dordrecht: Springer.

Ochs, E. (1979). Transcription as theory. In E. Ochs & B. Scheiffelin (Eds.), *Developmental pragmatics* (pp. 43–72). New York: Academic.

Tannen, D. (1979). Whats in a frame? Surface evidence for underlying expectations. In R. Freedle (Ed.). *New directions in discourse processing* (pp. 137–181). Norwood, NJ: Ablex.

Author Biographies

Laurie Katz (EdD, University of Massachusetts Amherst) is Professor in Department of Teaching & Learning at The Ohio State University. Her research focuses on teacher preparation, young children and families from birth—8 years of age, inclusive education and narrative styles and structures of young children.

Judith Green (Ph.D., University of California Berkeley) is Professor Emeritus of Education, University of California, Santa Barbara-Gevirtz Graduate School of Education. Her research focuses on discourse and ethnographic studies of knowledge construction in educational settings from Pre-K through Higher Education.

Chapter 17
Networked Teaching and Learning for Life-Long Professional Development

Mandia Mentis and Alison Kearney

17.1 Introduction

Our societies are in the midst of intense economic, social, and technological change, and around the world educators and policymakers are being challenged to ensure that education systems are cognizant of these changes and that education is relevant for the demands of twenty-first-century citizenship. In particular, the democratization and changing understandings of knowledge; the growing connectedness and diversity of societies; the need for life-long and life-wide learning; and the critical role that technology will play, have been shown to be some of the important considerations in the planning of twenty-first-century learning environments.

These changes have significant implications for teacher education and ongoing teacher professional learning. A reconceptualization of the design and delivery of teaching programs is required to prepare teachers for learning environments that are interconnected, technology-enabled, and information-rich. In a 2012 OECD report into preparing teachers and school leaders for the twenty-first century, Schleicher (2012) highlighted that, along with in-depth subject knowledge and a rich repertoire of teaching and learning strategies, twenty-first-century teachers will require strong skills in technology; the ability to be able to work in highly collaborative ways with other teachers, professionals, and organizations; and the skills and dispositions to be reflective practitioners. They will also need to be able to take responsibility for developing themselves professionally and be instruments of innovation.

This chapter provides a case study of a professional learning program that responds to these challenges by using a networked teaching and learning approach in

M. Mentis (✉) · A. Kearney
Massey University, Palmerston North, New Zealand
e-mail: m.mentis@massey.ac.nz

A. Kearney
e-mail: a.c.kearney@massey.ac.n

© Springer Nature Singapore Pte Ltd. 2017   253
M.A. Peters et al. (eds.), *A Companion to Research in Teacher Education*,
DOI 10.1007/978-981-10-4075-7_17

its design and delivery. It shifts from a traditional static approach of information transfer through formal, structured lessons to a more networked understanding of teaching and learning. This networked approach involves designing a technology-enabled community of inquiry and interprofessional practice for life-long learning. The interconnected, fluid, and complex nature of twenty-first-century teaching and learning is accommodated in this program through the three elements of technology-enabled, interprofessional, and inquiry-based. These three design elements will be detailed in this chapter following a brief introduction to, and description of, the context and structure of the program. An evaluation of each of the three design aspects will then be presented, using the combined data from three cohorts of teachers who graduated from the program. This data illustrates the teachers' perceptions of the importance of these three elements, their preparedness on entry into the program, and their sense of achievement on completing the program to learn and work through a technology-enabled community of inquiry and interprofessional practice. Conclusions are drawn and suggestions are made to keep advanced professional learning programs relevant for a changing educational landscape.

17.2   Specialist Resource Teacher Program

The Specialist Resource Teacher program was developed in response to a call from the New Zealand Ministry of Education for the provision of an advanced post-graduate course that would support both specialist and common core competencies for advanced specialty teaching areas within the workforce. The program is for experienced teachers and practitioners to gain further skills and knowledge to work in a variety of educational contexts alongside teachers, parents, students, and other professionals to improve educational outcomes for all learners.

This professional education program is a joint initiative funded by the New Zealand Ministry of Education and managed by a consortium partnership of two New Zealand universities, one in the North Island and one in the South Island. The program attracts teachers and practitioners geographically from all regions across New Zealand and from seven specialist areas including: Autism Spectrum Disorder; Blind and Low Vision; Complex Educational Needs; Deaf and Hearing Impairment; Early Intervention; Gifted and Talented; and Learning and Behavior. Graduates of the program become resource teachers in these specialist areas and contribute to the practice of Special and Inclusive Education in a range of contexts, including early years, primary, secondary and tertiary sectors, and government and nongovernment organizations.

The program is delivered as a postgraduate, part-time, flexible, and blended qualification, using both online and face-to-face learning environments, thus enabling teachers to participate anytime anywhere, while continuing to work and study from home regardless of location. It is highly practical and self-directed, and teachers are encouraged to focus their learning on their authentic casework. Generic core content across all specialist areas as well as specialist content is covered to facilitate a shared understanding of common knowledge and skills across and within specialist areas. This generic and specialized content was established prior to the start of the program through conducting a national survey of 92 stakeholders and 65 nominated individuals with interests in the specialist areas. Over 400 survey responses fed into the initial program design, and ongoing development occurs through consultation with seven Stakeholder Advisory groups, including a Māori,[1] Pasifika and Multiethnic Advisory Group that cross all specialist areas, ensuring relevance for the diversity of students from different backgrounds and with different needs across New Zealand.

The program is based on a technology-enabled Community of Inquiry and Interprofessional Practice model. These three design dimensions: technology-enabled; interprofessional; and inquiry-based will be discussed in the sections below, with descriptions of how each one of these is applied in the program. For each of the three dimensions, we report on data gathered from three cohorts of teachers who have graduated from the program. The teachers completed online surveys at the beginning of the first year and final year of their 2-year program. The surveys covered a wide range of questions, but of particular relevance to this chapter were those questions related to interprofessional practice and learning in a community of practice, technology-enabled learning, and inquiry learning. The survey at the beginning of year 1 asked participants to rate their perceptions of the importance of each of these aspects of the program on a 4-point Likert scale from very important (1) to not important (4), and to rate their sense of preparedness to address each of these aspects of the program from very prepared (1) to not prepared (4). The end of program survey repeated the importance scale and also asked teachers to rate how well they thought they had achieved in each of these areas from very well achieved (1) to not achieved (4).

Table 17.1 provides information on the number of teachers enrolled in the program in each year, the number who agreed to participate in the research and the number who completed the surveys.

For each cohort, demographic data were collected in the first survey. In relation to all three cohorts, the majority of teachers were aged between 40 and 55, were female, and identified as of New Zealand or European descent (Table 17.2).

Participants in the study represented all seven endorsement areas as shown in Table 17.3.

For the purposes of this discussion, data for all three cohorts have been combined. This is because there were no significant differences between the cohorts over the 4-year period of this project. Data from all three cohorts aligned in terms of their responses to the model of learning. Discussion of these three elements of interprofessional practice, inquiry-based learning, and technology-enabled teaching and learning will follow in the next sections along with the teachers' perceptions of the

---

[1]Indigenous people of New Zealand.

Table 17.1 Survey response rates

	Survey	Total enrolments	Research participants	Number of responses	Response rate (%)
Cohort 1	Beginning year 1	171	106	76	72
	End year 2		84	35	42
Cohort 2	Beginning year 1	146	112	65	58
	End year 2		90	46	51
Cohort 3	Beginning year 1	288	195	126	
	End year 2		161	60	

Table 17.2 Demographic data

	Mean age group	Gender %			Ethnicity %		
		Male	Female	Missing	European	Maori	Other
Cohort 1	40–55	10	78	12	70	13	17
Cohort 2	40–55	5	92	3	74	4	22
Cohort 3	40–55	8	90	2	68	17	15

Table 17.3 Participants across endorsement areas

	Cohort one % of total sample		Cohort two % of total sample		Cohort three % of total sample	
	Pre (N = 76)	End (N = 35)	Pre (N = 65)	End (N = 46)	Pre (N = 126)	End (N = 60)
Autism spectrum disorder	11.8	17.1	20.0	26.1	9.5	8.3
Blind and vision impairment	6.6	8.6	7.7	8.7	4.0	5.0
Complex educational needs	n/a[a]	n/a	n/a	n/a	6.3	8.3
Deaf and hearing impairment	9.2	5.7	29.2	23.9	2.4	1.7
Early intervention	10.5	5.7	13.8	15.2	7.1	10.0
Gifted and talented	0	0	6.2	0	3.2	1.7
Learning and behavior	60.5	62.9	20.0	26.1	67.5	65.0
Missing	1.3	0	3.1	0	0	0
Total	100	100	100	100	100	100

[a]The Complex Educational Needs Endorsement did not begin until 2011

importance of these dimensions, their preparedness on entering the program and their achievement on exiting the program to work and learning in technology-enabled.

17.3   Interprofessional Practice

With the growing worldwide emphasis on inclusive education systems, student populations within schools are becoming more and more diverse and can include students with highly complex learning, behavior, health, and/or social needs. Because of this complexity, it is not uncommon to find a range of professionals; for example teachers, psychologists, therapists, social workers, and specialist teachers, all providing some aspect of support to a student and his or her teacher. However, research shows that it is not enough for professionals to simply act independently and in isolation from each other. Effectively meeting complex needs will typically require a focus on interprofessional practice where teachers and professionals work together, communicating and sharing expertise, and delivering a coordinated and integrated service (Bridges et al. 2011; World Health Organization 2010).

The notion of interprofessional practice originated in the health sector and is based on an integrated and cohesive framework for collaboration among professionals (Geva et al. 2000). The literature provides multiple definitions of interprofessional practice, and while there are differences between them, there are also common elements. Interprofessional practice involves a team of professionals working together while bringing their own identity, skills, knowledge, and expertise for the benefit of end users. There is also general agreement that interprofessional practice involves cooperation and collaboration between team members who share a common purpose and mutual respect for the roles and identities of team members (Barr 2002).

However, while most descriptions of interprofessional practice emphasize aspects of collaboration, working together, sharing knowledge, expertise, and power; for some researchers the meaning goes much deeper than this. Trodd and Chivers (2011) describe interprofessional practice as an "ontological position" (p. 2) where professionals' identities are formed through their interactions with others. Now, more than ever, there is a need for teachers and other involved in education to work interprofessionally, however, in order to practice effectively interprofessionally, professionals need to learn how to do this, which involves learning together. Interprofessional education has been described as two or more professionals learning "about, from and with each other" (World Health Organization 2010, p. 13) and is seen as a critical component of interprofessional practice. This is because it fosters collaboration, enhances shared understandings between professionals about each other's roles, and promotes the practice of combining expertise for improved outcomes (WHO 2010; Barr and Low 2013).

Within the Specialist Teaching program, *interprofessional practice* involves a redesigning of traditional training models and a move toward an orientation where allied programs are integrated and aligned so that teachers and future practitioners can learn *with* each other, *from* each other, and *about* each other. This approach allows for interaction, communication, and collaboration across and within disciplines during the different courses of study to facilitate an understanding of the varied specialist qualifications thus enhancing future practice in multidisciplinary teams. The extent to which members of a team have a shared understanding will result in better outcomes in casework. Learners who engage in educational programs that strive to develop knowledge, skills, attitudes, and behavior across professional boundaries, will be able to respond to different knowledge bases, reflect on their values, and thereby improve provision of services across education teams.

Three of the four courses in the program are taught interprofessionally as one cohort, and the principles underpinning each broad domain competency in each course are then applied to the different specialist areas. The domain competencies include: culturally responsive practice; ethical and reflective practice; contextualized practice; interprofessional practice; and evidence-based practice. Teachers have different tasks specifically structured *within* their specialist area, for example, online forums to critique specialized practices, as well as *across* specialist areas, for example, co-constructed glossaries to compare practices, language, values, and approaches. The online environment allows for sharing of resources such as assessment tools, intervention packages or good readings, both *within* and *across* disciplines. Hence the motto of the program "learning with, from and about" is central to the learning design of both the face-to-face and online interaction. Teachers co-construct and collaborate *with* each other to explore their own specialist area in depth and share this with others, thus learning *from* each other *about* the different specialisms. This shared understanding of all the specialist areas impacts on future practice—as teachers who learn together interprofessionally, work together more effectively in interdisciplinary teams in later practice.

The graph below outlines teachers' perceptions of their preparedness (at the beginning of course) and their achievement (at the end of course) of key aspects of *interprofessional practice*.

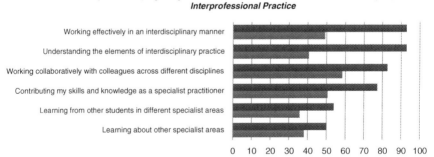

Preparedness (Beginning of Course) and achievement (End of Course) of key aspects of
Interprofessional Practice

At the beginning of the course, those aspects of interprofessional learning teachers felt most prepared to engage in were working collaboratively with colleagues across different disciplines (58.3% felt prepared or very prepared to do this), and contributing their skills and knowledge (50.6% felt prepared or very prepared to do this). Those aspects that participants felt least prepared to engage in were learning from other teachers in different specialist areas (only 35.8% felt prepared or very prepared to do this) and learning about other specialist areas (only 38% felt prepared or very prepared to do this). These areas also had the lowest levels of improvement with 53.9 and 50% of respondents respectively feeling they had achieved or well achieved these by the end of the program. Understanding the elements of interdisciplinary practice and working effectively in an interdisciplinary manner were the two aspects of interprofessional learning that most participants (92.9 and 92.9%, respectively) felt that had achieved or achieved well by the end of the course.

Participants were also asked to indicate the importance they placed on these key aspects of interprofessional practice both at the beginning of the program and at the end. The aspect of interprofessional practice thought most important at the beginning of the program was "working effectively in an interdisciplinary manner," where 86% of respondents thought that this was either important or very important. The aspect of interprofessional practice thought least important at the beginning for the program was 'learning about other specialist areas' with 58% of respondents rating this as important or very important. At the end of the program, these remained the participants' perceptions of the most and least important aspects of interprofessional practice however, the number of participants who thought them important or very important had grown to 71 and 72%, respectively. Also worth noting is that at the end of the program, participants' perceptions of the importance of all of these key aspects of interprofessional practice had increased. At the end of the program, participants were asked to describe those aspects of the program that had been most beneficial. The aspects of interprofessional practice that featured in their responses included opportunities to meet and learn with and about other professionals and to discuss aspects of their own practice with others, as indicated in the following student comment:

> (This course) has allowed me to expand my networks and learn from and alongside a broad range of people who are all passionate about and committed to ensuring that all children receive a quality education that responds to their needs and challenges them to be the best they can be. (Teacher feedback 2013)

Other comments from teachers about the beneficial aspects of the course included:

- *Working interprofessionally and having easy access to a range of specialist who expanded what I knew about learning.*
- *Having a range of local practitioners to discuss my day-to-day practice and study with.*
- *I learned so much about practice from other endorsement areas. This has encouraged me to consider further study in these areas.*
- *Working and learning alongside peers from the same and different endorsements helped me to shape my professional identity.*

17.4   Inquiry-Based Learning

Inquiry learning is a learner-centered, learner-directed pedagogy that involves students making decisions regarding what learning is important to them, what resources they will need, and what actions they will take to achieve their learning goals (Blessinger and Carfora 2014). Through the process of inquiry learning, students construct knowledge and understanding, becoming increasingly more self-sufficient and responsible for their own learning (Blessinger and Carfora 2014; Spronken-Smith et al. 2008). Advantages of inquiry learning include increased participation of students in the learning process, more active and participatory learning, a focus on authentic learning, better alignment to career aspirations, a focus on the skills required for higher order thinking, and the promotion of skills required for life-long learning, particularly around knowledge production (Blessinger and Carfora 2014).

In a study investigating an interdisciplinary inquiry-based learning project across an educational psychology and a social work program in Scotland, Hannah et al. (2014) found that inquiry-based learning facilitated the development of professional identities while fostering interdisciplinary learning and collaboration. In particular, respondents in the study reported an increased awareness and understanding of other professional roles, a valuing of differing perspectives, and an increased commitment to collaborative practice. Inquiry learning approaches have been shown to support interprofessional teaching and learning (Hannah et al. 2014), and promote higher level learning (Richmond et al. 2015).

In the Specialist Resource Teaching program, the rationale for including inquiry-based learning as a design element was to facilitate a student-centered and research-based approach to life-long educational development. This approach enables resource teachers to experience the processes of knowledge creation and equips them with the skills and values to think critically and adapt to change in their workplace. It facilitates the move to self-directed learning and the development of skills in self-reflection, as it is driven by interest and relevant work-related questions and problems. It aligns with a collaborative approach, community involvement, fieldwork, or practicum as well as an interprofessional focus.

Inquiry learning in this program was framed as being both "information-oriented" as well as "discovery oriented" (Levy 2009). As such the learning experiences ranged from structured inquiry (teacher-directed), scaffolded inquiry (teacher-guided), as well as open inquiry (learner-directed). Traditional training models were redesigned to enable the teachers to set their own learning agenda, depending on the context of their work environment, their interests, and their previous experience. Teachers set their own learning goals that meet the competencies of the program, thus individualizing their learning for their needs and settings. To facilitate this, the program uses a "flipped" delivery approach, whereby extensive curriculum content for all competency areas is open to all teachers at all times. This content is presented in the online learning environment (which uses *Moodle* software) and covers a greater depth and breadth than is required for any individual teacher or specialist area. It takes the form of online books, resource packages, professional readings, videos, podcasts, video interviews, databases, glossaries, and course updates. This content serves as both a resource and curriculum, as teachers select the specific information they need to meet their unique learning goal and fulfill their personalized assignments. Typically teachers begin each course by taking the online quiz as formative assessment to determine their areas of interest, gaps in knowledge and get an overview of the content area. They then generate their specific learning goals, and focus on relevant content to enable them to engage in online forum discussions, complete assignments as well as curate and collate artifacts as evidence of meeting the core competencies of the course. All teachers will have unique learning goals, cover different content areas, and develop artifacts that are relevant to their own individual work context and professional identity. This student-centered method enables the teachers to direct their own learning that is both linked to the specialist course competencies and relevant to their professional practice context, thus making their learning individualized and authentic. The online site enables a flipping of the curriculum whereby ongoing anytime, anywhere access to course material enables teachers to select relevant content when needed to complete their unique learning inquiry. The site remains open and available to teachers once they graduate, as alumni, enabling them to continually access updated information to inform their ongoing life-long learning and practice as part of the growing community specialist teachers.

Teachers' perceptions of their preparedness (at the beginning of course) and their achievement (at the end of course) of key aspects of inquiry learning are outlined in the figure below.

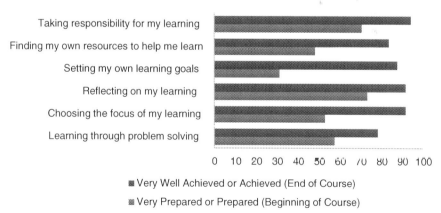

Preparedness (Beginning of course) and achievement (End of course) of key aspects of *Inquiry Learning*

At the beginning of the course, those aspects of inquiry learning teachers felt most prepared to engage in were reflecting on their learning (73.2% felt either prepared or very prepared to do this) and taking responsibility for their learning

(70.5% felt prepared or very prepared to do this). Those aspects that participants felt least prepared to engage in were setting their own learning goals (only 31.2% felt prepared or very prepared to do this) and finding their own resources to help them learn (only 48.1% felt either prepared or very prepared to do this). By the end of the course however between 83.5 and 94.2% of participants felt that they had either achieved or well achieved these practices.

Participants were also asked to indicate the importance they placed on these key aspects of inquiry learning both at the beginning of the program and at the end. The aspect of inquiry thought most important at the beginning of the program was taking responsibility for my learning where 98% of respondents thought that this was either important or very important. The aspect of inquiry learning thought least important at the beginning for the program was learning through problem solving with 84% of respondents rating this as important or very important. At the end of the program, these remained the participants' perceptions of the most and least important aspects of inquiry learning however, the number of participants who thought taking responsibility for their learning important or very important had decreased to 96%. The number of respondents who thought learning through problem solving was important or very important had increased to 86%. Other aspects of inquiry learning were also reported as very important or important by less respondents at the end of the program than at the beginning including reflecting on my learning (reducing by 4% of respondents), finding my own resources to help me learn (reducing by 3% of respondents), and setting my own learning goals (reducing by 1% of respondents).

At the end of the program, participants were asked to describe those aspects of the program that had helped them and had been most beneficial. Aspects of inquiry learning featured in these responses. These included opportunities to control the focus of their study, to be flexible, learn at times and rates that suited them and to be able to organize their own learning plan around their strengths and needs. The following participants statements highlight what was valued in the program:

- *Being able to tailor my program around my learning strengths and weaknesses*
- *Selecting my own learning areas, and being able to work at my own speed*
- *Making my own learning goals and choice of associated study*

Participants also noted the following aspects of inquiry learning that helped to shape their professional identity:

- *Learning to become more reflective*
- *Professional inquiry and self-reflection with different communities of practice*
- *Although I found it frustrating at times, the emphasis placed on being a reflective practitioner has really allowed me to identify where I am at and where I need to go next*
- *I did enjoy the self-directed learning (and) I have a greater confidence in myself as a learner and as a person who can shape my own learning*

17.5 Technology-Enabled

If ongoing professional learning and development courses are to be engaging and responsive, they will need to explore the affordances of new technologies that offer the potential for different and innovative ways to connect and network practitioners in interprofessional learning communities (Garrison and Anderson 2003). Two of these new technologies relevant for this discussion and used in the Specialist Teaching program are e-portfolios and digital badging.

An e-portfolio is a digitized collection of text-based, graphic, or multimedia artifacts or collections of work that demonstrate competence in various contexts (Lorenzo and Ittelson 2005). Barrett (2010) defines e-portfolios as an electronic collection of evidence that shows a learning journey over time, and can relate to specific academic fields or life-long learning. Evidence may include writing samples, photos, videos, research projects, observations by mentors and peers, and/or reflective thinking. For Barrett (2010), the key aspect of an e-portfolio is the reflection on the evidence. She identifies two "faces" of an e-portfolio: the Working Portfolio or "workspace", and the Presentation Portfolio or "showcase". The workspace is about process, where the reflection on the chosen artifacts of evidence occurs, and the showcase is about product, where the story or the narrative of learning is presented. These two "faces" combine to produce the individualized narrative of learning.

In the Specialist Teaching program e-portfolios are critical as the learning space of the course. The resource teachers create their own e-portfolios using *Mahara* software to document and reflect on their learning. Teachers' e-portfolios become their showcase and workspace for their developing professional identity and learning. They map their professional learning by exploring how their personal and cultural identity links to their specialist endorsement area. Each teacher's portfolio consists of artifacts as evidence of learning, personal reflections, and a professional philosophy, which combine to form their professional identity. The portfolio is begun during formal study, but continues into ongoing practice, to document life-long and life-wide practice. This results in a continuation of learning through formal coursework on into fieldwork placement after completion of the course and the ongoing curation of artifacts and evidence of learning, as well as narration by the teacher of the journey from novice to experience. The e-portfolios are also used for supervision and mentoring both within the course and for ongoing practice, as well as used for appraisals, accreditation, documenting ongoing competency as practitioners and as part of a résumé or curriculum vitae for job applications. As Wenger (1999) points out, portfolios are another digital tool to share resources and network within a community of practice as they act as vehicles for documenting developing professional identity and capturing the process of "becoming" a professional through "belonging" to a community of practice (Wenger 1999).

Digital badging is another digital technology that is changing the way we teach and learn. As Grant (2014) argues, the value of digital badging is that it offers us the chance to rethink what counts as learning and provides the potential to change our systems of credentialing, enabling new ways to recognize more diverse learning pathways, and opportunities for learners. While traditional formal qualifications are somewhat distant from the actual activities of learning, digital badges contain specific information about what was learnt, where and how. This meta-data that sits behind a digital badge image adds a transparency to credentialing, linking the actual evidence or artifact to the learning. As Grant (2014) posits, digital badging can be used to create a meaningful bridge between content and learning, and help learners develop a sense of personal reward, confidence, and connection to the learning process.

In the Specialist Teaching program, digital badging is used in two ways. The first is in the more formal part of the program, whereby each competency domain of the separate papers and courses are linked to specific domain badges. As teachers complete the required activities and demonstrate competence within a domain, the badge becomes available. This is useful as evidence for summative assessment as it documents learning against specific criteria. It is also accessible for teachers to save and display in their e-portfolios and on other social media sites used for their professional work such as blogs or *Facebook* pages. These badges provide documentation of the micro skills and knowledge gained and the teacher can decide how this information can be shared, stored, and viewed, as evidence of ongoing learning.

The second use of digital badging blurs the boundary between formal and nonformal courses. Course content from the formal qualification is packaged in a different way and offered as "short courses" open to any group of professionals and tailored to suit their needs. These ongoing professional learning "short courses" vary from a day workshop to part-time online courses over a few weeks. These courses are then digitally badged, and this nonformal credentialing enables the participant to make their learning more visible in their online portfolios, curriculum vitae, or social networking spaces.

As Grant (2014) points out, our twentieth century model of education is based on the view that teaching is essential for learning to occur, yet digital technologies have made it possible for us to learn anywhere, anytime, from anyone, on any device. Digital badging and e-portfolios are just two affordances of new technologies outlined here that shift our teaching and learning practices. These kinds of shifts are necessary for ongoing professional programs to remain meaningful and relevant in a twenty-first-century learning and teaching environment. Knowing how to use technology is becoming every more critical, and part of any professional education program should be to increase the digital capability of learners.

The Specialist Teachers preparedness to use technology-enabled learning such as e-portfolios and interacting with others online was assessed at the start of the program, and their achievement in using these tools was assessed as they graduated from the program. Their perceptions of preparedness and achievement are outlined below:

Preparedness (Beginning of course) and achievement (End of Course) of key aspects of **technology-enabled learning**.

Preparedness (Beginning of course) and achievement (End of Course) of key aspects of *Technology enabled Learning*

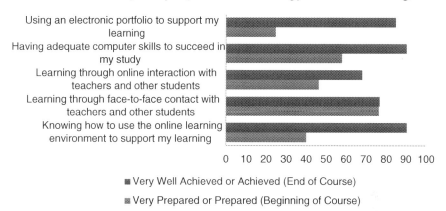

■ Very Well Achieved or Achieved (End of Course)

■ Very Prepared or Prepared (Beginning of Course)

At the beginning of the course, the aspect of blended learning teachers felt most prepared to engage in was learning through face-to face contact with teachers and other teachers (76.4% felt either prepared or very prepared to do this). There were a very similar percentage of respondents who felt they had either achieved or well achieved this at the end of the program (76.8). Out of all the aspects of pedagogy reported in this study, using an electronic portfolio to support learning was the least likely to be identified by teachers as something they were prepared or very prepared to do (24.9). However, it was also the aspect where there was the greatest change in teachers perceptions as at the end of the program 84.8% of respondents felt that they had either achieved or well achieved with the use of this tool. Another aspect of blended learning where teachers indicated a positive change in perceptions was knowing how to use the online learning environment to support their learning. At the beginning of the program, only 24.9% of teachers felt either prepared or very prepared to do this however by the end of the program 90.6% of respondents indicated that they had either achieved or very well achieved this.

Teachers in the program were also asked to indicate the importance they placed on these aspects of technology-enabled learning. At the beginning of the program, having adequate computer skills to succeed in study was rated either as important or very important by 97% of respondents, and the same number rated this as important or very important at the end. Knowing how to use the online learning environment to support learning was also rated as important or very important both at the beginning and end of the program (96 and 95% of respondents, respectively). In contrast, using an electronic portfolio to support learning was rated as very important or important by only 47% of respondents at the beginning of the program, however, by the end of the program, this had increased to 74%.

At the end of the program, participants were asked to describe those aspects of the program that had helped them and had been most beneficial. Aspects of blended learning featured in these responses. These included learning about technology and increasing their confidence and competence in this area, using online portfolios, opportunities to access the learning material at anytime, learning face-to-face and learning to use online technologies, as indicated in these responses to what was beneficial in the program:

- *Learning to be far more confident and competent using the computer and developing an e-portfolio*
- *The collaborative online environments* and *learning new technology*
- *Discussing my goals and endeavours with colleagues across the globe*
- *The online discussion forums*

Participants also noted the aspects of blended learning that helped to shape their professional identity:

- *The increased use of technology including developing my portfolio*
- *Interprofessional contact with my peers in the forum and face-to-face*
- *The online portfolio which I will now use for my ongoing professional needs.*

17.6   Conclusion

The findings of this case study are encouraging in a number of ways. First, it appears that designing and delivering a teacher professional learning program that is technology-enabled, interprofessional, and inquiry-based, enables teacher participants to develop confidence and competence in critical aspects of twenty-first-century teaching and learning. These include various networking skills including: collaborating across professional disciplines, connecting professional learning with authentic fieldwork, and integrating networks of knowledge into ongoing digital professional portfolios. Second, learning *through* technology-enabled learning environments emphasizing inquiry and interprofessional practice can assist teachers to learn *about* these concepts. Third, this program not only allowed teachers to learn the skills required for technology-enabled, interprofessional, and inquiry-based learning, but it also increased their sense of the importance of these elements thus increasing the likelihood that they will carry these into their practice. Finally, qualitative data from this study demonstrated that teacher participants began to incorporate these elements of the program into their professional identities. Using a more networked approach to teaching and learning show promise in promoting the particular skills required for life-wide and life-long learning for teachers in a time of transition.

References

Barr, H. (2002). *Interprofessional education: Today, yesterday and tomorrow*. A review commissioned by the Learning and Teaching Support Network for Health Sciences and Practice. London: CAIPE.

Barr, H., & Low, H. (2013). *Introducing interprofessional education*. Fareham, UK: CAIPE.

Barrett, H. (2010). Balancing the two faces of ePortfolios. *Educação, Formação & Tecnologias, 3* (1), 6–14.

Blessinger, P., & Carfora, J. M. (2014). Innovative approaches in teaching and learning: An introduction to inquiry-based learning for the arts, humanities, and social sciences. In P. Blessinger & J. M. Carfora (Eds.), *Inquiry-based learning for the arts, humanities and social sciences. A conceptual and practical resource for educators* (pp. 3–16). Bingley WA, UK: Emerald Group Publishing Limited.

Bridges D. R., Davidson, R. A., Odegard, P., Maki, I. V., & Tomkowiak, J. (2011). Interprofessional collaboration: Three best practice models of interprofessional education. *Medical Education Online, 16*, 1–10.

Garrison, D. R., & Anderson, T. (2003). *E-learning in the 21st century: A framework for research and practice*. London: Routledge Falmer.

Geva, E., Barsky, A., & Westernoff, F. (2000). *Interprofessional practice with diverse populations: Cases in point*. Westport Conn: Auburn House.

Grant, S. (2014). *What counts as learning*. Retrieved from http://dmlhub.net/sites/default/files/WhatCountsAsLearning_Grant.pdf

Hannah, E. F. S., Ingram, R., Kerr, C., & Kelly, T. B. (2014). Inquiry-based learning for interprofessional education. In P. Blessinger & J. M. Carfora (Eds.), *Inquiry-based learning for the arts, humanities and social sciences. A conceptual and practical resource for educators* (pp. 105–126). Bingley WA, UK: Emerald Group Publishing Limited.

Levy, P. (2009). *Inquiry-based learning: A conceptual framework*. University of Sheffield: Centre for inquiry-based learning in the arts and social sciences. Available from http://www.sheffield.ac.uk/cilass/resources/

Lorenzo, G., & Ittelson, J. (2005). An overview of e-portfolios. *Educause Learning Initiative, 1*, 1–27.

Richmond, A. S., Fleck, B., Heath, T., Broussard, K. A., & Skarda, B. (2015). Can inquiry-based instruction promote higher-level learning? *Scholarship of Teaching and Learning in Psychology*. Advance online publication. doi:10.1037/stl0000032

Schleicher, A. (Ed.). (2012). *Preparing teachers and developing school leaders for the 21st century. Lessons from around the world*. OECD Publishing. Available from http://www.oecd.org/site/eduistp2012/49850576.pdf

Spronken-Smith, R. A., Walker, R., Batchelor, J., O'Steen, B., Angelo, T., & Matthews, H. (2008). *Inquiry-based learning*. Report prepared for the Ministry of Education. Available from http://akoaotearoa.ac.nz/projects

Trodd, L., & Chivers, L. (2011). Introduction. In L. Trodd & L. Chivers (Eds.), *Interprofessional working in practice. Learning and working together for children and families* (pp. 1–4). Berkshire, England: Open University Press.

Wenger, F. (1999) *Communities of practice: Learning, meaning, and identity*. Boston. Cambridge University Press.

World Health Organization. (2010). *Framework for action on interprofessional education and collaborative practice*. Geneva, Switzerland: Author.

Author Biographies

Mandia Mentis is Associate Professor in the Institute of Education at Massey University, New Zealand, where she coordinates postgraduate Inclusive Education programmes. She has worked as a teacher and educational psychologist in primary, secondary, and tertiary settings. As co-director of the Equity through Education centre, her research inquires into innovative practices that promote diversity.

Alison Kearney is Associate Professor at the Institute of Education at Massey University in New Zealand where she teaches and researches in the areas of learning, specialist teaching, and educational inclusion and exclusion. She is the co-director of the Equity Through Education Centre at Massey University and editor of the New Zealand education journal, Kairaranga.

Chapter 18
Teacher Agency and Professional Learning Communities: What Can Learning Rounds in Scotland Teach Us?

Carey Philpott

18.1 Introduction

In recent years, there has been a significant and rapid rise, internationally, in researching and theorising teacher agency. Much of this research has been in the context of exploring teachers' responses to, and room for manoeuvre within, mandated educational reforms or forms of externally imposed accountability (Vongalis-Macrow 2007). Some of the research has considered the relationship between teacher agency and professional learning (Pyhältö et al. 2014) and some has been in the context of growing policy interest in mobilising teacher agency as a resource for school and system reform (Priestley et al. 2012). In each of these foci, reform and learning, both individual and collective, are seen as intertwined and as different facets of the same process.

In all of this literature, sociocultural models of agency are adopted in which agency is theorised as an interaction between personal capacity and disposition and the affordances or resources for agency of the particular sociocultural context. Furthermore, this sociocultural theorisation of teacher agency tends to view personal capacity and disposition as arising from earlier biographical trajectories through differing sociocultural contexts, and in relation to differing resources for agency, rather than in terms of innate or idiosyncratic personal differences. These latter might be a reality and have an influence on agency but they are elusive to theorisation. It is also important not to underplay the role of sociocultural factors in individual development. Emirbayer and Mische's (1998) conceptualisation of agency has been the single most frequently adopted in this work.

Carey Philpott—Deceased

C. Philpott
Leeds Beckett University, Leeds, UK

© Springer Nature Singapore Pte Ltd. 2017
M.A. Peters et al. (eds.), *A Companion to Research in Teacher Education*,
DOI 10.1007/978-981-10-4075-7_18

For Emirbayer and Mische agency involves the interplay of what they term a chordal triad of the iterational element, the projective element and the practical-evaluative element of agency. The iterational element is defined as "the selective reactivation by actors of past patterns of thought and action" (ibid, p. 971); the projective element is defined as "the imaginative generation by actors of possible future trajectories of action" (ibid, p. 971) and the practical-evaluative element is defined as "the capacity of actors to make practical and normative judgments among possible trajectories of action, in response to … presently evolving situations" (ibid, p. 971). Put in other terms these are: the way we have become habituated by past experience and resources to think and act in any given sociocultural context (iterational); whether we can envision possible future alternative ways of thinking and acting and what these are (projective); the capacity, resources or affordances in the current situation (practical-evaluative) that mediate past understanding and actions into future understanding and actions. At the extreme ends of a range of possibilities, we can either reproduce the iterational unchanged or we can think and act in new ways.

It is worth noting that each of these elements of agency could be personal or collective. That is we can consider the iterational, projective and practical-evaluative capacity of particular individual actors within a shared sociocultural context, which might differ depending on personal biographical trajectory; or we can consider the collective iterational, projective and practical-evaluative capacity of the sociocultural context and its members as a community. Emirbayer and Mische (1998, p. 971) note that the practical-evaluative element of agency "has been left strikingly undertheorized". One question that could be asked in relation to this is "what is it in the present situation (practical-evaluative) that influences how much agency actors exercise?"

In trying to understand what features of the interacting personal and sociocultural aspects of agency influence the likelihood of agentic action, some researchers have focused on identifying personal attributes that seem conducive to agency (van der Heijden et al. 2015) and some have focused on contextual factors (Bridwell-Mitchell 2015). However, both these approaches also recognise the symbiotic and reciprocal nature of the two aspects. Although for the purpose of analysis, it is a defensible strategy to foreground one aspect, this approach can run risks, particularly if we want to consider how we can enable serving teachers' agency in relation to either learning or reform. A risk of foregrounding the personal aspect is that, in the practical-evaluative present of exercising agency, the personal capacity or disposition for agency might be seen to be a given, already assembled by the past trajectory and, therefore, not amenable to change at this moment. If we want to consider how we foster and develop teacher agency in the present, we might feel there is not much we can do about the past. However, some research has taken on this agenda by considering how early teacher education can better develop the capacity and disposition for agency so that at present (practical-evaluative) moments in the future, future serving teachers will have pasts (the iterative aspect) that are more conducive to exercising agency (Lipponen and Kumpulainen 2011).

On the other hand, a risk of foregrounding features of the sociocultural context that are conducive to the exercise of agency is that we might slip into believing that if we create the right sociocultural context for teacher agency, teachers will utilise its resources and affordances, at least in ways consistent with their own personal disposition and capacity. However, this might not be the case. So what may be needed here is less a description of the "architecture" of a sociocultural context conducive to the exercise of teacher agency and more of a consideration of whether and how teachers collectively make use of the resources or affordances that are available to them.

At the same time as growing interest in teacher agency in relation to professional learning and reform, there has also been interest in professional learning communities as vehicles for both professional learning and school and system reform. Some academic literature has made explicit connections between professional learning communities and teacher agency, seeing professional learning communities as an important affordance for the development and exercise of teacher agency both in terms of learning and in terms of responding to, or driving, reform (Lipponen and Kumpalainen 2011; Riveros et al. 2012). A related approach, which has had some influence, is the idea of relational agency (Edwards 2015; McNicholl 2013) which grows out of cultural and historical activity theory to argue that agency can be best developed and mobilised by making use of others.

However, it has also been argued that evidence for the effectiveness of professional learning communities is scant and there is little detailed empirical evidence of what happens within professional learning communities (Riveros et al. 2012).

18.2   Learning Rounds, Instructional Rounds and the Scottish Context

The research reported here focuses on a form of professional learning community that has been popular in Scotland: Learning Rounds. Learning Rounds is a method for collaborative professional development in which educators come together to observe teaching and learning across a number of classrooms in a single school. In a post-observation debrief, they use notes and other forms of recording, such as diagrams, taken during the observations to build up a detailed evidence-based picture of teaching and learning in the school. The intention is to use this to develop understanding of the teaching and learning practice in the school and make plans for what needs to be done next to develop that practice. The aim of Instructional Rounds is system improvement rather than developing the practice of the particular teachers observed or of the observers.

In order to understand the discussion of data later in this chapter, it will be helpful to have a clearer view of some features of Learning Rounds in theory and practice. Learning Rounds is based on the Instructional Rounds practice developed in the United States of America (City et al. 2009). City et al. (2009) describe Instructional Rounds as a "four step process: identifying a problem of practice, observing, debriefing, and focusing on the next level of work" (City et al. 2009, p. 6). They state that a problem of practice "is not a whim and does not emerge from thin air. It comes from data, dialogue, and current work. The problem of practice is grounded in some kind of evidence, preferably shareable evidence … [it is] not just … a hunch" (City et al. 2009, p. 102). A "rich problem of practice" (ibid, p. 102):

- Focuses on the instructional core;
- Is directly observable;
- Is actionable (is within the school's or district's control and can be improved in real time);
- Connects to a broader strategy of improvement (school, system);
- Is high-leverage (if acted on, it would make a significant difference for pupil learning)
  (City et al. 2009, p. 102).

City et al., define the instructional core as "the teacher and the student in the presence of content" (ibid, p. 22). Instructional Rounds need to focus on the relationship between these three and how changes to any one of them require or create changes in the other two. Focusing on one without connecting it to the others is not considered to be effective.

The second step, observing, is intimately linked to the debrief step and City et al. (2009) consider most of requirements for observing in relation to debriefing. The debriefing step is subdivided into four stages: description, analysis, prediction and evaluation. City et al. (2009, p. 34) insist that it is always "Description before analysis, analysis before prediction and prediction before evaluation". They are particularly wary of the evaluation stage, stating that "[o]nly after people have developed the disciplines of description, analysis and prediction do we raise the issue of evaluation" (ibid, p. 34).

There are two other requirements for the description stage. The first of these is the "grain size" (ibid, p. 92) of the description. The finer grained the description, the more useful it is. The second requirement is that participants should not describe what they do not see, only what they do see (ibid, p. 94). This is because describing what we do not see is an indication of what we think is important (i.e. evaluative) rather than evidence of what is happening in the room.

Another element claimed to be necessary for the effective use of Instructional Rounds is a "theory of action" (City et al. 2009). A theory of action needs to be a "*statement of a causal relationship* between what I do … and what constitutes a good result in the classroom … [i]t must be *empirically falsifiable* [and] [i]t must be *open ended*" (City et al. 2009, italics in original). The open-ended requirement means that it must be able to be amended as more is discovered about the situation (s) being observed. In fact having a finished theory of action, according to City et al. (2009) is not the goal and once it is viewed as finished it "ceases to function as a learning tool and it becomes a symbolic artefact, useful primarily as a tool for legitimising … authority" (ibid, p. 53).

Although they claim to be based on Instructional Rounds, guidance for teachers in Scotland on Learning Rounds (National CPD Team 2011) differs in some respects from the practice outlined above. *The Learning Rounds Toolkit* (National CPD Team 2011) includes references to the importance of a "plan of action" (National CPD Team 2011, p. 9) emerging from the post-observation stage that relates to Instructional Rounds emphasis on a theory of action. However, it is worth noting that this is a *plan* and not a *theory*, so it could become a set of actions to be carried out rather than a developed understanding of the cause and effect of particular actions.

Most of the guidance on the practice of Learning Rounds focuses on the observation and the debrief (National CPD Team 2011). Perhaps the most conspicuous absence in comparison to Instructional Rounds is the lack of attention given to developing a "rich problem of practice". This is treated more briefly in Learning Rounds as "the theme of the observation is agreed by the group" (ibid, p. 9). The relative lack of attention given to this area, and to the importance of connection to a theory of action, could result in Learning Rounds practice in Scotland that focuses on observation and debrief at the expense of other equally important parts of the process.

Learning Rounds has been more than just a preferred method of professional development in Scotland. It has also been a part of the Scottish Government's declared intention to leave the details of curriculum development to teachers. The recently introduced curriculum, Curriculum for Excellence is intended to be less prescriptive than earlier Scottish curricula and this lack of prescription is intended to provide space for practitioners to develop practice through the exercise of their own agency. In 2006 the Scottish Executive (forerunner of the current Scottish Government) stated that Curriculum for Excellence

> aims to engage teachers in thinking from first principles about their educational aims and values and their classroom practice. The process is based upon evidence of how change can be brought about successfully – through a climate in which practitioners share and develop ideas. (Scottish Executive 2006, p. 4)

As such Learning Rounds can be seen, in potential at least, as an important affordance for teacher agency.

Despite the fact that Instructional Rounds has been sufficiently influential internationally to inform official teacher development and curriculum development policy and practice in Scotland, there is little peer-reviewed academic literature on the practice. The research reported here focuses on the ways in which Learning Rounds do (or do not) provide a practical-evaluative affordance for teacher agency and the extent to which that affordance is actually utilised for the exercise of teacher agency. This research seeks to make a contribution in three ways:

- Adding to an empirical understanding of what happens in professional learning communities
- Understanding how the practical-evaluative element of agency is (or is not) exercised in practice
- Considering what factors might affect the utilisation (or otherwise) of affordances for teacher agency.

18.3   Data Gathering and Method

Table 18.1 shows the four schools involved in the data gathering, their experience and training with Learning Rounds and the nature of the participants in the data. Each school was in a different local authority and they were chosen as both a convenience sample and a purposive sample. A convenience sample because they were known to be carrying out Learning Rounds at the time that we wanted to gather the data and a purposive sample because they represented four different Local Authorities and were, therefore, more likely to present a wider picture of practice than might have been found in a single Local Authority where experiences and training were more likely to be shared. Post-observation debriefing meetings were audio recorded and then transcribed. Each of these meetings was about an hour long. This is shorter than is typical for Instructional Rounds in the US and this is probably because the Learning Rounds model has been adapted to fit into the pattern of an average school day in Scotland without causing too much disruption by taking teachers away from their other work.

18.4   Findings

All four schools were making use of agreed foci for observations (see Table 18.1) and it is worth remembering that the *Learning Rounds Toolkit* emphasises agreeing a focus for observation rather than developing a problem of practice. The observation foci of the four schools overlapped and some foci recurred in all schools. Most of the recurring foci grouped around techniques associated with "assessment for learning" and this probably reflects teaching and learning techniques that have been considered to be good practice recently in Scottish education. The foci for all schools were multiple with some having a long list of different foci for the same observation.

Limitations of space mean findings from the data will only be summarised here. A more detailed presentation and discussion of this data can be found in Philpott and Oates (2015).

In three of the four schools studied (Schools B, C and D), there was scant evidence in the transcripts that Learning Rounds were being utilised as an affordance for teacher agency. This lack of agency seems to be attributable to several features in the data. None of the groups of teachers explicitly articulated a theory of action during the discussion (that is, articulated what their assumptions were about cause and effect in the classroom in relation to particular "problems of practice"). This resulted in an implicit theory of action that accepted externally produced models of good practice. For example, if peer assessment was used by the teacher this was taken as evidence of good practice. In places this seemed to slip into "audit" in which teachers seemed to be most concerned with "ticking off" whether they had seen certain strategies currently prescribed by the local authority or the

Table 18.1 Schools and participants represented in the data

Type of school	Experience with Learning Rounds	Preparation for Learning Rounds	Nature of participants	Coding in transcript	Focus of Learning Round observation
School A: primary school	None	Guidance from national CPD coordinator; information accessed on education Scotland website	Teachers including Head Teacher plus 3 Local Authority representatives	AA-depute head teacher (facilitator); AB-head teacher; AC-class teacher; AD-LA representative; AE-LA representative; AF-LA representative; AG-class teacher; AH-class teacher Transcript line numbers 1–370	Pupils' awareness of learning intentions and success criteria; differentiation; challenge and pace; independent learning
School B: secondary school with feeder primary school	Second time	Guidance from national CPD coordinator	Teachers including CPD coordinator	BA-teacher (facilitator) BB-teacher BC-teacher BD-teacher BE-teacher BF-teacher Transcript line numbers 1–312	Learning intentions Plenaries Formative assessment
School C: community secondary school	Third or fourth time for different participants	Some support at local authority level	Teachers including CPD coordinator	CA-teacher (facilitator) CB-teacher CC-teacher CD-teacher CE-teacher Transcript line numbers 1–312	Learning intentions Target setting Opportunity to work at increased pace Questioning

(continued)

Table 18.1 (continued)

Type of school	Experience with Learning Rounds	Preparation for Learning Rounds	Nature of participants	Coding in transcript	Focus of Learning Round observation
School D: community campus school (nursery, primary, secondary)	Fourth time	Visit to another school in another local authority that had experience	Teachers including CPD coordinator	DA-teacher (facilitator) DB-teacher DC-teacher DD-teacher DE-teacher DF-teacher DJ-teacher Transcript line numbers 1–285	Development of skills Pupil participation Questioning Behaviour management Group work Use of ICT Active learning Challenge and extension/differentiation Uniform Use of learning intentions

school. Arguably the implicit nature of this theory of action mean that it could not be challenged and, therefore became a finished theory of action which in the words of City et al. (2009, p. 53) is "useful primarily as a tool for legitimising ... authority". In this case, the authority of whoever had mandated the practices.

These limitations in the teachers' discussions were sustained by: observing what the teacher was doing more than what pupils were doing (that is, not focusing on the instructional core in City et al's (2009) terms); observing and recording in molar units, e.g. "peer assessment happened" rather than more fine grained observations; the large number of observation foci in some schools that led to an "audit" approach rather than sustained and detailed consideration of a single focus.

In contrast, in the fourth school, school A, there were emerging examples of teachers observing the effects of teachers' actions by focusing on pupils and making relatively fine grained distinctions about exactly how teachers carried out actions rather than just using molar categories. This led to the possibility that mandated views of good practice could be challenged or refined. However, in school A, these insights did not feed back into challenging or refining a theory of action as a theory of action was never explicitly articulated. As a result the nascent insights tended to peter out and return to an audit approach.

18.5   Discussion

This section will consider how the findings from the data on Learning Rounds in practice from the four schools relate to affordances for teacher agency.

Teachers did not explicitly articulate assumptions about cause and effect in the classroom so they had no falsifiable theory to test. This meant, in practice, that they were left with an implicit theory of action. The implicit nature of this theory of action meant that it was never the object of scrutiny and, therefore, potential challenge or revision. As a result it became a "finished" theory of action which in the words of City et al. (2009, p. 53) "ceases to function as a learning tool and ... becomes a symbolic artefact, useful primarily as a tool for legitimising ... authority". In this case, the authority of whoever had mandated the practices, whether this was government, local authority or school management. Explicitly articulating a theory of action would have made it available to scrutiny, which would have provided an affordance for teacher agency through evaluation of that theory.

The other constraint linked to the absence of an explicitly articulated theory of action is the lack of attention in the teacher observations to the effects of teacher actions on pupils' learning. This meant that the teachers had no evidence by which to judge the claims of mandated good practice. This led to accepting evidence of the use of mandated good practice as, by default, the same thing as good practice. The relative lack of fine grained data had a similar effect. Describing in molar units (e.g. pupils carried out peer assessment) rather than attending to the specific details of pupils' actions and interactions meant that teachers could not clearly discriminate the effects of procedures in the classroom. The point here is that robust empirical classroom evidence is an affordance for teacher agency as it enables teachers to authoritatively evaluate mandated practices.

McNicholl (2013) writes about the ways in which practitioner research can provide an affordance for agency as it gives teachers an authoritative basis for their views. This is related to Pyhältö et al. (2014) distinction between teachers who see themselves as objects or subjects of change. Teachers engaged in practitioner enquiry are the subjects of educational change not its objects. Vongalis-Macrow (2007) writes about the authority of teacher expertise being underutilised in educational change. Faced with apparently authoritative prescriptions from outside the classroom teachers may feel that their views lack authority. Robust empirical evidence can provide this authority. van der Heijden et al. (2015) also identify "mastery" or expertise as an important personal factor in the exercise of agency. Teachers' (and others) sense of their own expertise can be underpinned by robust empirical data. This links to Lipponen and Kumpulainen's (2011) argument about the importance of social capital for agency. Social capital comes from being recognised within a community as someone whose ideas have value. One form of this is epistemic agency, which is the recognition of an ability to generate valid knowledge.

If not explicitly articulating a theory of action is a constraint on teacher agency, so is the lack of alternative discourses to explain what was happening in the classroom. The only discourse that was apparent was policy discourse or policy discourse mediated through local authority or school mandates. Biesta et al. (2015) report a similar experience in their research on teacher agency. In one sense, explicitly articulating a theory of action would have opened up the possibility of alternative discourses once the initial discourse had been explicitly surfaced rather than being invisible and, therefore, possibly normalised. However, there remains a question of where alternative discourses would come from. Biesta et al. (2015) report that the Scottish teachers in their research had a very similar set of views about teaching, learning and education more broadly, even though they were from diverse locations and sectors. This was the same in the research reported here. This reduces the chances that alternative discourses will come from within the group; a condition that Bridwell-Mitchell (2015) identifies as an important affordance for practical-evaluative agency. City et al. (2009) suggest the use of external sources of understanding in Instructional Rounds such as academic readings and models. However, guidance on Learning Rounds (National CPD Team 2011) makes no reference to the value of these and they were not apparent in the examples of Learning Rounds recorded in this research. Similarly, Bridwell-Mitchell (2015) argues that, as well as diversity within the group, others' research can provide alternative repertoires.

An issue similar to the lack of alternative discourses from external sources (for example, educational research or theory) is the lack of alternative professional voices in the group. As previously reported, Biesta et al. (2015) found a relatively diverse group of Scottish teachers shared a very similar discourse with its origins in policy. This was also found to be the case here. Bridwell-Mitchell (2015) argues that the right balance of cohesion and, importantly, *diversity* in a community is necessary for practical-evaluative agency to be exercised. Diversity, in terms of discourse at least, seemed to be lacking here. One interesting similarity here is with some research into medical rounds where it is argued that the dominance of doctors in the process leads to a conceptualisations of patients' conditions and needs which are too narrow. It is suggested that the inclusion of other medical professionals in the process would give alternative and broader conceptualisations of patients' needs. A similar case could be made for Learning Rounds and professional learning communities more generally if they are to be resources for teacher agency. The careful and considered inclusion of people who are likely to have alternative experiences and perspectives could enhance the possibilities for agency.

The narrowness of shared professional perspectives is also linked to the ways in which teachers' agency can be limited in terms of scope. Pyhältö et al. (2014, p. 309) argue that a "central challenge" for teachers is to broaden the scope of their perceived educational expertise beyond the technical details of classroom interactions to include larger issues such as the goals and purposes of education. Likewise Biesta et al. (2015) point to a lack of discourses among teachers that construct education in terms other than the technical-rational concerns of "efficiency" to include questions of purpose and value. Vongalis-Macrow (2007, p. 436) similarly writes about the "diminution" of the aspects of teacher agency related to authority and autonomy and the increase of obligations which restricts teachers' agency narrowly to decisions about techniques for teaching and learning in the classroom.

The data discussed here suggests that, in their current form, Learning Rounds (and possibly by extension many professional learning communities) are technical-rationalist in that, at best, they focus on "what works" in technical terms rather than asking broader questions about the nature and purpose of education and the identities of those involved. As Edwards (2015) cautions, they may only be affordances for weak evaluation. This is evaluation only of the effectiveness of certain means to achieve ends given by others.

A related point is the persistence and influence of accountability. Priestley et al. (2012) argue that accountability is more of a constraint on teacher agency than the prescription of means. As long as the goals and measure of success are set by others and teachers are held to account in relation to these, the scope for teacher agency will be limited. So although Learning Rounds look to be a valuable affordance for teacher agency, as long as they are used in the service of achieving goals set and "measured" by others that agency will be constrained.

The limited scope of current Learning Rounds practice can also open up questions about who owns the process and how this relates to the exercise of agency. Vongalis-Macrow (2007) writes about teachers being given "professional makeovers" as new forms of professional development are imposed on them with little ownership. The Learning Rounds researched here were largely set up by the teachers involved. However, the nature and purpose of the Learning Rounds process can be seen as subject to definition by policy and by Local Authority and school management given the official endorsement and fostering of the process. As a result questions can be raised about the extent to which teachers own definitions of the process and its purposes even if they participate voluntarily. If teachers do not own Learning Rounds this may have a constraining effect on its ability to be an affordance for teacher agency with scope beyond the technical-rational. Philpott and Oates (2015) found that teachers participating in Learning Rounds often thought about them in terms of the procedures they had been taught rather than the underlying purposes of those procedures. This lack of ownership of purpose, which among its effects reduces the ability to evaluate the success of the practice and make informed revisions to it, is itself an constraint on agency.

Ownership of purposes and perceptions of the scope of those purposes is also connected to how understanding of Learning Rounds is developed in teachers. Philpott and Oates (2015) identify that in the USA teachers' use of Instructional Rounds was developed through long engagement with the academics who developed the process. In contrast, in Scotland most teachers were given a single training event or accessed online materials with no training. This can result in Learning Rounds practice being assimilated into existing school cultures (what City et al. (2009, p. 90A) call the "pull to the black hole") rather than reconstructing cultures with enhanced teacher agency. Philpott and Oates (2015) conclude that Learning Rounds could be enhanced through longer engagement between teachers and proponents of Learning Rounds as an affordance for teacher agency. A similar situation was found by Pyhältö et al. (2014) whose research suggests that agency could be developed through sustained collaborative engagement between teachers and academics.

18.6   Conclusion and Implications

If we want to enhance the role of Learning Rounds (and by extension other forms of professional learning community) as affordances for practical-evaluative teacher agency, we need to pay attention to a number of aspects:

- Teachers need to explicitly articulate the assumptions that exist about cause and effect in the classroom and use professional learning communities as a way of critically examining these assumptions.
- This requires that teachers generate a fine-grained and nuanced body of data about the effects of differing classroom practices.
- Professional learning communities should be constructed to ensure that a diversity of voices is present.
- Ways should be found to move beyond technical-rationalist foci for observation and discussion to questions about, for example, purposes, values, identities or relationships. Ensuring a diversity of voices could be one way to achieve this.
- "Academic" practices should be used as a resource for agency. This can be in terms of existing research and theory providing alternative discourses for observations, or in terms existing research and theory lending weight to the authority of teachers' interpretations as a counterbalance to the perceived

authority of policy prescriptions. Teachers' authority can also be underpinned through enhanced academic credentials for teachers or by teachers generating robust data. It should be noted that this is in contrast to those who have seen the academy as potentially producing a "rhetoric of conclusions" that can be inimical to teacher agency. It also runs counter to much current thinking about preferred models for professional learning which advocate teachers working with teachers often without a clear role for the academy. While it can be the case that certain forms of academic prescription and perceived authority can constrain teacher agency, properly utilised, academic knowledge, practices and qualifications can be an affordance for teacher agency as a counterbalance to the perceived authority or apparent monologue of policy.

- More time working collaboratively with informed facilitators of collaborative learning practices can enhance teacher agency in the longer term. This is in contrast to believing that handing the process over to teachers from the outset is a guarantee of ownership and teacher agency.
- It may not be possible to change affordances without changing identities. This is obviously a reciprocal relationship but this study suggests that the iterational aspects of identity and practice may prove resistant to changes in practical-evaluative affordances. We need to pay more attention to how we support identity shifts beyond just changing the architecture of present affordances. This might be through longer collaboration between teachers and others, more support of teachers' practitioner enquiry, greater prevalence of continuing academic study for teachers or some other means.

References

Biesta, G., Priestley, M., & Robinson, S. (2015). The role of beliefs in teacher agency. *Teachers and Teaching: Theory and Practice, 21*(7), 624–640.

Bridwell-Mitchell, E. N. (2015). Theorizing teacher agency and reform: How institutionalized instructional practices change and persist. *Sociology of Education, 88*(2), 140–159.

City, E. A., Elmore, R. F., Fiarman, S. E., & Teitel, L. (2009). *Instructional rounds in education; A network approach to improving teaching and learning.* Cambridge, MA: Harvard Education Press.

Edwards, A. (2015). Recognising and realising teachers' professional agency. *Teachers and Teaching: Theory and Practice, 21*(6), 779–784.

Emirbayer, M., & Mische, A. (1998). What is agency? *American Journal of Sociology, 103*(4), 962–1023.

Lipponen, L., & Kumpulainen, K. (2011). Acting as accountable authors: Creating interactional spaces for agency work in teacher education. *Teaching and Teacher Education, 27,* 812–819.

McNicholl, J. (2013). Relational agency and teacher development: A CHAT analysis of a collaborative professional inquiry project with biology teachers. *European Journal of Teacher Education, 36*(2), 218–232.

National CPD Team. (2011). *The learning rounds toolkit; Building a learning community.* Retrieved from http://issuu.com/nationalcpdteam/docs/the_learning_rounds_tool_kit__ updated_#download

Philpott, C., & Oates, C. (2015). What do teachers do when they do learning rounds? Scotland's experience of instructional rounds. *European Journal of Educational Research, 4*(1), 22–37.

Priestley, M., Edwards, R., Priestley, A., & Miller, K. (2012). Teacher agency in curriculum making: Agents of change and spaces for manoeuvre. *Curriculum Inquiry, 42*(2), 191–214.

Pyhältö, K., Pietarinen, J., & Soini, T. (2014). Comprehensive school teachers' professional agency in large-scale educational change. *Journal of Educational Change, 15,* 303–325.

Riveros, A., Newton, P., & Burgess, D. (2012). A situated account of teacher agency and learning: Critical reflections on professional learning communities. *Canadian Journal of Education, 35*(1), 202–216.

Scottish Executive. (2006). *A curriculum for excellence: Progress and proposals.* Edinburgh: Scottish Executive.

van der Heijden, H. R. M. A., Geldens, J. J. M., Beijard, D., & Popeijus, H. L. (2015). Characteristics of teachers as change agents. *Teachers and Teaching: Theory and Practice, 21*(6), 681–699.

Vongalis-Macrow, A. (2007). I, Teacher: Re-territorialization of teachers' multi-faceted agency in global education. *British Journal of Sociology of Education, 28*(4), 425–439.

Chapter 19
Supporting Mentoring and Assessment in Practicum Settings: A New Professional Development Approach for School-Based Teacher Educators

Simone White and Rachel Forgasz

19.1 Introduction

This chapter examines the professional development of an emerging occupational group in the Australian context—a group we call 'school-based teacher educators'—acknowledging and focusing on their learning about the complex work of teacher education, mentoring, supervising and assessing pre-service teachers. Teachers who work with pre-service teachers in schools—typically known as cooperating teachers or supervisors/mentors in schools—are noted for the vital role they play in the success or otherwise of that experience. The teacher education discourse and research literature highlight, however, that their work is plagued by role confusion, and lack of professional learning and preparation, as well as difficulty dealing with the complexity of making judgements and assessing pre-service teachers (Clarke et al. 2014).

While many teachers take on the important work of mentoring over their careers, to date there has been little attention paid to the professional development needs of this group, even as they are increasingly required to shift their focus as professional educators to include the work of teaching pre-service teachers about teaching (Loughran 2006) while also teaching their students. It is to their professional development that we turn our focus in this chapter. In this way, we endeavor to build on the understanding of what Boyd et al. (2014) describe as a 'layered pedagogy of teacher education'. By 'layering' they describe

S. White (✉) · R. Forgasz
Monash University, Melbourne, Australia
e-mail: Simone.White@monash.edu

R. Forgasz
e-mail: Rachel.Forgasz@monash.edu

© Springer Nature Singapore Pte Ltd. 2017
M.A. Peters et al. (eds.), *A Companion to Research in Teacher Education*,
DOI 10.1007/978-981-10-4075-7_19

that primarily the learning of children and young people is at the heart of all teacher education but with layers above that level, for example [focusing] on the learning of teachers and on the learning of teacher educators. (p. 7)

In this chapter, we explore these learning layers and consider their interrelationship; namely, that by learning more about teacher education and becoming a teacher educator, a mentor teacher can further contribute to not only the learning of the pre-service teacher but also to their own professional learning and thus the learning of their students. We consider the professional development of supervisors/mentors as akin to becoming teacher educators (albeit school-based) and argue that greater attention be paid to researching and understanding their learning processes as they move more towards becoming 'second order practitioners' (Murray 2002) without necessarily shifting the location of their work outside of the school as workplace.

To support our thinking, we draw from a particular study of 12 mentor teachers engaged in one such mentor professional learning program. We document their increasing awareness of the complexity and importance of teacher education and the ways in which their professional identities shifted towards the recognition of themselves as school-based teacher educators, working together with university-based teacher educators, within a particular school-university partnership model. Like Boyd et al. (2014) we found that the mentors involved explored, for example, 'explicit modelling' to make their tacit knowledge visible for the pre-service teacher and by doing so illuminated more about their own knowledge of practice and learning.

Before discussing the findings further, it is important to take a step back and to outline the Australian initial teacher education context and the current policy initiatives that led to such a program.

19.2   The Australian Initial Teacher Education Context

In the Australian context, initial teacher education is led by higher education providers (majority as Universities) in partnerships with schools. Teacher 'training'—or as we prefer, 'teacher education'—moved out of Teaching Colleges and into Universities in the late 1980s. Pre-service teachers now typically complete a four year undergraduate Bachelor of Education degree or a two year post-graduate Master of Teaching degree. They spend the majority of their time learning at the University site with mandated days spent in workplace learning (known as professional experience or practicum) in schools. Pre-service teachers are typically assigned a 'supervising or mentor teacher' (language used in Australia) who takes the main responsibility for mentoring and assessing their professional learning, while the University takes responsibility for assessing the course/program work and ultimately awards the degree. The majority of Universities have now moved their practicum assessment requirements to reflect the newly established national graduate standards outlined in the Australian Professional Standards for Teachers (2012).

Classroom teachers to date have little to no professional development before being assigned a pre-service teacher to mentor and assess and there is much criticism from teachers of the perceived lack of engagement or involvement from Universities in supporting them in their work. Teachers regularly inquire why faculty staff, teaching in the various courses, do not visit pre-service teachers during their practicum. The processes for selecting mentors and matching them to pre-service teachers are generally ad hoc. In some schools, teachers deemed as 'leading' or exemplary are chosen; in other schools, any teacher who is willing to 'offer up' their classroom is assigned a pre-service teacher. In some schools, teachers are weary of having what they perceive as the extra burden of taking a pre-service teacher in times of increasing accountability and standardized testing. Universities are thus often in competition with one another to secure placements for all of their pre-service teachers for the mandatory practicum days. This has led to something of a national crisis of an under supply of mentors and schools stretched to accommodate growing numbers of pre-service teachers. Despite this situation, the school site is increasingly viewed by politicians and principals alike as the best place to learn to teach, with increasing interest in school-based ITE models.

In keeping with international trends, the existing university-led model has come under increased scrutiny in Australia over the past decade. There have been calls for more alternative pathways (for example, 'Teach for Australia') and more 'practice' time in schools with greater emphasis placed on the role of the supervisor/mentor in improving initial teacher education. Following England's lead in earlier incentives for school-university partnerships, the Australian partnership policy agenda began in earnest through the *National Partnership Agreement on Improving Teacher Quality* (Council of Australian Governments 2008) which laid the groundwork for strengthening linkages between initial teacher education (ITE) programs and schools. More recently, the Australian Government has focused more attention on the practicum in school as the main site of learning about teaching, commissioning a review into ITE. The report from the review, entitled *Action Now: Classroom Ready Teachers,* was released in early 2015. Amongst many other recommendations, this report focused on the important work of the supervisor/mentor in improving initial teacher education. It states

> To ensure new teachers are entering classrooms with sufficient practical skills, the Advisory Group recommends ensuring experiences of appropriate timing; length and frequency are available to all teacher education students. Placements must be supported by highly-skilled supervising teachers who are able to demonstrate and assess what is needed to be an effective teacher. The advisory Group strongly states that better partnerships between universities and schools are needed to deliver high quality practical experience. (p. 7)

The emphasis on placements, partnerships and supervising teachers outlined in this report is not new in the international literature. The shift in emphasis towards 'partnerships' and more 'practical skills' is again consistent with changes that have occurred in other countries. In England, for example, government legislation from

1992 onwards made it mandatory for ITE providers to offer pre-service courses with schools. Conroy et al. (2013) describe the rise of 'teacher training schools' or 'professional learning schools' across a number of Countries as part of this 'practice-based' reform agenda and in the Australian contexts most Universities over the past decade have initiated various school-university partnership models under various state-based jurisdictional initiatives such as the Victorian *School Centres of Teaching Excellence* (Department of Education and Early Childhood Development 2012–2014) and more recently the Victorian *Teaching Academies of Professional Practice* (Department of Education and Training 2015–2016). While not yet officially mandated in policy, established school-university partnerships will likely emerge as an accreditation requirement for all providers of ITE across Australia.

Such school-university partnerships can have their own continuum of function; they can be rather loose connections with little real reciprocity or they can be fully functioning and evolving communities of practice in which schools and universities partner in a spirit of mutuality, joint enterprise and shared repertoire (Wenger 2000). To become such an evolving community of practice means that each and every site of learning—for example, the school, the classroom, and lecture theater —needs to offer opportunities for pre-service and mentor teacher reflection (theory) and engagement (practice) but not always at the same time. The opportunities to reflect and engage can be viewed in conflict or can be complimentary. For example, Wenger (2000) recommends reflective periods that 'can activate imagination or boundary interactions' (p. 229) that require alignment with other practices around a shared goal, and that these could be used to counteract the possible narrowness of engagement (practice) alone.

Such communities require that teacher educators (both school-based and university based), facilitate these kinds of reflective learning opportunities for pre-service teachers and with each other, moving between boundaries and across the multiple sites of learning. Focusing on the role and work of the supervising/mentor teacher and increasing the professional development of all mentors are understood as keys to strengthening school-university links and improving pre-service teachers' learning. In Australia, however, there are currently no formal professional development requirements for teachers to meet in order to take up the work of becoming a mentor/supervising teacher of pre-service teachers and little work is done to support their understanding of a 'pedagogy of teacher education' (Loughran 2006).

19.3 Mentors as School-Based Teacher Educators?

Teachers and teacher educators internationally are in the spotlight as attention focuses on the important role teachers can play in improving student learning. This includes mentors who are subjected to stronger critical examination as they are required to take on greater responsibility for improving pre-service teacher education at the same time as affecting improvement in their own students' learning. At the same time, a meta-analysis of international scholarship about mentors and mentoring revealed that for the most part:

> [C]o-operating teachers lack specific preparation to enable high quality and developmentally appropriate support for student teachers—they tend to be under-prepared for their work as mentors. For example, most feedback offered by cooperating teachers is observation-based feedback and therefore moving beyond reporting on, to inquiring into practice is unrealized in many practicum settings. (Clarke et al. 2014, p. 46)

This is hardly surprising given that most teachers would tend to prioritize the learning of their students over the learning of a pre-service teacher and that their own initial teacher education was focused on student learning and not on their possible future roles working as adult educators with pre-service teachers. Research into becoming a teacher educator is an emerging field. Most of the literature to date has focused on teachers who move from the classroom and into the university to do this work. Murray (2002) notes the shift that occurs from being a classroom teacher to a teacher educator located in a university as one of becoming a 'second-order practitioner'. In later work, Murray and Male (2005) describe second-order practitioners as teacher educators (usually university based) 'who induct their students into the practices and discourses of both school teaching and teacher education' (Murray and Male 2005, p. 126). In this way, they describe schools as first order teaching settings and universities as second order

> Where they once worked in the first-order setting of the school, they now work in the second-order setting of Higher Education (HE). (Murray and Male 2005, p. 126)

In our research into school-university partnerships, we note that the same kind of shift can occur for mentors of pre-service teachers too. Although this professional group does not change their location, they can nevertheless become 'second order practitioners' by working with pre-service teachers alongside university-based teacher educator colleagues. The additional complexity they face is that they do so while continuing in their roles as first-order practitioners with responsibility for teaching school students.

In this chapter, we now focus on a particular school-university partnership model that was designed to fill the mentor professional learning gap through the provision of university-led professional development of mentors. Now known as Men/tee, this partnership project was premised on the notion of (re)positioning mentors as school-based teacher educators, recognizing the important shift through partnerships of those who work alongside university-based teacher educators in pre-service teacher preparation.

In the following sections, we share findings regarding Men/tee participants' professional learning, and then go on to suggest recommendations for future professional learning models that encourage the repositioning of mentors in schools as school-based teacher educators.

19.4 Mentors Becoming 'Second Order Practitioners': The Men/Tee Initiative

Under the policy drive for partnerships noted earlier, different universities and schools across Australia have forged a variety of school-university partnership models. The Men/tee model involved the Faculty of Education at Monash University and one large Secondary school, Keymore College (pseudonym), which is based across two campuses in Melbourne, Victoria. Simultaneous to their work with a pre-service teacher in school over a five week teaching block, Men/tee mentors also participated in a weekly university-led professional learning community on the school site in order to develop their skills and practices as school-based teacher educators.

The aforementioned policy and practice imperatives are very much the same contextual drivers out of which Men/tee arose. In particular, three common practicum problems drove the project design. First was the persistent problem of finding placements for pre-service teachers. The second problem emerged as a consequence of changes that were made by the partner university to the provision of support to PSTs during their time in schools. The old model in which an academic made a site visit and observed every PST at least once during their final year of practicum was replaced by remote support such as email, phone and online discussion forums. In many ways, it might be argued that such an approach offers better support to PSTs since they receive consistent and ongoing contact and communication with the university over the course of their practicum. At the same time, physical absence from schools meant that this increased contact with PSTs was largely invisible to school-based personnel who instead read—and experienced—academics' physical absence as an indication of a decline in university support during the practicum. Men/tee sought to redress this problem by reintroducing an academic presence in schools during the practicum. Finally, Men/tee piloted a proactive response to practicum problems that often arise as a consequence of poor relationships between pre-service teachers and mentors and problematic mentoring practices.

The pragmatic priorities that drove this pilot were, therefore

1. To encourage schools to accept larger numbers of PSTs
2. To reintroduce the sense of a strong academic presence in schools
3. To better support pre-service teachers and their mentors in order to achieve quality practicum.

Altogether, Men/tee involved 17 mentors who worked with 17 PSTs over their final 5 week practicum block, 12 of whom participated in the research component. Over the course of the 5 weeks, a team of university-based teacher educators (including the authors) met weekly after school hours, with these mentors to engage them in professional learning about mentoring and about the principles that underlie a 'pedagogy of teacher education' (Loughran 2006). Hence the name Men/tee: Mentor/Teacher Educator Education. It is important to note that the professional development allocation time was recognized and supported by the school principal.

The structure of each professional learning session was essentially the same: we began with a research-informed concept/strategy about mentoring or initial teacher education; for example, the tacit nature of teacher expertise, explicit modeling, and structured observation. We explored each concept collaboratively, including through the provision of related research literature and resources that our mentors might use with their pre-service teachers. The following week's session began with a reflection on how the previous week's ideas had influenced their mentoring practices over the course of the week before moving on to the next idea.

19.5   The Men/Tee Study

Research data were collected from multiple sources to enable exploration of a range of questions about becoming and being a mentor and school-based teacher educator, including a pre-survey in the form of Clarke et al. (2012) Mentor Profiling Inventory, a post-program evaluation survey, field notes and recordings from each of the professional development sessions and semi-structured interviews with 12 of the 17 participants. Questions included, for example

- Which aspects of your recent mentoring experience were most rewarding? Most challenging?
- What changes (if any) did you make to your mentoring approach in response to the ideas explored during our PD sessions? With what effect?

Two main themes emerged through the reading and analysis of the transcripts. First, participants developed a new awareness of their roles and identities as mentors, as school-based teacher educators, and as 'expert' teachers. Second was their growing awareness of a 'pedagogy of teacher education' (Loughran 2006) and how to do the work of mentoring, including the articulation of a range of tools and strategies for undertaking that work.

19.5.1   Role and Identity Development

Those familiar with the research literature understand the significance of the mentor's role to pre service teachers' practicum learning. But our findings revealed that mentors themselves tend to undervalue the significance of the role. For example, Linda described her *realisation of the importance and seriousness of the mentor role*, where previously she had thought *it's just a pre-service teacher, it's not a big deal … but it actually is a big deal.*

Men/tee participants also began to understand more of the complexity of the role, especially in relation to the emotional work of mentoring. For participants such as Melanie, the importance of empathy and offering emotional support added a new dimension to her understanding of her role

> There was an emphasis on supporting them and I think it helped me ultimately be more sensitive towards the end, just a bit more sensitive to their whole experience and … how terrifying it was. You know, we kind of know about that, but we forget… Once you put us in touch with that, I was thinking, "Gee, it must be a very intimidating experience". So I was able to put myself in her shoes and understand how hard it would be and I tried to be a bit more perceptive of that.

For others, such as Greta, supporting personal growth was familiar but doing so in the context of ensuring that professional standards were being met added a new layer of complexity

> I often thought perhaps I was a little bit too sensitive, touchy feely, I don't know…not as academically rigorous or professionally rigorous as some… [Men/tee] allowed me to really identify the very important professional standards that had to be met and to be able to make sure that I am supporting the pre-service teacher with understanding [them]… So, not just supporting their personal growth, but also really reinforcing the professional expectations.

According to Bullough and Draper (2004), the complex and multifaceted nature of the mentoring role is a source of emotional labor but, as Maynard (2000) points out, so too is role confusion. Opportunities for mentors to share and compare their understandings of the nature of the role enabled some clarity to emerge, even in the context of complexity.

Apart from developing more nuanced appreciation of the complexity and significance of the mentoring role, some participants also made the critical identity shift from first-order to second-order practitioner. No longer thinking of themselves as coaches or guides who simply make space for pre-service teachers to practice teaching, participants such as Linda began to reconceptualise the mentor's role as that of school-based teacher educator. As part of her new understanding of her role, she described beginning to choose intentionally which aspects of teaching were important to teach her pre-service teacher

> I did start thinking along the lines of "okay, so what do you actually need in your toolbox to be a good teacher?" And I actually do think you need a certain amount of skills, like a ballet dancer has moves, like a tradesman has tools and knows what to do with them. I just really felt like that and all of a sudden it seemed quite clear that you actually do need some basic skills.

Linda's choice of metaphors illustrates the way in which she was beginning to think like a teacher educator. The image of the ballet dancer captures perfectly the sense in which skilled professionals can make something complex seem so deceptively easy to the untrained eye. She began to think of her own practice as a set of highly skilled maneuvres that need to be made explicit to pre-service teachers so that they see the complexity behind every seemingly simple pedagogical decision and action. Likewise, the notion of the tradesman with tools that serve particular and discrete purposes suggests the skilful and considered nature of teaching.

While Linda was focused on *what* to teach about teaching, Diana's shift to thinking like a 'second order practitioner' (Murray 2002) was characterized by a focus on a changing conception of *how* to teach about teaching. Diana explained

> I actually felt like I was thinking about what my role as a mentor was and was really conscious of every conversation and action I took. The constant reflection made me realise how much everything you do with your pre-service teacher influences them and helps shape them into becoming a better or worse educator.

In ITE, Loughran (2006) argues that teacher educators are always modeling whether they are conscious of it or not. Diana's comments above reflect precisely this kind of understanding of her potential influence as a school-based teacher educator.

The final point to make about participants' role and identity development is that their new understanding of their roles as mentors and school-based teacher educators also led to new understandings about their work and expertise as teachers. Paul simply stated: *I feel like I'm a lot better in terms of not only being a* mentor *but in my own teaching.* For Linda, too, professional learning about mentoring encouraged a deep layer of reflective learning about her own teaching

> Now I am aware of breaking down my teaching practice into parts that I could speak about to other people. I find I can justify my practice better to myself as my awareness of it grows, and I am deliberately trying new ways of doing things, to see the effect… I've got this real passion for teaching and I've kind of had that before but now I've really got it, I've really got a buzz. Like people get it in travel, I've got a teaching buzz.

Invited to consider the mentoring role as providing learning experiences about teaching, participants had to make explicit their tacit knowledge about teaching and learning, to articulate their wisdom of practice, first to themselves and then to their PST. Doing so created a heightened sense of identity and strengthened appreciation of their work as teachers.

19.5.2 Tools and Strategies for Effective Mentoring: A Teacher Educator's Approach

Existing university-led mentor professional development appears to take more of a 'training' approach in which mentors are offered opportunities to upskill in key aspects of mentoring such as coaching, providing feedback, and setting professional learning goals (Crasborn et al. 2008). Men/tee offered a departure from this approach. Much more than 'mentor training;' Men/tee was premised on the idea of deepening and indeed shifting participants' understandings of teacher education and of their role within it from that of mentor to school-based teacher educator. This involved engaging them in collaborative professional learning about teacher education itself, with a curriculum focused less on the skills of mentoring and more on exploring some of the key pedagogical approaches, processes and strategies used by teacher educators to teach about teaching. With access to new understanding about how to teach about teaching, participants described the new approaches they took to their mentoring work.

The fundamental concept that underpinned all Men/tee work was the idea of treating the practicum as a learning experience for pre-service teachers, rather than a teaching experience. In this sense, the program was premised on the conception of the practicum according to Dewey's (1904) laboratory model, as opposed to the apprentice model. For many Men/tee participants, the idea of the practicum as a learning experience was new. Seeing it as such encouraged them to begin to consider how they might deliberately engineer opportunities for their pre-service teachers to engage in particular kinds of learning about teaching. For example, new possibilities opened up for Norman as he considered the mentor report as a kind of curriculum framework for the practicum. He explains, *that was something I'd never done before; actually pick up the [mentor report] document and look at it.*

Liana was similarly affected by reframing the practicum from one of practicing teaching to one of learning about teaching. In Liana's case, it altered her approach to providing feedback to her pre-service teacher so that she was less focused on telling the pre-service teacher what was right and wrong and more focused on providing an educative opportunity for the pre-service teacher to learn through experimentation and reflection on aspects of his developing practice. She explains

> I used to write heaps of notes and go through them and it would take hours whereas now I'll say "Why don't we focus on this" and then we work on that and then talk about how well that did or didn't work and then make the next plan. So I'm possibly a bit more laid back and giving them a bit more space to investigate and to make minor mistakes without stopping them from making their mistakes before they've made them.

Liana's description of her changed approach reflects the shift from a technicist approach to a reflective understanding about how to teach about teaching (Loughran 2006) and marks a significant departure from the master-apprentice model that problematically typifies the approach taken by many mentors in schools.

Whereas an apprentice—or technicist—approach to teacher education assumes that pre-service teachers learn how to teach by mimicking the practices of experienced teachers in schools, a laboratory—or reflective—approach assumes that there is much more going on in teaching than what is outwardly visible. It therefore requires a unique range of pedagogical strategies to enable pre-service teachers to see the complex and often invisible work of pedagogical reasoning that underpins powerful practice by raising these invisible dimensions of teacher knowledge and action to the visible surface. In Men/tee, the introduction of two such interrelated pedagogical strategies influenced how participants undertook their mentoring work: structured observation and explicit modeling.

It is common during the practicum for pre-service teachers to 'observe' a range of experienced teachers at work, presumably with the expectation that this will contribute to their learning about teaching. But according to Loughran (2006), in many cases, pre-service teachers do not know what they should be looking at or what they should be looking for. Worse still, in their observations, pre-service teachers can see what they expect to see (Loughran 2006), thereby confirming a whole host of their unmediated assumptions about teaching and learning. In Men/tee, the problem of 'uneducative' and 'miseducative' observation was explored through collaborative inquiry and focused observation was introduced as a pedagogical strategy to counter it, including through the introduction of observation schedules. In the following excerpt, Caroline describes how she structured her pre-service teacher's observations of other teachers at work

> I said, "Okay, go down and look at year seven eight and nine. Look at how they start the lesson. Do they do much chalk and talk and then think about why or why not?" So it gave me the idea of giving a list of questions so that they actually had a structure to look at when they're observing... Then he'd come back and actually say to me, "yeah I noticed that you're right. They don't do much chalk and talk and they do more group activity." So I found that really good.

Here, Caroline demonstrates her understanding of the pedagogical potential of structured observation. In this case, she used it to create an experiential learning opportunity for her pre-service to understand how to balance direct instruction and activity-based learning. With his own lived experience 'that you're right' about the balance, the pre-service teacher was more willing to accept Caroline's critique of his practice in this regard.

As well as structuring their pre-service teachers' observations, Men/tee participants were also encouraged to deliberately and explicitly model particular aspects of teaching as part of their approach to mentoring. Like structured observation, this was a new approach for many participants. Caroline explained that *although you get them in the classroom, I'd never actually said specifically "come in and watch this here and how I do it." I'm just like, "come in and see what I do and learn from that ..."* Caroline's preexisting *'come in and see what I do and learn from that'* approach reflects a master-apprentice style of modeling whereby the apprentice is encouraged by the master to 'do as I do.' Explicit modeling differs substantially in that what is being modelled by the mentor is assumed to be neither self-evident nor able to be imitated through mimicry.

Explicit modeling encourages pre-service teachers to articulate their thought processes, to reflect on what they believe they have seen, and to integrate theory and practice in those reflections (Smith 2014, p. 25). Explicit modeling therefore creates opportunities for mentors to both explicate their intentions and to clarify pre-service teacher misconceptions. Here, Tim describes how he incorporated explicit modeling as a mentoring strategy

> I said [to the PST], "Alright, well you've got to be looking for who is listening, why are they sitting there, why is so and so sitting there, what am I doing with her, her and her or what am I doing with this kid or stuff like that." So I think it opened my eyes up to different challenges and different things that I should be pointing out to student teachers, whereas in the past I hadn't pointed it out to them.

Like Caroline, Tim indicates that, prior to Men/tee, he had not thought to make explicit to his pre-service teachers what he was modeling for them, or what he hoped they would see in their observations of his practice. Professional learning about explicit modeling as a teacher education approach enabled both Carline and Tim to realize, as Boyd et al. (2014) note, that pre-service teachers 'may be blissfully unaware that the teacher educator is modelling' (p. 56). As a consequence, they each developed strategies to draw out and make explicit the intended learning.

The program's structural approach of weekly professional learning meetings between mentors and university-based teacher educators emerged as another significant factor in influencing participants' mentoring work. Never before had they shared their mentoring experiences or had the opportunity to discuss together key ideas, concepts and strategies. The group quickly began to function as a professional learning community of reflective practitioners (Wenger 2000). As Norman explains

> That interaction and communication with other people.... I remember turning up and hearing other people's horror stories thinking "I have no problems, I'm on easy street." But there would've been times where I thought "oh my god, what am I doing?" So actually not having a student teacher in isolation to everyone else actually made me think about what was going on with her and her teaching and our relationship and I became a lot more self-conscious than what I would've been otherwise.

Here, Norman acknowledges the value of the mentor community as opposed to the 'isolation' in which mentoring usually happens. For him, being exposed to the approaches and strategies of his Men/tee peers pushed Norman's own thinking about how to approach his own mentoring work.

Similarly, Paul describes the satisfaction of being able to both offer and receive advice and suggestions about mentoring as a consequence of working as a part of a professional learning community of mentors

> I thought I was able to contribute to [colleagues'] development, to solving their problems and I learnt just as much from hearing what other people said about the issues they were having and how they were resolving it, and yeah, there were some wonderful suggestions put forward that I think made us all richer for the experience of having that discussion which we wouldn't have had otherwise.

Paul's and Norman's reflections on the positive influence of being part of a professional learning community of mentors recall the insights of self-study researchers who similarly describe the ways in which engaging with others as part of a community of teacher educators opened up new understandings of how to undertake the work of teacher education (e.g., Berry and Forgasz 2016).

19.6   Implications for Shifting Practice

The Men/tee project was only a small pilot, tested in the context of a single school-university partnership. Nevertheless, participants' professional learning experiences during the program give rise to a number of significant implications for the future design of school-university partnerships that encourage mentor teachers to make the transition to becoming school-based teacher educators. Moving away from a mentor training model is the first. The following features highlight the components that were identified as important in the design of the Men/tee pilot.

- Community: A professional learning community approach enables participants to learn from each other and to test ideas and strategies. It is recommended as the best way to foster professional learning.
- Context: Engaging mentors in professional learning about mentoring simultaneous to their mentoring work with pre-service teachers provides an immediate context in which new ideas and strategies for mentoring can be applied and subsequently reflected upon as part of the learning experience.
- Collaboration: Ongoing, collegial collaboration between school-based and university-based teacher educators is essential to enabling the development of a shared vision for pre-service teachers' practicum learning.
- Curriculum: Matching professional learning content with self-identified needs and interests generates learner consent. A developmental curriculum that links teacher education theory with the mentors' in-situ practicum experiences offers a powerful combination.
- Capacity: The provision of mentor and teacher educator education has the potential to contribute to improving not only the quality of participants' mentoring, but also their confidence and capacities as teachers.

19.7 Conclusion

The Men/tee project stemmed from many of the shifting and competing public and political forces in ITE and consideration of the best ways to prepare future teachers. The dual focus on participants becoming research-informed mentors *and* thinking of themselves as school-based teacher educators was a key feature of this mentor professional learning program which enabled the development of a shared vision for teacher education that cut across school and university boundaries. A limitation of the study was the absence of data on the professional learning of pre-service teachers and the implications for student learning within this partnership model. This is an area for future research, building on the recent Donaldson (2011) review which calls for "alternative models that help reduce 'unhelpful philosophical and structural divides, [that] have led to sharp separations of function amongst teachers, teacher educators and researchers" (p. 5). Our initial Men/tee findings do provide a platform for future investigation and highlight that by (re)positioning mentors as school-based teacher educators, together with university-based teacher educators, the enactment of teacher education can be improved. We therefore encourage the further development of school-university partnerships premised on educative partnerships between university and school-based teacher educators.

References

Berry, A., & Forgasz, R. (2016). Becoming ourselves as teacher educators: Trespassing, transgression and transformation In: *Professional learning through transitions and transformations* (pp. 95–106). Springer.

Boyd, P., Szplit, A., & Zbróg, Z. (2014). Teacher educators and teachers as learners: International Perspectives.

Bullough, R. V., Jr., & Draper, R. J. (2004). Mentoring and the emotions. *Journal of Education for Teaching, 30*(3), 271–288.

Clarke, A., Collins, J., Triggs, V., Nielsen, W., Augustine, A., Coulter., D., & Kinegal, J. (2012). The mentoring profile inventory: An online professional development resource for cooperating teachers. *Teaching Education, 23*(2), 167–194.

Clarke, A., Triggs, V., & Nielsen, W. (2014). Cooperating teacher participation in teacher education: A review of the literature. *Review of Educational Research, 84*(2), 163–202.

Cochran-Smith, M. (2005). The new teacher education: For better or for worse? *Educational Researcher, 34*(7), 3–17.

Conroy, J., Hulme, M., & Menter, I. (2013). Developing a 'clinical' model for teacher education. *Journal of Education for Teaching, 39*(5), 557–573.

Crasborn, F., Hennissen, P., Brouwer, N., Korthagen, F., & Bergen, T. (2008). Promoting versatility in mentor teachers' use of supervisory skills. *Teaching and Teacher Education, 24*(3), 499–514.

Dewey, J. (1904). *The relation of theory to practice in education. The third yearbook of the National Society for the Scientific Study of Education.* Chicago, IL: The University of Chicago Press.

Donaldson, G. (2011). *Teaching Scotland's future: Report of a review of teacher education in Scotland.* Edinburgh: The Scottish Government. APS Group. http://www.scotland.gov.uk/Resource/Doc/337626/0110852.pdf.

Janssen, F., Westbroek, H., & Doyle, W. (2014). The practical turn in teacher education designing a preparation sequence for core practice frames. *Journal of Teacher Education, 65*(3), 195–206.

Loughran, J. J. (2006). *Developing a pedagogy of teacher education: Understanding teaching and learning about teaching.* Taylor & Francis.

Maynard, T. (2000). Learning to teach or learning to manage mentors? Experiences of school-based teacher training. *Mentoring and Tutoring, 8*(1), 17–30.

Murray, J. (2002). *Between the chalkface and the ivory towers? A study of the professionalism of teacher educators working on primary initial teacher education courses in the English university sector.* Institute of Education, University of London.

Murray, J., & Male, T. (2005). Becoming a teacher educator: Evidence from the field. *Teaching and Teacher Education, 21*(2), 125–142.

Smith, H. (2014). Teacher education in Scotland: The challenges facing teachers and teacher educators within a rapidly changing education landscape. In P. Boyd, A. Szplit, Z. Zbrog (Eds.), *Teacher educators and teachers as learners: International perspectives* (pp. 21–38). Krakow, Poland: Libron.

Wenger, E. (2000). Communities of practice and social learning systems. *Organization, 7*(2), 225–246.

Author Biographies

Simone White is Professor and Chair of Teacher Education in the Faculty of Education at Monash University, Australia and currently the Immediate Past President of the Australian Teacher Education Association (ATEA). Simone's research, teaching and engagement are focused on the key question of how to best prepare teachers and leaders for diverse communities.

Rachel Forgasz is a teacher educator and researcher in the Faculty of Education at Monash University, Australia, where she is also a Fellow of the Monash Education Academy. She researches and writes about: embodied pedagogies, self-study, the emotional dimension of learning to teach, Professional Experience, and mentor professional learning.

Chapter 20
Research in the Workplace: The Possibilities for Practitioner and Organisational Learning Offered by a School-University Research Partnership

Leon Benade, Bill Hubbard and Leanne Lamb

20.1 Introduction

Educational research being 'done to' or 'about' teachers is the more likely con-vention than research 'done with' participants. There are many reasons for this condition, but arguably more important is the effect, which is the alienation of education practitioners from understanding some of the core processes affecting their daily work. Education (or 'learning' as some would prefer), we are told, is a lifelong activity; thus, it should not be assumed that teachers cease learning after graduation. Research *in* the workplace and *about* the workplace, carried out *with* teachers can make a material difference to the way they conceptualise their work, talk about their work, and thus to the way they go about their work. Education researchers are uniquely positioned to support teachers' work given their privileged access to flexible time, which their school-based colleagues are unlikely to share. In addition, they have access to resources not generally available to the public, and are able to harness and develop intellectual capital also not freely available to their school-based colleagues (in short, academics have the luxury of developing 'head space' on issues of significance). In their turn, schools offer education researchers a 'living lab', a 'chalk-face', or a 'trench' on the 'front line', so to speak. Schools provide education researchers what no university setting or any number of journal articles or books can

L. Benade (✉) · L. Lamb
Auckland University of Technology, Auckland, New Zealand
e-mail: leon.w.benade@aut.ac.nz

L. Lamb
e-mail: leanne.s.lamb@gmail.com

B. Hubbard
Rosehill College, Auckland, New Zealand
e-mail: b.hubbard@rosehillcollege.school.nz

© Springer Nature Singapore Pte Ltd. 2017
M.A. Peters et al. (eds.), *A Companion to Research in Teacher Education*,
DOI 10.1007/978-981-10-4075-7_20

offer—namely living practice where teachers and students can be observed in a naturalistic setting, providing a rich data source, to be complemented by the gathering of the views of the various stakeholders associated with schools. In short, the act of researching within a school setting opens the possibilities of broadening the work education of both teachers and education researchers.

20.2   A Personal Introduction

This chapter is simultaneously *about* school-university partnerships, it *describes* an instance of a specific school-university research partnership, and its *writing* is a living exercise in partnership. The literature review was written largely by Leanne, whose postgraduate study focuses on school-university partnerships. Leon and Bill worked closely in 2015 once the school agreed that Leon could conduct the next phase of his research there. While most of the participants in the study described in this chapter were conventional research participants, Leon and Bill collaborated on a practitioner conference presentation, while Leon and Leanne worked together on shaping the literature review. All have shared in writing this chapter.

This chapter presents a review of literature outlining the subject of school-university partnerships. A practitioner perspective is provided by Bill, followed by a researcher perspective, in which Leon outlines his larger research activity, following some of the usual conventions governing presentation of research. This provides a context for understanding the research conducted at Rosehill College.[1] The presentation of findings is however kept to a minimum, as the focus is to discuss the implications of the research process and findings for the development of practitioner research arising from school-university research partnerships.

20.3   An Introduction to School-University Partnerships

School-university partnerships are not simple in terms of structures, processes, and outcomes (Nelson 2006; Schuck 2012; Segedin 2011). Intersecting theory and practice, they are oriented towards building shared expertise (Tsui and Law 2007), are subject to shifting power relationships, and must be responsive to complex accountabilities. There are certain factors common to successful school-university partnerships—committed individuals who are flexible, and adaptive to emergent needs, whilst being cognisant of the overarching principle of reciprocity.

School-university partnerships, where interactions contribute to mutually beneficial outcomes, are relevant to the future of education in secondary and tertiary

---

[1]Although the terms of the ethics agreement was that the school and participants would not be mentioned by name, for the purposes of this chapter, the school has agreed to be named. Participant identities (apart from the co-authors) have, however, been kept anonymous.

contexts. The on-going education of teachers can link school improvement and academic research (Hargreaves and Fullan 2012), thus universities and schools develop collective responsibility for improving education, and generating professional capital. This process may challenge the common divide between teacher educators and teachers, and Hargreaves and Fullan (2012) advised stakeholders to aim "to do things that bridge the chasm [between school and university], reach for partnership, and replace polarization with interaction" (p. 153).

In the following review, some of the key debates emerging from the literature on school-university partnerships will be outlined. These include some of the challenges in establishing a partnership, notably in relation to negotiating the power relationships, and the challenge of developing flexibility. As a partnership, there is an expectation of a two-way, equal relationship, thus understanding the principle of reciprocity is important. Of most significance to practitioners and organisations, however, is what may be learnt.

20.4 Changing Power Relationships

The development of collaborative partnerships takes time and trust (Moss 2008; Schuck 2012), and must tolerate institutional (Schuck 2012; Tsui and Law 2007), political (Moss 2008), and financial (Gardner 2011; Walsh and Backe 2013) forces. As Walsh and Backe (2013) explain, while participants can be committed to the partnership, "they are not immune to competing professional pressures" (p. 604). Nevertheless, the appeal of co-construction rather than power (2013) supports collaboration, and helps to negate the influence of top-down power.

It is, however, in negotiating the relationship between school and university researcher that power dynamics are highlighted. Within a school-university partnership "trust, communication, and other ineffable partnership qualities" (Gardner 2011, p. 82) are paramount to success. Partnerships operate in a system where "challenges continually emerge" (Walsh and Backe 2013, p. 602), so the ability of participants to address these challenges as the partnership progresses is essential, requiring the skills of interaction, enabling "partners [to] enact collaborative implementation processes" (Gardner 2011, p. 74). Successful operational strategies include collaboratively negotiated planning for infrastructure and sustainability, allowing, however, that "the initial design of the partnership's infrastructure...often changes as the project and programs develop" (Walsh and Backe 2013, p. 601).

20.5 Reciprocal Benefit

When establishing school-university partnerships, discussion of mutual benefits and how institutions and individuals might benefit from the partnership, must take place. Reciprocal benefit may be achieved through developing sensitivity, respect, understanding, and "mutual informing and critiquing" (Moss 2008, p. 348). Equally, mutual benefit may be achieved through achieving partnership outcomes. Nevertheless, discussion and development of what is mutually beneficial and "the need for both institutions to benefit from the partnership" is the "most important challenge in establishing collaborative research partnerships" (Schuck 2012, p. 59), and cannot be rushed: in this regard, Tsui and Law (2007) acknowledged the process of building partnerships incrementally.

While partnership goals can vary, or conflict, (Edens and Gilsinan 2005), mutual purpose is a cornerstone for any partnership (Gardner 2011). A key purpose is establishing and sustaining partnership learning, and sharing the benefits associated with that learning. Deconstructing traditional academic boundaries (Carlson 2001) to "support reciprocity and the free exchange of ideas, connect theory and practice, promote collegiality and honest talk, and provide…supportive feedback" (Miller 2015, p. 25) fosters understanding of partnerships as learning systems.

20.6   Learning as a Profession

The majority of school-university partnerships are linked to teacher professional learning programmes which highlights "learning as a core component of partnerships" (Callahan and Martin 2007, p. 136). Teacher perceptions and understandings of themselves, as both learners and as professionals, are regarded as a dominant influence on school-university partnerships (Moss 2008; Nelson 2006; Segedin 2011). Segedin (2011) noted that participant teachers felt "accountable to be change agents in their school" (p. 54). Organisational learning from engagement with school-university partnerships is linked to participant experiences, and a willingness to change their practice.

20.6.1   Practice Context: Bill's Narrative

Periodically, transformations occur within the education sector that can test the capacity of even well-established systems. The advent of e-Learning, leveraged by the ubiquity of Internet access and affordable personal and mobile computing devices, has forced a rethink of many schooling conventions, and schools in New Zealand are no exception. Although there was much internal impetus for the uptake of e-Learning (using ICT to facilitate learning) at Rosehill College, the early uptake of e-Learning and Bring-Your-Own-Device (BYOD) by its contributing schools, created a tipping-point for Rosehill College.

The college, a state co-educational school, was established in 1970, and its current enrolment is 1755 students and 105 teachers. It has a historic tradition of embracing innovation and after considering the research and consulting the local community, a plan for a measured implementation of BYOD in 2014 was set in place between 2011 and 2013. A comprehensive programme of professional learning and development in 2013 supplemented existing teacher e-Learning competencies. In this way, the college laid the framework for the implementation of 1:1 BYOD, beginning with the 400 new Year Nine entrants of 2014.

Teaching in a BYOD environment for the first time can be demanding, and in our case, the implementation of BYOD was an opportunity to put some of the questions contained in the Teaching as Inquiry (TAI)[2] model to the test. Each day required a demanding evaluation of what worked, what did not work and a proposed resolution to take alternative action, if required.

Beyond my personal struggles in the classroom, as the Deputy Principal with overall responsibility for ICT, e-Learning and BYOD, I experienced a growing volume of unsolicited feedback from teachers, including their narratives and accounts about what was and was not working.

The senior leadership team of Rosehill College had long recognised that a comprehensive review process was a vital element to the long-term success of the implementation of a BYOD policy. Initially, however, time and attention had been devoted to developing physical infrastructure and teacher capability; planning for how to review and refine e-Learning/BYOD had not been really considered. Nor was there a planned process for integrating and understanding the data that was being informally generated.

By the second year of BYOD, in 2015, the school's computing infrastructure was able to provide a stable platform for the teaching and learning experience; teachers confidence of successfully working in a blended e-Learning environment was growing, and some parental requests for feedback on the progress of the BYOD implementation, and its effects on student learning, were being heard.

Leon Benade had included Rosehill College as part of his own on-going research into 'twenty-first century learning' in 2014, thus his request in 2015 to continue his research, with a focus on the school's BYOD implementation as a manifestation of twenty-first-century learning, was fortuitous indeed. Before considering the request, both parties had to determine that they had compatible goals (Gardner 2011; Schuck 2012), and to clarify the assumptions, parameters and intent of the research.

Once the research plan and the school's requirements were aligned, the work began. Early collaboration with Leon provided the school the confidence in his capacity and willingness to adapt his research to fit the needs of the school. Schools operate within tight operational budgets, and teachers have minimal free time,[3] thus imposing a researcher on teachers can be a risky undertaking. Leon's research style, however, accommodated flexibility and sensible changes to the research plan as we progressed together in Term Two of 2015.

---

[2]A model for practitioner reflection, advocated by The New Zealand Curriculum (Ministry of Education 2007).

[3]This echoes the institutional and financial pressures mentioned by Gardner (2011), Schuck (2012), Tsui and Law (2007), and Walsh and Backe (2013).

Despite the challenges of ensuring smooth communication between researcher and research participants, the school leadership team had significant confidence in the process, for several reasons. The questions the school wanted to ask cohered with the research questions. The school had confidence that the research plan had sound methodology, designed by a 'research professional'. I recognised the value of teachers and students speaking freely with an external person, who would preserve their anonymity. Relatedly, the school community would have greater confidence in the results established by an unbiased, independent researcher, who would also be able to locate these results in a larger national and global educational research context. Finally, from a purely pragmatic viewpoint, no one in the school would be able to devote the time and energy into both the research and analysis that is possible when working with a university researcher.

The research relationship described here has demonstrated the benefit of collaborations between schools and universities to confidently meet important educational challenges. An external researcher brings a collection of unique skills and resources to a school context that schools are unlikely to ever be funded for. Furthermore, the objective pair of eyes places the problem and the results of the research into a broader perspective.

From the view of a Deputy Principal with a complex task to complete, having the resources and skill of a university researcher has solved many problems. Our school-university partnership has suggested ways of giving TAI a wider scope, moving from practice in individual classrooms to collective practice. Given that teachers without postgraduate qualifications have had less exposure to conducting research, the school-university liaison gives such teachers opportunity to learn these skills from an accomplished practitioner.

20.7 Researcher Perspective

20.7.1 Background to the Research

Important features of the concept of 'twenty-first century learning' in New Zealand schools are the use of digital technologies and, increasingly, use of flexible spaces. It is claimed that the widening and deepening use of technologies, especially (but not only) mobile technologies will encourage (even demand) new pedagogies and, in turn, require teachers to take up an increasingly critical (self-reflective) orientation (Wright 2010). The promise of the introduction and use of digital technology to the classroom is for students to become better engaged, more highly motivated and able to engage in critical and collaborative learning (2010).

The research discussed in this chapter was developed from a larger, on-going study commenced in 2013. This qualitative study has focussed on the work of teachers and the strategic actions of leaders at a selection of New Zealand schools. In 2015, it has explored, interpreted and sought greater understanding of modern teaching and learning practices, and the transitions teachers and school leaders make as they grapple with the challenge of twenty-first-century learning, the development of flexible learning spaces and the rapidly changing nature of knowledge and learning in a digital age. Teachers and leaders were selected from the several case study schools that have participated since 2013. In 2015, data was gathered through interviews, focus groups and observations of teachers working in flexible spaces and/or implementing BYOD and/or e-Learning. The intent was to continue to encourage these participants to explore and reflect on their lived professional experiences in the context of twenty-first-century learning, but now with the focus being on their evolving understanding and experience of leading and managing their transition to modern teaching and learning practices. It was also important to understand the challenges and obstacles they have encountered in this transition process, and how they sustain fundamental pedagogical change.

Current Ministry of Education discourse and rhetoric is associated with the development of the 'twenty-first century skills' that are a springboard for lifelong economic success. The skills to be developed in young people are "resilience, adaptability, the ability to think critically and solve problems, team work, and the ability to independently find and use information" (Ministry of Education 2014, p. 30). An evaluation of practice in the selected case study schools should, therefore, be considered through the lenses of pedagogical principles that can be considered essential to the development of 'twenty-first century skills', such as: personalisation, interdisciplinary and project-based inquiry, student direction or agency, and collaborative practices (Pearlman 2010).

One of the case study schools that had participated in the earlier project was Rosehill College, and it was once again approached as it was in the second year of BYOD implementation. This made it an ideal case study in view of the likelihood of teachers living through the experience of implementing a significant new strategy, which, as suggested above, would be placing demands on their pedagogy and sense of professional identity.

20.7.2 Research Design

Initially, the design of the 2015 study was framed as a comparison of four case study schools. Each of the four schools presents as a 'case' of teachers experiencing transition. Within this design, it was intended that three teachers (or three teams of teachers) would be observed three times each, would participate in various informal debriefing discussions, and a final staff focus group. In addition, the principal would be interviewed.

Case study design is contentious, if only because there is no clarity over whether it is a methodology or an approach (Chadderton and Torrance 2011). Further, there are differences of opinion over where to draw the boundaries around a case, and whether understanding the 'case' develops from the constructed meanings of the participants, or from the account provided by the 'objective' researcher. To resolve some of these issues, Chadderton and Torrance (2011), opted for a specific definition, which "combines a policy focus…with a physical location…[and where] …reference to…individuals…[is] from the position of asking what does 'the case' look like for this [person]?" (p. 53).

Relevant ethical authorisations were obtained, thus permitting researcher observation of classes, including some unrecorded exchanges with students. The data gathered from observations and interviews would be analysed with the help of NVivo software. This selection process leads to the themes by which the researcher is able to gather the data to inform both description of what has been observed and heard, but also to engage with, and make sense of, the lived experience of the participants.

20.8   Research Reality: Leon's Narrative

20.8.1   Recruitment, Ethics and Design

Research as planned and research as executed may not necessarily cohere. First, there are several participant recruitment challenges. Finding schools whose principals and teachers are willing to engage in research is no easy task. Several emails are followed by telephone calls, further mails, and further, sometimes nagging, calls. Recruiting participants and participant schools can be time-consuming and characterised by rejection.

In the spirit of reciprocal partnership and attaining mutual ends (as indicated by Moss 2008 and Schuck 2012) I offered the schools who were willing to proceed, the opportunity for me, as the researcher, to 'dig deeper' into any aspect related to my research (on transitioning from traditional to modern teaching and learning practices) that the school was particularly keen to develop or understand. This idea was taken up by the senior leaders at Rosehill College, who saw an opportunity here for me to evaluate the implementation of the school's BYOD programme. Given that BYOD and e-Learning was what I was looking at anyway, this was a sensible suggestion.

An initial meeting took place with prospective teacher participants, to review the proposed ethics documentation (thus I could demonstrate 'consultation' to my ethics committee). The mechanics of dealing with the documentation exercised our collective mind, as at that stage, I had prepared for students to be treated as participants, despite their role being marginal in the observations—common sense prevailed at the ethics committee, however, and specific consents for students was eventually not required.

Design was the following challenge. I explained I was not a scientist seeking generalisable knowledge; rather I wanted to tap into what sense people were making of the way their work was evolving, and what kind of influence these changes were having on them. I also wanted to see them at work, so I could make sense of how differently they might be working. From this, I would reach some conclusions, possibly putting forward some explanations, and thus deepening the collective understanding of the profession of these changes and what they entailed. The difficulty that arose, however, is that rather than just three participants, I had seven who wanted to take part. I could have applied the rules I had put in place in my ethics application regarding participant over-subscription, but given my comments above regarding the challenge of recruiting, and, as the school was hoping I would provide an evaluative report, I made the decision to include all seven. I could not, however, observe each person three times (considering I had three other schools where I was observing). I recall discussing this problem with an experienced colleague around the coffee machine at work, and his advice was simple: separate this study out from the other three schools where the focus was more on the development of practice in flexible, shared spaces (which includes ICT and e-Learning too, of course). He was quite correct[4] and thus I adjusted the design for Rosehill College, specifically in regard to the number of observations.

Following Chadderton and Torrance (2011), the implementation of the BYOD policy became the 'case' in a specific physical setting (Rosehill College), thus removing the requirement to treat the college and its teachers as a case in comparison with other case study schools. The research could then focus on (a) what this implementation looks like for participants and (b) an evaluation of the implementation. Flowing from this shift in emphasis, a student survey, and focus groups of students and parents were arranged, of which more will be referred to below, suffice to say now that additional ethics approvals were required and sought.

20.8.2   Communication

Throughout the ethnographic phase, when I was visiting the school to conduct observations, the Deputy Principal and I met for informal updates. At the outset, he provided me with a timetable. As the school has a 6-day timetable, planning observations was challenging. Although the Deputy Principal often coordinated my visits, he reflected the pressures characteristic of his job position, requiring that I often negotiated directly with the teachers I was observing. I had their email addresses, thus would propose dates and times of visits. In some instances, however, negotiation occurred around programming clashes that challenged observations. These included whole-class assessments and end of term processes. Thus, any university researcher working in a school must recognise the "competing professional pressures" Walsh and Backe (2013, p. 604) referred to, and these demand a degree of mutual flexibility.

Both communication and partnership were highlighted by a decision made soon after the research process commenced. The Deputy Principal invited me to co-present with him at the 2015 National Association of Secondary Deputy and Assistant Principal's (NASDAP) Conference. This conference provided a stream dedicated to school-university research partnerships. This decision required us to plan and build the presentation over a number of months, developing our

---

[4]I am acknowledging here my colleague, Andy Begg, for his clear advice.

collaboration and communication. It created some new opportunities too. The Deputy Principal and I worked on a student survey he wanted to administer to the Year Nine and Ten cohorts on behalf of the school. We processed several iterations, the teacher participants had an opportunity to reflect on the items, and they provided useful feedback in regard to the length and complexity of the items. In this way, we were building the shared expertise referred to by Tsui and Law (2007). Sensing too that verbal feedback given to an outsider (rather than a staff member) would possibly be more forthright, the Deputy Principal and I discussed the possibility of focus groups of Year Nines, Tens and parents. These groups and the survey yielded valuable qualitative feedback that informs the programme evaluation dimension of the partnership. I will now briefly consider some of the findings relevant to the concept of an educative school-university partnership.

20.9 Key Findings that Bear on the School-University Partnership

The research literature on partnerships highlights the importance of reciprocity, and in this regard, the scope to share information and offer respectful critique (Moss 2008) is important. Ideally, teachers engaged in a school-university partnership should benefit by "learning [which is] a core component of partnerships" (Callahan and Martin 2007, p. 136). This learning may be derived from being directly part of the research (as the deputy Principal was), or by participating in focus group discussions (as the staff participants were). Another source of learning is to view some relevant findings, and for this purpose, just a small sample has been chosen. These are presented in three parts, the first being to share some critique, the second to consider what participants can learn by their response to change, and the third, to reflect on what motivates them to change. All of these may be considered as feedback, with some thoughts about next steps.

20.9.1 Some Critical Points

- *Teachers overestimate the digital capability of their students, and assume that young people necessarily know their way around computing and digital devices.* This plays out in the classroom when teachers tell students to seek the help of their peers. The staff focus group verified that certainly at the outset, teachers assumed more on behalf of students than was warranted. It was also confirmed that teachers call on students to help each other to master the required technical or computing skills. While these participants seem to believe they now no longer make these assumptions, the student focus groups indicated this continues to be the experience of students. Furthermore, some teachers may also assume that students will be 'naturally intuitive' in accessing, navigating and working in the digital elements of the e-Learning environment.

- *Teachers regard technology merely as a tool, rather than as way to revolutionise their pedagogy.* Interviews with key staff revealed this finding, suggesting the notion of technology as a 'digital pencil' persists. In this sense, technology has not been integrated into the fabric of the some teachers' thinking about their work; rather, it remains 'out there', as no more than a support for 'business-as-usual', thus resulting in minimal or limited pedagogical change.
- *While teachers understand the SAMR model, they find it challenging to get beyond substitution.* The Substitution Augmentation Modification Redefinition (SAMR) model (Puentedura 2013) provides a way of evaluating the degree of technology integration, and level of learner engagement with tasks requiring technology. At the lower levels of substitution and augmentation, learning is merely enhanced using technology, whereas, at the higher levels of modification and redefinition, transformative learning is made possible by technology. In an online survey of Year Nine and Ten students who voluntarily completed the survey ($n = 88$), 87.5% indicated that using a teacher made document was the activity that they most likely completed on their devices. In contrast, 72.7% indicated that creating new content was the activity they were least likely to complete with their devices. Observation data recorded wide use among the participant teachers of 'electronic worksheets', the simple substitution of a paper handout with one now on Google Classroom. There were, however, examples of up-scale teaching, including students creating their own documents, making Powerpoints, and creating Prezi presentations. For some teachers, however, there is simply not enough time for the development of redefinition tasks, not to mention unwillingness to take the risks associated with possible failure, should radically new tasks go awry.
- *The implementation of blended e-Learning is variable.* Observational data recorded mixed use of classroom strategies, including overuse of devices and non-use in one case. This may be what led some parents to suggest that the implementation among teachers is inconsistent. One of their critiques was based on their children's feedback indicating teachers sitting through classes while students worked quietly on tasks placed on Google Classroom. There was some evidence of this in the observational data, including several examples of front-of-the class teaching, despite the view of the parent focus group that such teaching was not occurring (notwithstanding that such teaching approaches are not desirable, if carried on for lengthy periods). In contrast, the best case observed example reflected minimal teacher talk time, constant teacher movement around class, the teacher checking in with the students, who were actively completing a challenging exercise using devices, Google Classroom and the Internet.

20.9.2 How Some Teachers Have Responded to Change

These views are drawn from responses made by participant teachers in their focus group (seven teachers in total) to questioning relating to how the implementation of BYOD has changed them. All noted personal change, or the demand for change. Some embrace this change, seeing in it the opportunities for developing their imaginative abilities. This change may go so far as to influence (positively) the very way some teachers think about their jobs and daily work. One of these changes is to think about, and put into action, more individualised teaching and less teacher talk. Ironically, it may be this kind of shift that has motivated some students and parents to imagine teachers have relinquished their responsibility to 'teach' and just become 'glorified baby-sitters'. On the other side of the ledger, teachers report the changes leading to a loss of professional identity, feelings of superfluity and confusion about their core purpose.

20.9.3 Why Are Teachers Willing to Change?

Data drawn from staff focus groups and interviews make it is clear that there are teachers who are motivated by their desire to make a difference in the lives of their students, no matter how difficult and challenging change may be. Some spoke of the significantly increased workload entailed by implementing BYOD and associated e-Learning strategies, with implications for personal health and well-being. Nevertheless, these teachers recognise that they must shoulder the responsibilities of writing, planning and creating new materials, and a view expressed by several is of this being an experience akin to the first year of teaching. Such teachers recognise themselves as "accountable to be change agents in their school" (Segedin 2011, p. 54). Still, the sense of not trying at all produces feelings of guilt and inadequacy, propelled by a view that working in a technology-rich digital environment requires teachers to be 'experts' who are constantly maintaining a position at the cutting-edge of new technologies and applications.

20.10 Concluding Discussion

Feedback from teacher participants indicated that not many of the critical findings (of which a selection have been presented here) came as a surprise. It will, however, be in the combination of some of these findings, or explanations, that new insights can emerge. For example, the strong view of some students and parents that the teachers were 'no longer teaching' (while potentially disparaging and hurtful to some teachers) might grow from a misunderstanding by the community of the differences in approach required by e-Learning. Particularly if teachers are attempting to work up the SAMR scale, there should be less teacher-direction and more student-led learning. On the other hand, simply placing worksheets on Google Classroom with instructions to students to source information does not constitute good practice. Looking ahead, then, a focus will be for the school to better communicate its intentions to parents and students, while simultaneously attempting to broaden good e-Learning practice across the school.

The shift from teacher-direction to greater student (or learner) agency and self-management of learning is one of the direct implications of the implementation of the BYOD policy at the school. This implication, however, challenges the conventional sense of teacher identity. Tsui and Law (2007) noted the significance of 'learning in boundary zones', which may be areas of difficulty or discomfort for practitioners. Crossing boundaries allows individuals to re-examine their own practices, and develop new learning (2007). This occurred as the researcher and practitioners negotiated meanings and made sense of the challenges confronting a group of teachers attempting to craft a new practice paradigm. In sum, the research partnership stands to promote wider learning between the school leadership, teachers, and the wider community, while a critical examination of emergent 'teacher' and 'learner' identities in a BYOD context will become a foundation for next-step planning in the school.

While some teachers may respond negatively to change, there appears to be enough reason to suggest that positive motivations to change can lead to actual changes in practice. The school leadership team may consider ways of conveying and sustaining positive narratives to teachers and community alike, this too based on further evaluative research. Simultaneously, however, enthusiasm and energy must be kept in balance, as the findings reveal significant levels of stress and work overload. This too, is in the hands of leadership and governance.

School-university partnerships present complex spaces for learning, where accepted expertise is challenged while, concurrently, promoting professional empowerment. They can be transformative because they promote development of beliefs, and practices, that enable deep learning, and sharing of practice (Tsui and Law 2007). The shared approach to examining practice and contribution to learning as a profession actively promotes the replacement of polarisation with interaction (Hargreaves and Fullan 2012). More interactional spaces in which educators are constructing shared meanings, and developing shared understandings of each other's contexts, support professionals to engage in using deeper twenty first century learning skills of communication, collaboration and critical thinking to create new understandings.

Sustaining a school-university partnership as a learning system means managing contradictions, negotiating new ways of understanding, and generating reciprocal benefits. The discursive comments above indicate fertile ground on which one such partnership can proceed.

References

Callahan, J., & Martin, D. (2007). The spectrum of school-university partnerships: A typology of organisational learning systems. *Teaching and Teacher Education, 23*(2), 136–145. doi:10.1016/j.tate.2006.04.038

Carlson, P. (2001). A grassroots approach to educational partnerships. *Technological Horizons in Education [T H E] Journal, 29*(3), 83–88. Retrieved from http://search.proquest.com

Chadderton, C., & Torrance, H. (2011). Case study. In B. Somekh & C. Lewin (Eds.), *Theory and methods in social research* (2nd ed, pp. 53–60). London, England: Sage Publications.

Edens, R., & Gilsinan, J. (2005). Rethinking school partnerships. *Education and Urban Society, 37*(2), 123–138. doi:10.1177/0013124504270654

Gardner, D. (2011). Characteristic collaborative processes in school-university partnerships. *Planning and Changing, 42*(1), 63–86. Retrieved from http://search.proquest.com

Hargreaves, A., & M. Fullan. (2012). *Professional capital: Transforming teaching in every school* [Kindle version]. Retrieved from Amazon.com

Miller, L. (2015). School-university partnerships and teacher leadership: Doing it right. *The Educational Reform, 79*(1), 24–29. doi:10.1080/00131725.2015.972810

Ministry of Education. (2007). The New Zealand curriculum. Wellington, New Zealand: Learning Media Ltd. Also available online at http://nzcurriculum.tki.org.nz/The-New-Zealand-Curriculum

Ministry of Education. (2014). *Aspiration and achievement—Education system. Briefing to incoming Minister.* http://www.education.govt.nz/assets/Documents/Ministry/Publications/Briefings-to-Incoming-Ministers/AspirationAndAchievementEducationSystem.pdf. Retrieved from http://www.education.govt.nz/ministry-of-education/our-role-and-our-people/briefings-to-incoming-ministers/

Moss, J. (2008). Leading professional learning in an Australian school through school university partnerships. *Asia Pacific Journal of Teacher Education, 36*(4), 345–357. doi:10.1080/13598660802375941

Nelson, A. (2006). *Characteristics of a school-university partnership: A grounded theory approach* (Doctoral dissertation). Order No. 3250140. Available from ProQuest Dissertations & Theses Global (UMI No. 305330749).

Pearlman, B. (2010). Designing new learning environments to support 21st century skills. In J. Bellanca & R. Brandt (Eds.), *21st century skills: Rethinking how students learn* (pp. 117–148). Bloomington, IN: Solution Tree Press.

Puentedura, R. P. (2013). *The SAMR Model explained by Ruben R. Puentedura* [Video file]. Retrieved from http://www.youtube.com/watch?v=_QOsz4AaZ2k

Schuck, S. (2012). The opportunities and challenges of research partnerships in teacher education. *The Australian Educational Researcher, 40*(1), 47–60. doi:10.1007/s13384-012-0069-5

Segedin, L. (2011). The role of teacher empowerment and teacher accountability in school-university partnerships and action research. *Brock Education Journal, 20*(2), 43–64. Retrieved from http://brock.scholarsportal.info/journals/brocked

Tsui, A., & Law, D. (2007). Learning as boundary-crossing in school-university partnership. *Teaching and Teacher Education, 23*(8), 1289–1301. doi:10.1016/j.tate.2006.06.003

Walsh, M., & Backe, S. (2013). School-university partnerships: Reflections and opportunities. *Peabody Journal of Education, 88*(5), 594–607. doi:10.1080/0161956X.2013.835158

Wright, N. (2010). *e-Learning and implications for New Zealand Schools: A literature review.* Retrieved from http://www.educationcounts.govt.nz/publications/ict/e-learning-and-implications-for-new-zealand-schools-a-literature-review/executive-summary

Author Biographies

Leon Benade is Director of Research in the School of Education of AUT University. He currently researches 'twenty-first century learning', the establishment of Innovative Learning Environments (ILE) and digital pedagogies. Related interests include teachers' work, education policy, ethics, critical pedagogy and teachers' critical reflective practice.

Bill Hubbard is currently serving as a deputy principal in a large New Zealand state co-ed secondary school. For the last 5 years, he has overseen leadership, teacher and infrastructure developments towards 1:1 student-owned digital device use. During 2017, he has been an Aitken Foundation Fellow at the University of Auckland Centre for Educational Leadership.

Leanne Lamb is Master of Education candidate at Auckland University of Technology. Her research interest is in partnerships. Leanne is a member of Auckland University of Technology's educational futures network, Edge Work, and works in partnership with New Zealand schools. She was the Director of e-Learning at Rosehill College before taking up a contract position in the School of Education of the Auckland University of Technology.

Chapter 21
A QUEST for Sustainable Continuing Professional Development

Birgitte Lund Nielsen

21.1 Introduction

Continuing Professional Development (CPD) can be a crucial factor in improving teaching, and student learning (Little 2006). Extant research suggests consensus pertaining to the core features of effective CPD including content focus, active learning, coherence, duration, collaborative activities and collective participation (Desimone 2009; van Driel et al. 2012). More typically, however, teachers experience professional development as episodic, superficial and disconnected from their day-to-day teaching and recurring problems of practice (Little 2006). Even when CPD-programs are designed according to the mentioned consensus criteria, there is often a lack of knowledge about the sustainability of the effects (Avalos 2011).

This chapter reports on a large-scale, long-term Danish CPD project called QUEST, which was designed with the overall purpose of developing a sustainable model for teacher CPD. Both the design of activities in the QUEST program and their content: approaches to science education created to enhance students learning of science, were informed by research. Furthermore, the outcomes of the CPD activities were closely followed and subjected to periodic formative evaluation, which made it possible to refine approaches iteratively based on teacher reflections and new enactments, student reactions, and whether interventions were shown to support schools in meeting their targets. In this chapter, the outcomes of the QUEST research are condensed with a particular focus on discussing general perspectives and implications in relation to teacher CPD and future research.

B.L. Nielsen (✉)
VIA University College, Aarhus, Denmark
e-mail: bln@via.dk

© Springer Nature Singapore Pte Ltd. 2017
M.A. Peters et al. (eds.), *A Companion to Research in Teacher Education*,
DOI 10.1007/978-981-10-4075-7_21

21.2   Background

Contemporarily it is widely acknowledged in the research literature that CPD, like other educational change processes, is best approached and studied as a complex system with multiple interrelations. Much research point to the importance of talking about teachers' professional *learning*, instead of *development* as a unidirectional (and passive) process whereby teachers are given new ideas, which are expected to change their knowledge and beliefs, and ultimately lead to new enactments in their classrooms (Luft and Hewson 2014). Professional learning can more likely be seen as a spiral in which reflection and new enactments might be triggered when teachers identify learning opportunities/positive learning outcomes for their students when being supported in implementing new approaches during the CPD (Clarke and Hollingsworth 2002; Nielsen 2012). Furthermore, extant research suggests that teacher efficacy, agency and empowerment can be crucial if changes are to be sustainable, and that individual and collaborative efficacy seems to interact (Bandura 1997). Educational change in general thus seems to depend on initiatives at different levels of the system, and the most successful implemented reform initiatives can be those that provide top-down support for bottom-up development (Darling-Hammond 2005).

21.2.1   CPD and Professional Learning Communities

In relation to bottom-up development, Luft and Hewson (2014) emphasize that it is crucial that CPD activities are embedded in the teachers' daily work, i.e., their classroom teaching, and their collaboration with colleagues. There has been a shift from mainly viewing CPD as an individualistic activity toward emphasizing a school's collective capacity (Little 2006). Research has steadily converged on the importance of teachers' joint work and shared responsibility in professional learning communities (PLCs) (Stoll et al. 2006). Collaboration among peers and within educational communities can take many forms. For Stoll et al. (2006), the key characteristics of a successful PLC are shared values and vision, focus on students learning, reflective professional inquiry, and collaboration and collective responsibility.

Learning communities can in principle be both a team of science teachers (for example) at a particular school, working collaboratively to reinforce, expand and challenge their notions about teaching science, or science teachers from a network of schools across a municipality (Luft and Hewson 2014). Little (2006, p. 4) talks about school districts as a context for professional learning and argues that teachers professional learning depends both on the school's internal resources and on its external connections and relationships. For the purposes of this chapter, "network" is used to describe collaboration across schools, and "PLC" is used to describe the science team at a local school, whatever initial level and kind of collaboration we saw compared to the characteristics of a successful PLC (Stoll et al. 2006). In the findings below the development at the various schools is however categorized and discussed according to some levels of PLC.

21.2.2   The QUEST Project

QUEST ("Qualifying in-service Education of Science Teachers") was a large-scale, long-term CPD project involving 42 schools from five municipalities in Denmark. All in all, the 4-year project, which ran from 2012 to 2015, involved 450 science teachers. QUEST activities were inspired by and designed according to the consensus criteria mentioned in the introduction. So, for example, activities supported both teachers' situated learning organized in PLCs at participating schools, as well as development organized by networks of schools. The overall purpose of QUEST was to develop a sustainable model for CPD, which would support professional capital and bottom-up development (Darling-Hammond 2005). A program of alternating network seminars and "collaborative inquiries" between seminars was designed as a means to stimulate collaboration among science teachers and embed the CPD activities in the teachers' daily work and experiences (Luft and Hewson 2014). This is called the QUEST rhythm (Fig. 21.1). Activities between seminars were organized by the local PLC, but involved also individual teachers trying new tools and refined approaches in their classrooms, and collecting "data" and artifacts

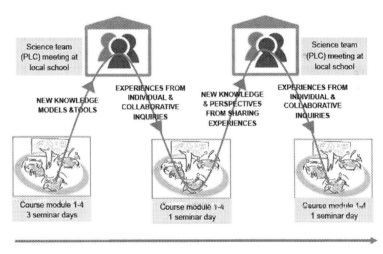

Period of 4-5 months

Fig. 21.1   The QUEST rhythm. In the first years, four consecutive course modules were organized and each of these followed this rhythm. In the last years, the institutionalization phase, course modules were substituted with network seminars organized by the local municipal consultants, but these still followed the rhythm

representative of their students' work. The facilitation of teacher inquiries was inspired by the models proposed by Timperley (2011). In practice various "levels of inquiry" were observed: the PLC might talk about this as "an assignment" from QUEST or in other instances we saw a more genuine inquiry and knowledge building cycle (see findings below).

The QUEST project was divided into two main phases, a 2½ year implementation phase and a 1½ year institutionalization phase. In phase 1, the implementation phase, the primary and lower secondary science teachers participated in one or more of four consecutive course modules, each following the QUEST rhythm (Fig. 21.1). The content of the course modules was informed by research about student learning in science (Bransford and Donovan 2005). For example, the teachers in module 1 worked with inquiry-based science education (IBSE), and in module 2 with the principles of addressing preconceptions and supporting students' knowledge of what it means to do science, e.g., by using tools like students' annotated drawings (Nielsen 2014). The course modules also addressed issues connected to learning progressions in science, and presented and supported the trial of concrete methods for collaborative teacher inquiries like lesson studies, peer-observation and video-clubs (Little 2006). The course modules in the implementation phase were organized as full-day seminars, where the participating teachers were introduced to and tried out new tools, materials, and approaches, followed by a period of individual and collaborative enactments in local practice, and culminating in the sharing experiences at the next meeting of the network (Fig. 21.1). In the implementation phase, this rhythm aimed to support teachers in developing individual and collective efficacy for continuously developing science teaching locally. This is in line with Bandura (1997) who emphasizes personal and social change as complementary and both teachers' personal and collective efficacy as crucial for changes to be sustainable. In phase 2, the institutionalization phase, support from the CPD providers was gradually withdrawn with the aim of empowering local schools and communities to engage in continuous development. Local municipal consultants, typically experienced science teachers working a day per week as a consultant, played an important role in this phase. But, as will be highlighted below, all municipal networks chose to continue to follow the QUEST rhythm to frame their activities.

The research questions guiding the research presented in this chapter are as follows:

- What are the teachers' perceived outcomes in relation to the teaching of science and to the collaboration with science colleagues?
- How does collaboration in the schools develop over time, and what kinds of supportive factors and challenges do the teachers emphasize?
- What examples are seen of teachers developing reflections about teaching science, and new enactments in own classroom?
- What kinds of student outcomes can be identified?
- What factors support sustainable development, characterized as a shared teacher focus on student learning in science, and the teachers' perceived individual and collective efficacy for continuingly developing their teaching of science?

21.3 Methodology

CPD can be evaluated at various levels: (1) participants' reactions/perceived outcomes, (2) participants' "learning"/reflections on course content, (3) organizational support and change, (4) participants' use of new knowledge and skills, and (5) student learning outcomes (Guskey 2000). The QUEST project's research addressed all these levels, but not all findings will be presented in detail in this chapter. The project used a mixed methods approach (Creswell and Clark 2007). Both quantitative and qualitative data were retrieved during and after each course module in phase 1, and the findings were used iteratively to inform the design of subsequent modules. A questionnaire with 5-point Likert-scale questions and open-ended categories focused on teachers' experiences from the course modules/network meetings, the local PLC, and trials in own classrooms was used to gather data on five occasions during the project. The data gathered from the questionnaire, along with notes made during observations of all course modules/network meetings were assembled in a case protocol for each of the schools. Nine schools were also selected for more in-depth case studies (diversity sampling: school size, town/rural etc.). In these schools, there were repeated classroom observations, interviews with teacher and students, and observation at PLC meetings.

Likert-scale questions from the questionnaires were analyzed by frequency, and open-ended reflections and the qualitative observation data, were categorized/coded through an iterative data-based process. Analysis of student outcomes was based both on repeated interviews at the case schools, and on results from the 9th grade examinations in Biology, Geography and Physics & Chemistry at QUEST schools and comparable schools. The examinations involve a multiple-choice test in the first two subjects, and an oral and practical exam in the Physics and Chemistry laboratory.

21.4 Findings and Discussion

Findings based on the quantitative teacher data are presented first; these are followed by an introduction to the qualitative data from participating schools, and finally some student data. The presentation of findings gradually moves into a discussion.

21.4.1 The Teachers' Perceived Outcomes

The overall benefits from the course modules in the first phase were rated quite highly by the participants. On average from all four modules 11% of respondents reported a very high degree of outcomes, 53% a high degree, 34% a medium degree, 2% a small degree, and 0% a very small degree. Likewise, the teachers were generally positive about the course content and referred to gaining new insight into student learning in science, and to trying out models, tools, and activities from the course modules in their own classrooms. These quantitative results were quite stable over the four modules.

The answers to whether the teachers experienced changes in the way the PLC cooperated locally were more divided, with great variation between schools, and with a positive trend from the first to the last course module. On average from the four modules 6% reported a very high degree of change, 29% a high degree, 43% some degree, 19% a small degree, and 3% a very small degree. Teachers' rating of the effect of QUEST on their teaching of science and collaboration with science colleagues is represented in Fig. 21.2.

Analysis of the quantitative data (Fig. 21.2) revealed a moderate positive correlation ($R = 0.553$) between how the teachers rated the effect from QUEST on the way they are teaching science, and their ratings of the effect from QUEST on the way they are collaborating with their science colleagues. This does not say anything about cause-effect, but social and individual changes seem to be mutually supportive. Below we will see that sharing experiences in the PLC might inspire teachers to make changes in their classrooms, while sharing ideas and approaches from individual classrooms, instead of just discussing purchases for the science lab, can help energize the PLC.

21.4.2   Development of Teacher Collaboration

The categorization of sustained development at the participating schools was based on teacher self-reports, reflections about collaboration, etc., assembled in the case protocols "following each school through the project" (Table 21.1). The investigation methods were data-based, but also included descriptors like shared responsibility and values used in the literature about PLCs (Stoll et al. 2006). The naming

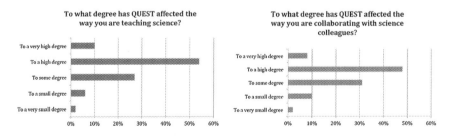

Fig. 21.2 The perceived effect on the teaching of science and collaboration with science colleagues after phase 1, with the four course modules

of the categories as basic, developing and integrated likewise was informed by former research (Timperley 2011).

The categories were iteratively developed, but applying the categories to the pre-data in retrospect, all the schools were at what corresponds to level 1 or 2 before the project. There was great variation, e.g., most of the schools in one municipality were at level 2, while all schools in another municipality were at level 1. Alongside the involvement in QUEST a great variation in development was observed. Implementing the local collaborative part of the QUEST rhythm was obviously easier for the schools that already had a culture of regular meetings at the start of the project, and these differences were still reflected in the municipalities' self-reports after ½ year. This variation did, however, become less pronounced over time, and when coding according to the categories in Table 21.1 after 2½ years (two coders) the main differences were between schools not so much between municipalities. The distribution was 8% at level 1, 34% at level 2, 48% at level 3, and 10% at level 4.

Data after 2½ years is used here since the last period of the QUEST project saw major national school reforms and municipal changes in school districts, school fusions, etc. In one municipality that took part in the project, for example, many science teachers were relocated to new schools. This resulted in a lot of "noise" in the open reflections that accompanied the final questionnaire, hence it mainly pre-reform data is discussed here. The institutionalization activities were, however, implemented and by the end of the project local network and PLC activities were stabilized in all five municipalities, despite the challenges posed by the reforms. These networks continued after the project had finished, and they also maintained

Table 21.1 Categories synthesizing the level of changes at the QUEST schools

Category	Description
1. Pre-PLC	Hard to arrange meetings. When meetings do happen purchases of materials and equipment for the science labs top the agenda. A limited amount of local trials with new tools and approaches. Individual teachers exchanging ideas, but no joint work
2. PLC basic	Regular meetings. Purchases of materials and equipment for the science labs still high on the agenda, but a culture of exchange of ideas, strategies, and teaching experiences are (slowly) developing. New tools and approaches are tried out in local classrooms, mainly by copying activities from the network seminars, and following concrete assignments
3. PLC developing	Exchange of ideas, materials and strategies are consolidated. Evidence informed discussions of student learning based on data from local inquiries. PLC meetings are typically active and with hands-on activities and discussions. Teachers report about positive outcomes from the meetings in relation to their own teaching. Both things indicate the gradual development of a shared responsibility
4. PLC integrated	Joint planning and discussions into student learning, like in an inquiry and knowledge building cycle (Timperley 2011). Not just copying activities from network seminars, but adjustment to the local context and collaborative redesign. New experiments going beyond but inspired by network seminars: generative changes, shared responsibility, and gradual development of a shared vision

the QUEST rhythm. So, it can be argued that the project achieved its goal of sustainability. A closer look at some of the qualitative data will further inform the discussion of factors supporting sustainable development, and illustrate the background for the descriptions in Table 21.1.

21.4.3 Changing Collaboration—Teacher Reflections

Teachers' self-reports about collaboration on average revealed a positive trend over time: the 26% of the teachers experiencing a small or very small degree of change in collaboration with science colleagues after the first half year, decreased to 12% experiencing a small or very small effect on collaboration with science colleagues after 2 years (Fig. 21.2). The same five categories could be used to condense the open-ended reflections about collaboration in the four questionnaires from the first 2½ years: (1) QUEST-rhythm, (2) Developing a shared focus on student learning, (3) Continuous external support, (4) The role as a resource-teacher among colleagues, and (5) School contextual factors/school leadership. An additional theme, (6) "Political reforms" was added for analysis of the last questionnaire. So, the teachers experienced some of the same *kinds* of supportive factors, positive outcomes and hurdles in relation to developing a local science PLC, but with a great variation in *weight*.

The QUEST rhythm was perceived as supportive of local changes both in schools where there was a high degree of change in the collaborative culture and at schools with slower or less significant changes. The teachers reported that the QUEST rhythm "forced them in a positive sense" to collaboratively try out and discuss new tools and approaches. To participate in QUEST the schools were urged to arrange two PLC meetings each semester, but it is one thing to meet up, quite another to take collective responsibility and agree on shared values. Some teachers had more or less regular meetings with science colleagues also before QUEST (level 2), but most of them reported a change in focus from purchases of materials and equipment for the science labs to how best to support student learning of concrete science content mediated by the "assignments" from QUEST, and by data and artifacts from trials in local classrooms. This teacher perspective is mirrored in the categories in Table 21.1. The teachers do *not* reflect on being presented to the idea of—and research documenting the value of—learning communities, or on discussing shared responsibility and vision (Stoll et al. 2006) per se. It is more the other way around; finding inspiration for your own teaching through collaborative CPD activities, sharing "student data", etc., can lead to the gradual development of a shared responsibility (level 3), and a shared vision (level 4): A potential positive spiral driven by teachers' experiencing positive outcomes.

The variation in change pace at the participating schools was evident in the quantitative data, but many teachers also explicitly reflected about changes taking time and the need for continuous support, e.g., explaining in their reports that it takes time to change the local collaborative culture, but that they "*are heading in the right direction*". Many teachers also emphasized the need for continuous support from the CPD providers, "*So the changes do not fall back*".

A central feature in QUEST was the expectation that the teachers participating in course modules/network meetings should share new input with the local PLC and should accept extra responsibility for implementing local activities that used the new tools and approaches. Some of the reflections about disseminating ideas in the local PLC revealed challenges, e.g., some teachers referred to "*reluctant colleagues*". But in the schools where two or more colleagues typically shared this role, and planned active meetings for their colleagues, there was evidence that those teachers who partook in the QUEST modules were able to contribute *positively* to collective agency (Bandura 1997). Active meetings could be about trying out some hands-on activities or equipment in the lab or outside in the school's surroundings, or joint planning of teaching, or working collaboratively to illustrate learning progression on a big poster or a smart board. Another point that was raised in the reflections was that it seemed that the role of resource-teacher for colleagues was a challenge if the trained teachers did not have the support of the school leadership. School leaders were seen to be quite important for the local development of a collaborative culture. Those who took a visible and active role in PLC meetings, etc., and were prepared to delegate leadership tasks and support teacher initiatives, giving staff some degree of autonomy, as illustrated in the case in the next section, were considered most helpful.

The last theme of political reforms deserves a long discussion in itself, but here there is only space to cover a few key points. First of all, participants in QUEST found that the top-down political reforms disturbed the gradual process in the longitudinal CPD project. For some teachers this "disturbance" was positive because the national reforms recognized the importance of teacher collaboration. For example, school leaders were now required to call PLC meetings and this meant that more staff were likely to attend meetings on a regular basis. Many teachers, however, felt a huge lack of motivation following the introduction of more top-down management. In general, the most positive views following the reforms came from teachers who experienced school leaders who listened to and supported teacher suggestions for how best to implement the new top-down political initiatives.

21.5   One Teacher's Journey Through QUEST

The differences in findings between schools highlight the important role school contextual factors can play in relation to the long-term effect of CPD. These findings also highlighted the need for in-depth knowledge at a school level about development over time and in individual teacher's classrooms, as recognized by van Driel et al. (2012) and Luft and Hewson (2014). A condensation of the reflections and new enactments of one of the case teachers is a useful way to illustrate how this can work in practice. In this case, the teacher in focus had 4 years teaching experience, and was classified as a novice teacher. From the beginning of the project, she was only teaching one class of primary science, alongside other classes with a more humanistic outlook. Although a diverse range of case teachers was followed in the full research design, here there is only space to consider the case outlined below. During the course of the project the case teachers were observed five times, they also participated in interviews. A combination of a rubric and a text memo was used for observations. Furthermore a group of students from each class was repeatedly interviewed.

From the quantitative study it appears that the case teacher emphasized that the QUEST interventions had a very high degree of effect on her own teaching and a high degree of effect on collaboration (Fig. 21.2). The school she worked in was categorized as level 3 (Table 21.1). So, this case study is situated in the data as positive teacher outcome and a school with a developing PLC. Although the school had not reached the point where it had the most sustained PLC activities.

In the first interview the teacher referred, in general terms, to supporting student interest as the most important issue in relation to teaching science, but found it hard to exemplify how this might be done in relation to her own teaching. In relation to QUEST she positively highlighted the importance of sharing concrete ideas for a more inquiry-based approach to teaching science, and to initiating a closer collaboration with the other primary science teachers at the school. Over the duration of the project the case teacher's reflections on teaching primary science showed that teaching was becoming *more confident and personalized*. She began to include experiences from inquiry-based projects in her own class, and her ideas about how best to support student learning and frame their inquiries became *more detailed*. Furthermore, over time, a closer connection between her reflections on the teaching of primary science and enactments in her own classroom could be identified. The development can be characterized more as an evolution than a revolution in relation to structuring student inquiries, but these small changes seemed rather important in relation to facilitating and mediating her students' learning activities and dialogues about science experiments: findings supported by the student data.

The case school was characterized by a school-leader, who took a rather hands-off approach, for example, he did never participate in PLC meetings. He however encouraged the case teacher and her colleagues from primary science to collaborate closer with colleagues from lower secondary science. Before QUEST only secondary science teachers met up, primarily in relation to purchases for the science lab. Framed by the QUEST project the local PLC grew to include both primary and lower secondary science teachers. Over the first years, the case teacher gradually developed a central role as a resource-teacher among colleagues from *both* primary and lower secondary. She was however one of the teachers who was moved to another school as a part of a municipal reform. But she managed to "persuade" the leader and her colleagues at the new school to also enter the QUEST network. At the end of the project, she was teaching science in six different classes at the new school. Furthermore, she was acting as a science resource-teacher, e.g., one observation was of her co-teaching with an experienced biology colleague in his class—on his request as he was trying out a more inquiry-based approach.

Decisive aspects for starting and sustaining a positive spiral in this case included (1) alignment between the teacher's beliefs and the approaches taken in the CPD program, e.g., in relation to inquiry-based science, (2) the experience of support to try out new approaches in her own classroom and in collaboration with colleagues, and (3) the responsibility handed over from the school leader, e.g., to develop the local science PLC to also involve primary science teachers. The case exemplifies the complex interplay between individual and collective agency among teachers (Bandura 1997), and contextual factors like leadership, in starting a positive spiral at a school participating in a CPD program. Teacher beliefs reveal understanding of knowledge and learning and how these *may* be enacted in classroom teaching, but not what the teacher actually *does*. Over time the case teacher expressed her beliefs more explicitly, allowed her beliefs to be affected by her own teaching experiences, and looked in detail at how her beliefs related to actual student learning, and eventually her beliefs became aligned to what she actually did in her teaching. Apparently she was empowered by the CPD, and she was able to use this newfound power in her new role in the PLC, where she *had to* be more explicit about her beliefs as she worked with her primary science colleagues to implement more active meetings. The case also exemplifies the importance of acknowledgement by colleagues and *vicarious reinforcement* (Bandura 1997), e.g., the co-teaching with an experienced colleague trying to develop his teaching.

21.5.1   Student Outcomes

The students in the case were followed from 4th to 6th grade, so they might be expected to develop, e.g., a more independent approach to science inquiries with fewer teacher-led interventions. Compared with other classes, the case teacher's class did seem to incorporate ideas introduced in the QUEST modules to a rather high degree. At the time of the first observation the case class would shift between whole-class teaching and group work. But parallel to the teacher following the CPD program and becoming more explicit and precise in her reflections about her own teaching, she also grew to be more explicit in her communication with the students. The framing around their group inquiries grew to be more transparent, e.g., when they were expected to generate and try out their own ideas in a group they knew that in 10 min they should share and ask questions. Furthermore they used tools for inquiry, like a rubric: What do we know? What do we want to know? What are possible explanations? How will we investigate? What did we learn?

From the interviews with the students, it generally seemed that they found *an open approach* motivating. But in the first round of interviews some students also said that there were situations when they did not quite understand what they were expected to do and why. Over time, the teacher was able to develop a more structured and guided approach, although this was still experienced by the students as more *open*. In the 6th grade, the class participated in, and actually won, a "science inquiry and invention competition" in the municipality. They described this experience as highly motivating and were enthusiastic about the fact that they "*had to think for themselves and find the solutions*".

The research design did not deliver any test data from these students or from other primary science classes, but exam results 2012–15 from the QUEST schools and a cohort of comparable schools were collected. First of all, it must be emphasized that on average there were no significant differences between students' exam results at the QUEST schools and schools not participating in the project. The two groups of schools followed the same average trend over the four years in all three subjects. This in many ways could have been expected, as student exam results depend on a very complex range of factors. What is interesting, however, is that there seems to be some (delayed) correlation between schools with the most sustained PLC activities (level 4 in Table 21.1) and a positive trend in student results. Table 21.1 represents analyses made by two researchers including the various sources of teacher data. A statistician carried out the analysis of student exams at a later date. If the full data set is considered, four of the QUEST schools showed a particular improvement in examination results, among those three of the four schools (the 10%) coded at level 4 (Table 21.1). The last school coded at level 4 in Table 21.1 was not in the data set as it was a school with only primary science, but the case school referred to above, coded at level 3, was the last of four QUEST schools with a particular positive development based on the statistics. It must be emphasized that the data samples are very small, so it is only possible to talk about a tendency, and it might be a covariation due to other causes than the CPD, but it is anyway interesting that the schools with the most sustained local PLC activities are also schools with improvements in examination results from below average, to average or above.

21.5.2 Summing up: Factors Supporting Sustainable Development

Changing the collaborative culture at a school is not without challenges and certainly takes a lot of time and effort, but explicitly framing such changes as part of a CPD program seems to be both possible and worthwhile. The analyses presented here show a positive correlation between perceived effect from a longitudinal CPD project on collaboration and on science teaching. Furthermore, the data indicates how the changes teachers make when participating in CPD can influence the students.

In relation to sustainability the overall conclusion is that the QUEST model so far has proved to be sustainable: the QUEST rhythm has been institutionalized and networking across schools and PLC activities continue in all five municipalities even though the project has come to an end. Based on the broad range of data, factors supporting sustainable development at schools participating in a large-scale, long-term CPD initiative seem to revolve around scaffolding teachers' collaborative inquiries. The QUEST rhythm provided such a scaffold. The majority of the teachers found that the project helped to support changes both in relation to new enactments in their individual classrooms, and in relation to collaboration in the PLC. Furthermore, the rhythm was identified as helpful both by teachers reporting a high degree of change, and also by teachers at schools with slower/less significant changes.

Based on the findings, the great variation among schools must once again be emphasized. In about 10% of the schools no significant changes were observed, despite the longitudinal, multi-perspective effort. Meanwhile in those schools where change did take place, it was generally found that the project had long-term support from the school leadership, and that the school followed a structured rhythm to support both local and municipal science networks (Darling-Hammond 2005). One finding of the QUEST project is that there is no simple fix for ensuring teacher and school development. However, it does seem that a positive spiral can be started both by collective enactive mastery experiences, like the shared initiatives by the primary science teachers at the case school, and by individual enactive experiences in the classroom, shared with and therefore inspiring colleagues (vicarious reinforcement).

The case study exemplified the complex interplay between individual and collaborative agency among teachers, and contextual factors like leadership, in starting a positive spiral. The case teacher grew to be an active learner and codesigner in her own and colleagues' CPD (Luft and Hewson 2014).

All in all, the research contributes to an in-depth understanding of how CPD can filter down to enhanced student learning through teacher reflection, new enactments and collaboration. Clearly, the effect is dependent on the design of the CPD, but also on school contextual factors such as leadership and teacher autonomy.

21.6   Perspectives- and CPD-Research Looking Forward

This companion aims to provide guidance for future research directions. Based on this chapter, there is clearly a need for more consideration of CPD and also more research into CPD. The importance of the consensus criteria for design of effective CPD: a clear content focus, active learning for the teachers, coherence, duration, collaborative activities, and collective participation, is confirmed by the research presented. Furthermore, following a simple CPD-structure like the QUEST rhythm has proved to be determent in relation to sustainability pertaining to the teachers developing a shared focus on student learning, and individual and collective efficacy in continuingly developing their teaching. Not all participating schools succeeded in developing a science teacher PLC with shared responsibilities, values and visions. The research illustrates that there is a need for a coordinated and sustained effort to start and reinforce a positive spiral. And that the important thing is not presenting the idea about PLCs to teachers, or implementing top-down reforms with a focus on PLCs. It is about acknowledging teachers as professional learners and designing CPD in which teachers' collaborative inquiries are scaffolded.

The results of the QUEST project reveal a need for continuing research into CPD and particularly into initiatives that acknowledge the complexity of the developmental process, taking into account organizational and school contextual factors, and the interplay between collaborative and individual professional learning.

References

Avalos, B. (2011). Teacher professional development in teaching and teacher education over ten years. *Teaching and Teacher Education, 27*(1), 10–20.

Bandura, A. (1997). *Self-efficacy—The exercise of control*. New York: Freeman.

Bransford, J. D., & Donovan, S. (2005). *How students learn—Science in the classroom*. Washington DC: The National Academic Press.

Clarke, D., & Hollingsworth, H. (2002). Elaborating a model of teacher professional growth. *Teaching and Teacher Education, 18*, 948–967.

Creswell, J. W., & Clark, V. L. P. (2007). *Designing and conducting mixed methods research*. Thousand Oaks: Sage Publications.

Darling-Hammond, L. (2005). Policy and change: Getting beyond bureaucracy. In A. Heargreaves (Ed.), *Extending educational change* (pp. 362–387). Dordrecht: Springer.

Desimone, L. M. (2009). Improving impact studies of teachers' professional development: Toward better conceptualizations and measures. *Educational Researcher, 38*(3), 181–199.

Guskey, T. R. (2000). *Evaluating professional development*. Thousand Oaks, CA: Corwin.

Little, J. W. (2006). *Professional community and professional development in the learning-centered school*. Washington: National Education Association NEA.

Luft, J. A., & Hewson, P. W. (2014). Research on teacher professional development programs in science. In N. G. Lederman & S. Abell (Eds.), *Handbook of research in science education* (Vol. II, pp. 889–909). New York: Routledge.

Nielsen, B. L. (2012). Science teachers' meaning-making when involved in a school-based professional development project. *Journal of Science Teacher Education, 23*(6), 621–649.

Nielsen, B. L. (2014). Students' annotated drawings as a mediating artefact in science teachers' professional development. *NorDiNa, 10*(2), 162–175.

Stoll, L., Bolam, R., McMahon, A., Wallace, M., & Thomas, S. (2006). Professional learning communities: A review of the literature. *Journal of Educational Change, 7*(4), 221–258.

Timperley, H. (2011). *Realizing the power of professional learning*. Maidenhead: Open University Press.

Van Driel, J., Meirink, J. A., van Veen, K., & Zwart, R. C. (2012). Current trends and missing links in studies on teacher professional development in science education: A review of design features and quality of research. *Studies in Science Education, 48*(2), 129–160.

Author Biography

Dr. Birgitte Lund Nielsen is Senior Associate Professor at VIA University College and Research Fellow at Aarhus University, Denmark. Her Ph.D. research focused on professional development for science teachers, and a continual research focus is teachers' professional learning communities, and how to mediate inquiries and dialogue, e.g., with classroom video.

Part IV
Global Education Reform and Teacher Education

Introduction

The nature, quality and effectiveness of teacher preparation increasingly have become a central focus for education policy worldwide in a fiercely argued debate among governments, think tanks, world policy agencies, education researchers and teacher organisations (see bibliography). Teacher education issues have taken on a special urgency for several reasons: the quality of teachers is widely perceived to be "the single most important school variable influencing student achievement" (OCED 2005: 2) and also claimed to be in part responsible for America's educational decline (NCTQ 2013) especially in a time of transition from industrial to information economy (Levine 2006, 2007); governments around the world under the influence of neoliberal policies have imposed market-based performance-oriented systems; a global reform movement has led to standardisation, greater managerialism and test-based accountability (Childs and Menter 2013); university-based teacher education is currently challenged by other models, many of which advocate for shorter or school-based training; edu-businesses and private sector interests alleged "producer capture" by teachers and increasingly seek to establish for-profit and not-for-profit schools and training programs; new clinical models based on the "practicum turn" have encouraged a shift in professional preparation from universities to a closer partnership with schools; there have been strong attacks on the quality of university-based teacher education programmes and on the professionalism of teachers; there have been systematic and ongoing doubts cast on the nature of the relationship between education theory and classroom practice; the "generic" teacher education model has been questioned in the face of increasingly diverse, ethnic, and especially urban, school populations (Hammerness and Axelrod 2013) with the attendant demand for "Context-Specific" Teacher Preparation.

There has been little sustained, long-term or systematic research to provide empirical support for the broad aspects of teacher education policy largely because such research has been chronically underfunded and based on traditional practitioner knowledge (Cochran-Smith 2008). Menter et al. (2010) in their exhaustive literature review found that "it is rare to find studies which establish causal links between curricular change, teacher education and improvements in educational standards", "The evidence on linkages between enhanced profession-alism and pupil outcomes was found to be limited, contradictory and somewhat inconclusive" and research "is rarely cumulative, long-term or large-scale". Many of the changes to teacher education are contentious and yet are occurring in rapid succession. These policies and movements have important consequences for edu-cation, teacher quality and the future of the teaching profession. At the same time, the policies and initiatives that support these changes seem to be based more on ideology, business interests and tradition than on research and empirical findings. There is a general need for a state-of-the-art Companion that assembles and assesses the extant research available on teacher education and make clear guidelines on future directions.

There are at present only a small number of handbooks or companions on teacher education research and they are now dated. There is the *Handbook of Research on Teacher Education* that was first published in 1990 and now in the third edition. The *International Handbook of Research on Teachers and Teaching* (Springer) Saha, Lawrence J., Dworkin, Anthony Gary (Eds.) was published in 2009. This collection has the potential to address an important need and gap in the market in a Companion that will be of value for teachers, teacher educators, poli-cymakers and politicians.

References

Brisard, E., Menter, I. & Smith, I. (2005). *Models of partnership in initial teacher education.* Edinburgh: General Teaching Council for Scotland.

Childs, A. & Menter, I. (2013). Teacher Education in 21st Century England. A Case Study In Neoliberal Public Policy, *Revista Española de Educación Comparada, 22*, 93–116.

Conroy, J., Hulme, M. & Menter, I. (2013). Developing a 'clinical' model for teacher education. *Journal of Education for Teaching, 39*(5), 557–573.

Darling-Hammond, L. & Lieberman, A. (Eds.). (2012). *Teacher education around the world: Changing policies and practices.* London, Routledge.

Department for Education. (2010). *The importance of teaching schools white paper.* https://www.gov.uk/government/uploads/system/uploads/attachment_data/file/175429/CM-7980.pdf

Department for Education. (2011). *Training our next generation of outstanding teachers: Implementation plan.* https://www.education.gov.uk/publications/eOrderingDownload/DFE-00083-2011.pdf

Donaldson, G. (2011) *Teaching Scotland's future, report of a review of teacher education in Scotland.* Edinburgh: Scottish Government. http://www.scotland.gov.uk/Resource/Doc/337626/0110852.pdf

Greenberg, J., McKee, A. & Walsh, K. (2013). *Teacher prep review: A review of the nation's teaching preparation programs* (Revised December 2013), Nation Council on Teacher Quality.

Hammerness, K. & Axelrod, Y. (2013). "Context-Specific" Teacher Preparation for New York City: An exploration of the *content* of context: A Report on the Second Year of Bard College's Urban Teacher Residency program. Paper presented at the   Annual Meeting of the American Educational Research Association San Francisco, CA   April–May, 2013.

Levine, A. (2006). *Educating school teachers.* Education for Schools Project, http://www. edschools.org/

Levine, A. (2007). *Educating researchers.* Education for Schools Project, http://www.edschools. org/

Chapter 22
Teachers, Curriculum and the Neoliberal Imaginary of Education

Steven Hodge

For Giroux (2004, p. 44) neoliberalism is 'the defining ideology of the current historical moment'. Neoliberalism is a family of economic, political and administration theories that share assumptions including the self-interested nature of individual motivation, the naturally curbing and coordinating influence of markets on self-interest, and the vital role of government in the promotion of a pro-market citizenry (Olssen and Peters 2005). Education policy shaped by these principles has entrenched and exacerbated social inequality on an unprecedented, global scale (Rizvi and Lingard 2010). Neoliberal education policy is associated with reduction of public expenditure on education, erosion of educator autonomy, centralisation of curriculum and a focus on high-stakes testing and league tables (Giroux 2004). For many education researchers, neoliberalism is a fundamental threat to the educational project.

Rizvi and Lingard (2010) coined the term 'neoliberal imaginary' to capture the broad acceptance and facility in neoliberal ideas and norms evident in the practices of contemporary society.[1] They argue (in contrast with Giroux) that neoliberalism is more than an ideology, that the grip of neoliberalism is facilitated and manifested in ways that do not refer to ideas. Discussing the globalisation of neoliberal education policy, they explain that

> If many of the recent claims about globalisation and its implications for practice are ideological, the question remains as to how it is that people internalize them. How do these claims become part of their world view, shaping the ways in which they think about their social relations and forge conceptions of their future? In short, how is ideology translated into actual material practices steering our sense of possibilities and conceptions of the future? (Rizvi and Lingard 2010, p. 33)

---

[1]Marginson (1997, p. 65) used the phrase 'market liberal imaginary' to refer to the utopian visions of economists Hayek and Friedman. This usage of imaginary contrasts with the concept of social imaginary in that it retains the sense of the productions of individual genius.

S. Hodge (✉)
Griffith University, Brisbane, Australia
e-mail: s.hodge@griffith.edu.au

© Springer Nature Singapore Pte Ltd. 2017
M.A. Peters et al. (eds.), *A Companion to Research in Teacher Education*,
DOI 10.1007/978-981-10-4075-7_22

333

In Rizvi and Lingard's view, the theory of social imaginaries offers a way to understand the translation of ideas—in this case neoliberal theory—into the bases of action, imagery, narrative and reflection in society. They draw on an emerging strand in social theory that has taken imagination out of its romantic, individualist framing to analyse collective thought and action (Appadurai 1996). The theory of social imaginaries has been elaborated by Canadian philosopher Charles Taylor, who used it to analyse the widely held sense of legitimacy surrounding modern democratic practices and acceptance of 'the economy' as an objective way of conceptualising social relations (Hodge and Parker 2017). Taylor says that by 'social imaginary',

> ...I mean something broader and deeper than the intellectual schemes people may entertain when they think about social reality in a disengaged mode. I am thinking, rather, of the ways people imagine their social existence, how they fit together with others, how things go on between them and their fellows, the expectations that are normally met, and the deeper normative notions and images that underlie these expectations. (Taylor 2004, p. 23)

Drawing on the theory of social imaginaries, Rizvi and Lingard (2010) seek to account for the infiltration of neoliberal ideas into educational practices. In this chapter I tackle an aspect of this broader phenomenon, employing Taylor's account of social imaginaries to analyse the impact of neoliberal theory on the curriculum work of teachers. In doing so I adapt Taylor's explanation of the process by which ideas are supposed to mesh with practices to analyse the extension of Public Choice Theory (a member of the neoliberal family) to authorise restriction of teacher control of curriculum. There is a history of controversy over educator control of curriculum (Apple and Teitelbaum 1986; Timmins 1996). What neoliberal theory— and Public Choice Theory in particular—offers is a new and potent rationale for limiting teacher autonomy. The neoliberal concept of the knowledge economy raises the stakes considerably in relation to curriculum. As knowledge becomes a new kind of commodity (Olssen and Peters 2005), curriculum stands out as a significant factor in economic calculation and form of investment. I go on to highlight implications of the transformation of the educational imaginary for teachers and curriculum, including the embedding of a 'moral image' of educators as self-interested, the obfuscation of the role of neoliberal theory in education, and the formation of a 'horizon' that stymies imagination and thought about alternatives to neoliberal educational practices.

22.1   Neoliberal Theory

Crucial to the analytic framework used in this chapter is the translation of what Rizvi and Lingard (2010) call 'ideology' and Taylor (2004) calls 'ideas' and 'idealisations', into the social imaginary. By taking this approach, the theory of social imaginaries departs from influential treatments of the formation of widespread ways of thinking and acting, such as that of Foucault. In Taylor's account, analysis of high theory authored by big-name intellectuals in history sheds light on contemporary modes of thought, whereas post-structural accounts eschew this strategy as an example of idealism—the view that ideas have independent force to shape history and society. But Taylor is at pains to forestall the charge of idealism. He makes the point that social imaginaries historically precede the emergence of any given theory, and offers an account of the 'infiltration' or 'penetration' of ideas into the social imaginary as an alternative to the binary of theory and practice. Taylor's account derives from detailed analysis of practices in the context of what he sees as the historically unique pervasiveness of theory in modernity. His analysis, then, can be seen as an attempt to explain the influence of theory on practices in a highly theoretical society while avoiding idealism (Hodge and Parker 2017). The process of penetration of ideas into the social imaginary is considered in more detail in the next section. In this section, neoliberalism as a set of ideas or ideology is summarised with a view to clarifying the theory that has shaped contemporary curriculum practice.

Sociological and social-theoretical accounts of neoliberalism highlight the fact that the term's reference is actually to a cluster or family of theories about economics and government. Olssen and Peters (2005) identify a set of theories including theories of human behaviour, markets and the role of government that have developed within the discipline of economics, as well as contemporary theories that reflect and articulate the neoliberal turn in contemporary economic and policy theory. What makes them a family rather than a mere bundle of theories is that they share certain assumptions and have overlapping foci. There are three basic assumptions evident in neoliberal theories.

A cardinal assumption of neoliberal theory is centuries old. This understanding of human nature was articulated by philosophers and political theorists in Britain and Europe in the 1600s. In an era of social upheaval, these theorists were concerned to bring an analysis of humans and their society to bear on the problem of political organisation. A key theorist of the early modern era, Adam Smith, analysed our individual nature and how we act in society. Smith's analysis produces one of the key assumptions of neoliberalism: the fundamentally self-interested nature of individual humans. He illustrates his thesis about humans with the example of some everyday occupations:

> It is not from the benevolence of the butcher, the brewer or the baker that we expect our dinner but their regard to their own interest. We address ourselves not to their humanity but to their self-love, and never talk to them of our own necessities but of their advantages. (Smith 1981, pp. 26–27)

This oft-quoted excerpt captures Smith's understanding of individual behaviour, which has been appropriated by economists and made into the cornerstone of neoliberal theory. Smith articulated another important assumption of liberal and neoliberal economics: the beneficent nature of markets. For Smith, it is the market that naturally curbs, coordinates and renders socially beneficial the sum of individual self-interested activity. The market stops individuals from pursuing their self-interest to the neglect or destruction of others, for the market will punish extremes of self-interest by engendering competition. Such is the responsive, almost intelligent effect of the market mechanism on self-interest that Smith called it 'the invisible hand'. Together, self-interested activity of individuals and the coordinating effect of markets comprise the engine of the 'wealth of nations'. Smith's understanding of the benevolence of the market mechanism has also come down to us as a fundamental assumption of neoliberalism.

Olssen and Peters (2005) emphasise the importance of another idea to the constitution of neoliberalism: that of government as a promoter of markets and market behaviours. They note that the liberal economic theory of Hayek, for example, argued for minimal government on the premise that any attempt to regulate or augment the free operation of markets can only be disabling to the natural engine of wealth and ultimately a threat to individual prosperity and freedom. However, other economists such as James Buchanan believed government could play a role in constructing and promoting markets, particularly where the market mechanism did not naturally take root such as public services. Buchanan's (1984) Public Choice Theory (PCT) is one of the distinctively neoliberal economic theories, and its object was to extend the reach of the market mechanism into the public sphere.

Buchanan and his colleagues had to take on an established way of thinking about public sector workers that positioned them as capable of serving the interests of others. For Buchanan (1984), part of the mission of PCT was dispelling what he called the 'romance' of this image of public sector workers. To do this, he called on that foundational premise of liberal economics, the self-interested individual, and argued that it makes more sense to view public servants as individuals who will take every opportunity to pursue their own interests, even at the expense of those they are paid to serve. With the assistance of analysis by his colleagues of the inevitable 'rent seeking behaviour' of these professionals, Buchanan demonstrated that in the absence of natural market mechanisms the public was at the mercy of that fundamental drive that public sector workers must exercise in virtue of being human.

22.2   Neoliberal Theory into Practice

Taylor (2004) describes the mechanisms by which early modernist theory was conveyed into the practices and imaginary of contemporary society. For Taylor, social imaginaries are transformed by ideas when theory is bundled with new or modified social practices. He is at pains to avoid the charge of idealism in his account. Idealism is the tradition that ideas have separate force in history to shape practices. For Taylor, however, practices always have ideas that are 'internal' to them that can be abstracted and elaborated in the form of theory. At the same time it is possible to repackage ideas with practices. Taylor's account of theory and practice, then, is modular—practices always contain ideas, but the connection between practices and ideas is not fixed and new permutations of theory–practice bundles are always possible. In his account of the 'penetration' of the political theories of Grotius and Locke into the social imaginary, Taylor describes historical changes that initially involved these and other theorists engaged in 'discursive practices' in which 'idealisations' of political order were formulated. Elite groups that were struggling to maintain control in conditions of upheaval used their power to modify and create institutions and practices to shore up their position. To make sense of these changes—to themselves and to those they wanted to convince— governing classes who were close to discursive practices drew on new outlooks provided by the theorists. According to Taylor, dissemination of these ideas involved simplification or 'glossing' to produce widely accessible 'outlooks' that could provide compelling reasons for new or modified practices. In the process, practices served to 'schematise' or refract and disseminate theory. In what Taylor (2004, p. 30) calls 'the dense sphere of common practice', theories take on localised forms with a life of their own, becoming tied more closely with practices, and articulated in the forms characteristic of a social imaginary, that is, as stories, images, proverbs and norms. It is possible for newly internalised ideas to be extracted and elaborated later on, producing new theories potentially consistent but not identical with the penetrating theory. In this way, through the process of first becoming associated with practices through the machinations of elite groups, then by being glossed and schematised, theories can come to infiltrate the social imaginary.

The previous section acquainted us with products of the discursive practices of neoliberal theorists. The conditions that spurred the theory-making of these econo- mists was the breakdown of 'welfare state' that had been guided by so-called 'welfare economics' (Timmins 1996). The same conditions provided impetus for elite groups to refashion and initiate practices and institutions. Globalisation pro- vided a stage for introducing new practices, and neoliberal theory, glossed and disseminated through the action of academic, pedagogic, policy and mass-media mechanisms, furnished the new outlook needed to make sense of the changes. The passage of key elements of neoliberal theory into educational practice has been analysed by education researchers including Marginson (1997), who drew attention to the process and outcomes of the implementation of market mechanisms. He explained how practices of dezoning, parental choice and new funding models were all strategies to implement educational markets. Marginson's analysis of New Zealand and Australian education systems suggests the process served to reduce government funding of schooling and entrench privilege. Another education researcher, Giroux (2004), described the inequitable results of the withdrawal of government funding and public influence on education. His arguments focus attention on the corporatisation of education in the US and some of the more severe consequences of neoliberal policy such as the criminalisation of young people from less privileged schools.

While marketisation and abrogation of Government responsibility for public education associated with neoliberal education policy produce shifts in the contexts of teaching, the infiltration of PCT into educational practice directly affects teacher work. The latter process can be considered in the light of Taylor's concepts of glossing and schematisation. In his sociology of school effectiveness, Angus (1993) cites examples of the application of PCT to school reform. For instance, Scheerens

(1992) articulates the value of PCT for identifying problems in schools and improving their 'effectiveness'. He joined other educational administration researchers in advocating the value of PCT's analysis of public sector organisations for improving schools. According to this gloss, teachers can be viewed as members of a 'professional bureaucracy', which explains some of the difficulties encountered by administrators seeking efficiencies in schools. Scheerens asserts that,

> There is little room for interference of the leadership with the work of the professionals [i.e. teachers], nor is work-related interaction among the professionals common; they operate autonomously and resist rationalization of their skills. Consequently it is hard for educational administrators to control the work of the professionals even when cases of dysfunction are clear. Professionals oppose strict planning and external evaluation of their work. (1992, p. 22)

Considering the challenge posed by teachers operating as professionals to school effectiveness, Scheerens presents a solution:

> The image of schools as professional bureaucracies explains the general resistance to change on the part of these organizations. Leadership, technological innovation and adaptation to environmental changes are not likely channels to make professionals alter their routines. The best approach to change, according to this organizational image, would be long-term alteration of the training programmes of teachers, with respect to teaching technologies and educational ideologies (for instance, when changing an orientation towards personal development into a more achievement-oriented mode). (1992, p. 22)

A different analysis and prescription is offered by Finegold and Soskice (1988) in relation to post-compulsory education and training (ET) in Britain. They elaborate the relevance of PCT in this context, as well as 'Agency Theory', a neoliberal administrative theory that advocates limiting the autonomy of 'agents' through prescriptive contractual arrangements that bind them to the interests of the paying 'principal'. Finegold and Soskice's analysis illustrates the glossing process, channelling the precepts of both PCT and Agency Theory to produce a succinct account of how to deal with the one-sided interests of educators:

> Running a complex ET system is a principal-agent problem. However clear the ideas of the Government (the principal) and however effective its own research and development activities, the co-operation of teachers and trainers as agents is essential to efficient course development, assessment, etc. But educators will have their own interests. (Japan is a case in point, where educationalists dominate the development of sixteen-eighteen education, business has no influence, and where rote learning still plays a major role.) A more effective solution is to balance the interests of educators against the interests of employers and those of employees. Hence the case for involving their representatives as additional agents, to bring about more balanced objectives. (1988, p. 47)

While Scheerens suggests that reforming initial training of educators will eventually bring 'achievement-oriented' professionals into the system, Finegold and Soskice advocated a more direct, structural 'solution' that involves 'balancing' the interests of educators with those of other parties. In effect, they propose a mechanism that mimics the dynamics of a market, which, since Adam Smith, has been considered the natural means for curbing and coordinating diverse interests.

Post-compulsory vocational education has been a traditional target for government reform efforts due to perceptions of a direct link with national economic performance. The analysis of Finegold and Soskice is a contribution to a neoliberal conceptualisation of reform in this area, and numerous policy measures have been put in place in countries like New Zealand, Australia and Britain to engineer clearer alignment between vocational education and economic goals. One of these policies involves the use of 'competency-based training' (CBT) to limit educator autonomy in relation to curriculum (Hodge 2016). The CBT approach hails from the US and Canada where it played a role in reforming teacher education (in the US) and served to sideline educators from the development of youth training programs (in Canada). CBT possess a unique structure that allows a sharp division of labour between representatives of employers and educators. This division of labour characterises implementations of CBT in countries, where it was a component of neoliberal reform. The division of labour here is striking because all responsibility for curriculum is transferred to employer representatives and responsibility for 'delivery' (a new instrumentalist term for teaching) is left with educators. CBT thus presents a mechanism for structurally limiting educator influence on curriculum.

The specific vocational goals of post-compulsory education perhaps make it appear that such control of curriculum by employers is justifiable, and that schooling presents a qualitatively different case. But control of curriculum has been a fraught issue for the whole educational project since the birth of humanism in ancient Greece and Rome. At stake is the reproduction of society itself. As early as Plato, intellectuals have articulated curriculum visions, with powerful institutions dictating their preferred interpretation of what is important to teach in different periods. Apple and Teitelbaum (1986) explain that teacher control of curriculum is a relatively recent practice, although powerful interests continue to attack this role. Their argument for teachers continuing to play a role in determining curriculum is that like other workers, to be effective teachers need to have a holistic grasp of the process in which they play a central part. This means actively contributing to the determination of curriculum that they are required to teach as well as facility in the more 'technical' activities of conveying curriculum and promoting and measuring learning with respect to it. In the West, mandated education levels for teachers are high meaning that teachers should be well equipped to contribute to the complex task of deciding what, of all that could be taught, should be taught at a particular time and place to particular students. Any attempt to separate conception and execution in the case of curriculum undermines and wastes this special form of expertise with demoralising consequences.

In the neoliberal era, control of curriculum is as contested as ever. Given the goal of neoliberal policy to foster a market-oriented, entrepreneurial citizenry (Olssen and Peters 2005), what educators teach is of utmost importance. Neoliberal reform has seen the strengthened resolve of governments to take control of school curriculum. Timmins (1996) traced the struggle over school curriculum in Britain, from a situation where politicians were assumed to have no authority to interfere with teacher control of curriculum to neoliberal reforms by the Thatcher government that resulted in strong centralisation of school curriculum. The general rationale of PCT applied in this instance, of the need to find ways to limit educator autonomy, while national economic and social imperatives underwrote the need for government influence in what had been described by politicians as 'the secret garden' of curriculum into which only teachers were allowed (Timmins 1996, p. 322). In the years since the first waves of neoliberal reform to education, curriculum has been centralised in states across the world and teacher influence reduced or curtailed. A contemporary example of this practice is the so-called 'C2C' ('Curriculum to Classroom') initiative in Queensland. Under this curriculum model, not only is curriculum centralised, but detailed programs and lesson plans are offered to teachers to spare them the effort of interpretation. Such 'teacher proof' curriculum models are common in nations that have embraced the neoliberal agenda.

22.3   Teachers, Curriculum and the Neoliberal Imaginary

Rizvi and Lingard's (2010) analysis of the spread of neoliberal policy uses the concept of social imaginaries to articulate a widespread acceptance of neoliberal ideas and norms that are not necessarily conveyed or located conceptually. Like Taylor (2004), Rizvi and Lingard (2010) distinguish between ideology and imaginaries. Ideology literally concerns the ideas and idealisations associated with practices, while a social imaginary, especially as it is defined by Taylor, embraces more. A distinctive sense of moral order is associated with an imaginary, a sense of how things should go on between people. An imaginary also forms the background of understanding that enables particular practices and self-interpretations. A social imaginary exhibits both moral and explanatory features. In the context of particular practices, the imaginary furnishes the broad sense of what is legitimate and why things are done in certain ways. Specific norms and understandings consistent with the imaginary form the immediate background of engagement in particular practices. It is at this latter level that 'ideas' feature. In the context of the present analysis of teachers and curriculum, the formation of a neoliberal imaginary related to practices is problematic at a number of levels.

A major problem with a neoliberal imaginary of education foregrounded by analysis in terms of the theory of social imaginaries is the wide acceptance of the neoliberal image of the educator. Taylor (2004) argued that for a theory to penetrate the social imaginary it must possess both explanatory and normative power. PCT clearly associates public sector professionals with a moral evaluation. It tells us that when people employed to serve others are given autonomy without market mechanisms to curb their interests, inefficiency and neglect inevitably result. Translated into educational practice PCT authorises an unmistakably moral interpretation of teachers' work. Curriculum practice in the neoliberal era implements and affirms the moral image of the educator as a kind of worker whose autonomy is suspect. In the context of these practices any attempt to exert professional autonomy can be interpreted morally, as can be measures to balance educator interests. Restricting teacher autonomy eventually seems to be the right thing to do to protect the interests of learners, parents, government and society.

A second problem with neoliberal education practice anticipated by the theory of social imaginaries is theoretical disjunction. When theories infiltrate the imaginary they do so via practices. Theories are glossed or simplified for learning and application. Generalisations, keyword vocabularies and fragments of arguments circulate and are on hand to give sense to new and modified practices. Teachers, students, parents and employers become acquainted with reasons for changes. Central concepts of neoliberalism such as global competition, knowledge economy, high skills equilibrium, small government, parental choice and industry leadership infiltrate the language of education and help to rationalise new practices. In addition, schematisation of theory into practice has the effect of translating between orders, from ideas to actions and arrangements. But schematisation also means the localisation and naturalisation of theory in the context of practice. Taylor (2004) explains that from such a setting ideas can be abstracted and formalised as people engaged in these practices seek better understanding or are invited or challenged to explain their actions. Prompted to theorise, those engaged in practices tap into the ideas Taylor believes are internal to practice. Through glossing and schematisation, changed education practices such as curriculum work are understood and explained in new ways that restate, diversify and reinforce neoliberal categories. Glossing and schematisation disconnect practices and thinking in relation to them from the infiltrating theory. The theoretical disjunction produced by the transformation of imaginaries entrenches the inaccessibility of first principles, making it difficult or impossible for those engaged in practices to directly interrogate and critique the infiltrating theory. Teachers and others close to neoliberal curriculum practice only have access to the theory that defines their practice in the form of glosses that do not expose the details and assumptions of the theory, or local interpretations of practice that has already been structured in accordance with the theory through schematisation. The theoretical disjunction produced by glossing and schematisation in curriculum practice effectively insulates the principles and assumptions of PCT from scrutiny by those most affected by the new arrangements.

A third problem of the penetration of neoliberal theory into the social imaginary is that imaginaries form a 'horizon' of possibility that limits as much as it enables thought and imagination. Social imaginaries are the background against which particular practices are engaged and understood. As the basis for understanding, actions and norms, the imaginary powerfully constrains generation of alternatives. With reference to the infiltration of theories of moral order into the imaginary of modernity, Taylor (2004, p. 17) explains that 'once we are well installed in the modern social imaginary, it seems the only possible one, the only one that makes sense'. The profound grip exercised by the imaginary on our everyday consciousness is such that imagining alternatives to the practices we engage in is difficult. According to Taylor, the social imaginary 'constitutes a horizon we are virtually incapable of thinking beyond' (2004, p. 185). In the context of education, the horizon-setting effect of the imaginary militates against coherent thinking about alternative curriculum practices while fostering a sense of resignation in the face of reforms such as we see in an instructional design manual for teachers:

> We will analyze our learners, and their context, but we aren't really going to analyze their needs. This is, in general, because within the classroom, there are requirements and those needs are often determined at a much higher, even a community or political, level. We all realize that there are some standards, for example, that we don't necessarily think make sense for a given developmental level, but they're there, and pretty immutable. (Carr-Chellman 2010, p. 3)

The horizon-setting feature of the neoliberal educational imaginary suggests that even if educators object to limitations on their autonomy, they may eventually be hard-pressed to articulate other possibilities since current practices are considered 'immutable'. The horizon-setting character claimed for social imaginaries suggests that Apple and Teitelbaum's (1986) critique of restrictions on educator control of curriculum needs to be amended. They argued that when teachers are removed from the curriculum making process their curriculum skills 'atrophy'. The theory of social imaginaries suggests that in addition to loosing a sense of the whole process and the skills to contribute to curriculum construction, educators can loose the ability to even conceive of an education practice in which they actively contribute to curriculum. In an era where centrally designed curriculum packages are implemented by technician teachers who work in an environment where such limited roles make sense and seem legitimate, it may be near impossible to think through to new ways of practicing curriculum.

22.4   Critiquing and Reimagining Curriculum in Neoliberal Times

The analysis presented here suggests that contemporary curriculum practice is a site for the glossing and schematisation of neoliberal theory, and a vector for embedding PCT's moral image of the educator. It also suggests that while neoliberal theory can inform change to practices and the imaginary, the theory itself is screened off from scrutiny by people engaged in those practices. A problematic implication of the theory of social imaginaries for the influence of neoliberal theory on education is that whatever transformations are brought about, the result may be the formation of a 'horizon' upon thinking and imagination that forestalls alternatives. In this final section, three research needs are sketched that are prompted by the foregoing explorations.

The first concerns the moral image of the educator that is circulated and potentially embedded in the social imaginary in the process of its transformation by neoliberal theory. Specifically, PCT—a key element of neoliberalism—harbours the valuation of public sector professionals, including educators, as given to the neglect of the interests of those they are paid to serve. In the case of educators, PCT implies that they will tend to neglect the interests of learners, parents, employers and governments. The theory of social imaginaries suggests that the moral charge that attaches to this understanding of educators can promote an image of educators as self-interested and whose professional autonomy needs to be circumscribed. This notion will come to seem normal, and efforts to curb the seemingly natural neglect and excesses of educators will seem legitimate. The moral image of the educator embedded by a neoliberal transformation of the imaginary demands research and critique. The analysis of PCT needs to be inspected closely to determine the interest structure of educators. What is to be noted is that the work of Buchanan and colleagues focussed primarily on bureaucracies. Potentially, teachers are not homogenous with this group. It may well be that a complex interest structure is at play in the formation of educator identities in which it becomes possible to conceive of a convergence of educator interests and those of learners and related groups. This can be both theoretical and empirical work, to interrogate and re-theorise the premises of PCT and to understand the reality of educator interests.

A second need for research is more generic. Strategically, it addresses the problem of theoretical disjuncture created by processes of glossing, schematisation and practice re-theorisation that accompany the transformation of imaginaries. In the case of the penetration of neoliberal theory into educational imaginary, the threat is that the guiding theory becomes cut off from consideration by people engaged in educational practices. Those most affected by neoliberal reforms may be unable to apprehend and challenge the assumptions and arguments of neoliberal theory because of the convoluted and segmented process of theoretical transformation. The process hides neoliberal theory behind glosses, and as the theory is schematised in social practices and infiltrates the social imaginary, those engaged in educational practices draw on the resources of the imaginary to understand their actions. Thus when they conceptualise their own practices it is a contextualised and normalised version of the penetrating theory they recreate. Research into this process is required to test the value of the theory of social imaginaries for analysing theory-led reforms, but also to promote collective remembrance of the aetiology of reform. By interrogating the process of the neoliberal transformation of the educational imaginary, educators and other affected groups have a chance of understanding and critiquing curriculum reform.

Perhaps the most stubborn effect to be anticipated from a transformed social imaginary is the construction of horizons on thought and imagination. If a neoliberal imaginary of education has indeed formed, then it will be difficult to imagine alternatives to the practices that have been affected by neoliberalism. With respect to curriculum practices it will seem legitimate to limit teacher control—given the moral image of educators that goes with the new imaginary—but if teachers object or feel alienated then responding by framing different ways of doing curriculum may not be an accessible option. Because educators have one foot in the area they teach and the other in the world of education, they have the perspective from which to understand and appraise what is important to teach and make the relevant decisions that lead to learner experience of curriculum. While it is no doubt true, as Apple and Teitelbaum (1986) argue, that curriculum skills atrophy when scope to contribute to this part of the educational process is denied teachers, another issue is imagining that this kind of contribution is possible and modes by which it can be exercised. Centralised and often commercial production of curriculum packages is only one way of constructing curriculum, but in the neoliberal era it may seem to teachers that there is no other way. To challenge the infiltration of neoliberal theory into education, then, it may be valuable for researchers to directly engage with the question of alternative ways of making curriculum. In particular, it may be worthwhile to examine ways to draw upon the dual expertise of educators—understanding fields of knowledge and understanding education—which is currently wasted by neoliberal models of curriculum. Imagining curriculum alternatives therefore stands to not only disturb the horizons set on thought and imagination by a neoliberal imaginary, but to realise the potential squandered in neoliberalism's drive to efficiency.

References

Angus, L. (1993). The sociology of school effectiveness. *British Journal of Sociology of Education, 14*(3), 333–345.

Appadurai, A. (1996). *Modernity at large: Cultural dimensions of globalization*. Minneapolis, MN: University of Minnesota Press.

Apple, M. W., & Teitelbaum, K. (1986). Are teachers losing control of their skills and curriculum? *Journal of Curriculum Studies, 18*(2), 177–184.

Buchanan, J. M. (1984). Politics without romance: A sketch of positive public choice theory and its normative implications. In J. M. Buchanan & R. D. Tollison (Eds.), *The theory of public choice II* (pp. 11–22). Minneapolis, MI: University of Michigan Press.

Carr-Chellman, A. (2010). *Instructional design for teachers: Improving classroom practice*. Florence, KY: Routledge.

Finegold, D., & Soskice, D. (1988). The failure of training in Britain: Analysis and prescription. *Oxford Review of Economic Policy, 4*(3), 21–43.

Giroux, H. A. (2004). *The terror of neoliberalism: Authoritarianism and the eclipse of democracy*. Boulder, CO: Paradigm Publishers.

Hodge, S. (2016). Alienating curriculum work in Australian vocational education and training. *Critical Studies in Education, 57*(2), 143–159.

Hodge, S., & Parker, S. (2017). Accounting for practice in an age of theory: Charles Taylor's theory of social imaginaries. In J. Lynch, J. Rowlands, T. Gale & A. Skourdoumbis (Eds.), *Practice theory and education* (pp. 39–54). Abingdon, UK: Routledge.

Marginson, S. (1997). *Markets in education*. St Leonards, NSW: Allen & Unwin.

Olssen, M., & Peters, M. A. (2005). Neoliberalism, higher education and knowledge economy: From the free market to knowledge capitalism. *Journal of Education Policy, 20*(3), 313–345.

Rizvi, F., & Lingard, B. (2010). *Globalizing education policy*. London & New York: Routledge.

Scheerens, J. (1992). *Effective schooling: Research, theory and practice*. London: Cassell.

Smith, A. (1981). *An inquiry into the nature and causes of the wealth of nations* (Vol. I). Indianapolis, IN: Liberty Classics.

Taylor, C. (2004). *Modern social imaginaries*. Durham, NC: Duke University Press.

Timmins, N. (1996). *The five giants: A biography of the welfare state*. London: Fontana Press.

Author Biography

Steven Hodge works at Griffith University (Brisbane, Australia) as a Lecturer in Professional, Vocational and Continuing Education. His overarching interest is in ideas and how they influence education. Steven's current focus on how occupational expertise is represented in standards and curriculum frameworks and how educators interpret standardised curriculum.

Chapter 23
Re-Casting Teacher Effectiveness Approaches to Teacher Education

Andrew Skourdoumbis

23.1 Introduction

This chapter explores the policy rationale coursing through contemporary teacher education. The argument developed in this chapter suggests that the field of teacher education is experiencing a steady reversal moving from a liberalizing curricular emphasis towards a singular reckoning, the focus now squarely on how to better the classroom instruction (teaching practice) of teachers as the only way to enhance student achievement. Like all things in this current period of late capitalism, teacher education too finds itself wedged by the push and pull of the economic realm. There is one certainty that this world poses, the heightened demands of official probing, the sort often favoured by the present-day controllers of finance capital.

An examination of the kind offered in this chapter first and foremost focuses on the 'perform or else' constancies confirmed by the rigours and procedures of performativity. A simple narrative fuels its existence, that of a 'knowledge economy'. School education is now overseen by a worldwide explosion in testing at national and international levels serving a singular objective, preparing students for a new world of work. School and teacher education are primed for the interventions they can help stimulate to cope with new economic global settings.

Late capitalism and globalization securitize school education and the curriculum that infuses it, narrowing it towards work-ready vocational skill sets and the vernacular of competencies. Use-value outcomes found in policy and curriculum papers often broadcast the multifarious and all-encompassing Education will respond to the challenges envisaged and will also 'as far as possible, anticipate the conditions in which young Australians will need to function as individuals, citizens and workers when they complete their schooling' (ACARA 2012: 7). The right type of teacher with the best preparation is needed.

A. Skourdoumbis (✉)
Deakin University, Burwood, Australia
e-mail: andrew.skourdoumbis@deakin.edu.au

© Springer Nature Singapore Pte Ltd. 2017   347
M.A. Peters et al. (eds.), *A Companion to Research in Teacher Education*,
DOI 10.1007/978-981-10-4075-7_23

With this in mind, the work of this chapter focuses on three aspects. First, the macro-structural context is sketched providing background to the global pressure points re-making teacher education: *performativity* and a *knowledge economy*. Second, implications for teacher education are considered as well as details of key policy aspects including how the work of teacher effectiveness research (TER) is used to inform and decide policy on teaching. Finally, the chapter outlines some possibilities for change in teacher education by discussing aspects of the capabilities approach (CA) and its relevance to teacher preparation.

23.2 Performativity and a Knowledge Economy

Performativity requires:

> a technology, a culture and a mode of regulation that employs judgements, comparisons and displays as means of incentive, control, attrition and change based on rewards and sanctions (both material and symbolic). The performances (of individual subjects or organizations) serve as measures of productivity or output, or displays of 'quality', or 'moments' of promotion or inspection. (Ball 2003: 216)

This is not simply about performance per se, the emphasis is of a 'doing' more akin to that of exploit, namely develop and utilize rather than merely 'do' or complete. Connected to the performative drive is a judgement component assessing efforts expended against yields obtained and efficiency is the benchmark of relevance.

A policy context global in reach underpinned by economic reform focuses on developing skills and learning that an education of a particular type musters. The global context is of a high-skill and knowledge-driven economy. A catalyzing competitive edge from within the scientific and technological fields squared with qualities of flexibility, innovation and design maintains the necessary and rapid momentum now needed in economies. Competing effectively denotes exploitation of commercial advantage sustained by the flexibilities offered by a more autonomous and highly trained workforce. In advanced societies, new technologies and an unrestrained globalization are the spin-offs of late post-Fordist capitalism. Knowledge is transformed in this process. The metamorphosis is elastic, responsive to the instabilities ever-present now in a perpetually anxious economy. Economic rejuvenation is knowledge and market centred, characterized by the 'rise in the importance of knowledge as capital' (Olssen and Peters 2005: 330).

Furthermore, performativity commoditizes knowledge and flexible, highly trained 'job-ready' workers are needed, amenable to the demands and complexities found in a performative and informational world. Human capital considerations are at work here. There is also a premium on the benefits of science. Science can produce, transmit and transfer knowledge. Moreover, a knowledge economy is readily discernible through quantification. Inputs, outputs, stocks and flows can all be measured and managed in organized interconnecting networks bounded by a complete scientific system. The performance orientation inside the knowledge economy has a pragmatic side. Economic optimization and certainty is sought via a mechanism on the hunt for instabilities and teaching of a particular type is favoured.

23.3 Implications: Putting Teacher Education to Work

The human capital considerations of performativity and a knowledge economy sustains much of the current policy reform process in teacher education. The human capital function is evident in the way in which international measures of student achievement are used as proxy measurements for the success of individual nation states' education systems (and by implication, the success of their teachers) and therefore are seen to be measures of the human capital produced by these countries. Teachers and the teacher education that they receive will need to be 'capable of preparing students to live, work and be successful in a society in which they will be required to solve problems, work collaboratively and think creatively and critically' (TEMAG Issues Paper 2014: 4). One way that current economies develop their economic competitiveness is to invest in their human capital linking policy narratives in teacher education with an emphasis on 'what works' so that schools and students perform and achieve.

A case in point is Australia where more than 40 reports on or about teacher education of various types have been undertaken in as many years (see Rowan et al. 2015). A policy constant by way of findings emanating from reports of this kind is the role of teachers in enhancing student achievement. The teacher is the variable of influence in improving student progress. In Australia as is likely elsewhere, the starting point is almost always not that teachers '*could* improve but that they *need* to *improve*' (Rowan et al. 2015: 278) reinforcing many of the alleged failings of an inadequate system of teacher education. The only reasonable thing to do is to tackle issues of teacher quality and so effective teaching requires working on teacher education. Areas to address include quality assurance issues regarding teacher education courses, improving the practical school placement experiences of pre-service teachers, enhancing entry requirements for teacher education candidates and focusing on classroom practices. Furthermore, while much of the policy rationale for teacher education reform is expressed in performance-orientated terms linking broader debates about the need for educational and economic change including teachers that are immediately 'classroom ready', a political motive is also at work. De-regulation pressures are ever-present. The dual aim of financial profit and that of different beginnings for teacher education align with an altered set of convictions, ones attuned to commodification objectives. Replete with specified objectives, teacher education is delineated between what is deemed effective and research informed, accompanied by 'real-world' practical integrations. The scope is simple enough to outline and understand. Basic necessities are needed, principal of which is a sound research base to determine the effectiveness of teacher education. Foremost amongst what qualifies for effectiveness in teacher education is teacher graduate quality and modelled, 'best-practice'. Reconstituting the question of student achievement so that it closely aligns with effective teaching removes ambiguity. The only relationship of interest and importance is between effective and quality teaching and the output(s) of student learning (achievement). While the stakes are raised for the individual classroom teacher, a higher purpose is served, holding to account the education and training that pre-service teachers receive. An aim is the universalization of teaching practice(s) captured and catalogued by the legitimations of TER.

Underlying the regulatory imperatives of an effective teacher education are the symbolic formalizations of an overseen—governed—'best-practice' teaching comprised of three elements. The first involves the facilitated evaluations of classroom performance made visible via comparison against system-devised benchmarks. Evaluative criteria promise causal educative connections between classroom teacher effects and student achievement. Models of effective instruction are the preferred guidelines of teaching practice, practically developed and tested, applicable anywhere and everywhere. Modelled effective instruction is then an objective truth that can be observed and described as it can be accessed from different vantage points, and it can also be replicated. Second, as an objective truth, a model of effective instruction is intelligible across observers as there is common agreement about it that thirdly must hold, irrespective and independent of any beliefs, desires and hopes.

The mathematical codifications of TER linearize the relationship between teaching and learning snap-freezing it into a document (a book, video, instructional material) so that teacher effects simply become variables in a pre-constructed programme of scientific inquiry. The aim of enhancing our influence and understanding over teaching and learning enables stronger and tighter policy control. The vagaries of teaching are presumably then minimized, as our power to predict dispenses with the unwanted and hindering. Hence, TER seeks out the logical, sequential and purposeful associations between the variables that evidently matter in teaching and learning. There is policy-maker appeal in this research as it 'treats schools and teachers as bearers of specific variables (attitudes, qualifications, strong leadership, etc.) to be correlated with pupil outcomes, measured on standardized tests as there is always a "best-practice" that can be instituted and audited from above' (Connell 2009: 217). Doubts over causal links between effective teaching and student learning wane as the precise and straightforward are captured, isolated and described by the singularities that define effective performance. In the teacher effectiveness approach to student learning, design and process trumps lived existence. Either specific nominated teacher characteristics (years of experience, credentials, planning and preparation) or conversely, teaching practices (time spent on task(s), form(s) of engagement, and so on) matter more than any contextual influences. In addition, any disparity between student achievement variation(s) across and between classrooms in the same school is attributed to teaching effectiveness or lack thereof. The social background of students can be 'controlled for' in the statistical regularities applied to evaluate performance. Standardized student test scores are proxies for evaluating teacher performance so that the measurement tool adopted comprehends the learning attained expressed as the valued-added component of formal instruction. In this precise world all is accounted for as the certainties of regression analyses and multiple rating categories that somehow account for the errors linked to statistical estimation can also distinguish between the learning attainment of individual students and the specific effect a teacher had on students. This is the preferred method of teacher effectiveness models of instruction, brevity rather than wholesome profundity so that everything in teaching can be narrowed and summarized boxlike.

Consequently, the twofold basis of teacher effectiveness approaches to student learning narrows towards (a) a production-function equation where achievement (output) equals countable although limited inputs and (b) directly matching specific styles of instruction (pedagogy) and designated knowledge domains (curriculum). Teacher effects on student learning can then be measured in one of two ways. The first is purely arithmetical, relying upon estimation of large scale surveys of student achievement. The second involves determining the achievement gained after a period of intervention, in other words, where student achievement is measured after a time of structured teaching, known as the value-added component. The foundationalist logic of TER now stands as a uniform authority on teaching practice and educational attainment. TER helps eliminate supposed risks linked to teaching and learning corralling school education towards the accepted 'basics'. But if anything, this current period in time is representative of an increasing uncertainty and so if education including teaching is to be a positive practice there needs to be some re-thinking about what it means to learn and what there is to learn.

23.4   Re-Casting Teacher Education: Capabilities

Capabilities is concerned with human development. Proposed by Sen (2008) and Nussbaum (1997, 2011) their distinctive takes on capabilities and the capability approach (CA) notwithstanding focuses on an approach to human development that accounts for differences in available resources. Sen takes a panoramic view of capabilities, concerned with broad-based social inequities in comparative terms. Capability for Sen is a 'kind of power' (2008: 336) and it would be wrong to view capabilities simply in terms of basic end point advantages or attributes. The key point for Sen in his conceptualization of capability is in terms of 'scope or room to' as opposed to a 'state of'. Conversely, Nussbaum itemizes capabilities suggesting that people require a basic list of things to attain human functioning. These things encapsulate and include (1) life, (2) bodily health, (3) bodily integrity, (4) sense, imagination, and thought, (5) emotions, (6) practical reason, (7) affiliation, (8) other species, (9) play, and (10) control over one's political and material environment (see Nussbaum 2006).

The relevance of the CA for education and schooling is in its enabling qualities. The approach conceptualizes education and schooling in terms that speculates on the freedom(s), and opportunities one has to lead a life that one values having due regard for the possibilities afforded to each individual to make informed and personal decisions. While economic and political considerations are important, the CA focuses on the potential an individual has in exercising how they personally shape their own lives and to develop it fully rather than be dominated by external influences.

Empowerment is then a fundamental aspect of capabilities. Terzi says as much when addressing capability and education. She suggests that

> ...capability to be educated, broadly understood in terms of real opportunities both for informal learning and for formal schooling, can be considered a basic capability in two ways. First, in that the absence or lack of this opportunity would essentially harm and disadvantage the individual. Second, since the capability to be educated plays a substantial role in the expansion of other capabilities, as well as future ones, it can be considered basic for the further reason that it is fundamental and foundational to the capabilities necessary to well-being, and hence to lead a good life. (2007: 25)

So, while the capability to be educated contains a demonstrable and concrete function, that of equipping an individual with particular skills and attributes that may lead to further education eventuating in some form of acquired credential for employment purposes, it also performs the role of aesthetic enhancement for the 'appreciation of' and the 'engaging in' the Arts.

The distinctive benefits of re-casting how we think about the field of teacher education then are threefold. First, recognizing that in a pluralist, democratic and cosmopolitan society geared for the complexities of the twenty-first century, education is a principal public good, the effect(s) of which are felt far into the future. Second, in parsing *capabilities* and learning, rather than simply focusing on validating standardized benchmarks, teaching practice is acknowledged as an activity with its own unique and contiguous features answerable to the family of practices that define it. Third, in prioritizing the achievement of students beyond system demarcated endpoints, their potential is nourished through the learning experiences that intrinsically motivate them.

Limited notions of achievement confine conceptions of teaching practice to arrays of specific teaching or instructional practices. Emphasizing how the pedagogic capacity of teachers can be enhanced to address the issue of student underachievement including strategies beyond the classroom is one way that the field of teacher education can transcend the restrictive accounts and singularities of teacher effectiveness studies. Delineating teacher capabilities so that student capabilities are advanced improves the field of teacher education providing it with more than a contemporary policy relevance. This is more than merely improving teacher quality and effectiveness. It is about identifying then fostering specific teacher capabilities needed to cope with the complex demands of teaching practice in multifaceted societies.

Australian schools like their OECD counterparts are demanding places. While the professional life of teachers is often described by a particular set of terms and qualities intrinsic to their daily practice; care, wisdom, resilience, respectfulness, trustworthiness, integrity, it also needs to incorporate a capacity for intellectual activity. This means at its most rudimentary that a capable teacher has the capacity to address the 'basics' that is literacy and numeracy. However, it also signifies a capacity for articulating and understanding how to recognize what counts as the major qualities needed of the fully developed person of today. In other words, there are moral and ethical considerations that require attention. Teacher capability in one sense then means an ability to frame and comprehend the complex social, economic and political demands of today as also educational ones. While much in the field of teacher education of late is concerned about the 'profession' and the skills and personal characteristics of what defines an effective teacher—the rational and cal-culable—less emphasis is on some of the core capabilities identified by Nussbaum: bodily health, bodily integrity, sense, imagination, thought and practical reason (see Nussbaum 2011). These if adequately recognized and developed within people, provide a foundation to lead a life centred on the self-definition bestowed by the choices made and valued by motivated and engaged individuals living in a more complex world. In many ways, these core capabilities resemble the 'education of sensibility' that Macmurray advocates, the 'development of our capacity for sense experience, and through this, the education of the emotions' (Macmurray 2012: 671). Learning is then not only about the narrow and standard where the differ-entiations of student achievement are extracted 'one off' as neutral markers of teacher performance. Learning becomes about an integration; mixing our humanity with what we see and hear rather than resembling a performative input and output mode of production.

Pedagogy matters in developing capabilities and teachers need the capacity to develop their teaching beyond contemporary standardized minimums. A requisite pedagogic practice emphasizing conceptual understanding is about the relational, a bridging of and between subject content (disciplinary) knowledge and the knowl-edge that comes from a disciplined contemplation. Learning in this 'aspect, is the cultivation of sensibility, by which is meant, or should be meant, the development of the capacity for fine sensory discrimination' (Macmurray 2012: 671). This means focusing teacher education on a quality teaching rationale that recognizes fine-grained subtleties and the uniqueness of context. Concentrating on the ways teachers teach their students effectively within a specific context, and the different ways teaching and learning occurs, potentially changes how we conceive engage-ment in schools, (i.e. situated learning). In other words, absent from a current teacher education is a 'learning to live in our senses' (Macmurray 2012: 672), or put simply, to draw more fully upon our imaginations.

Furthermore, a re-casting of teacher education towards capabilities opens debate and thought on the teacher as 'deliberate professional' (see Gale and Molla 2016). Teaching in a complex world is more than simply about delivering 'the basics'. Teachers and teaching contributes beyond the current policy inflections of maxi-mizing social and economic participation as there is also a well-being component. Teaching in this sense prioritizes a concern for learning needs that not only taps into the achievable present it also signals the evolving future. Teaching professionals at 'their most deliberative…are "transformative" in thought and deed, particularly in relation to social inequalities' (Gale and Molla 2016: 1). If as Connell suggests education is a 'process that creates social reality, necessarily producing something new' (2009: 225) then teacher education will play its part by including in its outline theorizations of teachers' roles outside the boundaries of school. In other words, while teachers need to constantly immerse themselves in considerations of 'learning environments' and what it means 'to learn', they too need to be 'critical' as part of 'deliberative action' (see Gale and Molla 2016) about what it means to be educated.

Firm foundations encapsulating the energy of education as a core human entitlement unencumbered by contextual influences means eschewing generic skill sets as the sine qua non of contemporary teacher education. Aligning teacher-student relations so that teaching and schooling makes significant differences to achievement merits understanding(s) of pedagogy beyond standardized midpoints. Embracing and enabling truly what one is 'able to do and to be' (see Nussbaum 2011) is about a teacher education that concerns itself with the human being as a 'dignified free being' (Nussbaum 2002: 123–124) supported by liberalizing and rich curricula highlighting both the complexities of and interconnections between education, schooling and the exigencies of past and contemporary society. There is a social justice element attached to this conception of a teacher education, one that treats individuals as holistic beings free from economic and serviceable endpoints. There is a deliberateness to the actions needed here on the part of teachers one that involves 'thoughtfulness and purposefulness: the careful consideration of circumstances or issues and weighing up of the relative merits of all available or known options and possible responses before making a judgment or decision' (Gale and Molla 2016: 2).

In a teacher education that addresses the capacity of teachers to make a difference, building teacher capabilities will both enhance their own understanding(s) of what it is to be agentic and how that may be relayed to their students. Teachers themselves are often very unevenly prepared (Bourdieu and Passeron 2000) so attending to evident educational inequality by developing teacher capabilities through a holistic understanding of knowledge; the informational—the basic 'facts' of contemporary schooling and educational practice, and the emotional—as a component of pedagogic work, broadens the scholastic options of their students.

Bourdieu and Passeron (2000) contend that the success of all school education and 'more generally of all …pedagogic work, depends fundamentally on the education previously accomplished in the earliest years of life, even…when the educational system denies this primacy in its ideology and practice by making the school career a history with no pre-history' (43). Confronting underachievement by bolstering the pedagogic capacity of teachers fortifies the scholastic connection between what is taught and learnt. Pedagogic mastery to enhance student achievement demands a richer set of learning opportunities than those currently on offer. The field of teacher education has a responsibility for improving teaching and it can do so more effectively if teachers actively engage in investigating problems of underachievement to produce local and specific solutions with an emphasis on engaging more of the most vulnerable students. Some of the core themes of a capabilities approach (Nussbaum 2011) currently missing from 'quality teaching' and teacher effectiveness pedagogies include broader conceptions of student functioning/achievement, for instance, 'being able to imagine, to think and to reason' and to 'engage in critical reflection about the planning of one's own life' (Nussbaum 1992: 222). These aspects are important considerations for the field of teacher education arguably heightening the productivity of pedagogic work. This is important as restrictive teacher quality and effectiveness pedagogies do not adequately serve the interests of students.

Developing in teachers the capacity for deep and disciplined thinking about the academic complexities of their work and its connections to learning means advancing issues around inequality beyond narrow school and teacher effectiveness interpretations (see Thrupp and Lupton 2006). Teacher education has a role to play here as it must. Primarily, a contemporary and relevant teacher education recognizes that to improve the achievement and capability of all necessitates strategies of intervention that professionally engages the capacities of teachers. Teacher capabilities, as alternatives to current reified multi-variate analyses potentially offers the field of teacher education a broader and more rounded conception of achievement promoting the human autonomy of students. This should form the new account of the 'pedagogic relation' (Bourdieu and Passeron 2000: 95) with potential to express complexities of student learning from within self-defining personal abilities and characteristics rather than skill development for vocations that in all likelihood will vaporize in the next global economic shock.

23.5 Conclusion

I have argued in this chapter that economic imperatives provide the policy rationale for change in teacher education at present. Throughout I have inferred that the field of teacher education is experiencing a period of transition brought about by a new sharper-edged phase of late capitalism. Performativity and the rapidly changing edifices of a knowledge economy necessitates educational responses and the field of teacher education is now jammed by significant policy pressures. At one level, there is a 'kind of crisis discourse—with an associated tendency to try and name and shame teacher education for its failings' (Rowan et al. 2015: 276). The obvious marker of the arguments mounted within the crisis discourse centre on poor teacher quality and inadequate or ineffective pre-service teacher preparation. However, a broader macro argument is also in play, one echoing the performative and efficiency driven policy rationales of a sharper economic station namely, stringent standards, stringent accountability and an acceptance of and adherence to market competition, de-regulation and 'more choice'. The policy imperative is then one of greater emphasis on classroom instruction as the answer to declining student achievement and performance. An overt policy storyline is at work namely that effective classroom instruction and teaching practice(s) not only correct for but overcome capital insecurities. In a world characterized by rising casualization and the cyclic shudders of capital, precise teaching practice(s) appropriately informed by a robust teacher education are increasingly considered the sole and only solid educational foundations needed to enhance student achievement and prepare students for the new world of work.

While this shift in emphasis for some is hardly novel, it does point to the deepening drift towards a narrow teacher effectiveness notion of student achievement. Teacher education need then only be studied insofar as it provides ready-made solutions to make teaching more effective for the productive economic benefits it will bestow a nation. This potentially sweeps aside or at a minimum trims how the field of teacher education treats (i) issues and questions of school student learning and achievement and (ii) the preparation of teachers. It also has far reaching implications for education policy as policy-makers tend to draw on a diminishing pool of new thinking not only about how to address inequity and social disadvantage in school education but perhaps more importantly, what counts towards the educated person.

The chapter has also located current teacher education policy transitions towards exacting theorizations of classroom instruction as indicative of a particular evaluative mindset, one that in policy terms, champions the scientific 'technical' study of teacher education as a formal 'evidenced based' system complete with its own quantitative appraisal mechanisms. An amplified meta-mathematics 'over-systematizes' teaching debilitating the field of teacher education by destabilizing conceptions of 'the teacher' as the embodied change agent that will make '*the*' difference in the end.

Be that as it may, I contend that something basic is missing, namely that those seeking to be teachers have the right to expect an actual and enlightening *teacher education* one that recognizes its especial significance to society. In other words, a teacher education in its broadest sense that at its core deals with the fundamental questions of learning and teaching as primarily ethical rather than purely economic questions. A way for this to occur is to broaden how we conceive of teacher education so that we look beyond narrow vocational interpretations of it.

Acknowledgements I want to sincerely thank Dr. Julianne Lynch for taking the time to read and offer detailed commentary on an earlier draft of this chapter.

References

Australian Curriculum Assessment and Reporting Authority (ACARA). (2012). *General capabilities in the Australian Curriculum*. Accessed from http://www.australiancurriculum.edu.au/GeneralCapabilities/Pdf/Overview

Ball, S. J. (2003). The teacher's soul and the terrors of performativity. *Journal of Education Policy, 18*(2), 215–228.

Bourdieu, P., & Passeron, J. C. (2000). *Reproduction in education, society and culture*. London: Sage.

Connell, R. (2009). Good teachers on dangerous ground: Towards a new view of teacher quality and professionalism. *Critical Studies in Education, 50*(3), 213–229.

Gale, T., & Molla, T. (2016). Deliberations on the deliberate professional: Relating thought and action, provoking critical reflection. In J. Lynch, J. Rowlands, T. Gale & A. Skourdoumbis (Eds.), *Practice theory: Diffractive readings in professional practice research*. UK: Routledge.

Macmurray, J. (2012). Learning to be human. *Oxford Review of Education, 38*(6), 661–674.

Nussbaum, M. C. (1992). Human functioning and social justice: Defense of aristotelian essentialism. *Political Theory , 20*(2), 202–246.

Nussbaum, M. C. (1997). Capabilities and human rights. *Fordham Law Review, 66,* 273–300.

Nussbaum, M. C. (2002). Capabilities and social justice. *International Studies Review, 4*(2), 123–135.

Nussbaum, M. C. (2006). *Frontiers of justice*. USA: Harvard University Press.

Nussbaum, M. C. (2011). *Creating capabilities: The human development approach*. Cambridge, MA: Belknap Press.

Olssen, M., & Peters, M. A. (2005). Neoliberalism, higher education and the knowledge economy: From the free market to knowledge capitalism. *Journal of Education Policy, 20*(3), 313–345.

Rowan, L., Mayer, D., Kline, J., Kostogriz, A., & Walker-Gibbs, B. (2015). Investigating the effectiveness of teacher education for early career teachers in diverse settings: The longitudinal research we have to have. *Australian Educational Researcher, 42,* 273–298.

Sen, A. (2008). The idea of justice. *Journal of Human Development, 9*(3), 314–332.

TEMAG. (2014). *Teacher education ministerial advisory group issues paper*. Canberra, Australia: Australian Government Publisher.

Terzi, L. (2007). Capability to be educated. In M. Walker & E. Unterhalter (Eds.), *Sen's capability approach and social justice in education* (pp. 25–43). Basingstoke: Palgrave MacMillian.

Thrupp, M., & Lupton, R. (2006). Taking school contexts more seriously: The social justice challenge. *British Journal of Educational Studies, 54*(3), 308–328.

Author Biography

Andrew Skourdoumbis is a Senior Lecturer in Education at Deakin University, Australia. His research interests include curriculum theory, policy analysis, teacher practice and educational performance. He investigates global reform efforts in education that impact teacher practice and the way that exacting methods of research govern teacher performance.

Chapter 24
The Paradox of Teacher Agency in a Glocalised World

Tom Are Trippestad

24.1 Introduction

The article presents the concept of rhetorical agency to understand, and analyses the parallel and paradoxical agencies teachers are offered, and limited by, under discourses of globalisation within education. The paper identifies typical arguments, reactions, narratives and metaphors of globalisation. It discusses some of the consequences these have on the premises of teacher agencies locally, nationally and globally. The article raises normative questions on the kind of agencies that are necessary for teachers in an open and glocalised world. It suggests new interpretations of the bildung—tradition as a constructive rhetorical agency to respond to and balance the needs of local, national and global interest in education.

24.2 Rhetorical Agency

In classical rhetoric theory, sovereignty is primarily located in the speaker. Rhetoric is considered an art and a craft of persuasion—to be used on an audience in a public sphere in order to achieve specific aims. Post-modern theories of the subject and modern approaches to discourse have resulted in many analyses of how the modern subject is far from being sovereign as speaker. The concept of *rhetorical agency* is an analytical compromise allowing both for analysis of deterministic perspectives on discourse; and for the agency of skillful and strategic rhetorical subjects. Agents are those with the ability to persuade others. In a rhetorical culture, agents exercise influence and yet they are also being acted upon by the rhetorical culture of the community. Agents are shapers being shaped.

T.A. Trippestad (✉)
Western Norway University of Applied Sciences, Bergen, Norway
e-mail: tat@hib.no

© Springer Nature Singapore Pte Ltd. 2017
M.A. Peters et al. (eds.), *A Companion to Research in Teacher Education*,
DOI 10.1007/978-981-10-4075-7_24

Rhetorical agencies are both limited and made possible by different discourses and their communicative practices (Trippestad 2014). Discourses represent fundamental conditions for communication and performance. Within them lie authority, genres, expectations and commonplaces that make communication effective and possible for the rhetorical agent. For an agent it is possible to choose strategically within the many possibilities of a discourse. Discourses can allow for rhetorical creativity and, therefore, for possibilities of developing or changing the discourse. A strategic agent can be enabled to strategically choose between discourses when discourses are recognised and their functions understood.

To be a rhetorical agent, as a teacher, means to have the ability and capacity to influence others. Yet there are limitations. Language, traditions, texts and communicative practices can all enhance or limit the capacity of a rhetorical to influence others. Teachers typically will be inscribed in a multitude of political and pedagogical discourses and therefore, express different and competing agencies in direct conflict with each other—sometimes undermining their possibilities and sometimes strengthening their positions as agents. This article tries to identify and discuss some agencies that are central to teaching in discourses of globalisation in influential educational texts. What controversies, dilemmas and paradoxes can be identified?

24.3   Global Teacher Agency and the Emerging of a New Open Society

Peters (2010) argues that an open science economy is emerging in the knowledge society where science and knowledge are emerging as global public goods. A new public sphere is in global creation. Open source models of knowledge, science and education have emerged as new and positive trends in the light of the crisis of neoliberal globalisation. Policies and innovations of open source, open access and open publishing are themselves subversive and are challenging commercial business models of authorship and publishing, and are raising new questions on content development processes. New digital technologies create changes in production and consumption. In the scholarly field, this open science economy allows for the integration of new electronic research models, open journals, cheap distribution and global access, to mention a few. It allows coproduction, real-time and dynamic update. According to Peters, this marks the existence of a new global public good that emerges out of global science and knowledge, which furthermore rests on an ethic of coproduction and sharing of goods, services, opinions and knowledge.

To be a rhetorical agent of science, of global sharing and the distribution of knowledge, is raising new ethical and democratic demands on teachers. It is an agency based on new technology, policies and economies of openness. Peters (2010) introduces the concept of "techno-political economy of openness" in his article. He promotes the importance of three elements, which are overlapping and historically related: politics of openness, economics of openness and technologies of openness. All of these elements have practical, political and normative implications in educational policy texts, and have shape the new rhetorical agencies of teachers.

Let me introduce an example from the Norwegian core curriculum that shows a combination of these concerns. The new global science and vastness of knowledge production and its distribution present new threats in the form of "Scientific analphabetism" or "Scientific Illiteracy". The government introduced vital curriculum goals to address the potential problems of globalisation and science dependency in society. Open technology, global mass culture, new economy and a politics of openness demand a new agency in teachers. A vital part of this rhetorical agency of teaching relates to the ethical and global democratic demands of educating pupils to be a part of an international culture of learning that equips them for new universal endeavours.

> The flows between nations – of ideas and instruments, of capital and commodities, of materials and machines – have become more extensive, formidable and inexorable. [...]
>
> A research-based society risks becoming increasingly driven by technology. The flow of technological facts and findings requires learning to avoid "scientific illiteracy" – the inability to comprehend words like "gene splicing", "ozone layer" or "immune system", and what social consequences they augur.
>
> Networks of information are continuously being augmented; networks that bind together firms and organizations, countries and continents, are constantly being built. [...]
>
> The international culture of learning links humanity together through the development and use of new knowledge to better the human condition. Adults living now and the young growing up today must acquire the vision and wisdom which [to] equip them for such universal endeavors, especially those that can help the world's destitute. (KUF 1993, pp. 27–28)

These curriculum demands for primary and secondary education in Norway also deeply affected teacher education. There was a strong government demand for the training and involvement of teacher students in scientific methods and theory, the use of modern technology, and the combining of national teacher training with studies abroad, all in an extended for of training to address these education challenges.

Together with the demand for the development of a global teacher agency, requiring sharing, global orientation and the use of new technology, a quite contradictory demand was also introduced which become, particularly during the 1990s, a demanding strongly government-controlled agency.

24.4   The State as a State of Mind: The Teachers as State Agents

A stronger emphasis on the teacher as a rhetorical agent was implemented in the national curriculum, together with the global agency. This was a controversial act. The agency of globalisation was challenging, but a rather free and open rhetorical

agency for the teachers to interpret and enforce, allowing them significant autonomy, although with little support and backup from the government. National
concerns, regarding globalisation in the 1990 s though, led to an impoverishing of
teacher agency through their losing autonomy to centralised control over curriculum, teaching methods and subject matters. Teachers were expected to be scripted
agents of a detailed national curriculum. A political counter-reaction to the politics
of openness was initiated in parallel to the need to master it goals. The double focus
on both a global and a national discourse created paradoxical agencies for teachers.
This paradoxical political reaction can be explained using Popper' (1995) classical
theory of the open society and the typical counter-reactions to it.

In *The Open Society,* Popper not only forms the arguments of the need for an
open society, he also identifies typical reactionary reflexes and the restorative
policies that can occur as a reaction against this openness and relativism (Trippestad
2009). These counteractions are also interesting when it comes to understanding the
kind of agency nation-states try to implement as a means of managing teachers'
reactions to globalisation and openness. Popper diagnoses typical destructive or
critical reactions to openness, which also seem to be traits that characterise educational policies in many countries during the 1990s and 2000s. The first reaction is
an attempt to arrest change by values and cultures of the past. The other
counter-reaction looks to control future development by planning, science and
carrying out social experiments on a grand scale. Often these two reactions combine. Popper names both these reactions as *utopian social engineering.* Utopian
social engineering uses strong regulations to control the way in which agents
implement their discourses. They are either obligated to play the role of rhetorical
agents of a tribal or nationalistic culture that involves the task of arresting development, or they are obligated to play the role of scripted rhetorical agents of a
quasi-scientific planning regime promising to lead countries into desired
future-states.

Popper claims utopian engineering to be an archetypical, philosophical, organisational and political reaction to Heraklit's influx: to the notion that all there is, is
in movement, is changing or is in a state of transition. Knowledge, power or
governing no longer express clear objectives or sovereign ground within the
epistemological domain. On the upside, this means a society is more open to debate,
democracy and individualism. But these paradigmatic intellectual changes also
mean that society is more uncertain of itself. So openness creates tensions and
feelings of risk in relation to a need for control. Such tensions can be easily
identified in Norwegian policies over the last 20 years. But they also seem to be
typical national responses to the openness of globalisation the world over.

According to an article by Wang Jianjun, these tensions seem to be an important
experience with the "reform and opening-up policy" in Chinese curriculum reforms

During the 30 years after the 'reform and opening-up policy' was announced in 1978,
curriculum reform in Mainland China has been continuously facing the tension between the
demand of change pushed by the changing domestic and international context, and the
cultural and ideological tradition – old and new. (Wang 2010, p. 1)

The attempt to arrest change is, according to Popper (1995) often based on a notion of development and change as a form of decay of an original shape or golden age of a society or a state. The typical goal of restorative policies is to bring society back to its original shape and/or its golden age. This is *the arrested state,* where there is an attempt to bring development and movement under control through the use of the historical ideals and values. The safety of religion, collectivism, law and order, myths, traditions and group commitments are typical ingredients in these attempts to master the feeling of risk and uncertainty that can preoccupy an open society.

In Norwegian educational policies of the late 1980s and 1990s, such reactions were typically a part of rhetoric, diagnosis and policymaking. As reactions to what Peters (2010) names as the exercising of technologies of openness, one sees emerging dramas and metaphors describing the existing conditions in policy documents as being representative of decay and threats. A clear withdrawal to religious and national metaphors, myths and authoritarian figures comes into play.

In a foreword to the book *Den digitale revolusjonen* (The Digital Revolution), Gudmund Hernes, the Church, Education and Science minister at the time, claimed that the geopolitical notion of the nation was weakened by the new technological revolution and the new global public. In his opinion, the significance of both time and place are reduced within the context in which opinion-making takes place. A political diagnosis within this regime reacted against exactly the state Peters names as a techno-political economy of openness.

> We are, in fact, in a new technological revolution, which again creates tension between the base and the superstructure. […] Technically, soon films, music, books, journals and paper can be directly distributed from producer to consumer. […] This reduces the economic significance of time and space. The systems that bind people together are not connected to physical space. People can, to an increasing extent, work anywhere; communicate independently of working hours, between organisations and across national borders. […] Funnily enough, it seems that people become more nationalistic the less the nation, as an organisation, is capable of being sovereign over the technology that shapes our lives. The problem is, therefore, how to gain sovereignty at a different level. (Hernes 1995, pp. 25–26, authors translation)

On the basis of the diagnosis that globalisation causes the formation of a heterodox situation at national level, an important political strategy that has to do with the will to gain central control over national identity and common culture emerges. This politics of the new knowledge society was, in part, understood as a state of mind.

Teachers were required to be obedient and loyal rhetorical agents for the new knowledge society. First, this rhetoric obligation could be seen in the demands made on teachers in higher education. It was a typical restorative and conservative knowledge reaction. Knowledge policy demanded focus on core knowledge to control and arrest the negative effects of influx. One of the most important dramas and threats is the notion of the knowledge explosion. The new and massive production of knowledge threatens basic understanding, classical science and the common reference ground.

But new data and aged facts do not mean that knowledge is something of the past. On the contrary, basic knowledge becomes more important. […] the basic theoretical doctrines are decisive – both for interpreting new information and to govern the search for new facts. […] Production of new knowledge makes it more necessary than ever to know these fundaments of understanding. The great stream of discoveries and findings demands basic knowledge – systems for understanding and action – now more than ever. Without this systemic knowledge, the knowledge explosion will lead to confusion and despair. The flow of ideas will be disorderly if the referential frames that can give them meaning are missing. (Universitet og Høyskoleutvalget and Hernes 1988, p. 9, authors translation)

A restorative and conservative view of knowledge, university ideas and a back-to-basics strategy was put forward to meet the knowledge explosion. It was both an orthodox and an idealistic reaction. The policy documents promote the importance of core knowledge, traditional values, classic science and religious ideas of the past as key elements for controlling the modern flow. In the rhetoric, we find metaphors of place, architecture and construction symbolising order, solidity and stability against all metaphors depicting shifts, disorder and movement that are a consequence of the knowledge explosion and knowledge society.

There was also a vital discourse on how new global mass culture and global media influence threatened national unity and common opinion-making.

The media technology cuts through national borders and spreads an international mass-culture. […] But when the world becomes one and the same public, that is related to a global monoculture, the question of national uniqueness and cultural preservation are raised in a new and radical way. […] In the same way the knowledge explosion demands stronger concentration on basis and core knowledge, and common scientific values, international-ization demands that we give importance to our own culture to preserve the diversity in the world community. (Universitet og Høyskoleutvalget and Hernes 1988, p. 16, authors translation)

Such a classical political reaction to influx can also be clearly identified in cur-riculum texts for primary and secondary education.

When transitions are massive and changes rapid, it becomes even more pressing to emphasise historical orientation, national distinctiveness and local variation to safeguard our identity. (KUF 1993, p. 29)

The central government took a firm grip on curricula, teaching methods and cur-riculum development in the 1990s. The motive for creating a common reference and grounds for association for all people through the national curriculum was clearly expressed and exemplified with the headline *Common References in a Specialized Society* in the core curriculum.

Common background knowledge is thus at the core of a national network of communi-cation between members of the community. It is the common frames of reference, which make it possible to link what one sees, reads or hears, to a shared, tacit mode of thinking. It makes it possible to fathom complex messages, and to interpret new ideas, situations and challenges. Education plays a leading role in passing on this common background infor-mation – the culture everybody must be familiar with if society is to remain democratic and its citizens sovereign. Education must, therefore, provide the fertile soil for cultivation of coherent knowledge, skills and outlooks. (KUF 1993, pp. 26–28)

The role of teachers as rhetorical agents of a national cultural state was emphasised. The nation state was to be understood as a state of mind. The political discourse set up a rhetorical agency in a detailed curriculum, which was bound by law. In the chapter *The Role of the Teacher and Educator*, the teacher is portrayed as an agent with both a capacity and the skills to persuade. Furthermore it was thought that this agency should be a national agency, using the capacity to forcefully deliver to pupils national traditions, myths, history, religion and heritage.

> The good teacher is master of the subject – his or her section of our common cultural heritage. [...] To explain something new implies mooring it to something familiar. This is accomplished by the teacher using expressions, images, analogies, metaphors and examples which convey meaning to the pupil. [...] A good portion of this the pupils have in common, from our broad cultural heritage which provides a sounding board for communication, dialogue and learning.
>
> The cultural baggage that learners carry with them, from the home, local community, or earlier schooling, determines which explanations and examples have meaning. Pupils from other cultures do not share the common Norwegian heritage. Good teachers, therefore, use many and varied images to make a point or demonstrate a common pattern, and draw material and illustrations from the diverse experiences of different pupils. Further, a good school places emphasis on broadening the pupils' common store of associations because it aids simple and succinct communication. (KUF 1993, p. 20)

While the global discourse is narrated as threatening, the national discourse is given rhetoric of stability, order and responsibility. The local is given mostly an instrumental value as pupils backgrounds need to be taken into consideration when explaining other and higher forms of knowledge, as building blocks toward a higher national—and then global—understanding, and as a mere pedagogical tool in the hands of the skilled teacher.

24.5   Teacher Agency as Structuring Well-Tempered Selves

The political concern regarding the riddle of globalisation versus the national and the local is not a typical Norwegian trait. Ken Robinson—government advisor, for different countries, on education and change—clearly expresses such concerns on behalf of a lot of governments in his famous animated speech in 2010.

> Every country on earth, at the moment, is reforming public education. There are two reasons for it. The first one is economic. People are trying to figure out: How do we educate our children to take their place in the economies of the 21st century? How do we do that given that we can't anticipate what the economy will look like at the end of next week? [...] The second one is cultural. Every country on earth is trying to figure out: How do we educate our children so they have a sense of cultural identity and so that we can pass on the cultural genes of our communities while being part of the process of globalisation? (Robinson 2010)

One answer to this riddle might come from the notion of shaping the pupils personalities or skills such that they are able to master the drift and shifts that characterise globalisation and the knowledge society. In Norwegian policies, this motive had already been expressed in the 1990s.

> Since the topography of society – its basis – split the nation, we in the council of the king need to unite. The grip of the statesman must be this; what is dissolved by the natural infrastructure, we need to correct by affecting the structure of the personality. (Hernes 1992, p. 36, author's translation)

New right wing governments and the new reform in 2006—*Kunnskapsløftet* ("The knowledge lift")—removed, in part, the detailed curriculum and decided to focus more on the development of basic skills and competencies of pupils. They gave schools more freedom to develop their own local curricula. A teacher agency of developing basic skills and competencies in pupils was demanded: An agency to develop skills to master and deal with the flow of globalisation under surveillance of national testing and accountability regimes.

Another, but similar master strategy of the global drift can be found in Britain. In his famous speech on Britishness, Tony Blair put forth "unchanging" values to master a changing world; a rediscovery (or reconstruction) of an open British identity and common self-interest as instrumental keys to release the potential and solve the problems of the nation state in a globalised world.

> We are living through a period of unprecedented change. [...] New ideologies of personal liberation and opportunities for self-fulfillment, made possible by social and economic change, are transforming traditional social structures and turning some inwards to themselves, rather than looking outward to the nation and the state. [...] What is the answer to such a challenge? Not to retreat into the past or cling to the status quo, even if it cannot sensibly be justified; but to rediscover, from first principles what it is that makes us British and to develop that identity in a way in tune with the modern world. [...]
>
> I believe few would disagree with the qualities that go towards that British identity; qualities of creativity built on tolerance, openness and adaptability, work and self-improvement, strong communities and families and fair play, rights and responsibilities, and an outward looking approach to the world – that all flow from our unique island geography and history. (Blair 2000)

Arguments such as these form teacher agencies that are quite paradoxical in terms of the sorts of personalities, skills and identities that teachers are to structure and implement in pupils. Let me give you an example from the Norwegian curriculum that is quite contrasting to the demand for stability, identity and community.

> Education shall qualify people for productive participation in today's labour force, and supply the basis for later shifts to occupations as yet not envisaged. It should develop the skills needed for specialized tasks, and provide a general level of competence broad enough for re-specialisation later in life. Education must ensure both admission to present-day working and community life, and the versatility to meet the vicissitudes of life and the demands of an unknown future. Hence, it must impart attitudes and learning to last a lifetime, and build the foundation for the new skills required in a rapidly changing society. (KUF 1993, p. 5)

While national cultural and identity politics seeks stability, roots, national feelings and community, the rhetoric of the market and the economy demand a flexible individual adapting to an ever-changing environment. Miller (1993) analyses these paradoxes in the formation of the individual in his book *The Well-Tempered Self*. According to Miller, we are in a cultural-capitalistic state which is dominated by two major discourses. First, a capitalistic-economic discourse that has change, development, profit and wealth as its themes. This discourse identifies and produces individuals who are utilitarian and selfish, who are trained to seek profit and are willing to adapt to the ever-changing environment of the market. Under metaphors of marketing, corporation, development, production and consumption, identities as worker, employer and consumer—a creative, flexible and changeable individual—are set up for the citizen to develop, in order to expand the economy.

On the other hand—there is a political discourse that tries to produce citizens who are moral, with feelings of community and societal spirit—both in the public sphere and in private life. Stability, cultural identity and recognition of the community of politics, its institutions and representations are central themes within this discourse. Miller (1993) points out that these paradoxical discourses have important functions in forming a well-tempered and docile self. According to Miller, the state needs to produce a sense of oneness among increasingly heterogeneous populations because political systems are under question by new social movements and the internationalising of cultures and economics. The state works to create loyalty to market economics, to parliamentary democracy and a sustainable society through the formation of cultural citizens who can be docile and efficient participants in this cultural-capitalistic state.

For Miller (1993), a key concept of this global cultural-capitalistic state is to implement a feeling of ethical incompleteness in the individual. The individual is trained to strive hard within different discourses and is invited to unite the contradictory discourses in his/her personality. The subject goes on an endless seminar with it selves and in their process of reflection will be managed to manage it (govermentalitè). Teacher agency, in light of these discourses, will be an agency of structuring personalities and skills to both the economic and the cultural-political discourses, and to train individuals in reflections to implement ethical incompleteness so that the individual is managed to manage him or herself in this mix.

24.6   The Teacher as a Bildung Agent

Influential sociologists have critically challenged the promotion of globalisation as being a mere positive force and constructive social process for most humans. Zygmunt Bauman (1998) claims that powerful stockholders from global economic, corporate and political institutions promote a globalisation of self-interest. Bauman points to the emergence of new inequalities and injustices. Globalisation can leave areas and people behind in disorderly, jobless and hopeless environments.

Globalisation can dismantle religious traditions and national institutions, often with devastating results on individuals, nations and groups.

Christopher Lasch (1995) claims that there is a threat to democracy and the nation state from modern elites that refuse to accept traditional limits being inflicted upon them. New economic and meritocratic elites create their own networks and intuitions, often with competing ambitions and goals for the nation, their culture and their people. The challenges of globalisation on the nation state are a concern needed to be considered carefully. As analysed by Benedict Anderson (1983) in his classic *Imagined Communities*, the nation, on the one hand, has created disasters like no other institutions in history. On the other, it has handled challenges of mass education, economy, health, identity, culture and community with a success like no other institution. A globalisation dismantling of nation-state institutions could have a devastating impact on important public welfare systems, identity and community makers.

Formulating our global experience so far: we have had a global discourse without necessary institutionalisation to deal both with its full potential and the problems it brought. The nation-state reacts to it in quite a schizophrenic way. Elites can misuse it. It can create an unbalanced and inharmonious globalisation, with the potential to leave large groups behind—challenging cultures, identities and nations —in a potentially destructive way. This is the challenge for creating global educational cooperation, sharing and understanding between countries, educationalists and cultures. A strong belief in globalisation underestimates the still important functions of the nation state. On the other hand, nation states react in a quite schizophrenic and insufficient manner to the many facets of globalisation.

Robertson (1995) introduces the concept of glocalisation in his classic *Glocalisation: Time, Space and Homogeneity–Heterogeneity*. According to Robertson the term "glocal" is a blend of both the local and the global. It sprung out of the business jargon of the 1980s. The idea of glocalisation is connected to micromarketing—tailoring and advertising goods on a global basis to increasingly differentiated local and particular markets. Robertson criticises the polarised concept of the global and the local, and invites the reader to a more dynamic understanding of the concept. I am here inspired by his challenge to see the local in the global and the global in the local.

A glocal educational teacher agency and philosophy must be built upon respect for the individual and the local, with an understanding and respect for the history, and the political and cultural institution of a country or state, while, at the same time, realising a common universal understanding, interconnectedness and the humanistic potential of globalisation. All these elements are necessary in an international corporation of education. *The Glocal Teacher* is a vision of such an educational institution. The philosophy of glocal teaching draws its influence from the bildung tradition in European educational philosophy, from public theory and from ancient roots in Greek philosophy.

The bildung tradition focuses on education along three normative lines (Slagstad et al. 2003). The first was the thought of an education that enabled the pupil to develop himself when encountering means that could have good educational effect on the character. The goal of education should be to get the individual to develop personal judgment, autonomy, self-decision-making and self-activation, and have the courage to use the judgment such that they are able to come out of self-inflicted and unenlightened helplessness and powerlessness. This thinking reminds us of the Confucian thought of the relationship shared by learning, reflecting and action.

The importance of stimulating teachers and students in such a way has been a trait developed through different periods in Chinese educational reforms and the results have been characterised by Xioawei Yang as representing an undoubted leap in quality

> The past thirty years witnessed a very clear picture of the teaching reform: the focus switched from knowledge and skills to the non-intelligence factors such as interest and affection (…) The fundamental value of teaching is to enhance every student's independent, initiative and healthy development, and every specific subject and comprehensive curriculum should demonstrate its unique irreplaceable values. In other words, every subject would produce a unique influence on individuals' spiritual growth, because it presents facts and knowledge, contains the methods and strategies of thinking, and brings students some unique experience during their learning. (Yang 2010, p. 5)

Xiaowei Yang promotes an even stronger emphasis on these internal aims of education as a key factor for lifelong learning that will be needed in the future. He says

> The public and parents value Enrolment Rate (升学率) so much that we accordingly tend to neglect the internal aim of education – to promote the foundational qualities of every individual and help them to acquire the ability to teach themselves. Therefore, we have to rethink the value orientation of the school reform, and re-examine the gains and losses of the teaching reform against it. In the future reform, we must pay more attention to the fostering of the non-intelligence factors and general abilities such as interest, aspiration, habits and character, which are beneficial to lifelong learning, so as to realise the potential role of the basic education as the foundation of students' lifelong learning and development (Yang 2009). This new orientation may become a new focus and direction of the teaching reform in mainland China. (Yang 2010, pp. 6–7)

The Chinese experience and results, as described by Yang (2010) should inspire Europe to revitalise its bildung tradition. The combination of spirit and knowledge, in the bildung tradition in Europe, was believed to be achieved through stimulating the individual in his local surroundings to meet and use art, tradition, history, music and literature in the development of a wise and comprehensive judgment. The local, by this thought, is a vital ingredient in a rhetorical teacher agency—to foster and inspire pupils to local self-empowerment, personal judgment and action in a global age. The local can be a window to the global. As stated by the English philosopher Francis Bacon (1605): A wider horizon is often seen by looking at the landscape through a small window than by standing in the wide landscape trying to see what is behind all the small windows. Sharing local knowledge openly and globally brings voice, variety and difference to globalisation.

The second principle of the bildung philosophy was enlightenment of the individual in relation to society as demos and ethnos—to the people, culture, history and the political institutions that one is a part of. This implies an agency of teaching through giving knowledge and skills to pupils to understand and cultivate one's own community and nation state—its traditions, language, music and art (Herder, Humboldt, Schleiermacher) and the political institutions, laws and contracts of society (Rousseau, Kant). This rhetorical agency needs to encourage the use of personal judgment, rationality and speech in respect and relation to a national, common cultural, public or political sphere. It is relevant to see how this might be a vital ingredient today in glocal teacher agency. This refers to an idea of an agency of preserving the variety of culture and traditions among nations in a global age, and also inspiring and training pupils for public life. It means an obligation to take care of well-functioning institutions and functions of the nation state, intrepid in the face of new challenges, and to develop them.

In a globalised age we are not only inhabitants of a nation state, but live also as world citizens in a globalised world. The teacher, therefore, must be an agent of the world citizen, ready to educate pupils of the common nature of the human being and his or her potential. A glocal agency must recognise common global threats and challenges, and create connectedness and understanding between personal, economic, cultural and national boundaries to develop mankind in a common respect for each other. This form of agency must be grounded in humanity and in the universal human condition.

The individual and the local can be found in the universal. In between nations and the state, we can find universal or commonly desired political or economic conditions or solutions. And in the global, the particular and the local can be focused on.

The glocal teacher, in the light of a bildung tradition and the globalisation era, must teach students the personal and the local, the polis and the common culture, and the global and the universal, to create a harmonious and balanced education. It means viewing the public, pupils and students positioned in a multitude of overlapping meanings and texts, technologies and messages implied in the personal, local and global, at the same time, empowering them to be meaning creators and to use their judgment in all spheres.

References

Anderson, B. (1983). *Imagined communities: Reflections on the origin and spread of nationalism.* London: Versto.

Bauman, Z. (1998). *Globalization: The human consequences.* New York: Columbia University Press.

Blair, T. (2000). *Tony Blair's Britain speech, Guardian 28.03.2010.* http://www.guardian.co.uk/uk/2000/mar/28/britishidentity.tonyblair

Hernes, G. (1992). *Læreboka fra godkjenning til forskning. Fra godkjenning til forskning.* Oslo: NFF Seminarrapport.

Hernes, G. (1995). Innledning ved statsråd Gudmund Hernes. In H. Gundersen (Ed.), *Den digitale revolusjonen.* Oslo: KUF.

KUF. (1993). *Core curriculum for primary, secondary and adult education Norway.* Oslo: The Royal Ministry of Education, Research and Church Affairs.

Lasch, C. (1995). *The revolt of the elites and the betrayal of democracy*. New York: W. W. Norton & Company.

Miller, T. (1993). *The well-tempered self: Citizenship, culture and the postmodern subject*. London: John Hopkins University Press.

Peters, M. A. (2010). The virtues of openness in higher education. In S. Marginson, P. Murphy & M. A. Peters (Eds.), *Global creation: Space, mobility and synchrony in the age of knowledge economy*. Peter Lang Publishing.

Popper, K. (1995). *The open society and its enemies* (Vol. 1). Plato, London: Routledge.

Robertson, R. (1995). Glocalization: Time–space and homogeneity. In M. Fetherstone, S. Lasch & R. Robertson (Eds.), *Global modernities*. London: Sage Publications.

Robinson, K. (2010). Changing educating paradigms. *RSA animate*. http://www.youtube.com/watch?v=zDZFcDGpL4U

Slagstad, R., Korsggaard, O., & Løvlie, L. (2003). *Dannelsens forvandlinger*. Oslo: Pax.

Trippestad, T. A. (2009). *Kommandohumanismen. En Kritisk analyse av Gudmund Hernes' retorikk, sosiale ingeniørkunst og utdanningspolitikk*. Ph.D. thesis, University of Bergen, Bergen.

Trippestad, T. A. (2014). The rhetoric of experience and the importance of teaching. In V. Ellis & J. Orchard (Eds.), *Learning teaching from experience. Multiple perspectives an international contexts*. London: Bloomsbury Academic.

Universitet og Høyskoleutvalget, & Hernes, G. (1988). *Med viten og vilje*. Oslo. Forvaltningstjenestene.

Wang, J. (2010). *Curriculum reform in mainland China 1978–2008: Change, maintenance and conflicts*. Shanghai: ECNU.

Yang, X. (2010). *Practise reform and theory reconstruction*. Shanghai: ECNU.

Author Biography

Tom Are Trippestad is a PhD in science theory, professor in pedagogy and former director of Centre of Education Research at Bergen University College. He has done research on education reforms and governance, rhetoric of reforms and teacher professionalism. He teaches pedagogy in teacher education in all levels.

Chapter 25
The Marketization of Teacher Education: Threat or Opportunity?

Geoff Whitty

25.1 Introduction

Teacher education has often been a target for reform. In recent decades, the dominant mantra as purveyed by OECD and McKinsey, and adopted by governments around the world, has been that improving the efficiency and equity of schooling depends on getting and keeping good teachers. This has pointed to a need to raise the quality of entrants to the teaching profession and improve the quality of teacher education programmes. The conventional wisdom has been that we should recruit better qualified students to teacher training courses, increase the length of teacher training courses, make teacher training courses more academically rigorous, incorporate teacher training colleges into universities and enhance government and/or professional regulation of the training system.

25.2 The Case of England

England has fitted this model from the 1970s onwards as most teacher training colleges were incorporated into multi-faculty higher education institutions and especially since 1984 when the then Conservative government of Margaret Thatcher established a Council for the Accreditation of Teacher Education (CATE) to review all initial teacher training providers and recommend whether they should receive accreditation to provide courses leading to Qualified Teacher Status

G. Whitty (✉)
University of Newcastle, Callaghan, Australia
e-mail: tedpggw@hotmail.co.uk

G. Whitty
Bath Spa University, Bath, England, UK

© Springer Nature Singapore Pte Ltd. 2017
M.A. Peters et al. (eds.), *A Companion to Research in Teacher Education*,
DOI 10.1007/978-981-10-4075-7_25

(QTS) (DES 1984). Her Majesty's Inspectorate of Schools (subsequently Ofsted) was charged with reporting to CATE on the quality of provision and whether courses met set criteria in terms of their content, a role that was significantly expanded over the subsequent 20 years under successive governments. From 1992 onwards, a succession of sets of competences and standards for trainees to meet were drawn up by government and its Teacher Training Agency (and successor bodies) and there was growing emphasis on partnerships between higher education and schools and increases in the time all trainees needed to spend in school. At the same time, a number of new routes to QTS were introduced. A combination of the teaching standards and the Ofsted inspection criteria ensured that all routes were, to a significant extent, preparing teachers for a common concept of professionalism.

With colleagues, I was involved during the 1990s in a research project, funded by the UK's Economic and Social Research Council, investigating the ways in which these reforms were being implemented and their impact on teacher professionalism. Among its first outputs, in 1992, was a topography of initial teacher education in England and Wales (Barrett et al. 1992). In what follows, I explore just how much the landscape of teacher education in England has changed in the subsequent 20 years. Since Wales has had a devolved administration since the late 1990s, its approach to education, including teacher education, has begun to diverge significantly from the English system described below.

When the New Labour government left office in 2010, there were three main routes into school teaching in England, all of which led to QTS, which (with some limited exceptions) was a requirement for anyone teaching in a publicly maintained school, including most Academies (autonomous schools rather like Charter Schools in the USA):

Partnerships led by higher education institutions (HEIs)
These provided both undergraduate and postgraduate qualifications. The former included three- and four-year BEd and BA(QTS) courses. The number of undergraduate trainees had decreased from 9,770 in 1998-99 to 7,620 in 2007-08. Most trainees, around 27,000 a year, now followed one-year postgraduate courses, called the Postgraduate Certificate in Education (PGCE).

School-centred initial teacher training schemes (SCITTs)
These were consortia of schools that offered training towards the PGCE. The consortium itself arranged the training and channelled the funding for placements, as compared with HEI-led partnerships, where the university arranged placements and channelled the funding to schools. Nevertheless, universities validated the SCITTs' PGCEs.

Employment-based routes (EBITTs)
These involved 'on-the-job' training and fell into three groups: the Graduate Teacher Programme (GTP), Overseas Trained Teacher Programme (OTTP) and TeachFirst, a scheme to bring high-flying new graduates into teaching in challenging schools. They all led to Qualified Teacher Status (QTS) and some, including TeachFirst after some initial hesitation, also led to a PGCE, an identical qualification to the other routes.

In total, in 2009–10, there were 234 providers offering routes into teaching, including 75 HEI-led partnerships, 59 SCITTs and 100 EBITTs. However, some of these providers had a very small number of trainees. HEIs were responsible for the vast majority of trainees: in 2009–2010, for example, they trained 78.7% of the recruits to teacher training programmes, compared with 16.7% in EBITTs and 5.6% in SCITTs.

25.3 Towards a Marketized Model?

The quality of most provision, as judged by Ofsted, was good (HMCI 2011). Indeed, it had only recently been claimed by a House of Commons select committee that England had some of the best qualified and best trained teachers ever. Even so, there were those who argued, not entirely unreasonably, that standards were still not good enough compared to the country's leading competitors internationally. In this vein, in 2010, the incoming Secretary of State for Education in the newly elected Coalition government, Michael Gove, decided that things needed to change.

His White Paper in 2010 on *The Importance of Teaching* proposed to

- Continue to raise the quality of new entrants to the teaching profession, by ceasing to provide Department for Education funding for initial teacher training for those graduates who do not have at least a 2:2 degree; expanding Teach First; offering financial incentives to attract more of the very best graduates in shortage subjects into teaching; and enabling more talented career changers to become teachers.
- Reform initial teacher training so that more training is on the job, and it focuses on key teaching skills including teaching early reading and mathematics, managing behaviour and responding to pupils' Special Educational Needs.
- Create a new national network of Teaching Schools, on the model of teaching hospitals, giving outstanding schools the role of leading the training and professional development of teachers and head teachers.

(Roberts and Foster 2015)

The government's implementation plan the following year announced:

- A significant expansion of the Teach First programme
- Launch of the School Direct programme and increased prioritisation of ITT funding on providers that are successful at involving schools in training programmes
- The launch of the Troops to Teachers programme for ex-service personnel
- Ongoing reform of Ofsted's inspection framework for ITT providers
- Making successful completion of professional skills tests (literacy and numeracy qualifications) a prerequisite for beginning an ITT course.
- More targeting of student financial support on student teachers in particular subject areas, and on those with higher pass marks for their first degrees.
- Launching a small number of University Training Schools, which will deliver three core functions: teaching children; training teachers; and undertaking research.

(Roberts and Foster 2015)

The Coalition government thus encouraged more school-led initial teacher training, including the creation of around 500 Teaching Schools, schools highly rated by

Ofsted in teaching and learning that could potentially take over leadership of teacher training from the universities. The extent to which, the scale on which and the speed at which this was likely to happen remained unclear but there was no doubt that this was the direction of travel favoured by the government and that some Conservative Ministers would have liked—and would still like—to see the majority of new teachers trained under school-led routes.

The key policy for realising this change was School Direct, a scheme which, in simple terms, involved training places being allocated to schools who then cashed places in with a university or another accredited teacher training provider to deliver a training package for a teacher. When the School Direct policy was first announced, it was going to be restricted to about 500 places and was designed to meet teacher supply needs that were not being met through existing mechanisms. Subsequently, it has been reinvented as the main vehicle for putting schools in the lead in teacher training and making universities more responsive to the needs of schools. Its projected share of postgraduate trainee numbers was increased to over 9,000 for 2013–2014, rising to over 17,000 for 2015–2016, as shown in the table below.

	2011–12	2012–13	2013–14	2014–15	2015–16
HE provider	28,669	28,841	26,790	23,095	22,224
School Direct	0	772	9586	15,254	17,609

(Quoted in Roberts and Foster 2015)

Even though, in these allocations of teacher training numbers, HEI-led partnerships still had a majority of places, some individual HEIs lost virtually all their own allocated student numbers and became dependent on gaining School Direct contracts for survival. However, the overall allocation figures were inflated by government to enable School Direct to grow where it could while allowing HEIs to maintain a presence in case the new approach failed to meet teacher supply needs. In practice, School Direct grew rapidly in some subjects and regions but not in others. In 2015, the new Conservative government abandoned the allocation system and proposed that all teacher training providers could recruit as many trainees as they wished until a national cap on numbers was reached. Whether this will result in meeting teacher supply needs remains to be seen. However, it seems to represent a further move away from centralised workforce planning towards a more marketized approach.

As a result of all these changes, the landscape of initial teacher education in England has become even more varied than it was in 2010. Although there is some dispute about what constitutes a 'route', a 'course', a 'qualification' and what is merely a 'funding mechanism', the Association of School and College Leaders identified what it called the following 'Routes into Teaching' by 2015:

SCITT http://tinyurl.com/k2wblyv
Led by a network of schools that have been given powers to run their own training independently
Course generally lasts a year

School Direct (Unsalaried) http://tinyurl.com/lx8fw46
Designed by a group of schools in partnership with a University or SCITT with the schools themselves recruiting
Generally lasts a year

School Direct (Salaried) http://tinyurl.com/mxuxpy8
As above
Earn a salary while training and school covers the cost of achieving QTS

Teach First http://tinyurl.com/mgswvba
Earn while you train and work in a challenging school in a low-income community
Minimum 2.1 degree. Two year course

Troops to Teachers http://tinyurl.com/ol8pxau
For Service Leavers in the two years before or the two years after leaving the Armed Forces
With a degree – one year course through SD Unsalaried, Salaried or University led PGCE
Without a degree – two year, school-based, salaried teacher training programme

Researchers in Schools http://tinyurl.com/lfxm4rt
For researchers who have completed or are finishing their doctorate
Two year salaried programme in six regions

Undergraduate route http://tinyurl.com/kvmaf7d
Study for a degree & teacher training at the same time. Minimum C at GCSE in English and Maths plus Science for Primary or Key stage 3 and 2 A levels (check with individual Universities)
Full time 3-4 years, part time 4-6 years

Postgraduate route (PGCE) http://tinyurl.com/ofl2jjz
If you already have a degree, one year course at a University or College with school placements

(Annex to ASCL 2015)

Small wonder that a review of initial teacher education conducted for the Coalition government during 2014 concluded that the system had become 'complex' and information about it 'confusing'—and therefore called for clearer information about choices on official websites. It also recommended the development of a 'framework of core ITT content' (Carter 2015).

Although the review found examples of good practice across all routes, Conservative Ministers often imply that professional wisdom lies exclusively in schools. An extreme version of this position was stated by Michael Gove just before he was moved away from Education to another post:

> In the past, the education debate has been dominated by education academics - which is why so much of the research and evidence on how children actually learn has been so poor. Now, thankfully, teachers are taking control of their profession's intellectual life, taking the lead in pioneering educational research and creating a living evidence base…

(Quoted in Whitty 2014)

Meanwhile, there was an additional development. The Coalition government decided that its autonomous so-called Free Schools would not have to employ qualified teachers and could instead employ whoever head teachers regard as most suitable. It subsequently made a similar change for Academies, which now constitute a majority of all secondary schools in England and an increasing proportion of primary schools. Thus, the officially prescribed training requirements will apply to a diminishing number of schools in future, as will the National Curriculum. There has also been a significant deregulation of training requirements in the further education sector. So it is plausible to see this as the start of a radical deregulation of teacher education, effectively ending even the core national professionalism associated with the pre-service award of QTS, creating a series of 'local professionalisms' associated with individual or groups of schools and leaving teacher supply and teacher quality to market forces (Whitty 2014).

A further development has been the emergence of what I have termed 'branded' professionalisms. Autonomous schools, called Academies and Free Schools in this English case, are increasingly being linked into chains, like the ARK and Harris Academy Chains. Some of these are seeking also to take on more responsibilities for teacher training either by becoming accredited providers themselves or by franchising other providers to train the particular sorts of teachers they want. This could produce distinctive ARK branded teachers or Harris branded teachers, to join an existing example of 'branded professionalism' in the form of Teach First teachers.

Interestingly, this all moves English teacher preparation towards the scenario favoured in the 1980s and early 1990s by New Right pamphleteers of both neo-liberal and neo-conservative varieties. As I said at the time in my inaugural lecture at Goldsmiths College in May 1991:

> The neo-conservatives regard most of the existing curriculum of teacher training as dispensable, so in their ideal world the prescribed curriculum would only be a good dose of 'proper subject knowledge'. The neo-liberals would allow schools to go into the market and recruit whomever they wanted, but would expect them in practice to favour pure graduates…over those who have 'suffered' from teacher training…
>
> There is general agreement amongst both groups that, say, two or three years of subject study in a conventional vein is sufficient academic preparation for would-be teachers and any training necessary can be done on an apprenticeship basis in schools…
>
> (Whitty 1991, p. 5)

Twenty years later, of course, the attack on mainstream teacher education came not from New Right think tanks but from government Ministers like Michael Gove, who seemed to have learned the script.

25.4   English Exceptionalism?

To date, the dominant orthodoxy described at the beginning of this chapter continues to hold sway in much of the world. However, some of the trends described here for England are beginning to emerge elsewhere in local form, suggesting that marketization or deregulation may be more than just an English or even just a New Right approach to teacher education.

Alternative routes have long been a feature of the teacher preparation landscape in the USA. After 1999, the number of US teachers licensed through these routes climbed steadily, so that by 2005 about one-third of all new teachers entered through such routes. Teach for America (the inspiration if not the model for Teach First in England) is now the major provider of new teachers in some US States. When he was Federal Education Secretary in Barak Obama's Democratic administration, Arne Duncan commented that teachers deserved better support and training than mainstream teachers colleges today provide. One of the strongest US examples of branded professionalism, the New York-based Relay Graduate School of Education, a collaboration by three Charter Management Organizations (the equivalent of English Academy Chains), explicitly positions itself as a response to 'a nationwide failure by most university-based teacher education programmes to prepare teachers for the realities of the twenty first century classroom' (Relay GSE publicity 2013).

The marketization of teacher preparation in the USA is certainly accelerating (Arnett 2015). In many cases, new routes can opt out of the mandates that govern traditional university-based provision. So far, though, deregulation has been less significant in the US than in England, not least because Charter Schools (the equivalent of English Free Schools and Academies) make up a much lower proportion of school provision and, in most States, they remain more subject to government regulation. Nevertheless, in 2015, a more radical proposal to deregulate entry to teaching was proposed by Scott Walker, the Republican Governor of Wisconsin, although it eventually had to be watered down in response to widespread public opposition.

25.5   Hybrid Systems

The reality in many countries is however likely to be the creation of hybrid systems with varying degrees of both marketization and central regulation. Many countries still conform to a model where schools and teachers appear to have been 'empowered' to develop their own 'local' professionalisms, but centrally specified competences and standards mean that local professional freedom is actually quite tightly constrained by the demands of the 'evaluative state' (Whitty 2000).

It seems unlikely that extreme deregulation will prevail even in England, particularly as current Ministers move on. Nevertheless, the chances of initial teacher education being maintained in all current higher education institutions are remote. Some will leave the scene as result of judgements about their quality or the impact of competition. It is also likely that some research-intensive universities will decide that the new arrangements for university involvement in teacher training will prove just too onerous to justify remaining in that area of work.

A few years ago, in January 2013, I predicted that, as a result of the developments discussed here, some English higher education institutions would abandon teacher education, some would embrace School Direct with enthusiasm, private 'for profit' providers as well as branded Academy chains would enter the field and compete nationally, some key 'full service' Education departments would remain in universities and new institutional, regional, national and international partnerships would develop. Most of these things have since happened, including the entry of Hibernia College Dublin into the online teacher training market in England, albeit with limited success, and interest in teacher education being shown by large global companies like Pearson plc.

David Bell, former Permanent Secretary at the Department for Education under Michael Gove, has offered his own reflections on the English education reforms of recent decades. He believes that England is probably moving towards a 'system of many small systems' in education:

> 'Messiness' in terms of structures will be a natural by-product of radical structural reform as we move from a standardised national system to a system of many small systems. I don't have a single, solution to offer, nor do I necessarily think there should be one, as the end-point of these school reforms hasn't been reached yet.
>
> (Bell 2012, p. 6)

He was thinking here of small systems of schools, such as Academy Chains and school federations, which might take on some of the functions of local authorities and might also choose to take a major role in teacher preparation, with or without substantial university involvement, as befits local circumstances. Interestingly, Bell's use of the term 'messiness' resonates with Stephen Ball's characterisation of post-modern education systems as 'untidy' (Ball 2011).

25.6 Global Trends

Although the new model being pioneered in England is unlikely to become the norm, the conventional wisdom is no longer sacrosanct. The alternative narrative that teachers learn best on the job will have significant implications for the many countries in the world where the orthodox trajectory is still a distant dream. Even some well down that path have begun to consider alternatives. For example, Hong Kong has recently retreated from the 'all trained, all graduate' policy that it introduced in 1997.

At the same time, some of the new approaches are gaining global traction, not only through the work of global companies like Pearson, but also philanthropic endeavours like the Gates Foundation and Teach for All, which brings together national initiatives like Teach for America, Teach First and Teach for Australia.

Meanwhile, the OECD has stimulated a developing discourse about 'clinical practice' models of teacher preparation amid concerns about how best to prepare teachers for contemporary schools in terms of the relationship between theory and practice. This is potentially much more constructive than the parochial debates in England and America about the institutional location and leadership of teacher education, although it has sometimes been used as ammunition in those debates.

OECD (2010) argued that

> the best-performing countries are working to move their initial teacher-education pro-grammes towards a model based less on preparing academics and more on preparing professionals in clinical settings, in which they get into schools earlier, spend more time there and get more and better support in the process. (p. 238)

In England, Michael Gove suggested that such approaches involved giving aspiring teachers 'the opportunity to work in a great school from day one, just like student medics in hospitals—learning from more experienced colleagues and immediately putting their new skills into practice'. Not only did this somewhat misrepresent the nature of medical training, it also ignored the extent to which the best such programmes entail not just 'clinical practice', but 'research informed clinical practice'. Indeed, in the same document cited above, OECD (2010) itself pointed out that 'some countries, notably Shanghai-China and Finland, provide teachers with the research skills needed to enable them to improve their practice in a highly disciplined way' (p. 239).

Clinical practice of this sort is one of the ways in which research literacy might be better incorporated into teacher education wherever it is located, as argued in a recent report from the British Educational Research Association and the Royal Society of Arts. Significantly, that report concluded by calling for an end to the false dichotomy between university and school-based approaches to initial teacher education (BERA 2014). And, in this spirit, a recent report on successful clinical practice models in the USA embraces both university- and non-university-based programmes (UTRU 2015).

25.7 New Opportunities?

Although marketization and globalisation are often seen as a threat to university-based teacher education, they may also open up some new opportunities. For years teacher educators have complained about increasing standardization constraining innovation and creativity, with unintelligent accountability systems replacing trust in professional judgement. Even the government in England says that the intention of its reforms is to enhance professionalism, so why not see whether the new-found freedoms can be used to further alternative educational projects? The development of research-rich teacher education programmes, such as those that involve research-informed clinical practice, could be one such case in point.

Additionally, there is an urgent need for evidence about the efficacy of the growing diversity of approaches to teacher education in relation to the challenges of preparing teachers for twenty-first century schools. Not only is the attack on conventional approaches to teacher preparation frequently ideologically driven and lacking in a strong evidence base, so too is its defence. Research on the impact of different modes of teacher education and their implications for teacher professionalism, along the lines of that carried out in England in the 1990s (Furlong et al. 2000), now needs to be undertaken as a matter of urgency in the changing landscape outlined in this chapter. The Institute for Fiscal Studies and the UCL Institute of Education have already embarked on a project to compare the costs and benefits of different models of teacher education in England (see Allen et al. 2014). Meanwhile, Bath Spa University and Birmingham University are engaged in broader comparisons of the nature and impact of different approaches. Similar studies are planned in Australia and in the USA, where colleagues at Teachers College Columbia University are undertaking some research specifically on the nature and impact of 'research-rich' programmes of teacher preparation.

References

Allen, R., Belfield, C., Greaves, E., Sharp, C., & Walker, M. (2014). *The costs and benefits of different initial teacher training routes*. London: Institute for Fiscal Studies.

Arnett, T. (2015). *Start-up teacher education: A fresh take on teacher credentialing*. San Mateo, CA: Clayton Christensen Institute for Disruptive Innovation.

ASCL. (2015). *Teacher supply and initial teacher education*. Leicester: Association of School and College Leaders.

Ball, S. J. (2011). Attempting a theory of untidiness: An interview with Stephen J. Ball. *Studia Paedagogica, 16*(2).

Barrett, E., Barton, L., Furlong, J., Miles, E., & Whitty, G. (1992). *Initial teacher education in England and Wales: A topography*. London: Goldsmiths College.

Bell, D. (2012). *Reflections on reform (tribal annual education lecture)*. London: Tribal.

BERA. (2014). *Research and the teaching profession: Building the capacity for a self-improving education system*. Final Report of the BERA-RSA Inquiry into the Role of Research in Teacher Education. London: British Educational Research Association.

Carter, A. (2015). *Carter review of initial teacher training (ITT)*. London: Department for Education.

Department of Education and Science. (1984). *Initial teacher training: Approval of courses (circular 3/84)*. London: DES.

Furlong, J., Barton, L., Miles, S., Whiting, C., & Whitty, G. (2000). *Teacher education in transition: Re-forming professionalism?* Buckingham: Open University Press.

HMCI. (2011). *Annual report of Her Majesty's Chief Inspector of education, children's services and skills 2010–11*. London: Ofsted.

OECD. (2010). *Strong performers and successful reformers in education: Lessons from PISA for the United States*. Paris: OECD.

Roberts, N., & Foster, D. (2015). *Initial teacher training in England.* Briefing Paper No. 6710, 7 July. London: House of Commons Library.

UTRU. (2015). *Clinically oriented teacher preparation.* Chicago, IL: Urban Teacher Residency United.

Whitty, G. (1991). *Next in line for the treatment? Education reform and teacher education in the 1990s.* London: Goldsmiths College.

Whitty, G. (2000). Teacher professionalism in new times. *Journal of In-Service Education, 26*(2), 281–295.

Whitty, G. (2014). Recent developments in teacher training and their consequences for the 'University Project' in education. *Oxford Review of Education, 40*(4), 466–481.

Author Biography

Geoff Whitty taught in schools before working in teacher education in universities. He joined the Institute of Education in London in 1992, serving as its Director between 2000 and 2010. He now holds a Global Innovation Chair at the University of Newcastle, Australia and a Research Professorship at Bath Spa University, UK.

Chapter 26
Postfeminist Educational Media Panics, Girl Power and the Problem/Promise of 'Successful Girls'

Jessica Ringrose and Debbie Epstein

26.1 Introduction

For the past 20 years, the story of 'failing boys' and 'successful girls' has been seen regularly in the media. In reaction, and in contrast, to feminist concerns around getting girls into 'masculine' subjects and higher education during the 1980s, we have since the 1990s we have been faced with an overarching story about boys' chronic underachievement and 'failure' at school. Debbie Epstein and colleagues began charting the dominance of this narrow understanding of gender and achievement in education in their now—'seminal' book Failing Boys? (1998). From the United Kingdom and elsewhere in the Global North to South Africa in the Global South, this trope can be found over and over again up to the contemporary moment.

In this chapter, we position the debates around 'failing boys' as a postfeminist educational media panic (Ringrose 2013). This is because these debates typically invoke and blame feminism for boys' demise, and call up a second, binary figure, the overly 'successful girl', who has put masculinity into crisis (Walkerdine et al. 2001). We use the framework of postfeminism to think about how stories of both crisis and celebration over girls' educational success continue to take shape. First, we explore how neo-liberal 'discourses' (that is ideas, ways of understanding the world, that often seem like common sense) of feminine educational success have influenced what we call a postfeminist media panic that constructs girls as wholly successful in the Global North, through a review of British policy on gender and education and news media reporting. We explain how the news media whips up

J. Ringrose (✉)
University College London, London, England, UK
e-mail: j.ringrose@ioe.ac.uk

D. Epstein
University of Roehampton, London, England, UK
e-mail: debbie.epstein@roehampton.ac.uk

© Springer Nature Singapore Pte Ltd. 2017
M.A. Peters et al. (eds.), A Companion to Research in Teacher Education,
DOI 10.1007/978-981-10-4075-7_26

sensationalism and panic in order to make the topic news worthy. Second, we explore the globalising reach of postfeminist notions of 'girl power' and the celebratory promise of how girls' educational success will enable wider transnational economic revolution, through a consideration of the corporate social media campaign, the 'Girl Effect', in the Global South. We argue this campaign also operates through media forms that generate the promise of salvation from difficult structural conditions. Through these examples, we argue binary understandings of gender formations (girls vs. boys) and the reductive marshalling of gendered 'affect' (for instance emotional tenors of crisis vs. celebration over girls) can be usefully challenged through an intersectional feminist approach.

26.2   Postfeminism: Neo-liberalism, Femininity and Education

Postfeminism has been theorised as a set of discourses and political practices grounded in assumptions that gender equity has now been achieved for girls and women in education, the workplace and the home (McRobbie 2004, 2008; Gill 2007; Gill and Scharff 2011). Angela McRobbie (2004: 4), a key figure in theorising postfeminism, suggests it is characterised by a set of discourses that 'actively draw on and invoke feminism … in order to suggest that equality is achieved, [and] in order to install a whole repertoire of meanings which emphasise that it is no longer needed, a spent force'. Postfeminist discourses also promote the idea that girls/women have now won total equality or have even surpassed boys/men, so that feminism is considered to have 'gone too far' and unleashed girls'/women's competitive and aggressive qualities and power (Ta 2004). Moreover, girls'/-women's over-success is positioned as having been won at the expense of taking away something from men (especially working-class men in the British context) (Walkerdine et al. 2001). Postfeminism as a concept describes, then, both the cultural diffusion of feminism into the public domain and a backlash against feminism, due to fears and anxieties over the shifting gender 'order'.

A key component of postfeminism is the positioning of girls as the primary benefactors and winners of globalisation in the twenty-first century (Harris 2004; Aapola et al. 2005). Anita Harris's powerful thesis in Future Girl is that girls and notions of girlhood have become a projective vehicle for contemporary desires about what is possible in the late-modern world of complex globalised de-industrialised societies—girls are, it seems, seen as bearing and being responsible for contemporary aspirations and emotions. Harris argues young women are 'constructed as ideal flexible subjects; they are imagined as benefiting from feminist achievements and ideology, as well as from new conditions (of education and work) that favour femininity and female success' (Harris 2004: 8). Davies and Bansel (2007: 248) suggest that neo-liberalism is characterised by 'the transformation of the administrative state, one previously responsible for human well-being, as well as for the economy, into a state that gives power to global corporations and instals apparatuses and knowledges through which people are reconfigured as productive economic entrepreneurs of their own lives'. The neo-liberal ethos is, they argue, to change, transform, adapt, reinvent and self-perfect towards the goal of marketability and consumption. These tenets, are, however, highly gendered; consider, for instance, the modern beauty industry and make-over television as an example of pedagogy around how girls and women (not exclusively but more so than men) are called upon to make-over their bodies and selves (Skeggs and Wood 2012). Thus, Gill and Scharff (2011: 7) suggest in their work on postfeminist 'new femininities' that postfeminism works in concert with neo-liberalism in relation to gender, suggesting that both discourses thrive on a current of individualism, seeing 'freedom' (economic, sexual, etc.) as now especially open to girls and women in the wake of feminist gains—think of the many advertising slogans, promulgated since the 1990s, about women and girls' 'having it all' which have been promulgated since the 90s.

In this chapter we discuss how, through ideas about feminine educational success, neo-liberal discourses have directly promoted and fed into postfeminist notions about female empowerment, through ideas about feminine educational success, with girls positioned as the chief benefactors of increased access and opportunity to educational—and therefore it is assumed economic—rewards (Harris 2004). One of the primary ways this works is through touting girls' academic successes over boys in schooling.

26.3 Constructing Boys' Educational Underachievement as a Fact

A widespread common-sense agreement about UK boys' educational 'underachievement' has continued to dominate contemporary UK policy debates on gender and education in the nearly 20 years since Epstein et al's Failing Boys (1998). Girls have been understood to have overtaken boys in several types of testing and performance audits that have become normative in neo-liberal schooling climates. Educational debates in the United Kingdom have been shaped by undisputed 'facts' of a gender gap, facing boys, a gap that varies little year to year (Skelton and Francis 2009):

- Girls outperform boys at ages 7, 11 and 14 in National Curriculum assessments in English; achievements in maths and sciences are broadly similar.
- Girls are more successful than boys at every level in GCSE.
- Girls are succeeding in 'boys' subjects' such as technology, maths and chemistry (adapted from Jackson 1998: 78).

As Arnot and Phipps (2003) suggested, these claims about statistical patterns of female performance were touted as one of the most significant transformations in the history of social inequality in the [UK United Kingdom]. In the UK the lasting impact of the failing-boys' panic in the United Kingdom was visible in the 4-year (2000–2004) Department for Education and Skills 4-year (2000–2004) project 'Raising Boys' Achievement Project', which was developed as a 'holistic' school resource, focused entirely on 'helping boys succeed'. The gender gap has thus come to refer in a 'common-sense' way to the 'disadvantage' facing boys. In the 2007 UK Labour governments' policy document, Gender and Education: The evidence on pupils in England (DfES 2007) is almost entirely preoccupied with boys' achievement and offering strategies for boy-tailored learning strategies in schools. Significant issues of behaviour and safety are raised in the report (school discipline problems, school-leaving and truancy) but only as key 'indicators' of racialised (black) and working class boys' 'failure to attain'. Every issue is reduced to the outcome of attainment. What happens conceptually is that gender—as a relation or as a culture or as an identity—is never able to be addressed; gender is only a measure/variable for what it can tell us (or not) about achievement. The assumed logic of the gender gap continued to dominate the UK Coalition government's Department for Education website guidance (2010), which assured the reader:

> The National Strategies, at primary and secondary … provide support for techniques to tailor teaching and learning to the needs and interests of boys … include[ing] setting clear objectives to help them to see exactly what they have to learn, and interaction with the teacher in the whole-class sessions keeps boys motivated and involved. (DfE 2010: OO)

In the next section we aim to show how the news media selectively picks up on these binary gender discourses about educational achievement that pit girls against boys, congealing into a dominant yet reductive pattern of gender stereotyping and the narrative of 'failing boys' and 'successful girls'. We want to pay attention to the psychosocial or affective anxieties (that is the public waves of feeling which enliven fantasies about the state of gender and education) that are generated in the news media (Skeggs and Wood 2012).

26.4   What Is a Postfeminist Educational Media Panic?

Segal (1994) talks about abiding 'gender anxieties' over shifting and destabilising feminine and masculine 'roles' and subject positions. This relates to transformations in contemporary, late-modern cultures characterised by de-industrialization and the partial break down in the conventional 'sexual contract' and gender roles in the private and public spheres, as theorised over twenty years ago by Pateman (1988). Blackman and Walkerdine (2000), drawing on Cohen discuss 'moral panics' as public anxieties generated when behaviours are found 'deviant'. Gender and queer theory shows us that gendered and sexuality behaviour is feared if it jars against (hetero) normativity (if it troubles or disturbs the normal heterosexual matrix or order) (Butler 1990). Moral panics as contagious and shared group anxieties are a useful framework for thinking about the affective dimensions and dynamics of how public discourses circulate and feed 'public feeling' around gender and sexuality (Cvetkovich 2012). Moral panics are largely constructed through the media, as we explore below, but come to shape and inform policies and practices around social issues like such as health or and education.

One of the primary sites where gender anxieties around girls' and women's 'appropriate' place in society circulate and take force is through representations of feminism in contemporary news media (Mendes 2011). These work to mould broader ideas about femininity, gender and education, 'shap[ing] public opinion by directing readers to adopt particular policy priorities and assign responsibility for political issues' (Cohen 2010: 106). Ringrose (2013) connects up these ideas of moral panics in the news media—which involve a battle of ideas over rightful 'female' and 'male' rightful places in the educational pecking order—and post-feminism—the idea that feminism has won equality for girls and women, but may have gone too far in the other direction at the expense of boys (see also Ta 2004). She Ringrose coined the notion of 'postfeminist panics' over educational issues. Assembling postfeminism, panic, education and the media together helps us understand how the power of some educational discourses (ideas) about particular groups of girls and women or boys and men grip the public imagination and individual psyches in ways that are often exploited in news media.

Instead of taking at face value the policy and educational discourse about failing boys and successful girls at face value, then the concept of postfeminist panic moves our attention to consider why particular concerns emerge and become remarkable, sensational and news worthy. In Postfeminist Education (2013), Ringrose considers in depth two further postfeminist panics in education. Besides the figure of the 'successful girl', she also discusses the construction and treatment of the 'mean girl' through popular culture and educational interventions on rela-tional aggression and bullying, and she explores the figure of the 'sexy girl' and the heightened public anxieties over the 'sexualisation' of girls at the same time that the topic of girls' sexualities and desires are a 'silenced' or 'missing' 'dilemma' at school and in sex-and-relationship education (Fine and McClelland 2006). Whilst there are many sorts of gendered and sexualised panics over, for instance, gay rights to marriage or women entering the priesthood, in this chapter we focus on the panic related to girls' and women's successes in education—waves of postfeminist anxiety that emerge when the naturalised 'gender order' in education is disturbed in ways, either explicitly or implicitly, attributed to feminism (McRobbie 2008).

26.5 Is the Future Female? UK News Media's Panic Over Girls' Success

As we saw above, in the nearly 20 years since Failing Boys? was published, the gendered postfeminist panic over girls' success has proliferated. In the Anglophone West, we have been faced with a 'postfeminist' onslaught in the news media of discourses about 'girl power' in the news media in the Anglophone West (Harris 2004; McRobbie 2004; Ta 2004). For instance, we have increasingly seen common-sense 'presumptions' that gendered equality in education and work mean the labour market, and schools and universities have been 'feminised'. In 1997 the UK left wing think tank, Demos, noted the 'future is female' (see, and cf., Segal 1994), suggesting women were set to enter the labour market in huge numbers and that the kinds of work which stress characteristics ascribed to femininity—service, empathy, communication, nurturance and, to be looked-at-ness would be the ones in demand (Walkerdine et al. 2001). Ten years later, Ian Pearson, 'futurologist' for British Telecom, Ian Pearson, confirmed the worrying trends in the 'gender order' (Connell 1987), with the headline: 'The future is female' (BBC News, 23 April 2007), which warned of a future dominated by female-oriented jobs that will 'displace' men. Similarly, Harvard psychologist Dan Kindlon's book, Alpha Girls: Understanding the New American Girl and How She is Changing the World (2006), outlines the mythical qualities of the new 'successful girl', suggesting the 'Alpha girl', as a new hybrid that embodies the best traits of masculinity and femininity, is poised to change the world, economically, politically and socially, as a new hybrid that embodies the best traits of masculinity and femininity. Kindlon suggests this new hybrid is somehow confident, assertive, competitive, autonomous, future-oriented and, risk-taking, as well as collaborative, and relationship-oriented, but not obsessed with boyfriends or her physical appearance. The UK broadsheet, The Times, carried an article based on the book and titled: 'Free at last: alpha teenage girls on top' (Allen-Mills 2006, 15 October), which stated

> [A]alpha girls [are] the new breed of … schoolgirl growing up free of gender stereotyping and ideological angst. They are the daughters of the feminist revolution, but they see no need to become feminists themselves because they know they are smarter than boys.

We can witness the formation of a 'figure' of feminine success evoked in such media representations, which shape how gender is understood as a binary construction where in which girls and boys are pitted against one another in abstract and decontextualised ways, and in which one gender's success means the other's failure in a kind of zero-sum game which requires one side to lose and the other to win.

In the article 'David Willets: feminism has held back working men' (Prince in The Daily Telegraph, 1 April 2011) the then Minister for Universities and Science in the UK Coalition government, is described as arguing in his recent book, The Pinch, that the rise of equal rights for women has left working-class men struggling:—'[A] as a result of better education for women, households now contain two people who are either both financially successful or struggling to get on'. Mr Willett's is also quoted as saying

> The feminist revolution in its first-round effects was probably the key factor. Feminism trumped egalitarianism. It is not that I am against feminism, it's just that it is probably the single biggest factor.

The minister argued that the feminist revolution was 'the single biggest factor' contributing towards economic decline in the United Kingdom, because women, who had previously had very few educational or vocational opportunities, were suddenly able to pursue a career. Instead of challenging inequality, feminism has 'trumped egalitarianism'. Moreover, middle-class women's 'assortative' mating rituals have meant they apparently 'choose' successful men, thereby worsening social divides. We find an excellent example of a postfeminist discourse wherein feminism is 'taken into account' (McRobbie 2008), whilst it is simultaneously blamed for social problems of women being overly—successful at the expense of (particularly working-class) men. This is a form of divide-and-conquer tactic that works effectively to divert our attention from issues of post-industrial decline in the UK United Kingdom as a result of late-modern global capitalism (shifting the jobs from UK manual labourers to more poorly paid developing-world workers) and the knowledge economy. Ignoring the Coalition government's 'wide-scale savage cuts in education, health and welfare ... on-going social and structural inequalities' and an associated increase in women's and children's poverty, this is an interesting strategy whereby feminism becomes the straw woman for economic and social demise. The postfeminist logics at work mean the Universities' minister of the United Kingdom was effectively blaming feminism for entrenching class divisions and hierarchies and even for overall economic decline in the United Kingdom.

Another aspect of the anxiety and panic over gender and education is that what is called the 'feminization' of schools and schooling, which is seen as negative and harmful (emasculating) for boys (Skelton and Francis 2009). The advent of more feminine modes of testing (fewer 'sudden death' exams), and 'softer' subjects (like sociology or drama) as spelling trouble for boys, has emerged repeatedly. In 2002 a columnist with The Daily Mail suggested that 'wholesale feminisation' had made the education system 'unfair and discriminatory against boys' (Phillips, 19 August 2002). Four years later, The Daily Mail published another story on how '[b]Boys are being failed by our schools', citing Dr. Tony Sewell who blamed a 'feminised' system and teachers who, instead of encouraging the development of 'male traits such as competitiveness and leadership ... celebrate qualities more closely associated with girls, such as methodical working and attentiveness in class' (Clarke, 13 June 2006). In addition to recommending recruitment of 'more male teachers, particularly to primary schools', Dr. Sewell is quoted as calling for the 'replacement of some coursework with final exams and a greater emphasis on outdoor adventure in the curriculum':

> We have challenged the 1950s patriarchy and rightly said this is not a man's world. But we have thrown the boy out with the bath water ... It's a question of balance and I believe it has gone too far the other way.

On 11 October 2008, The Daily Telegraph, in 'The future is female ...', similarly 'reveals' how women 'are poised to become the dominant force in the workplace over the next decade, paving the way for a dramatic feminization of society' (Sawer and Henry 2008). Although the article is about jobs, the educational discourse of

J. Ringrose and D. Epstein

failing boys is ushered into the dialogue by a psychologist quoted as imploring the government to take action with boys: 'Ministers must take note of these figures and do more to support boys at school to stop them falling off the ladder'. The statistics on the proportion of male primary teachers (13%) are also cited to underscore how 'many fear the imbalance has left young boys without positive role models'.

Similar headlines in 2010 proclaim: 'Eton head says UK education is failing boys', which cites the headmaster warning that the '… British system of education is failing to give boys the help they need and has become too focused on girls'. The headline statement is used to support a political goal of single-sex schools or classrooms because 'boys require a much more physical and active style of learning' (Ross in The London Evening Standard, 19 January 2010).

Another article, 'Girls think they are cleverer than boys from age four' (Shepherd in The Guardian, 1 September 2010), from a study on 'Gender expectations and stereotype threat', warns about the dramatic effects of teachers' poor expectations of boys, urging and urges teachers to stop using phrases like 'silly boys' and 'schoolboy pranks' for fear of its negative effects on boys' psyche and development. Robbie Hartley, the researcher, is quoted as saying 'gender bias' is normative, and educators have found it 'acceptable to pitch girls against the boys'. While it seems that Hartley is actually arguing against girl–boy comparisons in order to resist gender stereotyping, what is clear is that the broadsheet picks up and runs with the gender dichotomy, 'girls think they are cleverer than boys', as the sensational attention—grabbing headline.

These headlines are all examples of how the media works affectively to propel and renew gender binaries and hierarchies and to whip up anxiety and fear. The news stories position girls as being successful at the expense of boys—that is by taking something away something from boys and masculinity (Foster 2000). These binaries create stereotyping tropes that operate to mobilise affect and sentiment— we are invited to worry over boys as well as perhaps secretly celebrate an apparent victory for girls. These stories are useful emotively because they attract 'eyeballs' through familiar repetition and dramatic headlines provoking simplistic postfeminist notions where we see the damage wrought by empowered girls and women. But these media debates also have a much wider range of policy and practical effects/affects, which are explored in the next sections.

26.6 Questioning Postfeminist Panics in the Global North

In the period since the mid-1990s, education policy research has explored a terrain across the Global North that understands 'gender gaps' and sexism to refer almost solely to the need to help boys catch up to girls in school—with boys positioned as the new 'disadvantaged', a formation described by Lingard and his colleagues as a form of 'recuperative masculinity politics' (Lingard 2003; Lingard et al. 2009). Furthermore, a range of naturalised gender differences (like such as the belief that boys and girls learn differently) are re-asserted. These understandings are framed through by a narrow binary conception of gender, so that the unitary, essentialised category of 'girl' is simplistically pitted against the unitary, essentialised category of 'boy', which enables statistical claims to be made about girls' success. This stems from the particular logic of gender as binary quality residing in naturalised bodies, which can then be measured (Paechter 2006). Gender, taken as an essential quality residing in girl and boy bodies, can be added or subtracted—statistics can be formulated to (dis)prove gender parity in school and achievement in educational testing. This misses an understanding of gender as a socially constructed set of variable traits; rather than tying gender to naturalised 'sexed' bodies, it does not account for how femininity and masculinity are a set of qualities that are granted hierarchically valued attributes through historical and social processes, rather than tying gender to naturalised 'sexed' bodies (Butler 1993). It also radically decontextualizes gendered experiences of schooling and 'achievement' performance from a complex web of economic, cultural and material relations and conditions that shape educational outcomes.

Yet this focus on measuring gendered achievement in school as an essentialised variable has set the terms for a reactionary educational debate—failing boys/successful girls—educational debate and resulting in a set of policy formations for nearly two decades (Jackson 1998; Skelton and Francis 2009). As Epstein et al. asked nearly 20 years ago, and we have to keep asking still: 'which boys, which girls?' How do racialisation, class, economic background, neighbourhood, family context and multiple other axes of experience inform the (e)quality of educational experiences?

In the Global North the assumption that girls are 'not a problem' (and have no problems) in schooling spaces has resulted in the marked neglect of girls' experiences, and a failure to allocate resources to girls' needs in school (Crudas and Haddock 2005). For example, research has shown that many girls still face exclusion from schools, (Osler and Vincent 2003) not all girls are academically successful (Jackson 2006); for some girls (perhaps especially white, middle-class girls) striving for excellence can be damaging for their bodies and subjectivities (Evans et al. 2010); there are longstanding issues of gender and (hetero) sexualised-based bullying, aggression, harassment and violence facing girls (and some boys) at school (Duncan 2006; Keddie 2009; Payne 2012; Ringrose and Renold 2010); and the list could go on.

The dangerous mythologies of girls and women educationally 'on top' appears, however, to be continuing unabated, however, as seen in the massive uptake of the bestselling book, Lean In, where Sheryl Sandberg (2013) argues that sheer staying power has enabled female breakthroughs and triumph in the corporate world. Hooks (2013) launched a powerful black feminist critique of Sandler's thesis, pointing to the necessity for a sociological class/race/gender analysis of wealth, poverty and systemic obstacles missing from Sandler's arguments about particular (white, middle-class) women breaking through the corporate glass ceiling.

Hooks's critique is based upon anti-racist, postcolonial, black, subaltern and critical race feminist theories, and it is to here we need to (re)turn in order to think through the figure of the abstract (yet, white and middle-class?) girl who gains power through educational 'success'. Black feminists, for instance, have repeatedly illustrated the conceptual problems with gender analysis organised as a binary between an essential man/woman body that does not account for how gender is performed and experienced differently for different groups of women/men—so how is 'success' to be negotiated by black, female bodies (Mirza 1992). Such writers have consistently argued that different life and cultural experiences produce particular forms of masculinity or femininity, which people take up differently, and that such gender discourses are always differentiated by other 'intersecting' or 'articulating' axes of experience and identity/identification, such as race and intersectional analyses, derived from black feminism (e.g., Crenshaw 1991; Lykke 2010), insist that we engage with multiple social discourses, including those that are productive of social class/economic, race- and ethnic-based inequalities, so that we can understand how femininity is always racialised as white or black, or through ethnic and cultural categories. Feminisms must also be cognizant of the enormous economic disparities between the Global North and Global South, questioning any easy resolutions to the historical, social and political problems of 'development' and gender inequalities through education.

26.7 Questioning Postfeminist Promise in the Global South

In this final, brief section we aim to show how ideas about girls' success and girl power have spread out and been rearticulated in complex ways in non-Western contexts. We discuss how corporations and NGOs in the Global South are using postfeminist parables about the promise of girls' education as the route to economic and demographic salvation for the Global South (McRobbie 2008).

In the context of questions of gender and development, there has long been a trope in which educating women and girls has been regarded as a kind of 'silver bullet', which that could achieve a whole range of objectives, from preventing population growth (education as contraception), through the making of peace (women as doves) and to economic growth (women as workforce). What is shared by all these discourses is that educating girls and women is seen only in instrumental ways. In the 1990s the discourse of education as contraception for women was vigorously contested by a number of researchers in the area of gender, development and education (Unterhalter 2008). The contemporary version of this instrumentalist view of girls' education can be found amongst those NGOs and corporations that are using Western 'girl power' discourses to suggest that the liberation of girls is the human capital pathway to resolve national debt and find economic salvation (Koffman and Gill 2013; Switzer 2013).

One example of this we explore here is a global initiative, entitled 'The Girl Effect', promoted by a coalition of organisations, including Nike, the UN and the World Bank. This social media campaign is one of hopeful simplicities in which girls are positioned as an 'untapped resource' which can effect global change.

In brief, through a series of interactive websites, links, memes and short films, the campaign suggests that by investing in girls in the Global South through educational and entrepreneurial schemes for consumers in the Global North, Southern these girls will be economically empowered to save themselves and therefore their communities from pandemics crises such as starvation and disease. The promotional materials include statements like such as this: 'Girl Effect, noun: The unique potential of 600 million adolescent girls to end poverty for themselves and the world' (Koffman and Gill 2013: 88). Invest in a girl, the initiative suggests, and '"she will do the rest"', pulling herself, her family, her community and her country out of poverty.

The Nike Foundation has been publically criticised as oversimplifying a complex problem and shifting resources away from other approaches and from the company's own exploitative past labour practices. Feminist researchers suggest the 'Girl Effect' campaign relies on essentialist views of womanhood, depict women and girls in developing countries as "in need of saving". The campaign plays into stereotypes of women as natural caregivers and reinforced perceptions of 'women's work' and 'men's work', neglected crucial macro-economic issues, and prioritised the well-being of the economy over the well-being of women (Switzer 2013). Thus 'Girl Effect' combines the grammar of neo-liberalism, post feminism and the 'education as-development' imperative (Koffman and Gill 2013). Crucially, this type of campaign does not take into consideration men, boys and masculinity, and the relations of women and girls with their households and community often have the effect of overburdening women who are already responsible for childcare and all types of formal and informal labour. Girl's bodies become the locus of economic development as human capital investment in 'potential productivity'. Thus, we need to ask the following: Does the campaign address structural inequality and power imbalances? Does it focus on what girls can do for development, rather than what development can do for girls?

Switzer (2013) specifically explores how education enters into the 'Girl Effect' stories and the ways the idea of saving a nation through the human capital currently wasted in girls and women (constituted as too sexually reproductive too soon, and therefore as failed consumers) works in the campaign. The promotional materials position adolescent girls into 'diametrically opposed' figures, those who have access to schooling and therefore choice and autonomy (Global North) and those who are confined to 'reproductive peril' (Global South). Promoting institutional access to formal schooling for adolescent girls as a means for economic development serves neo-liberal aims to predict female productive and reproductive capacity by managing adolescent bodies and, thereby reifying postfeminist female exceptionalism as the singular 'solution' to global poverty. In so doing, the 'Girl Effect' narrative participates in the production of feminist development 'fables' by promoting a particular kind of (self)regulation—via formal schooling—of adolescent female sexuality, fertility and social reproduction. Girls' bodies become the locus of economic development as human capital investments in 'potential' productivity.

The 'Girl Effect' campaign aims to draw in successful Western successful consumer girls in as saviours of 'third world' girls (Koffman and Gill 2013)—the rich who can donate money to the cause. The campaign enacts 'a powerful fantasy for Western girls in particular to save "other girls" from patriarchal sexual slavery as "child brides", for instance, through a mechanics of erasure that ignores the politics of location of girlhood, leading ultimately to 'securing the status-quo" (Switzer 2013: 13). Through analysis of social media campaigns like the 'Girl Effect', we can see how affect is mobilised (powerful feelings are evoked) through fantasies about girls' successes, which comes in the wake of feminism and is therefore postfeminist. As Koffman and Gill (2013: 98) argue, the 'girl-powering' of development discourses have co-opted specific strains of feminist discourse. In emphasising the postfeminist idea that 'all the battles have been won' (for privileged women in the Global North) it further underscores the move to individualistic discourses that disavow structural or systemic accounts of inequality. Furthermore, capitalist pursuit of profit is described as being wholly compatible with feminist activism. Global corporations can safely claim that they are seeking to increase their company's profit and help girls at the same time.

26.8   Conclusion

In this chapter we have explored the global reach of the postfeminist figures of the failing boy and successful girl. In the Global North we find a simplistic story of losing boys and winning girls, a story which for two decades has manifested as a masculinity crisis over regarding boys and education in the West (Epstein et al. 1998; Ringrose 2013). The construction of naturalised, universal binary sex–gender differences is a key dynamic of postfeminist politics (Gill and Scharff 2011), which we have shown plays out through media debates on educational achievement. One of the most significant implications of the postfeminist discourse of successful girls is how it has shifted and reduced understandings of gender and education and caused a shift away from any feminist understandings of sexism as permeating the wider fabric of society—resulting in, to a recuperative masculinity politics focused on raising boys' achievement. We also illustrated the transfer and reconfiguration of postfeminist ideas about girls, education and 'girl power' into the Global South. We showed how the 'Girl Effect' media campaign re-formulates girls' presumed educational attainment and success in the Global North as the a magic bullet for economic prosperity in the Global South. It is implied that it is possible to solve 'Third World' debt and poverty by harnessing the economic capital waiting in the untapped, uneducated girl.

To counteract these reductionist postfeminist panics and promises, we have discussed the important tools of feminist intersectionality approaches for understanding power and difference. These perspectives are imperative in building 'educational feminisms' able to account for the intricate complexities of in how economic and material contexts shape gender in relation to class, race, sexuality, culture and more. Our hope is that these feminisms offer ways forward that resist being perpetually caught up in the gender binaries (girls versus boys)—and the affective turbulence of gendered crisis versus celebration surrounding girlhood and gender and education—operating in both the Global North and Global South through over-simplified postfeminist media panics versus fantasies of girl power, as we have explored.

References

Aapola, S., Gonick, M., & Harris, M. (2005). *Young femininity: Girlhood, power and social change*. Basingstoke, UK: Palgrave.

Allen-Mills, T. (2006). Free at last: Alpha teenage girls on top. October 15. http://www. timesonline.co.uk/tol/news/world/article600902.ece. Accessed July 15, 2008.

Arnot, M., & Phipps, A. (2003). Gender and education in the United Kingdom. *Paper commissioned for the EFA global monitoring report 2003/4, The leap to equality*. Available online at http://unesdoc.unesco.org/images/0014/001467/146735e.pdf

Blackman, L., & Walkerdine, V. (2000). *Mass hysteria*. London: Routledge.

Butler, J. (1990). *Gender trouble: Feminism and the subversion of identity*. New York: Routledge.

Butler, J. (1993). *Bodies at matter: On the discursive limits of 'sex'*. New York: Routledge.

Cohen, J. (2010). Teacher in the news: A critical discourse analysis of one US newspaper's discourse on education, 2006–2007. *Discourse, 31*(1), 105–119.

Connell, R. W. (1987). *Gender and power*. Cambridge: Polity.

Crenshaw, K. (1991). Mapping the margins: Intersectionality, identity politics and violence against women of color. *Stanford Law Review, 43*(6), 1241–1299.

Crudas, L., & Haddock, L. (2005). Engaging girls' voices: Learning as social practice. In G. Lloyd (Ed.), *Problem girls: Understanding and supporting troubled and troublesome girls and young women*. London: Routledge-Falmer.

Cvetkovich, A. (2012). *Depression: A public feeling*. London: Duke University Press.

Davies, B., & Bansel, P. (2007). Neoliberalism and education. *International Journal of Qualitative Studies in Education, 20*(3), 247–259.

Department for Education. (2010). *What is the department doing to address the gender gap?* http://www.education.gov.uk/popularquestions/schools/curriculum/a005576/what-is-thedepartment-doing-to-address-the-gender-gap. Accessed June 2011.

DfES. (2007). *Gender and education: The evidence on pupils in England*. London: Crown Copyright. http://www.ttrb3.org.uk/gender-and-education-the-evidence-on-pupils-in-england/

Duncan, N. (2006). Girls' violence and aggression against other girls: Femininity and bullying in UK schools. In F. Leach & C. Mitchell (Eds.), *Combating gender violence in and around schools*. Stoke-on-Trent: Trentham Books.

Epstein, D., Elwood, J., Hey, V., & Maw, J. (Eds.). (1998). *Failing boys? Issues in gender and achievement*. Buckingham: Open University Press.

Evans, J., Davies, B., & Rich, E. (2010). Schooling the body in a performative culture. In M. Apple, S. J. Ball, & L. A. Gandin (Eds.), *The Routledge international handbook of the sociology of education* (pp. 200–212). Abingdon: Routledge.

Fine, M., & McClelland, S. I. (2006). Sexuality education and desire: Still missing after all these years? *Harvard Educational Review, 76*(3), 297–338.

Foster, V. (2000). Is female educational 'success' destabilizing the male learner-citizen? In M. Arnot & J. A. Dillabough (Eds.), *Challenging democracy, international perspectives on gender, education and citizenship*. London: Routledge-Falmer.

Gill, R. (2007). Post-feminist media culture: Elements of a sensibility. *European Journal of Cultural Studies, 10*(2), 147–166.

Gill, R., & Scharff, C. (2011). Introduction. In R. Gill & C. Scharff (Eds.), *New femininities: Postfeminism, neoliberalism and subjectivity*. Palgrave: Basingstoke.

Harris, A. (2004). *Future girls: Young women in the twenty-first century*. New York: Routledge.
Hooks, B. (2013). *Dig deep: Beyond lean in*. Available online at http://thefeministwire.com/2013/10/17973/. Accessed November 19, 2013.
Jackson, D. (1998). Breaking out of the binary trap: Boys' underachievement, schooling and gender relations. In D. Epstein, J. Elwood, V. Hey & J. Maw (Eds.), *Failing boys? Issues in gender and achievement*. Buckingham: Open University Press.
Jackson, C. (2006). Wild' girls? An exploration of 'ladette' cultures in secondary schools. *Gender and Education, 18*(4), 339–360.
Keddie, A. (2009). 'Some of those girls can be real drama queens': Issues of gender, sexual harassment and schooling. *Sex Education, 9*(1), 1–16.
Koffman, O., & Gill, R. (2013). The revolution will be led by a 12 year old girl: Girl power and the global biopolitics of girlhood. *Feminist Review, 105*, 83–102.
Lingard, B. (2003). Where to in gender policy in education after recuperative masculinity politics? *International Journal of Inclusive Education, 7*(1), 33–56.
Lingard, B., Martino, W., & Mills, M. (2009). *Boys and schooling: Beyond structural reform*. Basingstoke: Palgrave Macmillan.
Lykke, N. (2010). *Feminist studies: A guide to intersectional theory, methodology and writing*. Abingdon: Routledge.
McRobbie, A. (2004). Notes on postfeminism and popular culture: Bridget Jones and the new gender regime. In A. Harris (Ed.), *All about the girl: Culture, power and identity*. London: Routledge.
McRobbie, A. (2008). *The aftermath of feminism: Gender, culture and social change*. London: Sage.
Mendes, K. (2011). *Feminism in the news: Representations of the women's movement since the 1960s*. London: Palgrave.
Mirza. (1992). *Young, female and black*. London: Routledge.
Osler, A., & Vincent, K. (2003). *Girls and exclusion: Rethinking the agenda*. London: Routledge-Falmer.
Paechter, C. (2006). Constructing femininity/constructing femininities. In C. Skelton, B. Francis, & L. Smulyan (Eds.), *The sage handbook of gender and education*. Thousand Oaks: Sage.
Pateman, C. (1988). *The sexual contract*. Cambridge: Polity Press.
Payne, E., & Smith, M. (2012). Rethinking Safe Schools approaches for LGBTQ students: Changing the questions we ask. *Multicultural perspectives, 14*(4).
Phillips, M. (2002). The feminisation of education. *Daily Mail*. http://www.melaniephillips.com/the-feminisation-of-education. Accessed November 17, 2013.
Ringrose, J. (2013). *Post-feminist education? Girls and the sexual politics of schooling*. London: Routledge.
Ringrose, J., & Renold, E. (2010). Normative cruelties and gender deviants: E performative e ects of bully discourses for girls and boys in school. *British Educational Research Journal, 36*(4), 573–596.
Ross, T. (2010, January 19). Eton head says UK education is failing boys. *London evening standard*. http://www.standard.co.uk/news/eton-head-says-uk-education-is-failing-boys-6730040.html. Accessed November 17, 2013.
Sandberg, S. (2013). *Lean in: Women, work and the will to lead*. London: Ebury Publishing.
Sawer, P., & Henry, J. (2008, October 11). The future is female, job figures show. *Telegraph*. http://www.telegraph.co.uk/news/uknews/3179265/The-future-is-female-job-figures-show.html. Accessed November 17, 2013.
Segal, L. (1994). *Is the future female? Troubled thoughts on contemporary feminism*. London: Virago.
Shepherd, J. (2010, September 1) Girls think they are cleverer than boys from age four. *The Gurardian*, http://www.theguardian.com/education/2010/sep/01/girls-boys-schools-gender-gap
Skeggs, B., & Wood, H. (2012). *Reacting to reality television: Performance, audience and value*. London: Routledge.
Skelton, C., & Francis, B. (2009). *Feminism and the schooling scandal*. London: Routledge.

Switzer, H. (2013). (Post)Feminist Development fables: The girl effect and the production of sexual subjects. *Feminist Theory, 14*(3), 345–360.

Ta, J. (2004). Girl power politics: Pop-culture barriers and organizational resistance. In A. Harris (Ed.), *All about the girl: Culture, power and identity* (pp. 69–78). New York: Routledge.

Unterhalter, E. (2008). Cosmopolitanism, global social justice and gender equality in education. *Compare, 38*(5), 539–554.

Walkerdine, V., Lucey, H., & Melody, J. (2001). *Growing up girl: Psychosocial explorations of gender and class*. Basingstoke: Palgrave.

Author Biographies

Jessica Ringrose is Professor of Sociology of Gender and Education, at the University College London Institute of Education. Her books include *Post-Feminist Education?: Girls and the sexual politics of schooling* (Routledge, 2013); *Deleuze and Research Methodologies* (EUP, 2013, edited with Coleman) and *Children, Sexuality and Sexualisation* (Palgrave, 2015, edited with Renold and Egan).

Debbie Epstein is Professor of Cultural Studies in Education in the School of Education at the University of Roehampton. She has pioneered educational research in the areas of sexuality, gender and race; school cultures; the spread and prevention of HIV, particularly in Southern Africa; wider questions of media texts and audiences; and aspects of pedagogy in the formal and hidden curricula.

Chapter 27
Helping Teachers and School Leaders to Become Extra-Critical of Global Education Reform

Martin Thrupp

Teacher education faces a big problem, or rather a series of interconnected ones. If teachers want to be of service to current and future generations, they need to understand our neo-liberal and globalising world and the positioning of educators within it. When teachers and school leaders are really well informed they will often challenge local elements of the global education reforms that pose a threat to public education systems (discussed in Part 4). But initial teacher education students and experienced teachers alike often find it difficult to tap into rigorous research ideas and findings given the abundance of material from neo-liberal advocacy groups and policymakers available through traditional or social media (Malin and Lubienski 2015). As well, since a lot of privatisation reform is quite subtle or 'hidden' (Ball and Youdell 2007), being aware of only the most obvious manifestations of reform will not be enough. Teachers could oppose reforms quite stridently but still not realise how they are gradually welcoming global education reform, sometimes referred to as the GERM (Sahlberg 2011), into their schools and classrooms.

There are great challenges for both initial and continuing teacher education to prepare teachers to be 'extra-critical', strongly searching rather that just a little bit so. In initial, teacher education the problems often start with finding space within reduced and increasingly managerial teacher education programmes to discuss the politics of education and probe the politically conservative perspectives that generations raised under neo-liberal governments increasingly manifest. Unless teachers are provided with the skills to question the politics of what they are reading, they may end up being influenced as much by the advocates of neo-liberalism as by those against the GERM. Once in the teaching workforce there are ongoing challenges for teachers to find space to think about the politics of their work, to interact with colleagues who have a less critical orientation, and to

M. Thrupp (✉)
University of Waikato, Hamilton, New Zealand
e-mail: thrupp@waikato.ac.nz

© Springer Nature Singapore Pte Ltd. 2017
M.A. Peters et al. (eds.), *A Companion to Research in Teacher Education*,
DOI 10.1007/978-981-10-4075-7_27

recognise and respond to how one's own practice may be being inadvertently hollowed out by the global education reform agenda.

In this chapter, I provide an overview of these concerns in one particular national and sector context, primary school teaching in New Zealand. Focussing on a specific context is helpful here because it allows us to consider how teachers respond to reform and take up the possibilities for contesting it alongside an assessment of the historical, social and political constraints and possibilities afforded by a particular setting. New Zealand is a small nation with only 4.5 million people and about 2000 primary schools and is a place where many global education reform developments are still relatively embryonic. This makes it much easier to see the interrelated issues affecting the potency of teacher education in New Zealand compared to larger systems with state or local authority level differences in policy and where there is often now a longer history of contested neo-liberal reform. The New Zealand history may be shorter but the education reform movement is gradually taking hold in New Zealand schools. The current Government led by Prime Minister John Key is into its third term and pushing on with a privatisation agenda as boldly but pragmatically as ever (Edwards 2015).

This chapter starts by considering some relevant features of the culture of primary teaching in New Zealand. Second, I note how changes in university-based initial teacher education provision and professional learning for practising teachers since the 1990s have reduced the opportunities for critically oriented discussion. Third, this has occurred against the background of a more general decline in the influence of universities on New Zealand teachers compared to the rise of business, philanthropic and media influences. Fourth, and related to all of the above, I discuss some specific examples of practices where New Zealand teachers are being critical but not critical enough. I conclude by noting actions that vigilant teachers can take, with or without the support of teacher educators.

27.1 Primary Teaching in New Zealand

During the decades after World War II, New Zealand primary teachers became acculturated into a distinctive and internationally regarded professional culture (Middleton and May 1997). This professional culture, many elements of which continue today (Fraser and Hill 2015), has been learner-centred with a broad and progressive approach to curriculum, pedagogy and assessment. It has been the result of educational politics and policies within a mostly public education system that, until recently, often sought genuine consultation with teachers and where teachers expected to be heard. Often their influence on policy has been through the New Zealand Educational Institute (NZEI), the sole teacher union for primary teachers and principals and one which most belong to.[1] Another significant

---

[1]Support staff in schools and early childhood teachers also belong to NZEI. There is another union for secondary teachers, the Post-Primary Teacher's Association (PPTA).

influence on the professional culture of New Zealand primary teaching has been the New Zealand Principals Federation (NZPF), most primary principals are members of this organisation as well. Teacher education mainly within Government-run teachers colleges (incorporated into universities since the 1990s) has also played an important role, as has the Government-run New Zealand Council for Educational Research (NZCER). That a single institution like the NZCER could be so influential reflects the intimacy of the New Zealand education system. Its small size has facilitated easy communication amongst schools, principals and teachers.

These features, along with being able to observe the experiences of other countries further down the track with global education reform, help to explain why New Zealand primary teachers have strongly fought the more obvious manifestations of GERM. Led by a generally unified NZEI and NZPF, primary teachers and principals have waged a number of feisty campaigns in recent years. One was against the introduction of a high stakes assessment system 'National Standards' from 2010, another fought against proposed increases in class sizes in 2011, and a third involved the rejection of a 2013 clustering initiative called 'Investing in Educational Success'. The class sizes campaign attracted public support and the Government quickly backed away from the proposal whereas the contestation of National Standards and Investing in Educational Success have been less successful in terms of shifting policy. The NZEI and NZPF have also campaigned more against global education reform more generally. As a result, most New Zealand primary teachers probably have some understanding of the GERM and concern about it.

Yet although the professional culture of New Zealand primary teachers has been robust, there are vulnerabilities. Teachers often fail to make connections between the global and the local whether through lack of analysis or through wishful thinking. Such lack of understanding may sometimes be self-serving within the context of a competitive, performative education policy environment but often it will be quite genuine. The shifts in teacher education as discussed below are unlikely to be helping. Another vulnerability is that teachers tend to give way where they believe others know better. As Locke and colleagues have noted, a teacher convinced that 'the authorative other knows best' is '…more likely to sacrifice autonomy out of deference to the expertise of the other and that other's judgement' (Locke et al. 2005, p. 564). Both of these vulnerabilities are relevant to the examples of New Zealand primary teachers not being critical enough discussed later.

27.2 Changes in University-Based Initial Teacher Education and Professional Learning for Practising Teachers

Nearly all primary initial teacher education (ITE) in New Zealand is still university-based but, in the same way that has been extensively documented in other countries such as England (see Furlong 2013), the proportion of programmes for primary teaching given over to papers most likely to raise education reform issues has been reducing. In the late 1990s, the New Zealand Ministry of Education began to fund three rather than four year teaching degrees for primary teachers and this become the norm for all institutions. In the process of reducing the degree, many papers that would have introduced students to political issues became optional or were dropped altogether. An example is that in the 1990s I used to teach a second year paper, 'Sociology of Education', at the University of Waikato. This paper no longer exists, a casualty of the reduction of teaching time.

On the other hand, the New Zealand situation has remained one where learning about educational policy and politics should still be an important part of ITE. One of the 'Graduating Teacher Standards' established by the New Zealand Teachers Council (now the Education Council of New Zealand) requires that beginning teachers 'have an understanding of education within the bicultural, multicultural, social, political, economic and historical contexts of Aotearoa New Zealand' (Education Council 2015). This means that all teaching degree qualifications in New Zealand should still include a component on social and political issues in relation to education. At the University of Waikato, for instance, this is explicitly provided through a second year paper on 'Social Issues in Aotearoa New Zealand Education' which is compulsory for most primary teacher education students. In this respect New Zealand teacher education is still a far cry from, for instance, the situation in England where most students pass through a one-year PGCE or through school-led initial teacher education programmes such 'School Direct' or 'Teach First'. In New Zealand there are one-year postgraduate courses and one university does sponsor a Teach First programme but most primary students still do a three-year undergraduate teaching degree.

Changing student perspectives are part of the picture as well. New Zealand university students today are encouraged to be more instrumental about their university education than their parents' generation through user-pays tertiary education fees introduced in the 1990s and by the secondary school assessment system of counting assessment credits towards their school-leaver qualification, the National Certificate of Educational Achievement (NCEA). Many New Zealanders under 30 have also known nothing other than neo-liberal policies, leading to some decidedly conservative positions on social and educational policy that need a careful response by their university teachers. For instance in 2011, I gave a lecture that criticised the contentious National Standards policy and a small group of students complained directly to the Minister of Education's office. Such incidents have served to teach academics to be careful in the political climate that has come to dominate New Zealand life.

University-based professional learning or continuing professional development for practising teachers has also become an increasingly difficult space within which to interrogate the GERM. New Zealand used to have a permanent advisory service based in universities but in recent years those working in this area are typically on one-year contracts and working within frameworks and within programme that are not intended to encourage critique. The focus of professional learning has also narrowed considerable with many curriculum areas no longer supported and a heavy emphasis on literacy. Those working in this uncertain environment are usually experienced teachers who have their own views and may pursue lines of argument or discussion that are more searching than might be expected given the nature of the programmes they are involved in. But university-based professional learning is also being sidelined by opportunities provided elsewhere as discussed below.

27.3   The Declining Influence of the University and the Rise of Other Influences

The changes to teacher education already mentioned are part of a more general decline in the influence of university-based teaching and research on New Zealand teachers when compared to business, philanthropic and media influences. On the university side there are numerous reasons for the decline. Faculties and schools of education have often had successive rounds of redundancies, are only rarely appointing new staff, and workloads have been climbing. Government policy is pushing universities towards STEM subjects and an increasing vocational emphasis. Research funding for university-based education research is falling away both in terms of the kinds of research that will be funded and the number of RFPs that are put up for tender. Staff are under pressure to publish, with the Performance Based Research Fund (PBRF) assessing academic staff on an individual basis in successive rounds since 2003 and requiring a high number of publication 'outputs' compared to other countries. Far from respecting their 'critic and conscience role', academics who speak out against social or economic policies have been publicly dismissed by politicians in. Education academics caught up in such insecurities and pressures are less likely to have time and enthusiasm for critique of GERM.

Meanwhile business and philanthropic or 'charitable' influences on teachers are on the rise. First, there are numerous small private providers and educational consultants that offer training or professional learning services to New Zealand primary schools. Second, there are larger education trusts like 'Cognition' and 'Core' providing various services including professional development for teachers and principals. These may technically be charities but act more like businesses and are able to influence education policy in powerful ways ('Phoncy Philanthropy' 2014). Third, there are those like the 'Next Foundation' and the 'Aotearoa Foundation' which are engaged in 'strategic philanthropy' or 'philanthrocapitalism'. For example, both of these foundations fund the 'Springboard Trust' which 'connects school principals with business mentors, enhancing their leadership and planning skills, achieving better educational outcomes for schools and their students, and dramatically improving life skills for young New Zealanders' (Springboard Trust 2015). The business networks seeking influence here are as palpable as those discussed in the UK context by Stephen Ball in *Education plc.* (Ball 2007). For instance, the chair of the Springboard Trust at the time of writing is not only CEO of a New Zealand bank but was previously a partner at management consulting firm, McKinsey & Co.

There are also other examples of how business is rising above universities in terms of influencing primary teachers and principals in New Zealand. Ministry of Education contracts are often being let to private education research companies and sometimes not even to educational researchers. An example is that Martin Jenkins, a firm of management consultations, has been recently contracted by the Ministry of Education to both evaluate New Zealand's first charter schools (called 'Partnership Schools' in New Zealand) and a new one-year graduate teacher education programme (the Master of Teaching and Learning). This sort of evaluation work would have previously been done either by university-based education researchers or researchers at NZCER. Business lobby groups are also starting to hold more sway. For instance, the Minister of Education recently launched a mathematics education report published by business think-tank 'The New Zealand Initiative'.

Such developments reach teachers through a mainstream media increasing orientated towards infotainment rather than serious journalism. Like many other countries, the media coverage of teachers and teaching in New Zealand is increasingly derisive or salacious. There are also right-wing blogs that have become notorious for attacking teachers and principals (e.g. 'Whaleoil'). The main lesson for teachers here is the importance of staying out of the news and senior staff in many schools are getting media training. Meanwhile the specialist education media, such as it was in a small country, has all but collapsed. *The New Zealand Education Review* (New Zealand's answer to the *Times Educational Supplement*) is down to five issues a year whereas for many years it was a weekly source of information.

27.4 Teachers Being Critical but not Critical Enough

Due to the kinds of developments discussed so far, the general climate for New Zealand teacher education and the culture of teaching is not conducive to creating a searching approach to global education reform. The NZEI and NZPF do a good job of informing members about GERM, there are lobby groups such as the 'Quality Public Education Coalition' and 'Save our Schools NZ', and of course teachers also learn much via the Internet about what is going on in other countries. But the concern has to be that many local developments in education are not sufficiently connected to the GERM agenda by most teachers. There are probably many examples that could be considered, but here I look at outsourcing of curriculum in the Health and Physical Education curriculum area, the approach of primary schools to the 'National Standards' and 'Investing in Educational Success' policies, and a new enthusiasm in New Zealand for 'Modern Learning Environments'.[2]

---

[2]O'Neill (2015) links 'Bring Your Own Device' (BYOD) to the GERM agenda.

27.4.1 Health and Physical Education

In the Health and Physical Education (HPE) area, Powell (2015) points to the ways New Zealand primary teachers and principals are encouraged to choose from an ever-increasing range of curricula and programmes provided by corporations (e.g. McDonald's, Honda, Macleans) and industry groups (e.g. United Fresh New Zealand Inc.), as well as charities and other 'not-for-profit' organisations (such as 'pokies' gambling trusts). Powell undertook qualitative research in three Auckland primary schools and shows how outsourcing teaching and curriculum saw teachers and principals inadvertently supporting the increased privatisation of education despite being opposed to GERM. He provides numerous examples of teachers justifying the marketing of products and services to schools:

> Obviously [corporations are] going to make dough out of [school-based programmes and resources] too, but if that's their prime purpose, well, we will see through it and wouldn't have them anyway. If it's only just for them, um, but if it's beneficial for kids, that's what it's got to be about, you know. Simple as that. (Dudley School principal, cited in Powell 2015, p. 103)

> Well, we have an expert to teach. It's a focus on that particular sport, and they can break down the skills probably better than [the teacher] … And a lot of the teachers don't have the skills nowadays, or the time to prepare what they should do, like in the old days they used to. (St Saviour's School teacher, cited in Powell 2015, p. 123)

Overall Powell's work illustrates that HPE in schools is a kind of 'Trojan Horse' of privatisation where corporations and their associated charities can get involved quite easily and where education reform is being made possible from the 'inside out' through the roles played by teachers and principals.

27.4.2 National Standards

New Zealand's National Standards were launched in October 2009 and involve schools making and reporting judgements about the reading, writing and mathematics achievement of primary aged children. These judgements are made annually against a four-point scale ('above', 'at', 'below', or 'well below' the standard).[3] The policy matches existing curriculum levels (and associated numeracy stages and literacy progressions) to these assessment times. This means that teachers are supposed to consider children's achievement against what is required for the curriculum levels, and use that understanding for making Overall Teacher Judgements (OTJs) about achievement against the National Standards. Since 2012, the results have been reported publicly (previously there was no public release of primary

---

[3]Judgements take place after one, two or three years at school in the junior school and then at the end of each year level in years 4–8.

achievement data) and now form part of the Government's wider data dissemination approach, the Public Achievement Information (PAI) pipeline.

Many, probably most, New Zealand primary teachers and principals were opposed to the introduction of National Standards for primary school achievement at the outset and as noted already, the NZEI and NZPF ran a major campaign against them when they were introduced in 2010. Despite this, and without much monitoring pressure from Government, by 2013 there was a shift towards the National Standards. The author's research (Thrupp and White 2013) has suggested several reasons for this. First, problems within the policy were disguised by components that teachers were connecting to previous practice without acknowledging the new 'high stakes' use of these practices in the National Standards. Second, National Standards intersected with a culture of commitment to high expectations and constant improvement so that the perspective essentially became that 'if we are going to do the Standards we are going to do them really well, in the same way we do our best at everything else'. Third, there was a loyalty to one's own particular school: that our school is 'boxing clever' or, as one teacher in the study put it, has 'nice' National Standards compared to other schools.

27.4.3 Investing in Educational Success

A school clusters policy, 'Investing in Educational Success' (IES) was introduced in 2014 and has also been controversial within the education sector. Supporters of the IES have seen it as new education spending on a relatively benign exercise in collaboration while critics have argued that the money is being squandered on payments for new leadership roles that could be better spent on reducing class sizes or provision for children with special needs. A further concern is that the new 'Communities of Learning' set up by IES represent another form of managerial control of schools. Clustering of schools may become viewed by governments as a better way to push neo-liberal reform along than with individual schools (e.g. federations of academies in England) and it may also encourages the 'superhead' culture of entrepreneurial and increasingly privatised school leadership. The policy was supported, after modifications, by the PPTA (secondary teachers union) but opposed by the NZEI, whose members voted overwhelmingly to reject it.

Yet despite the huge support amongst primary teachers and principals for the NZEI's opposition in 2014, over time a number of primary schools are becoming involved in local IES clusters. By August 2015 there were 42 Communities of Learning involving 333 schools, with most of these being primary schools. This has inevitably weakened the NZEI's position as it has tried to negotiate a more favourable alternative arrangement with Government, the 'Joint Initiative'. It seems many school principals and their boards of trustees are looking at their local situation and thinking that the threat represented by the IES may have been overstated or can be overlooked.

27.4.4 Modern Learning Environments

'Modern Learning Environments' (MLE's, also known as 'Innovative Learning Spaces') have become very popular in the New Zealand primary sector over the last few years. These involve creating new teaching and learning areas that are more flexible for several teachers working together, differentiated learning in small groups and using digital technologies. This is done either through new construction or through changing the architecture, layout and furniture in existing school buildings. Although there are likely to be some genuine educational benefits to the new arrangements, a dimension of MLEs often not considered by teachers and principals is the opportunities they open up for the private sector including consultants working in this area of 'future-focused education', furniture manufacturers, architects and construction companies/consortia. Moreover although some involved are supposedly not for profit or philanthropic, their outlook and networks may still align closer to GERM than to quality public education.

27.5 Conclusion

This chapter has repeatedly emphasised the need for teachers to think more critically on the assumption that this is necessary if they are to take action to contest, disrupt or undermine the more subtle elements of global education reform. Although New Zealand primary teachers can be admired for their public opposition to GERM, based on the examples given here there is room for more vigilance. Part of the problem could be that there is no single GERM, but rather many versions (GERMs). National contexts and trajectories of reform mean that governments push on different policies at different times in different countries. This sometimes makes GERM harder to recognise even if the overall direction is similar.

What teachers can actually do if they have greater understanding depends on the spaces available for agency in relation to particular issues. In some cases, it may be possible to individually or collectively reject some unwanted development, in other instances it may be about taking a more token approach, while sometimes it might prove necessary to go with a required reform but keep up a running critique of it. Furthermore, when teachers or principals seem to be supporting some manifestation of GERM, they may sometimes be doing so in a critically informed way in order to get purchase and influence the initiative: 'better to be in the tent' etc. Nevertheless there is a risk in being incorporated even as influence is being gained.

It is probably unrealistic to expect much leadership to come from university-based teacher educators given what is happening in New Zealand universities and their teacher education programmes. New Zealand education academics are becoming less outspoken for the reasons already mentioned and perhaps also a greater sense of déjà vu and fatigue as the Key Government moves through its third term. But one bright point on the horizon is that the next (2018) round of the PBRF will for the first time allow academics to credit activities that represent 'outreach and engagement'. Such activities may include contributing to public understanding, contributing to 'critic and conscience of society' debates, getting research into the media and presenting research to professionals. Perhaps as the academic performance measures change, academic critique of GERM will become more forthright.

In the meantime, teachers and their organisations are better to take the lead themselves, welcoming in those teacher educators who are interested in contesting global education reform. Indeed the NZEI Te Rui Roa has already set up an online resource 'Te Kete Aronui' which it describes as 'professional learning and development for members by members' but which includes some academic presentations and writing. In this kind of activity, a teacher organisation like NZEI will find itself competing for the attention of teachers alongside many others with a less-principled interest in influence. The key advantage teacher organisations must retain is the trust by members that their own representative organisations are committed to social justice.

References

Ball, S. J. (2007). *Education Plc. Understanding private sector participation in public sector education*. London: Routledge.

Ball, S. J., & Youdell, D. (2007). *Hidden privatisation in education*. Educational International.

Education Council. (2015). *Graduating teacher standards*. Retrieved from http://www.educationcouncil.org.nz/sites/default/files/gts-poster.pdf

Edwards, B. (2015). A tale of two governments. *New Zealand Herald*. Retrieved September 6, from http://www.nzherald.co.nz/nz/news/article.cfm?c_id=1&objectid=11508719

Fraser, D., & Hill, M. (Eds.). (2015). *The professional practice of teaching* (6th ed.). Melbourne: Cengage Learning.

Furlong, J. (2013). Globalisation, neoliberalism, and the reform of teacher education in England. *The Educational Forum, 77*(1), 28–50.

Locke, T., Vulliamy, G., Webb, R., & Hill, M. (2005). Being a 'professional primary school teacher at the beginning of the 21st century: A comparative analysis of primary teacher professionalism in New Zealand and England. *Journal of Education Policy, 20*(5), 555–581.

Malin, J. R., & Lubienski, C. (2015). Educational expertise, advocacy, and media influence. *Education Policy Analysis Archives, 23,* 6.

Middleton, S., & May, H. (1997). *Teachers talk teaching 1915–1995*. Palmerston North, New Zealand: Dunmore Press.

O'Neill, J. (2015). *Privatisation—Why BYOD is a GERM*. Workshop presented to NZEI Annual Conference, Rotorua, 27–30 September.

Phoney Philanthropy. (2014, November). *PPTA News* (*35*(10), *23*(6)). Wellington: PPTA. http://dx.doi.org/10.14507/epaa.v23.1706

Powell, D. (2015). *"Part of the solution"? Charities, corporate philanthropy and healthy lifestyles education in New Zealand primary schools* (Unpublished doctoral dissertation). Charles Sturt University: Bathurst, Australia.

Sahlberg, P. (2011). *Finnish lessons. What can the world learn from educational change in Finland?* New York: Teachers College Press.

Springboard Trust. (2015). Retrieved from http://www.springboardtrust.org.nz

Thrupp, M., & White, M. (2013). *Research, analysis and insight into national standards (RAINS) project* (Final report: National standards and the damage done). Wellington, New Zealand: NZEI.

Author Biography

Martin Thrupp is an education policy sociologist, with a particular focus on neo-liberal policy and its lived effects in contextually diverse schools. He is professor of education and head of Te Whiringa School of Educational Leadership and Policy at the University of Waikato.

Part V
Teacher Education as a Public Good

"A man without the proper use of the intellectual faculties of a man is, if possible, more contemptible than even a coward, and seems to be mutilated and deformed in a still more essential part of the character of human nature. Though the state was to derive no advantage from the instruction of the inferior ranks of people, it would still deserve its attention that they should not be altogether uninstructed (…). The state, however, derives no inconsiderable advantage from their instruction"

Adam Smith (1937), pp. 739–740.

Introduction

The notion of a public good originates quite recently in a paper by the economist Paul A. Samuelson in his 1954 article, "The Pure Theory of Public Expenditure."[1] It is a paper devoted to the analysis of optimal public expenditure leading to the distinction between *private and collective consumption goods* which turns on whether the consumption of a good is enjoyed in common or leads to the substraction of an individual's consumption. In this mathematic paper Samuelson attempts to define optimal conditions and notes the impossibility of a decentralized or market solution adding that it is not the economist's job to make normative judgments concerning the desirable states. His paper formalized the concept of public goods as goods that are non-rival and non-excludable, highlighting the market failure of free riding when he wrote: "it is in the selfish interest of each person to give false signals, to pretend to have less interest in a given collective consumption activity than he really has" (p. 388). Samuelson is credited with laying the foundations for the modern theory of public expenditure or public goods. He was one of the founders of neo-Keynesian economics and acted as an advisor to both John F. Kennedy and Lyndon B. Johnson. As well as his work on the optimal

---

[1]See http://www.econ.ucsb.edu/ ~ tedb/Courses/UCSBpf/readings/sampub.pdf.

allocation of resources in the presence of public and private goods he was highly influential in developing the field of welfare economics based largely on Keynes' ideas.

Given that a public good is a consumption good that individuals can enjoy without reducing its availability or enjoyment by others then the classic examples normally taken to exemplify this concept include education, high literacy levels, knowledge and information. Public education is deemed a public good: it is funded by the state because it is argued it has multiple societal benefits spread in terms of citizenship, employment, economic prosperity, innovation and creativity, health, social cohesion and mobility. Teacher education insofar as it is provided by the state, then, would also be seen to fall under this concept. If it is in the public good and public interest that the state provide for well-informed citizens for the smooth function of democratic governing, the general improvement of health and welfare of the general population, economic prosperity and so on then if also follows that the state needs to provide and ensure that teachers themselves are well educated. If the success, improvement, effectiveness and achievement of public education depends upon the quality of the teaching force then teacher education can be seen to be a significant part of the question of education as a public good. If teacher education can be seen to be part of a complex public good then clearly it is also the case that teacher education research can also be so regarded.

Froese-Germain (2013) of the Canadian Teachers' Federation author "Reframing Public Education as a Public Good" usefully refer to Keeping and King (2012) who state that "public education is a deliberate model of the best that a civil democratic society can be. This is not accidental, or occasional, or a matter of convenience. Public schools look and function like the democratic, civil, pluralist society of which they are an integral part." (p. 17).

Froese-Germain (2013: 1) refers to Keeping and King (2012: 17) to state the other characteristics of public education:

• All children have a right to be included in public education, and the community has a responsibility to be inclusive: every adult in a community has both a right and a responsibility to be involved in the education of all children, not just their own or their grandchildren's.

• Public education celebrates diversity. Children should be educated together, not in order to try to make them all the same, but so they may come to value everyone's unique individuality.

• Public education supports social mobility because a democratic society will fail if it does not constantly strive for greater fairness, ensuring that every child has the opportunity to benefit from its public education system, regardless of economic status.

Interestingly in this regard a recent paper by Dittmar and Meisenzahl (2016) that inquires into the origins and impacts of the state as a provider of public goods one of the first studies to examine the "new municipal legal institutions established Europe's first large scale experiments with mass public education" beginning in the 1500s demonstrate the positive impacts of educational public goods for city growth and human capital development:

Our research documents that the Reformation provides a canonical example of the emergence of state capacity and public goods institutions. The new institutions promoted economic inclusion and directly targeted welfare: they supported the provision of education and social services and set up anti-corruption safeguards (p. 2).

Meghnad Desai in "Public Goods: A Historical Perspective" indicates that the discourse has developed since Samuelson wrote his classic essay:

We now recognize a larger array of goods as public goods and differentiate among, for example pure, impure, and club goods and joint products as well as between public goods and externalities. At the same time, we have learned from the theory of public choice and new political economy as well as from bitter political experience that the provision of public goods does not take place in a neutral, politics-free public space. The issue of public or private goods is contested, as is the larger issue of the role of the state.[2]

Deasi also mentions the extension of public goods to global public goods, an important addition to the concept when we consider the global importance of education. As Irina Bokova, Director-General of UNESCO puts it in her Foreword the UNESCO's (2015) *Rethinking Education: Towards a Global Common Good*

The world is changing—education must also change. Societies everywhere are undergoing deep transformation, and this calls for new forms of education to foster the competencies that societies and economies need, today and tomorrow. This means moving beyond literacy and numeracy, to focus on learning environments and on new approaches to learning for greater justice, social equity and global solidarity. Education must be about learning to live on a planet under pressure. It must be about cultural literacy, on the basis of respect and equal dignity, helping to weave together the social, economic and environmental dimensions of sustainable development.[3]

As various commentators have pointed out the statist notion of public goods belongs to the era of the welfare state and has been strongly challenged by those belonging to neoliberal political economy that education is a mixed public good and that higher education is a private good with most benefits accruing to the individual. The neoliberals contest the welfare theory of public goods and argues that it needs to be revisited and updated in light of current political realities. They argue from an ideological commitment against the "big state" on efficiency grounds and from premises concerning political individualism that wants to protect "individual freedom" from state interference. Accordingly, neoliberal states around the world have introduced a set of policies designed to privatize public education systems by various means—through the state support for private schools, the introduction of Charter schools, establishment of student loans, the deprofessionalization of the teaching force and its reregulation, and through the privatization of teacher education, among many other measures.

[2]See http://web.undp.org/globalpublicgoods/globalization/pdfs/Desai.pdf.

[3]See http://unesdoc.unesco.org/images/0023/002325/232555e.pdf.

The UNESCO publication recognizes the limits of public good theory to argue for common goods in the era of globalization in part because it goes beyond the instrumental notion framed by individualistic consumption and more easily admits of conceptions of well-being within diverse communities. The "common good" emphasizes a participatory process served by collective responsibility and collective action aimed at enhancing the role of civil society.

The chapters in this part demonstrate the applications of some of these concepts and arguments. Poonam Batra in "Quality of Education and the Poor: Constraints on Learning" examines the arguments emerging in the 1980s and after that emphasized the role of education in reducing poverty and argues "that poverty research as well as educational research fail to capture the dynamics of how poor children experience schooling". Batra shows how children of the poor with access to school suffer from a deficit perspective that limits the conditions of capability.

References

Dittmar, J. E. & Meisenzahl, R. R. (2016). "State Capacity and Public Goods: Institutional Change, Human Capital, and Growth in Early Modern Germany," Finance and Economics Discussion Series 2016-028. Washington: Board of Governors of the Federal Reserve System. http://dx.doi.org/10.17016/FEDS.2016.028

Froese-Germain, B. (2013). *Reframing public education as a public good*. Retrieved from http://files.eric.ed.gov/fulltext/ED546892.pdf

Keeping, J. & King, D. (2012, Summer). "What happened to the 'public' in public education?" *Education Canada, 52*(3), 16–19. http://www.cea-ace.ca/education-canada/article/what-happened-%E2%80%9Cpublic%E2%80%9D-public-education

Samuelson, P. A. (1954). The pure theory of public expenditure. *Review of Economics and Statistics, 36*, 387–390.

Chapter 28
Quality of Education and the Poor: Constraints on Learning

Poonam Batra

28.1 Introduction

Poverty theorists have for a long time argued that developing human capacities through a concerted focus on basic education is a significant way to reduce poverty. The role of education in reducing poverty has been emphasised since the mid-1980s. In this frame, poverty has been defined in economic terms rather than as a measure of 'social disadvantage'. Drawing upon the human capital theory, it has since been emphasised that education is a critical instrument in reducing poverty. Investment in education is assumed to develop valued human capital which in turn enables the economic growth of a nation, leading to poverty reduction.

This view has been criticised for ignoring larger socio-structural factors that are known to be responsible for maintaining the 'cycle' of poverty. Failure to confront the structural dimensions of poverty and inequality has led governments to institute focussed policies and programmes with targets to alleviate some of the disadvantages children from impoverished environments face. For instance, international donor initiatives and major state policy in India and other countries have focused on various measures to attract and keep children in school. Some of these schemes, such as the mid-day meal scheme have played a critical role in providing nutrition supplements, increasing school enrolments and retaining children in schools.

With the increasing recognition of human development indices in assessing a nation's progress since Mahbubul Haq's Human Development Report (UNDP 1998), the human capital perspective was enlarged to include the idea of people's capacities and choice leading to differential emphasis and trajectories. Sen (1999) emphasised the need to view poverty within the frame of human capabilities rather than in terms of income alone. In Sen's view, 'poverty can be sensibly identified in terms of capability deprivation; the approach concentrates on deprivations that are

P. Batra (✉)
University of Delhi, Delhi, India
e-mail: batra.poonam@gmail.com

© Springer Nature Singapore Pte Ltd. 2017
M.A. Peters et al. (eds.), *A Companion to Research in Teacher Education*,
DOI 10.1007/978-981-10-4075-7_28

intrinsically important, (unlike low income, which is only *instrumentally* significant)' (1999: 87). Capability deprivation refers to deprivation of opportunities,
choices and entitlements, and therefore includes the idea of freedom. Nussbaum
(2011) proposes the view that the capabilities approach is also concerned with
social injustice and inequality, especially because entrenched discrimination and
marginalisation results in 'capability failures'. However, the mere physical provisioning of education for the poor is still seen as the *key* to reduce poverty even
within the frame of capability deprivation. The assumption is that policy measures
such as access to schooling, the provision of school choice and a central legislation
that ensures the right to free and compulsory education, are necessary and sufficient
conditions to help overcome capability deprivation.

This chapter argues that simplistic connections between educational provisioning and poverty miss the more important unheeded idea embedded in the construct
of 'capability deprivation'—that of foregrounding the criticality of the educational
process.

To begin with, the capability deprivation frame offers the possibility of developing a more nuanced understanding of how poverty may operate in the educational
space. Two aspects emanating from poverty research are worth engaging with: one,
that processes in the classroom and the school that promise to develop capability are
often projected in an over simplistic manner, ignoring the complexities of the
educational process and, two, it is assumed that enquiry into the educational process
is the sole preserve of educators. Questioning this, scholars have argued that
poverty research is noticeably blind to research that has consistently demonstrated
how schooling is more inclined to reinforce socialisation processes rather than
challenge power relations that maintain inequities in society (Stromquist 2001).

Educational research too has, for long, held the view that poverty essentially acts
as a barrier to schooling. Issues related to inequity, exclusion and inclusion in
education have been examined; but very little attention is paid to the processes that
influence teaching and learning in schools where children of the marginalised study.
It is often assumed that provisioning of education enables poor children to attend
school, learn and develop capacities and skills. This however has not been the case.
Educational policy initiatives have continued to pay limited attention to the school
and the classroom where capabilities are assumed to be developed and honed.[1]
Several testing initiatives[2] across the country have demonstrated consistently poor
performance of elementary school children in basic literacy and numeracy skills. It
can therefore be argued that provisioning alone, without adequate engagement with
the underlying processes of education that may foster or create further disadvantage, proves to be an ineffectual instrument of reducing poverty. This calls attention

---

[1]This is despite the fact that the curriculum discourse in India post NCF 2005 has repeatedly drawn
attention to the microcosm of the everyday classroom and the need to prepare teachers to speak to
that.

[2]ASER (2015) has revealed little improvement in children's learning achievement levels in the last
ten years. Other examples are the NCERT survey and surveys conducted by private organisations
such as Education Initiatives, based in Ahmedabad.

to the longstanding need for poverty and education researchers to work together to re-examine the relationship between poverty and education (Rose and Dyer 2008).

To take this argument further, a subtle and significant distinction needs to be established between the term 'educational deprivation' and the term 'capability deprivation' which scholars have tended to use interchangeably.[3] While educational deprivation is likely to conjure up an image of deprivation in terms of access to a school, capability deprivation inevitably draws our attention to the everyday school experiences of the poor and the marginalised. It foregrounds educational process as the site where capabilities are most likely to develop. This distinction makes it incumbent on policymakers to move beyond mere provisioning of education and to ensure that children participate and learn. Hence, the site of education induces an ineluctable engagement for the researcher as much as the policymaker.

The capability approach frame can be drawn upon to challenge yet another entrenched view—the view that poverty is essentially an individual condition. In an attempt to revive the 'culture of poverty thesis' of the late 1960s and early 1970s, more recent empirical research by Payne (2005) portrays the poor in monolithic and stereotypical terms of values and behaviours, arguing that poverty is no excuse for low performance. Critiquing Payne's research, Ng and Rury (2006) contend that efforts to educate poor children by locating the problem of poverty within the individual without regard to the larger social context in which they live, are misdirected.

It is evident, so far, that both educational research and poverty research fail to capture the dynamics of deprivation as both view poverty as extrinsic to the process of education. Micro-level narratives, analysis of processes of schooling, teaching and learning are required to understand how poverty influences and shapes children's experiences in school.

Having established the significance of viewing education of the poor in the extended frame of the capability approach, the central argument of this chapter is that conditions of capability deprivation are being engendered in the classroom every day, and that these pose severe constraints on learning for children from disadvantaged backgrounds; in particular, children of the poor. Primary field data and existing ethnographic accounts of classrooms have been drawn upon to argue how conditions of capability deprivation are being engendered in the everyday classroom.

Primary data used in this chapter comprises of responses of individual teachers to a set of open-ended questions with regard to children and their learning. Responses were sought from two groups of teachers prepared through two distinctly different pre-service teacher education programmes. The methodology used is elaborated in the section following the policy narrative on measures of reform and the quality debate. Secondary sources comprise of available ethnographic accounts

---

[3]Tilak (2005), for instance, uses the term 'educational deprivation' and argues how income poverty and educational poverty are mutually reinforcing.

of classrooms of select government schools attended by the poor in the hope to learn.

The argument is built using four dominant narratives that are seen to construct the everyday experiences of children from poor and deprived homes: (a) a policy narrative that seeks to create major shifts in educational thinking reflected in measures of reform and the quality debate; (b) a narrative of teacher perceptions and beliefs about children of the poor and their education; (c) a narrative of reforming children as the chief aim of education; and (d) a narrative of viewing children as 'non-epistemic' entities. Woven together, the narratives lend credence to the argument that conditions of capability deprivation, posing severe constraints on the learning of children of the poor, are indeed being fashioned in the classroom every day. The chapter also highlights possibilities of a 'counter-narrative' that emerges from teachers who are deliberatively prepared to engage with the complexities of diverse social and economic realities. Though the 'counter-narrative' is not the subject of this chapter, it points to the need to subvert processes that encumber the intellectual agency of teachers as a way to address the tension between education and social structure within the challenges of a market-based economy.

28.2 Educational Reform and the Quality Debate

The need to focus attention on issues of diversity amongst learners and on the prerequisite of preparing teachers to enable all children to learn assumed significance in the curricular discourse over the last decade, as a means of enhancing quality in Indian classrooms. Questions of knowledge and learning and the epistemic identity of children have taken centre-stage. Educators are being prompted to view children, foremost as learners, whose social identities are acknowledged and experiences drawn upon to engage critically with sociocultural and economic realities. Here, the aim and process of education converge and advance in considerable harmony. This discourse is accepted as formal state policy on school curriculum and the curriculum to prepare and develop teachers.[4]

Policy enforcement, however, is seen to lay renewed emphasis on large-scale testing as a means of enhancing quality of teaching and learning in schools. There is a growing belief and advocacy that frequent assessment of learning outcomes is necessary to effect quality education.[5] No attention is drawn to a fact well known to

---

[4]The National Curriculum Framework (for school education) (NCF) 2005. National Council for Educational Research and Training, New Delhi: NCERT; and The National Curriculum Framework for Teacher Education (NCFTE) 2009, National Council for Teacher Education (NCTE) (2009). New Delhi: NCTE.

[5]It is important to note that the most recent ASER (2015) Report advocates privatising school education by asserting that the Government of India's 'neglect of learning outcomes has definitely contributed to a growing divide in every village and community between those who access private schools or tutors, and those who do not' (Chavan 2015: 4). Yet, the state-wise analysis of ASER

educators, that poor learning achievements in the primary school is directly related to the quality of teaching-learning environments and the presence or absence of opportunities to learn. This lack of attention to the processes of education is a direct consequence of the trajectory educational reform has taken, including the assumed relationship between poverty and education, elaborated earlier in this chapter.

Educational reform in India since the mid-1990s—the first phase of liberalisation —focused on increasing access to schooling, fulfilling the demand for teachers by hiring professionally unqualified teachers[6] and making provisions for frequent in-service training. Most of these training programmes were designed to 'motivate' the 'unmotivated' teacher, as this was perceived to be the key to ensure quality education. Towards the end of a decade of such reforms, learning achievement levels showed little improvement and commissioned research concluded that teachers were responsible for the poor quality of education despite the huge amounts invested in 'motivating' a cadre of 'unmotivated' teachers. Continuing efforts at placing the onus of poor learning outcomes on school teachers led to the growing anti-teacher discourse, followed by a spate of policy measures to ensure teacher accountability and efficiency. Examining curriculum and pedagogic processes that prepare and support teachers have not been seen as possible areas of engagement and intervention with regard to the quality debate.

On the intervention of the Supreme Court via the Justice Verma Commission on Teacher Education (GoI 2012),[7] several fundamental flaws that plague the system of preparing teachers were identified. In its articulation of the kind of teacher required to teach children in their formative years, the Commission in its report draws attention to the classrooms in which opportunities for learning are relinquished every day. The quality debate is struggling to bring the focus back on this important aspect of school education which has virtually lost its significance in the cacophony of advocacy for frequent testing to ensure quality education in the era of market-based reforms.

Locating 'educative experiences' at the heart of quality education and the expanded understanding of poverty as capability deprivation—foregrounds the

---

(Footnote 5 continued)

data (by its own admission), shows that 'controlling for other factors reduces the government– private school learning gap considerably in all states … (and therefore) a smaller proportion of this gap is actually attributable to private schools themselves' (Wadhwa 2015: 20).

[6]Para-teacher is a term that refers to a cadre of school teachers hired to meet the demand for teachers. Para-teachers do not have any professional pre-service qualification and are paid consolidated salaries of amounts less than one-third of regular teachers' pay. Large numbers of para-teachers continue to pose a major challenge to providing quality education in several state government-run schools across the country.

[7]In May 2011, the Supreme Court constituted a high-powered Commission under former Chief Justice of India, Justice J.S. Verma, to address complaints of widespread malpractice, policy distortions and regulatory conflicts.

significance of turning attention to how children of the poor experience schooling. This, however, has not captured the imagination of either educational researchers or policymakers. Poverty theorists, too, rarely view as worthy of attention, school experiences and identities of children as tied into their socio-economic conditions and associated social milieu. Moreover, the simultaneous revival of the educational agenda in an era of reforms as framed in economic competitiveness rather than social justice has changed the very aims of education. Hence, the growing perception and belief that education should be about skill development, and in itself has little potential to enable social transformation, dominates current conceptions of quality education.

There appears to be collusion between how poverty and quality of education are conceptualised and positioned in a market-based economy. This is seen to shape the educational agenda of contemporary India. Viewed in the framework of 'delivery', quality education is posed as a system of efficiency and accountability measures, best standardised through regular testing of learning outcomes and technology-oriented solutions to the problem of teaching and learning. In this frame, the process of education is left vacuous and essentially unaddressed.

Equally important is the recognition that the dominant view of poverty as a barrier to education has led educational research to majorly focus on how poverty impacts learning. Some of these impact studies attribute the poor performance of children on basic tasks of literacy and numeracy to lack of resources, poor health and lack of home support—conditions associated with poverty. Poverty is thus taken to be a given—a factor outside the realm of schooling and one which impacts learning outcomes rather than shapes the everyday quotidian of the school. This also explains why such little effort has been made to investigate how children of the poor experience poverty in school.

28.3 Examining Conditions of the Production of Capability Deprivation

The central argument of this chapter, that children's learning is severely constrained by conditions of capability deprivation, engendered in the everyday classroom, derives from a meticulous analysis of teacher responses and ethnographic classroom accounts. Together, the field presents a coherent picture of a school and classroom setting in which opportunities to learn are forsaken every day.

Primary data was gathered to examine teachers' views about children—especially those who come from backgrounds of poverty—their learning and capacities to learn. Responses were sought from teachers teaching in elementary grades for over a decade, over a period of two months. The study included two groups of teachers—those who have undergone pre-service teacher education through the two-year Diploma in Education (DEd) offered by the District Institutes of Education and Training (DIETs), state institutions based outside the university system (henceforth referred to as Group 1); and those educated through a four-year integrated, interdisciplinary Bachelor of Elementary Education (BElEd) programme offered in undergraduate colleges of liberal arts and sciences (henceforth referred to as Group 2)—comprising a total of 82 elementary school teachers[8] teaching in 10 state-run corporation schools[9] across Delhi. The aim was also to explore whether teachers prepared differently develop alternate views of children from diverse backgrounds, and their learning.

Although both programmes prepare teachers for teaching at the elementary level, there are distinct differences in their curriculum and pedagogical approach. The two-year DEd programme offered by DIETs is typically designed to view children through the lens of universal characteristics and their education through techniques of pedagogy as derived from the basic principles of behaviouristic psychology, following the colonial model of training teachers. The four-year BElEd programme, on the other hand, views education as located in the larger socio-cultural, political and economic context in terms of understanding children, childhood and education; and evolving appropriate pedagogies through engagement with subject knowledge, and interdisciplinary perspectives on learners, processes of learning and aims of education; relying on theories of socio-constructivism and critical pedagogy. Responses from teachers were sought on several issues related to children's participation in school, their performance in class, engagement with processes of education and its connect with the larger socio-economic context of the children they teach.

Teacher responses were sought on specific classroom situations related to issues of children's work, how they conduct themselves in school, teachers' pedagogic approaches and teacher–student interactions. The majority of children taught by these teachers came from poor homes and from marginal social communities. Teachers were asked simple questions around everyday occurrences such as: why do children come late to school; why do children show little interest in classroom activities; why do girls and boys segregate themselves during assembly and other classroom activities? In each case, teachers were asked to think of ways in which they have handled or would handle such situations in class and the school. The second set of questions related to specific errors that children make in solving mathematical problems, tasks of reading, writing and their pace of completing given tasks. Teachers were asked to reflect on their pedagogic strategies—how they

---

[8]Teachers were selected on the basis of the pre-service teacher education programme they had been educated in. Fifty teachers had qualified with a Diploma in Elementary Education (DEd) offered by DIETs and 32 teachers had qualified with a Bachelor's Degree in Elementary Teacher Education (BElEd) offered by select constituent colleges of the University of Delhi.

[9]The majority of teachers interviewed were teaching in the corporation-run primary schools while others in composite state government-run schools of Delhi.

would adapt them to enable children to recognise errors and seek support to correct them, to read and write with fluency and to feel comfortable learning at their own pace. The third set of questions required teachers to reflect on specific aspects of the pre-service teacher education courses that provided them opportunities to develop professional capacities and sensibilities. Responses of teachers were analysed to reveal their views on poverty, the poor and their education, and their capacities to learn.

Teacher orientations, beliefs and assumptions revealed through primary data find resonance in the ethnographic accounts of classrooms studied by various researchers. Accounts of three specific ethnographic studies conducted in select state-run schools in Andhra Pradesh, West Bengal (Majumdar and Mooij 2011), and Delhi (Iyer 2013; Dalal 2014) were examined. The aim was to understand teacher orientations and assumptions about children from poor and socially disadvantaged backgrounds and their capacities to learn through classroom observations and expressed views.

The following section presents qualitative accounts of classrooms that reveal how teachers' unquestioning and entrenched views on poverty, their views about learners from poor and marginalised homes, and their views about knowledge and learning shape the classroom discourse. Analysis highlights how the poor continue to be marginalised from processes of learning despite having access to schooling.

28.4 Teachers' Perceptions of the Poor, the Disadvantaged, and Their Learning

Some of the key observations with regard to how teachers view children of the poor provide insight into how schooling is experienced by these children. Data gathered from two groups of teachers reveal significant differences in perception, views, conceptions and dispositions towards children and their education.[10] It is argued that these differences in turn significantly influence the ways in which children experience schooling. The views of teachers of both groups presented below have been analysed to understand how this is so.

28.4.1 Dominant Perceptions, Conceptions and Dispositions

The dominant tendency of teachers from Group 1 was to view children as lacking in something. For instance, most believe and assume that children who come late to school are disinterested in school and do not value time and studies. Most teachers

---

[10]Responses discussed present the dominant views of teachers of both groups, although some variations within each group were also observed.

think that punitive measures are necessary to coerce children to come to school on time. Even where teachers reflect on the possible role of extraneous factors beyond their control that could compel children to arrive late to school, their responses were generic and sweeping, attributing such behaviours to family background, unpleasant atmosphere at home, lack of support and families' disinterest in their children's education. The majority of teachers seems to hold the view that children are lazy, have bad habits and are disinterested, explaining students' perceived 'truant' behaviour as something internal to them. Teachers whose responses came across as 'sensitive' in actual effect reflect a patronising attitude towards children from poor and marginalised families, reaffirming the conviction that such children require 'corrective' measures.

Teachers continually doubt children asserting that they fail to perform because they do not value school, do not practice enough at home, lack concentration, have bad habits and often disrupt the class. Ethnographic accounts reveal that as a matter of routine and in the name of disciplining children, teachers often isolate such 'undisciplined' (read 'non-performing') children from the mainstream activities of the classroom, deny them the pleasure of participating in games and other activities by way of punishment, and keep them busy in meaningless tasks of 'copying' from the blackboard or the textbook. 'Class monitors' are 'used' to institute a system of regular 'surveillance' and are given a free hand to reprimand and hit children on the instructions of the teacher and the headmaster (Iyer 2013).

Any diversity amongst children in terms of the pace at which they complete a task or how they complete it is seen through the lens of individual ability. Children are classified as 'intelligent' and 'dull' where the 'dull' are further labelled as 'slow learners'. Teachers expect little participation from children who they label as 'slow learners' and in a sense have given up on them. Many teachers did not hesitate to refer to 'non-performing' children as lazy, inattentive, even unscrupulous and immoral.

Another dominant view amongst teachers is that the family backgrounds of such children interfere in creating conditions conducive to learning. Teachers carry preconceived notions about the effects of deprivation; openly attributing children's 'non-performance' and 'indiscipline' to the illiterate parent, their non-serious attitude towards education and their poor economic conditions. In a major ethnographic research undertaken in four countries of Latin America, Avalos (1986) had argued that explanations for failure could be traced to the teachers and the school conditions they create; and that school failure is produced within schools.

Persuaded by the deep-rooted belief that children need to be 'reformed', teachers often justify constant verbal abuse and frequent beating of children. Children too have internalised the view that beating is good for them (NCPCR 2009). As argued by Sarangapani (2003), the value congruence between teachers and students legitimises social control as the key function of education where teacher authority is perceived to have legitimate power. Teachers are seen to exercise authority by 'controlling their learning environments, restricting their movements and expression with the aim to improve their 'performance' in school. 'Performance' denotes a range of 'expected' behaviours, apart from doing well in class tests.

Children's errors in tasks of writing, reading and mathematical operations are attributed to cognitive 'deficiency' and disinterest. The appropriate strategy to deal with children's poor performance in the teachers' view would be to use methods of drill and repeated practice through frequent testing. Hidden in this view is the conviction that there are 'correct' ways of doing things, whether it is to pronounce words 'properly', solve arithmetical problems or behave as children, learners, boys and girls. Creative writing too, teachers say, should be assessed in terms of correctness in the formation of letters, correctness of content and spelling. Even where teachers acknowledge that differences in dialects may explain why children pronounce words differently, they continue to hold the belief that this difference indicates poor cognitive grasp and needs to be corrected; and can be corrected through regular practice and daily tasks of dictation. Delays in learning are attributed to differences in age, cognitive levels and 'IQ', which according to many teachers is hereditarily determined.

Teachers' conceptions about children from marginalised communities portray the poor in stereotypical terms of values and behaviour, thereby contributing to the positioning of poverty and associated behaviours as an individual condition. This understanding is part of the constructed discourse of the in-service programmes[11] for teachers since the late 1990s that aimed to address 'hard-spots' of learning amongst underperforming children in state-run schools.

Ethnographic accounts[12] reveal that children are acutely aware of the teacher's lack of confidence in them. Hence, they may be physically present in the classroom but are excluded from all classroom processes. The casual nature of classroom processes is particularly observed in poorer and more educationally backward areas and it is within the school that children learn their place in the social hierarchy at large (Majumdar and Mooij 2011). Immersed in an ambience of everyday exclusion, children seem to be learning from teachers that they are incapable of learning and that they themselves are responsible for failing to perform.

28.4.2 Changing Perceptions, Conceptions and Dispositions: Shaping the Possible

Teachers educated to engage with diversity in the everyday, were found to appreciate social and individual differences; share ways of encouraging children to participate; create fearless and non-threatening learning environments and opportunities for peer learning; and reach out to parents to ensure a continuity of positive

---

[11]The District Primary Education Programme (DPEP) funded by the World Bank between 1994–2003 in India, constructed such a discourse and designed training of teachers around this idea.

[12]These accounts were based on observations gathered from classrooms in state government-run schools in Andhra Pradesh. See Majumdar and Mooij (2011) for detailed classroom accounts and the analysis offered.

experiences between the home and the school. For them, enquiry into children's errors facilitates an understanding of their world and thinking patterns and creates a compelling need for epistemic engagement with children and conceptual knowledge. They question the prevalent notion of the 'educability' of children from disadvantaged contexts, and acknowledge the larger responsibility of educators in enabling social justice.

Teachers (Group 2) are acutely aware of the lack of opportunities that impede the learning experience of children from disadvantaged backgrounds. They recognise that children struggling with the standard language of the school are at a considerable disadvantage not because they lack in cognitive capacities but because they are coerced into making meaning using an alien language. They speak about the need to relate school knowledge to children's social milieu and to make teaching plans keeping in mind their contexts and needs. A candid sharing of these teachers suggests that many notions they held about children from poor and marginalised communities were systematically challenged during their pre-service education. Several activities involving field experiences and theoretical engagement compelled them to reflect on their socialisation, repeatedly acknowledge and counter the stereotypes they held. They spoke about the change they experienced in themselves —learning to take initiative, connect with the lives of children, question their own notions and biases, understand problems from different perspectives, learn to trust themselves, and express their arguments logically and with confidence.

These teachers believe that the onus of finding solutions to the problem of frequent absenteeism amongst children also lies with teachers who need to understand their everyday compulsions, often emanating from harsh socio-economic conditions, and involve them in school activities by making teaching-learning a worthwhile experience. Teachers acknowledge that many children arrive late to school because they are disinterested, but this disinterest they attribute to possible unattractive and irrelevant teaching-learning materials and pedagogic approaches that often make school learning a meaningless and often negative experience for them.

With regard to questions about children's errors and their inability to read and write with facility, teachers expressed a more nuanced understanding of the specific issues related to subject matter. For instance, they analysed children's errors in mathematics with specific reference to concepts and sub-concepts that children need to engage with. They could discern the difference between conceptual and procedural knowledge and the need to design learning activities based on this understanding. They reflected on the need to adapt curriculum sequencing and alter pedagogic strategies to address the specific cognitive needs of children who were seen as lagging behind. Solutions offered by these teachers lay in problematising the issue at hand and then looking for appropriate strategies related to curriculum design and pedagogy.

On evaluating creative writing, teachers gave priority to children's expression of ideas and their originality; the need to address the structure and rules of language without denigrating children and their home language. Teachers foregrounded the importance of involving children, encouraging them to talk and ensuring their participation by creating non-threatening and accepting learning environments. Teachers expressed the view that learning experiences would need to be adapted for children at different levels of learning. Whether children came from poor backgrounds or diverse abilities, the response of teachers indicated sensitivity, a sense of agency and competence in creating appropriately designed learning experiences.

Group 2 teachers are convinced that gender differences are socially constructed, hence teachers have a crucial role in enabling gender equality. This, they felt, must be addressed by way of school policy; for instance, involving children in gender-neutral ways and engaging with parents so as to consciously challenge processes of socialisation. In contrast, Group 1 teachers accept gender differences as 'naturalised', as part of socialisation at home and in society and therefore do not warrant change. Most teachers indicated helplessness, stating that not only does it have the sanction of society; it is also an expectation of school authorities that teachers actively discourage girls and boys to interact or sit together in class. Group 2 teachers who have engaged with questions of gender in school and society during their preparation to become teachers, argue that socialisation patterns of gender, class or caste need to be brought into the classroom for dialogue, enquiry and reasoning.

Field accounts illustrate that teachers who engage with the complexities of diverse social reality, develop insight into the lives of diverse people. They learn to introspect and reason, call into question hierarchies and inequalities by voicing their concerns, expressing dissent and reaching out to make a difference. While acknowledging that poverty creates limiting conditions, they do not see these conditions as determining how children learn and behave. Seeking to design educative experiences that draw all children in the processes of learning can also be attributed to the dispositions they develop, of valuing children from diverse contexts, relating to them as epistemic selves and having faith in their capacities to learn.

Ethnographic accounts of schooling resonate with the dominant views teachers hold about the poor and the marginalised, their social milieu, abilities and inabilities, providing substantive evidence to the argument that conditions which impede children's learning are engendered in the everyday quotidian of the classroom. So far, the paper has argued that this view dominates the narrative of teachers in classrooms where the poor come to learn. Underlying this view are two deeper narratives: that of reforming poor children as the chief aim of education-manifest in the everyday culture of schooling; and the construction of a totalitarian disbelief in the epistemic identities of children of the poor. Substantive evidence from classroom accounts, juxtaposed with the views expressed by teachers, makes this a compelling argument.

28.4.3 Reforming Children as the Aim of Education

Several teachers believe that children who fail to perform are 'cognitively deficient', even 'uneducable'. Teachers also attribute 'non-performance' of children to a lack of application of mind and hard work and inadequacies in their parental and community backgrounds. The aim of education in their view is to change behaviour using coercive methods to 'make' children perform. Iyer (2013) gives a lucid account of how teachers are routinely preoccupied with the need to 'reform' children. This they attempt to do through a strict regimen of everyday rituals in school. Biased and negative behaviour of teachers towards children, frequent corporal punishment and the sheer negation of children's identities are the usual norm —creating a classroom feared by most children, especially the marginalised.

A recent ethnographic study of a state-run school[13] comprising migrant and non-migrant families illustrates how children's experience of schooling is largely shaped by their specific class positioning. Teachers were observed reminding children of their lower class status during all major activities in school, including the distribution of incentives such as uniforms and money. Lack of discipline amongst children, their poor performance and frequent disruptions within the school were attributed to their social milieu. It was common to observe teachers 'demeaning children's work', 'ridiculing cultural difference', being openly 'disdainful about their expressed aspirations' and 're-inscribing social identities' (Dalal 2014).

The classroom ethos unfolded in these ethnographic accounts and the views expressed by individual teachers indicate how teachers construct the understanding that the chief aim of education is to 'reform' children of the poor. This idea of reform leads teachers to fastidiously control the way children behave, the way they talk, walk or play. The school is constructed by teachers as a space where children from poor and marginalised communities ought to be reformed to become 'clean, orderly, disciplined and obedient'. This understanding of teachers rooted in middle class values finds legitimacy in universalistic theories of child development and learning promulgated through teacher training programmes. Teachers often view the children they teach from the lens of an 'ideal child' and an 'ideal childhood'. The dominant perceptions teachers develop about children and their communities lead them to create a culture of exclusion and marginalisation of the poor. The dynamics of poverty hence shapes social relations between the teacher and the taught in a manner that produce and reproduce experiences of deprivation.

28.4.4 Children as Non-Epistemic Entities

Most 'failures' of children in terms of non-performance were attributed by teachers to inadequacies inherent in them, their parental and community backgrounds and social milieu. Children's errors are viewed as deficiencies in individual children,

---

[13]This ethnographic study is the work of a doctoral student who spent a year and a half in a state government-run primary school to investigate how children's identities are manifested and constructed in the everyday processes of the school. See Jyoti Dalal (2014).

indicative of degrees of 'educability'. Dalal (2014) also notes that children are continually referred to as belonging to a certain community, gender, caste, religion or class and are rarely addressed as learners.

The negative attitudes towards children, the lack of faith in their abilities to learn and the everyday focus on their class and social identities reveal that children are viewed as 'non-epistemic' beings. Viewing the classroom as a social and relational space, Majumdar and Mooij (2011) argue that the kind of relationship children share with teachers and the kind of interactions they have, shapes classroom processes—involving or excluding children from processes of learning. For instance, when teachers attribute lack of performance to aspects inherent in children and their social milieu, they provide sanction to class inequalities. Teachers are also seen to demean the poor backgrounds of children even while transacting text lessons. Dalal (2014) observed that during the teaching of a lesson in environmental studies (EVS), the text—written with the intention to include the experiences of children in the classroom discourse—was instead used to humiliate the social milieu of children. The examples given below illustrate this.

The chapter: 'The World in my Home' from the NCERT Environmental Science textbook engages with issues of diversity such as gender, caste divide and honesty. The text is written in a manner that seeks the participation of children, encouraging them to talk about their experiences. The first part of the chapter deals with a common scenario at home where a fight breaks out over the remote control of the television. The teacher reads the text and the questions that are aimed at engaging children in a conversation are as follows: "Do you have such fights at home?" Several children give mixed responses. The teacher ignores all of them and pronounces her judgment on the children and their families: "You people fight on anything and everything. What else do you do other than fight?"

She moves on to the nest section of the text which encourages children to be sensitive and truthful. The text alludes to the integrity of the main protagonist of the story, who pays the correct amount of money for an ice cream even though the shopkeeper asks for a lesser amount. The teacher reads the question given in the textbook: "Would you also do such a thing?" This time too she answers on her own: "No, you don't do this" Abhishek intervenes: "Yes madam, we do" Dismissing him she says: "You definitely cannot do this. I do not think there would be even one child in your neighbourhood who would do such a thing".

This classroom episode highlights how teachers tend to essentialise the values and behaviours of children who come from poor families. Teachers' orientations towards these children are driven by the stereotypical assumptions they hold about them and about poverty.

As argued elsewhere, an overwhelming emphasis on archaic concepts of the psychology of learning and individual differences during pre-service training constructs a frame within which students are perceived as dull, lazy and 'uneducable' even as they struggle with alienating aspects of school environments—be it the language or an irrelevant school curriculum. Concepts of 'slow learners' and 'low IQ', rampantly used in contemporary Indian classrooms, are 'naturalised' in the amalgamation of a folk and entrenched 'practical' discourse of pre-service teacher education (Batra 2014).

Primary research evidence and classroom accounts presented in this chapter help to take this argument further: that children are excluded from learning not because of the *absence* of conditions necessary for enabling school participation and learning but because of the *oppressive presence* of conditions of capability deprivation commonly observed in schools which children of the poor attend with hope. The most important amongst these is teachers' refusal to accept these children as being capable of engaging and learning. The dominant school ethos appears to be one where children of the poor and the marginalised are perceived with stigmatised identities and not recognised as epistemic entities.

There is need to understand why teachers' discourse about social and economic differences and children's specific learning needs continue to remain unchallenged and where the possibilities for change lie. Views of teachers educated to engage with questions of diversity, knowledge, learner and learning in interdisciplinary frames, discussed earlier, provide some insight into how this challenge could be addressed.

28.5   Conclusion

This chapter begins with the argument that poverty research as well as educational research fail to capture the dynamics of how poor children experience schooling. Poverty research is insensible to social research that demonstrates how inequities are reinforced in the classroom. Dominant educational research on the other hand, remains guilty of viewing poverty as a mere barrier to education and hence fails to enquire into how poverty shapes the everyday classroom.

Primary data gathered from teachers and ethnographic accounts of select state classrooms, makes a compelling case for viewing the education of the poor and the marginalised in the expanded framework of the capability approach, including how being poor shapes school experiences. Empirical accounts reveal how the poor continue to be marginalised from processes of learning despite having access to schooling. The dominant school ethos is one where children of the poor are viewed from a deficit perspective. Teachers' lack of faith in the educability of poor children and their entrenched views on what education must offer, excludes them from opportunities to learn.

Thus, conditions of capability deprivation are created in the everyday classroom. It is argued that collusion between the manner in which the quality of education and its relationship with poverty is conceptualised and positioned in the era of market-based reforms sets the conditions for the production of capability deprivation. The thrust on a universalised, standardised and outcome-based discourse of education redefines the very purpose of education, shifting the educator's gaze away from the classroom process. Precluding a focus on what happens inside the classroom renders teaching-learning processes irrelevant for research and meaningful policy intervention.

The consistently poor performance of children on tasks of basic arithmetic and reading as indicated in ASER Reports (2015) warrants the need to re-examine the processes of teaching and learning. The bulk of the children who underperform may well be those who attend school with an aspiration to make progress but are unyieldingly excluded from processes of learning within the space of learning. Capability deprivation, it is argued, is a direct consequence of exclusion that plays out in classrooms. Informed by the perspective of social justice and equality, the capabilities approach evinces the criticality of the educational process. Further research would be required to examine how the collusion between the conceptualisation of poverty and quality education also threatens to dilute the 'right to education' by institutionalising mechanisms that maintain conditions of capability deprivation in schools for the poor and marginalised.

References

ASER. (2015). *Annual status of education report (Rural) 2014, Provisional report, 13 January 2015*. New Delhi: ASER Centre.

Avalos, B. (1986). *Teaching children of the poor: An ethnographic study in Latin America*. Ottawa: International Development Research Centre.

Batra, P. (2014). Problematising teacher education practice in India: Developing a research agenda. *Education as Change, 18*(S1), S5–S18.

Chavan, M. (2015). Looking back and looking ahead. *Annual status of education report (Rural), 2014, Provisional report, 13 January 2015* (pp. 1–4). New Delhi: ASER Centre.

Dalal, J. (2014). *Delineating identity: Reflections on its construction and articulation in the school*. Unpublished Ph.D. dissertation. New Delhi: Central Institute of Education, University of Delhi.

GoI (Government of India). (2012). Vision of teacher education in India: Quality and regulatory perspective. *Report of the high-powered commission on teacher education constituted by the hon'ble supreme court of India*. New Delhi: Ministry of Human Resource Development, Government of India.

Iyer, S. (2013). An ethnographic study of disciplinary and pedagogic practices in a primary class. *Contemporary Education Dialogue, 10*(2), 163–95.

Majumdar, M., & Mooij, J. (2011). *Education and inequality in India: A classroom view*. London: Routledge.

National Council for the Protection of Child Rights (NCPCR). (2009). *Corporal punishment: Everyday reality of India's children report of the study commissioned by NCPCR*. New Delhi: NCPCR.

Ng, J. C., & Rury, J. L. (2006). Poverty and education: A critical analysis of the Ruby Payne phenomenon. *Teachers college record*. http://www.tcrecord.org.ID. Number: 12596. Accessed on February 10, 2015.

Nussbaum, M. C. (2011). *Creating capabilities: The human development approach*. Massachusetts: The Belknap Press of Harvard University Press.

Ruby, P. K. (2005). *A framework for understanding poverty*. Highlands TX: Aha Process, Inc.

Rose, P., & Caroline, D. (2008). Chronic poverty and education: A review of the literature. Working paper no. 131, Chronic Poverty Research Centre. www.chronicpoverty.org. Accessed on September 28, 2014.

Sarangapani, P. (2003). *Constructing school knowledge: An ethnography of learning in an Indian village*. New Delhi: Sage Publications.

Sen, A. (1999). *Development as freedom*. Oxford: Oxford University Press.

Stromquist, N. P. (2001). What poverty does to girl's education: The intersection of class, gender and policy in Latin America. *In Compare, 31*(1), 39–56.

Tilak, J. B. G. (2005). *Post-elementary education, poverty and development in India. Post-basic education and training, working paper series No. 6*. Edinburgh: Centre of African Studies, University of Edinburgh.

UNDP. (1998). *Human development report*. New York: Oxford University Press.

Wadhwa, W. (2015). Government vs private schools: Have things changed? *In annual status of education report (ASER) (Rural) 2014, provisional report, 13 January 2015* (pp. 19–21). New Delhi: ASER Centre.

Author Biography

Poonam Batra is Professor of Education at the Central Institute of Education, University of Delhi, India. Major areas of research and professional focus include public policy in education; curriculum and pedagogy; social psychology of education, teacher education and gender studies.

Chapter 29
The Future of Teacher Education: Evidence, Competence or Wisdom?

Gert Biesta

29.1 Introduction: The Fear of Being Left Behind

In recent years policymakers and politicians have become increasingly interested in teacher education. In England, for example, the government has published a policy framework for school education—a paper with the interesting title "The Importance of Teaching"[1]—which not only sets out the parameters for a significant transformation of state funded school education but also contains specific proposals for the education of teachers. In Scotland the government has recently commissioned a review of Scottish teacher education. This report, with the title "Teaching Scotland's Future",[2] also makes very specific recommendations about teacher education and about the further professional development of teachers. In addition, discussions about teacher education are increasingly being influenced by developments at European level, particularly in the context of the Lisbon strategy which, in 2000, set the aim of making the European Union into "the most competitive and dynamic knowledge-based economy in the world",[3] and the Bologna Process, aimed at the creation of a European Higher Education Area, a process that was inaugurated in 1999. In the wake of the 2005 OECD report on the state of teacher education—a report called *Teachers Matter: Attracting, Developing and Retaining Effective Teachers*[4]—

---

[1]http://www.education.gov.uk/b0068570/the-importance-of-teaching/. Retrieved 27 Feb 2011.
[2]http://www.reviewofteachereducationinscotland.org.uk/teachingscotlandsfuture/index.asp. Retrieved 27 Feb 2011.
[3]http://www.consilium.europa.eu/uedocs/cms_data/docs/pressdata/en/ec/00100-r1.en0.htm. Retrieved 27 Feb 2011.
[4]www.oecd/edu/teacherpolicy. Retrieved 27 Feb 2011.

G. Biesta (✉)
Brunel University, Uxbridge, England, UK
e-mail: gert.biesta@brunel.ac.uk

© Springer Nature Singapore Pte Ltd. 2017
M.A. Peters et al. (eds.), *A Companion to Research in Teacher Education*,
DOI 10.1007/978-981-10-4075-7_29

the European Commission produced a document in 2007 called *Improving the Quality of Teacher Education*[5] which proposed "shared reflection about actions that can be taken at Member State level and how the European Union might support these". As part of this process the European Commission also produced a set of "Common European Principles for Teacher Competences and Qualifications".[6] While none of these documents have any legal power in themselves, they do tend to exert a strong influence on policy development within the member states of the European Union—a point to which I will return below.

One could see the attention from policymakers and politicians for teacher education as a good thing. One could see it as the expression of a real concern for the quality of education at all levels and as recognition of the fact that the quality of teacher education is an important element in the overall picture. But one could also read it more negatively by observing that now that governments in many countries have established a strong grip on schools through a combination of curriculum prescription, testing, inspection, measurement and league tables, they are now turning their attention to teacher education in order to establish total control over the educational system. Much of course depends on how, in concrete situations, discourse and policy will unfold or have unfolded already. In this regard it is interesting, for example, that whereas in the English situation teaching is being depicted as a *skill* that can be picked up in practice (with the implication that teacher education can be shifted from universities to training schools), the Scottish discussion positions teaching as a *profession* which, for that very reason, requires proper teacher education, both with regard to teacher preparation and with regard to further professional development. While there are, therefore, still important differences 'on the ground', we are, at the very same time, seeing an increasing *convergence* in discourse and policy with regard to teaching which, in turn, is leading to a convergence in discourse and policy with regard to teacher education. The main concept that seems to be emerging in all of this is the notion of *competence* (see, for example Crick 2008; Mulder et al. 2007). Competence is an interesting notion for at least two reasons. Firstly, as mentioned, the notion of competence has a certain rhetorical appeal—after all, who would want to argue that teachers should *not* be competent? Second, the idea of competence focuses the discussion on the question what teachers should be able to *do* rather than that it only pays attention to what teachers need to *know*. One could say, therefore, that the idea of 'competence' is more practical and, in a sense, also more holistic in that it seems to encompass knowledge, skills and action as an integrated way, rather than to see action as, say, the application of knowledge or the implementation of skills. Whether this is indeed so also depends on the particular approach to and conception of competence one favours. Mulder et al. (2007) show, for example that within the literature on competence there are three distinctive traditions, the behaviourist, the

---

[5]http://ec.europa.eu/education/com392_en.pdf. Retrieved 27 Feb 2011.
[6]http://ec.europa.eu/education/policies/2010/doc/principles_en.pdf. Retrieved 27 Feb 2011.

generic and the cognitive, that put different emphases on the 'mix' between action, cognition and values. While some definitions of competence are very brief and succinct—such as Eraut's definition of competence as "(t)he ability to perform the tasks and roles required to the expected standards" (Eraut 2003, p. 117, cited in Mulder et al. 2007)—other definitions, such as, for example, Deakin Crick's definition of competence as "a complex combination of knowledge, skills, understanding, values, attitudes and desire which lead to effective, embodied human action in the world, in a particular domain" (Crick 2008, p. 313), become so broad that it may be difficult to see what is not included in the idea of competence.

What is worrying, therefore, is perhaps not so much the notion of competence itself—it is a notion with a certain appeal and some potential—but first and foremost the fact that the idea of competence is beginning to monopolise the discourse about teaching and teacher education. It is, therefore, first of all the convergence towards one particular way of thinking and talking about teaching and teacher education that we should be worried about. After all, if there is no alternative discourse, if a particular idea is simply seen as 'common sense', then there is a risk that it stops people from thinking at all. While, as mentioned, European documents about teaching and teacher education have no *legal* power—decisions about education remain firmly located at the level of the member states—they do have important *symbolic* and *rhetorical* power in that they often become a reference point that many want to orientate themselves towards, perhaps on the assumption that if they do not adjust themselves to it, they run the risk of being left behind. We can see a similar logic at work in the problematic impact that PISA (OECD's Programme for International Student Assessment) has had on education throughout Europe. What I have in mind here is not the fact that PISA is only interested in particular 'outcomes'—although there are important questions to be asked about that as well—but first of all the fact that PISA and similar systems create the illusion that a wide range of different educational practices *is* comparable and that, by implication, these practices therefore *ought to* be comparable. Out of a fear of being left behind, out of a fear of ending up at the bottom end of the league table, we can see schools and school systems transforming themselves into the definition of education that 'counts' in systems like PISA, the result of it being that more and more schools and school systems begin to become the same.

So this is what can happen when a particular discourse becomes hegemonic— that is, when a particular discourse begins to monopolise thinking and talking. It is not so much that the discourse has the power to change everything but rather that people begin to adjust their ways of doing and talking to such ideas. This then generates increased uniformity or, to put it form the other side, a reduction of diversity in educational thought and practice. The argument from biodiversity shows what is dangerous about such a development, as a reduction of diversity erodes the ability of a system to respond effectively and creatively to changes in the environment. Also, the fact that the move towards uniformity is more often than not driven by fear, that is driven by a lack of courage to think and act differently and independently, makes such developments even more worrying, as we all know that fear is not a very good counsellor.

But it is not only the tendency towards uniformity that is problematic here. It is also that through the discourse about competence, about the competent teacher and about the competencies that teacher education should develop in teachers, that a very particular view about education is being repeated, promoted and being *multiplied*. This is often not how ideas about the competences that teachers need, are being presented. Such competences are often presented as general, as relatively open to different views about education, as relatively neutral with regard to such views, and also as relatively uncontested. They are, in other words, presented as 'common sense'. One thing that is important, therefore, is to open up this common sense by showing that it is possible to think *differently* about education and about what teachers should be able to do, at least in order to move away from an unreflected and unreflective common sense about education. But I also wish to argue that the particular common sense about education that is being multiplied is problematic in itself, because it has a tendency to promote what I would see as a rather uneducational way of thinking about education. And this is the deeper problem that needs to be addressed in order to have a better starting point for our discussion about the future of teacher education. Let me try to explain what I have in mind.

29.2   The 'Learnification' of Education

There are a number of places where we could start, but I invite you to have a brief look at the key competences enlisted in the document from the Directorate-General for education and Culture of the European Commission, called "Common European Principles for Teacher Competences and Qualifications".

Making it work: the key competences

Teaching and education add to the economic and cultural aspects of the knowledge society and should therefore be seen in their societal context. Teachers should be able to:

Work with others: they work in a profession which should be based on the values of social inclusion and nurturing the potential of every learner. They need to have knowledge of human growth and development and demonstrate self-confidence when engaging with others. They need to be able to work with learners as individuals and support them to develop into fully participating and active members of society. They should also be able to work in ways which increase the collective intelligence of learners and co-operate and collaborate with colleagues to enhance their own learning and teaching.

Work with knowledge, technology and information: they need to be able to work with a variety of types of knowledge. Their education and professional development should equip them to access, analyse, validate, reflect on and transmit knowledge, making effective use of technology where this is appropriate. Their pedagogic skills should allow them to build and manage learning environments and retain the intellectual freedom to make choices over the delivery of education. Their confidence in the use of ICT should allow them to integrate it effectively into learning and teaching. They should be able to guide and support learners in the networks in which information can be found and built. They should have a good understanding of subject knowledge and view learning as a lifelong journey. Their practical and theoretical skills should also allow them to learn from their own experiences and match a wide range of teaching and learning strategies to the needs of learners.

Work with and in society: they contribute to preparing learners to be globally responsible in their role as EU citizens. Teachers should be able to promote mobility and co-operation in Europe, and encourage intercultural respect and understanding. They should have an understanding of the balance between respecting and being aware of the diversity of learners' cultures and identifying common values. They also need to understand the factors that create social cohesion and exclusion in society and be aware of the ethical dimensions of the knowledge society. They should be able to work effectively with the local community, and with partners and stakeholders in education—parents, teacher education institutions, and representative groups. Their experience and expertise should also enable them to contribute to systems of quality assurance. Teachers' work in all these areas should be embedded in a professional continuum of lifelong learning which includes initial teacher education, induction and continuing professional development, as they cannot be expected to possess all the necessary competences on completing their initial teacher education.[7]

There is, of course, a lot that can be said about this text, and I would say that documents like these do require careful and detailed critical analysis. For the purpose of my presentation I would like to make two observations. The first is that in this text school education is very much positioned as an instrument that needs to deliver all kinds of societal goods. Education needs to produce such things as social cohesion, social inclusion, a knowledge society, lifelong learning, a knowledge economy, EU citizens, intercultural respect and understanding, a sense of common values, and so on. In terms of its agenda this is a very functionalist view of education and a very functionalist view of what is core to what teachers need to be able to do. It paints a picture where society—and there is of course always the question who 'society' actually 'is'—sets the agenda, and where education is seen as an instrument for the delivery of this agenda. One can note that in this text the only 'intellectual freedom' granted to teachers is about *how* to 'deliver' this agenda, not about what it is that is supposed to be 'delivered'. (I put 'delivery' in quotation marks to highlight that it is a very unfortunate and unhelpful metaphor to talk about education in the first place.) This functionalist or instrumentalist view of education does not seem to consider the idea that education may have other interests—perhaps its own interests (I return to this below)—but predominantly thinks of the school as the institution that needs to solve 'other people's problems', to put it briefly.

My second observation concerns the fact that in this text education is predominantly described in terms of *learning*. We read that teachers are supposed to nurture the potential of every learner, that they need to be able to work with learners as individuals, that they should aim at increasing the collective intelligence of learners, that they should be able to build and manage learning environments, integrate ICT effectively into learning and teaching, provide guidance and support

[7]From http://ec.europa.eu/education/policies/2010/doc/principles_en.pdf. Retrieved 27 Feb 2011.

to learners in information networks, and view learning as a lifelong journey. For me this document is another example of what in elsewhere (see particularly Biesta 2004, 2006) I have referred to as the rise of a 'new language of learning' in education. This rise is manifest in a number of 'translations' that have taken place in the language used in educational practice, educational policy and educational research. We can see it in the tendency to refer to students, pupils, children and even adults as learners. We can see it in the tendency to refer to teaching as the facilitation of learning or the management of learning environments. We can see it in the tendency to refer to schools as places for learning or as learning environments. And we can see it in the tendency no longer to speak about adult education but rather to talk about lifelong learning.

Now one could argue that there is no problem with this. Isn't it, after all, the purpose of education that children and students learn? Isn't it therefore not reasonable to think of the task of teachers as that of supporting such learning? And does not that mean that schools are and should be understood as learning environments or places of learning? Perhaps the quickest way to make my point is to say that for me the purpose of education is *not* that children and students learn, but that they learn *something* and that they do so with reference to particular *purposes*. A main problem with the language of learning is that it is a language of *process,* but not a language of content and purpose. Yet education is never just about learning, but is always about the learning of something for particular purposes. In addition I wish to argue that education is always about learning from someone. Whereas the language of learning is an *individualistic* language—learning is after all something you can do on your own—the language of education is a *relational* language, where there is always the idea of someone educating somebody else. The problem with the rise of the language of learning in education is therefore threefold: it is a language that makes it more difficult to ask questions about content; it is a language that makes it more difficult to ask questions of purpose; and it is a language that makes it more difficult to ask questions about the specific role and responsibility of the teacher in the educational relationship.

All this is not to say that learning is a meaningless idea, or that learning has no place in education. But it is to highlight the fact that the language of learning is not an *educational* language so that when discussions about education become entirely framed in terms of learning, some of the most central educational questions and issues—about purpose, content and relationships—begin to disappear from the conversation and, subsequently, run the risk of beginning to disappear from the practice of education too. In my own work I have referred to this development as the 'learnification' of education (see Biesta 2010a). I have deliberately constructed an ugly word for this because, from the standpoint of education, I think that this is a very worrying trend. While, as mentioned, the idea of competence is therefore, in itself, not necessarily bad, I am concerned about the way in which it is multiplying a particular view about education through a particular language about education, the language of learning. This means that if we wish to say anything *educational* about teacher education, if, in other words, we wish to move beyond the language of learning, we need to engage with a way of speaking and thinking that is more properly educational. Once we do this we may find—and this is what I will be arguing below—that the idea of competences becomes less attractive and less appropriate to think about teacher education and its future. Let me move, then, to the next step in my argument, which has to do with the nature of educational practices.

29.3 What Is Education for?

Let me begin with a brief anecdote. In Scotland experienced teachers have the opportunity to follow a specially designed master's programme in order to obtain a higher qualification. Teachers who have successfully gone through this programme can call themselves 'chartered teachers' (just like, for example, chartered accountants or chartered surveyors). One of the things that the teachers studying on this programme need to be able to do is show that through the conduct of small-scale inquiry projects they can *improve* their practice. I have supervised a number of these projects, and what I found interesting and remarkable is that while most of the teachers were able to provide evidence about the fact that they had been able to *change* their practice, they found it quite difficult to articulate why such changes would count as an *improvement* of their practice. Quite often they thought, at least initially, that a change in practice is automatically an improvement, until I showed them that each time a practice has changed we can still ask the question why such change is an improvement, that is, why that change is *desirable* change, why the changed situation is *better* than what existed before. There is only one way in which we can answer this question, and that is through engagement with the question what education is *for*, that is, the question about the purpose of education. It is, after all, only if we are able to articulate what it is we want to achieve, that we can judge whether a change in practice gets us closer to this or further away from it.

As I have already said, the language of learning is utterly unhelpful here, because if we just say that students should learn—or that teachers should support or promote students' learning (which is actually how the job of teachers is being described in some Scottish policy documents)—but do not specify what the learning is supposed to achieve or result in, we are actually saying nothing at all. This shows something particular about educational practices, namely that they are *teleological* practices—the Greek word 'telos' meaning aim or purpose—that is, practices that are *constituted* by certain aims, which means, that if you take the orientation towards aims away, you take the very thing that makes a practice into an educational practice away. In my work—particularly the book *Good education in an age of measurement* (Biesta 2010a)—I have therefore argued that if we want to move back from 'learning' to 'education' we need to engage explicitly with the question of purpose. I have referred to this as the question of good education in order to highlight that when we engage with the question of purpose in education we are always involved in value judgements, in judgements, that is, about what is educationally desirable.

By arguing that there is a need to engage with the question of educational purpose, I am not trying to define what the purpose of education should be. But I do wish to make two points about how I think we should engage with the question of purpose. The first point is that educational practices, in my view, always serve more than one purpose—and do so at the very same time. The *multi-dimensionality of educational purpose* is precisely what makes education interesting. It is also, and this is my second point to which I will return below, the reason why a particular kind of judgement is needed in education. By saying that that question of educational purpose is multi-dimensional, I am trying to say that education 'functions' or 'works' in a number of different dimensions and that in each of these dimensions the question of purpose needs to be raised. In my own work I have suggested that we can distinguish three dimensions in which the question of purpose needs to be raised—or to put it in more simple language: I have suggested that educational processes and practices tend to function in three different domains. I have referred to these domains as *qualification, socialisation* and *subjectification* (see Biesta 2010a, and for a Swedish version Biesta 2011b; see also Biesta 2009). *Qualification* roughly has to do with the ways in which education qualifies people for doing things—in the broad sense of the word—by equipping them with knowledge, skills and dispositions. This is a very important dimension of school education and some would even argue that it is the only thing that should matter in schools. Education is, however, not only about knowledge, skills and dispositions but also has to do with the ways in which, through education, we become part of existing social, cultural and political practices and traditions. This is the *socialisation* dimension of education where, to put it in more general terms, the orientation is on the 'insertion' of newcomers into existing orders. Newcomers, here, can both be children and those who move from one country or one culture to another. We can also think here of the ways in which education introduces newcomers into particular professional orders and cultures. While some, as mentioned, take a very strict and narrow view of education and would argue that the only task of schools is to be concerned about knowledge and skills and dispositions—this is, for example, the view of education currently emerging in educational policy discourse in England—we can see that over the past decades the socialisation function has become an explicit dimension of discussions about what schools are for. We can see this specifically in the range of societal 'agendas' that have been added to the school curriculum, such as environmental education, citizenship education, social and moral education, sex education, and so on. The idea here is that education not only exerts a socialising force on children and students, but that it is actually desirable that education should do this.

Now while, again, some people would argue that these are the only two proper and legitimate dimensions that school education should be concerned about, I wish to argue that there is a third dimension in which education operates and should operate. This has to do with the way in which education impacts on the person. In the English language it is a bit of a struggle to find the right concept here, as I would argue that this dimension has to do with the subjectivity of the human person—a notion that probably works slightly better in the German language: 'Subjektivität' and 'Subjekt werden'—which is why I have referred to this dimension as the *subjectification* dimension of education. It is important to see that subjectification and socialisation are not the same—and one of the important challenges for contemporary education is how we can actually articulate the distinction between the two (for more on this see Biesta 2006). Socialisation has to do with how we become part of existing orders, how we identify with such orders and thus obtain an identity; subjectification, on the other hand, is always about how we can exist 'outside' of such orders, so to speak. With a relatively 'old' but still crucially important concept, we can say that subjectification has to do with the question of human freedom—which, of course, then raises further questions about how we should understand human freedom (for my ideas on this see, again, Biesta 2006; and also Chap. 4 in Biesta 2010a; and for a discussion in Dutch Biesta 2011a).

To engage with the question of purpose in education, so I wish to suggest, requires that we engage with this question in relation to all three domains. It requires that we think about what we aim to achieve in relation to qualification, socialisation and subjectification. The reason why engagement with the question of purpose requires that we 'cover' all three domains, lies in the fact that anything we do in education potentially has 'impact' in any of these three domains. It is important to acknowledge that the three domains are *not separate*. I tend to depict them through a Venn diagram of three overlapping areas.

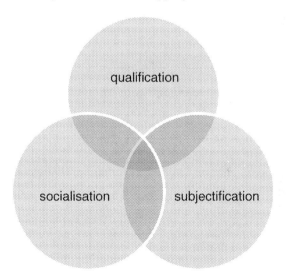

The overlap is important because on the one hand this indicates opportunities for *synergy*, whereas on the other hand it can also help us to see potential *conflict* between the different dimensions. An example of potential synergy is the way in which in vocational education the teaching of particular skills at same time functions as a way to socialise students into particular domains of work, into professional responsibility and the like. An example of potential conflict is that where a constant pressure on testing and exams, which is perhaps an effective way to drive up achievement in the domain of qualification, can have negative impact on the domain of subjectification if it teaches students that competition is always better than cooperation.

Given the possibility of synergy and of conflict, and given the fact that our educational activities almost always 'work' in the three domains at the very same time, looking at education through these dimensions begins to make visible something that in my view is absolutely central about the work of teachers, which is the need for making situated judgements about what is educationally desirable in relation to these three dimensions. What is central to the work of teachers is not simply that they set aims and implement them. Because education is multi-dimensional teachers constantly need to make judgements about how to balance the different dimensions; they need to set priorities—which can never be set in general but always need to be set in concrete situations with regard to concrete students—and they need to be able to handle tensions and conflict and, on the other hand, should be able to see possibilities for synergy. All this is at play in this simple distinction between 'change' and 'improvement'. Answering the question whether change is improvement is, therefore, not only a matter of assessing progress towards one particular aim. Because of the multi-dimensionality of education we always need to consider the possibility that gain with regard to one dimension may be loss with regard to another.

What is beginning to emerge from this line of thinking, as you will probably be able to see, is the idea that because education is a teleological practice and because the question of the 'telos' of education is a multi-dimensional question, judgement —judgement about what is educationally desirable—turns out to be an absolutely crucial element of what teachers do. Before I say more about this in order, then, to link this to the question of teacher education, let me make three brief further points about the approach to the question of purpose in education I have outlined above.

First: while I would argue that all education in some way impacts in the three domains—qualification, socialisation, and subjectification—different schools concepts do this in quite different ways. They have different priorities in relation to the three dimensions and these priorities, in a sense, characterise their educational outlook. It is at least crucial that schools are able to *articulate* their position, are able to articulate what their priorities are and what they want to stand for—and it is my experience that the distinction between the three domains and the representation of them in a Venn diagram provide a helpful set of tools which schools can use to become clearer about what it is they prioritise and what it is they ultimately stand for. Secondly: next to the question of the articulation of this—which is about providing clarity—there is of course also the question of the *justification* of a particular school concept, that is the justification of why a particular position and a particular way of prioritising is considered to be desirable. By being able to articulate one's position it becomes at least easier to see what it is that needs to be justified. Third there is, of course, the question whether some school concepts—or wider conceptions of education—are more desirable than others. My own humble opinion here is that education—if it is education and not, say, training or brain-washing—should always have an explicit concern for the person and the question of the freedom of the person, which, as mentioned before, leaves open what it means to be concerned about the person and about the freedom of the person.

(I have developed this in more detail in Biesta 2006 through the introduction of the ideas of 'coming into the world' and 'uniqueness'—see also Biesta 2010a, c.)[8]

29.4   Judgement and Wisdom in Education: Becoming Educationally Wise

If I try to bring the lines of my argument so far together, the point that is emerging is that the question is not so much whether teachers should be competent to do things—one could say that of course they should be competent—but that competence, the ability to do things, is in itself *never enough*. To put it bluntly: a teacher who possesses all the competences teachers need but who is unable to judge which competence needs to be deployed when, is a useless teacher. Judgements about what needs to be done always need to be made with reference to the purposes of education—which is why the language of learning is unhelpful as it is not a language in which the question of purpose can easily be raised, articulated and addressed. And since the question of purpose of education is a multi-dimensional question, the judgement that is needed needs to be *multi-dimensional*, taking into consideration that a gain with regard to one dimension may be a loss with regard to another dimension—so that there is a need to make judgement about the right *balance* and the right '*trade off*' between gains and losses, so to speak. Exerting such judgements is not something that is done at the level of school policy documents, but lies at the very heart of what goes on in the classroom and in the relationships between teachers and students—and this goes on again, and again, and again.

While some might argue that this is an argument for saying that teachers need to be competent in making educational judgements, I would rather want to see the capacity for judgement as something different from competences. Part of my argument for this is that if we would see the ability for educational judgements as a competence, it would be the one and only competence on the list. But we could also say that to the extent that there is something reasonable in the idea that teachers should be competent in doing certain things, there is always the further need to judge when it is appropriate to do what.

A similar argument for the absolutely central role of educational judgements can be made in relation to another tendency we can find in discussions about teaching

---

[8]In my view the priority of Steiner education lies with the person and with the freedom of the person. That does not mean that the other two dimensions—subjectification and socialisation—do not matter in Steiner education, but they do not simply matter in themselves but always as ways in which the person can 'encounter' the world and through this can also 'encounter' himself or herself. This suggests the importance of using the Venn diagram in a *dynamic* way, so that a particular school conception is not simply represented as a position in the diagram, but has to be identified through where its starting point is located and how, from this starting point, it relates to the different dimensions of education.

and teacher education, which is the idea that teaching should develop into a so-called evidence-based profession just as, for example, people have argued that medicine should develop into an evidence-based profession. This is a big and complicated discussion (for more detail see Biesta 2007, 2010b; in Swedish Biesta 2011b; in German Biesta 2010c), so let me try to capture the main issue here, which is the idea that rather than for education to rely on the judgement of professionals it should be based on strong scientific evidence about 'what works'. The idea is that such evidence can only generated in one way, viz. through large scale experimental studies where there is an experimental group who gets a particular 'treatment' and a control group who does not get this 'treatment', in order then to measure whether the 'treatment' had any particular effect. If it did, then—so the argument goes—we have evidence that the 'treatment' 'works' and therefore have an evidence base that tells us what to do. You may recognise these ideas from clinical trials used to test the effectiveness of certain medications and drugs—where there is often an experimental group who gets the real drug and a control group who gets the placebo. The same approach is also used in agriculture, for example to test whether particular chemicals have any effect on, say, the growth of potatoes.

There is a lot that can be said about this, such as the question whether teaching can be understood as a 'treatment'—which I have argued does not make sense—or that students can be compared to potatoes—which I have also argued does not make sense. But even if, for the sake of the argument, we would concede that it might be possible to conduct the kind of studies suggested above, the outcomes of those studies are limited in two ways. One point is that such studies at most give us knowledge about *the past*. That is, they give us knowledge about what may have worked in the past, but there is no guarantee whatsoever—at least not in the domain of human interaction—that what has worked in the past will also work in the future. This already means that such knowledge can at most give us *possibilities* for action, but not rules. While it may therefore have the possibility to *inform* our judgements, it cannot *replace* our judgements about what needs to be done. Judgement is also important because something that may work in relation to one dimension of education may actually have a detrimental effect in relation to another dimension. (An example of this is the whole medicalisation of education—partly in the domain of diagnoses such as ADHD and partly through the use of drugs such as Ritalin— which may perhaps have positive effects on cognitive achievement, but is most likely to have quite negative effects in the domain of subjectification.)

So just as competencies in themselves are not enough to capture what teaching is about, the idea of education as an evidence-based profession makes even less sense. What is missing in both cases is the absolutely crucial role of educational judgement. Particularly with regard to the latter discussion—that is, about the role of scientific evidence—this may remind you of a question that has been circulating in education for a fairly long time. This is the question whether teaching is an art or a science. I think that it is important to pose this question again in our times, not in the least because of the strong push to bring (a certain conception of) science into education, partly through the discussion about evidence, but also increasingly through neuroscience. One person who has very concisely and very convincingly argued against the idea of teaching as a science is the American psychologist William James (1842–1910), and I quote him here because it is perhaps better to hear this argument from one of the founding fathers of modern psychology than from me.

> Psychology is a science, and teaching is an art; and sciences never generate arts directly out of themselves. An intermediary inventive mind must make the application, by using its originality.
>
> The most such sciences can do is to help us to catch ourselves up and check ourselves, if we start to reason or to behave wrongly; and to criticise ourselves more articulately after we have made mistakes.
>
> To know psychology, therefore, is absolutely no guarantee that we shall be good teachers. To advance to that result, we must have an additional endowment altogether, a happy tact and ingenuity to tell us what definite things to say and do when the pupil is before us. That ingenuity in meeting and pursuing the pupil, that tact for the concrete situation, though they are the alpha and omega of the teacher's art, are things to which psychology cannot help us in the least. (James 1899, pp. 14–15)

While James provides a convincing argument why teaching should not and cannot be understood as a science—and actually needs tact, ingenuity and, so I wish to add, judgement—James has less to say about the positive side of the argument, that is, the idea that education should therefore be understood as an art. A thinker who I think has something very helpful and important to say with regard to this question is Aristotle (384–322 B.C), and the interesting question he allows us to ask is not whether teaching is an art or not, but *what kind of art* teaching is (see Aristotle 1980).

Aristotle's argument starts from the distinction between the theoretical life and the practical life. While the theoretical life has to do with "the necessary and the eternal" (Aristotle 1980, p. 140) and thus with a kind of knowledge to which Aristotle refers as science (*episteme*), the practical life has to do with what is 'variable' (ibid., p. 142), that is with the world of change. This is the world in which we act and in which our actions make a difference. What is interesting about Aristotle's ideas about our engagement with the world of change is that he makes a distinction between two modes of acting in the domain of the variable: '*poiesis*' and '*praxis*' or, in Carr's (1987) translation, 'making action' and 'doing action'. Both 'modes' of action require judgement, but the kind of judgement needed is radically different, and this is an important insight for the art of education. *Poiesis* is about the production or fabrication of things—such as, for example, a saddle or a ship. It is, as Aristotle puts it, about "how something may come into being which is capable of either being or not being" (which means that it is about the variable, not about what is eternal and necessary), and about things "whose origin is in the maker and not in the thing made" (which distinguishes *poiesis* from biological phenomena such as growth and development) (Aristotle 1980, p. 141). *Poiesis* is, in short, about the creation of something that did not exist before. The kind of knowledge we need for *poiesis* is *techne* (usually translated as 'art'). It is, in more contemporary vocabulary, technological or instrumental knowledge, "knowledge of how to make things" (ibid., p. 141). Aristotle comments that *poiesis* "has an end other than itself" (ibid., p. 143). The end of *poiesis* is *external* to the means, which means that *techne*, the knowledge of how to make things, is about finding the means that will produce the thing one wants to make. *Techne* therefore encompasses knowledge about the materials we work with and about the techniques we can apply to work with those materials. But making a saddle is never about simply following a recipe. It involves making judgements about the application of our general knowledge to *this* piece of leather, for *this* horse, and for *this* person riding the horse. So we make judgements about application, production and effectiveness as our focus is on producing something—or to be more precise: producing some *thing*.

But the domain of the variable is not confined to the world of things, but also includes the social world; the world of human action and interaction. This is the domain of praxis. The orientation here, as Aristotle puts it, is not towards the production of things but to bringing about 'goodness' or human flourishing (eudamonia). Praxis is "about what sort of things conduce to the good life in general" (ibid., p. 142). It is about good action, but good action is not a means for the achievement of something else. "(G)ood action itself is its end" (ibid., p. 143). The kind of judgement we need here is not about how things should be done; we need judgement "about what is to be done" (ibid.; emphasis added). Aristotle refers to this kind of judgement as phronesis, which is usually translated as practical wisdom. Phronesis is a "reasoned and true state of capacity to act with regard to human goods" (ibid., p. 143).

Two points follow from this. The first has to do with the nature education. Here I would argue, with Aristotle, that we should never think of education *only* as a process of production, that is, of *poiesis*. While education is clearly located in the domain of the variable, it is concerned with the interaction between human beings, not the interaction between human beings and the material world. Education, in other words, is a social art and the aesthetics of the social is in important ways different from the aesthetics of the material (which is not to say that they are entirely separate). This does not mean that we should exclude the idea of *poiesis* from our educational thinking. After all, we do want our teaching and our curricula to have effect and be effective; we do want our students to become good citizens, skilful professionals, knowledgeable human beings; and for that we do need to think about educational processes in terms of *poiesis*, that is, in terms of bringing about some*thing*. But that should never be the be all and end all of education. Education is always more than just production, than just *poiesis*, and ultimately education is precisely what production/poiesis is not because at the end of the day we, as educators, cannot claim that we produce our students; instead we educate them, and we educate them *in* freedom and *for* freedom. That is why what matters in education—what makes education educational—does not lie in the domain of *poiesis* but in the domain of *praxis*. (Which is one of the reasons why the whole idea of evidence-based practice in education does not really make sense, at it is based on a poiesis model, which might work for potatoes, but not for human beings.) It shows, in other words, why education is a social art and not a material art.

The second point I wish to make is that practical wisdom, the kind of wisdom we need in relation to *praxis* with the intention to bring about goodness, captures quite well what I have been saying about educational judgement. Educational judgements are, after all, judgements about what needs to be done, not with the aim to produce something in the technical sense, but with the aim to bring about what is considered to be educationally desirable (in the three—overlapping—domains I have identified). Such judgements are, therefore, not 'technical' judgements but they are value judgements—and perhaps we can even call them moral judgements. What Aristotle adds to the picture—and this is important for developing these views about education into views about teacher education—is that practical wisdom is not to be understood as a set of skills or dispositions or a set of competencies, but rather denotes a certain quality or excellence of the person. The Greek term here is ἀρετή and the English translation of ἀρετή is virtue. The ability to make wise educational judgements should therefore not be seen as some kind of 'add on', that is, something that does not affect us as a person, but rather denotes what we might call a holistic quality, something that permeates and characterises the whole person—and we can take 'characterise' her quite literally, as virtue is often also translated as 'character'.

The question is therefore not how can we learn *phronesis*. The question rather is, how we can become a *phronimos*; how can we become a practically wise *person*. And more specifically the question is: how can we become an *educationally wise person*. Now this, so I wish to suggest, is the question of teacher education, and in the final step of my lecture I will draw some conclusions and make some observations about what all this might mean for the future of teacher education.

29.5 Virtuosity: Becoming Educationally Wise

I have, finally, arrived at the central question of this paper, the question of teacher education. That it took me a while to get here has to do with the fact that in order to say anything about teacher education we first need to get a sense of how we wish to understand teaching—and here I have put forward what we might call a virtue-based conception of teaching, a conception that puts the ability for educational judgements at the very centre of the 'art' of teaching—and in order to do that, I had to say a few things about education so that we were in a position to speak about teaching in an *educational* manner, rather than just in terms of learning. Where I ended up with these reflections was with the conclusion that teachers need to develop the ability to make wise educational judgements. This, as I have indicated, should not be seen as a skill or competence but should rather be understood as a quality of the person. Where I ended up, in other words, is in arguing that the overarching aim of teacher education should be the question how teachers can become educationally wise. This is not about the acquisition of *phronesis*, but about how a teacher can become a *phronimos* or, to be more precise, how a teacher can become an *educational* phronimos, so to speak.

But how can we get there? One interesting observation Aristotle makes in relation to this is that he says "that a young man of practical wisdom cannot be found" (ibid., p. 148). What he is saying there is that wisdom is something that comes with age—or perhaps it's better to say that wisdom comes with *experience*. This is one important point for teacher education, to which I will return below. The second point that is relevant here is that when Aristotle comes to points where one would expect him to define what a practically wise person looks like, he doesn't come with a description of certain traits or qualities, but actually comes with examples—and one main example in Aristotle's writings is Pericles. Pericles, so we could say, appears in the argument as someone who *exemplifies* phronesis, he exemplifies what a practically wise person looks like. It is as if Aristotle is saying: if you want to know what practical wisdom is, if you want to know what a practically wise person looks like, look at him, look at her, because they are excellent examples.

If all this makes sense, it suggests three things for the education of teachers, and we could see this as three 'parameters' for our thinking about the future of teacher education.

It first of all means that teacher education is about the *formation of the person* (not, so I wish to emphasise, as a private individual but as a professional). It starts, to use the terms I introduced earlier, in the domain of subjectification. Teacher education is not about the acquisition of knowledge, skills and dispositions per se (qualification) nor about just doing as other teachers do (socialisation) but starts from the formation and transformation of the person, and it is only from there that questions about knowledge, skills and dispositions, about values and traditions, about competence and evidence come in, so to speak—*never the other way around*. What we are after in the formation of the person is educational wisdom, the ability to make wise educational judgements. Following Aristotle we can call this a virtue-based approach to teacher education. While we could say that what we are after here is for teacher students to become virtuous professionals, I prefer to play differently with the idea of virtue and would like to suggest that what we should be after in teacher education is a kind of *virtuosity* in making wise educational judgements.

The idea of virtuosity might help to appreciate the other two components of this approach to teacher education, because if we ask how we can develop virtuosity—and here we can think, for example, about how musicians develop virtuosity—we do it through practice, that is, through doing the very thing we are supposed to be doing, and we do it by careful study of the virtuosity of others. And these are precisely the two other 'components' of the approach to teacher education I wish to suggest.

The second component, therefore, is the idea that we can develop our virtuosity for wise educational judgement only by practising judgement, that is, by being engaged in making such judgement in the widest range of educational situations possible. It is not, in other words, that we can become good at judgement by reading books about it; we have to do it, and we have to learn from doing it. At one level you may argue that this is not a very original idea, i.e. that we can only really learn the art of teaching through doing it. But I do think that there is an important difference between, say, learning on the job (the picking-skills-up-on-the-job-approach the English government seems to be returning to), or reflective practice, or even problem-based learning. What I am after is what we might call judgement-based professional learning, or judgement-focused professional learning. It is not just about any kind of experiential or practical learning, but one that constantly takes the ability for making wise educational judgements as its reference point and centre.

The third component, so I wish to suggest, has to do with learning from examples. While on the one hand we can only develop virtuosity through practising judgement ourselves, I think that we can also learn important things from studying the virtuosity of others, particularly those who we deem to have reached a certain level of virtuosity.[9] This is not to be understood as a process of collaborative learning or peer learning. The whole idea of learning from studying the virtuosity of others is that you learn from those who exemplify the very thing you aspire to, so to speak. The process is, in other words, asymmetrical rather than symmetrical. The study of the virtuosity of other teachers can take many different forms. On the one hand this is something that can be done in the classroom through the observation of the ways in which teachers make embodied and situated wise educational judgements—or at least try to do so. We have to bear in mind, though, that such judgements are not always obvious or visible—also because they partly belong to the domain of what is known as tacit knowledge—so there is also need for conversation, for talking to teachers to find out why they did what they did. This can be done at a small scale—teacher students interviewing teachers about their judgements and their educational virtuosity—but it can also be done at a bigger scale, for example through life history work with experienced teachers, so that we not only get a sense of their virtuosity but perhaps also of the trajectory through which they have developed their educational virtuosity. (We also should bear in mind that, as with musicianship, in order to keep up your virtuosity you need to continue practising it.) And we can also go outside of educational practices and study images of teachers in literature, in film, in popular culture, and the like. We will, of course, encounter both success and failure, and we can of course learn important things about the virtuosity of educational wisdom from both.

These, then, are three reference points or three parameters for thinking about the future of teacher education: a focus on the formation and transformation of the person towards educational wisdom; a focus on learning through the practising of educational judgements; and a focus on the study of the educational virtuosity of others. This is what might follow if we approach the task of teacher education in educational way rather than with reference to a language of learning, and if we take the role of the teacher seriously rather than letting this be replaced by evidence and competence, also in order to capture that wise educational judgement is never the repetition of what was in the past, but is always a creative process that is open

---

[9]An interesting question here is whether we should only focus on those who exemplify educational virtuosity, or whether we can also learn from studying those who do not exemplify this virtuosity. The more general question here is whether we can learn most from good examples or from bad examples. With regard to educational virtuosity I am inclined to argue that it is only when we have developed a sense of what virtuosity looks like, that we can begin to learn from those cases where such virtuosity is absent.

towards the future for the very reason that each educational situation, each moment in the practice of education in which judgement is called for, is in some respect radically new and radically unique. If we recognise this as being at the very heart of educational processes and practices then, so I wish to conclude, we need teacher education that is neither orientated towards evidence, nor towards competence, but towards the promotion of educational wisdom.

Acknowledgements This text is based on my keynote presentation at the "2020 The Future of Teacher Education" conference, Vienna, 3–4 March 2011. I would like to thank the organisers of the conference for the invitation to share my ideas, and the audience for questions and insightful feedback that has helped me to develop my ideas further. A version of the presentation was published in 2012 in the open access journal *Research on Steiner Education 3*(1), 8–21.

References

Aristotle. (1980). *The Nicomachean ethics.* Oxford: Oxford University Press.
Biesta, G. J. J. (2004). Against learning. Reclaiming a language for education in an age of learning. *Nordisk Pedagogik, 23*(1), 70–82.
Biesta, G. J. J. (2006). *Beyond learning. Democratic education for a human future.* Boulder, CO: Paradigm Publishers.
Biesta, G. J. J. (2007). Why 'what works' won't work. Evidence-based practice and the democratic deficit of educational research. *Educational Theory, 57*(1), 1–22.
Biesta, G. J. J. (2009). Good education in an age of measurement: On the need to reconnect with the question of purpose in education. *Educational Assessment, Evaluation and Accountability, 21*(1), 33–46.
Biesta, G. J. J. (2010a). *Good education in an age of measurement: Ethics, politics, democracy.* Boulder, CO: Paradigm Publishers.
Biesta, G. J. J. (2010b). Why 'what works' still won't work. From evidence-based education to value-based education. *Studies in Philosophy and Education, 29*(5), 491–503.
Biesta, G. J. J. (2010c). Evidenz und Werte in Erziehung und Bildung. Drei weitere Defizite evidenzbasierter Praxis. In H.-U. Otto, A. Polutta & H. Ziegler (Hrsg.) (Eds.), *What works—Welches Wissen braucht die Soziale Arbeit?* (pp. 99–115). Opladen: Barbara Burdich.
Biesta, G. J. J. (2011a). De school als toegang tot de wereld: Een pedagogische kijk op goed onderwijs. In R. Klarus & W. Wardekker (Eds.), *Wat is goed onderwijs? Bijdragen uit de pedagogiek* (pp. 15–35). Den Haag: Boom Lemma Uitgevers.
Biesta, G. J. J. (2011b). *God utbildning i mätningens tidevarv.* Stockholm: Liber.
Carr, W. (1987). What is an educational practice? *Journal of Philosophy of Education, 21*(2), 163–175.
Crick, R. D. (2008). Key competencies for education in a European context. *European Educational Research Journal, 7*(3), 311–318.
Eraut, M. (2003). National vocational qualifications in England—Description and analysis of an alternative qualification system. In G. Straka (Ed.), *Zertifizierung non-formell und informell erworbener beruflicher Kompetenzen*, Münster, New York, München & Berlin: Waxmann.
James, W. (1899). *Talks to teachers on psychology: And to students on some of life's ideals.* New York: Henry Holt and Company.
Mulder, M., Weigel, T., & Collins, K. (2007). The concept of competence concept in the development of vocational education and training in selected EU member states. A critical analysis. *Journal of Vocational Education and Training, 59*(1), 65–85.

Author Biography

Gert Biesta (www.gertbiesta.com) is Professor of Education at the Department of Education of Brunel University London and NIVOZ Professor for Education at the University for Humanistic Studies, the Netherlands. In addition he is Visiting Professor for Education at NLA University College, Bergen, Norway. His work focuses on the theory and philosophy of education, education policy, and the philosophy of educational and social research.

Chapter 30
Attracting, Preparing, and Retaining Teachers in High Need Areas: A Science as Inquiry Model of Teacher Education

Cheryl J. Craig, Paige Evans, Simon Bott, Donna Stokes and Bobby Abrol

30.1 Introduction

In Organization for Economic Co-operation and Development (OECD) countries, teacher retention and attrition is an increasing problem. The theme appears often in the literature from the Netherlands, Australia, Canada, the United States, Israel and Norway, among other nations. Even Finland with its leading Programme for International Student *Assessment* (PISA) scores and focus on teacher professionalism has retention and attrition issues. According to a background Australian Organization for Economic Cooperation & Development (OECD) report, "… teaching is becoming … a career of 'movement in and out' and the 'out' may be permanent" (Skilbeck and Connell 2003, pp. 32–33).

Perhaps nowhere in the world is the teacher attrition problem more advanced than in the United States. Major urban centers like Houston and Philadelphia lose 50–70% of beginning teachers in 4–6 years, baby boomer teachers are retiring earlier than anticipated, and the most recent teacher satisfaction survey indicates that one-third of those teachers remaining in the workforce plan to leave soon

C.J. Craig (✉)
Texas A&M University, College Station, USA
e-mail: cheryljcraig@tamu.edu

P. Evans · D. Stokes · B. Abrol
University of Houston, Houston, USA
e-mail: pevans@uh.edu

D. Stokes
e-mail: dstokes@uh.edu

B. Abrol
e-mail: bobbyabrol7@gmail.com

S. Bott
Swansea University, Swansea, Wales, UK
e-mail: s.g.bott@swansea.ac.uk

© Springer Nature Singapore Pte Ltd. 2017
M.A. Peters et al. (eds.), *A Companion to Research in Teacher Education*,
DOI 10.1007/978-981-10-4075-7_30

(Craig 2014). Additionally, the cost of teacher attrition to the American economy exceeds $2.2 billion dollars per year. The cost to the state of Texas's economy alone is over $800 million (Keigher 2010, in Craig 2014). The aforementioned factors, among others, contribute to the U.S.'s teaching crisis. The annual replacement of one-third of the country's teaching workforce, mostly by new-comers, is an inadequate approach to meeting societal demands. Also, alternate forms of teacher certification/evaluation (26 competing service providers in Greater Houston alone) and value-added approaches to accountability appear not to be working. While Americans agree that teachers are vital to students' academic performance and the country's economic status, they are rancorously split about how to address the national teaching calamity and similarly at odds concerning what constitutes teacher quality.

Against this backdrop, a different model of secondary science teacher education has emerged within the existing higher education structure at the University of Houston. The model, *teach*HOUSTON, is a replication of the UTeach program birthed at the University of Texas at Austin. In this chapter, we feature the *teach*HOUSTON model for two important reasons. The first reason is that present-day population mix in Texas resembles the U.S. in 2040. Second, Greater Houston's teacher attrition rate, particularly where secondary content area teachers (mathematics, science, and special education) are concerned, is among the most concerning in the U.S. and in the developed regions of the world. It is therefore important to show how *teach*HOUSTON is successfully attracting, preparing and retaining secondary science teachers in what appears to be an against-the-odds situation.

We begin by briefly tracing the theoretical roots of teaching as inquiry and science as inquiry and then discuss science as inquiry as presented in the con-temporary literature and policy documents. After that, we further contextualize the Texas educational scene, and elucidate in fine-grained detail the *teach*HOUSTON programme. We conclude with a sampling of what *teach*HOUSTON graduates have to so say about their experiences of teaching and learning physics via the inquiry process. Finally, we share two figures: the first depicting the increasing number of Greater Houston secondary school students served by *teach*HOUSTON mathematics and science graduates instructing in their areas of specialization; and the second capturing *teach*HOUSTON's evolving approach to secondary science as inquiry teacher education in the form of a model.

30.2   Theoretical Roots of Teaching as Inquiry and Science as Inquiry

In North America, the origins of teaching as inquiry trace to John Dewey, and the origins of science as inquiry also trace to Dewey and Joseph Schwab as well. Dewey was the first to give mindedness to teachers and to see them as thinking, acting human beings. For Dewey, teachers were a great deal more than vessels through whom others' codified knowledge prescriptions passed through. Dewey maintained that learning is deep-rooted in the experiences a teacher/student enters into and the knowledge which arises from their inquiries. In Dewey's view, the inquiring mind is triggered by a perplexing experience or a discrepant event that leads the student/teacher to think reflectively and to engage in some type of action to resolve the problem. In this way, reflective thinking involves both the past and the future in that students/teachers build upon previous experiences and present knowledge to construct new knowledge to inform future experiences. Because of these baseline understandings, Dewey advocated for an experimental approach to science teaching. For him, the scientific process of inquiry was foundational to both the discovery, use and application of scientific knowledge.

Joseph Schwab, who was Deweyan in orientation, advocated for students learning scientific concepts through inquiry and reinforced the teaching of science as inquiry in the field of education. Schwab's personal experiences as a scientist and curriculum theorist convinced him that the inquiry approach was the most defensible one.[1] For Schwab, "scientific research has its origin, not in objective facts alone, but in a conception, a construction of the mind" (Schwab 1962, p. 12). In his iconic treatise on *Teaching science as inquiry*, he went on to say that

> ... the treatment of science as [i]nquiry is not achieved by talk about science or scientific method apart from the content of science. On the contrary, treatment of science as [i]nquiry consists of a treatment of scientific knowledge in terms of its origins in the united activities of the human mind and hand which produce it; it is a means for clarifying and illuminating scientific knowledge. (p. 102)

It was not surprising, then, that Schwab was highly critical of textbooks that presented scientific facts as "rhetoric of conclusions" (p. 24)—that is, irrevocable truths. Such assertions, in Schwab's view, are only tentative stories because they remain truthful only until new discoveries are made.

Having sketched the roots of teaching and learning as inquiry and science as inquiry in place, we now turn to contemporary literature and policy documents supporting science taught as inquiry.

30.3 Science as Inquiry: A Contemporary View

One of Dewey's most salient contributions to science education, as mentioned earlier, is the fact that he advocated an experimental approach to science teaching, which was then reinforced by Schwab who similarly favored the approach. Together, their influence is imprinted in the national standards and even in the

---

[1]Bobby Abrol, a Research Assistant on the evaluation team, created a digital story around Schwab's contributions titled *An Inquiry into inquiry*. The digital story can be viewed at https://www.youtube.com/watch?v=2vL5WieX2RY.

Texas Essential Knowledge and Skills (TEKS). The TEKS, for example, devote a significant portion of the objectives to the Nature of Science and process skills and the rest to content knowledge.

The teaching of science as inquiry embedded in the *teach*HOUSTON programme is also recommended by a myriad of resources including the *National Science Education Standards* (National Research Council [NRC] 1996); *Benchmarks for Science Literacy* (American Association for the Advancement of Science 1993); and *Rising above the Gathering Storm: Energizing and Employing America for a Brighter Economic Future* (National Academy of Sciences 2007). The National Science Education Standards (NRC 1996), for instance, defines inquiry as follows:

> Scientific inquiry refers to the diverse ways in which scientists study the natural world and propose explanations based on the evidence derived from their work. Inquiry also refers to the activities of students in which they develop knowledge and understanding of scientific ideas, as well as understandings of how scientists study the natural world. (p. 23)

The features of classroom inquiry and their variations as endorsed by the National Research Council are outlined in Table 30.1.

Despite the emphasis placed on the use of inquiry in science education being addressed in preservice and in-service science teacher preparation programmes, research has shown that the majority of teachers still fail to incorporate inquiry teaching methods into their teaching repertoires (Salish I Research Collaborative 1997). *teach*HOUSTON was initiated for this latter reason in addition to the urgent problems present in the Texas educational landscape, which we will discuss next.

30.4 The Texas Educational Landscape

As foreshadowed, the challenges of the Texas educational landscapes are mammoth, particularly since the largest, most well-known Houston area school district currently has 80% of its teachers with five years or less experience and 50% of its principals with five years or less experience. Also, in Texas as a whole, more than 30% of middle school (grades 6–8) mathematics and science teachers are teaching out of their specialty areas and 13.3% (mathematics) and 28.7% (science) high school teachers (grades 9–12) teachers are additionally instructing out of field. This phenomenon is more pronounced in secondary schools, which tend to employ the least qualified teachers to instruct the most disadvantaged youth. These campuses experience the greatest shortages, creating an achievement gap that Darling-Hammond (2011) perhaps more appropriately termed an "opportunity gap." A study conducted by Nelson et al. (2009) reported that underserved students are twice as likely to have teachers who are not certified in comparison to their white peers. Figures 30.1 and 30.2 illustrate the percentages of high full-time equivalent (FTL) school science and mathematics teachers in Texas who are assigned positions out of field in relation to the percentages of youths living in poverty.

Table 30.1 Essential features of classroom inquiry and their variations (National Research Council 2000, p. 23)

Essential feature	Variations			
1. Learner engages in scientifically oriented questions	Learner poses a question	Learner selects among questions, poses new questions	Learner sharpens or clarifies question provided by teacher, materials, or other source	Learner engages in question provided by teacher, materials, or other source
2. Learner gives priority to **evidence** in responding to questions	Learner determines what constitutes evidence and collects it	Learner directed to collect certain data	Learner given data and asked to analyze	Learner given data and told how to analyze
3. Learner formulate **explanations** from evidence	Learner formulates explanation after summarizing evidence	Learner guided in process of formulating explanations from evidence	Learner given possible ways to use evidence to formulate explanation	Learner provided with evidence and how to use evidence to formulate explanation
4. Learner connects explanations to scientific knowledge	Learner independently examines other resources and forms the links to explanations	Learner directed toward areas and sources of scientific knowledge	Learner given possible connections	
5. Learner communicates and justifies explanations	Learner forms reasonable and logical argument to communicate explanations	Learner coached in development of communication	Learner provided broad guidelines to use sharpen communication	Learner given steps and procedures for communication

More ··—Amount of Learner Self-Direction ··—— Less
Less ————··— Amount of Direction from Teacher or Material ————··— More

Fig. 30.1 Percentage of high school science teachers assigned out-of-field in Texas from 1999 to 2008 by student poverty (Fuller 2009)

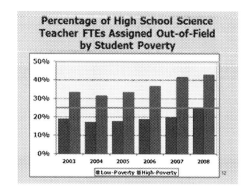

Fig. 30.2 Percentage of high school math teachers assigned out-of-field in Texas from 1999 to 2008 by student poverty (Fuller 2009)

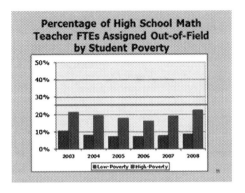

Percentage of High School Math Teacher FTEs Assigned Out-of-Field by Student Poverty

Attracting qualified teachers (teachers with subject matter credentials for their assigned teaching positions) to teach in high poverty schools is difficult due to the lack of funding, support and resources available. It additionally has been reported that low income students have only a 10% chance of having a good teacher in their overall K-12 education (Chenowith 2011).

30.5   The *teach*HOUSTON Programme and Its Evolution

As previously explained, the first iteration of the nationally recognized UTeach program, the *teach*HOUSTON programme at the University of Houston, began in 2007 as a collaboration between the College of Natural Sciences and Mathematics, the College of Education, and two local school districts,[2] and has since expanded to eleven local school districts.[3] The program's central aim is to address the shortage of qualified math and science teachers in the U.S. *teach*HOUSTON is directly aligned with the national goal of the *Prepare and Inspire* report (President's Council of Advisors on Science and Technology 2010) to train 100,000 new quality STEM middle school and high school teachers in the U.S. The programme emphasizes early and ongoing field-based teaching experiences while students are concurrently working to obtain a degree in math or science. The program provides secondary teacher certification for those completing a Natural Sciences and Mathematics degree. From the beginning to the end of their teacher education programme and beyond, *teach*HOUSTON graduates are charged with changing the face of public education.

The following percentages characterize *teach*HOUSTON graduates: 95% of the program's graduates are teaching in the Greater Houston area; 75% of the graduates

---

[2]Fort Bend and Spring Branch Independent School Districts.

[3]Aldine, Alief, Aldine, Cypress-Fairbanks, Deer Park, Fort Bend, Galena Park, Houston, Katy, Pasadena, and Spring Branch Independent School Districts.

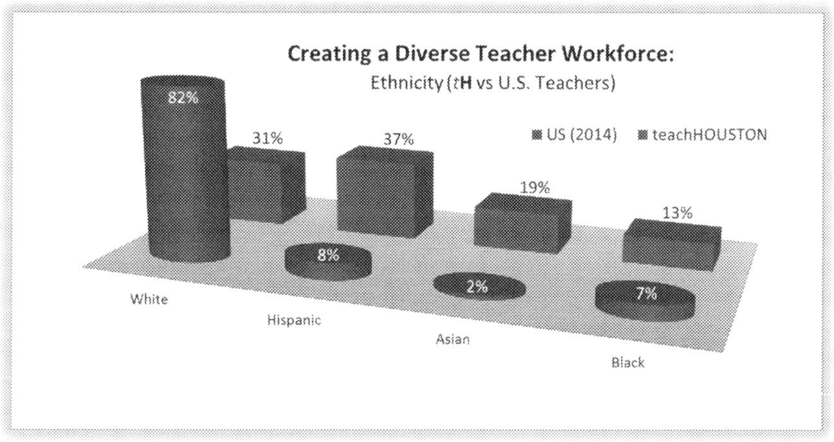

Fig. 30.3 Racial composition of *teach*HOUSTON graduates compared to the American teaching force

are teaching in high need schools; 90% of the graduates continue as public school teachers beyond two years; and the programme graduates one of the largest pools of chemistry teachers in the country (top 2% of universities nationally). Moreover, *teach*HOUSTON's graduates reflect the diversity of the University of Houston (37% Hispanic, 31% White, 19% Asian, and 13% African American) as compared to the cumulative U.S. teacher population (Boser 2014) (Fig. 30.3).

This is essential because students' academic achievement improves when minority teachers serve as role models for underrepresented students. The *teach*HOUSTON programme combines undergraduate degrees in science, computer science, or mathematics with learning how to teach (pedagogy), field-based training (practicums), and teacher certification. Key components of the program include

- **Strong collaboration** between the College of Natural Sciences & Mathematics and the College of Education to ensure the highest quality preparation both in subject matter and teaching skills. Preservice teachers receive their major in mathematics or science and their capstone (similar to a minor) along with their teacher certification with the teachHOUSTON programme that is housed in the College of Education.
- **Active recruitment** of science and mathematics majors early in their academic careers to take the two initial *teach*HOUSTON courses, STEP 1 and STEP 2. Students are immediately afforded the opportunity to try out teaching in public schools where they are placed with mentor teachers who are experts in their craft.
- **Early and intensive field experiences** throughout the programme, including the opportunity for students to teach lessons as early as their first semester, and become increasingly comfortable with teaching in a variety of school environments as they advance through the programme. Preservice teachers begin

teaching upper elementary students in their first field-based course and work with middle school students in their second field-based course. The third and fourth courses have a high school field experience followed by a semester-long experience of student teaching (ST) which is typically at the high school level.

- *Master Teachers* with extensive teaching and leadership experience in the public schools work at the University of Houston alongside students in the programme. The master teachers teach and coordinate field experiences associated with the *teach*HOUSTON programme. They work with students as they progress through the program and graduate, and then continue to work with them as new teachers for up to three years after they start full-time employment.

- *Mentor Teachers* currently teaching in public schools that work closely with *teach*HOUSTON students during their field experiences. Preservice teachers observe mathematics and science teachers who are highly recommended by their administrators. Additionally, mentor teachers work with preservice teachers to develop and teach two or three inquiry-based lessons during the semester for the four field-based courses that occur prior to the entire semester of student teaching. Constructive feedback is provided by the mentor teachers subsequent to each teaching experience

- *Faculty members* at UH who are actively engaged in research in mathematics and science, as well as the teaching and learning of mathematics and science. They focus on developing deep-level understanding of the subject area material and incorporating effective teaching approaches with a strong emphasis on the integration of technology.

- *Appealing student benefits* to encourage enrollment and retention, including paid internships that offer opportunities for education-oriented community outreach including summer STEM camps as well as scholarships limited to those in the *teach*HOUSTON program. The National Science Foundation Robert Noyce Scholarship and Internship program offers both internships and scholarships for preservice teachers. The Noyce Scholarship program provides junior and senior level physics and chemistry majors and minors, and post-baccalaureate students seeking teacher certification in physics or chemistry with $12,000/year Noyce scholarship. Students are eligible to apply for the scholarship for up to two years. All students accepting a Noyce scholarship are required to sign a contract that requires them to teach for two years in a high-needs school district for every year of scholarship support after graduation (certification for the post-baccalaureate scholars).

- *Informal experiences* to better prepare teachers to be effective in high need schools and provide opportunities for students to build skills and increase self-efficacy as educators. Overall teacher self-efficacy is increased through exposure to multiple forms of formal and informal teaching experiences and teacher-efficacy has been correlated to student achievement outcomes as well as to student self-efficacy. The Noyce summer internship program is a 6-week experience designed for incoming freshmen and sophomore mathematics and science majors who are interested in the teacher certification plan, but who are not yet eligible for the Noyce scholarship program. During this experience, 12 freshman and sophomore students work with science master teachers and recent *teach***HOUSTON** graduates in the ExxonMobil Bernard Harris Summer Science Camp (EMBHSSC) and receive a $2700 stipend. The EMBHSSC is a two-week, academic, residential camp organized to provide activities, experiments, projects, and field experiences for underserved students entering middle school (Grades 6–8). The camp encourages underrepresented youth to pursue mathematics and science in high school and to set goals and follow their dreams to enter higher education institutions and engage in STEM-related careers. The camp increases students' mathematics and science skills, introduces them to college life and stimulates their interest in science and engineering as a potential career path. Each day, campers attend classes that include problem solving, research and communication skills incorporated with biology, chemistry, physics, environmental sciences, earth sciences, engineering and design concepts, and field excursions. Interns help plan physics and chemistry lessons before the start of the camp and then assist in teaching these lessons with science master teachers during camp operation. Additionally, interns serve as camp counselors and interact with campers daily. Upon completion of the camp, the interns review and improve the science modules and make suggestions for modules to use for future camps. The summer internship program introduces students to teaching early in their academic careers and serves as a recruitment tool because the interns are eligible to be future candidates for the Noyce Scholarship Program.

- *Compact, time-sensitive degree plans* that allow most students to graduate within four years with a bachelor's degree in math or science *and* teacher certification. Two tracts, a Bachelor of Science (BS) and a Bachelor of Arts (BA) degree with a *teach***HOUSTON** options have been developed for biology, chemistry, physics, and mathematics majors. The BS degree programs include the prescribed courses for a typical math or science degree with many of the University required core courses scheduled to be taken over the summer sessions. Typically, a BA degree is pursued by students who intend to teach in the 7–12 arena; therefore, the designed BA degree plan with a *teach***HOUSTON** option is a viable alternative for students entering the program. It offers a less rigorous major course plan than does the BS degree with a *teach***HOUSTON** option. It includes the major courses necessary for adequate preparation of mathematics and science teachers; however, it eliminates some of the advance specialty major courses that are not required for teaching at the 7–12 level.

30.6   Required Coursework for *teach*HOUSTON Certification

Eight *teach***HOUSTON** courses are required for teacher certification including Step 1: Inquiry Approaches to Teaching; Step 2: Inquiry-Based Lesson Design; Knowing & Learning in Mathematics and Science; Classroom Interactions (CI);

Perspectives in Science and Mathematics; Research Methods; Multiple Teaching Strategies (MTS); and ST. These courses integrate the concepts of math and science with a technology-based curriculum which utilizes interactive, inquiry-based teaching tools. They cover (1) methods of teaching science and mathematics in schools; (2) a variety of theories and frameworks addressing how people learn mathematics and science; (3) multiple models of teaching, what each model requires of teachers, and the corresponding impact on interactions that occur in mathematics and science classrooms. The Step 1 and 2 courses, CI, MTS, and ST (described below in greater detail), incorporate field experiences which provide students the opportunity to implement instructional strategies and experience success and failure in a highly supportive setting. Students enrolled in field-based courses work with Mentor Teachers in local area schools. The remaining courses are focused on development and application of pedagogical content knowledge. Another course, Physics by Inquiry, was created in 2013 and addresses both physics content and instruction and counts as an upper level physics/science course on their degree plans.

In **Step 1**, students teach science or math lessons in elementary classrooms to obtain firsthand experience with implementing an inquiry-based curriculum in a diverse yet supportive environment. Most students have little prior experience with student-centered teaching and master teachers introduce students to the theory and practice behind excellent inquiry-based science and mathematics instruction; provide students opportunity to experience inquiry-based science and mathematics instruction; guide them through the process of preparing to teach lessons in elementary classrooms; and assess their progress toward course objectives.

Where **Step 2** is concerned, students work with master teachers to develop and teach inquiry-based lessons in middle school classrooms using research-based, recognized curricula and materials. In addition to the emphasis on writing innovative lesson plans, the Step 2 course focuses on the importance of using appropriate questioning strategies throughout the lesson. Students develop pre- and post-assessments for performance objectives created for their lesson plans. As a major project, students analyze and modify one of the lessons they taught, taking into account the results of the assessments, reflection on how successful the lesson was, feedback from their mentor teachers and the course instructor who observed the lesson. Additionally, technology is utilized to enhance lesson planning.

In **Classroom Interactions**, students participate in several learning activities which allow students to evaluate their own learning and understanding of a topic. Participating in learning activities also allows students to consider equity issues. For example, is it fair for only the fastest students to contribute to an activity? How would learning be different if all students were not only allowed but required to participate? Is it fair that some students are learning in a language that is not their first? The class considers the implications of deficit thinking in classroom outcomes. Students interview and observe classroom teachers and teach in high school classrooms. The first teaching experience is a one-day event; the second lasts 2 days. Both teaching experiences are videotaped. Students spend significant time preparing, practicing, and revising lessons for the teaching events. Master and mentor teachers work closely with students on lesson preparation and implementation. They assist with the development of sample activities linked to the content to be taught during the field experience.

With the **MTS** class, students experience and analyze a variety of MTS. Model lessons involving several of the strategies are presented to (a) demonstrate appropriate usage of the strategy and (b) allow students to experience effective implementation of the strategy. Some lessons are presented twice using a different teaching strategy each time. Attributes (strong and weak) of each strategy are addressed thus allowing for discussion of whether one strategy is more effective for the given topic than another. This leads to discussions of how to choose the best teaching strategy for the given material. Teaching strategies that are less familiar to most learners (i.e., inquiry, discovery, problem solving, and project-based approaches to teaching) are the focus of the course. Students observe exemplary high school teachers as well as develop and teach lessons in diverse, urban high schools. Students also develop and present a project-based instructional unit.

During **Student Teaching**, preservice teachers work with University Supervisors and Cooperating Teachers to design instruction appropriate for all students that reflects an understanding of relevant content and is based on continuous and appropriate assessments; create a classroom environment of respect and rapport that fosters a positive climate for learning, equity, and excellence; promote student learning by providing responsive instruction that makes use of effective communication techniques, instructional strategies that actively engage students in the learning process, and timely high-quality feedback; and fulfill professional roles and responsibilities and adhere to legal and ethical requirements of the profession. Student teachers start out the semester by observing and then gradually taking over all of the teaching and other responsibilities of a full-time teacher with guidance from University Supervisors and their Cooperating Teacher.

We will now catch a quick glimpse of what happened in one science as inquiry course and what sample *teach*HOUSTON student teachers had to say about their experiences.

30.7 *teach*HOUSTON Student Teachers' Responses to a Physics as Inquiry Course

The Physics by Inquiry Course (Physics 4342) is a laboratory-based course in which the *teach*HOUSTON students develop a deep understanding of physics concepts by experimenting and establishing scientific concepts based on a concrete experience.[4] The course is taught as a set of laboratory-based modules that provide

---

[4]Bobby Abrol, Ph.D. student and evaluation team member, designed a poster board presentation, *A true story of teaching and Learning physics as inquiry*" about *teach*HOUSTON students' experiences of learning Physics, which she presented at the Graduate Research and Scholarship

an inquiry approach to the introduction of physics. In small groups, students develop concepts based on inquiry experiments; use those concepts to develop rules and patterns; and determine equations that could be utilized to solve problems. Peer instruction and discussion as well as making predictions and analyzing results are essential components of the course; thereby, participants form their own mental models for understanding physics and chemistry concepts. This course was designed to augment the content knowledge of the preservice teachers while allowing participants to experience the process of inquiry learning.

Interviews and focus group discussions were conducted with those enrolled in the class. We now summarize what Katrina, Ryan and Jason had to say about their physics as inquiry experience in the *teach*HOUSTON course.

First, the three preservice teachers, consistent with their peers in the group of 12, said they developed their keen interests in science from teachers who had instructed them in the public schools. Each of them was able to name individual educators—and one could name a whole department of high school teachers—who sparked and nurtured their interests in science and science careers. However, teachers were not the only ones who fueled their passions for science. So, too, did family members (parents, aunts, uncles). Ryan, for example, communicated how sitting on his mother's lap with her chemistry book in hand constituted his first early literacy experience. Katrina likewise discussed how her father's attitude toward science had a major impact on her

> My dad is a … mad scientist. He's just one of those people who is naturally into science … I can't even count the times that I awoke [as a child] and did … experiments with him in the kitchen. He's a registered nurse … He has always told me I should be a science teacher … He's kind of my inspiration for anything I do that is science because he gets so excited about it. Science is his muse.

Jason was somewhat different from Ryan and Katrina in that his route to science and eventually teacher education was circuitous. Studying religion and majoring in youth ministry propelled him to become a science teacher. Jason's overarching interest, he said, was "to find answers to things that are really great mysteries—the metaphysical, in the case of religious studies, and the physical, where physics is concerned." However, Jason encountered an obstacle he could not overcome in his religious education: his need to counsel students about religious topics and having to "make up answers for them because [he] did not know [the answers] himself." This resulted in Jason doing a lot of "soul searching" about what he wanted to do with his professional life. He discovered "teaching was really his interest and what he enjoyed doing." He settled on teaching physics because he had always loved physics along with religion.

(Footnote 4 continued)

Program at the University of Houston, Houston, TX in 2014. She also created a digital story, *Teaching Inquiry-based Learning to Preservice Teachers,* from videotaped higher education classroom activities and interview transcripts. The digital story can be viewed at http://www.youtube.com/watchv=_1VJ4PthaXg.

Katrina, Ryan and Jason were appreciative of the inquiry approach to the teaching and learning of physics. Ryan, for example, shared the following about teaching and learning via the inquiry method:

> There's something amazing about seeing a student learn through inquiry ... It just gives me the chills. You know, it is like [experiencing] the dissention of the Holy Spirit, do you know what I mean? It's very freeing ... the Eureka moment. It lifts you up and you feel your whole body come alive. It's tingly and you want to learn and teach that way again and again and again. You want to start that fire again ... and you want to keep fanning the flames ...

As for Jason, he had already learned in his religious counseling education that "experience [needs to] come in the front door and theory [needs to] come through the back door." He understood that this theory–practice relationship would allow him to retain his interest in great mysteries of life "without imposing [not fully formed] answers on others." This way he could increase students' live chances in a non-authoritarian way.

All three *teach*HOUSTON preservice teachers credited their science and science teacher educators for having a significant impact on all of them. The transcripts of the interviews and focus group sessions were full of comments about their effects. Katrina, for example, said that their instructors would "guide us and scaffold us— but would not tell us the answer. It was a lot of guided questions. It was never direct teaching." Katrina "appreciated the approach" and said that she "would try to mimic it in her own teaching as well." As for Ryan, he was able to discern the differences between physics taught as theory in his high school classes and physics taught as inquiry class at university. In physics taught theoretically, he said that "the words

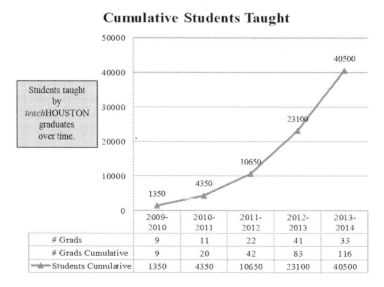

Fig. 30.4 Cumulative secondary science students taught by *teach*HOUSTON graduates (cumulative number of students taught is an estimate that assumes teachers will teach 150 students per year.)

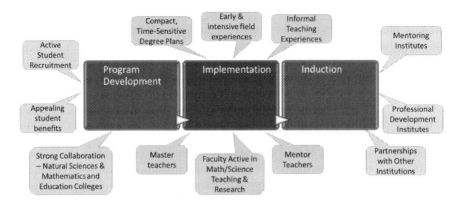

Fig. 30.5 Model of science as inquiry teacher education programme

are just words dancing around in your head … that may/may not mean something to you." But, in physics as inquiry, "you come to knowledge on your own … it comes from inside of you and grows to be solid and a part of you." Ryan went on to say that his teacher educators put him into "the flight zone" for which he had been searching his entire academic life and that he hoped, through his teacher educator models, to help high school students "get into that flight zone" and better the quality of their studies and their lives.

In these *teach***HOUSTON** students' words, we learn that "whether intended or not, teaching methods are learned by example. If the ability to teach by inquiry is a goal of instruction, [science professors/teacher educators] need to work through a substantial amount of content in a way that reflects this spirit" (McDermott et al. 2000, p. 413) as Katrina, Ryan and Jason made clear. Furthermore, the separation of science content from instruction in pedagogy is unnatural to those preparing to teach science as inquiry as the *teach***HOUSTON** students explained in their own words.

30.8 Conclusion

Since 2007, *teach***HOUSTON** has prepared an increasing number of secondary science teachers with urban teaching experiences who mostly will teach in metropolitan Houston schools. Figure 30.4, which follows, captures the growing number of largely underserved, minority middle and high school students who have been or will be taught by qualified *teach***HOUSTON** teachers with strong science content area knowledge and pedagogy:

Thus far, the *teach***HOUSTON** programme has successfully enabled the University of Houston to contribute significantly to the American effort to improve math and science education. As explained throughout this chapter, it has become increasingly difficult in the U.S. and internationally to recruit, train, and develop teachers with a long-term commitment to teaching, especially in the areas of mathematics and science content. Today, 80% of *teach*HOUSTON's 149 graduates work in the local, urban area with predominantly at-risk, minority students.

To conclude, we have distilled what has been learned about *teach*HOUSTON and its challenges and successes into a model of a science as inquiry teacher education programme (Fig. 30.5) that we hope will be of value to others addressing similar problems in the field and in the teaching of science internationally. As the figure shows, *teach*HOUSTON's future steps center on the fuller development of graduates' induction year (first 3–5 years of career) experiences, which presumably will also increase teacher retention in the urban area over time.

Acknowledgments A special thank you is extended to Dr. Liping Wei who also contributed to this project as a member of the evaluation team. We also acknowledge the contributions of Dr. Gayle Curtis who assisted with the creation of this chapter's figures.

References

American Association for the Advancement of Science. (1993). *Benchmarks for science literacy: A project 2061 report*. New York: Oxford University Press.

Boser, U. (2014). *Teacher diversity revisited, a new state-by-state analysis*. Washington, DC: Center for American Progress.

Chenowith, K. (2011). Turning obstacles into triumph. *U.S. News & World Report, 147*(7), 58–61.

Craig, C. (2014). From stories of staying to stories of leaving: A U.S. beginning teacher's experience. *Journal of Curriculum Studies, 46*(1), 81–115.

Darling Hammond, L. (2011). *The world is flat and the educational future: How America's commitment to equity will decide our future*. New York, NY: Teachers College Press.

Fuller, E. (2009). *Secondary mathematics and science teachers in Texas: Supply, demand, and quality*. Texas Instruments & TBEC.

McDermott, L. C., Shaffer, P. S., & Constantinou, C. P. (2000). Preparing teachers to teach physics and physical science by inquiry. *Physics Education, 35*(6), 411–416.

National Academy of Sciences. (2007). *Rising above the gathering storm: Energizing and employing America for a brighter economic future*. Washington, DC: National Academy Press.

National Research Council. (1996). *National science education standards*. Washington, DC: National Academy Press.

National Research Council. (2000). *Inquiry and the national science education standards; A guide for teaching and learning*. Washington, DC: National Academy Press.

Nelson, J., Palonsky, S., & McCarthy, M. R. (2009). *Critical issues in educations: Dialogues and dialects* (7th ed.). New York: McGraw Hill.

President's Council of Advisors on Science and Technology. (2010). *Prepare and inspire: K-12 education in science, technology, engineering, and math (STEM) for America's future*. Washington, DC; Executive Office of the White House.

Salish I Research Collaborative. (1997). *Secondary science and mathematics teacher preparation programs: Influences on new teachers and their students; Instrument package and user's guide*. Iowa City: Science Education Center, University of Iowa.

Schwab, J. (1962). The teaching of science as enquiry. In J. Schwab & P. Brandwein (Eds.), *The teaching of science* (pp. 3–103). Cambridge, MA: Harvard University Press.

Skilbeck, M., & Connell, H. (2003). *Attracting, developing and retaining effective teachers*. Canaberra, Australia: Commonwealth of Australia.

Author Biographies

Cheryl J. Craig is a Professor and Houston Endowment Endowed Chair of Urban Education at Texas A&M University, TX, USA. Her research focuses on what and how prospective and practicing teachers come to know, do and be in context. She is an American Educational Research Association (AERA) Fellow and an AERA Division B (Curriculum) Lifetime Achievement awardee. She is the evaluator of several National Science Foundation grants, including two Noyce grants awarded to *teach*HOUSTON.

Paige Evans is a Clinical Associate Professor in the teachHOUSTON program in the Mathematics Department at the University of Houston, TX, USA. She is the creator/instructor of the *Physics by Inquiry* course and the Principal Investigator of the NSF Noyce Grant UH-LIFE. She was the recipient of three Teaching Excellence Awards between 2013 to 2015.

Simon Bott is a Chemistry Professor at Swansea University, Wales, UK. He formerly was employed by the University of Houston, TX, USA. He was a Co-Director of *teach*HOUSTON from 2007 to 2016 and a Co-Principal Investigator of 2 Noyce Grants. At the University of Houston, he was named the 2012 Piper Professor and won eight other teaching and advising awards.

Donna Stokes is an Associate Professor in the Physics Department, University of Houston, Houston, USA. Her research focuses on structural/optical characterization of semiconductors for device applications. She also is involved in physics education research and is Principal Investigator for the Noyce Scholarship Program for the recruitment/retention/training of physics and chemistry teachers.

Bobby Abrol recently completed her Ph.D. in Curriculum and Instruction from the University of Houston, Houston, TX. While at UH, she worked alongside Cheryl J. Craig in the evaluation of the Noyce grant for the recruitment/retention/training of physics and chemistry teachers that was awarded to *teach*HOUSTON.

Chapter 31
Teacher Education, Research and Migrant Children

Nesta Devine, Jeanne Pau'uvale Teisina and Lorraine Pau'uvale

A companion to research in teacher education holds already a complex position with regard to research: it is concerned with both the process of educating teachers, and the matter of education itself; with the relationships with students; the processes of teaching and learning; and fitting in with the cultures of school and family and community and government. In our paper, we have tried to address these elements, by addressing teacher research from three angles: some issues which could be researched in order to improve teacher education (i.e. targeted at teacher educators); some issues which are best addressed by the student teachers doing some research while they are in the relatively safe environment of institutional teacher education; and some suggestions concerning research into the needs of migrant children which should inform teacher education and teacher practice.

31.1 Introduction

We have tried to follow the following organisation of our thoughts in this paper:
Teacher educator research

1. Teacher education teachers'—research into the ways of being of migrants, i.e. into sociological and nomadological research into migrant groups and their differences from each other as well as from the mainstream.

N. Devine (✉) · J.P. Teisina · L. Pau'uvale
Auckland University of Technology, Auckland, New Zealand
e-mail: nesta.devine@aut.ac.nz

J.P. Teisina
e-mail: jteisina@yahoo.com.au

L. Pau'uvale
e-mail: lorraine.pauuvale@yahoo.com.au

© Springer Nature Singapore Pte Ltd. 2017
M.A. Peters et al. (eds.), *A Companion to Research in Teacher Education*,
DOI 10.1007/978-981-10-4075-7_31

2. Teacher educators' research into perceptions, and changing behaviour of student and young teachers.

   Student teacher research

1. Student teachers research into the ways of being of migrant groups in the form of sociological or nomadological (Deleuze and Guattari 1986) inquiry.
2. Student teacher research into existing material on the beliefs and culture of migrant groups.

   General research which will benefit student teachers and migrant children.

1. Research into specific issues relating to a defined place—city, country, school or village—a sociology of interaction (not a 'deficit' account of migrant behaviours!).
2. A general approach to research which respects the 'other' and deconstructs the privileges associated with hegemonic social constructions.

31.2 The Matter of Research into Teacher Education Regarding the Teaching of Migrant Children

This paper explores how research and teacher education can better prepare migrant and non-migrant teachers to support migrant children. Our work is based on a phenomenological claim, because all three of us are migrants and researchers, and we draw on our experience and our research. The technique we used to background this paper, and in other related research, is 'talanoa', a Tongan convention of conversation which allows all participants to have their say in a supportive but purposeful context (Vaioleti 2006).

31.3 Consciousness Raising in Teacher Education

Ethnic and cultural diversity is changing the social landscape and hence the educational landscape all over the world. New Zealand has been the beneficiary of immigration for 1000 years approximately, with the numbers intensifying in the middle of the nineteenth century and again in the middle of the twentieth and early twenty-first century. Each wave of immigrants brings with it increasing social complexity, and an increasing challenge for the education system. Because of the rapid change of cultural contexts in the social landscape of our country, there is now an increased focus on the issues of diversity and multiculturalism in all walks of life and within different communities (Arndt 2012). We argue that the challenge of increasing diversity for the education system can be productively addressed by an attitude and practice of inquiry, that is, of research, at all levels of the system, but most importantly in initial teacher education.

Of course migrant students, like migrant teachers, are just students, and just teachers. The characteristics of good teaching do not change. Any research which aids better teaching of all children will assist migrant children.

Nonetheless there are some aspects of good teaching which can be reinforced for the benefit of migrant students.

Foucault makes the point that the laws of the land are established by the dominant group in a country (Foucault 1980). Sometimes these people are themselves migrant—as with William the Conqueror's invading forces—and are able to bring with them their language, cultural assumptions, mores—and perhaps their children require little extra assistance as 'migrants'. But successive waves of non-conquering migrant students do not enjoy the privileges of sharing hegemonic language, culture, "habitus" (Bourdieu 1977). For them, there is a transition period—quite possibly lasting their entire life times—when they have to negotiate the language and culture that are already established in the new land, while retaining to a greater or lesser degree, the cultural attributes of the homeland.

In some cases, the transition is abrupt: particularly in the case of refugees, there may be no going back, no cultural groups of compatriots, perhaps even no family. Such isolation is fortunately relatively rare, although not unknown, and is a little beyond the scope of this paper. Chain migration and resettlement patterns can result in lively immigrant communities.

But, typically, student teachers come from the dominant group. They tend (we apologise for the generalisation, but it is a useful one), to assume that the way they and their peers see the world is—not so much the right, but the *only* way, to see it. They often fear and/or distrust the immigrant groups (along with other minorities).

Hence it would be helpful for teacher educators to be familiar with some of the migrant groups in the community—both those their students come from and those they will teach.

31.4 Teacher Educators' Research into Perceptions, and Changing Behaviour of Student and Young Teachers

In our experience with student teachers, often they simply do not 'see' the immigrant children before them. They will make huge assumptions, considering Pacific children to be Maori for instance. Sometimes they take pride in this failure to 'see', considering it to be proof of their non-discriminatory values. They often believe that to acknowledge or discuss difference from the norm is somehow insulting—so closely is their own consciousness of status bound up in their belonging to a visibly privileged group. Wanting to believe that they are not prejudiced in any way leads them to a belief in 'sameness', a misrecognition of sameness as equality. This misrecognition is often founded on an ostensibly egalitarian view that every child is the same as—'as good as'—themselves, which is both wrong and defies the possibility that the migrant child takes pride in belonging to their own community of origin.

But it is also the case that their sense of personal security is bound up with belonging to that elite group, and that to abandon that privilege can be a frightening move for them.

Thus the teacher educator has to do two things at the same time: to encourage the respectful acknowledgement of difference; and to reassure the student stepping hesitantly into a world they do not know, that it is going to be all right: they will survive engagement with the Other without loss of mana or prestige.

Of course it is possible to lecture on such topics—endlessly—and of course students in seminars will—sometimes—discuss their fears and hesitations—and sometimes deny them—but what transpires in the classroom shows all too clearly the state of the student teacher's head. Sometimes, perhaps often, the clues lie in what is said, but more often it is in classroom actions and interactions. Who is asked the questions—and what kind of questions—whose waving hand is acknowledged and whose is not—who sits at the back of the classroom, and does the teacher ever venture down there? Who is regarded—to use the words of a teacher one of us worked with—as a 'waste of space'?

Teacher educators therefore can usefully be engaged in two kinds of research: one, into the characteristics of the migrant communities their students must engage with, to smooth the path to a recognition of difference, and two, into the issues presented by the student teachers themselves, on their nomadological journey from assumed privilege to conscious and deconstructed privilege as a means to developing the wherewithal to engage with the 'other'. Research of this kind could be most productive, particularly if it assists the teacher educator to hep their student teachers 'see' the migrant child as legitimately belonging to their own group *as well as* to the classroom group and to see and question the positions the student teachers start from.

If the focus is on research into student teacher engagement with migrants then it should take the form of investigating the attitudes they hold at the outset and (hopefully) the changes over time and exposure to migrant students. Many of the questions we might ask are both social and psychological: what supports/factors/circumstances might lessen their fear/make them feel more secure in a strange environment and reassure them that association with migrants is not going to cause them loss of face or status. Exasperating as it may be to devote more research time to an already privileged section of our society this may well be the most efficient way to ensure more equitable treatment of our children.

31.5   Student Teacher Research into the Ways of Being of Migrant Groups in the Form of Sociological or Nomadological Inquiry

How can student teachers, so anxious about 'control' and 'covering the syllabus' and generally about performing the role of teacher, learn to put aside their pre-conceived ideas of what they 'ought' to do; and instead take the more humble and successful position, of finding out what their migrant children (particularly) think and need?

We say *think*, because a modicum of research on the teacher's part into how their migrant children *think* will repay the teacher enormously. If the migrant children come, for instance, from a culture that values collective achievement over individual achievement then a number of the *techne* of conventional pedagogy may be called into question. For instance are classroom competitions which result in individual winners going to be counter-productive? Would the class work more comfortably and/or productively if the layout of the classroom was changed? Is the 'flexible learning environment' seen as stimulating? … or threatening?

If the focus of research is on what migrant children *need,* then the temptation is to focus on those attributes they do not have which would in fact turn them into members of the dominant cultural group. This is what Bishop et al. (2003) and Bishop and Glyn (1999) refer to as deficit thinking. The conceptual form of research which focuses on lack will inevitably lead to remedial action, whether it be teaching-to-the-test, or attacks on specific skills or forms of knowledge that define the difference between the migrant child and the mainstream. Such research may have very good short-term results—in improving the child's ability to communicate through English for instance—but may also have some undesirable long-term consequences. It has not been a satisfactory approach to the difference in achievement between Maori students and Pakeha students to date, although it has been used for many years. Alison Jones' (1991) research demonstrates the point: not only were teachers providing what they thought their migrant (Pacific) students needed, but students were active agents in articulating and enforcing the satisfaction of the same perceived 'needs', to the detriment of their educational achievements and future possibilities.

The complexity of migrant children's conceptual and philosophic background is itself a subject for research. It is a mistake to believe that all migrant children share the same socio-economic status for instance (see Wu 2008). As the circumstances of immigration and the consequent life patterns of families differ, so do their material and cultural positions in the new context. However, many immigrant children will not come from well off families. That does not mean that they are culturally poor. The research of Teisina (2011) and Pau'uvale (2011) into the philosophic background of Tongan immigrants shows a richness of concept and practice which is not understood by many teachers, but which can stand here as a model for the kinds of findings an investigation into an immigrant community might produce.

31.6   CASE STUDY: Tongan Concepts and Precepts

- *Faka'apa'apa* (respect, considerate, humility)—being aware of the Tongan customs and values in order to show respect towards the people. This will include wearing the right clothes to gatherings, how to speak to elders and those who are above the hierarchy of living in a Tongan community. If you show faka'apa'apa (respect) towards the people then there is a guarantee that it will be returned. Faka'apa'apa is about acknowledgement, it is about inducing a sense of belonging.

- **'Ofa** (love)—*'Ofa* is the philosophy underpinning Tongan society. If *"ofa* is included in our practices our children will feel it through the words and our approaches. If *'ofa* is lacking then relationships would be heading towards a negative path which Tongans would refer to as *anga ta'e'ofa (unkind/damaging/selfish)*. Showing *'Ofa fe'unga* (appropriate compassion, empathy, love for the context) is fundamental to maintaining integrity and at the centre of all research activities (Vaioleti 2006, p. 31).

- *Tauhi Vā* (maintaining and nurturing reciprocal relationships)—this is a vital part of the Tongan culture where the emphasis is on forming reciprocal relationships between the students and the teachers. The Tongan culture highly value *tauhi vā* because it is the connecting space between people rather than space that separates. It is about drawing the space closer to each other through reciprocal obligations and kindness.

- *Fetokoni'aki* (working together/collective)—In the Tongan culture there is no 'I' but a 'We' instead—because the emphasis is on working together and helping each other. In teacher education, and as teachers, we need to involve the collective throughout our practice to ensure that we maintain the reciprocity of *tauhi vā*. In this case our students are more likely to contribute meaningfully, willingly and accurately.

- *Use of the child's language*. An acknowledgement of the greetings such as 'mālō e lelei' will go a long way. It is important too for the teacher to say students' names in Tongan correctly. Some parents will be very shy to speak to the teacher in English. But the way in which the teacher approaches them —'mālō e lelei'—will help to get to know the parents, and they will open up, because this gesture of respect will incline them to trust you with their children. So it is with the children: as soon as you say mālō e lelei—oh wow! this Teacher is cool you know! they can speak my language!

- *Acknowledging culture*. Acknowledging their culture means respect for their culture. Very little knowledge will make an enormous difference. Teacher researchers are not expected to learn everything straight away. But those who have made the first move are more likely to go to a cultural event, which provides the opportunity to learn in more depth, and consequently develop deeper understanding of the significance of 'difference'.

In terms of difference or different world views, the place to start is probably by challenging the notion of the individual. Which would bring us to a notion of *tauhi vā*, and the importance of the collective, the family, the village (for further discussion of *tauhi vā* see Devine et al. (2012)).

Teisina (2011), Pau'uvale (2011) and Wu (2008), have all been able to engage with migrant communities in their own languages, and hence have been able to gather richer data than is likely to be available to the student teacher who is limited to English. The distance/difference between the English-speaking researcher and migrant participant will appear to be lessened when the research conversation is held in English. This apparent lessening in difference however is deceiving, as English simply will not have adequate translations for some concepts and the migrant children will have learnt (already) what they can say in English and what they cannot say—some ideas will remain obscure, incomprehensible, 'irrational' in terms of English language and research discourse. Some recognition of this recalcitrant problem of translation and articulation will assist the student researcher to lessen the impact, but collaboration with speakers of the migrants' language would probably assist more.

31.7 Pedagogic Tactics: How Do We Get Our Student Teachers to Engage with the Other?

This cannot be left to chance: the defence systems against vacating the assumptions of privilege are already highly developed and moreover, constantly reinforced by educational discourse—'ability'; excellence'; 'achievement'—all these terms contribute to the over-valuing of the already privileged and undervaluing of the migrant child's knowledge.

An interesting, exemplary process which might show what can be done, was developed as an inquiry assignment by Timote Harris and Timoti Vaioleti at the University of Waikato.

Secondary education students had to undertake, in pairs, to coach an adolescent student from a recent migrant or refugee family for 10 hours, in the family home. It sounds simple, but required a great deal of lecturer effort to find and match pupils with the ITE student in respect of disciplinary specialty. Then there was the matter of access and communication. Schools often do not know where these children are: they move frequently and often do not inform the school. For some of our ITE students, locating the child and getting access comprised much of the task. Supervisors had to acknowledge the difficulties and honour the efforts involved.

Some students would be scared off by dogs, peeling paint, tattoos or social taboos about gender interaction (hence we tried to send out mixed pairs). Often it was the students who had had the most difficulty overcoming their fears who reported the most dramatic changes in their own perceptions, once they had made the contact and established relationships with the family. While the target of assistance was ostensibly the teenager in the family, it was frequently the case that all the children of the family would gather around the table—with the mother. Often our students would devote a lot of their time to assisting the mother with English, with navigating social welfare or explaining cultural practices.

The endpoint of this research project—research in Dewey's (1915) sense, of an inquiry that changes things for the researcher as much as for the researched—was a one page summary of what the student teacher had learnt. In this case the 'research' was less in the report—although the reports were often deeply moving—than in the doing.

It is the case that in a very diverse society such as ours the student teacher cannot research all the different cultural groups with whom they must engage in the course of their professional lives. It is not necessary. If they can only learn to vacate the high ground of privilege or respectfully ask the oppressed (Freire 2000) they can transpose these skills time without number. It is the first time that is the hardest, and we as teacher educators have to engineer that happening while we are able to—or it may never happen.

31.8 Student Teacher Research into Existing Material on the Beliefs and Culture of Migrant Groups

One of the things that shocks the ITE researcher when they really begin to inquire, in a Freirean manner (Freire 2000), about the ways of seeing of their immigrant students, is the profundity of the difference, the distance between their own assumptions as to what matters and how the world is, and those of their migrant students. The research does not have to be extensive to yield this result—an interview with a very small group of students or parents will do it. The spoken answers however may well make more sense if they are read in conjunction with sociological, historical or anthropological academic work which may alert the student researcher to deeper meaning. 'Where we once belonged' for instance, the title of a book by Figiel (1996), a Samoan author, does not yield its full meaning unless read in conjunction with the Samoan view of collective life—as Tamasese et al. (1998) say 'The Samoan is not an individual'. Where '*we*' once belonged is an elegiac to the heroine's past, to a childhood where 'I' made no sense, except as part of 'we'.

31.9 Why Put in the Effort?

Despite the recruitment efforts of teacher education institutions, the students tend to come from a relatively narrow sector of society—for precisely the same reasons which justify our seeking a wider range.

It may be thought that the remarks concerning the 'normal' or mainstream ITE student will not apply to those from minority groups. This may or may not be not the case. Minority students who have (whether successfully or not) integrated their formal education into their own being have been subjected to 15 or 20 years or more of indoctrination into the beliefs that are problematic for mainstream teachers. Those who can resist are rare, and precious. The second problem is, that they may not generalise from their own experiences to those of other groups of people. Indeed it can become a matter of importance that 'other' groups remain further down the ladder. The third problem is that they are often having difficulties of their own, and if they are struggling themselves to survive in an alien environment, they cannot be held responsible for the well-being of all or any minority children in addition to the usual workload (see Brown et al. 2008).

Should the question be asked, why should teachers learn to engage pleasantly and productively (not just one or the other!) with migrant students the answers can be constructed in a number of ways.

For those who subscribe to religious beliefs there are any number of precepts about behaviour to the 'stranger at the gate'.

For those of a more philosophic turn of mind we might turn to Levinas. If the foundation of the 'self' is what we see mirrored in the other's face, then, as long as one is open to or attuned to his kind of notion of self, there is a clear pay-off, in terms of positive self-image, in treating others with respect (Levinas 1999).

Where this approach falls down is where an ITE teacher does not 'see' the migrant student and so is indifferent to the image of self reflected in that gaze. Understandably, the migrant students are likely to object to this little oversight and start to clamour, perhaps disruptively, for attention or withdraw from an indifferent engagement.

All of these reasons are to some extent self-interested. But the most instrumental, the most governmental reason of all is that given by the writers of *The Knowledge Economy* (1999). Here the WPAG argue that, given our unbalanced demographic, the overweighting, especially in the (quite near) future, of the aged in our population, we need well-educated, productive young people, and the major sources of such young workers are Maori (although their fecundity rates are falling to European levels), Pacific peoples (who still have high numbers of children under 15); and other migrants. This is true of New Zealand and even more true of other countries without comparable numbers of indigenous and migrant children—this is part of the reason Germany has welcomed the Syrian refugees. Despite the rumblings of those who feel that migrants represent competition for jobs and housing, the continued well-being of our ageing population depends on them—but only if teachers do their jobs well.

Finally, in our list of reasons why teacher educators and student-teacher researchers should engage in research of this kind in order to lift the quality of their teaching, we omitted the two most important reasons of all. One is that it is simply a matter of justice: it is the right thing to do. The other, is that the process, the becoming-other of this experience will be immensely joyful. Challenging, even frightening, but rich and satisfying.

So—to summarise—as this is a handbook for teacher education research.

Inquiry done with honest intention will probably yield life-changing, or at least pedagogy-changing results. The inquiry can be both theoretic and empirical: the most significant theoretic approach would be one that interrogates the totalising nature of any theory, pedagogic, political or social, and contemplates the possibility of respectful engagement with different ways of knowing the world (see for instance King 2003).

Empirical research can as productively be focused on student teachers and their attitudes, values and behaviours as on the target migrant community. Where empirical work is done with migrants it might well include the family as well as the student and for some cultural groups this will be more appropriate (and in the long run more helpful).

Academic sources can support but should not supplant the empirical research. One might bear in mind Levinas' insistence on the importance of the face-to-face encounter.

The point of research of this kind is not the academic output, but the *encounter*, including all the difficulties of fear, access, poor communication, language issues, cultural differences, visual symbols, social conventions … that stand in the way of good relationships and good teaching.

References

Arndt, S. (2012). *Foreigners, immigrants, otherness: A philosophical analysis of complications, delights and tensions*. Unpublished thesis, University of Auckland.

Bishop, R., Berryman, M., Tiakiwai, S., & Richardson, C. (2003). *Te Kotahitanga: The experiences of year 9 and 10 Māori students in mainstream classrooms*. Report to the Ministry of Education. Ministry of Education Te Tāhuhu o te Mātauranga.

Bishop, R., & Glynn, T. (1999). *Culture counts: Changing power relations in education*. London, UK: Zed Books.

Bishop, R., & Glynn, T. (2003). *Culture counts: Changing power relations in education*. Palmerston North, NZ: Dunmore Press.

Bourdieu, P. (1977). *Outline of a theory of practice*. Cambridge, UK: Cambridge University Press.

Brown, T., Devine, N., Leslie, E., Paiti, M., Sila'ila'i, E., Umaki, S., et al. (2008). *Pasifika Teachers in secondary education: Issues, possibilities and strategies*. Wellington, New Zealand: TLRI.

Deleuze, G., & Guattari, F. (1986). *Nomadology: The war machine*. (B. Massumi, Trans.). New York: Semiotext(e).

Devine, N., Teisina, J., & Pau'uvale, L. (2012). *Tauhi vā*, Spinoza and Deleuze in education. *The Journal of the Pacific Circle Consortium for Education, 24*(2), 57–68.

Dewey, J. (1915). *Democracy and education*. New York, NY: MacMillan.

Figiel, S. (1996). *Where we once belonged*. Auckland: NZ Pasifika Press.

Foucault, M. (1980). *'Two lectures' in power/knowledge: Selected interviews and other writings, 1972–1977*. Brighton, Sussex, UK: Harvester Press.

Freire, P. (2000). *Pedagogy of the oppressed*. New York, NY: Continuum.

Jones, A. (1991). *"At school I've got a chance" culture/privilege: Pacific Islands' and Pakeha Girls at School*. Palmerston North, NZ: Dunmore Press.

King, T. (2003). *The truth about stories*. Minneapolis, MN: University of Minnesota.

Levinas, E. (1999). *Alterity and transcendence* (M. B. Smith, Trans.). London, UK: The Athlone Press.

Pau'uvale, L. (2011). *Laulotaha; Tongan perspectives of 'quality' in early childhood education*. Unpublished thesis, AUT

Tamasese, K., Peteru, C., Waldegrave, C., & Bush, A. (1998). *O le Teao, the new morning*. The Family Centre, NZ: Christchurch.

Teisina, J. W. B. (2011). *Langangave 'a e kaufaiakoAkoteu Tonga nofo 'I Aotearoa. Tongan early childhood education: Building success from the teachers' perspectives*. Unpublished thesis, AUT.

Vaioleti, T. M. (2006). Talanoa research methodology: A developing position on Pacific research. *Waikato Journal of Education, 12*, 21–34.

WPAG. (1999). *The knowledge economy*. Wellington, New Zealand: Ernst and Young.

Wu, B. (2008). *Whose culture has capital?* Auckland, NZ: Peter Lang.

Author Biographies

Professor Nesta Devine of Auckland University of Technology, is interested in 'subjugated knowledges', feminist and post-structuralist thinking. She is an Associate Editor of *Educational Philosophy and Theory*, co-editor of the *New Zealand Journal of Teachers' Work*, and an editor of the *Bhutan Journal of Research and Development*.

Jeanne Pau'uvale Teisina was born in the islands of Vava'u and moved to New Zealand with her family in 1995. Her involvement in Tongan Early Childhood Centres has drawn her attention to the cultural problems inherent in the regulatory context of New Zealand Early Childhood Education. She is a currently doing her doctorate degree in Education at AUT University.

Lorraine Pau'uvale was born and raised in the Kingdom of Tonga. Lorraine graduated with a Master of Education and Master of Education Leadership in 2012. Her Master of education thesis is titled Laulotaha; Tongan Perspectives of 'Quality' in Early Childhood Education. This research focused on reclaiming an understanding of 'quality' from Tongan perspectives.

Chapter 32
Reforming Teacher Education in England—'An Economy of Discourses of Truth'

Meg Maguire

32.1 Introduction

Education policy works by producing sets of ideas that become part of the 'taken for grantedness' of the way things should be. This frequently involves the production of hard policy texts that represent and document and illustrate what has to be done or what is desirable to do. 'These textual artefacts are cultural productions that carry within them sets of beliefs and meanings that speak to social processes and policy enactments—ways of being and becoming—that is, forms of governmentality' (Ball et al. 2011: 122). But policy texts are constructions—constructions and productions of versions of 'truths'. As Foucault explains:

> Contrary to a myth whose history and functions would repay further study, truth isn't the reward of free spirit nor the privilege of those who have succeeded in liberating themselves. Truth is a thing of this world: It is produced only by virtue of multiple forms of constraint. And it induces regular effects of power. Each society has its own regime of truth, its "general politics" of truth; that is, the type of discourse which it accepts and makes function as true. (Foucault 1980: 131)

I start with a brief review of the main propositions for reforming English teacher education. Much of what is being enacted is an amalgam of long-standing policies and strategies that have been revisited and reworked to fit with discourses of markets, efficiency, competition and globalising 'necessities'. These policies are an attempt to displace and erase any alternative and 'counter memories' of becoming a teacher. However, despite all the rhetoric and activity around the 'new' reforms for

An earlier version of this chapter appeared in the *Journal of Education Policy*, Vol. 29, Issue 6, 2014, pp. 774–784

M. Maguire (✉)
King's College, London, England, UK
e-mail: meg.maguire@kcl.ac.uk

Teacher Education, one of the most intriguing things about all this 'policy noise' is the way in which many previous policy attempts for reforming the sector were resuscitated in the expanding policy textual portfolio of the conservative coalition (2010–2015)—*The importance of teaching: The schools White Paper 2010*, the follow up paper, *Training our next generation of outstanding teachers: An improvement strategy for discussion* (DfE 2011). These policies are being accelerated in England by the present Conservative government (2015 onwards).

This chapter is an attempt to 'think aloud' about the policy proposals in circulation in England that address pre-service teacher education. Rather than dealing with details of policy and points of specificity in practice, the focus is with how propositions are justified and the overall ways in which meanings are being managed; a fundamental aspect of policy analysis. What I concentrate on is the 'general politics' of truth, and the justifications (Foucault 1980: 131) that surround the reforms of teacher education in England.

32.2   The Case for Reform

The recommendations contained in the English policy documents focus on the alleged need to improve teacher quality through 'attracting and training even better teachers' (Foreword to the White Paper by Michael Gove 2010: 7). (Michael Gove was Secretary of State for Education in the 2010–2015 administration and was a key driver of policy change in education provision including teacher education reform). This improvement is to be managed in a variety of ways; one method being by not funding any recruits who have less than a second class honours degree (in England, a 2.2)—the assumption being that a 'better' class of degree leads to better teaching and that subject knowledge can be separated off from pedagogy. As an aside, the work of Darling-Hammond (2000: 167) in the US on this matter suggests that the relationship of subject knowledge to teaching effectiveness 'is curvilinear; that is, it exerts a positive effect up to a threshold level and then tapers off in influence'—an example of policy not necessarily reflecting evidence. Another method for improving teacher quality at the point of recruitment is through more rigorous 'basic skills' testing for intending trainee teachers—even though it might be expected that these allegedly 'better' qualified recruits would already have command of these skills. There are financial incentives for graduates in shortage subjects to encourage their recruitment into teaching. There are more diverse routes into school teaching.

Perhaps the most 'troubling' suggestion for those of us who work in Initial Teacher Training (ITT), or who work in Universities where this work is central to the mission of the Department, is the call for more training to take place 'on the job' in schools. This is despite the fact that in the main secondary route into teaching in England, the Post Graduate Certificate of Education (PGCE), 24 of the 36 weeks of the programme are already based in a variety of schools, and in the Primary PGCE, at least 18 weeks of the programme are spent in school placements. In the undergraduate degrees, at least 24 weeks, spread over the courses of study are spent in gaining experience in different schools. All these are partnership models between schools and educational institutions. The conservative coalition expanded the school-based routes (SCITT), despite the fact that the English Inspectors found the university-based courses to be generally of a better quality than those offered in schools. One way this was and is being managed is through extending the School Direct route, another school-led programme (see http://www.education.gov.uk/ get-into-teaching/teacher-training-options/school-based-training/school-direct). The conservative coalition envisaged a larger number of training schools, on the model of teaching hospitals, where schools would lead on pre-service and in-service professional development—and I will come back to these later on in this chapter.

One particular form of school-based training—the 'Teach First' scheme has been extended. This is the English version of a global travelling policy that originated in the USA as 'Teach for All' and which recruits 'outstanding graduates' from prestigious universities. These graduates teach in challenging schools for 2 years and are expected to progress onto leadership roles on other careers; hence the UK name, 'Teach First'. In England, a fast-track route, 'Teach Next', recruits professionals in other careers who want to move into teaching; and the 'Troops to Teachers' programme supports suitable candidates leaving the armed forces to move into teaching (http://www.education.gov.uk/get-into-teaching/troops-to-teachers.aspx). The numbers that are proposed for these routes are small (at least at the moment). However, the impact of these proposals for additional SCITT lies in the way in which they discursively break up, disturb, disrupt and displace current patterns of pre-service university-based teacher education and training—extending diversity—all part of a market economy. As another aside, some of these policy moves may be counterproductive in practice because of the way in which they may be encouraging high teacher turnover by design:

> Recruiting policies that tolerate and even encourage high numbers of young and inexperienced teachers to move in and out of the job within 3 – 5 years might keep down short-term costs, but they squander taxpayer's investments. They also sell disadvantaged students short by condemning them to inexperienced and less effective teachers who leave long before they reach their potential. (Hargreaves and Fullan 2012: 76)

32.3   Why Is English Teacher Education so Susceptible to Reform—or to 'Multiple Forms of Constraint'?

While there are many questions that can be raised about the substantive proposals for reforming teacher education provision in England, what I want to do now is consider two fundamental points. These are as follows; first, teacher education has *always* been regarded by various Governments as a 'suitable case for reform' and second, allegations of 'necessity' because of alleged low standards and matters of economic expediency have consistently driven policy attention in this sector.

The outcome is that, since its inception, teacher education has been continually worked on by policy-makers; it has been constantly reformed, and elaborated or cut back in different historic periods. Perhaps then it is not surprising that the conservative-led coalition government and the current Conservative government have maintained their crusade to reform teacher education.

But why has teacher education been susceptible to so much policy reforming unlike other professional education and training such as that provided for medical doctors or lawyers? Status and power differentials over time have something to do with the forms of 'multiple constraints' that have bedevilled the professional preparation of the schoolteacher in England. Teacher education has been a 'late arrival' to the academy as teaching was not initially a degree-level occupation and was mainly delivered by teacher training colleges. All this has affected its status. Teacher education itself is not of a piece but is marked by a hierarchy of status and prestige within which different programmes and institutions are differentially positioned. When Hencke (1978: 15) was investigating reforms to teacher education in a period of massive cuts and closures to the training colleges in the 1970s, he claimed that many of the problems that confronted this provision lay in what he called its 'unwholesome beginnings'. He argued that as teacher training started in Southwark, 'a slum district of London' rather than in Oxbridge, right from the start, it was denied status, resources and 'talent' in England. In the nineteenth century, teachers were only trained to teach in the state-provided elementary schools that predominantly served the working classes. The job of teaching, for it was not a profession, was a non-graduate, intermediate occupation. As Hencke (1978: 13) pointed out:

> Unlike theology, medicine or law, it (teacher training) has no historic claim to a university tradition of academic excellence or respectability. It has more in common instead with medieval craft guilds, whose apprenticeship system preceded modern technical education.

Since its inauspicious start, teacher education has been characterised by an almost continual set of conflicts, and an uneasy relation between the central and local state, (and different sets of 'stakeholders') over who should control and manage this provision, and by demands for reform from an increasingly professionalised and unionised teaching force as well as teacher educators. Many of these struggles and contestations have centred on the academic profile of the teacher and the moves to an all-graduate profession as well as the curriculum of teacher education and its relationship to school-experience; all these competing discourses, these 'multiple forms of constraint', have a long and enduring history and have been sedimented down and become reactivated at particular moments in time. One such perennial discourse in England concerns the role of school experience. For example, Andrew Bell, who with Joseph Lancaster set up the first apprenticeship style model—that of the pupil teacher—emphasised that teachers are formed through in-school experience and not by attending lectures. What we see here is the genesis of an on-going dispute between the place of theory and practice in pre-service teacher education.

Another 'multiple form of constraint' has been the need to manage teacher supply, recruitment and retention—the numbers game! Currently in England, there is an attempt to break the assumption that teacher supply is a responsibility and function of the state. However, at various times, over-supply has led to the closure of large numbers of teacher education colleges and high numbers of unemployed teachers, while undersupply and extreme shortages have resulted in 'quick fix' policies. There have been various schemes, driven in part by a shortage of recruits to teaching as well as difficulties in retention, to enlist the services of different constituencies, such as a scheme in 1993 for a so-called Mum's Army of primary teachers, which eventually transmuted into Teaching Assistants. And even further back, at the end of the Second World War, many ex-servicemen and women were successfully drafted into becoming 'Emergency Trained Teachers' because of staff shortages. Thus, it is evident that in England the construction of the teacher has always been context dependent—the teacher is constructed out of local histories, cultures and politics. The teacher is also constructed out of economics and expediency too.

One of the unintended consequences of all this diversity of routes into teaching is that it can contribute towards a loss of professional identity and a reduction in the power of teachers and teacher educators to influence professional development policy and practice. Hencke (1978: 124), writing of the reforms in the 1970s and the diversity of entrance routes at the time said: 'Nobody would dream of allowing practising lawyers, doctors, dentists, or architects to run their professions with such a variety of qualifications. It would be considered unprofessional and against the public interest'. Now while I do not whole-heartedly agree with what he is saying in terms of some routes into teaching, he does have a point.

One more reason why teacher education has always been relatively easy to position as in need of reform in England is that it has regularly been demonised since its inception in the nineteenth century and onwards, right up to the present times. These discourses of derision are built out of a 'type of discourse which it (society) accepts and makes function as true' (Foucault 1980: 131). Over time in England, the positioning of teacher education as 'flexible', as low status in the academy and as a (mainly) practical concern set alongside the positioning of teachers as semi-professional state workers, has contributed towards this susceptibility.

32.4 And Why More Reforms to Teacher Education Again?

The reform of teachers and teacher education has always been driven by more than pedagogical concerns about raising quality and helping children to learn, and improving the pre-service provision for teacher education, important those these are. While there have been persistent and long-standing concerns with supply and demand, social control and the need to respond to the 'needs' of the labour market, more recently, there have been complex sets of pressures in relation to claims about market forces and international competition. In an internationally competitive market place, education plays a critical role in helping each nation to create and maintain a competitive edge—or so the argument goes. Thus, in response to aspects of the globalisation discourse, attempts have been made to align educational provision to the 'needs' of capital in many international settings.

Many nations, aware of international comparisons such as TIMMS and PISA, have been spurred on to reform their educational provision and raise their measurable levels of attainment. What has emerged is a new set of public policy demands for efficiency, accountability, effectiveness and flexibility aimed at reforming public sector education provision. In consequence, education policy has been rearticulated and justified in terms of economic expediency and international competition. The outcomes can be seen in current preoccupations with raising standards and measured attainment, making state education more accountable in relation to internationally derived targets, and ensuring that curriculum, pedagogy and the teaching force are managed in order to 'deliver' these demands.

No politician wants to be seen as lacking in energy, commitment and policy ideas. This is true of all politicians, their advisors and policy entourages. As Edwards et al. (2002: 3) make clear,

> Governments, perhaps by their very function, are drawn irresistibly to certainties. They make policy. Politicians cluster round certainties like moths around a flame, accumulating them to create manifestos, policy documents and the paraphernalia of government.

Contemporary teacher education reform is predicated on a range of suppositions; that schools have failed in the past, due in some part, to inefficient and incompetent teachers, and that policy-makers and governments are best placed to determine what makes an 'effective' teacher and a 'good' school. One way of ensuring teacher quality is to reform teaching at source by regulating and controlling pre-service teacher education. Many nations including the US, UK, New Zealand, Australia, Canada and countries in Europe and in the Asian-Pacific region, seek to manage recruitment and pre-service training through the generation of lists of competencies that have to be met before the teacher can be licensed to practice in schools. And many of these competencies include prescriptions about what constitutes 'best practice' that intending teachers are expected to adopt and perform in the practicum element of their course. The emphasis in these restructured courses is arguably on 'teacher-proofing' classroom practice. Thus, the emphasis, more and more, is on successful in-school experience, technical skills such as teaching literacy through centrally prescribed methods, behaviour management, familiarity with testing regimes, etc. Other matters, for example, those of commitment, values and judgement are frequently sidelined, made optional or simply omitted; teacher education is constructed as a skill and any socio-cultural complexity is 'bleached' out of the agenda.

Another way of thinking about all these reforms that are detailed in the many policy texts and policy rhetoric that drive teacher education policy is that the teacher is being reconstructed as a state technician, trained by various 'providers' to 'deliver' a national curriculum in England's schools. Alongside this competency-based model of the technical skills-based teacher is a market model of the 'flexiblisation' of teaching work, a move towards individual contracts and pay negotiations including the use of non-qualified teachers and teaching assistants—where the teacher is positioned as part of the contracted labour force rather than as a professional partner in the process of education.

The current government is trying to ensure that market forces, competition and diversity are further inserted into pre-service (and in-service) teacher development. As Stuart Hall (2011: 9) has claimed, 'the long march of the neo liberal revolution' is continuing in 'our extraordinary political situation'. Hall believes that currently we are experiencing another conjunctural crisis. Drawing on Gramsci, Hall argues that new social settlements and 'the new social configurations which result, mark a new 'conjuncture''—where a number of contradictions in different sites (cultural, education, social as well as economic) come together to conjoin. To go back to my opening quote from Foucault, some of this conjuncture in society is evident in 'the type of discourse which it accepts and makes function as true' (Foucault 1980: 131). This 'truth telling' for a new conjuncture is amply illustrated in many of Michael Gove's earlier policy texts and speeches. One example will have to suffice:

> Every parent in the land knows that we need to improve our education system. We've got great teachers doing a fantastic job across the country, but they've been held back by a bureaucratic and dumbed-down approach which has seen us fall behind other nations. Labour spent money but far too much of it has gone on red tape, interference, quangos and politically correct pet projects. Teachers have been denied the powers they need to keep order, they've been restricted in the exams they can offer so children in state schools couldn't sit the more rigorous tests they have in the private sector and they've been judged not on how well they teach but how many bureaucratic boxes they tick. (Gove 2011a, b, article in the Sunday Express available on DfE website)

32.5 'Truth Being a Thing of This World'

Turning now to the provision of training schools, in which some schools will take the leading role in the education of pre-service and in-service professional development. I do not think that anyone would disagree with the proposition that experiences of learning alongside more expert practitioners in a classroom setting is anything other than a fundamental part of becoming a teacher. But it is not just about where teacher education is done, it is also about what is being done and how it is being done and who has the power to innovate. In the mid-1980s some universities set up PGCE programmes that were jointly planned by school-based mentors and university staff and that were research-informed (here I am thinking particularly but not exclusively of Sussex, Leicester and Oxford University). Projects such as IT-INSET, funded by the then Department of Education and Science (DES) in 1978 at the Open University, were alternative approaches to collaborative planning, teaching and the evaluation of learning jointly undertaken by classroom teachers, college tutors and trainee teachers working in teams— pre-service and in-service education—with the emphasis on theoretically reflexive school-based experience. (And as I have already noted, the current PGCE courses are significantly school-based and many Higher Education Institutes (HEIs) still manage to run imaginative and innovative programmes—or bits of their programmes that are like this!)

I am not concerned so much with the provision of training schools per se, although there is much that could be said about this move; but here I want to consider the manner in which a 'general politics' of truth has been assembled to support this particular policy. First, there is a *technology of erasure*—the erasure of the work of progressive and reforming teacher educationalists who have in different times attempted to produce new ways of using school-based experiences to produce new forms of teacher (and trainee teacher) knowledge. Some work that HEIs have done in the past and are still engaging in, may be key to a better alternative future. A paper by Ellis (2010) argues that we do not have a sufficient understanding of 'experience' in teacher learning. He argues that 'fitting in' and 'tapping into' classroom practices and school and department cultures may not extend and develop teacher knowledge. I think this is a fruitful avenue for greater reflection. Second, there is the normative assertion that underpins the move to school-based teacher education of teaching as a craft:

> Teaching is a craft and it is best learnt as an apprentice observing a master craftsman or woman. Watching others, and being rigorously observed yourself as you develop, is the best route to acquiring mastery in the classroom. (Gove 2010: 6)

In contrast, teaching is a complex undertaking, where interplay between experience, research evidence, knowledge of practice elsewhere as well as ethical-moral decision-making shape what the teacher does. This is far richer, complex and harder to bring off and while there is no reason why training schools will not be able to do this, there is a repository of expertise and resources in HEIs that could complement their work. As always, the devil is in the detail and in the ensuing practices. However, Gove commented on his reforms that:

> Higher education institutions will continue to make a significant and important contribution to teacher training. But we want schools to play a much bigger role. As employers, schools should have greater responsibility for recruitment; be more involved in the provision of quality placements; and have more say in the development of content for training... we will allow schools to recruit trainees and then to work with an accredited teacher training provider to train them to be qualified teachers. Schools will be expected to employ these trainees after graduation. (Gove 2011a, b)

In terms of the discussion I am rehearsing here about the legitimation of policy and the way that specific texts call up versions of what is to be enacted, I want now to briefly consider one of the key analogies that the Government uses to conjure up 'quality', and which is frequently used to advocate for reforms in training teachers. That is, the medical model. The argument goes that doctors are trained in teaching hospitals and this model can be distilled and reconstructed in the teaching schools.

Now, what is not ever mentioned is that becoming a doctor is a long and arduous process spread over many years. Second, it is not made clear that trainee-medics spend most of the first two years at their various universities. When they do start their hospital placements, they are still expected to attend classes and undertake academic study. In this most practical of training, theory, practice and the capacity to exercise professional judgements based on evidence-informed reflection are firmly welded together—as they need to be once the doctor is legally qualified to start to practice.

> Hospitals are large and patient care is one-to-one, so many trainees can be absorbed in the one institution. In schools, however, children are taught in groups of twenty or more, and parents are liable to grow restive if their child's education consists of wall-to-wall trainees. (Smithers and Robinson 2011: 32)

What the analogy between hospital teaching school and the training schools for teacher education attempts, is to couple together a long-standing and highly respected aspect of a high-status professional preparation with an aspect of current education policy and in this way, to lend virtue and legitimation to what is being proposed. This is not to say that training schools have nothing to offer; that would not be the case at all. But it is worth highlighting the contribution made by inno-vatory PGCE programmes that ask (to paraphrase Yandell 2010) not only how it is that teaching and learning are achieved by but 'how might it be otherwise'— questions that 'cut across any simple oppositions of university and school-based elements of the PGCE. However, what I am primarily concerned with here is the production of a 'general politics of truth' that endeavours to add legitimacy to some proposals rather than others.

32.6 'An Economy of Discourses of Truth'

There is so much more that could be said about the reforming of teachers and teacher education, related funding issues and the current dilemmas of high teacher turnover and recruitment problems in some subject areas and in some types of schools. However, I want to return to where I started, to Foucault and power, truth and policy:

> There can be no possible exercise of power without a certain economy of discourses of truth which operates through and on the basis of this association. We are subjected to the production of truth through power and we cannot exercise power except through the production of truth. This is the case for every society. (Foucault 1980: 39)

This paper has set out to 'think aloud' about the current policy proposals in cir-culation in England that address pre-service teacher education, how these propo-sitions are being justified and the overall ways in which meanings are being managed. In England, what we are seeing is the attempted erasure of the role of the university-based teacher educationalist as a knowing expert and the valorization of practical experience, craft and skills. This move has been somewhat easier to bring off in England, because teacher education has never enjoyed parity of esteem with other disciplines or professions. Teacher education has always existed in an uneasy alliance between the classroom and the lecture theatre; it has always existed in a constrained relationship with the state lying somewhere between a pattern of total domination to strong indirect influence at different moments in time.

These contemporary English reforms could be seen as an attempt to construct an even more competitive market in the supply of different types of (and no) teaching qualifications and perhaps a new hierarchy of teachers. What is also being advanced is a move away from the state control of teacher education towards a less/un regulated set of different providers; chains and clusters of schools run by sponsors and social enterprise organisations providing teacher training. In all this rush to reform, there are a number of dangers. One is the way in which individualism may triumph over concerns for the common good. Will the training schools be preparing teachers for all schools and all children, or just for their own? Will national concerns about the provision of a linguistically and ethnically diverse teaching force fall by the wayside in Schools Direct training routes? Localism may cost us dear! And what to make of the version of the teacher and the school that is being produced by these reforms? There are also more practical concerns; will these reforms really drive up standards and teaching quality; will these reforms actually produce the numbers of teachers needed; will these reforms tackle the issue of high turbulence and early drop-out in teaching numbers? Let us see see!

References

Ball, S. J., Maguire, M., & Braun, A. (2011). *How schools do policy: Policy enactment in the secondary school*. London: Routledge/Falmer.

Darling-Hammond, L. (2000). How teaching matters. *Journal of Teacher Education, 51*(3), 166–173.

Department for Education (DfE). (2010). *The importance of teaching: The schools white paper 2010*. UK: The Stationery Office Limited.

Department for Education (DfE). (2011). *Training our next generation of outstanding teachers: An improvement strategy for discussion*. UK: The Stationery Office Limited.

Edwards, A., Gilroy, P., & Hartley, D. (2002). *Researching teacher education: Collaborative responses to uncertainty*. London and New York: Routledge/Falmer.

Ellis, V. (2010). Impoverishing experience: the problem of teacher education in England. *Journal of Education for Teaching, 36*(1), 105–120.

Foucault, M. (1980). *Power/knowledge*. New York: Pantheon.

Gove, M. (2010). *Speech to the Annual Conference of the National College for Leadership of Schools and Children's Services*. Available at http://www.education.gov.uk/inthenews/speeches/a0061371/michael-gove-to-the-national-college-annual-conference-birmingham. Accessed February 17, 2013.

Gove, M. (2011a). *Speech to the National College/heads of the first 100 teaching schools*. Available at http://www.education.gov.uk/inthenews/speeches/a00198074/michael-gove-to-the-national-college. Accessed February 17, 2013.

Gove, M. (2011b). *Michael Gove writes on education reforms in the Sunday Express*. Available at http://www.education.gov.uk/inthenews/articles/a0061737/michael-gove-writes-on-education-reforms-in-sunday-express. Accessed March 28, 2013.

Hall, S. (2011). The neo-liberal revolution, soundings. *A Journal of Politics and Culture*, 48, 9–28.

Hargreaves, A., & Fullan, M. (2012). *Professional capital: Transforming teaching in every school*. London, New York: Routledge, Teachers College Press.

Hencke, D. (1978). *Colleges in crisis: The reorganization of teacher training, 1971–7*. Harmondsworth: Penguin.

Smithers, A., & Pamela Robinson, P. (2011). *The good teacher training guide 2011*. Centre for Education and Employment Research, University of Buckingham. Available at http://www.buckingham.ac.uk/wp-content/uploads/2010/11/GTTG2011.pdf. Accessed March 4, 2013.

Yandell, J. (2010). Sites of learning. In R. Heilbronn & J. Yandell (Eds.), *Critical practice in teacher education. A study of professional learning* (pp. 15–29), London: Institute of Education, Bedford Way Papers.

Author Biography

Meg Maguire's research focuses on sociology of education, urban education, policy and social justice. She has a long-standing interest in the lives of teachers. Meg is Professor of Sociology of Education at King's College London and is Lead Editor for the Journal of Education Policy.

Chapter 33
Teacher Educators' Responsibility to Prepare Candidates for Classroom Realities

John O'Neill

33.1 Introduction

School teaching in most countries is legislated as a form of professional practice and governed by specific system level preparation, registration and continuing certification requirements. Teacher education programmes offered in universities are required culturally to induct candidates into contributing discipline knowledge, and contractually to ensure functional preparedness and fitness to enter the profession. In this sense the candidates are consciously positioned both inside and outside the academy, having to negotiate the various and subtly different normative expectations of their in-university and in-school educators. In turn, university teacher educators must reconcile their own occupational tensions between dutiful promotion of and critical engagement with official government policy on curriculum, pedagogy and assessment matters.

In New Zealand over the last decade, the term "quality teaching" has emerged as a powerful touchstone around which to nurture a common set of premises about desirable teacher education practices and to encourage the adoption of officially preferred values, behaviours, competencies and dispositions among pre-service, novice and experienced teachers. Over that same period, the control agencies of teaching (the Ministry of Education [MoE], the Education Council [EC], the Education Review Office [ERO]) have proselytised this common language throughout the commission, execution and evaluation of teacher education policy initiatives in an effort to ensure greater predictability of teacher education workforce quality and supply. Teacher professional associations or unions meanwhile have tried to accommodate policy demands by linking "quality teaching" to the advancement of professional and industrial concerns about the materiality and performativity strands of state teachers' working conditions and lives.

J. O'Neill (✉)
Massey University, Palmerston North, New Zealand
e-mail: j.g.oneill@massey.ac.nz

© Springer Nature Singapore Pte Ltd. 2017
M.A. Peters et al. (eds.), *A Companion to Research in Teacher Education*,
DOI 10.1007/978-981-10-4075-7_33

Government and the national polity have also attempted to infuse the ideal of quality teaching throughout their engagement with mass media and popular cultural texts. This effort is reflected in diverse tactical efforts, for example: the direct association of the Prime Minister, not the Minister of Education, with a prestigious national annual awards ceremony for teaching excellence; and more broadly, the intentional deployment of "quality teaching" as a catch-all proxy or umbrella concept by ministers and officials whenever early childhood and compulsory schooling "problems" and their "solutions" are discussed.

In this sense, quality teaching may be regarded as a socially constructed discourse, worthy of critical analysis in its own right. This paper takes the now ubiquitous Quality Teaching Discourse (QTD) as a basis for asserting that teacher educators need to be reflexive about their responsibility as questioning mediators of official policy discourses. In New Zealand, tertiary education institutions enjoy a statutory responsibility to act as a "critic and conscience" of society. This obligation is vested in the staff who work in them. Accordingly, teacher educators in this instance are ethically obligated to understand how and why key ideals about the role of teachers in society become part of common understandings and practices, and the ways in which, in turn, this shapes the possibilities of their work with teaching candidates and of theirs with students in classrooms.

This stance would certainly constitute a form of teacher education scholarship but is it teacher education research in the sense expected of contributions to this volume? Lawrence Stenhouse is credited with the aphorism that research is simply systematic inquiry made public. In that sense, the tradition of education policy scholarship is systematic in its attempts to trace the historical, political and social trajectories of educational ideas (such as the QTD) and their practical effects in a particular time and place. The advent of the World Wide Web has produced, among other things, a viral spread of New Public Management (NPM) education policies across jurisdictions, the rise of social media as a highly influential public sphere, and the emergence of new policy governance networks comprising fluid, dynamic alliances of public, private and philanthropic actors. In response, policy governance scholarship has required immersion in the virtual field and attempting to keep track, and make sense of, these policy making moments as they unfold more or less in real time across traditional and new media.

Drawing on these forms of scholarship, this chapter, then, offers a personal analysis of the underlying meanings and purposes of what might otherwise be a taken-for-granted trope in contemporary teacher education discourse, namely that overcoming structural and often intergenerational structural inequalities is simply a case of "fixing-up" teachers. The first part of the paper identifies the key origins and features of the QTD in the local New Zealand context. The remainder of the chapter identifies other elements of the day to day work and working conditions of teachers which also need to be taken fully into account by both teaching candidates and teacher educators (i.e. partiality, performativity, materiality). In developing the analysis in this way, I claim to be modelling a reflexive approach to the work of teacher educators that is essential if: (i) teacher candidates are to be able to develop a critical understanding of education policy texts and the ways in which normative expectations of teacher's work may be quite at odds with classroom realities; and (ii) teacher educators are to be able to maintain a "safe" tertiary education space in which to interrogate increasing prescriptions/proscriptions of the state for the preparation of beginning teachers.

33.2   The Quality Teaching Discourse

Today, in Aotearoa New Zealand, the Quality Teaching Discourse (QTD) is hegemonic in official schooling policy texts. As such it is rarely questioned. QTD emerged from the former post-WWII "progressive sentiment" in education policy discourse according to which the ideal teacher was an "educated person" whose job it was to create classroom environments and programmes conducive to students' engagement and learning. This ideal was gradually displaced following the publication of the Education and Science Select Committee's 1986 report, *The Quality of Teaching,* by an ideal of the teacher who is held accountable (by self and others) for the measurable outcomes achieved by students.

New Zealand's growing participation in international studies of comparative student performance from the mid-1990s gave added impetus to the QTD policy agenda as information and communication technologies made it easier to produce periodic statistics to identify precisely which students were succeeding, or not, at national, institutional and classroom levels, and to disaggregate these data by class location, ethnicity and gender. Simple correlational analyses made it possible to identify examples of teachers or schools that had apparently "beaten the odds" of their socio-economic circumstances and thereby justified a new "state sponsored possibilism" (Nash 2003): the ideology that all students can succeed provided only that sufficient attention and commitment are given to improving the quality of teaching.

In recent years, the work of selected academic researchers has been variously co-opted, distilled and redeployed tactically by officials to justify numerous QTD teaching policy initiatives (e.g. Alton-Lee 2003; Bishop et al. 2007; Timperley et al. 2007; Hattie 2009). Within the QTD, policy and academic discursive strands have become mutually sustaining and practically indistinguishable over time: officials come to depend on their preferred academics, and vice versa. Together, groups of officials and academics acting on behalf of the State have developed QTD as, in effect, an intellectual project. Its purpose is to secure greater control over the ways in which teachers as an occupational group come to view their obligations to learners and to distract attention from the deteriorating material conditions of teachers' work. In a very real sense, these "intellectuals" are "functionaries" (Gramsci 1971, p. 12) of dominant groups within the state. In Gramsci's terms, they are "exercising the subaltern functions of social hegemony and political government" in order to maintain the trajectory of QTD via the "spontaneous" or unthinking consent of teachers in schools (p. 12).

The QTD may also be argued to be based on a "Janus-faced" polity ideology of the "responsible" teacher (O'Neill 2010). In this ideology, the teacher is simultaneously the cause of and the solution to schooling inequalities. On the one hand, responsible teachers are asserted to be sensitive to and appreciative of the cultural situatedness of individual learners. These teachers are claimed to actively assist learners in their classrooms to overcome the combined effects of structural socio-economic disadvantage and cultural invisibility (including class-ism and racial-ism). On the other hand, teachers who cannot do this are claimed to be solely responsible for the localised educational failure of *their* students. Teachers are further pathologised in QTD through the frequent assertion that the primary reason students fail is because their teachers subscribe, consciously or unconsciously, to a so-called "deficit theory" of poor and ethnic minority students' capacities to succeed at school (Persell 1981).

The term "responsible" therefore connotes a highly ambiguous and ambivalent stance among the politicians, officials and academics who sustain the QTD towards state school teachers. Overall, the QTD seeks to minimise the importance of contextual effects on learning outcomes, and maximise the importance of what teachers do. According to QTD, if classroom teachers exemplify the language, practices and relations of "quality teaching", then all students *shall* succeed.

However, in promoting this stance, the QTD not only ignores the well-established effects of non-classroom-related practices on students' learning *and* capacity for learning, it also ignores the material conditions in which classroom teachers work each day, and, more specifically, the ways in which these material conditions actively militate against the possibility of teachers engaging in the sorts of pedagogical work that is proselytised through the QTD. In other words, it is a poverty of *material conditions*, not a poverty of *teacher dispositions*, that is the significant education policy issue. Moreover, the QTD may be seen to be not only implausible but also untruthful. Comparative data such as that published annually by the OECD in its omnibus *Education at a Glance* report, consistently demonstrates that New Zealand teachers are under-resourced compared with their overseas counterparts, yet it comes from exactly the same policy texts and think-tank reports that officials use to promote the view that quality teaching is the major determinant of whether or not students succeed.

Socially critical commentaries from sections of the academy and organised labour in New Zealand have over the years attempted to maintain a discursive space in which issues of class and cultural location are seen to matter, and that teachers may only be held to account for their occupational behaviours and judgments, not student outcomes. Within QTD, however, as in neoliberal discourse generally, educational concepts and vocabularies have been appropriated, redefined and deployed towards technocratic, NPM ends. The plausibility, popular appeal and self-evident rationality of the QTD force its critics to engage in a tactical game to try and recapture colonised educational discourses. The danger in so doing is that academics (including teacher educators) and organised labour help to shore up the QTD rather than discredit it. But academics and organised labour also have a shared responsibility to ensure that comprehensive empirical data on the material conditions of classroom teachers' work are regularly gathered, analysed and publicly reported. In this way, the amounts and types of government investment in state education may properly be viewed as contributing factors to the quality of pedagogical relations in classrooms.

Under-resourcing materially affects what it is reasonable, and not, to expect classroom teachers to contribute to the reduction of structural educational inequalities in schooling. The collation, analysis and dissemination of empirical data from official and officially preferred sources thus facilitate a counter-hegemonic discursive process of demonstrating that teachers' responsibilities and accountabilities have increased over time, while the levels of state investment in resources to support teachers' expanded responsibilities have declined.

The QTD masks and distracts attention from the gradual but inexorable withdrawal of government from its statutory obligation to fully fund universal free schooling, which was a basic tenet of the progressive sentiment in education.

33.3 Partiality

The QTD is a highly selective and partial account of the language, practices and relations of classroom teaching. The issue of "quality teaching" is not centrally concerned with the "best" teachers in our schools, nor the "worst", but with the overwhelming majority of ordinary classroom teachers who strive every day to do meaningful work in demanding material conditions. Some days, they manage to promote meaningful learning in most or all of their classes, some days they do not. Over some terms and some years they contribute more to aggregated student outcomes than over some others. Ordinary teachers "perform" better on a daily, termly or annual basis with some of their students and classes than they do with others. That is simply the reality of school teaching where many factors outside the classroom teacher's control contribute directly and indirectly to the quality of students' personal and social learning (Snook and O'Neill 2014). Teachers can reasonably be expected to plan diligently, teach energetically and assess the artefacts of students' learning in a timely and constructive manner, but they cannot guarantee that their students will learn, nor that their students' learning outcomes will improve in line with official expectations or targets. Teachers can really only "add value" to the quality of their classroom relations with students, and this is consequently the only element of teaching performance for which they can reasonably be held accountable.

No-one could sensibly disagree with the assertion that the country needs the most competent teachers possible to support young people's learning in classrooms. Equally, no-one could sensibly disagree with the assertion that incompetent teachers should not be allowed anywhere near a classroom. That is not the issue. References in the QTD to "excellence" and "incompetence" with regard to the quality of teaching serve only to masque the material conditions that support or inhibit most teachers' capacities to do their job to the best of their ability (i.e. to create the optimum conditions in which students may choose to learn).

Even people who know a lot about schooling frequently disagree over (i) what is important in terms of students' learning; (ii) the extent to which teachers are responsible for students' learning; and (iii) how to optimise the quality of teaching and learning in classrooms. At heart, these can be reduced to a basic difference of policy priority: should teachers be held accountable for their actions as teachers (the quality of learning relations) or students' success in national credential assessments (the quality of learning outcomes). From each basic position, quite different teaching workforce policy solutions flow. A primary emphasis on the quality of teaching *processes* necessarily requires pro-active attention to the material conditions in which teachers work. It suggests the key question: To what extent do the conditions of teachers' work *facilitate* good pedagogical judgments to be made? Conversely, a primary emphasis on the quality of learning *outcomes* requires reactive attention to relative levels of educational success and failure, overall and between various groups of students. It suggests the key question: What is wrong with teachers and teaching that *produce* educational failure? Integral to the first position are practical considerations of the classroom and workgroup environments in which teachers actually attempt to meet the needs of learners on a daily basis (an ideology of feasibility as it were). Integral to the second position are abstract considerations of how teachers are exhorted to behave to ensure all students achieve desired outcomes.

The final report from the secondary teacher union's (NZPPTA) Quality Teaching Taskforce (QTT) (2012) rightly identified the iterative nature of productive relationships between teaching "quality", "development" and "performance". However, in seeking to shape popular debate, NZPPTA and other teacher unions need to be wary of following the same path as official policy discourse and, in doing so, unquestioningly to adopt the concepts, language and the assumptions that underpin it. QTD is based on a normative model of teacher learning and practice that depicts these productive relationships, wrongly and misleadingly, as linear. According to this model, if the desirable characteristics of quality teaching can be specified in sufficient detail, and teachers educated or re-educated so that they adopt these, teacher and student performance outcomes will inevitably improve. This is both wrong and unhelpful for the simple reason that the normative and pathological QTD model of occupational behaviour fails to account for the material conditions of teaching: the classroom environment in which teachers have to work each day. Indeed, the normative model of teaching quality asks us to ignore the material conditions in which teachers work and focus instead on what is presented as a generic, decontextualised "recipe" for teaching success.

In New Zealand's case, the quality teaching recipe has been energetically proselytised by the MoE, EC and ERO by drawing on the work of a limited number of preferred academics who are contracted periodically to contribute to the education policy development cycle: Adrienne Alton-Lee's "ten characteristics of quality teaching"; Russell Bishop and colleagues' Effective Teaching Profile (comprising "two understandings" and "six ways" in which "effective teachers relate and interact with Māori students on a daily basis"); Helen Timperley and colleagues' "effective contexts" for teacher professional learning "opportunities";

and John Hattie's league table of effective teaching characteristic "effect sizes". Unfortunately, these "characteristics", "understandings", "ways" and "effect sizes" are merely lists of ingredients, not recipes. There is no indication (by any of their respective proponents) of how much of each is required, nor in what order they should be combined in order to secure "quality" or "effective" teaching, nor how their relative weighting might need to be altered to suit the diverse material conditions of work that secondary teachers encounter both within a day, and from day to day, week to week or term to term. It is more than a little illogical that generic, decontextualised "teaching" solutions are proposed to meet the contextually specific "diversity" challenges posed by socio-economically and culturally located learners. This flawed logic has major implications for teacher education.

33.4   Performativity

From the early 1940s until the late 1980s, there existed a broad and productive accord between the teachers' professional associations, the Department of Education and the government of the day. The key premise of the accord was that the three "partners" would jointly develop manifestos around the quality of teaching and agree how best to promote these. Decisions around teacher quality, development and performance were, for the most part, matters of consensus arrived at through careful trial and error. Since 1989, in particular, the post-WWII partnership accord approach has been superseded by a NPM ideology. In this, an external audit and compliance culture (i.e. ERO, EC) has displaced one of apprenticeship and socialisation within the school (syndicate or subject department) and occupation (union, subject association). To borrow Roger Dale's terms, since the 1980s, teachers have moved from "licensed" to "regulated" autonomy. Regulated autonomy has resulted in specification of idealised performance "standards", the requirement for teachers to demonstrate performance against these standards, and to have that performance regularly evaluated and attested by the teacher's manager. Since the mid-1990s, the official criteria of teacher quality have increasingly been based on quantitative student outcomes (aggregate and specific "at-risk" or "underserved" groups) as opposed to the qualitative wisdom of occupational judgments made by teachers. Teachers now regularly engage in various rituals of performance: national assessment moderation, annual appraisal and periodic school inspections. Increasingly, hand-picked researchers have been co-opted to provide a veneer of scientific "evidence-based" certainty for pre determined policy choices. Or, as Alexander (2012) aptly put it recently, we are living through an era of *policy-based evidence* rather than *evidence-based policy*.

When rituals contribute materially and beneficially to the quality of teaching, development and performance of teachers, they may be justifiable in terms of the opportunity cost to learners, teachers and their line managers. When they do not, they are merely displays of performance, or "performativity"—performance for the sole purpose of being seen to have performed. Requiring teachers to engage in more individual and collective professional development, and more performance management—more performativity—will do little or nothing to improve the quality of teaching in classrooms for the simple fact that it does nothing to ameliorate the conditions in which ordinary teachers work. Teacher unions operate in both the industrial and professional domains. Over the years, matters such as class size, teaching hours, support for advanced credential acquisition, career pathways and remuneration have all been rehearsed for the most part in the industrial domain as part of collective contract negotiations. This conceptual separation is an unhelpful one. If the issue is quality of teaching, the debate needs to focus on making improvements to the material conditions in which teachers' work every day, not abstract and normative or idealised conceptions of "professional" development and performance. Just as teachers may reasonably be held to account for the quality of classroom relations, government must be held to account for the quality of material conditions in which New Zealand teachers work.

33.5 Materiality

Teaching as work has both symbolic and material elements. Symbolic elements are reflected in the demands made of teachers by society as a whole. Material elements are reflected in the resources allocated by the state to support achievement of those demands. QTD reifies the former and ignores the latter. The rationality and consequent credibility of QTD depends almost entirely on society's ignorance of the material conditions in which school teachers work in New Zealand. However, OECD and other readily available comparative international data demonstrate unequivocally, for example, that: (i) government spends less per student than other OECD countries; (ii) cumulative spending per student in compulsory schooling is lower; (iii) teacher: student ratios and average class sizes are higher; (iv) teachers teach more hours per week and per year; (v) teacher salaries compare well for the first fifteen years of a career but poorly thereafter; (vi) New Zealand teachers on average enjoy better classroom relations with their students and in students' eyes, are more responsive to their needs.

Four key trends stand out in the data.

- First, the material conditions in which New Zealand teachers are required to work daily cannot reasonably be argued to be conducive to them creating optimum learning relations in individual classrooms.
- Second, these same conditions are not conducive to facilitating the investigative and collaborative activities by teachers in and outside classrooms that are asserted by influential QTD private sector lobbyists (e.g. Jensen 2012) to have the greatest impact on learning.
- Third, according to feedback from New Zealand students towards the end of their compulsory schooling, as evidenced in the OECD's PISA online database, a sizeable minority of teachers need a mixture of education, support and

performance management strategies in order to develop basic competencies and dispositions necessary to create the same sort of optimum learning relations that already exist in the great majority of New Zealand school classrooms.

- Fourth, externally mandated assessment compliance workload is more likely to be increasing rather than decreasing over time. This reduces the time available to engage in pedagogically oriented activities that are argued to have the greatest impact on learning.

The first two of these trends cannot realistically be addressed through teacher development and performance management at the school level. They require significant additional investment by the state. The material conditions of teachers' work are the state's responsibility, not that of individual schools which have only limited local room for manoeuvre within the shrinking fiscal envelope determined by government.

The third trend is a shared responsibility of professional associations and the State on behalf of all teachers. However, the issue remains a chicken and egg conundrum: Do some teachers not create optimum learning relations because of the material conditions in which they work or because they do not know how, or because they choose not to? While the state presumes that teachers are culpable in this regard, the assumption is by no means a reasonable conclusion when all the relevant evidence is evaluated.

The fourth trend is a matter of priorities. Prior to the 1990s, it used to be the case in many OECD countries that teachers spent the majority of their time at work teaching. Periodic surveys since then have consistently demonstrated that ever larger proportions of teachers' time are spent in NPM compliance activities and meetings outside the classroom. To the extent that this increasing proportion of time is meaningfully devoted to activities that have a demonstrable beneficial impact on the quality of student learning, it is feasible to argue its merits despite the personal cost to teachers involved. However, it is far from clear that this is the case. Specifically, for example, the findings of a 2010 national assessment workload survey (NZPPTA 2010) suggest that a substantial proportion of this growing workload may be devoted to compliance and other rituals removed from the classroom that have limited or no demonstrable impact on the quality of teaching or learning. If the priority is the quality of teaching and learning, compliance costs must be reduced and empty performativity rituals eliminated from schooling.

33.6 Conclusion

Teachers' individual and collective capacity to create optimum learning conditions or "the quality of teaching" is a shared responsibility of state, teacher educators, professional associations or unions, schools and teachers themselves. Central to this is acceptance that conditions of work and quality of teaching are inextricably woven together, and therefore must be analysed in tandem. Teacher educators, in particular, need to introduce candidates to the contested nature of "quality teaching" and of the material conditions under which classroom teaching are facilitated and constrained. This in turn requires teacher educators to adopt a critical stance toward officially preferred discourses of teaching, such as the QTD, rather than simply take them as given.

Unless the State is prepared to invest sufficiently to create the material conditions for teachers' work that are necessary for them to be able to engage in activities that have a demonstrable impact on learning, nothing much is likely to change by way of students' learning outcomes. Paradoxically, in comparison with teachers in other countries, New Zealand school teachers on average do better in promoting optimum learning conditions for students, despite having fewer resources and less time to do so. Feedback from students would nonetheless suggest that a sizeable minority of teachers need structured support to adopt the basic pedagogical competencies necessary to optimise learning relations that are otherwise commonplace among the workforce as a whole.

Normative models of teaching such as the QTD are not only of limited use in the endeavour to improve the quality of teaching, they may adversely masque the material conditions of teachers' work that compromise this endeavour in practical concrete ways. It is unclear, in this regard, the extent to which the missing basic competencies are attributable to material conditions of work or personal occupational dispositions but, in any event, the QTD appears to have considered only the latter possibility, which is insulting both to teachers as persons and their professional commitments to learners.

Reflexive scholarship by teacher educators on the origins, purposes and effects of normative teaching discourses, and their own occupational positioning within these, are both equally important if teaching candidates are to receive a realist preparation for the local conditions in which they will develop their craft and professional identities.

References

Alexander, R. J. (2012). Moral panic, miracle cures and educational policy: What can we really learn from international comparison? *Scottish Educational Review, 44*(1), 4–21.

Alton-Lee, A. (2003). *Quality teaching for diverse students in schooling: Best evidence synthesis iteration (BES)*. Wellington: Ministry of Education.

Bishop, R., Berryman, M., Cavanagh, T., & Teddy, L. (2007). *Te Kōtahitanga Phase 3 Whānaungatanga: Establishing a culturally responsive pedagogy of relations in mainstream secondary school classrooms*. Report to the Ministry of Education. Wellington: Author.

Gramsci, A. (1971). *Selections from prison notebooks* (Q. Hoare & G. Nowell Smith (Eds., Trans.). London: Lawrence & Wishart.

Hattie, J. (2009). *Visible learning: A synthesis of over 800 meta-analyses relating to achievement*. London: Routledge.

Jensen, B. (2012). *Catching up: Learning from the best school systems in East Asia*. Carlton: VIC.: The Grattan Institute.

Nash, R. (2003). Inequality/difference in New Zealand education: Social reproduction and the cognitive habitus. *International Studies in the Sociology of Education, 13*(2), 171–194.

NZPPTA. (2010). *The cost of change: PPTA survey on NCEA workload*. Wellington: Author.

NZPPTA. (2012). *Quality teaching for excellence and equity: Report from PPTA's quality teaching taskforce*. Wellington: Author.

O'Neill, J. (2010). Teachers and teaching. In M. Thrupp & R. Irwin (Eds.), *Another decade of education policy: Where to now?* (pp. 1–20). Hamilton: Waikato University, Wilf Malcolm Institute for Educational Research.

Persell, C. (1981). Genetic and cultural deficit theories: Two sides of the same racist coin. *Journal of Black Studies, 12*(1), 19–37.

Snook, I., & O'Neill, J. (2014). Poverty and inequality of educational achievement. In V. Carprenter & S. Osborne (Eds.), *Twelve thousand hours: Education and poverty in Aotearoa New Zealand* (pp. 19–43). Auckland: Dunmore Publishing.

Timperley, H., Wilson, A., Barrar, H., & Fung, I. (2007). *Teacher professional learning and development: Best evidence synthesis iteration (BES)*. Wellington: Ministry of Education.

Author Biography

John O'Neill is Professor of Teacher Education and Director of the Institute of Education at Massey University. His research interests include the relationships between education policy and teacher learning, and the practical professional and ethical dilemmas such relationships produce.

Chapter 34
Complexity and Learning: Implications for Teacher Education

Mark Olssen

Although complexity research takes its origins from its applications in physics, chemistry and mathematics and the 'hard' sciences, undergoing its formative development in the early and mid-twentieth century, during the second half of the twentieth century it has exerted an effect on the social sciences as well. Today, while there exists a multitude of different approaches and research centres across the globe, complexity research is generating a quiet revolution in both the physical and social sciences. One interest in the approach is that it liberates philosophy and social science from the prison-house of a constraining scientific past based on the linear determinism, reductionism and methodological individualism. Another is that it presents a view of science that supports the social sciences claims that history and culture are important. Arguably, it permits an approach in the social sciences and philosophy that heralds the rise of a 'third-way' between the stark individualism of liberal philosophy, and what many consider to be the (equally) oppressive socio-logicism of 'thick' communitarianism.[1] As an offshoot of this, complexivists also claim their new approach reinstates, and possibly elevates, a previously marginalized cadre of scholars within the western intellectual tradition.[2] In this paper,

---

This paper is a revision of a paper that first appeared in *Access: Critical Perspectives on Communication, Cultural & Policy Studies* Vol. 30, Issue 1, pp. 11–24. The publisher of the journal is thanked for its reproduction in this context.

---

[1]My own work has promoted writers like Nietzsche and Foucault as representing a 'third-way' between Kant and Hegel in philosophy.
[2]Including John Stuart Mill, Alexander Bain, C.D. Broad, Samuel Alexander, Friedrich Hayek, Friedrich Nietzsche, Charles Babbage, George Herbert Mead, Charles Sanders Pierce, Martin Heidegger, Michel Foucault, Jacques Derrida and John Maynard Keynes.

M. Olssen (✉)
University of Surrey, Guildford, UK
e-mail: m.olssen@surrey.ac.uk

my purpose is to elaborate the normative possibilities of complexity theory for learning theory and teacher education.

34.1   An Introduction to the Science of Complexity

The core distinctiveness of complexity approaches can be seen most easily in relation to traditional mechanical models of science in relation to the particular ontology they presuppose. In Newton's science, the world is represented deterministically as a mechanical system, with parts comprised of particles subject to the unchanging influence of universal laws, and reducible to mathematical codification. Newtonian mechanics posited closed systems where time was 'reversible' which meant it was irrelevant to the laws, which were represented as capable of moving forwards or backwards, i.e. independently of time. Because Newton's model presumed a static, atemporal view of the universe, systems were assumed to be simple, i.e. not to be affected by outside events. Laws (for example, on temperature or the movement of the planets) were held to operate given constant conditions and not subject to interference. Hence, because the axioms of such systems were reducible to physics, once ascertained, the laws constituted a basis for prediction. Causation was represented in linear terms, much as Hume described the process, which requires that a trajectory is identified where a cause can be shown to precede the effect, where 'contiguity' operates in time, where a 'necessary connection' can be established.[3]

In a range of publications from 1980s to 2004, Ilya Prigogine developed a complexity formulation relevant to both the physical and social sciences. In works, such as *Order Out of Chaos* (1984), written with Irene Stengers, and *Exploring Complexity* (1989), written with Grégoire Nicolis, it is claimed that complexity theory offers a bold new and more accurate conception of science and the universe. They claim that complexity theory offers a more advanced formulation of science and is superseding standard traditional models including quantum mechanics and relativity which came to prominence at the beginning of the twentieth century as "corrections to classical mechanics" (Nicolis and Prigogine 1989, p. 5). Newtonian mechanics and quantum theory represented time as reversible, meaning that it was irrelevant to the adequacy of laws.[4] Complexity theory builds on and intensifies the '"temporal" turn' introduced by this 'correction'. Prigogine places central importance on time as real and irreversible. With Newton, say Prigogine and Stengers

---

[3]Always providing that Humean scepticism can be offset by the specification of the appropriate operational force—which enlightenment science was quick to do!

[4]If a film can represent motion running backwards in the same way as running forwards, then it is said in physics that time is reversible. The rotation of the hands of a clock is reversible, whereas tearing a piece of paper is irreversible. Prigogine does not deny that time reversibility has relevance but wishes to add that in many areas including life itself time is irreversible.

(1984), the universe is represented as closed and predictable. Its fundamental laws are deterministic and reversible.

Prigogine's revolution in response to the classical and quantum paradigms stated in formal terms was to challenge the *principle of ergodicity* which resulted in Poincaré recurrence. This was the principle which, in conformity with the law of the conservation of energy, that system interactions in physics would eventually reproduce a state or states almost identical to earlier initial states of the system at some point in the future.[5] It was based on such an approach that time reversibility had been defined as real, and time irreversibility an illusion. Prigogine challenged the applicability of these assumptions as relevant to classical or quantum measurement. If systems are never isolated or independent from their surroundings, then in theory even small perturbations or changes in the surroundings could influence the system functioning or trajectory. Even *very* small perturbations could cause *major* changes.[6] "The consequences of this way of thinking are profound", says Rae (2009, p. 113), for they replace assumptions of reversibility with irreversibility (p. 114), introduce notions of indeterminism into physics (p. 113), and project future states of affairs in terms of multiple 'consistent histories' (p. 122).[7] Although quantum theory had introduced notions of indeterminacy, through the interaction with measurement, for Prigogine, such an indeterminism is more centrally associated with 'strong mixing' in initial system interactions.[8]

What non-ergodicity means in less technical terms, as Stuart Kaufmann states, is that "at the level of the evolution of the species, of human economy, of human history, and human culture…the universe is vastly non-repeating, hence vastly nonergodic" (2008, p. 123). Such a message was popularized recently by Taleb (2007) in his book *The Black Swan* in order to underscore the centrality of uncertainty and non-predictability in both science and human affairs. Although Taleb claims that traditional predictive models can be applied when predicting variables, such as human weight, or height, and thus demonstrates the continued relevance of closed mechanical models, in relation to such phenomena as economies, the immune system, or the human brain and life itself, where a system of specific parts can generate complex outcomes, traditional models and outcomes can not be held to apply. One of Taleb's key points in his book is that algorithms cannot

---

[5]The amount of time taken for repeatability is known as 'Poincare cycle time'.

[6]This is the phenomenon of 'strong mixing' (see Footnote 10 for a definition).

[7]The main idea of the 'consistent histories' approach in Prigoginian physics is that new knowledge must connect with already consistent histories of possibilities to be taken as valid. It therefore is not just the results of 'measurements' as it was for the quantum theorists. Rae (p. 123) says that it thus "has the advantage of being more general as well as more objective". "The consistent-histories approach claims that we have reached the point where a purely mathematical map is unable to give a unique description of the physical universe. It can, however, provide a map book containing all possible histories and their probabilities. Perhaps this is the best we can expect to achieve" (p. 127). Prigogine, says Rae (p. 126), is also more materialist in that he is not simply concerned with how the world can be observed, but how it can be.

[8]'Strong mixing' refers to the effect of influences or instabilities on a system, which is frequently chaotic, small and arbitrary.

be utilized as the basis for predicting the future due to contingent contextual conditions which are ceaselessly changing and cannot be predicted in advance. Invisible causal generators comprising the system produce different outcomes at different locations in space and time. This raises the issue of unobservable generators which, as Blyth (2009, p. 450) puts it, "might produce different outcomes in the future than they did in the past". This means, says Blyth (p. 457), that:

> causes are inconstant; they change over time, and they are emergent. New elements combine to create causes of future events that were impossible before – not just impossible to foresee, since they did not exist in the prior period. In short, "the new" is not necessarily an informational problem.

Although regularity operates predictably for many purposes, it is thus never assured. The whole constitutes a context which is always changing, and where new and unique actions and events constantly *emerge*. For Taleb, this means that the world of the future is not simply *unknown*, but *unknowable*, and there is no basis for predictability of events, as either visible or invisible contingent factors may derail mechanical outcomes. In mathematical terms, somewhat similar thesis was formulated by writers like Alan Turing and Kurt Gödel.[9] Such a thesis will, as we shall see, have major implications for education.

Prigogine introduces the concept of *bifurcation* to explain the central importance of non-predictability and indeterminacy in science. When a system enters far-from-equilibrium conditions, its structure may be threatened, and a 'critical condition', or what Prigogine and Stengers call a 'bifurcation point' is entered. At the bifurcation point, system contingencies may operate to determine outcomes in a way not causally linked to previous linear path trajectories. The trajectory is not therefore seen as determined in *one* particular pathway. Although this is *not* to claim an absence of antecedent causes, it is to say, says Prigogine (1997, p. 5), that "nothing in the macroscopic equations justifies the preferences for any one solution". Or, again, from *Exploring Complexity*, "[n]othing in the description of the experimental set up permits the observer to assign beforehand the state that will be chosen; only chance will decide, through the dynamics of fluctuations" (Nicolis and Prigogine 1989, p. 72). Once the system 'chooses' "[it] becomes an historical object in the sense that its subsequent evolution depends on its critical choice" (p. 72). In this description, they say, "we have succeeded in formulating, in abstract terms, the remarkable interplay of chance and constraint" (p. 73).

---

[9]In 1931, Kurt Gödel, a 25-year-old mathematician, presented his 'incompleteness' theorem which demonstrated the mathematical inability to predict future events. Alan Turing's basic claim was that decisions regarding methodology in mathematics were always in excess of the programme or algorithm that generated them, and hence could not be determined axiomatically from such an algorithm. Turing also reiterated a point made by Heisenberg that "when we are dealing with atoms and electrons we are quite unable to know the exact state of them; our instruments being made of atoms and electrons themselves" (Turing, cited in Hodges 2000, p. 497). This means that there are limitations to what it is possible to compute and to know (Hodges 2000, pp. 493–545).

Fig. 34.1 Mechanical illustration of the phenomenon of bifurcation (from Nicolis and Prigogine 1989, p. 73)

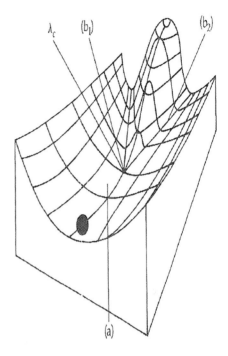

A schematic diagram of *bifurcation* appears in Fig. 34.1, reproduced from Nicolis and Prigogine (1989, p. 73). Highlighting their thesis of indeterminacy, Nicolis and Prigogine make the following comment upon the model:

> A ball moves in a valley, which at a particular point λ_c becomes branched and leads to either of two valleys, branches b1 and b2 separated by a hill. Although it is too early for apologies and extrapolations…it is thought provoking to imagine for a moment that instead of the ball in Figure [1] we could have a dinosaur sitting there prior to the end of the Mesozoic era, or a group of our ancestors about to settle on either the ideographic or the symbolic mode of writing. (p. 73)

Although, due to system perturbations and fluctuations, it is impossible to precisely ascertain causes in advance, retrospectively, of course, we find the 'cause' there in the events that lead up to an event, in the sense that we look backwards and point to plausible antecedent factors that contributed to its occurrence. While therefore not undetermined by prior causes, the dislocation of linear deterministic trajectories and the opening-up of alternative possible pathways that cannot be *pre-ascertained* in open environments, is what Prigogine means by 'chance'.[10]

In thermodynamics, Nicolis and Prigogine give the examples of thermal convection, the evolution of the universe itself, as well as climate and all physical processes. They were also aware that their conclusions extended to the social and human sciences, embracing life, biological organisms, and to social, economic and political processes, as an illustration of non-equilibrium developments in human development, learning and education. Central to such a model is the ability for new and novel developments to take place within systems through the emergence of new patterns and features. The model of explanation in complexity science places a greater importance on system affects and interactions, action from a distance, the unintended consequences of actions, the impossibility of predicting linear trajectories or the future, a restricted capacity of individual agents to understand system developments, and conveys new understanding of ignorance, restricted cognition, novelty, uniqueness and creativity of action in open environments.

Two key ideas of complexity theory include *self-organization* and *emergence*. The idea of self-organization entails that systems are not organized by anything external to themselves, in the sense of a foundation or essential principle, and it also explains how systems generate new patterns of activity through dynamic interactions over time.

Complexity theorists also typically represent the world as stratified, characterized by levels of systems or sub-systems, interconnected by interactions. Within complex systems, the interconnectedness of part and whole means that interactions of various sorts will define relations at various levels. Interactions also characterize relations within the world as we live it, both at the microscopic (organisms, cellular life) and macroscopic levels. In this sense, interactions can be of qualitatively different orders and types, both linear and nonlinear, and 'multi-referenential' in Morin (1977/1992, p. 47) sense. For Morin:

> Interactions (1) suppose elements, beings or material objects capable of encountering each other; (2) suppose conditions of encounter, that is to say agitation, turbulence, contrary fluxes, etc.; (3) obey determinations/constraints inherent to the nature of elements, objects or beings in encounter; (4) become in certain conditions interrelations (associations, linkages, combinations communications, etc.) that is to say give birth to phenomena of organization... (1977/1992, p. 47)

---

[10]At times Prigogine appears to suggest that the limitation is fundamentally epistemological, and concerned with measurement, as it was for Heisenberg. But, at other times, he notes that as fluctuations and perturbations occur in open environments are theoretically without limit in terms of their reinvestment within a system, the indeterminism is also ontological, not in the sense of there being no antecedent conditions, but in terms of there being alternative options available which can be determined by contingent variables. In this 'ontological' view, he seems to follow Neils Bohr.

It is through interactions at different levels that ontological emergence[11] takes place, and it is this that defeats the possibilities of reductionism.[12] At its most basic sense, emergence describes the constitution of entities through their synthetic combination in time and space. As a consequence, as Kauffmann (2008, p. 34) explains it, "[o]ntological emergence has to do with what constitutes a real entity in the universe: is a tiger a real entity or nothing but particles in motion, as the reductionists would claim?" Complexity theorists maintain, in opposition to classical physics, that many phenomena, including consciousness and life itself, must be considered as emergent, in the sense of being historically or cosmologically constituted as well as ontologically independent (in relation to its necessary genesis) from its physical basis.[13]

34.2 The Normative Consequences of Complexity for Learning and Teacher Education

Central to the complexity perspective on learning theory is its opposition to traditional empiricist and rationalist models which assume that learning is an individual matter which is linear and non-generative. The tradition of empiricism, associated with Bacon, Locke, Berkeley and Hume challenged Aristotle for being too unconcerned with the world and with sensory experience and too concerned with reasoning according to established and fixed principles. In Hume's *associationist* psychology, simple ideas (*hard, soft, round, square*) are formed through basic sense impressions, which through associations form the basis of composite ideas. Central to all empiricist approaches, whether Hume, or Locke, or John Stuart Mill, is the priority on experience as the basis of ideas, that complex ideas can be reduced to simple ideas, that basic sensations lie at the foundation of all ideas, and that the rules of getting from simple to complex ideas and upon which predictions are made are additive. Rationalistic approaches, as sponsored by Descartes, Spinoza and Leibniz, rejected the strong emphasis on sensory experience made by empiricism, and suggested instead that our knowledge of the world came from innate ideas, which made reliable reasoning possible. The differences between these two approaches were not as great as the similarities: both were reductionist. Complexity theories, while not denying a role for experience, including sensation, differ from

---

[11]Kauffman (2008, p. 34) also refers to "epistemological emergence", which he defines as "an inability to deduce or infer the emergent higher-level phenomenon from underlying physics".

[12]In physics, the reductionist programme maintained that all social, biological, chemical and physical reality could be explained by physics, ultimately reducing to particles and laws.

[13]Kauffman (2008, Chaps. 3–5) cites a 'quiet rebellion' within existing physics, and science more generally, as to adherence to reductionism. He notes various Nobel Laureates, such as Philip W. Anderson, Robert Laughlan, and Leonard Susskind, who all argue for versions of emergentism and against reduction to physical laws in order to explain life processes, biology or forms of social organisation.

both empiricist and rationalist approaches in that they are non-reductionist or holist. They emphasize that the system is more than the sum of its parts, and recognize system effects through 'downward causation' and nonlinear feedback loops, as well as contingent assemblages of time and place, as being central.

Learning must be seen, in this sense, as a goal-directed activity, related to the evolution and survival of life. It involves a qualitatively different type of thinking, one that recognizes uncertainty, unpredictability, novelty, openness, a balance between order and disorder, and which represents discursive elements, such as concepts and words, as conventional and historical. Due to human fallibility and limitations, the type of knowledge that complex learning results in is bereft of the arrogance of the enlightenment claim to know (*aude sapere*) according to the new found faith in reason. Rather, it is more modest, humble, less self-assured, recognising 'partial knowledge', 'human error', and limited cognition. At the same time, it also encompasses processes of creativity and of possibilities of unexpected developments within situations. Complex education implies, say Trueit and Doll (2010, p. 138), a view of "education as a journey into the land of the unknown taken by ourselves but with others". Yet, within this paradigm, many questions are unanswerable and remain an impenetrable barrier of the human condition. Matters of determinism-free will, the existence of God, and issues of a metaphysical nature unlinked to human concerns must remain beyond the limits of positive knowledge, and limits beyond which learning cannot form a bridge. Complexity's emphasis upon the nonlinearity, unpredictability and recursivity of educational processes, while not denying order, state that that the policy response to uncertainty and chance should be one of coordination through institutions. This entails managing elements within a system as well as recognizing the practical context in terms of which learning is situated.

How we characterize the processes of learning and teaching is thus important. In recent times, some educational literature has focussed upon what is termed 'complexity-reduction' which potentially creates the view that the task of education is to attempt to contain, reduce and even 'tame' the complex uncertainties of the world. The conservative politics of Burke comes to mind in such a situation. Burke endorses a conception of community as the taming of chaos, the ordering of life, and the constraint of danger.

In his article 'Five theses on complexity reduction and its politics', Biesta (2010, Chap. 2) utilizes the concept of 'complexity reduction' which to my mind may place too much emphasis on control. Whether Biesta would agree that he intends such a description to entail normative and political senses as I suggest above is perhaps problematic. For Biesta complexity reduction is inescapable. For him, as he states it in one place, it is a claim about *language use*. As he puts it:

> Learning is neither a noun nor a verb. To use the word 'learning' rather means that one makes a value judgment about change and identifies some changes as valuable. Such judgments can only be made retrospectively, which means that using the word 'learning' is itself a form of retrospective complexity reduction. (2010, p. 11)

Earlier in the same article, however, he seems to assert a different claim as a strict thesis about the use of words, and specifies it as a claim about how *systems function*. As he states:

> Complexity reduction has to do with reducing the number of available options-for-action for 'elements' within a system. Fast food restaurants are a good example of a system with reduced complexity, as the number of available option for action – both for customers and staff – are significantly reduced to make a quick and smooth operation of the system possible... Education, particularly in the form of organised schooling, is another prominent example of a system operating under conditions of complexity reduction. (p. 7)

Although Biesta may intend use of the term 'reduction' only in the sense of a Deleuzean *mot d'ordre*, to suggest that any attempt to codify reality entails a particular organization, there is a strong risk that it may begin to function as an inserted metaphysic. To my mind the concepts of 'organization' and 'management' better characterize the process by which discourses organize the world. I think of words, concepts and discourses as *organizing* complexity, and of actions (which are normative and end-orientated) as *managing* or (even) as *controlling* or *channelling* complexity. To speak of 'reduction' risks imposing an unnecessary direction or character to the ordering of diversity.

In this quest for "thinking complexly", Trueit and Doll (2010, p. 138), see education as a central institution in a way recognized by Dewey, who explored the role and function of education in adapting to and coping with uncertainties of the environment. For Dewey (1958, 1997), education was conceptualized, not as a discipline-based mode of instruction in 'the basics', but according to an inter-disciplinary, discovery-based curricula, defined according to obstacles in the existing environment. As Dewey says in *Experience and Nature*, "The world must actually be such as to generate ignorance and inquiry: doubt and hypothesis, trial and temporal conclusions...." (1958, p. 41). The rules of living and habits of mind represent a 'quest for certainty' in an unpredictable, uncertain and dangerous world (p. 41). For Dewey, the ability to organize experience proceeded functionally in terms of problems encountered which needed to be overcome in order to construct and navigate a future. This was the basis of his 'problem-centred' pedagogy of learning. While it could be seen to concentrate on transferable skills from a complexity perspective of coping with an environment, Dewey can be criticized for an overly functionalist concern with system adaptation, in the same way that structural-functionalist sociologists, like Talcott Parsons, or contemporary systems theorists, such as Niklas Luhmann can be. By focussing on a 'problem-centred' approach runs the risk, in other words, of neglecting the critical tasks of ideological reflexivity and criticism which are so important to the educative tasks of myth demystification and cleansing the discursive template of history from its distorted and ideological elements. There is little in Dewey, for instance, that suggests any parallel with Gramsci's distinction between 'good sense' and 'folklore' as the basis of a critical pedagogy and common sense. Dewey's functionalism is further reinforced through his utilization of terms, such as 'interaction' and 'growth' which run the risk of contributing to a naive enlightenment conception of 'progress', leading inevitably to the successful resolution of both individual and societal problems and leading, onward and upward, to ever higher levels of experience. Yet, while Dewey runs a risk, like Hegel, of being identified with a progressive evolutionary theory of history and development, unlike Hegel, Dewey posited no end point, or resting place; for the end of growth was more growth; and the end of learning was further learning. In terms of learning theory, Dewey used the concept of 'continuity' in order to theorise the link between existing experience and the future based upon the "interdependence of all organic structures and processes with one another" (1958, p. 295). Learning for Dewey thus represented a cooperative and collaborative activity centred upon experiential, creative responses to contingent sets of relations to cope with uncertainty in a never-ending quest. It is in this sense that the processes of iteration are central for Dewey. As such, Dewey's approach conceptualizes part and whole in a dynamic interaction, posits the learner as interdependent with the environment, as always in a state of becoming, giving rise to a dynamic and forward-looking notion of agency as experiential and collaborative. In such a model learning is situational in the sense of always being concerned with contingent and unique events in time.

It is through plan or pattern coordination that institutions function and that the learning experiences of future generations are embarked upon. Because in planning one must assume incomplete information due to the dispersal of knowledge across social systems, such coordination can be more or less exact or loosely stochastic and probabilistic in terms of overcoming uncertainty. Learning will be invariably situational and involve experiences that are always unique. It will involve what Aristotle called *phronēsis*, that is, practical judgement within a context. Such practical judgement is holistic and goal-orientated action sensitive to the exigencies of time and place. In elucidating the tasks of *phronēsis*, Aristotle emphasizes the integrity of the speaker, their skills as a communicator, the context of the message, as well as the interests and dispositions of the audience. Because learning is time-dependent, and individuals and communities are always experiencing unique features of their worlds, uncertainty cannot be eliminated. Hence, all that is possible is skills of coping, problem-solving, and pattern coordination in open-ended systems, where planning is formed around 'typical' rather than 'actual' features. Such plan or pattern coordination can only be a constructed and probabilistic order. Constructing plans becomes the agenda for teacher education both individuals and societies in Dewey's sense. Dewey ultimately held to the faith that despite unpredictability and uncertainty, the macro-societal (or macro-economic) coordination of core social problems was possible.

34.3 A Possible Ethical Theory for a Complex Global Society

Finally, what are necessary for a theory of learning in a complex world is a normative theory and a global ethic. As Cilliers (2010, p. viii) notes, "complexity leads to the acknowledgement of the inevitable role played by values…" If the world is complex and uncertain, the educational consequence suggests that education is ethical and political.

More than ever, today, individual aspirations can only be realized through the coordinated action of the local and the global. The good then, must recognize *survival*, but also *well-being*, of all life forms. Such a good need not be seen as in the classical era, as emanating from a teleology of nature, but rather as a shared or collective end as they expand or contract in different historical times.[14]

In addition to a new global ethics, complexity posits a model of the global citizen who has knowledge of global processes, procedures, and forces, well-developed *agentic* skills and abilities, as well as a multidimensional global identity which is both local and global. By *agentic* skills, I mean to refer to such things as the capacity to understand and access global knowledge systems; the awareness of multi-perspectival orientations to self and culture, based upon an understanding of diverse human experiences, as well as the ability to construct new ideas. Cognitively and intellectually, such an education must develop a knowledge and sensitivity to global concerns and issues; an awareness of emerging conflicts and disputes, issues and problems, as well as the capabilities for critical deconstruction and judgement in relation to historical documents, identities and systems.

Although for complexity uniqueness and uncertainty constitute core ontological postulates, we can still posit some educationally relevant universal postulates concerned with the ubiquity of certain types of experience that will need to be confronted, certain dispositions that will be important, and certain virtues and values that students will profit from. Such dispositions and virtues that constitute the ethics of life continuance might include a will to learn, to critically engage and inquire, to be receptive, to be open, and to actively negotiate the future. Virtues might include criticality, creativity, carefulness, care toward others and the environment, courage, self-discipline, equity, equality, integrity, caution, respect, flexibility and openness.

---

[14]In *Capitalism, Socialism, and Democracy*, Joseph Schumpeter says that while we must reject the classical conception of good, of old, there is nothing to "debar us from trying to build up another and more realistic one" (pp. 252–253). Despite his antagonism towards the classical doctrine of good, Schumpeter sees nothing amiss with representing aggregate human interests in history as common collective interests, by which he means "not a genuine, but a manufactured will. And often this artifact is all that in reality corresponds to the *volonté génerale* of the classical doctrine" (p. 263).

In previous work on an ethics of life continuance, I represent it as both deontological and consequentialist, and as simultaneously both objectivist and subjectivist. It is objectivist in terms of ethics in that some things are clearly better or
worse, right or wrong in terms of the values of what best continues life irrespective
of time or place and for all life forms. It is also subjectivist in that in a world of
infinite options and choices, each individual is also faced with innumerable personal ethical choices, conflicts and conundrums which they much resolve within the
contingent circumstances of the present. Although Anglo-American philosophy has
traditionally represented the objectivist and subjectivist approaches in ethics as two
mutually incompatible approaches, my suggestion here is that within a complexivist
understanding certain senses of both approaches can potentially cohere.

To reconcile deontology and consequentialism is far more difficult and must
necessarily await some later study. Indeed, despite its importance for teachers, it can
only be alluded to here in the most general of senses. We would start with the
proposition that life in a complex world is both gratuitous and contingent; that it has
no essential *raison d'etre*, a fact which a priori gives no moral justification for
privilege or hierarchy of value or precedence. We might acknowledge also that
complexity provides a cruel mathematics of existence and yet despite this life has
value to all beings that live, at least as judged by virtue of the fact that all forms of life
strive to survive and continue. This then can constitute a foundation for both an
individual and collective ethic of humanity. According to Doubrovsky (1960, p. 75),
this deontological view is essentially the message of Camus, in *L'Etranger*, where
"[t]hreatened with annilalation, life gathers and concentrates its force, becomes
conscious of itself and proclaims that it is the only value". This immanent value that
life affirms is the source of moral sentiment. It motivates for Camus the ethics of
rebellion. As Camus states, "il…fait intervener un judgement de valeur, si peu
gratuity, qu'il le maintient au milieu des périls" (Camus 1951, p. 28).[15] Bataille
makes a similar argument in arguing that moral sense arises from the
self-consciousness of life in a system of parts and whole where the 'sovereignty of
each individual' needs protection in order to survive. Morality is the protest of
fairness in a limited and dangerous world. It therefore constitutes as it were a
sentiment common to all men, which constitutes their humanity, a view also
admirably stated by David Hume. There is therefore a deontological dimension of
value adhering to life itself that propels ethics, establishes right, resists perfectibility
and rational becoming should they conflict with right, and yet acts for and simultaneously with the actions of life to survive in a view of becoming as the continuance
of life itself. Life therefore has value which it constructs and interpolates in the
course of it monitoring and critically evaluating the future horizon that both enables
it and threatens it. In a complex world human history can have no overall 'inner
logic' or 'overall design' or 'direction' in Hegel's sense which morally justifies them
(i.e., the end cannot justify the means), yet, nevertheless, the value of life requires a
context, a system, and a goal for life operates in time. Consequences and goals are

---

[15]He brings in a moral judgement, so un-gratuitous, that he maintains throughout his perils.

thus important although do not override the rights of life itself. These two domains are independent in the sense that conflicts can only be resolved through democratic deliberation in a public forum. While the moral value of life is determined by sentiment, it is reason, albeit now with a small 'r', and within a complex and uncertain world of risks, gambits and calculations, that guides life on its way.

References

Biesta, G. (2010). Five theses of complexity reduction and its politics. In D. Osberg & G. Biesta (Eds.), *Complexity theory and the politics of education* (pp. 5–14). Rotterdam, Boston, Taipei: Sense Publishers.

Blyth, M. (2009). Coping with the Black Swan: The unsettling world of Nassim Taleb. *Critical Review: A Journal of Politics and Society, 21*(4), 447–465.

Camus, A. (1951). *L'Homme Revolté*. Gallimard.

Cilliers, P. (2010). Foreword. In D. Osberg & G. Biesta (Eds.), *Complexity theory and the politics of education* (pp. vii–viii). Rotterdam, Boston, Taipei: Sense Publishers.

Dewey, J. (1958). [orig. 1925] *Experience and nature*. Mineola, NY: Dover Publications.

Doubrovsky, S. (1960). The ethics of Albert Camus. In G. Bree (Ed.) (1962), *Camus: A collection of critical essays*. Prentice Hall Inc.

Hodges, A. (2000). Turing: A natural philosopher. In R. Monk & F. Raphel (Eds.), *The great philosophers: From socrates to turing* (p. 493). London: Phoenix/Orion Books Ltd.

Kauffman, S. A. (2008). *Reinventing the sacred: A new view of science, reason and religion*. New York: Basic Books.

Morin, E. (1977/1992). *Method. Towards a study of humankind. Vol. 1: The nature of nature*. New York: Peter Lang.

Nicolis, G., & Prigogine, I. (1989). *Exploring complexity*. New York: Freeman.

Prigogine, I. (1997). *The end of certainty: Time, Chaos and the new laws of nature*. London: The Free Press.

Prigogine, I., & Stengers, I. (1984). *Order out of Chaos*. New York: Bantam.

Rae, A. (2009). *Quantum physics: Illusion or reality?* (Second, updated edition). Cambridge: Cambridge University Press.

Taleb, N. N. (2007). *The black swan: The impact of the highly improbable*. New York: Random House.

Trueit, D., & Doll, W. E. (2010). Thinking complexly. In D. Osberg & G. Biesta (Eds.), *Complexity theory and the politics of education* (pp. 135–152). Rotterdam, Boston, Taipei: Sense Publishers.

Author Biography

Mark Olssen FAcSS, is Emeritus Professor of Political Theory and Education Policy in the Department of Politics at the University of Surrey and Professor of Education at the Auckland University of Technology, New Zealand. He has published many books, book chapters and articles in academic journals, in Britain, America and in Australasia. Recent works viewable at: https://en.wikipedia.org/wiki/Mark_Olssen.

Chapter 35
The Prevailing Logic of Teacher Education: Privileging the Practical in Australia, England and Scotland

Trevor Gale and Stephen Parker

35.1 Introduction

Teacher Education (TE) in OECD nations is undergoing its most significant challenge since its relocation from colleges to universities. The focus of this change is the contribution that teacher education makes to the development of teachers for a new political and economic future. Today's teachers now need to produce students who perform highly on international rankings in PISA (and TIMSS, PIRLS, etc.) in a context of increased neo-liberal governance led by 'big data' and policy as numbers (Grek 2009). When students perform at levels below national aspirations, it is their teachers who are deemed to be at fault and it is their teacher education that needs to change.

This logic is particularly evident in nations such as Australia and the UK, with increasing emphasis on professional standards, measures of competency and teacher effectiveness. These have emerged in response to the perceived poor quality of teaching and teacher education[1] that have presumed to be responsible for declining achievement among Australian and UK school students relative to other 'reference societies' (Sellar and Lingard 2013). Along with the public perception that schooling does not do enough to teach the 'basics' of literacy and numeracy,

---

[1]The terminology for teacher education varies between nations. In Australia it is known as teacher education (TE), while in the UK the terms initial teacher education (ITE) or initial teacher training (ITT) are more common. Our preference is for 'education' rather than 'training' although for the purposes of this chapter we understand the terms synonymously in how they are used within quotations and the like.

T. Gale (✉) · S. Parker
University of Glasgow, Glasgow, Scotland
e-mail: trevor.gale@glasgow.ac.uk

S. Parker
e-mail: stephen.parker@deakin.edu.au

© Springer Nature Singapore Pte Ltd. 2017
M.A. Peters et al. (eds.), *A Companion to Research in Teacher Education*,
DOI 10.1007/978-981-10-4075-7_35

students' poor performances on international tests have created a sense of panic among policy makers and politicians. While their concerns are arguably based on a misreading or misuse of PISA and other data (Gorur and Wu 2015) and an ideological/cultural battle over the purposes and content of schooling, nevertheless they have had a significant impact on how TE is now conceived and implemented.

In this chapter, we compare and contrast these issues in three jurisdictions: Australia, England and, to a lesser extent, Scotland. The cases of Australia and England are arguably founded on similar philosophical accounts of the nature of teacher education, although England is further down the path of transforming these into changed practice. Australia is moving in similar directions, with a '(re)turn to the practical' and a shift away from teaching as a 'research-based profession and intellectual activity' towards a technicist craft-based occupation that relies on the application of particular clinical skills (Beauchamp et al. 2015: 160). While England has demonstrated a distinct move towards school-based ITE (Menter and Hulme 2011), in Australia TE remains the domain of universities, albeit increasingly delivered at postgraduate level and in partnerships with schools. On partnerships, Australia has much in common with Scotland (Menter and Hulme 2011; Donaldson 2011), although Scotland differs philosophically from Australia and England in its resistance to craft-based models and a concerted move towards greater research-informed teaching.

The chapter draws on key reviews of TE from each of these nations, including: the Teacher Education Ministerial Advisory Group (TEMAG) report *Action Now: Classroom Ready Teachers* (TEMAG 2014b) in Australia, the *Importance of Teaching* White Paper in England (DfE 2010), and *Teaching Scotland's Future* in Scotland (Donaldson 2011). We also draw on related reports and the public statements of politicians who advocate various policy moves. Indicative of the different approaches in these jurisdictions, the reviews in Australia and England identify the 'problem' of TE in similar ways with similarly narrowly conceived solutions. In contrast, the Donaldson Review has been described as "progressive, if not radical, and forward thinking" (Menter and Hulme 2011: 394), particularly in its propositions for reform even if starting with many of the same concerns as in Australia and England.

We identify four assumptions evident in and constitutive of the prevailing logic of TE in OECD nations (particularly Australia, England and Scotland):

1. Students are underperforming by international and community standards;
2. There is a direct cause–effect relation between student performance and teacher performance (i.e. teaching is all that matters);
3. Teachers' performance does not meet the required standards, partly because of the low quality of TE students and of TE itself; and
4. Better TE requires: more discipline depth, a proven approach, more time spent in schools and better school-university relations.

We draw on the above documents to show how the logic has shaped the ways in which TE policy is framed as responses to particular diagnoses. We also show that at each step there is research evidence questioning these diagnoses. We conclude that the most socially just way forward is to rework the prevailing logic of TE by shifting the focus to teachers' capabilities (Nussbaum 2011).

1. Students are underperforming

Recent years have seen the emergence of 'PISA shock' (Ertl 2006): the feeling among some OECD countries that they are falling behind the rest of the world in student achievement, as measured by the *Programme for International Student Assessment* (PISA) and other testing regimes. Christopher Pyne (former Australian Education Minister)[2] expressed his own PISA shock in the wake of the results released in late 2013, which he described as:

> the worst for Australia since testing began and shows that we are falling further behind our regional neighbours … Australia has lost more ground to other participating countries since the last test in PISA 2009. … we have dropped from fifteenth to nineteenth in mathematical literacy, tenth to sixteenth in scientific literacy and nineteenth to fourteenth in reading literacy. (Pyne 2013)

TEMAG in Australia reiterated these data a year later in its review of TE: "The declining performance of Australian students in international testing has recently driven increasing community debate about the quality of teaching" (2014b: 2). UK Prime Minister David Cameron and his then coalition partner and deputy Nick Clegg expressed similar dismay at the performance and global position of England's school students, using this as a justification for reform: "The only way we can catch up, and have the world-class schools our children deserve, is by learning the lessons of other countries' success" (Cameron and Clegg 2010: 3).

For Pyne, the PISA lesson for Australia is that "it matters more which teacher you are allocated as opposed to which school you attend", thus playing down the influence of socio-economic context in student achievement despite PISA and other data highlighting the growing tail of low achievement among low SES students (OECD 2013). PISA shock in Australia has "generated a narrative of decline in recent policy debate, particularly in relation to Australia being outperformed by its Asian neighbours" (Sellar and Lingard 2013: 478). Comparison with 'reference societies'—most notably Shanghai, Singapore, Korea and Japan—in which PISA results are strong, has led to "the use of policies in other systems to justify and legitimate the necessity of domestic reform" (Sellar and Lingard 2013: 467).

And yet for all of the faith placed in PISA results as a basis for reform, much of the research literature (e.g. Gorur 2015; Grek 2009; Sellar and Lingard 2013) has shown that PISA (and similar testing regimes) provides a questionable rationale for shaping policy. For example, PISA results are contextually dependent and thus 'lessons' from high performing nations or regions cannot be easily transferred

---

[2]In September 2015, there was a leadership coup in Australia within the ruling Liberal/National coalition of parties, resulting in a change in Australia's Prime Minister and members of the cabinet. Although different individuals now occupy the positions of Prime Minister and Minister for Education, the Government's education policies and sentiment remain unchanged.

between contexts. As Gorur and Wu argue (2015), even within national contexts PISA data can be read in different ways so that a nation's policy aspirations to be among the 'top five', for example, are insensitive to the elements that contribute to a country's average performance. Average scores in literacy, mathematics and science, used to justify the need for reform, do not reveal the many ways in which a country might already be performing. For example, Gorur and Wu show that some jurisdictions in Australia—e.g. the Australian Capital Territory (ACT)—show performance in reading on par with reference societies in Asia and Scandinavia.

In short, the assessment that students are underperforming is too gross to be meaningful in a policy and educational sense. Instead, national PISA rankings produce "statistical categories applied across the globe" which "contributes to the creation of a global commensurate space of measurement and equivalence, in turn *rendering it legible for governing* and helping to create a global education policy field" (Sellar and Lingard 2013: 466–467; emphasis added). Such measures and their interpretations do not just misrepresent student achievement and the relative positioning of nations. Their very existence creates 'calculable worlds' (Gorur 2015: 581) that help to construct policy problems and commensurate solutions for certain population groups.

2. Teaching is all that matters

The current TE logic connects this perception of student performance directly with the performance of their teachers. A key theme in Australian and English policy and official discourse is that the quality of teaching is the single most important factor in determining student achievement. The logic proceeds: "the curriculum has passed its use-by date; our students just do not measure up; schools are wasting opportunities; and it is the teachers who are to blame" (Skourdoumbis 2014: 113). There is a presumed linear, causal relationship between teacher performance and student achievement. Also implied is that good teaching in one school is also good teaching in another. It is a view that strips teaching of social context resulting in a reductive view of schools, students and teaching (Skourdoumbis and Gale 2013).

Thus informed, official statements in both Australia and England regard teaching as *the* "single greatest in-school influence on student achievement" (TEMAG 2014a: 3) and that *the* "most important factor in determining the effectiveness of a school system is the quality of its teachers" (DfE 2010: 19). The similarity in discourse across nations is striking, with the UK Prime Minister and (then) Deputy Prime Minister remarking that "no education system can be better than the quality of its teachers" (Cameron and Clegg 2010: 3) and the recent review of Australian TE commenting that the "quality of an education system simply cannot exceed the quality of its teachers" (TEMAG 2014a: 3).

There are two main critiques of this decontextualisation of TE. The first observes that teacher effectiveness models built on linear and exclusive student-teacher performance relations tend to ignore influences from outside classrooms and schools. Berliner refers to these influences as 'exogenous variable[s]' that are "outside the system being described" (2013: 240) and are "unexplained by the model" (2014: 4). Home, family and socio-economic influences are excluded, which "render unimportant, perhaps even invisible, the social and economic inequalities that really prevent some students from doing as well as others. As a result they help to perpetuate unequal schooling and unequal outcomes" (Thrupp and Lupton 2006: 312). As Mills and Gale (2010: 30) have argued "context is being forgotten in the rush to attribute student achievement solely to what teachers do." Even when acknowledged, teacher effectiveness models are not good at 'controlling' for these broader issues, partly because "researchers simply do not know all the variables that affect teachers in their classroom" (Berliner 2013: 240) and partly because these external influences interact with, and so cannot be divorced from, what teachers do in classrooms. Outside-school influences on achievement cannot be readily dismissed as simply 'background factors' or 'controlled' by statistical manipulation, as proponents of teacher effectiveness models suggest (Skourdoumbis and Gale 2013).

Yet even within schools, teachers are not the most significant influence. The relationship between teacher and student is far more complex (Berliner 2014). As with all social interactions, classroom interactions are never entirely unilateral. Interlocution with others is always party-dependent; it necessarily involves each party's changing understandings and perceptions of the context and of those with whom they engage. Interlocutors can 'speak back' to each other and change their position, disrupting the tentative understandings they might have of each other. The implications for teaching are that:

> the simple model of influence, Teacher—> Student, held so widely by the general public, and particularly by our politicians, is surely reciprocal, and more like this: Teacher <-> Student. And, 25–35 of such separate relationships need to be negotiated in every classroom. (Berliner 2014: 3)

Teaching–learning relations are further complicated by the combinations and permutations of Student <-> Student. Thus, the focus on teachers making *the* difference to student achievement (Skourdoumbis 2014) is reductive in its simplification of learning and in its disregard for external, out-of-school influences. Student performance can never be directly or exclusively attributed to teacher performance.

3. Teachers' performance is poor and TE is at fault

But once you accept that students are performing poorly at school and imagine a close relationship with the performance of teachers, it is then a logical step to argue that the education of teachers—specifically, teacher education—leaves a lot to be desired.

Official documents suggest that TE needs to be improved and entry standards need to be lifted. In England, "the current cohort of trainees is one of our best ever. But we have much further to go" (Cameron and Clegg 2010: 3). The imperative remains to "continue [to improve] the quality of teachers and teaching" (DfE 2010: 20). In Australia, these same sentiments are expressed more bluntly and with greater pessimism: "the Australian community does not have confidence in the quality and effectiveness of new teachers" (TEMAG 2014b: 1). TEMAG also claims that in their preparation:

> less than 10 % of time in compulsory subjects is devoted to equipping pre-service [primary] teachers with an understanding of how to teach reading. In a survey of secondary beginning teachers, only 10 % of all respondents indicated that their course prepared them 'very well' to teach literacy. (TEMAG 2014b: 19)

The assertion is that TE needs to change to ensure that all new teachers leave their training 'classroom ready' (TEMAG) and measure up against national accreditation requirements. This requires an increased focus on the content of TE courses, to emphasise "what is really important" (DfE 2010: 22), namely literacy and numeracy, and 'evidence-based' teaching practice (TEMAG 2014b). In contrast (and indicative of Scotland's distinctive approach), Donaldson (2011: 34) suggests that it is unrealistic to demand initial teacher education cover "all that would ever be required of teachers", acknowledging that much teacher knowledge is developed over time through experience and ongoing professional development.

Part of the diagnosis of the TE 'problem' is that its courses are not attracting the right people. A common concern in Australia, England and Scotland is with attracting suitable candidates—the 'most talented' (DfE 2010: 20)—into TE courses, with an emphasis on academic skills in combination with personal characteristics and traits believed to make good teachers (TEMAG). The UK government (DfE 2010: 20) has indicated it will cease "to provide Department for Education funding for initial teacher training [in England] for those graduates who do not have at least a 2:2 degree".[3] It has also proposed shifting a literacy and numeracy test for pre-service teachers from the end of their studies to the beginning, while also arguing for a more rigorous test and cutting down on opportunities to enter TE until a satisfactory mark is attained. The aim is to ensure "that all entrants to initial teacher education are the best fit for teaching. This includes the balance of academic skills and personal characteristics needed to be suitable for teaching" (TEMAG 2014b: xi).

The TEMAG report similarly determined that the application of existing professional standards are inadequate, unevenly applied or implemented too slowly; such that many graduate teachers lack essential skills, like "evidence-based teaching strategies and skills they need to respond to different student learning needs" (TEMAG 2014b: xi). In short, TEMAG asserts that not all graduates are 'classroom ready' but are victims of poor quality 'training' and/or were never suitable for teaching in the first place. These perceptions are reinforced by media sentiments that "low entry scores required to study teaching sent the message that 'if you're dumb you can be a teacher'" (Ferrari 2015).

---

[3]A '2:2 degree' is an expression used in the UK to mean a lower second-class honours undergraduate degree. Honours is incorporated within students' degrees, often spread over the final two years. In England, the undergraduate degree is taken over 3 years full time; in Scotland it is over 4 years full time.

Donaldson (2011: 27) also sees a need to assess TE students' academic skills and personal attributes on entry and rigorous "diagnostic assessments of their competence in both literacy and numeracy". Menter and Hulme (2011: 392) stress that these tests should be diagnostic "and not be used to exclude people from entry if there is evidence that they can become effective teachers." This would "allow for weaknesses to be addressed by the student during the course" (2011: 27), rather than demand students already possess these skills from the outset. Even the TEMAG report recommends a 'sophisticated' (2014b: 14) approach to entry with multiple pathways that still maintain high academic and personal standards. Yet, as noted above, these pathways still need to be only for those who are fit for purpose.

The contradictory messages in these issues are not exclusive to Australia. In examining the research literature for Donaldson's review of Scottish TE, Menter and Hulme (2010) question the efficacy of testing regimes for entry into TE programs. They note that such tests "are not reliable predictors of teacher quality. Many dimensions of effective teaching are not reliably predicted by tests of academic ability … Research on the impact of testing as a means of regulating entry to the profession is inconclusive" (Menter and Hulme 2010: 26, 27). In spite of this, Recommendation 5 of the Donaldson report identified the need for "diagnostic assessments of their [candidates'] competence in both literacy and numeracy" (Donaldson 2011: 85). In Donaldson's terms, the strategy to fix TE is first about getting the "right people in the right numbers" (20).

4. Proven approaches to TE are needed

In responding to the diagnosis of inadequate TE programs, there is a notable degree of commonality in the remedies proposed across the three jurisdictions. Irrespective of their geographies and philosophical orientations, they all seem to agree on what TE needs: greater disciplinary depth; the use of proven pedagogical approaches; more time spent in schools (although the Donaldson Review places less emphasis on this); and better school-university relations.

35.1.1   Greater Disciplinary Depth

All three reports (in Australia, England and Scotland) argue that pre-service teachers need to have both in-depth content and pedagogical knowledge. In Australia, the emphasis is twofold: on providing pre-service teachers with the skills to more effectively teach literacy and numeracy, particularly at secondary school level; and developing specialisations among primary teachers, particularly in science, mathematics and languages other than English (TEMAG 2014b). Among its priorities, the DfE White Paper includes improvement in the quality of new "teachers subject knowledge and academic preparation" (DfE 2010: 20). This is stated alongside other goals of literacy and numeracy, and strong interpersonal skills. Notably, England's White Paper also argues for the professional development of existing teachers to update and deepen their content knowledge.

Similarly for Donaldson, teachers need in-depth content and pedagogical knowledges that go beyond the overly vocational orientation of some undergraduate TE courses. While in Australia and England the move is towards making the theory acquired in TE subservient to practice through a greater emphasis on practical experience, the view in Scotland is that existing undergraduate TE programs are 'too narrowly vocational', which leads to "an over emphasis on technical and craft skills at the expense of broader and more academically challenging areas of study" (Donaldson 2011: 88). Donaldson's alternative is the concurrent study of traditional TE content with 'in-depth academic study' (88) and development of "high levels of pedagogical expertise" (84). Thus the focus is on broad and deep studies. Teaching is seen to be a research-informed, intellectual endeavour.

Yet while the case for teachers possessing greater disciplinary knowledge is significant, teaching requires more than just knowing the content to be taught. Teachers also require *pedagogical* content knowledge—i.e. knowledge about *how* the content is best taught not just knowledge of the content. Hence, "[m]ere content knowledge is likely to be as useless pedagogically as content-free skill" (Shulman 1986: 8). Pedagogical content knowledge relates content to pedagogy; it "embodies the aspects of content most germane to its teachability" (9). It includes:

> the most useful forms of representation of those ideas, the most powerful analogies, illustrations, examples, explanations, and demonstrations—in a word, the ways of representing and formulating the subject that make it comprehensible to others. Since there are no single most powerful forms of representation, the teacher must have at hand a veritable armamentarium of alternative forms of representation. (Shulman 1986: 9; emphasis added)

This is in contradistinction to the current emphasis in Australia and England on increased content knowledge, which assumes that the skills required to effectively deliver content are generic and transferable. Generic formulae for pedagogy are insufficient to respond to the varying and changing contexts and needs of the classroom and of disciplines. Pedagogical content knowledge not only varies between disciplines and subject areas, but also by year level, classroom mix and the socio-economic background of students. For example, the best way to teach Science or English literature may well be different, as is teaching in different contexts. Thus by diminishing the importance of pedagogic content knowledge and of school context in favour of greater discipline depth, the *teaching* of content is arguably reduced to a set of technical skills.

35.1.2 Proven Approaches

One of the remedies for the perceived flaws in TE—those that are espoused by TEMAG in Australia and the *Importance of Teaching* in England—is to return to approaches of previous eras and presumed to have been effective. As noted above, in Australia the concern among politicians is that TE and teaching have been infiltrated by leftist ideology (Gale and Cross 2007). For example, English is said to be dominated by postmodernist theory that undermines the essentials of literacy. The current focus on pursuing a 'back-to-basics' approach to teaching students not only centres on literacy and numeracy but also increasingly prescribes teaching methods reminiscent of a 'golden' past, far removed from the multiple literacies movement that alerts students to the politicisation of texts. In this vein, the Australian Government has lamented the decline of what it regards as effective and proven methods: especially 'phonemic awareness and phonics' (TEMAG 2015: 5) popular during the 1970s. Accompanying this is a predilection for direct instruction, especially in remote and disadvantaged schools. Former Minister Pyne has artic-ulated this preference thus: "I am personally very determined to drive an agenda in literacy that focuses on phonics" (Pyne, in Hurst 2013) and:

> I think a phonics-based, robust curriculum in primary years should be the norm across all schools in Australia … when parents discover the transformative impact… on their struggling child's learning ability there will be a revolution demanding that it be introduced beyond remote schools. (Pyne, in Walker 2014)

In England there is a similar assertion that "we do not have a strong enough focus on what is proven to be the most effective practice in teacher education and development" (DfE 2010: 19). This is championed as "focusing on core teaching skills, especially in teaching reading and mathematics and in managing behaviour" (DfE 2010: 9). As in Australia, the argument is that "systematic synthetic phonics is the proven best way to teach early reading" (DfE 2010: 22–23).

Yet critical research on literacy in schools suggests that when teachers are required to teach in prescribed ways for particular outcomes, other pedagogic approaches and teachers' professional judgments are squeezed out (Comber 2012). Students for whom prescribed approaches to teaching literacy are not effective, are difficult to accommodate when other ways of teaching are marginalised. Teachers' knowledge and experience in assisting these students are no longer valued as they do not contribute to mandated literacy teaching:

> Because NAPLAN [National Assessment Program: Literacy and Numeracy] is what counts, other curriculum areas and other literacy activities are sidelined … a disengaged student experiences a teacher who is unable to use her full repertoire to re-connect him with the educative process. It is not that she doesn't have the professional knowledge or experience, so often seen as the causes of student alienation. … Subsequently, a student, who most needs her expertise, becomes a problem in a different way. (Comber 2012: 129)

In contrast, these are the very knowledges and experiences that Donaldson wants teachers to evoke:

> The most successful education systems invest in developing their teachers as reflective, accomplished and enquiring professionals who are able, not simply to teach successfully in relation to current external expectations, but who have the capacity to engage fully with the complexities of education and to be key actors in shaping and leading educational change. (Donaldson 2011: 14)

35.1.3   More Time in Schools

Part of the policy emphasis on proven approaches to teaching is a belief that teaching is predominantly a practical vocation, which requires a specific skillset and increased time in schools to hone and develop these skills.

Recommendations with this focus in both Australia and England, are based on an "assumption that more time spent in schools inevitably—and unproblematically —leads to better and 'more relevant' learning" (McNamara and Murray 2013, in Beauchamp et al. 2015: 163). The final TEMAG report argues that there is a disconnect between what pre-service teachers are taught in universities and what they need to know and do in classrooms. This includes an "apparent disconnection between theory and practice" (2014b: 25). TEMAG also argues that there is inconsistency among TE providers regarding the extent and degree of integration with professional experience (school placements of pre-service teachers). Well-integrated professional experience components of TE are said to be "critical for the translation of theory into practice" (TEMAG 2014b: xi). The report recommends that there ought to be teacher placements of 'appropriate timing and length' and "early exposure of preservice teachers to school and classroom settings" (27). Although the timing and duration of placements is left to higher education providers, the implication is that current arrangements are insufficient with too little time spent in schools and an over-emphasis on theory.

The Australian Government's Response (TEMAG 2015) to the TEMAG report simplifies the call for improved professional experience placements. It notes that practical experience is essential for developing the skills and knowledge required to be an effective teacher, and that "high quality practical experience should be embedded in every teacher education course" (2015: 7). Similarly, England has taken a "turn to the practical" (Furlong and Lawn 2011: 6), evident in the UK Government's intention to "Reform initial teacher training, to increase the proportion of time trainees spend in the classroom" (DfE 2010: 9). This is in response to a perception that "Too little teacher training takes place on the job" (DfE 2010:19). McNamara and Murray (2013: 22; in Beauchamp et al. 2015: 163) argue that this emphasis on practical experience amounts to:

> an understanding of teaching as (a) essentially a craft rather than an intellectual activity; (b) an apprenticeship model of teacher training that can be located entirely in the workplace … [It] privileges performativity and 'practical' knowledge over theoretical, pedagogical and subject knowledge.

Teaching standards are "defined as regulatory rather than developmental in intent" (Beauchamp et al. 2015: 160). That is, standards are largely prescriptive and assume that a teacher should be expert from the outset ('classroom ready' in TEMAG terms), allowing relatively little scope for teacher development, enhancement or refinement over time.

In contrast to the Australian and English reviews, the Donaldson Review is more measured: envisaging teaching not in terms of technical skill or a clinical approach or simply more time spent in schools, but as an occupation responsive to the changing needs of young people in the modern age:

> The capacity of the teacher should be built not just through extensive 'teaching practice' but through reflecting on and learning from the experience of supporting children's learning with all the complexities which characterise twenty-first century childhood. The 'craft' components of teaching must be based upon and informed by fresh insights into how best to meet the increasingly fast pace of change in the world which our children inhabit. Simply advocating more time in the classroom as a means of preparing teachers for their role is therefore not the answer to creating better teachers. (Donaldson 2011: 4–5; emphasis added)

Further, the Scottish approach resists the current "over-emphasis on preparation for the first post" (Donaldson 2011: 5). Donaldson argues for continual refinement of teachers' skills through ongoing professional development, 'career-long growth' (2010: 5) and viewing teaching experience and capacity as a continuum. He also suggests that professional experience should not be limited to classroom time, but include time with parents and other professionals associated with schools in order for student-teachers to gain a more rounded experience.

35.1.4 Better School-University Relations

Along with this privileging of the practical, all three jurisdictions are concerned to develop greater integration and better relationships between universities and schools in delivering TE, although the basis for such concern varies. In Australia, the focus is on professional experience placements that enable pre-service teachers to translate "theory into practice". This assumes such translation does not already occur and that TE courses are too theory-heavy. Thus TEMAG calls for 'mutually beneficial' school-university partnerships that "set criteria for professional experience across a range of classroom situations" (2014b: xiii). This involves providing mentors to assist student-teachers and opportunities for them to "continually reflect on their own practice" (2014b: xiii).

The Donaldson Review similarly calls for more reflective practice but in concert with a more elaborate and integrated approach to school-university partnerships. In this account, professional experience should not just be better integrated with university studies but allow for "reflection on practice and its interpretation in ways which bring theoretical and research perspectives to bear in relation to actual experience" (Donaldson 2011: 7). Donaldson emphasises that partnerships should be collaborative and involve schools and local authorities in all aspects of TE. Such 'shared responsibility' (7), he argues, should be based on:

> a new concept of partnership among universities, local authorities, schools, national agencies and other services which embraces selection, course content and assessment, which sets practical experience in a much more reflective and inquiring culture and which makes optimum use of ICT for professional learning. (11)

But perhaps the most ambitious Donaldson proposal is for 'hub schools' that are "analogous to teaching hospitals" (7), in which schools, universities, local and national services authorities are jointly engaged. This intensification of partnerships is imagined to enable reciprocal relationships and collaborations between relevant institutions. For example, it would enhance support for student-teachers while at the same time facilitating research with positive effects on student learning. The greater integration of research and practice and greater capacity for partnership and collaboration has been positively received by the Scottish Government which, in response to Donaldson's recommendations, established the National Partnership Group to focus on "the new and strengthened partnership working to support delivery of effective teacher education and professional development in every school in Scotland" (Scottish Government 2011: 2).

This approach to partnerships stands in contrast to the predominantly practice-oriented positions advocated by policy within Australia and England. In these countries, improved relations and more time spent in schools are intended to temper the theoretical knowledge of TE courses with practical knowledge and to ensure compliance with professional standards. Whereas, Donaldson's proposals are more attune to the development of teaching as an intellectual endeavour, which includes but is not confined to practice.

35.2   Conclusion: Towards a New Logic?

In setting out this prevailing logic of TE we have also sought to show that it is flawed. It is premised on: (1) decontextualised testing regimes with narrow conceptions of what counts as literacy, numeracy and knowledge more generally, thus producing questionable representations of students' abilities; (2) a simplistic and exclusive belief in cause–effect relations between teaching and learning, dismissive of other sometimes more significant influences on student learning; and (3) a presumption that if the second is true, any problem with students' test results (identified in the first) must be the fault of poor teaching and, by implication, with teachers' own education. Having diagnosed the problem in this way, the solution is self-evident: (4) improved teacher education, which oddly means a return to a previous conception of teaching (e.g. direction, instruction, phonics, etc.), largely discredited in the research literature, and which reduces teaching to a collection of practical skills technically applied according to a predetermined formula.

The rationale for all this 'revisioning' is that Anglophone nations like Australia, England and, to a lesser extent, Scotland are struggling to retain their global economic dominance—in the wake of the industrialisation of China, India and other developing nations—and have pinned their future hopes on their ascendency in a global knowledge economy. For this to happen, it is reasoned, teaching and teacher education need to become more effective. Curriculum is thus narrowed, teaching is scripted, TE becomes an exercise in training. Pushed to the margins is any real sense that getting an education is of much value beyond what it contributes to national agendas. Absent from consideration is what a person is capable of doing and being, and the ways education can contribute to the development of students' capabilities so that they are able to live lives they have reason to value (Nussbaum 2011).

We think that having regard for the development of students' capabilities—specifically those that students need in order to live lives they value, rather than the narrow range of capabilities privileged by governments—is a more socially just place to start to reimagine what kind of teaching is required and thus what kind of teacher education. A capabilities approach to teaching and TE:

> has direct implications for curricular materials and pedagogical practices. Curricular materials, the quality of learning experiences and of learning outcomes, need to be evaluated against the capabilities of students (i.e. their substantive freedoms), not solely on the basis of economic returns such as employment and income or, more broadly, students' contributions to the national economy. The capability perspective ... recognizes that education generates economic and non-economic returns, promotes agency and supports social mobility. (Gale and Molla 2015: 825)

From a capability perspective, then, the issue is not simply how students perform on standardised literacy and numeracy tests, but what capabilities students need and desire in order to "form a conception of the good and to engage in critical reflection about the planning" (Nussbaum 1992: 222) of the lives they, their parents and communities have reason to value. A good life in this sense might not simply align with the aspirations of government and its conception of an educated person as possessing particular skills and knowledges (Gale and Molla 2015).

The questions for teaching and TE then become, what capabilities do teachers need themselves in order to enable their students to develop these capabilities? Such questions refocus the purpose, intent and content of TE education away from the performative aspects of mandated literacy and numeracy programs towards a more expansive view of teaching and its contribution to students' lives. It has as its starting point a different logic of teaching and TE, which is broadly educative and more socially just.

References

Beauchamp, G., Clarke, L., Hulme, M., & Murray, J. (2015). Teacher education in the United Kingdom post devolution: Convergences and divergences. *Oxford Review of Education, 41*(2), 154–170.

Berliner, D. C. (2013). Problems with value-added evaluations of teachers? Let me count the ways! *The Teacher Educator, 48*(4), 235–243.

Berliner, D. C. (2014). Exogenous variables and value-added assessments: A fatal flaw. *Teachers College Record, 116*(1), 1–31.

Cameron, D., & Clegg, N. (2010). Forward by the Prime Minister and Deputy Prime Minister. In Department for Education (England) [DfE]. (2010). *The importance of teaching: The schools white paper* (pp. 3–5). London: The Stationery Office.

Comber, B. (2012). Mandated literacy assessment and the reorganization of teachers' work: Federal policy, local effects. *Critical Studies in Education, 53*(2), 119–136.

Department for Education (England) [DfE]. (2010). *The importance of teaching: The schools white paper*. London: The Stationery Office.

Donaldson, G. (2011). *Teaching Scotland's future: Report of a review of teacher education in Scotland*. Edinburgh: Scottish Government.

Ertl, H. (2006). Educational standards and the changing discourse on education: The reception and consequences of the PISA study in Germany. *Oxford Review of Education, 32*(5), 619–634.

Ferrari, J. (2015). Unis tell 'dumb students to teach'. *The Australian*, February 24. http://www. theaustralian.com.au/higher-education/universities-tell-dumb-students-to-teach/story-e6frgcjx-1227236256612?sv=3f3296c215b903bb0afc382ae7db1529

Gale, T., & Cross, R. (2007). Nebulous gobbledegook: The politics of influence on how and what to teach in Australian schools. In A. Berry, A. Clemans, & A. Kostogriz (Eds.), *Dimensions of professional learning: Professionalism, practice and identity* (pp. 5–21). Rotterdam: Sense.

Gale, T., & Molla, T. (2015). Social justice intents in policy: An analysis of capability for and through education. *Journal of Education Policy, 30*(6), 810–830.

Gorur, R. (2015). Producing calculable worlds: Education at a glance. *Discourse: Studies in the Cultural Politics of Education, 36*(4), 578–595.

Gorur, R., & Wu, M. (2015). Leaning too far? PISA, policy and Australia's 'top five' ambitions. *Discourse: Studies in the Cultural Politics of Education, 36*(5), 647–664.

Grek, S. (2009). Governing by numbers: the PISA 'effect' in Europe. *Journal of Education Policy, 24*(1), 23–37.

Hurst, D. (2013). Say after the minister: Old is new again. *Sydney Morning Herald*, September 28. http://www.smh.com.au/federal-politics/political-news/say-after-the-minister-old-is-new-again-20130927-2ujhn.html#ixzz3oJuHsKF7

Menter, I., & Hulme, M. (2011). Teacher education reform in Scotland: National and global influences. *Journal of Education for Teaching, 37*(4), 387–397.

Mills, C., & Gale, T. (2010). *Schooling in disadvantaged communities: Playing the game from the back of the field*. Berlin: Springer.

Nussbaum, M. C. (1992). Human functioning and social justice: Defense of Aristotelian essentialism. *Political Theory, 20*(2), 202–246.

Nussbaum, M. C. (2011). *Creating capabilities: The human development approach*. Cambridge, MA & London: The Belknap Press of Harvard University Press.

Organisation for Economic Co-operation and Development [OECD]. (2013). *PISA 2012 results: Excellence through equity: Giving every student the chance to succeed (Vol. II)*. PISA: OECD Publishing.

Pyne, C. (2013). *PISA results show more work to be done*. Media Release, December 3. https:// ministers.education.gov.au/pyne/pisa-results-show-more-work-be-done

Scottish Government. (2011). *Continuing to build excellence in teaching—The Scottish government's response to teaching Scotland's future*. Edinburgh: Scottish Government. http://www.gov.scot/Resource/Doc/920/0114570.pdf

Sellar, S., & Lingard, B. (2013). Looking East: Shanghai, PISA 2009 and the reconstitution of reference societies in the global education policy field. *Comparative Education, 49*(4), 464–485.

Shulman, L. S. (1986). Those who understand: Knowledge growth in teaching. *Educational Researcher, 15*(2), 4–14.

Skourdoumbis, A. (2014). Teacher effectiveness: Making the difference to student achievement? *British Journal of Educational Studies, 62*(2), 111–126.

Skourdoumbis, A., & Gale, T. (2013). Classroom teacher effectiveness research: A conceptual critique. *British Educational Research Journal, 39*(5), 892–906.

Teacher Education Ministerial Advisory Group [TEMAG]. (2014a). *Issues paper*. Canberra: Australian Government. http://www.studentsfirst.gov.au/files/temag_issues_paper_-_april_2014_4.pdf

Teacher Education Ministerial Advisory Group [TEMAG]. (2014b). *Action now: Classroom ready teachers*. Canberra: Australian Government. https://docs.education.gov.au/system/files/doc/other/action_now_classroom_ready_teachers_print.pdf

Teacher Education Ministerial Advisory Group [TEMAG]. (2015). *Action now: Classroom ready teachers. Australian government response.* Canberra: Australian Government. http://docs.education.gov.au/system/files/doc/other/150212_ag_response_-_final.pdf

Thrupp, M., & Lupton, R. (2006). Taking school contexts more seriously: The social justice challenge. *British Journal of Educational Studies, 54*(3), 308–328.

Walker, J. (2014). Pyne eyes national direct instruction rollout. *The Australian*, July 2. http://www.theaustralian.com.au/national-affairs/pyne-eyes-national-direct-instruction-rollout/story-fn59niix-1226974451763

Author Biographies

Trevor Gale is Professor of Education Policy and Social Justice, Head of the School of Education at The University of Glasgow and founding editor of Critical Studies in Education. He is a critical sociologist of education, and draws on Bourdieu's thinking tools to research issues of social justice in schooling and higher education.

Stephen Parker is a Research Fellow in Education Policy and Social Justice at the University of Glasgow. His research interests include equity in access to higher education, policy analysis and social justice in education, and utilises a range of social theory and philosophical approaches.

Part VI

Research, Institutional Evaluation and Evidence-Based Research

Introduction

Education as a discipline is bedevilled by a series dualisms that makes life difficult: between theory and practice, research and policy, and research and practice. These dualism characterize most practice-oriented disciplines and demand careful analysis for even to list these "gaps" is not to identify their true nature which shifts according to the development of the discipline, the progress of science in general and the current interpretations proposed for "theory", "research", and "practice". The dualisms impact on "effectiveness", "efficiency", and "achievement" and are also driven by larger theoretical development in evaluation theory. One notable tendency has been the growth of the assessment and evaluation industries that have passed out of the public domain into the hands of private sector that increasingly make available technology-enabled systems and formats driven by data and recently by "big data" and "analytics".

One is tempted to argue that the technology-enabled development of evaluation that is used for assessing institutional or individual performance coincided with the rise of the accountability movement in the policy realm and neoliberalism more generally that demands "value for money" and insist on regular and ongoing audits.

Tracey Burns and Tom Schuller (2007) from OECD Centre for Educational Research and Innovation, write of "the (re)emergence of 'evidence'" in the form of evidence-informed policy research (EIPR) which they trace back to the growing recognition of the economic importance of education in knowledge-based economies, the concern with accountability in respect of educational expenditures and a concern about the quality and effectiveness of current educational research (p. 16). Their work explores the issues underlying the use of evidence in educational policy-making discussing what constitutes evidence for research in education in an attempt to link research and policy.

Of course what Burns and Schuller are presenting as "evidence" is a historically conditioned notion that is framed as a result of certain models of evidence and a view of what should constitute the relationship between research and policy. This is not the place to enter into a discussion of the philosophy of evidence except to say that the notion is closely related to the concept of "justification" and what it is rational to believe on the basis of evidence. Generally we would se the expression "objectivity" for evidence-based inquiry where there is intersubjective agreement among inquirers and the idea is that evidence thus can act as a neutral arbiter among theories determining which we should adopt.

Rarely does this sort of easy relationship between research and policy or theory and practice work in the real world especially in an ideological policy realm like education. For one thing the narrow inductivist model of inquiry that assumes evidence stands independently or prior to theory seems open to question in many grounds. The history of recent debates going back to Thomas Kuhn is that observation is theory-laden as is evidence (Kelly 2014). What constitutes "evidence" is often determined by the history of research practices.[1]

The term "evidence-based" in research, policy and practice in education, is an extension of evidence-based medicine, utilizing randomized controlled trials that emerged from the field of clinical epidemiology in the late 1980s. Introducing "current best evidence" and "five levels of quality evidence", including statistical validity and risk prediction, meta-analysis, systematic review, clinical relevance, currency, and peer-review, it was developed as a framework for public health policy in the 1990s with the establishment of the Cochrane Collaboration in 1993 and the Centre for Evidence Based Medicine. The same evidential model has been since generalized and applied to other areas of public policy including education.[2]

Evidence-based practice is an interdisciplinary approach, to mainly clinical practice that originated in medicine, utilizing randomized controlled trials that emerged from the field of clinical epidemiology in the late 1980s, but that have been utilized recently in psychology and education. The premise of evidence-based practice is that all practical decisions should originate from scientific studies and that studies are interpreted based upon standards and norms. Introducing "current best evidence" and "five levels of quality evidence", including statistical validity and risk prediction, meta-analysis, systematic review, clinical relevance, currency, and peer-review, it was developed as a framework for public health policy in the 1990s with the establishment of the Cochrane Collaboration in 1993 and the Centre for Evidence Based Medicine. The same evidential model has since been generalized and applied to other areas of public policy, including education (Bridges et al. 2009).

The history of evidence-based policy has evolved from evidence-based medicine, in which research findings are used to support clinical decisions, and evidence is gathered by randomized controlled trials (RCTs). In 1993, the Cochrane Collaboration was established in the UK. It works to keep all RCTs up-to-date, and provides Cochrane reviews of health policy. Research and policy advocacy pushed for more evidence-based policy-making, leading to the formation of the Campbell

---

[1]See http://coalition4evidence.org/468-2/publications/.

[2]The following section draws on Peters and Tesar (2016) "Bad Research, Bad Education: The contested evidence for evidence-based research, policy and practice in education."

Collaboration in 1999, and conducts reviews on the best evidence, analysing the effects of social and educational policies and practices. *Campbell Systematic Reviews* is a peer-reviewed online monograph series of systematic reviews, prepared under the editorial control of the Campbell Collaboration. Campbell systematic reviews follow structured guidelines and standards for summarizing the international research evidence on the effects of interventions in crime and justice, education, international development, and social welfare. More recently, it has been developed in a UK Cabinet policy paper (2012) "Test, Learn, Adapt: Developing Public Policy with Randomised Controlled Trials" published in collaboration with Ben Goldacre and David Torgerson, arguing that Randomised Controlled Trials (RCTs) should be used much more extensively in public policy. In March 2013, Teach First in the UK launched "a new vision for evidence-based practice in education and teaching", attended by Secretary of State for Education Michael Gove and introducing Ben Goldacre (2013), author of *Bad Science*, who presented "Building Research into Education".

The purpose of a systematic review is to sum up the best available research on a specific question. This is done by synthesizing the results of many studies. A systematic review uses transparent procedures to find, evaluate, and synthesize the results of relevant research. Procedures are explicitly defined in advance, in order to ensure that the exercise is transparent and can be replicated. This practice is also designed to minimize bias. Studies included in a review are screened for quality, so that the findings of a large number of studies can be combined. Peer review is a key part of the process; qualified independent researchers control the author's methods and results. A systematic review must have: clear inclusion/exclusion criteria, an explicit search strategy, systematic coding and analysis of included studies and meta-analysis (where possible). Campbell reviews must include a systematic search for unpublished reports (to avoid publication bias). Campbell reviews are usually international in scope, a protocol (project plan) for the review is developed in advance and undergoes peer review, study inclusion and coding decisions are accomplished by at least two reviewers, who work independently and compare results.

Davies (2003) develops a critique of new managerialism and of its implications for the professional work of scholars and teachers, and then critiques "evidence-based practice" as it is being developed for schools. Davies argues that it is only possible to make sense of the policies and practices of the evidence-based practice movement within the framework of new managerialism, and also explores some of the tensions and contradictions between managerialism and gender reform in educational contexts. Davies ends with a challenge to begin the work of generating the collective story through which we can dismantle the hegemony of new managerialism and engage in the transformative work that will afford us a different future. On the other hand, Clegg (2005) argues that a critical realist perspective can contribute to a critique of evidence-based practice, while at the same time not abandoning the idea of evidence altogether. The paper is structured around a number of related themes: the sociopolitics of "evidence-based"; epistemological roots and a critical realist critique; the debate in action, based on the recent systematic review of personal development planning; and theory to practice gaps. The advocacy of evidence-based practice is currently being used to undermine professional autonomy and to valorise the "gold standard" of randomized controlled trials. However, the paper proposes that evidence can properly be claimed for critique and emancipatory projects, and that its current discursive location at the core of New Labour thinking is not the only one available.

Biesta (2007) provides a critical analysis of the idea of evidence-based practice and the ways in which it has been promoted and implemented in the field of education, focusing on the tension between scientific and democratic control over educational practice and research. He examines three key assumptions of evidence-based education: first, the extent to which educational practice can be compared to the practice of medicine, the field in which evidence-based practice was first developed; second, the role of knowledge in professional actions, with special attention to what kind of epistemology is appropriate for professional practices that wish to be informed by research; and third, the expectations about the practical role of research implicit in the idea of evidence-based education. Evidence-based practice provides a framework for understanding the role of research in educational practice that not only restricts the scope of decision-making to questions about effectivity and effectiveness, but that also restricts the opportunities for participation in educational decision-making. He argues that we must expand our views about the interrelations among research, policy and practice, to keep in view education as a thoroughly moral and political practice that requires continuous democratic contestation and deliberation.

References

Biesta, G. (2007). Why "what works" won't work: Evidence-based practice and the democratic deficit in educational research. *Educational Theory, 57*(1), 1–21.

Bridges, D., Smeyers, P., & Smith, R. D. (Eds.) (2009) *Evidence based educational policy: What evidence? What basis? Whose policy?* Oxford, United Kingdom: Wiley Blackwell.

Clegg, S. (2005). Evidence-based practice in educational research: A critical realist critique of systematic review. *British Journal of Sociology of Education, 26*(3), 415–428.

Davies, B. (2003). Death to critique and dissent? The policies and practices of new managerialism and of 'evidence-based practice'. *Gender and Education, 15*(1), 91–103.

Peters, M. A. & Tesar, M. (2016) Bad research, bad education: The contested evidence for evidence-based research, policy and practice in education.

Kelly, T. (2014, Fall). "Evidence". In E. N. Zalta (Ed.), *The stanford encyclopedia of philosophy.* URL = http://plato.stanford.edu/archives/fall2014/entries/evidence/

Chapter 36
On the Role of Philosophical Work in Research in Teacher Education

David Bridges, Alis Oancea and Janet Orchard

36.1 Introduction

We work, as many scholars and international research associations do, including the American Educational Research Association and the European Educational Research Association, with an inclusive definition of research which we share with the editors of this International Companion. In 1969 two philosophers, Richard Peters and John White, first defined research in this way, as 'systematic and sustained inquiry' (Peters and White 1969). This is better known today in its slightly expanded form, attributable to Lawrence Stenhouse (1975), as 'systematic and sustained inquiry made public'.

On this view educational research is not limited to empirical inquiry, still less a particular form of empirical inquiry which may be put forward as a 'gold standard'. There is an important role for empirical evidence in teacher education: to help understand how things are and what has been; to fathom the consequences of different educational practices and interventions in the past. However, such evidence never provides a *sufficient* basis for policy formation. History, discourse analysis and deconstruction, socio-cultural theory, feminist sociology, psycho-analytic theory, all have a part to play too—and so does philosophy, for teacher education, at the level of policy, practice, or research, is 'based' in, or given direction by, values, whether it concerns its aims, aspirations, goals or, more

D. Bridges (✉)
University of East Anglia, England, UK
e-mail: db347@cam.ac.uk

A. Oancea
University of Oxford, England, UK
e-mail: alis.oancea@education.ox.ac.uk

J. Orchard
University of Bristol, England, UK
e-mail: janet.orchard@bristol.ac.uk

© Springer Nature Singapore Pte Ltd. 2017
M.A. Peters et al. (eds.), *A Companion to Research in Teacher Education*,
DOI 10.1007/978-981-10-4075-7_36

modestly, some specific improvement to be achieved. If teacher education is to be evidence-based, values will dictate what evidence may be relevant to a particular purpose. It cannot be a neutral technical exercise, but rather

> a deeply ethical, political and cultural one bound up with ideas about the good society and how life can be worthwhile. (Winch and Gingell 2006, Preface)

So there is work to be done establishing a coherent normative framework. This might include: substantive work rooted in what in more popular terms are described as 'philosophies of education', and in conceptions of individual and social well-being; analytic work which examines and critiques the views that are held or offered as the direction for educational improvement; phenomenological work which explores the meaning and significance of teaching experience. 'Evidence' always leaves you with the 'so what?' question, and this question can only be answered by reference to the sort of considerations indicated above.

Having taken a wide ranging and inclusive view of what might count as research, provided that in whatever form it is rigorous and disciplined, we take a similar view on philosophy itself. When the philosopher, A.J. Ayer was asked 'What is philosophy?' he gestured in the direction of a large study wall stacked with books. 'It's all that' was his reply. This ostensive definition (as philosophers might call it) is not very helpful to anyone unable to view the contents of Ayer's bookshelves. However, it does point to philosophy as consisting centrally of traditions of literature that have developed over at least 2000 years and which continue to be a crucial point of reference, not just because of what they reveal about the past, but also because of what they continue to contribute to contemporary thinking.

Some of this work provides systematic views of individual being, of the good life and of the good society; some is focussed on what we can know and how, feeding into a wide range of 'philosophies of X', including science, history, religion, education. Some philosophers strive to articulate aspects of existence in imaginative, new terms; others have a preference for plain language and conceptual analysis. We embrace all these traditions in examining the contribution of philosophy to research in teacher education.

Although this chapter is focussed on the distinctive contribution of philosophy to research into teacher education, it is our view that philosophy should not be something set apart from other forms of inquiry. We are all committed, as Sect. 36.4 will illustrate, to a research community in which philosophers work with other researchers in multidisciplinary teams—participating in field observation, interviewing and test construction as well as more strictly philosophical work. Such engagement provides a stimulus to philosophical work as well as a way of ensuring that the contributions of this work are absorbed into every phase of the research programme. Through this joint work, 'new knowledge emerges when people lose some part of their discrete professional/occupational identities, in the process of working on some common purpose' (MacLure, in Bridges 2017: 160).

So, with these preliminaries established, let us look more closely at philosophy's contributions to research in teacher education. Section 36.2 below illustrates some of the questions about the nature of teacher education, and in particular what kind of knowledge teachers need. It considers philosophy '*of*' teacher education which might be concerned with epistemological, ontological and ethical questions about teacher education. We discuss three epistemological questions around the kinds of knowledge teachers need, whether these relate to their subject or theoretical knowledge and ongoing questions around the theory practice relationship. Section 36.3 explores philosophy '*as*' teacher education research. Examples of teacher educators' own philosophical work lead us to argue for the importance of practical grounding in experience for both philosophical and empirical enquiry into teacher education. Finally, in Sect. 36.4 we reflect on the role of philosophy '*in*' inter or multidisciplinary teacher education research.

36.2 Philosophy of Teacher Education: Traditions of Philosophical Inquiry

Perhaps a central question for teacher education is: 'What sort of knowledge, understanding and practical competence do teachers need to develop?' This is another way of asking: 'What are the aims of teacher education?' though to pose the question as one about teacher *education*, as distinct from teacher *training*, is already to take sides in a debate that continues to run through the profession and receive philosophical treatment in the analytic tradition.

This question needs to be answered by reference to a teacher's individual circumstances—their prior knowledge and experience and their future aspirations. In the context of in-service teacher education the answers are likely to be diverse, depending on the positions that teachers occupy, the particular contexts in which they find themselves and their ambitions. For pre-service teacher education (on which we shall focus here) we tend to provide in any one country a relatively consistent programme modified primarily by reference to the age range that students plan to teach and their subject specialisms.

In designing a course of pre-service education, the teacher educator quickly encounters teasing and often controversial questions which have engaged philosophers among others for some time. In the space available we will consider briefly three such questions.

36.2.1 What Is the Importance of Subject Knowledge in the Preparation and Indeed the Continuing Development of Teachers?

It is sometimes argued that 'a good teacher can teach anything'. This relies on a view of teaching as a set of generic skills and an approach to the task that relies on individual and collaborative student inquiry-and resource-based learning rather than on any specialist expertise on the subject area provided by the teacher. The teacher, then, becomes 'a facilitator of learning', an authority on the social and intellectual processes of inquiry rather than an authority on the subject.

By contrast, most teacher education systems in the world require the equivalent of three years of full-time study at degree level of the subject/s that the individual proposes to teach (though sometimes less for primary teachers), even if subsequent professional training has a strong emphasis on, for example, interactive learning, group work, inquiry-based learning, etc. Why is this?

For some, the identification of the teacher with particular subject knowledge is a key to understanding the practice of teaching. MacIntyre and Dunne stand in this tradition when they write:

> a teacher should think of her or himself as a mathematician, a reader of poetry, an historian or whatever, engaged in communicating craft and knowledge to apprentices. (MacIntyre and Dunne 2002: 5)

Fordham extends the argument, which he says is interesting because:

> 'it situates subject expertise at the heart of the activity of teaching. Furthermore, it does not reduce subject expertise to a simplistic conception of subject knowledge: rather, it requires us to see teachers as members of an active and developing tradition that continues to negotiate notions of excellence and the goods that are internal to the practice'. (Fordham 2015: 1)

He goes further in suggesting that: a teacher being engaged in the practice of a discipline is a necessary condition of pupils learning that discipline (ibid: 11) and then 'that teaching is a form of disciplinary activity and the implications of this for how teachers are trained and evaluated are significant' (ibid: 11).

This brief summary of an argument illustrates that teacher education depends on a conception of what it is to be a teacher, of the nature of the authority that a teacher can exercise, the source of his or her legitimacy in the classroom and the location of the teacher in relation to the disciplined and professional practice of the subject that is taught. There are contributions from social epistemology and other sources to these questions, but, as the argument in the papers just referred to demonstrates, they are fundamentally philosophical ones.

36.2.2   What Kind of Theoretical Knowledge and Understanding (If Any) Do Teachers Need to Have and to Engage with in Their Own Terms?

Most teacher education programmes across the world include elements of educational theory, though in the UK these have been reduced to an absolute minimum by successive governments deeply sceptical of its value and of, perhaps, the critical ideological framing provided by some of the sources to which students have been introduced.

However, the nature of this theory varies enormously from country to country. In some post-Soviet countries like Kazakhstan, theory is mainly represented under the label of *Pedagogika*, though a substantial course in Educational Psychology sits alongside this. The contents of one authoritative textbook by Minbayeva on *Pedagogika* used in Kazakhstan, for example, gives an indication of the scope of this course, which focuses on particular educational thinkers, rather than an intro-duction to the disciplines as such. The whole text is formed around a requirement on students to learn and regurgitate what dozens of scholarly figures—from the West, from Kazakhstan and from the former Soviet Union-have said. There is no indication in the text of critical engagement with these sources or their applicability to the teaching practicum that awaits students.

'Pedagogy' remains a feature of teacher education in some western countries too the tradition of teaching about such thinkers, even from the western canon of Rousseau, Montessori, Froebel, Charlotte Mason and A.S. Neale (but with the possible exception of the enduring John Dewey) has been largely abandoned in favour of a more social scientific approach to teacher education. In the UK, in the 1960s and 1970s (and with the introduction of a four year Bachelor of Education degree) the 'great educators' tradition was largely replaced by a 'discipline' based approach to educational theory set out in Tibble's 1966 collection of essays on *The study of education*, which heralded the constitution of educational theory in terms of philosophy, history, psychology and sociology of education. Thus was the study of education defined for several generations of students in the UK and a wider sphere of influence, and, of course, these disciplines continue to feature in pro-grammes of many international education research conferences, in learned societies and in journals (many of which were founded during this period). This 'disci-plinarity' provided an academic edge to teacher preparation and it had the conse-quence of defining educational theory as essentially applied social science—but including philosophy and history—with its source in the academy. It also helped to equip student teachers with critical and analytic tools rather than just descriptive knowledge;

The international tendency towards the 'universitification' of teacher education tended to disseminate this approach to education theory very widely, even if dif-ferent elements tended to surface more powerfully is some places than other—critical theory, for example, in Australia, psychologically based theories of 'in-struction' in the USA.

In the meantime, however, there was developing a movement based in cur-riculum reform that turned this conception of educational theory on its head. For Lawrence Stenhouse, one of the leading figures in this movement, curriculum was a hypothesis that required testing in the classroom (Stenhouse 1975). This principle led directly to the development of classroom action research (notably by John Elliott) which took root in many parts of the world including the USA (where it had its origins in community action programmes), Spain and Australia, where, in par-ticular through Deakin University, it took distinctive radical form and became referred to as 'down under action research'. With this turn and also Schön's development of the idea of 'reflective practice', the source and authority for education theory shifted from the academy and academicians to the classroom and practising teachers:

> The rationale for involving teachers as researchers of their own practice is connected with an aspiration to give them control over what is to count as knowledge about practice. As action researchers, teachers are knowledge generators rather than appliers of knowledge generated by outsiders. (Elliot 1991: 133)

Education theory was, then, what teachers—individually and collectively—worked with and modified in the light of examined experience.

The point of this short historical review is to highlight the sort of debates which have taken place and continue to take place about the sources for teachers' professional knowledge, about what kind of theoretical foundations for their future roles should feature in programmes of teacher education. Our argument is that these debates are essentially philosophical in character and require on-going attention in philosophical insight and argument.

The 'great thinkers' approach invites us to identify with and to model ourselves on people who have developed both their thought and practice in the sphere of education, offering perhaps challenging and even eccentric models. The 'disciplines' approach teaches us the importance of developing concepts that help us to see what might otherwise have remained invisible in the school or classroom (how long did it take us to 'see' racism or sexism in our classrooms?) and forms of inquiry that enable us to look critically at a given set of beliefs and investigate the unknown. It is difficult to see how 'teachers as researchers' can really examine their classrooms without some of this conceptual apparatus or ethical direction. Similarly, it is argued that 'reflective practice' requires us to have something to reflect with as well as something to reflect on.

Philosophical considerations also underpin arguments about the relationship between theory and practice...

36.2.3   How Should We Understand the Relationship Between Theory and Practice?

Anyone who has been involved with the teaching of education theory will also be familiar with the complaint that it is not relevant to practice, or at least that its relevance is not made clear. In the UK this scepticism has led to the marginalisation of educational theory even on the most common route into teaching, the 36 week university-linked Postgraduate Certificate in Education. More radically, school-led 'Qualified Teacher Status only' teacher training programmes have been promoted in recent years, which prioritise direct immersion into schools so that research-based and conceptual deliberation about principles virtually disappears. It represents the victory of craft over theory.

But can teaching be a-theoretical? Surely any teacher has to work with some guiding principles, with some beliefs about what (s)he should be trying to achieve;

about what sorts of effects and consequences flow from acting in one way or another; about the grounds on which one may and may not deal with children, parents, colleagues in particular ways; about what sort of knowledge and what sort of practices might engage and even excite children with learning; and so forth.? Such sets of beliefs constitute educational theory, at least for that teacher.

If that is so, we are left with two particular questions. The first concerns the extent to which one teacher's beliefs might be broadly held in common with those of other teachers (or at least those working in the same school). Do such sets of beliefs begin to constitute the kind of shared professional knowledge and understanding which might allow teachers to work in concert and develop professional conversational communities rather than working as isolated individuals?

But the second question takes us beyond the social processes of the construction of the professional knowledge of teachers to the intellectual ones. Whatever beliefs teachers hold (and we all hold beliefs about education because we have all been through it in some form) do notwe want these to be *sound* beliefs in some sense? Thus Oancea and Orchard ask: 'How can they [teachers] have confidence in the quality of their pedagogical judgment and the soundness of their educational beliefs?' (2012: 580). One route to establishing their soundness is to test them out in the classroom and to see 'what works'. Another is to examine what wider sets of evidence might indicate to be 'best practice'. But as we (and others) have pointed out elsewhere 'what works' is parasitic upon 'what will count as working' (i.e. the normative frame one brings to the assessment).

'Best practice' is not discoverable by empirical investigation alone, but requires the application of some values, of educational aims or principles. Search for the 'soundness' of teachers beliefs leads us inexorably to the requirement that they are rigorously examined not only by reference to their experiential or empirical bases, but also by reference to their capacity to withstand critical argument, their amenability to what Phillips (2007) calls 'intelligent argumentation'. Such rigour and criticality are a *sine qua non* of the existence of the academy. But if the academy is to contribute to teachers' professional knowledge, it has to engage with teachers in a professional 'community of arguers' in which theory and practice both have their place.

While we have argued that many of the questions posed here are philosophical in character, many might also be informed by empirical inquiry. In the field of education—and educational research—philosophical and empirical enquiry need to sit alongside each other.

36.3 Philosophy as Teacher Education Research: Teacher Educators' Engagement in Philosophical Work

Readers may be forgiven for assuming at this point that the philosopher who researches teacher education is set apart from its practice. This is the way in which the popular stereotype of philosophy plays out; as idealised, and potentially interesting but self-indulgent, detracting from the core business of teacher quality and competence as the proper concern of research in teacher education.

But many of the philosophers who are engaged in researching teacher education are themselves teacher educators (for examples, see Heilbronn and Foreman-Peck (eds., 2015) or teachers, e.g. Fordham (2015)). Hogan's ontological interests in the transformative qualities of learning, or Higgins' ethical defence of the 'self-ful', self-cultivating teacher are examples of serious philosophical arguments that have arisen out of direct engagement with teachers' professional development.

Therefore, in this section, we consider philosophy as a mode of teacher education research and the potential difference that being a teacher educator might bring to the philosophical inquiry being undertaken. We distinguish between the potential for specialised philosophical thinking in teacher education and a more general form of philosophy undertaken by teachers and teacher educators. As philosophers who are teacher educators have demonstrated, this potential in each respect remains under-developed.

36.3.1 The Contribution of Teacher Education Practice to Philosophical Inquiry

Specialist philosophy is not for everyone but we have shown in the previous section that philosophy remains as relevant as ever to the education of teachers. Furthermore, there are teachers as well as teacher educators both willing and able in principle to engage with ideas of this nature and type. Positioned within teacher education, they are well-placed to identify valuable new areas for philosophical inquiry rooted in that experience, including the direct impact of policy initiatives, whether through philosophical or inter/multidisciplinary inquiry. Take the following two examples which are currently being investigated because a philosopher who is a practitioner has initiated them.

First, a prominent debate in teacher education at present concerns teachers' knowledge and understanding of the warrants of educational research. Tom Bennett (2013), a teacher whose first degree is in philosophy, has promoted the urgent need for teachers to be able to distinguish good educational research from bad, drawing on a long-standing debate about 'visual, auditory and kinaesthetic learning styles', once popular in teacher education programmes, and now downplayed, following widespread criticism. Bennett argues that teachers themselves should be equipped to distinguish authoritative from non-authoritative research during their initial training, to protect them from the imposition of popular fads and to enable them to identify 'quality' research most likely to impact positively on their practice.

Furthermore, the much neglected area of developing teachers' ethical sensitivity through professional learning is now being addressed by philosophers who are teacher educators (e.g. Orchard and Heilbronn 2014). The moral and ethical dimensions of teachers' classroom practice are recognised widely as critical to good teaching but given relatively little attention in professional formation programmes. Philosophical inquiry has a distinctive and valuable role to play in addressing this deficit, as Heilbronn's earlier work on professional judgement has also illustrated (see Heilbronn in Heilbronn and Foreman-Peck 2015).

Further, as part of an interdisciplinary initiative, philosophers of education have collaborated with other teacher educators to develop deliberative and dialogical approaches to reflecting on everyday decisions in classroom situations (see the chapter by Shortt et al. in Heilbronn and Foreman-Peck 2015). These could be general moral and ethical dimensions of teaching practice; for example, why teach these students, this content, in this context, and in this way? What course of action should I take in this situation? Or other, more specific concerns that might exercise teachers; are my students free to choose what they want? What's a fair way to divide the limited time I have to help my students?

We are not suggesting that only philosophers who are teacher educators research these areas well, or even that they have the best ideas. On the contrary, one distinctive feature of philosophy of education as a discipline is that it provides a means by which the researcher can 'conceive otherwise' in systematic and structured ways within the field. In a time of considerable flux in teacher education, one contribution that those philosophers who are not too intimately bound up in its practice might usefully make would be to initiate critical reflection on the nature and purpose of teacher education, leading to recommendations as to how it might change in the medium to long term future.

Nevertheless, where they are motivated to do so, and adequately equipped, it should be possible for those teachers and teacher educators to think philosophically about their own practice, as well as about the policy and theory which frame it. The problem is, however, few teacher education programmes allow either the intellectual space or an environment conducive to philosophical deliberation. Instead, we are faced at the macro level by a crowded teacher education system driven by instrumental, competence-based learning outcomes, focussed on 'doing' rather than 'thinking'; and at the micro level by set tasks and assignments which are not amenable to philosophical interpretation.

36.4 Philosophy in Teacher Education Research: The Role of Philosophers in Multidisciplinary Research Teams

Teacher education research is part of a wider landscape of shifting funding, structural and governance arrangements for education research more widely, and for publicly funded research and development more generally. This landscape is characterised by increasingly selective and concentrated funding, particularly in conditions of financial restraint. The allocation of funding has been supported by detailed assessments of research performance at organisational (for example in the UK Research Excellence Framework or Hong Kong's Research Assessment

Exercise), publication (for example, the Danish bibliometric points system), and mixed level (individual staff and organisation—for example, New Zealand's Performance-Based Research Fund). In several contexts, research funding is also conditional on evidence of actual or potential impact from research, a step up from past demands for relevance and usefulness (for example, the UK Research Excellence Framework gives significant weight to impact; the UK Research Councils and the European Commission also include impact in their evaluations).

As a result of these incremental changes in the wider environment, recent research policy in the UK and elsewhere, notably in the EU, has moved towards channelling a significant proportion of research funding into schemes driven by sets of 'societal challenges', practical problems, and ongoing policy priorities. Tackling these concerns is generally seen as requiring not only different and complementary skills and knowledge, often straddling not only sectors, but also disciplinary traditions. This trend has led to incentives (and even pressures, within particular financial and performance management contexts) for increased collaboration among higher education researchers and institutions nationally and internationally; as well as between them and researchers and practitioners from a wide range of other settings, including: schools, governmental and non-governmental organisations, for-profit consultancies and international organisations.

Incentives of this nature have been strengthened by the recent shift towards including consideration of 'impact' in the assessment of research. This may happen either at proposal stage (for example, by the UK Research Councils) or output stage (for example, as part of the UK Research Excellence Framework). An implication of this move has been that 'user engagement' and research 'co-design' have become common in many areas of research, including the engagement of practitioners in education research (on which see previous section above). And this provides a further incentive for the breakdown of the traditional disciplinary boundaries protected by the academy.

36.4.1 Collaborative Work in Teacher Education Research

Many, however, see education research as a field or subject connected with different disciplines, rather than as a discipline in its own right—that is, to use Hirst's (1974: 97) terms, "a conceptual and propositional structure" which is a (sub-set of) a particular form of knowledge. Academic educational research and teaching practice are framed by the structural organisation and discursive construction of education departments in higher education institutions. Education departments are a melee of subject specialisms, for example, psychology, sociology, economics, anthropology and the full range of school subjects. Philosophers are also part of the mix, but they are thin on the ground nowadays, presumably as a reflection of the fact that many education departments are now clearly oriented towards the social sciences, rather than the humanities, as their ideal "disciplinary matrices".

Other 'disciplinary' structures based, arguably, on themes rather than distinctive modes of inquiry, such as School Leadership, International and Comparative Education, or Higher Education, have increasingly shaped the organisational structure of university departments of education. Given these arrangements, working across specialisms and disciplines is likely to be part of the everyday practice of education researchers (both higher education and practice-based), as they interact with others within and beyond their own departments.

Thus, teacher education research is embedded in a complex, multidisciplinary and multi-institutional landscape of teaching and of teacher education. It therefore needs to work through networks that can enable the different elements of this landscape to be connected in new and productive ways, given the "collaborative" and "hotly contested" nature of the practice it expresses and supports. Particular challenges and opportunities in terms of the nature of collaborative work in teacher education research arise from the fact that many see this area of inquiry as a natural 'meeting' of disciplines, given the combination of subject and educational expertise involved in designing, offering and researching teacher education programmes.

Further, some see teaching itself either as a means towards the realisation of other practices, rather than being a coherent, socially established practice in its own right (MacIntyre and Dunne 2002, p. 5). Teacher educators themselves may have 'hybrid' or 'migrant' academic identities, having moved into teacher education from discipline specific degrees (e.g. in the sciences, in literature, in mathematics) and, in the process, reframed their knowledge in terms of pedagogically contextualised school 'subjects' and 'curriculum areas', which are different from 'disciplines' or even from university 'papers' or 'subjects'.

In principle, there are a number of different ways in which teacher education research can draw together different disciplines and sectors. While it is possible that collaborations across different areas of expertise may amount to fully integrated interdisciplinary or transdisciplinary research (such as bioinformatics or neuro-science), it is difficult to identify such areas in teacher education research specifically. Perhaps research on communities of practice may approach this model (Lave and Wenger 1991), or, similarly, narrative and ethnographic research. Although work in such areas may have roots in distinctive disciplines, it coalesces into a field of study in its own right, with philosophical contributions intertwined with other theoretical and empirical efforts directed at substantive, methodological and infrastructural development of that particular field.

In other, and arguably more numerous, cases, a research project involving team members from different disciplinary backgrounds may simply function as parallel disciplinary work, joined together by organisational arrangements rather than substantive and methodological integration. Such work may consist of parallel mini-projects, sometimes objectivised as 'work-packages', each of which is based on mono-disciplinary work and produces outputs separately from the others, with a minimum of integration across the entire study. In such cases, philosophical work may be carried out as part of a wider study and lead to important arguments and substantive proposals, but risks to remain largely insulated from other components of that study.

In most cases of collaboration, however, the work progresses through creative multidisciplinary and/or multi-institutional or cross-sectoral arrangements, whereby research involves constant dialogue among team members from different disciplines and sectors, leading to jointly produced outputs. Some of the work on subject pedagogies provides examples; see the contribution of philosophers of education to religious education, citizenship education and moral education, with clear significance to the education of teachers (illustrated, for example, by the *Learning to Teach in Subjects in the Secondary School* book series, edited by S. Capel and M. Leask).

36.4.2 The Contribution of Philosophers to Multidisciplinary Inquiry in Teacher Education

But what can philosophers bring to the mix of backgrounds and knowledge involved in collaborative multidisciplinary and/or cross-sectoral teacher education research?

First, they can contribute to developing and refining an understanding, among the research team and more widely, of the nature of interdisciplinarity, multidisciplinarity and disciplinarity. Such understanding would include not only the sociological aspects of different arrangements for academic work, but also the dynamics of knowledge involved in making particular claims about phenomena situated at the intersection of different areas of expertise or specialisms.

Second, philosophical analysis and the rich and diverse traditions of philosophical argument can provide conceptual and methodological tools to question the extent to which a multidisciplinary programme has developed a shared language to sufficient extent for meaningful communication to happen. For example, they may prompt more systematic and nuanced scrutiny of the claims being made and of the assumptions that each party brings to the use of inevitably normative terms (such as 'cohesion', 'inclusion', 'development', 'potential', 'ability', or 'assessment') in the development of research constructs and measures.

Third, philosophical resources and methods can be mobilised to bring wider perspectives to bear on these assumptions, for example by exploring and critiquing concepts such as learning, experience, values, or 'teacher education' itself (Oancea 2014), as well as by paying close attention to the ontological aspects of being a teacher, the ethical aspects of teachers' actions, and the epistemological aspects of teachers' knowledge (see, for example, the essays in Heilbronn and Foreman-Peck 2015). In doing so, philosophical inquiry can not only help increase conceptual rigour in multidisciplinary communication, but also, and importantly, to introduce different language or new substantive directions of argument, particularly at points when debates, research and action may be at risk of stalling.

And fourth, philosophers can draw on traditions of philosophical exploration of meaning, dialogue and communication (see, e.g. Habermas, Austin, Gadamer), in order to mind the conditions of the communicative situation that surrounds the multidisciplinary research process, and what Gadamer refers to as the complex 'fusion' of horizons that may occur through it.

36.5   Conclusion

Asking well-developed questions, challenging assumptions, making substantive and conceptual contributions, and minding communicative conditions and the wider frames for cross-disciplinary interaction are, of course, roles shared among different participants to a multidisciplinary research project. While the tools and questions of philosophy are "no privileged possession" of a particular section of academia (Floden and Buchmann 1990), philosophers are well-placed to take up such roles, in ways that connect fruitfully and critically with historical traditions of philosophical inquiry, and proceed with the rigour that a philosophical endeavour requires.

References

Bennett, T. (2013). *Teacher proof: Why research in education doesn't always mean what it claims, and what you can do about it*. London: Routledge.

Bridges, D. (2017). *Philosophy in educational research: Epistemology, ethics, politics and quality*. Dordrecht: Springer

Elliott, J. (1991). *Action research for educational change*. Milton Keynes: Open University Press.

Floden, R. E., & Buchmann, M. (1990). Philosophical inquiry in teacher education. In: W. R. Houston (Ed.), *Handbook of research on teacher education*. New York: Macmillan; London: Collier Macmillan.

Fordham, M. (2015). *Teachers and the academic disciplines*. Paper presented to the annual conference of the Philosophy of Education Society of Great Britain, March 28–29.

Heilbronn, R., & Foreman-Peck, L. (Eds.). (2015). *Philosophical perspectives on teacher education*. Oxford: Wiley-Blackwell.

Hirst, P. (1974). *Knowledge and the curriculum*. London: Routledge and Kegan Paul.

Lave, J., & Wenger, E. (1991). *Situated learning: Legitimate peripheral participation*. Cambridge: Cambridge University Press.

MacIntyre, A., & Dunne, J. (2002). Alasdair MacIntyre in dialogue with Joe Dunne. *Journal of Philosophy of Education, 36*(1), 1–19.

Oancea, A. (2014). Teachers' professional knowledge and state-funded teacher education: A (hi) story of critiques and silences. *Oxford Review of Education, 40*(4), 497–519.

Oancea, A., & Orchard, J. (2012). The future of teacher education. *Journal of Philosophy of Education, 46*(4), 574–587.

Orchard, J., & Heilbronn, R. (2014). *Developing ethical reflection on behaviour in the classroom* http://blogs.heacademy.ac.uk/social-sciences/2014/09/22/developing-ethical-reflection-on-behaviour-in-the-classroom-2. Accessed April 9, 2015.

Peters, R. S., & White J. P. (1969). The philosopher's contribution to educational research. *Educational Philosophy and Theory, 1*, 1–15.

Phillips, D. C. (2007). The contested nature of empirical research (and why philosophy of education offers little help). In D. Bridges & R. Smith (Eds.), *Philosophy, methodology and educational research* (pp. 311–332). Oxford: Blackwell.

Stenhouse, L. (1975). *An introduction to curriculum research and development*. London: Heinemann.

Winch, C., & Gingell, J. (2006). *Philosophy and educational policy: A critical introduction*. London: Routledge.

Author Biographies

David Bridges is Professor Emeritus of the University of East Anglia (where he was formerly Dean of the School of Education and Pro Vice Chancellor), Emeritus Fellow of St Edmund's and Homerton Colleges Cambridge and author, most recently, of *Philosophy in Educational Research: Epistemology, Ethics, Politics and Quality*.

Alis Oancea is Professor of Philosophy of Education and Research Policy, Director of Research (Education) and Pro-Proctor at the University of Oxford. Her published work explores the philosophical entanglements of different modes of research, of research policy and assessment, of teacher professionalism and educational practice, and of higher education.

Janet Orchard is a teacher educator in the School of Education, University of Bristol. Her recent publications include "The Contribution of Educational Research to Teachers' Professional Learning—Philosophical Understandings" (2014) and "What training do teachers need? Why teachers need theory" IMPACT 22 (Wiley Blackwell 2015). She co-edited *Learning Teaching from Experience: Multiple Perspectives, International Contexts* (2014).

Chapter 37
Relational Expertise: A Cultural-Historical Approach to Teacher Education

Anne Edwards

37.1 What Is the Problem?

Educational research should, by now, to be able to conceptualise teachers' professional learning with some confidence, after all, human learning is where much of our expertise lies. Yet the ideas underpinning learning to teach and further professional development are often either contested or obfuscated. Challenges that continue to surface include how student teachers are guided as learners in schools; how partnerships between schools and universities support student teachers' learning; how newly qualified teachers continue to learn; and how later continuing professional learning occurs. Each of those concerns has been thoroughly researched, often through careful studies of specific programmes located within different regional and natural policy environments. So much so, that the answer to each question is often "well it depends on whether...".

The "it depends" response has been taken as a weakness and opened the door to searches for simple certainties that can be inscribed in policy to save teachers from themselves. Therefore, as many have observed, teacher education has been configured almost everywhere as a policy problem, to the extent that research questions are frequently shaped by policy concerns, leading to a focus on policy solutions. These questions mean that the research is likely to promote teaching in terms of what Evetts has called "organizational professionalism", where being a professional involves following institutional rules, rather than in terms of "occupational professionalism", where one is held account to professional values and knowledge base of the profession (Evetts 2009).

In response to this reading of how teacher education research is being positioned, a set of theoretical tools will be offered. I shall argue that these tools can be used to understand and promote teachers' professional learning in different teacher edu-

A. Edwards (✉)
University of Oxford, Oxford, England, UK
e-mail: anne.edwards@education.ox.ac.uk

© Springer Nature Singapore Pte Ltd. 2017
M.A. Peters et al. (eds.), *A Companion to Research in Teacher Education*,
DOI 10.1007/978-981-10-4075-7_37

cation systems. The argument will point to how teachers' professional learning at every stage can be seen as knowledge work and how teaching can be defined as a knowledgeable and informed profession engaged in responsive work with learners, so meeting Evetts' criteria for an occupational profession. In doing so, I shall suggest that aspects of teacher education may need to be re-thought in order to create the conditions in which occupational professionalism can flourish.

The starting point is the premise that pedagogy, i.e. teaching to enhance learning, is a relational and therefore responsive activity. That view holds whether we examine relationships between student teachers, university tutors and school-based mentors; teachers' professional conversations with each other; or teacher and pupil interactions. In this chapter, the focus is the first two relationships, though the arguments presented are also relevant to the third. I shall first suggest that the relational aspects of professional learning will benefit from being labelled and valued and will do so by drawing on the ideas of *relational expertise, common knowledge* and *relational agency* (Edwards 2010, 2012) which have been developed within a cultural-historical account of learning.

37.2 Cultural-Historical Approaches to Learning

Cultural-historical accounts of learning draw on the work of Vygotsky. Writing in Russia in the 1920s and early 1930s, he was interested in how mind is shaped in different environments. In brief, how does culture enter mind, how do people take on what is important in the cultures they inhabit, how are concepts which carry what matters culturally acquired and used? This recognition that mind and action arise within societal conditions is the central thesis in the cultural-historical approach to human learning, with implications for how we think about, for example, concepts, practices, activities and actions. In this section, I focus on just four aspects of cultural-historical theory: concepts as cultural tools; the dialectical nature of human learning; mediation; and motives in practices, activities and actions.

Vygotsky saw concepts as tools, which have cultural origins and are used in ways which are valued by those who already inhabit cultural practices. For him learning was not simply a matter of internalisation; his view was that learning occurs through a process of internalisation and externalisation. In brief, a learner's ability to work with conceptual tools develops through a dialectical relationship between the learner and the practice, where learners refine their grasp of concepts using them as tools to work in and on the practice. The idea of the dialectic is important, not only because it emphasises externalisation and the impact of the learner on the world she inhabits, but also because it alerts us to the demands made on learners for how tools are used (Hedegaard 2012).

The dynamic iteration between what the learner brings to the practice and the demands in the practice is a key to how cultural-historical approaches to learning are able to avoid an analytic separation of individual and society. The dynamic also points to the role of the expert alongside the learner, helping them interpret the demands as well as respond to them. In brief, learners enter a potential learning situation and try to make sense of it using the knowledge they already have. But their agency and desire to make sense is only one side of the dialectic, they also need to pay attention to the demands. A situation will present a number of potential demands which can take learners' understandings forward; but only some, and perhaps none, of the demands will be recognised by the learner. What they recognise will depend on what they are able to interpret in the situation.

For example, a 6-year old might enjoy a visit to an ancient fort, may recognise that the walls she climbs over were built as a defence and might begin to consider why the walls were needed. The 16-year old, bringing more knowledge of the history of the fort, might examine how the walls were built in relation to the lie of the land, who the potential enemies were and might consider these aspects in relation to what weaponry was available at different periods in the fort's history. In both cases, it is possible that neither learner would recognise the conceptual demands I have just outlined. It is therefore useful to have someone at hand who can steer attention to what is important in relation to what the learners need to know, to help them connect their attempts at making sense of the environment with publicly validated knowledge. These demands are not random, but can be seen in terms of curricula or pathways towards expertise in a field.

There are therefore clear roles for teachers within cultural-historical approaches to pedagogy: helping learners to orient towards the demands; enabling them to use their existing understandings in interpreting them; challenging their interpretations; offering them fresh conceptual tools based in validated public knowledge; and ensuring they use those tools in further problem-solving. Mediating publicly accepted knowledge is therefore not simply a matter of informing or telling; rather, the Vygotskian dialectic acknowledges that learners recognise and respond to new challenges using conceptual tools, and the role of the teacher is to be at hand to increase the conceptual demand and offer conceptual support.

Vygotsky explained the role of the teacher as follows: "[the teacher] has to become the director of the social environment...where he (sic) acts like a pump, filling up the students with knowledge, there he can be replaced with no trouble at all by a textbook, by a dictionary, by a map, by a nature walk" (Vygotsky 1997, p. 339). Vygotsky's solution was the knowledgeable and "scientifically trained teacher" (p. 344) who can help the learner make connections while they work on tasks. The Vygotskian teacher is alongside the learner, sometimes close-by and sometimes at more of a distance, as the learner takes control. Teaching, including teacher education, is from this perspective, a relational activity, which involves recognising what learners bring to a potential learning encounter and calibrating the conceptual demands and tools offered to them in order to orient, guide and challenge them.

The relational interactions between teacher and learner occur in the practices that make up schooling and teacher education. These practices are cultural products with histories, values and purposes and are likely to differ between schools, and between schools and universities. Leont'ev, a colleague of Vygotsky's has helped us understand how purposes and motives are embedded in practices and are revealed in what we do in the activities that make up a practice (Leont'ev 1978). Key concepts for him were the *object of activity* and *object motive*. These can be seen as the task being worked on and the motive for action that it calls forth. The object motive arises through an interaction of the person with the task, where the actor interprets and responds to the demands of the task using the concepts that matter in the practice in which they are located. For example, a parent, a teacher and a football coach may see the same child in very different ways and therefore want to work on their developmental trajectory differently.

Like Vygotsky, Leont'ev was concerned with the connection between individual and society, recognising that the individual motives shaping actions on tasks arise at the level of society. Hedegaard has drawn on Leont'ev to create a useful heuristic (Fig. 37.1), which allows us to see the relationship between societal purposes, how they are mediated by the motives embedded in institutional practices and are played out or worked around in individual actions in activities (Hedegaard 2012).

The four analytic planes in Fig. 37.1 are: societal priorities reflected, for example, in policy documents; institutional practices such as those found in schools or university departments, each with their own motives or objectives; activity settings such as a classroom or team meeting where each activity will carry demands, which may or may not be recognised by participants; and the intentional actions of individuals in the activities.

If we use Fig. 37.1 to consider what teachers do in a teaching activity we can ask useful questions about the vertical alignment of motives, purposes and priorities in the third column. The answers can sometimes reveal considerable discrepancies between planes, for example where national policies based on high-stakes testing inhibit the use of teaching methods such as talk in group work in English language classes. If we also use the model to examine alignment in purposes across collaborating organisations such as a school-university partnership we are likely to find large horizontal discrepancies between what matters in institutional practices. For example, creating tomorrow's teachers might be the major motive in the initial teacher education (ITE) practices of the university department; while recruiting good science teachers might be the major motive for a school science department

Entity	Process	Dynamic
Society	Political economy	Societal needs/conditions
Institution (e.g. a school, department, team …)	Practice	Values/motives /objectives
Activity setting (e.g. a lesson, meeting …)	Activity/situation (with potential for individual learning)	Motivation/demands
Person	Actions in an activity (which may or may not give rise to learning)	Motive/intentions

Fig. 37.1 Planes of analysis (after Hedegaard 2012)

when involved in ITE. Student teachers will, I suggest, experience more coherence in ITE programmes where there is understanding of and mutual respect for these different motives, than where it is absent.

37.3 Relational Expertise, Relational Agency and Common Knowledge in Teachers' Learning

Over the last decade or so, I have drawn on cultural-historical theory to develop the idea of *relational expertise*, seeing it as a form of expertise which augments one's specialist expertise as, for example, a mathematics teacher or university tutor, and makes responsive collaboration possible (Edwards 2010, 2012). In brief, it involves the ability: to take the standpoints of potential collaborators; recognise what matters for them when working on an object of activity such as a learner's trajectory; make visible to them what matters for you in the task; jointly expand the interpretation of the task; and calibrate responses so that you can work together on it. This kind of work occurs at *sites of intersecting practices* (Edwards 2010), where people from different backgrounds or practices come together, suggesting that relational expertise is relevant for institutional collaborations such as school-university partnerships, for mentor-student teacher encounters and for teachers' interactions which aim at practice development.

Relational expertise enables the exercise of *relational agency* when people work together on a complex object of activity (Edwards 2010, 2012). Relational agency involves expanding the interpretation of a phenomenon by bringing to bear the different expertise or conceptual resources offered by collaborators. This expansion means that more aspects of the phenomenon are recognised and worked on. The wider interpretation is then responded to while drawing on the strengths of each collaborator. In ITE, the phenomenon to be worked on is likely to be the learning trajectory of a student teacher. The trajectory is likely to be enhanced if teacher mentor, university tutor and student teacher all bring to bear their knowledge to interpret its development and to negotiate how to support it.

These interpretations and negotiations are mediated by what I have termed *common knowledge* (Edwards 2010, 2012). The concept of common knowledge developed in my research on inter-professional collaborations, where I noticed that successful collaborations were mediated by a resource, which consisted of a mutual understanding of the motives of each collaborator. I came to describe common knowledge as a respectful understanding of different professional motives, what matters for one as a professional, which can mediate responsive collaborations on complex problems.

In this sense common knowledge is what most Vygotskians would recognise as a second stimulus. In brief, the first stimulus is the problem or phenomenon being worked on and the second stimulus is made up of the cultural resources or tools available to interpret and work on it. The second stimulus provides possibilities for action and enables an actor to control her behaviour as she tackles the problem.

Common knowledge, however, does not arise spontaneously; attention needs to be paid to the conditions in which it is built. My analyses of inter-professional collaborations suggest that it is created over time in interactions, which overtly emphasise the following:

- recognising similar long-term general goals, such as children's wellbeing, as some kind of affective or value-laden glue that holds all motives together;
- revealing values and motives in discussions, by legitimising asking for and giving reasons for interpretations and suggestions; and
- listening to, recognising and engaging with the values and motives of others, i.e. what matters to them.

I shall first consider the implications of the three relational concepts I have just outlined for ITE, while pointing to their potential for addressing some frequently found difficulties. One common difficulty is the difference in messages given by university and placement schools so that student teachers feel confused and torn between differing demands. For example, evidence from a doctoral study currently underway showed that while the university department in question saw the final school placement as the opportunity for student teachers to stretch themselves as learners, the placement schools tended, for a variety of reasons, to make relatively low demands on them over that period (Tan, work in progress). At a more detailed level Tan's study of how student teachers learn to use Assessment for Learning (AfL) while on placement in school, showed the difficulties arising for students when schools interpreted AfL in terms of summative assessment, while the university emphasised its formative aspects.

The gap between universities and school in ITE programmes has been long documented, with reflection on practice frequently being offered as a way of bridging that gap (Edwards et al. 2002). All these studies, implicitly at least, indicate the efforts that student teachers need to make to connect what they meet in university-based courses, with what they experience when working in classrooms. It is little wonder that each new cohort of student teachers, year on year, finds it difficult to make the connections. This failure provides a rationale for promoting school-based programmes and the risk of creating local dialects of professional practice which are not tested against publicly validated knowledge about teaching.

A cultural-historical approach to teacher education offers a way out of this impasse because it is premised in the view that: (i) informed actions arise in societal conditions and therefore students will learn to become occupational professionals in schools where national or state policy is mediated in ways that allow teachers' actions to be informed by powerful professional knowledge; and (ii) learning is evidenced and judged by how demands are interpreted as well as how they are addressed, i.e., assessment of performance is not enough. This analysis means that attention needs to be paid to the conditions in which student teachers' actions as beginning teachers arise, to ensure that they are informed by the best ideas and evidence available and that the demands presented to student teachers allow them to move forward as learners with the expert guidance and challenge of their mentors.

My argument is that both universities and schools should be involved in educating tomorrow's teachers as thoughtful and responsive professionals, but the nature of the relationship needs re-thinking, so that the role of universities in relation to schools is seen as one of intellectual and conceptual support at the institutional level (see Fig. 37.1).

As a first step, attention needs to be paid to building common knowledge as a resource for aligning and mutually informing the different practices in which student teachers are placed as learners. The work of teacher mentors is located within the institutional practices of their schools. Consequently, their actions in the activities of planning, teaching, etc. are likely, particularly in school practices that value organisational professionalism, to be given direction by what matters at the institutional plane. For example, Tan has found that most of the teacher mentors in his study made judgments about student teachers' progress in relation to the criteria used by Ofsted, the government inspectors who visit and grade schools (Tan, in progress), even though these criteria were not directly relevant to student teachers' progress through the ITE programme.

Some mentor-tutor links do draw on common knowledge as a resource and use it as a second stimulus to give student teachers a coherent experience. Douglas gives an example of one mentor who "…read academic literature out of interest and was aware of the research work happening at the university…[and] his confidence in adapting tasks to the needs of the student teacher came from a long-standing relationship with the department at the university and his work with the tutor." (Douglas 2010, p. 42); but he was a rare example in Douglas's study and was using common knowledge created when the ITE programme was initiated 20 years earlier.

Worryingly the "Work of Teacher Educators" (WOTE) project revealed that among the 13 UK teacher educators whose workloads were studied in detail, "relationship maintenance" with placement schools was by far the most time-consuming activity for most of the participants. The research team described this work as follows: "Relationship maintenance included building, sustaining and repairing the complex and fragile networks of personal relationships that allow initial teacher education programmes, school partnerships and, indeed, HE Education departments to function." (Ellis et al. 2014, p. 40). The mean amount of time spent on maintaining relationships with schools and mentors was 13.192 h in the data collection week, with a maximum of 31.0 h recorded, and it was frequently carried out at the expense of engaging in research. The team's argument, echoing Evetts, is that as a result teacher educators have become proletarianised. The consequence of spending so much time on "relationship maintenance" is that ITE is being sidelined in an academic world which increasingly values heavy hitting researchers. As a result, teacher education is in danger of being removed from the University sector in some countries, whether it is placed entirely in schools or privatised.

There is clearly work to be done to develop a less personal and more professional approach to understanding what matters for both mentors and university tutors, so that the relationships are no longer so time-consuming. I am suggesting that they are recast in terms of relational expertise aimed at building common knowledge, where schools also recognise what matters for university staff and the practices they inhabit. That common knowledge can be a resource ensuring that student teachers enjoy some coherence between the school and university elements in their training programmes.

Recently Sannino and Engeström have given account of how what they term the "relational infrastructures" of an intervention in an Italian primary school built a common understanding of the potential in a set of conceptual and material resources among teachers, student teachers and pupils (Sannino and Engeström in press). They argue that the intervention benefitted from having shared problems to work on, so that relational infrastructures were built slowly and arose from much sharing and mutual assistance as they tackled problems, such as how to teach fractions to young children. The processes in the intervention allowed for the building of common knowledge as a resource or second stimulus, which brought coherence to the demands placed on the student teachers, enabling student teachers and school-based teachers to see what the pupils were capable of doing.

In summary, once we see ITE as the formation of occupational professionals, we need to attend to how their professional agency is strengthened, while also connecting them to the publicly validated knowledge that marks the profession. In order to do, so we need to consider how we design learning environments and position mentors and university tutors within them, so that the environment itself is knowledge-rich, presenting demands which take forward the learning of beginning teachers.

I now turn to the relational work of established teachers by focusing on the development of knowledge-rich practices. Teachers' collaborative practice development is not a new idea, but we perhaps need to be clearer about how this is done.

Recently, Hermansen has examined knowledge work in teacher meetings aimed at implementing AfL. She has defined knowledge work in cultural-historical terms as "the actions that teachers carry out as they work with and upon the knowledge that informs their professional practice." (Hermansen 2014, p. 470). The knowledge work she traced over time involved teachers in recognising the histories in the practices they inhabited, and moving forward to a jointly produced and co-owned refreshed version of future practice.

The interactions she captured were typical of the relational work that so often is hidden and backstage. Yet it seems essential if teachers, as occupational professionals, are to recognise the potential in new tools and fashion them to fit the purposes of institutional practices, while also reshaping those practices. The new tools, a new form of assessment, were not taken as readymade and to be easily inserted established routines. Instead, their potentially disruptive qualities were acknowledged in the moves the teachers made towards the renewal of school practices. As they struggled to make sense of the potential in the new tools and to connect them to what mattered for them, they articulated the knowledge that motivated them as professionals. In the meetings that Hermansen recorded, the teachers first constructed common knowledge, which included their interpretations of what mattered in school practices, and then used that common knowledge to construct new understandings of the potential to be found in formative assessment as a pedagogic tool, which could inform future school practice.

Unfortunately, there is little evidence that this kind of knowledge work is commonplace in mentoring conversations with student teachers schools. It is, however, not impossible to achieve. Gonzales and Carter, for example, have argued that student teachers "… should have the opportunity to discuss openly their personal histories and understandings of teaching…to help them understand what drives their interpretations and decisions in classroom contexts." (Gonzalez and Carter 1996, p. 46). They also suggest that there is a role for the cooperating teacher (mentor) in enabling these discussions with them so that learners can connect their limited understandings quite overtly to the networks of concepts that comprise expert knowledge in teaching.

37.4 Cultural-Historical Approaches to Teacher Education

The suggestions made in the previous section involve just a few of the tools that the cultural-historical tool box offers teacher education to help it move on from weak "it depends" responses, without falling into the trap of thinking that the scientifically trained teachers that Vygotsky imagined (Vygotsky 1997) would be unthinkingly applying research findings as they planned and worked in classrooms. The actions of the Vygotskian teacher arise in social conditions, which are informed by publicly validated knowledge and these actions are evidence of a capacity to agentically externalise those understandings to interpret and shape those practices.

Van Huizen and his colleagues, arguing for a Vygotskian teacher education put the case as follows:

> …the close association of action and meaning in Vygotskian theory suggests that apprentices will have to orient themselves towards the meanings of teaching informing the practice in which they become participants. In particular, they will have to orient themselves towards a public standard of teaching that reflects the values and goals in the cultural and political setting of the schooling in which they are engaging. This orientation should not lead them to be recruited into any existing ideology, but clarify and define their own allegiance and commitment to teaching as the core of their professional identity. (van Huizen et al. 2005, p. 276)

Back in 2002, Peter Gilroy and David Hartley and I went a little further, by suggesting that a Vygotskian approach to learning, with its emphasis on externalisation aimed at improving the conditions in which we act, allows us to ask some fundamental questions about what kinds of teachers and learners does society need and therefore how should practices be changed. Our answers led us to call for a future-oriented teacher education which produces teachers who are able to hold an ethical commitment to societal wellbeing together with developing agentic problem-solving in learners. We suggested that this outcome could be achieved through what we described as "collaborative responses to uncertainty" (Edwards et al. 2002).

The uncertainty we observed was both the unwelcome churn of education policies and in the welcome responses that children make in classrooms. Our argument was that informed teachers could, if not trammelled by cultures of compliance, work agentically and collaboratively with university-based colleagues to address both kinds of uncertainty. Over the last 15 years cultural-historical accounts of teacher education have proliferated in encouraging ways. Many are captured in Ellis et al. (2010) where, in a number of contributions, Engeström's work on systemic change through the tools of activity theory was used powerfully to consider how teacher education systems could adapt to changing demands or partnerships be strengthened.

The potential of cultural-historical ideas for re-thinking teacher education is now also being recognised in the US. Zeichner, Payne and Brayko have, for example, drawn on cultural-historical activity theory (CHAT) to ask the question whose knowledge counts in teacher education. In an argument that resonates strongly with the relational approach advocated in the present chapter, they "… call for a rethinking of the epistemology of teacher preparation in the United States and for the development of new forms of shared responsibility for preparing teachers among colleges and universities, schools, and local communities" (Zeichner et al. 2015, p. 123). They suggest that the way to achieve this is through creating "new hybrid spaces in university teacher education where academic, school-based, and community-based knowledge come together in less hierarchical and haphazard ways to support teacher learning" (p. 3). In the final section of this chapter, I describe one example of a hybrid space, or site of intersecting practices, to illustrate how the ideas outlined so far may be put into action.

37.5   The Oxford Education Deanery: A New Hybrid Space

ITE has a long history at the University of Oxford, beginning in 1885 with the University Day Training College, its more recent history, as well as focusing increasingly on research, has included the Oxford Internship Scheme, a one-year post-graduate ITE programme for secondary school teachers based on a deep partnership with local schools. In 2013, this partnership was developed to create a new site of intersecting practices, The Oxford Education Deanery. The Deanery now includes collaborations in continuing professional learning and school development and in pedagogic research in schools as well as ITE.

When the Deanery was first discussed in early 2010, the landscape of English teacher education provision was complex, with an increasing number of routes towards qualification as a teacher, some of which with very little university involvement. But the policy context was not the original driver for the initiative. Instead, it was based on the view, rehearsed in this chapter, that both ITE programmes and schools would benefit from building stronger inter-institutional connections which would inform the practices in both the university department and schools.

The idea of the Deanery as a hybrid space was offered to Headteachers of partnership schools in February 2010. It was presented to them as a multilayered system of distributed expertise, where the three layers were: ITE, continuing professional learning and research. Its potential for enhancing the work of all partners was recognised immediately by the Headteachers and after three years of building common knowledge across the different practices involved, through meetings and discussion, the Deanery was officially launched in November 2013. All nine Oxford secondary schools signed up to it, and the intention is to involve all partnership schools over the next few years.

The Deanery was conceived as a site of intersecting, but different, practices with each bringing the specialist expertise it offers to local education. The objects of activity, when practitioners in the different practices have engaged in knowledge work together, have included the learning trajectories of student teachers on the post-graduate programme; newly qualified teachers in schools; changes in ways of teaching physics in a school science department; annual action research fellowships; collaboration to ensure that senior practitioners can bring their expertise to bear on university research on school exclusion; and the development of collaborative practices in schools.

Key to all of these, and the other activities also undertaken, is that attention is paid to what matters for all collaborators. School-based practitioners are participants in Deanery activities and their professional knowledge and motives count in that work. At the same time university tutors are explicit about what matters to them when collaborating with teachers and school leaders, and do not politely hold back if research-based knowledge might be useful to schools or the need to learn more about what matters for the school.

Some of the most interesting developments have been initiated by school-based colleagues. These include a 5-year jointly designed programme of support for newly qualified teachers and a version of the university's masters programme tailored to the needs of local schools. Each initiative has been developed by building and drawing on the common knowledge that consists of the professional motives that shapes each practice. Colleagues in both sets of practices have been adept at exercising relational expertise as they do so, taking time to be clear about each others' motives and ensuring that developments address what matters in each practice. The outcome has been an ability to exercise relational agency, to expand interpretations of the problems being worked on and ensure that relevant expertise is brought to bear.

These processes necessarily take time, and they do not fit well with the kind of business model that seeks profit in every transaction. Nonetheless, they appear to be meeting needs. The University is delighted with how the Deanery provides evidence of how it tries to be a local resource as well as a global player in research. Researchers in the Education Department have ready access to expert school-based practitioners for reference groups and advice on how schools are interpreting upcoming education policies and the intention is that student teachers will have smoother transitions when they move between university and school. Schools benefit from teachers being engaged with university research as action researchers, research collaborators and sounding boards for new research-based ideas. Examples of how research is taken into school practices have included changes in school policy for the support of beginning teachers and developments in carrying out observations of teaching and giving feedback to established staff across several schools.

The Deanery appears to have created a site where practices can intersect; where what matters for each participant, their knowledge and expertise, counts; and where interpretations of problems of practice, whether teaching or research, are expanded so that the resources of the wider set of practices are brought into play. Because teachers and tutors change responsibilities or move on, effort is needed to make sure that common knowledge continues to be built and used. A relentless commitment is needed; but this is not the work of the teacher educators described WOTE project. It is premised in a shared set of values about what matters in education locally as the glue that holds the practices together.

We have yet to assess the impact on student teachers, but would hope that the growing valuing of educational research in and across schools is mediating unwelcome aspects of national policies in schools and helping senior leadership teams in creating the conditions for teachers' knowledge work and occupational professionalism to flourish.

37.6 Putting Research into Action

This contribution to the collection has not been about applying research findings to educational practice. Instead, it has attempted to indicate how a set of concepts, rooted in cultural-historical theory and refined in a series of research studies, can be used as tools to question and consider how the conditions for creating and supporting teachers' occupational professionalism can be accomplished. In doing so it has begun to indicate how the same conditions can support future-oriented pedagogic research. Cultural-historical approaches to learning see concepts, such as the three at the core of this chapter, as tools to use to make the world a better a place. These tools get refashioned while used in different practices, making them useful in any educational context where the intention is to create and support thinking teachers and the research that informs their work. It is a distinctly modernist agenda, but then so is Education.

References

Douglas, A. (2010). What and how do student teachers learn from working in different social situations of development in the same school? In V. Ellis, A. Edwards, & P. Smagorinsky (Eds.), *Learning teaching: Cultural historical perspectives on teacher education and development* (pp. 30–44). London: Routledge.

Edwards, A. (2010). *Being an expert professional practitioner: The relational turn in expertise.* Dordrecht: Springer.

Edwards, A. (2012). The role of common knowledge in achieving collaboration across practices. *Learning, Culture and Social Interaction, 1*(1), 22–32.

Edwards, A., Gilroy, P., & Hartley, D. (2002). *Rethinking teacher education: An interdisciplinary analysis*. London: Falmer.

Ellis, V., Edwards, A., & Smagorinsky, P. (Eds.). (2010). *Learning teaching: Cultural historical perspectives on teacher education and development*. London: Routledge.

Ellis, V., McNicholl, J., Blake, A., & McNally, J. (2014). Academic work and proletarianisation: A study of higher education-based teacher educators. *Teaching and Teacher Education, 40*(2), 33–43.

Evetts, J. (2009). New professionalism and new public management: Changes continuities and consequences. *Comparative Sociology, 8*, 247–266.

Gonzalez, L., & Carter, K. (1996). Correspondence in cooperating teachers' and student teachers' interpretations of classroom events. *Teaching and Teacher Education, 12*(1), 39–47.

Hedegaard, M. (2012). The dynamic aspects in children's learning and development. In M. Hedegaard, A. Edwards, & M. Fleer (Eds.), *Motives in children's development: Cultural-historical approaches* (pp. 9–27). New York: Cambridge University Press.

Hermansen, H. (2014). Recontxtualising assessment resources for use in local settings: Opening up the black box of teachers' knowledge work. *The Curriculum Journal, 25*(4), 470–494.

Leont'ev, A. N. (1978). The problem of activity in psychology. In *Activity, consciousness and personality*. Upper Saddle River, NJ: Prentice Hall. Available online at http://Marxists.anu.edu.au/archive/leontev/works/1978. April 29, 2004.

Sannino, A., & Engeström, Y. (in press). Relational agency, double stimulation and the object of activity; An intervention study in a primary school. In A. Edwards (Ed.), *Working relationally in and across practices: Cultural-historical approaches to collaboration*. Cambridge: Cambridge University Press.

van Huizen, P., van Oers, B., & Wubbels, T. (2005). A Vygotskian perspective on teacher education. *Journal of Curriculum Studies, 37*(3), 267–290.

Vygotsky, L. S. (1997). *Educational psychology*. Boca Raton, FL: St. Lucie Press.

Zeichner, K., Payne, K., & Brayko, K. (2015). Democratizing teacher education. *Journal of Teacher Education, 66*(2), 122–135.

Author Biography

Anne Edwards is Professor Emerita at the University of Oxford Department of Education. She is co-founder of the Oxford University Centre for Socio-cultural and Activity Theory Research (OSAT) and holds honorary degrees from the Universities of Helsinki and Oslo. She has written extensively on learning in the professions.

Chapter 38
Researching Teacher Education Policy: A Case Study from Scotland

Aileen Kennedy

38.1 Introduction

Teacher education policy across the United Kingdom as a whole suffers from a lack of sustained and systematic research, both to inform its development and to evaluate its enactment, a point highlighted by Christie et al. (2012) in their report for the British Educational Research Association. In Scotland, a small country with a population of approximately 50,000 teachers, and eight universities offering teacher education, this situation is equally marked. While there are some exciting developments happening in Scotland in terms of teacher education policy, there remains very little research employing a policy studies approach. This chapter seeks to analyse what research there is with a view to identifying gaps and barriers that might support a more focused future research agenda. It should be acknowledged that the situation in relation to policy research in teacher education is mirrored in education research more generally, being limited in its impact due to its small-scale, fragmented and non-cumulative nature (Whitty 2006). This is exacerbated by the tendency for a significant proportion of teacher educators to focus on localised, action research type scholarly activity, compounded by a lack of funding from government and research councils (Brown 2008).

This chapter takes a case study approach in reviewing studies published after 2010 that focus on the analysis of teacher education policy in Scotland. 2010 is significant for Scotland as it marked the instigation of the widest ranging review and proposed policy reform of teacher education in recent history—'the Donaldson Review'. The chapter provides an overview of the range and type of policy studies carried out as well as providing an analysis of the methodologies employed, before providing an overall assessment of the current state of policy studies research in

A. Kennedy (✉)
University of Edinburgh, Edinburgh, Scotland, UK
e-mail: aileen.kennedy@ed.ac.uk

© Springer Nature Singapore Pte Ltd. 2017
M.A. Peters et al. (eds.), *A Companion to Research in Teacher Education*,
DOI 10.1007/978-981-10-4075-7_38

relation to Scottish teacher education policy, and suggesting some ways forward. First, however, the chapter provides a brief overview of the current policy context, by way of orientation.

38.2 The Scottish Policy Context

38.2.1 Public Policy Governance in Scotland

Scotland is part of the UK, but has had a devolved Scottish Parliament since 1999, one of its devolved functions being education (together with health, housing, justice, rural affairs and transport). While education was formally devolved at this point, there has traditionally always been separate education legislation for Scotland. Politically, there is a will to explore yet further separation from the UK as a whole, and in September 2014 a referendum on Scottish independence was held, resulting in a narrow majority (55%) against independence. The Referendum resulted in a process to devolve yet more powers to the Scottish Government, in particular, fiscal powers. This process is ongoing, although the Scottish Government already has responsibility for much of the public policy portfolio.

The Scottish Government is elected by a proportional representation system, rather than a 'first past the post' system, resulting in greater likelihood of a coalition Government. However, the current Government is a majority one, led by the Scottish National Party (SNP), a left of centre party with a strong social justice and anti-austerity ideology. Cairney and McGarvey (2013) note that the public sector in Scotland accounts for a much greater proportion of resource than it does elsewhere in the UK, and talk of the distinctive 'Scottish policy style' which privileges ideas of social justice and promotes a partnership approach to governance involving significant dialogue between Ministers, civil servants and relevant stakeholders in taking forward an outcomes-based approach which requires stakeholders to work together to address societal challenges. This way of working is very much reflected in the governance and control of teacher education, with key stakeholders (government, universities, employers, unions and special interest groups) being consulted and involved in most major policy developments. This background is important in seeking to understand the context in which policy studies might be carried out in Scotland, and what impact such studies might have. A more detailed exploration of the political and policy context for teacher education can be found in Hulmes and Kennedy (2015, forthcoming).

38.2.2 Teacher Education Policy in Scotland

In 2010, the Scottish Government commissioned a wholesale review of teacher education, to be led by recently retired senior chief inspector of Her Majesty's

Inspectorate, Graham Donaldson. The review, entitled '*Teaching Scotland's Future: Report of a review of teacher education in Scotland*', reported in 2011 making 50 recommendations, all of which were accepted by Government in whole, in part or in principle. Amongst other things, the recommendations called for: greater partnership between schools, local authorities and universities in supporting teacher education; a revised suite of professional standards, including a new 'standard for active registration'; the establishment of a new Scottish College for Educational Leadership; new forms of undergraduate initial teacher education encompassing a greater focus on disciplinary study outwith education; and all professional learning to be at Masters level (although notably, did not call for a Masters qualified teaching profession). The Report as a whole called for what Donaldson variously termed '21st century professionalism', 'extended professionalism', enhanced professionalism' and a 'reconceptualised model of professionalism', suggesting a radical change to teacher education and teachers' work in Scotland. It is also worth noting that this review of teacher education was taking place at a time of significant curriculum reform (see Priestley 2013) which positioned teachers as curriculum developers and encouraged much more professional autonomy than the previous curriculum structures required.

Shortly after the Donaldson Review of teacher education was commissioned, the Scottish Government invited Professor Gerry McCormac, Principal of the University of Stirling, to carry out a review of teacher employment in Scotland: '*Advancing professionalism in teaching: The report of the review of teacher employment in Scotland*', also published in 2011. Several of the recommendations in this report also had a bearing on teacher education policy, not least the controversial recommendation to discontinue the internationally admired Chartered Teacher scheme (for further discussion of the Chartered Teacher Scheme see Ingvarson 2009; McGeer 2009).

While some current teacher education policy initiatives can be traced clearly to either the Donaldson Report or the McCormac Report, other important developments are not as easily attributable to one particular policy review. For example, in granting the General Teaching Council for Scotland (GTCS) full independent status in 2012, the Scottish Government charged it with developing a system of 'professional reaccreditation' whereby registered teachers would have to prove their eligibility to remain on the register on a periodic basis. As a result of negotiations between and among the various stakeholders, this eventually became 'Professional Update'—a process whereby teachers are required to get their line manager to sign-off to say that they have undertaken appropriate professional learning activities over the past five years. While the genesis of Professional Update can be traced to a Scottish Government imperative, its links to other aspects of teacher education policy, such as the revised professional standards, locate it firmly within the post-Donaldson milieu of policy activity. The development of policy emanating from the Donaldson Review and Report has been based on a network governance approach, with multiple working groups, constituted by members drawn from all the key stakeholder groups, with an emphasis on consensus building (Kennedy and Doherty 2012).

38.3   Approach Taken

In identifying studies/articles for analysis in this chapter, a literature search was conducted using the search terms "policy", "teacher education" and 'Scotland", restricting publication dates to post-2010, and searching in peer-reviewed academic journals. This resulted in ten articles being identified which met the criteria set:

1. Gray, D. & Weir, D. (2014). Retaining public and political trust: teacher education in Scotland. *Journal of Education for Teaching, 40*(5), 569–587.
2. Humes, W. (2014). Professional update and practitioner enquiry: Old wine in new bottles? *Scottish Educational Review, 46*(2), 54–72.
3. Hulme, M. & Menter, I. (2011). South and North—Teacher education policy in England and Scotland: a comparative textual analysis. Scottish Educational Review, 43(2), 70–90.
4. Kennedy, A., Barlow, W. & MacGregor, J. (2012). 'Advancing Professionalism in Teaching'? An exploration of the mobilisation of the concept of professionalism in the McCormac Report on the Review of Teacher Employment in Scotland. *Scottish Educational Review, 44*(2), 3–13.
5. Kennedy, A. & Doherty, R. (2012). Professionalism and partnership: Panaceas for teacher education in Scotland? *Journal of Education Policy, 27*(6), 835–848.
6. Menter, I. & Hulme, M. (2011). Teacher education reform in Scotland: national and global influences. *Journal of Education for Teaching, 37*(4), 387–397.
7. Menter, I. & Hulme, M. (2012). Teacher education in Scotland—riding out the recession? *Educational Research, 54*(2), 149–160.
8. O'Brien, J. (2011). Continuing professional development for Scottish teachers: tensions in policy and practice. *Professional Development in Education, 37*(5), 777–792.
9. Reeves, J. & Drew, V. (2012). Relays and relations: tracking a policy initiative for improving teacher professionalism. *Journal of Education Policy, 27*(6), 711–730.
10. Watson, C. & Fox, A. (2015). Professional reaccreditation: constructing educational policy for career-long teacher professional learning. *Journal of Education Policy, 30*(1), 132–144.

An analytical frame was devised to ensure consistent analysis of key features in each article. The frame included the following aspects:

- Location of article, i.e. journal name
- Particular policy focus under investigation
- Motivation for/purpose of study
- Funding of study
- Methodological approach adopted
- Theoretical frame employed
- Anticipated/intended impact of study

- Inward/outward referencing, i.e. focus purely on Scotland (inward) or Scotland located within the wider global context (outward)

Each article was read in turn with responses noted against each of the above categories. In some cases the responses were explicit in the article, but in other cases they were either implicit or not discernable. The analysis below summarises the key aspects of each article in turn, in line with the categories in the analytical frame. It thereafter takes each aspect within the analytical frame and discusses the common themes, divergences and omissions.

38.4   Analysis

Gray and Weir (2014) set out to provide an account of 'key periods, players and events' (p. 569) in teacher education policy in Scotland from the 1960s to the current Donaldson Review period. There is no funding source acknowledged, and the article is entirely inward referencing in that it describes the Scottish context without reference or appeal to wider policy developments or influences elsewhere. There is no explicit outline of the methodological approach adopted, but it draws on research and policy literature in providing a chronological, historical account of CPD policy development. While the article is not structured around any one particular theoretical framework, the conclusions do draw on Zeichner's (2006) four tests of high quality public education. The 'insider' perspective from which the article is written (by two longstanding Scottish teacher education academics) is also defended explicitly in the article when the authors discuss the need for academics with intimate knowledge of the national education system in order to have influence on policy makers. There is no explicit claim made to intended impact of the article, but it does set out to illustrate the way(s) in which 'Scotland's teachers and their teacher education have retained well-deserved public and political trust' (p. 584), and in this regard is perhaps presented as an inward-referencing piece of self-promotion for the Scottish system, as opposed to an outward-referencing critique.

Humes (2014) focuses on Professional Update and practitioner enquiry, suggesting in the title that this is perhaps a repackaging of existing policy: 'Professional update and practitioner enquiry: Old wine in new bottles'? The intended impact of the article is made clear when Humes asserts that 'the paper concludes by arguing for greater intellectual freedom in defining what counts as legitimate professional learning and cautioning against the expectation that new systems and structures will by themselves bring about major shifts in attitude' (p. 54). He provides a challenge to what he perceives as a technicist, managerial and systems-focused approach to the development of teacher professional learning policy. This is a standalone piece of work, which does not acknowledge any external funding. The article uses discourse analysis, adopting a comparative historical perspective, although is limited in specific methodological detail. Theoretically, it draws on the notion of discourse as a discursive site that reflects changes in policy direction.

Hulme and Menter (2011) provide a comparative textual analysis of the most recent key teacher education policy reform reports in Scotland (*The Donaldson Report*) and in England (*The Importance of Teaching*). The article sets out to explore how policy formation in Scotland and England is premised on different sets of values and conceptualisations of professionalism. It does not make any explicit claims to intended impact, other than to highlight the differences in underpinning values in the two jurisdictions. It is outward looking in that it does not focus solely on Scotland, but there is no reference to teacher education policy outwith the UK. Interestingly, it is perhaps Anglo-centric in its presentation, despite being published in the 'Scottish Educational Review', as the presentation of the Scottish policy discourse is presented in reference to the English discourse, yet the same approach is not adopted vice versa. That is, the Scottish context is promoted as positive through more negative presentation of the English context. The methodological approach is very detailed and specific: it uses critical discourse analysis and corpus linguistic approaches to devise a 'text analysis protocol', aided by WordSmithTools software. In addition to the two main policy documents, consideration is also given to 'associated genre chain texts', that is, texts which provide additional perspectives on the two key reports analysed.

Kennedy et al. (2012) report on a critical discourse analysis of the 'McCormac Report': *Advancing Professionalism: A Report of a Review of Teacher Employment in Scotland* (Scottish Government 2012). The motivation for the work comes from a view that the title of the McCormac Report was perhaps misleading, or at least not particularly reflective of the real purpose of the review which was to look at teachers' pay and conditions rather than to look at how best to promote or advance teacher professionalism. The study adopts a critical discourse analysis approach focusing on three key ideas: professionalism, teacher flexibility and economic concerns, and the analysis is then considered in relation to Whitty's (2008) categorisations of professionalism, in coming to conclusions about the underpinning messages promoted through the report. That is, that managerial conceptions of professionalism are much more prominent than democratic or collaborative ones. This study was unfunded, carried out by an academic, and two teachers who were also doctoral students at the time. It is inward looking, focusing on the Scottish context only, but is explicit in its aspiration to highlight the semantic importance of the concept of professionalism in this particular policy text. It also makes a plea to stakeholders to be more critical about claims to enhance professionalism in policy discourse.

Kennedy and Doherty (2012) focus on the Donaldson Report, claiming that the prioritisation of 'partnerships' and 'professionalism' in the Report are presented as policy panaceas. This article also uses critical discourse analysis, adopting a sociocognitive approach to analyse how the terms 'partnership' and 'professionalism' are used in the Report. Theoretically, the piece draws on the concept of policy panaceas and McConnell's (2010) three dimensions for measuring policy 'success'. Again, this is a standalone, unfunded piece of work, which presents a plea to stakeholders to balance the focus on operationalising policy reform with a healthy critique of the panacea-type approach to solving policy problems. It also aspires to highlight the existence of a network governance approach to policy implementation. The article is mainly inward referencing, but does provide some contextual acknowledgement of global policy trajectories in teacher education.

Menter and Hulme (2011) provide an overview of key developments in teacher education policy leading up to the Donaldson Report, speculating on its possible impact. The purpose of the article is to explain a policy trajectory that differs significantly from elsewhere in the UK, with particular reference to England. This article is adapted from an earlier conference presentation, and claims to provide an account based on policy document analysis, the authors' own experiences as teacher educators and experience of working on the literature review commissioned as part of the Donaldson Review of teacher education in Scotland. Beyond this, there is little detail of the methodological or analytical approach adopted. The piece is mainly inward referencing, but provides some contextual acknowledgement of global policy trajectories in teacher education. It does not draw explicitly on any particular theoretical framework, rather claiming to provide an account of a particular national policy context, presumably for an audience unfamiliar with Scotland (the original conference presentation was made at the American Educational Research Association Conference).

In yet another unfunded piece of work, Menter and Hulme (2012) look at Scottish teacher education policy in general when they explore the extent to which the global financial crisis has impacted on policy development. The article reports on documentary analysis of policy and research literature in producing a plea for 'innovative responses to enduring challenges', highlighting the 'longstanding commitment to explicit values in Scottish culture and education' (p. 149). No further detail is given on any particular methodological or analytical approach to the task of documentary analysis. While the focus is clearly and exclusively on Scottish policy, the article is outward referencing in that it sets the Scottish case within the nested and intertwined structure of national, UK, EU and global policy, whilst simultaneously paying detailed attention to the particular cultural and historical context of Scotland.

O'Brien (2011) provides an overview and analysis of the development of CPD policy in Scotland, with a particular focus on the role of professional standards. It provides a historical reflection of CPD policy since the 1970s, but does not make explicit reference to a particular methodological or theoretical approach. While there is no explicit statement of the intended impact of the article, it uses the historical account to speculate on the possible outcome of the Donaldson Review at a time of economic austerity. Again, this is a standalone and unfunded piece of work.

Reeves and Drew's (2012) article takes the now discontinued Chartered Teacher scheme as its policy focus, drawing on empirical data from artefacts produced by chartered teacher students. The impetus for the article is to explore ways in which policymakers attempt 'to promote educational change' through teacher education policy. No funding source is declared, and the article contains both inward referencing in terms of the specific Scottish focus and outward referencing in terms of offering an analytical model that could be employed in other national settings.

The analysis of the empirical data focuses on 'the discursive and material relations created across social spaces in the designing of the CT programmes' (p. 712). Theoretically, the article draws on policy sociology in relation to interactions of knowledge and power in policymaking through the exploration of policy content and policy mechanisms, as well as drawing on organisational development theory. The aspiration for the impact of the article is that it provides an analytical framework (discursive analysis) that can aid understanding of the complexities of the policy process and enhance the critical awareness of those involved in the policy process.

Watson and Fox (2014) focus explicitly on the development of professional update policy, exploring how 'appraisal policies' work to create teacher subjectivities. The work is 'supported by Education Scotland', but no detail provided on what that support entailed. It employs discourse analysis of interviews with senior staff being prepared to carry out professional update interviews with their own staff members. Theoretically, the piece considers the data within the context of appraisal as a tool for accountability or for improvement. The article exposes what the authors claim to be an attempt on behalf of the General Teaching Council for Scotland (who have responsibility for overseeing the Professional Update process) to conflate accountability and improvement in a process that started off life as an accountability measure but is now presented to teachers as an improvement measure.

Taken together, the articles represent output from academics in five of the eight providers of teacher education in Scotland, published in five different academic journals. While the sample is undoubtedly too small to draw clear conclusions from, the fact that three of the articles are published in *Journal of Education Policy*, and three in *Scottish Educational Review*, perhaps points to the intention of the authors to contribute to the critique of national policy, as opposed to simply seeing their work as generic teacher education research.

In terms of policy focus, the articles provide a mix of specific policy initiatives and generic teacher education policy, with Menter and Hulmes writing from more of a Scotland/England comparative perspective. This can perhaps be explained by the fact that both Menter and Hulme have professional and personal connections with England as well as having spent considerable time working in Scottish universities.

In considering the intended purpose of the articles, the key purpose seems to be to provide a challenge to, or alternative reading of, perceived policy wisdom, often focusing on the ways in which specific language or terminology is used semantically to shape teachers' behaviour or compliance. Several studies also seek to provide frameworks to aid interrogation and understanding of policy/ies beyond superficial engagement.

With the exception of Watson and Fox's (2015) article on Professional Update, which acknowledges that it was 'supported by Education Scotland', the other nine do not acknowledge any funding source, suggesting that the majority of teacher education policy studies in Scotland are self-motivated, standalone pieces of work, carried out as part of academics' ongoing work rather than as part of specific funded projects.

The most popular methodological approach in the ten articles is discourse analysis, albeit not necessarily using exactly the same techniques; indeed some articles do not spell out the specific analytical technique in much detail. Other articles tend towards providing 'accounts' drawing on documentary analysis, but also containing significant experiential knowledge as well. Only two of the ten articles use empirical data beyond policy and research documentary evidence: Reeves and Drew (2012) analysing various texts relating to the development of their Chartered Teacher course, including policy and course documentation, teaching materials, students' assignments and evaluative feedback, and Watson and Fox (2015) analysing interview transcripts. The articles also revealed use of a comparative approach—both geographical (i.e. comparing Scotland and England) and historical.

Some of the articles made explicit mention of theoretical frames in which the work was situated, while others made no such statements. Across all ten, perhaps with the exception of Reeves and Drew (2012), the theoretical frame was seen as less important than the substantive discussion of policy itself. Thus, the building of a body of policy study theory does not seem to be a core purpose of the work analysed here, perhaps attributable to the individualised, small-scale and self-motivated nature of the studies, none of which were drawn from wider, theoretically driven research projects. This situation illustrates longstanding criticisms of UK education research more generally (Tooley and Darby 1998).

Some of the authors do not make explicit any particular intended impact of the article, rather providing accounts of policy development. Where intended impact of the article is stated, or even implied, in the majority of cases the intention is to promote critical engagement with the policy development under investigation, and to promote a more critical stance on policy; a traditional role of the academy. For example, Humes (2014) argues for 'greater intellectual freedom in defining what counts as legitimate professional learning' (p. 54), while Kennedy and Doherty (2012) 'conclude with a plea that as the rush to attend to the more tangible, operational aspects of the proposed reform [in the Donaldson Report] gather momentum, such a panacea approach to solving perceived problems needs to be critiqued openly' (p. 835). Similarly, Reeves and Drew (2012) conclude by suggesting that 'a discursive analysis of how a centrally mandated initiative is transmitted can help to promote an understanding of the complexities of this process and increase critical awareness of the issues at stake for those involved' (p. 711).

The majority of the articles reviewed are wholly or principally inward referenced in that they consider the Scottish context only. Hulme and Menter (2011) consider Scotland and England from a comparative perspective, but with little reference beyond the UK, while Reeves and Drew (2012) and Watson and Fox (2015) both use the Scottish 'case' to explore and illustrate wider global policy phenomenon. It appears, then, from this small sample of work, that the authors are committed to providing detailed accounts of the Scottish teacher education policy context, despite systemic pressure to publish 'international' research.

38.5 Discussion

The above analysis reveals a context in which individual academics are clearly motivated to contribute critical perspectives on the development of teacher education policy, with the aim of documenting developments and provoking critical interrogation within the national context. However, the small-scale, unfunded nature of the work reviewed suggests a lack of support from both Scottish Government and from research councils to conduct this kind of national-focused policy research.

None of the ten articles reviewed here are the result of commissioned research planned at the outset of policy development; rather they appear to be the result of academics' own intellectual curiosity and desire to provide a critical perspective on national policy development. It seems that, certainly in Scotland, research into education policy processes is not planned at the outset of policy developments. Indeed, the Royal Society of Edinburgh, Scotland's National Academy of Science and Letters, in a report on the development of the new school curriculum reform— Curriculum for Excellence—argued that the upcoming OECD review of progress would be difficult due to 'The absence of a systematic programme of independent evaluation of CfE [which] has been a long-standing and key concern of the education committee'. This lack of planning for research and policy evaluation is mirrored elsewhere in education policy in general in Scotland.

The Scottish Government's education research strategy seems currently to prioritise participation in large-scale surveys such as PISA, together with some small-scale evaluative commissions, having withdrawn some years ago from supporting researcher-initiated projects. In the field of teacher education, the most recent Scottish Government commissions have been the evaluation of routes to headship (published in 2014), which was led by commercial consultants Blake Stevenson Ltd., and the recently commissioned evaluation of the impact of the Donaldson Report, which has been awarded to Ipsos Mori Scotland, a commercial market research company. Neither of these commissions was planned at the outset of the respective policy developments. This perhaps signifies a desire on the part of the Scottish Government to prioritise the evaluation of what McConnell (2010) would term the 'programme' strand of policy rather than to focus on either the 'process' or the 'politics' of policy-making. It is evident that in awarding contracts to commercial companies, the focus is much more likely to be on the evaluation of tangible programme outcomes than it is on the detail of the policy-making process or the politics of the policy context. Interestingly, it is the process and politics aspects that appear to be prioritised in the articles reviewed in this chapter.

The brief of the Scottish Government-commissioned evaluation of the Donaldson Review is 'to gather teacher, headteacher and educational stakeholder views, in order to evaluate current provision and provide an insight into the extent of the impact of changes that have occurred in teacher education since 2011' (http://www.publiccontractsscotland.gov.uk/search/show/search_view.aspx?ID=AUG216 429&catID=). This suggests a focus on stakeholder perceptions of the policy reform in general, rather than any specific indicators of change in any particular aspects of the reform package. In choosing this focus, the evaluation will most likely steer away from any of the underpinning process or political aspects, and will not easily be able to gather rigorous evidence on particular impact of the reform. The generic terms of the evaluation brief mean that key issues such as the nation-wide change to undergraduate initial teacher education programmes may go un-researched. The Donaldson Report called for undergraduate initial teacher education to move away from a purely professional focus to include a much wider academic experience for students, studying a range of different university disciplines alongside the study of education and teaching. To research the impact of these new programmes on teachers, schools and pupils would undoubtedly require considerable resource—it could not be done on the same terms as the studies reviewed here, requiring some fairly significant and wide-ranging data collection moving well beyond documentary evidence or perception studies alone. So we are left with a situation where six universities have completely restructured their undergraduate initial teacher education programmes in response to the Donaldson Report, in partnership with key stakeholders (schools, employers and the General Teaching Council for Scotland), yet we have no way of knowing whether or not these changes to provision will result in a better learning experience for pupils. Unfortunately, this kind of research does not seem to have appeal to research councils, being policy-focused and nationally bound, and nor does it seems to be prioritised by Scottish Government.

The policy studies discussed in this chapter focus principally on critical interrogation of the policy discourse, on matters of values and principles and on the intellectual underpinning of policy ideas. There are some questions to be asked then, about how such critiques can be shared and debated with the wider policy community in order for the research to make a real impact. What is not apparent in the text of the articles themselves is the opportunity that academics in Scotland have to engage with the wider teacher education policy community. Being a small country, and one which currently promotes partnership working through a model of network governance (Kennedy and Doherty 2012), means that academics are regularly in meetings, seminars and events with other members of the policy community, and have the opportunity to form well-connected working relationships with each other. This allows academic opinion to be expressed as part of wider policy discussion, supporting informal and ongoing knowledge exchange and policy influence, albeit acknowledging that some academics fulfill this role more easily than others. While this natural forum for knowledge exchange exists, it must not be forgotten that, as Gray and Weir (2014) point out, 'education staff have to be careful not to criticise the government overtly since it still controls courses, the setting of intakes and the funding of most research relevant to teacher education' (p. 582).

Another concern around the production and use of teacher education policy research in Scotland is the issue of who carries this out. All of the authors of the articles reviewed in this chapter are (or were at the time of writing their papers) academics in Scottish universities providing teacher education, with the exception of Barlow and MacGregor who are secondary teachers and were engaging in doctoral studies at the time of co-authoring their article. All the authors have either only worked in the Scottish system or have spent significant chunks of their careers working in Scottish universities. This undoubtedly provides a detailed insider perspective that can reveal nuances of policy and practice not necessarily discernible to the outside eye. If we consider academic work to be primarily about objective, replicable, internationally relevant research, then much of the research reported here would not satisfy these criteria. However, the critical and informed interrogation of policy is a key duty of the academy, and the Scottish context, where the policy community is small enough for people to know each other by name, this kind of research and knowledge exchange undoubtedly has enormous capacity for impact. However, the pressure to perform well in the UK-wide 'Research Excellence Framework' (www.ref.ac.uk) forces universities to focus more on international research excellence and impact than on the interrogation and deeper understanding of national policy concerns, arguably skewing the generation of research to satisfy accountability purposes (Marginson 2015). As Gray and Weir (2014) describe, 'There is a steady trend of appointing people [academic staff in schools of education] whose research achievements are high so that they can maximise the university's academic status and income-generating potential, rather than people who have intimate knowledge of, and connection with, the national education system and can exert pressure on policy makers as a result of that' (p. 582). While the situation Gray and Weir describe is clearly a challenge, it must also be acknowledged that there are academics who can satisfy both of these demands, provided that performative pressures do not always force them to seek work internationally in order to progress there careers, and also that 'international' academics are not always seen as preferable to 'home-grown' ones.

In conclusion, from the analysis presented and discussed here, it seems that there are three main challenges to the development of a healthy, vibrant and sustained body of teacher education policy research in Scotland. First, policy research is not routinely planned at outset of the development of specific policy initiatives or reforms. When commissioned later on in the process it tends to focus on perceptions of the impact rather than of the process itself, or indeed of unintended consequences and potential alternatives, taking political goals as given (Sanderson 2002). Such commissions tend to be restricted to Government-initiated evaluations, rather than research that would support theory development or the accumulation of a significant body of policy study research; they also tend not to support research into the longer term impact of policy, instead pushing for indicators of immediate impact. Munn (2005) argues that such a conception of policy research suggests a narrow conception of policy itself, seeing it as a linear succession of events (formulation, implementation, evaluation) rather than as a complex, messy and iterative process. This type of policy evaluation research is therefore only one very narrowly construed approach to policy research, and not one that reflects the approaches and stances adopted by the authors of the articles discussed in this chapter. Second, teacher education policy in Scotland is not deemed attractive enough for funding councils: either the politics of teacher education are not interesting, significant or different enough to warrant investigation, or else the relatively small geographical boundary of Scotland is not deemed 'big' enough to warrant specific study. Alternatively, perhaps the academic community in Scotland has not yet advanced a convincing enough case for the development of new and innovative methodological approaches to the investigation of Scottish teacher education policy. Finally, the performative and accountability-focused Western university culture, of which the Research Excellence Framework is illustrative, does not provide a context supportive of small-scale, nationally focused policy studies—the kind of work discussed in this chapter does not seem to have an overt value in contemporary Western university cultures, and it therefore makes it difficult to see how such work—policy research in teacher education in Scotland—might be supported further without it having to lose its overt national focus.

References

Brown, S. (2008). Capacity and quality in education research in Scotland: A stimulus report. SFRE.

Cairney, P., & McGarvey, N. (2013). *Scottish politics* (2nd ed.). Basingstoke: Palgrave Macmillan.

Christie, D., Donoghue, M., McNamara, M., Menter, I., Moss, G., Noble-Rodgers, J., et al. (2012). BERA-UCET working group on education research: Prospects for education research in education departments in higher education. Available https://www.bera.ac.uk/wp-content/uploads/2014/01/FINAL-REPORT-FINAL-27-March-2012.pdf?noredirect=1

Hulmes, M., & Kennedy, A. (2015). Teacher education in Scotland: Consensus politics and 'the Scottish policy style'. In TEG (Eds.). *Teacher education in times of change*. Bristol: Policy Press.

Ingvarson, L. (2009). Developing and rewarding excellent teachers: The Scottish Chartered Teacher scheme. *Professional Development in Education, 35*(3), 451–468.

McConnell, A. (2010). Policy success, policy failure and the grey areas in-between. *Journal of Public Policy, 30*(3), 345–362.

McGeer, J. (2009). The Chartered Teacher scheme in Scotland: A survey of the views of teachers. *Professional Development in Education, 35*(1), 5–22.

Marginson, S. (2015). UK research excellence: Getting better all the time? *International Higher Education, 81,* 12–13.

Munn, P. (2005). Researching policy and policy research. *Scottish Educational Review, 37*(1), 17–28.

Priestley, M. (2013). The 3–18 curriculum in Scottish education. In T. G. K. Bryce, W. M. Humes, D. Gillies, & A. Kennedy (Eds.), *Scottish education fourth edition: Referendum* (pp. 28–38). Edinburgh: Edinburgh University Press.

Sanderson, I. (2002). Evaluation, policy learning and evidence-based policy making. *Public Administration, 80*(1), 1–22.

Tooley, J., & Darby, D. (1998). *Educational research—A critique: A survey of published educational research*. London: Office for Standards in Education.

Whitty, G. (2006). Education(al) research and education policy making: Is conflict inevitable? *British Educational Research Journal, 32*(2), 159–176.

Whitty, G. (2008). Changing modes of teacher professionalism: Traditional, managerial, collaborative and democratic. In B. Cunningham (Ed.), *Exploring professionalism* (pp. 28–49). London: Institute of Education, University of London.

Zeichner, K. (2006). Reflections of a university-based teacher educator on the future of college- and university-based teacher education. *Journal of Teacher Education, 57*(3), 326–340.

Chapter 39
Researching Practice as Education and Reform

Colleen McLaughlin

39.1 Introduction

This chapter explores the use of action research as part of formal policy makers' plans to implement change in education and begins by looking at past writings on this. It draws on work in reforming teacher education and teacher practices in Kazakhstan, South Africa and the UK. It shows how action research is well suited to developing teachers' learning and practice. It makes the case for engaging teachers in researching practices as part of reform attempts and shows the impact of this process on teachers' conceptions of themselves as teachers and on the process of teaching and learning. It details the emotional and professional challenges and the necessary supports needed if this process is to be as powerful as it might be.

39.2 The Union of Change and Action Research

The idea of linking action research to change is, to state the obvious, not a new one. Many would argue that action research has the notion of change conceptually embedded. Many key titles encapsulate the idea of action research as an educational change process, and contain the words action, research and change. Somekh (2009) articulates these connections well when she points out that action research is a methodology that suits those social scientists researching innovation and that, in particular the knowledge generated 'has the capacity to transform social practices,' and can help those involved in educational change 'gain access to the intimate and

C. McLaughlin (✉)
University of Cambridge, England, UK
e-mail: colleen.mclaughlin@sussex.ac.uk

© Springer Nature Singapore Pte Ltd. 2017
M.A. Peters et al. (eds.), *A Companion to Research in Teacher Education*,
DOI 10.1007/978-981-10-4075-7_39

passionate purposes of individuals whose lives and work construct these practices.'
(p. 3) These ideas also show the potential or the actual different uses of action
research. Some view it primarily as a collection of methods and some as a vehicle
for radical participatory change.

It was this issue of these different traditions that led Nofke (2009: 7) to undertake
an historical analysis and from this emerged her distinction between the professional, personal and political dimensions of action research. The professional
dimension is concerned with the nature of research as well as the debate around
who creates the knowledge. Key figures in the UK who engaged in educational
research of a professional nature are Lawrence Stenhouse, who argued that teachers
needed to research in order to understand classroom practice, and John Elliott, who
saw teacher research as able to generate alternative challenging knowledge and able
to promote a reflective professional able to theorise and engage in major curriculum
development. In Australia, Carr and Kemmis also focused upon transforming
educational research into a more critical and participatory tradition. The personal
dimension is where the transformation of individuals is emphasised, as well as the
collaboration with others, including university-based colleagues. Nofke would
argue that the political dimension is part of everything, as power is an inevitable
aspect of all three dimensions. However, the political dimension also alludes to
explicit political purposes such as the promotion of democratic practices in schools
or engagement with marginalised peoples. These three dimensions are also arenas
of change too and when a fairly large-scale educational reform is undertaken then
all of the three dimensions are engaged with—the professional, the personal and the
political. These three areas will be explored in more detail later in this chapter.

39.3 Change and Educational Reform

Fullan (2013) argues that not many large-scale reforms have been undertaken
successfully, although he says there are recent examples in the UK and elsewhere.
His analysis of the success of reform is that the major challenges are not around
policy formation but around the point of implementation of policy (Fullan 2013:
13). This is now well known. It is understandable since this is where the real change
is made possible or not. It is entirely dependent on the teachers' understandings,
values and practices, as well as their perceptions of the worthwhileness, or not, of
the change. For it is … 'the intimate and passionate purposes of individuals whose
lives and work construct these practices,' (Somekh 2009, p. 3) which will determine
what happens in the classroom. This does sometimes gets forgotten in our time of
global concerns.

We live in an era of international comparison tables, the search for the perfect
practice and major accountability measures. Most recent educational reform initiatives have been driven by policy makers and in a top-down fashion. Often in
these change or reform initiatives teachers are positioned as 'a problem' as Fullan
and Langworthy (2014) note, 'One of the most frequently cited barriers is the

perceived resistance of teachers to adopting new practices or tools (p. 49).' Yet this paradigm is being challenged in thinking about policy change and it is now seen that this language and positioning is unhelpful. There is a more collaborative approach being taken (Fullan 2013). This includes adopting different perceptions of the role of teachers and of the degree of involvement and autonomy they have in change and reform. It is these very international comparisons that are driving some of the shift in perceptions. In an analysis of what the United States of America can learn from the world's most 'successful' school systems Tucker (2011) writes about the positioning of teachers in relation to improvement and autonomy. 'In the United States, teachers are generally the objects of research rather than participants in the research process itself' (p. 20) and he notes that systems such as the Japanese, which are viewed as successful, are based on the view of the teacher as a competent professional. In discussing professional development through enquiry-based approaches, such as the use of research lesson study, he muses over what would happen should teachers be viewed as 'highly competent professionals who are expected to take the lead in defining what good practice is, advancing that practice and keeping up to date on the latest advancements' (p. 21). This argument is exactly that made by Stenhouse (1975) when he put forward a 'research model' of curriculum development.

> All well founded curriculum research and development, whether the work of an individual teacher, of a school, of a group working in a teachers' centre or of a group working within the coordination framework of a national project, is based on the study of classrooms. It thus rests on the work of teachers. It is not enough that teachers' work should be studied: they need to study it themselves. (Stenhouse 1975: 143)

Policy makers have also now theoretically accepted that teaching is best seen as a profession of lifelong learning and that the learning of teachers is linked to the development of practice. This is a shift in thinking, although maybe not yet in practice, and has also been linked to the international comparison game or the Global Educational Reform Movement, as Pasi Sahlberg has named it, brought about the primacy of the Finnish position in league tables. Finland has a tradition of focusing on high quality teacher preparation and professional development. The idea, if not the practice, has been picked up internationally.

So I have argued that action research is well suited to educational reform for it is the key to seeing the reform aims through to action and to discovering the professional and personal challenges in action: the very things that can blow a reform process of course if not attended to. However, the argument is not just for involving action research as a curriculum development tool or problem solving vehicle but also for the authentic engagement of teachers in the direction and content of the reform, for they are professionals and, as Stenhouse (1975) famously said, only they can bring about real change.

39.4 Teacher Learning

I have argued that at policy level there is a rhetoric that emphasises the importance of teachers' professional development and learning but at the same time research has begun to focus on the process of teacher learning and its characteristics and links to student learning. We have learned much more in the last decade about how teachers learn best and how this connects to curriculum and student development. The general consensus is that practice is inadequate and the understandings of policy makers underpinning practice have been 'too simplistic and [they] have not understood how learning is embedded in the professional lives, working conditions and contexts that teachers inhabit.' (Menter and McLaughlin 2015: 36). What has emerged from these studies is that teacher learning is highly situated in the context of the school and that this context exerts great influence over how or whether teachers learn. Our understanding of these factors is still limited but we know more than we did.

What we do know is that there are three significant elements in teacher learning: it is a complex dynamic phenomenon; rooted in the context, systems and in professional community (ibid, p. 39). The phenomenon is dynamic because all the influences on teachers' pedagogy are interacting during the process of learning about practice—the national policy context, the immediate school context and past experience and preparation. Opfer and Peddar (2011: 380) in their review of the evidence showed the interaction between teachers' beliefs, knowledge, past practice and experience. They called the interaction between these elements the learning orientation of the teacher. What is important in facilitating learning is that there is the creation of a gap or of some dissonance, for it is in trying to re-establish cognitive equilibrium that teachers learn (ibid). The other important element was the site of professional learning. The creation of collaborative learning is highly recommended. Collaboration is the process through which teacher learning can be empowered and so the creation of a professional learning community is important. It is also the place where teachers can gain support to shift their thinking and practice. We need to try things out to envisage different ways of working. We know that 'norms of collegiality and experimentation' (Little 2006: 15) rather than a culture of privacy and non-interference are strong facilitators of teacher learning and change, and translate into higher recorded student attainment. When the norms and the culture are directed towards teacher learning rather than the protection of past practice or non-interference, then we see that professional learning is constructive and can be powerful. Collaboration can be for good or ill. Teachers can collaborate in ways that are not good for student learning so it is not an uncritical area of work. It is the establishment of a teacher professional learning community that emerges as a key factor in developing learning.

Collecting data is a way to create safe disequilibrium. The data show us that our experience of our classrooms or systems is not always how others view it. This examination of data, focusing on the data rather than the person, is a way of generating gaps for learning and at the same time creating support for change within the group as well as critical examination. This is why action research can be so powerful.

This exploration of the research on teacher learning shows that it must be rooted in practice and in the community of school, as well as creating the conditions for disequilibrium and support. Cordingley (2015) has also shown us that these elements align with research on effective continued professional learning and development. Her and others' systematic reviews of the evidence have identified the need for external support to help teachers see the familiar differently, give access to specialist knowledge, for teachers to collaborate effectively, for there to be a rooting of the learning or enquiry in close observation of practice and in knowledge and evidence. Recent new reviews of research have shown 'an increasing emphasis on learning from looking at practice, from and through assessing pupil progress formatively and in fine-grained and contextualised ways and the development of theory or an underpinning rationale side by side with practice' (Cordingley 2015: 65). Just as others, including Cordingley, (BERA 2014) have shown that enquiry-based approaches including research lesson study, are particularly attuned to these processes, I argue that action research is very suited to engage with all of these elements and expand on this further.

39.5 Using Action Research as a Reform Strategy

Action research has been used as a reform strategy in education. In Namibia there was a concerted move from 1990 to transform teacher education (Zeichner 2001). A similar approach was taken in South Africa to the implementation of a revised post-apartheid national curriculum (Robinson and Soudien 2009). A further recent example has been my own involvement in a reform of the curriculum, assessment and pedagogy in Kazakhstan. Action research was used as part of the evaluation of the introduction of the new curriculum, although it diverted away from this. I will use these two examples—the South African one as described by Robinson and Soudien (ibid) and the one in Kazakhstan (McLaughlin and Ayubayeva 2015), which I describe in some detail, to examine the critical issues emerging and how we can refine this as a research and development method to facilitate and support educational reform.

39.5.1 The Kazakh Example—The Context and the Reform

Kazakhstan is, like many Central Asian countries, engaged in a rapid reform of its education system and has very high ambitions for its educational achievements. The government strategy for the reform of schooling has been to build a network of 20 'autonomous schools of innovation', 14 in the regional capitals and two additional schools in three cities with a population of more than one million. The schools were to be the drivers of modernisation in Kazakhstan. These schools had a new curriculum, new assessment practices, new pedagogies, international teachers working alongside local teachers, and the reform was undertaken in partnership with selected international strategic partners, e.g. Cambridge International Examinations, the CITO Pedagogical Measurements' Institution of the Netherlands and the Center for Talented Youth of Johns Hopkins University, USA (cf. McLaughlin and Ayubayeva 2015). The new curriculum was also being assessed and evaluated, and in 2011 a plan was developed to introduce action research to the teachers in these schools as part of the evaluation and development of the new curriculum and other practices. The action research project began in 2015 and now involves 500 teachers. So it is a fast paced reform drawing on international practice and the experience of the 20 schools is now being 'translated' to the rest of the school system. There is a big programme of continuing professional development through an organisation called the Centres of Excellence and the in-service education programme focuses upon the new pedagogy embedded in the curriculum. By the end of 2015, the three-month Centres of Excellence courses that have focussed on 'modern' approaches to teaching and learning will have reached some 60,000 teachers. The action research programme described in this chapter was located within these 20 schools of innovation, with links to the partner schools that were learning about the practices in the innovative schools.

The other important aspect of this discussion is the cultural history of the schools in Kazakhstan, since this so clearly affects the values, beliefs and past practices of the current schooling and is so central to teacher learning as I have already discussed. On the 16 December 1991, Kazakhstan became the last Soviet state to be granted independence. It had been part of the United Soviet Socialist Republics for more than 70 years. Naturally some of the current achievements, practices and beliefs are from the legacy of the Soviet era. These range from universal free education, universal levels of primary education, an emphasis on the wider goals of education in the form of 'vospitanie' or upbringing, adult literacy and gender parity, to a highly centralised system of education where policy is centrally dictated and state controlled, and with heavy reliance on textbooks and hierarchy. There were collaborative practices amongst teachers in the soviet era but other practices have become influential since independence. This first decade was labelled the 'post socialist education reform package' (McLaughlin and Ayubayeva 2015: 56) where practices were adopted and implanted in the Kazakh system. This was not successful and the teachers struggled to understand and implement the new proposals. The schooling system along with the economic system struggled in the nineties.

The second decade saw a shift in strategy to the internal growth of new ideas and hence the schools of innovation. This was a view of reform based on 'teachers' involvement in the process of curriculum development, development of the assessment system, and textbook writing (which was previously never the case) so that there would be better adaptation and implementation, thus allowing teachers to function as 'developers—implementers' … However, this is a huge intellectual and emotional challenge for the teachers for the reasons explained in the above section (ibid, p. 57).' More recently individualistic rather than community focused practices based on a competitive, neo liberal model have also been introduced. For example, in order to raise the low levels of teacher salary, teachers were rewarded for attending the previously referred to continuing professional development courses and, if they met the criteria of development judged through a system of 'attestation', they could if necessary double their salaries. So the values of individualism, competition and accountability are there too. This is a system that is also used in Ontario to facilitate teacher development. The aspiration to involve teachers in the development of the curriculum and practices was there when the action research project was introduced. The processes of critical thinking and reflection were central to many of the initiatives being introduced and it was in this context that the action research project began.

39.6   The Action Research Project in Kazakhstan

The project drew on two models that the facilitators from the University of Cambridge Faculty of Education had been involved in for many years. It was a schools-university partnership called SUPER (Schools-University Partnership for Educational Research) and the HertsCam project. Both involved teachers in researching their practice within a formal partnership facilitated by both university and school-based colleagues. The project in Kazakhstan set up the following structures. Each school was to appoint a senior member of staff, who with the school principal, (or Director in the Kazakh context), would be responsible for the coordination and development in the school as well as being the primary contact for the Cambridge team. There were teams of teachers who attended the first round of action research training and practice. They comprised the principal, the research coordinator and other interested teachers. Numbers in each team varied but the recommended team size was four. The project is now in its third year and from inception the plan was to develop facilitators of other groups from amongst the cohort so the first year was going through the action research cycle twice in the schools involved and setting up the processes and structures to facilitate the work. Schools in Kazakhstan were paired on a regional basis and the teams of facilitators from Cambridge University Faculty of Education consisted of university-based- and school based colleagues working together as critical friends to the Kazakh group. The second year saw the development of a the Research Coordinator group as more central to the sustainable future of the work and their development moved more centre stage with faculty colleagues moving to a more clearly support rather than teaching role. The action research questions and projects came from the teachers concerns with in the areas of curriculum and pedagogy.

39.7   The Action Research Project in South Africa

In 2004, the South African Government introduced a Revised National Curriculum, which was a second attempt to reform the national curriculum after criticism of the first. A generic five-day training was introduced and the whole approach was underpinned by 'a positive orientation to teacher development' (Robinson and Soudien 2009: 475). This included the incorporation of an action research approach or disposition to problem solving in the curriculum, although explicit development of the teachers in this area did not form part of the training—'action research never explicitly premised or preceded the training that was provided' (p. 473)—it was part of the plan. Action research and a more democratic approach to teacher involvement were deliberate parts of an attempt to build cohesion and social justice in the country as part of a reform. Both these initiatives were evaluated so we have data to draw on.

   Both of these initiatives shared the following aims: to facilitate teacher learning: facilitate curriculum development and to facilitate change in practice. The underlying premise is also that of developing teachers as practitioners capable of reflecting upon enquiring into and creating some new knowledge about their practice. How did action research as a strategy for bringing about fundamental change fare against these criteria?

39.8   Action Research as a Vehicle for Teacher Learning

The three characteristics discussed earlier as core to teacher learning were: that it is a complex dynamic phenomenon; rooted in the context, systems, and in professional community.

39.8.1   A Complex Dynamic Phenomenon

There was much evidence of the dynamism of the process and the learning. In the Kazakhstani example, the teachers reported shifts in their learning, but they were initially slow and the bigger change occurred in the second year or the second cycle of the action research, i.e. *this is a slow process that requires support and facilitation*. This is also supported by the work on effective professional development cited earlier. Evidence shows the need for a continuous, cumulative and planned process of teacher professional development that fits with teacher's own individual agendas (Cordingley 2015). The teachers reported learning about many aspects— learning about practice, about self as teacher and learner and learning about research (Chandler-Grevett et al. 2014). It was often a gradual movement and did not progress in a neat linear fashion. In the first stages, participants often talked about developing practice in ways that did not fit with the wider goals of the intended pedagogical changes but this shifted later. It was a slow shift to accommodate the challenge to past experience, values and beliefs. The evaluation report concluded that for those involved over two years there was evidence that action research had impacted

i. 'Upon ways in which they have designed and implemented their own teaching and learning so that they can describe positive differences that this has made to pupil outcomes;

ii. … Upon teaching and learning beyond the original remit of the action research project that they have designed and led;

iii. … Had some positive impact upon those teachers who have been trained more recently … and the way in which they can jointly impact teaching and learning in their shared environments to improve pupil outcomes;

iv. There is much evidence that the experience of the Cambridge training has had a considerable and positive impact upon teacher's capacities to think reflectively and reflexively.' (ibid, p. 2)

The South African example concluded that it needed to be a longer term, more sustainable enterprise and that it had been too one−off as an initiative.

However, motivation was assumed in both these projects. The curriculum advisers or facilitators in the South African example questioned that assumption they had made that all teachers would want to engage in such an activity. 'The biggest assumption we made was to say that teachers would be more than willing and excited by the possibility of developing their own curriculum within a national framework' (Robinson and Soudien 2009: 474). Many teachers did not want to share their work and did not now how to collaborative in constructive ways. This was true initially in Kazakhstan. The values of collaboration embedded in the project did not necessarily fit easily with a climate of individualism and competition and there were cultural clashes, but they did alter slowly.

39.8.2 Rooted in the Context, Systems and in Professional Community

It was stated earlier that the phenomenon is dynamic because all the influences on teachers' pedagogy are interacting during the process of learning about practice— the national policy context, the immediate school context and past experience and preparation. The work brings the participants and policy makers face to face with the reality of the context and the history relating to implementation. In South Africa, the authors concluded that 'all of the respondents were critical of the how it engaged with the realities that teachers brought with them from their pasts, citing difficult conditions, demoralisation inadequate and unequal resourcing and poor management ad leadership' (ibid: 473). They raise the very important question,

'How does an initiative which is about teacher improvement understand its own environment?'

In Kazakhstan, fundamental ways of thinking and seeing became enmeshed in the action research. The new pedagogy and the principles of action research challenged teachers' previous thinking in profound ways. The relationship between theory and practice was turned upside down. Teachers had been trained in the Soviet tradition where it was the norm to learn theory and then 'try (frequently in vain) to apply it to practice ...' In addition it challenged the notion that '... the academy ... is the source of this professional knowledge. Rather, [in the Action Research project] theory is generated out of practice, reflection upon that practice and inquiry into practice, and it is generated primarily not by academicians but by teachers' (Bridges et al. 2015: 16). This was not something that was explicit or recognised before the programme started. It also led to shifts in teacher's perceptions of their worth for they saw themselves as having elevated status as they could conduct research.

In both cases, there were issues related to power and traditional hierarchies of power. In societies where there are firm hierarchies of power the more democratic approaches in action research can cause shifts and dissonance. Bridges et al. (2015) cite this example from the retraining of teachers on the professional development course in Kazakhstan.

This said, one school director, who had not attended any of the CoE programme herself (because she was 'too old') found herself with 23 trained teachers from the level 3 programme who clearly had found new self-confidence

> I can share information from my own school. Twenty-three teachers were sent for Level 3 training. They came and they were boycotting saying that our experts said that we can do anything we want in this course and we are not going to listen to the director .... The director was having a hard time, she said they don't listen to me, they just go, they do whatever they want and now I don't know where to go and to whom to complain (Participant B, FG-CoE-trainers).' (Bridges et al. 2015: 16)

There was evidence in the Kazakhstan example that the action research had impacted upon the professional community and teachers talked of learning new ways of communicating with each other. These practices need to be synthesised with planned changes in leadership and internal structures.

> I cannot say that there is a global change, but gradually step-by-step we can notice different kinds of changes especially in the way of thinking of teachers. Teachers know they do not prepare for lessons individually but in groups and earlier teachers were ashamed to share their problems or talk about that aloud but right now if they have problems they can come to other teachers and ask advice and consult.

> (Deputy Principal and Teacher Researcher Coordinator B) (McLaughlin and Ayubayeva 2015: 63)

39.9 Action Research as a Vehicle for Curriculum Development

If curriculum development is to be about the rooting and development of ideas and practices, it has to be rooted in the reality of the lives of the teachers and the students in their contexts. The experience of both these examples is that action research engages with these realities and can either support the problem solving required to make the new practices embed, or it will founder. These realities must be faced in a supportive and constructive way. Robinson and Soudien (2009) argue that 'sustainable and meaningful change depends on teachers being able to identify with the principles and procedures of the change and to see its purpose in their own environment.' (p. 475)

39.10 Action Research as a Vehicle for Reform

The advantages of engaging teachers in action research as part of a national reform agenda is that there is more chance of it being a real and sustainable change. The issues of power and voice that were central to the South African example emerge again. The process must be planned from the inception of the reform and followed as in integral part of it. Robinson and Soudien (2009: 475) raise the questions 'How does the community of teachers participate in a national agenda of reform?' In the next section, I explore this question and look at what can be learned from these two examples and other current examples of reform in the UK and Canada.

39.11 Researching Practice as Education and Reform

The two illuminative cases have raised questions as well as providing some substance to support the argument that action research is a highly suitable strategy for the sustainable development of teachers' practice and for planned educational reform. There are two recent examples that have also exemplified this and are systematic and well-planned reform initiatives. Both included research or the use of data in their strategies: one used teacher enquiry and one made more general use of data. These two are the London Challenge initiative (Hutchings et al. 2012; Kidson and Norris 2014) and the reform of the Ontario schools (Fullan 2009). They show that the planning of all the elements discussed in this chapter is possible and key to remarkable progress.

The first important element is clear supported pathways for teacher learning. This involves professional development aligned to the teacher's needs and goals right from the beginning of the reform attempt. Action research where the teacher has limited autonomy is well suited to this. It requires skilful facilitation and the

Kazakhstani example suggests it should not be a quick process. We can refine and adapt action research to attune more harmoniously with the research on continuing professional development and teacher learning.

The second key element is the establishment of professional learning communities. This is something long advocated within the action research tradition but in the two examples of successful reform these were given prominence and influence over the reform implementation. It is in these communities that the assumptions about practice and conditions can be tested out. It is here too that the cultural assumptions and traditions will emerge. Edwards (2011) argues that using cultural historical analysis involves the explicit and transparent discussion of values, beliefs and traditions. This helps to ensure that there is a fit, or a fit can be found, between the ways of working with teachers and the traditions. It leads to a conscious process of planning based on reality rather than aspiration.

The use of action as a strategy for reform is a process of engaging in ways that are respectful of teacher autonomy in all the domains—the professional, personal and political dimensions of action research. It can be a transformative process for individual teachers who are making sense of and creating new practices, it is a deeply personal process which requires support and sophisticated facilitation and it can address some of the political aspects of reform, but only if it is integrated from inception and planned with the feedback being taken seriously to modify and amend from what is learned.

References

BERA-RSA (British Educational Research Association and The Royal Society for the Arts). (2014). *Research and the teaching profession. Building the capacity for a self-improving education system. Final Report of the BERA-RSA Inquiry into the role of research in teacher education.* www.bera.ac.uk/wp-content/uploads/2013/12/BERA-RSA-Research-Teaching-Profession-FULL-REPORT-for-web.pdf

Bridges, D., Yakavets, N., Shamatov, D., & Kurakvayev, K. (2015). *Pedagogics, teaching methods, practicum... and collaborative action research: Constructs and the construction of teachers' professional knowledge in Kazakhstan.* Presented at European Educational Research Association annual conference, Budapest, September 2015.

Chandler-Grevett, A., Daubney, A., & Webb, R. (2014). *Integrated programme of development. Strand 10/13 extension: Independent evaluation of action research element report* (Unpublished report). University of Cambridge, Faculty of Education: Cambridge, England.

Cordingley, P. (2015). 'Evidence about teachers' professional learning and continuing professional development. In C. McLaughlin, P. Cordingley, R. McLellan, & V. Baumfield (Eds.), *Making a difference: Turning teacher learning inside out.* Cambridge, England: Cambridge University Press.

Edwards, A. (2011). *Cultural historical activity theory.* British Educational Research Association on-line resource. https://www.bera.ac.uk/researchers-resources/publications/cultural-historical-activity-theory-chat. Accessed on November 16, 2015.

Fullan, M. (2009). Large scale reform comes of age. *Journal of Educational Change, 10,* 101–113.

Fullan, M. (2013). *Great to excellent: Launching the next stage of Ontario's education agenda.* Downloaded on November 5, 2015, from http://www.michaelfullan.ca

Fullan, M., & Langworthy, M. (2014). *A rich Seam: How new pedagogies find deep learning*. London: Pearson.

Hutchings, M., Greenwood, C., Hollingworth, S., Mansaray, A., Rose, A., Minty, S., et al. (2012). *Evaluation of the city challenge programme* (pp. 102–103). London Metropolitan University & Coffey International Development. Retrieved July 2, 2014, from https://www.gov.uk/government/publications/evaluation-of-the-city-challenge-programme

Kidson, M., & Norris, E. (2014). *Implementing the London challenge*. London: Institute for Government.

Little, J. W. (2006). *Professional community and professional development in the learning-centred school*. Washington: National Educational Association.

McLaughlin, C., & Ayubayeva, N. (2015). 'It is the research of self experience': Feeling the value in action research. *Educational Action Research, 23*(1), 51–67.

McLaughlin, C., Cordingley, P., McLellan, R., & Baumfield, V. (2015). *Making a difference: Turning teacher learning inside out*. Cambridge, England: Cambridge University Press.

Menter, I., & McLaughlin, C. (2015). 'What do we know about teachers' professional learning? In C. McLaughlin, P. Cordingley, R. McLellan, & V. Baumfield (Eds.), *Making a difference: Turning teacher learning inside out*. Cambridge, England: Cambridge University Press.

Nofke, S. (2009). Revisiting the professional, personal and political dimensions of action research. In S. Nofke & B. Somekh (Eds.), *The Sage handbook of educational action research*. London: Sage.

Opfer, D., & Peddar, D. (2011). Conceptualizing teacher professional learning. *Review of Educational Research, 81*(3), 376–407.

Robinson, M., & Soudien, C. (2009). Teacher development and political transformation: Reflections from the South African Experience. In S. Nofke & B. Somekh (Eds.), *The Sage handbook of educational action research*. London: Sage.

Somekh, B. (2009). Action research: A methodology for change and development. In S. Nofke & B. Somekh (Eds.), *The Sage handbook of educational action research*. London: Sage.

Stenhouse, L. (1975). *An introduction to curriculum research and development*. London: Heinemann.

Tucker, M. S. (2011). *Standing on the shoulders of giants: An American agenda for education reform*. Washington: National Center on Education and the Economy. UNESCO-OIE.

Zeichner, K. (2001). Educational action research. In P. Reason & H. Bradbury (Eds.), *Handbook of action research*. London: Sage.

Author Biography

Colleen McLaughlin is a Professor and Director of Educational Innovation at the University of Cambridge, Faculty of Education. She was Head of Department at the University of Sussex and Deputy Head of Faculty at Cambridge. She is currently interested in teacher learning, educational reform, how schools interact with children's emotional wellbeing and schools-university partnerships for educational research.

Chapter 40
Representing Teaching Within High-Stakes Teacher Performance Assessments

Kevin W. Meuwissen and Jeffrey M. Choppin

40.1 Introduction

Teacher education in the United States is contextualized by efforts among various actors—for instance, state policy makers, teacher educators, and researchers—to wrest control over the terms, conditions, and consequences of accountability in the field. A key mechanism in this campaign is teacher performance assessments (TPAs), which have evolved with the accountability movement to serve the roles of gatekeeping teachers' entry into the profession and evaluating the outcomes of teacher education. Tensions over TPAs as policy levers first emerged in California in the early 2000s, when—in response to a law mandating that teaching candidates pass a state-approved performance assessment for licensure—universities within the PACT consortium developed an alternative to the existing test that aimed to emphasize subject-specific student learning, position the TPA as a formative assessment tool, and preserve flexibility in teacher education programming.

Currently, deliberation on TPAs' dual roles as accountability levers in the policy context and formative tools in teacher education intensifies with their nationalization via the edTPA, an assessment which evolved from the PACT and increasingly is embraced as a state-level licensure mechanism (Meuwissen and Choppin 2015). It consists of three core competencies—planning, instruction, and assessment—that teachers must demonstrate via lesson plans, instructional videos, assessed samples of student work, and narratives that contextualize and interpret those artifacts. In 2013, the states of New York and Washington became the first to require that all teaching candidates complete and pass the edTPA as a mandate for initial state

K.W. Meuwissen (✉) · J.M. Choppin
University of Rochester, Rochester, USA
e-mail: kmeuwissen@warner.rochester.edu

J.M. Choppin
e-mail: jchoppin@Warner.Rochester.edu

© Springer Nature Singapore Pte Ltd. 2017
M.A. Peters et al. (eds.), *A Companion to Research in Teacher Education*,
DOI 10.1007/978-981-10-4075-7_40

certification. In 2014, we began to investigate preservice teachers' experiences with the edTPA during its first year of consequential use as a high-stakes test in these two states.

Several studies suggest that TPAs' enactments of planning, instruction, and assessment constitute ecologically and consequentially valid representations of practice (Sato 2014; Wei and Pecheone 2010). While we concur with this suggestion, we also found that the edTPA's situation in New York and Washington as a high-stakes accountability mechanism, evaluated by a private subcontractor outside of the teacher education context, forced candidates to make difficult choices about what to represent in their teaching and how to represent it, sometimes on questionable grounds. Our goals for this chapter are threefold. First, we describe the edTPA and the difficulties associated with positioning the assessment as a summative measure of high-quality teaching. Second, we draw from our research to illuminate specific challenges associated with candidates' efforts to represent of their teaching through the edTPA. Finally, we discuss the implications of our work for using TPAs as accountability and instructional improvement levers in and beyond policy contexts like those in New York and Washington.

40.2 The edTPA as a Tool for Measuring Quality Teaching

40.2.1 The edTPA and Its Proliferation Across the United States

The edTPA, designed by the Stanford Center for Assessment, Learning, and Equity (SCALE), includes a series of artifacts and written commentaries aligned with the core teaching practices of planning, instruction, and assessing student learning. We describe its specific components in Table 40.1.

Table 40.1 Components of the edTPA

Task	Artifacts	Narratives
1. Planning for instruction and assessment	Three to five consecutive lesson plans with relevant instructional materials and lessons	Context for learning commentary; planning commentary
2. Instructing and engaging students in learning	Two continuous, unedited instructional video recordings of ten minutes or less per recording	Instruction commentary
3. Assessing student learning	Three assessed work samples from focus students, at least one of whom has unique learning needs	Assessment commentary

At the secondary level, each of the three tasks includes five rubrics with five-point scales, totalling 15 rubrics and 75 points across the assessment. Because of strong foci in both mathematics and literacy at the elementary level, those edTPAs include subject-matter instructional components and rubrics for both domains. The commentaries range in allowable length from three pages for the *context for learning* commentary to 10 pages for the *assessment* commentary. Other more specific rules apply to the various components of the assessment: for example, the assessment handbook for secondary history/social studies indicates that lesson plans shall be no more than four pages in length, video clips featuring targeted groups of students shall include no fewer than four learners, and verbal feedback on students' work samples (if there is any) shall be recorded and submitted separately from the instructional artifacts (SCALE 2014). The rubrics emphasize character-istics of teaching that are widely considered to be indicative of effectiveness. These characteristics include drawing from students' prior knowledge and experiences as assets for planning and instruction, representing the subject matter in ways that meet different learners' needs, and using analyses of classroom interactions and assessment results to inform ongoing practice.

Presently, the edTPA fulfils multiple roles across the United States, proliferating at state levels as licensure requirements and local levels as teacher education pro-gram assessments. In 2015, the states of Wisconsin and Georgia joined New York and Washington in mandating the edTPA as a high-stakes, state-level certification test, with others (e.g., Illinois, Oregon, and Hawaii) following suit in subsequent years (AACTE 2015). By contrast, the Tennessee Board of Education approved the edTPA as an alternative to the state's written certification tests in 2013, upon the encouragement of several piloting universities. In more than a dozen other states where no policy exists for consequential use of the assessment (e.g., Pennsylvania, North Carolina, and Indiana), some teacher education institutions have adopted the edTPA as a program-level evaluation tool.

Alongside variations in its roles and uses, the edTPA's standards of performance and consequences fluctuate from place to place. For example, Washington's and New York's cut scores for passing are markedly different, generating a pass rate (and thus, a licensure eligibility rate) of approximately 98% in Washington and about 80% in New York in 2014. Further, some states and institutions of higher education have moved relatively quickly to require the edTPA's passage for cer-tification and graduation respectively, while others have taken several years to pilot the assessment and plan for its integration into their policies and programs. Taking into consideration the edTPA's substantive depth and complexity, its myriad functions and modes of implementation across the United States, and—as the following section explains—disparate positions on its suitability as a lever for change in teaching and teacher education, it is unsurprising that interpretations of the assessment's value and significance vary substantially.

40.2.2 The Difficulty of Representing High-Quality Practice in Assessments of Teaching

A central assumption underlying the edTPA's use as a professional gatekeeping mechanism is that an authentic assessment of practice can identify, ensure, and even elevate high-quality teaching. But quality in teaching is not easily defined and determined. Fenstermacher and Richardson (2005) explain that successful teaching does not necessarily equate to good teaching, as it is possible to successfully teach people to do things that are harmful, immoral, or pointless. For teaching to be of high quality, it must be both successful, in the sense that teachers help students develop consequential knowledge and skills, and good, in the sense that teachers and learners demonstrate ethics of care, civility, and responsibility throughout the process. They argue that these markers of quality are contingent upon several conditions beyond teachers' practice itself—specifically, students' commitments to the learning process, supportive social environments for professional growth, and the availability of resources that promote powerful teaching and learning.

Berliner (2005) similarly suggests that high-quality teaching is made of moral dimensions, like empathy, respect, and fairness toward others; psychological dimensions, like motivating students and interpreting their interactions; and logical dimensions, like defining and demonstrating subject-matter concepts and modeling learning tasks. Because these dimensions are inextricable from each other and from the environments in which they are enacted, Berliner indicates that measuring teaching practice judiciously is less a matter of documenting task completion—even if the tasks are highly authentic—and more a matter of assessing the construct of "underlying competencies that enable performance" (p. 212). Zeichner (2012) raises three points of caution related to Berliner's argument. The first point is that what constitutes a full representation of practice for experienced teachers differs from what constitutes a reasonable representation for novices with no independent classroom experience; in other words, the construct is provisional. The second point is that schools vary considerably in the extent to which they regulate or script instructional practice; and thus, teachers' capacities to choose particular pedagogical approaches may be variously encouraged or undermined. The third point is that a relatively narrow focus on techniques associated with planning, instruction, and assessment might overshadow cultural and political-institutional competence, which arguably impact the ways in which teachers respond to and act upon the conditions of their practice.

Studies abound in support of SCALE's indication that TPAs are credible assessments of teacher quality. Darling-Hammond et al. (2013) note that preservice teachers' performance on the PACT significantly predicts future effectiveness as determined by student achievement scores in mathematics and English language arts. From a different angle, Goldhaber and Anthony (2007) report that the National Board for Professional Teaching Standards' (NBPTS) certification assessment—another close relative of the edTPA—is useful for identifying effective teachers, though they found no evidence that participating in the NBPTS certification process significantly increases teacher quality. Wilson et al. (2014) corroborate those findings in their study of a Connecticut state portfolio assessment that resembles the edTPA; that is, TPAs can more powerfully predict teachers' contributions to student achievement and more accurately identify the characteristics of effective teaching than exclusively written alternatives.

Yet our chapter's central dilemmas remain, despite these studies. First, they do not address the problem of representing the complex dimensions of teaching in measures of quality, as Fenstermacher and Richardson (2005), Berliner (2005), and Zeichner (2012) do. And second, they do not explore how policy contexts in which TPAs are positioned as high-stakes tests might impact candidates' interpretations of quality and representations of practice via those assessments. Wei and Pecheone (2010) suggest that it may not be possible to disentangle the design principles and conceivable consequences of TPAs from the policy contexts in which they are situated—a position with which we agree. This means that the edTPA, as a policy tool for gatekeeping entry into the teaching profession, could impart a limited or potentially confounding definition of high-quality teaching and steer how teachers (and teacher educators) decide what dimensions of practice to prioritize or suppress.

In what follows, we draw from our study of candidates' experiences with edTPA implementation in New York and Washington States to discuss the tensions associated with representing teaching practice in the assessment. In short, we interviewed over 50 candidates seeking licensure in grade levels and subject areas across the K-12 spectrum about their knowledge of the edTPA and its place in their teacher education programs, their processes of completing it, and their viewpoints about its fairness, credibility, and consequences for teaching and teacher education. The tensions we identify in the next section center on two key questions: (1) how do candidates conceptualize, construct, and attempt to fully portray teaching within the context of the edTPA; and (2) how do the externality and ambiguity of the evaluation process impact candidates' choices about what elements of teaching should be discussed and demonstrated and what dimensions should be concealed or omitted?

40.3 Tensions Associated with Representing Teaching in the edTPA

40.3.1 *Conceptualizing, Constructing, and Fully Portraying Teaching Quality*

While most participants in our study perceived the edTPA to credibly identify and measure important professional competencies, some described tensions that mirror Berliner's (2005) and Zeichner's (2012) aforementioned concerns: respectively, (1) to what extent can a set of discrete tasks or exercises demonstrate the construct of teaching; and (2) what are the consequences for representing teaching in situations where practice is highly regulated? Candidates who defined quality predominantly by the effectiveness of instruction for facilitating subject-matter learning outcomes tended to be less critical of the edTPA's construct of teaching than those who spoke of two other crucial, if somewhat ineffable, elements: interpersonal-relational elements and political-institutional elements. For example, one participant who perceived that the edTPA deemphasizes the processes of building relationships, rapport, and motivation explained:

> I feel like the idea behind the edTPA is great – actually looking at my teaching rather than just what I say about my teaching – but I think what it actually ended up assessing was my ability to follow instructions… I was finding myself using techniques whether or not they were appropriate in the moment… because I was just so focused on writing about them [in the commentaries]. That was very teacher-centered. It wasn't about what the students need; it's about what I need for the assessment. (secondary English candidate)

Another candidate with a strong focus on inclusive education noted that high-quality teaching means "knowing how to… and being able to differentiate" instruction; but ultimately, that process involves extensive efforts to "connect with your students, form relationships with your students, [and] get to know them" over time. In other words, the moral and psychological dimensions of teaching may be underrepresented in the edTPA.

Still others indicated that the assessment largely ignores pedagogical autonomy within the political institution of schooling as a quality of teaching. Several years ago, the New York State Education Department (NYSED) released a set of instructional modules designed to operationalize its English language arts and mathematics standards for elementary teachers. Upon their release, educators widely critiqued the modules as being of varying quality and appropriateness. While NYSED portrayed them as flexible curricular guidelines, some school districts adopted the modules as instructional scripts on account of their purported alignment with standardized tests that would be used to determine teachers' and schools' performance ratings. Consequently, some New York candidates were compelled to use lessons that they had no agency in designing. While the edTPA's *context for learning* commentary provides an opportunity to explain such circumstances, one prospective teacher remarked:

> Some of the modules are very teacher-centered, with a lot of whole-class instruction. And to think that the political details of the War of 1812 are meaningful and developmentally appropriate to second graders is ridiculous. So edTPA is mandated by the state. But if I want to do well on it, and teach in ways that I know are beneficial for my kids, I have to find ways to teach outside of the modules, which also come from the state. (elementary candidate)

This candidate illustrates how policy conflicts can affect practice and suggests that high-quality teaching involves effective curricular and instructional gatekeeping, which Thornton (2005) defines as a process of mitigating the impacts of disparate policies via well-warranted pedagogical purposes and a deep understanding of how students learn. With regard to instructional design, the edTPA's emphasis on strategic, principled planning to support diverse students' content knowledge, learning needs, and language demands is indisputably important. Yet the questionable assumption that student teachers are in positions to make planning, instruction, and assessment decisions autonomously is baked into the edTPA, which generally remains silent on the impacts of external conditions and the practice of gatekeeping in deeply political school contexts.

Overall, candidates' degrees of unease with how their teaching was represented in the edTPA seemed to correspond with their perceptions that the aim of the assessment was to approximate the construct of teaching as fully as possible. By contrast, those who did not find the tensions of representation especially problematic tended to characterize the test as a device for sampling and demonstrating particular proficiencies in a bounded way. Berliner (2005) suggests that "we often confuse task-centered and construct-centered approaches to assessment," and that "when we evaluate quality in teaching, we are categorically not interested in a single performance," but in the confluence of pedagogical reasoning and practice over time, in context. In other words, candidates whose positions on assessing teaching quality were most aligned with Berliner's also were among the most apprehensive about the edTPA's design and potential consequences—particularly given its use as a high-stakes licensure exam, where entry into the profession is contingent upon an unknown external evaluator's interpretations of candidates' representations. In the next section, we discuss one key implication of the edTPA's role in New York and Washington States: test-takers' decisions about what elements of teaching to demonstrate or conceal often reflected the ambiguity, externality, and high-stakes nature of the evaluation process.

40.3.2   Choosing What Elements of Teaching to Demonstrate or Conceal

We begin this part of our discussion with comments by two candidates who were concerned about test evaluators' interpretations of the assessment criteria, relative to the different ways teachers might portray their practice:

> A lot of people are conflicted about what they think raters want to see… You're trying to figure out, do they want to see me diffuse a situation, or do they want to see me teach a perfect class? (elementary candidate)

> When you imagine that the scorers are looking for this perfect classroom, you focus on different things than you would if you thought the scorer was going to value reflection and improvement… I think that's one of the biggest faults in this whole process: you don't know what the scorer is looking for. When you're a candidate and you're completing this process [for certification], that's excruciating. (secondary music candidate)

These interview excerpts demonstrate candidates' hazards of applying particular selection criteria to their instructional artifacts and choosing what tone to strike when writing about those artifacts.

Note that the respondents in this case are imagining how raters might interpret their work products, not explaining how raters actually evaluate them. This seems peculiar, given that the edTPA's handbooks include at least 15 separate five-point rubrics that carefully describe performance expectations for planning, instruction, and assessment. As one preservice teacher noted, "I would expect the raters to just follow the rubrics and not impose any judgments on our artefacts and commentaries beyond what's in them." However, many more candidates implied that interpreting artifacts and commentaries via the rubrics inevitably involves reading subtext, searching for preferred descriptions, prioritizing certain competencies and activities as more significant than others, and even introducing personal beliefs or biases that make the precept of "not imposing judgment" impossible. Consider, for instance, the middle school science candidate who was concerned that a short video segment of one student playing with a pair of scissors might derail her entire portfolio, and then was surprised to learn that she had attained a mastery-level score of 56 out of 75. This illustrates the common lament that participants did not really know how evaluators would assess their representations of practice.

Generally, participants took one or more of the following four approaches when choosing what elements of teaching to demonstrate or conceal via their edTPAs: (1) a *rational approach*, whereby the candidate included only artifacts and explanations directly linked to the rubric criteria, forsaking additional contextualizing and supporting information; (2) a *sanitized approach*, whereby the candidate selectively edited potential artifacts to strike a "best practice" tone, emphasizing strengths and omitting faults; (3) a *confessional approach*, whereby the candidate treated the edTPA as a formative tool, including difficult predicaments and discussing how the process of learning from missteps made her or him a better teacher; and (4) a *misrepresentational approach*, whereby the candidate fabricated an image of teaching that met the edTPA's assessment criteria but did not approximate typical practice. Examples of these approaches are found in the following explanations:

Rational approach: "I cut things off for the edTPA because they only wanted a snapshot. I had to scaffold certain skills, and I kept working on them with my students [after the edTPA lessons], but I didn't feel like there was space to talk about that." (secondary science candidate)

Sanitized approach: "When you're just starting student teaching, that's when you're learning, and that's when you're making mistakes and figuring things out. But I basically feel like – any mistake that I made, I had to never show it in the edTPA… The first day I tried videotaping, one of my kids had the biggest meltdown that I have ever handled… You can't send that to the state." (elementary candidate)

Confessional approach: "I think it's important to demonstrate that you're not perfect. I think that probably pulls at the heartstrings of your rater, for lack of a better word. It says, 'Hey, listen; I know I'm not perfect, but I'm learning.' There's that human element to it." (elementary candidate)

Misrepresentational approach: "I think there's certainly areas where I kind of fudged it for edTPA, where I had to make it sound like I was doing something that I didn't really feel like I'd accomplished… It's not that edTPA doesn't align with what I want my practice to be… but I didn't really feel like I'd gotten there in those lessons." (English as a second language (ESL) candidate)

These approaches—perhaps with the exception of the confessional approach—are consequences of the high-stakes nature of the edTPA, and are consistent with the reactions of those subjected to high-stake assessments, in general. In this case, preservice teachers interpreted the assessment in terms of its functional or technical requirements, rather than as an instrument for documenting more comprehensively what it means to be a good and competent teacher. The primary goal of test-takers via the approaches described above is to anticipate the kinds of competencies envisioned by edTPA creators and those who evaluate the portfolios. The result is that candidates' edTPA portfolios end up being less an authentic indication of their practices than an indication of how they interpret and respond to required performance criteria. This narrows the range of practices reported by the candidates and evades the messier and more challenging aspects of teaching, especially ambitious teaching that aims for exceptional outcomes. In short, candidates' representations of teaching in the edTPA, and their approaches to constructing those representations, tended to reduce teaching quality to technical performance outcomes rather than the kinds of rich, complex dimensions of practice discussed by scholars like Fenstermacher and Richardson (2005), Berliner (2005), and Zeichner (2012). Only the confessional approach seemed to acknowledge this complexity; and those who took that approach often adopted a defensive stance in doing so, as evinced below:

> [The raters] don't know me, they didn't see me [student teach] for the whole eight weeks. They just have this [edTPA portfolio], and that's it. That's scary to me. Not to say that I don't have confidence in myself… but in terms of my teaching experience, I'll just tell you, yeah, I have a lot to learn; I'm brand new; who doesn't? I hope they're looking at [the portfolio] with the same sense, like, 'They're not going to be perfect; they're not going to be probably the best teacher I've ever seen. But I can see where they're going and where they're coming from.' Hopefully the commentary on the videos, the planning – everything – hopefully it shows how much thought went into my teaching.

40.4 Implications for TPAS in the Current Accountability Climate

More than 30 years ago, in perhaps the most comprehensive study of American schooling ever conducted, John Goodlad (1984) denounced the tendency for states to focus more on the accountability of individual teachers and administrators via carrot-and-stick policies than on collective educational commitments and dynamic professional growth. When policy messages and initiatives are more about failures than opportunities, he argued, policy makers often are left wondering why their supposedly sensible solutions to the problems at hand were met with such insipid and dissatisfactory outcomes. Even before Goodlad's study, political scientist Campbell (1976) warned against overusing measurements of social activity for the purposes of identifying and rectifying deficiencies within social systems. What has become known as Campbell's Law states that the more far-reaching an evaluation tool is for decision making, the more subject it will be to corruption pressures, and the more likely it will be to distort the processes it is intended to monitor.

We believe that Goodlad's and Campbell's warnings remain prescient today, at a time when the edTPA is touted by some state policy makers as a tool for halting alleged educational failures and ensuring teacher accountability in American schools. A former New York State Commissioner of Education, for instance, suggested that the edTPA would serve a productive role in weeding undistinguished teachers and teacher education programs out of the profession. Yet this particular rationale for implementing the edTPA is conspicuously absent in SCALE's and the American Association of Colleges of Teacher Education's (AACTE's) discussions of its potential uses, consequences, and benefits. In fact, at the 2014 annual meeting of the American Educational Research Association, Linda Darling-Hammond, a Stanford University faculty member and well-known proponent of the edTPA, called New York State's implementation model a case study in how not to carry out the assessment. Further, it has been almost two decades since the standards movement in American education began morphing into the accountability movement, and thus far, the track record for using high-stakes assessments to improve students' learning opportunities and teachers' practices is, itself, undistinguished.

The evidence we presented above demonstrates that New York and Washington candidates' conceptions of teaching quality are at least somewhat contingent upon what is named and prioritized in a high-stakes test that only partially captures the construct's dimensions. In light of this and other concerns, a robust discussion among American teacher educators and researchers about the appropriate place of TPAs in policy and practice is well underway. SCALE and AACTE persistently have propped up the edTPA as a valid, research-based mechanism for bringing teacher education institutions together around common standards and expectations for teaching; and scholars affiliated with those organizations have published widely on the benefits of edTPA for identifying high-quality practice and strengthening the evidentiary grounds for improving teacher education programs (Peck et al. 2014). But Cochran-Smith et al. (2013) explain that the policy contexts of the edTPA's implementation can overshadow the advantages of its use. They describe a situation in their home state of Massachusetts—not a test adoption state, but one that participated in nationwide piloting—in which teacher educators protested the proprietary nature of the assessment and the deprofessionalization associated with restricting teacher educators' support roles and subcontracting the evaluation process out to anonymous scorers working for a private entity. Cochran-Smith and colleagues call this circumstance ironic, given that "many of those in favor of the TPA as a national assessment… are leaders of the teacher education professionalization movement" (p. 18).

Let us look at this point by way of the question that centers our chapter: how might the edTPA's position in a policy context impact the ways candidates represent teaching within it? In New York and Washington, teacher educators, cooperating teachers, and candidates are exceedingly cautious about what and how much support is appropriate and allowed when dealing with the representation tensions we describe, given restrictions that accompany the edTPA's role as summative licensure exam (Meuwissen and Choppin 2015). While local uses for the purposes of formative assessment and program development might provide opportunities for teacher educators and candidates to work through the challenges of representing the psychological, moral, and logical dimensions of teaching together, a high-stakes policy context leaves the process of linking tasks with an underlying construct of teaching up to the novice teacher. Further, there is evidence that couching the edTPA within an accountability discourse can marginalize certain teacher-educational concerns—for instance, strong foci on understanding and addressing educational inequities and social injustices—and reframe professional practice as something that is highly controlled, rather than something that adapts to ambiguity and change within the relationships among teacher, student, subject matter, and social milieu.

In conclusion, it behooves us to continue looking hard, and in great detail, at the ways assessment mechanisms like the edTPA operate on images of high-quality teaching, and in turn, on networks of teachers, teacher educators, cooperating teachers, and K-12 students. We may find that they work very differently in one context—like program evaluation and reform—than they do in another—like licensing teachers and sanctioning underperforming schools of education—and thus, the ways stakeholders mediate those assessments could vary considerably from place to place. We must be careful when conducting these analyses, for it is tempting, given the edTPA's current roles in state policy and its association with a private company that manages the evaluation process, to impulsively connect the assessment with nebulous critiques of neoliberalism and corporatization in public education. But we also must be aware that it exists in the policy sphere on account of longstanding assumptions that learners in the United States are neither college- and career-ready nor particularly competitive on international achievement tests, and that improving teaching quality by tightening teacher evaluation standards is a pathway to solving that problem. That said, those who advocate for the edTPA as a tool for recognizing high-quality teaching and strengthening teacher education programming also must reconcile with its use as a new accountability lever within an old kind of governmentality.

References

American Association of Colleges of Teacher Education. (2015). *edTPA participation map*. Washington, DC: Author. Retrieved June 11, 2015, from http://edtpa.aacte.org/state-policy

Berliner, D. C. (2005). The near impossibility of testing for teacher quality. *Journal of Teacher Education, 56*(3), 205–213.

Campbell, D. (1976). *Assessing the impact of planned social change (Occasional paper #8)*. Hanover, NH: Dartmouth College Public Affairs Center.

Cochran-Smith, M., Piazza, P., & Power, C. (2013). The politics of accountability: Assessing teacher education in the United States. *The Educational Forum, 77*(1), 6–27.

Darling-Hammond, L., Newton, S., & Wei, R. C. (2013). Developing and assessing beginning teacher effectiveness: The potential of performance assessments. *Educational Assessment, Evaluation and Accountability, 25*(3), 179–204.

Fenstermacher, G. D., & Richardson, V. (2005). On making determinations of quality in teaching. *Teachers College Record, 107*(1), 186–213.

Goldhaber, D., & Anthony, E. (2007). Can teacher quality be effectively assessed? National board certification as a signal of effective teaching. *The Review of Economics and Statistics, 89* (1), 134–150.

Goodlad, J. (1984). *A place called school: Prospects for the future.* New York: McGraw-Hill.

Meuwissen, K. W., & Choppin, J. M. (2015). Preservice teachers' adaptations to tensions associated with the edTPA during its early implementation in New York and Washington states. *Education Policy Analysis Archives, 23*(102). Retrieved from http://epaa.asu.edu/ojs/article/view/2078

Peck, C. A., Singer-Gabella, M., Sloan, T., & Lin, S. (2014). Driving blind: Why we need standardized performance assessment in teacher education. *Journal of Curriculum and Instruction, 8*(1), 8–30.

Sato, M. (2014). What is the underlying conception of teaching of the edTPA? *Journal of Teacher Education, 65*(5), 421–434.

Stanford Center for Assessment, Learning, and Equity. (2014, September). *edTPA secondary history/social studies assessment handbook.* Stanford, CA: Stanford University.

Thornton, S. J. (2005). *Teaching social studies that matters.* New York: Teachers College Press.

Wei, R. C., & Pecheone, R. (2010). Assessment for learning in preservice teacher education: Performance-based assessments. In M. Kennedy (Ed.), *Teacher assessment and the quest for teacher quality* (pp. 69–132). San Francisco, CA: Jossey-Bass.

Wilson, M., Hallam, P. J., Pecheone, R., & Moss, P. (2014). Evaluating the validity of portfolio assessments for licensure decisions. *Education Policy Analysis Archives, 22*(6). Retrieved from http://epaa.asu.edu/ojs/article/view/955

Zeichner, K. (2012). The turn once again toward practice-based teacher education. *Journal of Teacher Education, 63*(5), 376–382.

Author Biographies

Kevin W. Meuwissen directs the University of Rochester's social studies teacher education program. His research examines the impacts of state and school politics on teacher education, and on teaching practices and professional development in secondary-level history and civics in the United States.

Jeffrey M. Choppin's research focuses on teachers' perceptions and uses of curriculum materials, most recently in relation to the context of enacting the Common Core State Standards for Mathematics. His research emphasizes how curriculum materials impact teacher learning and instructional practices, which has implications for policy makers and instructional leaders.

Chapter 41
Research and the Undermining of Teacher Education

Richard Pring

41.1 Introduction

Research is traditionally associated with universities—the sort of thing they do in addition to teaching. But we should not lose sight of the fact that increasingly research is conducted by institutions, independent of universities, established specifically for that purpose, although often in association with university members and contracting out some of its work to universities. In Britain, for example, the National Foundation for Educational Research has conducted significant research projects over many years. The Nuffield Foundation funds research activities in universities, whose proposals fit within the research interests established by the Foundation—for example, one million pounds for the research leading to a major report on 14–19 education and training.

But the influential McKinsey Report, *How the World's Most Improved School Systems Keep Getting Better,* has probably had more impact in recent years on Government education policy and on classroom practice than any university based research.

None the less, the importance of research as a central university activity, and the urgency of obtaining research funding from outside bodies, have increased significantly in the last few decades, both generally and specifically in university education departments.

However, it was not always thus. What follows is a brief account of the evolution of the significance of the financial importance of this research with particular reference to its impact on educational studies and on the preparation of teachers. Indeed, the concern raised by these developments is whether or not the preparation of teachers should or will remain within the university sphere.

R. Pring (✉)
Oxford University, Oxford, England, UK
e-mail: richard.pring@education.ox.ac.uk

© Springer Nature Singapore Pte Ltd. 2017
M.A. Peters et al. (eds.), *A Companion to Research in Teacher Education,*
DOI 10.1007/978-981-10-4075-7_41

41.2 The Evolving Nature of Universities and Higher Education

It was not always the case that universities should attach so much importance to a tradition of research. John Henry Newman's classic text, *The Idea of a New University,* argued that university is 'a place of teaching universal knowledge', and its objects are intellectual—the 'diffusion and extension of knowledge rather than the advancement'. There is an inheritance of knowing, reasoning, appreciating, which needs to be preserved and passed on to future generations. Scholarship is, of course, essential to such a preservation of that inheritance, but systematic research as presently understood (particularly in the need for research grants) found no place in Newman's university.

Furthermore, 'professional learning' (such as the preparation of teachers based on a core of knowledge) also was notable for its absence. Indeed, John Stuart Mill, at his inaugural lecture at St Andrews University in 1867, agreed that universities should not be places of professional education as

> their object is not to make skilful lawyers, or physicians, or engineers, but capable and cultivated human beings [for] what professional men should carry away with them from an university is not professional knowledge, but that which should direct the use of their professional knowledge, and bring the light of general culture to illuminate the technicalities of a special pursuit. (Mill 1867, p. 133)

Such a clear distinction, on the one hand, between teaching and research, and, on the other, between universities so conceived and professional preparation, affected profoundly what was regarded as the best preparation and continuing professional development of teachers for the best part of a century. Teacher training took place in 'training colleges', only marginally connected with the university system. That historical context provides the backcloth to the more recent evolution, first, of the place of such professional development in universities, and, second, of the nature of the research, mainly university based, into education and into the professional development of teachers.

In England in 1963, the major Robbins Report into Higher Education in effect challenged the rather elitist and exclusive nature of the university system, arguing, first, for much wider access, and, second, for a greater sense of relevance to the country's needs. Furthermore, it called for a unitary system of higher education, one which would elevate and include the many training colleges which focused on the training of teachers in two year courses. However, it took some years before such a unitary system was achieved, first, through Colleges of Advanced Technology and Polytechnics becoming universities, and, second, through Training Colleges (more recently called Colleges of Education) merging with existing universities or gradually evolving into universities.

41.3 The Increased Importance of Research

Until the 1980s roughly one-third of funding for all universities (a much smaller number than is the case now) was given for doing research, irrespective of its nature or quality. It was assumed that, in Newman's words, 'a place of teaching universal knowledge' required time and resources for scholarship and research generally conceived. But there was not universal pressure to seek research funding or to publish. That was radically changed upon the considerable expansion of universities just referred to. That 'one third' was removed from the funding of universities and would be returned proportionately to the assessment of the quality of the research conducted. Thus was established what was referred to as the Research Assessment Exercise (RAE)—the advent of 'quality measurement'. Quality was measured on a scale 5 (of international excellence) down to 1. There would be winners. Departments graded 5 and 4 would receive much more than the one-third removed. There would be losers. Departments graded 2 and 1 would receive much less. The RAE began in 1986 and has been conducted roughly every four years ever since.

The RAE became the Research Excellence Framework (REF) in 2010 with much more importance attached to the measured quality of publications on a scale 1–4 and on the 'impact' (also measured) of the research conducted on economic usefulness, government policy, social improvement, and so on. The quantum of money for the top grades has become focused more and more on fewer 'research universities'. Indeed, the distinction is made now between 'research universities' and 'teaching universities', reflecting profound differences in funding.

All this is most important in our understanding of the evolving nature of university departments of education and indeed of their continuing survival.

41.4 Evolving Nature of Educational Studies Within Universities

Educational studies had become, as explained above, a major 'discipline' within the university sector, with all teachers trained within universities either as post-graduate trainees or via the newly established professional degree, the B.Ed. Now being part of the university system, educational studies needed to gain greater 'academic respectability'. At a conference of the Association of Teachers in Colleges and Departments of Education in Hull in 1964, studies for the professional development of teachers were dismissed by Professor Richard Peters as 'so much undifferentiated mush'. Henceforth began a purposeful attempt to inject into the professional training and development of teachers an academic rigour that respectability in the eyes of the universities demanded. There was an exponential growth of theory in what were called the 'foundation disciplines'—the philosophy, sociology, psychology and history of education, and finally comparative and curriculum studies.

At the same time, there became a need to develop a research tradition within universities (though—most important—not necessarily within the relatively new education departments), which would inform policy makers on education, on the training of teachers and on their professional development.

Three examples illustrate this.

First, the Rutter Report (1979), in recognising the influence of social disadvantage, showed how certain kinds of intervention could make a considerable difference to children—thereby countering the pervasive influence of the view that the effects of social and economic disadvantage were so powerful that school could make little or no difference. Rutter and his team provided detailed case studies of twelve schools from similar social and economically disadvantaged areas and showed considerable difference in achievement, differences which could only be explained by the quality of the teaching in the school. This research gave rise to the development within education departments of further fruitful research into school effectiveness and school improvement. (see, for example, Mortimore and Sammons 1997).

Second, the establishment in the 1970s and 1980s of 'Educational Priority Areas' followed the research of Halsey (1972), on the relation of educational performance to social conditions. Thus began what was referred to as 'the political arithmetic' tradition in the sociology of education', namely, quantitative research which requires the gathering of hard data, especially in relation to gender, ethnicity and social class, and of discovering the correlation of such data with subsequent performance and achievement. There is, of course, a philosophical question about the extent to which strong correlations constitute causal relations, but, in the shaping of policy, such powerful connections clearly are, and need to be, influential.

Third, the long standing debate on selection for different kinds of school (in England, the selection for grammar schools of 20% of the 11 year-old age cohort) depended on the research, published through learned journals, on the nature of intelligence—its fixed or movable nature and its measurement. The research of Cyril Burt, itself arising from the research of Galton (whose laboratory was at University College London), pointed to the fixed hereditary nature of intelligence and of the accuracy of the IQ tests in determining what kind of education (and therefore school) a student should have after the age of 11. It was, however, the work of another psychologist, Philip Vernon, which demonstrated that, rather than the intelligence quotient being fixed, it could be raised by as many as 14 points through coaching, thereby undermining the basis for selection at age 11.

These three examples show how research has influenced educational policy, with implications for educational practice. But one interesting feature of these researches is that they did not arise from within education departments. Michael Rutter was Director of the Institute of Psychiatry, Halsey was Director of the Department of Social Policy at the University of Oxford, Heath was a Fellow of New College Oxford, Burt was an educational psychologist employed by the London County Council. Where major research, which guides educational policy, arises from within the distinctive disciplines of sociology or psychology, then there would seem to be no need for education departments to undertake such research. Such departments would need, so it seems, only to show the relevance of such research to educational practice through their teacher training and professional development courses. Education Priority Areas (EPAs) were established as a result of Halsey's research; Rutter and colleagues' research stimulated the school effectiveness and school improvement developments in schools and across schools; Burt's research and papers were influential in the creation of nation-wide IQ tests for entry into grammar schools—though rejected in most areas following Vernon's research. Hence, 'beware Chicago' where the once prestigious School of Education, by cutting itself off from practical work in schools in order to concentrate on its research, having joined the School of Social Sciences, eventually closed down.

41.5   Criticisms of Educational Research

Meanwhile there were increasing criticisms of educational research, which was gradually emerging in the relatively new University departments of education. Those criticisms had an impact in England on the political views about the purposes served by funding research within education departments of universities. That political understanding was forcefully expressed by Lord Skidelski in the House of Lords

> Many of the fruits of that research I would describe as an uncontrolled growth of theory, an excessive emphasis on what is called the context in which teaching takes place, which is code for class, gender and ethnic issues, and an extreme paucity of testable hypotheses about what works and does not work. (see Bassey 1995, p. 33)

Those doubts were reinforced by the Hillage Report, published in 1998 by the Department for Education and Employment. Many believed that the money given to universities for educational research was not well spent. Four reasons were given for this.

The first reason for the research money not being well spent was that much research is often tendentious or politically motivated and exclusive of those who do not share the ideological underpinnings of the research programme—much the point made by Lord Skidelski quoted above. Indeed, that was a major criticism made by Tooley and Darby (1998) in their analysis of research articles in four leading educational journals on behalf of Ofsted, the inspectorate of schools. This was inevitably refuted by many in the research community, but the dispute reflected the fundamental differences, often of a philosophical kind, which underpin the understanding of education—its nature and its aims—and thereby research into it.

The second reason given by Hillage was that educational research does not provide answers to the questions Government asks in order to decide between alternative policies on 'what works'. In response, however, there would seem to have been clear examples of where research did provide answers, such as in the examples given above. But, even then, there is inevitably political reluctance to accept 'what works' where that does not comply with the prevailing political ideology (as in the case of selection at age 11 for different kinds of schooling). More importantly, however, is the meaning of 'what works'. Unfavourable comparisons were made to medical research where such research not only identifies the cause of illness but also provides the appropriate cure.

The third reason given for the inadequacy of educational research was that it did not help teachers in their professional practice (for example, demonstrating the most appropriate teaching methods). Can there not, following the example of medicine, be a 'science of teaching'—that is, the creation of systematically tested hypotheses predicting exactly what will happen if one follows a particular course of action? For example, a National Strategy for reading in secondary schools was universally instituted, based on research, to improve the 'outputs' as measured on tests. A 328 page book, including 'booster classes', showed 'exactly how teachers should gear their teaching to the precise requirements of the tests' (Mansell 2007, p. 59). The difficulties here, however, are several. One is that such strategies are disengaged from the complex social conditions and relations within the teaching setting which require professional judgment on the part of the teacher, not simply the 'delivery' of a set of prescriptions irrespective of context and learners. In pursuit of a more scientific style of research, the science of 'deliverology' has arisen defined in terms of measurable targets and performance indicators (see www.kypost.com/dpp/news/state/institute-to-help-ramp-up-educational-improvement).

The fourth reason given by the Hillage Report was that educational research is fragmented—lots of bits and pieces which, though often addressing similar questions, start from different positions or use different samples, not creating a coherent and reliable basis for practice or policy. Again, adverse comparisons are made with medicine. Hargreaves (1996), drawing upon a North American critique of educational research and his own Leverhulme funded project, argued that, despite the enormous amount of money spent on research and the large number of people who claim to be active researchers, there was not the cumulative body of relevant knowledge which would enable teaching to be (like medicine) a research-based profession. For it to be so, it would be necessary to change, first, the content of that research, and, second, the control and sponsorship of it. Content would need to focus on the practice of teaching and learning in order to build up sufficient, well-tested bodies of knowledge to serve as guidelines for professional practice in, say, the teaching of reading or in the grouping of pupils in classrooms. Of course, such a corpus of knowledge would be complex and would need to be used flexibly because situations, context and personalities of both teacher and learner affect the relevance of the research conclusions. None the less, such a research exercise would seem possible. Teachers would need to be involved (as doctors are in the development of research-based medicine) in identifying research needs, in formulating the questions which respond to these needs and in collecting the data to make it 'rooted firmly in the day-to-day professional practices'. The relationship between 'professional researchers' and teachers would be more integrated in the setting of agendas and in the undertaking of the research. This was reiterating what Stenhouse (1975, Chap. 10) had argued, namely, that only the teachers could appreciate, and have access to, the complexity of data required to understand the interactions of the classroom.

These criticism of educational research (namely, not saying 'what works'; irrelevance to professional practice; fragmentation; politically biased or indeed motivated) were reiterated in the US. Hargreaves (1996) quoted Lortie as saying of the US,

> Teaching has not been subjected to the sustained, empirical and practice-oriented inquiry into problems and alternatives which we find in university based professions … [T]o an astonishing degree the beginner in teaching must start afresh, uninformed about prior solutions and alternative approaches to recurring problems …

The issues were thoroughly discussed in the pages of *Educational Researcher*. Kaestle (1993) asked the question, 'Why is the reputation of educational research so awful?' In a collection of papers addressing these matters, Goodlad put the problem bluntly:

> Criticism of educational research and statements regarding its unworthiness are commonplace in the halls of power and commerce, in the public marketplace, and even among large numbers of educators who work in our schools. Indeed, there is considerable advocacy for the elimination of the locus of most educational research - namely, schools, colleges and departments of education. (see Berliner et al. 1997, p. 13)

But the reasons seemed to lie not so much in the lack of an adequate knowledge-base. Indeed, Gage dismissed those critics who said that research had not provided the well-tested generalizations which can inform practice. But he did take researchers to task for their failure to develop an adequate theoretical framework within which well-established research might be brought to bear upon educational understanding and practice. There was a need for the 'meta-analyses' of existing research to meet the needs of those who wanted to know the evidence for supporting one policy rather than another, or one educational practice rather than an alternative. Berliner draws a similar conclusion: there was the body of knowledge, but it was not synthesized in a way which could relate to teachers' administrators and politicians.

In modern parlance, educational research was conducted without reference to possible or likely 'impact'.

41.6   But Different Kinds of Educational Research

The foregoing criticisms require certain broad distinctions.

First, there is the kind of research which, providing a broad picture of the effects of social conditions, draws conclusions for policy—given agreement on educational aims. Such research lies within the 'political arithmetic' tradition exemplified by the work of Halsey and Heath, referred to above. It would include also the longitudinal research such as the Youth Cohort Studies conducted at the London Institute of Education. It would include, too, the research behind the Assessment of Performance Unit which itself was inspired and based on the US' National Assessment of Educational Performance. Such research, on the basis of periodic stratified and light sampling of educational performance across the curriculum, was able to give a picture of educational standards and their change over time. However, one difficulty with instituting such research is the necessary size of the cohorts taking part and the consequent cost of conducting the research. It requires the financial support of foundations such as the Nuffield Foundation or the ESRC (Economic and Social Science Research Council) over a period of several years.

Second, the frequent reference to the comparative virtues of medical research has emphasized the need for a more systematic approach to observation through experimental and control groups—pioneered in medicine by Professor Arthur Cochrane in the United States, and replacing anecdotal case description (Cochrane 1972). Following this, the Cochrane Centre was established in Oxford to help policy-makers make decisions on proven effectiveness of evidence-based policy and practice within the social services. An essential element in this approach was the systematic review of existing research for the quality of its sampling and its methodology more generally. The compatibility or otherwise between different research findings would be analysed. Reports would be produced on what conclusions were to be trusted. Such a centre in education was established at the London Institute of Education. And an example would be Sylva and Hurry's research into intervention in reading difficulties which compared two different interventions with a control group, thereby concluding that, if one group scores significantly more high on reading after the period of intervention, then the intervention itself was a significant factor in the improvement.

Consequently, there have been initiatives, both in the UK and in North America, to learn from the developments in evidence-based health care and, through systematic reviews of research (especially randomized controlled tests) to answer specific policy and professional questions by reference to well-established evidence (see the series of papers in Thomas and Pring 2004).

Similarly, in response to the criticisms of educational research referred to, the Research Council (ESRC) funded UK's largest ever research investment in education, directed by Andrew Pollard at the Institute of Education, viz. 'Teaching and Learning Programmes 2002–9'. It addressed many of the criticisms referred to above, in particular 'quality criteria for the assessment of educational research in different contexts'.

A third distinction would be that the attraction of a more scientific model of research (a 'science of teaching') has created an approach to research into teacher effectiveness permeating the demands for greater accountability. Within the behaviourist tradition, research into 'effectiveness' has required precise behavioural outcomes together with the claimed practices which either do or do not lead to those outcomes. In hypothesizing and then measuring the outcomes, one can build up a body of theory on what teaching methods and approaches 'work'. Thus there has developed a science of 'deliverology', pioneered by Sir Michael Barber, and established in the US Education Delivery Unit. The research which incorporates the language of delivery and justifies the tools for 'delivering' outcomes, is to be found in the 2012 McKinsey Report, *How the World's Most Improved School Systems Continue to Get Better.*

Finally, however, the fourth area of criticism arising from Hillage Report was that so much research fails to address the problems which teachers daily face. It is as though the world of the educational researcher and the world of the teacher are far apart, or, even worse, impose a model of cause and effect which does not do justice to the complex world of the classroom, or to the different contexts in which teachers work. They ignore the values, aims and deliberation which permeate the thoughtful teacher's judgment. A powerful tradition therefore has emerged of teacher-initiated action research, pioneered in England by Laurence Stenhouse in the Centre for Applied Research in Education at the University of East Anglia. Research here refers to any 'systematic, critical and self-critical enquiry which aims to contribute to the advancement of knowledge' (Stenhouse 1975, p. 156). Such knowledge, geared to understanding particular practices (for example, how to promote discussion on controversial issues, or how to get across to young learners central but difficult concepts in biology), would give rise to tentative hypotheses which need to be tested out, and refined in the light of further experience. Moreover, it would be discovered that such practices worked in certain circumstances, and not in others—those differences being noted and entering into the more general knowledge or theory. A significant variable would be the teacher—his or her talent, temperament, and understanding. For that reason each teacher would need to develop a research perspective in his or her practice. For it to be a research per-spective there would need to be a critical reflection based on evidence. The nature of such action research is fully described by Elliott (1991) in his influential book, *Action Research for Educational Change,* in which there are many examples of action research in practice, especially in relation to the formulation of hypotheses, the gathering of evidence and the significance of supportive but critical commu-nities of teacher researchers.

41.7 Impact of Research Measurement

At the same time universities were, as explained above, changing in so far as research was becoming a much more important element in their responsibilities, and even-tually in their funding. Quality of research submitted for consideration was, under RAE, measured on a scale 5 to 1. Initially the judgment would be made by panels chosen for each university subject on a range of evidence including publications, research grants from external resources, number of research students successfully completing research degrees, proven influence on educational policy and practice, and the ethos of the respective departments. The transformation of RAE into REF put greater stress on the four best publications (measured on the scale 4 to 1) from those members of the respective departments chosen for submission. The overall research quality of the department would be calculated (again on a scale 4 to 1) on the measured quality of the publications of the academics submitted to the panel—who would most likely be fewer than the total number of academics within the department. Furthermore, under REF, 'impact measures' were introduced. League tables of university departments in the different subjects inevitably followed. Given so many universities, following the expansion in the 1980s and subsequently, and given an increased competitiveness between universities for students, one's place in the league table became important for reputation and funding.

Education, now being a 'discipline' along side all the others in the university, is subject to the same pressures. The funding arrangements were changing as funding was to be concentrated in fewer university centres for research. In 2001, 81 university education departments submitted altogether 2045 'active researchers' for the RAE. The 50 departments assessed as 3 (that is, at national levels of excellence) received no funding and the 18 rated 4 had their funding cut back.

Therefore, as the overall unit of resource has fallen, getting high grades in research, based mainly on publications, has become increasingly important and therefore consequences follow, namely,

- focus on internationally significant research (the 'big ideas' of universal application);
- publication of such research in journals high on the Social Science Citation Index;
- a new and inflated market in the appointment of academics who have so published;
- less significance given to more practically focused research which cemented the relationship between education and schools—the very fruitful 'action research' referred to above.

To aid this process, there has emerged a 'league-table' of journals, publication in which would be one 'impact measure' and therefore would contribute to the quality rating of the paper published. Thus, the 'Thomson Reuters Impact Factors', with reference to Taylor and Francis publications for 2014, measures the impact value of their many journals related to educational studies and research. For example, the citation index for the *British Journal of Educational Studies* was 0.444 whereas that for the *Oxford Review of Education* (a 'rival' journal) was 0.739, and for the Journal of Educational Policy, 1.318. It is clear therefore which journals one should strive to publish in if one is to be judged a researcher of international quality.

The effects of all this on the idea of the university and of the role of academics within them are several, affecting necessarily the nature of education departments and, for many, their survival.

First, there is a growing hierarchy within the university sector, at the top of which are the 'research universities', the departments within which (having being judged 'internationally excellent' in their research) are much better funded and more able to attract profitable overseas students—compared to other universities funded in effect as 'teaching universities'. Increasingly universities are, at a time when there is a declining 'unit of resource', to close down departments which are becoming a financial burden.

Second, within such university departments, there is an increased division between those who do research (and who need time and resources to research and to publish) and those who just teach (mainly those whose research was not judged good enough for submission to the REF subject panels). A recent example brought to my notice is that of a well researched paper, arising from work in several schools, concerning transition from primary to secondary school. Such research is relevant to current policy deliberations on an issue of importance. But it was judged internally not to be of 3* quality because, without international reference or significance. It was therefore denied permission to publish. This young lecturer therefore has to remain in a teaching only contract—lower pay and three hours only a week for engaging in research.

Third, research seeking assessment as internationally excellent is unlikely to be pursued in partnership with local schools, and thus to focus on the kind of school improvement arising from teacher based research. There becomes a growing gap between pursuing research of international significance and the original mission of education departments, namely, that of serving the schools and colleges through initial training and professional development of teachers—where theory (what universities are good at) is tested against practice (what schools are good at) and practice informed by theory. When the establishment of a department for the training of teachers was first mooted at the University of Oxford in the 1890s, against the views of many at that university, it was Mr. Haverfield of Christ Church who foresaw the possible integration between theory and practice and between the academic concerns of the university and the practical purposes of schools.

> The object seems to me to get the future teacher thinking about teaching; then being (on the whole) an educated and capable man, he will probably be able to take his own line. (Bryce report 1895, v. 167)

Fourth, the competition between universities for league-table rankings inhibits the collaboration between disciplines within and between universities. Better to keep the research and publication 'within house'.

The implications of all this for the role and funding of university department of education is considerable, leading to questions over the viability of some and over the relevance of many to initial training and professional development of teachers. Especially is this the case when the Government is supporting routes other than through universities for the training of teachers.

How far can the close relationship between departments of Education, rooted in the practice and experience of schools as well as relevant theory, now be maintained in the modern university, given the changing pressures on them? Should we not learn from Chicago? There the once prestigious School of education, under pressure to produce world-class research, found less and less time to be in schools. It joined the University's School of Social Sciences. The social scientists did not care much for the research of the erstwhile educationists. Educational studies, without friends in schools and without friends in the university, closed down.

References

Bassey, M. (1995). *Creating education through research.* Newark: Kirklington Moor Press.
Berliner, D. C. et al. (Eds.). (1997). "The vision thing": Educational research and AERA in the 21st century. *Educational Researcher, 26*(5), 12.
Bryce Report. (1895). *Secondary education,* London: HMSO.
Cochrane, A. (1972). *Effectiveness and efficiency: Random reflections on health services.*
Elliott, J. (1991). *Action research and educational change.* Milton Keynes: Open University Press.
Halsey, A. H. (1972). *Education priority.* London: HMSO.
Hargreaves, D. (1996). Teaching as a research-based profession. Teacher Training Agency Annual Lecture.
Hillage Report. (1998). *Excellence in research on schools.* University of Sussex: The Institute for Employment Studies.
Kaestle, C. F. (1993). The awful reputation of educational research. *Educational Researcher, 22*(1), 23.
Mill, J. S. (1867). Inaugural address at St. Andrews. In F. A. Cavanagh (Ed.). (1931). *James and John Stuart Mill on education.*
Mortimore, P., & Sammons, P. (1997). In J. White & M. Barber (Eds.), *Perspectives on school effectiveness and school improvement.* London: Bedford Way Papers.
Rutter Report. (1979). *15,000 hours: Secondary schools and effects on children,* London: Open Books.
Stenhouse, L. (1975). *An introduction to curriculum research and development.* London: Heinemann.
Thomas, G., & Pring, R. (Eds.). (2004). *Evidence based educational practice.* Open University Press: Milton Keynes.
Tooley, J., & Darby, D. (1998). *Educational research: An OFSTED critique.* London: OFSTED.

Author Biography

Richard Pring is Director of Department of Educational Studies, Oxford University 1989–2003, Director of Nuffield Review '14–19 Education and Training', 2003–2009. Publications since retirement: *John Dewey: philosopher of education for 21st century; Philosophy of Educational Research (3rd edition); Life and Death of Secondary Education for All; A Generation of Radical Educational Change* (edited).

Chapter 42
The Role of Comparative and International Research in Developing Capacity to Study and Improve Teacher Education

Maria Teresa Tatto

It has become fashionable among comparativists to argue that innovations in the "developing" world are due to policy borrowing and that little learning occurs at the local level. An important assumption of this view is that there are some who have the knowledge and expertise that is desirable and that others do not have it and thus see themselves in the role of borrowers. Rather than truly to innovate, it is argued, policy makers and educators too often look outside their locales for solutions to complex, unique, and local educational problems. In this chapter, I propose a different model based on my own work as a Mexican researcher working in Mexico and internationally, and as informed by my work in comparative research. I argue that international and comparative research that is collaborative, reflective, rigorous, capacity building, and policy oriented can allow learning at the ground level and produce useable knowledge for policy making and implementation and that this learning and development of expertise can occur within and across settings regardless of level of development.[1] Moreover, I propose that the mere act of engaging in comparative and collaborative reflective inquiry already constitutes an intervention and brings about learning and a notion of normativity to the phenomenon under study, thus challenging the notion that research does not have an effect and that policy is "packaged" and borrowed. The comparative and interna-

---

This chapter is a shortened and slightly edited version of the article Tatto, M.T. (2011). Reimagining the education of teachers: The role of comparative and international research. *Comparative Education Review*, 55, 495–516 (with permission).

[1]The idea of reflective learning is not new and has been extensively explored as a pathway to individual and organizational learning by Argyris and Schön (1978) and Schön (1983). What is new in my work is the idea of taking reflective learning to scale by using it as part of my approach to collaborative comparative research.

M.T. Tatto (✉)
Arizona State University, Tempe, USA
e-mail: teresa.tatto@asu.edu

© Springer Nature Singapore Pte Ltd. 2017
M.A. Peters et al. (eds.), *A Companion to Research in Teacher Education*,
DOI 10.1007/978-981-10-4075-7_42

tional dimension brings an added layer to what can be learned from research as it illuminates what is possible in other contexts from a scientific and humanistic perspective.[2]

The model I have developed for comparative education research could be understood as "a collaborative and reflective approach to policy-oriented inquiry." While these words may sound simple, the idea of conducting comparative research that is truly collaborative and reflective is a highly complex enterprise. It carries a strong commitment to the development of the capacity for true participation and reflective learning in the research process. It requires the construction of episte-mological communities of researchers operating within the frameworks of comparative inquiry. In addition, since the research is located within the policy realm, it requires the use of rigorous study methods.[3] Thus, the research questions are formulated considering a socially relevant problem or area of interest defined by enduring questions in the field and with high internal and construct validity.[4] The use of social science theory includes consideration of (a) the State as a key and relatively autonomous actor, "able to formulate independent goals and to shape societal outcomes" (Kjaer 2007, 126); (b) institutional theory, to understand negotiation of conflicting internal and external demands (Cummings 1999); and (c) governance theory, to understand the State's and organizations'/institutions' search for legitimate power, social exchange and cohesion, trust, and accountability (Kjaer 2007). Using social science methods includes understanding and applying multidisciplinary and systematic procedures and techniques adapted to diverse modes of inquiry taken from psychology, policy analysis, and evaluation research.[5] The analysis and the results, while open to public scrutiny, carry strong respect for and protection of participating individuals, and ways of seeing emerge from those who implement and receive the policy. For the field of comparative education, the ultimate goal is the development of "useful and concise theory" (Farrell 1979, 4).

This approach invites individuals and institutions and in some cases the State, to create a space for collaborative inquiry in interaction with external and internal

---

[2]Indeed, as Bereday (1977) pointed out, systematic and symmetric comparison of settings to elicit a balanced view of the similarities and differences comes close to "permitting inferences, predictions, and recommendations for policy" an approach that he called quasi-scientific. See Kazamias (1961) for an excellent argument on why the aims of comparative education must be seen as a combination of scientific and humanistic elements.

[3]Reflective researchers are especially vulnerable to criticisms by policy makers. To be taken seriously, their research needs to demonstrate rigor, especially if the aim is to develop bottom-up policy alternatives.

[4]Because my work is located in the policy analysis area, research questions are typically directed at finding whether or not policy has been successful at achieving a positive influence on identified social problems. Internal and construct validity are essential in this process, and I argue that these can only be achieved if the questions are defined by those who are intrinsically connected with the object of the research. For more on these important concepts consult Trochim (2006).

[5]There are numerous approaches to evaluation research. I follow the excellent foundations developed by Weiss (1972, 1997).

networks, local institutions, and individuals. Collaborative and reflective inquiry brings about learning (understanding what the concept is and why it is important, as well as considering whether we know enough); creates a new language and definitions for the specific field of study to serve in cross-national, cross-cultural communication; and develops collaborative capacity building, thus enabling individuals and institutions to play an active role in education and policy development and implementation. This approach, therefore, helps to create spaces for what I term the "collaborative construction" and "collaborative contextualization" of policy-usable knowledge.

In the rest of this chapter, I illustrate the application of this model to the international study of teacher education. While my foundational experiences began in Sri Lanka (see Fig. 42.1) and in Mexico (see Tatto 2001 for a summary of these experiences), I have chosen a large comparative study carried in collaboration with 17 countries between 2006 and 2013 to illustrate my approach to research.

42.1 Views on the Knowledge Teachers Need to Be Able to Teach Well

Beginning in the 1980s, there was a transformation in the dominant theories of teaching and teacher learning away from transmission views and toward a more cognitive, constructivist, or situated-learning orientation (e.g., Schön 1987). In the late 1990s and early 2000s, changing conceptions of what it meant to know and of what knowledge was valued in teaching had led to questions about the worth of traditional teacher education programs and about how to reform them (Day et al. 2000; Stuart and Tatto 2000). Internationally, there were debates about these issues as well (e.g., UNESCO 1996). New definitions of "good teaching" included knowing and managing disciplinary content, helping pupils develop intellectual tools, and making them aware of their own intellectual capacities during learning. The international and comparative research literature suggested that quality teachers may evolve from different models of teacher education and development including those based on spiritual, moral, and aesthetic conceptions of good teaching with a focus on learning (LeTendre and Rohlen 1999; Avalos 2000), and sensitive to the political aspects of teachers' lives (Liston and Zeichner 1991). Others called for attention to schools' culture as a key factor expected to facilitate self-regulatory processes to, in turn, influence effective teaching (Fuller and Clarke 1994); yet others took a more relativistic position, affirming that definitions of quality teaching and learning were very diverse and highly dependent on school context (Rust and Dalin 1990). In sum, while the field seemed open to considering alternative views on the knowledge needed for teaching and to modifying teacher education and development accordingly, few of these notions were sustained by convincing empirical evidence.

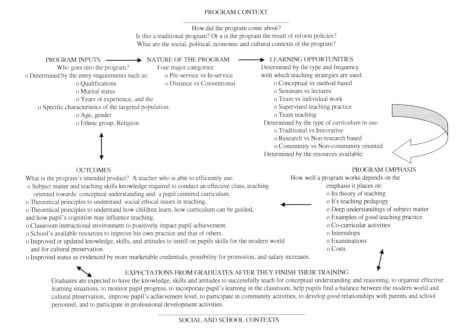

PROGRAM CONTEXT
How did the program come about?
Is this a traditional program? Or a is the program the result of reform policies?
What are the social, political, economic and cultural contexts of the program?

PROGRAM INPUTS ————————▶ NATURE OF THE PROGRAM ————————▶ LEARNING OPPORTUNITIES
Who goes into the program?   Four major categories: Determined by the type and frequency
o Determined by the entry requirements such as: o Pre-service vs In-service   with which teaching strategies are used:
            o Qualifications   o Distance vs Conventional   o Conceptual vs method based
            o Marital status   o Seminars vs lectures
            o Years of experience, and the   o Team vs individual work
    o Specific characteristics of the targeted population: o Supervised teaching practice
            o Age, gender   o Team teaching
            o Ethnic group, Religion   Determined by the type of curriculum in use:
                                                                                      o Traditional vs Innovative
                                                                                      o Research vs Non-research based
                                                                                      o Community vs Non-community oriented
                                                                           Determined by the resources available:

OUTCOMES   PROGRAM EMPHASIS
What is the program's intended product? A teacher who is able to efficiently use: How well a program works depends on the
o Subject matter and teaching skills knowledge required to conduct an effective class, teaching   emphasis it places on:
  oriented towards: conceptual understanding and a pupil centered curriculum.   o Its theory of teaching
o Theoretical principles to understand social ethical issues in teaching.   o It's teaching pedagogy
o Theoretical principles to understand how children learn, how curriculum can be guided,   o Deep understandings of subject matter
and how pupil's cognition may influence teaching.   o Examples of good teaching practice
o Classroom instructional environment to positively impact pupil achievement.   o Co-curricular activities
o School's available resources to improve his own practice and that of others.   o Internships
o Improved or updated knowledge, skills, and attitudes to instill on pupils skills for the modern world   o Examinations
  and for cultural preservation.   o Costs
o Improved status as evidenced by more marketable credentials, possibility for promotion, and salary increases.

EXPECTATIONS FROM GRADUATES AFTER THEY FINISH THEIR TRAINING
Graduates are expected to have the knowledge, skills and attitudes to successfully teach for conceptual understanding and reasoning, to organize effective
learning situations, to monitor pupil progress, to incorporate pupil's learning in the classroom, help pupils find a balance between the modern world and
cultural preservation, improve pupil's achievement level, to participate in community activities, to develop good relationships with parents and school
personnel, and to participate in professional development activities.

SOCIAL AND SCHOOL CONTEXTS

Fig. 42.1 Conceptual foundations underlying the actions of teacher education approaches in Sri Lanka (*Source* Tatto 1991)

42.2   An Evolving Theoretical Framework to Guide Studies

The diversity of views concerning the knowledge needed for teaching was related to the multitude of idiosyncratic views on teacher education and the general lack of an empirically validated teacher education *program theory*, that is, a more general theory postulating the links between teacher education, teaching quality, and pupil learning. Most of what was known about the effects of teacher education had been advanced by research on teaching framed within the process-product paradigm in areas studying pupil learning.[6] However, after Thomas Kuhn's *The Structure of Scientific Revolutions* (1962), these views began to change. In addition, under the increasing influence in education of the premises of social constructivism first initiated by Piaget (1967) and energetically brought into the 1990s by Von Glasersfeld (1995)[7] among others, accepted ideas about knowledge, teaching and learning, and knowledge for teaching began to be questioned.

[6]See Garrison and Macmillan (1984) for a critique of this approach.

[7]See a critique of Van Glasersfield's radical constructivism in Slezak (2000). For the origins of constructivist thought see also Vygotsky (1986) and Montessori (1961).

In the late 1990s and early 2000s, international researchers began to examine the effect of various classroom-level variables and school-level factors on student achievement including databases produced by the International Association for the Evaluation of Educational Achievement (IEA) studies such as TIMSS (e.g., Bos and Kuiper 1999; Keys 1999; Koller et al. 1999). These databases, however, lacked detailed information on the knowledge and skills that teachers of high-achieving pupils possessed and information on what characterized their teaching.[8] The results of the TIMSS Video Study (Stigler and Hiebert 1997; Stigler et al. 2000) began to open up the notion that teachers across cultures exhibited substantially different practices and depths of knowledge that seemed associated with the achievement levels of their pupils as measured in the TIMSS tests. Until then, the theoretical framework to guide studies of teacher education had not been based on assessing the expected knowledge for teaching that future teachers must acquire to teach well.[9]

42.3 The Use of Diverse and Increasingly Sophisticated Methods

Changing conceptions about knowledge, and how it is learned began to influence the design of education studies. Great advances were made in the conceptualization of teaching and learning as imbedded in hierarchical school and social contexts (e.g., Raudenbush and Bryk 1986; Riddell 1989), and these novel conceptualizations lead to changes in research design and analytic techniques. But while social science methods continued to evolve and provide a richer range of methodological approaches to address the research questions emerging in the field, research on teaching and teacher education was still limited. For instance, in a review of the international literature on teacher education research Tatto (2000) concluded that studies that considered teacher education mostly explored teaching effectiveness as related to pupil learning and included some information concerning teachers' preparation (e.g., whether or not they had credentials on specific subject matters and on pedagogy, or whether they had learned "on the job") but failed to provide important details on what teachers learned, how, why, and when. Particularly problematic were the methods used which used such indicators of teacher preparation as degrees, years of study, and kinds of courses taken but did not directly measure the actual knowledge teachers had acquired as a result of the experienced preparation. Most research on the effects of teacher education on teaching and, thus,

---

[8]An important reaction to the gap on the research on teacher education was the development of comparative descriptive studies of teacher education. The research done by the MUSTER project out of the University of Sussex in a number of African nations merits special recognition. See the work of Lewin and Stuart (2003) and other publications on the MUSTER website (http://www. sussex.ac.uk/education/research/cie/rprojects/muster/pubs).

[9]For an exception see Fig. 42.1 showing the resulting program theory and design guiding the Sri Lanka research by Tatto et al. (1993).

on pupils' learning outcomes included a number of variables that served as indicators of teacher characteristics such as gender, years of schooling, and degrees obtained, but for the most part ignored the process involved in learning to teach. Many large-scale international empirical studies used less-than-ideal proxies for what teachers knew, such as the number of years of teachers' formal education, the quantity of courses they have taken, or whether they attended formal teacher education or development programs (see Fuller and Clarke 1994). Studies specifically directed at exploring the impact of teacher education and development had failed to include measurements that could actually reflect what teachers knew (such as observations and tests of knowledge and skills).

In a review of the literature, Kennedy (1999) found that most studies included indirect measures—such as situated descriptions of teaching by teachers, including teachers' daily logs or vignettes, non-situated testimony about practice (e.g., teacher questionnaires and interviews that ask about teaching practices), or testimony about effects of policies or programs in which teachers are asked to judge how a policy affects teaching practice. She argued that as one is further removed from direct tests of knowledge and observations the larger is the risk of self-serving bias, lack of face validity, estimation errors, and reliability. More recent work explored relationships between time and learning, pupil cognition, and teacher cognition, and decision making. Many of these studies have, for the most part, ignored indicators essential to teachers' learning and teaching quality, such as the knowledge that teachers acquire as a result of teacher education and how it relates to curriculum and instruction, and to the values orientation of teachers and their pupils (Good and Brophy 2000).

Although still limited in scope, there were exceptions in the international mathematics research literature found in the works by Fuson and Kwon (1992), Fuson et al. (1997), LeTendre and Rohlen (1999), and Linn et al. (2000). Though less dominant, the comparative literature also provides examples of the application of ethnographic and ecological approaches to understanding teacher learning and quality (Ma 1999). A modest number of studies that linked teacher education with teacher quality and pupil learning used statistical analysis methods, such as HLM or ML3, to allow for analysis across the nested contexts of schooling; such methods later came into common use.[10] By the early 2000s, however, no large-scale studies had linked teacher education with teachers' acquired knowledge for teaching and with teacher quality and pupil learning.

In sum, the research on teacher education—while making important contributions to the field—was lacking in several aspects, ranging from the positing of valid and relevant research questions to how and whether the research was disclosed for examination by the users of the knowledge produced. The quality of educational research as an issue was widely acknowledged by the early 2000s, and the educational community, with the support of the National Academy of Sciences, agreed

---

[10]See Creemers and Reezigt (1996), Murnane et al. (1996), Raudenbush and Bryk (1986), and Riddell (1989).

upon principles of scientific inquiry in education. Important work has been done in this area by Shavelson and Towne (2002, 51–52). They agree that while "there is no universally accepted description of the elements of scientific inquiry," a way to proceed was to describe the scientific process in terms of six interrelated, but not necessarily ordered principles of inquiry:

- Pose significant questions that can be investigated empirically.
- Link research to relevant theory.
- Use methods that permit direct investigation of the question.
- Provide a coherent and explicit chain of reasoning.
- Replicate and generalize across studies.
- Disclose research to encourage professional scrutiny and critique.

In addition to the preceding principles, I suggested three more (Tatto 2001). The process should be aimed at the following:

- Reflection[11]
- Capacity building
- Policy building

These ideas have proven indispensable in my comparative education research and have guided the next stage of my work.

42.4   Designing and Implementing a Comparative Study of Teacher Education

International teacher education researchers have conducted a variety of case studies and descriptive studies focused on answering questions concerning *what* characterizes teacher education and *how* it is implemented (e.g., Craig et al. 1998). However, in 2000 there was scarce evidence based on empirical studies using representative samples to document the influence of teacher education and development on teacher learning, teaching practice, and pupil learning.

---

[11]The idea that the recipients of the policy should be active subjects (not the objects) in the research enterprise has guided my work since I began doing it in Mexico in 1978. These ideas further evolved as a result of my work with Carol Weiss and Noel McGinn and expressed in a paper that McGinn and I wrote early on in my doctoral program (McGinn and Tatto 1984).

42.4.1 Piloting the TEDS-M Study

In 2000, a comprehensive review of the research literature supported a call to the teacher education and development community to move beyond purely descriptive or explanatory studies towards more exploratory and evaluative, policy-relevant, and prospective studies to test the various hypotheses underlying teacher education and development (Tatto 2000, 2008). Subsequently, the National Science Foundation (NSF) encouraged and supported a proposal for such a study.[12] In 2003 the NSF supported a pilot study for the larger IEA TEDS-M. In collaboration with colleagues from Bulgaria, Taiwan, Germany, Mexico, South Korea, and the United States, we initiated an exploratory study of how lower-secondary mathematics teachers learn to teach mathematics content effectively as a result of their preparation.

The main findings from this pilot study indicated that the opportunities to learn provided by teacher education programs impacted what future teacher knew and believed when they left their teacher education programs. The future teachers in the particular programs selected for study in Taiwan and South Korea seemed to be most knowledgeable on questions asking them about mathematics and pedagogy concepts.[13] Contrary to expectations, however, the opportunities to learn provided to these highly knowledgeable future teachers were for the most part balanced across mathematics, mathematics pedagogy, and general pedagogy (including practical pedagogy). The future teachers from Mexico whose programs emphasized general pedagogy also did quite well in these questions, suggesting the importance of providing coherent opportunities to learn to future teachers. While much was accomplished in this pilot study, there were important limitations. For example, the study did not develop an assessment of teacher knowledge having instead a series of questions that covered some but not all of the knowledge domains expected from future mathematics teachers, these were then constituted as an ex-post-facto test of knowledge; the study was only limited to lower-secondary future teachers (e.g., we had no questions directed at future primary school teachers); and the study did not develop a sampling frame to help select representative samples of future teachers in participating countries to answer our surveys, and used instead a convenience sample. Thus, we learned little in P-TEDS about these three areas, which came to represent important challenges for TEDS-M.

---

[12]I am thankful to Larry Suter and Elizabeth VanderPutten of the NSF for their encouragement in this initial stage of the TEDS-M work. I am also thankful to Janice Earle and James Dietz for their support as NSF program officers for the P-TEDS and TEDS-M studies respectively.

[13]In the pilot study, we did not design a test per se; the questions that were developed were constituted into scales after the future teachers had answered them. Thus, the P-TEDS pilot study fulfilled its purpose, it made it possible to test different strategies for data collection, clarified whether it was possible to ask future teachers questions about their knowledge, and allowed us to learn whether our initial research questions were significant and could be investigated empirically in a larger study.

42.5   The TEDS-M Study Design

In 2005, two years after beginning the pilot study, we secured a larger grant from the NSF to carry out the IEA's First International Mathematics Teacher Education Study (TEDS-M).[14] The study sought to explore a key question that had not been answered satisfactorily in the United States or internationally: How are teachers prepared to teach mathematics in primary and lower secondary schools? And with what results?[15] The key research questions for TEDS-M focused on the relationships between teacher education policies, institutional practices, and future teacher mathematics and pedagogy knowledge[16]:

1. What is the national and policy context for mathematics teacher education?
2. What are the main characteristics of teacher education programs that provide mathematics preparation to future primary and secondary teachers? What opportunities to learn do they provide?
3. What is the level and depth of the mathematics and related teaching knowledge attained by prospective primary and secondary teachers?

See Fig. 42.2 for a visualization of the multilevel relationships we explored as we investigated teacher education outcomes. Consistent with IEA policy TEDS-M extended an open invitation to IEA countries and others not in the IEA network to participate in the study. In the end, 17 countries joined the study: Botswana, Canada, Chile, Georgia, Germany, Malaysia, Norway, Oman, Philippines, Poland, Russia, Singapore, Spain, Switzerland, Taiwan, Thailand, and the United States. These countries fall between medium and high on the Human Development Index (HDI) and varied in size, demographics, and wealth. The countries that participated in TEDS-M were a self-selected group, yet within the group are countries whose

---

[14]This project was funded by a major grant from the NSF (REC-0514431) and was sponsored by the IEA with leadership from Michigan State University in collaboration with the Australian Council for Educational Research (ACER). The final report of TEDS-M, which contains extensive descriptive information on the study findings, was published in Tatto et al. (2012) (see the IEA Publications website http://pub.iea.nl/ please click the 'online' link in the "Complete list of publications" box at the right and then search publications by selecting "a study/project" and then select the TEDS-M link. A copy of this publication can be obtained directly from the author).

[15]At the same time, another study sponsored by the OECD was launched. The study was named TALIS and, according to the OECD, "provided the first internationally comparable data on conditions affecting teachers in schools based on the findings of the OECD's survey in 23 participating countries" (http://www.oecd.org/edu/school/theexperienceofnewteachers-resultsfromtalis2008.htm). TALIS is very different from TEDS-M, but some countries did not participate in TEDS-M under the assumption that TALIS would answer the same or similar questions. It does not.

[16]For a complete description of the study design please consult the TEDS-M *Conceptual Framework* document which is housed at the IEA Publications website http://pub.iea.nl/ please click the 'online' link in the "Complete list of publications" box at the right and then search publications by selecting "a study/project" and then selecting the TEDS-M link. A copy of this publication can be obtained directly from the author.

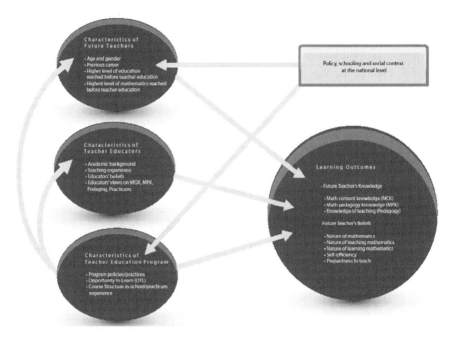

Fig. 42.2 The teacher education and development study conceptual framework (*Source* Tatto et al. 2008)

pupils vary substantially in mathematics achievement, thus allowing us to investigate a diverse set of education systems in terms of the variables of interest.

In 2008, the TEDS-M team and the national research center in each participating country collected data[17] from representative samples of (a) pre-service teacher education programs, (b) future primary teachers, (c) future secondary teachers, and (d) teacher educators in the participating countries. The database developed through the study involved 750 programs; 22,000 future teachers; and approximately 5000 mathematicians, mathematics educators, and general pedagogy educators.

---

[17]Questionnaires were developed to collect information on the systems of teacher education; the background and mathematics knowledge for teaching of future teachers; and background and other relevant information about teacher educators. Document analysis of the teacher education curricula and syllabi in the institutions studied in each country provided a "snapshot" of the intended curriculum.

42.5.1 Findings from TEDS-M

The TEDS-M study provided new insight into the nature of teacher education across the participating countries. Different from other IEA studies that have focused on primary and secondary education systems, this study of teacher education revealed that these systems are not standardized and are rather highly complex. The teacher education programs in the TEDS-M samples varied in terms of size and nature. Of the 750 programs studied about 45% (349 programs) exclusively prepared future teachers to teach primary pupils; about 30% (226 programs) exclusively prepared future teachers to teach secondary pupils; and the rest (176 programs) prepared future teachers to teach primary and secondary pupils (Tatto et al. 2012). The study found that opportunities to learn mathematics, mathematics pedagogy, and pedagogy depended at a general level on the grade level and the curriculum future teachers were expected to teach. For example, compared to the programs preparing lower secondary school teachers, the programs for future primary teachers gave more coverage to the basic concepts of numbers, measurement, and geometry and less coverage to functions, probability and statistics, calculus, and structure. Furthermore, the programs preparing upper secondary teachers tended to either require or provide on average more opportunities to learn mathematics than those programs that prepared teachers for lower secondary schools. The findings of this study thus reflect what seems in some countries to be a cultural norm, namely the idea that teachers who are expected to teach in primary—and especially lower primary—grades do not need much mathematics content beyond that included in the school curriculum. The pattern among secondary future teachers is characterized by more and deeper coverage of mathematics content; however, there was more variability in opportunity to learn mathematics content among those being prepared for lower secondary (known in some countries as "middle school") than among those being prepared to teach upper secondary (grade 11 and above).

Not surprisingly, therefore, we also found that knowledge for teaching mathematics varies considerably among individuals within countries as well as between countries. On average, future primary teachers prepared as mathematics specialists had higher mathematical content knowledge and mathematical pedagogical content knowledge than those prepared to be lower primary generalist teachers. And, on average, future teachers prepared as upper secondary teachers had higher scores in our assessments on both these measures than those being prepared to be lower secondary teachers. Additionally, primary-level and secondary-level teachers in high-achieving systems, such as those in Singapore, Taiwan, and the Russian Federation, had significantly more opportunities to learn university- and school-level mathematics than primary and secondary teachers in others countries (see Tatto et al. 2012 for a full report of the study findings).

In sum, the design of teacher education curricula can have substantial effects on the level of knowledge that future teachers are able to acquire via the opportunities to learn provided to them. Even within the same country, the design of the program according to level (primary or lower primary) may have important consequences on the differential achievement of future teachers.

42.5.2 Contributions of TEDS-M

TEDS-M constituted not only the first nationally representative, correlational, and cross-national research study on teacher education, but in higher education as well. In this regard, TEDS-M laid the foundation for future rigorous cross-national research in teacher education, providing common terminology, sampling methods, instruments, and analytical approaches that can be adapted and improved in subsequent teacher education studies as has been demonstrated by many researchers since the TEDS-M Database became publicly available. Importantly, TEDS-M also served to develop research capacity within the countries that participated in this study and has already contributed to this new line of research through the public dissemination of test items, the resulting database for secondary data analysis, and various technical reports.

The results of TEDS-M provide a baseline for further investigations in the countries that participated in the study. For example, content experts may look at the descriptions of the levels of knowledge acquired by future teachers graduating from their programs and investigate how changes in curriculum or other program features may lead to improved learning. Policy makers may also benefit from learning that encouraging more talented secondary school graduates to pursue teacher education studies can lead to graduates who have higher levels of both mathematics content knowledge and mathematics pedagogical content knowledge. One conclusion that can be drawn from TEDS-M is that the goal of improving future teachers' mathematics content knowledge and mathematics pedagogy knowledge through well-organized pre-service teacher education programs in higher education is ambitious, but achievable.

42.6 A New Study: FIRSTMATH

Despite the important insights derived from TEDS-M, we still do not know how much of what future teachers learn in pre-service programs will eventually contribute to make them successful teachers or whether success in teaching is only acquired in the first years on the job. FIRSTMATH[18] is a comparative study, launched in June 2011 designed to begin to address this question. The study is sponsored by NSF, and brings new and seasoned TEDS-M colleagues together in

---

[18]Funding for FIRSTMATH is provided by a grant from the National Science Foundation Award No. DRL-0910001. Principal Investigator: Maria Teresa Tatto.

the conceptualization and development phases. FIRSTMATH is studying novice teachers' development of mathematical knowledge for teaching and the influence on that knowledge of previous preparation, school context, and opportunities to learn on the job. FIRSTMATH is exploring the connections between pre-service preparation and what is learned on the job with respect to knowledge, skills, and curricular content and the degree to which standards, accountability, and other similar mechanisms may enhance the support that beginning teachers of mathematics receive during their first years of teaching.

We expect that the results of this study will provide needed empirical evidence about the influence of school context and on-the-job opportunities to learn on mathematics teachers' knowledge, as well as about the nature of the knowledge that is useful in and for mathematics teaching in diverse settings and school contexts. The study speaks to contentious policy issues about the relative cost-effectiveness of university-based and alternative certification programs. Understanding these effects has potential economic impact for thousands of school districts and other agencies concerned with teacher recruitment and retention and with developing quality mentoring, induction, and professional development programs for teachers of mathematics and other subjects.

42.7 Conclusion

The various research experiences described above, suggest that a comparative-collaborative-reflective approach to policy-oriented inquiry is uniquely positioned to create spaces for the collaborative construction and collaborative contextualization of policy-usable knowledge.[19] As comparative scholars, we must ask ourselves: What can we learn from doing collaborative and reflective education research and how can this learning be put to good use?

Following Sadler (1900; cited in Bereday 1964; Phillips 2006), there is a need to understand context and culture for the contextualization of policy making and implementation. Additionally, we need to pay attention to the unintended consequences of the myths around the so-called a-contextual "policy borrowing." I propose that we engage national and international networks in what I call the "collaborative and reflective construction of policy knowledge in context" through comparative international research. This approach supersedes the notion of policy borrowing because this joint work by definition brings about the re-contextualization of policy useable knowledge, an action that should not only explain what is, but must identify the factors within specific macro, meso and micro contexts that may lead to continuous educational improvement.

---

[19]The comparative research paradigm I propose already constitutes an intervention and alters the policy landscape as studies progress. This is true from the Sri Lanka studies to the TEDS-M study, where policy evolved as the research evolved. By definition, the research is reflective. That is, it conceptualized and developed by those who finally implement it.

To end I would like to invite you to engage in the development of epistemic communities of comparative education scholarship[20] around the principles and key social concerns of social justice[21] in education and development.

References

Argyris, C., & Schön, D. A. (1978). *Organizational learning: A theory of action perspective.* Reading, MA: Addison Wesley.

Avalos, B. (2000). Policies for teacher education in developing countries. *International Journal of Educational Research, 33*, 457–474.

Bereday, G. Z. F. (1964). Sir Michael Sadler's 'study of foreign systems of education'. *Comparative Education Review, 7*, 307–314.

Bereday, G. Z. F. (1977). Comparative analysis in education. *Prospects, 7*. http://collections.infocollections.org/ukedu/en/d/Jh1848e/2.html

Bos, K., & Kuiper, W. (1999). Modeling TIMSS data in a European comparative perspective: Exploring influencing factors on achievement in mathematics in Grade 8. *Educational Research and Evaluation, 5*, 157–179.

Brighouse, H. (2006). *On education.* New York: Routledge.

Craig, H. J., Kraft, R. J., & du Plessis, J. (1998). *Teacher development: Making an impact.* Washington, DC: U.S. Agency for International Development and World Bank.

Creemers, B. P. M., & Reezigt, G. J. (1996). School level conditions affecting the effectiveness of instruction. *School Effectiveness and School Improvement, 7*, 197–228.

Cummings, W. K. (1999). The institutions of education: Compare, compare, compare! *Comparative Education Review, 43*, 413–437.

Day, C., Fernandez, A., Hauge, T. E., & Moller, J. (2000). *The life and work of teachers: International perspectives in changing times.* London: Falmer.

Farrell, J. P. (1979). The necessity of comparisons in the study of education: The salience of science and the problem of comparability. *Comparative Education Review, 23*, 3–16.

Fuller, B., & Clarke, P. (1994). Raising school effectiveness while ignoring culture? *Review of Educational Research, 64*, 119–157.

Fuson, K. C., & Kwon, Y. (1992). Korean children's single-digit addition and subtraction: Numbers structured by ten. *Journal for Research in Mathematics Education, 23*, 148–165.

Fuson, K., Smith, S. T., & Cicero, A. M. L. (1997). Supporting Latino first graders' ten-structured thinking in urban classrooms. *Journal for Research in Mathematics Education, 28*, 738–766.

Garrison, J. W., & Macmillan, C. J. B. (1984). A philosophical critique of process product research on teaching. *Educational Theory, 34*, 255–274.

Good, T. L., & Brophy, J. E. (2000). *Looking in classrooms* (8th ed.). New York: Longman.

Haas, P. (1992). Introduction: Epistemic communities and international policy coordination. *International Organization, 46*, 1–35.

Kazamias, A. M. (1961). Some old and new approaches to methodology in comparative education. *Comparative Education Review, 5*, 90–96.

Kennedy, M. (1999). Approximations to indicators of student outcomes. *Educational Evaluation and Policy Analysis, 2*, 345–363.

Keys, W. (1999). What can mathematics educators learn from TIMSS? *Educational Research and Evaluation, 5*, 195–213.

Kjaer, A. M. (2007). *Governance.* Malden, MA: Polity Press.

---

[20]See Haas (1992) for an elaboration of the concept of epistemic communities.

[21]See Brighouse (2006).

Koller, O., Baumert, J., Clausen, M., & Hosenfeld, I. (1999). Predicting mathematics achievement on eight grade students in Germany: An application of parts of the model of educational productivity to the TIMSS data. *Educational Research and Evaluation, 5,* 180–194.

Kuhn, T. (1962). *The structure of scientific revolutions.* Chicago, IL: University of Chicago Press.

LeTendre, G. K., & Rohlen, T. P. (1999). *Teaching and learning in Japan.* Cambridge, UK: Cambridge University Press.

Lewin, K. M., & Stuart, J. S. (2003). Research teacher education: New perspectives on practice, performance and policy. MUSTER Synthesis Report no. 12882, Department for International Development (DFID), Sussex, UK. http://webarchive.nationalarchives.gov.uk/+/http://www.dfid.gov.uk/Documents/publications/researchteachedpaper49a.pdf

Linn, M. C., Lewis, C., Tsuchida, I., & Songer, N. B. (2000). Beyond fourth-grade science: Why do U.S. and Japanese students diverge? *Educational Researcher, 29,* 4–14.

Liston, D., & Zeichner, K. (1991). *Teacher education and the social conditions of schooling.* New York: Routledge.

Ma, L. (1999). *Knowing and teaching elementary mathematics.* Mahwah, NJ: Lawrence Erlbaum Associates.

McGinn, N. F., & Tatto, M. T. (1984). *Does research on education fit the development needs of Latin America?* Education Resources Information Center (ERIC: ED245397). Washington, DC: U.S. Department of Education, Institute of Education Sciences.

Montessori, M. (1961). Maria Montessori's contribution to the cultivation of the mathematical mind. *International Review of Education, 7,* 134–141.

Murnane, R., Mullens, J., & Willett, J. (1996). The contribution of training and subject matter knowledge to teaching effectiveness: A multi-level analysis of longitudinal evidence from Belize. *Comparative Education Review, 40,* 139–157.

Phillips, D. (2006). Michael Sadler and comparative education. *Oxford Review of Education, 32,* 39–54.

Piaget, J. (Ed.). (1967). Logique et Connaissance Scientifique. *Encyclopédie de la Pléiade.* Paris: Gallimard.

Raudenbush, S. W., & Bryk, A. S. (1986). A hierarchical model for studying school effects. *Sociology of Education, 59,* 1–17.

Riddell, A. (1989). An alternative approach to the study of school effectiveness in third world countries. *Comparative Education Review, 33,* 481–497.

Rust, V. D., & Dalin, P. (1990). *Teachers and teaching in the developing world.* New York: Garland.

Schön, D. (1983). *The reflective practitioner: How professionals think in action.* New York: Basic Books.

Schön, D. (1987). *Educating the reflective practitioner.* San Francisco, CA: Jossey-Bass.

Shavelson, R. J., & Towne, L. (Eds.). (2002). *Scientific research in education.* Washington, DC: National Research Council, National Academy Press.

Slezak, P. (2000). A critique of radical social constructivism. In D. C. Philips (Ed.), *Constructivism in education: Opinions and second opinions on controversial issues.* Chicago, IL: University of Chicago Press.

Stigler, J. W., Gallimore, R., & Hiebert, J. (2000). Using video surveys to compare classrooms and teaching across cultures: Examples and lessons from the TIMSS and TIMSS-R video studies. *Educational Psychologist, 35,* 87–100.

Stigler, J. W., & Hiebert, J. (1997). Understanding and improving classroom mathematics instruction: An overview of the TIMSS video study. *Phi Delta Kappan, 79,* 14–21.

Stuart, J., & Tatto, M. T. (2000). Designs for initial teacher preparation programs: An international view. *International Journal of Educational Research, 33,* 493–514.

Tatto, M. T. (2000). *Assessing what we know about teacher quality and development: Empirical indicators and methodological issues in comparative perspective.* Washington, DC: Board on Comparative and International Studies in Education, National Research Council, National Academy of Sciences.

Tatto, M. T. (2001). The value and feasibility of evaluation research on teacher preparation: Contrasting the experiences in Sri Lanka and Mexico. *International Journal of Education and Development, 22,* 637–657.

Tatto, M. T. (2008). Teacher policy: A framework for comparative analysis. *Prospects, 38,* 487–508.

Tatto, M. T., Nielsen, H. D., Cummings, W. C., Kularatna, N. G., & Dharmadasa, D. H. (1991). *Comparing the effects and costs of different approaches for educating primary school teachers: The case of Sri Lanka.* BRIDGES research report series (10). Cambridge, Massachusetts: Harvard Institute for International Development.

Tatto, M. T., Nielsen, H. D., Cummings, W. C., Kularatna, N. G., & Dharmadasa, D. H. (1993). Comparing the effectiveness and costs of different approaches for educating primary school teachers in Sri Lanka. *Teaching and Teacher Education, 9*(1), 41–64.

Tatto, M. T., Schwille, J., Senk, S., Ingvarson, L., Peck, R., & Rowley, G. (2008). *Teacher education and development study in mathematics (TEDS-M): Conceptual framework.* Teacher Education and Development International Study Center, Michigan State University, East Lansing, MI, and IEA.

Tatto, M. T., Schwille, J., Senk, S. L., Ingvarson, L., Rowley, G., Peck, R., et al. (2012). *Policy, practice, and readiness to teach primary and secondary mathematics in 17 countries. Findings from the IEA Teacher Education and Development Study in Mathematics (TEDS-M).* Amsterdam: International Association for the Evaluation of Student Achievement.

Trochim, W. M. K. (2006). Internal validity. In *Research methods knowledge base.* http://www.socialresearchmethods.net/kb/intval.php

UNESCO. (1996). Learning: The treasure within. Retrieved from http://unesdoc.unesco.org/images/0010/001095/109590eo.pdf

Von Glasersfeld, E. (1995). *Radical constructivism: A way of knowing and learning.* London: Falmer Press.

Vygotsky, L. S. (1986). *Thought and language* (A. Kozulin, Ed. and Trans.). Cambridge, MA: MIT Press.

Weiss, C. (1972). *Evaluation research: Methods of assessing program effectiveness.* New Jersey: Prentice Hall.

Weiss, C. (1997). *Evaluation* (2nd ed.). New Jersey: Prentice Hall.

Author Biography

Maria Teresa Tatto is the Southwest Borderlands Professor of Comparative Education at the Mary Lou Fulton Teachers College, and Professor in the Division of Educational Leadership and Innovation at Arizona State University. She is the principal investigator for the Teacher Education and Development Study in Mathematics, and for the First Five Years of Mathematics Teaching Study, both designed to explore the connections between pre-service preparation and what is learned on the job during the first years of teaching. She is a former President of the Comparative and International Education Society, and studies the effects of educational policy on school systems.

Chapter 43
The Place of Research in Teacher Education? An Analysis of the Australian Teacher Education Ministerial Advisory Group Report *Action Now: Classroom Ready Teachers*

Martin Mills and Merrilyn Goos

43.1 Introduction

In 2014, the Australian Commonwealth government appointed the Teacher Education Ministerial Advisory Group (TEMAG) to investigate and make recommendations regarding initial teacher education in Australia, with the view to better preparing new teachers for the classroom. In early 2015 the TEMAG report, *Action Now: Classroom Ready Teachers,* was released. An overriding concern within this document was the need for pre-service teachers to be 'classroom ready' upon graduation. In this chapter, we provide a critique of the notion of classroom readiness. Underpinning our critique is the assumption that teaching is an intellectual exercise requiring constant informed and complex decision making. These decisions require knowing about curriculum, pedagogy and assessment and a knowledge and understanding of students and their backgrounds (the disciplines of sociology and psychology, are of course important here). However, none of this decision making work occurs in a vacuum, the social, political and cultural context within which teachers operate both enables and constrains what teachers are able to do. We want to suggest in this chapter that the concern articulated through the TEMAG document about classroom readiness fails to take context into account and that the absence of a concern with attributes associated with 'research literacy' will do little to support pre-service teachers' ability to pro-actively engage with the students (and their communities) when appointed to their first school.

M. Mills (✉) · M. Goos
University of Queensland, Brisbane, Australia
e-mail: m.mills@uq.edu.au

M. Goos
e-mail: m.goos@uq.edu.au

© Springer Nature Singapore Pte Ltd. 2017
M.A. Peters et al. (eds.), *A Companion to Research in Teacher Education*,
DOI 10.1007/978-981-10-4075-7_43

We are worried that the way in which the TEMAG recommendations may be taken up, and the standards that they may impose, will lead to a very narrow view of what constitutes the 'ideal teacher'. This is not to say that we are opposed to standards: depending upon the standard, they can play a role in ensuring that teacher education is valued within universities and that teaching is regarded as a high status occupation (Reid and Brennan 2013). What we are concerned about is standardisation. The tone of the government's response to the report, the report itself and the broader set of discourses about teachers' work and teacher education all appear to work with antiquated notions of the teacher as craftsperson (see Hoskins and Maguire 2013, for critique). Whilst there are clear elements of 'craft', if teaching is to be regarded as a profession and activity that has major responsibilities for the cohesiveness and inclusiveness of society as well as its economic prosperity, then attention has to be paid to what constitutes teachers as intellectual workers. We argue in this chapter that an important aspect of this construction of a teacher is someone who is 'research literate', that is, is a competent consumer of research who is also able to undertake and utilise their own research (BERA/RSA 2014).

This chapter then provides an analysis of the TEMAG report with a particular focus on the constructions of 'research' within the document and the ways in which such constructions align with its notion of 'classroom readiness'. In the chapter, we argue that in terms of research, the TEMAG report has a focus on 'research as evaluation'. For example, within the report it is noted that 'there is a lack of research into the effectiveness of initial teacher education in Australia' and argued that there should be 'a national focus on research into teacher education, including into the effectiveness of teacher preparation and the promotion of innovative practice' and that teacher education providers should be expected to demonstrate 'better evidence of effectiveness'. There is also a use of 'research as justification' for programme content. For example, the report authors claim that 'the theory, methods and practices taught to pre-service teachers need to be clearly based on evidence linked to impact on student learning outcomes' and that programmes should be based on 'solid research evidence'. Within the report there is a virtual silence about 'teacher as researcher' except where the ability to undertake research is interpreted as 'data literacy'. In exploring the notion of 'classroom readiness', we argue that such readiness requires teachers to have an understanding of what constitutes 'educational research' and an ability to undertake this type of research, where educational research refers to research that makes a difference (see Furlong 2013). In this regard, we are very much in support of the work conducted by BERA and the RSA in the UK that argues for the need for teachers to be 'research literate'.

43.2 Context

Whilst not wishing to provide a detailed history of the Australian education system, some points of note need to be outlined. Australia is a federation of States and Territories, and education is constitutionally the responsibility of these jurisdictions.

This has meant that the States and Territories have had responsibility for curriculum, assessment, reporting to parents, university entrance, and teacher education and teacher registration. However, as Lingard and Sellar (2013) indicate, since the 1970s there has been a growing federal involvement in education, and whilst the 1980s saw the creation of the first national education policy, which related to the education of girls (AEC 1987), it was also the decade when human capital theory began to drive future national reforms. Major reforms through to the current day have been concerned with ensuring that Australia can compete economically with countries globally, but especially in the region, and that the country is ready for the 'Asian Century'. These concerns have been reflected in, for example, the instigation of a national curriculum, first raised in the 1980s but pursued most vigorously from 2007 onwards, and a national approach to the accreditation of pre-service teacher education programmes. However, the complexities of State-Commonwealth relations, and differing and changing political parties holding government across the Commonwealth, State and Territory jurisdictions over this period, has meant that such reforms are neither seamless nor uniform (see, for example, Lingard and McGregor 2014). However, where there has been bi-partisan support and uniform implementation has been the introduction of national literacy and numeracy testing and the making 'transparent' of the results on these tests, along with various other accountability measures. In regards to these trends, the former Commonwealth Labor government introduced a website, MySchool, to enable parents to compare *all* registered schools in Australia on a range of measures, but importantly, on national literacy and numeracy tests, and also to see how schools compared with 'like schools'. This has clearly had an impact on individual schools (see Hardy and Boyle 2011, for discussion). However, the national tests have also led to systemic reforms in individual States and Territories. For example, in Queensland, after that State appeared to perform poorly against other States on the literacy and numeracy tests, the State Labor government commissioned an inquiry into how these scores could be improved (Masters 2009) and then introduced an audit of teaching and learning practices in all government schools to improve practice (see Mills et al. 2014). Many of these current, and other, educational reforms in Australia, as in many other countries of the global North, constitute what Shalberg (2011) has referred to as the Global Education Reform Movement, with the apt acronym GERM.

Within this GERM, there has been a focus on accountabilities, often of a very narrow form, a valorisation of the market, an emphasis on outcomes on national and international tests, especially as they compare to other jurisdictions. Within the Australian strain of the GERM, teacher education has come under the spotlight as failing to ensure that education systems across the country, and the teachers within them, are producing students who are capable of competing with the highest performers on the world stage. Underpinning many of the claims about the failings of teacher education (and teachers in general) is the assumption that teachers make *the* difference in relation to student academic outcomes: in many instances, politicians and the media, and many within the policy space, have used the work of Hattie (2012) to confirm this. Whilst we want to acknowledge the important work done by teachers, and indeed by those who educate them, such an assumption washes out considerations of students' life circumstances, for example, poverty, various forms of discrimination, such as institutional racism, and the resourcing of schools. We of course do not want to claim that such factors abrogate teachers' and schools' responsibilities to cater to the needs of *all* students. Thus, we would argue that the issues are more complex than simply reforming teacher education and that without broader redistributive and social equity policies any gains from improving teacher education will be limited.

That said, we do have suggestions for teacher education. Many of these contrast with those outlined in the TEMAG report, *Action now: Classroom ready teachers.* We are of the view that if teacher education is to play a role in improving the quality of practice in schools and of the education system generally, we need programmes that develop the capacities of graduate teachers to recognise and develop responses to the factors that extend beyond the classroom context. Here we draw heavily on BERA and RSA (2014) report on teacher education, *Research and the Teaching Profession*, to argue that teachers need to be research literate and that this consideration has to be central to any reforms in teacher education.

43.2.1   Research and the Teaching Profession: Building the Capacity for a Self-improving Education System

The BERA and RSA (2014) report in the UK, *Research and the Teaching Profession: Building the capacity for a self-improving education system*, was the product of a national inquiry into the place of research in teacher education. The inquiry collected evidence in the form of seven academic papers, 32 submissions from a variety of sources in domains such as teacher education, schools and policy, consultations with key figures in the field of teacher education, and feedback from a reference group and 'Special Advisors'. In the Foreword to the report, John Furlong, the Chair of the steering group, stated of the inquiry: 'Our organisations have come together to consider what contribution research can make to the development of teachers' professional identity and practice, to the quality of teaching, to the broader project of school improvement and transformation, and critically, to the outcomes for learners: children, young people and adults, especially those for whom the education system does not currently 'deliver' (p. 3). The findings of this report offer much to systems that are concerned with ensuring that they meet the needs of all the students in their schools, especially marginalised students, that want to keep improving and responding to new social and cultural demands, which see education as more than an economic driver and that value the work of teachers.

The report concluded that research contributes to teacher education in four ways: the content of teacher education programmes being grounded in research-based knowledge and scholarship across a range of disciplines; research on teacher education being used to inform the structure of teacher education programmes; ensuring teachers and teacher educators are 'discerning consumers of research'; and enabling teachers and teacher educators to undertake their own research and evaluate and respond to the findings of that research. The report goes on to argue that what is needed to ensure that all students, but especially those from marginalised backgrounds, have high quality educational experiences and that their academic and social outcomes from schooling are maximised, are schools (and other education institutions) that are research-rich environments, teachers who are research literate and collaborative partnerships between universities and education institutions. Further, the report argues that when a research-rich environment exists in schools and within teacher education provision then a 'self-improving education system' will exist. We take this as our starting point in considering TEMAG's *Action now: Classroom ready teachers.*

43.3 TEMAG: Background and Findings

TEMAG was commissioned to make recommendations on improving the preparation of new teachers, especially with regard to the mix of academic and practical skills needed for the classroom. According to the Minister, the inquiry was not politically motivated, but instead was intended to address the decline in the performance of Australian students in international assessments such as PISA and TIMSS. Ministerial advisors also pointed out that this 'problem' of declining student performance had not been solved by the 100% increase in Commonwealth funding for schools over a period of time when school enrolments had only risen by 17%. Inquiries into teacher education in Australia are not a new phenomenon—indeed it has been widely reported that in the preceding decade there had been more than 40 inquiries into different aspects of teacher education, which had done little to bring about significant change (see for example, Rowan et al. 2015). What is new has been the unrelenting critiques of (perhaps more appropriately referred to as 'attacks' on) teacher education and blaming teacher preparation programmes for Australia's supposed declining ranking on international tests and for putting Australia at risk of not being able to compete on the international economic stage. Despite the Minister's claims about TEMAG not being politically motivated, these arguments behind its creation have been driven by a concern, somewhat media driven by, for example, focussing on low entry standards, and hence, supposedly poor quality pre-service programmes, and has served to construct the notion of an underperforming teacher education sector as a 'truth', requiring political intervention. This political intervention has been enthusiastically embraced.

TEMAG was chaired by Professor Greg Craven, Vice-Chancellor of the Australian Catholic University, and included seven additional members: two Professors of Education, a university Deputy Vice-Chancellor (Education), a school principal and a deputy principal, the Chief Executive Officer of an educational consultancy firm, and the Chief Executive Officer of a state-based association of independent schools. It could be argued that this membership over-represented some stakeholder groups and under-represented university academics who were practising teacher educators. This under representation speaks to the devaluing of academic knowledge about teacher education and creates the impression of 'doing to' teacher educators rather than 'doing with'.

The Executive Summary of *Action now: Classroom ready teachers* refers to the need to improve the quality of teachers in Australian schools by focusing on when teachers 'are first prepared for the profession' (p. xi). It is clear that initial teacher education providers are being held accountable for producing 'classroom ready' graduates, and there is an implied criticism that this is not already happening in Australian university programmes.

The report delivered six key findings:

(1) National standards are weakly applied in accrediting initial teacher education programmes and assessing the classroom readiness of graduates.
(2) There is a need to lift public confidence in initial teacher education, especially in terms of entry requirements.
(3) There is evidence of poor practice in a number of programmes, which do not provide graduates with adequate content knowledge or evidence-based teaching strategies.
(4) There is insufficient integration of university-based teacher education providers with schools and systems in the professional experience component of initial teacher education.
(5) There is insufficient professional support for beginning teachers.
(6) There are gaps in workforce planning data, and insufficient information on the effectiveness of initial teacher education programmes.

This set of findings works to undermine much of the current practice in teacher education, and in some respects targets issues that are often outside the domain of university programmes. For example, the responsibility for accreditation and quality assurance of programmes (findings 1 and 3) is shared by universities and the national regulatory body, the Australian Institute for Teaching and School Leadership (AITSL), currently chaired by John Hattie. Also, while entry requirements for initial teacher education are set by universities, these requirements are influenced not so much by trends in workforce supply and demand or by academic prerequisites considered necessary for successful university study, but by financial considerations in maximising enrolments. The fourth finding works to highlight that somewhat old tension between theory and practice which suggests that there is too much theory in teacher education and that the real world experience of the classroom requires that more attention be paid to practice. This is not to say that partnerships between schools and universities are unimportant; however, concerns with such partnerships need to go beyond the organisation of the professional experience component of initial teacher education. Such partnerships also need to attend to concerns with the intellectual enterprise of teaching as a research endeavour.

Whilst the latter two of these findings clearly relate to education departments, and other employing agencies, by linking the last of these to the 'effectiveness of teacher education programmes' the blame for poor workforce planning is attached to the university sector. Ironically, the finding of a lack of 'public confidence in initial teacher education' will not be helped by this report.

The recommendations from the report are telling in their grounding in an accountability regime influenced by the GERM. On the basis of these findings, the report recommended a number of proposals to bring about structural and cultural change in initial teacher education in Australia:

(a) A strengthened national quality assurance process, requiring universities to provide evidence of the impact of their initial teacher education programmes on pre-service teachers and their students' learning.
(b) Sophisticated and transparent selection for entry to teaching, which addresses both the academic skills (including literacy and numeracy) and personal qualities needed for success in a teaching career.
(c) Integration of theory and practice, by establishing mutually beneficial partnerships between universities and schools that offer professional experience placements.
(d) Robust assurance of classroom readiness, entailing rigorous assessment of graduates' knowledge and teaching practices against a national assessment framework.
(e) National research to inform innovative programme design and delivery, and collection of national workforce data to build capacity for workforce planning.

Terms such as 'quality assurance' in relation to programmes, 'sophisticated and transparent selection' in regards to entry into programmes, and 'robust assurance' and rigorous assessment' in relation to the assessment of graduates' teaching capacities all point to a strengthening of accountability regimes in teacher education. This is illustrated in the media release by the Commonwealth Education Minister, Christopher Pyne, when announcing the TEMAG report and the government's response which emphasised that the focus would be on universities being held to account. He stated in this media release: 'The report sets high expectations for everyone involved in initial teacher education including universities. It also makes a clear case that providers be held accountable for the quality of the teaching graduates they produce'. He went on to say: 'I hope my state and territory colleagues will join with us to make sure all beginning teachers have the skills they need and deserve to deliver positive education outcomes for students'. The media release was highly selective in listing the following as key recommendations:

• A test to assess the literacy and numeracy skills of all teaching graduates
• A requirement for universities to demonstrate that their graduates are classroom ready before gaining full course accreditation
• An overhaul of the in class practical element of teaching degrees
• A specialisation for primary school teachers with a focus on STEM and languages
• A requirement that universities publish all information about how they select students into teacher education programmes.

The first of these was not actually a recommendation of the TEMAG report, since the proposed literacy and numeracy test had already been planned as yet another accountability measure of initial teacher education. It could be argued that most of the other recommendations highlighted in the Minister's media release served to reassure the public that the government was taking strong action (and 'Action now') about the supposed low standards for programme entry and exit.

43.4 TEMAG and 'Classroom Readiness'

Core to the report's findings is the notion of pre-service teachers' levels of 'classroom readiness'. However, the notion of classroom readiness is open to debate. In one sense, this concept plays into the increasing vocational orientation of university programmes that prepare graduates for specific professions (such as law, accounting, engineering, etc.), so that a university education is seen as no more than advanced training for employment. On the other hand, the requirement to be classroom ready at graduation suggests that there is no need for further learning or development throughout a career. Neither of these interpretations sits well with the view that teaching is a profession involving lifelong learning.

Because classroom readiness is so prominent in shaping the key directions proposed by the TEMAG report, it is worth examining the report's recommendations to discover how classroom readiness is conceptualised—especially in relation to the role of research in teacher education. This analysis has three parts: (1) *what* is required to be classroom ready, for example, in terms of knowledge, understanding, skills, dispositions; (2) *how* is classroom readiness to be determined; and (3) against what *standards* is classroom readiness to be measured?

43.4.1 Classroom Readiness—What?

The TEMAG recommendations are not explicit in setting out what is required to be classroom ready. Instead, there are references to equipping pre-service teachers with various kinds of skills. For example, Recommendation 15 states that higher education providers should equip pre-service teacher with 'data collection and analysis skills to assess the learning needs of all students', while Recommendation 16 asks providers to equip pre-service teachers with 'the skills to effectively engage with parents about the progress of their children'. Knowledge and understanding of two types are mentioned that could be part of the 'what' of classroom readiness. Recommendation 17 requires higher education providers to 'equip all primary and secondary pre-service teachers with a thorough understanding of the fundamentals of teaching literacy and numeracy', and Recommendation 18 involves a departure from the practice of most Australian teacher education programmes in calling for providers to 'equip all primary pre-service teachers with at least one subject specialisation, prioritising science, mathematics or a language'. Thus, 'classroom ready' teachers appear to be those who can work with data, engage with parents, and can teach literacy and numeracy, preferably with a subject specialisation.

How do these recommendations position teachers and teacher educators in relation to the role of research, especially by comparison with the conclusions of the BERA and RSA (2014) report discussed earlier? One could argue that the *content* and *structure* of programmes with the above characteristics should be informed by research-based knowledge and scholarship, but there seems to be little expectation that pre-service teachers (or even teacher educators) should be engaged with and *discerning consumers of research*. The contribution of research is at the level of programme and course design, and not necessarily in the enactment of teaching and learning in these courses, so that research remains invisible to those who should be engaging with it.

43.4.2   Classroom Readiness—How?

Given the lack of elaboration in the TEMAG recommendations on what classroom readiness means, it is not surprising to find little explication of how classroom readiness of graduates is to be recognised. Recommendation 26 calls for AITSL to 'develop a national assessment framework…to support higher education providers and schools to consistently assess the classroom readiness of pre-service teachers throughout the duration of their programme'. Recommendations 27 and 28 go on to ask for development of Portfolios of Evidence that assist pre-service teachers to collect 'sophisticated evidence of their teaching ability and their impact on student learning'. Although it will be the responsibility of AITSL to develop the assessment framework, universities are currently considering ways by which graduates and programmes could demonstrate impact, and how to plan for collecting evidence of impact. The role of research in this process might well be limited to informing *programme structure*, although there are signs that the need for evidence of impact could become a catalyst for embedding small-scale research projects or action-research inquiry into initial teacher education programmes.

43.4.3   Classroom Readiness—Standards?

If classroom readiness is to be assessed in some way, then the evidence collected by pre-service teachers needs to be compared against some specified standard of knowledge, skills and capabilities to be demonstrated by graduates. Recommendation 29 of the TEMAG report calls for AITSL to review the Graduate level standards in the Australian Professional Standards for Teachers 'to ensure that knowledge, skills and capabilities required of graduates align with the knowledge, skills and capabilities beginning teachers need for the classroom'. It is therefore relevant to examine the place of research in the Standards framework.

The Australian Professional Standards for Teachers (available at http://www. aitsl.edu.au/australian-professional-standards-for-teachers/standards/list) are structured around the three domains of Professional Knowledge, Professional Practice, and Professional Engagement, across four career stages, Graduate, Proficient, Highly Accomplished and Lead teacher. At the Lead teacher stage there is occasional reference to use of 'research-based' learning and teaching programmes and to analysing current research to improve students' educational outcomes. Both of these kinds of statement, found in the Professional Knowledge and Professional Practice domains of the Standards framework, assume that teachers can engage with and be *discerning consumers of research* in ways alluded to by the BERA-RSA inquiry. Within the Professional Engagement domain, Lead teachers are expected to *engage in their own research* as a form of professional learning to improve practice, which aligns with the fourth way in which research can make a contribution to teacher education, identified by the BERA-RSA report.

Although the Lead teacher stage seems far removed from the aims and activities of initial teacher education programmes, and thus might account for the lack of reference to research in the TEMAG report, some elements of the Australian Professional Standards for Teachers contribute to a developmental trajectory for graduate teachers that could lead them towards the richer interpretations of 'research' outlined in the BERA-RSA report (see Standards 6.2 and 6.3, for examples). However, it remains to be seen whether AITSL takes up and strengthens these existing threads within the professional standards framework in order to highlight the need for research literacy amongst Graduate teachers.

43.5   TEMAG and the Assumed Role of Research in Initial Teacher Education

One of the key proposals of the TEMAG report related to the need for national leadership in research on teacher education, especially in relation to the effectiveness of teacher preparation. Recommendation 34 called for the reconstitution of the functions of AITSL to provide such a national focus. However, this move—with its implied top-down approach to researching programme effectiveness—we would argue, will not on its own support teacher educators or pre-service teachers to conduct their own research that investigates the effects of their educational practices.

There are two other research-related strands within the TEMAG report recommendations. The first of these is seen in Recommendations 6 and 14, which require higher education providers to ensure that programmes have evidence-based pedagogical approaches and deliver evidence-based content. Clearly, the assumed role of research here is to inform *programme content and structure*. The second strand is seen in Recommendation 15, which calls for providers to equip pre-service teachers with data collection and analysis skills to assess the learning needs of all students. While this approach could position teachers as *discerning consumers of research*, it limits research literacy to data-driven approaches that might not engage teachers with richer forms of research inquiry.

As discussed in the previous section on classroom readiness, there is implied support in the TEMAG report for research to inform the *content* and *structure* of initial teacher education programmes, with little evidence to support the notion that pre-service and graduate teachers, or teacher educators themselves, should engage with and be *discerning consumers* of research. At best, research engagement is conceptualised in terms of teachers collecting and analysing student achievement data in order to adjust and improve teaching strategies. While this could create a *data-rich* environment that supports school improvement, such an approach would not necessarily immerse teachers in a *research-rich* environment that draws on multiple forms evidence from multiple sources.

43.6 Classroom Readiness and Research Literacy

One of our great concerns with the TEMAG's focus on classroom readiness is that it fails to take into account context. Contained within this failing is a standardised notion of the 'ideal teacher' who can operate within any context. We are not suggesting that teacher education does not need to reform or that the various programmes throughout Australia currently prepare teachers to walk into any classroom, in any location, conditions or situation, in which they might find themselves when they first begin their careers. However, we would argue that a standardised notion of classroom readiness being articulated through the particular recommendations being taken up by government will also not adequately prepare pre-service teachers for the diversity of experiences they are likely to face in Australia. In the Australian context, as in most other national contexts, a 'one size fits all' model of teacher education is clearly not appropriate. If we were to take our own State of Queensland, schools in rural and remote areas are vastly different from those in urban areas, and even within these different locations, schools serve vastly different populations, shaped around socioeconomic status, and the race and ethnic background of students. Teaching, for example, in the remote Indigenous community of Aurukun is vastly different from teaching in any school in suburban Brisbane. Preparing teachers for any possibility is extremely difficult. However, we maintain that a concern in teacher education with research literacy will go some way to supporting newly qualified teachers in diverse locations.

There has to be an awareness in pre-service teacher education programmes then that not all schools are alike and that ensuring that pre-service teachers are 'classroom ready' in any context requires that they have the abilities to adapt and apply knowledges. For example, there are some clear indications that teachers who will be working in communities with highly marginalised young people do need some special attributes, knowledges and skills, and that teacher education programmes can be a place where they develop these (see, for example, Lampert and Burnett 2014). However, we propose that supporting teacher adaptability, especially in relation to supporting the most highly marginalised students within a school, requires enabling teachers to become competent consumers of research, to use this research to apply it to their own contexts and to delve deeper into that context through sound research skills.

We have shown that the TEMAG report did nod towards the need for teachers to be able to understand and analyse data in their school contexts. However, as was noted in the BERA/RSA report, 'many of those who contributed to the Inquiry are deeply concerned by the emergence of an environment, often narrowly data-driven, that appears to militate against teachers' engagement in more open forms of research and enquiry' (2014, p. 11). The same concerns most likely apply in the Australian context as well. It appears that governments, and by implication TEMAG, want teachers to be proficient in analysing data that relate to academic outcomes, and principally academic outcomes on standardised tests, both national and international. The perverse effects of such a focus, for example, the thinning down of pedagogies, the narrowing of curriculum options, high suspension rates, etc. have been well documented (Lingard and Sellar 2013). These perverse effects are likely to be amplified when teachers' research skills are focussed on improving their 'data literacy' in relation to test scores. Here the teacher is likely to become primarily concerned with using this limited 'data' in order to construct themselves as a 'good teacher', and by corollary, teacher education will become focussed on pre-service teachers' learning how to construct such an image (Mills and Mitchell 2013). Teacher education institutions' reputations depend on pre-service teachers' ability in this regard.

Other concerns about research in the TEMAG report are also limiting in their scope and appear to be tied into notions of accountability. Aspects of the GERM are clearly present in this report. For instance, universities are required to provide evidence about the quality of their programmes in relation to teacher aptitudes, how they have selected students for their programmes and the extent to which they have assessed pre-service teachers' classroom readiness. Putting teacher education institutions under such a microscope is also likely to impact upon practice, especially when 'classroom readiness' is interpreted in narrow ways, such that the disciplinary depth of educational research may well be reduced in the programme. We do not have a problem with accountability. However, we are concerned with issues of accountability to whom and for what. At the moment the 'who' is very much government and governments whose views on the purposes of education tend to restricted to human capital understandings. As such the 'what' often relates to schools, their teachers and teacher education institutions being able to demonstrate what they have done to support improvements in student academic performance, especially as it relates to international economic competitors. Ironically, we are of the view that this is a self-defeating approach. In contrast, and in line with the BERA/RSA report, we contend that the education system would be improved by supporting schools to become 'research-rich' environments.

Our focus in this chapter has been on the need for pre-service teachers to become 'research literate' as part of becoming what TEMAG has referred to as 'classroom ready'. However, this cannot be a completed project that ends on graduation. There is a need for newly qualified teachers to be able practice this research literacy in on-going ways in schools which value and encourage 'research-rich environments' (not just data rich!). The role for teacher education in this project is to develop and refine pre-service teachers' research literacy, their ability to consume, adapt and undertake research, which will require that through their degrees they are taught how to read literature, how to be discerning in the selection of research evidence, how to ask the right research questions, how to conduct research and how to analyse findings in ways that lead to informed decision making. For this focus on research to create what the BERA/RSA refer to as a self-improving system there does have to be a relationship between schools and universities. However, again this relationship needs to go beyond that encouraged in the TEMAG report. Collaborative partnerships between universities and schools based on mutual respect where each is seen as having the potential to inform theory and practice in the other will have benefits for all young people in schools. At the current moment, the TEMAG report sees this relationship as primarily a technical one related to the organisation of professional experience within teacher education. Here again we find ourselves in accord with the BERA/RSA report, which states:

> Evidence gathered in the course of this Inquiry underlines the need to go much further, to progress from being data-driven to being research-rich and from being isolationist to being collaborative. This requires a much stronger relationship between schools and colleges, and between practitioners in schools and colleges and those in the wider research community'. (2014, p. 24)

It is also critical that teacher education occurs in a research rich environment. The TEMAG report stresses the need for teacher education courses to provide pre-service teachers with 'adequate content knowledge' and 'evidence-based teaching strategies'. We agree these are important. However, the environments in which teacher education occurs need to involve the academics teaching into courses for pre-service teachers in undertaking and disseminating research that is not simply instrumental, but also informed by attempts to tackle the big questions in education related, for example, to its purpose, to its relevance to contemporary youth, to addressing the issues of the day (climate change, marriage equality, global terrorism), and to what counts as 'powerful knowledge'. Without encouraging pre-service teachers to question assumptions and supposed education 'truths', and providing them with the tools to undertake such questioning, schools are unlikely to become part of a 'self-improving system'.

References

Australian Education Council. (1987). *National policy for the education of girls in Australian schools*. Canberra: Australian Government Printing Service.

BERA/RSA. (2014). *Research and the teaching profession: Building the capacity for a self-improving education system*. London: BERA.

Furlong, J. (2013). *Education—An anatomy of the discipline: Rescuing the university project.* Abington: Routledge.

Hardy, I., & Boyle, C. (2011). My school? Critiquing the abstraction and quantification of education. *Asia-Pacific Journal of Teacher Education, 39*(3), 211–222.

Hattie, J. (2012). *Visible learning for teachers: Maximizing impact on learning.* London: Routledge.

Hoskins, K., & Maguire, M. (2013). Teaching the teachers: Contesting the curriculum. In L. Beckett (Ed.), *Teacher education through active engagement: Raising the professional voice* (pp. 71–82). London: Routledge.

Lampert, J., & Burnett, B. (2014). Teacher education for high-poverty schools: Keeping the bar high. In S. Gannon & W. Sawer (Eds.), *Contemporary issues of equity in education* (pp. 115–129). Newcastle Upon Tyne, UK: Cambridge Scholars Publishing.

Lingard, B., & McGregor, G. (2014). Two contrasting Australian curriculum responses to globalisation: What students should learn or become. *The Curriculum Journal, 25*(1), 90–110.

Lingard, B., & Sellar, S. (2013). 'Catalyst data': Perverse systemic effects of audit and accountability in Australian schooling. *Journal of Education Policy, 28*(5), 634–656.

Masters, G. N. (2009). *Improving literacy, numeracy and science learning in Queensland primary schools.* Melbourne: Australian Council for Educational Research.

Mills, M., & Mitchell, J. (2013). Where is pedagogy in teaching and teacher education? The production of pre-fabricated teachers. In L. Beckett (Ed.), *Teacher education through active engagement: Raising the professional voice* (pp. 83–95). London: Routledge.

Mills, M., Monk, S., Keddie, A., Christie, P., Renshaw, P., Geelan, D., et al. (2014). Differentiated learning: From policy to classroom. *Oxford Review of Education, 14*(3), 331–348.

Reid, J., & Brennan, M. (2013). The standards cage: A contradictory politics of control. In L. Beckett (Ed.), *Teacher education through active engagement: Raising the professional voice* (pp. 110–124). London: Routledge.

Rowan, L., Mayer, D., Kline, J., Kostogriz, A., & Walker-Gibbs, B. (2015). Investigating the effectiveness of teacher education for early career teachers in diverse settings: The longitudinal research we have to have. *Australian Educational Researcher, 42,* 273–298.

Sahlberg, P. (2011). *Finnish lessons: What can the world learn from educational change in Finland?* New York, NY: Teachers' College Press.

TEMAG. (2015). *Action now: Classroom ready teachers.* Canberra: Department of Education.

Author Biographies

Martin Mills is Professor of Education and Head of School at The University of Queensland. He is a former President of the Australian Association for Research in Education (2014-2016). His research areas include social justice issues in education, school reform, including alternative education and social cohesion.

Merrilyn Goos is Professor of Education at The University of Queensland, Australia. Her research interests include mathematics teacher education, numeracy education in school and non-school contexts, interdisciplinary boundary practices, and teaching and learning in higher education.

Chapter 44
Educating the Educators: Policies and Initiatives in European Teacher Education

Jean Murray, Mieke Lunenberg and Kari Smith

44.1 Introduction

Education policy commonly emphasises the potential to make improvements to schooling by reforming teacher education (Darling-Hammond and Lieberman 2012). Initial Teacher Education (ITE) or pre-service, in particular, is widely seen as a 'lever' to change and improve school systems. These policy documents often emphasise the importance of changes to the recruitment criteria and structures of teacher education, including the curriculum of programmes and its assessment modes, but they rarely focus on teacher educators and their centrality to all aspects of work in the sector. Professional voices, in contrast, clearly recognize teacher educators as the 'linchpins in educational reforms' (Cochran-Smith 2003: 3) with distinctive expertise and professional learning requirements (Boyd et al. 2011; Goodwin and Kosnik 2013). But, despite this long-term professional consensus, teacher educators' places in the teacher education system remain largely 'hidden' in policy documents.

Between 2010 and 2013, however, a European Commission initiative began a series of consultations and peer learning activities to investigate how policy makers across the European Union 28 member states might implement improvements to their national teacher education systems, thereby contributing to pan-European prosperity. This initiative, as it progressed, influenced the content of a number of key European policy documents and finally resulted in the publication of a

J. Murray (✉)
University of East London, London, UK
e-mail: j.m.f.murray@uel.ac.uk

M. Lunenberg
University Amsterdam, Amsterdam, Netherlands
e-mail: mieke@lunenberg.info

K. Smith
Norwegian University of Science and Technology, Trondheim, Norway
e-mail: Kari.Smith@iuh.uib.no

© Springer Nature Singapore Pte Ltd. 2017
M.A. Peters et al. (eds.), *A Companion to Research in Teacher Education*,
DOI 10.1007/978-981-10-4075-7_44

report—*Supporting Teacher Educators for Better Learning* (European Commission 2013). For the first time in the pan-European policy agenda, this report, issued with advisory status across all member states, positions teacher educators themselves as a major factor in achieving improvements in teacher education and consequently, schooling. The report, explicitly states, for example, that '(r)eforms that enhance the quality of teacher educators can make a significant improvement to the general quality of teaching and therefore raise pupil attainment' (p. 1). The report then goes on to identify the need for 'competences' to be identified at national level and for systematic and sustained professional learning opportunities to be provided for all teacher educators, as we describe in more detail below. The definition of the occupational group given in the report is inclusive, seeing teacher educators as all those who 'guide teaching staff at all stages in their careers, model good practice, and undertake the key research that develops our understanding of teaching and learning' (p. 2). One implication of this definition is that across Europe, teacher educators work in schools and/or in Higher Education Institutions (HEIs) of some kind—most commonly, universities, polytechnics or colleges of higher education.

This chapter starts with a brief analysis of policies and practices for teacher educators' professional development with particular reference to this seminal European report and to other European policy documents which it informed, particularly *Supporting the Teaching Professions for Better Learning Outcomes* (EC 2012). We then aim to capture something of the variable impact of the 2013 report on the member states and the reasons for that variability. This is achieved through three sections on the 'state of play' for teacher educators' professional development in the Netherlands and England (both EU member states) and Norway (a member of the European Economic Area [EAA] and therefore closely associated with the EU and its policies); these accounts are contextualised within the broad changes to each teacher education system since 2010.

We then move to consider broader issues through a focus on Info-TED—a pan-European organisation which essentially aims to make the aspirations of the European Commission report into reality, albeit through a different approach to professional learning for teacher educators. At this point, we should acknowledge our own positions as founder members of the group. Drawing on the group's vision, the questions we address in this chapter are: what makes for high quality professional learning for teacher educators? What is the contribution of nation-specific provision? And what might pan-European learning opportunities for professional development look like?

44.2 Competences and Teacher Educators' Professional Learning

The European report of 2013 adopts the view that identification of teacher educators' 'competences' is essential in order to build robust selection and recruitment procedures and to provide the basis for high quality professional learning. There is also a clear focus on these competences being nationally defined and specific.

Countries which have not already done so need to define explicitly what competences are required by any professional involved in the initial or continuous education of teachers, in whichever institutional setting they may work. (European Commission 2013: 7)

In the report such definitions of 'competence-based criteria' are seen as providing the basis for selection and recruitment procedures and the subsequent crafting of 'specific professional development opportunities' (p. 6). These are also seen as nationally defined. The competences which teacher educators are said to need reflect their multi-faceted and complex roles (Davey 2013: 79). They include those related to knowledge of: the first order field of schooling; the second order field of teacher education (Murray 2002); research (or 'knowledge development' as it is termed in the report); the educational systems in which they work; leadership skills; and more general abilities to integrate knowledge. A further area is the need for 'transversal competences' which enable teacher educators to work across and between schools and HEIs. This competence is seen as central as it supports the required 'active collaboration' (European Commission 2013: 2) between all those educating teachers, in whichever setting they work—a collaboration which is acknowledged as essential for high quality teacher education.

This analysis of teacher educators' competences is broadly akin to other definitions of expertise in teacher education, particularly those of the Dutch Association of Teacher Educators (VELON). Many of these definitions also use the language of competences or the closely related concept of 'standards'. These competences are then also used as the basis for providing professional learning. In educational research, there have been criticisms of this kind of approach (for example, Kelchtermans 2013) which is seen as generating quality control instruments, failing to capture professional complexity and holding professionals accountable in inappropriate ways. Nevertheless, this inter-linking of competence and professional learning is also seen in many professional initiatives in European nations.

In 2002, for example, VELON established a professional standards framework for teacher educators and embedded these in a procedure that enables teacher educators to show how they meet those standards. Teacher educators, voluntarily, composed a structured portfolio that was discussed with peer assessors; they were then accredited as members of VELON for 4 years. Studies into the portfolios that teacher educators constructed in this registration procedure showed that they were predominantly practice oriented, with the theoretical underpinning of actions and thoughts rarely made explicit. The reason given for this lack of theoretically underpinning was that teacher educators found it hard to locate relevant literature in the abundance of research about teacher education. This has led to new initiatives, as detailed later in this chapter.

Other professional interest groups including ATE in the USA, Mofet in Israel and VELOV in Flanders also have standards for teacher educators, which have been developed through intra-professional initiatives. These standards cover broadly similar areas to those of VELON, although the Flemish (and Dutch standards) start with principles, responsibilities and practice, whereas the American and Israeli standards are described in terms of ideal behaviours.

Other definitions of teacher educators' expertise draw on the concept of 'professional knowledge domains' rather than competences or standards. Goodwin and Kosnik (2013) in North America, for example, define five knowledge domains for teacher educators: personal knowledge, autobiography and philosophy of teaching; contextual knowledge and understanding learners, schools, and society; pedagogical knowledge of content, theories, teaching methods, and curriculum development; sociological knowledge of social diversity, cultural relevance, and social justice; and social knowledge and skills including co-operation, working in democratic groups and conflict resolution. Davey (2013) in New Zealand identifies three broad areas of comprehensive and 'nested' propositional or content knowledge as central for teacher educators: subject knowledge, including pedagogical content knowledge; knowledge of a range of educational and pedagogical theories and the ability to enact these through practice; and a working knowledge of schools, schooling and the teaching profession in its national context.

Particularly notable here is VELON which, to complement its standards, has also developed a web-based knowledge base, with the aim of supporting teacher educators in finding relevant literature to underpin practice and reflection (Lunenberg et al. 2014). Ten domains are identified in all, starting with four core domains of knowledge—the profession of teacher educator, pedagogy of teacher education, learning and learners, and teaching and coaching—then two domains that focus on programme-specific and subject-specific knowledge, and finally four domains offering an introduction to extended knowledge on the context of teacher education, the organisation of teacher education, curriculum development and assessment in teacher education, and research by teacher educators.

In a short section on professional development, the European Report (2013) stresses the need for 'the constant updating of teacher educators' knowledge, skills and attitudes' through a coherent continuum of professional development opportunities from initial training through systematic induction to further learning (p. 17). Emphasis is also placed on the establishment of new ways of working in professional learning between stakeholders in order to overcome 'divides' between HE and teaching staff.

Professional associations at national level are seen as crucial in taking forward CPD initiatives. But, as the report emphasises, perhaps the most powerful influence on teacher educators' professional learning is the provision made by the institutions which employ them. This provision in the HEIs usually focuses around the three key commonly defined areas of academic work—teaching, research and service to the institution (this last area often encompassing management skills). As the report states, there are, of course, a number of 'recurring problems' around this model: 'insufficient funding, lack of incentives, few research opportunities in professional development and little coordination between institutions' (p. 17). In addition, these professional learning programmes often change, of course, as institutional priorities and teacher education policies shift, as further sections of this chapter illustrate.

Professional learning provision in the 2013 report is then seen as nationally and institutionally organized, involving a wide range of modes and foci. There is only one short mention of professional development through 'mobility opportunities' across the EU; this is in contrast to a later (European Commission 2015) report which places heavy emphasis on European mobility for school teachers and the cross-national learning developments it can bring. There are few specific details of what good quality learning provision looks like, and there is little emphasis on listening to teacher educators' voices and working from their self-identified needs. The report works rather on defining professional learning from nationally defined competences which in turn reflect national (and often institutional imperatives); this leaves a vacuum which other associations and researchers have filled, however.

A survey in the Netherlands of teacher educators' professional development in schools and universities (Dengerink et al. 2015) showed different learning needs and preferences at different career stages and locations for work. In their early years in teacher education, for example, inexperienced teacher educators struggled to find their way and form new identities; many wanted coaching or supervision to support them. More experienced educators preferred to pursue individual and communal interests in enquiry-based learning. School-based teacher educators predominantly wanted professional development on co-operation with the teacher education institution and on coaching, while the focus of university-based teacher educators was mainly on developing their personal pedagogy. In terms of *how* to learn, teacher educators preferred informal learning (reading, attending events, practitioner research initiatives and focused discussions with peers). School-based teacher educators mainly wanted to learn 'together with colleagues in their own region', who were also involved in partnership between schools and universities, while university-based wanted to learn individually or with colleagues within their own institution and, as their experience grew, also with colleagues from other HEIs.

A recent study by the Info-TED group of over 700 Higher Education-based teacher educators from across Europe showed that, whilst 72% recorded some degree of satisfaction with the professional learning opportunities they had received to date, 97% also showed degrees of interest in furthering their learning. As in the Dutch survey, here the results showed that 'intentional' or 'facilitated' informal learning with colleagues was the preferred mode of learning; the desired foci included current policy developments and best practice in pedagogy, curriculum development, research skills, scholarly writing and using new technologies and social media. Learning could be best achieved by informal and 'facilitated' collaboration with colleagues, targeted mentoring from experienced colleagues, and attendance at conferences and workshops. Analysis of this large-scale study is still in the early stages, but the results undoubtedly indicate valuable directions for the design of teacher educators' professional learning.

44.3   Three European Case Studies

44.3.1   The Netherlands

As described above, in the Netherlands a strong focus on the professional development of teacher educators was initiated by VELON in 2002, and has continued to this day. Indeed, the VELON model exerted a powerful influence on the EC work of 2010–2013 and on the final report. It is not surprising then to find that the report has had some influences on professional learning provision in the country, although national policy changes in schooling and HE have also been powerful influences.

The VELON definition of teacher educators has long been an inclusive one, with school-based teacher educators joining the registration and recognition procedures soon after their initiation. In 2012, the professional standard framework was revised and an explicit connection between the framework and the knowledge domains, described earlier, was established. In the same year a professional learning programme for teacher educators started—and has now been carried out five times—in which the registration procedures are incorporated. In the modules of this programme, several aspects of a teacher educators' work are analysed, practically as well as theoretically, with HE-based and school-based teacher educators learning and working together (Lunenberg et al. 2014).

Participating in these and other professional development activities was then initiated, led and owned mainly by VELON members, creating a powerful, communal and intra-professional initiative for those teacher educators who chose to be involved it. This situation, however, is changing. In 2013, the Dutch Ministry of Education presented a report entitled '*Teachers' Agenda 2013–2020: The Teacher Makes the Difference*'. The report accorded with the European Commission report of 2013 in viewing improvement in the quality of teacher educators as one of the key ways to further improve teacher education. Some main themes in this report are: the continuation of the quality development of teacher education; further development of the co-operation between HEIs and schools; and increasing the number of teachers with a masters degree. In this context, VELON has been asked to further develop its registration procedure, in co-operation with national commissions for teacher education institutions. The aim is that, in 2017, all teacher educators, working in teacher education, wherever they work, will go through the registration procedure; being accredited in this way will then offer all teacher educators professional development and this, in turn, will improve quality.

The Associations of Universities and Universities of Applied Science support this initiative, financed by the Ministry of Education. The new registration procedure has only just been presented and includes a variety of routes, with HEIs offered the opportunity to organize most of the registration process themselves. This offers also the possibility to combine the registration process with the procedure for the Basic Qualification for Teachers in Higher Education (Basiskwalificatie Onderwijs (BKO); comparable to the English Higher Education Academy [HEA] Professional Standards Framework). It will be interesting to follow this development, because while it may seem positive that HEIs will incorporate the registration procedure in their human resource policy, these changes also imply a power shift from VELON as the—until now leading—professional community to the HEIs, which may also affect the quality and focuses of teacher educators' professional learning.

In the Netherlands HEIs still have the overall responsibility for the quality of the programme, including the practicum, but schools also have powerful voices. According to the Ministry of Education, most formally recognized co-operations between HEIs and schools are smoothly organized, the communication is stream-lined, student teachers feel welcome and many mentors and school-based teacher educators are trained (this last factor is due in part to the way in which school-based teacher educators were incorporated in VELON and its professional development activities at a very early stage). In reality, however, there is a huge variety among the partnerships with regard to the quality of the coaching in schools and the assessment of school-based work. The Ministry concludes that the implementation of a systematic quality circle for partnerships is missing and that more attention to quality control is needed.

To support already certified teachers to study for a masters degree, the Ministry of Education provides grants. The increasing focus on enhancing the academic quality of student teachers, however, has proved to be more complicated. Teachers for the higher secondary level are already educated at universities to obtain a master degree, and in the universities teacher education research traditions are strong. Teachers for primary schools and for the lower level of secondary schools are educated at Universities of Applied Science and obtain an under-graduate degree. At these institutions research programmes in teacher education are still scarce and small, and most teacher educators do not have a research background (often their master thesis represents their most recent research experience). This evokes questions when they are requested to supervise their students' research projects. There are, however, two interesting developments here. Since 2008 several universities and teacher education institutions for primary education have started collaborative programmes for primary schools (these are also designed to attract more male teachers). Since 2010 universities have also offered under-graduate teacher education students an educative minor that leads to a degree for the lower secondary level. The involvement of teacher educator researchers in these programmes offers a more productive context both for their own professional development and for the development of the academic quality of their students. For the majority of Dutch teacher educators, however, professional development activities involving research are still limited.

In sum, in the Netherlands three issues about teacher educators' professional learning ask for attention. First, while the organisation of the co-operation between schools and HEIs is well organized, the implementation of a systematic quality circle for partnerships is still missing. Second, the professional development of both school-based and HE-based teacher educators has been initiated by teacher educators themselves and further developed by the active role of VELON. The focus of these initiatives was on pedagogical practice, and less attention has been given to the professional development of the research qualities of teacher educators.

Moreover, until now participation in professional development activities has been voluntary. This situation, however, is changing. Influenced, among others, by the increasing attention for the professional development of teacher educators in Europe, the Dutch government has decided that from 2017 on all teacher educators, school-based as well as institution-based will be obligated to become registered. On the one hand, this decision requires that HEIs and schools have to incorporate this in their training provision; on the other hand, it means a power shift away from the professional community, VELON.

44.3.2 Norway

As in many other countries, Norway's ranking in international tests caused what has become known as 'PISA shock' or 'Pisa hysteria'. Subsequently, Norwegian teacher education has been subject to multiple reforms which reflect political trends striving to make the Norwegian schooling system competitive against international indicators. The assumption here is that international competitiveness is necessary to maintain the high standard of living currently enjoyed in Norway.

Some initiatives within the new reforms are to make elementary (primary) school teacher education more specialized (Ministry of Education and Research 2010), and to strengthen teachers' subject competence. Similar messages are reinforced by the new government's policy paper (Ministry of Education and Research 2014), including increased funding for the in-service education of teachers focusing on subject matter knowledge, especially mathematics and Norwegian. Other intentions are to increase the length of the practicum during teacher education and to provide strengthened support during induction. The most recent and radical initiative, however, was officially launched by the government in 2014. It states that from 2017 all ITE will consist of five year masters programmes, requiring a research dissertation. This reform means that student teachers training to teach in elementary and lower secondary schools will have the same academic level of education as their counterparts in the upper secondary sector, although they will take different majors. It seems that here Finland is the 'light house' for Norwegian policy makers, as it is for many other European countries. In the same policy document (Teacher Empowerment, (author translation)) in 2014 the formal education of school leaders will be continued and strengthened. Here Norway follows similar international trends mentioned in international documents coming from the OECD and the European Commission (2012, 2013).

The good news is that in Norway most (but not all) initiatives are accompanied by government funding, for example, funding has been provided for the further education of teachers, mentors and school leaders. Research has been prioritized through support for research and development (R&D) projects in education, and the establishment and continued funding of the National Research School in Teacher Education (NAFOL) (Östern and Smith 2013). These initiatives highlight the need for Norwegian teacher educators—both mentors working in schools and HEI-based—to be involved in research. In research and development projects the two types of teacher educators work together for school improvement; such projects are most often part of joint activities framed by partnership schemes between schools and HEIs. Moreover, when all teacher education moves to masters level from 2017, all teacher educators will be required to have research competence, preferably a doctorate, to be able to supervise the students' master dissertations.

There have been two, major government supported projects in teacher educators' professional learning: mentor education and NAFOL. As previously mentioned, the practical component of ITE is increasing, meaning that student teachers will spend more time in schools under the guidance and support of their mentors. For nearly a decade mentor education has been supported by the government and all teacher education institutions offer mentor education programmes of 30 ECTS. Commonly, programmes are structured so that the first module (worth 15 points) focuses on mentoring student teachers, whereas the second module (same value) focuses on mentoring novice teachers and other colleagues. Mentor education is usually placed at masters level, meaning it is research informed; engaging in action research or self-study of personal mentor roles or activities is a frequent requirement in these courses. Norway still has a long way to go before all school-based teacher educators are educated as mentors, but the process has started and will hopefully continue.

The second government-funded initiative, NAFOL, is a network of 23 Norwegian HEIs who work together to strengthen the research competence of the country's teacher educators. The initial project period starting in 2010 was judged so successful that the project, originally intended to finish in 2016, has now been extended to 2021. NAFOL's first priority is to support all teacher educators in their work towards a doctorate in *teacher education* itself, rather than in an academic discipline. The main goal is to develop a generation of researching teacher educators in Norway who identify themselves as teachers of teachers and also produce new knowledge about teaching and teacher education, with direct relevance to the field. The second goal is to empower teacher educators in supervising students' research projects at under-graduate and masters levels. However, not all teacher educators are motivated to engage in the demanding process of studying for a doctorate; NAFOL therefore also offers seminars and courses to practise teacher educators who want to update and expand their research competence in other ways. This too is an essential part of the process of developing research-based teacher education in Norway.

In Norway then new developments in the structures of ITE are accompanied by acknowledgement of the need for teacher educators to be prepared to undertake new responsibilities. Research is introduced to partner schools within the framework of joint research and development projects with HEIs, and an increasing number of school-based teacher educators undertake mentor education. Finally, the political claim for a research-based teacher education in Norway has gone beyond rhetoric to implementation through the establishment and continuation of NAFOL. Teacher education in Norway is certainly on the move, and research on the professional learning initiatives for teacher educators will hopefully contribute new knowledge of the field useful to international colleagues.

44.3.3 England

A period of sustained economic downturn, from which the UK is only now emerging, has had significant effects on provision for teacher educators' professional learning in England since 2010. Wide-ranging, politically enforced changes to schooling, caused by concerns about the international competitiveness of the English education system, have meant that state schools are in the process of radical change and fundamental fragmentation. There have also been significant changes or 'reforms' to ITE and serving teachers' Continuing Professional Development, with market-led models put in place and schools given considerably more responsibility for leading teacher education and research in both areas. All of these factors have impacted on teacher educators and the provision for their professional learning.

One clear consequence of the switch to a 'school-led' system of ITE has been the emergence of a new occupational sub-group of school-based educators with growing confidence and authority in their 'second order practice' (Murray 2002). The emergence of 'Teaching Schools' as recognized centres of excellence, with government funding available to support school-led ITE programmes and school-focused research and development projects, has greatly increased the professional learning opportunities available to school-based educators. Some (but by no means all) of these educators still work in partnerships with HEIs to implement and develop their ITE and research programmes. Such partnerships often bring further professional learning opportunities for all the educators, as detailed below.

A further consequence of the 'reforms' has been the closure of some university programmes and subsequent redundancies for a number of HE-based teacher educators. The absence in England of a strong professional interest group or national community of teacher educators, like VELON in the Netherlands or VELOV in Flanders, has been notable in recent attacks on HE-based pre-service programmes and on many teacher educators. This has often resulted in communal senses of marginalisation and powerlessness to defend the value of teacher educators' work. Despite these factors though, at the time of writing, most teacher educators in England are still based in or closely linked to a HEI.

Institutional provision for the professional development of HE-based teacher educators is very important. Provision varies greatly, but, in general, academic development programmes have been influenced by a growing acknowledgement of the importance of high quality of teaching in Higher Education. This has led to widespread generic teacher training and induction programmes for all new academic staff. In some institutions, all academics, including teacher educators, are also required to go through the various procedures around accreditation against the generic Higher Education Academy (HEA) Professional Standards Framework. All of this provision though, offers limited potential for the development of teacher educators' pedagogy and research development, unless programmes or accreditation procedures allow space for personal practice and enquiry as a teacher of teachers. Many programmes have, however, succeeded in using these generic university or HEA procedures to create strong, valid and focused platforms for the development of such pedagogical enquiry.

The economic downturn brought widespread austerity and many cuts in education budgets, including a reduction in funding for the Higher Education sector. Of particular relevance here was that funding for the HEA was reduced. This was particularly significant for teacher educators' professional development as it meant the closure of ESCalate—the education specialist area which had supported many initiatives for teacher educators. These had included the production of induction guidelines (Boyd et al. 2011), professional training events and the provision of small-scale grants to research practice. Some of these initiatives, including national induction programmes, have managed to continue drawing on other funding sources, but many have disappeared.

A further negative influence on provision for teacher educators' professional learning has been the effects of repeated national research audits. As indicated earlier, these have re-defined what is meant by 'research', and narrowed the criteria for 'what counts' as a valid research output and who is acknowledged to be a researcher. This in turn has limited some universities' formal support for practice-based research and for the development of teacher educators as active researchers. Since many teacher educators come into Higher Education without a doctorate or sustained experience of research, the lack of professional development in this area may mean that opportunities to participate fully in academic life as both researcher and teacher become restricted. But, again, it should be noted that generic university programmes may offer opportunities for the development of high quality practitioner or pedagogical research.

As Boyd et al. (2011) have argued, most professional learning for teacher educators happens, not through formal provision and organized programmes, but through informal workplace learning. This includes learning from and in the daily arenas of practice and from the face-to-face and virtual networks or communities to which teacher educators belong. An example of this kind of creative, informal learning opportunity is that in some of the new school-led pre-service routes HE-based educators are now working in ways which simultaneously develop their own professional learning and that of the school-based educators with whom they were working. In these instances, mutually beneficially development of shared practices and second order knowledge (Murray 2002) of how student teachers learn creates important, if tacit and often under-valued forms of professional learning for both groups of teacher educators.

In England, then, professional development provision for school-based teacher educators has expanded since 2010, whilst that for HE-based teacher educators has been reduced and diversified by the economic downturn and recent 'reforms' to ITE. Because of this, HEI provision has been become more important for the latter group. Despite all the weaknesses of this institutional model, identified above, most HEIs are still able to create some formal and informal learning opportunities for the teacher educators working within them. Professional associations and learned societies, including the much reduced HEA, still also offer some formal learning events. Most professional learning opportunities involve a focus on good practice in teacher education, pedagogy and pedagogical research, with outputs from the last activity being devalued in some HEIs by the re-definitions of research and research outputs reinforced by national research audits.

44.3.4   Teacher Educators' Professional Learning Across the National Cases

Important professional learning provision for teacher educators exists in all three national cases, often implemented within the employing institutions, particularly HEIs. Changes in this provision are also commonly led by major developments in teacher education nationally, as well as by institutional imperatives and intra-professional initiatives. All three countries have seen an increase in the importance of school-based teacher educators and subsequent provision for their professional learning. This is particularly strong in Norway through government-funded mentor development programmes. Both the Netherlands and England have notable histories of professional learning development for school-based teacher educators, and in England new learning opportunities are opening up. In all three countries, there is a clear acknowledgement, though, that this provision needs to be extended further.

There are no professional standards or competences specific to teacher educators in either Norway or England. In the Netherlands, VELON as a powerful, professional group has been able to establish and implement standards and then deploy these as the basis for communal learning, owned by the profession. But government changes to that established system mean that power over professional learning will shift more to institutions in the future. Provision here, as in England, tends to have strong focuses on pedagogy and practice rather than research development. There is some provision around research, of course, but in the Netherlands, even though institutional changes now require teacher educators employed to be more actively engaged in research, provision is still limited. In England, whilst school-based teacher educators may have new opportunities to engage in research, such opportunities, particularly in practitioner research, are in decline in some (but by no means all) HEIs. Norway is distinctive in its strong focus on the development of research skills through NAFOL and research and development projects between schools and HEIs. We should note here, of course, that different understandings of research are operating across the three cases, reflecting the valuation of different educational research practices, paradigms and outcomes.

Our brief case studies show that existence of nationally agreed standards or competences is not essential as the basis for the provision of professional learning opportunities. Professional groups, where they exist, are powerful actors in national provision but government funding facilitates large-scale and sustainable projects such as those found in Norway and to a lesser extent in the Netherlands. This direct funding supplements and strengthens institutional provision in these countries. In England, however, where professional learning is often dependent only on institutional provision, the position is more fragile, especially for HE-based educators. Whilst all three countries have the same avowed intentions for high quality teacher education and schooling, they have initiated very different ways of achieving and sustaining this excellence through the degrees of attention given to their professional learning for teacher educators. Such nationally specific provision is clearly important, but what spaces are there for systematic and sustainable pan-European learning? To consider this issue, we now turn to analyze the work of Info-TED.

44.3.5 Info-TED and Its Vision for Teacher Educators' Professional Development

Info-TED is a pan-European organisation which aims to bring together, exchange and promote research, policy and practice about teacher educators' professional development in order to develop the professional identities and knowledge bases. The group works from the conviction that educating teacher educators cannot be an ad hoc process, involve only narrow responses to national or institutional imperatives. As Vanassche et al. (in press) state, this learning is definitely not only about

> 'instrumental knowledge (i.e., 'how to'-questions: how to teach; identifying the most effective approaches)' (rather) 'it must also address 'what'-questions (i.e., selecting curriculum materials), 'why'-questions (i.e., defining goals and purposes), and 'who'-questions (i.e., expertise and professional responsibility of teacher educators)'. (Vanassche et al., in press: page number not yet known)

Practice is conceptualized as the starting point for professional development, rather than rather than standards or competence profiles which may attempt to provide a 'blueprint' (Kelchtermans 2013).[1] In order to conceptualise and map professional learning, the first stage of our work has involved the development of a conceptual model (see Fig. 44.1). This provides a common language with which to describe, communicate and discuss the diversity of pan-European teacher education. This is our attempt to visualize what we understand about teacher educators' professional development. Full details of the model can be found on the group's website, but in summary teacher educators' practices are seen as situated in personal, institutional, national and international policy contexts. Also presented on the left-hand side of our model is a non-exhaustive list of possible content domains (including social and technological change, social diversity and communications between teacher educators and other stakeholders, such as policymakers) which could be consideration when crafting teacher educators' professional learning opportunities.

In the group's approach then, high quality professional learning provision is required to grow and sustain teacher educators' expertise through the development of

---

[1]There is, of course, a distinct irony here in that the very act of creating a language and such a model implies a normative stance. We acknowledge this irony and the tensions between this stance and our practice-based intentions.

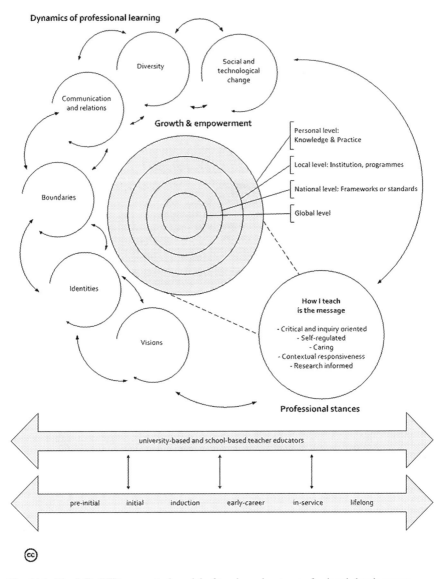

Fig. 44.1 The InFo-TED conceptual model of teacher educator professional development

distinctive and contextually relevant professional repertoires. This process occurs alongside understanding of the social and educational positioning of the occupational group, the complex roles and multi-faceted work required of it and the multiple identities often necessarily generated by teacher educators as they practice. This development of understanding also includes teacher educators becoming aware of the working conditions in which they enact their practice—and the expansive or restricted learning opportunities (Boyd et al. 2011) offered there. Here then practices and contexts are central to learning, as is the development of personal and communal awareness and a shared, public and critical language about teaching teachers.

But in addition to strengthening the necessary focus and specificity of professional learning tailored to individual, institutional and national needs, Info-TED also aims to generate awareness of the learning potential of analyzing the differences and commonalities in practices (for teaching and research) in the many policy and institutional contexts for teacher education across Europe. We are particularly interested in the reciprocal benefits of working in national *and* international contexts since as Stevenson (2015: 758) states:

> Recognising what is similar, and what is different, as well as to what extent and in what ways, professional learning policy and practice travel across borders becomes increasingly important given the way global pressures drive national, regional and local experiences. None of these are simple processes. Globalisation may tend to homogeneity, but the centrality of local experience remains critical.

Info-TED then brings together teacher educators across Europe to exchange practices, ideas and visions, developing our senses of the collective identities which bind us as a professional group, within supportive and collaborative learning communities. Our plans are to develop an electronic learning platform and a teacher educator academy will enable us to create the structures and contents for these pan-European learning opportunities in ways which are systematic, sustainable, inclusive and open to all teacher educators across Europe. The group is also taking clear stands in the debates on teacher educators' professional learning within our own nations and across Europe, continuing to voice our communal messages to educational policy makers and other stakeholders. The long term aims here, as ever, are to achieve higher quality and more holistic learning for teacher educators, as part of achieving improved learning opportunities for student teachers and for the schools and children they will go on to serve across Europe. And, although the work has a distinct European focus, we hope that the on-going work of the group has clear relevance for teacher educators across the rest of the world, who may be aiming to collaborate across national groups to achieve excellence in the provision of professional learning opportunities and to make their communal voices heard.

References

Boyd, P., Harris, K., & Murray, J. (2011). *Becoming a teacher educator* (2nd ed.). Bristol: The Higher Education Academy/ESCalate.

Cochran-Smith, M. (2003). Learning and unlearning: The education of teacher educators. *Teaching and Teacher Education, 19*(1), 5–28.

Darling-Hammond, L., & Lieberman, A. (Eds.). (2012). *Teacher education around the world.* London: Routledge.

Davey, R. (2013). *The professional identity of teacher educators: Career on the cusp?* London: Routledge.

Dengerink, J., Kools, Q., & Lunenberg, M. (2015). What and how teacher educators prefer to learn. *Journal of Education for Teaching, 41*(1), 78–96.

European Commission. (2012). *Supporting the teaching professions for better learning outcomes: Rethinking education: Investing in skills for better socio-economic outcomes.* Accessed at http://eur-lex.europa.eu/LexUriServ/LexUriServ.do?uri=SWD:2012:0374:FIN:EN:PDF

European Commission. (2013). *Supporting teacher educators for better learning outcomes.* European Commission.

European Commission. (2015). *Strengthening Teaching in Europe: New evidence from teachers compiled by Eurydice and CRELL,* June 2015. http://ec.europa.eu/education/library/policy/teaching-professionpractices_en.pdf. Accessed August 2015.

Goodwin, A. L., & Kosnik, C. (2013). Quality teacher educators = quality teachers? Conceptualising essential domains of knowledge for those who teach teachers. *Teacher Development, 17*(3), 334–346.

Kelchtermans, G. (2013). Praktijk in de plaats van blauwdruk. Over het opleiden van lerarenopleiders. [Practice instead of blueprint. Educating teacher educators]. *VELON Tijdschrift voor Lerarenopleiders, 34,* 89–99.

Lunenberg, M., Dengerink, J., & Korthagen, F. (2014). *The professional teacher educator. Roles, behaviour, and professional development of teacher educators.* Rotterdame: Sense Publishers.

Murray, J. (2002). Between the chalkface and the ivory towers? A study of the professionalism of teacher educators working on primary initial teacher education courses in the English education system. *Collected Original Resources in Education, 26*(3), 1–530.

Norwegian Ministry of Education and Research. (2010). Rammeplan for lærerutdanningen 1 til 7, og 5 til 10 [Regulations on curriculum for primary and secondary education for steps 1 to 7 and steps 5–10].

Östern, A. L., & Smith, A. (2013). Response of the National Graduate School for Teacher Education NAFO, to the call for a more research based teacher education in Norway. In A. L. Östern, K. Smith, T. Ryhaug, T. Krüger, & M. B. Postholm (Eds.), *Teacher education research between national identity and global trends* (pp. 13–28). Trondheim, Norway: Akademia Publishing.

Stevenson, H. (2015). Professional learning in global times. *Professional Development in Education, 41*(5), 757–758.

Vanassche, E., Rust, F., Conway, P. Smith, K., Tack, H., & Vanderlinde, R. (in press). InFo-TED: Bringing policy, research, and practice together around teacher educator development. In C. Craig & L. Orland Barak (Eds.), *Advances in research on teaching. International teacher education: Promising pedagogies* (Part A). New York: Emerlad.

Author Biographies

Jean Murray is a professor of education in the Cass School of Education at the University of East London. Her research focuses on teacher education policies and practices. Jean has published extensively, taught at all levels of higher education and acted as an educational consultant for governments, NGOs and universities.

Mieke Lunenberg is a teacher and researcher at VU University Amsterdam where her focus is on the professional development of teacher educators. She has published extensively on this theme. Mieke has also been internationally invited to give lectures and workshops about the professional development of teacher educators.

Kari Smith is a Professor Norwegian University of Science and Technology and is Head of the Norwegian National Research School in Teacher Education. Her research interests are teacher education, professional development, mentoring novice teachers, and assessment for and of learning. She has published widely and has given multiple invited talks internationally.

Chapter 45
Making Connections in the UK and Australia—Research, Teacher Education and Educational Improvement

Ian Menter

45.1 Introduction

In this chapter I seek to explore the relationships between teacher education, research and educational improvement. My exploration is based on a deep commitment to a research-based approach to teacher education, indeed on my commitment to teaching as an enquiry-based profession and also to the improvement of educational experiences for all learners. This is not therefore a dispassionate perspective. It is one based on many years working in schools and universities and working with other teachers and researchers. However, even if it is not dispassionate, I will nevertheless seek to provide the evidence to support the case I am developing, in the true spirit of critical enquiry.

The other key point to be made by way of introduction is that while education systems may still be largely based around nation states or states within nations, there is nevertheless an increasingly global element in education policy processes and to some extent that is also echoed in educational practices. Some of the most visible aspects of these developments may be associated with the attempts at international comparisons in educational achievement, such as PISA, TIMMS and PIRLS. One of the most perceptive accounts of these developments has been offered by Sahlberg (2011), who continues to be somewhat mystified by the success of Finland in these league tables, but is able to offer some partial explanations against the backdrop of his wonderfully suggestive acronym, the GERM. The Global Education Reform Movement is the process which has led to the following

This chapter is based on a talk given at the inaugural conference of the Peter Underwood Centre on Educational Underachievement at the University of Tasmania, Hobart, in June 2015.

I. Menter (✉)
University of Oxford, Oxford, UK
e-mail: ian.menter@education.ox.ac.uk

© Springer Nature Singapore Pte Ltd. 2017
M.A. Peters et al. (eds.), *A Companion to Research in Teacher Education*,
DOI 10.1007/978-981-10-4075-7_45

characteristics (or symptoms) being seen in many education contexts around the world:

- Standardization
- Increased focus on core subjects
- Prescribed curriculum
- Transfer of models from the corporate world
- High-stakes accountability policies (Sahlberg 2011: 99–106).

It becomes clear in Sahlberg's book that Finland's success is built against a very different background from many other developed nations, including England or even the wider UK, which is a much more stratified society than Finland, with many institutions of privilege for the privileged.

45.2 Teaching and Teachers

The overall theme for this symposium is 'Education underpinning social and economic transformation'. Teachers have a major role to play in supporting these aspirations for the transformative effects of education. However, from the outset we must remember the clear caveat stated by Basil Bernstein more than 40 years ago—'Education cannot compensate for society' (Bernstein 1970). Nevertheless as others have pointed out, 'School Matters' (Mortimore et al. 1988) and 'Teachers Matter' (Day et al. 2007). It is now a truth almost universally acknowledged that the single biggest element in educational success and indeed in educational improvement is the quality of teaching and of teachers. That is the conclusion of the McKinsey Reports (Barber and Mourshed 2007) and it is also what emerges from the TALIS studies (OECD 2009).

In England, we had a White Paper as long ago as 1983 called 'The Quality of Teaching' (DES 1983). In 2010, we had another White Paper called 'The Importance of Teaching' (DfE 2010). The recognition that teaching is important has led to some greater efforts to identify what it is that may make teachers more or less successful. But of course there is a rather important prior question that may get in the way of answering this directly. That is, what do we mean by 'educational success' or indeed by 'good teaching'?

It is often suggested that the measure of a successful education system is to be located in indicators of social and economic development. But few would deny the simultaneous importance of cultural and intellectual development. Indeed, in these times of 'the knowledge economy', much of the key debate concerns how these different purposes of education relate to each other and should be balanced. One of the key British thinkers on the development of twentieth century democracy, Raymond Williams, suggested that you could understand the development of education in Britain as a continuing struggle between the interests of three influential forces within society:

- the old humanists;
- the public educators; and
- the industrial trainers (Williams 1961/2011).

In so far as these social forces coincide with, respectively, the cultural, the social and the economic purposes of education, we can still see these tensions being played out, albeit on a more global scale, in the education systems of developed nations today.

So, it seems logical to expect that the shape and form of teacher education will be deeply influenced by the agreed purposes of education. If we do wish to see education, at least in some significant part, as an engine of social and economic transformation, then what kinds of teachers do we want and how should we prepare them?

Many of the debates about the form and structure of teacher education pro- grammes have centred on questions about the nature of teaching and what forms of knowledge, skills and experience are required in order to fulfil this definition. In a review of literature of teacher education in the twenty-first century, a team of us at the University of Glasgow (Menter et al. 2010) suggested that it is possible to identify four paradigms of teaching, each of which will lead to rather different approaches to the formulation of pre-entry programmes.

1. The effective teacher—with an emphasis on technical skills
2. The reflective teacher—with an emphasis on values and review
3. The enquiring teacher—with the adoption of a research orientation
4. The transformative teacher—with the adoption of a 'change agency' approach.

Moving from the first to the fourth, each paradigm incorporates those with a lower number but builds upon it. These might be seen as positions on a spectrum of professionalism which, using the terminology developed in the 1970s by Hoyle (1974) moves from 'restricted' professionalism at one end to 'extended' profes- sionalism at the other.

At the restricted/effective end of the spectrum, there is a view that the best place to learn to teach is alongside an experienced and successful teacher, through an apprenticeship model. This is sometimes depicted as a 'craft' view of teaching. The skills of teaching are learned by observation and by imitation and in turn by being observed and receiving feedback from the experienced teacher. On this model, knowledge of the subject content of the teaching is assumed to be present, in other words the trainee is already well versed in the subject and all they require is enthusiasm and an ability to learn from observation and feedback. If this is a limited view of becoming a teacher for a secondary school teacher of a particular subject it is even more challenging for the elementary or primary school teacher whose subject knowledge will need to range right across the school curriculum. This position has been well exemplified by a recent Secretary of State for Education in England, Michael Gove, in his foreword to the Government White Paper mentioned above:

> Teaching is a craft and it is best learnt as an apprentice observing a master craftsman or woman. Watching others, and being rigorously observed yourself as you develop, is the best route to acquiring mastery in the classroom. (DfE 2010)

But if we are indeed looking to education leading transformation, we surely need a more ambitious view of teaching and teacher education. To what extent one needs to adopt a transformative model of teaching in order to promote education as a transformative force is a key question for discussion at this symposium.

45.3 The Reform of Teacher Education

In his account of the lessons from Finland, Sahlberg (2011) is in no doubt that the standing of the teaching profession, the commitment to high-quality teacher education and continuing development and the reasonable remuneration of teachers are among the factors that are likely to have had a positive influence—even if he is no more able than the rest of us to demonstrate more than a correlation between these features. As we shall see, actually demonstrating a causal link, let alone a full explanation of this relationship, continues to be a very significant.

I have often made the argument that in order to understand a particular teacher education system as it currently exists it is necessary to consider the history, culture and politics of that society (see TEG 2016). I would now add very wholeheartedly that the economy of the society is also an important factor in shaping the system. So, if we need to look at all four of these to understand a teacher education system, we may also expect the system to have an influence on the future economy, culture and politics of that society. In other words, there is a dynamic relationship between teacher education and society. Teacher education is both shaped by but also influences the society. Indeed that is why a maxim that is important to me, especially in undertaking comparative work in teacher education research, is 'by their teacher education ye shall know them'.

For, through reviewing and analyzing a nation's teacher education system we are appraising what it is that teachers should know, what they should be able to do and how they should be disposed, in order to help in the formation of the future adult citizens of the society, in perhaps 10–20 years time. Teacher education may be taken to be highly symbolic of how a society sees its future and is therefore highly indicative of its underlying values. Perhaps it is a realization of this that has turned teacher education into such a centre of political interest in the past 20–30 years in many countries. It should therefore be no surprise that across the globe we have seen increasing numbers of reviews, reports and reforms of teacher education over recent. In my travels around the UK, as well as in the USA, Austria, Norway, Turkey and recently Russia there are major reforms going on in teacher education. And of course the same is true in Australia, of which more towards the end of this paper.

The big questions in teacher education that are both enduring—that is, they have historical manifestations—but are at the same time also highly contemporary, include the following:

- The background and experience of recruits into teaching
- The relationship between theory and practice
- The nature of professional knowledge
- The sites of learning
- The respective contributions of the school and of the university
- Curriculum and assessment within teacher education
- The continuum of professional learning
- Assessing the effectiveness of teacher education (see Menter 2015).

It may be useful here to offer a brief summary of what has been happening in the UK to give a sense of how some of these major issues have been debated. 2010 was a very interesting year for us. There was a general election held in May, which led to the creation of the Coalition Government, a partnership between the Conservatives and the Liberal Democrats. Michael Gove was appointed by Prime Minister David Cameron as Secretary of State for Education. Remember, however, that Gove's jurisdiction for education was not UK wide, it covers only England. Since the devolutions of the late 1990s, Scotland, Wales and Northern Ireland had full responsibility for education policy including teacher education policy.

In England then, one of the first White Papers that the Coalition Government produced was 'The Importance of Teaching' (DfE 2010). This set out a clear view of the nature of teaching and indeed of teacher education, as demonstrated in these extracts:

> We do not have a strong enough focus on what is proven to be the most effective practice in teacher education and development. We know that teachers learn best from other professionals and that an 'open classroom' culture is vital: observing teaching and being observed, having the opportunity to plan, prepare, reflect and teach with other teachers'

> [We will] reform initial teacher training so that more training is on the job, and it focuses on key teaching skills including teaching early reading and mathematics, managing behaviour and responding to pupils' Special Educational Needs.

We thus see Mr. Gove fully supporting a simple craft view of teaching and an apprenticeship model of teacher education—actually he persisted in calling it teacher training—and we now see the dominance of his 'School Direct' approach to teacher education. This school-led model has led to a small number of universities withdrawing altogether from teacher education and to a number of others seriously questioning whether it is worth their while to maintain their involvement.

However, only 2 months later, a report was published in Edinburgh, called 'Teaching Scotland's Future' (Donaldson 2010). This had been written by a leading educational professional rather than by a politician, namely the recently retired Chief Inspector of Education, Graham Donaldson. This set out a very different view of teaching and teacher education when compared to Michael Gove's model in England. Donaldson emphasised:

- teachers "as reflective, accomplished and enquiring professionals who have the capacity to engage fully with the complexities of education and to be key actors in shaping and leading educational change" (p4);
- teaching as a profession based on high-quality provision;
- the key role that universities have to offer in the development of teachers;
- teaching as a complex and challenging occupation which requires a strong and sophisticated professional development framework throughout every stage of the career;
- the link between teaching and leadership—good quality education is based on both, throughout the career.

Not surprisingly, in the light of these values, Donaldson not only endorsed the importance of higher education and research in teacher education, he was gently critical that universities were not even more broadly engaged in teacher education.

Therefore we have seen in the last 5 years somewhat different policy trajectories in the teacher education being offered in these two component nations of the United Kingdom (see TEG 2016). We should also note that processes of review have been underway in Northern Ireland and Wales as well and these have generally been aligned towards the Scottish view of teaching and teacher education, thus making England sometimes seem something of an outlier within the UK (see Teacher Education Group 2016). However, the push for school-based teacher education is not only alive in England, we see similar developments in many US states.

45.4   The BERA-RSA Inquiry

It was because of concern about the potential impacts on the educational research infrastructure of government policies concerning teacher education across the four nations of the UK, that BERA decided in 2012 to set up an inquiry into the relationship between teacher education and research. It came as something of a shock to many of us who had been working in university-based teacher education for a number of years that the importance of the links between higher education and teacher education were not widely understood. Indeed retrospectively and in spite of many years of pamphleteering and campaigning against university-based teacher education by right wing think tanks and their associates, we can see now that there had been a failure to resist or respond positively to defend the sector (Childs and Menter 2013). But yet, the evidence to demonstrate the importance of HE and research in teaching was not immediately to hand. There were no studies that convincingly demonstrated that educational outcomes were improved through teacher education with high levels of university input or indeed of research input.

Thus the Inquiry, which was then established in a partnership with the Royal Society for the Arts (RSA) set out to answer the following questions, more or less ab initio:

1. What is the role of research within initial teacher education (ITE) and how does it contribute to programmes of continuing professional development and learning (CPDL)?
2. What is the impact of research-informed teacher education on the quality of teaching and how far does research-based teaching improve learning outcomes for students?
3. How far does current provision across the UK meet the requirements of research-informed teacher education and research-based teaching? What are the barriers to creating research-rich environments at a school and system level and how may these be overcome?

A total of seven papers were commissioned from a range of leading scholars (BERA-RSA 2014a). A review of more and less successful education systems and their approach to teacher education was carried out by Maria Teresa Tatto and she found that there was at least *prima facie* evidence of a positive linkage between enquiry-oriented approaches to teacher education and successful outcomes—she looked at Finland, Singapore, the USA and Chile.

Two of my colleagues at Oxford, Katharine Burn and Trevor Mutton were asked to look at research-based clinical practice models of initial teacher education. They looked at approaches in Scotland, Australia, the Netherlands and elsewhere, as well as our own Oxford internship scheme, and found that models which sought to integrate theoretical and experiential learning in a systematic way, provided a firm basis for teachers' continuing professional learning and for the creation of teachers who could work in a range of contexts and situations.

Overall the Inquiry came to the following conclusions (BERA-RSA 2014b):

– Internationally, enquiry-based (or 'research-rich') school and college environments are the hallmark of high performing education systems.
– To be at their most effective, teachers and teacher educators need to engage *with* research and enquiry—this means keeping up to date with the latest developments in their academic subject or subjects and with developments in the discipline of education.
– Teachers and teacher educators need to be equipped to engage *in* enquiry-oriented practice. This means having the capacity, motivation, confidence and opportunity to do so.
– A focus on enquiry-based practice needs to be sustained during initial teacher education programmes and throughout teachers' professional careers,… [this needs to be] embedded within the lives of schools or colleges and become the normal way of teaching and learning, rather than the exception—[that is, teachers should be equipped with] 'Research Literacy'.

The report made recommendations for each of the four UK jurisdictions but also some more general recommendations, as follows:

– With regard to both initial teacher education and teachers' continuing professional development, there are pockets of excellent practice across the UK but good practice is inconsistent and insufficiently shared. Drawing on the evidence, the inquiry concludes that amongst policymakers and practitioners there is considerable potential for greater dialogue than currently takes place, as there is between teachers, teacher-researchers and the wider research community.

– Everybody in a leadership position—in the policy community, in university departments of education, at school or college level or in key agencies within the educational infrastructure—has a responsibility to support the creation of the sort of research-rich organisational cultures in which these outcomes, for both learners and teachers, can be achieved.

While visiting Australia in 2014 I became aware of the moves that were developing there to look at the organisation and delivery of teacher education. To be frank, there was considerable anxiety at that time that the outcomes of the processes of review established by Minister Pyne might bear a considerable similarity to the developments in England. My reading of the report (TEMAG 2014), is that this has not in fact been the case.

The key issues for teacher education (as delineated above) are all in there and the awareness of the political significance of teacher education is clearly flagged, as well as the influence of 'the GERM'. The report is not at all uncritical of current practice however and suggests that there are some serious weaknesses that must be urgently addressed. On the key issue of who should be responsible for high-quality teacher education, the report is clear:

> Higher education providers and the teaching profession must together embrace the opportunity to full participate in a reformed, integrated system of initial teacher education. This participation will be essential in embedding the reforms necessary to deliver high-quality teaching in every Australian school. (TEMAG 2014: xi)

The report identifies four 'fundamental principles' on which the group's deliberations are based: integration, assurance, evidence and transparency. Five proposals then follow from these principles:

1. a strengthened national quality assurance process;
2. sophisticated and rigorous selection for entry into teaching;
3. integration of theory and practice;
4. robust assurance of classroom readiness;
5. national research and capability.

On the third of these there is talk of structured and mutually beneficial partnerships between schools and higher education in order to provide the necessary 'real opportunities for pre-service teachers to integrate theory and practice'.

And on point 5, the report elaborates:

> Better evidence of the effectiveness of initial teacher education in the Australian context is needed to inform innovative program design and delivery, and the continuing growth of teaching as a profession. (xii)

Not only that but there is a clear recommendation as to where the leadership for this research should lie:

The AITSL [Australian Institute for Teaching and School Leadership] should expand its functions to include provision of leadership in national research on teacher education effectiveness, to ensure that the Australian teaching profession is able to continually improve its practice.

This is profoundly encouraging. Of course much will depend on the level of political support that the recommendations get—and we know politicians change and move on. However, what has been provided here is a clear evidence-based report that offers an overall strategy for transformation and improvement.

45.5   Conclusion

As we see in the TEMAG report, it remains crucially important to enquire into the relationship between educational outcomes and the nature of teacher education and professional development. This remains a greatly under-researched and underexplored aspect of education. We may have some *prima facie* evidence now that enquiry-oriented teaching is strongly associated with more successful education systems, but we still not really understand why that is.

Trust, respect, conditions and salary are all important and can play a part in the recruitment and retention of teachers who can make a big contribution and improve young people's life chances. The standing of the profession is likely to improve as the research and practice communities move closer together. Research literacy should be an entitlement for all teachers and should be developed throughout their careers. In the same way that other professions develop their expertise, this is likely to be best achieved through ever closer working with researchers and university-based colleagues who can ask the right questions and support teachers in identifying answers.

Making connections in the way suggested in the TEMAG report is crucial to positive development. We see here an opportunity to enrich and indeed embed the relationships between policy, practice and research. We see a commitment to critical reasoning as an underlying principle for teaching and for education, a commitment that is endangered in England, as demonstrated by Furlong's recent analysis (Furlong 2013).

It is very reassuring to see examples of researchers and policymakers seeking to learn from each other without blindly imitating. Education systems and teacher education systems each have their own histories and trajectories and each seeks to meet the needs of a distinctive culture and society at particular points in time. So the connections are important—global connections and internal connections—in all three overlapping worlds of policy, practice and research. Through such connections, we can seriously seek to transform our world—both locally and internationally—through education.

References

Barber, M., & Mourshed, M. (2007). *The McKinsey report: How the world's best performing school systems come out on top*. London: McKinsey and Co.

BERA-RSA. (2014a). *The role of research in teacher education. Reviewing the evidence. Interim report of the BERA-RSA inquiry*. Author: London. Retrieved from https://www.bera.ac.uk/wp-content/uploads/2014/02/BERA-RSA-Interim-Report.pdf

BERA-RSA. (2014b). *Research and the teaching profession. Building the capacity for a self-improving education system. Final report of the BERA-RSA Inquiry into the role of research in teacher education*. Author: London. Retrieved from https://www.bera.ac.uk/wp-content/uploads/2013/12/BERA-RSA-Research-Teaching-Profession-FULL-REPORT-for-web.pdf

Bernstein, B. (1970). Education cannot compensate for society. In D. Rubinstein & C. Stoneman (Eds.), *Education for democracy*. Harmondsworth: Penguin.

Childs, A., & Menter, I. (2013). Teacher education in the 21st century in England: A case study in neo-liberal policy. *Revista Espanola de Educacion Camparada (Spanish Journal of Comparative Education), 22*, 93–116.

Day, C., Sammons, P., Stobart, G., Kington, A., & Gu, Q. (2007). *Teachers matter: Connnecting lives, work and effectiveness*. Maidenhead: McGraw-Hill.

Department for Education (DfE). (2010). *The importance of teaching. White paper*. London: DfE.

Department for Education and Science (DES). (1983). *Teaching quality. White paper*. London: HMSO.

Donaldson, G. (2010). *Teaching Scotland's future: A report of the review of teacher education in Scotland*. Edinburgh: Scottish Government.

Furlong, J. (2013). *Education—An anatomy of the discipline: Rescuing the university project?*. Oxon: Routledge.

Hoyle, E. (1974). Professionality, professionalism and control in teaching. *London Education Review, 3*(2), 13–19.

Menter, I. (2015). Teacher education. In J. D. Wright (editor-in-chief), *International encyclopedia of the social & behavioral sciences* (2nd ed., Vol. 24, pp. 51–55). Oxford: Elsevier.

Menter, I., Hulme, M., Elliot, D., & Lewin, J. (2010). *Literature review on teacher education in the 21st century*. Edinburgh: The Scottish Government.

Mortimore, P., Sammons, P., Stoll, L., Lewis, D., & Ecob, R. (1988). *School matters—The junior years*. Wells: Open Books.

Organisation for Economic Cooperation and Development. (2009). *Teaching and learning international survey—Creating effective teaching and learning environments: First results from TALIS*. Paris: OECD.

Sahlberg, P. (2011). *Finnish lessons: What can the world learn from educational change in Finland?*. New York: Teachers College Press.

Teacher Education Group. (2016). *Teacher education in times of change*. Bristol: Policy Press.

Teacher Education Ministerial Advisory Group. (2014). *Action now: Classroom ready teachers*. Retrieved from https://docs.education.gov.au/system/files/doc/other/action_now_classroom_ready_teachers_accessible.pdf

Williams, R. (1961/2011). *The long revolution* (New edn.). Cardigan: Parthian Books.

Author Biography

Ian Menter is a Fellow of the Academy of Social Sciences in the UK and was President of the British Educational Research Association (BERA), 2013–15. He is Emeritus Professor of Teacher Education at the University of Oxford and was a member of the Steering Group of the BERA Inquiry into Research and Teacher Education (2014).

Part VII
Pedagogy in Action

Introduction

Pedagogy in action is a theme that emerges out of decades old notion of reflective practice that discussed the relationship between theory and practice, theories of pedagogical praxis and forms of action research. It is a term that now encompasses a wide range of methodologies including: "experience-based education", "new pedagogies", "pedagogies for deep learning", "supportive classroom environment", "community engagement", "new literacies", "critical pedagogy", "complexity pedagogy", "action research pedagogies".[1] Smith (2012) writes:

> In recent years interest has grown in 'pedagogy' within English-language discussions of education. The impetus has come from different directions. There have been those like Paulo Freire seeking a 'pedagogy of the oppressed' or 'critical pedagogy'; practitioners wanting to rework the boundaries of care and education via the idea of social pedagogy; and, perhaps most significantly, governments wanting to constraint the activities of teachers by requiring adherence to preferred 'pedagogies'.

A large part of this movement is to begin to theorize pedagogy from the action side of the theory–action divide and to "walk the talk" so to speak. Smith (2012) writes of "exploring pedagogy is as the process of accompanying learners; caring for and about them; and bringing learning into life".

The notion of practitioner and practitioner cultures has fast become part of a set of ideological dogma ever since Donald Schön first popularized the term in his 1983 book *The Reflective Practitioner: How Professionals Think in Action*. He stipulated that the capacity to reflect on action so as to engage in a process of continuous learning is one of the defining characteristics of professional practice. Schön (1987; 26) advances the concept of reflection-in-action in this formulation:

---

[1]See, for example, Connecting Theory to Classroom Practice, http://serc.carleton.edu/sp/index.html; Maggie Ryan, https://prezi.com/eo3qcgzsh_pz/pedagogy-in-action/; Understanding New Literacies for New Times: Pedagogy in Action, https://www.youtube.com/watch?v=QcITZSlDlas; Emergence: Complexity Pedagogy in Action, https://www.hindawi.com/journals/nrp/2015/235075/; Action Research Pedagogy, https://ecommons.cornell.edu/handle/1813/8326.

In an action-present – a period of time, variable with the context, during which we can still make a difference to the situation at hand – our thinking serves to reshape what we are doing while we are doing it. I shall say, in cases like this, that we reflect-in-action.

The simple theory was devised around an understand of learning systems and drew on Ashby's (1960) seminal work on cybernetics and the concept of feedback or what he later called in work with Chris Argyris "double loop learning" differentiating it from "single loop learning".

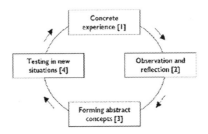

Schön had trained as a philosopher and completed his philosophy degrees at Yale completing his Ph.D. at Harvard on Dewey's theory of inquiry. From the 1970s Schön devoted himself to the question of what makes professional practice effective. Working with Chris Argyris at Harvard in the field of organizational learning he went on to co-author a series of books that developed an epistemology of professional practice based on the concept of knowledge-in-action, including *Theory in Practice: Increasing Professional Effectiveness* (1974), *Organizational Learning: A Theory of Action Perspective (1978),* and *Organizational Learning II: Theory, Method, and Practice* (1996).

Beginning with the practice of design in architecture (the reflective practicum in design studio) he extended his interests to professionals in education, management, medicine, psychotherapy, law, city planning, and engineering. Reflection-in-action is what professionals bring to their everyday practices and theories-in-use are tacit theories of action based on forms of tacit knowledge.

Schön's ideas developing in the early 1970s were based and brought together into a new frame and focus the ideas of cybernetic epistemology explored earlier by the likes of Gregory Bateson, W. Ross Ashby, and Gordon Pask, all part of the cybernetics group who developed their ideas at the Macy Conferences in New York during the period 1946–53 bringing together and applying cybernetics, information theory, and computer theory and constructing a distinctive American social science in the Cold War. As Steve Heims (1991: 271) puts it:

Feedback has come to mean information about the outcome of any process or activity. No single word for that general idea seems to have existed in the English language before feedback was introduced in the context of cybernetics.

The notion of the feedback mechanism was used to describe the process of social adaptation, of economic activity based on the idea of "information", of organizational performance, and of learning and education. These cyberneticians thought of their work as scientific and apolitical yet this cybernetics systems thinking encouraged both a naturalization of the social sciences (a reduction to biological systems) and a bio-mechanization that strongly supported a picture of biological roots and foundations of consciousness likening the mind to a network and an information-processing system.

Schön's work serves in part as a basis for a series of related developments in the area of professional development and learning: "situated learning", "communities of practice" (Lave and Wenger 1991), "situated cognition" (Greeno 1998), "experiential learning" (Kolb and Fry 1975), and "communities of inquiry" (Lipman 2003). Most of these concepts and movements flow out of a combination of Deweyan pragmatism and Piagetian psychology. Wenger (2006) uses the concept of "communities of practice" to refer to "groups of people who share a concern or a passion for something they do and learn how to do it better as they interact regularly". It is basically an anthropological notion that emerged from the study of apprenticeships. Wenger's (1998) influential notion is based on a social theory of learning that rests on four premises: we are social beings; knowledge is a matter of competences with respect to valued enterprises; knowing is a matter of participating in the pursuit of these enterprises; and meaning is learning to produce.

Key Characteristics of a Community of Practice

- Sustained mutual relationships—harmonious or conflictual
  - Shared ways of engaging in doing things together
  - The rapid flow of information and propagation of innovation
  - Absence of introductory preambles, as if conversations and interactions were merely the continuation of an ongoing process
  - Very quick setup of a problem to be discussed Substantial overlap in participants descriptions of who belongs
  - Knowing what others know, what they can do, and how they can contribute to an enterprise
  - Mutually defining identities
  - The ability to assess the appropriateness of actions and products
  - Specific tools, representations, and other artefacts
  - Local lore, shared stories, inside jokes, knowing laughter
  - Jargon and shortcuts to communication as well as the ease of producing new ones
  - Certain styles recognized as displaying membership A shared discourse reflecting a certain perspective on the world
  - Source: compiled from Wenger (1998, pp. 125–126).

The CoP approach is one among a number of practice-based approaches to learning and knowledge generation. Gherardi (2006, p. 38), in her recent review of such approaches, identifies three types of relations established between practices and knowledge. The first of these is a relation of containment, with knowledge as a process that takes place within situated practices. The second is a relation of mutual constitution, with the activities of knowing and practising tangled together and shaping each other. The third is a relation of equivalence, such that practising is the same as knowing in practice, whether the subject is aware of it or not. Gherardi (2006, p. 39) goes on to outline four main reasons for adopting a practice-based approach to learning and knowledge, which can be summarized as follows:

- To go beyond problematic dualisms like mind/body, actor/structure, human/ non-human.
- To question the primacy of the actor and the individual action as the building blocks of social phenomena.
- To see reason as a practice phenomenon and depict language as a discursive activity.
- To pay due attention to the materiality of the social world.

References

Argyris, C. & Schön, D. (1996). *Organizational learning II: Theory, method, and practice*. San Francisco: Addison-Wesley.
Bamberger, J. & Schön, D. (1991). Learning as reflective conversation with materials. In F. Steier (Ed.), *Research and reflexivity*. London: Sage.
Gherardi, S. (2006). *Organizational knowledge: The texture of workplace learning*. Oxford: Blackwell Publishing.
Greeno, J. G. (1998). The situativity of knowing, learning, and research. *American Psychologist, 53*(1), 5–26.
Kolb. D. A. & Fry, R. (1975). *Toward an applied theory of experiential learning*. In C. Cooper (Ed.), *Theories of group process*. London: John Wiley.
Lave, J. Wenger, E. (1991). *Situated learning. Legitimate peripheral participation*. Cambridge: University of Cambridge Press.
Lipman, M. (2003). *Thinking in education* (2nd ed.). Cambridge: Cambridge University Press.
Schön, D. & Rein, M. (1994). *Frame reflection: Toward the resolution of intractable controversies*. New York: Basic Books.
Schön, D. (1983). *The reflective practitioner: How professionals think in action*. NY: Basic Books.
Schön, D. (1984). *The design studio: An exploration of its traditions and potentials*. London: RIBA.
Schön, D. (1987). *Educating the reflective practitioner: Toward a new design for teaching and learning in the professions*. San Francisco: Jossey-Bass.
Schön, D. (1987). The crisis of professional knowledge and the pursuit of an epistemology of practice. In R. Christensen & A. J. Hansen (Eds.), *Teaching by the case method*. Boston, MA: Harvard Business School.
Schön, D. (1990). Causality and Causal Inference in the Study of Organizations. University of Sourthern California Colloquium on the Epistemology of Social Sciences.
Schön, D. (1992, March). Designing as reflective conversation with the materials of a design situation. *Knowledge-Based Systems, 5*(1). Butterworth-Heinemann Ltd.
Schön, D. (Ed.) (1991). *The reflective turn: Case studies in and on educational practice*. New York: Teachers College.
Smith, M. K. (2012). 'What is pedagogy?', *The encyclopaedia of informal education*. Retrieved from http://infed.org/mobi/what-is-pedagogy/
Wenger, E. (1998). *Communities of practice: Learning, meaning, and identity*. Cambridge, MA: CUP.
Wenger, E. (2006). *Communities of practice: A brief introduction*, at http://www.ewenger.com/ theory/index.htm

Chapter 46
'If I Could Not Make a Difference Why Would I Be a Teacher?' Teaching English as an Additional Language and the Quest for Social Justice

Ghazala Bhatti and Gail McEachron

46.1   Introduction

This chapter is about the education of children and young people who find themselves in countries where learning English is an absolute necessity. Their inclusion is not possible without the pivotal role played by teachers who can make a real difference, and whose values can be seen as social justice in action (Griffiths 2003). The chapter is in two parts; the first considers policy and practice in relation to English as an Additional Language (EAL)[1] mostly from a British perspective, with reference to some research findings in the United States (US). The second is based on a research project in Henrico County US involving Bath Spa University (BSU) in the United Kingdom (UK) and in Bristol, UK involving students from the College of William and Mary (WM) in US. Data was collected in schools by student researchers in both countries (see McEachron et al. 2015 for further details). This chapter sheds light on teaching opportunities in classrooms. Elaborating on the pedagogical process, it shows how reflexivity can deepen our understanding of EAL teaching. Reflexivity is the process of becoming self-aware. It is a 'researcher's ongoing critique and critical reflection of his or her own biases and assumptions and how these have influenced all stages of the research process. The researcher … critiques impressions and

---

[1]EAL is used for consistency and also when English may be a third or fourth language. Terminology differs according to the number of languages students speak as well as the policy context in each country. For ease of reference, EAL/ESL have been used according to the context.

G. Bhatti (✉)
Bath Spa University, Bath, England, UK
e-mail: g.bhatti@bathspa.ac.uk

G. McEachron
College of William and Mary, Williamsburg, USA
e-mail: gamcea@wm.edu

© Springer Nature Singapore Pte Ltd. 2017
M.A. Peters et al. (eds.), *A Companion to Research in Teacher Education*,
DOI 10.1007/978-981-10-4075-7_46

hunches, locates meanings, and relates these to specific contexts and experiences'
(Mills et al. 2010, p. 789).

46.2 Impact of the Global on the Local

EAL teaching and learning is important in all English speaking countries. Current
events like the Syrian crisis have highlighted the high risk this fleeing segment of
humanity will undertake to escape war, persecution and poverty. This century will
continue to face serious questions about human rights and social justice, as it
witnesses a further rise in the number of school age children in English speaking
countries. Schools are responsible for meeting educational, psychological, social
and cultural needs. Whether they are in Australia or US, refugees and asylum
seeking children have to utilize educational opportunities alongside second and
third generation of once-migrants-now-settlers/citizens. Inclusive education remains
a dream for young people facing exclusion because of learning disabilities, or
ethnicity (Gobbo 2015). This raises fundamental questions about the importance of
inclusion and the kind of society we wish to live in (Clough and Corbett 2000).
Better EAL teaching can optimize inclusion and educational opportunities for all.

Schools have to educate *everyone*. Local authorities in UK 'have a legal duty to
ensure that education is available for all children of compulsory age…irrespective of
a child's immigration status, country of origin or rights of residence in a particular
area' (Department for Education 2012, p. 1). This sounds just and egalitarian, but are
schools equipped to handle this diversity and 'super diversity'? Vertovec (2007)
defined super diversity as 'a term intended to underline a level and kind of complexity surpassing anything previously experienced in a particular society' (p. 1024).
Are all teachers fully aware and prepared for these global challenges? They are
expected to be well-informed, innovative and culturally responsive. The reality is
that most teachers in countries like UK and US are monolingual, while a rising
percentage of the student population is bilingual or multilingual. Young people want
to make a positive contribution and not become a burden on their parents or society.
To do so effectively, they must manage well in English. Our research in UK and US
schools looked at how schools support EAL/ESL (English as a second language)[2] in
Henrico County in US and Bristol in UK.

46.3 EAL and the Role of Policy

It takes 5–7 years for EAL learners to become fully fluent (Demie 2013). This
implies a long-term commitment to language provision. It is useful to consider the
role of policy before focusing on classroom-based observations. EAL is treated as a

---

[2]ESL is mostly used for bilingual speakers where English is a second language.

special educational need (SEN) by some schools. There is greater awareness of this injustice to children in states with a high percentage of EAL/ESL students in US. Students speak many languages and intensive EAL/ESL support is provided in Virginia where this research was conducted.

> Awareness of the representational patterns of ELLs (English Language Learners) at the national, state, regional, district, and campus levels continues to be the first step in providing students who are ELLs an education that meets their academic needs...

> Changing demographics ...have brought ... increased diversity ... With increased diversity comes the concern of disproportionate representation of students of colour in special education programs. (Linn and Hemmer 2011, p. 70)

Resourcing EAL/ESL classes adequately requires political and financial commitment. In Virginia, there is an awareness of EAL/ESL entitlement for migrants and refugees. EAL teachers are in demand, and universities provide EAL/ESL programmes and degrees for teachers and pre-service teachers.[3]

> The schools are expected to navigate federal, state and local policies...any student identified as limited English proficient (LEP) must have a Home Language Survey that identifies the student as bilingual and a score showing limited proficiency in one or all (of) listening, speaking, reading, writing. (McEachron et al. 2015, p. 67)

What happens inside classrooms depends on national and local policy. In UK the post-1990s period has not seen a commitment to EAL policy, though Wales enjoys a bilingual status. Several changes have affected schools and impacted EAL teaching. These are briefly outlined here. There is an inspection of and competition between schools. League Tables depict the 'good' and 'failing' schools. The latter are then put under 'special measures'. Well-resourced schools in affluent neighbourhoods are unlikely to experience 'special measures'. Power for decision-making and resource allocation has been devolved to schools in the state sector. Parents can 'choose' the best schools, or over-subscribed schools can 'choose' parents and children. Programmes to teach EAL in England are not offered in all universities. It is possible to research this subject at Masters and Doctoral level in universities in UK, which also offer Teaching of English to Speakers of Other Languages (TESOL). However, this is not accessed by EAL teachers. They are not required to obtain Masters level qualifications to teach in schools.

---

[3]At WM, ESL Dual Endorsement Programme students earn licensure to teach ESL in one year by taking five courses and completing 150 h of field experiences working with ELLs. This is in conjunction with another teacher preparation programme in which they are enrolled (Elementary, Secondary or Special Education). There is no equivalent programme in British Universities.

46.4 EAL in England

In England, there is no pre-service teacher education provision specifically for EAL (Costley 2014; Leung 2016; British Council EAL Nexus undated). The National Association for Language Development in the Curriculum (NALDIC), the subject association for EAL, campaigns for bilingual students and their teachers and provides short courses. Reviewing EAL provision over the past 40 years Leung (2016) cites over a million children in England for whom English is not a first language. Referring to 2013 National Curriculum Leung states that the onus for differentiating instruction is on the teachers.

> The brevity … of the statements on EAL in the 2013 National Curriculum signals an assumption that learning English through participation in the school curriculum is by now a universal principle, and that teacher diligence in its application is the main issue. (Leung p.164)

Leung (2016) discusses long-standing ideological and pedagogic debates which define 'equality of access'.

> The conceptual melding of first and additional language development removed the need for differentiated pedagogy and curriculum provision. In other words, the responsibility of society is to ensure equality of access. Beyond that, it is up to individuals to avail themselves of the opportunities available. (p. 166)

EAL was 'mainstreamed' in policy documents so that the focus is on teaching English. EAL is 'currently conceptualised as a 'mainstreamed' area of the school curriculum'.

No prescribed EAL curriculum was evident in the data we collected in UK schools, whereas the schools in US were following the Virginia Standards of Learning curriculum and guidelines accompanied by teaching materials such as the World-class Instructional Design and Assessment (WIDA). Reviewing 60 years of research in English language teaching in England, Costley (2014) explains how withdrawing children from mainstream classes in the 60s and 70s for EAL instruction was abandoned. After the Swann Report (1985) withdrawal policy was equated with unequal treatment. Everyone was entitled to the same language provision. This influential idea remains embedded in language teaching policy. However, in practice

> At the heart of National Curriculum ideology is the belief in the 'one-size fits (and is appropriate for) all' perspective, large numbers of EAL learners have for some time been identified as underachieving in schools across the country. (Costley 2014, p. 287)

Teachers learn to teach Standard English. No guaranteed funding from central government can be reserved for EAL. From 1966 to the mid-1990s some allocated funds were available under the Section 11 of Local Government Act. Now students are expected to adapt to the English education system and blend in with their peers. More resources for EAL and clear policy based on research evidence can help schools cope with 'one size fit all' provision (Costley 2014).

46.5 Latest Research in UK

Strand et al's (2015) statistical analyses of National Pupil Database (NPD) and the Longitudinal Study of Young People in England (LSYPE) from 2013, focused on Key Stage 2 and Key Stage 4 results and asked:

- Who are the most at-risk groups of learners with EAL and what are the predictors of low attainment for these learners?
- What are the most promising programmes and interventions to address EAL achievement gaps on the basis of causal evidence?

Key findings emphasized that 44% of 5-year olds achieved a good level of English. There was no evidence that a 'high proportion of EAL students impacted negatively on the attainment of students who spoke English as their first language' (p. 6). Studies about EAL were identified to address above questions. Of 29 studies that demonstrated an impact, 27 were conducted in the US and one in UK. Clearly more research is needed to look at interventions to accelerate English language acquisition.

Murphy and Unthiah's (2015) systematic review considered these questions:

- What intervention research has been carried out since the year 2000 which has aimed at improving English language and/or literacy skills in children with EAL?
- What is the strength of evidence of this research?

They looked for the 'most appropriate (interventions) to implement in the UK context to better support developing language, literacy, and in turn academic performance, of children with EAL' (p. 2). More studies were aimed at primary schools. 'None of the interventions received uniformly high ratings on methodological criteria. Some interventions for enhancing vocabulary could be implemented in UK' (pp. iii–iv). Further research into developing English vocabulary, word-level skills and alphabetic knowledge was recommended to 'equip teachers and schools with credible evidence upon which to develop effective support for children with EAL' (pp. 34–39).

Arnot et al's (2014) research involved two schools. Provision for new EU accession countries in English schools was studied to:

- Identify the contribution that primary and secondary schools make to address the language development, social integration and academic achievement of EAL students.
- Understand school practice regarding the above three factors from the perspective of school management, teachers, children and parents to address diversity in a constructive way.

No written language policy existed in either school. In the primary school, children were encouraged to speak English as soon as they could manage. Secondary school EAL students were trying to achieve learning targets for different subjects. Some teachers thought only English should be spoken in class. Others felt multilingualism helped all students. Both schools used 'mainstreaming approach' placing students in mainstream classes irrespective of their language skills. Some extra tuition was provided when students were withdrawn. Students' prior learning was not known, and teachers were not well-informed about social backgrounds or about parents' pre-migration social position. Arnot et al. concluded: 'All teachers should receive training in the second language acquisition process in order to discern the sometimes subtle differences between typical language development and the presence of concomitant learning difficulties' (p. 112). The executive summary recommends a nuanced and deeper engagement with what is in the students' best interest, and that schools should develop school-wide language policy including using home languages in the classroom.

This confirms Costley (2014) and Leung's (2016) acknowledgement of a policy and curriculum vacuum for EAL. UK researchers have often documented the need to do more than 'mainstreaming'. This is also related to our research schools. In US, teachers had to work towards state and federal tests (McEachron et al. 2015). Henrico County had clear EAL/ESL policies, syllabi and curricular priorities to guide teachers. This was not the case for schools in Bristol. We were interested in discovering what was happening in classrooms and how that information could help make sense of EAL teaching in different locations. The impact of policy on practice was implicit in the data.

46.6 Impact on Schools

Schools which are working without critical self-awareness or knowledge of research-based evidence will struggle to recognize bilingualism and multilingualism as strengths. They may be under-resourced or unable to see how bilingual or multi-lingual children acquire English. Safford and Drury (2013, p. 70) refer to teachers' 'monolingual mind set' and ask why bilingualism is a 'problem'. They suggest that policies and practices that place 'bilingual learners in a monolingual curriculum and assessment structure' are not helpful. According to Driver and Ullmann (2011) schools cannot help students with EAL who also have Special Educational Needs. Teachers' Knowledge of the students' background, cultural responsiveness and acknowledgement of diversity is crucial for meeting students' expectations and needs. Our interest in EAL led us to be mindful of these issues in UK and US schools.

46.7 Teaching EAL in the Global Classroom: A Transnational Study in US and UK

Our commitment to intercultural education, social justice and work with pre-service teachers led us to design a small project 'Teaching EAL in the Global Classroom' (McEachron et al. 2015). The research involved five UK teachers in two UK schools, four UK university students, five US teachers in two US schools and four US university students. This chapter offers reflections on data gathered during student researchers' detailed observations of teaching and learning. Our universities are committed to broadening and deepening students' understanding of global educational issues. We encouraged our students to work with us as student researchers. They were a team of eight researchers (seven pre-service teachers) for whom we acquired funding for two weeks' intensive data collection. The study provided students with the opportunity to gain comparative knowledge about EAL in their own and another country. The two main questions were (McEachron et al. 2015, pp. 59, 62):

- According to databases, how does the academic performance of language minority groups compare to the academic performance of non-linguistic minority groups at the elementary and secondary levels of education?
- According to language support teachers and university students, what are the strengths and weaknesses of the instructional practices for language minorities who are learning English in the United Kingdom (Bristol) and the United States (Henrico)?

Ethical clearance was obtained from both universities' ethics committees. Student researchers were required to study background information and the context of the schools before commencing field work. One primary/elementary and one high school were selected in each country. BSU students study modules which challenge them to engage with issues of ethnic and linguistic diversity and the inclusion of vulnerable learners. Unless they choose to study inequality in their undergraduate modules and write dissertations on the topic, and unless they attend placements in multi-ethnic urban settings in North and North East Somerset in England, not all students will have much experience of diverse classrooms. This is not the case everywhere in UK, and certainly not in London. It is possible for some BSU students to attend all white schools, then an almost all white university, to have studied 'diversity' but not have first-hand experience in multi-ethnic settings. In WM the foundations coursework includes topics on multiculturalism and cultural responsiveness. Students have access to diverse placements. They work with Asian-Americans, African-Americans, Hispanic-Americans and students from the Middle East. Each student researcher had a unique educational biography in terms of schooling and elective modules studied at university. What brought them together was curiosity about EAL and a commitment and willingness to learn more about inclusion and diverse classrooms. Prior to this study all except one, had visited at least three other countries and studied at least one foreign language at school.

It was envisioned that participation in research would extend student researchers' experiences and challenge their thinking. The study was set up to ensure they would focus on significant aspects of social justice in school settings. They were taught qualitative research methods and particularly participant and non-participant observation, which helped them think critically about their own assumptions about EAL. They were expected to use observation protocols, prompts, fieldwork journals and have focus group discussions amongst themselves. They had never participated in research where they had to collaborate closely with seven other peers. They were asked to keep a journal two weeks before, during and after travelling to the research sites. Detailed field notes were kept in response to the observation protocol and prompts. They were also encouraged to use their own initiative and collect data which was relevant to EAL but not mentioned in the protocol (see McEachron et al. 2015 for details).

Each student researcher collected data individually, followed by discussion with the teacher. This could be a conversation or an interview, depending on researcher/teacher interaction. Every evening they met as a focus group of eight researchers to critique and share their cumulative experiences. The notes from focus groups, chaired by a different student researcher each time, were shared via Google Doc [4]. As two principal researchers we also met the teachers to thank them for hosting our students. Notes from these meetings and conversations about teaching and learning in EAL classrooms were also documented. This led to very rich data.

46.8 EAL in Real Classrooms

What follows is a selection of data on EAL teaching in Bristol and Henrico County collected within 9 days of immersion in one classroom by each student researcher. It demonstrates the usefulness of reflexivity for enhancing a deeper understanding of the pedagogical process. The *student researcher's*, the *teacher's*, and the principal researcher's perspectives set out together illuminate the complex realities of the EAL classroom. A selection of quotations from fieldwork is presented. Why were teachers teaching students with EAL? What were they trying to teach? How did they feel about the presence of student researchers?. The following themes were generated during coding and analysis.

46.9 Ethnicity, Language and Allegiance

Lydia (BSU researcher in Henrico County high school)

> Issues surrounding race and ethnicity were rarely discussed by teachers but it was expressed by the students via jokes and mocking of accents between Spanish/Nepali male students. This evidenced a kind of hierarchy between the ethnicities, as Spanish and Nepalese are the most common spoken languages in the ESL classrooms at X High. I did observe that student/student interaction was predominantly between members of the same spoken language and ethnicity (minimal interaction between Nepali and Spanish speakers in the lower sets, yet the upper ESL level classes would often interact regardless of language spoken)

> Religion was not discussed or evidenced during my observations, yet an emphasis on patriotism and unity was expressed by the ritual pledging allegiance to the flag, as well as

---

[4]Google Docs are web-based programs created by Google, Inc.

the subtle reminders that the students are 'American now' (Mrs R). I did observe some resistance by the students as they had to be told to stand and pledge, whilst others simply stood and did not verbally pledge allegiance. This raised questions of how the students feel, with regards to culture and religion which do not appear to be inclusive or incorporated.

Teacher: 'We do allegiance. That is normal. It is about acceptance. About inclusion. The quicker we can move with school routines the easier it will be for all (students)'

It seems that the researcher heard something which the teacher did not. Should Lydia have reported the 'mocking of accents'? Did she discuss this with the teacher? Could she do so immediately after the class? Does the school have a policy about this, and did the students know what would happen if they departed from acceptable conduct? Also, the students who were more confident in English did not need to 'mock accents' and they conversed with each other.

It is difficult to know whether the students were at ease during the allegiance ritual. They were being socialized into a new routine and it is impossible to ascertain through observation what they felt. There could be a link between EAL proficiency and non-compliance. Could incomprehension of the English language cause the behaviour interpreted as resistance by Lydia? Within the curriculum religion is discussed more often in UK than it is in the US. Lydia noticed this. Some schools in UK teach comparative religion and discuss major world religions. Allegiance to the flag or overt patriotism does not happen in UK schools. This raises questions about formal and informal ways in which schools transmit values like loyalty and faith. The situation is complicated when teachers are uncertain whether English is an Additional Language or a Second Language as some students speak more than two languages outside school.

46.10 Classroom Environment and Differentiation

Ben (BSU researcher in Henrico County high school)

After my first three observations in this classroom TA (teacher) asked me what I felt were the main differences between hers and the EAL/ESL classrooms I had taught in UK. I mentioned the common theme in my experience of European EAL/ESL classrooms was language specific instructional EAL posters, such as those featuring a list of the main irregular verbs (listing the infinitive, past simple and past participle of each verb) or ones which explained how and when to use different tenses (such as past vs. present perfect). Within a few days TA told me she had ordered an irregular verb poster, for her room, and in week 2 of my observations this had been placed on the wall.

TA frequently interacted with a wide range of pupils… Typically she would lead the class from the front, and use concept checking questions for grammar rules or vocabulary (or to check students understood the task). These would either be answered on 'first to respond' basis (the strongest students in class raised their hand) or TA would direct the questions to a specific student. When she was directing the questions, she would often turn to a student who hadn't spoken aloud in English, that day. This came across as being a very inclusive strategy (although in some circumstances it was a challenge for the weaker students: they may have lacked the confidence or ability to do so, or been nervous in front of their peers).

TA showed no favouritism towards gender or ethnic background of student, during her frequent interactions, and treated all the students with … respect and attention … Her interaction gave her classes a very relaxed, almost semi-formal feeling, and the students responded extremely positively towards this environment.

Teacher: 'Differentiation is my biggest challenge because of the mixed abilities in my classes. For example one girl can barely speak, is having to learn phonetics, and in the same class there is another girl who can already write detailed paragraphs. Meeting the needs of every child is my biggest challenge'.

Ben had taught EAL and was able to document minor details about the environment which were geared towards helping students learn. His observation of the style and quality of the teacher's interactions capture the atmosphere in the class, her informal and accessible manner and the underlying respect for students. This teacher seems very open to new ideas. Her own appraisal of her biggest challenge— differentiating work for students shows how well she knew her students, their difficulties and capabilities.

46.11   Teaching for Tests

Amy (BSU researcher in Henrico County Elementary School)

I sat with JR who had two fifth grade boys at level 1 English. JR told me they are exempt from every test except for science, therefore, the lesson was spent going through a practice science test paper. JR knew it was a lost cause and struggled to keep one of the children engaged but there wasn't much he could do as the child knew very little English. … he said 'it's just one of those things' and continued to teach as much as he could to the children, despite the fact that he knew they couldn't understand much. I felt so frustrated… as I felt that time spent was wasted on the science paper that could have been used to teach and learn English. The fact that they even have to sit the test in the first place is ridiculous.

I didn't realise testing in Virginia was a major thing. I always thought in England that testing was over the top but here in America it really is beyond anything I could have ever imagined.

Teacher: 'It feels kind of strange trying to explain honestly why we must test kids who we know just can't do it! It doesn't help their self-esteem, but we have to play this test game.'

Formal testing is a stressful, labour intensive, time-consuming activity, not just the process of testing itself, but also the preparation and time leading up to tests. Data collection coincided with the testing period. Amy was frustrated on behalf of the children who were clearly not ready. Amy values children's entitlement to an appropriate education, but depending on local policy on testing, this is something over which teachers quite often have no control. It seems unfair that students are set up to fail in summative assessments. It seems that it is the teachers who are being tested on their teaching. They feel the pressure to produce good results, even though they know that testing will not encourage learning in every case. This seems unfair for children and teachers in schools which lack expertize in EAL, or are inadequately equipped for EAL. Yet it is important to have base line data on the proficiency levels so that students' needs and successes are documented. How to do this in a humane way remains a challenge for educators.

46.12   Literacy and Library

Lexi (WM researcher in Bristol secondary school)

> Students read from a PowerPoint that BJ had written. I was pleased to see that the simple sentences were designed to reflect the cultural backgrounds of the students. The sentences were along the lines of "My name is Hamza. I am from Somalia and now I live in Bristol." This class also uses a lot of manipulatives to support their literacy instruction.

> In "Reading" I noted that the library had a diverse selection of books. One student was reading about a girl moving to Ghana and another had a book with a girl with a headscarf on it. There is a section of bilingual dictionaries from countries that the students represent. Underneath the dictionaries is a "countries" section with books on at least thirty different countries. These were non-fiction books with facts and maps about the countries. I noticed the students in the Early Literacy class using Accelerated Readers. The books represent a wide range of language ability from beginner (something you might find in kindergarten) to fluent independent reader. After reading, the students take a quick quiz on a computerized program called Accelerated Reader.

> Teacher: 'It is all about valuing children and working with what they bring. We have their languages in our library books, but really we could be doing more. We need more resources... Are we burdening them by expecting what we do from them? We must find new ways to teach...what are we teaching them? What do they learn?'

Lexi focused on diversity and cultural responsiveness. Somalia is used an example by the teacher who wanted to teach sentence construction. This was also about including the student, though Lexi does not comment that actual details about Hamza are used to help him make sentences, rather than using a fictional character. This is an example of culturally and socially inclusive practice. Yet, there is self-doubt, ambiguity and uncertainty in the teacher's comments. 'What do they learn?' alludes to learning beyond EAL. In this secondary school 'learning' is more than what is learnt inside the classroom.

Lexi: from research journal:

> The school has limited influence over the students' life outside of the classroom. I spoke with one student from Iran who currently lives with a foster family...because of the variety of first languages among students here (I have heard a teacher quote 60), it is hard to attend to the development of students' reading, writing, speaking, and listening in their first language.

> Teacher: 'We do try our best to draw children out and connect them to each other, but there is just so much the school can do. I know that keeping first language is very important; I wonder whose responsibility it is to deal with this?'

This teacher is knowledgeable and committed but is still unsure about the situation with regard to EAL. If a student's home cannot support what is happening in school, then it is the child who must deal with conflicting expectations from parents who might speak in one language and wish to maintain one cultural tradition at home and teachers who may speak another language and may belong to a different culture. The cultural and linguistic demands such situations create have been recorded in school-based ethnographies (Bhatti 1999).

EAL classes can open up opportunities. An important role that teachers play is to offer stepping stones from uncertain first steps to independent learning. Some of this can happen through collaborative work among students which can build their confidence.

46.13 Collaborative Writing

Aaron (WM researcher in Bristol primary school)

> The students began the writing by filling out a pre-writing graphic organizer. Then, in an effort to elicit more specific details, they acted out their story in the school garden to their classmates. Finally, they wrote a draft. Completing the writing process showed cultural responsiveness and sensitivity to diverse learners. Some students might be culturally disposed to sharing stories orally, some students may have the natural gift of acting, some students may be more adept at writing (both academically and linguistically), some ELLs (English language learners) may be still developing their writing skills but can communicate well orally.

> The teacher showed sensitivity to her students, differentiating instruction to support linguistic, academic, and character diverse students, in writing lessons…Students had to learn the phrases and practice them at home. Students who have the language as their first language serve as tutor to help with pronunciation. The teacher uses the phrases learned to greet parents in their first language. Although this language learning is not a part of national curriculum, it is a part of the teacher's curriculum and evidence of instruction can be seen in the nature of application in the classroom… (it is not uncommon for students to speak 3–5 languages in this classroom as indicated by the teacher).

> Teacher: 'I wonder how I can teach more effectively… I wonder if Tim would respond better to a book on helicopters (than farm animals)… It is good to teach for the sake of teaching… if only we didn't have all the other boring stuff (record keeping, tests etc) …It is amazing how having an enthusiastic university student can remind me why I became a teacher… like a ray of sunshine.'

This teacher clearly enjoyed teaching her class. She wanted to teach to the best of her ability, which was not always easy. In her day-to-day working life routines could become tedious. Affirmation of past aspiration is acknowledged in this conversation with one of the principal researchers. While tedious routines and form filling became part of her daily work, the enthusiasm of university students reminded her of her past unencumbered self. Her own curriculum is holistic and wider than the national curriculum as noted by this observant student researcher.

46.14 Classroom Climate and Language Learning

Rachel (WM student researcher in Bristol secondary school)

> The teacher had asked the students to come up with questions. We sat around the table and each student pulled a question from a bucket... Some students were shy, but overall the room felt very comfortable and they respond well... I felt that having students develop the questions kept them more engaged and interested in the responses. One student asked What is the American dream? I felt that was quite a profound question and made me reflect a lot on the values that are expressed when we respond with things like 'owning your own home, becoming self-sufficient, getting a university education.'

> I observed two students... brother and sister from Somalia. When I introduced myself, the teacher pulled out a map for me to point to Virginia. It was obvious that they had never seen a map or had very little experience because they could not pinpoint Somalia on it (they pointed to China and Russia). The students had never been to school before, so there was a lot of emphasis on literacy skills...I wrote in the protocol that I worry how this might affect the language acquisition process.

> Teacher: 'I have this dilemma- what to assume? There is a whole world in my little class. This is the first school after the refugee camp! BUT tell you what- If I could not make a difference why would I be a teacher?'

These views provide insight into the nature of the challenge—the teacher's moral and pedagogical responsibility on the one hand, and the level of children's comprehension on the other. Nothing could be taken for granted including looking at a simple map. The researcher could not ascertain what was understood. Can some lines and colours on piece of paper symbolize a real country that had been left behind? The students did not know enough English to wonder or ask abstract questions. The researcher clearly sensed this in her 'worry' about language acquisition in relation to the cultural context and has captured how profound ideas can be lost in translation or in silence. The teacher's dilemma is an admission of the daunting task. There is a 'whole world' of children from different cultural, linguistic and geographical locations in class. Yet remarkably in her very next sentence there is an uplifting optimistic assertion—the desire to 'make a difference'.

46.15 Concluding Remarks

The above themes provide a glimpse at teaching opportunities and what happens inside real classrooms. Where there is no clear policy on EAL or guidance for effective pedagogical practices, teachers invent their own ways to impart knowledge. In Bristol, teachers without any formal training on EAL were guided by prior experience of teaching EAL. Aaron's observation of the 'teacher's curriculum' showed how the teacher was drawing on her skills and resourcefulness. As a contrast, where there was clear guidance for teachers' work, as observed by Amy, the teacher, despite being frustrated by the limitations of testing new students, was encouraged by the support from the school division and the Virginia Department of Education, knowing that ESL pedagogy was sanctioned.

Linn and Hemmer (2011) were mindful of conflating SEN and EAL. We did not find any evidence to ascertain what was happening in the four schools with regard to SEN and EAL. The findings of this study support the research by Costley (2014), Leung (2016) and Arnot et al. (2014) who argue that more targeted focus on policy and on collecting sufficiently detailed information about students' learning needs and achievements can improve learning experiences. During these times of super diversity teachers have to maintain self-awareness and criticality, so that the judgements which guide their actions in class are infused with reflexivity and thoughtfulness. Teachers' ability to respond to the children was affected by how well resourced the school was and how helpful and inclusive EAL policy was in each country, and most importantly, what they as individual teachers brought to their teaching.

Student researchers' presence provided opportunities for teachers to share their experiences, hopes, regrets and doubts. 'Modelling' their skills for future teachers and student researchers from another country made the 'familiar unfamiliar' (Hammersly and Atkinson 1983) and opened up creative spaces for real dialogue. Schools are places of transformation and hope. Teaching EAL requires spontaneity, cultural responsiveness and optimism, but most importantly it requires pedagogical and curricular expertise. A teacher's commitment to social justice in action (Griffiths 2003), is mediated by this pedagogical and curricular expertise. Clearer EAL policy, better understanding of linguistic diversity and initial and continuing professional development opportunities for teaching EAL can make a real difference to the lives of students who are living in, or will be migrating to English speaking countries. Greater diversity in the teaching force can enhance schools' capacity to empathize, understand and support more students' learning. Leadership at government and school levels is crucial for ensuring that *all* school students are perceived as young people who possess energy, potential and promise. This journey of hope and transformation begins in schools and in faculties of education in universities that prepare and inspire teachers of the future. The decision Britain has taken to leave the European Union might heighten the concern for the quality and content of education. Anti-immigration sentiment should not overshadow research that demonstrates the importance of the need to advance EAL policies.

Acknowledgements We would like to thank The Institute for Education, Bath Spa University with its affiliation to GALA (Global Academy of Liberal Arts) and The Reves Center for International Studies at The College of William and Mary for their interest in this project and the award of research grants.

References

Arnot, M., Schneider, C., Evans, M., Liu, Y., Welply, O., & Davies-Tutt, D. (2014). *School approaches to the education of EAL students: Language development, social integration and achievement*. Cambridge: Bell Foundation.

Bhatti, G. (1999). *Asian children at home and at school: An ethnographic study*. London: Routledge.

British Council EAL Nexus. https://eal.britishcouncil.org/

Clough, P., & Corbett, J. (2000). *Theories of inclusive education*. London: Paul Chapman.

Costley, T. (2014). English as an additional language, policy and the teaching and learning of English in England. *Language and Education, 28*(3), 276–292. doi:10.1080/09500782.2013.836215

Demie, F. (2013). English as an additional language pupil: How long does it take to acquire English fluency? *Language and Education, 27*(1), 59–69.

Department for Education (DfE). (2012). *A brief summary of government policy in relation to EAL learners*. London. Retrieved from http://www.naldic.org.uk/Resources/NALDIC/Researchand-Information/Documents/Brief_summary_of_Government_policy_for_EAL_Learners.pdf

Driver, C., & Ullmann, P. (2011). EAL and SEN. *NALDIC Quarterly*—NQ 8.4.

Gobbo, F. (2015). People 'of Passage': An intercultural educator's interpretation of diversity and cultural identity in Italy. In P. Smeyers, P. Bridges, N. C. Burbules, & M. Griffiths (Eds.), *International handbook of interpretation in educational research* (pp. 505–528). Dordrecht: Springer.

Griffiths, M. (2003). *Action for social justice in education*. Buckingham: Open University Press.

Hammersley, M., & Atkinson, P. (1983). *Ethnography principles in practice*. London: Tavistock.

Leung, C. (2016). English as an additional language—a genealogy of language-in-education policies and reflections on research trajectories. *Language and Education, 30*(2), 158–174. doi:10.1080/09500782.2015.1103260

Linn, D., & Hemmer, L. (2011). English language learner disproportionality in special education: Implications for the Scholar-Practitioner. *Journal of Educational Research and Practice, 1*(1), 70–80.

McEachron, G., Bhatti, G., Crushcov, B., Hartley, A., Heideman, R., Hogg, L., et al. (2015). Teaching English as an additional language in the global classroom: A transnational study in the United States and United Kingdom. *Global Education Review, 2*(2), 59–83.

Mills, A.J., Durepos, G., & Wiebe, E. (2010). Reflexivity. In D. L. Bergoray & E. M. Banister (Eds.), *Encyclopedia of case study research*. London: Sage. doi:10.4135/9781412957397.n290

Murphy, V. A., & Unthiah, A. (2015). *A systematic review of intervention research examining English language and literacy development in children with English as an Additional Language (EAL)*. Oxford: Bell Foundation.

Safford, K., & Drury, R. (2013). The 'problem' of bilingual children in educational settings: Policy and research in England. *Language and Education, 27*(1), 70–81. doi:10.1080/09500782.2012.685177

Strand, S., Malmberg, L., & Hall, J. (2015). *English as an additional language (EAL) and educational achievement in England: An analysis of the national pupil database*. Oxford: Bell Foundation. www.educationendowmentfoundation.org.uk

Swann, M. (1985). *Education for all: The report of the committee of inquiry into the education of children from ethnic minority groups*. London: HMSO.

Vertovec, S. (2007). Super diversity and its implications. *Ethnic and Racial Studies, 30*(6), 1024–1054.

Author Biographies

Ghazala Bhatti is a Senior Lecturer at the Institute for Education, Bath Spa University. She is a founding member and convenor of the network for Social Justice and Intercultural Education for European Conference on Educational Research. Her research interests include language, ethnicity, gender and social class and how they affect educational experiences.

Gail McEachron is a professor at the College of William and Mary. Her research interests include international/multilingual education. She directed the English as a Second Language Dual Endorsement Program for the past five years and is currently conducting case study research with individuals she began interviewing 25 years ago.

Chapter 47
Imperatives for Teacher Education: Findings from Studies of Effective Teaching for English Language Learners

Alison L. Bailey and Margaret Heritage

47.1 Introduction

The teacher is the key actor in addressing the learning needs of students who are acquiring English as an additional language in school. This chapter examines the role of the teacher in addressing these needs and the imperatives for teacher education in fulfilling that role. While this chapter focuses on how best to support teachers in the United States (U.S.) in this endeavor, the issues we raise are relevant to a broader range of contexts in which teachers, worldwide, face similar realities. First, we discuss current contexts for the education of students acquiring an additional language in school. This is followed by a consideration of factors that impact the preparedness of teachers to effectively meet the needs of students who are learning English as an additional language. We then draw from two research studies to suggest potential ways forward in improving teacher education programs in the U.S. Finally, we propose some directions for future research to inform teacher-preparation programs.

47.2 Current Context

We begin by considering current educational contexts of learners who are schooled in a second or additional language, specifically with reference to three main issues: (1) mobility of populations; (2) linguistic and academic achievements of English language learners (ELL students); and (3) teacher preparedness and effectiveness.

A.L. Bailey (✉)
University of California, Los Angeles, CA, USA
e-mail: abailey@gseis.ucla.edu

M. Heritage
WestEd, San Francisco, CA, USA
e-mail: mheritag@ucla.edu

© Springer Nature Singapore Pte Ltd. 2017
M.A. Peters et al. (eds.), *A Companion to Research in Teacher Education*,
DOI 10.1007/978-981-10-4075-7_47

47.2.1 Mobility of Populations

Recently, a leading article in the *Economist* noted, "The rise of Latinos is a huge opportunity. The United States must not squander it" (The Economist 2015, March. p. 15). In the context of a "graying population," a phenomenon also found across many European countries and Japan, the article argued that the U.S. is advantaged by the influx of young, energetic, language-minority adults. This perspective reorients much of the current, frequently negative, perceptions of language-minority groups in America.

While concerns about an influx of language-minority adults and children have been expressed in many quarters, as Europe faces the greatest resettlement of refugees since World War II, a counter argument to their arrival has also been mounted: these new arrivals will add energy and commitment to Europe's increasingly aging population.

This mobility of populations, which has characterized the last four decades in many countries, is likely to increase, particularly as developed countries continue to draw on a workforce from less-developed countries, for example, Turkish guest workers in Germany and the Netherlands, Filipino and Indonesian workers in Hong Kong, China, and South-East Asian workers in the Arabian Peninsula. Consequently, teacher education programs across many parts of the world will need to ensure that their graduates are fully equipped with the knowledge and skills required to meet the needs of students who are new to their countries.

47.2.2 Linguistic and Academic Achievements of English Language Learners

Close to 4.5 million school-age children in the U.S. are formally tested for English proficiency and found eligible for English language support services to access the curriculum. These students are designated English language learners in the U.S. and are the fastest growing segment of the nation's school-age population (Flores et al. 2012). Between the years 1980 and 2009, the percentage of U.S. school-age children who spoke a language other than English at home increased from 4.7 to 11.2 million, or from 10 to 21% of the school-age population [National Center for Education Statistics (NCES 2015)] and the number is expected to continue to rise.

As measured by standardized assessment, educational outcomes for ELL students are persistently poor. For example, the most recently available National Assessment of Educational Progress (NAEP) statistics for the U.S. show 33% of all fourth-grade students performing below the "basic" designation on the 2013 reading assessment. In other words, students did not reach "partial mastery of fundamental skills." Worse, 69% of ELL students performed below the basic level. Similarly, poor results are found in the NAEP mathematics results, which indicate that 17% of fourth-grade students overall performed below the basic level (i.e., had not reached "partial mastery of prerequisite knowledge and skills that are fundamental" for mathematics), whereas 41% of ELL students' performed below the basic level (NCES 2013).

This differential in achievement is also found internationally. In so much as we can compare students who are tested in a language they speak at home with students who are tested in a language they do *not* speak at home, results of the 2012 administration of the Program for International Student Assessment (PISA) are also suggestive of a linguistic basis for the academic achievement gap. The international mathematics average for 15-year-old students tested in a language they speak at home was 501, whereas the average was 462 for students tested in a language that differs from the one they speak at home (NCES 2014).

ELL students in the U.S. who are not proficient in English by the end of first-grade show achievement gaps with English-speaking peers in reading and mathematics, although the gap in reading narrows over time, while continuing to widen in mathematics (Halle et al. 2012). In terms of linguistic outcomes for ELL students, the same factors that characterize the heterogeneity in this group also account for differences in their rate of English acquisition. Being older at school entry, having a higher family income, more parent education, greater participation in cultural activities by the family, and parent beliefs that language is not a barrier to their involvement in school are associated with the more rapid progression in English proficiency (Halle et al. 2012).

There is increasing concern for students who spend considerably longer periods of time designated as needing language services. As many as 60% of U.S.-born ELL students remain designated as ELL in a state-wide, incoming high school cohort after presumably 9 years of education in U.S. schools (Slama 2012). In California, in order to bring attention and resources to this situation, students are officially classified "Long-Term ELLs" if they spend more than 6 years receiving ELL language support services. The rate of English acquisition, however, also appears strongly correlated with the type of program in which students are enrolled (e.g., English immersion, bilingual, dual-immersion). Slower rates of acquisition (e.g., up to 6 years) may be seen in programs that include the use of the student's first language but such programs ultimately better position students for academic attainment in reading and mathematics and successful reclassification to fluent English proficiency status (Umansky and Reardon 2014).

47.2.3 Teacher Preparation and Effectiveness

According to available nationwide statistics reported in 2002 by NCES, only 12.5% of the approximately three million teachers in the U.S. received eight or more hours of training to work with ELL students, despite the fact that 42% of them had taught ELL students. In 2008, the National Clearinghouse for English Language Acquisition (NCELA) concluded that teacher preparation in the U.S. is woefully lacking in meeting the needs of large numbers of ELL students. Given the current upward trend in student demographics reported above, the situation may be worse today. While more recent nationwide statistics are elusive, Reeves, 2006 cited in Rubinstein-Avila and Lee (2014) found that as many as 90% of surveyed secondary teachers (i.e., those teaching students 12–18 years old) who have a single-subject credential (e.g., biological sciences, mathematics) had no preparation at all for working with ELL students. General education teachers with ELL students in their classrooms report feeling most prepared when they demonstrate an understanding of the interconnected nature of language and content-area knowledge (Bailey and Osipova 2016), and possess "knowledge of teaching and learning, deep content knowledge, experience, and full certification in the field" (Gándara et al. 2005, p. 3).

47.3   New Educational Aspirations

To compound the current situation of general education teachers being underprepared to support the language learning needs of their ELL students, new demands for these teachers have been added by the most recent reform effort in American education: the introduction of college and career readiness standards (CCRS) in English language arts (ELA) and mathematics as well as Next Generation Science Standards. A response to ongoing globalization, the CCRS describe the competencies U.S. students need to have when they graduate from high school in order to be productive citizens and effective contributors to economic vitality. For the most part, the CCRS call for more rigorous learning and higher achievement than prior standards. Alongside the CCRS, new English language development (ELD) standards for ELL students have been introduced. Additionally, the federal government has funded the development of associated accountability assessments. These assessments, administered annually for students in grades 3–11, are intended to gauge student achievement of the new standards.

   While the new standards represent challenges for all students and their teachers, the challenge for ELL students is particularly significant. Already, ELL students have to learn subject-matter content while simultaneously acquiring a new language. Moreover, the CCRS place a strong emphasis on extensive language use to engage in deep and transferable content learning, and analytical practices. For example, in terms of analytical practices, the mathematics CCSS require students to explain, conjecture, construct viable arguments and critique the reasoning of others. And among the ELA analytical practices are engaging with complex texts; writing to inform, argue, and analyze; working collaboratively; and presenting ideas (Heritage et al. 2015).

   In general, across the U.S., language support for ELL students is seen as the purview of language specialists teaching English-as-a-second-language (ESL) classes. Typically, these teachers and their subject-matter counterparts do not spend time planning how they will complement each other in their respective classrooms. While ESL teachers have knowledge of language development, they often lack subject-matter knowledge. The situation is reversed with subject-matter teachers; they have content knowledge but not a level of knowledge of language development sufficient to support the ELL students in their classrooms. The results of this bifurcation are vividly illustrated by the results of the first year's administration of the new CCRS-aligned assessments. For example, in California, 65% of ELL students did not meet the standards in either mathematics or ELA (California Department of Education 2015).

With the expectations of the new standards, this current bifurcation must change, particularly with respect to subject-matter teachers. No doubt, it is desirable for students who are new to the country or enter school speaking little or no English to receive ELD instruction. However, once students have acquired some English, their continued language development must become the responsibility of every subject-matter teacher if ELL students are going to be able to engage successfully with language in the service of content learning. Clearly, supporting all teachers to take responsibility for ELL students represents a number of challenges for teacher education programs, a topic to which we now turn.

47.4 Current Challenges in Preparing Teachers of ELL Students

With the rising population of ELL students in the U.S. and their stubbornly persistent low educational outcomes, it is imperative that not just ESL teachers are trained to support ELL students, but also that general education teachers have the knowledge and skills to work with this population of students. Additionally, as pre-service teachers cannot learn all they possibly need to know about effectively teaching ELL students, continuing in-service support will need to be available for both ESL and general education teachers. In this section, we discuss current challenges to preparing teachers of ELL students.

To date, little attention has been paid in teacher education to the knowledge and skills that general education teachers need to have in order to teach ELL students effectively. Indeed, in many states, the examination teacher candidates are required to pass for completion of the state-approved teacher-preparation program does not assess teacher knowledge and skills relevant to teaching ELL students (Samson and Collins 2012). Extrapolating from the current context in the U.S. discussed earlier, as well as some key emerging findings from the research cited earlier, it seems reasonable to assume that prime among the knowledge and skills teachers need are (1) a deep knowledge of content and ELD standards; (2) a strong understanding of oral language development and an awareness of similarities and differences between first and second language development; (3) knowledge and skills to teach subject-matter and language simultaneously; and (4) the skills to assess students' developing understanding and language and act on evidence. However, there remain challenges in the present educational and policy environments to ensuring that both pre-service and in-service teachers receive the support they need in these core areas.

47.4.1 Limitations of Standards

While policymakers and education leaders in the U.S. have set great store by the new standards for improving educational outcomes across the board, currently, there are limitations in the standards to achieving this aspiration. The new content standards, specifying what all students need to know and be able to do, better reflect a progression of learning than prior ones did. The standards also integrate content and language to a greater extent than ever before. However, while this inter-grade-level clarity and the emphasis on language are welcome, the standards do not describe the intra-grade development of content learning, nor the development of the underlying and relevant language skills necessary for reaching content goals. The new ELA standards take account of the content standards but they focus primarily on scholastic contexts, for example, mathematics, English language arts, and literacy uses in history and science. While the English Language Proficiency Development Framework (CCSSO 2012) focuses on making the CCRS useful for understanding the language needed for content-area tasks, it was not designed to help teachers understand the linguistic content of the CCRS, for instance, the development of cohesive devices and sophistication of sentence structure. Pre-service preparation will necessarily involve assisting candidate teachers to acquire detailed knowledge of how content and language learning progress beyond that currently described in the standards. At present, there is an absence of such progressions—a void that vitiates effective preparation for teachers of ELL students.

47.4.2 Language Knowledge—The Cinderella of Pre-service?

Concerned about the importance of language to learning and the lack of breadth and depth in courses on language for pre-service teachers, Wong Fillmore and Snow (2002) laid out what they believed was important for all teachers to know about language. They proposed that teachers need to understand the structural differences among languages, as well as cultural patterns for discourse among different language communities. They argued that teachers also need to know how English proficiency develops in native speakers and in speakers who are learning English as an additional language. Furthermore, Wong Fillmore and Snow emphasized the necessity for clear communication with students, which requires teachers to know how to structure their own speech for maximum clarity.

Since Wong Fillmore and Snow published their paper, the demands on teachers have grown even greater in terms of number of ELL students and communicative demands of the CCRS. However, as we discussed earlier, a range of studies has indicated that mainstream teachers of ELL students still do not receive adequate preparation in their pre-service courses and few in-service teachers have professional learning opportunities related to working with ELL students. Not only do teacher candidates—and, indeed, in-service teachers as well—require knowledge of language per se, they also have to develop the skills to teach language and content simultaneously if their ELL students are going to meet the expectations of the new standards. To address this challenge, teacher education programs will need to make some significant changes—and soon—in their course offerings. And, since most in-service teachers have not received adequate preparation, in-service programs must provide in-depth opportunities for acquiring the necessary knowledge and skills.

Neglect of language learned in tandem with content knowledge in the preparation of teachers could prove particularly damaging for the content instruction of ELL students, and consequently warrants closer scrutiny in this context. The opportunity for ELL students to learn content area material and to be exposed to the cognitively demanding language of academic contexts can be seen as part of the larger concern for educational equity and access (e.g., Gándara et al. 2005).

47.4.3 Assessment

Over the last few decades in the U.S., assessment-based accountability has been the centerpiece of educational reform efforts. With the intention to erase persistent achievement gaps among students, all students in grades 3–8 were tested annually to gauge their achievement of standards. Students who were designated ELL were also administered additional annual tests to determine their progress in English until they achieved proficiency across the listening, speaking, reading, and writing modalities. While some have argued the benefits of accountability tests (along with the attendant sanctions for poorly performing schools), researchers have concluded that achievement gaps were not closed and that many of the consequences of high-stakes accountability tests have been negative (see Heritage 2014 for a full discussion).

With the introduction of CCRS, annual summative assessment remains an integral part of teachers' and students' school experience. While the assessments are intended to reflect better models of learning than prior assessments, the dominant role they still retain in American education means that teachers' focus remains primarily on annual summative assessments, including a concentration on "teaching to the test."

So where does this current situation leave teacher education programs and what challenges ensue from a continued emphasis on annual summative assessment? In this context, we discuss two issues: (1) assessment literacy and (2) the practice of formative assessment in supporting ongoing learning.

Smith et al. (2014) observed that when entering their teacher education programs, candidate teachers in New Zealand seem to view assessment "as a broad concept, mainly summative in nature" (p. 313). U.S. teaches likely have similar views. After all, throughout their own schooling many, if not most, will have experienced assessment solely in the form of grades and annual assessments. If teachers are to be able to make sound decisions from assessment information, shaping pre-service teachers' understanding of the varied types and uses of assessments within the system will need to be a goal of teacher education programs.

One of the consequences of both a long-term emphasis on accountability assessments and a lack of attention to teachers' assessment literacy is that the practice of formative assessment (in other countries often referred to as assessment for learning) remains underdeveloped among U.S. teachers. Research and theory on formative assessment point to the benefits of this practice for student learning (e.g., Black and Wiliam 1998) and in some countries, such as a number of jurisdictions in Canada, there are well-developed frameworks of assessment for learning from which other educational systems might benefit. Teachers graduating from teacher education programs in the U.S. are largely underprepared to engage in formative assessment in support of ongoing learning. This situation is further exacerbated for teachers of ELL students, who must attend to both content and language learning. The absence of language and content progressions noted earlier, combined with a lack of training in how to gather and interpret evidence of language and content learning day-by-day, results in newly qualified teachers entering the profession without core knowledge and skills to support their ELL students' ongoing learning.

47.5   A Way Forward

Given the paucity of support for mainstream U.S. teachers of ELL students, and the pressing need for improvement in teacher education programs in the areas discussed above, in the next section we consider some possible ways forward. We first report on a study of sixth-grade teachers that focuses on their explanations, a high-use pedagogical function for achieving new standards, of the key principles underlying mastery in Algebra I (Bailey et al. 2011). We then describe how, in a subsequent study, teachers' formative assessment and their resulting instructional decision-making can be assisted by an empirically derived learning progression of students' mathematical explanations. Both studies contribute to our understanding of teachers' language knowledge and use, and have the potential to lead to innovative ways to address professional preparation for teachers' work with ELL students.

47.5.1   Clarity in Teacher Explanations

If teachers are to communicate clearly with their students, they must know how to structure their own speech for maximum clarity. However, our understanding of the language that teachers use in teaching needs to extend beyond emphasis on single words and proper grammatical usage to also include a more complex view of the language associated with subject-matter teaching.

The 104 teachers in this study came from urban and suburban school districts in the greater Los Angeles area. The average number of years teaching was 7.2 years (SD = 6.1) ranging from one to 38 years. While 87 teachers had a general teaching credential, only 15 were credentialed in mathematics. During an online survey of their pedagogy, teachers were asked to explain the distributive property (Task 1), use of the distributive property to add fractions (Task 2), and why denominators stay the same when adding fractions with the same denominators (Task 3).

47.5.2 Associations Between Quality of Mathematics and Language Features

There were significant associations between the quality of mathematics demon-strated by the teachers and the language and discourse features of the explanations they gave in their written responses to Task 1. Mathematics quality required teachers to demonstrate accuracy, precision and appropriateness of the mathematics content in their explanations (dichotomously coded present or not), as well as the depth and type of knowledge being conveyed (scaled 1–3). Teachers with accuracy and depth of knowledge of mathematical concepts always elaborated their expla-nations by including two or more of the language and discourse features (di-chotomously coded elaborated-unelaborated). These features were explicitly providing a definition of one or more instances of the key terminology; sequencing with discourse connectors (e.g., *then, as, finally*); using real-life or analogous examples that clarified the mathematical concepts; using mathematical examples that explained how the problem would be worked out; and referencing multiple modes of communication, such as how the teacher would use a manipulative, graphic, etc. Those teachers showing conceptual knowledge (but not integrated with procedural knowledge) used fewer mathematical examples in their explanations.

For Task 2, teachers with accuracy and depth of knowledge of mathematical concepts included elaborated mathematics examples in their explanations. Task 3 had the largest number of significant associations with the inclusion of appropriate examples or analogies related to the use of elaboration in mathematics examples. There were also positive associations between the integration of procedural and conceptual understanding and the provision of elaborated definitions, the use of real-life examples, and the use of elaborated mathematics examples.

47.5.3 Intersection of the Quality of Mathematics and Teacher Explanations

Table 47.1 shows the contingencies between high language/discourse quality (i.e., two or more elaborated features) and high mathematics quality (i.e., highest possible ratings).

Table 47.1 Distribution of teachers by quality of mathematics and language/discourse features in explanations

Mathematics	Language/discourse quality—high			Language/discourse quality—low		
	Task 1	Task 2	Task 3	Task 1	Task 2	Task 3
Quality—high	4	1	1	8	10	8
Quality—low	19	10	6	72	56	89

Note Task 1 ($n = 103$); Task 2 ($n = 77$); Task 3 ($n = 104$)

Very few teachers exhibited high-quality explanations from both mathematics and linguistic perspectives. Task 1 showed a few teachers with this profile, but for Tasks 2 and 3 only one teacher demonstrated competencies in both areas. The example below is taken from a teacher's response to Task 1.

> To distribute is to share or spread things out. In the distributive property, you share or spread a number out with other numbers and functions. For example, in $3(2 + 6)$, you could add what's in parentheses first, where $2 + 6 = 8$, then $3(8) = 24$... or you can distribute the 3 to the 2 first, where $3(2) = 6$, then distribute the 3 to the 6, where $3(6) = 18$. Then add the two products, where $6 + 18 = 24$. In either case, the answer is 24.

A modest number of teachers had low language and discourse quality, yet demonstrated a sound knowledge of mathematics in their explanations. The example below is taken from a teacher's response to Task 2.

> In adding fractions with the same denominator, determine the smallest unit fraction and distribute this with the sum of the numerator. For example, when adding $5/8 + 3/8$, the smallest unit fraction is $1/8$. $1/8$ is distributed over the sum of 5 and 3, which are the numerators of the fractions. The problem looks like this $1/8(5 + 3)$. You can take the sum of 5 and 3, which is 8 and multiply it by $1/8$, giving you $8/8$ or 1 whole, or you can take $1/8 \times 5$ which is $5/8$ and $1/8 \times 3$, which is $3/8$ and since the denominators are the same, we are adding eighths, giving us a total of $8/8$ or 1 whole.

Some teachers were capable of well-structured explanations but this did not guarantee good quality mathematics knowledge being conveyed in their explanations, although this varied by task. Below is an example from a teacher's response to Task 3.

> I would explain that the numerators tell you how many of the denominators you have and the denominators are like what you have. For instance $3/5$ means I have three of something that is "cut" into fifths and $1/5$ means I have one of that same something cut into fifths. So if I have three of the something and 1 of the something then I have 4 of these somethings in all. Thus if I have 3 fifths and 1 fifth, then I would have 4 fifths in all. I would write the explanation just like I just did. I would also use manipulatives to show what I was talking about. The point being that "something" which is fifths in this case does not change. It's still the same thing.

By far the majority of explanations fell into the lowest ratings for quality of both mathematics and language/discourse features on each task. Below is an example from a teacher's response to Task 3.

> I would explain what the information represents i.e. the denominator (sic) represents how many pieces the object/s are divided into and does not change. The numerator tells how many pieces or objects there are and can be added together or subtracted from one another.

What might account for these profiles? Although there were very few teacher background characteristics (e.g., number of years teaching) that were related to teacher language use, we found that mathematics-specific background characteristics (e.g., mathematics credential, teaching Algebra I) were associated with more elaborated language and discourse features in the teachers' explanations. There is some suggestion in these findings that a well-crafted linguistic pedagogy can be foundational to quality mathematical explanations, but the overwhelming evidence is one of neglects of the skills to communicate mathematics clearly and convey sound mathematics content in the preparation of the teachers in this sample. These data offer a rare glimpse into both the mathematical knowledge *and* linguistic pedagogies of teachers. Possessing the linguistic acumen to produce clear (i.e., well-organized and sufficiently elaborated) explanations of content should be a fundamental prerequisite of teaching ELL students who need skillfully tailored interactions to meet their language-learning needs.

47.5.4 Responding to Content and Language Learning Needs

The second study we report on, The Dynamic Language Learning Progressions (DLLP) Project, is part of a larger effort to improve the instruction and assessment of ELL students by providing teachers with the opportunity to increase their own knowledge of how explanation discourse develops in concert with student academic learning. There have been prior efforts to create language progressions in New Zealand where the Ministry of Education developed progressions to guide teacher instructional practices. Our work builds on these international efforts and extends them by adopting an empirical approach. Extensive samples of authentic student language were collected over time and analyzed across a number of different domains to provide first-hand evidence of how school-age language develops. We describe lessons learned from a case study implementation of the DLLP with six teachers.

Language learning progressions derived from a longitudinal corpus of oral language were developed to provide an empirical basis for teachers' understanding of language development in the content areas (Bailey and Heritage 2014, Bailey et al. 2015). Multiple language samples, elicited in both academic and non-academic tasks, were generated from 324 elementary (K-6 grade) students who were ELL students with a wide range of English proficiency, as well as English-only and English proficient students. The progression of oral explanations is organized by discourse-, sentence-, and word-level characteristics and comprises high-leverage features that were selected because of their prominent role in academic contexts (e.g., sophistication of vocabulary and sentence structures, coherence and cohesion, relationships between ideas). To support teachers' instruction and formative assessment, descriptions of the features at four phases of

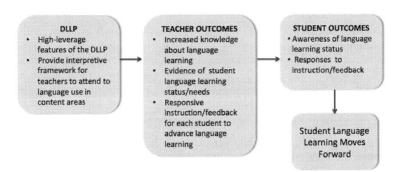

Fig. 47.1 Theory of action for the DLLP

development were created: *not yet evident* (i.e., not used by a student), *emergent* (i.e., intermittent use, inaccurate), *developing* (i.e., greater frequency of use, broadening repertoire of forms but could still be used inaccurately), and *controlled* (i.e., broad repertoire of forms and accurately used most of the time).

Our theory of action (see Fig. 47.1) hypothesizes that with the information generated by placing students on a progression based on evidence obtained during teaching and learning, teachers can engage in contingent pedagogy, building on individual student's current language to advance language learning within whatever pedagogical tradition or theoretical perspective a teacher prefers to adopt (Bailey and Heritage 2014). As a result, teachers will be more able to effectively meet the ongoing language learning needs as students engage in content learning.

Six teachers were recruited from a university elementary school serving 4–12 year olds with diversity in language backgrounds. The teachers ranged in teaching experience from 4 to 21 years. All reported that they had participated in a university-level language or linguistics courses, and four teachers reported having professional development training related to language. Three teachers taught in a Spanish–English dual-language program, and three taught in English-medium classrooms.

The teachers participated in focus groups, intended to support professional learning, nine times during an 18-month period of implementation. The teachers were first introduced to the DLLP and the high-leverage features, and in subsequent focus groups they shared their experience of implementation. Verbatim transcripts of the video-recorded meetings were coded to generate organizing themes for teachers' perspectives on professional learning related to using the DLLP.

47.5.5 Initial Challenges

Initially, the teachers found it very difficult to observe language while simultaneously attending to content learning. Eventually, they found a way to manage this; they decided to focus on one language function of their choice, in one specific content area, also of their choice. Gradually, they developed skills necessary for a dual focus on language and content. Reflecting on her implementation, one teacher stated

> I think the idea of starting small. I think what helped us was focusing on one particular content area and really just trying to flesh it out. Trying to understand the balance between teaching to content and teaching to language. Not just how you are going to teach it but how you to look for the evidence.

At the end of the study, teachers were asked to comment on the value of their learning. One teacher made a statement with which all the others agreed:

> I didn't have this level of knowledge [about language] – definitely not. I've always been told that language development is important – I remember learning that throughout my teacher education program that I went through, but it was not explicitly taught like this. I gained a much deeper understanding of that progression and all the different elements to look at.

At the beginning of the study, the teachers were also challenged by keeping track of evidence. However, they each developed a method for attending to and documenting student oral language during content instruction, often through a process of trial and error, which best suited their situation. For example, one primary teacher developed a note-taking template, which she placed on a clipboard and used for conferences with individuals and groups and observations throughout the lesson. The template headings were *date, language feature, student language, language feature modeled, student response, next steps.* In the context of mathematics talk, the teacher noted for one ELL student "still using simple sentence structures to explain how he solved a problem." In the *next steps* section she recorded "provide more opportunities for the use of complex sentences, model for support (partnering with Sean), work on paraphrasing with prompts."

We concluded from this small-scale implementation that the DLLP approach has the potential to increase teacher knowledge of language, make teachers more sensitive to language in the classroom, including their own linguistic pedagogies, and make them better able to formatively assess and plan instruction. These lessons learned are currently informing professional development designed to bring to scale the use of the DLLP for the purpose of formative assessment and adaptive instruction with ELL students.

47.6   Directions for Future Research

While we view the studies discussed as suggesting potential ways forward in the content of teacher education programs, we also realize much research remains to be done. Below, we suggested four fruitful areas for further investigation:

1. Research to develop language progressions for additional important language functions, for example, progressions for arguing from evidence in order to

provide support for teachers' knowledge of language, and for use in planning instruction and engaging in effective formative assessment;

2. The DLLP approach could be used in teacher pre-service programs to prepare teachers to work with ELL students and in ongoing professional learning. Particularly needed are experimental studies that focus on instruction, especially outside of English language arts and the elementary grades; and the results of such studies will need to be translated into pre-service and ongoing professional learning programs;
3. Studies of the unique linguistic pedagogies that may be necessary for additional content areas (e.g., science, social studies, the arts).
4. Studies that investigate what novice teachers entering the profession from pre-service programs need to know in order "to hit the ground running" in classrooms with ELL students.

47.7 Conclusion

There seems little doubt that, in many parts of the world, preparing teachers to effectively teach students who are learning an additional language has to be a priority. If it is not, then these children will likely be disadvantaged in their access to college and careers, no matter where they live. In addition to the poor life-long outcomes in terms of earnings for linguistic-minority students, societies that do not recognize the potential advantages of this population of students will not reap the economic benefits of their abilities and talents. In this chapter we have explored the charge of educating linguistic-minority children in the context of the U.S., raising issues related to the challenges for teacher-preparation programs as well as possible ways forward. We believe that many of the issues we have raised are pertinent beyond the U.S. Every country with linguistic-minority students has a duty to prepare teachers to work effectively with all students in their classrooms—no segment of the population can be left out. Teacher-preparation programs right across the world must equip their teachers with the knowledge and skills to be effective with their linguistic-minority students so they are ready to provide their students with the educational opportunities they need and deserve.

References

Bailey, A. L., & Heritage, M. (2014). The role of language learning progressions in improved instruction and assessment of English language learners. *TESOL Quarterly, 48*(3), 480–506.
Bailey, A. L., & Osipova, A. (2016). *Children's multilingual development and education: Fostering linguistic resources in home and school contexts.* Cambridge, UK: Cambridge University Press.

Bailey, A. L., Blackstock-Bernstein, A., & Heritage, M. H. (2015). At the intersection of mathematics and language: Examining mathematical explanations of English proficient and English language learner students. *Journal of Mathematical Behavior, 40,* 6–28.

Bailey, A. L., Hart, E., & Heritage, M. (2011, April). *The dual roles of the linguistic and mathematical features of pre-algebra explanations.* Roundtable paper presented at the American Educational Research Association Annual Conference, New Orleans, LA.

Black, P. J., & Wiliam, D. (1998). Assessment and classroom learning. *Assessment in Education: Principles Policy and Practice, 5,* 7–73.

California Department of Education. (2015). *News release #15-69.* Retrieved from http://www.cde.ca.gov/nr/ne/yr15/yr15rel69.asp.

Council of Chief State School Officers. (2012). *Framework for English language proficiency development standards corresponding to the common core state standards and the next generation science standards.* Washington, DC: CCSSO.

Flores, S. M., Batalova, J., & Fix, M. (2012). *The educational trajectories of English language learners in Texas.* Washington, DC: The Migration Policy Institute.

Gándara, P., Maxwell-Jolly, J., & Driscoll, A. (2005). *Listening to teachers of English language learners: A survey of California teachers' challenges, experiences, and professional development needs.* UC Berkeley: University of California Linguistic Minority Research Institute.

Halle, T., Hair, E., Wandner, L., McNamara, M., & Chien, N. (2012). Predictors and outcomes of early versus later English language proficiency among English language learners. *Early Childhood Research Quarterly, 27*(1), 1–20.

Heritage, M. (2014). The place of assessment to improve learning in a context of high accountability. In C. Wyatt-Smith & V. Klenowski (Eds.), *The enabling power of assessment* (pp. 337–354). New York, NY: Springer.

Heritage, M., Walqui, A., & Linquanti, R. (2015). *English language learners and the new standards: Developing language, content knowledge, and analytical practices in the classroom.* Cambridge, MA: Harvard Education Press.

How to fire up America. (2015, March 14). *The Economist* (p. 15).

National Center for Education Statistics. (2002). *1999–2000 schools and staffing survey: Overview of the data for public, private, public charter and bureau of Indian affairs elementary and secondary schools.* Washington, DC: U.S. Department of Education, Office of Educational Research and Improvement.

National Center for Education Statistics. (2013). *NAEP data explorer.* Available at http://nces.ed.gov/nationsreportcard/naepdata/dataset.aspx

National Center for Education Statistics. (2014). PISA data explorer. Available at http://nces.ed.gov/surveys/pisa/idepisa/

National Center for Education Statistics. (2015). *The condition of education 2015* (NCES 2015-144). Available at http://nces.ed.gov/pubsearch/pubsinfo.asp?pubid=2015144

Rubinstein-Avila, E., & Lee, E. H. (2014). Secondary teachers and English language learners (ELLs): Attitudes, preparation and implications. *The Clearing House: A Journal of Educational Strategies, Issues and Ideas, 87*(5), 187–191.

Samson, J. F., & Collins, B. A. (2012). Preparing all teachers to meet the needs of English language learners: Applying research to policy and practice for teacher effectiveness. *Center for American Progress.*

Slama, R. B. (2012). A longitudinal analysis of academic English proficiency outcomes for adolescent English language learners in the United States. *Journal of Educational Psychology, 104*(2), 265.

Smith, L., Hill, M., Cowie, B., & Gilmore, A. (2014). In C. Wyatt-Smith & V. Klenowski (Eds.), *The enabling power of assessment* (pp. 303–317). New York, NY: Springer.

Umansky, I. M., & Reardon, S. F. (2014). Reclassification patterns among Latino English learner students in bilingual, dual immersion, and English immersion classrooms. *American Educational Research Journal, 51*(5), 879–912.

Wong Fillmore, L., & Snow, C. (2002). What teachers need to know about language. In C. A. Adger, C. E. Snow, & D. Christian (Eds.), *What teachers need to know about language* (pp. 7–54). Washington, DC: Center for Applied Linguistics.

Author Biographies

Alison L. Bailey is Professor of Human Development and Psychology at UCLA. Bailey is a developmental psycholinguist working on issues germane to linguistic and educational development. She serves on the National Assessment of Educational Progress Standing Committee on Reading and the Classroom Assessment Taskforce of the National Council on Measurement in Education.

Margaret Heritage joined WestEd as Senior Scientist in October 2014 after 12 years as an Assistant Director at the National Center for Research on Evaluation, Standards and Student Testing, UCLA. Heritage's current work focuses primarily on formative assessment and innovative ways to support teachers' classroom assessment practice.

Chapter 48
University Coursework and School Experience: The Challenge to Amalgamate Learning

Allie Clemans, John Loughran and Justen O'Connor

48.1 Introduction

The theory-practice gap has long been recognized as a point of contention in teacher education. Bridging that gap has often been seen as difficult almost regardless of contextual perspective—i.e., from both the world of academia and that of schools. Recognizing and responding to the oft' bemoaned theory-practice gap demands a rethink of the ways in which the dynamics between the university coursework and professional experience components of teacher education are conceptualized and made tangible.

Schön's (1983) work on reflective practice offers one way of beginning to confront the 'gap' through his focus on the knowledge of practice. Schön's efforts lauded the work of those engaged in the world of practice, a world he described as situated in the 'swampy lowlands'. By focusing on practitioner knowledge and expertise, he cast new light on how skilled practitioners acquired (and developed) their knowledge. Importantly, he showed that knowledge of practice took an equally important but different form from the more highly valued knowledges which typically existed in the 'ivory towers' of academia.

A. Clemans (✉) · J. Loughran · J. O'Connor
Monash University, Clayton, Australia
e-mail: allie.clemans@monash.edu

J. Loughran
e-mail: john.loughran@monash.edu

J. O'Connor
e-mail: Justen.oconnor@monash.edu

© Springer Nature Singapore Pte Ltd. 2017
M.A. Peters et al. (eds.), *A Companion to Research in Teacher Education*,
DOI 10.1007/978-981-10-4075-7_48

48.2   Teacher Education: Developing Teachers
in an Integrated and Holistic Manner

> Since the time teacher education emerged as an identifiable activity, there have been few
> periods when it was not being critiqued, studied, rethought, reformed, and, often, excori-
> ated. (Cochran-Smith 2004, p. 295)

There is no shortage of criticism about teacher education—what it does, how it does
it and what it produces in terms of a 'teacher product'. Typically the theory-practice
gap comes into focus as a root cause of the 'ills of teacher education' as the nature
of what it means to learn theory is contrasted to the need to be able to do practice.
Therefore, the thoughtful interplay of theory and practice inevitably demands
careful consideration in shaping the thinking about, and practice of, students of
teaching. Hence, teacher education must be constructed as an integrated and holistic
venture in order to create opportunities for growth and development in education
rather than to maintain (or even reinforce) the status-quo.

It has been well-documented over the years how teacher education can be
viewed as a series of discrete and disjointed course work units (Darling-Hammond
2004) broken up by practice teaching opportunities in schools—with the practicum
typically being more highly valued by students of teaching—creating a fragmented
view of knowledge; a view that yet again plays out through notions of the
theory-practice divide:

> Sometimes the divide appears in the prevailing curriculum of teacher education, separated
> into domains of knowledge: educational psychology, sociology of education, foundations,
> methods of teaching and the academic disciplines corresponding to school subjects. These
> knowledge chunks are complemented by experience: supervised practice, student teaching
> and practice itself. In all of these, the gap between theory and practice fragments teacher
> education by fragmenting teaching. (Ball 2000, p. 242)

Addressing fragmentation is important, but not easy. For example, Mullen (2000),
in researching learning to teach through the experiences of a school-based teacher
education unit, found that the participating students of teaching did not view their
experience as 'learning to teach', rather they were 'doing teaching'.

48.3   Learning to Teach

It is not unusual to find teacher education programmes organized in ways that can
be interpreted as attempting to 'front load' students of teaching with as much as
possible in order to 'prepare' them for what it means to manage the initial experiences associated with beginning to teach. Such structures bow to the somewhat
superficial expectation that teaching can be 'scripted' and that students of teaching
might best be prepared for practice if they are familiar with that script.

Teacher education should be structured and conducted in such a way as to
support a process of knowledge growth through practice and so learning from

experience matters; such learning can be not be mandated or prescribed. Munby and Russell (1994) captured the essence of this issue through the distinction between the authority of position and the authority of experience.

> The authority familiar to students entering teacher education is the authority they have been subjected to, the authority that has told them what to do and what to believe. The authority these same individuals expect to experience when they become teachers is the authority they have seen their teachers wield. In this light, teacher education looks like a transition from being under authority to being in authority. (Munby and Russell 1994, p. 92)

If teaching truly is a profession, and if expertise is encapsulated in an unstated but observable knowledge-in-action (Schön 1983), then learning to teach carries demands and challenges that must be recognized—not just in rhetoric but also in reality. If learning to teach is about recognizing and responding to the dilemmas of practice that emerge in experience, then embracing the uncertainty of practice and beginning to conceptualize teaching as problematic lies at the heart of what it means to develop knowledge-in practice. In order for teacher education to be a collaborative and supportive enterprise, it must weave coursework and school experience together in purposeful and connected ways.

Perhaps it is in coming to see teaching as a complex and sophisticated endeavour (Loughran 2013) that Professional Experience can genuinely be placed at the centre of teacher education programmes. In so doing, professional experience might act as a catalyst for the generation of knowledge about practice and thus challenge notions of a theory-practice divide. However, such a view is predicated on professional experience being something very different from that of the more traditional, long-standing approach to a school practicum; an approach that has perhaps been more akin to an apprenticeship model of 'teacher training', or socialization into teaching which reinforces, rather than challenges, the status-quo.

As numerous reviews and reports consistently suggest teacher education changes dramatically when professional experience is seen as the centre of learning about teaching. Thus, locating professional experience at the centre of learning to teach is a positive and productive way of developing quality in teacher education.

48.4 Putting Professional Experience at the Centre

Within the teacher education programme in which we are involved, crafting a model to broaden out the positioning of professional experience arose as a consequence of a set of adverse conditions. First, in the midst of a growing competitive higher education landscape, a shortage of opportunities to secure professional placements for students of teaching created an increasingly stressful and frustrating situation. It meant that successful placements were secured on the basis of timing rather than intention, that is, success lay with the university that got in earliest to secure a placement. Under such conditions, there was little consideration of intentionality about the learning experience envisaged for students of teaching through their placement. Second, perceptions as to that which constituted the placement experience among schools and academics were hampered by narrow and prescriptive views based on 'how things had always been'. This included, for example, perceptions that a student placement could be a burden for the supervising school teacher, that a student of teaching should be placed with one teacher, and that it was classroom experience alone that constituted a legitimate placement experience. Just as Billett (2009) noted, there was a pressing need to re-imagine the purpose of professional experience and its function:

> … there are important and urgent issues associated with understanding, identifying and utilising the educational worth of authentic experiences, and proposing how the integration of these experiences might best proceed within university courses. (Billett 2009, p. 828)

Re-imaging professional experience led to serious questioning of: (i) the purpose of professional experience; (ii) the choice of 'provider' with whom a 'placement' was secured; and, (iii) the need to build reciprocal partnerships between academic and placement partner interests based on shared expectations about the nature of the learning experience for students of teaching. It was this approach that influenced the strategic direction for teacher education programmes in the Faculty by placing professional experience at the centre of the enterprise. Professional experience came to be understood not as the aspect that was solely about a placement or practicum, professional experience was about the integrated learning 'horizontally and vertically throughout the program' (Smith et al. 2014, p. 6)—which included extending beyond the placement component as it purposely permeated the academic components as well.

The repositioning of professional experience was driven by a need to broaden understandings of that which constituted professional experience in teacher education programmes. Its purpose was framed as building the professional readiness of students of teaching but also to provide experiences which would allow them to exceed a state of readiness and launch them towards their future participation as educational professionals.

Overall, the purposes driving the repositioning of professional experience to the centre of teacher education was in order to better prepare them to develop as multidimensional educational professionals who could demonstrate their knowledge, skills and ability in ways that highlighted their employability through articulation and demonstration of:

- professional practice and the standards which informed it;
- integration of theory and practice;
- valuing of lifelong learning;
- informed decision-making;
- collaborative approaches to work; and,
- commencement-readiness (Smith et al. 2014, p. 6).

48.5 The Approach

The approach taken to enacting this shift in the nature and positioning of professional experience at the centre of teacher education was through the notion of reciprocal partnership. In so doing, the intention was to transcend the view that higher education and school relationships commonly reinforced the essence of the theory-practice divide, or arguments through which such conceptions competed for legitimacy and dominance. The approach developed was therefore based on a view that "both practice and academic settings provide[d] particular kinds of experiences and potential contributions to students' learning … [and that] Each of these settings affords particular potentials for the learning of occupational practice" (Billett 2009, p. 835).

Both academic and workplace spaces need to be valued for the opportunities they present for students to learn to develop knowledge and practice of teaching in different but complementary ways. Genuine reciprocal partnerships between universities and schools matters in order to make clear that knowledge and practice of teaching needs to be critiqued and developed within and across contexts. Doing so is demanding but was conceptualized as being manifest on three fronts:

1. *Developing graduate excellence*

> For Australian universities to effectively engage with the graduate employability agenda…
> it will involve partnerships between faculties, careers services and employers to develop
> and implement programs addressing the issue of career management competence, including
> career building and self-management skills. Universities must remove the division between
> themselves and the demands of the world of work in order to enable graduates to adapt to
> the turbulent years to come. (Bridgstock 2009, p. 40)

Placing professional experience at the heart of teacher education carries an intention that the development of knowledge and practice of teaching should frame learning as career-building. As recent literature makes clear, employability is increasingly a key measure of the impact of teacher education, hence professional experience must explicitly foster a clear focus on what that means and how it might be enacted. With that intention in mind, the need for professional experience to be understood as supporting the purposeful development of knowledge and practice of teaching in ways that might better prepare students of teaching for diverse workplace environments became a priority (rather than simply experiencing different placement settings).

2. *Developing teaching and curriculum excellence*

> Within the curriculum and pedagogic practices of contemporary higher education it is,
> therefore, important to advance approaches that can support the effective integration of
> practice-based experiences. A helpful starting point is to acknowledge that both kinds of
> settings make particular contributions to students' learning. (Billett 2009, p. 838)

Enhancing professional readiness demands an approach to developing curriculum and practice in teacher education that fully embraces a full range of opportunities for connecting knowledge development across learning environments in a coherent and holistic manner. It follows that a key consideration for integrating practice-based experiences in higher education curricula is to utilize their key contributions and, if possible, redress or prepare students for the potential limiting experiences that they might encounter (Billett 2009).

To do as Billet (2009) suggests requires serious consideration of three key issues. The first is the need to position expert teachers in schools and other educational settings as school-based teacher educators who, through their leadership and mentoring, are able to significantly contribute to the learning of students of teaching beyond 'just supervising' classroom teaching. As research suggests, positioning expert teachers in this way creates a positive influence on participants' professional learning (both individually and collectively) as well as enhancing organizational capacity.

Second, there is a need to identify the distinctiveness of that which is able to be offered in the overall development of professional readiness among students of teaching through intentionally integrating theory and practice prior to, during and as a consequence of, professional experience. That means creating opportunities for school-based educators to co-teach with academics in the academic setting and leads to the third issue—making clear to all participants (teachers, academics and students of teaching) the inherent value in academic and school-based educators working together in complementary ways within and across workplace settings.

In conceptualizing learning about knowledge and practice of teaching through a reciprocal relationship, positively responding to the three issues (above) ensures that the learning of students of teaching can be more than the sum of each partner's sole contributions. More so, new possibilities for knowledge development of both university and school based educators emerges which similarly leads to positive gains for their practice in their workplace settings.

3. *Developing research excellence*

Research was crucial to professional experience being positioned at the centre of teacher education partly in response to the traditional university expectation of the search for new knowledge. Through the repositioning of professional experience, the ensuing collaborative endeavours created new possibilities for the production of new knowledge of relevance to all parties involved through the exploration of questions such as, "How do we build and contribute to the evidence base around the contribution of Professional Experience to graduate work-readiness?" and, "How does an (integrated approach to) Professional Experience shape the nature of learning about knowledge and practice of teaching?"

At the same time, recognition of the need to generate data around the effectiveness of practice-based learning as experienced by students of teaching was seen as important in informing the ways in which the nature of the professional experience was conceptualized and enacted. Research therefore needed to be viewed as not only facilitating knowledge engagement and production with partners but to also enable evidence-based and practice-based decision making.

In summary, placing professional experience at the centre of the learning of students of teaching was built on the basis of a partnership designed to foster collaboration whilst addressing particular imperatives as different teaching and learning possibilities were envisaged and achieved. Being cognisant of the distinctive needs of each partner, the partnership itself was fuelled by a recognition of the legitimacy of practice-based learning which itself was reliant on inquiry into practice and the knowledge forms and learning spaces in which it was conducted. Following is a brief example of how the approach to Professional Experience (described above) was initiated and activated.

48.6   Activating Professional Experience Through a Partnership

Activating this approach to professional experience is exemplified in the partnership between an Education Faculty and a Secondary School in Victoria, Australia. The Midland School-University partnership[1] was developed to provide a cohort experience for a group of students of teaching that might provide an intentional and consistent learning experience for the group while at the same time positively contributing to the school in which it was based.

> From their third week at university, the entire first year cohort of around 100 Bachelor of Education students attended Midland School for one day a week across a ten week period. The pre-service teachers completed a core undergraduate unit on the campus, undertook a school induction programme, learnt about what being a teacher meant, experienced the rhythms of work within a school and practised their teaching in numeracy, literacy and sport education curriculum.

> The numbers involved in having an entire cohort on the Midland campus meant that issues requiring serious consideration naturally extended beyond the logistics of parking and signing into the school. How participating teachers might prepare for working with, and assessing, the progress of large numbers of students of teaching through the professional experience required ongoing consideration. There was a need to develop a model that was not cumbersome for mentor teachers as they had up to six students of teaching to mentor but at the same time they needed to be comfortable with the sense of accountability associated with assessing progress in relation to the professional standards they were required to meet. (see AITSL professional standards, www.aitsl.edu.au)

> At the same time, the scale of the endeavour afforded significant benefits for resourcing and evaluation. Students of teaching ended their day of professional experience with their core university unit taught in Midland school. This offered time for university academics to facilitate the collective stories of practice accumulated during the day and to debrief and support the students of teaching around their practice and subsequent knowledge

---

[1]The school name is a pseudonym designated for this study.

development. Having university and school-based teacher educators in the same space as the students of teaching at the same time enabled the integration of theory and practice through practice in the site of practice. The immediate value to learning about teaching and learning was qualitatively different to that of the more traditional separation of university and school, teacher mentor and academic and students of teaching needing to bridge the divide in an individual and largely unsupported manner.

Collaboration and support was explicit as students of teaching worked in an environment in which academic and school-based knowledge and practice was wrapped around them. During their professional experience they participated in a literacy and numeracy programme which was a particular focus for Midland school. The students of teaching supported the programme in classrooms. They worked with individual school students to differentiate their learning, tailoring to the individual needs of students in ways that classroom teachers could not do on their own. This meant that school students received personalized feedback and support at their point of need in ways that were highly valued from both the student and teacher's perspective.

The nature of the professional experience initiated collaboration through research and evaluation that informed practice and fostered school improvement. The data gathered through the collaboration was used for what could be described as more traditional academic research as well as to form an evidence-base around which school improvement was based. Evaluation of the school students' progress around literacy and numeracy during the time in which the students of teaching actively participated in classrooms led to what the school described as significant improvement. Research interviews with stakeholders in the school signalled a positive reception across the school community about the nature of the professional experience and the overall value to all concerned.

The growth in the confidence of the students of teaching through the professional experience was significant. They built strong relationships and saw, first hand, the power of attending to relationships as the basis of better understanding the what, how and why of teaching and learning. Many of the students opted to take on extra-curricula roles and volunteered to continue their involvement with Midland school following the official completion of the experience.

The brief explanation of the approach to placing professional experience at the centre of teacher education (above) is designed to illustrate how meaningful change around developing the professional experience of students of teaching entails more than a rationalization of existing structures, imperatives and practices within a University. It reaches into the structures, imperatives and practices of schools as partners but equally requires an eye on both spaces and a vision for making the most of the resultant intersections. Through the manner in which the example above was conceptualized, developed and implemented, five insights emerged that distinguish the learning that emerged from the experience. They are outlined below:

1. *Boundaries are reframed as intersections within teacher education*

Traditionally professional experience has been positioned as somewhat of an 'add-on' in teacher education programmes. Alternatively, professional experience can be repositioned as the spine central to supporting a programme. If so, then it becomes possible to meaningfully span entrenched academic and professional divisions and invite students of teaching to engage in, and through, professional experience rather than to be corralled by each as boundaries.

Placing professional experience at the centre of the programm illustrates the priority afforded to experience and forces a consideration of how things from either side should feed into, and inform knowledge and practice development. In consideration of the 'traditional' features of teacher education (e.g. Foundation studies and teaching methods) the pairing of discipline studies (for example, science, physical education, history, etc.) with curriculum and pedagogy studies provides support for bridging theory and challenging the more typical fragmented connections or worse, 'siloed' forms of knowledge and practice. In so doing, curriculum and pedagogy studies are able to move beyond being positioned as 'method' units and become more interwoven with professional experience informing and responding to the knowledge based of discipline (Foundation) units.

Through intersections, boundaries serve to foster what Bernstein (2000) identified as possibilities to become key to transformative ideas and practice in education. Reframing boundaries as points of 'intersection' creates 'nodes of connection' so that new ways of working with them in partnership can strengthen education, engagement and research imperatives within a university as well as impact on the teaching profession and the organizational capacities of schools. Instead of conceptualising professional experience as something to be negotiated in isolation of other academic imperatives and disconnected from theory, placing professional experience at the centre of teacher education demonstrates how working in partnership at the intersections yields multiple opportunities.

2. *Professional knowledge grows through early and consistent practice*

The example of professional experience implemented at Midland school shows how students of teaching were transitioned into the role of teacher (they were not simply neophyte observers) in which they assumed responsibility for planning and implementation from early on in their first semester as students of teaching, reconceptualizing notions of what it means to be prepared to teach. The Midland school example suggests that a carefully considered cohort experience situated in a planned curriculum and supported through a structured partnership facilitates powerful teaching and learning experiences that extend beyond the students of teaching themselves. Participants' professional knowledge of practice grew through on-the-job learning experienced as existing in a two-way relationship with university coursework such that practice supported theory which supported practice.

3. *Purposeful partnerships yield significant outcomes*

Without intentional partnerships, students of teaching can find themselves spread thinly across many professional experiences as they are positioned as observers of practice whilst not necessarily having a specific lens through which to make those observations meaningful in terms of theory or practice. The Midland School-University partnership showed how moving beyond uncritical observation of practice can foster learning about practice by engaging in teaching and learning in focused ways. Additionally, forming a significant and purposeful partnership enabled dimensions to be included in the experience that was not possible on a smaller scale. In terms of the Midland school, the cohort was prepared by the University for a particular school approach and university academics partnered with the school in order to provide mentoring for teachers and students of teaching to support the project at the school 'at scale'. As a consequence, students of teaching seamlessly transitioned into 'University studies' at the school at the end of their teaching day with a focus on interrogating and extending their learning from daily practice. Crucially, the scale of the partnership facilitated an investment in the outcomes that flowed from the experience for all partners at a quantitatively different level to anything experienced (or even envisaged as possible) before.

4. *Viewing students of teaching as assets*

In many ways, extending the third insight above, the Midland school partnership targeted the enhancement of school student learning as much as it did the learning of the students of teaching. As a consequence, students of teaching were viewed as valuable assets to be supported by their teacher mentors because they were helping to 'deliver' on school objectives in ways that was not possible in their absence. The large cohort of students of teaching created: very favourable student–teacher class ratios; enhanced prospects for genuine differentiated teaching; opportunities to implement specific teaching procedures; and, efficiencies for assessment and evaluation not possible without the increased teaching capacity. The professional experience through the midland school-university partnership allowed for a strategic alignment with a pedagogic need that was important to the school and made student–teacher's feel valued.

5. *There is value in embedded research in professional experience*

The professional experience at Midland School was supported by (in part) a research agenda of the school (interest in the impact of a targeted numeracy programme by its teachers) whilst also creating valuable data about the nature of the professional experience approach. With research as an explicit aspect of professional experience, researching teaching and learning becomes more realizable through practice. In so doing, teachers, schools and students of teaching begin to recognize the research-rich environments in which they work and how important inquiry is to the ongoing development and valuing of teachers' professional knowledge of practice.

6. *Learning from experience*

Forming meaningful partnerships in teacher education requires moving beyond universities and schools negotiating a 'professional experience placement' for students of teaching. Facilitating learning by school-based educators, academics and students of teaching creates possibilities for professional learning, curriculum development and a renewed focus on teacher education practices. Under such conditions, opportunities for theory and practice to inform one another reinforces the value of reciprocal partnerships and the importance of data as an evidence base.

When students of teaching are viewed as assets in the education system, their participation can generate powerful professional learning opportunities. With carefully organized support structures, a partnership model that values students of teaching can serve to respond to perceived issues in teaching and learning. Working with colleagues and through cohorts and teams means that the well-noted 'isolatedness of teaching' can be addressed and can serve to 'push back' against the organizational and structural features of schools as workplaces that may encourage individualism as the default approach to practice.

Placing professional experience at the centre of teacher education encourages new ways of bridging the theory-practice divide. In the Midland school-University partnership, theory and practice was seen as intertwined and in a dynamic relationship, eschewing the notion of a divide needing to be bridged. Conceiving of professional experience as the backbone of teacher education led to a partnership that resulted in understanding the traditional boundaries between schools and universities as points of intersection that led to reframing of purposeful and reciprocal relationships to make the most of the learning they offered.

When the relation of theory to practice was highlighted by Dewey (1904), he similarly noted the way a connection between learning and work (professional experience) built a sense of vocation. He believed, however, that it was not the role of learning to adapt to industry but to position individuals to engage with work and practice and, ultimately, transform it. Re-thinking the relationship between theory and practice within the context of teacher education offers possibilities for transforming learning about practice by students of teaching. Placing professional experience at the centre of the enterprise offers ways of going beyond re-thinking to catalyze action. That could be what is needed if teacher education reform is to move beyond rhetoric and become reality.

References

Ball, D. L. (2000). Bridging practices. Intertwining content and pedagogy in teaching and learning to teach. *Journal of Teacher Education, 51*, 241–247.

Bernstein, B. (2000). *Pedagogy, symbolic control and identity. Theory, research, critique* (Revised ed.). Oxford: Rowman & Littlefield.

Billett, S. (2009). Realising the educational worth of integrating work experiences in higher education. *Studies in Higher Education, 34*(7), 827–843. doi:10.1080/03075070802706561

Bridgstock, R. (2009). The graduate attributes we've overlooked: Enhancing graduate employability through career management skills. *Higher Education Research & Development, 28*(1), 31–44. doi:10.1080/07294360802444347

Cochran-Smith, M. (2004). The problem of teacher education. *Journal of Teacher Education, 55*(4), 295–299.

Darling-Hammond, L. (2004). "Steady work": The ongoing redesign of the stanford teacher education program. *Educational Perspectives, 36*(1), 12.

Dewey, J. (1904). The relation of theory to practice in education. In C. A. McMurry (Ed.), *The relation of theory to practice in the education of teachers (Third yearbook of the National*

Society for the Scientific Study of Education, Part 1) (pp. 9–30). Bloomington, IL: Public School Publishing.

Loughran, J. J. (2013). Pedagogy: Making sense of the complex relationship between teaching and learning. *Curriculum Inquiry, 43*(1), 118–141.

Mullen, L. (2000). Preservice teachers' articulations of "learning to teach": Competing perspectives on teacher education. Retrieved April 2, 2015, from http://search.proquest.com/docview/62319178?accountid=12528

Munby, H., & Russell, T. (1994). The authority of experience in learning to teach: Messages from a physics method class. *Journal of Teacher Education, 4*(2), 86–95.

Schön, D. A. (1983). *The reflective practitioner: How professionals think in action.* New York: Basic Books.

Smith, C., Ferns, S., & Russell, L. (2014). The impact of work integrated learning on student work-readiness. NSW: Department of Education, Office for Learning and Teaching.

Author Biographies

Associate Professor Allie Clemans has worked as the Director of Professional Experience in the Faculty of Education at Monash University in Australia. This role involves the development of professional partnerships to support the professional readiness of graduates. She has published in the area of professional learning, lifelong learning and employability.

John Loughran is the Foundation Chair in Curriculum & Pedagogy and Dean of the Faculty of Education, Monash University. John was the co-founding editor of Studying Teacher Education and an Executive Editor for Teachers and Teaching: Theory and Practice.

Dr. Justen O'Connor utilizes systems thinking, strengths-based approaches to explore curriculum and pedagogy associated with health, physical education, sport and lifetime physical activity. Dr. O'Connor has been involved in, and led research projects including: Sports without Borders; Physical activity and wellness opportunities for children placed in care; and, re(connecting) children to place through active travel.

Chapter 49
Co-configuring Design Elements and Quality Aspects in Teacher Education: A Research Agenda

Jon Magne Vestøl and Andreas Lund

49.1   Introduction

The teaching profession and, consequently, teacher education is characterized by increasing transformation and complexity: The turnover rate of what is considered valid knowledge within specific disciplines escalates, knowledge is increasingly distributed between agents and (most often digital) artifacts with implications for how we assess competence, learning communities are heterogeneous and multi-cultural, and higher education (HE) institutions and schools seek new types of partnerships in order to draw on diverse but complementary sources of knowledge. The implication is that teacher education, as a specific field within the larger field of HE, needs to be future oriented, innovative, expansive, research informed and relevant in ways that may not be found in existing practices. As Ellis and McNicholl (2015) observe, "Around the world, ITE [Initial Teacher Education] continues to be in a state of almost continual reform, even crisis" (p. 6).

If this is the case, and there are strong indications it has been for some time (Ellis and McNicholl 2015), it will have implications for how we envisage teacher education but also for our research agenda and how we conduct research on teacher education; in particular how we capture emerging practices and how such practices are constructed and enacted by agents involved: student teachers (individually and collaboratively), teachers and supervisors in HE, mentors and teachers in schools, and—at least to some extent—policy makers at various levels. In order to examine and further cultivate emerging practices where they indicate promise and relevance we propose a research agenda that rests on *design* principles (Hauge et al. 2007;

J.M. Vestøl (✉) · A. Lund
University of Oslo, Oslo, Norway
e-mail: j.m.vestol@ils.uio.no

A. Lund
e-mail: andreas.lund@ils.uio.no

© Springer Nature Singapore Pte Ltd. 2017
M.A. Peters et al. (eds.), *A Companion to Research in Teacher Education*,
DOI 10.1007/978-981-10-4075-7_49

Lund and Hauge 2011) and *co-configuration* (Engeström 2004); i.e. an agenda that involves participants from various contexts such as outlined above, and where participants can construct meaningful learning practices and objects that can be adapted across such contexts. Co-configuration, thus, is sensitive to changing needs in the environment as well as of the participants involved. It will not result in a 'finished' model but rather serve to socially and collaboratively develop functional procedures, rules and infrastructures that prepare student teachers and teacher educators for making informed decisions about learning and teaching.

From a Vygotskyan and Cultural-Historical Activity Theory perspective we approach expansive, future-oriented co-configuration through three concepts that we will argue have explanatory power when studying and, when relevant, supporting phenomena that are currently evolving. First, we use the notion of *design* (Hauge et al. 2007; Lund and Hauge 2011) in order to operationalize a research agenda. Design is a dialectic concept that unifies intended designs, designs for teaching, with the appropriated and enacted designs, designs for learning. Second, we adopt the Vygotskyan principle of double stimulation (Lund and Rasmussen 2008) where the first stimulus is a problem, a challenge, or alternatives to navigate, and where the second stimulus consists of available cultural resources to (ideally) be productively employed by the agent. Third, we use the concept of transformative agency (Sannino 2014) in order to further unpack the relationship between agents and tools and how understanding this relationship is vital for constructing objects that are not always given but in the making. As we indicated above, we argue that this is what characterizes teacher education in an increasingly multi-cultural and technology-rich world.

Empirically, we use two cases or activities as carriers of more fundamental principles connected to design, double stimulation and transformative agency. The first case involves the design of an exam for student teachers integrating different types of knowledge, use of a digital video clip, and allowing for unlimited use of material and social resources. The second case presents an introduction to research and development (R&D)-based practices for student teachers. The cases were not developed for the purpose of the present study but are derived from projects included in the activity of ProTed—the first Norwegian Centre of Excellence in Teacher Education. We read the cases in a retrospective perspective to identify the aspects within the cases that serve as carriers of the principles we focus on in this article. The aspects identified may serve as examples of important and necessary trajectories of change to be examined in teacher education. Although there is some previous research which has focused on change (or expansion) within teacher education (Ellis and McNicholl 2015) such change has not, to the best of our knowledge, been studied with respect to the interaction between teaching and learning designs and what is at stake at the interface of the two.

49.2   Selected Relevant Previous Research

Early in 2015, Marilyn Cochran-Smith and colleagues mapped the landscape of research on teacher education by reviewing more than 1500 studies published between 2000 and 2012 and from diverse parts of the world (Cochran-Smith and Villegas 2015; Cochran-Smith et al. 2015). From a position where research on teacher education is seen as a "Historically Situated Social Practice" (Cochran-Smith and Villegas 2015, p. 7) they identify three major research programmes: (1) Research on teacher preparation and accountability, effectiveness and policies; (2) Research on preparation for the knowledge society; and (3) Research on teacher preparation for diversity and equity. These are clusters with numerous sub-categories involved. On the whole, the authors find "that sociocultural perspectives have been widely taken up by teacher education researchers" (Cochran-Smith et al. 2015, p. 113), and in particular concerning category 2. We argue that the present chapter primarily belongs in the second category, not least because this category has strong links to the learning sciences and changing conceptions of how people learn and construct new knowledge, but that the other two are not excluded.

However, the articles referred to above do not review the various methodological approaches in the studies (although they offer a brief historical overview) but state that their review "is deliberately inclusive of multiple—sometimes competing—research approaches and agendas", adding up to "a 'sprawling' field of research" (ibid., p. 8). This lack of methodological consensus is in itself interesting as it indicates a potentially productive diversity as well as potentially new spaces for methodological approaches, which is where the present chapter aims to make a contribution. Still, it is relevant to note that as for the second category on research on teacher preparation for the knowledge society, the authors identify the following six methodological clusters (p. 13):

- Preparing teachers to teach science subject matter
- The influence of coursework on learning to teach
- The influence of fieldwork on learning to teach
- Content, structures and pedagogy of teacher preparation for the knowledge society
- Teacher educators as teachers and learners
- Teacher preparation and learning to teach over time

At the end of the second article, Cochran-Smith et al. conclude by listing their findings. Of particular interest to the present study is the need for "studies that investigated how preparation influenced the candidates' practice", and that "few studies connected aspects of teacher preparation/certification to students' learning" (ibid., p. 117). The authors point to "research questions developed jointly by school and university" as a way of establishing or strengthening such connections. The above clusters and findings can also be used as a backdrop for the present approach, although—as we aim to demonstrate—we will focus on the interplay involved between intended and enacted designs or interventions and how agents face alternatives, or even conflicts, that require decision-making through co-configuration of work.

A complementary study to that of Cochran-Smith and colleagues, but with a specific focus on methodological approaches was done by Menter et al. (2010). These authors reviewed 446 studies on, in and about teacher education in the UK between 2000 and 2008, thus dovetailing in time with the mapping undertaken by Cochran-Smith et al. Menter et al. summarize their classification of research methods in the UK in a table where qualitative, small-scale studies based on reflection and interviews dominate. Large-scale studies, longitudinal studies and quantitative or mixed-method approaches are under-represented (Menter et al. 2010, p. 131). Based on this, and other systematic summaries, the authors conclude that what is missing is potential cumulative impact, there is relatively little attempt to theorize approaches (resulting in methodological weaknesses), little evidence of engaging in multiple methods or mixed methods, and that practitioner research in teacher education is a neglected area. The consequence is a lack of coherence and, we would add, a healthy knowledge base for the field. Although the UK may differ from other countries regarding teacher education programmes and policies (duly noted by the authors) we recognize observations such as "...teacher education research appears to be a relatively under-developed area, without a strong theoretical or methodological tradition" (p. 124).

From policy levels, but also from researchers, the response has been to require research that can demonstrate "what works" and teacher education accountability often embedded in effect sizes or mathematical tags that amount to audits. However, such research, even at its best, is restricted by being fundamentally retrospective and not focusing on many challenges that emerge when the turnover rate of valid knowledge increases rapidly, when knowing and learning (and teaching) is distributed over multiple agents and artifacts, and when increasingly heterogeneous groups of learners defy educational models where "one size fits all". The present chapter, therefore, offers a different response than merely quantifying or measuring processes (although this may be fine depending on the research question). As neither the overviews offered by Cochran-Smith or Menter point to methodological approaches that aim to capture how student teachers (or teachers) face complexity, transformation, potential expansion, and how they exercise agency when facing alternatives or dilemmas, we will in the following propose a design approach for examining such processes as future-oriented capacity building. We first discuss our conceptual framework before we present two cases, which will finally be discussed and related to further research on teacher education.

49.3   Researching Teacher Education as a Design Concept

49.3.1   *Design*

The notion of design is hard to delimit since it is found in connection with, e.g. artfully shaping objects, guiding architecture and as a particular type of intervention research. Other scholars have also used the notion of design when analyzing what teaching entails in the knowledge society and in particular in technology-rich environments (Laurillard 2012). All these aspects (and more) can be found in our use of the term. However, our main rationale for a design approach is found in the increasing complexity of learning and teaching environments and trajectories and how teacher educators and student teachers can prepare for this through co-configuring designs for teaching and designs for learning. Like Vygotsky (1978), we consider learning and teaching to be two mutually constitutive aspects of education as well as personal development. However, Vygotsky had the Russian word *obuchenie* at his disposal to capture the dual aspects, while English (as well as Norwegian and most other European languages) does not afford a similar term but dichotomize the *obuchenie* activity into learning and teaching. This becomes evident in the following quote from Cole (1996):

> In general, the Russian word, obuchenie, refers to a double-sided process, one side of which does indeed refer to learning (a change in the psychological processes and knowledge of the child), but the other of which refers to the organization of the environment by the adult, who, it is assumed in the article under discussion, is a teacher in a formal school with power over the organization of the children's experience. (p. 292)

It is the reciprocity of learning and teaching, the tensions and potential synthesis that we also seek to put into operation in our notion of design (Hauge et al. 2007; Lund and Hauge 2011). We distinguish between Designs for teaching and Designs for learning, partly for analytical purposes and partly because this duality shows how the latter might be a volitional transformation of the former—not least as a result of using powerful cultural tools. In our approach to design, we acknowledge that the two design types for all practical purposes are mutually constitutive of the learning activity, we just do not have a singular concept for this.

Design for teaching is basically the teacher educators' responsibility and emerges through interpreting curricula and competence aims, but may well involve students in the process. However, the intentionality behind this aspect of the design is primarily that of the teacher educator and the larger teacher educational policies. Thus, there is an institutional dimension to designs for teaching. *Design for learning* refers to the enacted design; what actually happens when student teachers (but also teacher educators) engage in joint construction of the (learning) object. While designs for teaching delimit the activities, designs for learning are context sensitive and respond to, for example immediate opportunities, learner initiatives and serendipity. Also, designs for learning open up for using student teachers' social and cultural experiences, their life worlds. Thus, the combination of the two design aspects has the potential to build conceptual bridges between student teachers' life worlds and institutional goals.

Without going into further detail, our notion of design draws on Cultural-Historical Activity Theory since this is a theory of transformation, it connects the individual to the collective, mind to social and material context, and identifies a potentially shared object of activity as a collective motive for learning and development (Engeström et al. 1999). What has recently attracted increased interest is how individual agency relates to the collective and contextual dimensions of this perspective. The following section addresses this issue.

49.3.2 Double Stimulation

As the complexity of learning environments increases there is a need to capture the relationship between tasks, available resources and agency together with the institutional affordances that are regulated by, e.g. white papers, exam guidelines or less formal contextual conventions. In our use of design, this relationship amounts to the most common use of a unit of analysis. In particular, we have examined how the use of available cultural resources (material, social, linguistic) is intrinsically linked to task challenges and responses, and how such resources are appropriated and put to use by learners (Lund and Rasmussen 2008). Thus, the notion of double stimulation can explain how subjects convert external means into object-oriented activity. If available resources or tools do not facilitate the untangling of the problem at hand it is simply not relevant for participants to pick them up. This relationship is at the heart of Vygotsky's (1978) notion of double stimulation, a principle for studying cognitive processes and development and not just results. In a teacher education setting, typically the first stimulus would be the problem, challenge, task or assignment to which student teachers are expected to respond. The second stimulus would be the available mediating tools or cultural resources. However, it is important to note that Vygotsky described this relationship in dynamic terms and where the second stimulus is not a discrete end point for this process but, "Rather, we simultaneously offer *a second series of stimuli* that have a special function. In this way we are able to study the process of accomplishing a task by the aid of specific auxiliary means" (p. 74, emphasis in the original). Note that Vygotsky identifies the second stimulus in the plural—a series—as if he somehow anticipated learning environments of high complexity.

However, we deviate somewhat from Vygotsky's notion in two respects. The first is related to Vygotsky's conception of the second stimulus as being "neutral"; that the available cultural tools (at least those used in his experiments) do not carry any cultural-historical connotations or content. In current learning environments including schools and teacher education we encounter a series of technological means. Although such means may appear to be content neutral, they hold inscriptions that point to certain organizational principles or activity, for example, regarding division of labour and the conventions or rules that are enacted in or around them. For example, wikis make more sense for collaborative than individual activity and will be equipped with preventive measures against vandalism. The implication is that the relationship between agent and tool is not unidirectional and the resources may not unconditionally yield to the will of the agent. The second problem pertains to Vygotsky's emphasis on individual internalization. We argue for the need of a sociogenetic perspective; how we come to knowledge by taking part in collective activities that evolve over time, and where language and material artifacts function as collective structural resources. From this perspective, double stimulation is also conceptualized as capturing the complexity of learning and teaching in collectively oriented and learning environments with a plethora of available and sophisticated resources. But this also involves a capacity to choose among alternatives, select and make decisions that impact on the activity and the object. This is where transformative agency emerges.

49.3.3 Transformative Agency

As in the case of double stimulation, transformative agency can best be characterized as principles that emerge when piecing together fragments in the works of Vygotsky and his contemporaries. Transformative agency emerges as a capacity in humans when they seek to alter the circumstances they face by assessing alternatives, overcoming potentially conflicting motives or making decisions with the help of second stimuli (Sannino 2014). Thus, transformative agency is a volitional action although inscriptions or even prescriptions in available resources may impact on the course of action taken when complex choices are involved. In the context of teacher education, we find that principles of double stimulation and transformative agency have explanatory power when examining situations where people face concrete challenges by seeking to transform the situation, creating new conditions, breaking away or expanding the object of the challenge. It is a process intimately linked to meaning-making in a complex world. Such transformative agency, we argue, is increasingly required from teachers who face a rapid turnover of valid disciplinary knowledge, new insights in learning and cognition, ethical and cultural judgment, and increasingly distributed and collaborative practices where humans as well as non-humans are involved.

In the following, we apply the principles of design, double stimulation and transformative agency to examine two cases that indicate dynamic and future-oriented practices in teacher education and, thus, a particular type of knowledge production. For the researcher, the linking of the principles emerges as opportunities to study transformation of contexts as well as of the agents who populate them.

49.4   Empirical Contexts and Cases

Two empirical cases will be presented here as a basis for further elaboration of how the described concepts could be put to work in the context of a scientific examination. Both cases relate to the work of the Norwegian ProTed Centre of Excellence in Teacher Education, a collaboration between the University of Oslo and the University of Tromsø—The Arctic University of Norway. The mandate of the centre is to develop and improve the 5-year programmes at master's level that recently were introduced as the backbone of teacher education in Norway. Vital to these programmes is the integration of scientific disciplines, school subjects and pedagogy and subject didactics ('professional knowledge'). Fieldwork is essential with 100 days of practice over the five years and the education programmes should reflect a strong research base as well as give student teachers opportunities to engage in research-oriented practices. To integrate these components into a coherent programme has proved to be challenging.

Case 1 from 2013 presents a digital home exam in the sixth term of the integrated 5-year teacher education for level 8–13 at the University of Oslo (UiO). In this exam, the students analyze and reflect on a video from a classroom situation. Case 2, also from 2013, presents an introduction to R&D among first- and second-year students of the integrated 5-year teacher education programmes for level 1–7 and 8–10 at the University of Tromsø—The Arctic University of Norway (UiT). In this introduction, the students collect and analyze empirical data from their fieldwork at practice schools.

In different ways these two cases illustrate how empirical sources, theoretical perspectives and elements from research methodology create complex, demanding, and productive learning contexts which raise challenges as to how a scientific examination of these situations may be conducted. The following case presentations are based on traditional research methods such as interviews with university teachers (case 2) and analyses of exam texts and interviews with staff members and students (case 1). The aim of the case presentations is, thus, not to introduce or develop new research methods as such but to suggest a conceptual and analytical framework for interpreting and understanding the educational and transformative processes displayed through the cases.

49.5   Case 1: Digital Exam

The first case presents a new type of video-based exam that was introduced in teacher education at the University of Oslo. The nucleus of the exam's teaching design was an intended object of integration expressed through a task in which the students were asked to apply knowledge from pedagogy, subject disciplines and practice in the analysis of a classroom situation presented in the form of a video. Since this was an exam design, there was a sharper distinction between the teaching design and learning design than in educational activities where teachers and students tend to collaborate more closely. On the other hand, the teaching design afforded a space of freedom for the students; they could explore the video case and integrate knowledge from different sources, angles, and perspectives, i.e. a series of second stimuli.

Organizational aspects were also of importance for how the teaching design's intended integration was appropriated and transformed by the students into an accomplished integration in the learning design. The students were given a strictly limited time for the analysis of the case and the production of their text. However, since the task was known in advance the students—albeit to a varying degree—took the opportunity to prepare themselves by working out templates of knowledge integration related to different themes and situations. Thus, the instructions combined with the restricted time limits served as tools for stimulating the students to process integration in advance. When the video case was introduced in the exam situation the students renegotiated the suggested object and developed or expanded the object in a variety of more selective and specific directions (Vestøl 2014).

While some students based their knowledge integration in a concept or central issue from their *scientific subject* which they subsequently elaborated in light of pedagogical concepts and practical knowledge, others chose a concept or issue from *pedagogy* which they then related to a subject topic and practical knowledge. Some students were interested in an observed phenomenon of *educational practice* (from the video case) which they sought to clarify through the use of pedagogical concepts and link to aspects of subject knowledge, while others undertook an *exploration* of concepts or issues of importance and relevance that were not particularly well developed in the study literature and sought to clarify the meaning and importance of such issues and concepts by relating them to elements from different knowledge domains.

This range of knowledge integration trajectories indicates a diversity of interactions between the task and instruction as stimulus 1 and the responses afforded by a series of stimuli 2. According to interview data some of this diversity may be rooted in the ways student teachers prepared for dealing with knowledge integration during the weeks before the exam when (some) students developed maps and sketches of concepts based on stimuli 2 (literature). In the exam situation, the video case as an additional stimulus 2 was given a vital function, and although the interviews did not investigate the impact of the video case in detail the informants gave accounts of how the video case contributed to the work process:

> Student 1D: I think that the video gives us the possibility to interpret it ourselves; a written [case] is sort of a fulfilled interpretation of the situation
>
> Student 2A: I think it was very good to have something that concrete and practical as a basis for the writing since it made it sort of easier to get started with a real discussion
>
> Student 2D: […] I am very much in favour of having a digital home exam because it is a good way of uniting theory and practice, it is not only theoretical because you see a classroom […]

Two aspects are emphasized by these students: the physicality or practicality of the case and the openness for interpretation. This indicates that the video case as stimulus 2 contributed to the variety of trajectories for knowledge integration found in the students' exam papers and thus played a central role in the way the exam design presented a teaching object that was both open and directional in terms of stimulating the development of a certain variety of learning objects. Through the variety of trajectories the teaching design was transformed in ways that were possibly intended but not foreseen in detail by the designers of the exam. This means that the student teachers' object constructions through transformative agency added new aspects of insight to the intended object of the exam design. In the interplay between the various stimuli of the digital exam we thus see transformative agency in terms of an interpretive space that opens towards practical dimensions as well as a variety of trajectories. This space could easily remain black-boxed without a scientific examination that identify and unpack the processes within.

49.6   Case 2: Introducing R&D

The second case focuses on the increasingly required research orientation in teacher education. In this case, it pertains to integration of systematic observation and analysis of practice in a campus course focusing on discipline specific knowledge. While case 1 showed a situation where the teaching design and learning design are separated in time, case 2 shows how designs for teaching and learning may interact closely over time.

Organized as a part of a teacher education course on Norwegian at the Arctic University of Norway in Tromsø (UiT) the project, 'Introduction to R&D', gave student teachers in their first and second year a basic experience in the use of research procedures. In the initial phase of the introduction the students were presented with guidelines for observation and interview, which served as stimulus 1 as they had to acknowledge what such approaches entailed or demanded. Based on templates from the course literature, the guidelines were refined in cooperation between students and university teachers to be applied by the students in the field work during the internship.

During periods of internship practice the students observed and interviewed their supervisors, generating data which served as a stimulus 2. While the observations focused on aspects of the supervisors' classroom conversation issues such as topics suitable for discussion, types of questions used and on who were talking, the interviews emphasized the goals for the conversation and the criteria used for evaluating the conversation.

After the internship, the data were analyzed during a two-week intensive work period. Through the work, the students developed skills in interpreting and systematizing data by developing categories and reducing the information into a particular format. The analysis took place through explorative plenary conversations and several stages of group work where the students worked closely together in cooperation with the supervisors. First they mapped and systematized the whole material and then they formed new groups to choose specific questions to look into more closely. There was a clear distinction between the initial mapping of the material and the subsequent investigation based on research questions: While there was some interplay between the teaching and learning designs in the preparatory phase, such interplay grew more intense during the phase of analysis. Early in the process of the analysis one of the university teachers (H) on one occasion took an observatory role and watched her colleague (K) working on the material together with the students. H described in the interview how the cooperation initiated a change in participant roles:

> H: I was sitting there […] and it became very clear to me that K did a fantastic job first asking simple questions that the students were able to find answers to and which K knew the answers to herself […] but after maybe five-ten minutes the conversation had arrived at a point where neither K nor the students or anyone else in the room had the answer. And in this way something developed […] which made the ownership of the project, of the knowledge of the empirical data …, that it turned into something much more shared than we have seen in other situations. […] It turned more into a sort of explorative or investigative perspective.

This apparently seamless interplay between teaching and learning designs suggests a form of transformative agency where the learning process transcends the traditional academic divisions of labour between university teachers and students. For some of the student groups this transformation was extended into a subsequent presentation phase as these students presented their project at a national Norwegian teacher education conference together with their university teachers. The project was also partly addressed in the exam task of a home exam where the students wrote about classroom conversations. In this way, we see how the transformation of the knowledge materialized in ways that were partly accustomed to traditional practice and partly transcended such practice by actively engaging student teachers in research-oriented activities.

According to the university teachers, the outcome of the introduction to R&D contributed to the students' understanding of both classroom practices and research practices. Although the results of the students' analyses showed that the internship supervisors had not a very precise understanding of the goals of the classroom conversation, the findings contributed to the students' awareness and sharpened their focus on how to develop classroom conversations that are really focused on subject topics. In addition the project gave the students first-hand experience with how developmental work depends on an attitude of inquiry as well as an attitude towards transforming their practices in light of insights gained form research-oriented activities.

49.7 Designs for Co-configuration

Surveys of research as well as trends in teacher education point to the need to examine emerging practices and how student teachers cope with complex situations and challenges. Thus, gap spotting in the literature as well as well as problematization of certain issues amount to the rationale for the type of research outlined in the present chapter. Both cases demonstrate how research can address co-configuration; how professional practices involve collaboration between teacher educators and student teachers and where student teachers through transformative agency and their learning designs participate in co-designing the education they also receive. The cases indicate how teaching designs can open up opportunities for students' learning designs to unfold.

In Table 49.1, we summarize the two cases in light of the conceptual framework we have used in order to, despite risks of reductionism, model our approach:

Table 49.1 Overview of research aspects of the two cases

Case aspects	Example 1: digital exam	Example 2: introduction to R&D	Research implications
Essence	An exam as a teaching design is transformed into a learning design as students face challenges by invoking a series of stimuli 2 (video case, literature and practice experience)	An R&D approach as a teaching design is transformed into a learning design as students and university teachers collaborate by invoking a series of stimuli 2 (classroom observations, interviews and field notes)	Focus on how a teaching design is transformed into a learning design mediated by a series of stimuli 2
Subjects	Academic, administrative and technical staff members design the activity. Students are testing technical solution, and interpreting and reflecting on the video case and writing the exam papers	Academic staff members design the activity in cooperation with students and school teachers. Students collect data, analyze data and write and present reports together with university teachers	Focus on co-configuration of work between participants

(continued)

Table 49.1 (continued)

Case aspects	Example 1: digital exam	Example 2: introduction to R&D	Research implications
Main object	Integrated knowledge production as an intended object realized in a multifaceted way	Knowledge production based on scientific analysis of classroom practices as an intended object. Realized as a co-constructed effort	Focus on capturing instantiations of the object as well as the processes leading up to them
Stimulus 1	Task and instructions requiring capacity to integrate knowledge sources and interpret classroom situations in light of scholarly literature. Task made available from the start of the semester	Suggested projects intended to develop analytical and research competence. Guidelines for observation and interview made available from the start	Focus on the possible expansive aspects of stimulus 1
Stimulus 2	The digital video case presented at the exam and the study literature and internship practice experience available to the students	The empirical classroom observations, interviews and field notes and transcript data resulting from this	Focus on the interplay between stimulus 1 and 2: to what extent student teachers' agency exploits and develops the expansive potential of stimulus 1 by using a series of stimulus 2
Transformative agency: the transformation of teaching design into learning design	The students' transformation of knowledge integration into a variety of integration types	The students' and university teachers' transformation of scientific approaches into co-constructed professional competence	Focus on the dynamic zone of interaction between teaching and learning design and stimulus 1 and stimulus 2

A persistent issue in research on HE is probing "how we know what we know" (Silverman 1987). The present chapter has tried to expand on this line of query by asking how we can know what we *ought to know* and *how to study* such phenomena. We have argued that this is crucial for teacher education in times of fundamental challenges for the teaching profession. As a response we have proposed a research agenda and approach that involve co-configuration and co-design of activities and practices and that through the lenses of double stimulation and transformative agency makes it possible to make emerging challenges visible for scientific examination. In particular, we have sought to demonstrate how the notion of design as a dual activity involving teaching as well as learning lends itself to analyzing how transformation of practices can be linked to the interplay between these two dimensions. This does not in any way mean that we propose a predetermined or 'fixed' model. However, we sincerely hope that the present chapter can stimulate a discussion on how best to conduct research on future-oriented teacher education that involves making informed decisions in increasingly complex and dynamic educational environments and trajectories.

References

Cochran-Smith, M., & Villegas, A. M. (2015). Framing teacher education research: An overview of the field, part 1. *Journal of Teacher Education, 66*(1), 7–20. doi:10.1177/0022487114549072

Cochran-Smith, M., Villegas, A. M., Abrams, L., Chavez-Moreno, L., Mills, T., & Stern, R. (2015). Critiquing teacher education research: An overview of the field, part 2. *Journal of Teacher Education, 66*(2), 109–121. doi:10.1177/0022487114558268

Cole, M. (1996). *Cultural psychology. A once and future discipline.* Cambridge, MA: The Belknap Press.

Ellis, V., & McNicholl, J. (2015). *Transforming teacher education: Reconfiguring the academic work.* London, Bloomsbury Academic.

Engeström, Y. (2004). New forms of learning in co-configuration work. *Journal of Workplace Learning, 16*(1/2), 11–21.

Engeström, Y., Miettinen, R., & Punamäki, R. (Eds.). (1999). *Perspectives on activity theory.* Cambridge: Cambridge University Press.

Hauge, T. E., Lund, A., & Vestøl, J. M. (2007). *Undervisning i endring: IKT, aktivitet, design* [Teaching in transformation: ICT, activity, design]. Oslo: Abstrakt forlag.

Laurillard, D. (2012). *Teaching as a design science. Building pedagogical patterns for learning and technology.* New York, Routledge.

Lund, A., & Hauge, T. E. (2011). Designs for teaching and learning in technology rich learning environments. *Nordic Journal of Digital Literacy, 6*(4), 258–271.

Lund, A., & Rasmussen, I. (2008). The right tool for the wrong task? Match and mismatch between first and second stimulus in double stimulation. *International Journal of Computer-Supported Collaborative Learning, 3*(4), 25–51.

Menter, I., Hulme, M., Murray, J., Campbell, A., Hextall, I., Jones, M., et al. (2010). Teacher education research in the UK: The state of the art. *Revue Suisse des sciences de l'education, 32*(1), 121–142.

Sannino, A. (2014). The emergence of transformative agency and double stimulation: Activity-based studies in the Vygotskian tradition. *Learning, Culture, and Social Interaction.* doi:10.1016/j.lcsi.2014.07.001

Silverman, R. (1987). How we know what we know: A study of higher education journal articles. *Review of Higher Education, 11*(1), 39–59.

Vestøl, J. M. (2014). Kunnskapsintegrasjon og profesjonsutvikling i lektorutdanningen [Knowledge integration and professional development in teacher education]. In E. Elstad & K. Helstad (Eds.), *Profesjonsutvikling i skolen* (pp. 114–130). Oslo: Universitetsforlaget.

Vygotsky, L. S. (1978). *Mind in society: The development of higher psychological processes.* Cambridge, MA: Harvard University Press.

Author Biographies

Jon Magne Vestøl is a Professor at the Department of Teacher Education and School Research, University of Oslo, Norway. Among his research interests are: design and quality aspects of teacher education, knowledge integration in teacher education and cultural and ideological aspects of pupils' learning.

Andreas Lund is a Professor at the Department of Teacher Education and School Research, University of Oslo, Norway and former Director of the ProTed Centre for Excellence in Teacher Education. Among his research interests are: teaching and learning in technology-rich environments, collective cognition, and sociocultural and activity theoretical perspectives.

Chapter 50
Theorising Teacher Practice with Technology: Implications for Teacher Education Research

Julianne Lynch

This chapter engages with contemporary theorisations of technology practice to discuss implications for teacher education and education research. First—drawing on the example of Australia—it characterises trends in government policy, where technological innovation is positioned as an economic imperative, a panacea for educational ills, and as a catalyst of educational change. Within this context, teachers are often positioned as lacking knowledge, skills and requisite attitudes for the correct and effective implementation of new technologies. This deficit approach to teacher practice also underpins much of the existing research into teacher technology practices, with many studies seeking to develop principles of best practice while also diagnosing inadequacy in teachers. The chapter offers a critique of such approaches to research by drawing upon three interrelated theoretical distinction:

1. Between different conceptions of technology practice—one focused on inputs and outputs (Lynch 2006); the other drawing on sociomaterial theorisations of practice (Fenwick 2012), together with de Certeau's notion of *reuse*;
2. Between different conceptions of professional practice—one focused on tech-norationalist conceptions of teaching (Connell 2009); the other drawing on contemporary practice thinking to support more expansive and productive views (Lynch et al. 2017); and,
3. Between axiologically distinct education research traditions (Biesta 2015)—one focused on developing and auditing technical solutions to educational problems; the other focused on developing understandings of the complexity and subsequent unprogrammability of educational practice.

Calling on these theoretical distinctions, the paper takes an explicit position on the nature of teacher practice with technology—as involving an ongoing, impro-

J. Lynch (✉)
Deakin University, Warrnambool, Australia
e-mail: julianne.lynch@deakin.edu.au

© Springer Nature Singapore Pte Ltd. 2017
M.A. Peters et al. (eds.), *A Companion to Research in Teacher Education*,
DOI 10.1007/978-981-10-4075-7_50

vised and often playful negotiation and remix of materials and techniques—and asks: what are the implications for how we research educational technology practice and for how we practice teacher education?

50.1   Introduction

'New technology' is not new. Over the last six or more decades (arguably since the establishment of formal schooling much earlier than that), wave after wave of 'new technology' have emerged: television, video cassettes, microcomputers, laptops, the internet and, most recently, portable, mobile (and even wearable) devices. In this chapter, I provide a critique of dominant views of teachers' technology work with reference to the assumptions underpinning much policy on and research into educational technology. First, I characterise approaches to understanding teachers' technology practices found in public policy and mainstream educational technology research. I then argue that sociomaterial understandings of practice offer alternative conceptual tools that are more likely to support and promote teacher innovation with technology. To do this, I draw upon a selection of concepts and analyses that have influenced my practice as a teacher educator and educational technology researcher and which inform a discussion of the practice of teacher education and implications for teacher education research.

50.2   Ed-tech Policy Discourse: Example of Australia

Per capita, Australia is an international leader in the uptake of new information and communication technologies, both in schools and more generally in the community. Australian government policy relating to technology in schools is similar to that found in other economically similar countries in terms of discursive politics and funding foci. Jordan (2011) provides an analysis of two decades of Australian national policies on school education and information and communication technology (ICT), identifying a persistent determinist view of technology, coupled with an instrumentalist view of teachers and teaching. Jordan argues that these are key features of an official discourse in support of ICT in schools. More recent government reports perpetuate this discourse, with the Australian Government Digital Education Reference Group stating:

> Achieving enhanced education outcomes in Australian schools is increasingly linked to the pace of digital education uptake. Investment in digital education is helping to reshape how students learn and even what they learn through powerful 21st Century tools. Schools must be encouraged to see the opportunities that such tools provide to support improving learning and teaching. (Australian Government Department of Education and Training 2013, p. 5)

Three features of this statement are typical of national school education ICT policies. First, there is an assumption that the technological innovation—presented as an unfolding of successive cycles of technological development—takes place at some location spatially and temporally outside of the site of use. It belongs to some other place and time, and teachers and students are persuaded to take it up. Second, and consistent with the determinism identified by Jordan (2011), it is the technology that has the agency—it will reshape how people do things. The subtext (sometimes explicit) of this discourse is that the development of new skills and greater effectiveness in schools is an imperative, linked to both educational and economic outcomes that are interrelated, with education servicing a changing economy. Third, schools—and, by implication, teachers—do not comprehend the opportunities that new technologies bring or the associated imperatives.

As demonstrated by Jordan (2011), these assumptions are not new. New technologies are usually positioned by government policies as a catalyst of educational change and innovation—good medicine for an ailing school education sector that must serve the needs of the economy. Across the last several decades of policies surrounding new technologies in schools, the most predominant characterisation of the relationship between schools and 'new technology' is that technology is an alien thing, a thing that needs to be 'introduced' via some artificial means. The technoschool hybrid has been storied as something surgically created—an implant that is inserted or an appendage that is sutured on, in the most part under duress, needing persuasion, inducement and preparations by others (preparation of technologies, of ways of operating, and of teachers). Within this discourse, teachers are positioned as lacking knowledge, skills and requisite attitudes for the correct and effective implementation of new technologies. Teachers are not innovators; they feature as reluctant and ill-prepared receivers of innovation. Jordan (2011, p. 247)—pointing out the contrast found in such policy documents between how students are represented ("as tech-savvy, and as expectant of using ICT in their learning") and how teachers are represented ("as lagging behind")—provides a critique of these assumptions as both inaccurate and as producing flawed policy in terms of guiding future directions.

These discursive politics can also be found in common approaches to educational technology research.

50.3 Approaches to Educational Technology Research

Education research is a multidisciplinary undertaking that encompasses a multitude of subfields, and is influenced by and employs diverse approaches to inquiry. Biesta (2015) provides a useful heuristic for thinking about trends in education research, arguing that two distinct traditions have emerged that differ in terms of their ontological assumptions and axiological intent: that is, two traditions in research that are distinct in the assumptions they make about the nature of reality, and in their purpose and the type of value they seek to produce. One tradition is focused on developing and auditing technical solutions to educational problems. Biesta terms this tradition the *technological view of education*. He does this without any intention to allude to educational technology, but instead to put to work a Classical machine metaphor to convey the ontology upon which such purposes are based. From Biesta's technological view, education is seen "as a machinery where there are inputs, mediating variables and outcomes" (p. 16). Accordingly, from this view of education, research ought to focus on determining which and in what manner inputs and variables can be manipulated to produce particular outcomes. In relation to technology usage, I have previously termed this an *input–output* approach (Lynch 2006, p. 32), where there is an assumption that a technological artefact "can be inserted into an educational setting to create a particular effect." Similarly, Bigum (2000) discussed what he termed category-based approaches to investigating educational innovation, where inquiry seeks to develop predictive models. Such approaches are attractive because they appear to be 'scientific', to allow for gen-eralisation and replication, and to be fundable and assessable in straightforward ways.

In contrast, Biesta's second tradition is based on an understanding of education as "open, semiotic and recursive" (Biesta 2015, p. 16), consistent with ontologies of immanence that preclude the pre-programming of results. This research tradition focuses on developing understandings of the complexity of educational practice. Biesta—perhaps unhelpfully for our purposes—terms this second tradition a *non-technological view of education*. It is worth taking a moment to consider this metaphor in relation to the focus of this chapter to see how else a machine metaphor might be conceived and utilised. As argued in Lynch (2006), an input–output approach is just one way of conceiving of a technological artefact, and I want to argue here that machines and their usage look different when we start from an ontological basis that recognises the indeterminacy of technology and its emergence through practice. In a move to reclaim a more nuanced and generative under-standing of the term *technology*, I will proceed here to employ Biesta's distinction, but to refer to the first of these views as consistent with at *technicist view of educational technology* and the second as consistent with a *sociomaterial view of educational technology*, where the latter recognises that technological artefacts emerge through practice and in relation with other entities.

The distinction between technicist and sociomaterial views is useful when characterising different conceptions of teaching. A focus on developing solutions is aligned with a technicist view of teaching, where teaching practice and the effects it produces are conceived in linear ways, where particular outcomes can be pro-grammed into the system, and where risks can be contained. This view of teaching aligns with a view of teacher professionalism as entailing a suite of profession-specific competencies (Connell 2009). Thus, technicist views of edu-cation provide for the positing of context-specific capabilities, strategies and resources that might be assembled to constitute a best practice, and that might be supported in equally linear ways via the production of classroom-ready teaching graduates by teacher education facilities, or the provision of skills to practising teacher via in-service training. Technicist views of education, teaching, teachers and teacher education—and the managerial policies and practices they support—have attracted much academic critique, not to mention professional suspicion and contempt. Amongst complaints of their implicit scientism and Classical logics, they are seen as driven by new managerialist (Davies 2003) motives rather than foundational and contemporary knowledges associated with the discipline of education, and, as failing to adequately account for the complexities of professional practice.

In contrast, sociomaterial views of education (where my own biases reside) derive from a recognition that "teaching's daily reality is an improvised assemblage" (Connell 2009, p. 219). Teaching is understood as a highly complex, non-linear undertaking, where there are no straightforward formulas, solutions or sets of actions that will translate into particular effects or *outcomes*. This view understands teaching practice to emerge as an assemblage of sociomaterial actors in ways that are difficult to capture and contain within the logics of competency-based frameworks. Instead, sociomaterial views support understandings of quality professional practice as alert to emergent opportunities, where resources are deployed in inventive, improvised ways that cannot be pre-programmed.

The bulk of published research into educational technology is based on assumptions aligned with a technicist view of education, with a focus on determining relationships between inputs and outputs, and on how mediating factors—such as teacher competency and teacher behaviours—might be directed to support desired outcomes. Selwyn (2010)—also citing on Biesta—provides a critique of the emphasis on *effective learning* found in educational technology research, as well as the related emphasis on the 'state of the art' in educational technology resources and practices. In the former, we see an abstract focus on how people learn with technology and a neglect of the social, political, economic, cultural and historical-material specificities of technology usage. In the latter we see the development of visions of perfect systems that fail to account for the actualities of schools and classrooms. Such approaches are dogged by the realities of education where a 'best practice' will not necessarily translate into predicted learning outcomes or even be seen as desirable within a particular educational setting. The discursive politics of such inquiries is rarely helpful. Technicist approaches to educational technology research position practising teachers and students and their everyday classrooms as inadequate. They favour the reproduction of knowledge and skills (and indeed existing power relations) despite an often-stated focus on innovation, and they fail to connect to what might be innovative in the everyday. These approaches emerge from undisclosed normative politics and agendas of reproduction that foreground deficiencies and failure, and that blind us to emergent practices and the small 'i' innovation that is the mainstay of contemporary classrooms.

50.4 Alternate Understandings of Teacher Technology Practice

Education researchers working with practice theory draw on theoretical resources that are diverse in their genesis but often cognate in their onto-epistemological sensibilities (Lynch et al. 2017). Practice theory provides alternatives to technicist understandings of practice. Through dialogues between onto-epistemological considerations and close-up empirical engagements, research informed by practice theory supports the production of new understandings of what professional practice is, how it comes to be, and how it might change (Lynch et al. 2017). One manifestation of practice theory that has proved efficacious in relation to understanding technology practices is the sociomaterialism described by Fenwick (2012), where:

- Practice is understood as material, embodied and relational;
- Practice formations are understood as contingent, requiring ongoing sociomaterial negotiations; and,
- Enquiries into practice resist the bracketing off of particular entities and locales as taken for granted or as mere context to the matter in focus, and instead seek to trace the sociomaterial movements that together work to constitute, for example, a technological artefact as practised.

From this view of practice, all entities—human and nonhuman—are understood as emerging in relation with diverse arrays of sociomatter—with people, with tools, with texts, with happenings past and future. Within educational technology research, sociomaterial approaches lead us to examine how new materials and tools become configured through practice within institutionalised settings such as schools and classrooms: that is, how they manifest in relation with other elements, how these relations are enacted and maintained and how reconfiguration occurs. Such approaches bring into view how the introduction of new technologies into classrooms necessarily articulates with other aspects of classroom practice (including more traditional information and communication technologies) in complex ways, thus highlighting the artificiality of a distinction between teachers' technology work and their other work.

Close attention to the specificity of practice and the ongoing co-constitution of entities supports new understandings of innovation as an everyday occurrence that affirms the productive everyday work of teachers and students. These alternative understandings are quite distinct from technicist conceptualisations of innovation as introduced into a field of practice from elsewhere. Influential cultural theorist, Michel de Certeau, provides a conceptualisation of everyday practice that is useful here, where the everyday usage of cultural products is seen as a productive re-deployment, characterised by microinnovations. Within de Certeau's conceptualisation, usage of machines, tools, techniques and ideas is never a straightforward implementation—a transference of some imagined, ideal usage into a particular site —but instead is always a creative act: what de Certeau (1984 trans) termed *reuse* (see especially Chap. 3—*Making do': Uses and tactics*—and also the final chapter in de Certeau's 1974 (trans) book *Culture in the Plural*). This framing of usage provides us with an understanding of everyday practice as necessarily and always innovative—involving an ongoing, improvised and often playful negotiation and remix of materials and ideas—and an understanding of innovation as a prolific and ubiquitous phenomenon.

The language frequently used in government educational technology policies and interventions—for example, metaphors such as 'road maps' and 'blue prints'— is flawed from a sociomaterial view of educational technology. This language implies that a pathway to a particular vision can be mapped out in advanced and specified in detailed and predictable ways, that practice flows in a linear manner from policy, and that practice can be measured and tracked in non-problematic ways. Sociomaterial views of innovation suggest that we need new ways of thinking about educational change and technology that are quite distinct from the technological determinism that infuses education policy and the discursive politics that position teachers as underprepared or resistant receivers of innovation. Rowan (2012) offers an alternative view of change in her discussion of equity reform, arguing that microinnovation and iterative change in schools is a more likely scenario than large-scale reform by external intervention. Rowan puts teachers at the centre of this type of change, which she argues occurs when teachers employ axiological dispositions based on suspicion of essentialist claims and recognition of the active production of meanings. Within this view, meanings are not produced by individuals but are co-produced and "policed" (p. 57) in multiple ways. Because they are produced, they are contingent (rather than essential), but because their production is brought about via complex, interrelated entities and operations, these meanings are difficult to change. Consistent with an understanding of innovation as everyday, Rowan advocates change via a "ceaseless introduction of difference" (p. 61), a characterisation not dissimilar to the everyday proliferation of difference observed by de Certeau.

While most research literature focusing on new technologies in education can be characterised as technicist in its assumptions and as perpetuating reductive and misleading views of teacher technology practice, close-up enquiries into educational practices do attest to the existence and value of everyday innovation; though often such enquiries do not take new technology as their starting points. For example, Handsfield et al. (2010) undertook a microethnographic approach to investigating preservice teachers' literacy education pedagogy, focusing on what they term "the microscopic and everyday" (p. 405) and drawing on theoretical resources provided by Bakhtin and de Certeau. Their combination of "syncretic theoretical framing and micro-level analytical approach" (p. 408) supported an analysis of the interactions between structuring forces and everyday micro-level operations, such as teachers' creative adaptation of curriculum resources and policy narratives. Similarly, Lynch and Herbert (2015, p. 300) drew upon de Certeau's conceptualisation of everyday practice to recast what might have been seen as teachers' failure and resistance to innovate in science education. Instead, they refigure divergence from top-down initiatives as evidence of teachers' "tactical redeployment of available discursive (and material) resources". This supports a conceptualisation of teachers' everyday professional practice, where microinnovation is a defining characteristic. Focusing on the development of a web-based authoring system for use in teaching and learning at one university, Bigum (2000) drew on the theoretical resources of actor–network theory to trace the ways that human and nonhuman actors are translated via a series of mutual negotiations as they make alliances with other actors. Bigum (2000, p. 20) argues that, although their promise of abstraction and generalisation make causal models of innovation attractive, they are of little practical value when innovations are necessarily "messy, always involve compromise and translation and are fundamentally political".

50.5 Considering Teacher Education

I have provided a critique of technicist conceptions of teacher technology practice, and argued in support of sociomaterial views where practices cannot be contained within a set of predetermined skills or recipes for producing particular effects or *outcomes*. So what are the implications of sociomaterial conceptions of teacher technology practice for teacher education? Within a sociomaterial ontological framing, it might seem contradictory to offer a 'roadmap' for teacher education, so I offer instead some principles for consideration, principles that I see as having potential to support generative practices within teacher education. A technicist approach to teacher education would prescribe a set of skills to be transferred to preservice teachers—those skills seen as the currency of the contemporary ICT tools and processes. Explicit teaching of particular skills has long been recognised as inadequate within an ICT context: even within computing degrees, university educators have long sought to develop undergraduates' understandings of key principles rather than specific skills that in the context of rapid technological change will soon become redundant. Understandings of how ICT skills are commonly learnt have also changed—no longer do teachers step students through operations necessary to make a particular device or piece of software work, and no longer are instructional manuals seen as a useful resource. We develop skills in the use of these tools *by using them*, and it is through this usage that the characters of tools are co-produced (Lynch 2006). This understanding about the development of ICT skills is recognised in much of the educational technology literature that focuses instead on *technology integration*, in that it emphasises that preservice teachers' operational skills ought to be developed in the context of curriculum-based teaching and learning. This can be seen when ICT skills are incorporated into curriculum methods courses so technology use with respect to particular areas of school curriculum and particular pedagogical approaches can be modelled and learnt. However, from a sociomaterial view, concepts like *technology integration* and the goals and assumptions of pedagogies seeking to model particular usages are equally flawed. These approaches seek to reproduce curriculum and curriculum-associated teaching methods, where technological innovation is seen as a diffusion of ways and means of doing the same, but better and quicker. Not surprisingly, these approaches produce familiar criticisms and discursive positionings of teacher educators as both unprepared and unwilling to change from old ways to new.

So how can teacher education programmes prepare teachers for an unprogrammable technological practice? Here I offer two tentative and interrelated points for consideration, as well as a source of contradiction or doubleness that questions the whole enterprise of preparing teachers to use technology. First, in an effort to move ourselves (teacher educators) and our preservice-teacher students beyond the technicist assumptions that tend to dominate popular understandings and expectations of teacher preparation, sociomaterial approaches can be supported by opportunities for explicit engagement with ontological questions. It is very easy to be seduced into conversations about the latest device or the latest app, but this sort of conversation needs to be complemented by substantive conversations about the nature of technology and the nature of technology practice. My first point is to suggest that teacher education programmes engage preservice teachers in robust, philosophical debate of questions such as: what is technology? and what is innovation? These types of questions lead us to consider both ontological assumptions and institutional and historical settings in ways that offer a critique of dominant positionings of technology, teachers and innovation.

It is one thing to consider in abstract terms the implications of ontologies of emergence, but it is more powerful to consider this with reference to specific examples of situated, emergent practice. My second point for consideration is that teacher education programmes provide opportunities for preservice teachers to practice technology—this is not a practising of particular operational skills (though even that would evidence instances of microinnovation if we looked closely enough), but a usage of materials and tools in ways that make visible the *reuse* of technological artefacts. Engaging in both usage *and* explicit examination of usage as *reuse* may well support the development of operational skills and indeed knowledge about technology integration as it is commonly understood, but more importantly it supports the recognition and affirmation of innovation in the everyday. Teacher educators and preservice teachers may well engage in practices that are novel in obvious ways (e.g. using a new device within an established curriculum area), but we should also be invited to notice the novel in the everyday. This type of work provides both critical and productive spaces, where preservice teachers in dialogue with teacher educators can develop their own critiques of commonly held assumptions and their own ways of introducing difference into institutionalised ways of doing teaching and learning. This type of work can also be complemented by opportunities for inquiry into the everyday microinnovations of others—for example, that of children's everyday use of technologies in schools and in homes.

These points taken together might support preservice teachers to develop their own practice-oriented thinking and indeed their own teaching-with-technology practice. However, there is a contradiction that emerges when these two points are considered side by side and indeed with the whole concept of teacher technology practice. The types of engagements that I suggest here—those concerning ontological questions around technology—almost always lead us to an understanding that new technologies are not substantively different to not-so-new technologies. Teaching has always been a mediated practice that connects all manner of technology—inscribing devices, techniques and routines, voice and gesture, furniture and architecture. The closer we look at so-called new technologies, the more meaningless conceptual boundaries between new and more traditional technologies become, and the term technology itself starts to fade away. Philosophically speaking, this understanding poses a challenge to treating educational technology as a special domain within teacher education programmes. Yet the history of teacher education (and of previously institutionalised tools and techniques) is present in the logics and structures of such programmes (particular materials, tools and techniques are privileged over others and marked for deliberate reproduction), and the symbolic force of popular representations of 'new technologies' cannot be ignored within this arrangement. Equally, the special status ascribed to new technologies in government education policies and in popular discourse does sociomaterial work that is part of teaching practice assemblages, even when those assemblages involves critiques of and resistance to dominant positionings.

50.6 Conclusion

In this chapter, I have outlined a number of distinctions that are useful for framing a critique of educational technology policy and of common approaches to educational technology research, and for positing more generative approaches to understanding technology, teaching and innovation, including considerations for teacher education practices.

In the case of Australia, we see a high level of uptake of new technologies in schools and in the wider community. Studies that look very closely at the technology practices of teachers and students identify a proliferation of everyday innovation, yet government policies evidence old policy discourses that fail to acknowledge the everydayness of innovation, and that suggest views of teachers as ill-prepared and unwilling to engage with new technologies. Most existing educational technology research reflects this positioning of teachers, together with an externalised conception of innovation. Practice theories suggest ways of understanding the complexity of technology usage, where technology is indeterminate, emergent, and dynamically realised through practice and in relation with a mesh of both traditional and new arrangements. Sympathetic research methodologies involve both sophisticated ontological work and close-up analysis of empirical data, which together produce new ways of understanding and new ways forward for supporting teachers in their classroom work.

In research undertakings, the term *technology* should never be taken for granted because, more often than not, it *is*. In policy documents, in curriculum frameworks, in research literature, and in everyday professional talk, terms like *technology*, *technology integration* and *educational technology* are used without interrogation. If these terms make their way into research conversations, research instruments and research data without explicit examination of what the referent might be and where the problematics might lay, then research risks perpetuating undisclosed and unexamined assumptions. Similarly, following capital 'I' innovations into teaching and learning settings usually produces research findings that are referenced to those innovations (as degrees of success or failure) rather than to the practices of teachers and their students. This is not to say that policies and reform agendas developed by governments, professional bodies, and universities can or should be ignored. In current times, these policies tend to present technology, teaching and teachers in technicist ways. Analyses of the material-discursive work of policy texts are useful because these texts are a material part of teacher education practice. Combining close-up analyses of activities (what is done and what is said in specific situations and particular locations) with analyses of how these activities relate to material and discursive strategies to manage and govern professional practice can help us to tease out tensions between continuity and change, and to understand how innovation occurs often despite such strategies.

But could policy also be otherwise? Saltmarsh (2015, p. 32) argues that the "proliferation of heterogeneous practices calls instead for a conception of cultural policy that creates space for others to operate and flourish." In relation to educational technology, such policy would effect a dispersal of the discursively constructed centre of innovation as outside of schools and classrooms, recognising that innovation and change involves multiple sociomaterial negotiations that do not flow in one direction from top to bottom. Such policy would also be respectful of teachers' extant abilities and commitments and the productive cultures already found in schools, and would support visions of innovation as messy and unprogrammable and as central to the everyday work of teachers and schools.

References

Australian Government Department of Education and Training. (2013). *Beyond the classroom: A new digital education for young Australians in the 21st century.* Report of the Digital Education Advisory Group, May 31st, 2013. Commonwealth of Australia: Canberra, Australia.

Biesta, G. (2015). On the two cultures of educational research, and how we might move ahead: Reconsidering the ontology, axiology and praxeology of education. *European Educational Research Journal, 14*(1), 11–22.

Bigum, C. (2000). Actor-network theory and online university teaching: Translation versus diffusion. In B. A. Knight & L. Rowan (Eds.), *Researching futures oriented pedagogies* (pp. 7–22). Brisbane, Australia: Post Pressed.

Connell, R. (2009). Good teachers on dangerous ground: Towards a new view of teacher quality and professionalism. *Critical Studies in Education, 50*(3), 213–229.

Davies, B. (2003). Death to critique and dissent? The policies and practices of new managerialism and of "evidence-based practice". *Gender and Education, 5*(1), 91–103.

de Certeau, M. (1984). *The practice of everyday life* (S. Rendall, Trans). Los Angeles: University of California Press.

Fenwick, T. (2012). Matterings of knowing and doing: Sociomaterial approaches to understanding practice. In P. Hager et al. (Eds.), *Practice, learning and change: Practice-theory perspectives on professional learnings* (pp. 67–82). Dordrecht: Springer.

Handsfield, L. J., Crumpler, T. P., & Dean, T. R. (2010). Tactical negotiations and creative adaptations: The discursive production of literacy curriculum and teacher identities across space-times. *Reading Research Quarterly, 45*(4), 405–431.

Jordan, K. (2011). Framing ICT, teachers and learners in Australian school education ICT policy. *Australian Educational Researcher, 38*(4), 417–431.

Lynch, J. (2006). Assessing effects of technology usage on mathematics learning. *Mathematical Education Research Journal, 18*(3), 29–43.

Lynch, J., & Herbert, S. (2015). Affirming irregular spaces in a schoolwide curriculum initiative: A place for the animals. *Curriculum Inquiry, 45*(3), 285–303.

Lynch, J., Rowlands, J., Gale, T., & Skourdoumbis, A. (2017). Introduction: Diffractive readings in practice theory. In J. Lynch, J. Rowlands, T. Gale, & A. Skourdoumbis (Eds.), *Practice theory and education: Diffractive readings in professional practice*. London: Routledge.

Rowan, L. (2012). Educated hope, modest ambition and school-based equity reforms: Possibilities and perspectives for change. In L. Rowan & C. Bigum (Eds.), *Transformative approaches to new technologies and student diversity in futures oriented classrooms: Future proofing education* (pp. 45–63). Dordrecht: Springer.

Saltmarsh, S. (2015). Michel de Certeau, everyday life and cultural policy studies in education. In K. N. Gulson, M. Clarke, & E. Bendix Petersen (Eds.), *Education policy and contemporary theory: Implications for research*. Florence, KY, USA: Taylor and Francis.

Selwyn, N. (2010). Looking beyond learning: Notes towards a critical study of educational technology. *Journal of Computer Assisted Learning, 26*(1), 65–73.

Chapter 51
Capturing Science PCK Through Students' Experiences

Pernilla Nilsson

51.1 Introduction

During the last decades, there has been a growing interest within teacher education programmes regarding the effectiveness of how to prepare beginning teachers for their future profession. The inherent complexity of teacher knowledge, and hence teacher learning, has been well documented in the education research literature (e.g. Van Driel and Berry 2012). For example, educational researchers in different content areas have raised concerns of the often-experienced lack of connection between the content and curriculum of methods courses and the acquisition of knowledge that is essential for promoting students' understanding. Thus, in order to create conditions for substantial learning, a significant challenge is to provide beginning teachers with both content knowledge and pedagogical skills to make the content visible and to adjust it to students' learning needs. To meet this challenge, more knowledge is needed about how students experience classroom teaching so that they may become resources not only for developing teachers' practice but also for the way teacher education in designed and conducted. For example, Ireson and Hallam (2005) and Pietarinen (2000) noted the importance of using students' perceptions of teaching indicating that students' academic self-perceptions, together with their perceptions of teaching, contribute to the affective value of schools. What is a significant educational situation for a teacher may only be partly so for a student. In this context, it is reasonable to suggest that students' perceptions of which aspects within a teachers' professional knowledge that make difference for their learning, might inform the way teacher knowledge is captured and understood.

P. Nilsson (✉)
Halmstad University, Halmstad, Sweden
e-mail: Pernilla.Nilsson@hh.se

© Springer Nature Singapore Pte Ltd. 2017
M.A. Peters et al. (eds.), *A Companion to Research in Teacher Education*,
DOI 10.1007/978-981-10-4075-7_51

In order to teach in ways that promote students' understanding, Shulman (1986, 1987) claimed that teachers need pedagogical content knowledge (PCK), a special kind of knowledge that teachers have about how to teach particular content to particular students. PCK was originally developed to represent one of the professional knowledge bases that an expert teacher possesses, and was later described as representing "the blending of content and pedagogy into an understanding of how particular topics, problems, or issues are organised, represented, and adapted to the diverse interests and abilities of learners, and presented for instruction" (Shulman 1987, p. 8). Among researchers, there is a common assumption that high level of PCK will predict high level of student achievement and some researchers stress that PCK makes the greatest contribution to explaining student progress.

But how do teachers know if their teaching is appropriate in order to promote students' understandings? Schneider and Plasman (2011) noted that "science teachers' knowledge of students' thinking about science includes teachers' ideas about students' initial science ideas and experiences (including misconceptions), the development of science ideas (including process and sequence), how students express science ideas (including demonstration of understanding, questions, responses), challenging science ideas for students, and appropriate level of science understanding" (p. 537). Teachers' learning about their students' ideas and that these ideas are not accurate prompt them to revisit their own ideas and teaching practices. Some teachers are interested in learning what students find interesting so they could gain students' attention at the beginning of a lesson (Schneider and Plasman 2011). However, most research on teachers' PCK is built around efforts to capture teachers' reflections on their own teaching practice and less on the relation between teachers' teaching and students' learning of science. It might well be argued that in the research literature there is a lack of research that includes students' conceptualizations of PCK and what aspects within a teachers' professional knowledge make difference for their learning of science.

This chapter intends to capture PCK through a group of secondary science students' experiences and reflections on a lesson of genetics. Yerrick et al. (2011) argued that the voices of children are conspicuously lacking in the research literature. "It is a rare account when challenged students can voice any preference or offer input regarding their view of a science teacher's expertise. Yet, though they may not be invited to speak often on such matters, they have unique, important, and often impassioned perspectives on who can teach them" (p. 14). With its particular focus on identifying the *students'* experiences of aspects within a science teachers' teaching that promote their learning, the chapter brings new dimensions to earlier research on science teacher PCK. The chapter presents empirical data to discuss what aspects within their teacher's teaching the students identify as important for their learning of science and how these aspects might be conceptualised as components of PCK. As such, investigating students' experiences might improve our understanding of students' thinking about themselves as learners, as well as of teachers' knowledge of how to represent and formulate the subject to make it comprehensible for others (i.e. their PCK).

51.2 Pedagogical Content Knowledge to Promote Students' Learning

As PCK is deeply rooted in a teachers' everyday work, it is reasonable to suggest that it encompasses both theoretical dimensions as well as experiences gained from ongoing teaching activities and interactions with students. Shulman (1987) argued that developing PCK involves a considerable shift in teachers' understanding "from being able to comprehend subject matter for themselves, to becoming able to elucidate subject matter in new ways, reorganise and partition it, clothe it in activities and emotions, in metaphors and exercises, and in examples and demonstrations, so that it can be grasped by students" (p. 13). As such, the relation between teachers' teaching and students' learning is explicitly focused. Magnusson et al. (1999) described PCK as consisting of five components; (1) Orientations toward science teaching; (2) Knowledge and beliefs of science curriculum, including national, state and district standards and specific science curricula; (3) Knowledge and beliefs of student understanding of specific science topics; (4) Knowledge and beliefs of assessment in science; (5) Knowledge and beliefs of science instructional strategies for teaching science. Magnusson et al. (1999) stated that the "development of PCK is not a straightforward matter of having knowledge; it is also an intentional act in which teachers choose to reconstruct their understanding to fit a situation" (p. 111). More recently, Park and Oliver (2008) noted that the development of *one* component of PCK might simultaneously encourage the development of others, and ultimately enhance the overall PCK—suggest introduce later when you explore the idea? Because PCK includes teachers' understanding of how students learn, or fail to learn, specific subject matter, the development of PCK is an important goal to focus on in professional development programmes (Van Driel and Berry 2012). Therefore, if we can identify PCK as the knowledge that teachers use in the process of teaching, our understanding of what 'good science teaching' looks like and how to develop this more consistently might be enhanced.

According to Park and Oliver (2008), PCK development means the development of single components of PCK or the integration of these components linking them with one another. Park et al. (2011) developed an instrument, the PCK rubric, to measure the level of a teacher's PCK based on observations of the teachers teaching and pre-/post-observation interviews. Their instrument was initially grounded in the Parks and Oliver's (2008) pentagon model in which PCK was defined as an integrated knowledge of five components; Orientations to Teaching Science, Knowledge of Students' Understanding in Science, Knowledge of Science Curriculum, Knowledge of Instructional Strategies and Representations for Teaching Science and Knowledge of Assessment of Science Learning. Park and Oliver (2008) noted that on one hand, the development of one component of PCK might simultaneously encourage the development of others, and ultimately enhance the overall PCK. However, for the students to learn a specific content, it might well be asserted that a teachers' PCK must be built around an integration of all aspects of teacher knowledge in highly complex ways. "Thus, lack of coherence among the components would be problematic within an individual's developing PCK and increased knowledge of a single component may not be sufficient to stimulate change in practice" (p. 266). Park et al. (2011) PCK rubric was designed to measure only two key components (i.e. knowledge of student understanding with respect to a certain subject matter (KSU) and knowledge of instructional strategies and representations of the subject matter (KISR) among the five components). Taken into account the specific design of *this* particular project, it might be reasonable to suggest that these two components are the ones that students' participation will inform the most. Teachers need to understand what students already know about a topic, what those students are likely to have difficulty with in learning the topic, and what concepts that need to be challenged (Park et al. 2011).

51.3 Design of the Project

The study presented in this chapter is conducted in a secondary science classroom (year 9, 15 year) in which an experienced science teacher taught a lesson of genetics. The lesson lasted for about 1 hour and the students should learn the difference between dominant and recessive characteristics. They should also work with punnet squares to find out if two brown-eyed parents can have blue-eyed children. The teacher had participated in a three years professional development project and had, through earlier research (Nilsson 2014), been documented as possessing a high level of PCK.

The lesson was video recorded and the video was reflected with the approach of a video club (Sherin and Han 2004; Van Es and Sherin 2008). In general, video clubs are used to stimulate teachers' reflections and interpretations of their own teaching, to build on each other's ideas and to support the development of a shared language in a team of teachers. Sharing of classroom videos in so-called video clubs might help teachers shift the focus towards the relation between their own teaching and their students' thinking and learning (Sherin and Han 2004; Van Es and Sherin 2008). As such, involving teachers in video clubs provides shared reflections on authentic clips from own and colleagues classrooms. Sherin and Han (2004) emphasise the opportunities in engaging teachers in activities where they do not have to respond immediately to the situation, and where reflection and fine-grained analysis can be supported by repeated watching of certain interactions. They report on results from teachers that indicate that the discourse changed over time from a primary focus on the teacher to increased attention to students' actions and ideas, and that the teachers' analyses of student ideas grew to be increasingly detailed. van Es and Sherin (2008) focus on the challenge for teachers to develop a professional vision (i.e. teachers' ability to notice and interpret significant features of a practice) and claim that learning to notice, the development of professional vision, consists of three main aspects: (1) identifying what is important in a teaching situation, (2) using what one knows to reason about the situation and (3) making connections between the specific events and broader principles of teaching and learning.

There have been a large number of studies on in-service teachers' video clubs (Sherin and Han 2004; van Es and Sherin 2008), but less research on how students can collaboratively analyse video from their own school experiences. Therefore, this study might provide a methodological contribution to the way teacher knowledge (i.e. PCK) is captured and enhanced.

In the video clubs for this particular project, the students were encouraged to focus on what happened during the lesson, how the teacher made their learning possible and how the teacher communicated the content in a way that made it accessible for them as learners. During the video clubs, 12 students (three groups of four students) participated voluntarily in the collaborative reflections. In order to stimulate the students' reflections, a research assistant (a student teacher) participated to ask questions (e.g. what within the teachers' teaching actions help or constrain your learning processes and why?), and to challenge the students' ideas when analysing the video. The research assistant was familiar with the students and she had carefully explained to them that her intention was not to assess or "judge" the teacher, but to learn more about how the teacher's way of handling the content also had an impact on the students' learning.

The video clubs were held in a separate room in the school and the atmosphere was relaxed. The reflections in the video club were conducted as a semi-structured interview, which both allowed the research assistant to ask prompting and challenging questions and provided an open space for the students' own thoughts and reflections. The video clubs lasted for about two hours and all three sessions were video recorded and transcribed verbatim to provide a deep analysis of the aspects that the students brought up in their reflections. The qualitative data obtained from the video clubs provided insights into the students' experiences of what aspects within their teacher's teaching that helped them in their learning. The video clubs were conducted after the school day. Hence the students participated during their free time. Therefore, it was decided that only one lesson should be video recorded. However, even though the study covered only one particular lesson, it still provided the opportunity to make an in depth analysis of both the video-recorded lesson and the 6 hours of video clubs.

51.4   Analysis

Data analysis involved two steps: *First*, and most importantly, the video-recorded lesson was analysed with a sharp focus on how the teachers enacted the specific content in the lesson and how the teacher strove to make learning possible for students. *Second*, the transcribed tape recordings from the three video clubs were analysed through content analysis (applied in the way described by Miles and Huberman 1994) in order to identify aspects that the students identified as being important for their learning. A content analysis of this kind is based on the view that it facilitates the production of core constructs from textual data (e.g. a systematic method of, data reduction; data display; and, conclusion drawing and verification). In this way, the primary mode of analysis was the development of categories from data into a framework that captured the key themes of how the students described aspects of PCK.

51.5   The Lesson

When starting the lesson the teacher introduced a "warm-up-task". The task was designed around the question "Discuss which characteristics are inherited and which are acquired among humans. Give examples, first individually and then together with a peer." As soon as the students entered the classroom they started to discuss the task with lots of engagement. The teacher was walking around in the classroom and reasoned with the students about what is inherited and what is achieved. After 10 minutes the teacher closed the door and introduced the lesson. He formulated the aim of the lesson on the whiteboard and explained to the students that they were going to focus on dominant and recessive genes. He continued with presenting the different concepts that they were going to work with during the lesson; dominant and recessive characteristics, allele, homozygote, heterozygote and cross-schemes. The three goals formulated on the whiteboard were:

- To learn the difference between dominant and recessive characteristics.
- To learn some examples of dominant and recessive characteristics.
- With the help of a punnet square, to discuss if two brown-eyed parents can have a blue-eyed child.

During the lesson and while explaining to the students, the teacher completed a concept map on the whiteboard. Through the concept map he wanted to help the students to see the linkages between the concepts and provide examples of different characteristics. Further to the concept map, he also drew two different cross-scheme for blue and brown eyes.

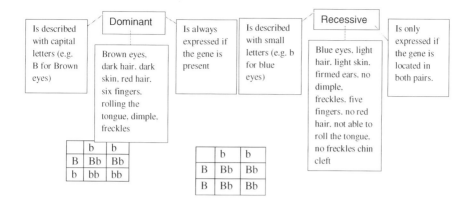

Before the lesson ended the teacher asked the students to discuss (individually and in pairs) if two brown-eyed parents can have a blue-eyed child. He also asked the students to draw a cross-scheme that showed how brown, respectively, blue eyes are inherited.

51.6 Students' Experiences and Perceptions of Their Learning from the Lesson

The result highlights several aspects that the 12 students identified as important for their learning of science. For example, the teachers' ability to link the content to students' everyday experiences (which might differ from the teacher's everyday experience); to highlight similarities and differences between the concepts; to use knowledge of students' previous understandings and engagement in the teaching activities; and, the teachers' subject matter knowledge and enthusiasm for the content.

51.6.1 Linking the Content to Students' Everyday Experiences

Being confronted by why something is important to teach can have important benefits not only for what is taught, but also how that teaching is conducted; another crucial aspect of a PCK. An important factor that the students raised was how the teacher helped them see the connections between the various science concepts and phenomena and their everyday life experiences. A common problem in science education is that the students do not always find science as meaningful and relevant. In the lesson, the teacher used analogies and examples from his own family, friends and from famous sportsmen such as Zlatan Ibrahimovic.

Student 9: Yes there are good examples, so it's not something totally weird, which you cannot relate to.
Student 7: And it's good when he takes "familiar" examples such as Zlatans nose. Yes, we all know how it looks like.

The teachers' way of providing meaningful metaphors and analogies that are connected to everyday life seemed to be an important aspect that made difference for the students' learning of science. The students also stressed the importance of providing examples that were relevant for them as learners. According to them, too often teachers try to give examples that they think connects to students' everyday but instead the examples are grown out of the "world of adults" (*student 7*). All three groups highlighted that this particular teacher was well aware of them, both as individuals and as learners, and in such way he most often managed to connect the examples to their interests and previous knowledge. The way he used his knowledge of the students both as learners (i.e. students' preconceptions and learning difficulties) and as individuals (i.e. their interests outside school) provides evidence of how his knowledge of students' understanding was integrated in his classroom practice.

Student 9: He makes it so simple; he is really committed and takes examples from our lives that we all can relate to. That makes sense.
Student 4: It's difficult if you just get the facts, and no examples … and to know how everything is interrelated.
Student 5: Well the teacher may present the main points and just when he takes those examples he tends to build on the examples and go a little bit further. If we understand some aspect that are not really connected to science and then pull these ideas into the natural sciences as an example, it is easier to understand how it is connected.

Most importantly, students expressed that the teacher helped them see how science connects to their everyday life, which stretched beyond the traditional notion that science is merely a subject in school.

Student 5: Yes, he normally manages to highlight the most important aspects within the content and when he brings in the different examples from the real world we understand much better. If we understand the context outside the science area and then takes the science into our already perceived understanding, it is easier to get a connection. Yes, he normally manages to do all these things.

The students also highlighted how they experienced the way the teacher brought up examples from his own personal life as engaging. For example, when he talked about his own child and how she had inherited his characteristics they expressed that they could better relate to the scientific concept.

Student 7: When he takes a personal example you can see that he feels confident as a teacher.
Student 4: It is difficult to understand if we just get the facts and no concrete examples. Then it is so much more difficult to understand how everything is connected to the real world.

51.6.2 Focusing on Similarities and Differences Between Concepts and Phenomena

In science teaching, many teachers emphasise the importance of taking one thing at a time and thus reduce the complexity, which is especially common in science education. On example might be that in order to understand the greenhouse effect you need to know about the gas carbon dioxide and how the gas is created in a car. Normally, students are taught about the gas carbon dioxide first and then, often much later, about the green house effect. The same applies to atoms and ions. Normally atoms are taught in year six and ions in year eight. This view was challenged in the students' reflections as they highlighted that the meaning of phenomena to a large extent is determined by how the specific phenomena differ from another phenomena (e.g. the difference between an atom and an ion). Several of the students emphasised that they found it easier to understand the science concepts when the teacher specifically focused on the similarities and differences between concepts instead of presenting the concepts alone.

> Student 3: Well now he compares the different concepts.
> Student 2: You can clearly see the differences and similarities.
> Student 1: Yes, you see concretely what belongs to what and what differs the concepts from each other.
> Student 3: Yes, it's great when he contrasts the two… like what are the differences between recessive and dominant genes?

Consequently, for a teacher it may be better to contrast things with each other and focusing on the differences between them, than to take them one at a time. Instead of first teaching about the atom, then introducing the molecule and then the ion to help students finally understand what happens within a chemical reaction between sodium and chloride, these can be taught together at the same time, focusing on the similarities and differences between the concepts. The students also highlighted that the way the teacher carefully chose his examples also helped them in their learning.

> Student 1: In this lesson we talk about eye colour and he (teacher) explains how the colour appears. It is good that he keeps up to one aspect and follows the common thread and that he does not start to talk about plenty of different characteristics. Then he will probably loose us.

As was indicated, the students' emphasised that the way the teacher organised the content within his teaching made difference for how the content was understood, hence an important aspect of PCK.

51.6.3   Using Knowledge of Students' Previous Understandings and Engagement in the Teaching Activities

Knowledge of students' previous conceptions is as an issue to which teachers should pay attention but which is often experienced as a demanding challenge. Knowing about difficulties and limitations is only a starting point for actually being able to recognise and work with them in the teaching activity. Further, being able to plan teaching activities around students' thinking and commonly held ideas about the topic (i.e. knowledge of student understanding with respect to a certain subject matter) is at the heart of this aspect of PCK. One aspect that the students raised as important for their learning was the teachers' knowledge of their thinking and previous understandings, and how he used different activities to engage them in their learning. In the video club, one of the students mentions that the teacher always makes effort into learning about their thinking and previous understandings.

> Student 6: One thing that I really appreciate with our teacher is that he often gives us different questions on papers to find out what we know about different phenomena. This is a really good way for him to learn more about our thinking and what he needs to do to make us understand better. When he collected all our papers he also understood what he needed to work with.

This indicates that the way the teachers strove to consider students' previous interests, engagement and motivation were aspects emphasised as important for students' learning.

Being able to build on students' engagement in discussions and argumentations about different science concepts is indicative to a teacher's knowledge of instructional strategies and representations of the subject matter (KISR) and hence, an important aspect of PCK. In their reflections the students highlighted how they became engaged in their science learning when the teacher encouraged them to discuss and communicate different concepts.

> Student 1: Yes, it's a sort of discussion then, it's fun because it makes the lesson interesting.
> Student 3: Yes, it is interesting when we talk and really argue about the different things. It is when you are forced to argument you really need to be aware of what the concept actually stands for.
> Student 1: I think this is better than if the teacher just stands and writes at the whiteboard, so it is better that we get the possibility to reason.
> Student 3: Then you remember it better too.

These active elements of the lesson was a natural feature, the teacher alternated video, group discussions and regular lecturing at the whiteboard. Everything the teacher did was conscious and his purpose was that he wanted to reach out to as many students as possible. The teacher was also very careful with providing different forms of explanations in order to meet the students' learning needs.

> Student 5: It is good to discuss the different concepts because the more you talk the more you learn about it.

However, the students expressed how they experienced difficulties when one concept has more than one name. Very often the teacher wants to meet students learning difficulties through making them aware of several synonyms of one particular concept. However, in the video club one student expressed how he experienced this as confusing.

> Student 1: It can be good to know that there are two words for the same concept but in the same time it might be confusing if he (teacher) does not explain this explicitly.

In summary, the teachers way of making the reason about different phenomena provided them with opportunities to exchange experiences, to share each other's ideas and to listen to each other's explanations. Through their communication they became more engaged both in terms of their learning of the science content and the activities provided in the lesson.

51.6.4 Subject Matter Knowledge and Enthusiasm for the Content

Seeing teaching and content as being in a dynamic relationship is certainly indicative of understanding knowledge of practice through the lens of PCK. In order to do that, a teacher needs to master the content in a way that also makes him/her confident in providing metaphors and various explanations for the students. All three groups of students emphasised the teachers' subject matter knowledge as an important aspect for their learning of the content. In the discussions, all groups noted that some teachers are more focused on *how* to do things (e.g. group works, discussions) and on the national tests, that on discussing the actual content (in this case genetics). In their reflections, the students highlighted that this particular teacher always had a strong focus on the content to be taught and they experienced that he had good subject matter knowledge. In order to discuss with the students, link the concepts to everyday experiences and provide accessible explanations the teacher used his subject matter knowledge in a way that the students' experienced as making them feel confident. However, two students (student 1 and 2) highlighted the importance for the teacher not only to know about the content but also to be able to keep the focus on the specific content to be learnt and not involve too many issues at the same time.

> Student 3: I just want to say one thing; it's so good when the teacher knows the content in such detail… then he can explain better and you just feel safe because you know that he will be able to explain in many different ways…
> Student 1: But in the same time, I think that sometimes he explains too much and involves too many things so even though you as a teacher are aware of the content you still need to be able to sort out those things that we must learn. Giving too much information can also be a little bit messy.

The students also felt that when the teacher showed interest and had a positive attitude towards his subject they became more engaged.

> Student 8: He is nice, positive and structured. I really appreciate that he always explains to us what is the aim of the lesson and what we should achieve.
> Student 9: He is really determined and committed and he makes all of us really engaged in our own learning.

Further, a well-structured lesson with a clear formulated and communicated goal (i.e. science Big Idea) made it easier for them to understand the specific content. Some students highlighted that they often experience that teachers present so many different things in one lesson so that they seem to loose the aim and the specific goals for learning. In terms of the teachers' PCK, the teachers' content knowledge as well as his enthusiasm seemed to be important both for the students' interest for science and for their attitudes towards their own learning processes.

51.7 Discussion—Learning About Teaching from Students

As Shulman noted PCK is "… the most powerful analogies, illustrations, examples, explanations, and demonstrations—in a word, the ways of representing and formulating the subject that makes it comprehensible for others" (Shulman 1986, p. 9). This project pays attention to how specific content becomes (or not) comprehensible for students through capturing a teachers' PCK through students' voices. As noted, listening and paying attention to students' views and experiences might the chapter strives to give a new perspective to science teacher knowledge and how to involve the learner into capturing a teacher's PCK. Shulman (1986) noted that two main components of teacher knowledge is (a) knowledge of instructional strategies incorporating representations of subject matter and responses to specific learning difficulties and (b) knowledge of student conceptions with respect to that subject matter. Both these components are strongly supported within students' reflections in the video clubs. The students noted that the teacher must be able to quickly pick up his/her subject knowledge when students ask questions and give different analogies and examples that give students a context.

The teacher picked up example after example and enriched the science content with different analogies and metaphors in order to promote students' understanding of the subject area. The teacher had the "fingertip feeling" when he wove together the context and content, in a very skilful way. Further, his affective skills (engagement, personality and joy) relates well with Shulman's (2015) notion that "The affective aspects of teacher understanding and action are important both because a lot of what teachers 'know and do' is connected to their own affective and motivation states, as well as their ability to influence the feelings, motives, persistence, and identity formation processes of their students (p. 9)".

Regardless of how researchers and teachers identify PCK, the importance of providing students with opportunities to identify that which makes it easy or difficult to learn is crucial. As noted by Yerrick et al. (2011) good teachers know that each student has a story to tell. In research, students' stories are understood to contain windows of students' culture, prior experiences and genres of discourse that need to be considered when teaching science. "Such a perspective informs educators not only about how children learn best but also what children expect from the teachers why they would allow others to teach them" (p. 33).

As the students noted, in order to promote their learning and engagement, there is a need to keep the content on a level that anyone can understand but still challenge those who are knowledgeable. Most importantly, students expressed how science education connects to their everyday life, which stretched far beyond the traditional notion that science is merely a subject in school. In using the students' views to capture that which makes it easy or difficult to understand makes an important contribution to the research field of teachers' PCK as well as to the practice of science teaching in secondary school. As such, the study presented in this chapter responds to the urgent call to focus direct attention on the relation between science teacher knowledge (framed by PCK) and the students' learning of science.

The varied perspectives on PCK have in many ways, however, strengthened the value of the construct, in particular for implementation in teacher development programmes. In the context of teacher education, this might imply that beginning teachers need to identify aspects in their own teaching that make difference for their students' learning of particular content, and consequently, come up with an approach to challenge students' needs. As indicated in this study, students feel supported when their teachers listen to them and help them to learn and understand. Shulman (1987) described PCK as "the capacity of a teacher to transform the content knowledge he or she possesses into forms that are pedagogically powerful" (p. 15). Therefore, as noted by Driel and Berry (2012) "the development of PCK goes beyond the acquisition of instructional strategies and techniques, per se, to include an understanding of how students develop insights in specific subject matter" (p. 27). Thus, one primary challenge for the teacher is to seek commitment from students' experiences and perceptions about their own learning.

51.8 Conclusion

As indicated in this chapter, students have several ideas about what is effective concerning teaching and learning of science and thus, they are ready to participate in developing classroom teaching. Pietarinen (2000) indicated that students expect that the teacher's choice of methods should pay attention to both the former and future learning environments of the individual student and to the character of the social community. Students do value the subject matter taught, the teachers' command of their subject, and the teaching methods they employ. But they are often dissatisfied with the teachers' ability to show flexibility (Pietarinen 2000). It might well be argued that a sign of teachers' professionalism is to be able to analyse students' experiences to develop teaching strategies that meet students' needs. It is especially important that teachers should attempt to situate the content of their lessons within the context of *students'* everyday life, both at school and out of school. The qualities required of teachers should thus include more reflection and evaluation of the practical experiences of the teaching and of supporting the students' skills together with the students. As such, teachers might cultivate the ability to view the classroom as a pedagogical environment for developing PCK from a perspective that reflects the experience of the students.

References

Ireson, J., & Hallam, S. (2005). Pupils' liking for school: Ability grouping, self-concept and perceptions of teaching. *British Journal of Educational Psychology, 75*(2), 297–311.

Magnusson, S., Krajcik, J., & Borko, H. (1999). Nature, sources, and development of Pedagogical content knowledge for science teachers. In J. Gess-Newsome & N. G. Lederman (Eds.), *Examining pedagogical content knowledge* (pp. 95–132). Dordrecht: Kluwer Academic Publishers.

Miles, M., & Huberman, A. (1994). *Qualitative data analysis* (2nd ed.). CA: Sage Thousand Oaks.

Nilsson, P. (2014). When teaching makes a difference: Developing science teachers' pedagogical content knowledge through learning study. *International Journal of Science Education, 36*(11), 1794–1814.

Park, S., Jang, J.-Y., Chen, Y.-C., & Jung, J. (2011). Is pedagogical content knowledge (PCK) necessary for reformed science teaching? Evidence from an empirical study. *Research in Science Education, 41,* 245–260.

Park, S., & Oliver, J. S. (2008). Revisiting the conceptualisation of pedagogical content knowledge (PCK): PCK as a conceptual tool to understand teachers as professionals. *Research in Science Education, 38,* 261–284.

Pietarinen, J. (2000). Transfer to and study at secondary school in finnish school culture: developing schools on the basis of pupils' experiences. *International Journal of Educational Research, 33*(4), 383–400.

Schneider, R. M., & Plasman, K. (2011). Science teacher learning progressions: A review of science teachers' pedagogical content knowledge development. *Review of Educational Research, 81*(4), 530–565.

Sherin, M. G., & Han, S. Y. (2004). Teacher learning in the context of a video club. *Teaching and Teacher Education, 20,* 163–183.

Shulman, L. S. (1986). Those who understand: Knowledge growth in teaching. *Educational Researcher, 15*(2), 4–14.

Shulman, L. S. (1987). Knowledge and teaching: Foundations of the new reform. *Harvard Educational Review, 57*(1), 1–22.

Shulman, L. S. (2015). PCK: Its genesis and exodus. In A. Berry, P. Friedrichsen, & J. Loughran (Eds.), *Re-examining pedagogical content knowledge*. Oxford: Routledge.

Van Driel, J. H., & Berry, A. (2012). Teacher professional development focusing on pedagogical content knowledge. *Educational Researcher, 41*(1), 26–38.

van Es, E. A., & Sherin, M. G. (2008). Mathematics teachers' learning to notice in the context of a video-club. *Teaching and Teacher Education, 24*(2), 244–276.

Yerrick, R., Schiller, J., & Reisfeld, J. (2011). "Who are you Callin' expert?": Using student narratives to redefine expertise and advocacy lower track science. *Journal of Research in Science Teaching, 48*(1), 13–36.

Author Biography

Pernilla Nilsson is a professor in Science Education, Halmstad University, Sweden. Her research focuses on teachers' and student–teachers' development of Pedagogical Content Knowledge in science education, working with Content Representations (CoRe), Learning Study, video and digital portfolios to stimulate reflection and help teachers and student teachers engage in their professional learning.

Chapter 52
Teacher Sense-Making in School-Based Curriculum Development Through Critical Collaborative Professional Enquiry

Mark Priestley and Valerie Drew

52.1 Introduction

The success or otherwise of mandated curriculum reform policy has been widely discussed within the literature (e.g. Cuban 1998). A major issue is the 'implementation gap' (Supovitz and Weinbaum 2008) between policy intention and classroom practice, due to the potential for teachers to significantly modify the intrinsic logics of the curriculum policy to match the institutional logics of the setting where it is enacted (Young 1998). In recent years, educational policy has evolved, at least in part to deal with the above phenomenon. There has been a shift from input regulation of the curriculum—tight front-end prescription of the curriculum—to output regulation (Kuiper and Berkvens 2013)—for example, through inspections and the evaluative use of examinations data; this has ostensibly afforded teachers greater autonomy in curriculum making. Combined with this shift has been the development of a discourse that 'teachers matter' (OECD 2005), characterised by talk of lifelong professional learning, teachers as a Master's level profession, teacher autonomy and teachers as agents of change.

Education policy in Scotland powerfully exemplifies these trends. *Curriculum for Excellence* (CfE) strongly emphasises the key role of teachers in shaping curricular practices:

> In the past, national curriculum developments have often been supported by central guidelines, cascade models of staff development and the provision of resources to support the implementation of guidance by teachers. Our approach to change is different. It aims to engage teachers in thinking from first principles about their educational aims and values and their classroom practice. The process is based upon evidence of how change can be

M. Priestley (✉) · V. Drew
University of Stirling, Stirling, Scotland, UK
e-mail: m.r.priestley@stir.ac.uk

V. Drew
e-mail: v.m.drew@stir.ac.uk

© Springer Nature Singapore Pte Ltd. 2017
M.A. Peters et al. (eds.), *A Companion to Research in Teacher Education*,
DOI 10.1007/978-981-10-4075-7_52

brought about successfully – through a climate in which reflective practitioners share and develop ideas. (Scottish Executive 2006, p. 4)

There has been a strong push to raise the quality—and capacity—of the teaching profession. For example, the educational policy context in Scotland is presently shaped by the influential report *Teaching Scotland's Future* (TSF) (Donaldson 2010). TSF advocates the development of new forms of 'partnership working' between universities, schools and local authorities to take forward the implementation of CfE. Reflecting the language of CfE, it espouses particular ways of thinking about career-long professional learning which seek to promote an understanding of teachers as 'reflective and enquiring teachers who are engaged in continuous improvement' (p. 15) and 'have the capacity to engage fully with the complexities of education and to be key actors in shaping and leading educational change' (p. 19).

Such rhetoric offers a tantalising glimpse of a transformation of the professional role of teachers in a new 'flipped system' (Evers and Kneyber 2015).[1] However, we would caution that such developments may be highly problematic for a number of reasons. First, the shift to output regulation has been associated with the development of performative cultures, with the attendant risk that consideration of educational purpose is supplanted by a short-term instrumentalism in schooling (Ball 2003). Second, the rhetoric that teachers matter has tended to lead to an over-emphasis on the importance of individual teacher capacity and a concomitant neglect of the structural and cultural conditions which frame teaching, and which indeed make effective teaching possible (see Priestley et al. 2015). Third, and linked to the abovementioned caveats, the siren call for greater teacher autonomy conflates the related concepts of teacher autonomy and teacher agency. The former—commonly understood as a comparative lack of regulation of teachers' work—is arguably an insufficient condition for teacher professional action in, for example, curriculum making. Autonomy may lead to reproduction of habitual patterns of behaviour and the continuation of poor practices as readily as it might lead to constructive educational change and the development of what might be termed a good education. For instance, in the case of CfE, research suggests a tendency for schools to audit current practices against curriculum outcomes, often leading to strategic compliance rather than engagement with the 'big ideas' of the curriculum, accompanied by poor understanding of its values, purposes and principles (Priestley and Minty 2013). Agency, conversely, following the ecological approach developed by Priestley et al. (2015), is dependent not only on high teacher capacity, but crucially on the availability of resources—cultural, relational and material—that facilitate effective practice. Such resources might include constructive collegial and external support for innovation, conceptual framings for educational practice, research findings and intelligently framed educational policy.

---

[1]The authors draw upon the metaphor of the flipped classroom—where processes are turned around to give primacy to learners—in calling for a system where the primary role in shaping curriculum and pedagogy should rest with teachers, rather than politicians and administrators.

In the context described above, there has been a resurgence of interest in the methodology of [collaborative] professional enquiry and similarly termed processes such as practitioner enquiry/inquiry or research[2] (Butler et al. 2015), most of which have their origins in Action Research. Such approaches offer considerable potential to facilitate engagement with educational policies and principles, and to afford teacher agency. As a result, professional enquiry is becoming an increasingly popular framework or methodology for professional learning in the twenty-first century as a means of engaging members of the education community to work in partnership to explore aspects of mutual interest or concern with 'the ultimate aim of improving educational outcomes for students' (DeLuca et al. 2015, p. 640). The remainder of this chapter describes a particular school/university partnership to develop CfE. This programme developed a systematic approach to curriculum development, utilising a collaborative professional enquiry methodology, and at the time of writing draws upon empirical evidence from three cohorts of participating teachers. In this chapter, we first draw upon literature related to professional enquiry, identifying some of the benefits and criticisms of this approach. We then set out the key features of the programme in question, illustrating how it has addressed some of the critiques in the literature. We conclude by reflecting upon the outcomes of the programme, and the benefits experienced by the participating teachers and school leaders.

52.2   Professional Enquiry—Some Themes from the Literature

According to Butler et al. (2015, p. 2), 'inquiry-based approaches, […] have potential to impact not only teachers' learning but also their practice in classrooms', thus offering a promising alternative to top-down dissemination and implementation of educational policy. These authors point to the potential for such approaches to actively engage teachers, encourage risk-taking and foster persistence as teachers undertaken innovation; thus, professional enquiry is now widely seen as a powerful means of fostering both teacher professional learning and innovation. Nevertheless, we note that many authors have problematized the approach—and indeed, in formulating and developing the programme described in this chapter, we have attended to some of these critiques. Space precludes a detailed examination of these critiques, but we highlight some of the key criticisms in the following paragraphs.

A fundamental tension in professional enquiry relates to its purpose. Such approaches can be driven by a deep concern with educational purposes, principles and values; or they can be reduced to more instrumental and/or short-term concerns,

---

[2]Please note that we employ the spelling most commonly used in Scotland, namely 'enquiry', throughout this paper, except where quoting directly from other authors using the alternative spelling 'inquiry'.

for example as a narrow mechanism for implementing policy or developing new technical approaches. A key question therefore lies in whether professional enquiry pays attention to the 'big ideas' of the curriculum (Priestley and Minty 2013) and how it will 'take into account ethical, political and moral concerns?' (Klein 2012, p. 8). This is fundamentally about asking *critical questions that matter*. This issue links to a number of practical concerns. First, there is the question of whether professional enquiry can interrupt current, habitual and often deep-grained practices and ways of seeing the world of schooling, or whether such processes simply provide a mechanism for reinforcing existing ways of thinking, through the development of groupthink and the reinforcement of dominant, mono-cultural discourses. The outcome would seem to be dependent on the processes that are undertaken during the enquiry (i.e. whether they surface values and beliefs and challenge assumptions), the contextual conditions framing the enquiry and the resources that become available to stimulate such interruption (Somekh and Zeichner 2009).

Second, and linked to this, are issues of power and control. Put simply, one might pose the question 'whose enquiry?' Recent research suggests that successful innovation needs to create a culture of enquiry that respects the voices of teachers and their professional knowledge (Zeichner 2002). Professional enquiry can be undermined by authoritarian leadership which takes a different world view to that adopted by teachers undertaking the enquiry, for example, exposing tensions between the bottom-up elements of professional enquiry and top-down, often externally driven school improvement agendas. It is also weakened in situations where teachers find that their colleagues either do not share their zeal for the enquiry, or feel threatened by it. Moreover, genuine innovation is not fostered by disingenuous attempts to use professional enquiry as a control mechanism to narrowly implement mandated policy (Somekh and Zeichner 2009); instead, a culture of enquiry needs to attend to school micro-politics, and to question the notion of leadership as only hierarchical.

Third, many authors have pointed to the practical constraints on professional enquiry resulting from limitations in space and time. Professional enquiry requires space for dialogical working, and a sustained period for engagement. This is essential if teachers are required to make sense of new and complex ideas, engage with research findings, change their emotional and cognitive attachments to former patterns of thinking and practice and enact and evaluate new ways of doing. Thus, DeLuca et al. (2015) emphasise the need to protect sanctioned time; Zeichner (2002) has highlighted the need for collaboration over a substantial period—at least a year—during which teachers are able to collaborate in a safe and supported environment; and Meirink et al. (2010) have stressed the particular importance of an extended period of engagement during the initial stages of an enquiry to enable teachers to make sense of and align goals.

A further practical issue relates to the knowledge and skills possessed by teachers undertaking professional enquiry. In particular, this applies to skills of data collection and analysis (Zeichner 2002). Teachers are not professional researchers, and masy lack the requisite skills, including an ability to determine what counts as baseline evidence, or evidence of a successful enquiry. Finally, while such weaknesses can be mitigated by the provision of external support (e.g. from university researchers) there remains the thorny question of what happens once funding ends, the supported project comes to a close, and the school is left to work alone. The literature on educational change is replete with example of projects that have thrived during the pilot phase, before quickly fading away once support was withdrawn.

The above issues are neatly summarised by DeLuca and colleagues in their extensive critique of collaborative inquiry. They suggest that future research should seek to clarify some of these issues through focusing on: devising educational questions for collaborative enquiry, articulating how 'enquiry' differs from research; the nature of the contribution of collaborative enquiry to professional learning; and the sustainability of the processes and methods of enquiry within professional practices (DeLuca et al. 2015). All of these issues have the potential to impact upon the effectiveness and sustainability of innovation fostered by professional enquiry approaches.

52.3 Critical Collaborative Professional Enquiry (CCPE)

52.3.1 The Development of CCPE

Since 2012, the education researchers at the University of Stirling have developed a distinctive approach to collaborative enquiry, which we term Critical Collaborative Professional Enquiry, or CCPE. This methodology is influenced in part by the insights generated in the literature on professional enquiry, plus our own research in this field, and draws upon twelve years of development of Master's programmes in Professional Enquiry in Education. This programme, developed in partnership with a Scottish local authority, was at the time of writing entering its fourth cohort, and utilises a collaborative professional enquiry 'lite' methodology; effectively a streamlined programme that introduces the key elements of the Master's programme compressed into a shorter timeframe. Thus, academic research is both influenced by and influencing day-to-day practices and experiences; the emerging outcome has been the development of a pragmatic approach underpinned by significant empirical insights,

The introduction of 'Critical' in the title has two functions: firstly it draws attention to the purposes and value of CCPE methodology in professional practice as a means of promoting social justice and equity through education; and secondly it signals the importance of engaging critically with concepts and ideas in research and academic readings, to critique policies and practices throughout the enquiry process. Collaborative denotes the collective nature of the endeavour and the networked responsibility of the group members to contribute to all aspects of the enquiry process. The 'Professional' in CCPE is used to signify the fundamental role of professional judgement underpinning the methodology in surfacing values and challenging assumptions in the endeavour to improve outcomes for all concerned. The importance of professional judgement is highlighted by Biesta (2009, p. 186) who states that judgements made by teachers are 'not simply of a technical or instrumental nature' but 'always involve an evaluation of the means themselves and hence require *value judgments* about the desirability of the ways in which particular ends and means might be achieved' (emph. in original). Finally the term 'Enquiry' rather than 'research' is deliberately utilised in CCPE, seeking to avoid conflation with the role of the researcher, whose prime responsibility may be considered to be predominantly focused on reporting the outcomes of research, whereas a 'practitioner' researcher's key responsibility is on improving outcomes for their students and colleagues. Thus, the methodology is designed to encompass elements identified as pertinent to improving teacher learning, namely: collaborative action, critical reflection and self-evaluation, and teacher leadership (Reeves and Drew 2012).

52.3.2   Developing a Robust Model for Enquiry

The programme, that forms the focus of the remainder of this chapter, originated through dialogue between Local Authority Education Officers and University researchers about how they might work in partnership, to address some of these complex and intertwining issues arising from the implementation of CfE in primary and secondary schools. It was significant, that local authority officers were at the time experiencing similar problems associated with curriculum development to those reported in University of Stirling research, conducted in another local authority (see Priestley and Minty 2013). These problems included poor understanding of the principles and purposes of CfE and superficial and/or strategic compliance with the new curriculum. Conversations between the researchers and local authority officers identified the strong potential of CCPE to 'interrupt' habitual practices in a manner which would be consonant with CfE. The programme was designed to take cognisance of the critique described previously, relating to some of the perceived limitations of or concerns with practitioner research.

Foremost among these was the need to connect the purposes of the curriculum (and other big ideas of education) through the methodology of professional enquiry, since in previous partnership working, this had led in some cases to the development of instrumental (and even trivial) development of practice linked to teachers' short-term classroom concerns, for instance relating to the behaviour of individual students rather than educational purposes and principles. The new programme thus explicitly linked CCPE to the notion of CfE as a process curriculum (see Priestley and Humes 2010), where fit-for-purpose practices are explicitly derived from broad purposes of education, in this case the attributes and capabilities of CfE.[3] It highlighted the following processes:

- Stage 1: a conceptual phase which involved developing nuanced understandings of different curriculum development models, engaging with the 'big ideas' of the curriculum in Scotland, considering the fitness for purpose of content, pedagogy and assessment, and addressing contextual conditions (including identification of barriers and drivers to innovation).
- Stage 2: undertaking Critical Collaborative Professional Enquiry (CPE), comprising three phases: focusing, interrupting and sense making (adapted from an earlier model in Drew et al. 2008) to trial new ways of developing school-based curriculum development with an impact for teachers' professional learning and outcomes for students.

These stages are described more fully in the next section.

A second concern related to the sustainability of innovation. The view was taken at the outset that, while this type of in-the-field partnership working was a slimmed down version of CCPE, being necessarily less intensive than university-based Master's level study, it should not be less robust or conceptually rigorous. Therefore, the programme ran for an extended period, comprising seven workshops over an academic session (approximately nine months), with sufficient time (and space) between sessions for participants to work with colleagues in schools to develop and evaluate their practice. The role of the external partner (university researchers) throughout the programme was crucial in this process, to both facilitate collaboration and to interrupt current processes and practices through challenging assumptions and taken for granted practices and policies thus developing the criticality. These roles could fall into tension at times, as some of the activities tended to highlight difference and diversity in values and beliefs, so it was important to create a safe practical and emotional communicative space for this work (Eady et al. 2014). Criticality was promoted through the pedagogies devised by tutors to facilitate the programme, and enhanced through the central role of reading in the programme. Participants were expected to engage with research and other academic texts to critique policies, practices and ideas, and to facilitate the development of a conceptual framework to inform their planned interruption to practice. Thus, another major role for researchers was to source and if necessary provide access to suitable academic resources to inform developments in practice. This was a time-consuming task, but one which was essential if the programme was to interrupt

---

[3]The Four Capacities of CfE have become a sort of mantra for the new curriculum, widely visible as slogans on posters in schools, but often stripped of meaning. In fact, they form a useful starting point for curriculum planning, being broken down into a set of key competencies known as attributes and capabilities, which define the skills and knowledge to be acquired by an education person. See: http://www.educationscotland.gov.uk/learningandteaching/thecurriculum/whatiscurriculumforexcellence/thepurposeofthecurriculum/index.asp.

habitual practices.[4] A related issue, highlighted in the literature and encountered in previous work, lies in the ability of participants to take their innovations back into school in the face of scepticism from colleagues, and more particularly competing management imperatives. The programme sought to address this through the selection of participants; it was emphasised from the outset that schools should send between four and six participants, reflecting a range of levels of experience and seniority, and as a minimum including at least one member of the senior management team. In some cases, head teachers participated.

Finally, and in recognition of the difficulties faced by some teachers in identifying and handling data, one session focused on developing research literacy, including addressing questions of what constitutes evidence. This session also focused on the notion of impact, suggesting how teachers might recognise and develop opportunities for their innovation to impact upon students, and also how they might identify ways of evidencing such impact.

52.3.3 Stage One: Conceptual Development

The aim of the first stage is to engage practitioners critically with the principles and purposes of current curricular policy in Scotland, addressing the issue, highlighted by research, that many teachers have a poor understanding of these. The emphasis at this stage is not on change per se, but on engagement, with the aim of developing 'good' educational practices from the conceptual framing provided by the new curriculum. Underpinning this activity is an assumption that existing practices might be fit-for-purpose, but that participants do not necessarily know whether this is the case unless they are critically evaluated against the benchmarks provided by the CfE attributes and capabilities; conversely, such an evaluation might lead to significant change in practices.

The initial sessions of the programme thus focus on a number of conceptual issues that form the foundation for the second, more practically focused CCPE stage. The participants first engage with some models or starting points for curriculum development, exploring the implications of treating CfE as either a content-led, outcomes-led or process-led curriculum (see Priestley and Humes 2010). Second, they examine how school-based curriculum development might proceed from the assumption that CfE is a process curriculum. This involves a number of steps. The first is a process of constructing meaning in relation to the big ideas of CfE and consideration of other purposes, principles and values of education. Within our programme cohorts, this has led to discussion of the difference between purposes and methods, often leading to an epiphany as participants realise

---

[4]This job was made considerably easier in 2013–14, when the General Teaching Council for Scotland subscribed to an EBSCO database, enabling teachers to access a range of research articles in peer-reviewed journals.

that they have been conflating the two, treating particular methods of educating (such as active learning methodologies) as ends in themselves, rather than as means of addressing broader educational aims. Second, this theory-focused discussion is then led into more practical dialogue about fitness-for-purpose, primarily focusing on two issues: fit-for-purpose knowledge/content (something that has been comparatively neglected in CfE; e.g. see Priestley and Minty 2013) and fit-for-purpose pedagogy. Typically, assessment is also discussed at this stage, and concrete ideas about curriculum development start to emerge. Third, participants are encouraged to think about barriers and drivers to their planned innovation, stimulating discussion about how, for example, accountability practices and school systems might impede their plans. At this stage, the value of the participation of senior school managers, both as participants and as critical colleagues, is clearly evident; there appeared to be less likelihood of participants being subsequently blocked in taking forward their planned innovations, if senior management had been involved in the process (Drew et al. 2016).

52.3.4   Stage Two: The 'How' of CCPE

The conceptual stage described above provides a firm foundation for professional enquiry rooted in educational purpose (and indeed participants are required to show how their subsequent enquiries relate back to the big ideas). There are many frameworks and/or models for collaborative professional enquiry, but authors tend to agree that there is no one or correct way of implementing this process or methodology (Klein 2012). However, in their review of 42 studies of collaborative inquiry, DeLuca et al. (2015, p. 640) noted that, while the models and frameworks they examined involved between three and eleven phases, there were three 'core and interconnected structural features', namely 'dialogic sharing, taking action and reflection'. The CCPE model for SBCD involves three phases: focusing, interrupting and sense-making; these encompass these common structural features, and this process is deliberately designed to surface and address issues of social justice and engagement in critique of policies and practices.

During the first phase, the participants begin the process of school-based curriculum development (SBCD) through the CCPE methodology by engaging in professional dialogue to identify an area of interest or concern in their practice related to content, pedagogy or assessment. Since this discussion draws upon participants' experiences and practices, it surfaces questions about personal and professional values and beliefs, and thus the process requires high levels of trust and collegiality amongst participants. Throughout this stage the participants develop the focus of the enquiry through engaging critically with ideas in research and academic readings, as they begin to form the enquiry question that will guide their innovation. All group members are expected to take responsibility for engaging critically with readings and reporting on their responses to these to their group. The ideas and concepts originating from the readings are thus shared and used to begin to draft a conceptual framework, a visual representation of how the group is making connections between the concepts and demonstrating how these will be used to inform the invention of new ways of working which constitute an interruption to practice. By the end of this phase the CCPE group generate and agree a broad 'critical' question for their enquiry and devise a collaborative plan for implementing the critical enquiry through interrupting practice through these new ways of working. Throughout the enquiry the participants are provoked to attend to principles of fairness, social justice and sustainable practices, underpinned by their codes of professional ethics to meet the demands of critical enquiry.

In Phase Two of CCPE, groups undertake critical collaborative enquiry to implement and trial new approaches designed to interrupt professional practices and impact positively outcomes for young people. They continue to critique and refine or modify their conceptual framework during this phase, through ongoing critical engagement with reading and professional dialogue, both within the CCPE group and with other members of the educational community including the University researchers and colleagues. The process of engaging in systematic generation of empirical data (both process and outcomes) takes place throughout all three stages but is perhaps most prevalent during this stage as the practitioners implement the interruption in practices, and begin to notice changes in their knowledge, understanding and practices, as well as the impact on their students.

In Phase Three, there is a focus on collaborative sense-making through critical analysis of data and interpretation of evidence, as the CCPE group begin to evaluate the impact of the interruption and draft a 'report' for dissemination to their educational community. However, this sense-making process permeates all three phases, as participants invoke professional judgement to make sense of the data generated throughout the enquiry and use this to evidence their claims and assertions about the contribution of the process to: developing pupils' attributes and capabilities; enhancing their professional learning in relation to development of educational practices; and identifying messages for the wider school community.

52.4 Discussion: Findings and Implications

We lack the space here to provide a detailed account of the empirical research associated with the programme. Instead we offer a brief overview of the main findings, which are reported in more detail in Drew et al. (2016). These were generated through a variety of methods and activities aligned to the methodology of CCPE, from three cohorts (approximately 25 teachers in each) across the three year project. Methods included participant observation and artefacts generated in workshops, mid/end of programme feedback, group presentations on final session, and field notes and cohorts' questions on the presentations. The data also included transcripts of six formal telephone interviews and 25 programme evaluation questionnaires.

52.4.1 Findings

We found that involvement in this programme exerted a powerful effect on the teachers who participated. In turn, this opened up new ways of working in school, through CCPE with the potential for enhanced practice and outcomes for children. We found significant evidence of enhanced understandings of the new curriculum, addressing one of the major concerns that had originally stimulated the programme development. In a sense this is not surprising; research (e.g. Priestley and Minty 2013) had already suggested that schools have not provided adequate spaces for sense-making as the new curriculum was introduced, and the programme established such spaces, through the setting up of structured dialogue for this purpose. Enhanced understandings were seen in relation to three main areas: first, participating teachers appeared to have a better grasp than previously of the core aims and principles of the new curriculum; second, participants developed better understanding of the potential links between purposes and practices; third, there was an increased familiarity with related and relevant concepts such as metacognition. Enhanced understandings of the substantive conceptual issues, related to the curriculum and its development, were manifestly accompanied by enhanced understandings of processes for school-based curriculum development; this includes a deeper familiarity with the principles and practices of CCPE and its potential contribution to school-based curriculum development, as well as new knowledge of appropriate models for curriculum development. Accompanying this better knowledge and understanding of professional principles and processes has been increased confidence exhibited by many of the participants.

Enhanced understanding and increased confidence have led to the emergence of more tangible outcomes. The project has stimulated the development of new and innovative pedagogical practices (in response to the demands of the new curriculum), which had not previously been considered. These include a primary school where there was a systematic development of a culture of questioning by children, notable in that it greatly extended opportunities for children's voice and participation in the classrooms. In some cases these changes were radical; in another primary school, innovation in pedagogy was noted with surprise by an external inspector, who complimented the school on their practice, and inquired into its origins and the processes by which collaborative inquiry had stimulated innovation

As we indicated in the earlier part of this chapter, radical changes are not uncommon in the pilot phase of a project such as this. Sustainability is a different matter altogether. While it is too early to judge definitively, there is emerging evidence that this programme has improved the sustainability of innovation in some of the schools. This is especially evident in schools where there is not only evidence of innovation, but also of sustained engagement with CCPE methodology. In some schools we have witnessed school leaders, who had been participants in the programme, actively pursuing systematic professional enquiry with colleagues, drawing upon CCPE principles as a means of developing educational practices for curriculum development. At least three head teachers (evidenced through interview data) have opened new spaces by using this framework to inform professional learning in their school.

There is some evidence that participating teachers have affected the cultures of their schools, introducing more democratic practices than previously. There are two aspects to this trend, which is slight but nonetheless discernible in the data. First there is some evidence of increasing concern for social justice in educational practice, and an increasing desire and ability to justify such practice in terms of values and principles. This contrasts to some extent with the schools researched by Priestley et al. (2015), where teachers were often unable to articulate long-term purpose for their practices, instead tending to justify them in terms of more instrumental and short-term imperatives such as keeping classes busy. Thus, our data show teachers utilising increasing levels of social justice oriented language, and a tendency for them to become more child-centred, seeking students' opinions and developing a more inclusive culture. The previously mentioned example of innovation in questioning is a notable example of this trend. Of course we would not claim to be the sole influence behind these trends; CfE advocates this sort of practice, and Scottish schools have been gradually moving in this direction for at least a decade. More likely is the influence of CCPE in stimulating greater engagement with such discourses, which in turn has had a knock-on effect on practices. A second 'democratic' trend relates to an interruption of traditional hierarchies within schools. The programme facilitated collaborative working for all involved—teachers, leaders and researchers—and emphasised the importance of professional dialogue. This in turn has provided opportunities for developing leadership skills, and affected working practices across the participating schools.

Finally, the data surfaces a great deal amongst our cohorts about developing criticality: how engaging in reading challenges and interrupts current perspectives; how it opens up new ways of thinking, generating the ability to more readily consider multiple possibilities; and how it helps to develop new conceptual frameworks to inform new ways of working.

52.4.2   Implications

This CCPE programme established by the university with the local authority has been an exciting project for the majority of participants. From the point of view of the participating teachers, it has opened up new possibilities for innovative working which, in contrast to established patterns driven by accountability practices, is more in tune with their values as professionals which brought them into teaching in the first place—as has been pointed out to us on several occasions. From the point of view of the university researchers, the programme has developed new insights about how teacher agency can be stimulated and developed. The ecological model of teacher agency (Priestley et al. 2015) suggests that agency is something that is achieved, rather than an innate capacity or quality of the individual. Agency emerges, unique in every situation, is shaped by influences from the past and present, and can be more or less oriented to the future. In terms of curriculum development, agency is achieved to a high degree when teachers with high levels of skill and knowledge and particular orientations to professional practice (the international dimension of agency—formed by past experience) are able to form expansive aspirations about future directions in curriculum making (the projective dimension of agency). In turn, agency is always acted out in the present, afforded by the availability of resources and limited by practical constraints, and shaped by judgment, for example, evaluation of risk (the practical evaluative dimension of agency[5]).

This theoretical framing chimes well with the findings from our empirical research, and with the processes and outcomes of CCPE. As we noted in the introduction to this chapter, current policy, in its valorisation of the central role of the teacher, tends to over-emphasise the important of raising individual capacity, while neglecting the cultural and structural dimensions of schooling that powerfully shape agency. CCPE potentially addresses all three dimensions. Our data suggest that the participating teachers have acquired an enhanced understanding of both concepts and processes involved in school-based curriculum development, so as a form of professional learning it clearly raises individual and collective capacity. Structurally, CCPE offers access to resources—cognitive and relational, which have opened up new possibilities and new practices. On a cultural level, CCPE has clearly, in the case of the participating schools, stimulated changes, as evidenced by the witnessed shift in power dynamics and leadership practices, and a shift towards emphasising children's voice. We suggest that such changes to the individual, structural and cultural dimensions of teachers' work, have enhanced their agency as they grapple with the complexities of developing a new curriculum through: engendering an ability to envisage a wider repertoire of pedagogical possibilities and practices in their day-to-day practice; affording additional resources to support their agency; and stimulating change to the cultures that frame their work.

Acknowledgements We wish to acknowledge the enthusiastic participation of around 75 teachers and senior managers over the three years of the project. We also wish to offer our thanks and appreciation to East Lothian Council, particularly Allson Wishart for her support in making this programme happen.

---

[5]For an extended discussion of these dimensions of agency—the chordal triad—see Emirbayer and Mische (1998).

References

Ball, S. J. (2003). The teacher's soul and the terrors of performativity. *Journal of Education Policy, 18*, 215–228.

Biesta, G. J. J. (2009). Values and ideals in teachers' professional judgement. In S. Gewirtz, P. Mahony, I. Hextall, & A. Cribb (Eds.), *Changing teacher professionalism* (pp. 184–193). London: Routledge.

Butler, D., Schnellert, L., & MacNeil, K. (2015). Collaborative inquiry and distributed agency in educational change: A case study of a multi-level community of inquiry. *Journal of Educational Change, 16*, 1–26.

Cuban, L. (1998). How schools change reforms: Redefining reform success and failure. *Teachers College Record, 99*, 453–477.

DeLuca, C., Shulha, J., Luhanga, U., Shulha, L. M., Christou, T. M., & Klinger, D. A. (2015). Collaborative inquiry as a professional learning structure for educators: A scoping review. *Professional Development in Education, 41*, 640–670.

Donaldson, G. (2010). *Teaching Scotland's future: Report of a review of teacher education in Scotland*. Edinburgh: Scottish Government.

Drew, V., Fox, A., & McBride, M. (2008). Collaborating to improve learning and teaching. In J. Reeves & A. Fox (Eds.), *Practice-based learning: Developing excellence in teaching* (pp. 52–66). Edinburgh: Dunedin Academic Press.

Drew, V., Priestley, M., & Michael, M. K. (2016). Curriculum development through critical collaborative professional enquiry. *Journal of Professional Capital and Community, 1*, 92–106.

Eady, S., Drew, V., & Smith, A. (2014). Doing action research in organizations: Using communicative spaces to facilitate (transformative) professional learning. *Action Research, 13*, 105–122.

Emirbayer, M., & Mische, A. (1998). What is agency? *The American Journal of Sociology, 103*, 962–1023.

Evers, J., & Kneyber, R. (Eds.). (2015). *Flip the system: Changing education from the bottom up*. London: Routledge.

Klein, S. R. (2012). Action research: Before you dive in, read this! In S. R. Klein (Ed.), *Action research methods: Plain and simple* (pp. 1–20). London: Palgrave Macmillan.

Kuiper, W., & Berkvens, J. (Eds.). (2013). *Balancing curriculum regulation and freedom across Europe*, CIDREE Yearbook 2013. Enschede, The Netherlands: SLO.

Meirink, J., Imants, J., Meijer, P., & Verloop, N. (2010). Teacher learning and collaboration in innovative teams. *Cambridge Journal of Education, 40*, 161–181.

OECD. (2005). *Teachers matter: Attracting, developing and retaining effective teachers*. Paris: OECD.

Priestley, M., Biesta, G. J. J., & Robinson, S. (2015). *Teacher agency: An ecological approach*. London: Bloomsbury Academic.

Priestley, M., & Humes, W. (2010). The development of Scotland's curriculum for excellence: Amnesia and déjà vu. *Oxford Review of Education, 36*, 345–361.

Priestley, M., & Minty, S. (2013). Curriculum for excellence: 'A brilliant idea, but'. *Scottish Educational Review, 45*, 39–52.

Reeves, J., & Drew, V. (2012). Relays and relations: Tracking a policy initiative for improving teacher professionalism. *Journal of Education Policy, 27*, 711–730.

Scottish Executive. (2006). *A curriculum for excellence: Progress and proposals*. Edinburgh: Scottish Executive.

Somekh, B., & Zeichner, K. (2009). Action research for educational reform: Remodelling action research theories and practices in local contexts. *Educational Action Research, 17*, 5–21.

Supovitz, J. A., & Weinbaum, E. H. (2008). Reform implementation revisited. In J. A. Supovitz & E. H. Weinbaum (Eds.), *The implementation gap: Understanding reform in high schools* (pp. 1–21). New York: Teachers College Press.

Young, M. D. F. (1998). *The curriculum of the future: From the "new sociology of education" to a critical theory of learning.* London: Routledge.

Zeichner, K. M. (2002). Teacher research as professional development for P–12 educators in the USA. *Educational Action Research, 11,* 301–326.

Author Biographies

Mark Priestley is Professor of Education in the Faculty of Social Sciences at the University of Stirling. His research interests relate to the school curriculum, curriculum change, curriculum development and the professional work of teachers. Recent publications include Teacher Agency: An Ecological Approach (Bloomsbury Academic), co-authored with Gert Biesta and Sarah Robinson.

Dr. Valerie Drew is a Senior Lecturer in Professional Education and Leadership in the Faculty of Social Sciences, University of Stirling, UK. Her research interests are concerned with professional learning, educational leadership, professional enquiry and curriculum development.

Chapter 53
Flows of Knowledge in Teaching Teams: A Collaborative Approach to Research in Early Childhood Education

Marek Tesar, Andrew Gibbons and Sandy Farquhar

The aim of this chapter is to theorise and propose ways to consolidate and build knowledge about the nature and impact of teacher education on teaching team relationships in Early Childhood Education (ECE). ECE teacher education provides a critical opportunity to study and practice being in a teaching team. In this chapter, we explore the nature of early childhood (EC) teaching teams with a focus on 'knowledge'. The 'knowledge relationships' within teaching teams are complex elements of the EC curriculum that have received little sustained, critical attention in educational research. Two aspects of team relationships are of particular value here because of their capacity to enrich the experiences of teachers and children in ECE: (1) the ways in which new and/or beginning teachers are welcomed into the knowledge community of an EC centre; and (2) the ways in which the sharing and construction of knowledge in a teaching team impacts on teaching and learning in the EC curriculum. These two elements are of significance to teacher education in terms of both how the student experiences the study of teaching as an experience in preparation for being a teaching team member, and how that experience translates into being in a teaching team.

The chapter contributes to two essential and ongoing wider research needs identified in Aotearoa New Zealand: the nature and promotion of twenty-first century teaching and learning environments—environments characterised in relation to open, dynamic, and collective knowledge environments; and the experiences of beginning and new teachers as they enter their teaching teams ('new teachers'

M. Tesar (✉) · S. Farquhar
University of Auckland, Auckland, New Zealand
e-mail: m.tesar@auckland.ac.nz

S. Farquhar
e-mail: s.farquhar@auckland.ac.nz

A. Gibbons
Auckland University of Technology, Auckland, New Zealand
e-mail: andrew.gibbons@aut.ac.nz

© Springer Nature Singapore Pte Ltd. 2017
M.A. Peters et al. (eds.), *A Companion to Research in Teacher Education*,
DOI 10.1007/978-981-10-4075-7_53

refers to teachers who are new to the centres, and 'beginning teachers' to those who are at the start of their teaching career).

In addition, the chapter proposes further research into the development of a collaborative teaching, learning and researching model in teacher education, based on sharing knowledge/professional practices between new and beginning, and experienced teachers. It draws upon current scholarship on pedagogy, professionalism and leadership in ECE which advocates for effective models of development to emanate from within the profession, grounded in the local contexts and aspirations of Aotearoa New Zealand teachers, and critically attuned to the complexities of communities (Dalli et al. 2012). Building on existing scholarship, the chapter further develops knowledge of the effectiveness of teaching teams in supporting beginning and new teachers, through responsive communities of support as outlined in the Education Council website, the governing and regulatory body of New Zealand teachers. This knowledge is strategically important for centre staff, management and the profession, in terms of promoting the best ways to embrace the new knowledge and practices that beginning and new teachers bring to the teaching and learning community, and for teacher education alike. Data from a recent study of the experiences of newly qualified early childhood teachers, and their relationship with 'knowledge', is woven through the chapter. The teachers' experiences are explored in relation to the concept of 'flows of knowledge'. This concept is developed out of the literature on 'future-focused' education (Bolstad et al. 2012). We argue that the study of flows of knowledge is a vital contribution to the study of education in teacher education programmes.

53.1   Teacher Knowledge and Knowledge Environments in the Twenty First Century

Relationships among adults have a significant impact on the learning and development of the child. One of the theories employed by the New Zealand early childhood curriculum *Te Whāriki* is Bronfenbrenner's ecological systems theory, which raises and guides a critical awareness of the impact of adult relationships on the curriculum (Ministry of Education 1996). This chapter has an interest in one element of the relationships among adults: the knowledge relationship. It is concerned with what happens to a teaching team when beginning teachers arrive at their centre with the knowledge that they have gained through their studies. How does knowledge develop as the team grows and/or changes? How does the teaching team adapt to this new knowledge that originates from the experiences of teacher education? How do the beginning and new teachers share (or perhaps keep silent about) these knowledge encounters? And, importantly, how does this process of adaptation impact on the early childhood curriculum?

These questions and concerns interest us as teacher educators and researchers because very little is known about such knowledge relationships, and yet they are essential to the quality of the curriculum and to children's learning. The quality of the curriculum is an ongoing concern for policy, theory, and practice—as is clearly evident in recent media coverage. See for example the series of articles on the quality of ECE in Aotearoa New Zealand, beginning with the article *Early Childhood Services Red-Flagged* (Johnston 2015). This series of articles raised significant concerns about teacher knowledge of the curriculum, of child development, and of culturally responsive practices. Such concerns raise points that are often associated with the benefits of teacher education for quality ECE experiences for all learners.

The research conducted by organisations such as the Organization for Economic Cooperation and Development [OECD] suggests that early childhood teaching teams regularly change as a result of high levels of workforce attrition. There is little research into these changing knowledge environments. Clearly, however, it is of significant value to provide evidence of how teachers can be attuned to and promote strong collaborative knowledge environments, and then draw on this evidence within teacher education. It is not only changing staff roles that impact on the knowledge environment, we are also concerned with how stable teaching teams construct and share knowledge in times of constant change. How is the ongoing professional learning of teachers integrated into the collective knowledge of a teaching team, and what is the relationship with teacher education?

In teaching, strong teams respond to fast flows of information from multiple sources (academic journals, government publications, professional development providers, and more) designed to inform teacher knowledge. Significantly though, little is known about how teachers negotiate that flow, how they incorporate it into their team, and how the flow of knowledge impacts on the team dynamics. Following discourses of educational futures (see, for instance, Bolstad et al. 2012) and the strategic direction for twenty-first century learning (New Zealand Parliament 2012), an essential dynamic of future teaching teams will be their professional capacity to make sense of these flows and respond to the values and aspirations of the teaching community.

We are intrigued with the ways knowledge is shared, shifted and constructed during the daily work of early childhood teachers—specifically with how teacher education impacts upon the experience of these flows of knowledge, how both beginning and experienced teachers reflect upon and discuss construction and sharing of knowledge, how knowledge relationships and environments are formed and altered, and how these relationships and environments impact on the curriculum. Such knowledge might include knowledge of child development, subject knowledge, pedagogical content knowledge and knowledge of the children and families. Teacher education is a critical space for engaging collaboratively in exploring what flows of knowledge generate, and what knowledge relationships, and knowledge environments, *do* to the curriculum (Bolstad et al. 2012). These are the concerns that, we argue, would benefit from further research.

53.2   Starting Strong: Critical Perspectives on the ECE Teaching Profession

'Starting Strong' is a theme used in a series of international reports by the OECD. The reports highlight the emphasis on early childhood professional knowledge and its relationship to quality ECE. The Starting Strong reports consolidate and build on existing professional knowledge and practice and align with current scholarship on pedagogy, professionalism and leadership in ECE (Dalli 2008; Osgood 2012; Woodrow 2008). This scholarship consistently advocates for effective models of development to emanate from within the profession, grounded in the contexts and aspirations of teachers, and critically attuned to the complexities of centre communities (Dalli et al. 2012). The idea of starting strong is a metaphor that may also be applied to the ways in which teaching teams work in early childhood centre communities, and the ways in which teacher education supports the professional work of teaching teams.

In Aotearoa New Zealand, the situating of professional development within centre communities is arguably evident in new strategic directions for initial teacher education (Education Council 2016) that focus on the role of mentor teachers during the practicum components of a teaching qualification. The emphasis here appears to be on continuing to address perceived dissonance between theory and practice (Gibbons et al. 2015). This concern was central to government-funded research partnerships known as Centres of Innovation (COI). The development of the COI programme reflected the importance of early childhood teachers and researchers strengthening their professional connections (see for instance Meade 2010). COI research focused on teacher-led participatory action-research models that developed pedagogical and research capacity and capability. In addition, professional development through the Educational Leadership Programme has been instrumental in putting forward a distributed leadership model focussing on centre practices and innovative education and the idea of teacher-led participatory models influenced by Kaupapa Māori models of sharing knowledge and responsibility based on concepts of Ako and Ata. Other countries have developed unique initiatives in terms of policy discourses in early childhood education (see, for example a series of articles in the special issue of *International Journal of Early Years Education* (Calder 2015).

Arguably, the early childhood profession is a site of active, free and open discussion and dissonance on the nature and role of the teacher. Different perspectives on the importance of qualifications and the necessary knowledge within a teaching qualification entail complex negotiations that are regularly repositioned, rearticulated and reconceptualised. This complexity requires care in making assumptions about what being a teacher means, and what being *new*, or a *beginner*, or an *expert* means, within a teaching team. Hence opportunities to discuss, for instance, tensions between theory and practice are valuable for teaching teams. They are valuable as they 're-place' the teacher in her teaching (Duncan 2004; Middleton and May 1997; Osgood 2012) and promote a critical awareness of how such debates and perspectives impact on the centre's teaching and learning. The student teacher's study of these elements of being in a teaching team, sharing and constructing knowledge, will impact on the individual teacher's experiences, as well as those of her future colleagues and wider centre community.

When studying 'flows of knowledge' within teaching teams, we cannot bypass the notion of 'working conditions', as the quality of EC care and education is closely associated with the nature and quality of working conditions. One critical element of the work environment that teacher education should be concerned with is the knowledge environment, through which teachers construct, understand, share and develop their professional knowledge in sustained, collective and collaborative professional relationships.

As noted above, teachers having recently completed their teacher education, may arrive with new knowledge, ideas and tensions that are different to those already circulating in their workplace. Such a condition thus requires negotiation in terms of making meaning of the new knowledge in relation to the existing knowledge, its value to the centre community, its impact on the curriculum, on children's learning and its impact on the sense of collegiality and security of the teaching team. The ways in which such negotiations might occur should be a central element in the study of teaching, to enable student teachers to practice the negotiation of knowledge in peer groups.

The focus on beginning/new teachers acknowledges the additional challenges of being new to a profession and new to the centre: establishing relationships (with children, teachers, parents and the teaching communities); establishing personal support systems and networks; locating oneself in a workplace with a wide-ranging ethos; engaging in professional processes such as registration, induction and mentoring programmes; and becoming part of teaching teams (Dall'Alba 2009; Sumsion 2002; Woodrow 2008). Because all of these factors and how they are processed have a direct impact on the knowledge environment, and a further direct impact on the quality of children's learning, this provocation and reconceptualization for teacher education has specific influence on centre management, for pedagogical leadership in teaching teams, and for mentoring beginning, new, and newly qualified teachers as they develop their knowledge and practice of teaching and learning, and are welcomed to the teaching profession.

53.3 Newly Qualified Teachers in Aotearoa New Zealand

Our study with newly qualified teachers (Farquhar and Tesar 2016a) explored the complexities of teacher identity, professionalism, relationship building and what it means for teachers to transition from their teacher education programme to the early childhood centre. The narratives of early career teachers, as explored through focus groups and interviews, allowed deep understanding into these teachers' relationships with knowledge. For example, Diana, an early career teacher, reported the following encounter of beginner and experienced teacher, and her understanding of what a 'flow of knowledge' looks like for her:

One thing that really frustrated me is you know we have to do learning stories for the children and the fact that we actually had to see the children's learning. I am not very confident in doing things like that ...I put something forward to ...these experienced fully qualified teachers, they said to me no it is fine and I thought you know ...you are supposed to be my mentor and explaining to me how am I supposed to see this learning taking place ... how can I do it if you are not telling me, giving me critical feedback ... with regards to my teaching and learning as well as my explaining to the parents what the child is learning.

Anxieties about the role of mentors reflect complex professional tensions for teaching teams. Such anxieties are also indicative of a deep commitment to professional development, as well as increasing governance of teacher competence through systems of professional evaluation. Both possibilities have important implications for teacher education as it supports beginning teachers in entering into a mentoring relationship, and understanding the ways in which their own concerns and expectations impact on the dynamics of the mentoring, and wider team relationship. Opportunities to experience different mentoring roles during teacher education may provide graduates with the opportunity to see the ways in which different knowledge about professional practice might be experienced and shaped.

In the following conversation Fiona talked about a struggle to transfer knowledge from her teacher education into practice:

... we have got all this knowledge but to put it into practice is sometimes quite difficult. And I have noticed some of the readings I have done the people feel the same way. This knowledge that you have for three years you can't really put into practice ..., it just becomes like a daily routine that you don't actually think like, you are not actually having all your knowledge that you have learnt, in your actual environment that you are working.

Leanne and Judy shared similar experiences:

In a way we were sheltered but also it gave us the knowledge to be able to see what is actually happening, actual working, though we don't always put that knowledge into practice but you can see it ... I struggle to verbalise, I am a visual person ... all that knowledge and backup that should bring it out, I struggle so bad to bring that out ... (Leanne).

I understand that a lot of the everyday, you know, aspects of practice, you know, to do with being just logical and practical and yeah basically that, just that it doesn't take studies to sort of, you know, quickly work out what is the best sort of thing to do here with this number of children and we've got this basin and these many people need to wash their hands and you know the logistics. So that side of it definitely seems to outweigh, yet there's not, yeah, enough of the other professional sort of expertise sort of coming into it. Maybe I guess I've come to sort of doubt my own abilities when it comes to the practical side of it. I feel like maybe I've got all this knowledge but because of my limited experience I kind of have got a lot to learn in that way, or that maybe I'm not suited to the job because sometimes that side of it sort of, I get sort of, I feel like I am told off quite a lot over sort of decisions (Judy).

Each of these three conversations might indicate a problem with flows of knowledge in the sense of the flow being somewhat one directional. In other words, the knowledge learned during teacher education is knowledge, whereas daily practice is in some way not knowledge. This is not to suggest, as Judy recognises, that a simple knowledge over practice hierarchy exists. Of more concern are the distinctions between studied theory and practiced theory and the importance of student discussions with their peers and lecturers. Importantly, such discussions can be constructed in 'daily' contexts, such that the knowledge flows might become more evident. Drawing centre community knowledge into teacher education enables student teachers, lecturers, and experienced teachers to engage productively with feelings of being undervalued, wrong, or, as Judy puts it 'told off'.

In the following conversation, Kylie shares an example of an open 'flow of knowledge' between teachers:

> Just a teacher that is fluid, you know, prepared to go whatever direction, prepared to change … I've had some really awesome associate teachers that I have been able to be open with and bounce ideas, but they've also been strong enough that they can turn around and say no I don't agree with you and give you a reason why. And I love that. I love the fact that … you can learn from that … I think that makes a strong teacher, is someone that is prepared to be open and change but I think also that has the knowledge there, and experience is still quite cool. They've got the experience, the knowledge, they have been through a lot and you are prepared to listen to them as well.

The ways in which knowledge is experienced and shared during teacher education can have a significant influence on this openness to critique. Student teachers arrive with many different attitudes to and experiences of education. Teacher education provides a space and time to make sense of these varied experiences and consider how they will impact on teaching team dynamics—particularly beginning and experienced teacher relationships. However, teacher education also runs the risk of reinforcing negative attitudes and experiences, particularly where assignments and assessment entrench highly individualising educational practices and so limit the scope for open discussion.

Annie adds a different perspective about knowledge flows:

> I think it was very different obviously for people who had come in who had been teaching … they came in with invaluable knowledge … we could then use their experiences to try and think about putting the theory together. But I hadn't been teaching. I had my experience as a parent, and I kept putting the theory to my experience as a parent, which is quite different.

Annie's observation provides an important socio-political context to our discussion of the influence of teacher education in early childhood teaching teams and to the value of a wide range of lived experiences. When professional qualification requirements and standards change, as they have in Aotearoa New Zealand, relationships between teacher education institutions and teaching teams change, and relationships within teaching teams change—as Annie is well aware. While teacher education institutions have a role to play in promoting their contribution to the teaching profession, they also have a role to play in a kind of critical reflexivity that is sensitive to the impact of changing policies for centre communities. Such an openness may promote a more critical understanding of flows of knowledge and of the limitations of study.

What has intrigued us about these narratives of newly qualified teachers are the relationships between the flow of knowledge from teacher education into practice.

What we have identified in these narratives is that for the flow of knowledge to be effective and useful, we need to examine flows among experienced and new/beginner teachers. Each narrative attends to how knowledge is a shared experience—revealing a flow (or lack of flow) among teachers in teaching teams. The narratives also highlight the challenge for teacher education in addressing perceived gaps between study/research and practice—gaps which, we argue, affect all members of the team, and which could usefully be addressed through teacher education and through research that better addresses the dynamics of team relationships. We now ask teacher education might adopt new, open, collaborative approaches to the flow from practice into teacher education?

53.4   The Study of Flows of Knowledge

Based on our research above, it is critical to study how knowledge is experienced in a teaching team. For teacher education, this means exploring the ways in which student teachers experience being in a team, and reflect on how knowledge flows within and among teaching teams. Our thinking builds on the position that teaching practice benefits from ongoing reflection on, and negotiation of, knowledge as a collaborative, dynamic and open experience of 'doing'. While much research is focused on particular aspects of quality teaching like enhancing pedagogy or developing content, our thinking leads us to a deeper view on engaging with both experienced and new/beginning teachers in meaningful knowledge experiences, and with their impact on practice. The focus on knowledge flows relies on a shared approach to knowledge as part of collegial, team experience in ECE.

The study of teaching practice and practitioner research has a critical role for student teaching teams as they engage in a study of knowledge. Our concern is how to align teacher education with practitioner research in ways that support flows of knowledge within the profession, through a research method that is fundamentally concerned with relationships in teaching and learning. We are interested in an approach that synthesises study and research around notions of team and knowledge, a 'critical ecological ethnography' (Dalli et al. 2012; Farquhar and Tesar 2016b) that aligns with the increasing complexity of praxis in EC settings, as argued above. Thus, in early childhood teacher education and in early childhood centres, we suggest that understandings about flows of knowledge in regard to child development, teaching practice, education policy and constantly shifting socio-cultural demographics are particularly important. Sharing experiences from future research partnerships will provide evidence of what is perceived to lead to effective teaching teams—what challenges might be addressed and what practices might be promoted to enhance team support for new teachers.

We argue that an applied approach to the study of these matters promotes a deeper understanding of the impact of teaching team dynamics on teaching practices, and on the richness of the curriculum that is constructed within each centre. This includes how teaching networks impact on learning networks, and how teacher openness to *one another's* knowledge influences their openness to the knowledge of the children with whom they work. The influence extends to the hidden curriculum, in that children learn about knowledge and about learning through 'collective pedagogy' (Fleer 2010) and through their observations of relational engagements among teaching teams in their educational settings.

Such a design in future teacher education would carefully connect the practices of research, teaching and learning through an inter-subjective knowledge construction, resonant with *Te Whāriki's* socio-cultural emphasis on sharing narratives of teaching and learning, and with a pedagogy of listening. Furthermore, it reflects the crucial importance of mutual trust in the sharing of perspectives, enabling voices to be heard and attention to be paid to how engaging in the research impacts on the 'feeling' of being a professional (Dall'Alba 2009). A critical ecological ethnographic approach generates space for professional dialogues, enabling rich understandings of how knowledge construction occurs, how it is experienced by the community, and how talking about it can change experiences. Studying flows of knowledge in teaching teams should be seen as an ongoing network of relationships among student teachers, graduate teachers and teacher educators. As part of a shared commitment to teaching and learning, such study should be sustained well beyond the point of a student teacher's graduation. As a research method, the next section of the article proposes critical ecological ethnography as a means to support and guide these spaces, relationships, and networks.

53.5 Researching Flows of Knowledge

In this final section, we address the role of research in making sense of how teaching teams experience flows of knowledge. Our thinking leads us to a combination of two methodologies: critical ecology and ethnography. Both methodologies require a sensitive involvement of any outsider researchers within everyday centre life, fostering a close professional relationship within the centre.

The critical ecological methodology developed in *Early childhood grows up: Towards a critical ecology of the profession* (Dalli et al. 2012) demonstrates the importance of working closely with early childhood centre communities to share in-depth knowledge about how these communities work and how they are experienced. Through a critical ecology the research design requires an "alertness to the challenges in its settings and to the strengths that can be brought to bear to make the present better" (Dalli 2010, p. 70), to respect and consider the setting and both its wider and intricate contextual elements. The central elements of a critical ecology are drawn into ethnography enabling the use of various lenses to understand the micro and macro influences of the teaching team's experiences of sharing and constructing knowledge. The ethnographic approach places the teacher education researchers in their own community of interest, based on the aspiration to reduce barriers to observation and discussion of phenomena, and to increase sensitivity to the meaning of the shared experiences. The choice of ethnography as a method reflects and values the complexity of the research focus and the importance of narratives to provide 'thick descriptions' to engage in close, shared conversations, and to negotiate emerging conversations about possibilities for changes to the ways in which knowledge is shared and constructed. Close partnerships between teacher educators and teaching teams, as both researchers and teachers, is supported by an ethnographic approach and its openness and 'non-interventionist' code.

Thus, we propose a method to negotiate and research the concept of flows of knowledge to strengthen and grow connections between teacher education and early childhood centre communities. The role of research is critical, although there is a shift in emphasis away from research institutions, favouring instead the generation of knowledge within centre communities in a mutually beneficial flow of knowledge between research institution and centre. Teacher education institutions benefit significantly from involvement that has wide-ranging practical benefits for the design of 'their' programmes. They have a critical role to play in reconceptualising and informing collaborative research in centre communities.

Collaborative research in teaching teams requires a research design that is qualitative and interpretive, involving a process of observation, reflection and discussion of the teaching team's day-to-day construction, sharing and experience of knowledge in an early childhood centre. Through the sharing of critical discussions and different narratives of experience, teachers enrich their teaching teams and the centre community (Dalli et al. 2012). The approach builds on the ongoing development of skills in collaboration that are regarded as important for early childhood centre communities, and it aligns with current research and scholarship in the field of teachers' work which call for a rich, deep understanding of how teachers work together and share ideas and narratives about themselves and their teaching practices (see for instance Dalli et al. 2012; Osgood 2012).

Both methodologies have strong associations with cultural research models relevant to the local communities. While it is important to avoid regarding these approaches as synonymous, the essence of respecting voice, 'natural' settings, complex influences and shared experiences make this approach sensitive to social and cultural difference. The methodological emphasis is on research as a professional collaborative practice rather than as a top-down approach of knowledge production and reproduction in the academy being transferred/applied to teachers' pedagogical practice. The ground-up approach puts into practice the tenets of critical theoretical, narrative and dialogical approaches to building collaborative inquiry (Woodrow 2008). The combination of these two methodologies is closely aligned to 'symbolic interactionism' and focuses on how the research and teaching partners make sense of their environment, creating a synergy between the research focus and the research design, and providing a robust platform for the analysis of findings as teachers and researchers construct, discuss and reconstruct the data. In the sense of critical ecological ethnography, such a study depends on partnerships within each centre being strengthened, professional relationships being negotiated and knowledge of the centre community being enriched.

53.6   Concluding Comments

In this chapter, we have argued for the importance of researching and uncovering flows of knowledge within ECE teaching teams, by focusing on the existing capacities of early childhood centres to develop and grow capability from the 'ground-up'. It is through such a connectedness between teacher educators and teachers working alongside one another that new, beginning and experienced teachers in these centres will be able to theorise their flows of knowledge. Thus, we promote an integrated and research-oriented model of pedagogical leadership, through the construction and maintenance of supportive knowledge-sharing environments. Our argument is grounded in a desire to build upon New Zealand-based research evidence, drawing on inclusive and participatory models of early education, and focussing on the richness of sharing knowledge to enhance teaching practice between participants in a centre community.

The nature of knowledge communities embraces teacher–learner relationships through engagements with teachers' understanding of their teaching environment, relationships within their centres, and their own learning. Networks of co-constructing learners are critically influenced by the ways teacher knowledge is constructed in EC teaching teams and negotiated in teacher education, requiring a complex awareness of the influence of teacher–teacher relationships on teacher–learner relationships. A critical and reflective approach to knowledge of the learning and teaching environment demands a collective experience in an ECE setting, in which teachers have an awareness of the 'other' in their centre. It is increasingly understood that dualisms like child/adult are rather limiting, although they may currently be promoted through teacher education. What we envisage is a ground-up research study to explore, challenge and impact on practices in early childhood centres and on teacher education programmes, through a critical ecological ethnography. We have outlined ways in which such a model might shape further understandings and strategies for sharing and developing knowledge. However, such a model can enhance practices only through careful and extensive development and dissemination to both professional and academic communities, to benefit learners, teachers, teacher educators and the wider community and society in Aotearoa New Zealand and overseas.

References

Bolstad, R., Gilbert, J., McDowall, S., Bull, A., Boyd, S., & Hipkins, R. (2012). *Supporting future-oriented learning and teaching: A New Zealand perspective*. Report prepared for the Ministry of Education. Wellington, New Zealand: New Zealand Council for Educational Research and Ministry of Education. Retrieved from www.educationcounts.govt.nz/publications

Calder, P. (2015). Policies and discourses in early childhood education and care. *International Journal of Early Years Education, 23*(3), 227–229. doi:10.1080/09669760.2015.1074561

Dall'Alba, G. (2009). Learning professional ways of being: Ambiguities of becoming. *Educational Philosophy and Theory, 41*(1), 34–45.

Dalli, C. (2008). Pedagogy, knowledge and collaboration: Towards a ground-up perspective on professionalism. *European Early Childhood Education Research Journal, 16*(2), 175–185.

Dalli, C. (2010). Towards the re-emergence of a critical ecology of the early childhood profession in New Zealand. *Contemporary Issues in Early Childhood, 11*(1), 61–74. doi:10.2304/ciec.2010.11.1.61

Dalli, C., Miller, L., & Urban, M. (2012). Early childhood grows up: Towards a critical ecology of the profession. In L. Miller, C. Dalli, & M. Urban (Eds.), *Early childhood grows up: Towards a critical ecology of the profession* (pp. 3–19). London, England: Springer.

Duncan, J. (2004). Misplacing the teacher? New Zealand early childhood teachers and early childhood education policy reforms, 1984–96. *Contemporary Issues in Early Childhood, 5*(2), 160–177. Retrieved from doi:10.2304/ciec.2004.5.2.4

Education Council. (2016). *Strategic options for developing future orientated initial teacher education*. Wellington, New Zealand: Author. Retrieved from https://educationcouncil.org.nz/sites/default/files/Strategic%20options%20REVISED%2029%20JUNEpdf.pdf

Farquhar, S., & Tesar, M. (2016a). Theorising what it means to be pedagogical in (the) early years (of) teaching. In J. M. Ioriro & W. Parnell. *Disrupting through imagination: Rethinking early childhood research* (pp. 26–36). New York NY: Routledge.

Farquhar, S., & Tesar, M. (2016b). Focus groups as temporal ecosystems for newly qualified early childhood teachers. *Contemporary Issues in Early Childhood, 17*(3), 261–274. doi:10.1177/1463949116660949

Fleer, M. (2010). The re-theorisation of collective pedagogy and emergent curriculum. *Cultural Studies of Science Education, 5*, 563–576.

Gibbons, A., Farquhar, S., & Tesar, M. (2015). The politics and practices of early childhood teacher education: Critical provocations for meaningful mentoring. In C. Murphy & R. Smith (Eds.), *Mentoring in early childhood: A compilation of thinking, pedagogy and practice*. Wellington, New Zealand: NZCER Press.

Johnston, K. (2015). Early childhood services red-flagged. *The New Zealand Herald*. Retrieved from http://www.nzherald.co.nz/nz/news/article.cfm?c_id=1&objectid=11435235

Meade, A. (2010, November). *The contribution of ECE centres of innovation to building knowledge about teaching and learning 2003–2010*. Paper presented to TLRI Early Years Symposium. Wellington, NZ. Retrieved from http://www.tlri.org.nz.ezproxy.aut.ac.nz/sites/default/files/pages/AMeade-ECE-Paper2010.pdf

Middleton, S., & May, H. (1997). *Teachers talk teaching 1915–1995: Early childhood, schools and teachers colleges*. Palmerston North, New Zealand: Dunmore Press.

Ministry of Education. (1996). *Te Whāriki: He Whāriki Matauranga Mō Ngā Mokopuna o Aotearoa, early childhood curriculum*. Wellington, New Zealand: Learning Media.

New Zealand Parliament. (2012). *Inquiry into 21st century learning environments and digital literacy: Report of the Education and Science Committee*. Retrieved from http://www.parliament.nz/en-nz/pb/sc/documents/reports/50DBSCH_SCR5695_1/inquiry-into-21st-century-learning-environments-and-digital

Osgood, J. (2012). *Narratives from the nursery: Negotiating professional identities in early childhood*. Abingdon, England: Routledge.

Sumsion, J. (2002). Becoming, being and unbecoming an early childhood educator: A phenomenological case study of teacher attrition. *Teaching and Teacher Education, 18*, 869–885.

Woodrow, C. (2008). Discourses of professional identity in early childhood: Movements in Australia. *European Early Childhood Education Research Journal, 16*(2), 269–280.

Author Biographies

Marek Tesar is a Senior Lecturer in childhood studies and early childhood education at the University of Auckland. His research focuses on childhood, philosophy of education, policy and methodology. Marek's scholarship and activism merge theoretical work with a practical impact on the mundane lives of children and their childhoods in Aotearoa New Zealand and overseas.

Andrew Gibbons is an early childhood teacher educator. He has published widely on topics including the role of technology in education, NZ ECE policy directions in the past two decades, the educational implications of the work of Albert Camus, the philosophy of education and approaches to early childhood curriculum.

Sandy Farquhar is Senior Lecturer at the University of Auckland. Her research is in philosophy of childhood, teacher identity and policy. She is particularly interested in philosophical inquiry, metaphor and narrative theories. Sandy has authored many articles/book chapters, and co-edited two issues on philosophy of early childhood in *Educational Philosophy and Theory*.

Chapter 54
Conquering Content: A Key to Promoting Self-efficacy in Primary Science Teaching

Anne Hume

54.1 Introduction

At a time when nations are calling for scientifically literate citizenry to achieve economic, societal and environmental goals (Slavin et al. 2014), international studies report concern about primary students' growing disinterest in science and falling rates of achievement (e.g. Tytler et al. 2008). Inquiry-based learning in real life contexts is widely promoted as a means for gaining primary students' interest and enabling their engagement in authentic scientific processes and argumentation as they develop understanding of key science ideas and vocabulary (e.g. Nowicki et al. 2013). Unfortunately, it is reported that these approaches/practices are not commonplace in primary classrooms (Slavin et al. 2014).

54.2 Barriers to Inquiry-Based Learning in Primary Science

The reasons why inquiry-based learning in science, indeed science itself, has a low profile in primary science classrooms needs further research (Slavin et al. 2014), but some factors clearly have a bearing. First and foremost, are the very high expectations that an overcrowded curriculum places on primary teachers, requiring them to have the professional knowledge and capabilities to teach numerous subjects to a diverse range of learners (Nowicki et al. 2013) Added pressures come from the

A. Hume (✉)
University of Waikato, Hamilton, New Zealand
e-mail: annehume@waikato.ac.nz

© Springer Nature Singapore Pte Ltd. 2017   799
M.A. Peters et al. (eds.), *A Companion to Research in Teacher Education*,
DOI 10.1007/978-981-10-4075-7_54

restricted time made available within school programmes for science teaching and learning because other subjects take precedence within the current political climate. Thus few opportunities exist for teachers to develop rich pedagogical knowledge (PCK), that is, the very special, often tacit form of professional knowledge a teacher possesses that enables him/her to successfully teach certain topics to particular groups of students. PCK encompasses teachers' personal orientations towards science and science teaching (beliefs and attitudes) and knowledge of their learners' characteristics, which in turn impact on what content they select to teach for a particular topic, the specific instructional strategies they choose to use and how they monitor students' learning (Magnusson et al. 1999). New curriculum imperatives such as inquiry learning in science requires sophisticated PCK since

> ... teaching elementary science via inquiry is a highly complex task, requiring a high level of planning and preparation as well as on-the-spot decision-making to meld multiple factors including the instructional context, knowledge of how children learn, how learners are likely to think and what they will find confusing, pedagogical knowledge, and science content knowledge. (Nowicki et al. 2013, p. 1138)

Crucial sources of this PCK are science content knowledge and classroom teaching experience, both of which are known to be limited for many primary teachers (Fleer 2009). The underdeveloped science content knowledge (CK) and PCK of many primary teachers leads, not surprisingly, to low levels of confidence in teaching science and even avoidance (Tytler et al. 2008), which compounds the problem. This avoidance behaviour of some teachers can be linked to self-efficacy beliefs, which involve judgments about one's ability to carry out a particular task effectively (Bandura 1997) and are both domain- and context-specific. In the context of this study self-efficacy relates to a teacher's belief in his/her ability to teach science effectively.

For science educators searching for ways to bring about reform in primary science education increasing science teaching self-efficacy amongst teachers becomes a key goal because it is known "teachers with high science teaching self-efficacy belief develop a lasting interest in science, a positive desire to help students, and a willingness to improve their science teaching" (Velthius et al. 2015, p. 217). They invest time, set goals, and display resilience and persistence when things do not go smoothly. Thus when considering professional learning opportunities to foster strong self-efficacy beliefs for science teaching, it is important to find the sources of these beliefs. Clearly since strong CK is a prerequisite for strong PCK (Magnusson et al. 1999), it is not surprising that various studies have shown the amount of content or subject matter knowledge is an important predictor for science teaching self-efficacy (e.g., Rohaan et al. 2012). However, some authors warn against the acquisition of formal science knowledge as a sole means of improving primary teachers' attitudes towards science teaching and point to better understanding of the nature of science and PCK development as essential components of teachers' professional knowledge for teaching inquiry-based science (e.g., Fleer 2009). Nowicki et al. (2013) add that teacher learning might prove more efficient if situated in teachers' daily practice, and "in concert with good quality materials may be the most efficient method for mitigating elementary teachers' lack of academic preparation in science" (p. 1151).

In his pioneer work into self-efficacy beliefs, Bandura (1997) identified four sources that can influence and/or these beliefs: mastery experience, for example, successful teaching episodes in the past which are direct results of the individual's own effort and abilities; vicarious experience, like observing a mentor or teaching colleague successfully accomplish a task; social (or verbal) experience, such as feedback from others that praises and acknowledges an individual's teaching performance; and physiological states, for example, feelings of excitement or anticipation that are aroused by the prospect of a teaching activity. The instances above denote positive influences and are likely to build high levels of self-efficacy—the converse, when such experiences are a negative influence, is likely to result in low self-efficacy beliefs. Bandura (1997) thought that enactive mastery was the most influential source because it provided the most convincing evidence for the individual that he/she could succeed or not at the task. The more successful this experience, the more likely the person will repeat or extend the experience and each successive proficient performance is confirmatory and becomes a new source of self-efficacy—a cycle of self-reinforcement.

With this understanding Velthius et al. (2015) advocate professional development that includes opportunities for primary teachers to gain experience from all four of Bandura's sources of influence, as they are coached and assisted during implementation of what they have learned to their own classrooms. Their school-based strategy, featuring a teacher design team (TDT) comprising three teachers with varying levels of experience and interest, showed promising increases in the teachers' self-efficacy, especially where support of implementation by the expert facilitator resulted in authentic task-specific mastery experiences. A TDT is a group of teachers collaborating together to design and enact classroom programmes from a common science curriculum. Expectations are that the teachers themselves lead the changes, make the necessary connections between the reform intentions and their own practices in their classrooms, develop and use new curriculum materials to influence teacher practice and ultimately engage in curriculum redevelopment school-wide. Teacher interaction and work in the team is expected to contribute to their professional learning by raising their awareness of diverse pedagogical approaches, deepening their science content knowledge and changing the way they interact which contributes to organisational levels at the school-cultural and school-structural levels. Velthius et al. (2015) noted the teachers in their study learned only the science knowledge and pedagogy needed to improve their own practice—their learning was highly contextual. The expert facilitator at times acted as a trigger causing teachers to reflect on their practice from another perspective or maintain their focus, and for some teaching when necessary.

54.3   The Context of This Study

This study occurred under the umbrella of a formal collaboration between the
Faculty of Education in a New Zealand (NZ) university and the schools it worked
with to deliver the school-based part of an Initial Teacher Education (ITE)
programme—the Collaborative University School Partnership (CUSP). In the
CUSP partnership the Faculty of Education staff worked with the school's mentor
teachers to co-construct a more seamless, coherent and relevant school-based
experience for pre-service teachers enrolled in the first year of a primary teacher
undergraduate programme. In science, if the school-based component was to successfully complement the university-based programme then the associate teachers
needed strong PCK for science inquiry learning to support their students' active
engagement with ideas and investigations where the students are thinking and
working scientifically (Tytler et al. 2008). Evaluation of the first trial of the new
science school-based ITE suggested the PCK of many associate teachers did not
support achievement of the aims and practices of reform-based science education,
as modelled by lecturers. For example, the associate teachers experienced difficulties in understanding the science tasks set by the university for the school-based
component; there was general absence of authentic scientific inquiry learning
opportunities in the associate teachers' science programmes and pedagogies; and
the science teaching and learning had a low profile in schools' science programmes.
Anecdotal evidence from the pre-service teachers suggested many found themselves in situations where their associate teachers seemed either reluctant to collaborate on the science tasks, or happy to let them take sole responsibility for
planning and teaching the science lessons. These situations resulted in significant
numbers of pre-service teachers being unable to work collaboratively with their
associate teachers designing reform-based science pedagogies.

54.4   The Response to the Challenge in the Science
Curriculum Area Within CUSP

The teacher educators recognised this situation might be symptomatic of the wider
issues in science education around falling levels of student engagement and
achievement in science. In the NZ context these falls are also beginning in the
primary sector of schooling and are being attributed to: the low status of science in
NZ primary school curricula generally; the widespread lack of knowledge and
confidence in teaching science amongst primary teachers; and minimal systemic
support for NZ science teaching (Bull et al. 2010). However, research findings into
teachers' professional learning in science education also pointed towards possible
ways to redress the situation by strengthening teachers' PCK, and the teacher
educators saw opportunities to take affirmative action under the CUSP umbrella.
To explore possibilities, one of the university lecturers approached the Principal of

a CUSP school with a proposal for enhancing teachers' science PCK through a small research project. The Principal was very positive about such a project and invited the lecturer to meet with her and the school's Science Curriculum Leader.

54.5 The CUSP School's Response

In her introduction to a potential research project, the teacher educator acknowledged the experience and expertise of the school's mentor teachers around education for the twenty first century and pedagogy for student-centred inquiry learning as strengths in the schools' educational programmes. Within the context of CUSP, she then raised the school-based learning experiences for pre-service teachers in science as an issue and identified them as an area for enhancement. She revealed how few pre-service teachers reported seeing classroom teachers modelling science teaching on their teaching practice, while other pre-service teachers found working with their associate teachers problematic in science compared to other subject areas. It appeared many associate teachers were less certain about their role in providing and supporting pre-service teachers' learning opportunities in science education, especially when it came to assisting with classroom planning and teaching episodes around science inquiry learning. The teacher educator shared key research findings from national and international sources with the Principal and the Science Curriculum Leader that might shed light on the pre-service teachers' practicum experiences in science.

In response the Principal and science curriculum leader openly recognised and accepted the need to strengthen science education in their school. They appreciated such moves would in turn increase their teachers' capabilities as associate teachers. In particular, the school leaders wanted to support their teachers' science pedagogy, and more closely align the school science education programme with the intent of the recently revised New Zealand Curriculum (NZC) (MoE 2007) and with twenty first-century learning principles that were a focus in the school's futures-focused curriculum plan. After further discussions, the school leaders came to the view that improvements in science education were best addressed through enrichment of all associate teachers' PCK at the school and redevelopment of the school science plan. At this point in the discussion, the teacher educator thought it opportune to introduce the notion of a collaborative research project featuring an intervention known as Content Representation (CoRe) design as a means for enhancing teachers' science PCK and initiating curriculum redevelopment.

The teacher educator explained that a CoRe, as originally developed by Loughran et al. (2006), is a strategy for making key features of the pedagogical content knowledge (PCK) of an individual teacher, or group of teachers, obvious to others (see Table 54.1). This exposure of the knowledge underpinning the teaching of certain science content to specific groups of students is achieved via the use of a framework or template, which teachers are asked to fill in. It contains what the

Table 54.1 Template for a content representation (CoRe), as developed by Loughran et al. (2006)

Pedagogical questions/prompts	Big idea 1	Big idea 2	Big idea 3
What you intend the students to learn about this idea			
Why is it important for the students to know this?			
What else you know about this idea (that you do not intend students to know yet)			
Difficulties connected with teaching this idea			
Knowledge about student thinking which influences teaching about this idea			
Other factors that influence your teaching of this idea			
Teaching procedures (and particular reasons for using these to engage with this idea)			
Ways of ascertaining student understanding or confusion about the idea			

teachers consider are the big ideas of the topic to be learned by students, and a series of questions/prompts that reveal the reasoning and actions of these teachers as they help students to develop understanding of the big ideas.

The teacher educator pointed out that not only did CoRe design have a proven record for exposing the PCK of experienced science teachers, but it was also proving effective in her experience for enhancing both pre- and in-service teachers' capabilities in science teaching. She found CoRe design, when done collaboratively and facilitated by an expert, helped address a significant cause of teachers' trepidation about teaching science, that is, lack of deep and coherent understanding of science content. This mastery of content for primary science can be achieved in CoRe design via the initial focus on establishing key science ideas for a given topic and the essential content students needed to learn for understanding of these ideas. The pedagogical prompts in the body of the CoRe then help teachers to consider, share and debate how best to scaffold students' learning of this core content. The teacher educator also saw its potential for assisting teachers in 'bigger picture' school-wide curriculum design if the intervention was introduced within a whole school science curriculum redevelopment. The Principal recognised the potential of the intervention and quickly accepted the opportunity to collaborate. Within a week a plan was negotiated that involved five university researchers (including the teacher educator as Principal Investigator) and all 25 teachers at the school. Together, they worked as a team in a school-based research project featuring CoRe design.

54.6 Methodology

The university researchers knew from research that most successful teacher development programmes take place inside school-based professional learning communities (PLCs) and use collaborative models of inquiry involving cycles of research and development where teachers shift their primary purpose from teaching to learning. In these PLCs teachers participate as self-regulated learners with opportunities to engage in deep discussion, open debates, and the exploration and enrichment of possibilities for action. Characteristics of successful PLCs include: shared values and vision; collective responsibility; reflective professional inquiry; collaboration, and group; as well as individual learning (Bolam et al. 2005).

Fortunately as a member of CUSP, the school in this partnership project had an established culture of collaborative professional learning. Since the research focus was on an identified practice-based problem, the study employed a pragmatic methodology featuring a Design-Based Research (DBR) approach (Anderson and Shattuck 2012). The DBR approach has the potential to enrich a PLC experience by offering a bridge between research and practice in education via a collaborative partnership between researchers and practitioners. Adopting this approach the project team was able to negotiate the study through all its phases "from initial problem identification, through literature review, to intervention design and construction, implementation, assessment, and to the creation and publication of theoretical and design principles" (Anderson and Shattuck 2012, p. 17). On a pragmatic level, the teachers' key intent was to trial the CoRe design intervention as a precursor to planning, implementing and evaluating a series of related science lessons featuring inquiry-based learning. The findings were to inform their planning of a whole school science education programme, to be called the Science Implementation Plan (SIP), at the end of the year of which teachers at the school had authorship and ownership. The teachers at the school would have authorship and ownership of the plan. For their part, the researchers focused on the impact of CoRe design on the teachers' PCK in science because they sought to increase the impact, transfer, and translation of their research around science PCK enhancement through CoRe design into teaching practice. They hoped working with teachers to build new theory and develop design principles that guide and improve the teachers' practice would inform education research generally. It was anticipated that the richer science PCK of the mentor teachers would in turn enhance the learning opportunities of the pre-service teachers on teaching practice in their classrooms under the CUSP project umbrella. The strength of the partnership lay in the underlying synergy of the purposes and goals each partner sought to achieve by participating in the project.

The initial research design (including purpose and goals, relevant literature, professional learning opportunities, data gathering, discussion of findings and time) was co-developed by the university researchers and the Principal and Science Curriculum leader from the partner school. As the plan unfolded classroom teachers made the pragmatic research decisions related to the day-to-day implementation of the plan, for example, the topics for CoRe design, unit planning processes, and the timing and nature of classroom implementation of unit plans and reflective/evaluative opportunities with researchers. The researchers in turn facilitated workshops that introduced teachers to: key features of inquiry-based learning in science; high quality resources to support inquiry learning; and the process of CoRe design. They also acted as mentors providing feedback to teachers as they implemented their professional learning in classrooms. The project took place over a year and involved distinct phases over two cycles or iterations.

54.7 The Lead-Up to the Development of the School's Science Implementation Plan (SIP)

While most teachers were experienced and skilled in student-centred pedagogy and inquiry learning, the school's self-review processes had revealed teachers were not so in science. The existing school science plan was over 20 years old and few teachers looked to it for guidance in their science lessons. Consequently science was taught on a rather ad hoc basis in the school and topics linked to chemistry and/or physics concepts typically did not feature strongly in classroom programmes.

CoRe design brought the teachers' focus back on students' learning of science concepts and processes as outlined by the NZC (MoE 2007), and acted as a catalyst for rich professional learning at a number of levels within the school-based PLC of teachers, when supported by knowledgeable facilitators and high quality resources. Teachers spoke of the CoRe design process deepening their science content knowledge by its emphasis on conceptual understanding. Here a teacher reflects on the former superficiality of the science content in her lessons.

> The CoRe was a new way of planning, like it made me focus on concepts of water and then hone in on what we wanted … The CoRe made me realise how I gloss over things. (Year 3/4 teacher, focus group interview)

Interestingly, while researchers were only invited into a total of 5 lessons for observations in this first cycle, in the follow-up focus interviews teachers at all levels reported positive experiences of teaching their science units and the student interest and learning that happened. Teachers in one of the Junior School groups, i.e. the Year Two Group who were teaching 6 years old, based their CoRe around big ideas in the Primary Connections Unit 'All Mixed up' (an early Chemistry topic). They felt well supported by their CoRe and the resource. An experienced teacher in the group commented:

> The structure, the link between the CoRe and the 'All mixed up' (Primary Connections unit) gave us confidence. (Junior School Teacher, Year 2, Focus group interview)

She had invited a researcher to observe her science lesson and was surprised and encouraged by students' enthusiastic responses to the investigations into everyday phenomena, and the scientific understanding they gained. As a mentor teacher, she saw the potential in the resource materials for developing the professional knowledge and capabilities of student teachers. She recognised how the resource had scaffolded her own scientific understanding and that of her students.

Slow to start, I felt this is going to be too boring, I was wrong. The first two lessons getting their ideas was not exciting, but actually it did hook the kids in. …You couldn't go wrong. The student teachers could take this lesson and do well. It gave me the background knowledge, broke it down into the children's thinking, and gave you scope to move sideways. …After you (researcher observer) came in and observed my sifting lesson, I really thought the kids had not really quite grasped it, which I was quite surprised about, so I did another lesson, but with different substances as a whole class lesson. I linked it back to noodles and rice, and suddenly I saw little light bulbs going on everywhere and "Oh, of course!" I also used a steamer with holes and the kids recognized this. (Junior School Teacher, Year 2, Focus group interview)

To the research team and Principal of the school perhaps the most gratifying outcomes of the project were the improved dispositions of teachers towards science teaching and the positive responses of their students. It appears that both mastery and social experiences (Bandura 1997) were sources of self-efficacy beliefs, as these comments show:

T7. I would not consider myself a teacher of science or a good teacher of science or a natural teacher of science so it [CoRe design] helped me engage with the material. It helped me think more deeply about the material. I felt I actually learnt a lot myself which actually improved me as well so with that, and with what the children brought as well, we just all learned heaps, and the markers were there too which kept me on track.

T3: I'm not naturally predisposed to teach science; the way we planned it has given me more confidence to do that…I knew the [resource]was there but I have more confidence to source things from the [resource]and other places. In the past I have been flailing around in the dark about the scientific concepts…I have more confidence to go out and teach that, and seeing the results from children, and the continuing conversations [with colleagues and researchers], have shown me I've done something right. (Middle School Teachers, Focus Group interview)

Principal: The teachers are saying they are confident in (1) that they have a plan to share with the students so they know where they are going and how that links with what everybody else is doing and (2) they know how they are linking enviro (environmental science) and science now, it wasn't clear before that, it felt too fragmented. And they have a planning model – the CoRe design – so they are now confident they can talk to students about 'this is the big idea that we are working on and this is how this impacts into the plan and this is the process we are going to use'. They are quite clear that they now have a much more focused way of talking to students about science education in the school. (Principal interview)

To provide more constructive feedback to individual teachers re their classroom practice (and to bring greater reliability to research data) the researchers designed an Observational Protocol to use during classroom observations. In conversations after lessons, this protocol enabled the researchers to provide individual teachers with more consistent and focused feedback on their classrooms actions and those of their students that were pertinent to their PCK development for teaching inquiry-based science. When collated, the data from completed observational protocols allowed trends in teachers' PCK for science inquiry learning to be identified and fed back to the teachers for discussion. This collated data provided key direction for the project team when establishing the set of contextualised design principles for the redevelopment and implementation of school's science education plan.

The input of the researchers in the process was openly acknowledged and valued by the teachers, especially the clarification of scientific ideas and feedback on teachers' classroom implementation of their professional learning related to inquiry learning in science. Although somewhat misunderstood during the first cycle of the study, most teachers came to recognise CoRe design in the second cycle as a useful tool for collaborative thinking and sharing of teaching expertise and knowledge within the teaching teams before conventional unit planning began. These experiences ultimately led to school-wide ownership by teachers of the need for a conceptually based science education plan for the school promoting learning in ways that mirrored authentic scientific inquiry.

Teachers welcomed the redevelopment of the SIP and made a number of suggestions and recommendations about its structure and content. The researchers also made observations from the project findings, which they raised for the school to consider when developing the plan and meeting teachers' professional learning needs.

54.8 The Design of the School's Science Implementation Plan

Late in the year of the project, a group of interested teachers known as the Science Development Group (SIG) met on three separate days to design the school's SIP. It was notable that while the research team and the Principal did provide some 'seeding' ideas and broad direction for the plan, the SDG effectively took over the planning process. On the basis of findings from the project, including their colleagues' views on what form of guidance they sought as teachers of science, this lead group with input from researchers designed a detailed set of principles, which were to underpin future science programmes in the school. They included:

- Collaborative CoRe design and unit planning as a means of strengthening teachers' science content knowledge, PCK and feelings of self-efficacy.
- A school-wide science implementation plan with a conceptual framework that provides direction and guidance for students' learning progressions in science as they move through their six years of primary schooling.
- Pedagogies where students engage in inquiry-based learning that mirrors authentic scientific inquiry.
- The development and fostering of scientific capabilities and dispositions in students (i.e. engage with science and ask questions, design investigations, gather and interpret data, use evidence, critique evidence, and interpret representations).
- School-wide assessment of sufficient depth to allow students to show that they can perform in increasingly more complex ways from school entry to Year Six. Evidence in any year to include a range of data to exemplify conceptual development, and science capabilities and dispositions linked to the school's SIP.

After the 3-day planning session in November, the Principal encapsulated how these principles and the collaboration with the researchers underpinned the construction of the school's SIP and teachers' professional learning.

> The three days spent by the development team in designing a new school implementation plan were a real gift to the school. The strong partnership that had developed with the researchers became a true collaboration. The researchers provided really helpful analysis and expert support. Rarely do lead teachers have such quality time for reflection, professional learning support and co construction of school curriculum. Working together where everyone contributed; being able to clarify progressions for concept development in science in the New Zealand curriculum for our implementation plan; making resource links and a purchasing plan; exploring and capturing examples of assessment practice from online sites such as the MOE, NZCER and the old NEMP exemplars were integral to the completion of our work for the year. (Principal's written exit comments)

The SIP combined flexibility of contexts, content and delivery with a structured progression of conceptual development through the schooling levels. The recommended pedagogy featured inquiry-based learning that mirrored authentic scientific inquiry. The draft SIP was aligned with the school's mission statement and vision and was to be introduced to and trialled by the teaching staff during the following year.

54.9 Conclusions

This study illustrates how a partnership, forged between university researchers and teachers around a shared and authentic problem of practice, produced solutions that provided the necessary knowledge, vision and will to move education practice forward in their context. From the findings in this DBR study, teachers and researchers together generated five generic principles (Yang and Hannifin 2005) for strengthening teachers' PCK and primary science education programmes in the study school. In this process the intervention of CoRe design proved to be a mediating tool for 'teaching science content' by giving purpose to teachers' exploration of high quality resources, i.e. the Science Learning Hub and the Primary Connections Programme resources. Through facilitated discussions around these resources, with the emphasis on identifying and understanding big science ideas and student-centred inquiry activities for constructing these ideas, teachers learned the necessary content for effective primary science teaching—the intervention immersed teachers simultaneously in content learning and pedagogical reasoning, the foundations for strong PCK. These teachers were then able to implement their new knowledge directly into their teaching in a supportive and reflective environment that provided the four main sources of influence on self-efficacy beliefs—mastery experience, vicarious experience, social experience, and physiological states (Bandura 1997). As a result teachers' positive dispositions towards science teaching were increased, and they were more confident and proactive in their attempts to create purposeful and meaningful science learning experiences for their students. Evidence from these teachers' classrooms verified that their students were engaging in science inquiry with interest and enthusiasm—certainly students were not turning away from science. Such teachers clearly have greater potential to be effective mentor teachers in the provision of school-based ITE in science. Such a partnership experience and the outcomes can serve as a model for other primary schools, given the support of school leadership and outside expert input where deemed appropriate.

References

Anderson, T., & Shattuck, J. (2012). Design-based research: A decade of progress in education research? *Educational Researcher, 41*(1), 16–25.

Bandura, A. (1997). *Self-efficacy: The exercise of control*. New York, NY: Freeman.

Bolam, R., McMahon, A., Stoll, L., Thomas, S., & Wallace, M., et al. (2005). *Creating and sustaining effective professional learning communities* (Research Report RP637). Nottingham UK: Department for Education and Science, DfES Publications.

Bull, A., Gilbert, J., Barwick, H., Hipkins, R., & Baker, R. (2010). *Inspired by science*. A paper commissioned by the Royal Society of New Zealand and the Prime Minister's Chief Science Advisor. Accessed on the 20/03/2013 from http://www.nzcer.org.nz/pdfs/inspired-by-science.pdf.

Fleer, M. (2009). Supporting scientific conceptual consciousness or learning in 'a roundabout way' in play-based contexts. *International Journal of Science Education, 31*(8), 1069–1089. doi:10.1080/09500690801953161.

Loughran, J., Berry, A., & Mullhall, P. (2006). *Understanding and developing science teachers' pedagogical content knowledge*. Rotterdam, The Netherlands: Sense Publishers.

Magnusson, S., Krajcik, J., & Borko, H. (1999). Nature, sources and development of pedagogical content knowledge for science teaching. In J. Gess-Newsome & N. G. Lederman (Eds.), *Examining pedagogical content knowledge* (pp. 95–132). Dordrecht, The Netherlands: Kluwer.

Ministry of Education (MoE). (2007). *The New Zealand curriculum*. Wellington: Learning Media.

Nowicki, B. L., Sullivan-Watts, B., Shim, M. K., Young, B., & Pockalny, R. (2013). Factors influencing science content accuracy in elementary inquiry science lessons. *Research in Science Education, 43*(3), 1135–1154. doi:10.1007/s11165-012-9303-4.

Rohaan, E., Taconis, R., & Jochems, W. (2012). Analysing teacher knowledge for technology education in primary schools. *International Journal of Technology and Design Education, 22*, 271–280.

Slavin, R. E., Lake, C., Hanley, P., & Thurston, A. (2014). Experimental evaluations of elementary science programs: A best-evidence synthesis. *Journal of Research in Science Teaching, 51*(7), 870–901.

Tytler, R., Osborne, J. F., Williams, G., Tytler, K., & Cripps Clark, J. (2008). *Opening up pathways: Engagement in STEM across the primary-secondary school transition. A review of the literature concerning supports and barriers to science, technology, engineering and mathematics engagement at primary-secondary transition*. Canberra: Commissioned by the Australian Department of Education, Employment and Workplace Relations.

Velthuis, C., Fisser, P., & Pieters, J. (2015). Collaborative curriculum design to increase science teaching self-efficacy: A case study. *The Journal of Educational Research, 108*, 217–225.

Yang, F., & Hannifin, M. J. (2005). Design-based research and technology-enhanced learning environments. *Educational Technology Research and Development, 53*(4), 5–23.

Author Biography

Anne Hume is Director at the TEMS Education Research Centre at the University of Waikato and lectures in science education at undergraduate, graduate and postgraduate levels. Her research interests centre on PCK development for pre-service and in-service teachers and teacher educators in science education.

Chapter 55
Mentoring of Newly Qualified Teachers in the Educational Sense

Hannu L.T. Heikkinen

The importance of lifelong learning in teachers' professional development has become increasingly topical issue globally. In teaching, especially the transition from education to occupation seems to be more challenging compared to other fields. It is evident that under the rapidly changing circumstances teachers' professional knowledge has to be constantly renewed, and especially in the phase of transition from teacher education to working life, new approaches are needed. In the modern world, the role of teacher has been challenged in many ways. We may say that even some of the fundamental presuppositions of knowledge construction and learning have changed due to the rapid expansion of information and communication technologies in our everyday life and the practices of working life, which in turn have an effect to learning processes in schools and universities.

Many different kinds of systems have been introduced in order to promote the professional learning and well-being of newly qualified teachers, with varying success (e.g. Tynjälä and Heikkinen 2011). We may ask, however, if the growing concern about attrition of new teachers is essentially an educational concern. It seems that much of the debate of teacher induction and mentoring has been motivated by interests that are preset somewhere outside the educational field, such as politics, production or economic life. On this basis, I introduce the idea of *induction and mentoring in the educational sense,* beginning by drawing on the recent discussions on lifelong and lifewide learning to introduce the counterdirectional trends of *informalization* and *formalization* of learning in modern working life.

In its most profound sense, the idea of lifelong learning has its roots in the philosophical ideas of *paideia* in Ancient Greek philosophy and *Bildung* in German human philosophy *Geisteswissenschaft* (Heikkinen 2015). These notions frame the examination of *education* versus *schooling* (Kemmis 2014). In terms of teacher education in its pure sense, the aim is to support professional learning and

H.L.T. Heikkinen (✉)
University of Jyväskylä, Jyväskylä, Finland
e-mail: hannu.l.t.heikkinen@jyu.fi

© Springer Nature Singapore Pte Ltd. 2017
M.A. Peters et al. (eds.), *A Companion to Research in Teacher Education,*
DOI 10.1007/978-981-10-4075-7_55

well-being at work by promoting teachers' autonomous professional agency. But if we want to promote the autonomous agency of new teachers, we find ourselves in a dilemma: how to act as a person (a teacher educator) so as to make another person (a student teacher or a new teacher) autonomous. But this is not quite enough; the ultimate aim of a teacher educator is to help the prospective teacher to make their pupils autonomous and critical thinkers. This is what I call the *second order paradox of teacher education* (Heikkinen et al. 2011).

55.1 Formalization and Informalization in Professional Learning

In contemporary research and policies on adult education, the concepts of *lifewide* and *lifelong* learning have been widely used and sometimes regarded as synonyms. However, there is an important conceptual distinction between the two. The concept of lifelong refers to the time span of learning; the learning process continues throughout the lifetime of the learner. Lifewide learning, in contrast, means that learning takes place broadly in different settings, such as work, human resource development processes, during free time, in family life, or hobbies (European Commission 2001; Tynjälä and Heikkinen 2011).

In the daily activities and practices of teacher education and professional development, it is sometimes difficult to distinguish between the above types of learning. For example, in many occupations active information retrieval is essential. The internet, social media and the various portable devices to make use of them, such as smart phones and tablets, have also become increasingly crucial tools for professional development. Formal education also frequently applies methods that resemble informal learning. For instance, training events that include pair or group discussion enable people to better link their everyday or work-life experiences to the phenomena being addressed. It is also increasingly common to integrate work-based learning, projects, and portfolio work into formal education. Social media has also changed the forms of learning and contributed to the blurring of formal learning boundaries. For example, it is common for university course participants or workers in the workplace to form a group on Facebook, WhatsApp or other social media platforms. This communication, while often highly casual, typically involves a broad exchange of ideas relevant to work or course work. With such discussion groups it is often quite difficult to distinguish what is learning that complies with the course curriculum, and what is something else.

The role of formal learning has changed both in schools and in contemporary working life. We have witnessed a trend in formal learning towards a kind of informalization of learning, i.e. a move towards more non-formal and informal learning. The lines between informal, formal and non-formal learning have been blurred.

The informalization of learning is a reflection of a contemporary pedagogical trend, constructivism. The idea of constructivism is based on the metaphor of knowledge construction, which is done by the learner and scaffolded by the teacher. The basic assumption is that knowledge is not transferred from one person to another, but that the learners construct their knowledge on the basis of their prior views, knowledge, and experiences. In terms of mentoring, the constructivist approach is a marked departure from traditional mentoring, which has been described as the transfer of (tacit) knowledge from a more experienced person to another. This traditional understanding of mentoring is clearly rooted in a different understanding of learning that is contradictory to a constructivist understanding.

However, the lines between formal, informal and non-formal learning are also being blurred for another reason—coming from an altogether opposite direction. In parallel with the discussion of the informalization of learning, there has been another discussion of the *formalization* of learning. This discussion is related to the notion of *recognition of prior learning*, which has been promoted in formal education, especially in the vocational education sector. A practical reason for this in vocational education is that it would simply be a waste of resources for both the learner and the school to invest time in training skills or knowledge that they already possess. It is better to offer opportunities to demonstrate and build on what they have already learned in their work and everyday lives. Skill demonstrations and portfolios are used for this purpose. Thus, two opposite processes seem to be at play within professional learning, and they are sometimes difficult to distinguish from each other. As a consequence of these interconnected processes, formal, informal, and non-formal learning converge (Fig. 55.1).

Whereas in traditional approaches it has been typical to distinguish between formal in-service training and informal job-embedded learning, in the modern approaches it is recognized that formal forms of learning are integrated with informal learning. In informal learning, the learning experiences which often are implicit are explicated to a conscious and conceptual level. The greater understanding of common challenges helps the teachers to face new situations and develop new solutions.

55.2 Induction and Mentoring in the Educational Sense

Induction and mentoring are not the same everywhere. Mentoring practices are rooted in the general practices, or *metapractices* (Kemmis and Grootenboer 2008), that take place in schools and educational systems in various national settings. Drawing on the theory of practice, we may say that different countries have different *ecosystems of practice*, or *practice architectures*, which form the preconditions for the activities and actions that are possible or desirable in the given social setting (Kemmis and Heikkinen 2012). These different national arrangements and practice traditions prefigure (enable and constrain) the actual daily practices in schools and educational institutions.

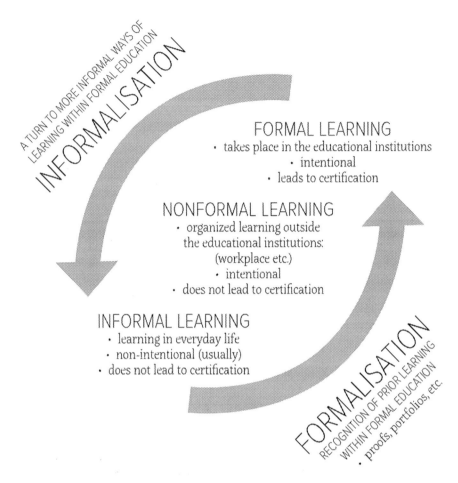

Fig. 55.1 The dialectics of formalization and informalization of learning (Heikkinen et al. 2012; Heikkinen 2015)

An important precondition for the various mentoring practices is the question of whether education is understood as a value and aim in itself, or as something that serves other external aims and purposes. At a general level, we may make a distinction between *education* in its pure meaning, and *schooling,* which is something narrower than education. This distinction between *education* and *schooling* has an important effect on the practices of teacher induction and mentoring (Heikkinen et al. 2014; Kemmis 2014).

Education in its most profound sense is something that enables self-cultivation and aspirations for the good life of individuals and society. 'Education is (…) an initiation into the kinds of practices that foster the good life for each person and the good for humankind (Kemmis 2014, 15).' It is a process of identity work that is not limited by preset targets or standards, but engages people in discussion of the values and aims of (good) human life. Education is about actualizing the unique potential in every human being in society; it is a process of individual and collective self-formation; it is personal as well as collective identity work (Kemmis 2014, Swachten in this volume). Education takes place not only in schools or classrooms, i.e. *formal* settings, but also in *non-formal* settings, such as the human resource development processes of workplaces, and *informal* settings, such as the everyday life of a family or a community. Schooling, in contrast, is a practice that takes place in the formal settings of educational institutions. It is taken for granted that schooling is intended to be educational, but it sometimes actually turns out to be the opposite. Schooling can also be *non-educational*, even *anti-educational*, if it does not promote people's aspiration for self-cultivation (Kemmis 2014, 45).

Schooling, instead, is rooted in instrumental thinking; a means-ends rationality according to which schools are understood primarily as servants of preset aims, targets or values that have been discussed and decided outside of education. In this paradigm, teachers and schools have been commonly viewed as servants of something other, such as the nation state, where the teacher's task is to build national identity and to serve the administration of society. This civil servant metaphor has gradually been replaced with neoliberal metaphors; teachers are no longer regarded as servants of the state, but of production and the economy. In contemporary Western (and nowadays global) discourse on education, economic imperatives play a central role. Teachers are expected to produce workers, consumers, (inner) entrepreneurs, active economic agents and actors who adapt to market trends. Both of these servant metaphors share a common feature: teachers serve an external party that exploits teachers, education, and upbringing as a medium. This thinking has been globalized through the New Public Management doctrine, which uses market forces to hold the public sector accountable and the satisfaction of preferences as the measure of accountability (Kemmis 2014; Lapsley 2009).

Since the emergence of nation states in the modern age, education has been used as an instrument for reproducing national values, collective identities and even patriotism (McDonough and Cornier 2013). But education is also seen as a servant of larger collective identities, such as Europe. Concerns regarding the emergence of a so-called *European dimension* of education have become heightened in the wake of recent European Commission white papers and other EU policy documents that reveal an EU vision for education that is shaped by economic targets and aims; the European Union wants to be the most competitive knowledge-based economy in the world by the year 2020 (European Commission 2010). In line with this objective, performance in education should be improved.

Consequently, much effort has been invested in developing vocational education and training. Contemporary aspirations for lifewide and lifelong learning are also rooted in the interest of developing labour skills; 'students' have been reconceptualized as 'lifewide consumers of education' (Siivonen 2010). Interestingly, the social impact of education has also often been reduced to the concept of 'human capital', the primary purpose of which is to enable economic growth (Schultz 1971). In short, economic discourse has colonized education discourse in many ways. This can also be seen beyond the contemporary discussions of mentoring and teacher induction.

All in all, the emphasis on schooling instead of education has come about through a neoliberal development in education which in practical terms has led to a considerable shift in focus towards the pursuit of economic objectives. As Stephen Kemmis (2014) puts it, the instrumental view pays little attention to what makes human beings human or what the good life might be. In the neoliberal discourses about accountability and effectiveness, there is little discussion of the aims or values of education. It has actually been claimed that education has been reduced to another element of production; '*producing people who are little more than the bearers of useful skills of production, good consumers, and good providers and clients of commercial and administrative services* (Kemmis 2014, 47)'. Drawing on this, we may examine also the practices of teacher education, induction and professional development of teachers in terms of *schooling* versus *education*. Induction of new teachers in the *schooling* sense has much to do with formal organization and administration, arrangements and institutions, agreements and qualifications, directives and formal standards as well as support systems, such as reduction of teaching load or organization of support. Mentoring in the schooling sense focuses mainly on the tools, methods and instruments of mentoring rather than its aims and values. Consequently, this may also mean that mentoring in the schooling sense is motivated by external aims and values, which can also make it non-educational or even anti-educational. The global tendencies towards accountability, standardization and neoliberalism underpin *schooling* instead of *education* in mentoring practices as well as other practices in schools.

Teacher retention rate and educational system effectiveness are often measured purely in terms of their impact on the economy. Teacher attrition, especially during early career years, is a serious problem in many western societies, with problems in the induction phase leading to increasing numbers of young teachers leaving the profession. In the US, for example, it has been estimated that up to 50% of teachers leave within the first five years (Ingersoll 2003). The economic impact of this problem seems to be the central motive behind various attempts to introduce extensive induction programmes for new teachers (e.g. Bickmore and Bickmore 2010; Devos 2010; Howe 2006; Lambson 2010; Marvel et al. 2007; Nasser-Abu Alhija and Fresko 2010; Scheopner 2010).

The *education* element of teacher induction, in contrast, involves teachers and other educational professionals in reflection and discussion about the values and aims of (teacher) education, i.e. human and professional growth. Mentoring in the educational sense is rooted in communication and interaction between teachers and other educational professionals. Induction and mentoring in an educational sense has much to do with the aspiration for the good life and happiness, identity construction and everyday social relations.

Induction and mentoring in the educational sense also means communication and dialogue between more and less experienced workers. There is a major difference here between traditional mentoring and the modern approaches. Traditionally, mentoring has been understood as the transmission of (explicit or tacit) knowledge from a more experienced worker to a less experienced one. Modern approaches, in contrast, are based on the idea that the relationship between the mentor and the mentee is reciprocal and both parties have something to offer. Mentors do not 'transfer' the correct view or knowledge but rather construct meanings and interpretations together with others. A dialogic relationship is based on the assumption that the other is recognized as an equal, which enables reciprocal exchange of ideas and joint construction of knowledge, from which both parties learn. In a mentoring dialogue, both parties participate in verbalizing their conceptions and experiences. In international research literature, the interactive and communicative character of mentoring is highlighted through such expressions as *co-mentoring, mutual mentoring, collaborative mentoring, peer collaboration, critical constructivist mentoring, dialogic mentoring, peer mentoring* and *peer group mentoring* (Bokeno and Vernon 2000; Heikkinen et al. 2012; Musanti 2004).

The communicative character of mentoring in the educational sense may also be conceptualized through Jürgen Habermas' theory of communicative action (1984). Mentoring in the educational sense can be understood as communicative action, whereas mentoring in the schooling sense is rather strategic action. In strategic action, other persons are regarded as objects of speech, whereas in communicative action others are regarded as equal subjects of communication whose interests and opinions are taken into account genuinely and authentically. Communicative action is a process where two or more individuals interact and coordinate their action based upon agreed interpretations of the situation and, more generally, of the values and aims that are valued in society and thus form the background and motivation for social practices. Communicative action respects the right of all participants to express themselves in everyday interaction between the parties regarding the virtues and values of the good life. Strategic action, in contrast, is instrumental action toward other people; purely goal-oriented behaviour where other persons are not equal subjects of human interaction but rather recipients of the message. In strategic action, the concern is to find methods and means to promote aims that are predetermined, either democratically through communicative action in society or in some non-democratic or authoritarian manner. Strategic action is typical of interaction between persons whose positions and relations are determined within social *systems*, whereas communicative action takes place in the *lifeworld* of society (Habermas 1984, 18–95). Mentoring in the schooling sense clearly represents the *system* of mentoring and *strategic action* in human relations, whereas mentoring in the educational sense represents the *lifeworld* dimension of mentoring, which promotes *communicative action* toward others and reflection on the basic values and ends of mentoring.

55.3 The Dilemmas and Paradoxes of Teacher Autonomy

The above mentioned understanding of *education* in its pure form—not that of *schooling*—means that in mentoring practices the aims and values of teachers' work are problematized and critically reflected upon, and not taken as givens embedded in the traditions of education and society. From this point of view, the main purpose of education is to emancipate from irrationality and immaturity; to empower people to use their own reason, as the enlightenment philosopher Kant (1803/1964) put it (see also Hamilton 1999). It follows, therefore, that mentoring meetings should include an aspect of critical reflection. Mentoring in the educational sense is based on a collective aspiration for good life and happiness, and promotes the identity construction of teachers and other educational professionals as individuals and educational communities.

Professional autonomy is both a prerequisite and an aim of the practices of induction and mentoring in the educational sense. High professionals are autonomous agents whose decisions are not made by following orders from somewhere outside the professional field, but are based on mutual understanding of right and wrong, achieved through collective will-formation among the professionals. In other words, professional autonomy is guided by professional ethics.

Professional autonomy is thus social in nature. It is achieved within a social process of collective will-formation, not through individual will-formation. In this respect, there seems to be some confusion regarding the concept of autonomy, which is sometimes misunderstood as individualism. It has been suggested, for example, that teachers in Finland are too autonomous. I would argue that they are not too autonomous in the truest sense of the word, but some teachers may well be too individualistic.

So as to justify my statement, I have to go back to the etymological origins of the word autonomy. The word stems from the Ancient Greek words *auto* and *nomos*, meaning *self* and *law* or *rules*, respectively. Literally speaking, the word means operating 'according to laws that one has made for oneself'. But this simple translation does not reveal the social aspect of autonomy; originally the word referred to social rather than individual practices. In Ancient Greece, this expression was used for a town-state (*polis*) that instituted its own laws. In such an autonomous *polis,* laws were discussed and established by its own citizens. If, however, the town was ruled by laws that had been constituted by another *polis*, in which case the town or village was described as *hetero nomos*, literally meaning that someone else (another *polis*) has instituted the laws. This is the origin of the word *heteronomy,* the opposite of *autonomy*. The original use of the word autonomous implies *interaction and collective will-formation in a social sphere*, whereas individualism refers to action based on the will of a particular individual (Heikkinen et al. 2011). In terms of the aforementioned theory of communicative action (Habermas 1984), we may say that in its original meaning autonomy is rooted in communicative action between participants in society.

Professional autonomy requires capacities and skills for critical thinking. A useful distinction can be drawn here between *critical thinking in the strong sense* and *in the weak sense*, which adds another dimension to the concept of autonomy. Critical thinking in the weak sense is an attitude based on egocentric and biased beliefs; being critical towards others without reflecting or questioning one's own presumptions, actions or behaviour. This is what we often mean when we say that someone is a critical person who readily points out flaws, weaknesses and shortcomings in the world around them, but not so readily in themselves. Critical thinking in the strong sense, instead, starts from self-criticism, where one's own assumptions and beliefs are reflected on, re-examined and questioned (Paul 1994).

Applying this idea, we can draw an important distinction between autonomy in the strong sense and in the weak sense. The autonomy of a professional community in a weak sense means that the community takes a self-centred view of the broader society, which means that collective will-formation takes place only within a limited community and does not take into account the broader social context. Such a professional community focuses on promoting the private interests of the members of the profession. This manifests in strategic action towards others, lobbying and persuading other parties to accept the demands of the professionals. This kind of professional autonomy is typically represented by labour unions.

Professional autonomy in the strong sense is rooted in discussion of the values of the profession and its role in society as a whole. One might say that the will-formation process is based on rather general and public interests and, ultimately, the good of society or humanity. Professional autonomy is realized through communicative action, which is oriented towards mutual understanding and unforced consensus between all possible parties concerned. The main distinctions between individualism and autonomy in the weak sense and in the strong sense are indicated in Table 55.1.

But how to promote autonomy through education? How can we act as a person (a teacher educator) so as to make another person (a student teacher or a new teacher) autonomous? Here we meet a classic problem, *the pedagogical paradox*, first formulated by philosopher Immanuel Kant in his lectures on pedagogy (1803/ 1964, 718): 'How to cultivate freedom through coercion?' The essence of the pedagogical paradox is that we face the problem of assuming the existence of something for which education is the precondition. How it is reasonable to assume that in order for education to be possible the individual must be free,

Table 55.1 Individualism and autonomy in the weak sense and in the strong sense (Heikkinen 2014, 2015)

Individualism	Autonomy	
	Weak autonomy	Strong autonomy
– Personal, individual will-formation	– Social will-formation within a limited community	– Collective will-formation
– Promotion of personal interests	– Promotion of collective interests of the community – Lobbying	Promotion of generalized interests
– The good of the individual	– The good of the professional community	– The good of society and humanity
– Strategic action: oriented to success of the individual	– Strategic action: oriented to success of the profession	– Communicative action: oriented to mutual understanding and unforced consensus

and simultaneously, in order for the individual to become free education is necessary? How can one become something that one already is? In general terms the pedagogical paradox arises when a teacher declares that education should foster autonomy in the sense of a free essence, but on the authority of the teacher. The paradox precipitates a clash between a person's internal regulation (*Selbstbestimmung*) and external regulation (*Fremdbestimmung*). Following the Kantian ideas of Enlightenment, education in general should aim at *maturity* (*Mündigkeit*) and autonomy, which means that everyone should be able to use their own reason: 'Enlightenment is man's emergence from his self-imposed immaturity. Immaturity is the inability to use one's understanding without guidance from another (Kant 1784/2011).

Following this Kantian idea, teacher educators actually face not only the traditional pedagogical paradox, but an also an even more complex pedagogical dilemma: their task is to educate teachers and also inherently the pupils of the prospective teachers. The pedagogical paradox for teacher educators thus becomes a *second order paradox*, as their purpose is not only to promote the autonomy of the upcoming teachers but also the autonomy of the upcoming teachers' future students. Philosophically, this is an intellectual dilemma that cannot be solved through rational thinking. In everyday life, however, we have to do our best to find a way forward.

References

Bickmore, D., & Bickmore, S. (2010). A multifaceted approach to teacher induction. *Teaching and Teacher Education, 26,* 1006–1014.

Bokeno, R. M., & Vernon, W. G. (2000). Dialogic mentoring. *Management Communication Quarterly, 14,* 237–270.

Devos, A. (2010). New teachers, mentoring and the discursive formation of professional identity. *Teaching and Teacher Education, 26,* 1219–1223.

European Commission. (2001). *Making a European area of lifelong learning a reality.* Communication from the Commission. COM (2001) 678 final. Brussels: Commission of the European Communities.

European Commission. (2010). *Developing coherent and system-wide induction programmes for beginning teachers: A handbook for policymakers.* European Commission Staff Working Document SEC (2010) 538 final. Brussels: Commission of the European Communities.

Habermas, J. (1984). *Theory of communicative action volume one: Reason and the rationalization of society.* Boston, MA: Beacon Press

Hamilton, D. (1999). The pedagogic paradox (or why no didactics in England?). *Pedagogy, Culture & Society, 7*(1), 135–152.

Heikkinen, H. (2014). *Drawing a line between autonomy and individualism: Practices of teacher induction and continuing professional development of teachers in Finland.* An invited visiting lecture presented in Department of Education, University of Oxford, October 28, 2014.

Heikkinen, H. (2015). Learning at work and around the coffee mugs: Induction and mentoring in the educational sense. In H. Heikkinen, L. Swachten, & H. Akyol (Eds.), *Bridge over troubled water. New perspectives on teacher induction* (pp. 95–118). Ankara: Pegem Akademi.

Heikkinen, H., Jokinen, H., & Tynjälä, P. (2012). Teacher education and development as lifelong and lifewide learning. In H. Heikkinen, H. Jokinen, & P. Tynjälä (Eds.), *Peer-group mentoring for teacher development* (pp. 3–30). Milton Park: Routledge.

Heikkinen, H., Moate, J., & Lerkkanen, M.-K. (2014). Education with a big E. In H. Heikkinen, J. Moate, & M.-K. Lerkkanen (Eds.), *Enabling education. Proceedings of the Annual Conference of the Finnish Educational Research Association FERA 2013*. (pp. 7–12) Jyväskylä: Finnish Association for Educational Research 66.

Heikkinen, H., Tynjälä, P., & Kiviniemi, U. (2011). Integrative pedagogy in practicum: Meeting the second order paradox of teacher education. In M. Mattsson, T. V. Eilertsen, & D. Rorrison (Eds.), *A practicum turn in teacher education* (pp. 91–112). Rotterdam: Sense.

Howe, E. R. (2006). Exemplary teacher induction: An international review. *Educational Philosophy and Theory, 38*, 287–297.

Ingersoll, R. (2003). *Is there really a teacher shortage?* A report co-sponsored by the Center for the Study of Teaching and Policy and the Center for Policy Research in Education. Seattle, WA: University of Washington, Center for the Study of Teaching and Policy.

Kant, I. (1784/2011). *An answer to the question: What is enlightenment?* Retrieved from http://www.english.upenn.edu/ ~ mgamer/Etexts/kant.html

Kant, I. (1803/1964). Über Pädagogik. In I. Kant (Ed.), *Schriften zur Anthropologie, Geschichtsphilosophie, Politik und Pädagogik* (pp. 711–761). Frankfurt: Suhrkamp.

Kemmis, S. (2014). Education, educational research and the good for humankind. In H. Heikkinen, J. Moate, & M.-K. Lerkkanen (Eds.), *Enabling education. Proceedings of the Annual Conference of the Finnish Educational Research Association FERA 2013* (pp. 15–67). Jyväskylä: Finnish Association for Educational Research 66.

Kemmis, S., & Grootenboer, P. (2008). Situating praxis in practice: Practice architectures and the cultural, social and material conditions for practice. In S. Kemmis & T. Smith (Eds.), *Enabling practice. Challenges for education* (pp. 37–62). Rotterdam: Sense.

Kemmis, S., & Heikkinen, H. (2012). Future perspectives: Peer-group mentoring and international practices for teacher development. In H. Heikkinen, H. Jokinen, & P. Tynjälä (Eds.), *Peer-group mentoring for teacher development* (pp. 144–170). Milton Park: Routledge.

Lambson, D. (2010). Novice teachers learning through participation in a teacher study group. *Teaching and Teacher Education, 26*, 1660–1668.

Lapsley, I. (2009). New public management: The cruellest invention of the human spirit? *Abacus, 45*, 1–21.

Marvel, J., Lyter, D. M., Peltola, P., Stirizek, G. A., & Morton, B. A. (2007). *Teacher attrition and mobility: Results from the 2004–2005 teacher follow-up survey.* Washington, DC: Government Printing Office.

McDonough, K., & Cornier, A.-A. (2013). Beyond patriotic education: Locating the place of nationalism in the public school curriculum. *Social Justice, 8*, 135–150.

Musanti, S. (2004). Balancing mentoring and collaboration. *Curriculum and Teaching Dialogue, 6*, 13–23.

Nasser-Abu Alhija, F., & Fresko, B. (2010). Socialization of new teachers: Does induction matter? *Teaching and Teacher Education 26*, 1592–1597.

Paul, R. (1994). Teaching critical thinking in the strong sense. In K. S. Walters (Eds.) *Re-thinking reason: New perspectives in critical thinking* (pp. 181–198). Albany: SUNY Press.

Scheopner, A. J. (2010). Irreconcilable differences. Teacher attrition in public and catholic schools. *Educational Research Review 5*, 261–277.

Schultz, T. (1971). *Investment in human capital. The role of education and of research.* New York: Macmillan.

Siivonen, P. (2010). *From a "student" to a lifelong "consumer" of education? Constructions of educability in adult students' narrative life histories.* Jyväskylä: FERA.

Tynjälä, P., & Heikkinen, H. (2011). Beginning teachers' transition from pre-service education to working life. *Zeitschrift für Erziehungswissenschaft 14*(1), 11–34.

Author Biography

Hannu L. T. Heikkinen is a professor in the Finnish Institute for Educational Research, University of Jyväskylä, Finland, where he is head of research in 'Education and the World of Work'. He is also an adjunct professor of Charles Sturt University, Australia; University of Tampere, Finland; and the Åbo Akademi University, Finland. He is specialized in research on continuing professional development of teachers, especially on mentoring.

Chapter 56
Building Teacher Confidence in Inquiry and Assessment: Experiences from a Pan-European Collaboration

Odilla E. Finlayson and Eilish McLoughlin

56.1 Introduction

There is widespread concern about the outcomes of science education in schools with too few young people selecting to study science once it is no longer compulsory in their school system. Research suggests that the main factor determining attitudes towards school science is the quality of the educational experience provided by the teacher and so clearly, any changes to science learning in the classroom must begin with the teacher (Tucker 2011). In recent years, there has been much research and interest worldwide from educators, governments and employers on the skills and competencies needed by school leavers and graduates to succeed in life, career and citizenship (so called Life-long Learning Skills and 21st Century Skills). These skills extend beyond those of basic reading, writing and arithmetic to encompass skills of critical thinking and problem-solving, effective communication, collaboration, creativity and innovation, digital competence and learning to learn. The key challenge for educationalists is to recognise these skills and to develop and implement strategies to incorporate their development in science education (Barth 2009).

Crucial to the development of key skills and competencies in young people is their engagement in the education process. Methodologies such as inquiry-based science education (IBSE) have been highlighted as having the potential to increase student engagement in science at primary and second level and provide such development opportunities (Rocard 2007). IBSE is an approach to teaching and learning science that is conducted through the process of inquiry. The term inquiry

O.E. Finlayson (✉) · E. McLoughlin
Dublin City University, Dublin, Ireland
e-mail: odilla.finlayson@dcu.ie

E. McLoughlin
e-mail: eilish.mcloughlin@dcu.ie

© Springer Nature Singapore Pte Ltd. 2017
M.A. Peters et al. (eds.), *A Companion to Research in Teacher Education*,
DOI 10.1007/978-981-10-4075-7_56

has figured prominently in science education, yet it refers to at least three distinct categories of activities—what scientists do (e.g. conducting investigations using scientific methods), how students learn (e.g. actively inquiring through 'thinking and doing' into a phenomenon or problem, often mirroring the processes used by scientists), and a pedagogical approach that teachers employ (e.g. designing or using curricula that allow for extended investigations).

The US National Science Education Standards (NSES) (National Research Council 2000) recognised inquiry as both a learning goal and a teaching method. To that end, the content standards for the Science as Inquiry section in the NSES include both abilities and understandings of inquiry. The NSES identifies five essential elements of inquiry teaching and learning that apply across science education, namely: (i) Learners engage in scientifically oriented questions; (ii) Learners give priority to evidence in response to questions; (iii) Learners formulate explanations from evidence; (iv) Learners connect explanations to scientific knowledge; and (v) Learners communicate and justify explanations. However, the use of the term inquiry was discontinued in defining the updated US framework for science education in 2013, Next Generation Science Standards (NGSS) (National Research Council 2013). The NGSS developers recognised that there was a widespread lack of understanding of the meaning of inquiry and defined a new term 'science and engineering practices'. In addition, the NGSS framework has focussed on and articulated the associated goals of assessment of these practices:

> "In the future, science assessments will not assess students' understanding of core ideas separately from their abilities to use the practices of science and engineering. These two dimensions of learning will be assessed together, showing students not only "know" science concepts, but also that students can use their understanding to investigate the natural world through the practices of science inquiry, and can solve meaningful problems through the practices of engineering design."

It is generally accepted that there is a wide variation in school cultures and classroom settings around the world in terms of inquiry teaching methods and approaches to assessment. Educational assessment is a well-defined field of research and practice which deals with collecting, analysing and utilising data on students' learning outcomes (Black et al. 2003). The large-scale international assessment projects such as PISA have directed the attention of decision-makers to the importance of assessment, and in many countries changes in national assessment systems have been implemented. This process has increased the level of expertise in assessment among teachers as well. However, large-scale assessments provide system-level feedback, and the related analyses tend to have little impact on everyday classroom practices. One of the reasons behind this limited transfer is that immediate classroom-level assessment requires the use and deployment of different methods and instruments in the learning context. A broader concept of assessment is required to capture the breadth and extent of student learning, i.e.

"Assessment is a term that covers any activity in which evidence of learning is collected in a planned and systematic way, and is used to make a judgment about learning. If the purpose is to help in decisions about how to advance learning and the judgement is about the next steps in learning and how to take them, then the assessment is formative in function. If the purpose is to summarise the learning that had taken place in order to grade, certificate or record progress, then the assessment is summative in function". (Harlen and Deakin Crick 2002, p. 1)

Several barriers to implementing IBSE-oriented assessment have been identified by practitioners, e.g. lack of time to develop and implement IBSE assessment; high content requirements in national curriculum; external tests not focused on assessing inquiry skills and lack of familiarity with formative-assessment tools for IBSE (SAILS 2013). Therefore, to effectively implement change in classroom practice towards IBSE, the pedagogy of inquiry learning has to align with national curricula and assessment strategies. Teachers must be well prepared to implement and understand the benefits of such strategies. If any curricular/pedagogical change is to be successfully sustained, the three areas of curriculum, assessment and teacher education need to be considered together. Teachers need to realise that IBSE pedagogy is both feasible and valued within the curriculum and assessment process as defined at national level. The consideration of these identified barriers is important when developing professional development programmes to support teachers in implementing changes in their pedagogic and assessment practices. However, addressing these barriers and supporting teachers changing their practices necessitates collaboration between teachers and teacher educators—so as to provide opportunities for teachers to trial new approaches and reflect on their experience with other practitioners.

The SAILS project team (SAILS 2012) have adopted the approach that to successfully change inquiry and assessment practices in the classroom requires sustained collaboration that is relevant and beneficial to all parties. The project team has produced a collection of SAILS Inquiry and Assessment Units—which showcase the benefits of adopting inquiry approaches in classroom practice, exemplifies how assessment practices are embedded in inquiry lessons and illustrates the variety of assessment opportunities/processes available to science teachers. In particular, the SAILS Units provide clear examples for teachers of how inquiry skills (i.e. developing hypotheses, working collaboratively, forming coherent arguments and planning investigations) can be assessed, alongside content knowledge, scientific literacy and scientific reasoning and illustrate the benefits of various types of assessments. The project team have developed and implemented Teacher Education Programmes (TEPs) to support teachers in using and assessing student learning in an inquiry classroom, as exemplified through the SAILS Units. The approach adopted by this project team and the impact of this approach on teachers confidence and competence in Inquiry and Assessment will be discussed in the following sections.

56.2   Collaborative Co-creation of Inquiry-Based Science Education and Assessment (IBSEA) Resources

Taking into consideration the diverse experiences of teacher cohorts across the twelve European countries participating in SAILS, i.e. their range of experiences in inquiry and its assessment and cultural differences in implementation, it was deemed necessary by the project team that exemplary materials for appropriate types of assessment for use in the science (Physics, Chemistry and Biology) classrooms at both lower and upper second level needed to be developed. Therefore, a range of Inquiry and Assessment units—SAILS Units—were developed by the project team, which provided sufficient flexibility so as to be usable by all the project team, to support teachers in adopting both inquiry and assessment.

The process adopted for the development of the SAILS Units is outlined in Fig. 56.1 and is discussed below.

As shown in Fig. 56.1, initially three pilot units were developed which presented an inquiry approach to teaching the topic and identified assessment opportunities within the unit. These opportunities were based on who assessed, when assessment was possible and ideas of how evidence of the assessment could be obtained (see Table 56.1). The pilot units were then distributed to all countries where each country trialled the material with groups of expert inquiry teachers. Following piloting, improvements were made to ensure that the material was applicable in different countries.

On the basis of discussion and dialogue between the project team and their expert groups in each country, thirty five further units (Draft Units) were suggested by the project team. However, nineteen of these draft units were selected for further development in terms of inquiry and its assessment. The units were selected based on having a diverse range of topics which covered the disciplines of science, the range of second-level education, relevance to curricula as well as the range of inquiry skills and different modes of assessment.

Each country led on the development of one or two units and coordinated the trialling of each of these units in at least three other countries. Thereby each final SAILS unit was informed by the project team and teachers from at least 4 different

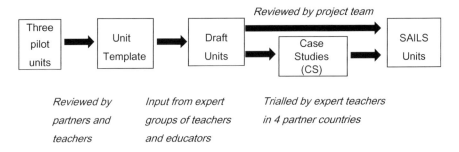

Fig. 56.1 Process adopted for the development of SAILS Inquiry and Assessment Units

Table 56.1 Assessment opportunities within SAILS inquiry and assessment units

Who assesses	When assessed	Evidence of assessment	Outcome of assessment
Teacher	Before an activity	Observations	Formative
Peer—student	During the activity	Dialogue (teacher/student, student/student)	Diagnostic
Student (self)	At end of activity	Student artefacts (concept map, graph, plan, drawing ...)	Summative

countries. Each of the teacher experiences was written up as a case study and the information summarised in the final SAILS Units. The purpose of the case studies was to provide real examples of how teachers implemented the inquiry activity and adapted the assessment to suit their own classrooms. Each case study was completed as a narrative detailing the following:

(i) **How was the learning sequence adapted?** *Teachers' reasons for their approach. What questions they used? How did the learners respond? What did the teacher notice?*

(ii) **How were the skills assessed?** *How did they plan to make their judgements (during/after the inquiry)? What model of assessment was used?*

(iii) **Criteria for judging assessment data:** *What were the teachers looking for in terms of satisfactory response to the inquiry? What were their expectations?*

(iv) **Evidence Collected:** *Teacher opinion, Observer notes, Sample Student artefacts.*

(v) **Use of Assessment Data** *What did the teachers do next? How did they feed back to their learners? How did doing the inquiry affect their planning and decisions about next steps in learning?*

A specific example of a pilot unit that was developed into a SAILS Unit was on the topic of Reaction Rates. The Reaction Rates Unit uses effervescent vitamin C tablets to introduce students to the concepts of gas production in the reaction of acid with carbonate, rates of reaction and factors influencing reaction rate. Three main activities aimed at lower second level are included, although these can be further extended and adapted for upper second level. This topic was chosen as rate of reaction has relevance in everyday life—from cooking, to taking medicines to aging! Usually this topic is investigated in schools using the effect of hydrochloric acid on marble chips—both of these materials are mainly unfamiliar to the students when they are starting their studies in chemistry. Therefore, the context as outlined of effervescent vitamin C tablets was chosen as it is familiar to the students and is non-threatening in that students can safely handle these materials. This unit focusses on the inquiry skills of planning and carrying out an investigation including identifying variables (relevant and irrelevant), handling a complex system to reduce number of variables, determining relationship between variables.

Table 56.2 Inquiry Skills assessed in the four case studies (CS1–CS4) of Reaction Rates Unit

CS1	Critique experimental design, Experimental problem-solving
CS2	Planning, Critiquing experimental method
CS3	Planning investigation, Working collaboratively, Data interpretation
CS4	Planning and implementing investigation, Graphical representation, Cause–effect relation, Coherent arguments from evidence

Reasoning skills of determining causality and proportional reasoning with graphical representation were also included in an extension to this unit.

The Reaction Rates Unit was trialled by teachers in four countries; Table 56.2 summarises the inquiry skills focussed on in each of the four case studies, all emphasising a focus on planning and carrying out investigations. In these case studies, the teachers also collected evidence of their students' learning showing different assessment methods, for example gathering individual input to group work using placemats (Murdoch and Wilson 2014), examining peer feedback to student generated plans for investigations, using student's drawing artefacts to monitor their design of an experiment, and using assessment rubrics. Teachers also identified areas in the lesson where unexpected behaviours occurred, e.g. one teacher indicated that the students were more unsure about their content knowledge in the inquiry lesson than she expected them to be. Likewise, other teachers indicated that students were eager and motivated by the inquiry activities. Recognising the range of assessment opportunities within a lesson was important in building teacher confidence in the wider use of assessment, particularly for formative-assessment purposes.

56.2.1 *Impact of Collaboration for Developing IBSEA Resources*

The development process for the final SAILS Units allowed for input and collaboration across all the partner countries and between teachers and educators. Initial discussions on the nature of the inquiry process and of its assessment required all of the project team to develop their understanding of inquiry and assessment within different contexts and national constraints.

Having diverse expert teachers, who were familiar with inquiry practices and who trialled units with their class groups, provided the project team with a very rich and fruitful resource for further discussion and clarification of ideas. An important part of combining the case study narratives was the discussion between the project team of similarities and differences between the narratives in each country. The mutual respect within the project team on the narratives presented and also the discussion of the cultural differences, language differences, etc., provided all participants the opportunity to share their understanding and develop their knowledge of different views of inquiry and its assessment.

The Units developed were available for use by teachers and educators in teacher education programmes (TEP) as exemplar materials showing the range of implementations and how evidence of learning had been determined in the case studies. Parallel to the development of the SAILS units, the programme for teacher education was also undergoing development.

56.3 Development of Pan-European Teacher Education Programmes in IBSEA

In recent years, developments in teacher education have been organised under several conceptual frameworks. These include improving the scientific foundations of teaching, developing teachers' knowledge and skills alongside providing them with materials and tools, and preparing teachers for identifying and applying research results and carrying out teaching experiments to improve their own work. Many professional development programmes are designed to attempt to change a teacher's attitudes and beliefs towards certain methods of teaching or a new curriculum. The presumption is that once a teacher's attitudes and beliefs have changed, specific alterations will occur in their classroom practices or behaviour, leading to improved student learning (Guskey 2002). An alternative approach is to rearrange the processes involved in teacher change. This alternative approach suggests that a professional development programme should attempt to change the teachers' classroom practices from the outset. This would then lead to a change in students' learning outcomes, which would give rise to a change in the teacher's beliefs and attitudes towards this new teaching method, material or curricula. The assumption in this case is that significant change occurs in teachers' attitudes and beliefs once they have gained evidence of the success of a new approach in the form of improvements in student learning (Guskey 2002). The teacher educators from across the SAILS collaboration, adopted this assumption in the development of Teacher Education Programmes (TEP) in inquiry and its assessment. The overall objective of this collaboration was to increase teacher's confidence and competence in adopting inquiry approaches to teaching science and also in assessing the skills and competences developed by their students in the classroom.

The four-year collaboration between teacher educators participating in the SAILS project facilitated the continual exchange of ideas and resources between science teachers and educators. Across the fourteen project teams in twelve European countries, a diverse range of national systems of education and different pressures and influences on these systems were highlighted, i.e. traditional approaches to teaching and learning in science, lack of time to develop and implement IBSE assessment, high content requirements in national curriculum, external tests not focused on assessing inquiry skills. An integral aspect in the development of TEP was to recognise the differences and diversity across the twelve participating countries and through ongoing discussion and dialogue to develop a common approach for TEPs that was relevant in all contexts. Therefore, the design of the SAILS TEP aimed to:

- Accommodate the diverse range of teachers participating in the programmes, based on teacher subject specialism, prior experience with IBSE and with assessment;
- Take account of the time available for in-service teachers to participate in continuing professional development programmes;
- Take account of the structure of the programmes that was suitable in each country, e.g. summer school/winter school versus a series of workshops over time versus one-day programmes;
- Align with the nature of typical pre-service initial teacher education programmes in each country;
- Suit the various cultural and educational practices of each participating country.

The SAILS TEPs in Inquiry-Based Science Education and Assessment (IBSEA) was developed over three sequential stages (0,1,2) of design and implementation.

- The focus of the initial STAGE 0 TEP was on introducing teachers to IBSE, helping teachers implement inquiry-based activities in the classroom and addressing key issues such as classroom management strategies, problem-solving, carrying out investigations, etc. As teachers in each country had different prior experiences of inquiry and assessment, each partner country was given the scope within STAGE 0 TEPs to develop and implement work-shops that best met the professional- development needs of their cohort of teachers. Discussions between educators following the implementation of STAGE 0 TEPs across ten countries identified four common features—namely, some teachers were introduced to IBSE for the first time; teachers were given the opportunity to experience active hands-on inquiry activities; teachers were engaging in reflective and plenary discussions with each other and teachers were introduced to the assessment of inquiry skills.
- The objective of STAGE 1 TEP was to include the assessment of inquiry skills as a core aspect of the TEP and to provide teachers with the opportunity to deepen and extend their understanding of the range of assessment approaches that can be used in classroom practice. Through discussion at project team meetings, it was clear that there were differences in teacher's understanding of the role of assessment in IBSE and in particular the distinction between for-mative and summative assessment. The project team agreed to adopt Harlen and Deakin Crick's (Harlen and Deakin Crick 2002, p. 1) interpretation of assess-ment "...*term that covers any activity in which evidence of learning is collected in a planned and systematic way, and is used to make a judgment about learning*". It was then discussed and agreed that any assessment activity could be used to inform learning in an ongoing manner, i.e. formatively (Black and Wiliam 1998), or it could be used as a diagnostic of learning or in a summative manner, e.g. to evaluate student learning at the end of a topic.

- The final stage of TEPs (STAGE 2 TEP) aimed to integrate education about inquiry practices with the assessment of these practices; i.e. teachers were introduced to inquiry and its assessment within the TEPs. Inquiry methodologies explored in the TEPs were those that are used to develop not only students' content knowledge, but also skills that students develop through engaging in inquiry practices, such as developing hypotheses, planning and carrying out investigations, forming coherent arguments and working collaboratively, and therefore the assessment of these skills is essential to ensure student development.

Almost 700 in-service teachers participated in STAGE 2 TEPs across the twelve participating countries—none of this group of teachers had attended any prior SAILS TEP. The teachers were mainly involved in teaching the science disciplines of biology, chemistry and physics, but also the additional subjects of general science, technology and mathematics. Teachers from both lower and upper second level schools attended. The in-service teachers taking part in the STAGE 2 TEPs self-reported on a range of experience with inquiry. For instance, teachers in Greece, Hungary and Poland had very little experience with inquiry before the TEPs, teachers in Sweden mostly had some experience with inquiry, while those from Belgium and the United Kingdom were a mixture of some and very experienced teachers in IBSE. Based on educators experiences of implementing Stage 0 and Stage 1 TEPs, the final TEPs were designed to incorporate three core elements:

I. Experiencing Inquiry and Assessment,
II. Trialling IBSE and Assessment in the Classroom,
III. Developing IBSE and Assessment Resources.

I. Experiencing Inquiry and Assessment

All TEPs incorporated activities that gave teachers the opportunity to experience inquiry as a learner. Teachers were also provided with inquiry-based resources that they critiqued and discussed how they would implement and adapt in order to meet the needs of their classroom curriculum. Teachers across all twelve countries, through experience with inquiry activities, recognised the value of IBSE as a teaching methodology and became motivated to try IBSE in their classrooms.

Teachers experienced the assessment of inquiry learning through several different approaches, e.g.

- Teachers completed an inquiry activity followed by a discussion of the learning that occurred and the opportunities for assessment of that learning;
- Teachers received "assessment feedback" from the educators during/after they had carried out an inquiry activity;
- A variety of assessment tools (such as extracts of written student work, self- and peer assessment instruments, assessment rubrics) were introduced, discussed and trialled in relation to an inquiry activity;
- Teachers peer assessed the work of their colleagues;

- Teachers designed an assessment instrument and described the success criteria they would adopt as evidence of inquiry learning;
- Teachers participated in lectures and seminars which presented a theoretical basis for formative and summative assessment.

Teachers across all twelve countries, through experience with these assessment activities, recognised opportunities for and the value of different assessment strategies and appreciated the richness in diversity of implementation in classroom practice.

II. Trialling IBSE and Assessment in the Classroom

The focus of this element was to facilitate teachers obtaining first-hand experience with their own students conducting inquiry activities and considering the impact of this approach on their student's learning. Teachers were supported to trial inquiry and assessment activities or adapt their own lessons towards an inquiry pedagogy in their classrooms. Educators used the SAILS units to exemplify inquiry and assessment approaches in the classroom. Additionally, teachers were encouraged to trial different assessment methods with their students and in particular to trial assessment to collect evidence of student learning during the inquiry activity.

Following trialling in the classroom, the teachers were given an opportunity to reflect on the implementation in their classroom through discussion with other teachers and educators. Teachers were also encouraged to bring evidence of their students' learning to share during these follow-up discussions. If these were not available, then examples from the SAILS units were used as the basis for plenary discussions. The key aspects raised during these discussions were:

- Identification of the skills that were assessable in an inquiry activity;
- Difficulties that were overcome during implementation (e.g. group work, time, etc.);
- Different assessment methods and their applicability for different groups of students;
- Preparation of students for different modes of assessment;
- What feedback should be given to students and where to next?

III. Developing IBSE and Assessment Resources

A significant aspect of all TEPs was to support teachers in the development of their own inquiry activities/lessons. The ability of teachers to develop their own resources was considered as a critical element for the preparation of teachers to adopt an inquiry-based pedagogy and use a variety of assessment strategies to assess the extend and breath of their student learning. With the support of their peer group and teacher educators, teachers (individually or in small groups) decided on a topic area and developed their own inquiry resources and assessment strategies for use in their classroom. Teachers developed these inquiry and assessment resources and in some cases, trialled them in the classroom, and were facilitated to share their resources and experiences with their peer group. In this way, teachers were supported in not only implementing assessment strategies in their classrooms, but also in developing and adapting other resources to suit their needs.

56.3.1 Impact of Collaboration for Developing SAILS TEPs

All of the SAILS project team implemented STAGE 2 TEPs with teachers across the twelve European countries and adapted the SAILS TEP framework to suit their own professional development programmes as appropriate to the backgrounds and cultural contexts of the participating in-service and pre-service teachers.

All national TEPs consisted of a number of workshops; however, the format of the workshops varied between countries to suit the needs of the teachers. In most countries, the workshops were provided as one-day or half-day sessions with some time in between in order to allow teachers to implement what they had learned in the workshops within their own teaching and then to share their experience and challenges. Teachers were encouraged to do some work such as developing their own inquiry and assessment materials in between or after the workshops and/or to implement particular aspects of the TEPs within their own classroom practice. In some countries, the sessions were concentrated in winter or summer schools, in order to attract teachers from around the country (e.g. Poland, Ireland and Turkey). No distinguishable differences were evident in the impact that different workshop formats and timing had on the participating teachers.

As documented in SAILS report (SAILS 2015), teachers from across the twelve European countries with different histories of curriculum, assessment and pedagogy have successfully adapted their teaching approaches to give students a more active role in the science classroom. For example, teachers organised experimental work so that the students posed their own questions, decided on appropriate methods they would use to collect and analyse the data in their investigations. Teachers also reported on facilitating their students to work together collaboratively and to use a variety of modes to communicate their ideas to others. Teachers highlighted the practices of students engaging with one another to discuss their scientific reasoning as they carried out their inquiry activities and that for many students, taking on the responsibility of inquiry increased their engagement in the classroom. SAILS TEPs supported these teachers in using assessment strategies to make judgments and give feedback to their students on how to improve their learning.

Evaluation data was collected using pre- and post-questionnaires from 305 participating teachers from across the twelve countries that participated in STAGE 2 TEPs (SAILS 2015). Female teachers outnumbered the male teachers in the overall cohort (29% Male, 71% Female). They ranged in the years of their teaching experience from less than 5 years' experience (20%), 5–10 years (22%), 11–20 years (27%) to more than 20 years' experience (29%). Pre-questionnaire data indicated that the teachers self-rated their prior experience in inquiry as none/hardly any knowledge about IBSE (29%); some knowledge about IBSE but no practical experience with IBSE in class (28%); some/limited experience with IBSE in class (28%) and good knowledge of and regularly use IBSE in class (4%). As evidenced by the analysis of questionnaires, all participating teachers' understanding of inquiry and their confidence with assessing inquiry practices in the classroom increased significantly. This occurred regardless of the prior experience level of the teachers in inquiry and of their number of years teaching experience.

56.4   Conclusions and Implications

The primary objective of the SAILS collaboration was to support teachers across Europe to not only teach through inquiry but also to be confident and competent in assessment of inquiry skills and competencies. The SAILS project has achieved this objective through a unified approach of implementing three key components for transforming classroom practice, i.e. teacher education, curriculum and assessment development around an IBSE pedagogy. The SAILS TEPs in inquiry and assessment have increased teachers' confidence in changing their classroom practice, have demonstrated the value of an inquiry approach on students' learning, and have described appropriate strategies for assessing inquiry skills and competences.

This sustained collaboration has resulted in the production of a collection of SAILS Inquiry and Assessment Units—which showcase the benefits of adopting inquiry approaches in classroom practice, exemplify how assessment practices can be embedded in inquiry lessons and illustrate the variety of assessment opportunities/processes available to science teachers. In particular, the units provide clear examples for teachers of how inquiry skills (developing hypotheses, working collaboratively, forming coherent arguments and planning investigations) can be assessed, alongside content knowledge, scientific literacy and scientific reasoning and illustrate the benefits of various types of assessments. These SAILS Inquiry and Assessment Units have been trialled in over 100 second level classrooms, each unit across at least three different countries. Feedback from teachers has been collected in the form of case study reports. As demonstrated in the case studies, the SAILS units can be used to focus on the main skills identified but also can be adapted to focus on particular skills that the teacher may wish to develop. The assessment criteria can also be modified to suit the student age and their experience level with inquiry.

The evaluation of the SAILS TEPs indicated that by explicitly addressing the key barriers in implementing IBSE-oriented assessment practices in classrooms as perceived by the teachers, the SAILS approach has equipped teachers to actively engage in the transformation of traditional approaches to teaching and assessing science towards IBSE and formative-assessment practices in their own classrooms and schools. However, several challenges need to be faced by teachers to develop their own assessment strategies and this remains the major impediment for teachers in implementing alternative assessment approaches in their classrooms.

In conclusion, the key outcomes from this pan-European collaboration are that teaching and assessment should be considered as a dynamic and iterative process in order to effectively support inquiry learning in the science classroom. Learning science through inquiry can result in better understanding and more broadly applicable scientific knowledge, along with transferable skills and competencies. With time and appropriate support, teachers can develop their confidence and competence in adopting inquiry and assessment of inquiry learning in classroom practice. These key outcomes are best achieved when teacher education, curriculum and assessment practices are addressed through sustained collaboration between teachers and educators and across borders, both classrooms and countries.

Acknowledgement SAILS project (2012–2015) received funding from the European Union's Seventh Framework Programme for research, technological development and demonstration under grant agreement no 289085.

References

Barth, P. (2009). What do we mean by 21st century skills. *American School Board Journal, 196* (10), 27–29.

Black, P., Harrison, C., Lee, C., Marshall, B., & Wiliam, D. (2003). *Assessment for learning: Putting it into practice*. Buckingham, U.K.: Open University Press.

Black, P., & Wiliam, D. (1998). Assessment and classroom learning. *Assessment in Education: Principles, Policy & Practice, 5*(1), 7–74.

Guskey, T. R. (2002). Professional development and teacher change. *Teachers and Teaching: Theory and Practice, 8*(3/4), 381–391.

Harlen, W., & Deakin Crick, R. (2002). A systematic review of the impact of summative assessment and tests on students' motivation for learning. In *Research evidence in education library, Issue 1*. London: EPPI-Centre, Social Science Research Unit, Institute of Education.

Murdoch, K. & Wilson, J. (2014). *Helping your pupils to work cooperatively*. London: Routledge.

National Research Council. (2000). *Inquiry and the national science education standards: A guide for teaching and learning*. Washington, D.C.: National Academy Press.

National Research Council. (2013). *Next generation science standards: For states, by states*. Washington, DC: The National Academies Press.

Rocard, M. (2007). *Science education NOW: A renewed pedagogy for the future of Europe*. Brussels: European Commission. Retrieved from http://ec.europa.eu/research/science-society/document_library/pdf_06/report-rocard-onscience-education_en.pdf. Accessed July, 2016.

SAILS. (2012). *Strategies for assessment of inquiry learning in science*. http://sails-project.eu/. Accessed July, 2016.

SAILS. (2013). *Report on IBSE teacher education and assessment programme—STAGE 1*. Strategies for Assessment of Inquiry Learning in Science. http://sails-project.eu/sites/default/files/outcomes/d4-2.pdf. Accessed July, 2016.

SAILS. (2015). *Report on IBSE teacher education and assessment programme—STAGE 2. Strategies for assessment of inquiry learning in science*. http://sails-project.eu/sites/default/files/outcomes/d4-3.pdf. Accessed July, 2016.

Tucker, M. (2011). *Standing on the shoulders of giants: An American agenda for education reform*. Washington, DC: National Center on Education and the Economy.

Author Biographies

Odilla Finlayson Ph.D. is a member of Centre for Advancement of STEM Teaching and Learning (CASTeL) and Senior Lecturer in Science Education in the School of Chemical Sciences, Dublin City University. Research interests in engaging pedagogies for science teaching and assessment. Co-ordinator of FP7 SAILS (2011–2015).

Eilish McLoughlin Ph.D. is Director of the Centre for Advancement of STEM Teaching and Learning (CASTeL) and Senior Lecturer in the School of Physical Sciences at Dublin City University. Eilish's research interests are in conducting evidence-based research on STEM curriculum, pedagogy and assessment and research informed STEM teacher education.

Author Index

© Springer Nature Singapore Pte Ltd. 2017
M.A. Peters et al. (eds.), *A Companion to Research in Teacher Education*,
DOI 10.1007/978-981-10-4075-7

Printed in the United States
By Bookmasters